ANNUAIRE EUROPEEN
EUROPEAN YEARBOOK

ANNUAIRE EUROPEEN

VOL. XXII

EUROPEAN YEARBOOK

PUBLIE SOUS LES AUSPICES DU
CONSEIL DE L'EUROPE

PUBLISHED UNDER THE AUSPICES OF
THE COUNCIL OF EUROPE

LA HAYE / THE HAGUE
MARTINUS NIJHOFF
1976

L'Annuaire européen vise à encourager l'étude méthodique des organisations européennes et de leurs activités. Il est publié sous la responsabilité d'un Comité de rédaction, organe officieux et apolitique auquel il n'appartient pas d'exprimer une opinion sur un aspect quelconque des affaires internationales.

The aim of the European Yearbook is to promote the scientific study of European organisations and their work. It is published under the responsibility of an Editorial Committee, which is an unofficial and nonpolitical body precluded from expressing an opinion on any aspect of international affairs.

ISBN 978-94-015-1199-5 ISBN 978-94-015-1197-1 (eBook)
DOI 10.1007/978-94-015-1197-1

Pour toutes communications
relatives à la rédaction de cet Annuaire
écrire à l'adresse suivante:
Editorial communications should be addressed to:

The General Editor
European Yearbook
Council of Europe
67006 Strasbourg Cedex
France

TABLE DES MATIERES

ARTICLES

SECTION DOCUMENTAIRE

TABLE OF CONTENTS

ARTICLES

DOCUMENTARY SECTION

SECTION BIBLIOGRAPHIQUE

BIBLIOGRAPHICAL SECTION

ARTICLES

CUMULATIVE LIST OF ARTICLES PUBLISHED IN VOLUMES I TO XX

Over a period of twenty years there have been published in the first twenty volumes of the European Yearbook nearly 150 articles by ministers, senior officials and other experts on different aspects of European cooperation and integration, including the structure, functions and activities of the different European organisations. This has been done in accordance with a decision of the Committee of Ministers of the Council of Europe in 1953, which authorised the publication of a Yearbook designed to promote the scientific study of European organisations and their work.

In order to facilitate consultation of these articles, a cumulative list has been prepared, classified under the following headings:

A. European Integration in general
B. OEEC/OECD
C. Council of Europe
D. European Communities
E. Western European Union
F. European Free Trade Association
G. Other European Organisations
H. Other Aspects of European Cooperation.

LISTE RECAPITULATIVE DES ARTICLES PUBLIES DANS LES VOLUMES I A XX

Sur une période de vingt ans près de 150 articles ont été publiés dans les volumes I à XX de l'Annuaire Européen. Ecrits par des ministres, de hauts fonctionnaires et d'autres experts, ils ont traité des différents aspects de la coopération et de l'intégration européennes en s'attachant notamment à la structure, au fonctionnement et aux activités des diverses organisations européennes. L'Annuaire se conformait ainsi à la décision du Comité des

Ministres du Conseil de l'Europe qui, en 1953, avait approuvé le projet de publication d'un ouvrage consacré à l'étude scientifique des organisations européennes et de leur oeuvre.

On trouvera ci-après une liste récapitulative des articles établie en vue de faciliter leur consultation. Les articles y sont repertoriés selon la classification suivante:

A. Intégration européenne en général
B. OECE/OCDE
C. Le Conseil de l'Europe
D. Les Communautés européennes
E. L'Union de l'Europe occidentale
F. L'Association européenne de libre échange
G. Autres organisations européennes
H. Autres aspects de la coopération européenne.

A. EUROPEAN INTEGRATION IN GENERAL
INTEGRATION EUROPEENNE EN GENERAL

B. O.E.E.C./O.E.C.D.
O.E.C.E./O.C.D.E.

C. COUNCIL OF EUROPE
CONSEIL DE L'EUROPE

D. EUROPEAN COMMUNITIES
COMMUNAUTES EUROPEENNES

E. WESTERN EUROPEAN UNION
UNION DE L'EUROPE OCCIDENTALE

F. EUROPEAN FREE TRADE ASSOCIATION ASSOCIATION EUROPEENNE DE LIBRE-ECHANGE

G. OTHER EUROPEAN ORGANISATIONS
AUTRES ORGANISATIONS EUROPEENNES

H. OTHER ASPECTS OF EUROPEAN CO-OPERATION AUTRES ASPECTS DE LA COOPERATION EUROPEENNE

EUROPEAN POLITICAL COOPERATION

by

GARRET FITZGERALD*

INTRODUCTION

European Political Cooperation (EPC), which began in 1970 is a separate and additional framework of cooperation between the Nine member States of the Communities under which the Nine agree to consult on, and so far as possible, to coordinate and act in common on foreign policy matters. The commitments subscribed to in this framework are parallel to, but distinct from, those which the member States have undertaken in legal form under the various EEC treaties – though their long-term goal like that of the EEC proper is European Union.

Political cooperation is essentially intergovernmental in character, and is concerned with questions external to the Nine which present a common interest. It is not concerned with political issues internal to the Community. As the Danish Minister for Foreign Affairs, Mr. Hartling, observed in the Folketing on 18 March 1971, "there are cogent reasons for pointing this out because much of what takes place within the Communities – the expansion of the institutions, the establishment of economic and monetary cooperation, the formulation of the common commercial policy vis-à-vis third countries, to mention but a few examples – is also of central political importance." It may unfortunately be a source of some confusion to the public that the term European political cooperation, therefore, has this special meaning.

The procedures of political cooperation were from the outset characterised by a pragmatic and flexible approach to the development of foreign policy coordination between the Nine. As the Second Report on political cooperation puts it: "what is involved in fact is a new procedure in international relations and

* **Irish Minister for Foreign Affairs, member of Dáil Éireann (the Irish Parliament), former member of Seanad Éireann (the Irish Senate), Chairman of the Council of the European Communities, January to June, 1975.**

an original European contribution to the technique of arriving at concerted action."

It should be said nonetheless that while the present structure of European political cooperation is a comparatively recent development, it incorporates a number of the ideas and concepts which had emerged during the earlier stages of development of the Community, and which to some extent may be considered to have paved the way for the activities which are the subject of this article.

1. THE HAGUE SUMMIT

The meeting of the Heads of Government and Foreign Ministers of the Six at the Hague in December 1969 marked the successful completion of the transitional phase of the Common Market, as envisaged by the treaties, and the point of departure for negotiations leading to the enlargement of the Community. Looking back the Heads of Government and Foreign Ministers considered that "never perhaps have independent States carried their cooperation so far," and noted that the Community had now reached a turning point in its history. "Entry upon the final stage of the Common Market not only means confirming the irreversible nature of the work accomplished by the Communities but also means preparing the way for a united Europe capable of assuring its responsibilities in the world of tomorrow and of making a contribution commensurate with its tradition and its mission. Thus, the Heads of Government wish to reaffirm their faith in the political finalities which give the Community its whole sense and meaning."

It was in the context of these objectives that the Heads of Government instructed the Ministres for Foreign Affairs "to study the best means of achieving progress in the domain of political unification in the perspective of enlargement, and to make proposals before the end of July 1970."

2. THE LUXEMBOURG REPORT

In accordance with this mandate, the Ministers held a first meeting on 20 January 1970 at which it was agreed that each

Government should draw up a document setting out its proposals. At their meeting on 2 March 1970 the Ministers decided to set up an ad hoc committee of officials, under the chairmanship of a Belgian, the Vicomte Davignon, with a specific mandate to draw up a report which would synthesize the different proposals.

Among the questions which had to be decided was how far the long-term objectives could be defined, involving some reference to the final shape that political unification might take, or how far a pragmatic approach should be adopted. A further issue was how to arrive at a definition of the fields covered by political unification and the extent to which efforts should be concentrated on cooperation on certain questions of foreign policy. Another problem was the degree to which the applicant States could participate in the work of political cooperation.

The report of the ad hoc committee (known as the Luxembourg or Davignon report) was submitted on 20 July 1970 and adopted by the Foreign Ministers meeting in Luxembourg on 27 October. Expressive of European ideals, it was at the same time pragmatic in its concrete proposals. The first part of the Report, after recalling the spirit of the Hague communiqué, made three important points: first, that "in the spirit of the preambles of the Treaties of Paris and Rome, form should be given to the will for political union which has not ceased to sustain the progress of the European Communities"; secondly, that "the implementing of common policies already instituted, or about to be, requires corresponding developments in the political sphere, so as to bring closer the time when Europe could speak with one voice"; and thirdly, that "Europe must prepare itself to exercise the responsibilities which its increased cohesion and growing rôle make a duty as well as a necessity to assume in the world." It went on: "the present development of the European Communities imposes on the member States the necessity of increasing their political cooperation, and, in a first stage, to endow themselves with the means of harmonizing their views on international matters." Their first efforts would therefore be concentrated on the coordination of foreign policies and the Ministers expressed their conviction that progress along this road would promote developments in the Communities.

In the second part of the Report the Ministers announced the decision of the Governments to cooperate in the field of foreign policy. The objectives of this cooperation would be "to ensure, through exchanges of information and regular consultations, a better mutual understanding of the major problems of international politics" and "to strengthen their solidarity by promoting a harmonisation of view points, the coordination of positions, and, where it appears possible and desirable, common actions." With regard to the subjects of the consultations, the governments would consult on "all important questions of foreign policy," and the member States could propose questions of their choice for consultation.

The Luxembourg Report established the broad guidelines for the organisation of European political cooperation. At the apex of the system were the twice yearly meetings of the Foreign Ministers. In exceptional circumstances their meeting could be replaced by one of the Heads of Government. Ministerial meetings were to be prepared and followed through by a Political Committee, consisting of the Political Directors (the senior officials with responsibility for political affairs in the national Foreign Ministries). The Political Committee would meet at least four times a year. It would also have the power to set up working groups and expert groups for specific tasks and problems. To ensure coordination of these activities, the country occupying the Presidency of the Communities (which rotates every six months in alphabetical order) would also preside over political cooperation meetings. The Presidency would organize the meetings, which would be held in its capital, and provide the Secretariat. It would also have the responsibility for organizing immediate consultations in times of crisis. A further provision to ensure the smooth running of the machinery was the nomination of a "correspondent" in each foreign Ministry, who would be the focal point for communications between the capitals.

The Report also set out arrangements relating the activities of political cooperation to those carried out within the Community framework. The Commission was to be invited to make known its views on subjects which might affect the activities of the EEC. The European Parliament, and through it public opinion, was to be associated with the work of political cooperation by a twice-yearly *colloque* between the Ministers and the Political Affairs Committee of the Parliament held in an informal manner "to permit a free exchange of opinion." The Report emphasised the correlation between membership of the Communities and participation in political cooperation. At the same time it was recognised that the applicant countries Denmark, Ireland, Norway and the United Kingdom wished to be consulted and kept informed on political cooperation developments, in which they might be participating fully in a relatively short time. It was decided that a Ministerial meeting of the Ten would be held soon after meetings of the Ministers of the Six. The Presidency would pass on information of interest to the applicant countries after Political Committee meetings and communicate their reactions.

Part III of the Luxembourg Report provided for constant review of the procedure. The Political Committee were to furnish a report at the six-month Ministerial meetings. The President in Office would report once a year to the European Parliament on how the work of political cooperation had evolved. Finally, the Ministers proposed "to continue their work on the best manner of achieving progress in the field of political unification," and to present a second report in two years time, which would contain an assessment of the results achieved in foreign policy consultations.

3. THE RESULTS OF POLITICAL COOPERATION UP TO THE PARIS SUMMIT, OCTOBER 1972

The first Ministerial meeting under the new procedures took place in Munich on 19 November, followed on 2 December by a meeting of the Foreign Ministers of the Ten in Brussels. In accordance with the provisions of the Luxembourg Report, subjects of common interest were selected as suitable for consideration within the framework of political cooperation.

One of the first subjects discussed was that of the Conference on Security and Cooperation in Europe (C.S.C.E.). In some ways this was an ideal subject with which to inaugurate the political cooperation procedure. The Conference was a new development, unique of its kind in the history of European relations since the war. Unlike many other international issues on which each of the member States had long established national policies, the C.S.C.E. posed a number of new problems in a framework yet untried. Faced with the complex and challenging problems of the C.S.C.E., the Nine were and have been able to evolve a common position and indeed a common identity in preparing their approach to the Conference. At this stage they were discussing the necessary prerequisities for the Conference, its scope and procedure. A sub-committee was set up by the Political Committee in February 1971 to prepare an analysis of the possible implications for European unification of the Security Conference and also to study economic and trade aspects; subsequently, an ad hoc group was set up to concentrate on the economic aspects, while the sub-committee continued to study the more general questions.

Another issue which, from the start, featured frequently on the agenda of EPC meetings was that of the Middle East. A group of experts was set up to study and report on some of the principal problems. On the basis of this work, the Political Committee drew up a report which was submitted to the Ministers for approval at their meeting on 12–13 May. After the meeting of the Ten on 18 May 1971 Mr. Schumann, the French Foreign Minister, announced their common agreement that U.N. Security Council resolution 242 formed a basis and framework for an overall settlement, and that in particular a partial solution in regard to the opening of the Suez Canal should be studied and encouraged as a contribution towards an overall settlement. This and other conclusions of the report were to be communicated to the U.N. Secretary General U Thant, as a contribution to the Jarring mission.

During the remainder of 1971 there were also consultations and exchanges of views on problems in Asia, the Indian sub-continent and the Mediterranean Basin. Under the Italian Presidency, it was decided to set up two new working groups, one concerned with cooperation in the event of natural catastrophes and another for the Mediterranean.

A further area to which political cooperation was extended was that of preparation of the U.N. General Assembly: a decision was made to transfer consultations formerly held in the WEU framework before General Assembly sessions to that of political co-operation. In 1973 it was decided to supplement the consultations already taking place between the Permanent Representatives in New York by meetings of the directors of the U.N. sections in the Foreign Ministries to discuss particular points on the agenda and to report to the Political Committee. During this period, the internal procedures of EPC continued to develop to take account of the changing needs. There were more frequent meetings of both the Political Committee and the Correspondents – the former meeting at almost monthly intervals.

To an increasing extent, too, the Embassies of the member States were involved in the work of political cooperation, both in the other capitals of the Community and in third countries. In the case of the latter, the Luxembourg Report provided for regular consultations on problems of common interest, and the submission, if requested, of common reports.

The first annual report to the European Parliament was made by Mr. Schumann, the French Foreign Minister, on 10 June 1971 (ahead of schedule). The primary purpose of the report was to inform the Parliament of how political cooperation was functioning in practice. Mr. Schumann said that the Six did not pretend to have given their cooperation its final shape, still less its ideal shape, and he stressed the scope for development. On 18 November the first *colloque* was held between the President in office, Sr. Moro and the Political Affairs Committee of the Parliament.

Arrangements for consultation with the applicant countries were simplified when, from the beginning of 1972 after signature of the treaties of accession, the applicants began to take part in the various committees. By the middle of April 1972 all were participating fully.

The Political Committee had been keeping a close watch on the evolution of political cooperation and furnishing periodic balance-sheets to the Ministers, conscious of the fact that a Second Report was due to be prepared in the course of 1972. Towards the end of 1971, it was decided to defer this Report until after the treaties of Accession had been ratified. From the end of 1971 preparations were beginning to be made for the Paris summit held in October 1972.

4. THE PARIS SUMMIT, OCTOBER 1972

The Conference of Heads of State or Government held in Paris on 19–20 October 1972 marked the enlargement of the Community. In their Declaration the Heads of Government sought to identify the principal objectives for the future which would match their intention "to transform, before the end of the present decade the ensemble of their relations into a European Union." The Heads of Government declared that "the time has come for Europe to recognize clearly the unity of its interests, the extent of its capacities and the magnitude of its duties. Europe must be able to make its voice heard in world affairs, and to make an original contribution commensurate with its human, intellectual and material resources. It must affirm its own views in international relations, as befits its mission of openness, progress, peace and cooperation." They also stated that "European construction will allow Europe to affirm its personality while remaining faithful to its traditional friendships and to the alliances of the Member States, and to establish its position in world affairs as a distinct entity."

On political cooperation, the Heads of Government considered that "it had begun well and should be still further improved." They agreed that "consultations should be intensified at all levels and that the Foreign Ministers should in future meet four times a year instead of twice for this purpose." The Communique also stated that the object of this cooperation was "to deal with problems of current interest, and as far as possible to formulate common medium and long-term positions." On matters having a direct bearing on Community activities close contact should be maintained with the institutions of the Community. To give effect to these decisions, the Heads of Government requested the Foreign Ministers to produce, not later than 30 June 1973, a second report on methods of improving political cooperation, as envisaged in the Luxembourg Report.

5. THE SECOND REPORT

The preparation of the Second Report was carried out during the Belgian Presidency in the first six months of 1973. It was finally approved by the Foreign Ministers at their meeting on 23 July 1973 in Copenhagen, and agreed by Governments.

The Second Report was conceived as complementing rather than replacing the provisions of the Luxembourg report. It reaffirmed the broad objectives of political cooperation as set out in that Report and in the Paris Communiqué. Much of its content was devoted to considering the procedural improvements needed to enable the intensification of EPC activities, called for by the Heads of Government, to take place, and also to an assessment of the results already achieved.

In their assessment of these results, the Ministers were able to report substantial progress. They affirmed that "the mechanisms introduced by the Luxembourg Report, which were pragmatic in nature, have proven their flexibility and effectiveness." They considered it important, in particular, that a habit of consultation had become established, and this in turn created "an impulse towards coordination which has had a profound effect on the relations of the member States with each other and with third countries. European collegiality is thus tending to become a major factor in international relations."

The Report contained a number of provisions relating to changes in the organisation and procedures of political cooperation in order to handle the increasing workload and its widening scope. Apart from the quarterly Ministerial meetings already agreed at Paris it was now agreed that the Ministers could consult on particular subjects when meeting on other occasions. The Political Directors would continue to meet within the Political Committee "in order to prepare the Ministerial meetings and to carry out the tasks which are entrusted to them by the Ministers."

The frequency of their meetings would be regulated "to correspond to the requirements of the intensification of the work." The Group of Correspondents would have the task of following the implementation of political cooperation and studying problems of organization and of a general character.

A section was devoted to the working groups, and it was made clear that one of their purposes was to promote contacts between corresponding sections of the Foreign Ministries. The undertaking of in-depth studies on medium and long-term policies was to be entrusted either to the experts'' groups or to special study groups.

The principal rôle of embassies of the Nine in the other Member States was to receive briefings from the Ministry of Foreign Affairs of the host country on any matter of interest to the community. Occasionally, they might also be asked to have consultations on specific subjects. In addition, a correspondent was to be nominated in each of the embassies to ensure the necessary contacts (the subsequent creation of a direct communication link between the Foreign Ministries of the Nine has helped considerably in this respect).

The particular responsibilities of the Presidency in the absence of a permanent Secretariat were given recognition in the Second Report. The task of the Presidency was "to ensure the collegial implementation of the decisions of Ministerial and Political Committee meetings," and to propose on its own initiative or on the initiative of a Member State consultations at the appropriate level. It also maintained liaison through the Ambassadors of Member States in between Political Committee meetings. Because of its heavy administrative load, other States could give it assistance for particular tasks (in practice this last provision has seldom been invoked).

To meet the desire of the European Parliament for closer consultations the number of *colloques* was increased from two to four annually, corresponding to the increase in the number of Ministerial meetings. In preparation for the *colloques* the Political Committee would draw the Ministers' attention to resolutions adopted by the Parliament on foreign policy questions.

The section of the Report dealing with the priorities to be determined in respect of the subjects for consideration reflected the widening range of matters being raised in the political cooperation framework. The purpose of the consultations was "the search for a common approach on specific issues" and the subjects chosen "should have a bearing on the interests of Europe in fields where the adoption of a common position had become necessary or desirable." A significant inclusion was the undertaking that on these questions each State would commit itself as a general rule not to fix its own position definitively without consulting its partners in the framework of political cooperation.

The final section concerned the relationship between political cooperation activities and work carried out in the framework of the Community. The distinction between political cooperation, "which deals with problems of international relations on an intergovernmental basis" and Community activity "which arises from the legal commitments entered into by the member States in the Treaty of Rome" was drawn and it was stated that "the purpose of both is to contribute to the development of the process of European unification." The detailed arrangements for liaison in matters affecting the Community were repeated. The Commission would continue to be invited to make its opinion known on matters of concern to it, in accordance with existing practice. The Council was to be informed of relevant decisions but also the Ministers could ask the organs of political cooperation to prepare studies on political aspects of problems being examined in the Community. These would be forwarded to the Council.

In presenting the annual report to the European Parliament in October 1973 the Danish Foreign Minister, Mr. Andersen, insisted on the real progress that had been made in comparison with what might have been expected in 1970. The Second Report represented "a very flexible formula, having the advantage that it does not exclude any sort of future progress on which States may agree, but avoids setting targets which could appear unrealistically high or remote at the present time," and the Minister added his personal assessment that this pragmatic way of proceeding would definitely prove most fruitful in the long run.

The Second Report remains the main authoritative source on the objectives, organisation and procedure of European political cooperation; while its provisions have subsequently, in specific instances, been modified or expanded (e.g. by the Communiqué of the Heads of Government at their Conference in Paris, December 1974), the text as a whole continues to serve as the basic guideline for EPC activities.

6. THE COPENHAGEN SUMMIT AND THE EUROPEAN IDENTITY

During the latter part of 1973 several important foreign policy questions of direct concern to the Nine came to the fore, providing the procedures as set out in the Second Report with their first major testing period. In particular, three developments should be mentioned: first, the holding in July 1973 of the First stage of the Conference on Security and Cooperation in Europe, and the commencement, in September in Geneva, of the Second stage; secondly, the response of the Nine to the invitation by the United States to consider jointly means whereby the relationship between the Nine and the U.S. could be defined and formalised; and, thirdly, the Middle East war of October 1973 and its consequences. Each of these issues was examined in the political cooperation framework and common positions were adopted. In this process a need was increasingly felt to attempt to define in more concrete terms the identity of the Nine in their relations with other countries. A document on the European Identity was drawn up. This was submitted to the Heads of State or of Government at their meeting in Copenhagen on 14 December 1973.

The object of the document on European Identity was stated as that of enabling the Nine "to achieve a better definition of their relations with other countries and of their responsibilities and the place which they occupy in world affairs." The document went on to identify the fundamental elements of the European Identity, which included the determination shared by the Nine "to defend the principles of respresentative democracy, of the rule of law, of social justice – which is the ultimate goal of economic progress – and of respect for human rights." It then reaffirmed that "the Nine have the political will to succeed in the construction of an united Europe." Referring to the difficulty for any of the Nine to solve alone current international problems, it stated: "international developments and the growing concentration of power and responsibility in the hands of a very small number of great powers mean that Europe must unite and speak increasingly with a single voice if its wants to make itself heard and play its proper rôle in the world."

The second part of the document was devoted to a consideration of the European identity in relation to the world. As the Community progressed towards a common policy in relation to third countries it would act in accordance with the following principles:

"(a) The Nine, acting as a single entity, will strive to promote harmonious and constructive relations with these countries. This should not however jeopardise, hold back or affect the will of the Nine to progress towards European Union within the time limits laid down.

(b) In future when the Nine negotiate collectively with other countries, the institutions and procedures chosen should enable the distinct character of the European entity to be respected.

(c) In bilateral contacts with other countries, the Member States of the Community will increasingly act on the basis of agreed common positions."

The document went on to state, with specific reference to each of the major areas – other European countries and countries associated with the Community, the Mediterranean and African countries, the Middle East, the United States, Japan and Canada, the USSR and the countries of Eastern Europe, China and other Asian countries, Latin America and the developing countries in general – the relationships which the Nine envisaged with the countries of that area.

The document ended with a reaffirmation of the overall objective of political cooperation between the Nine. "In their external relations, the Nine propose progressively to undertake the definition of their identity in relation to other countries or groups of countries. They believe that in so doing they will strengthen their own cohesion and contribute to the framing of a genuinely European foreign policy."

At their meeting in Copenhagen, the Heads of Government also agreed that they should meet more frequently, whenever circumstances required: the initiative for calling the meetings was left to the Presidency. Another decision was that the Foreign Ministers should consider the means by which a common position could be more speedily adopted in times of crisis. Procedures have been worked out subsequently in the political cooperation framework to meet this need. The Heads of Government also expressed the hope that the development of political cooperation would make it possible "to assess crisis situations with the aim of foreseeing them and of defining common positions to meet them."

7. RECENT DEVELOPMENTS

While it would be beyond the scope of the present article to set out in detail on particular issues the manner in which the Nine have jointly responded to all the major world questions in the period since the Copenhagen Summit, it is useful nevertheless to mention some of the main subjects of their cooperation in the past year.

The major problem of the Middle East has been the subject of frequent consultations between the Nine since the October 1973 war. A common position of the Nine on the conflict was elaborated after the Ministerial meeting in Brussels on 6th November 1973 in a statement which set out the principles on which, in the view of the Nine, a peace settlement should be based. These principles included in particular: the inadmissibility of the acquisition of territory by force; the need for Israel to end the territorial occupation which it has maintained since the conflict of 1967; respect for the sovereignty, territorial integrity and independence of every state in the area and the right to live in peace within secure and recognized boundaries; recognition that in the establishment of a just and lasting peace account must be taken of the legitimate rights of the Palestinians. This statement continues to reflect the basic position of the Nine on the Middle East question. The difficult situation in the region, coupled with its geographical proximity to and importance for Europe, make the Middle East an area of particular concern to the Nine and one on which there will be a continuing need for regular consultation between them.

In March 1974, the Nine agreed to begin a comprehensive dialogue with the Arab countries, an initiative which offered the prospect of a new and constructive dimension to the relations between Europe and the Arab world. The dialogue is a long-term undertaking which will embrace a wide area of practical cooperation in the economic, cultural and technical fields. It was proposed that the dialogue would be directed through a joint Euro-Arab Commission at official level under which five working committees at expert level would examine projects in the fields of agriculture, industry, infrastructure, financial cooperation and cultural, technical and scientific cooperation. While the Commission has not yet been convened, a Coordinating Group consisting of the nine member States and representatives of the Commission is undertaking the preparatory work in the different fields on the European side. At the meeting of European and Arab experts scheduled for June 1975, it is expected that there will be a detailed discussion of the concrete content of the dialogue.

Another major political issue affecting the Eastern Mediterranean area is that of Cyprus. Following the coup on the island on 15 July, 1974, the Nine reacted rapidly: on 16 July a joint communique was issued in which the Nine reaffirmed their attachment to the independence of Cyprus and their opposition to any intervention or interference tending to upset it. On 22 July, a further joint statement was issued, asking that the ceasefire should be effectively applied, that there should be cooperation with the U.N. forces and that the constitutional order should be restored in Cyprus, with which the existing *de facto* Government was incompatible.

The continuing crisis on the island led the Nine early this year to consider at length what contribution they could make to facilitate a negotiated solution which would be both equitable and durable. Following the meeting of the Foreign Ministers in Dublin on 13th February, a communication was addressed to the Governments of Cyprus, Greece and Turkey, indicating that the Nine were ready to hold discussions with "representatives of all the interested parties." The Cyprus question was subsequently referred to the Security Council and it was considered within the Nine that the most constructive approach would be to give full encouragement to the efforts of the U.N. Secretary-General, who, under the Security Council's resolution of 12th March, was requested by the Council to undertake a new mission of good offices on the Cyprus problem. The Heads of Government of the Nine at their meeting in Dublin on 10th and 11th March, had adopted a statement expressing the hope that in the context of the discussions then being held at the Security Council in New York, there would be an early resumption of negotiations on the question of Cyprus.

The deteriorating situation in the Portuguese territories in Africa had been kept under review for some time. At their meeting on 10 June 1974, the Foreign Ministers of the Nine welcomed the political developments in Portugal which opened the way to democratisation and which promised to bring to an end the protracted armed conflicts in Portugal's African colonies. In August 1974 the nine Governments announced their recognition of the independence of Guinea-Bissau.

The Nine were prompt to express their support for the new regime in Greece which displaced the colonels and which promised a return to democracy. At their meeting in Paris on 16 September 1974 the Foreign Ministers also made a joint statement welcoming the restoration of political and individual liberties and the process of democratisation in that country.

A topic of particular concern during the first half of 1974 was that of improving arrangements for consultations between the Nine and other countries, especially the U.S., on those issues where the Nine seek to adopt a common position. In April the Foreign Ministers agreed at Gymnich near Bonn on pragmatic arrangements for consultation through the Presidency, in each case where the issue is raised by one of the Nine and where there is a consensus in favour of such consultations.

The C.S.C.E. which was the first subject of political cooperation and which has been of major importance throughout, is now approaching its final phase. Day by day contact between the delegations of the Nine in Geneva, with frequent meetings also of both the Sub-Committee and the ad hoc group, had made it possible to harmonize successfully the various attitudes of the member States so that over the period of the Conference the Nine have pursued an agreed policy and presented common proposals on most of the political, economic and humanitarian issues involved.

The scope of consultations and coordination of foreign policy among the Nine has been extended to cover international issues in all parts of the world. An Asia group was set up in January 1973 to study problems in the Far East. A working group on Latin America was created towards the end of 1973, devoting particular concern to the Chilean refugee problem. The Nine agreed on a joint approach to the Chilean Government on humanitarian questions and all arranged to admit numbers of refugees from Chile to their countries.

The *Paris summit* of December 1974 marked a further stage in the development of political cooperation, emphasising the global nature of issues confronting the member States of the Communities and the need for an overall approach to the problems involved in the construction of Europe and the external problems facing Europe. Henceforth the Heads of Government were to meet at least three times a year, accompanied by their Foreign Ministers, thus intensifying consultation among the Nine on important world issues at the highest levels. The Heads of Government also confirmed that the Ministers for Foreign Affairs might meet within the framework of political cooperation on the same occasion as their meeting in the Council. These measures were intended to ensure "the overall cohesion of the activities of the Communities and the work on political cooperation."

Having in view progress towards European Union, the Paris Communiqué also reaffirmed the determination of the Nine progressively to adopt common positions and put into practice coordinated diplomatic action in all areas of international affairs affecting the interests of the European Community." The coordinating role of the Presidency, acting as spokesman for the Nine, was emphasised. And the important decision was taken to reply to questions from the European Parliament on political cooperation activities having regard to the increasing role of political cooperation in the construction of Europe.

The first meeting of Heads of Government under the new arrangements was held in Dublin under the Irish Presidency in March 1975, and the C.S.C.E. and Cyprus were political cooperation subjects discussed.

8. CONCLUSION

Looking back, the distance travelled since the modest beginning, made in 1970, can be seen to be considerable. The procedures established at the outset have provided a solid framework for the necessary adaptation and improvements which now allow coordination of policies and action on a wide range of world issues.

While the member States of the Communities do not adopt a collective or identical position on all international issues, their approach to these issues is without question showing an ever increasing convergence and on many international problems, and at the United Nations, they now speak more and more with one voice.

The scope of activities under way in political cooperation has expanded regularly since the beginning and is continuing to expand. The existing machinery has enabled this work to go forward in an effective manner; but it has, of course, its limitations. And without doubt, as political cooperation continues to intensify in harmony with the goals which the member States have set themselves, new procedures, imaginative and practical, will be required.

At the negotiating table, in international fora, in crisis situations the Nine are learning to develop the means and the habit of speaking and acting as one on the basis of an identity which derives partly from a shared heritage but mainly from their common interests as members of the European Communities. Internally, political cooperation has already added importantly to the cohesion of thought and action of the member States. The search to define together a new relationship with other areas of the world has in turn helped to mould a new identity among the Nine. Externally, political cooperation continues to face the Nine with the challenge of playing an open and constructive rôle in Europe and the world, consistent with the aims set at the Hagues summit of 1969 of promoting the relaxation of international tensions and a rapprochement among peoples.

These two facets of the process will continue to characterize the contribution which political cooperation has to make towards the overall goal of European unification.

RESUME

La coopération politique européenne (CPE), qui a commencé en 1970, constitue un mode distinct et complémentaire de coopération entre les neuf Etats membres des Communautés. Elle implique, de la part des Neuf, une consultation mutuelle en matière de politique étrangère et, autant que possible, une coordination des points de vue et des actions dans ce domaine. Cette coopération se développe parallèlement aux engagements juridiques pris en vertu des traités de Paris et de Rome. Elle a un caractère intergouvernemental et porte sur des questions qui, tout en étant extérieures au fonctionnement des Communautés, présentent un intérêt commun.

Les procédures mises en oeuvre sont pragmatiques et souples; elles représentent une contribution européenne originale à la technique de la mise au point d'une action concertée.

1. LE SOMMET DE LA HAYE

Au Sommet de La Haye de décembre 1969, les chefs d'Etat ou de gouvernement ,,ont réaffirmé leur foi dans les finalités politiques qui donnent à la Communauté tout son sens et sa portée" et ont chargé les Ministres des Affaires étrangères ,,d'étudier la meilleure manière de réaliser des progrès dans le domaine de l'unification politique, dans la perspective de l'élargissement, et de faire des propositions à ce sujet avant le mois de juillet 1970."

2. LE ,,RAPPORT DE LUXEMBOURG"

En mars 1970, les Ministres ont institué un Comité de fonctionnaires, présidé par un Belge, le Vicomte Davignon, et chargé de synthétiser les différentes propositions des gouvernements. Le rapport de ce comité, présenté en juillet 1970, a été approuvé par les ministres des Affaires étrangères, en octobre, à Luxembourg. Dans la première partie du rapport, on peut lire que le développement des Communautés impose aux Etats membres de renforcer leur coopération politique; ceux-ci devraient s'attacher surtout à coordonner leurs politiques étrangères, ce qui donnerait une impulsion aux Communautés. En second lieu, les Ministres ont annoncé l'intention de leurs gouvernements de coopérer dans le domaine de la politique étrangère, en vue de favoriser une harmonisation de leurs positions et, lorsque cela paraitra possible et souhaitable, de mener une action commune pour ce qui est de toutes les questions importantes de politique étrangère. A cette fin, les Ministres se réuniront deux fois par an; un Comité politique, composé des Directeurs des Affaires politiques des Ministères des Affaires étrangères préparera leurs réunions auxquelles il donnera les suites voulues; il siégera au moins quatre fois par an, et pourra créer des groupes de travail spécialisés. Le pays assumant la présidence des Communautés (qui change tous les six mois) présidera les réunions organisées dans le cadre de la CPE et en assurera le Secrétariat; des ,,correspondants" seront désignés, dans chaque ministère des Affaires étrangères, pour faciliter les communications entre les capitales. La Commission sera consultée sur les questions touchant la C.E.E., et un Colloque réunira, deux fois par an, les Ministres et la Commission politique du Parlement Européen. En outre, une fois par an, le Président fera rapport au Parlement sur l'évolution de la coopération politique.

3. BILAN DE LA PERIODE ALLANT DE NOVEMBRE 1970 A OCTOBRE 1972

La première réunion des six Ministres tenue conformément à la nouvelle procédure eut lieu à Munich en novembre 1970; elle fut suivie, deux semaines plus tard, d'une réunion des Ministres des Dix à Bruxelles. On commença par discuter de la Conférence sur la sécurité et la coopération en Europe, évènement unique et sans précédent, qui posait des problèmes entièrement nouveaux. Les Neuf purent définir une position commune à la CSCE; un sous-comité du Comité politique avait été créé spécialement à cette fin. On fit de même pour le Moyen-Orient; en mai 1971, les Neuf annoncèrent qu'ils avaient arrêté une position commune, sur la base de la Résolution 242 du Conseil de Sécurité, et ils formulèrent en même temps des propositions pour la réouverture du Canal de Suez. Firent également l'objet de consultations, en 1971 et 1972, divers problèmes concernant l'Asie – notamment l'Inde – et le Bassin méditerranéen, la question de la coopération en cas de cataclysme, et celle de la préparation des sessions de l'Assemblée Générale de l'ONU (préparation précédemment assurée dans le cadre de l'U.E.O.).

Le Comité politique, les correspondants et les ambassadeurs des Etats membres dans les pays tiers se réunirent plus fréquemment. En juin 1971, M. Schumann, Ministre français des Affaires étrangères, présenta le premier rapport sur la coopération politique au Parlement Européen, et en novembre, M. Moro, le Ministre italien, ouvrit le premier colloque avec la Commission politique du Parlement Européen. A partir de janvier 1972, les Etats candidats participèrent aux divers comités.

4. LE SOMMET DE PARIS, OCTOBRE 1972

Les participants au sommet de Paris, qui a consacré l'élargissement de la Communauté, ont déclaré que l'Europe devrait être capable de faire entendre sa voix dans les affaires mondiales et de fournir une contribution à la mesure de ses ressources humaines, intellectuelles et matérielles. Ils ont estimé que la CPE avait bien débuté, mais qu'il fallait encore l'intensifier; à cette fin, ils ont chargé les ministres des Affaires étrangères de se réunir quatre fois (et non plus deux fois) par an et, en outre, d'établir, pour juin 1973, un deuxième rapport sur le renforcement de la coopération politique.

5. LE DEUXIEME RAPPORT

Ce rapport établi au cours du premier semestre de 1973 et adopté en juillet à Copenhague,

1) se félicitait des progrès réalisés à la suite du rapport de Luxembourg, et relevait que ,,la collégialité européenne tend à devenir une ligne de force dans la politique internationale";

2) établissait des procédures pour les réunions trimestrielles – préparées par le Comité politique – des ministres des Affaires étrangères;

3) élargissait les attributions du Groupe des correspondants et des groupes de travail spécialisés;

4) complétait les dispositions relatives à l'information des ambassadeurs auprès des Etats membres, et prévoyait l'établissement de communications directes entre les ministères des Affaires étrangères;

5) élargissait les fonctions de la Présidence, compte-tenu de l'absence d'un Secrétariat permanent;

6) prévoyait quatre colloques par an avec la Commission politique du Parlement. La distinction était maintenue entre la coopération politique, qui traite sur le plan intergouvernemental de problèmes de politique internationale, et les activités communautaires, qui découlent du traité de Rome; la Commission continuerait d'être consultée sur les questions ayant une incidence sur les activités communautaires.

6. LE SOMMET DE COPENHAGUE ET L'IDENTITE EUROPEENNE

Ces arrangements furent mis à l'épreuve à l'occasion de trois événements qui survinrent pendant la deuxième moitié de 1973: l'ouverture de la CSCE; une demande des Etats-Unis tendant à définir les relations entre les Etats-Unis et les Neuf; les conflit du Moyen-Orient en octobre 1973. A la suite de ces événements, une Déclaration sur l'identité européenne fut adoptée lors du Sommet de Copenhague de décembre 1973.

Cette déclaration énonçait les fondements de l'identité européenne, au nombre desquels figure la détermination des Neuf de sauvegarder la démocratie représentative, le règne de la loi, la justice sociale et les droits de l'homme. Elle réaffirmait la volonté politique des Neuf de mener à bien la construction européenne et ajoutait que la concentration croissante des pouvoirs entre les mains des super-puissances implique que l'Europe s'unisse et parle d'une seule voix, si elle veut jouer le rôle mondial qui lui revient. La Déclaration poursuivait en disant que, lors des négociations qui mettront en présence les Neuf, collectivement, et d'autres pays, les Neuf respecteront le caractère spécifique de l'entité européenne, et que dans leurs contacts bilatéraux, les pays membres de la Communauté se baseront dans une mesure croissante sur des positions communes établies entre eux. A la lumière de ces principes, elle définissait les rapports que les Neuf envisagent d'entretenir avec chacune des principales régions du monde.

7. DEVELOPPEMENTS RECENTS

Dans le cadre du système de coopération politique ainsi instauré entre eux, les Neuf se sont fréquemment concertés et ont, dans une large mesure, adopté des positions communes: tel a été le cas à propos du Moyen-Orient, depuis la guerre d'octobre 1973 (déclaration de Bruxelles de novembre 1973) ; à propos d'un dialogue avec les pays arabes (position définie en mars 1974, s'accompagnant, notamment, de la proposition d'instituer une Commission mixte euro-arabe) ; à propos de Chypre, après le coup d'Etat de juillet 1974 (deux déclarations communes au courant de ce mois, suivie d'une communication commune, adoptée à Dublin, en février 1975, à l'adresse des trois gouvernements intéressés) ; à propos des événements survenus dans les territoires portugais d'Afrique (reconnaissance simultanée de l' indépendance de la Guinée-Bissau, août 1974) ; à propos, enfin, du nouveau régime démocratique de la Grèce (déclaration commune en septembre 1974). Des groupes distincts ont été créés en 1973 pour procéder à des consultations sur les problèmes de l'Extrême-Orient et de l'Amérique latine; une démarche commune a été entreprise auprès du Gouvernement chilien, au sujet de questions humanitaires, et il a été décidé d'admettre les réfugiés chiliens dans tous les pays de la Communauté. Des consultations ont eu lieu en permanence sur la CSCE, et elles ont conduit à formuler des propositions communes sur la plupart des questions soulevées lors de cette Conférence.

Le Sommet de Paris de décembre 1974 a marqué une nouvelle étape dans la coopération politique; il y a été décidé que les chefs de gouvernement se réuniraient, trois fois par an, en conseil européen, accompagnés de leurs ministres des Affaires étrangères, lesquels continueraient, par ailleurs, de se rencontrer dans le cadre de la CPE. Il y a encore été décidé, pour promouvoir l'union européenne, d'arrêter des positions communes et de mettre en oeuvre une diplomatique concertée dans tous les domaines qui affectent la Communauté. La première réunion organisée selon cette nouvelle procédure s'est tenue à Dublin en mars 1975; les discussions ont porté sur la CSCE et sur Chypre.

8. CONCLUSION

De grands progrès ont été accomplis depuis 1970. On observe une convergence croissante des politiques des Neuf sur de nombreux problèmes internationaux, y compris ceux qui sont discutés aux Nations Unies. Les Neuf apprennent à se doter des moyens et à prendre l'habitude de parler et d'agir collectivement, comme les y engagent les intérêts communs qui sont les leurs en tant que membres des Communautés européennes. Les efforts des Neuf pour redéfinir, ensemble, leur relations avec les autres régions du monde ont contribué à forger entre eux une nouvelle identité; la coopération politique apporte sa propre contribution à l'oeuvre globale d'unification européenne.

LES PERSPECTIVES ENERGETIQUES A MOYEN ET A LONG TERMES

par

GERARD ELDIN*

S'il est un domaine dans lequel les prévisions sont aléatoires, c'est bien celui de l'énergie. Qu'il s'agisse de l'évaluation des réserves de combustibles fossiles, des perspectives de l'offre et de la demande, et, plus encore, de l'avenir de la technologie, on n'en finirait pas de dénombrer les erreurs de diagnostic et de pronostic.

Cependant, la prévision est une nécessité: pour les entreprises de ce secteur qui ont à prendre des décisions portant sur des investissements particulièrement coûteux et amortissables sur de longues périodes de temps; pour les Gouvernements aussi, eu égard au rôle essentiel de l'énergie comme facteur de croissance et de puissance, et aux problèmes que son utilisation peut poser pour la société.

Il faut donc tenter de prévoir, même s'il est difficile de prédire. Ici, comme dans d'autres domaines, la prévision ne doit pas être un but en soi, mais être asservie à sa fonction la plus noble qui est de mieux informer l'action, étant entendu que la décision politique peut elle-même puissamment influer sur l'avenir prévisible.

C'est à cette catégorie de prévisions qu'appartient le dernier essai en date à l'OCDE, publié récemment sous le titre „Perspectives énergétiques jusqu'en 1985"[1]. Cet exercice ne se situe pas, en effet, dans la ligne des prévisions précédentes, compte tenu des particularités de la situation actuelle, dominée par la substantielle augmentation des prix du pétrole. Sur la base de diverses hypothèses concernant le prix du pétrole, il met en évidence un certain nombre d'évolutions spontanées résultant du jeu des forces du marché, et vise à explorer les marges d'action dont disposent

---

* M. Gérard Eldin, Secrétaire Général adjoint de l'Organisation de Coopération et de Développement Economiques, s'exprime ici en son nom personnel et les opinions qu'il avance ne sauraient engager l'OCDE.

[1] Perspectives énergétiques jusqu'en 1985 – un rapport du Secrétaire Général – OCDE, Paris, 1974.

les responsables pour agir sur la production, la consommation et les échanges d'énergie.

A partir de cette évaluation, le rapport tente de répondre aux deux principales questions que les Gouvernements des pays membres de l'OCDE se sont posées au début de la crise énergétique, à savoir: comment et à quel prix l'approvisionnement en énergie de nos économies peut-il être assuré au cours des 10 années à venir? et quelles sont les implications économiques et monétaires de la structure d'approvisionnement envisagée?

Dès le moment où cet exercice a été entrepris (environ un an avant le déclenchement de la crise de septembre 1973) la nécessité avait été reconnue de compléter la prévision à moyen terme par une étude à plus long terme intéressant la recherche et le développement en matière d'énergie. Cette étude vient également d'être publiée.[1]

En se fondant principalement sur ces travaux de l'OCDE, on voudrait ici présenter quelques données et réflexions sur les perspectives énergétiques à moyen et long terme. Ce découpage temporel s'impose, tant pour des raisons pratiques (notamment le fait que la plupart des prévisions d'ensemble s'arrêtent en 1985) que pour des raisons de fond, à savoir que les facteurs qui déterminent l'évolution des dix prochaines années ne sont pas les mêmes que ceux qui conditionnent l'avenir plus lointain, à l'horizon de la fin du XXème Siècle ou de la première moitié du XXIème Siècle.

PERSPECTIVES 1985

La crise du pétrole

Il est significatif que tous les exercisces de prévision effectués depuis la guerre dans les pays occidentaux concernant le marché de l'énergie aient reposé sur l'hypothèse d'un potentiel de production quasi-illimité à moyen terme, et n'aient fait qu'une place très réduite aux considérations de prix. Les dernières vingt cinq années resteront, en effet, dans l'histoire économique comme une sorte d'âge d'or – d'autres diront „âge d'imprévoyance" – caracté-

[1] Science et Technologie pour l'Energie, OCDE, Paris, 1975.

risé par l'existence d'une énergie disponible sans limites et à bas prix. Tout au plus, était-il alors nécessaire de faire des ,,études de marché" destinées à évaluer le volume et la structure de la demande et à adapter la production des autres sources d'énergie à celle, dominante, des hydrocarbures.

Cette période a pris fin du jour où, au ,,marché d'acheteurs," a succédé un ,,marché de vendeurs," et où les pays producteurs de pétrole, groupés au sein d'un cartel efficace, ont pris conscience du pouvoir que leur donnait le contrôle d'une ressource essentielle pour l'économie mondiale. En nationalisant les puits, en contrôlant la production et les échanges, ils pouvaient aussi, semblait-il, fixer unilatéralement les prix de manière à maximiser la rente pétrolière et à ménager leurs ressources pour l'avenir. Mais la hausse importante des prix du pétrole ne peut pas ne pas fortement réagir sur la consommation et sur le développement de sources alternatives.

Il est pertinent d'examiner en quoi le marché du pétrole s'est comporté différemment de celui des autres matières premières.

Tout d'abord, au cours de la décennie 1960–70, son rythme de production et, dans une large mesure, son prix, étaient soumis au contrôle d'un nombre relativement restreint de compagnies pétrolières internationales qui possédaient des concessions pour la mise en valeur des réserves mondiales prouvées, situées principalement au Proche-Orient, et dont le volume augmentait rapidement. La stratégie des ,,majors" a été fondée sur les bas prix résultant de la compétition entre pays producteurs. Ainsi a été assurée une exploitation aussi rapide que possible des gisements, permettant de bénéficier au maximum des économies d'échelle, tant en nature de production que de transport. Ce n'est que lorsque le boom économique a atteint son point culminant, entre 1970 et 1973, avec un essor explosif et simultané de la demande dans presque toutes les économies industrielles, que la situation s'est inversée. Du fait, notamment, que les Etats-Unis étaient passés de la position d'exportateur net à celle d'importateur net, (on prévoyait avant la crise que, vers 1985, les Etats-Unis importeraient 50% de leur consommation de pétrole), toutes les conditions étaient réunies au milieu de 1973 pour qu'une pression considérable à la hausse soit exercée sur le prix du pétrole à mesure que le groupe des pays de l'OPEP éprouvait sa force et sa cohésion. La plupart des observateurs, dans les pays industrialisés, s'attendaient donc à une série de hausses de prix pendant le reste de la décennie, mais nul n'avait prévu qu'elle serait aussi forte et aussi brutale.

A la faveur d'une conjoncture politique très particulière (la guerre du Kippour), les pays de l'OPEP ont réussi, on le sait, à imposer des prix f.o.b. du pétrole variant entre 8 dollars environ et plus de 13 dollars le baril, suivant la qualité, la teneur en soufre et la proximité des marchés, et suivant qu'il s'agissait de brut concession ou de brut participation. Compte tenu du degré plus élevé de participation qui a été progressivement imposé par les pays producteurs, le prix du pétrole brut importé a continué à augmenter au cours de l'année 1974 pour atteindre le niveau de 10 à 11 dollars le baril à la fin de l'année.

Si donc il a pu surprendre par son ampleur, ce retournement était loin d'être imprévu. Les experts les plus perspicaces – au sein des compagnies pétrolières, des administrations nationales et des organisations internationales – n'avaient pas ménagé les mises en garde à partir de 1970–71. C'est aussi dans cette optique que le Secrétaire Général de l'OCDE invitait, dès 1972, les pays membres à réviser leur évaluation des perspectives énergétiques.

On s'attachera, dans les pages qui suivent, à présenter la problématique, les résultats et les implications pour la politique énergétique de cette évaluation.

La problématique des prévisions à moyen terme

On a observé, jusqu'à présent, dans les pays industrialisés, une étroite corrélation entre la croissance de la demande globale d'énergie et celle du produit intérieur brut (PIB), de sorte que la plupart des prévisions de la consommation d'énergie reposaient sur des hypothèses de croissance probable du PIB et de ses divers éléments constitutifs. Le rapport de la consommation d'énergie au PIB a varié à un rythme relativement lent. Cependant, la baisse du prix réel de l'énergie, et notamment du pétrole, a incité à utiliser des méthodes de production et à adopter des modes de vie relativement dispendieux en énergie. Ce phénomène, associé à un accroissement rapide de la demande d'énergie électrique, à fait augmenter le rapport de la demande d'énergie au PIB dans les principaux pays industrialisés, notamment depuis 1965.

Le quadruplement brutal du prix du pétrole (et l'augmentation consécutive des prix d'autres formes d'énergie dans les pays de l'OCDE), a modifié les perspectives, non seulement quant à la relation entre la consommation d'énergie et la croissance économique, mais encore à l'égard de la croissance de la production elle-même.

Selon les prévisions établies avant la hausse du prix du pétrole, le taux de croissance moyen du PIB des pays de l'OCDE jusqu'en 1985 devait être de l'ordre de 5% par an. Les hypothèses retenues dans la dernière étude ont, en fait, pris en compte des taux un peu plus faibles pour la période 1980–85 que pour la période 1971–80, notamment pour le Japon et pour la Communauté Economique Européenne. Néanmoins, ces hypothèses sont entachées d'une incertitude notable que seule une nouvelle évaluation détaillée des perspectives de croissance permettra de réduire.

Ainsi qu'on l'a déjà noté, les études effectuées dans le passé ne faisaient généralement pas intervenir de manière explicite le prix de l'énergie comme facteur de la demande d'énergie, l'influence de ce dernier étant incorporée implicitement dans le rapport de la consommation d'énergie au PIB. Toutefois, lorsque les rapports entre les prix de l'énergie et ceux d'autres produits ou facteurs se modifient de manière importante et brutale (comme c'est actuellement le cas), ce paramètre prend une importance centrale.

Dans la mesure où les mécanismes du marché jouent librement, la hausse des prix du pétrole brut fait monter les prix des produits dérivés du pétrole et le prix des formes d'énergie concurrentes, à l'égard desquels le prix du pétrole apparaît comme un prix directeur. Lorsque les prix de l'énergie augmentent beaucoup plus rapidement que les autres prix, on peut s'attendre à ce que des efforts soient entrepris pour introduire plus d'efficacité dans l'utilisation de l'énergie et réduire les gaspillages. A court terme, les économies seront sans doute faibles, étant donné qu'il faut utiliser les installations consommatrices d'énergie, mises en place à l'époque de l'énergie bon marché. A moyen terme, et plus encore à long terme, ou peut, en revanche, escompter un renouvellement du capital qui permettra de réaliser des économies substantielles d'énergie, d'autant plus grandes que l'on aura sans doute mis au point, dans l'intervalle, de nouvelles techniques à cet effet. Cet aspect des projections a été traité dans l'étude de l'OCDE, par l'application de relations globales d'élasticité, ajustées pour tenir compte de diverses contraintes d'ordre technique et politique. L'analyse de la demande a naturellement été diversifiée par nature d'utilisation et par produit.

En ce qui concerne l'offre, les projections globales résultent de l'agrégation de bilans énergétiques établis pour chaque région dans les diverses hypothèses de prix. On a pu ainsi bénéficier d'un ensemble de travaux menés au plan national. Sans entrer dans la technique des prévisions, disons seulement que les productions indigènes des différentes catégories d'énergie ont été ajustées entre elles au moyen d'un certain nombre de paramètres, notamment les coûts de production estimés, compte tenu naturellement des programmes d'investissement dàjà décidés ou en cours de réalisation.

Enfin, les importations de pétrole par les pays de l'OCDE ont été traitées comme un paramètre résiduel, obtenu par différence entre la demande et la production indigène d'énergie pour chaque zone et dans les différentes hypothèses de prix. On a donc admis implicitement que les pays consommateurs pourraient obtenir tout le pétrole dont ils auraient besoin au prix du marché.

Trois séries de bilans énergétiques ont été établies, correspondant à trois hypothèses:

- une hypothèse de base, fondée en grande partie sur les prévisions établies avant la crise d'octobre 1973;
- une hypothèse fondée sur un prix du pétrole f.o.b. de 6 dollars le baril, en dollars 1972;
- une hypothèse fondée sur un prix du pétrole de 9 dollars, sous les mêmes spécifications.

Les experts ont estimé que ces valeurs de 6 et 9 dollars constituaient des limites raisonnables entre lesquelles les prix effectifs du pétrole en 1980 et 1985 pourraient se situer, compte tenu des coûts des énergies de substitution.

Les résultats les plus intéressants sont peut-être ceux qui correspondent à l'hypothèse forte, car 9 dollars 1972 correspondaient à environ 10.80 dollars aux prix de fin 1974, soit un niveau peu différent de celui qui était effectivement pratique à cette époque.

Quelques résultats

Les projections font ressortir que, dans cette hypothèse:

1. La consommation globale d'énergie augmenterait au taux annuel de 3,5 à 4% jusqu'en 1985, en réduction sensible sur la croissance prévue antérieurement, qui était de l'ordre de 5%.

2. La zone de l'OCDE couvrirait, au moyen de sa production propre, près de 80% de ses besoins en énergie en 1985, contre 65% en 1972, alors que la poursuite de la tendance passée aurait conduit à un taux d'auto-approvisionnement de 55% seulement en fin de période.

3. Cependant, l'amélioration du bilan des échanges énergétiques serait très inégale selon les grandes régions. Tandis que les Etats-Unis retrouveraient vers 1985 une position d'exportateur net, les pays européens membres de l'OCDE dépendraient encore des importations pour près de 60% de leurs besoins, et le Japon pour 80% environ. L'Europe et la Japon connaîtraient donc une diversification de leurs approvisionnements, sans accéder, cependant, à l'indépendance énergétique.

4. Une modification sensible de la structure par produits de la consommation d'énergie se produirait au cours de la période étudiée, dans le sens d'une réduction de l'importance relative du pétrole, de l'apparition de l'énergie nucléaire comme facteur d'appoint important et d'un arrêt de la régression du charbon.

Part en % des différentes formes d'énergie dans la consommation globale des pays de l'OCDE

	1972	*1985* (hypothèse 9 dollars)
Charbon	19,3	18,3
Pétrole	55,4	43,5
Gaz naturel	21,5	22,0
Energie nucléaire	1,0	13,4
Energie hydro et géothermique	2,8	2,8
Total	100,0	100,0
Electricité (% de la consommation finale)	22,4	17,7

5. Enfin, le ralentissement de la croissance de la consommation d'énergie et l'accroissement de la production dans la zone de l'OCDE se traduiraient par une réduction en volume des importations de pétrole, dont le niveau pourrait, dès 1980, être inférieur à celui de 1972 (1100 millions de tonnes contre 1200 environ), et se stabiliser ensuite. Pour l'ensemble de la période étudiée, il y aurait donc stabilisation des importations alors que l'on prévoyait avant la crise une augmentation de plus de 100%.

Incertitudes et marges de souplesse

Est-il besoin de dire que de telles prévisions fondées sur des calculs économétriques et postulant, de ce fait, le libre jeu des forces du marché, sont entachées d'une grande marge d'incertitude?

A cet égard, deux questions viennent immédiatement à l'esprit:

- quelles sont les chances que les hypothèses économiques retenues se réalisent effectivement?
- dans quelle mesure une politique active de l'énergie peut-elle influer sur ces résultats?

En ce qui concerne les hypothèses économiques, on a déjà noté que le taux de croissance retenu dans les calculs avait toute chance de pécher par excès, ne serait-ce qu'en raison de la perte, en 1974 et 1975, de deux ans de croissance pour la plupart des pays de l'OCDE. Il s'y ajoute que la hausse brutale des prix de l'énergie est suceptible, par les effets structurels qu'elle engendre, de conduire à une réduction du taux de croissance global au moins pendant la phase d'ajustement. La prise en considération de ces phénomènes n'altère pas, cependant, le sens des prévisions: elle conforte, au contraire, la conclusion selon laquelle les pays de l'OCDE devraient largement s'affranchir, d'ici à 1985, de la dépendance dans laquelle ils se trouvent vis-à-vis des pays producteurs de pétrole. L'analyse de sensibilité effectuée par les experts de l'OCDE montre que, si le niveau de la PIB devait, en 1985, être inférieur de 5% au niveau prévu, les importations de pétrole pourraient elles-mêmes être réduites d'environ 10% (11% dans l'hypothèse de 6 dollars et 8.2% dans l'hypothèse de 9 dollars).

Il est plus difficile de dire si, dans le domaine des prix, l'hypothèse „haute" (9 dollars 1972 le baril), constitue un plafond ou, au contraire, la perspective la plus réaliste. On se bornera à noter que, depuis le début de 1975, le prix du pétrole a connu une réduction en valeur réelle. En effet, la quasi stabilité du prix nominal du pétrole s'est accompagnée d'une certaine dépréciation du dollar et surtout d'une augmentation non négligeable des prix dans la zone de l'OCDE.

La poursuite de ce phénomène de réduction du prix du pétrole en valeur réelle, rendu possible par la remarquable détente du marché – elle-même imputable à la conjoncture économique et à des conditions climatiques exceptionnellement favorables dans les pays consommateurs – pourrait conduire à un niveau réel de prix plus proche de 6 dollars le baril que de 9 dollars, en fin de période. Il convient, cependant, de tenir compte, non seulement des réactions probables des pays exportateurs qui ont, jusqu'à présent, été capables d'ajuster la production au niveau de la demande, mais aussi du fait que le coût des énergies de substitution aura tendance à augmenter en dollars courants, constituant un frein à la baisse du prix du pétrole.

Une politique active de l'énergie

Une politique active de l'énergie peut contribuer à créer les conditions dans lesquelles les effets de marché se feront pleinement sentir. Elle peut même, dans une certaine mesure, les accentuer.

En dehors des dispositions qui peuvent se révéler nécessaires pour faire face à une réduction brutale des approvisionnements (stockage – système de répartition, etc.), les deux domaines principaux dans lesquels cette politique peut s'exercer dans le but de réduire la dépendance énergétique sont l'utilisation rationnelle de l'énergie et le développement des sources d'énergie nationales. Ce sont, par excellence, les objectifs de l'Agence Internationale pour l'Energie, créée en novembre 1974, à laquelle participent dix-huit pays Membres de l'OCDE.

Utiliser plus rationnellement l'énergie

L'utilisation rationnelle de l'énergie vise à réduire la quantité d'énergie consommée, sans diminution appréciable du PIB et sans détérioration marquée du niveau de vie général ou du niveau de confort individuel. Elle peut prendre la forme d'une réduction des gaspillages (définis comme des usages inutiles), d'un accroissement des rendements de conversion de l'énergie et des utilisations finales, et d'un changement de modes de vie.

Il est à noter que, dans le passé récent, les usages qui se sont le plus développés sont ceux qui ont le rendement le plus faible (transport automobile et climatisation de l'air). Ainsi définie, l'utilisation rationnelle de l'énergie se distingue assez nettement des limitations de la demande imposées par les pouvoirs publics dans des situations d'urgence. Parmi les domaines dans lesquels l'utilisation rationnelle de l'énergie peut avoir les incidences les plus importantes, on peut citer le chauffage et la climatisation des immeubles, le chauffage et le refroidissement de l'eau, la chaleur industrielle, le transport et la conversion de l'énergie électrique.

Le ralentissement, grâce à des mesures d'économie, de la croissance de la demande d'énergie totale est, à divers égards, plus avantageux que l'accroissement de la production nationale d'énergie, et ce, pour les raisons suivantes:

- il comporte des délais de mise en oeuvre plus courts, et donc incidences plus rapides sur les importations d'énergie;
- il est moins coûteux, à résultat égal, pour la collectivité que le développement de sources alternatives d'énergie;
- il exerce des effets positifs sur l'environnement.

Les économies totales d'énergie susceptibles d'être réalisées dans les pays de l'OCDE, sans que l'on ait recours à des mesures exceptionnelles de restriction autoritaire de la demande, ont été estimées, dans le Rapport sur les Perspectives Energétiques 1985, à 15–20% des besoins d'énergie primaire antérieurement prévus pour 1985, soit un chiffre de l'ordre de 900 millions à un milliard de tonnes d'équivalent-pétrole.

On estime que la réduction de la consommation résultant d'une politique d'économies pourrait être de 15% environ pour l'industrie, de 15 à 20% pour les transports et de 20 à 25% pour le secteur résidentiel et commercial.

Ces chiffres pré-supposent, de la part des gouvernements, une volonté soutenue, non seulement d'accepter les conséquences de la hausse des prix de l'énergie, mais aussi d'exploiter toutes les possibilités existantes. Au delà des économies à courte échéance, trois domaines méritent de retenir particulièrement l'attention:

- les économies de chauffage résultant d'une meilleure isolation thermique des bâtiments,
- la modification des sytèmes de transport et notamment le développement du transport en commun dans les grandes agglomérations,
- les techniques de récupération de chaleur, tant dans l'industrie et les foyers domestiques qu'à la sortie des centrales électriques classiques et nucléaires.

Malgré l'intérêt primordial qui s'attache à une politique d'économie d'énergie, il est permis de se demander si le public acceptera facilement le changement d'habitudes qu'elle implique, particulièrement dans les pays qui ont atteint un taux très élevé de consommation d'énergie par habitant.

Développer des ressources alternatives

Les possibilités de développement des ressources énergétiques intérieures de la zone de l'OCDE sont considérables, même si l'on s'en tient à la technologie existant actuellement. Ainsi, en prenant pour base 1972, on estime que, d'ici à 1985, la production de pétrole et de gaz pourrait doubler, celle de charbon augmenter de 65% (et davantage s'il est possible de lui trouver des débouchés); celle d'énergie hydro-électrique et géothermique de 67%; quant à la production d'énergie nucléaire, elle pourrait être multipliée par 20 et fournir jusqu'à 34% de l'électricité produite en 1985. Là encore, le potentiel disponible est très variable entre les différents pays de la zone de l'OCDE, qui sont très inégalement dotés en ressources naturelles.

Ainsi, les Etats-Unis – qui sont encore au premier rang des producteurs de pétrole – peuvent compter à moyen terme sur la récupération des huiles secondaires et tertiaires, sur les gisements de l'Alaska et sur le développement des groupes „offshore." A plus long terme, ils disposent d'énormes gisements de schistes bitumineux qui continuent de poser cependant des problèmes techniques d'exploitation, ainsi que de charbon qui, pour une large part, est disponible dans des mines à ciel ouvert.

De même, le Canada bénéficie de virtualités importantes tant en ce qui concerne le pétrole et le gaz naturel que l'exploitation des sables asphaltiques de l'Alberta, l'uranium, le charbon bon marché et l'énergie hydro-électrique abondante.

En Europe, c'est surtout de l'exploitation des gisements de la Mer du Nord que l'on attend une certaine amélioration du bilan énergétique, qui bénéficiera principalement à la Norvège et au Royaume-Uni. Bien que les prévisions demeurent incertaines, elles ont, depuis quelques années, été constamment révisées en hausse et l'on peut avancer que la contribution de la Mer du Nord pour le pétrole pourrait se situer aux environs de 300 millions de tonnes en 1985, ce qui correspond à la production de pétrole de l'Iran en 1974.

Notons encore le potentiel, non négligeable, de l'Australie en ce qui concerne le pétrole (2,3 milliards de barils de réserves prouvées), et surtout le charbon.

Les pays qui ne disposent pas de ressources fossiles abondantes devront, à l'évidence, faire une part plus grande à l'énergie nucléaire. Tel est, par exemple, le cas de la France, qui prévoit de couvrir près d'un quart de ses besoins d'énergie en 1985 par l'énergie nucléaire.

L'éventail des mesures que les pouvoirs publics pourraient prendre afin de favoriser l'accroissement de la production intérieure d'énergie est beaucoup plus large que dans le cas des économies d'énergie, de même qu'est beaucoup plus grande la complexité des interactions susceptibles de se produire entre les objectifs consistant à accroître la production et d'autres objectifs en matière de politique économique.

Le développement de sources nouvelles d'énergie va requérir, dans les années qui viennent, des investissements massifs dont on peut redouter qu'ils excèdent, dans certains cas, les moyens des entreprises privées.

Dans l'étude sur les Perspectives 1985, les besoins cumulés en capital nécessaires, dans l'hypothèse 9 dollars, à la production d'énergie „intérieure" – qui comprennent des investissements pour le renouvellement des équipements, la conversion, le transport et la distribution – ont été estimés à 1.100 milliards de dollars (en dollars de 1972) pour la période 1974–1985. De ce fait, la part de la formation brute de capital fixe consacrée à l'énergie serait très sensiblement accrue.

Une des conditions pour que ces investissements se réalisent est que les perspectives de prix soient relativement bien assurées. Il y a là un dilemme car, si des mesures n'étaient pas prises pour assurer la rentabilité des investissements sur une période convenable, une brusque diminution des prix du pétrole pourrait compromettre les efforts entrepris dans certains pays pour accroître leur potentiel de production et entraîner un gaspillage de capitaux. Aussi, les investisseurs privés hésitent-ils à s'engager, sachant que les coûts de production du pétrole dans les zones les mieux placées, notamment au Proche-Orient, demeurent très bas, et que les pays producteurs disposent d'une très large marge de manoeuvre dans la fixation de leurs prix. Ils veulent, en effet, obtenir l'assurance que le facteur de risque lié à leurs investissements n'excédera pas sensiblement celui qui caractérise la plupart des investissements commerciaux. Aussi bien, des garanties pourraient se révéler nécessaires pour que les investissements se réalisent avec toute l'ampleur désirable. Parmi les instruments susceptibles d'être utilisés à cet effet figurent des mesures de nature à influer sur les échanges dans le domaine de l'énergie, l'établissement d'un „prix minimum de sauvegarde" pour le pétrole importé, des garanties applicables aux prix à la production d'énergie d'origine domestique, et des mesures visant à assurer une distribution équitable de la rente tirée des ressources énergétiques. Un effort de très grande ampleur devra également être fait sur le plan de la recherche et du développement, tant dans le domaine des technologies de production et de transformation que dans celui de la protection de l'environnement.

Comme le délai nécessaire à la production d'énergie à partir de la plupart des sources nouvelles varie entre cinq ans environ et plus de dix ans, il est, en définitive, peu probable que l'action menée en vue d'accélérer le rythme de développement permette de dépasser sensiblement les niveaux de production envisagés dans les projections, mais elle permettra d'utiliser plus complètement ce potentiel.

En résumé, les perspectives énergétiques à moyen terme ne sont pas des perspectives de pénurie, mais des perspectives de restructuration du marché impliquant une politique plus active des pays de l'OCDE, sur le plan national, et un renforcement sensible de la coopération entre eux, dont la création de l'Agence Internationale pour l'Energie est la manifestation la plus évidente.

D'ici à 1985, les grands pays importateurs d'énergie ont encore devant eux quelques années difficiles. Jusqu'en 1978, ils doivent surtout compter sur une politique très stricte d'économies pour éviter que la reprise économique, au sortir de la plus grande récession de l'après-guerre, ne provoque de nouvelles tensions. A partir de là, la situation devrait s'améliorer progressivement. Il est clair, cependant, que, malgré tous les efforts pour développer d'autres formes d'énergie, le pétrole restera encore, au cours de cette période, la principale source – couvrant, en 1985, près de 45% des besoins de la zone OCDE – et donc que l'évolution de ce marché particulier demeurera une variable stratégique.

Au cours de cette période de transition, les pays industrialisés devront maîtriser les conséquences économiques de la hausse des prix du pétrole: ajustements structurels résultant d'une nouvelle structure des coûts, accroissement massif des besoins d'investissement dans les industries productrices d'énergie, et surtout, déséquilibres des balances de paiements dûs au fait que les pays producteurs seront dans l'incapacité de dépenser, sous forme d'importation supplémentaires, la totalité de leurs revenus. Ces problèmes sont d'une ampleur sans précédent. Ils impliquent, en particulier, un endettement croissant des pays de l'OCDE d'ici à 1980. Néanmoins, ils ne paraissent pas impossibles à maîtriser. Les études les plus récentes permettent d'envisager, avec un degré raisonnable de certitude, que la balance globale des opérations courantes de la zone de l'OCDE pourrait revenir à l'équilibre aux alentours de 1980 et s'améliorer ensuite.

Est-ce à dire que le problème énergétique aura trouvé, en 1985, sa solution définitive et qu'il sera alors oublié? Il serait bien présomptueux de le dire. En effet, la restructuration du marché énergétique qui est envisagée pour la zone de l'OCDE est fondée sur un effort difficile d'économies, sur l'exploitation accélérée de sources coûteuses et sur le maintien d'un volant important d'importations de pétrole (entre 1 et 1,5 milliard de tonnes en 1985, dans l'hypothèse d'une continuation des politiques énergétiques actuelles).

Si l'on retient un horizon plus lointain, d'autres facteurs doivent être pris en considération.

PERSPECTIVES AU DELA DE 1985

Les limites du développement énergétique

Au delà de 1985, la prévision doit céder le pas à la prospective car les incertitudes non seulement s'ajoutent mais se cumulent. Du point de vue qui nous intéresse ici, il n'est plus possible d'extrapoler des tendances, car ce n'est plus seulement l'approvisionnement en énergie qui est en question mais, semble-t-il, la croissance économique elle-même.

La parution, en 1972, du rapport „Halte à la Croissance,"[1] préparé par une équipe du M.I.T. pour le Club de Rome, a marqué un certain tournant dans la conception des stratégies à long terme du développement mondial. Dans ce rapport, les limites physiques du globe étaient évaluées à l'aide de calculs complexes et la croissance exponentielle des sociétés industrialisées était jugée comme incompatible avec la nature finie des ressources naturelles de notre planète. Si justifiés que puissent paraître le sceptiscisme et les critiques avec lesquels la vision apocalyptique du Club de Rome a été accueillie par les différents milieux, il n'en reste pas moins qu'aucune perspective à long terme ne peut plus ignorer ce cri d'alarme, même si la croissance de la civilisation industrielle se heurte d'abord aux limites liées à ses choix économiques et politiques bien avant d'être confrontée à l'épuisement des ressources de la planète.

La crise de l'énergie qui a suivi l'embargo pétrolier d'octobre 1973 a donné aux prévisions du Club de Rome une résonance nouvelle, bien que cette crise, on l'a vu, résultât de décisions politiques plutôt que d'une pénurie réelle. En matière d'énergie précisément, le rapport du M.I.T. prévoyait qu'au rythme de croissance du passé, et en supposant une multiplication par cinq des réserves connues, certaines sources d'énergie seraient épuisées relativement vite: d'ici 49 ans pour le gaz naturel, 50 ans pour le pétrole et d'ici 150 ans pour le charbon.

Pour l'énergie d'origine nucléaire, il est vrai que le rapport admettait que les réserves de matières fissiles seraient presque

[1] Meadows, Randers et Behrens, *Halte à la Croissance*, Fayard, Paris 1972. Traduit de *The Limits to Growth*, Universe Books, New York 1972.

illimitées grâce à l'utilisation des réacteurs surrégénérateurs et à l'extraction d'uranium à partir des roches à faible teneur, mais il estimait que des quantités considérables d'énergie nucléaire ne pourraient pas, à elles seules, résoudre le problème énergétique, car d'autres goulets d'étranglement pourraient bien apparaître du point de vue des ressources financières et des besoins en personnel hautement qualifié que leur mise en oeuvre pourrait requérir.

Les hypothèses retenues dans l'étude du M.I.T. appellent un examen critique, aussi bien du côté de la demande que du côté de l'offre. En premier lieu, rien ne permet d'affirmer que les besoins en énergie vont continuer à croître au même rythme que par le passé. Il paraît, au contraire, plus vraisemblable que la crise pétrolière ouverte en septembre 1973 marque un tournant important. Au cours des 25 années qui l'ont précédé, le monde a connu une diminution relative des prix de l'énergie, due à l'exploitation massive et rationnelle de gisements de pétrole particulièrement abondants et accessibles. De ce fait, la part du pétrole n'a cessé de croître et de nombreuses sources d'énergie concurrentes ont été éliminées.

Cette période d'énergie bon marché a été aussi une période de forte croissance, notamment grâce à la substitution de l'énergie à la main-d'oeuvre par la mécanisation et l'automatisation. Bien que ce ne soit évidemment pas le seul facteur déterminant, on peut penser que le coût nettement plus élevé de l'énergie jouera dans le sens d'une modération de la croissance économique, au même titre, par exemple, que la protection de l'environnement. Au reste, les tensions qui ont accompagné la période de croissance économique élevée pourraient bien conduire plusieurs pays à rechercher, à l'avenir, une expansion plus modérée.

La demande d'énergie pourrait, dans ces conditions, s'établir sur une pente plus modérée, d'autant plus que la recherche d'un haut rendement énergétique continuera à être encouragée par la tendance du marché.

Or, un point de moins en taux de croissance de la demande d'ici à la fin du siècle conduirait, par exemple, à „économiser" en fin de période une quantité d'énergie équivalente à la consommation actuelle, ce qui est évidemment énorme.

En supposant que la consommation mondiale d'énergie continuera à croître à un taux de 4,7% par an d'ici à la fin du siècle, elle se situerait, en l'an 2000, aux alentours de 20 milliards de TEP,[1] soit environ 4 fois la consommation de 1970, ce qui représenterait, pour les 30 dernières années du siècle, une consommation cumulée de 330 milliards de TEP.

Ce chiffre est impressionnant, parce qu'il est plus de trois fois supérieur aux réserves mondiales connues de pétrole (90 à 100 milliards de tonnes), et deux fois supérieur aux réserves mondiales cumulées de pétrole et de gaz naturel.

Il l'est déjà moins si on le rapproche des réserves mondiales de charbon, de schistes bitumineux et de sables asphaltiques, et des possibilités quasi-illimitées qu'offre l'énergie nucléaire, avec la technique des réacteurs à neutrons rapides (surrégénérateurs).

Réserves mondiales (prouvées et probables) de combustibles fossiles

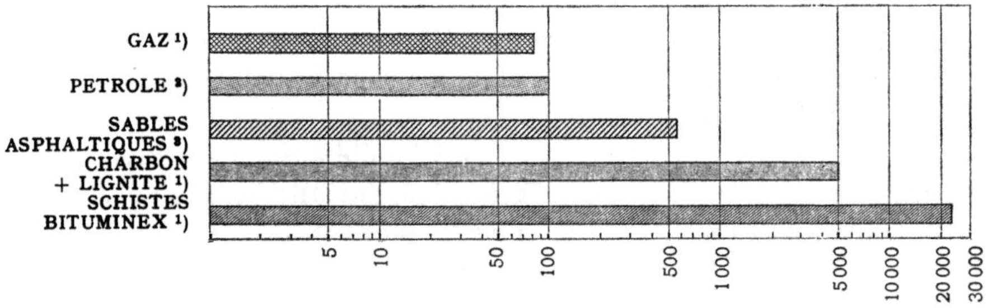

Sources: 1. OCDE, Perspectives Energétiques jusqu'en 1985.
2. Oil + Gas Journal, décembre 1974.
3. EDF, juin 1974.

Il ne fait guère de doute que l'ère du pétrole-roi touche à sa fin. La plupart des experts s'accordent pour dire que, dès avant la fin du siècle, la production mondiale commencera à décliner. Ainsi, à l'échelle de l'histoire, l'exploitation de cette ressource aura été à la fois très rapide et très intense.

De son côté, le charbon, s'il est abondant, a l'inconvénient d'être mal réparti et ne pourra couvrir une part importante des

[1] TEP: Tonne d'équivalent-pétrole.

besoins énergétiques que s'il peut être converti économiquement sous forme liquide ou gazeuse.

Quant aux schistes bitumineux et aux sables asphaltiques, ils constituent un réservoir d'énergie très considérable, en particulier pour les Etats-Unis, le Canada et l'Amérique Latine. Mais leur exploitation requiert d'énormes investissements et n'est pas sans poser des problèmes pour l'environnement.

En ce qui concerne l'énergie nucléaire, l'ensemble des réservées prouvées de minerai d'uranium (U_3O_8) exploitable au prix de 15 dollars par livre, est évalué à 1 million de tonnes, ce qui devrait suffire pour alimenter pendant une vingtaine d'années les réacteurs en service en 1980. Il faudra cependant, d'ici la fin du siècle, accélérer le rythme de découverte de nouvelles ressources, utiliser des minerais à plus faible teneur et disposer de capacités suffisantes d'enrichissement du minerai, en attendant l'introduction de réacteurs sur-régénérateurs.

L'expérience passée devrait d'ailleurs, en ce qui concerne l'évaluation des ressources, nous inviter à la fois à la modestie et à un certain optimisme.

Si l'on s'en tient aux combustibles fossiles, notre connaissance de la géologie, de la géophysique et de la géochimie des ressources est très limitée, non seulement pour le pétrole et le gaz, mais plus encore pour ce qui concerne les autres ressources. De plus, il est vraisemblable que les ressources les moins exploitées à présent, celles des fonds marins, représentent un potentiel énorme pour l'avenir. Rien que pour le pétrole et le gaz, certains experts estiment que les ressources sous-marines et celles des zones arctiques dépassent en quantité ce qui a été et ce qui sera découvert sur les continents. En troisième lieu, on peut escompter que l'innovation scientifique et technologique permettra de mieux exploiter des roches et des minerais jusqu'ici négligés en raison de leur faible teneur, ou de révéler et d'exploiter, par des techniques avancées de détection et de forage en profondeur, des zones sédimentaires inexploitées.

Au total, il ne semble pas qu'une pénurie globale soit à redouter au cours des 25 prochaines années, bien que des phénomènes limités de désajustement puissent se produire, tant que l'énergie nucléaire n'aura pas atteint un stade de développement lui donnant toute la souplesse nécessaire.

Mais la disponibilité matérielle d'énergie n'est pas le seul facteur qui conditionne le développement futur. D'autres contraintes apparaissent, qui sont de nature écologique et sociologique.

Le développement énergétique se heurte, en effet, à cette autre limite qu'est la préservation du milieu naturel. Faisant abstraction du problème esthétique posé par les centrales électriques classiques ou nucléaires, et du problème posé par les décharges de chaleur dans l'air et dans l'eau, deux types principaux de pollution sont inhérents aux différents combustibles fossiles et nucléaires, à savoir la pollution atmosphérique et la radioactivité.

En ce qui concerne la pollution atmosphérique, deux problèmes méritent d'être mentionnés. Le premier est bien connu: c'est celui qui résulte des émissions de soufre dans l'atmosphère. Déjà, les combustibles à faible teneur en soufre bénéficient d'une prime sur le marché. Mais, en raison de leur rareté, il faudra de plus en plus recourir à des hydrocarbones qui sont dans la nature, associés au soufre. Il ressort de l'étude de l'OCDE[1] que si la désulfurisation du pétrole et du charbon n'était pas plus largement pratiquée en 1985 qu'en 1972, les émissions de dioxyde de soufre pourraient augmenter de plus de 20% dams les pays européens de l'OCDE. Un effort considérable et coûteux devra être entrepris dans ce domaine.

Une incertitude plus fondamentale est celle qui a trait aux émissions de gaz carbonique dans l'atmosphère. Certains experts[2] ont noté que si l'on voulait et pouvait satisfaire aux besoins énergétiques dans l'avenir par les seuls combustibles fossiles, les émissions de gaz carbonique dans l'atmosphère, qui à présent s'élèvent déjà à 18 milliards de tonnes, pourraient atteindre des niveaux dangereux pour le milieu naturel, voire pour le climat, notamment par „l'effet de serre" qu'elles sont susceptibles de créer. Or, il semble qu'on connaisse mal la capacité d'assimilation des mécanismes régulateurs: photosynthèse et surtout absorption du gaz carbonique par les océans. Il s'agirait donc de veiller à ce qu'on ne dépasse pas le seuil critique avant que la consommation de combustibles fossiles ne régresse. Si ce risque devait se confirmer, ce serait une raison de plus pour accélérer cette évolution vers le nucléaire et résoudre ainsi ce problème.

---

[1] Perspectives énergétiques jusqu'en 1985, *op. cit.* p. 89.

[2] Voir, par exemple, C. Destival, *Revue Française de l'Energie*, n° 249, 1973.

Les incertitudes qui s'attachent aux applications de l'énergie nucléaire suscitent pourtant plus d'inquiétudes en raison des effets possibles des radiations, et les controverses qui opposent souvent les experts ajoutent à la difficulté d'une analyse objective. Ces inquiétudes, en partie fondées sur des réactions irrationnelles et mal informées (l'assimilation de l'énergie nucléaire à la bombe atomique) ne sont pas pour autant dénuées de tout fondement. Si le problème de la radioactivité émanant des centrales nucléaires en fonctionnement normal ne doit pas être exagéré (il est, en effet, très inférieur aux seuils dangereux), on ne peut pas absolument écarter le risque de fuites accidentelles ou provoquées dans une intention malveillante (sabotage – attentat – guerre).

Plus troublant encore est le problème de l'élimination des déchets radioactifs, dont il faut bien admettre qu'il n'a pas encore trouvé de solution définitive.

Les déchets fortement radioactifs, c'est-à-dire les produits de fission césium 137 et strontium 90, et surtout le plutonium et les autres éléments transuraniens émanant notamment des réacteurs sur-régénérateurs, doivent être isolés de la biosphère pendant de très longues périodes de temps, soit pluxieurs centaines d'années pour le césium 137 et le strontium 90, et des centaines de milliers d'années pour le plutonium. Si l'on considère que 2800 GW de puissance installée minimum sont prévus pour l'an 2000 dans le monde, il convient de se préoccuper, dès maintenant, des quantités de déchets qui existeront à la fin du siècle, et qui se chiffreront par millions de tonnes.

Diverses solutions ont été proposées à cet égard, telles la concentration des déchets sous forme solide et leur enfouissement dans des mines de sel, mais il ne peut s'agir que de solutions provisoires. En ce sens, le développement de l'énergie nucléaire constitue un pari, qui relève de calcul de probabilités. Ce pari comporte un acte de foi sur la capacité future de la technologie à donner des réponses plus satisfaisantes à des problèmes qui ne sont encore résolus qu'imparfaitement.

En dépit de l'élément de risque qu'il comporte, comme bien d'autres activités humaines, le nucléaire est cependant la seule source d'énergie alternative qui soit suffisamment mûre au plan industriel pour pouvoir prendre à moyen terme le relai des combustibles fossiles pour la production d'électricité. C'est donc la voie dans laquelle toutes les grandes nations industrielles se sont engagées, non sans avoir pesé soigneusement les risques auxquels on a fait référence. La question de l'attitude du public à l'égard de l'énergie nucléaire ne se réduit pas aux problèmes que pose objectivement son développement à très grande échelle. Le rapport „Science et technologie pour l'Energie"[1] note, à cet égard, comme un fait significatif que d'autres technologies énergétiques, qui sont potentiellement dangereuses pour la santé et l'environnement, n'aient jamais suscité de la part du public les réactions qu'ont provoqué les risques des technologies nucléaires.

Quelques hypothèses sur l'avenir à plus long terme

Le débat actuellement engagé autour de l'énergie nucléaire confirmera vraisemblablement le rôle essentiel que celle-ci est appelée à jouer dans la perspective du déclin du pétrole. Pour la zone de l'OCDE entre 1975 et 2000, les prévisions actuelles indiquent une multiplication par 30 de la production d'origine nucléaire, exprimée en GWe[2] de puissance installée. Au delà de cet horizon, on ne peut que formuler des hypothèses.

Le recours aux sources d'énergie „naturelles"

Compte tenu des risques que comportera l'utilisation de l'énergie nucléaire à grande échelle, la technologie de l'utilisation des sources d'énergie naturelles revêt une particulière importance.

En raison de son abondance et de sa „propreté," *l'énergie solaire* paraît la seule capable de fournir une alternative à l'énergie nucléaire: notre planète reçoit en effet chaque année, sous cette forme, l'équivalent de 70.000 milliards de tonnes de pétrole, soit plus de 1000 fois la consommation mondiale d'énergie à l'heure actuelle. Mais l'exploitation de cette ressource, qui a le grand avantage d'être renouvelable ,se heurte à deux obstacles de taille: son intermittence – qui pose des problèmes de stockage difficiles – et sa faible intensité.

Jusqu'à présent, seules des applications à petite échelle ont at-

---

[1] Science et Technologie pour l'Energie, *op. cit.*

[2] GWe: Gigawatt (électrique)
1 Gigawatt = 1.000 Megawatts

teint le stade économique: elles concernent le chauffage de l'eau et, à un degré moindre, la climatisation.

Pour les applications à grande échelle, diverses filières sont à l'étude, dont les principales portent sur la conversion thermique et sur la conversion photo-voltaïque. Si les recherches en cours ne permettent pas d'envisager une exploitation économique à brève échéance, on peut cependant penser que la fabrication en masse de cellules solaires poly-cristallines pourrait permettre à l'avenir de réduire sensiblement les coûts d'équipement. L'énergie produite serait exceptionnellement propre. Encore faudrait-il que le problème du stockage fût résolu dans des conditions économiques.

Une autre source, elle aussi, très abondante et géographiquement disséminée, la *géothermie*, fondée sur les échanges de chaleur avec le sous-sol, pourrait être exploitée, soit par récupération de vapeur humide, soit par l'extraction de la chaleur contenue dans les roches chaudes et sèches existant à de grandes profondeurs. Bien que sous sa forme de vapeur sèche elle ait produit, depuis des années, de l'électricité dans des installations de petite taille et à des prix rentables (un million de KwH produits en 1972), il est difficile, dans l'état actuel de nos connaissances, de prédire l'avenir de l'énergie géothermique. Pour la vapeur humide, il faudra résoudre les problèmes sérieux de corrosion, d'affaissement et de pollution qui compliquent l'exploitation de cette forme d'énergie géothermique. Pour les roches chaudes, la technologie n'en est qu'à ses débuts et elle promet d'être aussi difficile que coûteuse. Le potentiel de ces gisements, et surtout de ceux des roches chaudes, est suffisamment important pour que les recherches méritent d'être poursuivies et activées dans ce domaine.

Quant aux autres sources naturelles, elles sont, ou bien trop dispersées pour fournir autre chose qu'une source d'appoint (énergie éolienne, énergie des marées et des courants), ou bien trop mal maîtrisées (photosynthèse) pour être exploitées économiquement à brève échéance.

La percée technologique de la fusion thermonucléaire

Découverte avant la réaction de fission, étudiée depuis plus de 20 ans, la fusion nucléaire contrôlée n'a pu encore être pratiquement réalisée. En dépit des difficultés qui tiennent aux très hautes températures mises en jeu, certains experts américains prévoient que la fusion contrôlée par confinement magnétique pourrait être une réalité vers 1990, mais, en raison de progrès spectaculaires obtenus dans la fusion par laser, celle-ci serait, aux dires de certains experts, réalisée plus facilement.

La fusion nucléaire contrôlée apparaît avec l'utilisation de l'énergie solaire, comme une des „voies royales" qui pourraient mettre le monde à l'abri de la pénurie d'énergie sans créer de risques inacceptables pour l'environnement. Mais il est douteux qu'elle puisse recevoir des applications industrielles avant l'an 2000.

Il serait présomptueux de vouloir tirer de ce rapide tour d'horizon un tableau précis des perspectives énergétiques à long terme. Tout au plus, peut-on avancer quelques conclusions plus qualitatives que quantitatives:

1. La première est que le monde ne paraît pas menaçé d'une pénurie majeure d'énergie d'ici la fin du siècle. Jusqu'à présent, l'humanité a toujours trouvé la réponse à ses besoins croissants d'énergie. A l'utilisation du bois, des cours d'eau et des vents, a succédé celle de la houille. A l'âge de la houille a succédé celui du pétrole. Au delà du pétrole, il n'y a pas, semble-t-il, de solution unique. Ni le charbon, ni l'énergie nucléaire, ni la captation des énergies naturelles ne peuvent prétendre à l'exclusivité. L'inégale répartition des ressources et les problèmes d'environnement impliqueront, au contraire, une certaine diversification.

2. En revanche, il est clair que, sauf innovation radicale, les futures ressources en énergie coûteront de plus en plus cher, à mesure que s'épuisent les gisements à haute teneur; que des investissements de plus en plus complexes doivent être réalisés et que se renforcent les contraintes écologiques. Ce renchérissement a cependant un effet positif dans la mesure où il incite à limiter les gaspillages, notamment le gaspillage de pétrole. (N'oublions pas, en effet, que ce dernier n'est pas seulement une source de chaleur, mais aussi une matière première noble).

3. Il est vraisemblable – mais non certain – que la courbe de la demande mondiale d'énergie tendra à s'infléchir par rapport

aux tendances récentes sous l'effet de trois phénomènes:

Une certaine modération de la croissance économique; une modification structurelle de la production qui sera, moins que par le passé, dépendante de l'industrie; un effort généralisé de rationalisation des utilisations de l'énergie pour l'industrie, le chauffage et les transports.

4. Le problème de l'énergie est devenu, du fait de la raréfaction des ressources, de plus en plus international et de plus en plus inséparable des autres problèmes qui conditionnent l'avenir de notre société, à savoir la préservation de l'équilibre économique et monétaire (comme le prouve la crise actuelle), et la préservation de l'équilibre écologique.

5. Il en découle que les conditions dans lesquelles l'énergie est produite et utilisée ne sont plus seulement l'objet des politiques nationales mais devient un sujet d'intérêt commun à tous les pays, qu'ils soient producteurs ou consommateurs. Au surplus, l'effort de recherche et le développement des sources d'énergie de demain demandera des ressources humaines et financières qui ne sont à la portée d'aucun pays isolé.

C'est dire que la manière dont l'équation énergétique sera résolue sera grandement fonction de la coopération internationale.

SUMMARY

For all the uncertainties involved, i.e. in the evaluation of fossil fuel reserves, supply and demand prospects and, still more, future technological achievement, forecasting in the matter of energy is a patent necessity. Firms concerned with oil production are obliged to prepare investment programmes that are particularly costly – and, inevitably, long-term. Governments are dealing here with an essential factor of growth and power and must cope somehow with the complex problems which the use of energy poses for contemporary society. Such forecasting is not, however, synonymous with prediction; it is closely linked with the action process, inasmuch as this or that political decision may well, itself, exert a potent influence on the foreseeable future. The forecasting work of the OECD in this field belongs to this category, as for example its latest survey "Energy Prospects between now and 1985,"[1] This study by the Secretary-General of the Organisation, incidentally, differs from previous surveys by the fact of its taking account of the peculiar hazards of the present situation,

[1] OECD, Paris, 1974.

dominated as it is by the substantial increase in oil prices. It is indeed an attempt to provide answers to the two principal questions with which the Governments of the member states were faced at the onset of today's energy crisis: how can energy supplies be secured in the next decade and at what price; and what are the economic monetary implications of the supply structure envisaged? The Report should be read in conjunction with the recently-published longer-term study concerned with research and development – "Science and Technology for Energy"[1] – which was put in hand by the Organisation simultaneously a year or so before the advent of the oil crisis in September 1973. The purpose of the article is to supply a commentary on these two OECD reports.

Prospects for 1985

It is significant that all the forecasts made about the energy market since the War in the countries of the West postulated an almost unlimited medium-term production potential – and paid very little attention to the price factor. 'This golden age,' so to speak, of the oil industry – or, as some would say, this improvidence – came to an abrupt end once a sellers' market replaced the buyers' market; when, in other words, the oil-producing countries, forming up into an effective cartel, became fully conscious of the enormous power they could wield thanks to their control of an essential element of world commerce. By nationalising the oil wells, by controlling production and trade, they were in a position, it seemed, both to maximise their oil revenues and to husband their resources for the future. It remains true, as M. Eldin points out, that the substantial rise in prices cannot fail to have repercussions on consumption and also encourage the development of alternative sources of energy.

There is, of course, one reason why the oil market has behaved somewhat differently from that of other raw materials. In the sixties the rate of production and, to a large extent, the prices charged were under the control of a relatively small number of international oil companies owning concessions for the exploitation of the proven world reserves of oil, which were located for the most part in the Near East and were rapidly increasing all the time in volume. Competition between the producer countries kept the companies' prices down; and the swiftest possible exploitation of the existing oil deposits ensured maximum benefits through economies of scale. When, however, the economic boom reached its peak, with demand soaring simultaneously in almost all the industrial economies, in the period between 1970 and 1973, that situation was turned upside down. The United States, for instance, from being a net exporter of oil, became a net importer. Circumstances were conducive to rising prices in the seventies, as the oil-producing countries came to realise their combined strength; but no one anticipated such a drastic change – such an explosion – as has occurred.

[1] OECD, Paris, 1975.

Profiting by special political developments, e.g. the Yom Kippur war, the oil-producing States in concert have succeeded in imposing on the rest of the world oil prices f.o.b. ranging between 8 and 13 dollars a barrel. By the end of 1974 10 or 11 dollars a barrel was the norm. It should perhaps be noted that in 1972 the Secretary-General of OECD had sensed the way the wind was blowing – and had made a point of requesting member countries to revise their estimations of energy resources and requirements.

Medium-term Forecasting

The shattering fourfold increase in oil prices (and the consequent increase in the prices of other forms of energy in the OECD countries) has visibly affected the close correlation between the increase in the world total demand for energy and the increase in the gross domestic product. As far as future prospects were concerned, the reversal of the position undermined the relationship of energy consumption and economic growth but also had its effect on the incidence of the increase in production itself.

Now, in a free market the substantial rise in the price of oil as a raw material has, of course, meant a rise in the price of petroleum products and of other competing forms of energy. And when it happens that energy prices increase much more rapidly than other prices, it is only to be expected that efforts will be made to bring about a more effective use of energy and to cut down waste. In the short run, it is true, there will be very little saving, since there is no choice but to utilise energy consumption plans installed at a time when energy was cheap. As far as the medium-term, still more the long-term context is concerned, however, capital renewal should make it possible to effect substantial economies, all the more so because in the meantime new techniques to this end will no doubt have been introduced. The OECD Report duly provides for this contingency. It takes account, too, of the world projections arrived at by adding together the energy totals for each region corresponding to such and such prices. Also the oil imports of the OECD countries have been treated as a residual parameter – with the implicit assumption that consumer countries can rely on obtaining all the oil they need at the market price. The author illustrates his point by giving figures corresponding to the three postulated sets of circumstances.

Some Consequential Data

From these projections the following conclusions are drawn:

1) that from now until 1985 world consumption of energy is likely to increase at an annual rate of 3.5- 4 per cent, whereas the increase originally estimated was of the order of 5 per cent.

2) that in 1985 the area comprised in the OECD may expect to cover by its own production nearly 80 per cent of its energy requirements, as compared with a 1972 figure of 65 per cent, whereas earlier anticipations, for 1985, were for a figure of something like 55 per cent.

3) The upward movement indicated by the above figures, however, is likely to vary considerably according to the region. The United States, for

example, by 1985 might expect to have regained its exporter status, while the European members of the OECD would be still dependent to the extent of nearly 60 per cent on imports- in the case of Japan it would be 80 per cent.

4) One may expect, within the period in question, a diversification of energy supplies, in the sense of a relative diminution in the importance of oil itself, the introduction of nuclear energy as a prime factor, and a check to the rundown of coal supplies. (Figures are given for 1972 and 1985.)

5) One consequence of the slowing-up in the increase of energy consumption and of the increase in production, throughout the area covered by the OECD, is bound to be a reduction in volume of oil imports and a stabilization at a figure well below the more than 100 per cent increase which had been foreseen before the crisis.

Uncertainties and Flexibility of Margins

The author is at pains to emphasise that these assessments, arrived at on the basis of economic criteria, are necessarily speculative. But one firm conclusion at least can be drawn: that between now and 1985 the OECD countries ought largely to have ceased being dependent, as they are now, on the oil-producing countries. It is difficult to forecast the level of oil prices. What we can say is that already by the beginning of 1975 a reduction in real value has taken place; and that, because of the prevailing market trends, and exceptionally propitious climatic conditions in the consumer countries, the real price level seems likely to be eventually nearer six dollars a barrel than the higher 9 dollar figure forecast in 1972. Other factors, however, that need to be taken into account are the probable reactions of the exporting countries, which have so far been able to adjust production to the level of demand, and the fact that the cost of alternative energy supplies will tend to increase in dollars at the existing exchange rate, this in itself constituting a check on the lowering of oil prices.

An Active Energy Policy

There is naturally a lot of talk these days about countries undertaking "an active energy policy" in order to cope with the drastic reduction in supplies. This means essentially two things: a rational use of energy and the development of national energy resources. These are, of course, the objectives par excellence of the International Energy Agency created in November 1974 and grouping 18 member states of the OECD.

The rational use of energy implies a reduction of the quantity of energy consumed without appreciable diminution of the gross domestic product and without any conspicuous deterioration in the general standard of living or the level of individual comfort. The various means to achieve this end are a reduction of wastage, an increase in output as a result of conversion programmes and a certain amount of change in our way of life. It is worthy of note perhaps that in the recent past expansion has taken place chiefly in respect of the least profitable uses of energy such as motor transport and air conditioning. (Rational use in the sense indicated here is something quite apart from limitations in demand imposed by emergency situations.) Considerable savings can be effected no doubt in respect of water heating and water cooling, industrial heating, transport and the conversion of electrical power. Economy measures of this kind, causing a slowing-down of growth in total energy demand, is more beneficial, be it said, than any increase in domestic energy production, and this for a number of reasons (which the author details). The total saving for OECD countries should amount, according to the Report on Energy Prospects for 1985, to some 15–20% of the energy requirements previously estimated for that year. This is, however, always supposing that Governments show a firm determination not only to accept the consequences of the rise in energy prices, but also to exploit all existing possibilities. One cannot help wondering whether, in fact, the public will readily accept the changes of habit that such a policy involves, especially in those countries where there is a very high rate of consumption per inhabitant.

The Development of Alternative Resources

As for the expansion of energy resources, there are here indeed abundant possibilities. Between now and 1985 the production of oil and of gas could well be doubled (as compared with the 1972 figures), the production of coal could be stepped up by some 65 per cent or more, of hydro-electric and geothermic energy, some 67 per cent. Nuclear energy could conceivably be increased twenty times: by 1985 it could supply up to 34 per cent of the electricity figure. But it goes without saying that the coefficient of development will vary considerably according to the country.

The United States, for example, has immense development potential in respect of oil, bituminous schists (shale) and coal; Canada has vast resources of oil, natural gas, uranium, cheap coal and hydro-electric power. In Europe, the horn of plenty, it is generally assumed, will be the North Sea oil supplies, to the tune of some 300 million tonnes by 1985 (an amount roughly equivalent to oil production in Iran in 1974). If some countries, like France, are relatively deficient in fossil fuels, they will no doubt make up for this by concentrating their effort on nuclear energy. The fact remains that any such expansion of supplies will require massive investment, likely in many cases to exceed the capacity of private enterprise.

Obviously, one of the requisite conditions for such investment is that there should be relative stability of prices. Firms engaged in the oil industry are at the mercy of the big low-cost production countries, particularly those of the Middle East. Hence the present groping for guarantees of some kind such as establishment of a "minimum safeguard price" for imported oil, price guarantees with regard to domestic production and measures designed to promote an equitable distribution of the profits from energy resources.

In the medium-term context, then, there is no prospect of actual shortage: what is necessary is a re-structuring of the oil market through a more active policy on the part of the OECD countries at national level, together with an appreciable extension of co-operation by means of the newly-created International Energy Agency. Somehow, during the transition period, means will have to be found to overcome the economic consequences of the higher oil prices, and there will necessarily be structural adjustments to meet the huge investment requirements and the balance of payments problems of the producing countries. Although this may well mean, up to 1980, a steadily increasing indebtedness for the OECD countries, thereafter, according to the forecasts, it should be possible to achieve a world balance. Beyond 1985, however, there are other factors that must be taken into account.

Prospects beyond 1985

When we come to look more than ten years ahead, accurate forecasting is very difficult. Uncertainties accumulate, and a mere extrapolation of existing trends will not supply the answer. Beyond 1985 it is no longer the supply of energy which is in question but, so it would seem, economic growth itself. For, whether we like it or not, we shall have to take some account of the considerations put forward in the study by the "Club of Rome," which appeared in 1972 under the title "The Limits of Growth." The experts responsible for this MIT Report were at pains to demonstrate the finite nature of the resources of our planet, quite apart from the limits inherent in mankind's economic and political decisions. The Report predicts that on the basis of the growth rate of the past, and if the volume of known reserves be multiplied by five, certain energy sources could fairly soon be exhausted: natural gas in 49 years, oil in 50 years, coal in 150 years. On the other hand, it visualises almost unlimited quantities of nuclear energy – which, however, might not provide a solution for our problem, as there are likely to be fresh bottlenecks in respect of financial resources and on account of a lack of sufficient highly-qualified personnel to operate the reactors.

The MIT Report, let it be said, is open to criticism, with regard to demand as well as supply considerations. In the first place, there is no certainty that energy requirements are going to go on increasing at the same rate as in the past. On the contrary, it would seem more likely that the oil crisis that burst upon us in September 1973 will prove to have a turning point. There is the demonstrable fact that, because of the relative depreciation of energy prices during the preceding 25 years, due to the massive and rational exploitation of particularly abundant and accessible oil deposits, the use of oil was maximised at the expense of other forms of energy. Cheap energy in its turn encouraged mechanisation and automation resulting in ever-increasing economic growth. It may well be, then, that the much higher cost of energy today will have the effect of moderating that growth development – which will also be affected by the new factor of concern for the protection of the environment. In other words, the demand for energy could well ease up; and even a 1-point reduction in the growth rate of demand could lead by the end of the century to the "saving" of an amount of energy equivalent to the total amount of today's consumption. That means quite a lot of energy. The author then proceeds to give figures (with a table) which show indeed cumulative oil consumption in the year 2000 amounting to more than three times the known oil reserves, twice the combined reserves of oil and natural gas. However, to offset this, one must bring into the balance the total world reserves of coal and asphaltic gravel, plus, of course, the almost unlimited potential of nuclear energy.

Eventually, then, oil is likely to be dethroned. Most experts indeed are agreed that by the end of the century the world production of oil will be beginning to decline. As for coal, there is certainly plenty of this source of energy available, but it has the disadvantage of being unevenly distributed, and it can supply energy requirements on any significant scale only if it can be converted economically into liquid fuel or gas. In the USA, Canada and Latin America there is an abundance of bitumen and asphaltic gravel. Not only, however, will the exploitation of these forms of energy require substantial investment, but also they raise certain environmental issues. Nuclear energy, on the other hand, will certainly abound – indeed its potential still remains relatively untapped. If one adds the oil and gas resources under the seas and in the arctic zones, obviously one can say that there is not going to be any dearth of energy supplies.

Nevertheless, actual material availability is not the only factor determining the future. Other constraints, ecological and sociological, are now surfacing. Protection of the environment, conservation of nature, set bounds to energy development. Aesthetic considerations aside, two principal types of pollution have to be reckoned with, atmospheric pollution and radioactivity.

The sulphur content of certain fuels, we know, is already causing concern. Another, more fundamental, hazard arises from the emission of carbonic gas in the atmosphere, specifically from the fossil fuels. Here there is unquestionably a danger to the natural environment, indeed the climate may well be affected, and this particularly because of the possible "hothouse" effects. There are, of course, certain regulating mechanisms e.g. photosynthesis and absorption of the carbonic gas by the oceans, but not enough is known about the assimilation capacity of these relief measures. And the dangers in this respect constitute yet another reason for accelerating the switch to nuclear energy.

Then, however, we are up against the radioactive effects, still very much a subject of controversy. When nuclear power stations are functioning normally, there may well be no particular cause for concern; but one cannot entirely exclude the risk of accidental leaks or leaks deliberately contrived (sabotage, criminal intent, war). Finally, there is the question of radioactive waste, a problem which has not yet found an adequate solution. The author gives some startling figures of the experts' findings in this field. It can be said that so far mankind has found only temporary expedients for dealing with this problem: we shall have to pin our faith to future technological developments.

Whatever the risks involved, it remains true that nuclear energy is the only alternative source sufficiently developed industrially to replace fossil fuels in the medium term for electricity production. Which is why – despite public mistrust – all the major industrial States have embarked on the development of nuclear power. It happens, as the OECD's "Science and Technology" Report points out, that the technological developments which are likewise potentially dangerous for health and the environment have never provoked in the public such sharp reactions as this nuclear technology risk.

The Long-term Future

All things considered, we may take it that, as and when the importance of oil declines, nuclear energy will have an essential role to play. At the same time, because of the risks involved, we may expect further development in the use of natural forms of energy. And first and foremost in this category comes solar energy. The fact is that our planet receives every year in solar energy the equivalent of 70,000 milliard tonnes of oil i.e. more than a thousand times the amount of the world's energy consumption today. But exploitation of this energy source is up against two major obstacles: its intermittent character, with consequential storage problems, and its meagre intensity. Up to now only small-scale applications of this resource have proved economic, such as water-heating and, to a lesser extent, air-conditioning. Solar heat does, of course, have the great advantage of cleanliness.

Another source, likewise abundant and also widely distributed from a geographical point of view, is *geothermy*. But there are serious problems of corrosion and pollution to be overcome before geothermy is an economic proposition.

Finally, a word must be said of the possibility of thermonuclear fusion, which was indeed a subject of research before nuclear fission. Certain American experts set great store by this, and they report spectacular progress in fusion by laser beams. Controlled nuclear fusion, then like the use of solar energy, is capable of rescuing the world from energy shortage and without involving unacceptable risks for the environment. But it is unlikely to have any industrial application before the year 2000.

What, then are the conclusions to be drawn? They are admittedly qualitative rather than quantitative:

1) There would seem to be no real danger of a major energy shortage between now and the end of the century. History is likely to repeat itself, so that oil will come to be supplemented or replaced by various alternative forms of energy.

2) It is clear nevertheless that the future energy resources will be more and more costly; that the investment pattern will be more and more complex; and that future development of energy resources will be subject to ecological constraints. The increased costs will not necessarily be a bad thing because they will stimulate us to limit wastage, particularly the waste of oil.

3) It is probable, though not certain, that the curve of world energy demand will show a tendency to recede by comparison with recent trends,

and this for three reasons: a certain attenuation of economic growth; structural modification of the production process, which will be less dependent on industry; and an overall endeavour to rationalise the use of energy for industry, heating and transport.

4) One thing is certain. Because of increasing scarcity the problem of energy becomes more and more an international one – and it is more and more bound up with other problems determining the future of our society such as the maintenance of economic and monetary equilibrium (as the present crisis has demonstrated) and the preservation of an ecological balance.

5) Hence the emphatic conclusion that energy production and use are no longer merely matters of domestic policy, they have become a subject of common concern to all countries. What is more, it is plain that research and development in relation to the energy sources of tomorrow will demand human and financial resources byond the capacity of any single country. In short, the ultimate means of resolving the energy equation will be largely a function of international co-operation.

NEW FEATURES OF THE INFLATIONARY PROCESS

by

GUIDO CARLI *

1. INFLATION 1968–74: NEW FEATURES

It may be a common place, but it has to be emphasised at the outset that the most obvious, and the most immediately disturbing, new features in the inflation of recent years are indeed its steady acceleration and its spread to economies of varying types. If we consider all the OECD states it will be found that, apart from the slight exception in 1972, the growth of the implicit deflator increased uninterruptedly from 3.5 per cent in 1968 to 12.5 per cent in 1974. The deceleration process of the past few months is still too recent and beset with uncertainties, given the high costs in terms of unemployment and loss of income, to justify hopes of a clear reversal of the trend. Moreover, there has been a marked tendency for the phenomenon to spread, not only because it has affected all countries regardless of their stage in development or the degree of stability in prices earlier recorded but also in the sense that differences in inflation rates as between the individual economies have progressively diminished, in relation to the rising mean rate, more than the synchrony of the cyclical trends might lead us to expect.

The other peculiar and no less disturbing characteristic of the present inflation is the fact that it is accompanied by a persistant failure to make full use of the productive factors and by a less sustained development rate. From 1969 aggregate industrial production in the 7 main OECD countries has increased at constantly lower rates than the long-term trend line. With the exception of Japan (1969–70) and Federal Germany (1970–71) the gap between real and potential income has remained negative whilst the unemployment rate and the proportion of idle manufacturing

---

* Governor of the Bank of Italy.

I should like to thank Mr Ciocca, Mr Caranza and Ms Pierellifor their assistance. G.C.

capacity, measured against the peaks of the economic cycle, have exceeded the values for the sixties and late fifties. The term "stagflation" thus seems an appropriate description of recent experience in the main developed countries.

The third characteristic element of present-day inflation is to be found in the changes in comparative prices of goods and factors and in the income redistribution processes associated with such changes. From the early fifties, the ratio of world prices of manufactures to those of primary commodities showed a rising tendency, which was reversed shortly around 1968–69, when quotations for commodities began to increase practically without exception at an accelerating pace, so that they doubled in price by the end of 1973. The higher costs of raw materials and labour have exercised continuous pressure on the profitability of enterprises in the industrial countries. In some cases, there seems to be ample documentary evidence for a decreasing or stagnating trend in the profit rate on capital invested.[1] In more general terms we find a relative decrease in self-financing and risk capital and a corresponding tendency on the part of firms to incur debts, mainly on a short-term basis. Without underestimating the part which prospects of inflation and considerations of cost and risk may have played in determining such tendencies, they reflect, particularly in some less stable economies, more precarious balances between returns and costs and bear witness to a lesser degree of solidity in the financial structures of the enterprise. These phenomena were also reflected in the early stages in less encouraging trends (second half of the sixties) and subsequently (1973–74) in dullness or slumps on the main international stock exchanges. In the United States, in particular, there was a clear reversal around 1965 of the previous trend towards increasing the ratio of the valuation of real assets made by operators on the equity and bond markets to that based on replacement cost (current prices for capital goods). The decrease in that ratio has been almost continuous over the last ten years and reveals a disturbing deterioration in the prospects for profits in that economy, if Keynes is correct in his assertion that "... there is no sense in building up a new

[1] See for the United Kingdom, J. L. Walker, "Estimating Companies' Rate of Return on Capital Employed," *Economic Trends*, November 1974; for the United States, W. Nordhaus, "The Falling Share of Profits," *Brookings Papers*, 1974, No 1.

enterprise at a cost greater than that at which a similar existing enterprise can be purchased."[1]

Lastly, it should be pointed out that the acceleration of the inflationary process has been accompanied by the crisis in the international monetary system which dates from the devaluation of the pound (18 November 1967) and/or the introduction of a two-tier gold market (18 March 1968), with the subsequent alterations in parities and the general currency float, before and after the formal declaration of the non-convertibility of the dollar (15 August 1971).

2. INFLATIONARY FORCES AND MECHANISMS

In recent years there have been frequent analyses based on "monetarist" arguments in an attempt to explain, in particular, inflation after 1965–66.[2] Although worthy of closer consideration, these analyses fail to convince for a number of reasons. They seldom seek to examine the postwar inflationary process, including the "dollar shortage" phase and that preceding the birth and expansion of the Euromarket, whilst they wrongly attribute an exogenous and therefore causal character to the increasing deficit in the United States balance of payments and accordingly to the creation of international liquidity. Furthermore, they assume an excessively limited capacity on the part of the monetary authorities in the advanced countries to offset the undesirable effects of influxes of funds on the domestic creation of the monetary base. But, above all, such interpretations, centred on the hypothesis of an imbalance between overall monetary demand and aggregate offer, cannot easily be reconciled with the phenomena of stagnation of production and the incomplete use of resources, nor do they make it possible to offer a uniform interpretation of the changes observed in relative prices and distribution of income.

On the other hand, a more promising approach is an analysis

---

[1] Quoted by J. Tobin, "Monetary Policy in 1974 and beyond," *Brooking Papers*, 1974, page 223.

[2] See, for example, R. W. Mundell, "World Inflation and the Eurodollar," *Note Economiche*, 1971, pp. 5–23.

starting from these changes themselves and indicating the increasing difficulties which the price system encounters, because of the rigidity and imperfections of the markets, in ensuring that they occur without pressures on the average level of commodity prices. In such a scheme money is given an essentially permissive role, financing a process which derives its momentum from structural and compositional phenomena and in which that momentum is transmitted by a mechanism of one-way change in respect of the prices concerned. In sectors in which there is excess demand (as a result of changes in choices and preferences and/or increased production costs) monetary prices tend to increase more rapidly than they decrease in sectors where there is excess in supply.

A logical scheme of this type has the further advantage of being applicable not only to the acceleration of recent years but also to the longer-term inflationary trends recorded since the Second World War.[1] In the last resort, these can be traced back to the changes in composition which accompanied the major processes of industrialisation and tertiarisation of the economies which took place within the context of a steady pressure on productive resources favoured by full employment policies and the sustained expansion of world trade. Later bouts of inflation were due to the somewhat unbalanced character of the growth process, since pro-

---

[1] In fact, if we replace the primary sector, whose importance has considerably decreased, by the tertiary sector as the one whose productivity has not succeeded in keeping pace with the manufacturing sector, the inflationary trends of the last 20 years show, in their mechanisms and in some of their manifestations, aspects surprisingly like those of the "secondary" inflationary phases (covering 20-year periods) of world prices recorded between 1790 and 1940–50, described and interpreted in structural terms by a number of authors: "When industrial capacity tends to grow more quickly than the output of primary products, a shortage of these products is felt, and their prices rise, in terms of money, and also relatively to the price of industrial effort (terms of trade) ... When a phase of shortage of primary products sets in, the industrial economies experience a rise in wholesale prices. This spreads through the economy: rises in the cost of raw materials raise the prices fixed for final products; the rise in the cost of living moves wage-earners to press for rises in money wages; with more or less lag, other money incomes are raised to maintain customary differentials, and this causes further rises in costs and prices ... It must not be thought that this process is necessarily inhibited by the supply of money. There is no doubt that a restricted supply of money can stop prices from rising, but the evidence shows that actual restrictions have not usually been severe enough to do so ... The resistance to adaptation has been sufficient only to raise the long-term rate of interest gradually as the upward trend goes on (Gibson paradox)" E. H. Phelps Brown; S. A. Ozga "Economic Growth and the Price Level," *Economic Journal*, 1955, pp 13–14.

For other not exclusively monetarist interpretations of long-term price movements, see G. Maynard, *Economic Development and the Price Level*, Macmillan, London, 1962; P. Vilar, *Sviluppo economico e analisi storica*, Laterza, Bari, 1970.

ductivity increased at markedly different rates as between the production sectors, or, within them, between the branches comprising them. A noteworthy example of this was the difference between the growth in productivity in the manufacturing industry and the services sector and, within the former, the more than average performance of the chemical industry.

In the face of a rigidity in wage differentials, which in all probability has been accentuated recently, such movements have exercised continuous pressures in the direction of "creeping" inflation. It is also probable that the degree of monopoly has itself increased on the average, if we consider the various economies as a whole. In contrast with two elements which indicate the contrary – keener international competition connected with the increased integration of the economies and the apparently constant degree of concentration in the various industrial sectors – there is the, to my mind, overriding factor represented by the swifter expansion of the more highly concentrated manufacturing branches and by the tertiary sector (characterised by dominant forms of monopolistic competition) with the corresponding loss of importance of the branches or sectors in which competition is keener (including agriculture). The rigidity of prices, particularly downwards, has thus been steadily intensified.

With regard to the financing of the inflationary process, it should be pointed out that the growing demand for international liquidity connected with the increase in the global product, in transactions between countries and in prices, has been satisfied with relatively light pressures on long-term interest rates. After the post-war readjustment, the yield on long-dated government securities in the main countries rose on average between 1955 and 1966 from about 4.5 to 6 per cent. The appearance in the sixties of international money and capital markets strengthens the impression of a relatively sustained supply of international liquidity, elastic to interest rates and thus able to adapt itself endogenously to demand.

The other way in which the international monetary system has permitted inflationary trends to prevail is connected with the processes for readjusting the balance of payments and is directly ascribable to the increased importance of full employment as one of the aims of economic policy: "The result is that international adjustment through changes in relative costs and prices typically involves more upward adjustment in surplus countries than downward adjustment in deficit countries."[1] On the other hand this "inflationary" functioning of the Bretton Woods system accentuated the contradictions of a purely technical nature inherent in the gold exchange standard, and due to the difficulties of striking a balance between confidence in the reserve currency and the "adequate" creation of international means of payment. These contradictions were clearly foreseen by a number of experts[2] and they have constantly sharpened, the objective of securing confidence in the dollar progressively giving way to the need for the creation of liquidity: between 1950 and 1967 the official reserves of the United States fell by more than a third, whilst the balance of payments deficit increased to a marked degree.[3]

In recent years, marked by a progressive acceleration in price increases, the mechanism of the inflationary process does not seem to have changed. It is still bound up with the rigidity with which the system responds to changes in relative prices and proportions – particularly to changes which, in spite of the increased forecasting ability of the modern state and the big concern, are largely unexpected. On the other hand, the essence and nature of the basic forces are different. Within the individual countries, "the antithesis between capital and labour has become more acute and cannot always be explained according to the conventional model of the class strugggle ... The total demands of capital and labour on the national product tend to exceed its dimensions; inflation has become the means whereby aggregate demand is adjusted to those dimensions." At the same time "the acquisition of independence by nations formerly subjected to colonial domination produces a redistribution of income between countries not unlike that taking place within each nation as a result of rivalry between institutions or groups. The relations governing trade in raw materials and finished products are modified, and larger proportions of the income of the processing countries have to be

---

[1] IMF "Annual report for 1964," page 4.

[2] See in particular R. Triffin, "The Return to Convertibility," *BNL Quarterly Review*, 1959, pp 3–57.

[3] In the same period liabilities to all foreigners trebled, whilst liabilities to foreign official agencies increased by about 80 per cent between 1959 and 1967. See "International Economic Report," 1973, page 19.

transferred to countries from which they obtain their supplies."[1]

These two types of stimulus have gone hand in hand in recent years, and their combined effects on relative prices and distribution and hence, through the mechanism described, on the inflationary process have been quantitatively higher than those hitherto recorded over the long term.

Furthermore, although the nature of such stimuli is clearly complex – the socio-political aspects probably predominate owing to historically significant changes in previous equilibria – it is still possible and desirable to define the more strictly economic factors which have contributed to these developments.

During the sixties the labour market was characterised by a situation of relative shortage. From the structural point of view and by comparison with the preceding decade this was true both in Europe and in the United States, although for different reasons. In Europe the supply of "surplus" labour, which had promoted sustained growth with relatively stable prices in countries such as the Federal Republic of Germany, Italy, the Netherlands and Switzerland, dried up in the sixties. The absorption of structural unemployment, the administrative obstacles to immigration and its increasing cost (including political) and dwindling of agricultural manpower reserves were responsible for reducing the elasticity of the labour supply which for some European countries had already led to a marked slowing down in the growth of the labour force. The Kindleberger-Lamfalussy argument – that the European situation of a large surplus in the labour supply was already changing in the very early sixties[2] – although put forward somewhat in advance of the facts, was later increasingly proved correct.

Moreover, for demographic and institutional reasons, the annual growth rate of the labour force in the United States was on average higher in the sixties than in the preceding decade (1.8 and 1.1 per cent respectively). The moderating effect which might have resulted from this was however more than offset by an accentuation of the sectorial imbalance between labour supply and

[1] Banca d'Italia, Relazione 1973, pp 398–399.

[2] *Cf.* C. P. Kindleberger, *Europe's Postwar Growth. The Role of Labour Supply*, Harvard University Press, Cambridge (Mass.), 1967 A. Lamfalussy, *Les marchés financiers en Europe,* Presses Universitaires de France, Paris, 1968.

demand in relation to the composition by sex, age and colour and to vocational qualifications within these groups. It is also widely held that the tensions on the American labour market, having increased in recent years, will persist for the remainder of the seventies.[1] In terms of effects, these structural changes in the relation between labour supply and demand, together with more strictly social and political factors, have helped to produce a general "worsening" in the Phillips curves and, from the point of view of the trade unions, have led to a more energetic and continuous campaign of claims.

Cyclical and speculative factors, as well as more structural elements, contributed to the exceptional increase in the prices of raw materials after 1968 and the distinct improvement in the terms of trade for such commodities as opposed to manufactures. Among the structural factors reference need only be made, apart from the policy of rationing and high prices pursued by the OPEC countries, to the more general and increasingly oligopolistic nature of the commodity markets, due to the greater presence of multinational companies, the formation of cartels in the producer countries themselves, the greater dependence of the United States on external energy sources and the tendency – never before so pronounced – on the part of the Soviet Union to make up the domestic food deficit by imports.

At the beginning of the period under consideration the cyclical and speculative components influenced the phase of American expansion in 1965–68 and above all in 1972–73. Within these years we find the ascending phase of a cycle which has revealed a degree of synchrony between the main economies which had not been seen since the first half of the fifties. The absence of correlation in this period between prices and the quantity of imported raw materials, on the one hand, and the trend in industrial production in the importing countries, on the other, shows the existence of strong speculative factors confirmed by observation of the spot and forward prices on the main commodity exchanges.

Expert opinions are divided when assessing the respective importance of these forces: some stress the importance of secondary and cyclical factors; others postulate a fundamental imbalance

[1] See OECD "United States," Paris, June 1973, pp. 24–37.

between the supply of and demand for resources; yet others fearlessly go to the extreme of predicting conditions of "zero growth." What seems to emerge from the debate, however, is that in view of the undoubted influence of medium- and long-term factors on the increased prices of commodities in recent years, it is unlikely that the situation existing in the first 20 years after the war whereby such prices acted essentially as a check on world inflation, will recur.

In the light of the origin and nature of these inflationary forces, the coexistence of rising prices, reduced profit margins and slower income growth can be placed in its right perspective. In fact, we have seen the end of the expanding phase of a large cycle which began in the early fifties and continued until the late sixties, thanks to particularly favourable conditions in respect of the supply of labour and raw materials.[1] The pressure on profit margins, the reduction in available income as a result of a deterioration in the terms of trade, and monetary and fiscal policies aimed at offsetting inflation and the adverse balance of payments contributed, particularly in 1973 and 1974, to check the growth of demand and start the downward phase of the cycle.

The crisis in the international monetary system reflected these basic phenomena, and the present pattern of flexible exchange rates which is the ultimate outcome of that crisis can be regarded as the only one able to permit adequate freedom to economies which had to pass through a delicate transition phase in the search for new and more lasting foundations. In particular, increasing inflation exercised strong pressures on the creation of international liquidity, leading the United States, which was now the only reserve currency country, to break its links with gold, thus eliminating the main restrictive factor affecting the supply of liquidity. The result was an increase in the endogenous character of the creation of the world money supply through the normal channels of financial intervention and interest rates (which rose sharply). For a number of years no attempt was made to check the strictly domestic – and therefore "exogenous" in relation to the rest of the world economy – factors which caused the American balance

[1] See in this connection J. R. Hicks, "Real and Monetary Factors in Economic Fluctuations," *Scottish Journal of Political Economy*, November 1974.

of payments to show a deficit, and that, too, facilitated the financing of world inflation. The "Triffin problem" was consequently aggravated: between 1967 and 1971 (declaration of inconvertibility) the ratio of the USA's total reserves to its liabilities fell from about a half to around a quarter. The lack of confidence in the key currency increased accordingly.

Inflationary trends also exercised more direct pressures in the direction of exchange flexibility. On the one hand, inflation at rates which more than doubled, thus affecting export prices themselves, presented enormous management problems for economic policies aimed at maintaining the prices in every country in line with those of competitors and were thus an inducement to "isolate" export prices. On the other hand, the growing disparities in absolute terms of inflation rates in the various countries increasingly induced creditor nations to protect themselves against imported inflation and debtor nations to restore the balance of their accounts with foreign countries by depreciating their own currency.

This last point raises the question of the mechanism of the international transmission of inflationary thrusts and that concerning the distinction between countries "exporting" (those responsible) and countries "importing" (the victims) inflation. The preceding analysis has, however, emphasised the dissemination and universal nature of inflationary forces. That makes it possible to give the problem of transmission its true proportions and consequently to restate it radically. Empirically, moreover, the transmission mechanism based on the prices of goods in international trade seems to have assumed a more important role than that of the pure Keynesian mechanism (based on an excess demand for exports) and that of the monetary mechanism (based on an excessive creation of money through the external component). In recent years, indeed, the OECD countries have become considerably more open. But the degree of openness still differs widely from one country to another.[1] Together with the dimensions of the economy and the degree to which national and foreign pro-

[1] The extremes are represented by the Netherlands and the United States with a degree of openness (measuredly the ratio of average exports and imports of goods and services to national income) equal to 50 per cent and 6 per cent respectively in the early seventies.

ducts can be substituted for one another, that means that the ability to contain the internal effects of changes in world prices or determining such changes is greatest in the case of the United States, Federal Germany and the United Kingdom, average for countries like France and Japan and least for small, very open economies like those of Austria, Holland, Switzerland and Norway.

3. IMPLICATIONS AND DIRECTION OF ECONOMIC POLICY

Accordingly, the system must provide adequate answers to the demands made on it. A new equilibrium is sought by means of complex substitution procedures aimed at a far-reaching reallocation of resources allowing for their changed conditions of relative scarcity. The reply is undoubtedly already being given, as is confirmed by the trend of investment in plant and equipment during the present recession. Such investment seems to be relatively sustained, considering the slackness of demand and the checks resulting from particularly restrictive monetary policies. Moreover, in a number of countries, there are reports of programmes for the reorganisation of production which will imply a high rate of capital accumulation. In response to the pressures on profit margins resulting from higher costs of labour and raw materials, enterprises – after a first phase of uncertainty and pessimism – are therefore reacting "physiologically," i.e. investing in production techniques which permit savings on factors of production in short supply.

The system's automatic reply should however be stimulated and sustained by suitable economic policies which avoid the two extremes of excessive laxity and excessive restriction.

Permissive monetary policies might divert firms from the correct line – namely that of investment and reorganisation – by arousing the facile hope of being able to achieve a new business equilibrium, as indeed happened during some phases of recent inflation, by adjusting prices upwards. Moreover, an attempt to secure greater flexibility in the prices system through the continuation of the already excessively long phase of serious recession which began in the first half of 1973 would clearly be disrupting and too extensive.

In the long run, the second of the two extremes seems to be the more dangerous. Assuming bouts of inflation are absorbed or brought under control, a problem of aggregate demand and the reflation of the economies might arise, and this would be dealt with in the first phase by reorganising the international monetary system and controlling the processes for creating and distributing liquidity.

In fact "... if the international economy is to be effectively 'reflated', there must, one would think, be a more or less dependable international money in terms of which the 'reflation' is to be carried out. It is now not obvious that such a money exists ..."[1]

The collapse of the international capital market during the summer months revealed the inability of the present world monetary structure to ensure an adequate framework for financing disequilibria in the balance of payments. The Euro-dollar market seems to have come out of the crisis somewhat shaken up. This has probably contributed to consolidating the structure, but it is equally likely that it will involve a loss of elasticity in the global dollar supply, although it was precisely the increase in that supply which made it possible in the last decade to create international liquidity on a scale in keeping with the expansion of world trade.

In fact, throughout that period the ratio of official reserves to world imports showed a declining trend; but, if the index of relative scarcity is calculated by putting aggregate international liquidity (i.e. including liquid resources held by commercial banks and the public), as numerator, the basic trend seems on the whole stable. An excessive creation of international liquidity occurred in the three years 1970–72. The consequent loss of control over the world money supply was the price paid by the monetary authorities of industrial countries for defending to the bitter end an out-dated system of exchange ratios. But the relative "abundance" of international liquidity (confirmed by both the indices referred to above) decreased in 1973 and even more in 1974. There was a similar trend in the ratio of money to income calculated for the main industrial countries taken together. If this trend continued to predominate, it might compromise not only a rapid

[1] J. R. Hicks, *op. cit.*, page 214.

recovery from the present recessive phase but also the possibility of readjusting production ratios within individual countries and between groups of countries as a result of changes in the terms of trade. A new equilibrium would be reached at lower levels of economic activity, at a disproportionate economic and social cost, as is clear if we consider that already the loss of potential production in the OECD countries in the 1974–75 recession will probably be greater than the aggregate financial surplus which it is estimated that the OPEC countries will accumulate between now and 1980, namely about 200–300,000 million dollars (at 1974 prices).[1]

The alternative of absorbing the present imbalances in international trade and payments through increased imports by developing countries financed by the surplus funds of the oil-producing nations, seems a far more sensible alternative. A new expansionary phase in world trade would constitute a decisive element in sustaining demand in industrial countries and offset the downward trend in their economies observed in recent years. A gradual process of adjustment to changed world economic relations could also enable the industrial countries to defend the high growth rates of the post-war period.

To that end, however, the creation and distribution of international liquidity must be controlled by the authorities in a coherent manner.

During the second half of 1974 the authorities diverted part of the monetary flows from private to public channels, either by direct credit agreements between countries or through the oil facility system of the International Monetary Fund. But the problem is to expand that intervention systematically. Machinery for regulating the world money supply, conditioned as at present by the monetary policies of one or two large countries and aimed mainly at achieving objectives of domestic economic policy, may have an adverse effect – particularly in a period characterised by far-reaching changes in the structure of the world economy.

---

[1] See Morgan Guaranty Co., World Financial Markets, January 1975, and T. D. Willett, "The Oil Transfer Problem," *Department of Treasury News*, January 1975.

RESUME

1. L'inflation de 1968 à 1974: Caractéristiques nouvelles

Dans les dernières années l'inflation a été caractérisée par son accélération constante et par sa diffusion. Simultanément, on a constaté un sous-emploi constant des facteurs de production et un affaiblissement des taux de croissance. En troisième lieu, l'évolution des prix relatifs des biens et des facteurs a entraîné une redistribution des revenus: l'accroissement des coûts des matières premières et de la main-d'oeuvre a exercé une pression constante sur la rentabilité des entreprises, ce phénomène se reflétant dans la morosité des principales bourses internationales. Enfin, l'accélération du processus inflationniste s'est accompagnée d'une crise du système monétaire international qui remonte à la dévaluation de la livre en 1967, à l'introduction du double marché de l'or en 1968 et à la non-convertibilité du dollar en 1971.

2. Les forces et les mécanismes inflationnistes

Pour l'explication de l'inflation récente, les arguments monétaristes ne sont guère convaincants. Fondés sur l'hypothèse d'un déséquilibre entre la demande monétaire globale et l'offre correspondante, ils sont difficilement conciliables avec la stagnation de la production et le sous-emploi des ressources. De même, ils ne permettent pas d'interpréter l'évolution relative des prix et des revenus.

Il est plus intéressant de partir de cette évolution elle-même en montrant les difficultés croissantes qu'éprouve le système des prix à empêcher que cette évolution n'aboutisse à des pressions sur le niveau général dex prix. Dans les secteurs où il existe un excès de demande, les prix augmentent plus rapidement qu'ils ne diminuent dans les secteurs caractérisés par un excès de l'offre. La rigidité des salaires exerce une pression constante en faveur d'une inflation rampante. De même, l'expansion plus rapide des industries hautement intégrées et du secteur tertiaire où règnent les monopoles accentue la rigidité des prix, particulièrement à la baisse.

Les politiques visant à l'amélioration de la balance des paiements, liées à l'importance attribuée au plein emploi, impliquent plus d'ajustements à la hausse dans les pays excédentaires que d'ajustements à la baisse dans les pays déficitaires. Ce fonctionnement inflationniste du système créé à Bretton Woods s'explique par la difficulté de concilier la confiance dans la monnaie de réserve avec une création suffisante de moyens de paiement internationaux: la première nécessité a progressivement cédé le pas à la seconde.

Ces dernières années, le processus inflationniste est resté lié à la rigidité avec laquelle le système répond à l'évolution des prix relatifs, notamment lorsque cette évolution est inattendue. La demande totale de capitaux et de main-d'oeuvre tend à dépasser les possibilités du produit national et l'inflation est devenue le moyen par lequel la demande globale s'ajuste à ces possibilités. D'autre part, on assiste à une redistribution des revenus entre pays, une part plus large du revenu des pays transformateurs devant être transférée aux pays fournisseurs de produits primaires. Ces deux influences se sont manifestées avec une ampleur inconnue jusqu'à présent.

Dans les années 1960, le marché du travail a été caractérisé par une pénurie relative qui a réduit l'élasticité de l'offre. Cette situation a été aggravée par un déséquilibre sectoriel de l'offre et de la demande de main-d'oeuvre en ce qui concerne sa composition par sexe, âge, nationalité et qualification professionnelle. Il en est résulté des revendications syndicales plus actives et constantes.

Des facteurs cycliques et spéculatifs ont contribué à l'augmentation exceptionnelle des cours des matières premières après 1968 ainsi qu'à l'amélioration sensible des termes de l'échange en leur faveur. Il ne faut guère s'attendre à un retour de la situation qui a caractérisé les vingt premières années après la guerre où la détérioration des termes de l'échange des producteurs de matières premières freinait l'inflation mondiale. Nous avons assisté à la fin de la phase d'expansion d'un long cycle qui a commencé vers 1950 pour se poursuivre jusqu'à la fin des années 1960 grâce à des conditions particulièrement favorables de l'offre de travail et de matières premières.

L'inflation accrue a, de son côté, exercé une forte pression sur la création de liquidités internationales obligeant le dollar à rompre ses liens avec l'or, ce qui éliminait le principal facteur restrictif affectant l'offre de liquidités. Entre 1967 et 1971, le rapport des réserves totales des Etats-Unis à leurs engagements est tombé de la moitié à un quart environ. La méfiance envers le dollar s'est accrue en conséquence.

Les tendances inflationnistes ont également exercé une pression directe en faveur de la flexibilité des changes. Leur effet sur les prix à l'exportation posait d'énormes problèmes d'administration monétaire qui incitaient à isoler ces prix. D'autre part, les disparités des taux d'inflation selon les pays ont incité les nations créditrices à se protéger de l'inflation importée en dépréciant de leur propre monnaie. Bien entendu, la mesure dans laquelle l'inflation peut être transmise dépend du caractère plus ou moins ouvert de l'économie nationale du pays considéré.

3. *Conséquences et orientations économiques*

En réaction aux pressions qu'exerce sur leurs marges de profit l'élévation des coûts de la main-d'oeuvre et des matières premières, les entreprises investissent aujourd'hui dans des techniques de production permettant d'économiser les facteurs de production dont l'offre est déficiente. La nécessaire reflation de l'économie doit cependant passer par la réorganisation du système monétaire international et le contrôle des processus de création et de distribution des liquidités. Mais il faudrait pour cela pouvoir compter sur l'existence d'une monnaie internationale inspirant confiance . . .

La perspective la plus raisonnable est celle d'une absorption des déséquilibres actuels des échanges et des paiements au moyen d'importations accrues des pays en voie de développement financé par les excédents des pays producteurs de pétrole. Une telle formule viendrait soutenir la demande dans les pays industriels et compenserait la tendance récessionniste observée ces dernières années. Il faut cependant se garder des effets négatifs que peut avoir un mécanisme de régulation de l'offre mondiale de monnaie qui resterait conditionné comme à présent par les politiques monétaires d'un ou deux pays dominants et qui viserait principalement des objectifs de politique économique nationale. Ce danger est particulièrement réel dans la période actuelle caractérisée par le bouleversement des structures de l'économie mondiale.

LA CHARTE SOCIALE EUROPEENNE: DIX ANNEES D'APPLICATION

par

FADIL H. SUR*

La Charte Sociale Européenne, le premier traité international régional protégeant les droits fondamentaux sociaux et économiques de l'individu, est le „pendant" de la Convention Européenne des Droits de l'Homme,[1] et présente un intérêt tout particulier pour la construction européenne. L'année 1975 marque le dixième anniversaire de son entrée en vigueur, le 26 février 1965.[2]

Il serait peut-être utile, à cette occasion, de faire le bilan provisoire de cette décennie en insistant particulièrement sur le fonctionnement dans la pratique des mécanismes institués par la Charte et rechercher certains de ses effets sur la législation et pratique des Etats Contractants.

I. QUELQUES FAITS

La Charte Sociale Européenne est également le premier traité international protégeant les droits économiques et sociaux, ayant un effet contraignant sur les Etats qui l'ont ratifiée et munie d'un système de contrôle international. Signée à Turin le 18 octobre 1961 par douze Etats membres du Conseil de l'Europe, la Charte

---

* Directeur des Affaires économiques et sociales du Conseil de l'Europe, ancien Professeur d'économie et de finances à l'Université d'Ankara, ancien membre du Conseil d'Administration du B.I.T., Docteur *honoris causa* de l'Université de Hacettepe, Ankara.

[1] Le Comité des Ministres, dans son message spécial du 20 mai 1954 adressé à l'Assemblée Consultative déclarait: „Notre Comité s'efforcera d'élaborer une Charte Sociale Européenne ayant pour objet de fixer les objectifs sociaux que les membres s'efforcent d'atteindre et de guider l'action du Conseil dans le domaine social. Cette Charte constituerait dans ce domaine le pendant de la Convention Européenne des Droits de l'Homme et des libertés fondamentales."

[2] Cet exposé constitue dans l'esprit de son auteur un complément à l'excellent article publié par M. Finn Tennfjord, en 1961, dans le volume IX de l'Annuaire européen. L'auteur voudrait rendre hommage à la mémoire de Finn Tennfjord, son collaborateur le plus proche et ami personnel, disparu prématurément en 1967.

Sociale est entrée en vigueur le 26 février 1965, après sa ratification par cinq Etats:[1] Royaume-Uni, Norvège, Suède, Irlande et République Fédérale d'Allemagne; cinq autres Etats ont ratifié plus tard, le Danemark, l'Italie, Chypre, l'Autriche et la France, de telle sorte que le nombre des Parties Contractantes est actuellement de dix.

La Charte se compose d'un Préambule, de cinq parties et d'une Annexe.

Le *Préambule* met en lumière deux aspects fondamentaux: l'objet de la Charte et son champ d'application *ratione personae*. Le but de la Charte consiste dans „la jouissance des droits sociaux, sans discrimination fondée sur la race, la couleur, le sexe, la religion, l'opinion politique, l'ascendance nationale ou l'origine sociale" et: toutes les catégories de la population, tant rurale qu'urbaine, doivent bénéficier de la promotion du bien-être visée par les dispositions de la Charte.

La *première partie* contient l'énumération des droits et principes fondamentaux dont la réalisation est reconnue comme objectif d'une politique que les Parties Contractantes poursuivront par tous les moyens utiles, sur les plans national et international.

La *seconde partie* définit la portée des droits énumérés en première partie et leur donne la forme d'engagements formels. Elle comporte une énumération des mesures par l'application desquelles les Parties Contractantes s'efforcent de garantir et de réaliser les 19 droits fondamentaux[2] fixés dans la première partie. Ces mesures sont au nombre de 72.

---

[1] Elle est entrée en vigueur, conformément à l'article 35, § 2, le 30e jour suivant la date du dépôt du cinquième instrument de ratification ou d'approbation, à savoir celui de la République Fédérale d'Allemagne, survenu le 27 janvier 1965. Voir les Annexes I et II, pour les dates de ratification et d'entrée en vigueur, les articles et paragraphes ratifiés.

[2]

- Article 1er: Droit au travail.
- Article 2: Droit à des conditions de travail équitables.
- Article 3: Droit à la sécurité et à l'hygiène dans le travail.
- Article 4: Droit à une rémunération équitable.
- Article 5: Droit syndical.
- Article 6: Droit de négociation collective.
- Article 7: Droit des enfants et des adolescents à la protection.
- Article 8: Droit des travailleuses à la protection.
- Article 9: Droit à l'orientation professionnelle.
- Article 10: Droit à la formation professionnelle.
- Article 11: Droit à la protection de la santé.
- Article 12: Droit à la sécurité sociale.

La *troisième partie* fixe les conditions matérielles nécessaires à la ratification de ce Traité. Il en résulte que la première partie doit être acceptée dans son ensemble en tant que déclaration d'intention. De plus, les Etats doivent être liés par cinq des sept articles qui constituent le noyau de la Charte[1] et un nombre supplémentaire d'articles ou de paragraphes numérotés de la Partie II, de sorte que le total des engagements acceptés ne soit pas inférieur à 10 articles ou à 45 paragraphes numérotés.[2]

La quatrième partie de la Charte institue un système de contrôle international de son application de par des Etats contractants. Les rapports biennaux sont présentés par ceux-ci et quatre organes prennent part au contrôle:

- un Comité d'experts indépendants, composé de sept membres, élus par le Comité des Ministres du Conseil de l'Europe;
- un Comité gouvernemental,[3] formé d'un représentant de chacun des Etats contractants. Ce Comité invite deux organisations d'employeurs et deux organisations internationales de travailleurs au plus à envoyer des observateurs, à titre consultatif, à ses réunions;
- l'Assemblée Consultative;
- le Comité des Ministres.

La cinquième partie de la Charte contient certaines dispositions concernant les dérogations en cas de guerre ou de danger public; la possibilité d'apporter des restrictions à l'exercice des droits garantis; les relations entre la Charte et le droit interne ou les accords internationaux; la mise en oeuvre au moyen des conven-

---

- Article 13: Droit à l'assistance sociale et médicale.
- Article 14: Droit au bénéfice des services sociaux.
- Article 15: Droit des personnes physiquement ou mentalement diminuées à la formation professionnelle et à la réadaptation professionnelle et sociale.
- Article 16: Droit de la famille à une protection sociale, juridique et économique.
- Article 17: Droit de la mère et de l'enfant à une protection sociale et économique.
- Article 18: Droit à l'exercise d'une activité lucrative sur le territoire des autres parties contractantes.
- Article 19: Droit des travailleurs migrants et de leurs familles à la protection et à l'assistance.

[1] A savoir les articles 1 (Droit au travail), 5 (Droit syndical), 6 (Droit de négociation collective), 12 (Droit à la sécurité sociale), 13 (Droit à l'assistance sociale et médicale), 16 (Droit de la famille à une protection sociale, juridique et économique) et 19 (Droits des travailleurs migrants et de leurs familles à la protection et à l'assistance).

[2] En Annexe 2 figure un tableau récapitulatif des acceptations des divers articles de la Charte Sociale par les Parties Contractantes.

[3] Pour l'appellation, voir le réglement intérieur du Comité gouvernemental.

tions collectives; l'application territoriale; les amendements et les clauses finales.

Enfin, l'*Annexe* spécifie la portée de la Charte en ce qui concerne les personnes protégées; et une interprétation de certains articles.

Une fois la Charte entrée en vigueur, le Comité des Ministres du Conseil de l'Europe a mis en place, conformément à l'article 25 „le Comité d'Experts," en désignant sept membres sur une liste d'experts indépendants de la plus haute intégrité et d'une compétence reconnue dans les matières sociales internationales, proposés par les Parties Contractantes.[1]

L'Organisation Internationale du Travail a désigné, suivant l'article 26, un représentant qui participe, à titre consultatif, aux délibérations de ce Comité.

Cette première instance de contrôle est désignée dans les documents, et donc dans cet article également, comme „Comité d'Experts Indépendants de la Charte Sociale."

Le Comité des Ministres a approuvé d'autre part le questionnaire à adresser aux Gouvernements dont le projet a été préparé par le Comité d'Experts Indépendants. A titre d'exemple, nous citons les questions relatives à l'Article 2 § 1 (Droit à des conditions de travail équitables):

A. Prière d'indiquer les dispositions législatives et réglementaires applicables à la durée du travail, journalier et hebdomadaire.

B. Prière d'indiquer les règles concernant la durée normale du travail et les heures supplémentaires qui figurent en général dans les conventions collectives. Quel est le champ d'application de ces règles?

C. Prière d'indiquer la moyenne de la durée effective du travail pour chaque grande catégorie professionnelle.

D. Prière d'indiquer la mesure dans laquelle la durée du tra-

---

[1] Le Comité se compose actuellement des personnes suivantes: M. Pierre Laroque (Français, Président du Comité), Président de la section sociale du Conseil d'Etat; le Professeur L. E. Troclet, Professeur de droit social international (Belge, Vice-Président du Comité), Ministre d'Etat; le Professeur G. Kojanec, Professeur de droit international privé (Italien, Rapporteur Général du Comité); M. B. Bull (Norvégien), Maire d'Oslo, ancien Président de la Cour Suprême du Travail de Norvège; le Professeur B. Zanetti, Professeur de droit du travail (Suisse); M. A. N. Loizou (Chypriote), juge à la Cour Suprême de Chypre; le Professeur H. Armbruster, Professeur de Droit public (Allemand).

vail a été réduite par la législation, par les conventions collectives ou dans la pratique, notamment en raison de l'augmentation de la productivité pendant la période considérée.

E. Dans le cas où certains travailleurs ne sont pas couverts par des dispositions de cette nature, établies soit par la législation, soit par les conventions collectives, soit par d'autres mesures, prière d'indiquer la proportion de travailleurs qui n'est pas couverte (*cf.* Article 33 de la Charte).

Voici un autre exemple, l'Article 5 (Droit syndical):

A. Prière d'indiquer si la loi interdit à certaines catégories de travailleurs, et dans l'affirmative auxquelles, de constituer des syndicats ou d'y adhérer ou les soumet à certaines restrictions à cet égard et, notamment s'il existe des dispositions législatives ou réglementaires spéciales applicables à la constitution d'organisations par les fonctionnaires et d'autres personnes employées par les autorités publiques centrales ou locales.[1]

B. Prière de donner des indications sur les mesures de caractère général ou particulier qui s'appliquent aux organisations de travailleurs et d'employeurs, notamment les lois sur les associations et les réunions, les lois sur la sécurité de l'Etat, etc. ... Indiquer, en particulier, les conditions d'enrégistrement ou autres que les organisations de travailleurs et d'employeurs doivent remplir lors de leur constitution et les dispositions auxquelles elles doivent se conformer au cours de leur existence.[1]

C. Prière d'indiquer les mesures destinées à garantir la liberté syndicale et notamment à protéger les organisations de travailleurs contre toute ingérence des employeurs.

D. Prière d'indiquer, le cas échéant, les dispositions législatives concernant l'affiliation des organisations de travailleurs et d'employeurs à des fédérations nationales et à des organisations internationales de travailleurs et d'employeurs.[1]

E. Prière d'indiquer dans quelle mesure les garanties prévues par cet article s'appliquent aux membres des forces armées et de la police.[1]

La deuxième instance de contrôle „le sous-comité du Comité Social Gouvernemental" „composé d'un représentant de chacune

---

[1] Si votre pays a ratifié les Conventions internationales du Travail n° 87 (Liberté syndicale et protection du droit syndical), il suffira de fournir un résumé des rapports adressés jusqu'à présent au B.I.T. sur l'application de cette Convention.

des Parties Contractantes" a également commencé à fonctionner.[1] Cet organe est appelé „Comité gouvernemental de la Charte Sociale" dans les documents du Conseil de l'Europe et donc dans notre article.

Le Comité Gouvernemental a invité (article 27 § 2) une organisation internationale d'employeurs et deux organisations de travailleurs, en l'espèce l'Organisation Internationale des Employeurs, la Confédération Internationale des Syndicats Libres, la Confédération Mondiale du Travail à envoyer des observateurs, à titre consultatif, à ses réunions.

Le premier cycle de contrôle commança lorsque par lettre en date du 31 janvier 1968, à laquelle il joignait le questionnaire, le Secrétaire Général du Conseil de l'Europe invitait les Etats ayant ratifié la Charte Sociale (à savoir l'Italie, la Suède, la Norvège, le Danemark, le Royaume-Uni, l'Irlande et la République Fédérale d'Allemagne) à présenter avant le 1er juillet 1968 leur premier rapport qui devait porter sur la période allant de la date d'entrée en vigueur de cet instrument à l'égard de chacun d'eux au 31 décembre 1967.

Le Secrétaire Général a assuré la transmission de ces rapports au Comité d'Experts Indépendants.

Dans ses Conclusions I adoptées au cours de deux réunions en décembre 1968 et mai 1969, le Comité d'Experts indépendants préconisait l'adresse de 57 recommandations aux Etats intéressés. Toutefois, le Comité gouvernemental, dans son rapport adopté le 4 décembre 1970 (CG/Ch. Soc (70) 24 déf. page 2) demandait instamment qu'aucune des 57 recommandations proposées par les Experts Indépendants ne soit à ce stade, envoyé aux gouvernements."[2]

---

[1] Les membres de ce Comité sont les suivants: M. F. Kanler (Autriche), Conseiller ministériel au Ministère des Affaires sociales; M. Vakis (Chypre), Directeur du Département des Affaires sociales du Ministère du Travail; M. P. Juhl-Christensen (Danemark), Vice-Président du Comité, Chef du Département au Ministère des Affaires sociales et du Travail; Mme M. T. Tarkoy-Pezet (France), Division des Relations Internationales au Ministère du Travail et de la Santé Publique; M. F. Thomas (R.F.A.), Conseiller Ministériel au Ministère du Travail et des Affaires sociales; Mr. J. Downey (Irlande), Administrateur principal au Ministère du Travail; M. A. Caracciolo (Italie) Directeur de Section, Ministère du Travail et de la Prévoyance sociale; Mr. H. Havie, (Norvège) Directeur adjoint, Ministère de l'Administration locale et du Travail; Mr. S. E. Heinrici (Suède), Chef de Division au Ministère des Affaires sociales; M. J. E. D. Slater (Royaume-Uni) Président du Comité, Chef de Département au Ministère de l'Emploi.

[2] Doc. 2888 révisé, 1970.

L'Assemblée Consultative, qui avait obtenu la transmission du Rapport du Comité Gouvernemental, en plus des conclusions des Experts Indépendants, (Décision des Délégués des Ministres, 193e réunion) proposait, dans son Avis n° 57 (1971) adopté le 14 mai 1971 (7e séance) „qu'en raison des circonstances particulières qui ont marqué à ce premier stade le contrôle de l'application de la Charte le Comité des Ministres transmette globalement les conclusions des Experts Indépendants aux Etats concernés, en attirant leur attention sur les observations y contenues, ainsi que sur les propositions de Recommandations ...."

Par sa résolution (71) 30, adoptée le 12 novembre 1971 par les Délégués des Ministres, le Comité des Ministres, considérant „qu'il ne serait pas opportun pour lui d'émettre à ce stade un jugement ...," décidait de suivre l'avis du Comité Gouvernemental en n'adressant pas à ce stade de Recommandations aux Parties Contractantes, et de transmettre tout simplement à ces Parties les rapports des trois premiers organes de contrôle.

Une nouvelle ratification de la Charte étant intervenue (Chypre), *le 2e cycle de contrôle* qui portait sur les années 68–69 concernait huit Etats, dont les 2e rapports et le premier rapport pour Chypre devaient être soumis au Secrétariat du Conseil de l'Europe avant le 1er juillet 1970. Ces rapports furent examinés par le Comité d'Experts Indépendants au cours de trois réunions tenues respectivement en octobre 1970, mars et juillet 1971. La version finale des Conclusions II fut adoptée le 4 novembre 1971 et préconisait encore l'envoi d'un certain nombre de recommandations aux Etats intéressés.

Le Comité gouvernemental, dans son second rapport (CG/Ch. Soc (72) 40) estimait „que en tout état de cause, c'est seulement le Comité des Ministres qui peut décider de l'opportunité et du contenu de telles recommandations." De plus, en raison du laps de temps écoulé entre le dépot du rapport national et la saisine du Comité des Ministres, la situation incriminée dans un Etat donné pouvait avoir subi des modifications et le Comité était d'avis qu'„il serait inopportun que le Comité des Ministres envisage d'adresser des recommandations à des Etats déjà engagés dans un processus de révision d'une législation" contraire à la Charte d'après les Experts Indépendants.

L'Avis (64 (1973)) adopté par l'Assemblée le 26 septembre 1973

(10e séance) précisait qu'il est loisible au Comité d'Experts Indépendants „de présenter des propositions de recommandations..." et que „l'article 29 de la Charte devrait en principe trouver application lorsqu'une disposition de la Charte n'a pas été observée.

Toutefois, l'Assemblée estimait que dans certains cas il n'était peut-être pas opportun d'adresser des recommandations formelles et que „le Comité des Ministres pourrait alors ... transmettre [aux Etats intéressés] les observations des experts à titre de suggestions ...."

Elle décidait donc de proposer au Comité des Ministres qu'il:

"adresse aux Etats intéressés des recommandations portant sur l'application de quelques dispositions particulièrement importantes de la Charte, soit de l'article 1, paragraphe 2, de l'article 2, paragraphes 1, 3, 4 et 5, de l'article 3, paragraphe 2, de l'article 5 et de l'article 6, paragraphe 4 ..." et

"transmette pour le surplus les propositions de recommandations émises par le Comité d'experts indépendants aux différents Etats intéressés sous forme de suggestions ...."

Mais le Comité des Ministres par sa Résolution (74) 16, adoptée le 29 mai 1974, se contentait d'attirer „l'attention des Gouvernements des Etats ayant ratifié la Charte sur les observations formulées" ... [dans les rapports des différents organes de contrôle] „notamment en ce qui concerne les actions nécessaires en vue de rendre les législations et les pratiques nationales conformes aux obligations découlant de la Charte."

Pour *le 3 cycle de contrôle* qui couvrait les années 70–71, le Secrétariat Général invitait les sept premiers Etats à avoir ratifié la Charte à présenter leur 3e rapport biennal avant le 1er juillet 1972; Chypre devait soumettre son 2e Rapport et l'Autriche, qui avait ratifié la Charte le 29 octobre 1969, présentait son 1er Rapport biennal. Dans ses conclusions III, le Comité d'Experts indépendants s'abstenait de proposer toute recommandation, fait que le Comité Gouvernemental relevait „avec satisfaction" dans son 3e rapport (CG/Ch. Soc (74) 14).

Quant à l'Assemblée Consultative, dans son Avis 71 (1975) adopté le 22 avril 1975 (3e séance) elle exprime sa „vive déception que le Comité des Ministres n'ait pratiquement donné aucune suite aux propositions les plus importantes ..." contenues dans son avis précédent et insiste pour le Comité des Ministres:

„adresse des recommandations en vue d'une stricte application de la Charte
„invite les Etats intéressés à mettre leur législation et leur pratique en harmonie avec les dispositions de la Charte ..." et
„transmettre à titre de suggestion aux Etats intéressés les autres observations du Comité d'Experts Indépendants."

Ce dernier ne s'est pas encore prononcé (fin juin 1975) alors que *le 4e cycle de contrôle* (période du 1er janvier 1972 au 31 décembre 1973) a déjà commencé pour le Comité des Experts indépendants qui examine à l'heure actuelle les 4e rapports des huits premiers Etats ayant ratifié la Charte, le 3e Rapport de Chypre et le 2e rapport autrichien (lettre de demande des rapports du 20 décembre 1973 – date de soumission: avant le 1er juillet 1974).

II. QUELQUES OPINIONS

Après avoir décrit brièvement, pour ainsi dire de l'extérieur, certains faits concernant la Charte Sociale Européenne, nous arrivons à la partie de cette étude où nous essayerons de résumer les opinions et les conceptions des instances de contrôle et émettre quelques appréciations personnelles.

1. Le rôle des organes de contrôle

Un domaine dans lequel l'incertitude quant à la portée exacte des dispositions de la Charte s'est manifestée est celui relatif au rôle des organes chargés du contrôle de l'application de la Charte, et notamment du Comité d'Experts Indépendants et du Comité gouvernemental.

Les dispositions pertinentes de la Charte se bornent en effet à indiquer que le premier de ces organes doit examiner les rapports des Etats Contractants (ainsi que toutes observations émanant des partenaires sociaux) et transmettre ses conclusions au second, auquel il incombe de présenter un rapport au Comité des Ministres en y annexant les conclusions des Experts indépendants.

En l'absence d'indications plus précises quant à la nature du *mandat* des deux comités d'experts, ceux-ci ont été amenés à formuler eux-mêmes leur conception de leur propre rôle.

C'est ainsi que le premier des organes de contrôle mentionné dans la Charte, à savoir le Comité d'Experts Indépendants relève qu'il a été conçu comme „le cadre nécessaire pour une interprétation objective des dispositions liant les Etats et pour une évaluation de leur application, qui ne soient pas celles des intéressés eux-mêmes," en raison de qualités telles que l'„indépendance" „la plus haute intégrité et compétence," l'„impartialité" qui caractérisent par définition ses membres. Selon les Experts indépendants, leurs conclusions ne devraient donc pas être remises en cause, sauf si „pour des raisons impérieuses," le Comité des Ministres, l'Assemblée Consultative ou les Experts gouvernementaux devaient sur la base de sérieuses motivations ou de faits nouveaux contester une interprétation ou une appréciation émanant des Experts indépendants eux-mêmes.[1] L'Assemblée Consultative est également d'avis que „les interprétations données par les experts indépendants doivent être considérées comme des avis particulièrement autorisées, dont on ne saurait s'écarter, sauf raisons impérieuses."[2]

Ayant ainsi défini son propre rôle, ce comité a avancé une conception quant à la nature du mandat du Comité Gouvernemental. Après avoir souligné que ce comité est „composé de représentants des Parties Contractantes appartenant aux administrations sociales nationales," et qui „a été institué pour assister le Comité des Ministres dans tous les travaux qu'il consacrera à des questions relatives à la Charte,"[3] le Comité d'Experts Indépendants souligne que, „compte tenu de sa nature, la mission du Comité Gouvernemental semble devoir être, sur la base des rapports biennaux des Etats Contractants et des conclusions des experts [indépendants], de promouvoir la collaboration internationale entre ces Etats, en appréciant en particulier les préoccupations sociales communes auxdits Etats, et la suite à donner aux constatations et propositions du Comité d'Experts [indépendants], en recherchant le moyen de favoriser une évolution des législations et institutions sociales des Etats Contractants, là où elles révèlent des

[1] Conclusions III des Experts indépendants de la Charte Sociale Européenne – Introduction générale, paragraphe 9 et 14 – Strasbourg 1973.

[2] Avis n° 64 (1973) § 6 et surtout Avis n° 71 (1975) § 5.

[3] Ainsi s'est exprimé le Comité Gouvernemental dans son deuxième rapport (CG/Ch. Soc. (72) 40, paragraphe 21).

insuffisances, et en soumettant, le cas échéant, au Comité des Ministres des projets de recommandations."[1]

Il apparaît ainsi clairement que le Comité d'Experts Indépendants se considère comme la seule instance technique mandatée pour remplir une fonction purement juridique dans le cadre de l'application de la Charte Sociale, fonction qui s'exprime par un avis de conformité ou de non-conformité des législations et pratiques nationales avec les normes définies dans la Charte. Il est à souligner qu'une évolution s'est produite dans la conception du Comité d'Experts Indépendants de son propre rôle, dans la mesure où cet organe ne propose plus au Comité des Ministres, comme il l'avait fait lors des deux premiers cycles de contrôle biennaux, d'adresser des Recommandations aux Gouvernements des Etats dont les législations ne sont pas jugées conformes aux obligations découlant de la Charte. Cette évolution est significative car elle ne fait que confirmer le contenu purement juridique de l'action des Experts indépendants, toute recommendation aux Gouvernements des Etats membres du Conseil de l'Europe ayant une nature politique. D'autre part, le rôle du Comité Gouvernemental n'est, selon les Experts indépendants, qu'incidentellement juridique, sa nature d'organe subsidiaire du Comité des Ministres le rendant plus adapté à seconder une action politique en vue de la réalisation des objectifs de la Charte Sociale, qui s'identifient, dans le domaine des droits sociaux et économiques de l'homme, avec les objectifs de l'Organisation même.

Le Comité Gouvernemental pour sa part, tout en reconnaissant le rôle purement et *uniquement* technique des Experts indépendants, considère que sa propre nature de conseiller du Comité des Ministres sur toutes les questions afférentes à la Charte Sociale, y compris les interprétations et appréciations du Comité d'Experts Indépendants, comporte nécessairement un travail d'évaluation, et donc de confirmation ou contestation des conclusions de ce dernier. Il estime, en d'autres termes, que parmi ses prérogatives d'ordre institutionnel figure également une compétence juridique, dans l'acception technique du terme, sans aucune limitation, et qu'il incombe *aux deux comités* de formuler des conclusions sur la mesure dans laquelle les Parties Contractantes satisfont à leurs

---

[1] Conclusions III des Experts indépendants, paragraphe 11.

engagements. Le Comité Gouvernemental se reconnaît toutefois également un rôle politique car il estime que dans ses avis au Comité des Ministres il pourra indiquer les circonstances dans lesquelles des recommandations pourraient être envisagées.

Ce serait une erreur, nous semble-t-il, que de considérer cette confrontation dialectique entre les deux comités d'experts comme stérile. Elle a en effet été nécessaire voire positive dans la mesure où elle a permis l'instauration d'un dialogue entre ces deux organes, au cours duquel chacun d'entre eux a examiné à fond sa „raison d'être," ses fonctions, et son rôle dans le contexte de la mise en oeuvre de la Charte Sociale, compte tenu des conceptions de l'autre organe sur son propre rôle. Ceci a permis, au cours des trois premiers cycles de contrôle, un rapprochement progressif très important des positions respectives.

Les deux comités concordent en effet aujourd'hui sur la nature uniquement „technique" des conclusions des experts indépendants, sur la nécessité d'interpréter certaines notions de caractère général telles que „la durée raisonnable du travail journalier et hebdomadaire" ou „le niveau de vie décent," compte tenu du contexte économique et social des Etats en cause, de la conscience commune des populations concernées, des situations conjoncturelles et du fait que les Gouvernements doivent choisir des priorités. Quant à l'opportunité d'adresser des recommandations aux Gouvernements des Parties Contractantes, les deux comités sont de l'avis que le Comité des Ministres modulera son action en fonction des circonstances politiques, économiques ou sociales, ou du fait qu'un Gouvernement intéressé a manifesté son intention de modifier sa législation dans le sens nécessaire pour se conformer à la Charte. Le fait d'avoir manifesté leur accord pour que le Comité des Ministres fasse usage de son pouvoir discrétionnaire dans le choix des moyens et des méthodes susceptibles de solliciter et encourager les Parties Contractantes à appliquer correctement et intégralement les dispositions acceptées de la Charte, représente une preuve de la sensibilité acquise progressivement par les deux comités instantés par la Charte, et notamment par les experts indépendants, vis à vis des implications d'ordre politique inhérentes au contrôle de l'application de cet instrument.

L'Assemblée Consultative et le Comité des Ministres, les deux autres organes de contrôle de la Charte, se situent, d'après le Comité d'Experts Indépendants, au niveau de la politique européenne en général. Ils sont donc qualifiés, l'un et l'autre, pour se saisir des conclusions du Comité d'Experts Indépendants et des propositions de politique sociale du Comité gouvernemental dans le cadre de l'ensemble de la politique européenne, dont les aspects sociaux ne sauraient être dissociés de ses aspects économiques et politiques. Le Comité des Ministres est d'ailleurs seul compétent pour prendre des décisions, soit pour émettre des recommandations, soit pour entreprendre des actions inspirées des conclusions et propositions qui lui sont présentées.[1]

C'est ainsi qu'au terme des deux premiers cycles de contrôle de l'application de la Charte, couvrant respectivement les périodes de 1965 à 1967 et de 1968 à 1969, le Comité des Ministres a tenu compte des incertitudes quant à la portée exacte de certains engagements contenues dans la Charte, et au rôle respectif des organes chargés du contrôle de son application, qui ont caractérisé la première phase de la mise en oeuvre du Traité, et a décidé qu'il était prématuré d'adresser des recommandations aux Gouvernements des Etats dont la législation ne semblait pas, aux yeux des Experts Indépendants, entièrement conforme aux obligations découlant de la Charte. Le Comité des Ministres est toutefois convenu d'adresser aux Parties Contractantes les conclusions des deux comités instantés par la Charte et l'Avis de l'Assemblée Consultative, attirant l'attention des Gouvernements intéressés sur le contenu de tels documents, ,,notamment en ce qui concerne les actions nécessaires en vue de rendre les législations et les pratiques nationales conformes aux obligations découlant de la Charte.''[2]

On pourrait peut-être considérer que si, d'une part, le Comité des Ministres entend attirer l'attention des Gouvernements sur l'ensemble des documents mentionnés dans les résolutions, d'autre part, la référence explicite aux ,,actions nécessaires en vue de rendre les législations et les pratiques ... etc.'' ne peut que viser les Conclusions des Experts Indépendants, car c'est le seul document qui propose que les Gouvernements intéressés soient invités à entreprendre un certain nombre d',,actions'' en vue de la pleine

[1] Conclusions III, Intr. pp. XIV § 13.
[2] *Cf.* Résolutions (71) 30 et (74) 16 du Comité des Ministres.

application de la Charte.[1] Cette interprétation du contenu de la Résolution (74) 16 signifierait, en d'autres termes, que tout en évitant d'addresser lui-même des Recommandations au Gouvernements concernés, le Comité des Ministres considère que les ,,actions'' préconisées par les experts indépendants sont de nature à permettre aux législations nationales de se conformer aux obligations découlant de la Charte. Cette interprétation semble d'ailleurs confirmée par le libellé de la Résolution (71) 30 indiquant *expressis verbis* que ,,les conclusions du Comité d'Experts Indépendants ... fournissent des éléments utiles et susceptibles de contribuer à la pleine mise en oeuvre des principes énoncés dans la Charte,'' tandis que aucun commentaire n'est fait au sujet des conclusions du Comité Gouvernemental.

Cette confirmation implicite de la part du Comité des Ministres de l'autorité du Comité d'Experts Indépendants sans pour autant infirmer celle du Comité Gouvernemental, trouve par ailleurs sa justification dans la nécessité de faire progresser par tout moyen approprié l'application des principes contenus dans la Charte. Dans cette optique, les Conclusions des Experts Indépendants (qui, lors des deux premiers cycles de contrôle, préconisaient expressément l'envoi de Recommandations aux Gouvernements des Etats dont la législation n'était pas jugée conforme aux dispositions de la Charte) sont plus ,,constructives'' car elles recommandent l'adoption des mesures nécessaires à assurer une pleine application de la Charte, et il est logique que, tout en ayant à l'esprit les observations du Comité Gouvernemental, les Gouvernements des Etats intéressés soient invités à considérer les Conclusions des Experts Indépendants dans une optique constructive, la seule susceptible de leur permettre une mise en oeuvre progressive et sûre de la totalité des dispositions acceptées de la Charte Sociale.

L'Assemblée Consultative, quant à elle, ayant proposé[2] lors du premier cycle de contrôle, l'envoi aux Gouvernements des Parties Contractantes des conclusions des deux comités d'experts, en dehors de toute recommandation, aurait souhaité au terme du

---

[1] Bien entendu, les avis de l'Assemblée vont également dans ce sens; mais ils se basent presque exclusivement sur les appréciations des experts indépendants.

[2] Avis n° 57 (1971).

deuxième cycle de contrôle[2] que le Comité des Ministres adresse aux Gouvernements des Etats intéressés „des recommandations portant sur l'application de quelques dispositions particulièrement importantes de la Charte." Ces dispositions concernent notamment l'abolition du travail forcé, la durée du travail et du congé payé annuel, la réduction de la durée du travail (ou l'octroi de congés payés supplémentaires) dans le cas d'occupations dangereuses ou insalubres, le repos hebdomadaire, l'exercice du droit syndical et le droit de grève.

Cette proposition de l'Assemblée ayant été formulée en pleine conscience du fait que „l'envoi d'une Recommandation est une mesure très importante," et que „la décision ordonnant un tel envoi ne saurait être prise à la légère et qu'elle doit faire l'objet d'un examen approfondi,"[2] il est possible de constater que les deux organes politiques intervenant, chacun selon ses prérogatives, dans la procédure de contrôle de l'application de la Charte, à savoir le Comité des Ministres et l'Assemblée, ont formulé deux jugements de fond divergents quant à la nature des mesures à prendre pour assurer la pleine application du Traité. Il faut toutefois considérer que l'envoi de Recommandations n'est préconisé par l'Assemblée, au stade actuel, que lorsque „il est clair que l'Etat auquel elle est destinée n'a pas observé l'une ou l'autre des dispositions qu'il a acceptées."[2] et uniquement pour des dispositions très importantes, telles que celles mentionnées ci-dessus. L'Assemblée considère en effet que „dans le cas où les Etats qui n'ont pas respecté en tous points l'une ou l'autre des obligations qui leur incombent aux termes de la Charte s'efforcent visiblement de remédier aux lacunes de leur législation et aux défectuosités de leur pratique, il n'est peut-être pas indiqué de leur adresser des Recommandations formelles ... mais sans doute serait-il possible de leur transmettre les observations formulées par le Comité d'Experts [Indépendants], tout au moins sous forme de „suggestions."[3] Si ces „suggestions" devaient rester sans suite, l'Assemblée estime que le Comité des Ministres devrait décider, à

---

[1] Avis n° 64 (1973).

[2] Document 3276 révisé de l'Assemblée Consultative, point 12 de l'exposé des motifs.

[3] *Ibid.* point 13.

la majorité des deux-tiers prévue par la Charte, d'avoir recours aux recommandations.

Au terme de cette analyse du rôle des divers organes de contrôle de l'application de la Charte, nous pouvons conclure que les premiers trois cycles biennaux (le quatrième étant en cours) ont permis aux organes mêmes, grâce à un travail d'analyse de définir la sphère de leurs compétences respectives et de dissiper en grande partie les incertitudes qui ont caractérisé les premières années de la mise en oeuvre du système de contrôle international de l'application de la Charte.

Toutefois, ainsi qu'on le verra ci-après, cette recherche au niveau des instances chargées du contrôle de l'application de la Charte n'a pas empêché à ce traité de produire des effets très importants sur le plan de la pensée juridique, des législations, des pratiques et de la conscience commune.

2. *Quelques résultats*

Cherchons maintenant à formuler quelques réflexions sur les résultats obtenus par l'élaboration et la mise en oeuvre de la Charte Sociale Européenne.

Une grande partie des effets de la Charte se produisent probablement déjà avant sa ratification,[1] car ratifier cet instrument signifie essentiellement être déjà en mesure d'honorer les obligations découlant des dispositions acceptées. Certains Etats membres économiquement et socialement avancés sont peut-être déjà, au moment de l'élaboration d'une Convention internationale, dans l'heureuse situation d'avoir atteint en grande partie le niveau des normes adoptées. D'autres doivent faire un effort plus ou moins considérable pour y adapter leurs législations nationales. Avant ou pendant les procédures de ratification d'un traité international, la comparaison entre la législation nationale et les normes internationales finalement adoptées, permet aux gouvernements et aux parlements de tirer des enseignements et de modifier ou compléter éventuellement la législation nationale. On pourrait même dire que l'effort à entreprendre est même plus

[1] Cette affirmation vise essentiellement les Etats qui ratifient la Charte longtemps après sa conclusion ou qui envisagent de la faire prochainement.

considérable dans les Etats membres les moins développés, l'instrument international reflétant souvent l'état, dans ses grandes lignes, de la législation des Etats développés qui jouent un rôle important dans l'élaboration de ces instruments.

Une fois la ratification accomplie, un certain nombre de modifications supplémentaires sont encore rendues nécessaires à cause d'une évaluation inexacte ou incomplète de la portée de certaines dispositions de la Charte, de la part de ces Etats. Elles témoignent de la volonté des Etats d'honorer leurs engagements, mais cette même volonté se serait manifestée peut-être avant la ratification si toutes les implications de cet acte avaient été complètement clarifiées. Peut-être les Etats qui ratifient tardivement voient mieux les implications que ceux qui ont ratifié les premiers.

Par contre, d'autres modifications des législations des Parties Contractantes n'interviendront qu'assez longtemps après la ratification de la Charte; elles ont pour but de donner application aux dispositions de nature ,,dynamique'' prévoyant une amélioration progressive, dans le temps, des législations. Il s'agit, par exemple, des obligations de réduire progressivement la durée du travail (article 2, § 1), d'élever le niveau du régime de sécurité sociale (article 12, § 3), etc.

Evaluer les ,,résultats'' de la mise en oeuvre de la Charte Sociale signifie finalement déterminer la mesure dans laquelle les dispositions de ce traité ont été respectées, dans le système juridique, social et économique de chacun des Etats membres du Conseil de l'Europe.

Il n'est donc malheureusement guère possible d'estimer de façon complète l'importance de l'effort accompli par les différents Etats en vue de la ratification de la Charte. On ne peut se baser que sur quelques indices imparfaits, tels que le nombre et la nature des dispositions acceptées par chaque Etat Contractant, et la mesure dans laquelle ces dispositions sont réellement appliquées. Considérons ces deux points:

a) Taux d'acceptation de la Charte Sociale

Les dix-neuf articles de la Partie II de la Charte comportent, ainsi qu'on l'a dit au début de ces considérations, soixante-douze paragraphes représentant autant d'engagements juridiques de caractère international.

Si les dix Etats Contractants avaient accepté chacun la totalité de ces dispositions, l'ensemble des engagements souscrits serait au nombre de 720. Cela n'a évidemment pas été possible, car le total de ces engagements est de 593, ainsi que le montre la liste ci-après:

Autriche	62
Chypre	34
Danemark	44
R.F.A.	67
France	70
Irlande	63
Italie	72
Norvège	60
Suède	59
Royaume-Uni	62
Total	593

La première constatation qu'on peut faire en examinant ce tableau est que, dans l'ensemble, les dispositions de la Charte ont été acceptées dans une proportion de 82%, et que, pour les huit Etats ayant accepté le plus grand nombre d'engagements, ce chiffre moyen atteint la valeur de 89%. Si d'une part il est indéniable que ce procédé statistique ne serait significatif, dans le sens où nous entendons l'utiliser, que si le quotient choisi tenait compte de la totalité des Etats Membres du Conseil de l'Europe et non seulement des Parties Contractantes (le dénominateur étant dans ce cas représenté par le produit 72 × 18 au lieu de 72 × 10), d'autre part il serait absurde de considérer que les Etats qui n'ont pas encore ratifié la Charte ne seraient en mesure de satisfaire à aucune de ses obligations. Le cas de la France est, à ce sujet, assez significatif dans la mesure où cet Etat a attendu douze ans avant de ratifier la Charte, mais a finalement accepté 70 dispositions sur 72.

Il est donc légitime de limiter notre analyse aux seuls Etats Contractants, ce qui nous permet de constater que, dans l'ensemble, la Charte a été acceptée dans une très large mesure.[1] On ne

[1] Pour tous les Etats concernés, sauf un, cet engagement se situe bien au-dessus du minimum de 10 articles ou 45 paragraphes nécessaires pour accéder à la ratification de la Charte (voir Annexes I et II).

saurait sous-estimer l'importance de ce fait, car, indépendamment de toute considération ultérieure quant à l'application réelle des dispositions acceptées, il donne la mesure de la volonté des gouvernements de progresser sur la voie tracée par la Charte Sociale. Le premier „résultat" directement mesurable produit par la Charte est en effet représenté par cet engagement international, de nature à la fois juridique et politique, à appliquer et respecter les dispositions de la Charte, engagement qui n'aurait évidemment pas été souscrit, la Charte n'eût-elle pas existé.

Il serait naturellement souhaitable qu'en raison de la place particulièrement importante occupée par la Charte Sociale dans le contexte des objectifs généraux du Conseil de l'Europe, la totalité des Etats membres puissent, dans un avenir assez rapproché, ratifier ce Traité.[1] La plupart des incertitudes qui ont marqué les premières phases de la mise en oeuvre de la Charte, et qui sont inévitables lorsqu'il s'agit d'un instrument d'une telle complexité, ont en effet été dissipées, ce qui devrait encourager certains des huit Etats n'ayant pas encore ratifié la Charte[2] à faire un effort dans ce sens. Il est indéniable toutefois que la volonté politique d'agir dans le sens préconisé par la Charte est déjà présente auprès de tous les gouvernements car la procédure de ratification du Traité se trouve dans une phase assez avancée en Belgique, en Islande et au Luxembourg, tandis que tous les autres Etats examinent sérieusement la possibilité d'entamer une telle procédure dans un proche avenir.[3]

Pour permettre à la Charte d'atteindre complètement ses objectifs, il serait en outre nécessaire que les Etats contractants n'ayant pas accepté la totalité des dispositions du Traité (seule l'Italie a réalisé cet exploit), s'efforcent d'élever progressivement le nombre des obligations acceptées.[4] Du point de vue formel, cette opération est des plus simples, car, ainsi qu'on l'a souligné précédemment, elle ne comporte qu'une notification au Secrétaire

---

[1] Avis n° 64 (1973) et exposé des motifs de l'avis page 1.

[2] Il s'agit des Etats suivants: Belgique, Grèce, Islande, Luxembourg, Malte, Pays-Bas, Suisse, Turquie.

[3] Ainsi le Parlement Européen a demandé à trois reprises aux Etats membres des Communautés européennes n'ayant pas encore ratifié la Charte de „procéder sans tarder à une ratification même partielle de la Charte Sociale Européenne" (voir Rés. du Parlement Européen du 14/5/63, du 2/7/68 et du 30/4/73).

[4] Ces engagements ultérieurs font partie intégrante de la ratification et portent les mêmes effets dès le 30e jour suivant la date de la notification (Article 35).

Général du Conseil de l'Europe. Pendant la période considérée, aucune notification d'acceptation n'est encore survenue.

b) Taux d'application de la Charte Sociale

Toute évaluation en termes quantitatifs de la mesure dans laquelle la Charte Sociale est appliquée par l'ensemble des Etats Contractants et, individuellement, par chacun d'entre eux, ainsi que toute analyse comparative de l'évolution de cette mesure au cours des trois premiers cycles de contrôle ne saurait théoriquement se faire sans disposer de données exactes, définitives et homogènes quant au nombre des dispositions appliquées et à celui des dispositions non appliquées.

Le tableau qui suit, tiré des „Conclusions III" du Comité d'Experts indépendants, nous permet de formuler quelques considérations préliminaires quant à la possibilité d'effectuer de telles comparaisons et d'en tirer des conclusions significatives. Sont exclues de ce tableau les données relatives à Chypre et à l'Autriche dont les rapports ont été examinés au cours du deuxième et du troisième cycle seulement. Il y a lieu en outre de rappeler que les trois cycles de contrôle couvrent respectivement les périodes 1965–1967, 1968–1969, et 1970–1971. Le total des dispositions acceptées par les sept Etats considérés est de 427, mais en raison de la présence du même engagement dans le texte de deux dispositions différentes[1] ce chiffre est ramené à 414.

	Cycles		
Engagements	1er cycle	2e cycle	3e cycle
Engagements satisfaits	228	283	313
Engagements non satisfaits	56	61	60
Engagements à propos desquels le Comité n'a pu se prononcer	130	70	41
Totaux	414	414	414

[1] Notamment le paragraphe 4 de l'article 1 (Droit à l'orientation, la formation et la réadaptation professionnelles) qui fait double emploi avec l'article 9 (Droit à l'orientation professionnelle), l'article 10 (Droit à la formation professionnelle) et l'article 15 (Droit des personnes physiquement ou mentalement diminuées à la formation professionnelle et à la réadaptation professionnelle et sociale).

Ce tableau nous permet de constater qu'au cours des trois premiers cycles de contrôle le nombre des engagements non satisfaits est demeuré relativement constant, et que, par contre, celui des engagements satisfaits et des engagements à propos desquels le Comité d'experts indépendants n'a pu se prononcer sont caractérisés par une allure inverse, croissante pour le premier et décroissante pour le second. On peut donc en déduire qu'au cours du deuxième et du troisième cycle, ce Comité a été en mesure, grâce à l'amélioration progressive de la qualité des rapports nationaux, de se prononcer sur une grande partie des cas douteux, et que, pour la plupart de ces cas, la ,,conclusion'' a été dans un sens favorable aux Etats considérés.

Quant à l'objet de notre recherche, à savoir le taux d'application de la Charte, le tableau nous indique que les résultats des trois premiers cycles de contrôle sont caractérisés par une marge relativement élevée d'incertitude représentée par le nombre d'obligations au sujet desquelles aucune décision n'a pu être prise. Ces obligations représentent en effet 30% du total des obligations acceptées, pour le premier cycle, 16% pour le deuxième et 9% pour le troisième cycle. A première vue on pourrait considérer que tout résultat ayant une possibilité d'erreur de 9% ou plus ne saurait être considéré comme significatif et en conclure qu'aucune indication valable quant au taux d'application de la Charte n'est disponible après le troisième cycle de contrôle. Si toutefois on considère que parmi les 41 obligations au sujet desquelles un doute persiste quant à leur application, après le troisième cycle de contrôle 28 concernent l'Italie (70%), la marge d'erreur possible n'est plus que de l'ordre de 3%.

Ceci nous permet peut-être d'affirmer que, pour ce qui concerne les Conclusions des experts indépendants, une appréciation suffisamment exacte de la mesure dans laquelle la Charte a été appliquée par les sept Etats considérés n'est possible que pour la période couverte par le troisième cycle de contrôle, à savoir les années 1970–1971, et que par conséquent il faut être très prudent lorsqu'on entreprend une comparaison quant au taux d'application de la Charte, entre les résultats des trois cycles.[1]

[1] Le Comité gouvernemental, dans son deuxième rapport (CG/Ch. Soc (72) 40) et le Comité d'experts indépendants dans ses Conclusions III estiment respectivement que le passage du premier au deuxième cycle a été marqué par ,,un net accroissement

On parvient à cette même conclusion si l'on considere la qualité implicitement „expérimentale" et provisoire des deux premiers cycles de contrôle qui ont été caractérisés souvent par la présentation de rapports nationaux au contenu approximatif et dans une large mesure incomplet, par une certaine divergence dans l'interprétation des obligations découlant de la Charte donnée par les autorités nationales et par les instances internationales chargées du contrôle de l'application du Traité, et finalement par un conflit de compétence entre deux de ces instances. La conjugaison de ces trois phénomènes sont les effets sur le fonctionnement du système de contrôle se sont manifestés à des degrés différents selon les Etats et le cycle de contrôle considérés, donne aux résultats quantifiables des trois cycles un caractère plutôt hétérogène, ce qui confirme nos conclusions quant à la comparabilité et à la signification de ces données tant au sens absolu que relatif.

des résultats positifs de la mise en oeuvre de la Charte" et par „une évolution particulièrement positive de la mise en oeuvre de la Charte," en raison de l'augmentation de la proportion des dispositions considérées comme respectées par rapport au nombre total des dispositions acceptées. Ce que ces comités ont sans doute voulu indiquer par l'expression „résultats de la mise en oeuvre de la Charte" sont les résultats de la mise en oeuvre du système de contrôle de l'application de la Charte qui, du fait de l'amélioration qualitative des rapports nationaux et d'une meilleure compréhension de la portée exacte des dispositions de la Charte de la part des autorités compétentes nationales, a pu fonctionner d'une manière relativement plus complète. En effet il serait peut-être arbitraire de considérer qu'une augmentation du nombre des dispositions considérées comme respectées, accompagnée d'une diminution pratiquement équivalente du nombre des cas „douteux" coïncide nécessairement avec une meilleure „mise en oeuvre" de la Charte par les Etats Contractants. Pour éviter toute confusion semantique, il y aurait lieu, par conséquent, d'indiquer comme „résultats de l'application de la Charte" l'ensemble des mesures d'ordre législatif, réglementaire, administratif ou autre, prises individuellement ou collectivement par les Etats Contractants pour donner effet aux dispositions du Traité. L'instauration et le fonctionnement du système de contrôle international de l'application de la Charte, bien que rentrant dans cette définition considérée au sens large, est toutefois susceptible de produire des „résultats" propres qu'il convient de distinguer du point de vue conceptuel dans le but de mieux apprécier les différents aspects de la dynamique fonctionnelle qui caractérise la mise en oeuvre de la Charte. Le système de contrôle remplit, en effet, les fonctions suivantes: il permet de connaître la mesure dans laquelle le Traité est appliqué par les Etats Contractants; il permet aux organes responsables du contrôle d'interpréter les dispositions de la Charte et d'élaborer une „Jurisprudence" internationale indispensable pour une application correcte et homogène de cet instrument; Il permet d'orienter et de stimuler l'action des gouvernements en vue d'une application exacte et intégrale de la Charte. Comme „résultats de la mise en oeuvre du système de contrôle international de l'application de la Charte,"il y a lieu, par conséquent d'indiquer d'une part l'accomplissement des objectifs correspondant aux trois fonctions mentionnées ci-dessus (résultats „primaires" au sens chronologique du terme) et, d'autre part, l'ensemble des mesures (législatives ou autres) mises en oeuvre par chaque Etat Contractant pour modifier la situation interne à la suite de la connaissance des conclusions des organes de contrôle ou de l'envoi d'une recommandation de la part du Comité des Ministres (résultats secondaires).

Le troisième cycle, par contre, a été caractérisé par une nette amélioration qualitative des rapports nationaux qui ont pu être élaborés en tenant compte de la „Jurisprudence"[1] et des observations des organes de contrôle, et par un rapprochement marqué des positions respectives de ces organes, ce qui a exercé une influence positive sur l'ensemble du système de contrôle, et a permis une réduction sensible du nombre des cas „douteux" ou controversés. Nous pouvons donc accepter les données relatives au troisième cycle de contrôle comme susceptible de fournir des indications suffisamment précises de la mesure dans laquelle les experts indépendants ont estimé que la Charte est appliquée par six des sept Etats considérées.[2] Si l'on fait abstraction de l'Italie, pour la raison évoquée précédemment, le total des engagements acceptées par les six Etats est au nombre de 342 dont 281 (83%) ont été considérés comme entièrement respectés et 49 (14%) comme insuffisamment observés, tandis que pour 13 dispositions (3%) le Comité d'experts indépendants n'a pu se prononcer faute d'informations suffisantes. En incluant l'Italie dans cette analyse, ces proportions deviennent respectivement 77%, 14% et 9%.[3]

Indépendamment du degré de certitude de ces données, il est possible de faire une constatation importante, à savoir que, dans la meilleure des hypothèses qui se réaliserait si tous les cas „douteux" cachaient des situations conformes aux dispositions de la Charte, les experts indépendants ont estimé qu'au cours de la période couverte par le troisième cycle de contrôle la proportion des dispositions non entièrement ou complètement appliquées était

---

[1] Voir à ce sujet: H. Wiebringhaus „Jurisprudence du droit social européen" dans *Rivista di diritto Europeo*, Roma, 1972.

[2] Il s'agit, répétons-le, des Etats suivants: Danemark, Irlande, Norvège, République fédérale d'Allemagne, Royaume-Uni, Suède.

[3] Etant donné la nature particulière des résultats quantifiables des trois premiers cycles de contrôle, nous avons, aisnsi que nous venons de l'indiquer, été obligés de limiter notre analyse aux seuls résultats du troisième cycle, pour en tirer des conclusions valables quant au taux d'application de la Charte. Nous devrions, par conséquent, à la rigueur, prendre en considération également les données relatives à Chypre et à l'Autriche dont les deuxième et le premier rapports respectivement ont été examinés par le Comité d'Experts indépendants, au cours du troisième cycle de contrôle. Toutefois, la marge d'incertitude qui caractérise encore l'examen des premiers rapports soumis par tout Etat Contractant et qui s'identifie dans le nombre relativement élevé de cas „douteux" (23% des dispositions acceptées pour Chypre et 25% pour l'Autriche) nous conseille d'attendre les résultats des prochains cycles de contrôle avant d'essayer d'évaluer la mesure dans laquelle ces Etats appliquent la Charte sociale.

de l'ordre de 14% pour l'ensemble des Etats considérés. Ce chiffre n'est toutefois pas suffisamment représentatif en raison de la présence de variations individuelles très sensible entre les Etats concernés.

Le tableau suivant nous montre la proportion de pareilles dispositions par rapport au total des dispositions acceptées par chaque Etat[1]

Danemark	4%
Irlande	33%
Italie	15%
Norvège	10%
République féd. d'Allemagne	7%
Royaume-Uni	21%
Suède	5%

Tout jugement de valeur quant au taux „global" ou „général" d'application de la Charte devient ainsi très difficile, sinon pratiquement impossible. L'analyse doit donc se porter sur le plan individuel, le mieux susceptible de fournir des indications significatives quant à l'état d'application de la Charte sociale.

Le tableau ci-dessus nous permet de constater que pour trois Etats considérés l'application de la Charte a atteint un niveau très élevé, tandis que pour les autres des difficultés plus ou moins importantes semblent subister. Aucun Etat n'est, apparemment, complètement en règle avec les dispositions de la Charte qu'il a acceptées. L'on peut aussi constater qu'à l'exception de la République Fédérale d'Allemagne, les Etats caractérisés par la proportion la plus élevée des dispositions non appliquées, sont ceux qui ont accepté le plus grand nombre d'engagements. Cette corrélation peut être significative dans la mesure où elle montre que certains Etats, estimant leur législation en conformité avec l'interprétation qu'ils donnaient aux différentes dispositions de la Charte, se sont „exposés" outre mesure, tandis que d'autres ont préféré adopter une attitude plus „prudente."

La position des Etats Contractants à l'égard des dispositions

[1] Ces proportions ont été élaborées sur la base des informations figurant dans les Conclusions III du Comité d'Experts Indépendants. Les chiffres ont été arrondis à la valeur inférieure.

non appliquées cependant mérite quelques considérations supplémentaires.

On ne peut en effet douter de la „bonne foi" des Etats contractants au moment du choix des dispositions à accepter, notamment lorsque le nombre de ces dispositions dépasse largement, comme c'est le cas en général, le minimum nécessaire pour pouvoir ratifier le Traité. Il s'ensuit que les „lacunes" dont la présence au plan législatifs des Etats contractants a été à jour grâce à l'efficacité du système de contrôle international, loin de correspondre à des actes intentionnels visant à maintenir certaines incompatibilités avec les dispositions de la Charte, sont en réalité dues à un prolongement de situations préexistantes à la ratification du Traité, dont non-conformité potentielle avec les exigences de la Charte a été de toute évidence ignorée ou sous-estimée.

Quant à la nature des dispositions que les Experts indépendants ont considéré comme n'étant pas complètement appliquées par l'un ou l'autre des Etats contractants, il y a lieu de remarquer qu'il s'agit de la plus grande partie des dispositions de la Partie II de la Charte à l'exception des articles 9 et 10 (Droit à l'orientation et à la formation professionnelle), l'article 11 (Droit à la protection de la santé), l'article 14 (Droit au bénéfice des services sociaux), l'article 15 (Droit des personnes physiquement ou mentalement diminuées à la formation professionnelle et à la réadaptation professionnelle et sociale) et l'article 16 (Droit de la famille à une protection sociale juridique et économique), soit six articles ou 13 paragraphes, au sujet desquels, toutefois, le Comité d'experts n'a souvent pu se prononcer faute d'informations suffisantes.

c) La jurisprudence de la Charte Sociale

Déjà la ratification ou l'acceptation de la Charte nécessite une interprétation. Certains pays ont affirmé qu'ils avaient accepté la Charte parce qu'ils l'ont interprétée d'une certaine façon et que, à la lumière de cette interprétation, sont convaincus que leurs législations et pratiques étaient en conformité avec le libellé du Traité. „Or il est évident," ainsi que cela a déjà été souligné avec force dans l'Avis n° 57 (1971) de l'Assemblée Consultative, que la Charte Sociale ne saurait être interprétée par chaque pays selon un angle différent. La création même du Comité d'experts démontre que l'on a voulu qu'une interprétation uniforme, conforme à la lettre et à l'esprit de la Charte, puisse présider à l'application de la Charte chez toutes les Parties Contractantes."[1]

Or, il est encore trop tôt pour affirmer que ce but soit atteint. Toutefois, des progrès sont accomplis notamment grâce à l'action du Comité d'Experts Indépendants en ce sens. Le Comité Gouvernemental ainsi que l'Assemblée Consultative y ont également contribué et on peut dire qu'un accord s'est réalisé entre les divers organes de contrôle, sur l'interprétation de plusieurs articles.

C'est surtout le Comité des Experts Indépendants qui, en examinant les rapports biennaux, en application des articles 21 et 24, est appelé à interpréter les dispositions de la Charte. Il a, dans les Conclusions III, dégagé les principes de ses méthodes de travail:[2] „La Charte Sociale ... est un instrument juridique qui doit être interprété selon les règles normales d'interprétation des traités internationaux." ... „Lorsqu'un paragraphe est clair et précis, il doit être appliqué tel quel ...."

„Mais un grand nombre de dispositions de la Charte sont d'un caractère très général: l'article 2, paragraphe 1, oblige les Parties Contractantes à prévoir une *durée raisonnable* du travail journalier et hebdomadaire, ... „Or, ces dispositions bien que de formulation très générale, comportent des engagements juridiques." Le Comité d'Experts Indépendants est donc tenu d'en déterminer le contenu „et la portée juridique de l'engagement pris" ... Dans cet examen, le Comité s'attache à rechercher la réalité, et ne se contente pas des textes. C'est pourquoi il demande des données statistiques dans la mesure où elles peuvent être établies.

Selon le Comité d'Experts Indépendants, le degré d'exécution des engagements pris doit souvent être apprécié en fonction de facteurs économiques et sociaux. Lorsque les termes de la Charte ont un caractère très général et font appel à des notions telles que la „durée raisonnable" du travail ou „niveau de vie décent," il faut tenir compte non seulement des circonstances économiques et sociales propres à chaque pays et de la situation moyenne des pays membres du Conseil de l'Europe, mais aussi de ce qui est habituellement „décent" dans la conscience commune des popu-

---

[1] Assemblée Consultative, exposé des motifs, Doc. 3276 révisé § 19.

[2] Conseil de l'Europe, Comité d'Experts Indépendants de la Charte Sociale Européenne, Conclusions III, Strasbourg 1973, pp. XV-XVII.

lations de ces pays regardé comme „normal," „raisonnable." Enfin, de nombreuses dispositions de la Charte ont un caractère dynamique, comportant l'engagement des Parties Contractantes de faire progresser leurs législations et d'améliorer la situation des populations. Le rôle, dans ces cas, des organes de contrôle prévus par la Charte est de relever les progrès accomplis ou à accomplir sur le plan national.

Ces considérations ont recueilli la complète approbation de l'Assemblée Consultative.[1]

Voyons rapidement quelques exemples d'interprétation choisis parmi les „cas" de non-conformité.

Droit du travailleur de gagner sa vie par un travail librement entrepris (Article 1, paragraphe 2)

Les Experts indépendants ont interprété cette disposition comme comportant deux obligations différentes, à savoir l'interdiction du travail forcé et l'élimination des causes directes ou indirectes de discrimination dans l'emploi. Pour ce qui concerne la première de ces obligations, tout en constatant que le travail forcé a été aboli en tant que tel par la législation de tous les Etats Contractants, les Experts ont néanmoins estimé que cette forme de travail subsistait, sous une apparence plus ou moins déguisée, dans la marine marchande de plusieurs pays[2] à l'égard des marins coupables de désertion, désobéissance ou autre faute grave. Les mesures de contrainte ou les peines privatives de la liberté appliquées en pareilles circonstances ont été considérées par les Experts indépendants comme contraires à la disposition susmentionnée de la Charte.

Les membres du Comité gouvernemental, pour leur part, après avoir exprimé quelques réserves quant à la possibilité de qualifier de „travail forcé" l'application de réglements que les marins connaissent avant leur engagement et auxquels ils ont librement souscrit, estiment que des sanctions pénales infligées aux gens de mer doivent pouvoir se justifier lorsqu'elles sanctionnent des actes qui mettent en danger la sécurité du navire ou la vie ou la

---

[1] Rapport sur le 3e cycle de contrôle de l'application de la Charte Sociale Européenne (Rapporteur: M. Büchner), paragraphe 4.

[2] Chypre, Danemark, République Fédérale d'Allemagne, Irlande, Italie, Norvège, Suède et Royaume-Uni.

santé des personnes à bord. Le Comité gouvernemental a souligné que cette interprétation est conforme à celle donnée par l'O.I.T. à propos des Conventions Internationales du Travail n° 29 et 105.

Après avoir pris connaissance de ces observations, les Experts indépendants, tout en confirmant leur précédente jurisprudence en la matière, ont apporté quelques précisions à leur conception de la notion ,,travail forcé'' et estimé que des mesures pénales pourraient se justifier dans les cas précis mis en relief par le Comité gouvernemental.

L'Assemblée Consultative, quant à elle, dans son Avis n° 64 (1973) relatif à la période 1968–1969 avait proposé au Comité des Ministres l'envoi de recommandations aux Etats intéressés, car elle estimait que la disposition en question est parmi celles qui revêtent une importance particulière. Mais, dans son Avis n° 71 (1975), tout en exprimant sa ,,vive déception'' que le Comité des Ministres n'ait pas donné suite à sa proposition, l'Assemblée ne la réitère pas, sans doute en raison du fait qu'entre temps tous les Etats en cause ont soit modifié leurs législations sur la marine marchande, soit engagé une procédure en vue de les modifier.

Droit des travailleurs masculins et féminins à une rémunération égale pour un travail de valeur égale (Article 4, paragraphe 3)

Lorsqu'on examine les premiers rapports biennaux soumis par les Etats contractants ayant accepté cette disposition, et les observations du Comité gouvernemental sur ce point, on s'aperçoit que ces Etats, ou tout au moins ceux d'entre eux qui ont ratifié la Convention n° 100 de l'O.I.T. relative à l'égalité de rémunération entre la main-d'oeuvre masculine et féminine, ont interprété le paragraphe 3 de l'Article 3 de la Charte comme leur imposant des obligations comparables à celles découlant de ladite Convention mais en aucun cas supérieures à celles-ci, et qu'en conséquence, pour ce qui concerne le secteur privé, l'Etat n'est pas tenu d'intervenir directement dans les négociations entre les partenaires sociaux pour la fixation des salaires.

Les Experts indépendants ont, de leur côté, été d'avis que cette disposition oblige les Etats contractants qui l'ont acceptée à reconnaître non seulement en droit mais également en fait le principe de l'égalité de rémunération pour un travail de valeur égale. Ceci ne saurait se faire, selon ces Experts sans l'établissement par les gouvernements des Etats intéressés de „critères d'évaluation objective des travaux, fondés sur des méthodes appropriées (commissions d'études, enquêtes, etc.)."[1] La Charte, en effet, abandonne sur ce point aux gouvernements le choix des moyens à mettre en oeuvre pour réaliser l'égalité de rémunération entre travailleurs masculins et féminins (lois, réglements, conventions collectives ou autres mesures), à la seule condition que l'égalité soit réalisée dans la pratique. Le Comité a d'ailleurs fait remarquer que, à ce sujet, les dispositions de la Charte sont plus contraignantes que celles de la Convention n° 100 de l'O.I.T. dans la mesure où l'article 4 de la Charte prévoit expressément l'engagement de *reconnaître* le droit des travailleurs masculins et féminins à une rémunération égale pour un travail de valeur égale, et d'assurer[2] l'exercice de ce droit, alors que la Convention n° 100 comporte seulement l'engagement de *promouvoir* l'application de ce principe et d'*assurer* cette application *pour autant qu'elle soit compatible avec les méthodes suivies pour la détermination des taux de rémunération.* Or, le passage final de l'Article 4 de la Charte indique clairement que si l'exercice du droit n'est pas assuré par la voie de conventions collectives librement conclues, il doit l'être par des méthodes légales de fixation des salaires ou de toute autre manière appropriée aux conditions nationales. Après avoir constaté dans ses Conclusions I que dans aucun des Etats concernés,[3] malgré des efforts substantiels, l'engagement n'était intégralement respecté, le Comité constate dans ses Conclusions III un nouvel effort de la part de la République Fédérale d'Allemagne (qui procède à une évaluation de toute une catégorie de postes de travail), de la Norvège (création dès mars 1972 d'un „Conseil pour le statut d'égalité") et de la Suède, en vue d'une pleine application du principe de l'égalité de traitement.

Quant à l'Assemblée Consultative, elle s'est prononcée dans son Avis n° 64 (1973) sur cette question en partageant le point de vue des experts indépendants quant à l'interprétation des obligations découlant de l'acceptation du paragraphe 3 de l'article 4. Considérant toutefois l'importance des efforts déployés par les Etats

[1] Conclusions I du Comité d'experts indépendants.
[2] *Cf.* le passage final de l'Article 4.
[3] Il s'agit de la République Fédérale d'Allemagne, de l'Italie, de la Norvège et de la Suède.

concernés, l'Assemblée propose au Comité des Ministres de se borner à „suggérer aux Etats intéressés de poursuivre leurs efforts en la matière, afin d'aboutir à la pleine application de l'article 4, paragraphe 3 de la Charte."

Le Comité des Ministres pourrait prendre une décision à ce sujet au cours de l'année 1975.

Voyons un troisième cas, encore davantage controversé:

Droit des travailleurs et des employeurs à des actions collectives en cas de conflit d'intérêt, y compris le droit de grève, sous réserve des obligations qui pourraient résulter des conventions collectives en vigueur (article 6, paragraphe 4)

Lors de l'examen des premiers rapports gouvernementaux, le Comité d'experts indépendants a donné les interprétations suivantes au contenu de ce paragraphe:[1]

1. Cette disposition vise à la fois le droit de grève et le droit de lock-aout, bien que ce dernier ne soit pas mentionné explicitement;

2. Elle ne garantit le droit à des actions collectives qu'en cas de conflits d'intérêt, à l'exclusion donc des conflits de nature juridique (quant à l'existence, la validité ou l'interprétation d'une convention collective ou dans d'autres cas de différends juridiques entre travailleurs et employeurs);[2]

3. L'imposition d'une période de „temporisation" pendant la durée d'une négociation (ou d'une conciliation ou d'un arbitrage) ne constitue pas une restriction au droit de grève qui soit incompatible avec la Charte.

4. La suppression complète ou partielle du droit de grève des personnes employées dans des services publics essentiels pourrait être compatible avec la Charte, compte tenu de l'Article 31,[3] dans la mesure où la vie de la Communauté dépend des services en cause. Il en est de même pour les dispositions législatives pré-

---

[1] Voir Conclusions I, pages 39–40.

[2] Toutefois, sont compatibles avec la Charte des restrictions au recours à des actions collectives, même en cas de conflit d'intérêt, si elles sont imposées par une convention collective.

[3] L'article 31 règle la possibilité d'opérer des restrictions à l'exercice effectif des droits et principes prévus aux Parties I et II de la Charte. Des restrictions autre que celles expressément mentionnées dans la Charte sont admises lorsqu'elles sont prescrites par la loi et sont „nécessaires dans une société démocratique pour garantir le respect des droits et des libertés d'autrui ou pour protéger l'ordre public, la sécurité nationale, la santé publique ou les bonnes moeurs."

voyant le règlement obligatoire des conflits d'intérêts qui sont de nature à exposer l'économie nationale à des dangers sérieux.

5. Le droit de grève peut être restreint ou supprimé, sans que cela soit considéré contraire à la Charte, pour certaines catégories de hauts fonctionnaires, les membres de la police et des forces armées et les juges.

6. Le Comité a enfin considéré que le principe selon lequel l'exercice du droit de grève entraîne la rupture du contrat de travail n'est pas compatible avec les obligations découlant du paragraphe 4 de l'article 6.

Le Comité a estimé que les législations des Etats Contractants donnent en général suffisamment application à cette disposition. Il a toutefois remarqué que, en République fédérale d'Allemagne, l'ensemble des fonctionnaires publics sont exclus de l'exercice du droit de grève et que la législation allemande interdit toute grève qui n'a pas pour but la conclusion d'une convention collective ou qui n'est pas menée par un syndicat; qu'en Irlande les employés de l'Etat et des services publics, les personnes employées à des activités non lucratives et les travailleurs qui ne sont pas membres d'un syndicat ne bénéficient pas d'une protection suffisante de leur droit de grève; qu'en Italie, le lock-out est considéré comme un délit civil et, enfin, qu'au Royaume-Uni une grève peut entraîner la rupture du contrat de travail.[1]

Le Comité gouvernemental a estimé qu'en raison de la nature particulière et de la complexité des problèmes qui se posent dans le domaine des relations industrielles, il y a lieu de les examiner plus en détail à la lumière d'informations supplementaires à fournir par les gouvernements et, éventuellement, par les personnes intéressées elles-mêmes, avant de se prononcer sur ce point. Il a mis en relief que le Gouvernement de la République fédérale avait annoncé, avant de ratifier la Charte, son interprétation du champ d'application personnel du paragraphe 4 de l'article 6; qu'en Irlande les fonctionnaires et employés de l'Etat et le personnel des entreprises non lucratives bénéficieront en fait du droit de grève; et que l'Italie considère que dans la conjoncture économique actuelle l'introduction du droit au lock-out „équivaudrait à une regression sur le plan social."[2]

---

[1] Cette possibilité n'existe plus depuis l'entrée en vigueur de „l'Industrial relations Act, 1971" qui prévoit le maintien du contrat de travail en cas de grève ou de lock out.

[2] cf. CG/Ch. Soc (72) 40, p. 16 – 2e rapport du Comité gouvernemental.

Examinant la position des Etats intéressés par rapport au paragraphe 4 de l'article 6 de la Charte, l'Assemblée Consultative s'est ralliée à l'interprétation que les Experts Indépendants en ont donné à l'exception de la question relative à l'inclusion du droit au lock-out, sur laquelle elle n'a pas jugé utile, dans les circonstances de l'époque, de se prononcer. Dans son avis n° 64 (1973) et dans l'exposé des motifs correspondant, se référant à la déclaration faite avant la ratification de la Charte par le Gouvernement de la République fédérale d'Allemagne, l'Assemblée souligne que „les obligations d'un Etat sont déterminées, en vertu de son instrument de ratification de la Charte, par les engagements qu'il assume aux termes de l'article 20 de cette dernière, elles ne peuvent l'être par des déclarations faites par lui avant sa ratification." Elle propose l'envoi d'une recommandation au Gouvernement de ce pays, d'une simple „suggestion" au gouvernement irlandais car la situation juridique concernant le point en question „n'est pas absolument claire," et de ne rien faire à propos de l'Italie „jusqu'à ce que la situation quant aux règles de droit régissant le lock-out en Italie sont clarifiée ...."

Le Comité des Ministres n'a pas adressé de recommandations au Gouvernement de la République Fédérale d'Allemagne. Dans sa Résolution (74) 16, il a décidé, ainsi que nous l'avons indiqué précédemment, de transmettre aux gouvernements des Etats contractants les conclusions des deux comités concernés et l'avis de l'Assemblée en attirant leur attention sur les observations formulées dans ces documents.

Ces trois exemples nous offrent un portrait suffisamment précis de la complexité du fonctionnement du système de contrôle international instauré par la Charte Sociale et du dialogue constructif qui s'est instauré entre les différents organes et qui s'exprime par une recherche allant au-delà du contenu purement juridique de la Charte pour essayer d'atteindre les objectifs réalistes visés par chacune de ses dispositions. L'efficience de ce contrôle se manifeste à deux moments différents d'abord lorsqu'il révèle, souvent aux yeux mêmes des intéressés, l'existence de certaines aberrations de droit et de fait dans les systèmes juridiques internes des Etats contractants, favorisant ainsi une prise de conscience au niveau national et international de la nécessité de faire évoluer les législations dans le sens préconisé par la Charte; ensuite, lorsqu'il stimule, encourage et oriente de par la force morale qui le caractérise, l'introspection, la critique dialectique au niveau politique, doctrinaire et social et, souvent sans même faire appel à la recommandation – instrument politiquement délicat – l'action des gouvernements et des parlements nationaux. Certes, il est des domaines où cette action se caractérise par une „prudence" qui est fonction du niveau de radicalisation du problème dans le tissu juridique et social d'un peuple, et de la propension des gouvernements à assimiler le fruit de conceptions plus avancées, muries en dehors des conditionnements historiques et culturels et des contraintes économiques et sociales qui ont marqué l'évolution et la consolidation des systèmes juridiques nationaux.

Mais la Charte, en tant que synthèse de ces systèmes, en même temps qu'„ordre nouveau" est un instrument relativement très récent. L'avenir nous confirmera sans doute qu'elle aura pu prévaloir contre les inerties qui accompagnent inévitablement tout changement véritable.

d. Les dispositions de la Charte qui n'ont pas été acceptées

En tant qu'instrument cadre, la Charte Sociale étend son champ d'application matériel, ainsi qu'on l'a vu, à l'ensemble des principes et des droits susceptibles de constituer le fondement d'une politique sociale axée dans le sens de la justice sociale.

Pour déterminer la mesure dans laquelle de ces principes et de ces droits sont respectés par les législations des Etats contractants, nous avons fait recours aux deux paramètres d'application des dispositions acceptées et nous avons pu en tirer certaines conclusions. Le second de ces instruments analytiques revêt évidemment un caractère très relatif tout comme les conclusions auxquelles il nous a conduit. Il est clair, en effet, que toute tentative d'évaluation dans l'absolu, du degré d'application de la Charte ne saurait se faire sans prendre en considération également le nombre et la nature des dispositions que les Etats contractants tant dans leur ensemble qu'individuellement n'ont pas été à même d'accepter.

Cette nécessité d'une évaluation globale des rapports entre d'une part chacun des principes et chacune des dispositions du „droit social européen" consacré par la Charte et, d'autre part, les principes et les dispositions correspondantes mis en oeuvre sur le plan interne par les Etats contractants, indépendamment du degré d'acceptation du Traité, avait évidemment déjà été perçu par les auteurs de la Charte qui ont prévu, parallèlement au système de contrôle de l'application des dispositions acceptées, une procédure permettant aux mêmes organes de contrôle d'examiner la situation existante dans ces Etats par rapport aux dispositions qui n'ont pas été acceptées. La méthodologie adoptée est essentiellement la même que celle prévue pour le contrôle de l'application des dispositions acceptées, car elle prévoit qu'à des intervalles appropriés et sur demande du Comité des Ministres les Etats contractants présenteront au Secrétaire Général du Conseil de l'Europe des rapports relatifs aux dispositions qu'ils n'ont pas acceptées. Ces rapports seront examinés par le Comité d'Experts indépendants qui transmettra ses conclusions au Comité gouvernemental auquel il incombe d'en faire rapport au Comité des Ministres. L'Assemblée et les partenaires sociaux exercent dans ce contexte les mêmes fonctions que celles prévues dans le cadre du contrôle de l'application des dispositions acceptées et le Comité des Ministres a lui aussi la possibilité d'envisager toute forme d'action dans le but d'encourager les Etats Contractants à poursuivre leurs efforts en vue d'une application intégrale du Traité.

Ce système, dix ans après l'entrée en vigueur de la Charte, n'a pas encore été mis en oeuvre car, malgré la sollicitation provenant du Comité d'Experts indépendants et de l'Assemblée, le Comité des Ministres n'a pas à ce jour jugé opportun d'inviter, conformément à l'article 22 de la Charte, les Etats Contractants à présenter des rapports sur les dispositions qu'ils n'ont pas acceptées.

Les Experts indépendants attachent, cependant, une grande importance à la mise en oeuvre „immédiate" de la procédure prévue à l'article 22 de la Charte[1] car ils estiment qu'il ne leur sera pas possible de porter un jugement valable sur l'ensemble de la politique sociale d'un Gouvernement ainsi que sur l'application de certaines dispositions de la Charte sans connaître les raisons qui ont empêché ces gouvernements d'accepter certaines autres obligations.

Quant à l'Assemblée, elle considère que l'application de l'article

[1] *Cf.* Conclusions I, point 14; Conclusions II point 10; Conclusions III, point 33.

22 „ne devrait pas souffrir de nouveaux retards" car elle est de nature à permettre aux différentes instances de contrôle d'apprécier les difficultés qui empêchent l'acceptation de certaines dispositions de la Charte de la part des Etats Contractants.

Ayant constaté que dans leurs Conclusions II les Experts indépendants attirent „l'attention des autorités du Conseil de l'Europe sur certaines dispositions de la Charte qui n'ont été acceptées que par un très petit nombre d'Etats ou qui n'ont été respectées que par de très rares Parties Contractantes, voire par aucune"[1] l'Assemblée propose au Comité des Ministres, qu'elle considère comme juridiquement obligé de donner application à l'Article 22, de demander aux Parties Contractantes intéressées de soumettre leur premier rapports portant sur les dispositions suivantes, qui concernent essentiellement les femmes, les enfants et les jeunes:

Article 4, paragraphe 3:	droit des travailleurs masculins et féminins à une rémunération égale pour un travail de valeur égale
Article 7, paragraphe 1:	âge minimum d'admission à l'emploi
Article 8:	droit des travailleurs à la protection.

Nous ignorons les raisons qui motivent l'attitude réservée adoptée à cet égard par les Gouvernements des Etats membres du Conseil de l'Europe qui, au niveau du Comité des Ministres, n'ont pas encore pris la décision de mettre en application les dispositions de l'Article 22 de la Charte. On peut essayer d'imaginer que l'une des raisons réside dans les difficultés qui ont marqué les premières phases de la mise en oeuvre du système de contrôle international et qui pourraient avoir conduit le Comité des Ministres à ne pas compliquer encore davantage la tâche des organes de contrôle et à attendre que la situation ne soit clarifiée, avant de procéder à la mise en oeuvre de l'Article 22. Le Comité des Ministres examinera vraisemblablement à nouveau cette question au cours de l'année 1975 dans le cadre d'un ensemble de propositions formulées par le Comité gouvernemental dans le but de simplifier certaines modalités de la procédure de contrôle de l'application de la Charte et au sujet desquelles il serait prématuré de se prononcer au stade actuel.

[1] *Cf.* Conclusions II, point 9.

e. Le rôle des partenaires sociaux

Un rôle important est dévolu aux partenaires sociaux dans le contrôle de la Charte Sociale Européenne du fait de leur intervention, tout d'abord au niveau national, puis de leur participation à la procédure internationale de contrôle. Il est en effet prévu à l'article 23 de la Charte – ainsi que dans le formulaire qui sert de base à la rédaction des rapports gouvernementaux – que copies des rapports biennaux des gouvernements seront adressées à celles des organisations nationales qui sont affiliées aux organisations internationales d'employeurs et de travailleurs qui sont invitées, conformément à l'article 27, § 2, à se faire représenter aux réunions du Comité gouvernemental. A l'heure actuelle, ces organisations sont, comme nous l'avons indiqué précédemment, l'Organisation internationale des employeurs, la Confédération internationale des syndicats libres et la Confédération mondiale du travail.

Il est non seulement obligatoire pour les gouvernements d'adresser copies des rapports biennaux à ces organisations nationales, mais ils sont également tenus de transmettre au Secrétaire Général du Conseil de l'Europe toutes observations éventuellement formulées sur ces rapports par ces organisations (article 23, § 2).

Le second stade auquel les partenaires sociaux sont appelés à jouer un rôle très utile est celui de l'examen des conclusions des experts indépendants par le Comité gouvernemental de la Charte sociale. Bien que les observateurs des organisations internationales de travailleurs et d'employeurs n'y siègent qu'à titre consultatif, ils sont appelés à mettre en lumière les réactions des organisations nationales et internationales tant aux rapports biennaux et aux conclusions des experts indépendants qu'aux observations des différents gouvernements, telles qu'elles sont présentées au sein du Comité gouvernemental. Ce dernier d'ailleurs annexe à ses rapports les observations faites par les représentants des organisations internationales qui, de ce fait, sont portées à la connaissance de toutes les instances de contrôle.

Dans un troisième temps enfin, les partenaires sociaux sont appelés à collaborer aux travaux de l'Assemblée Consultative. En effet, ils participent en tant qu'observateurs aux réunions de la Commission des Affaires sociales et de la Santé publique de l'Assemblée Consultative, chargée de préparer les documents qui serviront à l'Assemblée à exercer ses fonctions en tant que troisième instance de contrôle.

Les partenaires sociaux ont commencé, quoique lentement, à prendre la place qui leur revient dans le mécanisme de contrôle de la Charte Sociale Européenne. Certaines organisations nationales envoient leurs observations et il est à souhaiter que d'autres suivront bientôt. En ce qui concerne les organisations internationales, celles-ci ont pris leur place dans le Comité gouvernemental et fournissent une contribution précieuse au mécanisme de contrôle.

CONCLUSION

Il ressort des pages qui précèdent que la Charte Sociale européenne est un instrument de progrès social et de coopération internationale qui tend à harmoniser l'ensemble des normes de la politique sociale des Etats démocratiques en Europe occidentale. Fruit d'un compromis, elle n'est certes ni parfaite, ni complète, mais a le grand mérite de contenir des éléments de dynamisme et de progrès intrinsèques et de provoquer des améliorations constantes. En effet, un grand nombre des mesures spécifiques telles que le statut européen de l'agriculteur, les instruments concernant les jeunes au travail et les handicapés, les personnes âgées, etc. ... – pour ne citer que quelques exemples dans le cadre des Conventions et Résolutions du Conseil de l'Europe – sont venus compléter et étayer les dispositions de la Charte Sociale. D'autre part, de nouveaux problèmes et aspirations se sont fait jour, telle la participation des travailleurs à la gestion de l'entreprise qui n'est pas visée par les dispositions de la Charte.

En tout état de cause, la Charte Sociale s'est fait une place dans la nouvelle Europe qui aspire à son unité. Elle joue un rôle important dans la réalisation d'une plus grande justice sociale. Elle mérite d'être mieux connue et surtout mieux soutenue par l'opinion publique en général et les partenaires sociaux en particulier.[1]

---

[1] Pour une bibliographie relative à la Charte Sociale voir ci-dessous dans la Section Bibliographique sous la rubrique „Conseil de l'Europe."

ANNEXE I

A la date du 30 juin 1975, l'état des signatures et ratifications se présentant comme suit:

ETATS	SIGNATURE	RATIFICATION	ENTREE EN VIGUEUR	NOMBRE DE § ACCEPTES
AUTRICHE	22 juillet 1963	29 octobre 1969	28 novembre 1969	62
BELGIQUE	18 octobre 1961			
CHYPRE	22 mai 1967	7 mars 1968	6 avril 1968	34
DANEMARK	18 octobre 1961	3 mars 1965	2 avril 1965	44
FRANCE	18 octobre 1961	9 mars 1973	8 avril 1973	70
REP. FED. D'ALLEMAGNE	18 octobre 1961	27 janvier 1965	26 février 1965	67
ISLANDE	non signée			
IRLANDE	18 octobre 1961	7 octobre 1964	26 février 1965	63
ITALIE	18 octobre 1961	22 octobre 1965	21 novembre 1965	72
LUXEMBOURG	18 octobre 1961			
MALTE	non signée			
PAYS-BAS	18 octobre 1961			
NORVEGE	18 octobre 1961	26 octobre 1962	26 février 1965	60
SUEDE	18 octobre 1961	17 décembre 1962	26 février 1965	59
SUISSE	non signée			
TURQUIE	18 octobre 1961			
ROYAUME-UNI	18 octobre 1961	11 juillet 1962	26 février 1965	62
				593

La Charte n'est donc pas encore ratifiée par la Belgique, la Grèce, l'Islande, le Luxembourg, Malte, les Pays-Bas, la Suisse et la Turquie; toutefois la Belgique, le Luxembourg, les Pays-Bas et la Turquie l'ont déjà signée.

Chaque paragraphe de la Charte étant considéré comme comportant un engagement particulier, les dix Etats ayant ratifié l'instrument sont donc liés à l'heure actuelle par 593 engagements sur 720. Les chiffres correspondants étaient de 427 pour le premier cycle et de 461 pour le deuxième cycle.

ANNEXE II

TABLEAU RECAPITULATIF DES ACCEPTATIONS DES DIVERS ARTICLES DE LA CHARTE SOCIALE

Dispositions de la Charte	Autriche	Chypre	Danemark	Rép. Féd. d'Allemagne	France	Irlande	Italie	Norvège	Suède	Royaume-Uni
1 (1)	■	■	■	■	■	■	■	■	■	■
1 (2)	■	■	■	■	■	■	■	■	■	■
1 (3)	■	■	■	■	■	■	■	■	■	■
1 (4)	■	■	■	■	■	■	■	■	■	■
2 (1)				■	■	■	■	■		
2 (2)	■		■	■	■	■	■	■		■
2 (3)	■		■	■	■	■	■	■	■	■
2 (4)	■			■		■	■	■		■
2 (5)	■		■	■	■	■	■	■	■	■
3 (1)	■	■	■	■	■	■	■	■	■	■
3 (2)	■	■	■	■	■	■	■	■	■	■
3 (3)	■	■	■	■	■	■	■	■	■	■
4 (1)	■		■	■	■	■	■	■	■	■
4 (2)	■		■	■	■	■	■	■		■
4 (3)	■			■	■		■	■	■	
4 (4)					■	■	■	■		■
4 (5)	■			■	■	■	■	■		■
5	■	■	■	■	■	■	■	■	■	■
6 (1)	■	■	■	■	■	■	■	■	■	■
6 (2)	■	■	■	■	■	■	■	■	■	■
6 (3)	■	■	■	■	■	■	■	■	■	■
6 (4)		■	■	■	■	■	■	■	■	■
7 (1)					■		■			
7 (2)	■			■	■	■	■	■	■	■
7 (3)	■			■	■	■	■	■	■	■
7 (4)	■			■	■	■	■		■	
7 (5)	■			■	■	■	■	■		■
7 (6)				■	■	■	■	■		■
7 (7)	■			■	■		■	■	■	
7 (8)	■			■	■	■	■	■	■	■
7 (9)	■			■	■		■		■	■
7 (10)	■			■	■	■	■	■	■	■
8 (1)	■		■	■	■	■	■		■	■
8 (2)	■				■		■			
8 (3)	■			■	■		■		■	
8 (4)	■				■	■	■			■

Dispositions de la Charte	Autriche	Chypre	Danemark	Rép. Féd. d'Allemagne	France	Irlande	Italie	Norvège	Suède	Royaume-Uni
9	■	■	■	■	■	■	■	■	■	■
10 (1)	■	□	■	■	■	■	■	■	■	■
10 (2)	■	□	■	■	■	■	■	■	■	■
10 (3)	■	□	■	■	■	■	■	■	■	■
10 (4)	■	□	■	□	■	■	■	■	■	■
11 (1)	■	■	■	■	■	□	□	■	■	■
11 (2)	■	■	■	■	■	□	□	■	■	□
11 (3)	■	■	■	■	■	■	■	■	■	■
12 (1)	■	■	■	■	■	■	■	■	■	■
12 (2)	■	■	■	■	■	□	■	■	■	□
12 (3)	■	■	■	■	■	■	■	■	■	□
12 (4)	■	■	■	■	■	■	■	■	□	□
13 (1)	■	□	■	■	■	■	■	■	■	■
13 (2)	■	□	■	■	□	■	■	■	■	■
13 (3)	■	□	■	■	■	■	■	■	■	■
13 (4)	■	□	■	■	■	■	■	■	■	■
14 (1)	■	■	■	■	■	■	■	■	■	■
14 (2)	■	■	■	■	■	■	■	■	■	■
15 (1)	■	■	■	■	■	■	■	■	■	■
15 (2)	■	■	■	■	■	■	■	■	■	■
16	■	□	■	■	■	■	■	■	■	■
17	■	□	■	■	■	■	■	■	■	■
18 (1)	■	□	■	■	■	■	■	□	■	■
18 (2)	■	□	■	■	■	■	■	□	■	■
18 (3)	□	□	■	■	■	■	■	□	■	■
18 (4)	■	□	■	■	■	■	■	□	■	■
19 (1)	■	■	□	■	■	■	■	■	■	■
19 (2)	■	■	□	■	■	■	■	■	■	■
19 (3)	■	■	□	■	■	■	■	■	■	■
19 (4)	□	■	□	■	■	■	■	■	■	■
19 (5)	■	■	□	■	■	■	■	■	■	■
19 (6)	■	■	□	■	■	■	■	■	■	■
19 (7)	□	■	□	■	■	■	■	■	□	■
19 (8)	□	■	□	■	■	■	■	□	■	■
19 (9)	■	■	□	■	■	■	■	■	■	■
19 (10)	□	■	□	■	■	■	■	■	■	■

■ accepté □ non accepté

ANNEXE III

QUELQUES EXEMPLES DES PROGRES PRATIQUES REALISES DEPUIS LE PREMIER CYCLE DE CONTROLE

- Au Royaume-Uni, la Loi du 25 juillet 1970 permet de rendre la réglementation britannique applicable aux marins plus conforme à l'Article 1er de la Charte;
- en Irlande, la Loi sur les délais minima de préavis et les conditions d'emploi (1973) (n° 4 de 1973), entrée en vigueur le 1.9.1973, prévoit des délais de préavis de licenciement proportionnels à la durée du service ininterrompu effectuée par le salarié;
- encore en Irlande, un projet de loi est en préparation qui reprend quasi-textuellement les termes du paragraphe 6 de l'Article 7 de la Charte garantissant l'inclusion des heures de formation professionnelle des jeunes travailleurs dans la durée normale du travail;
- en Suède, une nouvelle législation a été introduite qui, conformément à la Charte, interdit désormais d'employer des mineurs, encore soumis à l'obligation scolaire, à des activités agricoles;
- en République Fédérale d'Allemagne, la législation sur les jeunes travailleurs va être soumise à révision et sera complétée afin de prévoir, conformément à la Charte, un contrôle médical périodique pour les jeunes travailleurs de moins de 18 ans;
- en Irlande, également une nouvelle législation est actuellement en préparation pour réglementer le travail des enfants encore soumis à l'obligation scolaire dans tous les secteurs de l'économie;
- en Italie, la Loi n° 1204 du 30 décembre 1971 a prolongé la durée du congé-maternité et a amélioré de manière très substantielle le montant des indemnités de maternité de plusieurs catégories de travailleuses;
- un relèvement similaire des taux de prestations est également intervenu en Irlande;
- à Chypre, est entré en vigueur le 1er janvier 1973 la ,,Social Insurance Law'' 1972, qui apporte des améliorations substantielles quant au niveau des prestations de sécurité sociale, au champ d'application personnelle et aux risques couverts;
- en Irlande, une Loi de 1972 (Local Election Act 1972) a aboli une disposition de la Loi de 1898 qui exigeait des personnes ayant bénéficié de prestations d'assistance un délai de 12 mois avant de pouvoir participer aux institutions d'assistance;
- au Danemark, à la suite d'un assouplissement de la réglementation, le renouvellement des permis de séjour et de travail intervient, sans condition aucune, après deux années de résidence;
- en Suède, le renouvellement du permis de travail a été facilité après un an d'activité professionnelle, et l'octroi du permis de résidence, qui don-

ne libre accès au marché du travail, intervient après deux ans de résidence au lieu de cinq;

- en République Fédérale d'Allemagne, où le regroupement familial n'est autorisé en principe et en l'absence d'accords internationaux particuliers qu'après trois années de résidence du travailleur migrant, il vient d'être décidé de ramener ce délai à un an pour tous les travailleurs ressortissant des autres Etats ayant ratifié la Charte;
- au Royaume-Uni, les autorités de l'Irlande du Nord envisagent de modifier la législation en vue de faciliter l'accès des étrangers à des logements sociaux.

Par ailleurs, le lien créé par la Charte entre les Parties Contractantes a trouvé récemment une confirmation. A la suite de la crise du pétrole l'interdiction de recrutement des travailleurs étrangers décrétée par le Gouvernement de la République fédérale d'Allemagne, ne s'applique toutefois pas aux ressortissants des Parties Contractantes liées par la Charte.

SUMMARY

The European Social Charter, the first regional international treaty protecting the fundamental social and economic rights of the individual, entered into force on 26 February 1965.

It would be useful, on this 10th anniversary of the entry into force of the Charter, to review its achievements, particularly with regard to the working of its organs and its impact on the national legislation of the Contracting Parties.

I. SOME FACTS

Signed in Turin on 18 October 1961 by 12 member states, the Social Charter now has 10 Contracting Parties: Austria, Cyprus, Denmark, the Federal Republic of Germany, France, Ireland, Italy, Norway, Sweden, the United Kingdom.

The Charter has a preamble and is divided into 5 parts, with an Appendix.

The Preamble declares that the aim of the Charter is the enjoyment of social rights without any discrimination and by all categories of the population, rural and urban.

The *first part* lists 19 fundamental rights and principles which the Contracting Parties accept as the aim of their policy.

The *second part* sets out more specific obligations, and also the conditions for ratification, namely the acceptance of the whole of the first part and in the second part, of five out of seven specified articles (1, 5, 6, 12, 13, 16, 19), and either ten complete articles or 45 numbered paragraphs.

The supervision of the implementation of the Charter by the Contracting

States is carried out, in the first place, by a Committee of Independant Experts made up of 7 highly competent persons who examine and state their conclusions about the biennial reports of the States concerned. The International Labour Office is represented on this Committee in a consultative capacity.

A second organ of supervision is the Governmental Committee of the Social Charter, composed of one representative from each of the Contracting States. Observers from the International Union of Employers, the International Confederation of Free Trade Union and the World Labour Confederation have been invited to attend.

The reports of both organs are then transmitted to the Consultative Assembly for opinion and to the Committee of Ministers for decision.

The Contracting States submitted in 1968 their first reports on the period running from the entry into force of the Charter to the end of 1967.

Following examination of these reports, the Committee of Independant Experts proposed that Recommendations be addressed to the States concerned.

The Governmental Committee in its report, did not share this view, and the Consultative Assembly, in its Recommandation n° 57 (1971) thought that at this stage only the conclusions of both organs should be sent.

The committee of Ministers (Resolution (71) 30) felt that recommendations should not be addressed at this stage and decided simply to transmit the reports of the other 3 organs.

In their Conclusions on the 2nd biennial reports (1968–1969) of the Contracting States (including a 1st report by Cyprus, which had meanwhile ratified the Charter) the Committee of Independant Experts again proposed that a number of recommendations be addressed to the Contracting States concerned.

The Governmental Committee disagreed, maintaining that by the time the Committee of Ministers took cognisance of the matter, the Contracting States might have taken measures to amend their legislation.

The Consultative Assembly (Recommandation (64) 1973) proposed that recommendations should be addressed on the more important provisions of the Charter.

The Committee of Ministers, however, (Resolution (74) 16) limited itself to drawing the attention of the Contracting States to the observations made in the reports of the three organs.

The Committee of Independent Experts made no recommendations on the 3rd biennial reports (1970–1971) (including a 1st report by Austria which ratified in October 1969) and the Governmental Committee expressed its satisfaction at this fact.

The Consultative Assembly, however, showed disappointment (Recommendation 71 (1975)) at the lack of follow-up to the more important proposals and insisted that the Committee of Ministers should address recommendations for a strict application of the Charter by the Contracting States. No reply has been made to this request at the time of writing.

Meanwhile, the Committee of Independent Experts has started examining the fourth biennial reports (1972–1973).

II. VIEWS

1. The role of the Contracting organs

In the absence of clear terms of reference of the Committee of Independent Experts and of the Governmental Committee, each of these organs has formed its own views on its rôle.

The Committee of Independent Experts maintains that its purpose is to interpret objectively the provisions of the Charter and to assess, in an independent manner, the extent of their application. Their conclusions should not therefore be put in question, except for very serious reasons.

The Consultative Assembly shares this view.

The Committee of Independent Experts also believes that the purpose of the Governmental Committee is to promote international collaboration on common social problems and to follow up its own proposals.

The Committee of Independent Experts therefore considers it is the sole technical body empowered to assess the conformity or otherwise of the national legislations with the provisions of the Charter. This view is confirmed by the recent tendency of the Committee of Independent Experts not to make recommendations: such measures are considered to be of a political nature and therefore fall more within the competence of the Governmental Committee as a subsidiary body of the Committee of Ministers.

The Governmental Committee recognises the purely technical role of the Committee of Independent Experts, but maintains that its role of adviser to the Committee of Ministers involves an assessment of the conclusions of the Independent Experts and consequently their approval or rejection.

This argument has proved fruitful in that today both agree that the conclusions of the Independent Experts are "technical," that certain notions require a broad interpretation and that the Committee of Ministers should take action according to circumstances and to the political implications.

The Committee of Independent Experts, moreover, thinks that the Consultative Assembly and the Committee of Ministers are both competent to take cognisance of their conclusions, the latter being the sole body competent to take decisions.

Thus, for the 1st and 2nd Biennial Reports, the Committee of Ministers deemed it advisable at that early stage not to address recommendations to the Contracting States and instead transmitted to them the conclusions of the two expert committees (Resolution (74) 16) and of the Consultative Assembly, drawing their attention particularly to the action needed to conform with the Charter. This step is an implicit confirmation of the authority of the Committee of Independent Experts which alone found such action to be required.

On the other hand, the Consultative Assembly, which on the 1st biennal reports did not propose the addressing of any recommendations, when it came to the 2nd biennial reports requested the Committee of Ministers to make recommendations on the more important provisions.

It seems that the Committee of Ministers and the Consultative Assembly differ on the measures to be adopted for securing the implementation of the Charter. The Consultative Assembly, however, envisages recommendations only on very important provisions of the Charter when the Contracting States have clearly not observed them.

It may be concluded that the first 3 biennial reports have helped to define the competence of the respective organs of supervision and to dissipate many of the uncertainties which arose during the first years of application.

2. *The Results*

Ratification of the Charter may follow or be accompanied by changes in domestic legislation. This is particularly true of the less developed State, as the Charter reflects to a great extent the legislation of economically and socially advanced countries.

Following ratification, modifications may be necessary to bring fully into line with the provisions of the Charter legislation which, at the time of ratification, was thought to conform with the Charter.

Further modifications occur in order to apply the "dynamic" provisions which require progressive improvements.

No full assessment can be made of the results of the Charter. We can however follow as indicators the number of provisions accepted and the extent to which they are applied.

a) Rate of acceptance of the Social Charter

The 19 articles of the Charter contain in all 72 provisions. The ten Contracting States have, on average, accepted 82% of this total; and for the 8 Contracting States which have accepted the largest number of provisions, the percentage rises to 89.

The first tangible result is therefore the legal and political undertaking of the Contracting States to apply and respect the provisions of the Charter.

As the Social Charter ranks high in priority in the objectives of the Council of Europe, it would be desirable if all member states ratified it. The process of ratification is well advanced in Belgium, Iceland, and Luxembourg and the other member states are seriously examining the possibility of ratifying the Charter.

It would be equally desirable for the Contracting States (other than Italy which has already done so) to accept the totality of the provisions of the Charter. Formally, this acceptance involves only a notification to the Secretary General of the Council of Europe.

b) Extent of the application of the Social Charter

Precise and comparable statistical data would be necessary for a quantitative assessment of the extent of the application of the Charter and for a comparative analysis.

The only data of this kind available, the findings of the Committee of Independent Experts, shows that during the period covered by the first three biennial reports, the number of unimplemented obligations remained constant, while the number of implemented obligations increased. The number of obligations on which the Committee could not reach a conclusion decreased.

Another factor which seems to emerge is the relatively high level of uncertainty represented by the number of obligations on which the Committee reached no conclusion – 30% for the 1st biennial reports and 16% and 9% for the 2nd and 3rd biennial reports respectively. The last figure falls to 3% if one considers that 70% of the obligations on which the Committee reached no conlusion concerned only one country, Italy.

It follows that an exact assessment is possible only for the 3rd biennial reports. The period covered by the first two biennial reports was marked by ambiguity in the interpretation of the provisions and divergence of views on the precise functions of the organs of supervision. Consequently, data for this period are heterogeneous and not comparable.

Data for the period covered by the third biennial reports are, however, sufficiently reliable for assessing the extent of the Charter's application.

The equality of the national reports improved and the two organs of supervision narrowed their differences. The number of doubtful and controversial questions was consequently reduced.

The following analysis excludes Italy for the reasons already mentioned, as well as Austria and Cyprus whose 1st and 2nd reports respectively still contain a relatively high rate of "doubtful" cases. France ratified in 1973.

For the remaining six Contracting Parties 83% of the provisions were fully observed; 14% were considered not to be properly observed and no conclusion could be reached on 3%.

If Italy is included, the rates are respectively 77%, 14% and 9%.

No safe view can be reached on the global application of the Charter. As to individual countries, Denmark, the Federal Republic of Germany and Sweden have reached a very high level of application. No country is completely in line with the provisions of the Charter which it has accepted. With the exception of the Federal Republic of Germany, the States which have the highest rate of non-observation are the ones which have accepted the largest number of provisions; this probably results from varying degrees of optimism or prudence displayed in interpreting the provisions of the Charter at the time of its ratification.

The majority of the provisions have been the object of findings of non-observance by the Committee of Independent Experts in the case of at least one State. Exceptions are Article 9, 10, 11, 14, 15, 16; however the Committee often could not express an opinion on their application for lack of information.

c) Jurisprudence on the Social Charter

Clearly, the ratification or acceptance of the Charter implies an interpretation by the Contracting State. The Charter however should be interpreted in a uniform manner and the creation of a Committee of Experts was intended for this purpose.

This aim has not yet been reached but progress has been registered.

It is mostly the Committee of Independent Experts that is required to interpret the provisions of the Charter.

The rules followed are those applied in the interpretation of international treaties. If the meaning is clear the provision is applied as it stands. If not, the Committee must discover the legal extent of the obligation.

When general terms such as "reasonable working hours" and "a decent standard of living" are used, account must be taken of the economic and social situation of each of the States and of what is commonly regarded in the Council of Europe member states as "normal," "decent," and "reasonable."

With regard to the "dynamic" provisions intended to improve national legislation, the role of the organs of supervision is to throw light on the action which needs to be taken in the national context.

There follow a few exemples of the interpretation of provisions that have not been applied by the Contracting States.

Right of the worker to earn his living in an occupation freely entered upon (Article 1, para. 2)

The Committee of Independent Experts have interpreted this provision to include the prohibition of forced labour. Consequently, the practice in many countries of composing coercive sanction on merchant seamen for desertion or disobedience has been considered to be in violation of it.

The Governmental Experts maintained that certain considerations, such as the safety of the ship and its crew, could justify coercive sanctions against seamen.

The Independent Experts subsequently considered that penal sanctions could in such a case be justifiable. The Consultative Assembly, in its Recommendation on the 1968–1969 reports, requested that recommendations be addressed to governments on this matter; but when examining the 1970–1971 reports it did not repeat its request, as the States concerned had already either amended or planned to amend their legislation.

Right of men and women workers to equal pay for work of equal value (Article 4, para. 3)

Many of the Contracting States have interpreted this provision as an obligation similar to that undertaken under ILO Convention n° 100 and therefore not binding the State to intervene in the private sector.

The Independent Experts have held that this provision obliged the States to recognise not only in law but also in fact the principle of equal pay for equal work, leaving to them the choice of means for achieving it. It was noted in the last cycle that efforts towards this end were being made by the Federal Republic of Germany, Norway and Sweden.

In view of this the Consultative Assembly has proposed that the States concerned should be encouraged to continue their efforts in this direction.

Right of workers and employers to collective action in cases of conflicts of interest, including the right to strike, subject to obligations that might arise out of collective agreements previously entered into (Article 6, para. 4)

The Committee of Independent Experts considered that this provision was in general observed in the Contracting States. Some rules, however, seemed to be in violation of the provision: suppression of the right to strike for all public officials (Beamte) and limitation of the right to strike according to the purpose of the strike and its authors (Federal Republic of Germany), insufficient protection for civil servants and workers not belonging to a trade union (Ireland), prohibition of lock-out (Italy), striking considered as terminating the employment contract (United Kingdom).

The Governmental Committee considered that, due to its complexity, the matter needed detailed study.

The Consultative Assembly requested that a recommendation be addressed to the Federal Republic of Germany and a suggestion be made to Ireland. They felt no action should be taken as regards Italy.

The Committee of Ministers transmitted to the governments conclusions of the two organs of supervision and the Recommendation of the Assembly.

These three examples give us an insight into the complexity of the mechanism of supervision. The value of this mechanism is shown at two points: firstly, when the gaps in national legislation are revealed, creating an awareness of the need to change it; subsequently, when this mechanism, through its moral force, stimulates the critical analysis of a situation and directs the action of governments.

d) The provisions of the Charter that have not been accepted

To assess correctly the degree of application of the Charter it is equally important to consider the number and nature of the provisions which have not been accepted. The Charter in fact provides for a system of examining the existing situation in the Contracting States regarding those provisions they have not accepted. The procedure is exactly parallel to that followed for the accepted provisions.

This procedure has never been put into effect as the Committee of Ministers has not so far considered it opportune to do so.

The independent Experts urge its immediate application, because they believe that it is impossible to assess properly the social policy of a Government without knowing the reasons for its not accepting certain provisions.

The Consultative Assembly is of the same opinion and has proposed to the Committee of Ministers that it requests the Contracting States to submit their first report on the following Articles: Article 4, 3 – right to equal pay for equal work by men and women; Article 7, 1 – minimum age of admission to employment; Article 8 – right of employed women to protection.

It is possible that the Committee of Ministers has so far not put this procedure into effect to avoid complicating the work of the organs of supervision and to wait until all difficulties inherent in the first years of application of the treaty are overcome.

The matter will probably be examined again in the course of 1975.

e) The role of employers and workers

The international organisations of workers and of employers represented on the Governmental Committee as well as their affiliated national organisations play an important role both nationally and internationally in the mechanism of supervision of the European Social Charter.

The Contracting States are bound to send these national organisations copies of their biennial reports and they in their turn should send their observations to the Secretary-General of the Council of Europe.

Moreover the international organisations which participate as observers are called upon to state their views on the reports of the Independent Experts and the observations of the various governments. The Governmental Committee appends these observations to its reports.

Finally, these international organisations participate in the work of the Consultative Assembly when it is acting as one of the organs of supervision.

CONCLUSION

It results from what we have said that the European Social Charter is an instrument of social progress which is not perfect but contains intrinsic dynamic elements which make it a continuing stimulus to improvement over the whole range of social policy in the democratic States of Europe.

Many specific measures have come to complement the Social Charter – the European Convention on the Social Protection of Farmers, legal instruments concerning the young workers and the disabled, etc. On the other hand, new aspirations not provided for in the Charter arise, such as workers' participation in management.

The Social Charter has its place in a new Europe striving for unity. It should be better known and more widely supported.

THE EUROPEAN ORGANISATION FOR THE SAFETY OF AIR NAVIGATION – EUROCONTROL

by

RENE BULIN*

ITS ORIGINS

The safety of air navigation, in its broader sense, is often brought to the attention of the public at large, especially in the event of breakdowns in aviation safety. Nevertheless most attention has been directed at aircraft in operation and little is generally known of the organisation and systems which have been installed to ensure a safe, orderly and expeditious flow of traffic through the airspace, not only with a view to collision avoidance but also to enable operators to operate at greatest economic benefit with minimum inconvenience to passengers.

This particular aspect of air safety has been in Europe, as in the rest of the world, primarily a national responsibility. Since the second world war the standards applied and the safety requirements explicit in those standards have been coordinated through the International Civil Aviation Organisation (ICAO). The standards arrived at have been translated into specific facilities through the medium of large regional meetings, and embodied in Regional Plans covering most of the world. While these plans list the facilities which individual countries provide or intend to provide in order to meet their ICAO obligations, they do not set an upper limit on the lengths to which a nation may go in the pursuit of air safety and several countries have always operated air navigation and air traffic systems well in advance of ICAO requirements.

Even so, the growth and changing composition of air transport in Europe in the 1950's led to increasing problems. The major new factor was the introduction into civil air transport of the jet engine and this had several effects. One of these was to take civil

* Director General of EUROCONTROL.

air transport into the upper regions of the airspace above the maximum altitude of conventional piston engined aircraft (about 20,000 feet) which had hitherto been the preserve of military aviation. Secondly it sent aircraft through the sky at such speeds that they might well remain in the airspace of a particular country only for a matter of minutes and considerably shortened the decision-making time available to the air traffic control apparatus. Thirdly, the economic advantages of the new breed of aircraft pointed to a rapid increase in the amount of air traffic.

New operating techniques had to be introduced employing advanced technologies especially in the application of real-time automated systems, involving exceptionally complex, technical problems and demanding considerable investment for both development and acquisition. Costs were found to escalate rapidly and began to give real concern to the countries providing air traffic control services, at that time still wholely financed by the taxpayer. For obvious reasons this concern was most strongly felt by the smaller countries whose geographically confined airspace were crossed by the new fast aircraft in a matter of minutes.

All this was happening at a time when, in other contexts, the process of Europeanisation was taking root. In the air traffic control field, the fact that the new breed of aircraft operated mainly in an airspace where no services had been previously provided, except to military aircraft, appeared to certain states to offer a unique opportunity for organising the services on a joint European basis, over a wide area unrestrained by national frontiers.

As early as 1957 certain states were enquiring into the possibility of organising air traffic control for their airspace based on this concept and in January 1958 the problem was officially discussed for the first time at the IVth European Mediterranean Regional Air Navigation Conference of I.C.A.O. at Geneva. In the months following this conference, representatives of the Federal Republic of Germany, Belgium, Luxembourg and the Netherlands prepared the common ground for a coordination of their air traffic control services on a four-state basis.

On 30th and 31st July 1958, the Directors General of the Civil Aviation Administrations of the countries concerned met in Luxembourg. Administrative, financial and technical problems with which the participating countries would be confronted when implementing the common project were examined. France and Italy, who had in the meantime expressed their desire to participate, were also represented.

Meanwhile the project was taking shape and included the preparation of an International Convention setting up an Agency which would be charged with the common execution of air traffic services in the upper airspace of all represented countries.

This Agency was to be responsible for both the control of air traffic over the territories of the six countries, including the operation of its own air traffic control centres and other installations, and for the establishment of uniform training standards for all air traffic control personnel. Furthermore, the Agency was to operate an experimental centre for the evaluation of new equipment and procedures for air navigation and air traffic control, thus permitting a constant adaptation of its services to the ever-changing requirements of air traffic.

The Directors General of Civil Aviation met in Bonn (28–30 October 1958), Paris (27–29 January 1959), and Rome (6–9 March 1959). During the discussion of the first draft of the International Convention, they drew attention to the importance of the text being of an open nature in order to enable other States wishing for accession to become members at a later date. Moreover, the Convention was to allow for close cooperation between the founder States and any other States not yet able to adhere to it.

In autumn 1959 the United Kingdom of Great Britain and Northern Ireland expressed the wish to participate in the creation of EUROCONTROL.

The ministers responsible for civil and military aviation in the seven countries (Federal Republic of Germany, Belgium, France, the United Kingdom, Italy, Luxembourg and the Netherlands) met in Rome on 9th June 1960 to examine the draft Convention and agree on the Organisation which was to be set up.

Prior to the signing of the Convention in 1960 a preliminary diplomatic conference was held in Paris on 28th September 1960 to discuss modifications and amendments to the Convention. However Italy until then had participated in the preparatory work to a very large extent, decided for internal organisational reasons to postpone its accession – a decision which was deeply regretted by the other partner states.

On 13th December 1960 the plenipotentiaries of the Federal Republic of Germany, the Kingdom of Belgium, the French Republic, the United Kingdom of Great Britain and Northern Ireland, the Grand Duchy of Luxembourg and the Kingdom of the Netherlands held a diplomatic conference in Brussels under the presidency of the Belgian Minister for Communications at which the International Convention relating to Cooperation for the Safety of Air Navigation was signed.

THE TRANSITIONAL PERIOD: THE ASSOCIATION

The EUROCONTROL Convention was to be ratified by the Contracting Parties. However as the number of turbine-engined aircraft was increasing at an extremely rapid rate, it was essential that the measures designed to ensure the safety of the movements of such aircraft in the upper airspace be studied as a matter of urgency. The six Member States therefore signed a protocol to cover the interim period, taking note of the formation of an Association for improving air traffic control methods and equipment which was to be the forerunner of EUROCONTROL.

The purpose of the Association was to undertake immediately the study of the solutions which could be applied to the problems of air traffic control in the upper airspace when the Organisation was formed, prepare the corresponding plans and assess their effective value. To this end the signatory states set up a provisional commission consisting of two representatives from each Government for the purpose of providing the necessary resources in personnel, equipment and installations required for the studies. The share of the costs was to be calculated proportionately to the value of their respective Gross National Products.

THE CONVENTION

The Convention was ratified by the Contracting Parties and entered into force on 1st March 1963.[1] It remains effective for a

[1] The text of the Convention is published in *European Yearbook* Volume XXI, Chapter 15 at pp. 691 to 715.

period of twenty years from this date and is automatically prolonged for periods of five years providing no Contracting Party, at least two years before the expiry of the initial period, expresses its intention of denouncing the Convention.

The EUROCONTROL Convention set down in considerable detail the objective measures the contracting parties had decided upon to resolve the problems mentioned earlier. These were quite far-reaching in their implications. The essential political decision was embodied in Article 1 which stated that the contracting parties agreed to strengthen their cooperation in matters of air navigation and in particular to provide for the common organisation of air traffic services in the upper airspace.

In order to achieve this aim the signatory states set up the European Organisation for the Safety of Air Navigation EUROCONTROL. The executive responsibility for control services in the upper airspace of all the Member States would be entrusted to EUROCONTROL taking the form of collective responsibility of all the Member States acting through the Organisation. Air traffic was defined as comprising civil aircraft and those military, customs and police aircraft which conformed to the procedures of the International Civil Aviation Organisation. The level at which the "upper airspace" would begin was not defined in the Convention but was left to the unanimous decision of the national ministers in their capacity as members of the Permanent Commission, the governing body of the Organisation which is described later. This has since been generally established at 25,000 feet although some countries have adopted the level of 20,000 feet, a small anomaly which is of little practical import. Therefore in theory at least, there would be no interface between the upper airspace of individual countries allowing services to be organised with regard solely to technical and economic parameters and overcoming the problem of fast high-flying aircraft passing through individual national airspace in quick succession.

The other problem, which was mentioned earlier, namely the burden imposed on the smaller countries in particular by the increasing complexity and cost of air navigation services, was to be met in two ways. EUROCONTROL would be empowered to install, on a joint basis, the necessary air traffic control centres serving, where necessary, the airspace of more than one state. It would be able to establish common air traffic research and experimental centres for the development and testing of new systems and equipments and set up schools for the advanced and specialist training of air traffic services personnel.

As regards costs, these were to be met by a system of joint financing of the EUROCONTROL Organisation covering both capital and operating expenditure. It was calculated that it would be less expensive for one organisation to operate over a large area than if individual states carried out independent parts of the same task. A form of financial equity was to be obtained by states contributing to the Organisation's budgets broadly in proportion to their gross national product and to the services provided by the Organisation to the aircraft on their national register. To be more specific contributions to the Investment Budget, or expenditure relating to the execution of the equipment programme, would be proportional to the respective values of their Gross National Products as compiled from the statistics of the Organisation for European Economic Cooperation (OEEC).

With regard to the operating budget (expenditure relating to personnel, maintenance and operation of installations, etc.), in respect of upper airspace control, the costs would be divided in accordance with a more complex formula which took account not only of the gross national products but also of the value of the services rendered by the Organisation to civil aircraft registered in each of the Contracting Parties.

Even so the Convention also made provision for the possibility of the introduction of a system of remuneration for services rendered to users of the airspace and for such charges paid to the Organisation by the corresponding categories of users to be deducted from the contributions of the Contracting Parties.

Where the Convention was less specific was with regard to the combination of civil and military air traffic in the upper airspace. As with traffic in the lower airspace, that part of military air traffic not flying in accordance with ICAO rules, remained a national responsibility. The Convention simply stated that EUROCONTROL, in adopting its measures and in installing and operating its facilities, would do so in cooperation with the national military authorities. In practice, the interests of national defence are safeguarded by national military representatives serving on the governing bodies of the Organisation.

Nevertheless the Convention contributes to a significant evolution in international law; its scope is wider than that normally conferred by "conventions" and creates an "institution" with executive powers. Far from being a mere instrument of cooperation between States, the Organisation which it established is a "Public Service" and as such operates for the direct benefit of airspace users. By making it responsible for the control of air traffic in their sovereign airspace, moreover, the Member States conferred on the Organisation the status of an international public service.

In 1965 Ireland asked to adhere to the Convention and on 1st January 1964 became the seventh Member State.

THE ORGANISATION

The Organisation as laid down by the Convention comprises two bodies:

- the Permanent Commission for the Safety of Air Navigation;
- the Air Traffic Services Agency.

The Permanent Commission, the deliberative body, is composed of two representatives from each Member State, normally speaking the Ministers or Secretaries of State having responsibility for civil and military aviation.

The aim of the Commission is to promote in cooperation with the national military authorities the adoption of measures and the installation and operation of facilities designed to ensure the safety of air navigation and an orderly and rapid flow of air traffic, within defined airspace under the sovereignty of the Contracting Parties or in respect of which the air traffic services have been entrusted to the Parties under international agreements.

For this purpose the Permanent Commission is responsible for:

a. the study, on the basis of ICAO standards and recommended practices and having regard to the requirements of national defence, of the standardisation of national regulations governing air traffic and the standardisation of the operation of the services responsible for ensuring the safety and regulation of air traffic;

b. the promotion of a common policy to be followed with respect to radio aids, telecommunications, and corresponding airborne equipment, designed to ensure the safety of aircraft;

c. the promotion and coordination of studies relating to air navigation services and installations in order to take account of technical developments and if necessary, the study of amendments to the Regional Air Navigation Plans to be submitted to the I.C.A.O.;

d. the determination of the configuration of the airspace in respect of which the air traffic services are entrusted to the Agency;

e. the determination of the policy to be followed by the Agency in respect of remuneration for services rendered to users, and, where applicable, the approval of the tariffs and conditions of application of charges established by the Agency;

f. the study of measures designed to facilitate the financing of investments required for the functioning of the Agency or more generally of the services of the Contracting Parties which participate in the work of ensuring the safety of air navigation;

g. the exercise of the power of general supervision over the activities of the Agency.

The Commission acts through a system of recommendations, decisions, directives and conclusions.

Recommendations to the Member States relate to the standardisation of national regulations governing air traffic, the standardisation of the operation of air traffic services, the promotion of a common policy with regard to radio aids and of studies of technical developments relating to air navigational services and installations.

Decisions concern important matters of general policy. These include the configuration of the upper airspace for which air traffic services are to be entrusted to the Agency and whether any one of the Contracting Parties may transfer its responsibilities for its lower airspace to the Organisation or to another Contracting Party. Other fields in which formal decisions by the Permanent Commission are necessary relate to the power to conclude, on behalf of the Organisation, agreements with international organisations, Member States of the Organisation or other states which are necessary for the execution of the tasks entrusted to it and for the conclusion of agreements between the Organisation and any State not party to the Convention but which is desirous of using the services of the Agency.

Directives to the Agency apply to the remuneration for services rendered to users by the Agency, the tariffs and conditions of application of such charges, the financing of investments, and the entering into contracts of a purely administrative, technical or commercial nature by the Agency with the appropriate technical services, public or private of the Contracting Parties, of non-Contracting States or of international organisations.

Conclusions are formulated with respect to deliberations concerning the powers of general supervision of the Agency.

The voting system adopted for these matters is notable for the balance it achieves between the Member States. On the one hand it was necessary to give greater weight to countries making the heaviest financial contributions and this was done by allocating a number of votes to each State in relation to its Gross National Product. On the other hand, the interests of States having a low weighting factor had to be safeguarded and for this reason it was stipulated that an absolute majority of weighted votes would only be valid if the proposal was accepted by more than half the States. A unanimous vote is also required for certain matters covered by specific provisions of the Convention or the Statute of the Agency annexed thereto.

The Air Traffic Services Agency is responsible to the Permanent Commission for the executive work of the Organisation, including the control services for the upper airspace. It is administered by a Committee of Management, which is similarly organised to the Permanent Commission but at the level of officials, and a Director General. The Director General heads the team of international civil servants, known as the General Directorate, responsible for the day-to-day running of the Organisation with all the current operational planning, engineering, experimental, financial and administrative activities which that entails.

The Committee of Management meets rather more frequently than the Commission and fortunately their decisions do not require unanimity, these being taken by a variant of weighted majority voting.

The role of the Agency consists in providing air traffic services in the airspace defined by the Commission and in installing facilities required to ensure efficient and smooth operation of such services. To this end, the Agency cooperates closely with national civil and military authorities in order to satisfy as efficiently and economically as possible the needs of the air traffic under its control.

OPERATION

EUROCONTROL was set up on 1st March 1963 following ratification of the Convention.

The first task was to establish the Organisation's Headquarters in Brussels as required by the Convention and assume planning and control responsibilities. Initially, however, the embryo Agency had neither the operational equipment nor the staff with which to provide air traffic services from its own resources. It therefore entered into bilateral agreements with each of its Member States which, perforce, had established national systems in the meantime to meet their ICAO commitments, under which they would provide the General Air Traffic services in their upper airspace on the Agency's behalf with their own equipment and personnel, being remunerated for these services through the operating budget.

Belgium became the first country – in 1964 – to hand over the responsibility for the direct provision of upper airspace air traffic services to EUROCONTROL and the General Directorate continued with its planning to assume its responsibilities in the remaining airspace. However, differences in time-scale emerged between the planning of the General Directorate and the speed at which certain Member States were prepared to hand over their control responsibilities. These States, at the time when the EUROCONTROL Organisation was getting under way, were building up new air traffic control systems to meet their ICAO commitments, embracing both the upper and lower airspace, and, in the case of the United Kingdom, integrating civil and military control functions. By 1966 both France and the United Kingdom took the view that their national plans had advanced to the extent that it would be impractical and uneconomical for them to transfer the direct execution of upper airspace responsibilities to the Agency.

This led the Permanent Commission to adopt the recommendations contained in a report of a high level study group set-up to investigate the impasse, known as the "Moroni Report," whereby it was agreed that for the foreseeable future at least, the Convention could be applied in different ways in the various regions.

The outcome was that the Agency would concentrate its activities of providing direct control services to the upper airspace traffic in the BENELUX/Federal Republic of Germany Region, whilst France and the United Kingdom would continue in the interim period up to about 1980 to implement their own national schemes, excercising air traffic control in the upper airspace on a national basis on behalf of and under the responsibility of EUROCONTROL.

This interpretation of the Convention carried two financial corollaries. Firstly investments relating to the BENELUX countries and the Federal Republic of Germany and for Ireland would continue to be funded directly by the Organisation through its investment budget in accordance with the terms of the Convention, whereas France and the United Kingdom would finance investments in their own countries, leasing back to EUROCONTROL the upper airspace element of these investments over the period of their operation. Secondly the reimbursement of the operating costs of upper airspace control would be cancelled and the corresponding costs should be borne on a national or regional basis, although financial compensation from the Operating Budget was provided in the case of Ireland on account of its special position.

A further principal feature of the "Moroni Agreement" was that a fundamental study of the best system of air traffic control over Europe after 1980 should be one of the essential fields of the Organisation's future activities.

The Organisation's future activities would therefore be mainly:

- the development of common operational methods and procedures and the coordination of upper airspace ATC systems for the various participating countries;
- priority implementation of plans for the organisation of upper airspace control over the BENELUX/Federal Republic of Germany Region and plans for Ireland;
- studies relating to organisation and operation in member countries or regions expressing such a need;
- a fundamental study of the best system of Air Traffic Control

over Europe after 1980 bearing in mind the fact that such a system, if approved, might well begin to be implemented soon after 1975;

- with regard to the BENELUX/FRG Region, EUROCONTROL would assume the responsibility of operating services in respect of new Centres and of certain centres in advance of the establishment of these new Centres;
- the development and execution of an agreed programme of work for experimentation and its coordination with the programme of the member countries;
- the planning of equipment standardisation for the future;
- the preparation of operational plans in collaboration with the regions or countries concerned and the examination of existing national plans with a view to reaching agreement;
- the consideration of possibilities of identifying items of equipment required in common by more than one country/region so that the practicability and desirability of standardisation and central purchasing could be fully considered;
- coordination, insofar as they relate to EUROCONTROL, of proposals submitted by Member States to I.C.A.O. regarding standards and recommended practices and the regional navigation plans of this Organisation.

ACTIVITIES

It is within these terms of reference that the principal activities of the Agency have been pursued.

The first completely new facility to be built and commissioned by EUROCONTROL was its Experimental Centre at Brétigny, near Paris. The need for such a centre was recognised when the Convention was being written, and planning in fact started during the period of the Association before the Convention was ratified. Inaugurated in 1967, the Centre has developed into a highly technical complex for Agency planning in the determination of air traffic systems, air navigation and the application of new technology to the air traffic control problem as well as providing the means whereby technicians and controllers could become familiar with the new tools which they would shortly be using operationally. The basic means for studying and testing the operation of present and future systems of air traffic control is the digital computer driven dynamic Air Traffic Simulator. Facilities include an Experimental Data Processor and Display System for experimenting with automated processing and display of information more suited to the increasing tempo and complexity of air traffic and for the development of the complex computer programmes that such automated systems demand.

The Convention foresaw the need to establish schools to provide air traffic services training in keeping with the rapid development of control methods and procedures and to bring experienced controllers up to date on the radical changes that automatic data processing techniques have brought to air traffic control centres. It was in this context that the Permanent Commission in December 1967 decided to set up the Institute of Air Navigation Services in Luxembourg. Construction began early in 1969 and training started on 5th January 1970. While the emphasis on the Institute's work is placed on advanced and conversion training, and courses for instructors with a view to standardising ATS training at national level, plus the organisation of international symposia, a significant place is reserved for the ab initio training of controllers and ATS assistants particularly in the case of staff earmarked for EUROCONTROL's own ATC centres.

The main preoccupation of the Agency, however, was in the provision of the air traffic services which, under the "Moroni Agreement," were to be limited in the first instance to the BENELUX/Federal Republic of Germany Region. The complexity of the traffic and its rapid rate of growth in this region had already encouraged the Permanent Commission to approve in 1964 the setting up of a new international control centre at Maastricht in the Netherlands. The initial concept for this centre was to provide a fully automated and coordinated service to aircraft flying in the upper airspace of Belgium, Luxembourg, the Netherlands and the Federal Republic of Germany. Building started in 1966, systems planning got underway and contracts were laid in 1968 for the main data processing and display equipment (MADAP). The centre became operational in 1972 when the provision of services for the upper airspace of Belgium and Luxembourg (known as the Brussels upper information region UIR) was undertaken from the centre. Services for the northern sectors of the Federal Republic were transferred to the UAC Maastricht in February 1974. Those for the Netherlands are to follow later once that country is in a position to effect the transfer. The Maastricht Centre is the most advanced control centre in Europe, if not in the world, and its implementation has led to a marked improvement in the air traffic services in the airspace concerned.

It was during the build-up phase of the UAC Maastricht that its role underwent a fundamental change. Both civil and military traffic had far exceeded that forecast for the Federal Republic of Germany. This combined traffic density together with airspace limitations and a complex route structure necessitated the co-locating of the civil and military control functions in the Federal Republic. This requirement was most urgent in the southern part of Germany so that subsequent to a declaration of intent by the Governments of the BENELUX countries and the Federal Republic of Germany on their plans for the development of the air traffic control services in their region, the Permanent Commission decided that a second centre would be installed for the southern part of the German upper airspace from which the civil and military air traffic services would be jointly provided. In line with this policy the military authorities of the Federal Republic decided to transfer their air traffic control facilities providing services to operational air traffic for the northern part of the German upper airspace to Maastricht, so that civil and military services would be jointly provided for this area also. The transfer is due to take place in 1975 and measures to this end are well advanced.

The second centre built at Karlsruhe is currently being equipped, the systems used being similar to those installed at Maastricht. It is due to become operational in 1976 after suitable operational trials starting in 1975.

The Agency has also built and is about to commission a new upper area control centre at Shannon, the first stage of which is due to enter into operation in 1975. This centre will serve the upper airspace over the national territory of Ireland and its territorial waters and those international waters which have, by agreement in the International Civil Aviation Organisation, been assigned to Ireland for the provision of the necessary services.

In the field of air navigation EUROCONTROL has set up

secondary surveillance radar installations at Leerdam in the Netherlands, and at Brussels and Shannon. A fourth station is being installed on Mount Gabriel near Cork in Ireland, which will be remoting data to both the centre at Shannon and the London Air Traffic Control Centre at West Drayton. This station will give upper airspace coverage in the South West Atlantic approaches to Europe particularly for the projected supersonic transport routes as well as giving dual coverage to the SSR installation at Shannon. It forms a typical example of EUROCONTROL's role in rationalising the air traffic control facilities covering more than one state in the interests of both economy and operational efficiency.

Apart from such concrete evidence of its activities EUROCONTROL has played an important part in coordinating the air traffic control systems of its Member States and through a variety of working groups and specialist panels it has served to align the views of its members on various ATC matters coming up in other international contexts and particularly vis-à-vis I.C.A.O. It has become common practice for proposals involved and agreed within EUROCONTROL to be presented to I.C.A.O. by the EUROCONTROL Organisation on behalf of its seven Member States.

The Agency has been particularly active in the study and development of future ATC systems, including work on the development of the system of control of supersonic civil transport aircraft. Studies and simulations have been carried out within EUROCONTROL, in conjunction with national administrations as well as the aircraft manufacturers, to explore the long-term possibilities and in preparation for the initial operations proving flights starting shortly.

Work has progressed on harmonising the use of secondary surveillance radar, including requirements for the carriage of airborne transponders and procedures for their use and on the automatic exchange of data between computers in adjacent centres. Conflict detection has been another field of study towards developing techniques for the automatic prediction of aircraft profiles, the automatic detection of conflict between aircraft and the automatic resolution of such conflict. Operational research has assisted with the application of fast-time simulation models providing objective quantitative data to assist in ATC planning and the development of long term traffic forecasting models. Experimental work is also being directed towards the improved organisation of traffic flow over large areas.

Whilst this work has been principally for the purposes of the Organisation and its Member States, effort has also been given over to meeting certain requirements of non-Member States and international organisations. Thus the Institute has accepted students from national administrations of many non-Member States as well as from the private sector and students sponsored by I.C.A.O. in the execution of the United Nations Technical Aid and Development Programmes. Similarly the Experimental Centre has undertaken special studies and carried out simulation exercises for states outside the Organisation such as Italy, Switzerland and Spain.

This latter task falls within the provisions of the agreements of cooperation that the Organisation has concluded with Denmark, Norway, Sweden, Switzerland, Austria, Italy, Spain, Portugal and the Federal Aviation Administration of the U.S.A. These agreements were designed essentially to facilitate the reciprocal exchanges of information relating to air traffic control with a view to increasing efficiency in this field.

On the other hand not all the efforts aimed at the adoption of solutions to problems open to positive joint action have enjoyed immediate success and proposals for the standardisation and pooled purchasing of equipment for a single centre to supervise the European strategic flow of air traffic and for some intra-European rationalisation of "social" conditions of service, have still not reached fruition. A notable exeption is the very considerable exercise in cooperation which has led to the creation of a regional route charges system implemented by EUROCONTROL.

Two facts pointed to the suitability of EUROCONTROL as the principal agency for the collection of charges in respect of en route services. The first was that provision existed in the EUROCONTROL Convention for the levying of such a charge, although this provision, like most of the rest of the Convention, extended only to the upper airspace. The other fact was the principle adumbrated by I.C.A.O. that en route charges should, as far as possible, be imposed on a regional basis so that operators would be faced with only one charge per flight. One of the first conclusions reached was that, pace the Convention, it would be impractical to confine such a charge to the upper airspace parts of flights. The only workable system was to have the upper-airspace charge equated to a lower-airspace charge so as to avoid any need to ascertain, and base calculations upon, the exact point at which aircraft crossed the interface. Ministers were accordingly asked whether they would agree to reflect, in the lower airspaces for which they were individually responsible, the exact pattern of charges which, as a Commission, they were prepared to levy in the communal upper airspace. This of course involved in the majority of cases their undertaking to introduce the necessary legislation in their respective countries, where this was necessary, and meant the drawing up and unanimous acceptance of an elaborate Multilateral Agreement.

Having got this far the role of the General Directorate became clearer, for it could not collect lower-airspace charges as a matter of principle. The agreed answer was for it to act as an agent of the Member States in the collection of charges both in the lower and upper airspace. This is the pattern which has been successfully implemented via a series of bilateral arrangements between each country and the Agency. The basic decision of the creation of a collection system of user charges was taken in May 1969 and the multilateral agreement was signed on 8th September of the following year. The system came into operation on 1st November 1971; indeed it is by now not only functioning efficiently in the EUROCONTROL area and collecting in addition on behalf of four other European States, namely Austria, Portugal, Spain and Switzerland, but it has also strongly influenced the pattern for en route charges recommended to States generally by the E.R.F.A. (Economics of Route Facilities and Airports) Conference of I.C.A.O. The measure of cooperation achieved in this system is illustrated by the fact that all the numerous complex decisions required in order to set it up have been taken unanimously.

CONCLUSION

Viewing air traffic control from a European angle therefore one sees seven countries acting together in an International Organisation, with two other countries, Portugal and Spain, possibly joining soon. Two further countries are closely involved with EUROCONTROL in the running of a common en route charges system and certain other countries have concluded cooperation agreements with the Agency, which provide in the main for mutually beneficial exchanges of information. In the European countries outside EUROCONTROL the air navigation and allied services remain a national responsibility. In the first part of its life EUROCONTROL has built up an international experimental centre, an international training centre, an international upper area control centre with another two on the way and a central route charges office. If the initial period was the hardest in this field as in certain others, the Organisation has by now established itself on the European scene, and can be expected to absorb greater responsibility both downwards into the lower airspace and also geographically with the absorption of other Member States into its future framework.

RESUME

La sécurité de la navigation aérienne a été dès l'origine en Europe comme dans le reste du monde une responsabilité nationale, cependant depuis la seconde guerre mondiale les normes en vigueur et les critères qu'elles prescrivent ont été coordonnés au sein de l'Organisation de l'Aviation Civile Internationale (O.A.C.I.). Les normes ainsi arrêtées ont été traduites à la suite des délibérations de grandes réunions régionales par des installations qui ont été reprises dans des plans régionaux couvrant la majeure partie du monde. Si ces plans énumèrent les moyens que chaque pays met ou entend mettre en oeuvre pour respecter ses obligations envers l'OACI, ils n'imposent aucune limite aux mesures qu'un Etat peut prendre pour promouvoir la sécurité aérienne; aussi un certain nombre de pays ont-ils toujours exploité des systèmes de navigation aérienne et de régulation de trafic bien en avance par rapport aux exigences de l'O.A.C.I.

Malgré cela, l'augmentation du volume de trafic au-dessus de l'Europe et les changements qui se sont opérés dans sa composition ont posé au cours des années "50" des problèmes d'une acuité croissante. Le principal élément nouveau intervenu à cette époque a été la mise en service pour le transport aérien civil d'aéronefs à turboréacteurs. L'une des diverses conséquences de cette mutation fût de faire passer les vols de transport commercial dans les régions supérieures de l'espace aérien c'est-à-dire au-dessus de l'altitude maximale des avions à hélices classiques (soit quelque 20.000 pieds) où n'évoluait jusqu'alors que l'avion militaire. Une autre conséquence a été que la vitesse des aéronefs lancés dans l'espace était telle qu'il pouvaient ne rester dans l'espace aérien d'un pays déterminé que quelques minutes, ce qui réduisait considérablement les délais dont le système de contrôle pouvait disposer pour les prises de décisions. De plus, les avantages économiques de la nouvelle génération d'aéronefs ont conduit inévitablement à une augmentation rapide du nombre de vols.

Il a fallu alors mettre en oeuvre des nouvelles méthodes d'exploitation faisant à des techniques de pointe, notamment par la mise en oeuvre de systèmes automatisés en temps réel, ce qui donna lieu à des problèmes techniques d'une exceptionnelle complexité et exigeant des investissements très importants tant pour le développement que pour l'acquisition des matériels. L'escalade rapide des coûts devint un réel sujet d'inquiétude pour les Etats assurant les services de contrôle de la circulation aérienne lesquels étaient à l'époque financés exclusivement par les contribuables. Cette inquiétude fût particulièrement ressentie par les petits pays dont les espaces aériens étaient traversés en quelques minutes.

Toutes ces évolutions se produisaient à un moment où, sur d'autres plans, le processus d'unification européenne commençait à se préciser. Dans le domaine du contrôle aérien, le fait que les nouveaux types d'aéronefs évoluaient principalement dans un espace aérien où aucun service n'avait été fourni jusqu'alors sauf aux avions militaires, créait selon certains une occasion unique d'organiser les services requis sur un plan communautaire européen dans une vaste région affranchie des servitudes liées aux frontières d'Etats. En 1957, la Belgique, le Luxembourg, les Pays-Bas et la République fédérale d'Allemagne commençaient à débattre des possibilités de coordonner leurs systèmes de contrôle de la circulation aérienne. Par la suite la France, l'Italie et le Royaume-Uni vinrent s'ajouter à ces pays en vue de préparer une Convention internationale ayant pour objet la création d'une agence qui serait chargée d'assurer au nom de la communauté les services de la circulation aérienne dans l'espace supérieur des Etats représentés.

Le 13 décembre 1960 les plénipotentiaires de la République fédérale d'Allemagne, du Royaume de Belgique, de la République française, du Royaume-Uni de Grande-Bretagne et d'Irlande du Nord, du Grand-Duché du Luxembourg et du Royaume des Pays-Bas signèrent la Convention internationale de coopération pour la sécurité de la navigation aérienne, l'Italie ayant décidé entre-temps de remettre à plus tard son adhésion à cette Convention. Le 1er janvier 1965, l'Irlande a adhéré à la Convention devenant ainsi le septième Etat membre.

La Convention devait être ratifiée par les parties contractantes. Cependant, vu l'augmentation extrêmement rapide du nombre des avions à turbines exploités par les compagnies aériennes, il est apparu indispensable d'étudier d'urgence les mesures propres à assurer la sécurité de leurs déplacements dans l'espace aérien supérieur. Les six Etats signataires ont en conséquence signé un protocole couvrant la période intermédiaire et constitué une Association pour le perfectionnement des méthodes et de l'équipement du contrôle de la circulation aérienne, qui devait précéder l'Organisation européenne proprement dite. Le but de cette Association était d'entreprendre immédiatement l'étude des solutions susceptibles d'être appliquées aux problèmes de contrôle de la circulation aérienne dans l'espace aérien supérieur lorsque l'Organisation aurait été créée, de préparer les plans correspondants et d'en expérimenter la valeur pratique.

LA CONVENTION

La Convention, après avoir été ratifiée, entra en vigueur le 1er mars 1963 pour une période de 20 ans, sa durée devant être automatiquement prolongée par périodes de 5 années à moins qu'une partie contractante n'ait manifesté au moins 2 ans avant l'expiration de la période en cours, son intention de mettre fin à la Convention.

La Convention EUROCONTROL définit d'une manière très détaillée les mesures concrètes que les parties contractantes avaient arrêtées pour remédier aux problèmes qui s'étaient présentés jusqu'alors. Ces mesures comportaient des incidences très profondes. La principale décision d'ordre politique est énoncée à l'Article 1 au terme duquel les parties contractantes sont convenues de renforcer leur coopération dans le domaine de la navigation aérienne et notamment d'organiser en commun les services de la circulation aérienne dans l'espace supérieur. A cet effet, les Etats signataires ont institué l'Organisation européenne pour la sécurité de la navigation aérienne EUROCONTROL. Il s'agissait de confier à EUROCONTROL la responsabilité de l'exercice des services de contrôle dans l'espace supérieur de tous les Etats membres c'est-à-dire que ces services deviendraient la responsabilité collective de tous les Etats membres réunis au sein de l'Organisation. Il fût décidé d'entendre par "circulation aérienne" les aéronefs civils ainsi que les aéronefs militaires, de douane et de police qui se conforment aux procédures de l'Organisation de l'Aviation Civile Internationale. Dès lors, du moins en théorie, il ne devait plus y avoir de démarcations entre les espaces supérieurs des divers Etats participants et l'on pouvait organiser les services dans une très large région en tenant compte uniquement de considérations techniques et économiques.

La charge de la complexité et du coût des nouveaux systèmes à mettre en oeuvre devait recevoir une double solution. D'une part, l'Agence EUROCONTROL était habilitée à mettre en place à l'échelon communautaire les centres de contrôle nécessaires desservant le cas échéant l'espace aérien de deux ou plusieurs Etats, d'autre part elle allait pouvoir créer des centres de recherches communs pour la réalisation et l'expérimentation de nouveaux systèmes ainsi que des écoles pour la spécialisation et le perfectionnement du personnel des services de la circulation aérienne.

Quant aux coûts, il était entendu qu'ils seraient financés par un système commun de l'Organisation EUROCONTROL s'appliquant tant aux investissements qu'aux dépenses d'exploitation. On estima que le fonctionnement d'une seule et même Organisation sur une vaste région serait moins onéreux que l'exécution par les divers Etats d'éléments indépendants d'une même tâche. Dans un souci d'équité financière, il fût convenu que les Etats contribueraient au budget de l'Organisation grosso modo en fonction de leur produit national brut et de l'importance des services fournis par l'Organisation aux aéronefs immatriculés sur leur territoire.

En tout état de cause, la Convention ménageait également la possibilité d'instaurer un système de rémunération des services rendus aux usagers de l'espace aérien. Le contrôle dans l'espace aérien supérieur des aéronefs ne se conformant pas aux règles de l'O.A.C.I., il n'a pas été couvert par les dispositions de la Convention et est resté, même que le trafic dans l'espace aérien inférieur, une responsabilité nationale, la Convention indiquant simplement qu'EUROCONTROL devait coopérer avec les Autorités militaires nationales pour arrêter les mesures à prendre dans le domaine de la circulation aérienne. Dans la pratique, les intérêts de la Défense nationale ont été sauvegardés par les représentants militaires de chaque Etat siégeant dans les instances qui administrent l'Organisation.

L'Organisation créée par la Convention comporte deux organes: la Commission permanente pour la sécurité de la navigation aérienne et l'Agence des services de la circulation aérienne.

La Commission permanente, organe délibératif, se compose de deux représentants de chaque Etat membre qui sont normalement les Ministres ou Secrétaires d'Etat ayant respectivement dans leurs attributions, l'aviation civile et l'aviation militaire. La Commission traite des aspects politiques des tâches de l'Organisation encore que la Convention précise un certain nombre de matières qui requièrent l'approbation de la Commission et dans certains cas exige l'unanimité des votes.

L'Agence des services de la circulation aérienne rend compte à la Commission permanente des missions exécutives de l'Organisation. Elle est administrée par un Comité de gestion dont la composition est analogue à celle de la Commission permanente mais au niveau des hauts fonctionnaires, et par un Directeur Général. Le Directeur Général dirige une équipe de fonctionnaires permanents responsables de la planification opérationnelle et technique et des tâches financières et administratives que cela implique.

FONCTIONNEMENT

La première tâche de l'Organisation fût d'établir son siège à Bruxelles ainsi que la Convention l'avait prévu et de prendre en charge ses responsabilités de planification et de contrôle. Au début de son existence cependant, l'Agence EUROCONTROL n'avait pas encore d'équipements opérationnels ni les personnels qui lui auraient permis d'assurer les services de la circulation aérienne par ses propres moyens. Elle a donc dû conclure des accords bilatéraux avec chacun des Etats membres qui possédaient déjà leurs systèmes nationaux pour répondre aux normes de l'O.A.C.I., afin qu'ils assurent les services de contrôle dans l'espace supérieur au nom de l'Agence avec leurs propres équipements et personnels, ces services étant rémunérés par la voie du budget de fonctionnement.

La Belgique fût le premier pays, en 1964, à transférer ses responsabilités pour l'exécution directe du contrôle de la circulation aérienne à l'Organisation. En 1966 cependant, la France et le Royaume-Uni considérèrent qu'en raison du développement de leurs plans nationaux qui couvraient l'ensemble des espaces supérieur et inférieur et, dans le cas du Royaume-Uni en raison de l'intégration des fonctions de contrôle civil et militaire, il leur devenait pratiquement et économiquement impossible de transférer à l'Agence leurs responsabilités d'exécution du contrôle.

Ceci a amené la Commission permanente à approuver un certain nombre de recommandations reprises dans un rapport qu'un groupe d'étude de très haut niveau avait élaboré, connu sous le nom de ,,Rapport Moroni.'' Le résultat de ces recommandations fût que l'Agence devrait concentrer ses activités d'exécution directe des services de contrôle dans l'espace supérieur de la région de la République fédérale d'Allemagne, d'assurer des tâches de planification pour l'Irlande tandis que la France et le Royaume-Uni continueraient jusqu'aux environs de 1980 à agir au nom d'EUROCONTROL dans leurs espace supérieur conformément à leur planification nationale.

Cette interprétation de la Convention a eu deux conséquences financières:

1° Les investissements effectués directement par l'Organisation devaient continuer à être financés par l'intermédiaire du budget de l'Organisation tandis que la France et le Royaume-Uni finançaient eux-mêmes leurs investissements et obtenaient l'amortissement de ceux-ci pendant la période de leur utilisation opérationnelle dans la mesure où ils étaient utilisés pour les besoins de l'espace supérieur;

2° Les frais de fonctionnement des services de contrôle dans l'espace supérieur devaient être supportés sur une base nationale ou régionale.

D'autre part, l'Organisation devait poursuivre ses activités en matière de développement de méthodes et de procédures opérationnelles communes, la coordination des sytèmes intéressant l'espace supérieur et la préparation des plans opérationnels en coopération avec les Etats intéressés, la standardisation des équipements, les études et expérimentations ainsi qu'une étude fondamentale du meilleur système de contrôle du trafic aérien qui pourrait être mis en oeuvre dans l'espace européen après 1980.

ACTIVITES

C'est donc sur la base qui vient d'être indiquée que les principales activités de l'Agence se sont poursuivies.

En dehors du siège où sont centralisés les services d'études, de planning opérationnel et technique et d'administration générale, la première installation complètement nouvelle qui a été réalisée par EUROCONTROL a été son Centre expérimental à Brétigny près de Paris. Inauguré en 1967, ce Centre est devenu un complexe de haute technicité pour l'étude des systèmes de circulation aérienne et de l'application des nouvelles techniques aux problèmes du contrôle.

En décembre 1967, la Commission permanente a décidé la création de l'Institut des services de la navigation aérienne à Luxembourg. Ouvert en janvier 1970, cet institut est particulièrement chargé de la formation avancée et spécialisée du personnel des services de la navigation aérienne, contrôleurs et techniciens, dans la perspective des changements intervenus dans les méthodes et les procédures, par suite de l'introduction des techniques de traitement automatique des données dans les centres de contrôle.

La principale préoccupation de l'Agence était cependant de fournir des services de contrôle, lesquels suite au Rapport „Moroni" étaient limités tout d'abord à la Région Benelux-République fédérale d'Allemagne. Pour cette région, EUROCONTROL a créé deux centres de contrôle:

- le premier à Maastricht aux Pays-Bas est entré en exploitation en 1972; il fournit des services automatisés aux aéronefs dans l'espace supérieur de la Belgique, du Luxembourg et de la partie nord de la République fédérale d'Allemagne. Les services de contrôle pour l'espace supérieur des Pays-Bas seront transférés à ce centre à une date qui doit encore être précisée. Entretemps, le contrôle de la circulation opérationnelle militaire dans l'espace supérieur du nord de l'Allemagne sera assuré par la „Bundeswehr" depuis le centre de Maastricht à partir d'octobre 1975.
- le second à Karlsruhe est en cours d'installation pour entrer en exploitation en 1976. Il fournit les services de contrôle aux aéronefs tant civils que militaires dans l'espace supérieur de la partie sud de la République fédérale.

L'Agence a aussi installé un nouveau centre de contrôle de l'espace supérieur à Shannon qui entrera en exploitation, dans une première phase, en 1975 pour desservir l'espace supérieur de l'Irlande et la zone Atlantique ouest limitrophe.

EUROCONTROL a encore mis en place des radars secondaires de surveillance à Leerdam aux Pays-Bas, à Bruxelles et à Shannon. Une quatrième station est en cours d'installation au Mont Gabriel dans le sud de l'Irlande dont les données radar seront déportées au Centre de Shannon ainsi qu'au Centre de Londres.

Un autre exemple important de coopération entre les Etats membres a été la création à Bruxelles par les soins de l'Agence, d'un service central des redevances de route qui a la responsabilité de la perception de redevances pour l'usage des installations et services de navigation aérienne tant dans l'espace supérieur que dans l'espace inférieur. Ce système mis en place par les sept Etat membres d'EUROCONTROL et grâce auquel les usagers de l'espace aérien participent d'une manière uniforme et progressive au financement des services dont ils bénéficient a été adopté également par quatre pays non-membres de l'Organisation : l'Autriche, la Suisse, le Portugal et l'Espagne qui ont confié à l'Agence la perception des redevances pour leur compte.

Si les Etats membres peuvent se féliciter des résultats concrets de la mise en oeuvre de la Convention du 13 décembre 1960, il faut bien reconnaître cependent que certaines réalités ont empêché son application intégrale. L'état d'avancement de planification nationale, les différences de conditions des services des personnels de contrôle, les difficultés qui se sont présentées en matière de standardisation et d'achat en commun des équipements sont des exemples de problèmes où des solutions au niveau européen doivent encore porter leurs fruits.

CONCLUSION

En tout état de cause, on peut considérer que dans la première décennie de son existence, l'Organisation a pu se développer au bénéfice de tous. Sept Etats membres oeuvrent ensemble pour la sécurité de la navigation aérienne; deux autres pays ont demandé à rejoindre EUROCONTROL et l'Organisation a conclu des accords de coopération avec huit Etats européens et avec la Federal Aviation Administration des Etats-Unis. Dans les domaines de la fourniture des moyens modernes de contrôle de la circulation aérienne, le développement de systèmes à moyen et long terme, l'harmonisation des procédures, la formation des personnels et enfin le système des redevances qui aide les Etats à financer l'infrastructure des services de contrôle, EUROCONTROL s'est installée sur la scène européenne. L'Organisation a pu ainsi gagner une expérience suffisante pour assumer dans l'avenir encore d'autres responsabilités tant dans l'espace inférieur qu'en étendant géographiquement son aire d'activité par l'adhésion d'autres Etats membres.

SECTION DOCUMENTAIRE
DOCUMENTARY SECTION

MEMBRES DES ORGANISATIONS EUROPEENNES fin 1974
***MEMBERS OF EUROPEAN ORGANISATIONS* end 1974**

	Commission Centrale pour la Navigation du Rhin/ *Rhine Commission*	Benelux/ *Benelux*	Union de l'Europe Occidentale/ *Western European Union*	O.C.D.E.[1]/ *O.E.C.D.*	Conseil de l'Europe/ *Council of Europe*
Allemagne (Rép. Féd.) *Germany (Fed. Rep.)*	■		■	■	■
Autriche *Austria*				■	■
Belgique *Belgium*	■	■	■	■	■
Chypre *Cyprus*					■
Danemark *Denmark*				■	■
Espagne *Spain*				■	
Finlande *Finland*				■	
France *France*	■		■	■	■
Grèce *Greece*				■	■
Irlande *Ireland*				■	■
Islande *Iceland*				■	■
Italie *Italy*			■	■	■
Luxembourg *Luxembourg*		■	■	■	■
Malte *Malta*					■
Norvège *Norway*				■	■
Pays-Bas *Netherlands*	■	■	■	■	■
Portugal *Portugal*				■	
Royaume-Uni *United Kingdom*	■		■	■	■
Suède *Sweden*				■	■
Suisse *Switzerland*	■			■	■
Turquie *Turkey*				■	■
Yougoslavie *Yugoslavia*				associé associated	

[1] Also U.S.A., Canada, Japan, Australia and New Zealand. Yugoslavia is a full member for certain matters and has observer status in other matters.
Aussi Etats-Unis, Canada, Japon, Australie et Nouvelle Zélande. La Yugoslavie est membre à part entière pour certaines matières et observateur pour d'autres.

[2] Greece and Turkey have associate status.
La Grèce et la Turquie sont associées.

Communautés européennes/[2] *European communities*	Commission int. de l'état civil/ *Int. commission on civil status*	Conseil nordique/ *Nordic Council*	Conf. eur. des ministres des transports/*Eur. Conf. of Ministers of Transport* [3]	C.E.R.N.[3]/ *C.E.R.N.*	Commission eur. de l'aviation civile/*European Civil Aviation Conference*	Conf. eur. des administrations des postes et des télécommunications/ *Eur. Conf. Posts and Telecommunications Administrations*	Association européenne de libre-échange/*European Free Trade Association* [4]	Org. eur. de recherches spatiales/ *Eur. Space Research Organisation*	Org. eur. pour la mise au point[5] de lanceurs d'engins spatiaux/*Eur. Launcher Development Organisation*
								obser-vateur observer	
									obser-vateur observer
									obser-vateur observer
							associé associated		
associé associated									
								obser-vateur observer	
								obser-vateur observer	
									obser-vateur observer
associé associated				obser-vateur observer					
				obser-vateur observer					

[3] Turkey and Yugoslavia have observer status; also Poland.
La Turquie et la Yougoslavie sont observatrices; la Pologne également.
[4] Finland has associate status.
La Finlande est associée.
[5] Also Australia. Denmark has observer status.
Aussi l'Australia. Le Danemark est observateur.

COMMISSION CENTRALE POUR LA NAVIGATION DU RHIN

A. COMPOSITION ET PERSONNEL DE LA COMMISSION CENTRALE EN 1974

M. Walter Müller, avocat et notaire, a été nommé, le 28 octobre 1974, Commissaire de Suisse, en remplacement de M. Mangold.

M. Kurt Waldner, Directeur de l'Office de la Navigation Rhénane, a été nommé le 28 octobre 1974, Commissaire-suppléant de Suisse.

M. J. L. Schoenmaekers, Directeur à l'Administration de la Marine et de la Navigation Intérieure, a été nommé le 1er décembre 1974, Commissaire de Belgique, en remplacement de M. François.

En conséquence, la composition de la Commission Centrale était la suivante, à la fin de l'année 1974:

Allemagne

Commissaires:	MM. Thierfelder,
	Rümelin,
	Beck,
	Huber,
Commissaires-suppléants:	MM. Hoffmann,
	Hübener;

Belgique

Commissaires:	MM. Frey,
	Schoenmaekers,
	Erkens,
Commissaire-suppléant:	M. Woestijn;

France

Commissaires:	MM. de Lacharriere,
	Denoueix,
	Graff,
	Bernheim,
Commissaires-suppléants:	MM. Bonet-Maury,
	Dobias;

Grande-Bretagne

Commissaires:	Mlle Bristow,
	M. Eaton;

Pays-Bas

Commissaires:	MM. Riphagen, Président,
	Posthumus,
	van Til,
	van der Noordt,
Commissaires-suppléants:	MM. Nieuwenhuijsen
	Glazenburg;

Suisse

Commissaires:	MM. Schaller,
	Diez, Vice-Président,

CHAPTER I

CENTRAL COMMISSION FOR THE NAVIGATION OF THE RHINE

A. MEMBERSHIP AND STAFF OF THE CENTRAL COMMISSION IN 1974

On 28 October 1974 Mr. Walter MÜLLER, attorney at law and notary, was appointed Commissioner for Switserland in succession to Mr. MANGOLD.

On the same date, Mr. Kurt WALDNER, Director of the Rhine Navigation Office, was appointed Deputy Commisioner for Switzerland.

On 1 December 1974, Mr. J. L. SCHOENMAEKERS, Director in the Ocean and Inland Navigation Administration was appointed Commissioner for Belgium in succession to Mr. FRANÇOIS.

The membership of the Central Commission at the end of 1974 was accordingly as follows:

Germany

Commissioners:	Mr. THIERFELDER,
	Mr. RÜMELIN
	Mr. BECK,
	Mr. HUBER,
Deputy Commissioners:	Mr. HOFFMANN,
	HÜBENER;

Belgium

Commissioners:	Mr. FREY,
	Mr. SCHOENMAEKERS,
	Mr. ERKENS,
Deputy Commissioner:	Mr. WOESTIJN

France

Commissioners:	Mr. DE LACHARRIERE,
	Mr. DENOUEIX,
	Mr. GRAFF,
	Mr. BERNHEIM,
Deputy Commissioners:	Mr. BONET-MAURY,
	Mr. DOBIAS;

Great Britain

Commissioners:	Mrs. BRISTOW,
	Mr. EATON;

Netherlands

Commissioners:	Mr. RIPHAGEN, President,
	Mr. POSTHUMUS,
	Mr. VAN TIL,
	Mr. VAN DER NOORDT,
Deputy Commissioners:	Mr. NIEUWENHUIJSEN,
	Mr. GLAZENBURG;

Switzerland

Commissioners:	Mr. SCHALLER,
	Mr. DIEZ, Vice-President,

MÜLLER,
ZURBRÜGG,
Commissaires-suppléants: MM. WALDNER,
WYSS.

Le Secrétariat était, à la même date, composé comme suit:

Secrétaire Genéral:	M. R. DOERFLINGER
Secrétaire Général-adjoint:	M. H. WATERMANN
Ingénieur en Chef:	M. J. DUBOIS.

La Chambre des Appels comprenait, à la fin de l'année 1974, les membres suivants:

Juges	*Juges-suppléants*
MM. BONET-MAURY	MM. DE JONG
MÜLLER	SCHMITZ
QUANJARD	SMEESTERS
ROYER	WEIRICH
SPECHT	ZURBRÜGG

B. ACTIVITE DE LA COMMISSION CENTRALE

1. SESSIONS PLENIERES ET REUNIONS DE COMITES TENUES AU COURS DE L'ANNEE

a) La *Commission Centrale* a tenu deux sessions ordinaires, les 24 et 25 avril et les 13 et 14 novembre, sous la présidence de M. RIPHAGEN, à Strasbourg.

b) Les Comités se sont réunis comme suit:

le *Comité économique et le Comité restreint économique*, sous la présidence de M. VAN DER NOORDT, les 23 avril et 12 novembre, à Strasbourg;

le *Comité ad hoc chargé de procéder à l'étude des problèmes contenus dans l'inventaire adopté par la Commission Centrale lors de sa sessions d'octobre 1972 ainsi qu'à l'examen des différentes solutions susceptibles d'y être apportées*, sous la présidence de M. DE LACHARRIERE, les 25 avril à Strasbourg et 8 octobre à Paris;

le *Comité des douanes*, sous la présidence de M. HÜBENER, le 12 septembre à Strasbourg;

le *Comité du droit fluvial*, sous la présidence de M. FREY, les 13 et 14 mars et le 17 septembre à Strasbourg;

le *Comité du Rapport annuel et des Statistiques*, sous la présidence de M. MANGOLD, le 22 avril, sous la présidence de M. HÜBENER le 12 novembre à Strasbourg;

le *Groupe des Statisticiens*, sous la présidence du Secrétaire Général-adjoint, les 19 et 20 février à Strasbourg, les 17 et 18 septembre à Bâle;

le *Comité du Règlement de police*, sous la présidence de M. BECK, le 18 janvier, le 6 mars, le 23 avril, le 17 septembre, le 12 novembre à Strasbourg;

le *Comité du Règlement de visite*, sous la présidence de M. GRAFF, le 16 janvier, le 5 mars, le 23 avril, le 18 septembre réunion avec le Groupe préparatoire pour la révision du Règlement de visite et des représentants du Consortium de la navigation rhénane et du Comité international de prévention des accidents du travail de la navigation intérieure (CIPA), la 19 septembre, le 28 octobre, le 12 novembre à Strasbourg;

le *Comité des questions sociales, de travail et de formation professionnelle*, sous la présidence de M. GLAZENBURG, le 17 janvier, le 18 juin, le 15 octobre, le 13 novembre, à Strasbourg;

le *Comité des matières dangereuses*, sous la présidence de M. GRAFF, le 7 février, sous la présidence de M. DENOUEIX, le 4 avril à Strasbourg;

le *Comité technique permanent*, sous la présidence de M. ZURBRÜGG le 12 mars, le 23 avril, le 17 septembre, le 22 octobre, le 12 novembre à Strasbourg;

	Mr. MÜLLER,
	Mr. ZURBRÜGG,
Deputy Commissioners:	Mr. WALDNER,
	Mr. WYSS.

At the same dates the Secretariat had the following members:

Secretary General:	Mr. R. DOERFLINGER
Deputy Secretary General:	Mr. H. WATERMANN
Chief Engineer:	Mr. J. DUBOIS.

The Chamber of Appeal comprised the following members at theend of 1974:

Judges	*Deputy Judges*
MM. BONET-MAURY	Mr. DE JONG
MÜLLER	Mr. SCHMITZ
QUANJARD	Mr. SMEESTERS
ROYER	Mr. WEIRICH
SPECHT	Mr. ZURBRÜGG

B. ACTIVITIES OF THE CENTRAL COMMISSION

1. PLENARY SESSIONS AND COMMITTEE MEETINGS

a) The *Central Commission* held two ordinary sessions in Strasbourg, on 24–25 April and 13–14 November at which Mr. RIPHAGEN took the chair.

b) Committee meetings were as follows:

Economic Committee and Restricted Economic Committee in Strasbourg on 23 April and 12 November, Chairman: Mr. VAN DER NOORDT;

Ad hoc Committee to study the problems contained in the inventory adopted by the Central Commission at its October 1972 session and to investigate the various possible solutions, in Strasbourg on 25 April and Paris on 8 October, Chairman Mr. DE LACHARRIERE,

Customs Committee on 12 September in Strasbourg Chairman Mr. HÜBENER;

River Law Committee, on 13–14 March and 17 September in Strasbourg, Chairman Mr. FREY;

Committee on the Annual Report and Statistics in Strasbourg, on 22 April, Chairman Mr. MANGOLD, and 12 November, Chairman Mr. HÜBENER;

Group of statisticians on 19–20 February in Strasbourg and 17–18 September in Basle, Chairman the Deputy Secretary General;

Police Control Committee, on 18 January, 6 March, 23 April, 17 September and 12 November in Strasbourg, Chairman Mr. BECK;

Inspection Regulations Committee, Chairman Mr. GRAFF, on 16 January, 5 March, 23 April, 18 September, with the Preparatory Group on Inspection Regulations Revision and representatives of the Rhine navigation Consortium, and the International Committee for the Prevention of Accidents at Work on Inland Navigaton, 19 September, 28 October and 12 November in Strassbourg;

Committee on Social Questions, Labour and Training Chairman Mr. GLAZENBURG, on 17 January, 18 June, 15 October amd 13 November in Strasbourg;

Committee on Dangerous Substances, in Strasbourg, on 7 February, Chairman Mr. GRAFF, and 4 April, Chairman Mr. DENOUEIX;

Technical Committee, Chairman Mr. ZURBRÜGG, on 12 March, 23 April, 17 September, 22 October and 12 November in Strasbourg;

Restricted Committee on Navigation, Chairman the Chief Engineer, on 28–29 March in Gottlieben, 21–22 May in Mainz, 29–30 August in Basle and 4–5 December in Koblenz;

le *Comité restreint de navigation*, sous la présidence de l'Ingénieur en chef, les 28 et 29 mars à Gottlieben, les 21 et 22 mai à Mayence, les 29 et 30 août à Bâle, les 4 et 5 décembre à Coblence;

le *Groupe de travail des matières dangereuses*, sous la présidence de M. SCHNAPAUFF, les 5 et 6 fevrier, les 2, 3 et 4 avril, les 5, 6 et 7 juin, les 12, 13 et 14 août à Strasbourg, les 7, 8, 9 et 10 octobre à Bâle, les 2, 3 et 4 décembre à Bonn;

le *Groupe de travail ,,Guide de radiotéléphonie"*, sous la présidence de M. WIEDEMANN, les 10 et 11 janvier à Coblence;

le *Groupe préparatoire pour la révision du Règlement de visite et Groupe restreint*, sous la présidence de l'Ingénieur en chef respectivement de M. GAUTSCHI, les 14, 15 et 16 janvier, les 19, 20 et 21 mars, les 28, 29 et 30 mai, les 27 et 28 août à Strasbourg, les 16, 17 et 18 octobre à Bonn, les 29 et 30 octobre, les 16, 17, 18 et 19 décembre à Strasbourg.

Réunion du Centre administratif de la sécurité sociale pour les bateliers rhénans les 26, 27, 28 et 29 novembre à Strasbourg, sous la présidence de M. SCHWARTZ.

c) La Chambre des Appels s'est réunie, sous la présidence de M. ROYER les 7 mai, 16 et 17 décembre à Strasbourg.

2. RELATIONS AVEC D'AUTRES ORGANISATIONS INTERNATIONALES

a) Le Comité restraint économique s'est entretenu avec les Représentants du Consortium de la navigation rhénane et de l'Union Internationale de la Navigation Fluviale de problèmes économiques relatifs à la navigation rhénane et plus particulièrement au projet de réglementation d'immobilisation temporaire de la cale, le 14 février à Duisbourg, sous la présidence de M. VAN DER NOORDT.

b) Le Secrétaire Général a participé à titre d'observateur aux négociations entre les Parties Contractantes de la Convention révisée pour la navigation du Rhin, les Parties Contractantes de la Convention sur la canalisation de la Moselle ainsi que la Communauté Economique Européenne sur la mise en oeuvre d'une réglementation relative à l'immobilisation temporaire de bateaux.

c) Le Secrétariat a représenté la Commission Centrale:

- au Comité des Transports Intérieurs de la Commission Economique pour l'Europe des Nations Unies à Genève et à ses Groupes de travail et Groupes d'experts, soit:
  - au Groupe de travail des transports par voies navigables;
  - au Groupe d'experts sur l'unification des prescriptions techniques relatives aux bateaux et des documents de bord;
  - au Groupe d'experts pour l'unification des règles de route et de signalisation en navigation intérieure;
  - au Groupe d'experts des transports de marchandises dangereuses;
  - au Groupe d'experts du droit fluvial;
  - au Cycle d'étude relatif aux équipements portuaires sur les voies navigables;
- au Programme des Nations Unies pour l'environnement;
- à l'Association Internationale du Registre des bateaux du Rhin;
- à la Conférence Européenne des Ministres des Transports;
- à l'UNIDROIT;
- à l'Agence Internationale de l'Energie Atomique;
- au Comité d'experts en matière de sécurité sociale du Conseil de l'Europe;
- à la réunion des experts gouvernementaux sur le contrôle technique des bateaux naviguant sur les voies d'eau intérieures organisée par la Commission des Communautés Européennes.

d) La *Commission des Communautés Européennes* a été représentée

Working Party on Dangerous Substances, Chairman Mr. SCHNAPAUFF, on 5–6 February, 2–4 April, 5–7 June, 12–14 August in Strasbourg, on 7–10 October in Basle and on 2–4 December in Bonn;

"Guide to Radio-telephony" Working Party, Chairman Mr. WIEDEMANN, on 10–11 January in Koblenz;

Preparatory group on Inspection Regulations Revision, and Restricted Group, Chairman the Chief Engineer or Mr. GAUTSCHI, on 14–16 January, 19–21 March, 28–30 May and 27–28 August in Strasbourg, on 16–18 October in Bonn and on 29–30 October and 16–19 December in Strasbourg.

Meeting of the Administrative Centre for Social Security for Rhine Boatmen on 26–29 November in Strasbourg, Chairman Mr. SCHWARTZ.

c) The Chamber of Appeal met on 7 May and 16–17 December in Strasbourg under the chairmanship of Mr. ROYER.

2. RELATIONS WITH OTHER INTERNATIONAL ORGANISATIONS

a) On 14 February at Duisburg, the Restricted Economic Committee held talks with representatives of the Rhine Navigation Consortium and the International Union on River Navigation about economic problems in connection with Rhine navigation, more particularly with the draft regulations for the temporary immobilisation of carrying capacity, the chair being taken by Mr. VAN DER NOORDT.

b) The Secretary General attended, as an observer, the negotiations among the Contracting Parties to the revised Convention on Rhine navigation, the Contracting Parties to the Convention on the Canalisation of the Moselle and the European Economic Community on the implementation of regulations concerning the temporary immobilisation of vessels.

c) The Secretariat represented the Central Commission at the following meetings:

- The Inland Transport Committee of the United Nations Economic Commission for Europe, Geneva, and the following of its working parties and groups of experts:
  - the Sub-committee on inland waterway transport;
  - the Group of Experts on the unification of technical standards relating to ships and of ships' papers;
  - the Group of Experts on the unification of inland navigation traffic rules and signs;
  - the Group of Experts on the transport of dangerous substances;
  - the Group of Experts on river law;
  - the Study Cycle on port facilities on inland waterways;
- the United Nations Environment Programme;
- the International Association for the Rhine Ships' Register;
- the European Conference of Ministers of Transport;
- UNIDROIT;
- the International Atomic Energy Agency;
- the Council of Europe Committee of Experts on Social Security;
- the meeting of governmental experts on the technical supervision of boats navigating on inland waterways, organised by the Commission of the European Communities.

d) *The Commission of the European Communities* was represented at the April session by Mr. D'ELBREIL and Mr. GRAFF and at the November session by Mr. VENTRELLA, Mr. HAZELOOP and Mr. MASSE.

à la session d'avril par MM. D'Elbreil et Graff et à la session de novembre par MM. Ventrella, Hazeloop et Masse.

La *Commission Economique pour l'Europe des Nations Unies* a été représentée à la session d'avril et de novembre par M. Adossides.

3. TRAVAUX DE LA COMMISSION CENTRALE

a) *Questions générales*

Unification du droit fluvial

La Commission Centrale a chargé le Comité du droit fluvial de poursuivre la recherche de solutions permettant, en ce qui concerne la Convention relative à la limitation de la responsabilité des propriétaires de bateaux de navigation intérieure (CLN), de dégager une position commune des Etats membres sur la question de la limitation de la responsabilité en matière de pollution ainsi qu'en matière de créances des personnes transportées en vertu d'un contrat de transport de passagers ainsi que l'examen des problèmes que pose, notamment au regard de l'unité du régime de la navigation du Rhin, l'élaboration de la Convention sur le contrat de transport des marchandises (CMN), ainsi que celle relative au contrat de transport de voyageurs et de bagages en navigation intérieure (CVN).

Elle a prévu que le Comité consultera sur ces questions les représentants du Consortium de la navigation rhénane ainsi que de l'Union Internationale de la Navigation Fluviale.

Elle a enfin donné mandat au Comité d'examiner les bases et les limites juridiques de la compétence de la Commission centrale relativement aux dispositions adoptées par elle et concernant les matières dangereuses.

Problèmes découlant de l'évolution de la navigation rhénane

La Commission Centrale a pris acte de la communication concernant l'état des travaux du Comité ad hoc chargé d'examiner les problèmes découlant de l'évolution de la navigation rhénane.

Elle a prié son Président de prendre contact avec le Président de la Commission Internationale pour la protection du Rhin contre la pollution afin d'examiner avec lui les possibilités d'un approfondissement, en vue de la lutte contre la pollution du Rhin, de la collaboration entre les deux institutions, compte tenu notamment de l'élaboration par la Commission Internationale d'un programme à long terme qui concerne également la navigation rhénane.

Protocolle additionnel à la Convention révisée pour la navigation du Rhin signée à Mannheim le 17 octobre 1868

La Commission Centrale a pris acte de la ratification par la Grande-Bretagne, les Pays-Bas et la Suisse du Protocole additionnel à la Convention révisée pour la navigation du Rhin signé à Strasbourg le 25 octobre 1972.

b) *Questions économiques*

Mesures d'assainissement du marché de la navigation rhénane

Comme les années précédentes, la Commission Centrale a été informée par son Comité économique de l'évolution de la situation économique de la navigation rhénane. A ce sujet, les communications fournies par le Consortium de la navigation rhénane ont constitué des éléments d'appréciation supplémentaires.

Dans ce contexte la Commission Centrale a constaté que pour l'année

The United Nations Economic Commission for Europe was represented at the April and November sessions by Mr. Adossides.

3. WORK OF THE CENTRAL COMMISSION

a) General questions

Unification of river law

With regard to the Convention relating to the limitation of liability of the owners of inland navigation ships (CLN), the Commission instructed the River Law Committee to continue to seek ways of enabling member states to adopt a common attitude on the limitation of liability in matters of pollution and of claims by persons transported under a passenger transport contract. It also instructed the Committee to look into the problems arising from the drafting of the Conventions on the contract for the carriage of goods by inland waterway and on the contract for the carriage of passengers and luggage by inland waterway, particularly in the light of unity in the system of Rhine navigation.

The Committee would consult the representatives of the Rhine Navigation about these matters.

Lastly, it instructed the Committee to consider the legal bases and limits of its (the Commission's) competence concerning the provisions adopted by it in connection with dangerous substances.

Problems stemming from Rhine navigation trends

The Commission took note of the communication concerning the progress made by the ad hoc Committee examining the problems stemming from Rhine navigation trends.

It requested its Chairman to contact the Chairman of the International Commission for the Protection of the Rhine against Pollution, with a view to discussing with him the possibility of closer co-operation between the two bodies against pollution of the Rhine, having regard in particular to the International Commission's work on a long-term programme which affected Rhine navigation.

Protocol to the revised convention for Rhine navigation signed at Mannheim on 17 October 1868

The Commission took note that Great Britain, the Netherlands and Switzerland had ratified the Protocol to the revised Convention for Rhine navigation, signed at Strasbourg on 25 October 1972.

b) Economic questions

Measures to reorganise the Rhine shipping market

As in previous years, the Commission was informed by its Economic Committee about the economic trends of Rhine shipping. Communications from the Rhine Navigation Consortium provided additional information in this respect.

The Commission noted that in 1974 there had been an increase of about 5% in the goods transported by Rhine shipping, but that considerable changes had taken place both in the type of goods transported and in transport links.

1974 un accroissement d'environ 5% des marchandises transportées par la navigation rhénane a été noté mais que d'importants changements s'y sont produits tant en ce qui concerne la nature des marchandises transportées que les relations de transport.

Elle a en outre remarqué qu'en raison des actions de déchirage poursuivies en République fédérale d'Allemagne et, dans une mesure limitée aux Pays-Bas, le tonnage total des bateaux utilisés dans navigation rhénane a quelque peu baissé mais que par suite de la mise en service de nouvelles unités plus rationnelles, la capacité effective est restée au moins identique. Par ailleurs, du fait de niveaux d'eau favorables, la capacité de la flotte a pu être beaucoup mieux utilisée qu'en 1973. En conséquence, une forte pression sur les frets provoquée par la surcapacité s'est fait ressentir à nouveau; en raison d'une forte augmentation des coûts, la rentabilité de la navigation rhénane est demeurée insatisfaisante.

La Commission Centrale a, de ce fait, attiré l'attention des Gouvernements sur la nécessité de poursuivre et d'accentuer les actions de déchirage entreprises et de parvenir le plus tôt possible à l'organisation de l'immobilisation temporaire de bareaux.

Réglementation concernant l'immobilisation temporaire de bateaux

La Commission Centrale, après s'être informée sur les développements de ce problème, a pris connaissance avec intérêt de la nouvelle proposition de la Commission des Communautés Européennes tendant à résoudre les questions restant encore ouvertes. Elle a exprimé l'espoir qu'un accord puisse rapidement intervenir, au sein du Conseil des Communautés Européennes, sur la mise en oeuvre de la réglementation d'immobilisation temporaire de bateaux de navigation intérieure, dont l'importance et l'urgence n'ont jamais été contestées.

A cet effet, elle a recommandé aux délégations de mettre tout en oeuvre afin que les négociations, auxquelles participent les Parties Contractantes de la Convention révisée pour la navigation du Rhin et de la Convention sur la canalisation de la Moselle ainsi que la Communauté Economique Européenne, puissent aboutir à bref délai.

Application éventuelle de la réglementation de la TVA à la navigation rhénane

La Commission Centrale a été informée que la proposition de sixième directive du Conseil des Communautés Européennes en matières d'harmonisation des législations des Etats membres relatives aux taxes sur le chiffre d'affaire est actuellement en discussion. Elle a fait savoir au Président du Conseil des Communautés Européennes que l'application des dispositions qui y sont contenues poserait un problème de compatibilité avec les dispositions de la Convention de Mannheim et affecterait considérablement la position de la navigation rhénane; ce projet impliquerait en effet la suppression d'exonérations existantes et constituerait une discrimination par rapport à d'autres modes de transport exonérés. En conséquence, la Commission Centrale a exprimé le souhait qu'une coopération soit instituée avec les Communautés Européennes en ce qui concerne les délibérations se tenant de part et d'autre sur cette question.

Application des règles de concurrence dans le secteur des transports

La Commission Centrale s'est informée du développement des délibérations au sein des Communautés Européennes sur les problèmes intéressant particulièrement la navigation rhénane, notamment dans les domaines des règles de concurrence pour les transports et de l'imputation des frais d'infrastructure. Elle a prié son Comité économique de suivre l'évolution de ces questions.

It also noted that, because of breaking-up operations in the Federal Republic of Germany and to a lesser extent in the Netherlands the total tonnage of vessels engaged in Rhine navigation had decreased slightly, but that following the coming into service of new and more rational vessels, actual capacity had remained at least the same. Furthermore, thanks to favourable water levels it had been possible to make much better use of the fleet than in 1973. Consequently there had again been strong pressure on freight rates because of over-capacity, and with the considerable increase in costs the profit margin of Rhine navigation had remained unsatisfactory.

Accordingly, the Commission drew the attention of governments to the need to pursue and intensify breaking-up programmes and organise the temporary immobilisation of vessels as soon as possible.

Regulations for the temporary immobilisation of vessels

Having informed itself on developments in this matter, the Commission noted with interest the new proposal by the Commission of the European Communities for solving the remaining problems. It expressed the hope that agreement would soon be reached in the Council of the Communities on implementation of the regulations for temporary immobilisation of inland waterways vessels, the importance and urgency of which had never been in dispute.

To that end it recommended that delegations should do all in their power for early completion of the negotiations in progress among the Contracting Parties to the revised Convention for Rhine navigation and to the Convention on the Canalisation of the Moselle and the Economic European Community.

Possible application of VAT regulations to Rhine shipping

The commission was informed that the proposed 6th Order of the Council of the European Communities, on harmonisation of the legislation of member states on turnover taxes, was at present under review. It informed the President of the Council that application of the proposed Order would raise a problem of compatibility with the Mannheim Convention and would considerably affect the situation of Rhine navigation, in that it would involve the abolition of existing exemptions and thus discriminate in favour of other extempted forms of transport. Accordingly, the Commission expressed the desire for co-operation with the European Communities with regard to the discussions taking place on this subject on both sides.

Application of rules of competition in the transport sector

The Central Commission was informed of the progress of discussions in the European Communities on matters of particular concern to Rhine shipping, notably in respect of rules of competition for transport and the apportionment of infrastructure costs. It asked its Economic Committee to keep in touch with developments in these matters.

c) *Questions sociales*

Accord révisé en 1963 concernant les conditions de travail des bateliers rhénans – Conférence gouvernementale

La Commission Centrale après avoir entendu l'exposé du représentant des Communautés Européennes sur leurs projets d'harmonisation des conditions sociales dans la navigation fluviale et consciente de l'importance d'une réglementation appropriée des conditions de travail pour la navigation rhénane a chargé son Comité des questions sociales, de travail et de formation professionnelle d'examiner les possibilités de mise en vigueur du Protocole additionnel de travail des bateliers rhénans. Le Comité entendra à cet effet tels représentants des employeurs ou des travailleurs qu'il jugera opportun.

d) *Questions douanières*

En ce qui concerne le régime du transit communautaire institué dans les Pays membres des Communautés Européennes, la Commission Centrale a pris acte avec satisfaction de l'entrée en vigueur du règlement relatif aux transports avec la Suisse à partir du ler janvier 1974.

La Commission Centrale a pris acte de ce qu'un nouveau système de clôture douanière dit système ,,Bröhl'', a été homologué d'un commun accord par les Etats intéressés. Elle a invité les gouvernements des Etats contractants à rappeler aux bateliers du Rhin qu'ils doivent se conformer, dans la conduite du bateau, lors du passage du secteur douanier de Neuburgweier, aux besoins de la douane.

e) *Questions relatives au Rapport annuel*

La Commission Centrale, sur la base des propositions de son Comité du Rapport annuel et des Statistiques, a approuvé plusieurs modifications essentielles concernant la partie économique et la statistique des flottes de son rapport annuel.

f) *Questions réglementaires*

La Commission Centrale a adopté le texte d'un *guide de radiotéléphonie pour la navigation rhénane*, destiné en premier lieu à l'usage des bateliers. Ce guide définit les divers services radiotéléphoniques et les règles particulières s'y appliquant ainsi que les données techniques des matériels. Il fournit, en outre, à l'utilisateur toutes les informations concernant les liaisons qu'il peut établir en tout point du bassin rhénan ainsi que la procédure à suivre pour l'établissement de ces liaisons. Il contient enfin une rubrique comportant les renseignements relatifs aux différents services radiotéléphoniques du point de vue géographique avec les cartes correspondantes.

La Commission a adopté à titre d'essai une *réglementation visant à instaurer le principe de la navigation à droite* sur le secteur du Rhin compris entre Duisbourg et la frontière germano-néerlandaise.

Par ailleurs, étant donné l'intérêt économique que peut présenter l'exploitation de *grands convois poussés de six barges*, la Commission Centrale a recommandé que soient intensifiés et autant que possible élargis les essais portant sur l'exploitation de ces convois. Elle a en outre décidé d'instituer un Groupe de travail chargé d'étudier les problèmes posés sur le Rhin par *la navigation des bateaux de sport motorisés*.

La Commission Centrale a arrêté les principes d'un nouveau *Règlement relatif à la délivrance des patentes de batelier du Rhin*, notamment

c) *Social questions*

Agreement on the working conditions of Rhine boatmen as revised in 1963 – Governmental Conference

After hearing the statement by the representative of the European Communities on their plans to harmonise social conditions in inland waterway navigation, the Commission instructed its Committee on Social questions, Labour and Training, having regard to the importance of appropriate regulations on working conditions in Rhine shipping, to consider the possibility of applying the protocol to the Agreement, revised in 1963, on the working conditions of Rhine boatmen. To that end the Committee will hear such representatives of employers or workers as it thinks fit.

d) *Customs questions*

With regard to the Community transit system introduced in the member states of the European Communities, the Commission noted with pleasure that the regulations on transport to and from Switzerland had come into force on 1 January 1974.

The Commission took note of the fact that a new customs enclosure system, "Bröhl" system, had been approved by the states concerned. It called on the governments of the Contracting States to remind Rhine boatmen that they were required to comply with customs requirements when taking their vessels through the customs sector at Neuburgweier.

e) *Questions concerning the annual report*

On the basis of proposals from its Committee on the Annual Report and Statistics, the Commission approved a number of basic amendments to the section of its annual report dealing with economics and statistics of fleets.

f) *Questions of regulations*

The Commission adopted the text of a *radio-telephone guide for Rhine navigation*, mainly intended for boatmen. This guide describes the various radio-telephone services and the specific rules for them and gives technical details of the equipment. It also gives full information on all the connections possible at each point in the Rhine basin and how to obtain them. Lastly, it contains a section giving geographical information on the various radio-telephone services together with the relevant maps.

The Commission adopted experimentally *regulations introducing the principle of keeping to the right* in the sector of the Rhine between Duisburg and the German-Netherlands frontier.

In view of the potential economic advantage of using *pushboat convoys of 6 barges*, the Commission recommended that experiments with such convoys should be stepped up and if possible extended. It also decided to set up a working party to study the problems caused by *the use of motorised pleasure boats* on the Rhine.

The Commission established principles for new *regulations on the issue of Rhine boatmens' certificates*, including a compulsory examination for all prospective boatmen.

The Commission added to the *Regulations for the transport of dangerous substances on the Rhine* new provisions requiring the completion of a check list before the loading and unloading of tankers. The model list was en généralisant l'obligation d'un examen pour les candidats bateliers.

La Commission a introduit dans le *Règlement pour le transport de matières dangereuses sur le Rhin* (*ADNR*) de nouvelles prescriptions relatives à l'établissement d'une *liste de contrôle* à remplir avant les opérations de chargement ou de déchargement de bateaux-citernes. Le modèle de cette liste a été ajouté comme appendice à l'ADNR. Ces mesures ont pour but essentiel de contribuer à l'augmentation de la sécurité lors des chargements et des déchargements de matières dangereuses.

g) *Questions techniques*

En ce qui concerne les questions techniques, la Commission Centrale a constaté que compte tenu du contrôle approfondi et régulier de leur état, les *écluses de Kembs* sont capables de maîtriser aussi bien le trafic actuel que le trafic prévisible à l'horizon 1985. Elle a toutefois invité le Comité technique permanent à étudier la mise en place de mesures destinées à accélérer le déroulement des opérations d'éclusage et d'étudier l'amélioration de la capacité des écluses.

Elle a en outre pris acte du rapport du Comité technique permanent sur les plans et documents relatifs aux ouvrages de navigation de la *chute d'Iffezheim* et pris connaissance du programme des travaux révus au cours de l'année 1974 pour *l'aménagement du Rhin entre Lauterbourg/Neuburgweier et St. Goar.*

La Commission Centrale a en outre approuvé sous certaines conditions les projets suivants:

- *construction de ponts-routes* à Arnhem, Huningue-Weil, Weisenthurm-Neuwied et Düsseldorf-Flehe,
- *construction d'un port de transbordement* du p.k. 321,60 au p.k. 322,20, rive droite du Rhin;
- *extension de la zone portuaire de la Rheinumschag Gmbh à Breisach* du p.k. 226,23 au p.k. 226,30 et du p.k. 226,85 au p.k. 227,58.

4. CHAMBRE DES APPELS

La Chambre des Appels a rendu en tant que juridiction de dernier ressort, cinq jugements en matière civile.

appended to the Regulations. The basic aim of these measures is improved safety when dangerous substances are being loaded and unloaded.

g) *Technical questions*

The Commission noted that, in view of the thorough and regular checks on their condition, the *Kembs locks* would be capable of handling present and foreseeable future traffic until 1985. However, it requested the Technical Committee to study the introduction of measures to speed up operations at locks and improvement of their capacity.

It also took note of the report by the Permanent Technical Committee on plans and documents concerning navigation works at the *Iffezheim fall* and examined the programme of work as reviewed in 1974 for improvement in the stretch of *the Rhine between Lauterbourg/Neuburgweier and St. Goar.*

The Commission also approved the following projects subject to certain conditions:

- *the building of road bridges at Arnhem,* Huningue-Weil, Weisenthrum-Neuwied and Düsseldorf-Flehe,
- *the building of a transshipment installation* between km-post 321,60 and km-post 322.20 on the right bank of the Rhine;
- *extention of the Rheinumschlag Gmbh port area at Breisach* from km-post 226.23 to km-post 226.30 and from km-post 226.85 to km-post 227.58.

4. CHAMBER OF APPEAL

The Chamber of Appeal, as appeal court of the last instance, pronounced judgment in 3 civil cases.

CHAPITRE II

UNION ECONOMIQUE BENELUX

A. RAPPORT ANNUEL AU CONSEIL INTERPARLEMENTAIRE CONSULTATIF DE BENELUX

Le Conseil interparlementaire consultatif de Benelux, instauré en 1956, se compose de 49 membres dont 21 sont choisis par et parmi le Parlement belge. Selon ces mêmes modalités, le Parlement luxembourgeois y délègue 7 de ses membres, tandis que le Parlement néerlandais y est représenté par 21 membres. Le Conseil est habilité à se concerter et à émettre des avis aux trois gouvernements au sujet de problèmes ayant directement trait à l'Union économique entre les trois Etats, au rapprochement culturel et à la coopération entre les trois pays dans le domaine de la politique extérieure. Le Conseil s'occupe également de l'unification du droit des pays du Benelux.

Annuellement, les trois gouvernements soumettent au Conseil un rapport commun traitant de chacun de ces problèmes. Ce rapport est publié.

Les trois gouvernements viennent de présenter au Conseil interparlementaire consultatif de Benelux le dix-huitième rapport commun sur la réalisation et le fonctionnement de l'union économique entre les trois Etats. Ce rapport couvre la période du 1er juillet 1973 au 30 juin 1974. Il comporte une introduction qui, en termes généraux, donne un aperçu de l'évolution de l'union. Viennent ensuite quatre chapitres, à savoir: I. Réalisation de l'union dans le domaine économique; II. Réalisation de l'union en matière sociale, de santé publique, d'environnement et de circulation des personnes; III. Réalisation et fonctionnement de l'union en matière fiscale et financière; IV. Réalisation de l'union dans le domaine agricole.

Ces subdivisions correspondent à la répartition des taches entre les diverses commissions permanentes constituées au sein du Conseil. Le texte complet du rapport commun est disponible au Secrétariat général de l'Union économique Benelux, rue de la Régence 39 à 1000 - Bruxelles.

Nous publions ci-après le texte intégral de l'introduction au dix-huittième rapport. A l'intention du lecteur, nous avons en outre extrait certains points d'actualité des différents chapitres du rapport.

INTRODUCTION

L'année sous revue a vu se produire sur le plan mondial une série d'événements qui ont amené les gouvernements à s'interroger sur le contenu à donner à la coopération internationale. Les difficultés dans le secteur énergétique, les problèmes monétaires, l'inflation et la crise agricole sont de telle nature qu'il n'est pas possible d'y remédier ailleurs que sur le plan international. En outre, il n'est pas rare que des contradictions se manifestent. La coopération monétaire en est un exemple frappant. Il n'empêche que, même sur ce terrain difficile, le Benelux a réussi à sauvegarder son unité. Soucieux de l'avenir de l'Europe, les gouvernements des pays du Benelux ont joint leurs efforts pour renforcer la coopération européenne. L'effet positif de ces efforts a de nouveau démontré de façon péremptoire toute l'importance du Benelux, ainsi que le rôle de nos trois pays dans la construction de l'Europe. Pour qu'ils puissent continuer à remplir ce rôle, les trois pays du Benelux ont besoin que la coopération entre eux soit renforcée.

En vue de la réalisation de cet objectif, la préparation d'une concertation au plus haut niveau a été entamée depuis un certain temps; cette

CHAPTER II

BENELUX ECONOMIC UNION

A. ANNUAL REPORT TO THE BENELUX INTERPALIAMENTARY CONSULTATIVE COUNCIL

The Benelux Consultative Interparliamentary Council, which was established in 1956, has 49 members, 21 of whom are chosen by the Belgian parliament from among its own ranks. The Luxembourg parliament appoints 7 of its members in the same way, and the Dutch parliament is represented by 21 members. The Council is empowered to deliberate and submit opinions to the 3 governments on problems directly related to the Economic Union between the three states, cultural rapprochement and co-operation between the three countries in foreign policy. The Council also deals with unification of law in the Benelux countries.

Each year the three governments submit to the Council a joint report on each of these problems. This report is published.

The three governments have just submitted to the Benelux Interparliamentary Consultative Council the 18th joint report on the achievement and operation of the economic union among the three states. This report covers the period 1 July 1973 to 30 June 1974. The introduction surveys the way in which the union has evolved in general terms, and is followed by four chapters, viz: I. Achievements of the Union in the economic field; II. Achievements of the Union in the social, public health and environment fields and in the movement of persons; III. Achievements and operation of the Union in fiscal and financial matters; IV. Achievements of the Union in agriculture.

These subdivisions correspond to the apportionment of tasks among the various standing committees set up within the Council. The full text of the joint report is available on request from the Secretariat General of the Benelux Economic Union, Rue de la Régence 39, 1000 – Brussels.

The full text of the introduction to the 18th report is published below, together with a number of topical points taken from the various chapters of the report.

INTRODUCTION

During the year under review, a series of events took place throughout the world which prompted governments to reconsider the matters on which international co-operation was required. Difficulties in the energy sector, monetary problems, inflation and the agricultural crisis are such that the only possible remedies to them are international ones. Moreover, contradictions are not uncommon. Monetary co-operation is a striking example. Yet even in this difficult field, the Benelux has managed to preserve its unity. The governments of the Benelux countries, in their concern for Europe's future, have joined forces in order to strengthen European co-operation. The positive fruit of their efforts has once again convincingly demonstrated the full importance of the Benelux, and of the rôle which our three countries are playing in the unification of Europe. But if they are to continue fulfilling that rôle, co-operation among the three Benelux countries must itself be reinforced.

In order to achieve that aim, preparations were embarked upon some time ago for concertation at the highest level to determine the pace at which the Benelux Economic Union is to develop in forthcoming years.

concertation déterminera à quel rythme l'Union économique Benelux se développera au cours des prochaines années. Outre la consolidation de l'acquis actuel et la poursuite de la suppression des formalités aux frontières communes, cette concertation aura pour l'objectif l'accélération de la mise en œuvre de la nouvelle priorité que constitue la coordination des politiques.

Comme le mentionnait le rapport précédent, les pays du Benelux s'efforcent de conférer une teneur tangible à ce développement. A cet effet, des propositions ont été élaborées en ce qui concerne la coordination des politiques de l'environnement, de l'infrastructure des transports et de l'aménagement du territoire.

D'autres possibilités de coordination sont également examinées dans le secteur financier, le secteur économique et le secteur social, notamment à l'égard de la politique industrielle, de la politique énergétique et de la politique des prix.

Les gouvernements ne se cachent pas que la réalisation de la coordination et de l'intégration Benelux dans ces secteurs constituera une tâche ardue et longue. La réalisation de ces objectifs nécessitera des efforts de la part de toutes les parties intéressées. La tradition de trente années de coopération en Benelux rend les gouvernements confiants pour suivre la voie qu'ils se sont tracée.

Il faut constater que le processus d'intégration Benelux a quelque peu marqué le pas au cours du dernier exercice. Ainsi, la suppression des formalités à la frontière nécessite plus de temps que l'on ne l'avait prévu. C'est notamment le cas de l'harmonisation des taux d'accise. L'adaptation des taux de la TVA n'a pas encore pu être achevée au cours de la période sous revue, pas plus d'ailleurs que les consultations relatives à l'introduction du document unique.

Toutefois, si l'opération de l'ouverture des frontières rencontre certaines difficultés, l'harmonisation des législations visant à l'élimination des entraves commerciales, a atteint dans une très large mesure, sa phase terminale. Conformément à la décision du Comité de Ministres du 18 octobre 1972 et à l'avis du Conseil consultatif économique et social, les travaux d'harmonisation en la matière ont généralement été arrêtés. Ce n'est que dans le cas où une entrave commerciale réelle existe ou apparaît – entrave qui n'est pas susceptible d'être éliminée dans un délai raisonnable par la Communauté européenne – que les travaux d'harmonisation seront poursuivis en Benelux. Un nombre fort limité de matières seulement satisfont à cette exigence et l'on peut en conséquence constater qu'un chapitre important de l'intégration Benelux vient de se terminer.

L'installation de la Cour de Justice Benelux dont l'une des tâches consiste à promouvoir l'unité juriqidue lors de l'interprétation de règles communes, signifie un pas important dans la direction de l'unité Benelux en matière de législation et de jurisprudence.

CHAPITRE I

REALISATION DE L'UNION DANS LE DOMAINE ECONOMIQUE

La conversion de la *politique commerciale commune* du Benelux en politique C.E. s'est poursuivie, mais la phase de transition n'est toujours pas révolue.

En ce qui concerne l'abolition ou, le cas échéant, l'harmonisation des restrictions quantitatives restantes, appliquées à l'égard de certains pays tiers, la Communauté n'a progressé que laborieusement. Les Etats membres continuent dès lors à appliquer, après consultation dans le cadre de la C.E., le régime de politique commerciale de façon autonome, notamment

Besides consolidating what has already been achieved and further eliminating formalities at the common frontiers, it will be the purpose of that concertation to speed up the implementation of a new priority: policy co-ordination.

As was stated in the preceding report, the Benelux countries are endeavouring to give tangible substance to that development. To this end, proposals have been put forward for the co-ordination of environment, transport infrastructure and regional planning policies.

Other possibilities for co-ordination are also being examined in the financial, economic and social sectors, especially in respect of industrial policy, energy policy and price policy.

The governments are fully aware that the attainment of co-ordination and integration among the Benelux countries in these sectors will be a long, arduous task. The achievement of these goals calls for efforts on the part of all concerned. Yet the tradition of 30 years' co-operation in the framework of the Benelux is a source of confidence to the governments in pursuing the path they have marked out.

It must be said that the process of integration in the Benelux has been marking time somewhat over the last financial year. The elimination of frontier formalities, for example, is taking longer than had been expected. This is particularly so in the case of harmonising excise duty rates. It has not yet been possible to bring the VAT rate into line over the period under review, nor to complete the consultation on the introduction of a single form.

However, while the opening up of the frontiers is encountering a number of difficulties, the harmonisation of legislation designed to remove obstacles to trade has in very large measure entered its final phase. In accordance with the decision of the Committee of Ministers of 18 October 1972 and the opinion of the Economic and Social Consultative Council, most of the harmonisation work in this sphere has been brought to an end. Only in cases where there is, or appears to be, a real obstacle to trade – one which is not likely to be removed within a reasonable time by the European Community – is harmonisation work to be continued within the Benelux. This is true of only a very small number of questions, and it is therefore fair to say that an important chapter in Benelux integration has come to an end.

The establishment of the Benelux Court of Justice, one of whose tasks is to promote legal unity in the interpretation of common rules, constitutes an important step forward towards Benelux unity in matters of legislation and court practice.

CHAPTER I

ACHIEVEMENTS OF THE UNION IN THE ECONOMIC FIELD

The changeover from the *common Benelux commercial policy* to a European Communities policy has gone ahead, but the transition period is not yet complete.

The Community has made headway only laboriously in abolishing or, as appropriate, harmonising the remaining quantity restrictions applied to certain outside countries. Thus the member states, after consultation within the framework of the European Community, are continuing to apply their commercial policy arrangements on an independent basis, par-

parce que, depuis le 1er janvier 1973, ils ne sont plus habilités à négocier avec les pays à commerce d'Etat.

La marge restreinte pour opérer de manière autonome dans le cadre de la C.E. a été utilisée par les pays du Benelux pour adapter et proroger certains accords commerciaux du Benelux avec des pays de l'Europe orientale. Dans certains cas le Benelux a dû recourir à la clause de sauvegarde prévue par l'article 115 du Traité de Rome, pour des produits importés via la libre pratique des autres Etats membres et dont les montants excédaient la hauteur des contingents Benelux en vigueur.

Il est incontestable que le secteur des *communications* s'est signalé particulièrement à l'attention au cours de la période écoulée. En effet, le 28 novembre 1973 s'est tenue à Ostende la 4ème Concertation portuaire Benelux entre les ministres du Verkeer en Waterstaat, des Communications et des Travaux publics et des autorités portuaires belges et néerlandaises. Les conclusions de cette concertation ont conduit à une initiative du Benelux tendant à la mise en œuvre d'une politique portuaire communautaire. Le 10 juin 1974, le ministre belge des Communications a soumis, au nom également de ses collègues néerlandais et luxembourgeois, la proposition du Benelux au président de la Commission des Communautés européennes et l'a commentée verbalement lors de la réunion du Conseil des C.E. (transports) du 27.6.'74

Les travaux de la liaison Escaut-Rhin ont, dans les grandes lignes, progressé favorablement selon les prévisions, de sorte que la date repère fixée pour la mise en utilisation de la voie navigable – c'est-à-dire 1975 – est maintenue.

L'autoroute E-3 a été entièrement ouverte au trafic en juillet 1973.

En ce qui concerne la teneur concrète qu'il convient de donner à la *coordination des politiques économiques*, l'étude de divers secteurs a été entreprise en vue d'arrêter une manière pratique de procéder (politique des prix, politique industrielle). Dans d'autres cas, les partenaires du Benelux ont eu des consultations préalables pour aboutir à une position Benelux commune dans le cadre de la C.E. (politique d'approvisionnement en énergie, questions d'organisation de l'économie et de concurrence, politique de la consommation, politique des classes moyennes).

Par suite de l'évolution rapide de la situation énergétique, les consultations au sujet de la politique d'approvisionnement en énergie ont été intensifiées. C'est ainsi que les mois de décembre et de janvier ont été marqués par des consultations intensives sur la situation née de la crise pétrolière, les mesures prises dans les pays concernés, l'approvisionnement de l'industrie pétrochimique, et les conséquences de la crise pour le trafic intra-Benelux et pour la politique commune aux frontières extérieures. En raison de l'interdépendance des économies, on est parti du principe que les livraisons aux industries des pays partenaires devaient être limitées dans la même mesure que les livraisons aux industries nationales.

Les aspects Benelux de certains problèmes d'actualité ont été examinés. Parmi ceux-ci, il y a lieu de citer: la reconnaissance réciproque de diplômes, les heures de fermeture des magasins, les ventes à prime, en solde et en liquidation, les ventes à perte, la reconversion d'indépendants, les implantations périphériques de commerces de détail, le franchisage, les métiers d'art, etc.

La Convention Benelux en matière de dessins ou modèles est entrée en vigueur le 1er janvier 1974. De ce fait, la Loi uniforme sera d'application à partir du 1er janvier 1975. Dans cette perspective, le Bureau Benelux des Dessins ou Modèles a entamé ses travaux afin de prendre les dispositions préparatoires qui s'imposent.

En ce qui concerne *l'aménagement du territoire*, une procédure de consultation à suivre lors de la préparation des plans régionaux et de secteur a été définie. Une décision concernant la coordination de ces plans dans les ticularly because they are no longer empowered, since 1 January 1973, to negotiate with countries where trade is state-controlled.

The small margin for autonomous operation within the context of the European Community has been used by the Benelux countries to adapt and extend certain Benelux trade agreements with Eastern European states. In certain cases, the Benelux has had to resort to the safeguard clause provided for in Article 115 of the Treaty of Rome in the case of products imported freely through other member states in amounts exceeding the prevailing Benelux quotas.

There can be no doubt that the *communications* sector has stood out particularly in the course of the period under review. On 28 November 1973, the 4th Benelux Ports Conference between the ministers of transport, waterways, communications and public works and the Belgian and Dutch port authorities, took place in Ostend. The conclusions of that conference led to a Benelux move towards the implementation of a Community ports policy. On 10 June 1974 the Belgian Minister of Communications, also acting on behalf of his Dutch and Luxembourg colleagues, submitted the Benelux proposal to the President of the Commission of the European Communities, and commented verbally on it at the meeting of the EEC Council (transport) on 27 June 1974.

Work on the Schelde-Rhine link has, broadly speaking, progressed well according to plan, and the target date for putting the waterway into service – 1975 – is accordingly maintained.

The whole of the E-3 motorway was opened to traffic in July 1973.

As for the tangible substance to be given to *co-ordination of economic policies*, studies have been undertaken in a range of sectors in order to decide on practical machinery (pricing policy and industrial policy). In other cases, the Benelux partners have held prior consultations in order to define a common Benelux position within the framework of the European Community (energy supply policy, questions of economic organisation and competition, consumer policy, policy on tradespeople and shopkeepers).

Rapid developments in the energy situation have led to an intensification of the talks on energy supply policy. Thus December and January were marked by intensive consultations on the situation brought about by the oil crisis, the measures taken in the states concerned, supply arrangements for the petrochemical industry, and the effects of the crisis on intra-Benelux traffic and common policy at the external frontiers. By reason of the interdependence of the different economies, the principle was adopted that supplies to industries in the partner states should be subject to the same limits as those to home industries.

The Benelux aspects of certain topical problems were examined. Among these were the mutual recognition of qualifications, shop-closing hours, gift offers, sales and closing-down sales, loss leaders, reconversion of self-employed persons, out-of-town shopping centres, franchises, handicrafts etc.

The Benelux Convention on patterns and designs entered into force on 1 January 1974. The uniform law will accordingly be applied from 1 January 1975 onwards. With this in view, the Benelux Patterns and Designs Office has begun work on the preparatory arrangements that are necessary.

Where *regional planning* is concerned, the consultation machinery to be employed in the preparation of regional and sector plans has been decided. A decision on the preparation of such plans in frontier regions was signed during the period under review. In addition, a map of the recreational amenities available in the central part of the Benelux, together with directives on the subject, have been prepared in order to serve as guidelines for all future projects affecting this region. Publication of these documents is expected shortly.

régions frontières a été signée au cours de la période sous revue. D'autre part, une carte établissant un inventaire des possibilités récréatives dans la région centrale du Benelux ainsi que des directives en la matière ont été élaborées afin de servir d'orientation pour tous les projets futurs concernant cette région. La publication de ces documents est envisagée dans un proche avenir.

CHAPITRE II

REALISATION DE L'UNION EN MATIERE SOCIALE, DE SANTE PUBLIQUE, DE L'ENVIRONMENT ET DE LA CIRCULATION DES PERSONNES

Le Groupe de travail ministériel des Questions sociales s'est réuni à deux reprises au cours de la période sous référence. Après avoir examiné les problèmes sociaux qui se posent dans le cadre de la coopération au Benelux, les ministres ont procédé à un échange de vues au sujet du développement financier du Fonds social européen et de l'exécution du programme d'action sociale européen.

Le Groupe de travail ministériel a décidé que seront étudiés un certain nombre de problèmes d'actualité tels que la résorbtion des conséquences de l'inflation sur les prestations de la sécurité sociale et l'harmonisation des régimes de sécurité sociale différents d'après les groupes professionnels.

La politique du marché de l'emploi menée dans les pays du Benelux a fait l'objet d'une analyse comparative approfondie et à cette occasion a été examiné si l'expérience acquise dans un pays déterminé ne pourrait pas contribuer utilement à la politique du marché de l'emploi dans les autres pays. Quelques suggestions ont été formulées se rapportant principalement aux services de l'emploi. Il sera vérifié à l'échelon national si et dans quelle mesure ces suggestions peuvent être suivies.

A la fin de la période considérée, un rapport au sujet de l'automatisation dans les pays du Benelux a été présenté. Ce rapport donne un aperçu de l'évolution du parc d'ordinateurs des pays du Benelux de 1970 à 1973 et souligne en particulier le rôle des pouvoirs publics en matière d'automatisation. L'influence de l'ordinateur sur l'emploi direct d'une part, et sur l'emploi indirect de l'autre est également traitée dans ce rapport. En outre, un certain nombre de considérations sont consacrées aux aspects humains et psychologiques de l'introduction de l'automatisation.

En ce qui concerne les marchés régionaux de l'emploi, une procédure a été instaurée qui rend plus importante et plus efficace la compensation entre la demande et l'offre de maind'œuvre entre le Luxembourg belge et le Grand-Duché de Luxembourg.

Le président du Comité de Ministres a signé quelques recommandations concernant les prescriptions de sécurité pour une série de machines. D'autre part, les Pays-Bas ont ratifié par la Loi du 6 février 1974 la Convention Benelux concernant les machines dangereuses.

Pour ce qui est des *problèmes de l'environnement*, la comparaison des réglementations nationales concernant la pollution de l'eau et de l'air a été entamée afin d'être en mesure d'examiner ensuite les possibilités d'harmoniser ces dispositions. Cette harmonisation sera fondée, le cas échéant, sur la réglementation la plus stricte. Le rapport comportera également une description de l'infrastructure existante ou à créer pour contrôler la pollution.

Entre-temps des contacts réguliers se sont poursuivis entre les techniciens des laboratoires des trois pays. Les groupes régionaux examinent deux fois par an les résultats des prélèvements d'eau effectués dans les régions frontières et recherchent des solutions en commun aux problèmes du pollution de l'eau, de l'air et du sol.

CHAPTER II

ACHIEVEMENTS OF THE UNION IN THE SOCIAL, PUBLIC HEALTHS AND ENVIRONMENT FIELDS AND IN MOVEMENT OF PERSONS

The Ministerial Working Party on Social Questions met twice during the period under review. After examining the social problems arising in the context of Benelux co-operation, the ministers held an exchange of views on the financial development of the European Social Fund and the implementation of the European programme of social action.

The Ministerial Working Party decided that a number of topical problems are to be investigated; they include absorbing the effects of inflation on social security benefits, and harmonising the various social security schemes for different occupational groups.

A detailed comparative analysis was conducted of the employment policy pursued in the Benelux countries, and the opportunity was taken to consider whether the experience acquired in one country might not make a useful contribution to employment policy in the others. A number of suggestions, mainly related to employment services, were put forward. Checks will be made at national level to see whether and to what extent these suggestions can be adopted.

At the end of the period under review, a report was presented on automation in the Benelux countries. The report surveys developments in computer facilities in the Benelux countries between 1970 and 1973, with particular emphasis on the rôle of the public authorities in automation. The influence of computers on direct employment on the one hand and indirect employment on the other is also dealt with in this report. In addition, consideration is given to the human and psychological aspects of introducing automation.

Where regional labour markets are concerned, a procedure has been established which makes for greater and more effective compensation between the supply and demand of labour as between the Belgian province of Luxembourg and the Grand Duchy of Luxembourg.

The Chairman of the Committee of Ministers has signed a number of recommendations relating to safety regulations for certain machines. In addition, the Netherlands ratified the Benelux Convention on Dangerous Machinery in the Act of 6 February 1974.

As regards *environmental problems*, a start has been made on a comparative study of national regulations on water and air pollution, so that the possibilities of harmonising these regulations can later be examined. Such harmonisation will be based on the most stringent regulations. The report will also include an account of the infrastructure which either exists or needs to be established in order to monitor pollution.

In the meanwhile, regular contacts have been maintained between laboratory technicians in the three countries. Twice a year, the regional groups examine the results of water samples taken in the various frontier regions, and look for common solutions to the problems of water, air and soil pollution.

Near the frontier between Belgium and Luxembourg, Belgium has installed non-automatic sulphur and smoke monitoring equipment, which is operated by technicians from Luxembourg.

Près de la frontière belgo-luxembourgeoise, la Belgique a installé des appareils non automatiques pour la détermination du soufre et de la fumée, appareils dont le contrôle est assuré par les services grand-ducaux.

En ce qui concerne *la circulation des personnes*, les principaux problèmes traités au cours de la période sous revue, sont la présence dans le Benelux d'étrangers de pays non-C.E., la délivrance et la suppression de visas, les documents de voyage, le contrôle des personnes aux frontières extérieures, l'éloignement d'étrangers indésirables, les réfugiés et demandeurs d'asile, ainsi que la collaboration au niveau international.

CHAPITRE III

REALISATION ET FONCTIONNEMENT DE L'UNION EN MATIERE FISCALE ET FINANCIERE

Pour les grandes lignes de l'évolution en matière de territoire douanier commun, harmonisation des accises et de la taxe de transmission/TVA., on est prié de se référer à l'introduction du présent rapport annuel.

Le 17 septembre 1973, le florin a été réévalué de 5 %, les Gouvernements du Benelux s'étant concertés à ce sujet au préalable. Malgré une situation monétaire internationale extrêmement instable, le ,,petit serpent Benelux" s'est maintenu dans le ,,serpent C.E. aminci": les Pays-Bas et l'U.E.B.L. sont restés fidèles à la Convention Benelux d'août 1971, qui limite les marges de fluctuation entre les deux monnaies à 1,5 % de part et d'autre du taux-pivot. Après la réévaluation du florin, il a fallu soutenir cette monnaie dans le cadre de l'arrangement Benelux précité, mais ces interventions, qui se sont poursuivies jusqu'à la mi-décembre 1973, n'ont eu qu'une ampleur limitée.

CHAPITRE IV

PARACHEVEMENT ET FONCTIONNEMENT DE L'UNION DANS LE DOMAINE AGRICOLE

Dans le cadre de *la coordination de la recherche agronomique* des consultations ont été consacrées, pour le secteur phytosanitaire, à la lutte intégrée dans les vergers et dans les cultures céréaliaires et, dans le secteur vétérinaire, à la lutte contre la leucose bovine et les maladies respiratoires des veaux. Par ailleurs, le rapport annuel fait apparaître que la collaboration en *matière vétérinaire* se concrétise de plus en plus, ce qui ressort notamment de la mise en concordance des réglementations en divers domaines.

B. COUR DE JUSTICE BENELUX

Le traité relatif à l'institution et au statut d'une Cour de Justice Benelux, signé à Bruxelles le 31 mars 1965, est entré en vigueur le 1 janvier 1974.

Le texte du traité a été publié dans l'Annuaire Européen Volume XIII, 1965, pp. 259–266. La Cour a tenu une première Audience Solennelle à Bruxelles le 11 mai, 1974.

As regards the *movement of persons*, the main problems dealt with in the period under review are the presence in Benelux of aliens from non-EEC countries, the issue and withdrawal of visas, travel documents, checks on persons at external frontiers, the removal of undesirable aliens, refugees and persons seeking asylum, and international collaboration.

CHAPTER III

ACHIEVEMENTS AND OPERATION OF THE UNION IN FISCAL AND FINANCIAL MATTERS

For the broad lines of development in respect of the common customs territory, harmonisation of excise and turnover tax/VAT, the reader is referred to the introduction to this annual report.

On 17 September 1973, the guilder was revalued by 5% after prior consultation among the Benelux governments. Despite a highly unstable international monetary situation, the "Benelux worm" was maintained within the "narrow European Community snake": the Netherlands and the Benelux Economic Union continued to observe the Benelux Convention of August 1971, limiting the fluctuation margin between the two currencies to 1.5% on either side of the pilot rate. After the guilder had been revalued, it had to be supported within the framework of the above-mentioned Benelux arrangement, but these interventions, which continued until mid-December 1973, took place on a limited scale only.

CHAPTER IV

COMPLETION AND OPERATION OF THE UNION IN THE AGRICULTURAL FIELD

Co-ordination of agronomic research has entailed consultations, in the phytosanitary sector, on integral pest control in orchards and cereal crops and, in the veterinary sector, on the control of bovine leucosis and respiratory diseases in calves. Furthermore, the annual report reveals increasingly practical co-operation in veterinary matters, as particularly evidenced by the bringing into line of regulations in various fields.

B. BENELUX COURT OF JUSTICE

The treaty on the establishment and statute of a Benelux Court of Justice, signed in Brussels on 31 March 1965, entered into force on 1 January 1974.

The text of the treaty was published in the European Yearbook, Volume XIII, 1965, pp. 259–266 (in French only). The Court held its first Ceremonial Sitting in Brussels on 11 May 1974.

TEXTE DES ALLOCUTIONS PRONONCEES A L'OCCASION DE LA PREMIERE AUDIENCE SOLENNELLE DE LA COUR DE JUSTICE BENELUX

Allocution de Monsieur l'Avocat général Frédéric DUMON
Chef du Parquet de la Cour de Justice Benelux

Dès le début de cette première audience solennelle qui brille d'un éclat particulier, l'honneur m'échoira de prier des magistrats des Courts suprêmes de nos trois pays ainsi que les greffiers de la haute juridiction nouvelle de prêter le serment ou de faire la promesse qui les investira des fonctions de juges, avocats généraux et greffiers d'une juridiction commune aux Pays-Bas, au Luxembourg et à la Belgique chargée d'exercer, au nom des trois nations, la fonction juridictionnelle sur le fondement de règles de droit communes à ces trois pays.

Ces règles de droit, comme toutes les normes qui régissent des Etats démocratiques, naissent du concours étroit et nécessaire d'une part des exigences, souhaits, conceptions ou opinions de nos populations et d'autre part des initiatives et décisions de nos autorités politiques tenant compte des nécessités et des possibilités politiques, économiques et sociales; ces normes se développent et se précisent, ensuite, par le fait de l'exercice de la fonction juridictionnelle.

Nation, nécessités et possibilités, décisions des autorités politiques et jurisprudence; sources matérielles et formelles du droit.

Dans nos sociétés actuelles les intérêts, les activités et même la satisfaction ou l'épanouissement des sentiments et attachements humains ne peuvent plus être entravés, limités ou arrêtés par les frontières géographiques; les individus exigent de pouvoir user de leur liberté et de pouvoir épanouir ou étendre leurs possibilités et leurs activités intellectuelles, culturelles, sociales et économiques dans des espaces plus vastes.

Ils ne renient pas pour autant leur propre nation, l'attachement à leur histoire ou à leur culture – de même que les liens familiaux continuent durant toute notre vie à réchauffer nos sentiments les plus intimes – mais ils réalisent qu'un rapprochement des peuples est incompatible avec des nationalismes injustifiés qui contrecarrent le bien-être intellectuel et matériel et en même temps menacent la paix.

Ces exigences, désirs et nécessités constituent le fondement c.-à-d. les sources matérielles des institutions ainsi que des autres règles de droit et programmes des Communautés Européennes et de l'Union économique Benelux qui poursuivent le développement harmonieux des politiques économique, financière et sociale, la libre circulation des personnes, des biens, des capitaux et des services, objectifs qui ne peuvent être atteints si des législations nationales différentes et contradictoires, dès lors paralysantes, maintiennent leur empire et si les jugements et arrêts nationaux ne ,,circulent'' point librement c.-à-d. si leur autorité prend fin aux frontières nationales.

Les Communautés Européennes et peut-être encore plus l'Union Benelux et c'est là me paraît-il une des justifications encore actuelles et notamment l'utilité évidente de cette Union Benelux, ont favorisé et même réalisé l'harmonisation et l'unification de règles de droits nationaux; des traités, conventions et protocoles qui sont déjà en vigueur et d'autres qui vraisemblablement seront ratifiés d'ici peu ont de surcroît aboli les frontières nationales pour l'application de certaines dispositions nationales, pour l'intervention de fonctionnaires et même de magistrats et de juridictions nationales et aussi en ce qui concerne l'autorité ou la force exécutoire de certains jugements et d'arrêts nationaux.

Tout cela a été décidé et a fait l'objet de normes qualifiées règles juridiques communes dont l'interprétation uniforme par toutes les juridictions des trois pays sera rendue possible grâce à la Cour de Justice Benelux.

TEXT OF ADDRESSES DELIVERED AT THE FIRST CEREMONIAL SITTING OF THE BENELUX COURT OF JUSTICE

Address by the Solicitor-General, Frédéric DUMON Chef du Parquet of the Benelux Court of Justice

At the very beginning of this exceptionally resplendent ceremonial sitting, the honour falls to me of calling upon judges from the supreme courts in our 3 countries, and the registrars of this new judicial authority, to take the oath or make the promise that will invest them with the offices of judges, public prosecutors and registrars of a court which is common to the Netherlands, Luxembourg and Belgium and is responsible for exercising jurisdiction, on behalf of those 3 nations, on the foundation of the rules of law they have in common.

These rules of law, like all the other standards by which democratic states are governed, derive from the close and necessary interplay of the requirements, wishes, ideas and opinions of our peoples on the one hand and, on the other, of the initiatives and decisions of our political authorities, account being taken of political, economic and social exigencies and possibilities; and they are subsequently developed and clarified through the exercise of the judicial function.

Nations, needs and possibilities; the decisions of political authorities and the judgments of the courts: these are the material and formal sources of law.

In present-day societies, people's interests and activities, and even the satisfaction and fulfilment of their feelings and attachments, can no longer be impeded, curbed or confined by geographical frontiers; individuals demand the opportunity to use their freedom, to develop or extend their potential and their intellectual, cultural, social and economic activities in a broader framework.

This does not mean denying their own country, their attachment to their history or culture – just as family ties continue throughout life to animate our innermost feelings – but they realise that rapprochement between peoples is incompatible with unwarranted nationalistic attitudes which run counter to intellectual and material well-being, and are at the same time a threat to peace.

These requirements, wishes and needs constitute the foundation – that is to say, the material sources – of the institutions and other rules of law and programmes of the European Communities and the Benelux Economic Union, whose goals are the harmonious development of economic, financial and social policies and the free movement of persons, goods, capital and services: goals which cannot be attained if different and contradictory, and therefore paralysing, systems of national legislation continue to hold sway and if national judgments and decisions do not have freedom of movement, that is to say if their authority stops at national frontiers.

The European Communities, and perhaps even more the Benelux Union – and this strikes me as a continuing justification of the Benelux and a mark of its obvious utility – have promoted, and indeed achieved, the harmonisation and unification of national rules of law; treaties, conventions and protocols which are already in force, together with others which are likely to be ratified shortly, have in addition abolished national frontiers as regards the application of certain national regulations, intervention by officials and even judges and national court authorities, and also as regards the authority or enforceability of certain national judgments and decisions.

All this has been decided and laid down in standards referred to as common legal rules, whose uniform interpretation by all judicial author-

Regles juridiques communes auxquelles les individus et les autorités des trois pays sont soumis ou le seront et qui, il importe me paraît-il de le souligner, *réalisent une véritable dénationalisation du droit.*

Les nombreux et délicats problèmes qui devaient recevoir une solution pour que les objectifs de l'Union Benelux puissent être réalisés furent aperçus et souvent maîtrisés avec un esprit particulièrement entreprenant grâce à l'affinement et au perfectionnement de la méthode classique de l'élaboration des conventions internationales comme d'ailleurs cela avait été déjà fait, dans une certaine mesure, par les Etats scandinaves et au sein du Conseil de l'Europe: préparation par des experts, fonctionnaires et spécialement par la si méritoire Commission Benelux pour l'Unification du Droit, coopération entre les fonctionnaires des trois Etats, interventions fréquentes et agissantes des Ministres, dialogue avec le Conseil interparlementaire consultatif Benelux, même avec les chambres législatives nationales et le tout couronné par des exposés des motifs communs, soigneusement élaborés et motivés, des trois Gouvernements souvent soumis aux parlements nationaux, exposés des motifs qui constitueront, par excellence, pour notre Cour une source précieuse et adéquate d'interprétation.

Concernant la nature et les caractéristiques des institutions de l'Union Benelux, je me bornerai – bien que ces caractéristiques auront nécessairement une incidence sur l'application par les juridictions des règles décidées par ces institutions – à considérer qu'on peut y découvrir des éléments d'une confédération, d'une union d'États et même d'une fédération; spécialement en ce qui concerne celle-ci en raison de l'existence et des pouvoirs de la Cour de Justice Benelux: ses arrêts interprétatifs lieront, en effet, directement, in specie, les juridictions nationales – les arrêts de sa chambre chargée du contentieux relatif aux fonctionnaires de l'Union économique Benelux formeront directement titre exécutoire sur le territoire des trois pays.

Les cours et tribunaux parachèvent, affinent, précisent, harmonisent, coordonnent les règles issues à la fois des coutumes, des sources écrites – lois et conventions internationales – et des principes généraux du droit.

Œuvre créatrice immense, combien complexe et délicate, trouvant toutefois – ce qu'a actuellement tendance à perdre de vue une certaine doctrine – des limites en raison des missions et responsabilités normatives appartenant dans nos Etats aux autorités politiques responsables directement devant les populations.

Vingt conventions, traités, protocoles Benelux contenant des règles communes dont l'interprétation coordonnée est confiée à la Cour sont déjà en vigueur, treize autres sont signés, quatre le furent encore ce matin, en ce Palais d'Egmont qui nous accueille.

Ils contiennent d'innombrables règles susceptibles d'être appliquées, après interprétation, par toutes les juridictions de nos trois pays; il importe que les sujets de droit, avocats, autorités, magistrats des Pays-Bas, du Luxembourg et de la Belgique soient conscients de cet afflux Beneluxien dans nos trois droits positifs.

Vous apercevez, Messieurs, à la fois l'étendue et les difficultés d'une interprétation de règles communes qui sont introduites dans des droits nationaux, demeurant encore différents dans de nombreux domaines, échappant dès lors à votre pouvoir d'interprétation, et qui coexistent de surcroît avec des règles de droit des Communautés européennes dont l'interprétation coordonnée, comme la détermination de leur portée, appartiennent à la Cour de Justice de ces Communautés.

Ceux qui ont créé le Benelux ont compris, comme l'avaient fait les auteurs des traités de Rome, qu'il ne suffit point d'établir des règles communes aux fins de réaliser progressivement l'harmonisation et l'unification des droits nationaux si une juridiction commune n'est pas investie de la mission d'assurer l'unité d'interprétation desdites règles communes. Ainsi ities in the 3 countries is to be made possible thanks to the Benelux Court of Justice. These are common legal rules by which individuals and authorities in the 3 states are or will be bound and which, I think it is important to emphasise, *represent a genuine denationalisation of law*.

The many tricky problems that had to be solved if the aims of the Benelux Union were to be achieved were identified and frequently overcome in an extremely forward-looking spirit, through the refinement and perfection of the traditional method of drafting international conventions, as had in fact already been done to some extent by the Scandinavian countries and in the Council of Europe. The process entailed preparatory work by experts, government officials and especially the meritorious Benelux Commission for the Unification of Law, co-operation between officials in the 3 countries, frequent active ministerial intervention, dialogue with the Benelux Consultative Interparliamentary Council, and even with national legislative chambers – all this effort culminating in carefully drafted and reasoned joint explanatory memoranda by the 3 governments, often submitted to the national parliaments, and which will provide the Court with an outstanding body of source material for interpretation purposes.

As far as the nature and characteristics of the Benelux institutions are concerned, and although these characteristics will necessarily affect the manner in which courts apply the rules drawn up by the institutions, I shall confine myself to the consideration that they can be seen to contain the component parts of a confederation, a union of states, or even a federation – the last-mentioned particularly by reason of the existence and powers of the Benelux Court of Justice. Its judgments will be directly binding *in specie* on national courts: the decisions rendered by the chamber dealing with disputes relating to officials of the Benelux Economic Union will be directly enforceable throughout the territory of the 3 states.

The courts finalise, refine, clarify, harmonise and co-ordinate rules which derive variously from custom, written sources (laws and international agreements) and general principles of law.

It is an immense, complex and delicate creative job of work which does nonetheless – though there is a certain doctrine tending to overlook the fact at the present time – have its limitations by reason of the normative tasks and responsibilities devolving on the political authorities directly responsible to the population in our countries.

There are already in force 20 Benelux conventions, treaties and protocols containing common rules for whose co-ordinated interpretation the Court of Justice is competent, and a further 13 have been signed – 4 of them this very morning here in the Egmont Palace.

They contain countless regulations which may be applied, after interpretation, by the courts throughout our 3 countries; it is important that members of the public, barristers, official bodies and judges in the Netherlands, Luxembourg and Belgium should be aware of this Benelux contribution to our 3 systems of positive law.

You will perceive, Gentlemen, both the scope and the difficulties of interpreting common rules inserted into national bodies of law which are still at variance in many fields and thus lie outside your powers of interpretation, and which into the bargain exist side by side with the Economic Community's rules of law, whose co-ordinated interpretation and the determining of whose scope are the task of the Communities' Court of Justice.

Those who created the Benelux Union understood, as did the authors of the Treaty of Rome, that the formulation of common rules is not enough to ensure the gradual harmonisation and unification of national systems of law, without common jurisdictional machinery competent to see that there is unity in the interpretation of those common rules. Thus were sont nées d'abord la Cour de Justice des Communautés Européennes, qui a, en quelques années, créé une jurisprudence prestigieuse, puis la Cour de Justice Benelux.

C'est que, si objectives et détachées des tendances et opinions personnelles, philosophiques, politiques et sociales, que soient, comme elles doivent l'être, les décisions des magistrats, il est impossible, en l'absence d'une juridiction commune régulatrice, d'éviter les interprétations différentes, voire divergentes, de règles communes, recréant ainsi la diversité que celles-ci avaient voulu abolir.

Les causes de ces interprétations différentes sont multiples: méthodes, concepts et raisonnements différents, appréhension et compréhension non identiques des problèmes, habitudes et traditions propres aux pouvoirs judiciaires nationaux, qualités et caractères différents des hommes et des femmes que sont les magistrats. Ces caractères, qualités et personnalités ont d'ailleurs souvent joué un rôle combien bénéfique dans la formation et l'évolution des jurisprudences nationales.

Il m'est un agréable devoir de rappeler ici le rôle éminent à la Cour supérieure de justice du Luxembourg notamment des présidents Hansen et Faber, des procureurs généraux Welter et Huss, du président Rodenbourg, à la Cour de cassation de Belgique notamment du premier président Soenens, des procureurs généraux Leclercq, Cornil, Hayoit de Termicourt et Ganshof van der Meersch et du premier avocat général Mahaux et au Hoge Raad der Nederlanden, des Présidents Visser et Donner, des procureurs généraux Besier et Langemeijer et du Président Wiarda, actuellement aussi Président de la Cour de Justice Benelux.

La science du droit, l'expérience, le dévouement et la personnalité de notre Président comme ceux aussi des autres membres de la Cour sont le garant d'une uniformité d'interprétation efficace et adéquate dans nos trois pays de règles communes qui existent pour accroître le bien-être de nos sociétés et qui sont le garant aussi de la naissance et du développement d'une protection juridictionnelle des fonctionnaires de l'Union économique Benelux, mission qui est aussi confiée à notre Cour.

On est tenté de comparer notre Cour, et même de l'assimiler au Parlement de Malines, plus tard le Grand Conseil, qui dit le droit dans nos provinces de 1473 à 1794.

Certes, le Parlement de Malines eut un certain temps le ressort territorial qui est actuellement celui de notre Cour; certes aussi, notre robe rappelle dans une certaine mesure celle des parlementaires, mais les points de divergence sont importants. Notre Cour n'est point une juridiction d'appel, mais une juridiction ne connaissant généralement que du droit, elle est gardienne de règles communes, alors que le Parlement de Malines interprétait et appliquait des coutumes différentes.

Notre Cour n'a point été instituée pour affirmer une souveraineté nationale aux dépens d'une autre ou pour cloisonner le développement des droits. Bâtie sur les aspirations de nos Nations contemporaines, elle existe pour servir un droit nouveau, commun aux trois Nations membres de Communautés plus larges encore, et dont le fondement est le progrès humain et social, la coopération, la collaboration, la compréhension et la confiance.

Allocution de clôture du Président de la Cour de Justice Benelux, Monsieur G. J. WIARDA

En ma qualité de Président de la Cour qui s'est préparée aujourd'hui par la prestation du serment à entamer ses travaux, j'ai le privilège de prendre la parole en dernier au cours de cette audience solennelle.

Je ne voudrais pas manquer d'exprimer tout d'abord notre reconnaisborn, first the Court of Justice of the European Community, which has built up a formidable body of case law in the space of a few years, and now the Benelux Court of Justice.

The fact is that however objective and detached from personal, philosophical, political and social tendencies and opinions the decisions of the courts may be, it is impossible in the absence of a common controlling jurisdictional authority to avoid different, and even divergent, interpretations of common rules, thus restoring the diversity they were designed to abolish.

There are a multitude of causes for these differing interpretations: methods, conceptions and reasoning differ; problems are not understood and assessed in the same way; national judiciaries have their own habits and traditions; the men and women who constitute the bench have different qualities and characters. Indeed, these characters, qualities and personalities have often played a beneficial part in the shaping and development of national court practice.

It is both a duty and a pleasure for me to mention here the outstanding services rendered at the High Court of Justice in Luxembourg by its Presidents Hansen and Faber, Public Prosecutors Welter and Huss and President Rodenbourg; at the Belgian Court of Cassation by its first President Soenens, Public Prosecutors Leclercq, Cornil, Hayoit de Termicourt and Ganshof van der Meersch and the senior Solicitor General Mahaux, and at the Netherlands Supreme Court by Presidents Visser and Donner, Public Prosecutors Besier and Langemeijer and President Wiarda, who is now also President of the Benelux Court of Justice.

The legal knowledge, experience, dedication and personality of our President, and indeed of the Court's other members, are a guarantee of the proper and effective uniformity of interpretation in our 3 countries of common rules which exist to enhance the well-being of our societies, and will also ensure the creation and development of jurisdictional safeguards for the officials of the Benelux Economic Union, a task for which the Court is likewise responsible.

There is a temptation to compare this Court, and even to equate it, with the Parliament of Malines, subsequently the Grand Council, which administered the law throughout these provinces from 1473 to 1794.

It is true that the Malines Parliament did for a time enjoy the geographical competence now allotted to this Court; and admittedly, our robes are somewhat reminiscent of those worn by the members of that parliament. But the differences are important. Our Court is not an appeal court but one which, as a general rule, is concerned only with points of law; it is the guardian of common rules, whereas the Malines Parliament interpreted and applied different customs.

This Court has not been established to assert national sovereignty at the expense of another state, or to develop law along separate, self-contained channels. Built upon the aspirations of our countries in the present day, it exists to serve a new system of law common to the 3 nations that are members of still larger communities, and whose foundations are human and social progress, co-operation, collaboration, understanding and trust.

Closing Address by the President of the Benelux Court of Justice, Mr. G. J. WIARDA

In my capacity as President of the Court which has prepared for the inception of its activities today by the swearing in of its members, it is my privilege to speak last at this ceremonial sitting.

To begin with, I must not fail to express our gratitude to all those who sance à ceux qui nous ont appelés, mes collègues et moi-même, à remplir la mission pour laquelle la Cour est instituée, je veux parler ici des membres du Comité de Ministres de l'Union économique Benelux; ma gratitude s'adresse également à ceux qui ont créé cette mission.

La mission dont je parle consiste à contribuer, comme cela a déjà été relevé aujourd'hui, à la réalisation de l'un des objectifs les plus considérables que se sont fixés les pays réunis par leur coopération dans l'Union économique Benelux: l'unification du droit, là où elle est possible et utile; notre contribution reviendra à promouvoir une application aussi uniforme que possible des règles juridiques communes actuelles et futures de la Belgique, du Luxembourg et des Pays-Bas.

La destination qui nous est donnée, nous la devons à l'établissement du Traité relatif à l'institution et au statut d'une Cour de Justice Benelux; l'élaboration de ce Traité a nécessité le concours d'un grand nombre d'organes du Benelux et d'organes nationaux mais je crois que personne ne m'en voudra ou me taxera d'exagération si, en songeant à ceux qui ont présidé à la naissance de la Cour de Justice Benelux, je relève en particulier la Commission Benelux pour l'étude de l'unification du droit, qui fut le creuset même de la Cour de Justice.

La mise en place de la Cour de Justice Benelux est l'exemple le plus récent de ce que la coopération d'Etats nationaux dans un cadre institutionnalisé peut conduire à une nouvelle forme de juridiction supranationale.

L'observateur est frappé par la variété de ces formes.

Notre Cour de Justice a peu en commun, si ce n'est peut-être le caractère international, avec le premier exemple en date, la Cour internationale de Justice de La Haye dont la compétence se limite à trancher les litiges entre Etats.

La Cour européenne des droits de l'homme à Strasbourg, et nous sommes heureux qu'elle soit représentée ici en la personne de Monsieur Ganshof van der Meersch, ressemble davantage à notre Cour de Justice. Un point de comparaison qui saute immédiatement aux yeux est la situation de ces Cours par rapport aux formes de coopération interétatique dont elles sont nées. Quelle que soit l'étroitesse des relations de la Cour européenne des droits de l'homme avec le Conseil de l'Europe et l'importance de liens de la Cour de Justice Benelux avec l'Union économique Benelux, la Cour de Strasbourg n'est pas une institution proprement dite du Conseil de l'Europe ni la Cour de Justice Benelux une institution proprement dite de l'Union économique Benelux. Un autre parallèle qu'il est possible d'établir entre ces deux Cours se situe au niveau de leur champ d'activités qui est axé sur l'application du droit commun créé par des traités passés entre Etats.

Pour la Cour de Strasbourg, il s'agit des règles inscrites dans le Traité concernant la sauvegarde des droits de l'homme, règles qui constituent l'héritage commun des Etats groupés au sein du Conseil de l'Europe; pour le Cour de Justice Benelux, il s'agit de certaines règles juridiques communes egalement créées par traités dans le domaine du droit civil, du droit commercial, du droit pénal, du droit fiscal et du droit administratif. D'autre part, de grandes différences peuvent être decelées; la Cour de Strasbourg en effet, est appelée à prendre une décision définitive dans des cas individuels dont l'origine est une plainte contre un Etat déterminé; la Cour de Justice Benelux pour sa part – abstraction faite de la juridiction administrative qui lui est reconnue pour les personnes au service de l'Union économique Benelux – ne peut être saisie que de demandes de décisions préjudicielles relatives à l'interprétation des règles juridiques unifiées et la décision définitive incombe au juge national.

Sous ce dernier aspect, on note une plus grande similitude avec la Cour européenne de Luxembourg – et nous sommes heureux qu'elle soit repréhave called upon my colleagues and myself to discharge the function for which the Court has been created – by which I mean the members of the Committee of Ministers of the Benelux Economic Union; my thanks are also due to those who created that function.

The function to which I refer is that of contributing, as has already been said today, to the attainment of one of the most substantial aims which the countries united through their co-operation in the Benelux Economic Union have set themselves: the unification of law, wherever possible and useful. The essence of our contribution will be to promote the greatest possible uniformity in the application of the common legal rules, both present and future, adopted by Belgium, Luxembourg and the Netherlands.

We own the mission that has been assigned to us to the drawing up of the Treaty on the establishment and statute of the Benelux Court of Justice. A great many Benelux bodies and national bodies were involved in the preparation of that treaty, but I believe that nobody will hold it against me or accuse me of exaggeration if, in referring to those who presided over the creation of the Benelux Court of Justice, I make special mention of the Benelux Commission for the Study of the Unification of Law, which was the very crucible in which the Court of Justice took shape.

The establishment of the Benelux Court of Justice is the most recent example of co-operation between nation states within an institutional framework leading to a new form of supra-national jurisdiction.

The variety of forms which such co-operation can take is striking to the onlooker.

This Court of Justice has little in common, except perhaps for its international nature, with the first example of the kind, namely the International Court of Justice at the Hague, whose competence is limited to disputes between states.

The European Court of Human Rights at Strasbourg – and we are delighted that it should be represented here today in the person of Mr Ganshof van der Meersch – bears more similarity to our own Court of Justice. One point of comparison which is immediately apparent is the situation of the two courts in relation to the forms of inter-state co-operation from which they emerged. However close the relation between the European Court of Human Rights and the Council of Europe, and however strong the links between the Benelux Court of Justice and the Benelux Economic Union, the Strasbourg Court is not, strictly speaking, a Council of Europe institution, nor is the Benelux Court of Justice, strictly speaking, an institution of the Benelux Economic Union.

Another parallel that can be drawn between the two courts is their field of activity, which is centred on the application of a common body of law created by treaties between states.

Where the Strasbourg Court is concerned, the rules are those enshrined in the Convention for the Protection of Human Rights, and these rules are the common heritage of the Council of Europe's member states; in the case of the Benelux Court of Justice, they are certain common legal rules, also laid down by treaties, in the fields of civil law, commercial law, penal law, fiscal law and administrative law. On the other hand, there are major differences: the Strasbourg Court is called upon to take final decisions on individual cases originating in complaints against specific states; as for the Benelux Court of Justice – apart from the administrative jurisdiction it enjoys in respect of persons employed by the Benelux Economic Union – only requests for interlocutory decisions regarding the interpretation of the unified legal rules can be referred to it, the final decision lying with the national courts.

In the latter respect, there is greater similarity with the European Court in Luxembourg – and we are happy that it should be represented here by sentée ici en la personne de ses juges Donner, Mertens de Wilmars et Pescatore – la Cour de Luxembourg dont la tâche par ailleurs beaucoup plus étendue, comprend également des décisions préjudicielles à prendre à la demande du juge national. Au chapitre des différences toutefois et mis à part les missions de la Cour de Luxembourg dans d'autres domaines que la prise de décisions préjudicielles, il convient de faire remarquer que la Cour de Luxembourg, contrairement à celle de Strasbourg et à celle de Bruxelles, est bien une institution du cadre de coopération où elle est née, la C.E.E. et que ses décisions préjudicielles n'ont trait qu'au droit communautaire. La Cour de Justice Benelux, elle, s'occupera de règles juridiques touchant un nombre extrêmement varié de domaines qui n'ont parfois qu'un rapport éloigné avec les objectifs proprement dits de l'Union économique Benelux.

Il se justifie, à mon sens, de dire que la Cour de Justice Benelux est la première Cour de justice supranationale qui, abstraction faite à nouveau de la juridiction administrative, se voit conférer une mission dont l'essence même consiste à veiller à ce que l'application de règles juridiques uniformes communes à un certain nombre d'Etats se fasse également d'une manière tout aussi uniforme.

Il n'est évidemment pas fortuit que ce premier exemple tire son origine du cadre de coopération étroite entre la Belgique, le Luxembourg et les Pays-Bas. C'était là le lieu privilégié pour soumettre l'unification du droit à la pierre de touche d'une jurisprudence unificatrice.

Il n'est pas exclu qu'une réminiscence d'un passé lointain ait contribué à faire naître l'idée que c'était précisément entre nos trois pays que cette pierre de touche pouvait et devait trouver sa place. Je songe ici au grand Conseil de Malines dont on vient de fêter le souvenir. Quelle coïncidence remarquable: la proclamation du grand Conseil comme ,,court souverain'' dont la juridiction s'étendait à certaines régions de l'empire des ducs de Bourgogne réunissant à peu près la Belgique, le Luxembourg et les Pays-Bas, devait être suivie 500 ans après, presque jour pour jour, de l'entrée en vigueur d'un Traité instituant la présente Cour. Ceux qui ont participé à la cérémonie de commémoration du grand Conseil, se souviendront à cet égard du discours de M. Huss qui est beaucoup à l'origine de cette Cour et qui souligna cette coïncidence.

Les circonstances politiques d'il y a 500 ans qui entraînèrent la naissance d'un instrument qui aurait pu, si la situation politique d'alors s'était perpétuée, réaliser dans une large mesure l'unification du droit dans nos pays, ne sont évidemment comparables à aucun égard avec les conditions politiques que nous connaissons aujourd'hui.

Cela est certain mais il n'empêche que je pense pouvoir déclarer que ni l'instauration d'un grand Conseil comme juridiction commune à nos pays ni la présente Cour bien modeste, mise en place 5 siècles après n'auraient été bien pensables si les pays concernés n'avaient pas toujours été appelés à s'entendre en dépit de tous les aléas de l'Histoire, des conflits, des malentendus et des oppositions d'intérêt. Ce ne serait pas faire preuve de réalisme que de s'identifier au grand Conseil de Malines mais il n'en reste pas moins que les membres de la présente Cour de Justice peuvent regarder comme un privilège l'occasion qui leur est donnée d'exprimer dans la sphère qui leur est propre la cohésion de nos pays.

Il est temps de clore cette session solennelle. Permettez-moi de terminer en formulant l'espoir que les paroles bienveillantes prononcées ce matin dans cette enceinte et desquelles nous sommes profondément reconnaissants, accéderont à la réalité des faits et que l'activité de notre Cour se révélera précieuse pour l'évolution du droit de nos pays. La réalisation de cet espoir est notamment tributaire de l'évolution future de l'unification du droit dans nos pays et de la mesure dans laquelle l'interprétation des règles juridiques uniformes sera confiée à la Cour de Justice; de ce point

Judges Donner, Mertens de Wilmars and Pescatore – the Luxembourg Court, whose function is in fact much more extensive and also includes the rendering of interlocutory decisions at the request of national courts. However, where the differences are concerned, and disregarding the Luxembourg Court's functions in fields other than interlocutory decisions, it should be noted that the Luxembourg Court, unlike the courts in Strasbourg and Brussels, is actually an institutional part of the co-operation machinery from which it derives, namely the EEC, and that its interlocutory decisions relate only to Community law. The Benelux Court of Justice, for its part, will be concerned with legal rules affecting an extremely wide range of fields, sometimes only very distantly related to the goals of the Benelux Economic Union as such.

It is, I think, fair to say that the Benelux Court of Justice is the first supra-national Court of Justice which, once again disregarding its administrative jurisdiction, has been entrusted with a task whose very essence consists in ensuring that uniform legal rules, common to a certain number of states, are also applied in a manner which is equally uniform.

It is of course not by chance that this first example should originate in the close co-operation between Belgium, Luxembourg and the Netherlands. This was the ideal setting in which to test the unification of law against the touchstone of unifying court practice.

It is not inconceivable that a memory from the distant past may have contributed to the birth of the idea that this testing-ground could and should be the co-operation between our three particular countries. I am referring to the Grand Council of Malines, which has just been commemorated. What a remarkable coindicence it is: the proclamation of the Grand Council as a "sovereign court" with jurisdiction extending to certain parts of the empire of the Dukes of Burgundy, roughly covering Belgium, Luxembourg and the Netherlands, was to be followed 500 years afterwards, practically to the day, by the entry into force of a treaty establishing this Court of Justice. Those who attended the ceremony commemorating the Grand Council will remember the address by Mr Huss, who is closely connected with the establishment of this Court and who emphasised the coincidence.

The political circumstances of 500 years ago led to the creation of an instrument which, if the political situation at the time had remained unchanged, could have achieved a large measure of legal unification in our countries; but of course those circumstances are in no way comparable with the political conditions in which we live today.

While there can be no doubt about that, I think it is nevertheless fair to say that neither the establishment of a Grand Council as a common jurisdictional authority over our countries, nor this extremely modest Court established five centuries afterwards, would have been conceivable unless the countries concerned had always stood to gain from agreements with each other, in spite of all the ups and downs of history, conflicts, misunderstandings and clashes of interest. To equate ourselves with the Grand Council of Malines would be unrealistic; but the fact remains that the members of this Court of Justice may regard it as a privilege to have this opportunity of expressing the cohesion between our countries in a context which is theirs alone.

It is time to bring this ceremonial sitting to a close. Allow me to conclude by expressing my hope that the kind words that were said this morning in this Chamber, and for which we are profoundly grateful, will be translated into reality and that the work of our Court will prove to be of value to the development of law in our countries. The fulfilment of that hope depends mainly on future developments in the unification of law in our three states and on the extent to which the interpretation of the uniform legal rules is entrusted to the Court of Justice; in this connection, the de vue, les protocoles que viennent de signer les trois Ministres de la Justice me semblent constituer un excellent présage.

Nos travaux seront en outre largement conditionnés par la fréquence à laquelle les juridictions nationales s'adresseront à la Cour. Sous cet aspect également, il nous est peut-être donné de voir un heureux présage dans le fait que M. l'Avocat général Berger du „Hoge Raad der Nederlanden" dans ses conclusions données la semaine passée à l'occasion d'une affaire civile soumise à la Cour suprême néerlandaise, a proposé à celle-ci de demander une décision préjudicielle à notre Cour à l'égard du point de droit à trancher dans l'affaire en instance.

Si la Haute Cour des Pays-Bas se range à ces conclusions, l'activité pratique de notre Cour Benelux pourra être entamée immédiatement.

C. SECRETARIAT GENERAL

Secrétaire général: Dr. C. D. A. baron van Lynden

DIVISION A: (Questions sociales, Santé publique, Communications, Classes moyennes, Aménagement du territoire, Agriculture, Questions juridiques)

Administrateur principal:	J. L. Antheunissen
Administrateurs I:	Mme M. L. Demesmaeker-Willems
	J. Rousseau
	H. Roovers
	Mme M. F. de Meeûs d'Argenteuil
	J. N. Schleimer

DIVISION B: (Comité de Ministres, Conseil de l'Union économique, Politique commerciale, Affaires économiques, Douanes et finances, Budgets, Statistiques, Adjudications publiques)

Administrateur principal:	L. Geysemans
Administrateurs I:	M. A. van der Velden
	R. G. C. Oldeman
	J. Dessens
Administrateurs:	Mlle L. Nile
	J. Schotte

DIVISION C: (Affaires administratives, Comptabilité, Personnel, Relations publiques, Tourisme)

Administrateur I et chef de division:	Ph. Golenvaux
Administrateur I et chef de la comptabilité:	E. Tobac
Administrateur Relations publiques:	Mme J. E. S. Larive

DIVISION F: (Circulation des personnes, Etablissement et Unification du droit)

Administrateur I:	Mme A. Russel-D'Hooghe
Administrateur I:	G. Moreau

Secrétariat du COLLEGE D'IMPULSION:

Administrateur principal:	P. Van der Meiren

Greffe de la COUR DE JUSTICE:

Administrateur principal et greffier en chef:	G. Russel

Adresse: UNION ECONOMIQUE BENELUX, SECRETARIAT GENERAL, 39 rue de la Régence, 1000 Bruxelles protocols which the three Ministers of Justice have just signed seem to me to augur extremely well.

Our work will also be largely determined by the frequency with which national courts refer cases to the Court of Justice. From this angle too we may perhaps regard it as a happy omen that Mr Berger, Solicitor-General at the Supreme Court of the Netherlands, in his conclusions last week on a civil case referred to the Dutch Supreme Court, proposed that it should request our Court of Justice for an interlocutory decision on the relevant point of law.

If the Supreme Court of the Netherlands takes up that suggestion, the practical work of this Benelux Court can begin immediately.

D. PUBLICATIONS DU SECRETARIAT GENERAL

Revue ,,Benelux'' (trimestriel)

Abonnement annuel	200 F	ƒ 15,—
Par numéro	70 F	ƒ 5,—

Farde documentaire

Cette farde contient une documentation assez exhaustive en matière économique, juridique et statistique gratuit

Brochure ,,Que signifie le Benelux''?

Une brochure qui trace les grandes lignes de l'organisation et du fonctionnement de l'Union économique Benelux gratuit

Statistiques

Des statistiques comparatives régulièrement mises à jour concernant le commerce extérieur, l'économie, les finances, etc., des trois pays gratuit

Publications diverses

Des brochures et articles ayant trait à des matières plus spécifiques peuvent être obtenus sur demande

Textes de base Benelux

Tous les traités et conventions Benelux, les décisions et recommandations prises par le Comité de Ministres et les autres décisions officielles de l'Union économique Benelux sont publiés dans l'édition à feuilles mobiles ,,Textes de base Benelux''. Editée après la signature du Traité d'Union Benelux en 1958, cette publication comporte à présent dix tomes. L'abonnement donne droit à environ 8 mises à jour par an, au prix de 1 F le feuillet imprimé.

Loisirs sans frontières

Cette brochure consacrée au tourisme dans les pays du Benelux est une publication commune du:
- Commissariat général au Tourisme de Belgique
- Office National Néerlandais du Tourisme
- Office National du Tourisme Luxembourgeois gratuit

BUREAUX DE VENTE ET D'ABONNEMENTS

Pour la Belgique:
Moniteur belge
40, rue de Louvain, 1000 Bruxelles

Pour les Pays-Bas, le Luxembourg et les pays tiers:
Staatsdrukkerij en Uitgeverijbedrijf
Afd. Uitgeverij - gironr. 425.300
Chr. Plantijnstraat / NL - 's-Gravenhage

CHAPITRE III

UNION DE L'EUROPE OCCIDENTALE

A. CHRONOLOGIE DES PRINCIPAUX EVENEMENTS INTERESSANT LES ACTIVITES DE L'U.E.O. EN 1974

29 et 30 janvier: Réunion des adjoints aux Directeurs nationaux de l'armement, tenue à Paris sous les auspices du Secrétariat International du Comité Permanent des armements.

11 mars: Réunion du Conseil au niveau ministériel à La Haye, sous la présidence de M. Max van der Stoel, Ministre des Affaires étrangères des Pays-Bas et Président en exercice du Conseil.

11 mars: Rencontre entre le Conseil des Ministres et le Comité des Présidents de l'Assemblée tenue à l'issue de la réunion ministérielle du 11 mars 1974 à La Haye.

24 au 26 avril: Réunion du Comité de l'Administration publique à Bruxelles.

18 au 21 juin: Première partie de la XXème session ordinaire de l'Assemblée.

25 au 27 septembre: Réunion du Comité de l'Administration publique à La Haye.

4 au 15 novembre: Vingt-troisième rencontre multilatérale de fonctionnaires de pays membres organisée sous l'égide du Comité de l'Administration publique à Edinbourg.

2 au 6 décembre: Deuxième partie de la XXème session ordinaire de l'Assemblée.

D'autre part, dix-sept réunions ont été tenues en 1974 par le Conseil au niveau des représentants permanents à Londres.

B. TEXTES DE BASE

(Conventions, recommandations et réponses du Conseil, etc.)

1. Les principaux textes de base de l'Union de l'Europe occidentale sont le Traité de Bruxelles révisé et ses Protocoles, signés à Paris le 23 octobre 1954.[1]

2. Recommandations adoptées par l'Assemblée au cours de sa XXème session ordinaire et réponse du Conseil: [2]

Recommandation No 246 sur les activités politiques du Conseil

Recommandation No 247 sur l'application du Traité de Bruxelles

Recommandation No 248 sur l'Agence spatiale européenne

Recommandation No 249 sur les relations de l'Assemblée avec le Conseil

Recommandation No 250 sur l'amélioration du statut du personnel de l'U.E.O.

Recommandation No 251 sur les obstacles à un accord entre l'Europe et les Etats-Unis sur les solutions des problèmes économiques et politiques actuels

Recommandation No 252 sur la consultation et les décisions au sein de l'Alliance atlantique

---

[1] *Annuaire Européen*, Vol. I p. 206; Vol. II p. 312.

[2] *Cf.* Section C reproduisant les textes de ces Recommandations et réponses à l'exception de la Recommandation No 250 qu'il n'a pas paru utile de reproduire, eu égard à son caractère particulier.

CHAPTER III

WESTERN EUROPEAN UNION

A. CHRONOLOGY OF PRINCIPAL EVENTS RELATING TO THE ACTIVITIES OF W.E.U. IN 1974

29th and 30th January: Meeting of the deputy National Armaments Directors, held under the auspices of the International Secretariat of the Standing Armaments Committee in Paris.

11th March: Meeting of the Council of Ministers at The Hague under the chairmanship of Mr. Max van der Stoel, Minister for Foreign Affairs of the Netherlands and Chairman in Office of the Council.

11th March: Meeting between the Council of Ministers and the Presidential Committee of the Assembly held at The Hague after the ministerial meeting of 11th March.

24th to 26th April: Meeting of the Public Administration Committee in Brussels.

18th to 21st June: First part of the XXth Ordinary Session of the Assembly.

25th to 27th September: Meeting of the Public Administration Committee at The Hague.

4th to 15th November: Twenty-third multilateral course for government officials of member countries, organised under the auspices of the Public Administration Committee in Edinburgh.

2nd to 6th December: Second part of the XXth Ordinary Session of the Assembly.

In addition, the Council at permanent representative level held seventeen meetings in London in 1974.

B. BASIC DOCUMENTS

(Conventions, recommendations from the Assembly and replies by the Council, etc.)

1. The principal basic documents of Western Europe Union are the modified Brussels Treaty and its Protocols signed in Paris on 23rd October, 1954.[1]

2. Recommendations adopted by the Assembly during the XXth Ordinary Session and replies by the Council:[2]

Recommendation 246 on the political activities of the Council

Recommendation 247 on the application of the Brussels Treaty

Recommendation 248 on the European Space Agency

Recommendation 249 on relations between the Assembly and the Council

Recommendation 250 on improving the status of W.E.U. staff

Recommendation 251 on obstacles to agreement between Europe and the United States on solving present economic and political problems

Recommendation 252 on consultation and decisions in the Atlantic Alliance

Recommendation 253 on a European policy on the peaceful uses of nuclear energy

---

[1] *European Yearbook*, Vol. I p. 207; Vol. II p. 313.

[2] *Cf.* Section C which gives the texts of these Recommendations and replies, except for Recommendation 250, which it was not considered necessary to reproduce, in view of its special nature.

Recommandation No 253 sur une politique européenne d'utilisation pacifique de l'énergie nucléaire

Recommandation No 254 sur la sécurité et la Méditerranée

Recommandation No 255 sur les obstacles à l'union politique de l'Europe

Recommandation No 256 sur la sécurité européenne et la situation en Méditerranée orientale

Recommandation No 257 sur l'état des activités européennes en matière aéronautique

Recommandation No 258 sur les assemblées nationales et l'Assemblée de l'U.E.O.

Recommandation No 259 sur les techniques de pointe au Canada – Conséquences pour l'Europe.

3. Questions écrites posés au Conseil par des membres de l'Assemblée: le Conseil a répondu à dix-sept questions écrites, numérotées de 135 à 151.

4. Vingtième rapport annuel du Conseil à l'Assemblée sur les activités du Conseil du 1er janvier au 31 décembre 1974.[1]

C. RECOMMANDATIONS DE L'ASSEMBLEE ET REPONSES DU CONSEIL

RECOMMANDATION NO 246
SUR LES ACTIVITES POLITIQUES DU CONSEIL

L'Assemblée,

Considérant que les activités politiques du Conseil sont restées fort réduites en 1973;

Prenant note des informations fournies sur des affaires traitées dans le cadre d'autres institutions;

Regrettant, toutefois, que les réponses données à certaines recommandations – notamment à la Recommandation No 241 – demeurent très insuffisantes;

Rappelant le voeu qu'elle a déjà exprimé dans les Recommandations Nos 19 et 103 à propos de la désignation du Secrétaire général;

Constatant que les progrès réalisés vers une union politique de l'Europe, tant dans le domaine des institutions que dans celui de l'élaboration d'une politique commune, sont restés faibles et aléatoires,

RECOMMANDE AU CONSEIL

1. De poursuivre ses efforts pour améliorer son dialogue avec l'Assemblée en vue de veiller à l'application du Traité de Bruxelles modifié dans tout ce qu'il implique;

2. De fournir à l'Assemblée des indications plus précises sur les relations bilatérales entre ses membres et les pays tiers;

3. Suivant l'exemple de l'OTAN et du Conseil de l'Europe, d'appeler, de préférence, aux fonctions de Secrétaire général de l'U.E.O., après consultation du Comité des Présidents de l'Assemblée, une personnalité politique.

---

[1] *Cf.* Section D reproduisant un extrait du Chapitre I du Rapport annuel concernant les relations entre le Conseil et l'Assemblée et un extrait du Chapitre II relatif aux activités du Conseil.

Recommendation 254 on security and the Mediterranean
Recommendation 255 on obstacles to European political union
Recommendation 256 on European security and the situation in the eastern Mediterranean
Recommendation 257 on the state of European aviation activities
Recommendation 258 on national parliaments and the W.E.U. Assembly
Recommendation 259 on advanced technology in Canada – the consequences for Europe

3. Written questions put to the Council by members of the Assembly: the Council replied to seventeen written questions, numbered from 135 to 151.

4. Twentieth Annual Report of the Council to the Assembly on the Council's activities for the period 1st January to 31st December, 1974.[1]

C. RECOMMENDATIONS OF THE ASSEMBLY AND REPLIES OF THE COUNCIL

RECOMMENDATION 246 ON THE POLITICAL ACTIVITIES OF THE COUNCIL

The Assembly,

Considering that the political activities of the Council were very limited in 1973;

Noting the information given on matters dealt with in other bodies;

Regretting, however, that the replies given to certain recommendations – particularly Recommendation 241 – are still quite insufficient;

Recalling the wish already expressed in Recommendations 19 and 103 concerning the appointment of the Secretary-General;

Noting that progress towards the political union of Europe in institutional matters and in the preparation of a common policy has been slight and uncertain,

RECOMMENDS THAT THE COUNCIL

1. Pursue its efforts to improve the dialogue with the Assembly in ensuring the full application of the modified Brussels Treaty;

2. Give the Assembly more details concerning bilateral relations between its members and third countries;

3. As in NATO and the Council of Europe, preferably appoint a political personality as Secretary General of W.E.U. after consulting the Presidential Committee of the Assembly.

[1] *Cf.* Section D which contains an extract from Chapter I of the Annual Report dealing with relations between the Council and the Assembly and an extract from Chapter II dealing with the activities of the Council.

REPONSE

A LA RECOMMANDATION NO 246

1. Ainsi qu'il l'a souligné dans sa réponse à la recommandation No 249, le Conseil s'attache au maintien de relations etroites et satisfaisantes avec l'Assemblée.

2. Le Conseil estime que donner sur les relations bilatérales des indications plus précises que celles normalement fournies au Chapitre II du Rapport annuel souleverait des objections diverses, tant pratiques que de principe.

3. Le Conseil demeure de l'avis que le choix d'une personnalité politique pour les fonctions de Secrétaire général de l'U.E.O. ne s'impose pas dans les circonstances actuelles. La comparaison avec l'OTAN et le Conseil de l'Europe ne semble d'ailleurs pas justifiée en la matière.

RECOMMANDATION NO 247
SUR L'APPLICATION DU TRAITE DE BRUXELLES

L'Assemblée,

Se félicitant de ce que le Conseil reconnaisse qu'il conserve toutes les compétences que lui accorde le traité, comme le montre le compte rendu complet des activités qui lui incombent en vertu du même traité, qui figure au rapport annuel, qu'elles soient exercées directement par le Conseil ou au sein d'autres organismes;

Consciente de ce que, dans sa réponse à la Recommandation No 209, le Conseil déclare ,,qu'il continuera de faire tout en son pouvoir pour faire en sorte que les dispositions du Traité de Bruxelles modifié relatives au contrôle des armements soient observées aussi complètement que possible", mais consciente également ,,des difficultés qui s'opposent à cet objectif";

Consciente, toutefois, de ce que le Conseil n'a pas accepté les propositions de l'Assemblée tendant à faciliter cette observation complète en supprimant les discriminations contenues dans le traité, soit par voie d'amendement, soit par des initiatives ex gratia de la part des Etats membres;

Demandant, par conséquent, une déclaration publique et sans équivoque sur la mesure dans laquelle les dispositions du Traité de Bruxelles modifié relatives au contrôle des armements sont ou non appliquées, et insistant sur l'entrée en vigueur de la Convention établissant une garantie d'ordre juridictionnel;

Félicitant l'Agence pour le contrôle des armements de la manière dont elle s'est acquittée, dans des conditions difficiles, des tâches limitées qui lui ont été confiées par le Conseil;

Rappelant qu'elle a porté le plus haut intérêt à l'utilisation du Comité permanent des armements en tant qu'organisme de coordination et d'étude chargé de détecter les doubles emplois et de proposer des solutions pour les éliminer dans les autres organismes internationaux s'occupant de la standardisation et de la production en commun des armements,

RECOMMANDE AU CONSEIL

1. D'inclure dans ses rapports annuels un compte rendu plus clair et plus détaillé de ses activités concernant les niveaux des forces des Etats membres, notamment les renseignements donnés en réponse à la Question écrite No 130;

REPLY

TO RECOMMENDATION 246

1. As stated in their reply to Recommendation 249, it is the Council's aim to maintain a close and satisfactory relationship with the Assembly.
2. The Council consider that to provide more details concerning bilateral relations than those normally given in Chapter II of the Annual Report would give rise to a number of objections, both practical and of principle.
3. The Council remain of the opinion that the appointment of a political personality as Secretary-General of W.E.U. is not called for in present circumstances. Moreover, comparison with NATO and the Council of Europe does not appear justified in this context.

RECOMMENDATION 247
ON THE APPLICATION OF THE BRUSSELS TREATY

The Assembly,

Welcoming the Council's recognition that it retains all its responsibilities under the Treaty, as exemplified by the full account in the Annual Report of activities under the Treaty, whether now exercised within the Council or in other bodies;

Aware that the Council's reply to Recommendation 209 states that: "the Council will continue to make every effort to ensure that the provisions of the modified Brussels Treaty relating to the control of armaments are observed as fully as possible," but aware also of: "the difficulties in attaining this aim";

Aware, however, that the Council has not accepted the Assembly's proposals to facilitate full observation by eliminating the discriminatory provisions of the Treaty, either through amendment or ex gratia acts of the member states;

Calling, therefore, for a clear public statement of the extent to which the arms control provisions of the modified Brussels Treaty are applied or not applied, and insisting on the entry into force of the Convention on the Due Process of Law;

Congratulating the Agency for the Control of Armaments on the way in which it has carried out, in difficult circumstances, the limited tasks assigned to it by the Council;

Recalling that it has expressed the greatest interest in the use of the Standing Armaments Committee as a co-ordinating and review body responsible for detecting and making proposals for eliminating duplication in other international bodies concerned with the standardisation and joint production of armaments,

RECOMMENDS THAT THE COUNCIL

1. Include in its Annual Reports a clearer and more detailed statement of its activities concerning the levels of forces of member states, in particular the information given in reply to written question 130;

2. D'inclure dans ses rapports annuels un compte rendu fourni, complet et clair concernant tous les aspects des dispositions du Traité de Bruxelles relatives au contrôle des armements qui ne sont pas pleinement appliqués, et de respecter l'engagement qu'il a pris dans sa réponse au paragraphe 2 de la Recommandation No 222, de fournir chaque année, dans son rapport annuel, certains éléments d'information particuliers;

3. De continuer à insister sur l'entrée en vigueur de la Convention établissant une garantie d'ordre juridictionnel signée le 14 décembre 1957;

4. De soumettre à l'Assemblée, lors de la deuxième partie de sa présente session, un rapport intérimaire sur les travaux du Conseil permanent concernant le mandat du Comité permanent des armements.

REPONSE

A LA RECOMMANDATION NO 247

1. Dans l'établissement de ses rapports annuels, le Conseil s'attache à fournir à l'Assemblée une information aussi claire et aussi détaillée que possible sur ses activités concernant les niveaux des forces des Etats membres. Cependant, l'Assemblée comprendra que, ainsi qu'il a été indiqué à plusieurs reprises, la communication de ces informations est soumise à certaines règles restrictives, en raison notamment du caractère secret de certains des renseignements militaires dont il s'agit. Quant aux informations données en réponse à la question écrite No 130, le Conseil accepte de les inclure désormais dans ses rapports annuels.

2. Il ressort de ce qui précède que le Conseil donne à l'Assemblée tous les renseignements qu'il peut lui communiquer, compte tenu des restrictions imposées. En ce qui concerne les aspects des dispositions du Traité de Bruxelles modifié relatives au contrôle des armements qui ne peuvent pas être plainement appliqués, l'attention de l'Assemblée est appelée sur les observations présentées par le Conseil dans ses rapports annuels.

3. Comme l'Assemblée le sait, les difficultés qui font obstacle à l'entrée en vigueur de la Convention établissant une garantie d'ordre juridictionnel demeurent.

4. L'Assemblée n'ignore pas que le Conseil a entrepris il y a quelque temps un examen des activités du Comité permanent des armements. Bien qu'il ait consacré beaucoup de temps et d'attention à l'examen de ce problème complexe, et qu'il ait étudié plusieurs solutions possibles, le Conseil n'a pas encore pu arrêter de conclusions définitives.

Dans ces conditions, le Conseil estime qu'il n'est pas en mesure de présenter un rapport provisoire sur son étude des activités du Comité permanent des armements. Il se réserve de faire rapport à l'Assemblée dès qu'il aura obtenu des résultats plus substantiels.

En attendant, l'Assemblée peut être assurée que le Conseil est soucieux d'éviter tout double emploi entre les travaux du Comité permanent des armements et ceux des autres instances internationales dans le domaine de la standardisation et de la production en commun des armements.

RECOMMANDATION NO 248
SUR L'AGENCE SPATIALE EUROPEENNE

L'Assemblée,

I. Prenant acte des parties du Dix-neuvième rapport du Conseil concernant les questions scientifiques, techniques et aérospatiales, et considérant le temps pris par le Conseil pour répondre aux recommandations relatives aux politiques aéronautique et nucléaire;

2. Include in its Annual Reports a prominent, full and clear statement of all aspects of the arms control provisions of the Brussels Treaty which are not fully applied, and respect the undertaking given in reply to paragraph 2 of Recommendation 222 to include in their Annual Report each year certain specified material;

3. Continue to press for the entry into force of the Convention on the Due Process of Law, signed on 14th December, 1957;

4. Submit to the Assembly at the second part of the present Session an interim report on the examination by the Permanent Council of the work of the Standing Armanents Committee.

REPLY

TO RECOMMENDATION 247

1. In drawing up their Annual Reports, the Council make every effort to provide the Assembly with as clear and detailed information as possible on their activities concerning the level of forces of member states. The Assembly will realise however that, as stated on previous occasions, in providing this information, certain limitations have to be taken into account, in particular the secret nature of some of the military information involved. As to the information given in reply to written question 130, the Council are prepared to furnish this in their future Annual Reports.

2. It will be clear from the foregoing that within certain limitations, the Council provide the Assembly with as much information as they can. With regard to those arms control provisions of the modified Brussels Treaty which cannot be fully applied, the Assembly's attention is drawn to the Council's statements in their Annual Reports.

3. As the Assembly is aware, the problems which prevent the entry into force of the Convention on the Due Process of Law still exist.

4. As the Assembly is aware, the Council have been engaged for some time in a review of the activities of the Standing Armaments Committee. Although the Council have devoted considerable time and effort to this complicated question and made a study of several possible solutions, they have not yet been able to reach definite conclusions.

In these circumstances, the Council are of the opinion that they are not in a position to submit an interim report on their examination of the activities of the Standing Armaments Committee. They will bear in mind the possibility of reporting to the Assembly as soon as more substantive results have been obtained.

In the meantime, the Assembly may rest assured that the Council are anxious to avoid any duplication of the work of the Standing Armaments Committee with that of other international fora in the field of the standardisation and joint production of armaments.

RECOMMENDATION 248
ON THE EUROPEAN SPACE AGENCY

The Assembly,

I. Taking note of the parts of the Nineteenth Annual Report of the Council on scientific, technological and space questions and considering the time taken by the Council in answering the Assembly's recommendations on aviation and nuclear policies;

II. Se félicitant du projet de convention portant création d'une Agence spatiale européenne;

Notant qu'il ne s'est pas révélé possible d'insérer les activités spatiales européennes dans le cadre des Communautés européennes et, partant, dans celui de la future union politique européenne, mais considérant qu'il aurait été possible de tirer un meilleur parti de la situation en encourageant une participation plus large à l'Agence;

Regrettant qu'en raison des retards apportés à nommer le directeur général et les autres hauts fonctionnaires, l'Agence spatiale européenne n'ait pu commencer ses travaux le 1er avril 1974;

Instruite du projet de résolution sur l'établissement de relations entre l'Agence et le Conseil de l'Europe, annexé à l'Acte final;

Consciente de la nécessité, mise en relief par la crise de l'énergie, d'accélérer l'étude, la recherche et le développement dans le domaine des satellites européens de détection des ressources terrestres, afin d'effectuer, notamment, le relevé des dépôts de concentrés de minéraux,

RECOMMANDE AU CONSEIL

I. De répondre d'une manière appropriée et plus rapidement aux recommandations de l'Assemblée sur des questions d'actualité telles qu' „une politique aéronautique pour l'Europe" et „les politiques nucléaires";

II. D'inviter tous les pays libres d'Europe occidentale à adhérer ou à s'associer à l'Agence spatiale européenne et à ses activités scientifiques et technologiques ou à la réalisation de ses satellites d'applications;

De souligner auprès des gouvernements intéressés les raisons politiques pour lesquelles il convient de fournir, sans perdre de temps, à l'Agence les moyens de remplir sa tâche et de les inviter à procéder à la nomination immédiate d'un directeur général et d'autres hauts fonctionnaires, afin de faire en sorte que le programme soit exécuté comme prévu;

De s'efforcer d'inclure, dans la convention susmentionnée, un engagement de l'Agence spatiale européenne à coopérer avec les assemblées du Conseil de l'Europe et de l'Union de l'Europe occidentale, ainsi qu'avec les parlements nationaux des pays membres, et à leur soumettre un rapport annuel pour information, ou pour avis, et s'il n'est pas possible d'inclure cette disposition dans la convention, d'amender la résolution en conséquence;

D'insister auprès du Conseil de l'Agence spatiale européenne pour qu'il mette en oeuvre son programme sans oublier d'encourager dans le proche avenir, dans le cadre de son programme de satellites d'applications, la recherche et le développement relatifs aux satellites de détection des ressources terrestres.

REPONSE

A LA RECOMMANDATION NO 248

1. Sur le fond et les délais des réponses aux recommandations de l'Assemblée, le Conseil appelle l'attention de celle-ci sur sa réponse à la Recommandation No 249.

2. Le Conseil accueillerait avec faveur une plus large participation aux travaux de l'Agence spatiale européenne, comme proposé au premier alinéa du paragraphe II de la Recommandation. A la Conference spatiale européenne, qui donnera naissance à l'Agence spatiale européenne, participent tous les gouvernements membres des Communautés européennes

II. Welcoming the draft Convention for the establishment of a European Space Agency;

Noting that it did not prove possible to bring the European space activities into the framework of the European Communities and, hence, into that of the future European political union, but considering that the situation might be turned to better account by promoting a wider membership of the Agency;

Regretting that through delays in nominating a Director-General and other senior officials the European Space Agency could not start work on 1st April, 1974;

Aware of the draft resolution on the establishment of relations between the Agency and the Council of Europe, appended to the final act;

Conscious of the need made evident by the energy crisis to accelerate study, research and development on European earth resources satellites to conduct surveys, inter alia, for deposits of concentrated minerals,

RECOMMENDS THAT THE COUNCIL

I. Answer in an appropriate manner and with greater alacrity the Assembly's recommendations on topical questions such as "an aviation policy for Europe" and "nuclear policies";

II. Invite all free western European countries to join or be associated with the European Space Agency and its scientific and technological work or its application satellites;

Convey to the governments concerned the political reasons for losing no time in providing the Agency with the wherewithal to fulfil its task and urge the immediate appointment of a Director-General and other senior officials in order to ensure that the programme will be executed as foreseen;

Seek to include in the above-mentioned Convention a commitment by the European Space Agency to co-operate with the Assemblies of the Council of Europe and Western European Union as well as with the national parliaments of the member countries, and to submit to them an annual report for information or an opinion and, if it is not possible to include this in the Convention, to amend the resolution accordingly;

Urge the Council of the European Space Agency to implement its programme without forgetting to promote in the near future, in the framework of its application satellites programme, research and development of earth resources satellites.

REPLY

TO RECOMMENDATION 248

1. On the substance and speed of replies to Assembly Recommendations, the Council draw attention to their reply to Assembly Recommendation 249.

2. The Council would welcome wider participation in the European Space Agency as suggested in the first subparagraph of paragraph II of the Recommendation. Those participating in the European Space Conference, from which the European Space Agency will be formed, include all member governments of the European Communities (with the exception of Luxem-

(à l'exception du Luxembourg) et plusieurs autres gouvernements. Le projet de convention portant création d'une Agence spatiale européenne prévoit l'adhésion de membres nouveaux ou de membres associés, ainsi que la participation d'Etats non membres à des programmes particuliers.

Le Conseil regrette avec l'Assemblée les retards apportés à la désignation du Directeur général et des autres hauts fonctionnaires de l'Agence spatiale européenne. Ces questions, ainsi que plusieurs autres en suspens, font actuellement l'objet de négociations à la Conférence spatiale européenne.

Quant à la coopération avec les organes parlementaires, le projet de résolution No 5, annexé au projet d'Acte final de la Conférence des plénipotentiaires chargée d'établir l'Agence spatiale européenne, prévoit le maintien des dispositions qui ont été appliquées jusqu'ici pour le CECLES et pour le CERS. L'examen parlementaire des travaux de ces organisations était facilité par l'envoi de leurs rapports annuels, pour information, au Conseil de l'Europe, où ils faisaient l'objet d'un débat à l'Assemblée consultative. Le projet de convention et le projet de résolution sont le fruit de négociations approfondies entre tous les Etats membres de la Conférence spatiale européenne, dont certains ne font partie ni des Communautés européennes, ni du Conseil de l'Europe, ni de l'Union de l'Europe occidentale. En conséquence, le Conseil ne croit pas qu'il serait souhaitable de les amender.

Le programme adopté à la réunion ministérielle de la Conférence spatiale européenne, le 31 juillet 1973, pour la création de l'Agence spatiale européenne, la participation au programme américain post-Apollo par la construction du laboratoire spatial européen (SPACELAB), la conception et la construction d'un satellite maritime européen d'essais orbitaux (MAROTS) et la mise au point d'un lanceur de fusée européen (ARIANE) est déjà en cours d'exécution. L'importance de la recherche et du développement relatifs aux satellites de détection de ressources terrestres est reconnue par la plupart des Etats membres de la Conférence spatiale européenne, dont plusieurs développent leurs propres moyens d'investigation des ressources terrestres. La question des satellites de ressources terrestres sera vraisemblablement examinée par le Conseil de l'Agence spatiale européenne en même temps que les futurs programmes de satellites d'application.

RECOMMANDATION NO 249
SUR LES RELATIONS DE L'ASSEMBLEE AVEC LE CONSEIL

L'Assemblée,

Considérant que la plupart des réponses du Conseil aux recommandations adoptées par l'Assemblée, lors de la deuxième partie de la Dixneuvième session, sont parvenues à l'Assemblée à une date ne permettant pas aux commissions de les examiner lors de la préparation de la première partie de la Vingtième session;

Constatant l'insuffisance de la réponse à la Recommandation No 241;

Constatant qu'aucune réponse n'a été donnée à la Recommandation No 242;

Se réservant d'utiliser la procédure prévue à l'article V (h) de sa Charte,

RECOMMANDE AU CONSEIL

1. De répondre désormais aux recommandations de l'Assemblée dans un délai de huit semaines;
2. De fournir à ces recommandations des réponses substantielles sur l'ensemble des points à propos desquels les sept pays membres peuvent parvenir à un accord.

bourg) and several other governments. The draft European Space Agency Convention contains provision for new membership, associate membership and participation by non-member states in particular programmes.

The Council share the Assembly's concern about the delay in the appointment of a Director-General and other senior officials to the European Space Agency. Negotiations on this and other outstanding issues are at present taking place at the European Space Conference.

As for co-operation with parliamentary bodies, draft Resolution No. 5 appended to the draft Final Act of the Conference of Plenipotentiaries set up to establish the European Space Agency is designed to maintain the arrangements which have applied hitherto to ELDO and ESRO. Parliamentary discussion of the work of these organisations was facilitated by an arrangement by which their annual reports were sent for information to the Council of Europe where they were debated in the Consultative Assembly. The texts of the draft Convention and the draft Resolution are the product of much negotiation between all the member states of the European Space Conference, some of whom are members of neither the European Communities, nor the Council of Europe nor Western European Union. Consequently, the Council do not consider it desirable to amend them.

The programme agreed at the ministerial meeting of the European Space Conference on 31st July, 1973 for creation of the European Space Agency, participation in the United States Post-Apollo Programme by the construction of the European Space Laboratory (SPACELAB), design and construction of a European Maritime Orbital Test Satellite (MAROTS) and development of a European heavy rocket launcher (ARIANE), is already well under way. The importance of the research and development of earth resources satellites is recognised by most member states of the European Space Conference, several of which are developing their own earth resources surveying facilities. It is expected that earth resources satellites will be discussed when future programmes for applications satellites are discussed in the Council of the European Space Agency.

RECOMMENDATION 249
ON RELATIONS BETWEEN THE ASSEMBLY AND THE COUNCIL

The Assembly,

Considering that most of the replies of the Council to the recommendations adopted by he Assembly at the second part of the Nineteenth Session reached the Assembly at a date which did not allow the Committees to examine them when preparing for the first part of the Twentieth Session;

Noting the inadequacy of the reply to Recommendation 241;

Noting that no reply has been given to Recommendation 242;

Reserving the right to use the procedure provided for under Article V (h) of its Charter,

RECOMMENDS THAT THE COUNCIL

1. Reply henceforth to recommendations of the Assembly within eight weeks;
2. In respect of such recommendations, furnish substantial replies to all the points on which the seven member countries are able to reach agreement.

REPONSE

A LA RECOMMANDATION NO 249

Dans l'allocution qu'il a prononcée le 18 juin devant l'Assemblée au nom du Président du Conseil en exercice, M. Roy Hattersley a assuré celle-ci du désir du Conseil d'entretenir avec elle le dialogue le plus étroit possible. En même temps, il a souligné que ce serait une erreur que de sous-estimer la tâche de formuler des vues communes sur les divers et importants problèmes dont s'occupe l'Assemblée (se référant en particulier, sur ce point, à la Recommandation No 242), et la difficulté de fournir des réponses aux recommandations avec toute la célérité que non seulement l'Assemblée, mais le Conseil lui-même, désirerait.

Le Conseil a procédé sans retard à un examen soigneux des divers points soulevés au cours des récents débats de l'Assemblée, et notamment des moyens qui permettraient d'améliorer la procédure de ses réponses aux recommandations de l'Assemblée. Il a conclu à regret qu'il serait irréaliste de sa part de s'engager à répondre à toutes les recommandations dans un délai de huit semaines. Il prendra néanmoins toutes dispositions en son pouvoir pour que des réponses à toutes les recommandations parviennent à l'Assemblée dans les plus brefs délais et, en vérité, dans un délai bien inférieur à huit semaines chaque fois qu'il est possible. Il aura également le souci de rendre ses réponses aussi substantielles que possible.

Le Conseil désire réaffirmer toute l'importance qu'il continue d'attacher au maintien de relations étroites et satisfaisantes avec l'Assemblée.

RECOMMANDATION NO 251
SUR LES OBSTACLES A UN ACCORD ENTRE L'EUROPE ET LES ETATS-UNIS SUR LES SOLUTIONS DES PROBLEMES ECONOMIQUES ET POLITIQUES ACTUELS

L'Assemblée,

Considérant qu'une étroite entente entre l'Europe et les Etats-Unis est indispensable à la solution des problèmes politiques, économiques et monétaires contemporains ainsi qu'à la sécurité du monde occidental;

Estimant que la proposition du Président Kennedy de fonder la Communauté atlantique sur deux piliers doit être le fondement des relations entre les membres européens et nord-américains de l'Alliance;

Regrettant que l'Europe ne soit pas encore parvenue à harmoniser suffisamment ses vues pour constituer un véritable partenaire des Etats-Unis;

Redoutant que cette situation affaiblisse encore l'influence de l'Europe dans le monde et puisse accroître, entre les deux rives de l'Atlantique, une méfiance réciproque qui a parfois pris des proportions redoutables au cours des derniers mois;

Considérant qu'une déclaration de principes ne peut, en aucun cas, se substituer à une consultation institutionnalisée entre la Communauté européenne et les Etats-Unis qui constituent les deux piliers de l Alliance;

Considérant que le développement des relations américano-soviétiques rend urgente la mise en place de consultations approfondies, au sein de l'Alliance, sur ce sujet;

Constatant qu'en vertu du Traité de Bruxelles modifié l'U.E.O., demeure la seule organisation proprement européenne compétente en matière de défense;

Souhaitant organiser et développer, dans le domaine parlementaire, ses relations avec les membres nord-américains de l'Alliance atlantique,

REPLY

TO RECOMMENDATION 249

In his speech on behalf of the Chairman in Office of the Council on 18th June, Mr. Roy Hattersley assured the Assembly of the Council's wish to maintain the closest possible dialogue with the Assembly. At the same time, he stressed that it would be a mistake to underestimate the task of formulating common views on the various important problems with which the Assembly is concerned (in this context, he referred specifically to Recommendation 242), and the difficulty of furnishing replies to recommendations with the speed which not only the Assembly, but the Council themselves, would wish.

The Council have given urgent and serious thought to various points which were raised in the course of the Assembly's recent debates, and in particular to possible ways of improving their procedure for replying to the Assembly's recommendations. They have concluded, with regret, that it would be unrealistic to give an undertaking to reply to all recommendations within eight weeks. They will nevertheless take all steps they can to ensure that replies are sent to the Assembly in the shortest possible time, and indeed wherever practicable, well within eight weeks. They will also be concerned to make these replies as substantial as possible.

The Council wish to reaffirm the high importance which they continue to attach to the maintenance of a close and satisfactory relationship with the Assembly.

RECOMMENDATION 251
ON OBSTACLES TO AGREEMENT BETWEEN EUROPE AND THE UNITED STATES ON SOLVING PRESENT ECONOMIC AND POLITICAL PROBLEMS

The Assembly,

Considering that close understanding between Europe and the United States is essential for the solution of present-day political, economic and monetary problems and for the security of the western world;

Believing that President Kennedy's proposal to base the Atlantic Community on two pillars should be the basis of relations between the European and North American members of the Alliance;

Regretting that Europe has not yet managed to harmonise its views sufficiently to form a real partner for the United States;

Fearing that this situation may further weaken Europe's influence in the world and augment the reciprocal mistrust on either side of the Atlantic which has sometimes attained dangerous proportions in recent months;

Considering that a declaration of principles can in no event replace institutionalised consultations between the European Community and the United States, which form the two pillars of the Alliance;

Considering that the development of American-Soviet relations makes it urgent to initiate detailed consultations on this subject in the Alliance;

Noting that in accordance with the modified Brussels Treaty W.E.U. is still the only truly European organisation with responsibilities in the defence field;

Wishing to organise and develop its relations with the North American members of the Atlantic Alliance in the parliamentary field,

RECOMMANDE AU CONSEIL

1. De porter son attention sur les incidences que les problèmes soulevés par la coopération entre l'Europe et les Etats-Unis pourraient avoir sur la sécurité européenne et de les inscrire à l'ordre du jour de ses travaux, ce qui constitue l'une des tâches essentielles que le Traité de Bruxelles lui a assignées;

2. D'une manière plus générale, d'examiner régulièrement les problèmes soulevés par la sécurité de l'Europe et de discuter en temps voulu, au sein de l'Alliance, les solutions qu'il envisage de leur apporter;

3. A cette fin, de se réunir, à la veille de chaque réunion du Conseil de l'Atlantique nord, en vue de préparer les délibérations avec les autres membres de l'Alliance atlantique.

REPONSE

A LA RECOMMANDATION NO 251

Le Conseil estime avec l'Assemblée qu'une entente étroite entre les membres de l'Alliance, notamment entre les Etats-Unis et leurs Alliés européens, est indispensable à la sécurité de l'Europe occidentale.

De l'avis du Conseil, l'évolution de l'Europe vers l'unité politique n'est nullement incompatible avec le maintien de la solidarité au sein de l'Alliance. Au contraire, ainsi qu'il est indiqué au paragraphe 9 de la Déclaration atlantique, il est également reconnu que les progrès ultérieurs vers l'unité, que les Etats membres de la Communauté européenne sont déterminés à faire, devraient, le moment venu, avoir un effet bénéfique sur la contribution à la défense commune de l'Alliance de ceux d'entre eux qui en sont membres.

Dans cette déclaration, les Alliés se sont fixés une règle de conduite pour l'avenir. A cet effet, ils ont réaffirmé qu'ils étaient résolus à se tenir pleinement informés et à renforcer la pratique de consultations franches et menées en temps opportun.

La sécurité des membres de l'Alliance atlantique est indivisible. Il est donc nécessaire que les questions touchant la sécurité et la défense des Alliés soient examinées conjointement par ces derniers. L'organe compétent en la matière est le Conseil de l'Atlantique nord. Cela n'empêche pas les Alliés européens de se concerter entre eux, dans certains cas appropriés, avant que ces questions soient traitées par le Conseil de l'Atlantique nord. Dans le passé, certains Alliés européens se sont réunis dans le cadre des organes compétents pour procéder à un échange de vues sur ces questions. Le Conseil continuera d'examiner tous les problèmes relevant de sa compétence en vertu du Traité de Bruxelles, et ce faisant, il coopérera étroitement avec les organes de l'Alliance atlantique, conformément à l'article IV du Traité.

RECOMMANDATION NO 252
SUR LA CONSULTATION ET LES DECISIONS AU SEIN DE L'ALLIANCE ATLANTIQUE

L'Assemblée,

Inquiète de l'insuffisance de la consultation et des décisions communes au sein de l'Alliance atlantique en diverses occasions au cours des dix-huit derniers mois;

Consciente de ce que, à plusieurs reprises, ni les Neuf ni les Etats-Unis n'ont été disposés à accepter la consultation;

Persuadée qu'un mécanisme ne peut à lui seul garantir la consultation si la volonté de se consulter est absente,

RECOMMENDS THAT THE COUNCIL

1. Consider what repercussions the problem raised by co-operation between Europe and the United States might have on European security and include these matters on its agenda as being one of its main duties under the Brussels Treaty;

2. In a more general respect, consider regularly the problems raised by the security of Europe and discuss accordingly in the Alliance the solutions it proposes;

3. To this end, meet prior to each meeting of the North Atlantic Council with a view to preparing the discussions with the other members of the Atlantic Alliance.

REPLY

TO RECOMMENDATION 251

The Council share the Assembly's view that close understanding between the partners of the Alliance, especially between the United States and its European Allies, is essential for the security of western Europe.

In the opinion of the Council, Europe's development towards political unity is by no means inconsistent with the maintenance of solidarity within the Alliance. On the contrary, as stated in paragraph 9 of the Atlantic Declaration, it is also recognised that the further progress towards unity, which the member states of the European Community are determined to make, should in due course have a beneficial effect on the contribution to the common defence of the Alliance of those of them who belong to it.

In the Atlantic Declaration, the Allies have given themselves a practical guideline for their future action. To this end, they have reaffirmed their resolve to inform each other fully and to intensify the practice of frank and timely consultations.

The security of the members of the Atlantic Alliance is indivisible. It is therefore necessary that questions affecting the security and defence of the Allies should be treated by them jointly. The appropriate organ for this is the North Atlantic Council. This does not preclude the European Allies concerting their point of view in appropriate cases before such questions are dealt with by the North Atlantic Council. In the past, a number of European Allies have already met, within the framework of the relevant bodies, for a specific exchange of views on such questions. The Council will continue to discuss all problems which fall within their sphere of competence under the Brussels Treaty and, in doing so, co-operate closely with the organs of the Atlantic Alliance in accordance with Article IV of that Treaty.

RECOMMENDATION 252

ON CONSULTATION AND DECISIONS IN THE ATLANTIC ALLIANCE

The Assembly,

Concerned at the inadequacy of consultation and joint decision in the Atlantic Alliance on various occasions during the past eighteen months;

Aware that at different times there has been unreadiness to consult both on the part of the Nine and the United States;

Believing that machinery alone cannot ensure consultation if the will to consult is lacking,

RECOMMANDE AU CONSEIL

1. D'améliorer la consultation au sein du Conseil de l'Atlantique nord grâce à la participation des directeurs politiques au moins deux fois par an, et à la poursuite, au sein de ce conseil, d',,échanges de vues et d'informations aussi complets que possible et (d')une étroite consultation et coopération dans un esprit de confiance mutuellle sur tous les problèmes d'intérêt commun"[1] indépendamment des zones géographiques où pourraient surgir ces problèmes;

2. D'inviter le Conseil de l'Atlantique nord à attacher une plus grande importance à l'article 2 du Traité de l'Atlantique nord;

3. D'inviter les Neuf à procéder à des consultations avec les Etats-Unis à propos des problèmes d'intérêt commun à un moment où l'élaboration d'une décision sera suffisante pour permettre aux Neuf de défendre un point de vue commun, sans toutefois que la décision des Neuf ait été définitivement arrêtée au préalable;

4. De veiller à ce que les voies bilatérales d'information et de consultation avec les Etats-Unis restent ouvertes.

5. De veiller, grâce à tous les processus de consultation qui viennent d'être mentionnés, à ce qu'aucune concession ne soit faite qui serait contraire à l'intérêt vital de l'Europe dans les trois conférences Est-Ouest – C.S.C.E., M.B.F.R. et SALT – quelles que soient les pressions exercées en faveur d'un accord.

REPONSE

A LA RECOMMANDATION NO 252

1. Le Conseil peut assurer l'Assemblée que l'importance d'une étroite consultation et coopération est pleinement reconnue au sein de l'Alliance, comme en témoigne le paragraphe 11 de la Déclaration d'Ottawa. Des fonctionnaires de haut rang et des experts venus des capitales assistent aux réunions du Conseil de l'Atlantique nord chaque fois que cela parait utile à leurs autorités.

Le Conseil fait remarquer que l'importance de l'article 2 du Traité de l'Atlantique nord est pleinement reconnue aux paragraphes 11 et 12 de la Déclaration d'Ottawa, selon laquelle les gouvernements Alliés s'attacheront notamment à écarter les sources de conflit entre leurs politiques économiques, et où ils rappellent leur attachement aux principes de démocratie, de respect des droits de l'homme, de justice et de progrès social.

2. Pour ce qui concerne le problème distinct des relations entre les Neuf et les Etats-Unis, le Conseil est heureux d'informer l'Assemblée que des arrangements pratiques et de caractère ,,informel" ont été élaborés pour la consultation entre les Neuf et les Etats-Unis, et sont déjà entrés en application. Une telle consultation ne diminue en rien l'importance des voies bilatérales d'information et de consultation entre chacun des Neuf et les Etats-Unis.

Le Conseil peut assurer l'Assemblée que d'étroites consultations se tiennent régulièrement entre les Alliés participant à la Conférence sur la sécurité et la coopération en Europe, ainsi qu'aux négociations sur les réductions mutuelles et équilibrées de forces. Les autorités américaines informent également leurs Alliés européens, au sein du Conseil de l'Atlantique nord, de l'évolution des entretiens sur la limitation des armements stratégiques. Dans ces diverses négociations, les gouvernements européens directement intéressés font valoir constamment les intérêts vitaux de l'Europe en la matière.

---

[1] Communiqué du Conseil de l'Atlantique nord, 11 décembre 1973.

RECOMMENDS TO THE COUNCIL

1. To improve consultation in the North Atlantic Council through the attendance of political directors at least twice a year, and by maintaining in that Council "the fullest possible exchange of views and information, and close consultation and co-operation, in a spirit of mutual trust, on all problems of common concern"[1] irrespective of the geographical areas in which the problems may arise;

2. To urge the North Atlantic Council to pay more attention to Article 2 of the North Atlantic Treaty;

3. To invite the Nine to hold consultations with the United States on matters of common concern when the formulation of decisions is sufficiently advanced to allow the Nine to defend a common point of view but before the Nine have finalised their decision;

4. To ensure that bilateral channels of information and consultation with the United States remain open;

5. To ensure through the foregoing processes of consultation that no concessions are made that are contrary to the vital interest of Europe in the three East-West conferences C.S.C.E., M.B.F.R. and SALT, whatever pressures for agreement there may be.

REPLY

TO RECOMMENDATION 252

1. The Council can assure the Assembly that the importance of close consultation and co-operation is fully recognised within the Alliance, as paragraph 11 of the Ottawa Declaration on Atlantic Relations makes clear. Meetings of the North Atlantic Council are attended by senior officials and experts from capitals as and when their authorities consider this to be useful.

The Council point out that the importance of Article 2 of the North Atlantic Treaty was fully recognised in paragraphs 11 and 12 of the Ottawa Declaration, which states that Allied Governments will work to remove sources of conflict between their economic policies and recalls their dedication to the principles of democracy, respect for human rights, justice and social progress.

2. As regards the separate problem of relations between the Nine and the United States, the Council are glad to inform the Assembly that informal practical arrangements for consultation between the Nine and the United States have been worked out, and are already being put into effect. Such consultation in no way derogates from the importance of the bilateral channels of information and consultation between individual members of the Nine and the United States.

The Council can assure the Assembly that there are close and regular consultations between the Allies taking part in the Conference on Security and Co-operation in Europe and in the negotiations on mutual and balanced force reductions. The United States authorities also keep the European Allies informed, in the North Atlantic Council, of the progress of the strategic arms limitation talks. In all these negotiations, Europe's vital interests in the matter are constantly stressed by the European governments directly concerned.

---

[1] North Atlantic Council communiqué of 11th December, 1973.

RECOMMANDATION NO 253
SUR UNE POLITIQUE EUROPEENNE D'UTILISATION PACIFIQUE DE L'ENERGIE NUCLEAIRE

L'Assemblée,

Regrettant qu'après près de vingt ans d'activités nucléaires dans le cadre européen, il ne se soit pas révélé possible d'élaborer une politique nucléaire industrielle commune;

Consciente de la tendance actuelle, notamment depuis la crise du pétrole, à rechercher des solutions aux problèmes énergétiques dans un cadre national, sans tenter de parvenir à une solution européenne;

Consciente également de ce qu'aucune décision obligatoire ne peut être attendue d'organisations internationales telles que les Nations Unies;

Consciente de la nécessité de prendre, dans une plus large mesure, des décisions politiques communes quant au type de réacteurs que devraient adopter les services publics nationaux;

Considérant que ces décisions politiques seront fondées sur l'avis des agences nationales de l'énergie nucléaire;

Considérant que les industriels ne peuvent agir de concert si aucun accord politique n'est conclu,

RECOMMANDE AU CONSEIL

De prier instamment les gouvernements des Etats membres:

1. De réunir, dans le cadre approprié, les directeurs des agences nationales de l'énergie nucléaire et des services publics en vue de définir une politique commune et de faire des recommandations à leurs gouvernements respectifs sur le choix de réacteurs à moyen et à long terme;
2. De rechercher un accord politique sur le choix des réacteurs à construire pour les services publics à moyen et à long terme;
3. D'encourager la formation d'un nombre réduit de grands groupements industriels dans le domaine nucléaire et d'étendre la concurrence à l'ensemble de l'Europe;
4. De créer les conditions propres à stimuler le développement industriel de groupements européens à l'échelle européenne plutôt que nationale;
5. De faire en sorte que l'Europe conserve, dans le domaine nucléaire, une indépendance suffisante qui lui permette d'élaborer sa propre stratégie industrielle et d'exporter des centrales nucléaires et d'autres produits de l'industrie nucléaire de fabrication européenne;
6. D'entreprendre une action commune en vue d'informer l'opinion publique de la nécessité et des conséquences d'une large utilisation de l'énergie nucléaire et des solutions de rechange qui s'offriraient au cas où cette large utilisation serait impossible.

REPONSE

A LA RECOMMANDATION NO 253

Si la solution des problèmes énergétiques est, depuis la fin de la seconde Guerre mondiale notamment, un souci permanent pour l'Europe, elle est devenue aujourd'hui un véritable défi dont dépend dans une large mesure l'avenir économique de notre continent.

Pourtant l'Europe ne manque pas d'atouts ni même d'espoirs dans ce domaine. Ceux-ci reposent présentement, entre autres choses, sur les récentes découvertes de pétrole et de gaz naturel en Mer du Nord et sur les perspectives, à relativement court terme, de programmes considérablement renforcés de production d'énergie nucléaire.

RECOMMENDATION 253
ON A EUROPEAN POLICY ON THE PEACEFUL USES OF NUCLEAR ENERGY

The Assembly,

Regretting that after nearly twenty years of nuclear activities in the European framework it has not proved possible to formulate a common industrial nuclear policy;

Aware of the present tendency, particularly since the oil crisis, to seek solutions to energy problems within a national framework without attempting to find a European solution;

Aware also that no binding decisions can be expected from international organisations such as the United Nations;

Conscious of the need to reach to a greater extent common political decisions on the type of reactors which the national utilities should adopt;

Considering that political decisions will be based on the advice of the national nuclear energy agencies;

Considering that industrialists cannot act in concert unless political agreements have been reached,

RECOMMENDS THAT THE COUNCIL

Urge the governments of member countries:

1. To convene the heads of national nuclear energy agencies and of public utilities to meet within the appropriate framework with a view to determining a joint policy and making recommendations to their respective governments on the choice of reactors for the medium and long term;
2. To seek political agreement on the choice of reactors to be built for the utilities for the medium and long term;
3. To promote the formation of a limited number of large-scale industrial nuclear groupings and to extend competition to the whole of western Europe;
4. To establish incentives for industrial development for European groupings on a European rather than national scale;
5. To ensure that Europe has sufficient independence in the nuclear field so that it may elaborate its own industrial strategy and be free to export European-made nuclear power plants and other nuclear industrial products;
6. To initiate joint action to inform public opinion of the necessity and implications of the wide-spread use of nuclear power and the alternatives if this is denied.

REPLY

TO RECOMMENDATION 253

The need to find a solution for the energy problem, which has been a matter of constant concern to Europe, particularly since the Second World War, has now developed into an outright challenge on which the economic future of our continent largely depends.

Europe is not, however, without assets and hopes in this field. At the moment, these include the recent discoveries of oil and natural gas under the North Sea and the prospect of significantly augmented nuclear energy programmes in the fairly near future.

Or, si la coopération entre pays européens reste à mettre en place en ce qui concerne le pétrole et le gaz, elle connaît déjà des réalisations non négligeables – encore qu'imparfaites et certainement susceptibles d'améliorations – dans le domaine nucléaire, en particulier dans celui de l'utilisation pacifique de l'énergie nucléaire.

C'est ainsi que de nombreux efforts ont été faits, au cours des dernières années, pour promouvoir sinon une politique nucléaire industrielle commune, du moins une certaine concertation des politiques nationales. Dans sa réponse à la recommandation No 235, le Conseil a mentionné le rôle joué par l'EURATOM. Les efforts de concertation se manifestent notamment à l'occasion des contacts réguliers qui existent désormais au niveau des responsables européens tant politiques qu'industriels ainsi qu'entre les agences nationales de l'énergie nucléaire et au sein des instances de coopération européenne que sont la Société Européenne Nucléaire ou l'Agence de l'O.C.D.E. pour l'Energie Nucléaire.

Cette concertation s'est d'ailleurs traduite dans les faits par un certain nombre d'actions conjointes, réalisées dans des domaines limités, certes, mais dont l'importance est loin d'être négligeable et qui permettent d'envisager l'avenir de façon encourageante, telles que les centrales nucléaires communes (franco-belge), UNIREP, EURODIF, URENCO, l'Institut Laue-Langevin de Grenoble pour la construction et l'exploitation d'un réacteur à haut-flux, l'accord EDF-RWE-EWEL pour le réacteur Super-Phénix, les accords franco-italiens sur les réacteurs à neutrons rapides, l'UNIPEDE, le programme européen de fusion à Culham, le programme Allemagne/Bénélux pour la mise au point, à Kalkar, d'un réacteur rapide, le programme HTR DRAGON à Winfrith, la participation d'intérêts français, allemands, italiens et espagnols à l'exploitation de mines d'uranium au Niger, etc.

Sans doute peut-il apparaître comme souhaitable de favoriser plus activement encore des actions de ce genre. Il ne faut cependant pas oublier qu'en l'état actuel des choses, cette démarche, qui peut paraître à certains comme encore trop limitée et trop prudente, correspond à une approche pragmatique et réaliste de la situation qui seule a permis d'enregistrer les succès mentionnés plus haut. Il est probable, en effet, que la fixation d'objectifs trop ambitieux, impliquant des procédures autoritaires et moins respectueuses des intérêts de chaque pays ou de chaque industrie, ait conduit à des blocages sinon à l'échec des tentatives de coopération dans ce domaine.

L'expérience des dernières années montre à cet égard que ce sont essentiellement des préoccupations d'environnement ou d'ordre économique et industriel qui ont prévalu au moment du choix par chaque pays d'un type de réacteur et qu'il ne faut pas surestimer l'avis que peuvent fournir les agences nationales de l'énergie nucléaire.

Enfin, il semble que la conclusion d'accords politiques soit une condition nécessaire, mais qu'elle ne soit nullement suffisante s'il n'existe pas au préalable chez les industriels la volonté de coopérer. Il va de soit que cette volonté sera stimulée par de tels accords politiques.

Enfin, sans contester le rôle essentiel des réacteurs dans la chaîne de l'énergie nucléaire, le garant d'une certaine indépendance de l'Europe dans le domaine nucléaire n'est pas principalement constitué par les réacteurs mais par l'approvisionnement en uranium et par les moyens d'enrichir ce dernier. L'importance du problème de l'approvisionnement en uranium n'avait pas échappé aux promoteurs d'EURATOM. Mais l'Agence d'approvisionnement instituée par le Chapitre VI du Traité, inadaptée à ses objectifs, fait actuellement l'objet de propositions de révision. Les réacteurs ne représentent, en effet, que la technologie du savoir-faire. Cette technologie, une fois détenue, que ce soit par un développement européen ou par le biais des licenses, demeure un acquis. En revanche, si l'on ne dispose pas

While co-operation between European countries is still to be established in the case of oil and gas, achievements in the nuclear field, and particularly in the peaceful use of nuclear energy, are already substantial even if imperfect and open to improvement.

Over the last few years, for example, many attempts have been made to promote if not a common industrial nuclear policy, at least some concertation of national policies.

Reference to the part played by EURATOM is made in the Council's reply to Recommendation 235. Efforts in this direction are made in particular through the regular contacts which are now taking place between political and industrial leaders in Europe, between national nuclear energy agencies and in European co-operative fora such as the European Nuclear Energy Society and the Nuclear Energy Agency of the O.E.C.D.

This concertation of policies has already produced practical results in the shape of a number of joint actions which are limited in scope no doubt, but are by no means unimportant and are encouraging for the future. These include, for example, shared nuclear power stations (Franco-Belgian), UNIREP, EURODIF, URENCO, the Laue/Langevin Institute at Grenoble for the construction and operation of a high-flux reactor, the EDF-RWE-EWEL Agreement on the Super Phénix reactor, the Franco-Italian Agreements on fast neutron reactors, UNIPEDE, the European fusion programme at Culham, the Benelux/German programme for the development of a fast reactor at Kalkar, the "DRAGON HTR" programme at Winfrith, the participation of French, German, Italian and Spanish interests in mining uranium in Niger, and so on.

It may seem that such measures should be even more actively encouraged. It should not be overlooked, however, that in present circumstances, this line of action, which some may consider to be too limited and over-cautious, represents a pragmatic, realistic approach to the situation which has offered the only means of achieving the successes enumerated above. It seems likely that the setting of over-ambitious targets involving authoritarian procedures paying less attention to the interests of individual countries or industries, might have blocked attempts to co-operate in this field, or even led to their failure.

In this respect, the experience of the last few years shows that economic, environmental and industrial considerations have largely decided each country's choice of a type of reactor and that the advice which national nuclear agencies can give should not be overestimated.

It would appear that while the conclusion of political agreements is an essential condition, it is by no means sufficient if industrialists are not already willing to act in concert. Their willingness to do so would of course be encouraged by such political agreements.

Lastly, while the vital role of reactors in the nuclear energy process cannot be disputed, the main guarantee of a measure of European independence in the nuclear field lies not in reactors but in supplies of uranium and in the means of enriching it. The importance of the problem of uranium supplies was appreciated by the founders of EURATOM. But the supply Agency set up under Chapter VI of the Treaty is not suited to its aims, and changes have now been proposed. Reactors are no more than a product of technical "know-how." Once access to this technology is obtained, either by developments in Europe or through licences, it remains a permanent acquisition. If, however, no reliable supplies of uranium are available, Europe is still and will remain dependent in the nuclear energy field, even if it possesses original reactor techniques.

d'un approvisionnement assuré en uranium, l'on est et l'on sera dépendant dans le domaine de l'énergie nucléaire même si l'on dispose d'une technique originale de réacteurs.

RECOMMANDATION NO 254
SUR LA SECURITE ET LA MEDITERRANEE

L'Assemblée,

Déplorant la reprise des hostilités au Proche et au Moyen-Orient en 1973 et exprimant sa sympathie à toutes les populations concernées;

Considérant qu'il convient que l'Europe fasse connaître son point de vue et fasse entendre sa voix par l'intermédiaire de la Communauté européenne, et souscrivant, par conséquent, au communiqué publié le 13 octobre par les neuf gouvernements et à la résolution adoptée le 17 octobre 1973 par le Parlement européen;

Donnant son adhésion pleine et entière aux Résolutions 338, 339 et 340 du Conseil de sécurité;

Rappelant le paragraphe 8 de sa Recommandation No 227;

Inquiète des conséquences stratégiques que pourrait avoir l'intervention de l'Union soviétique au Moyen-Orient;

Ayant étudié les problèmes de sécurité qui se posent dans l'ensemble de la Méditerranée, et en particulier, l'attitude des pays riverains de la Méditerranée occidentale, et espérant que, le moment venu, l'Espagne pourra être associée à la défense de l'Europe;

Accueillant avec satisfaction à cet égard le pas décisif sur la voie de la démocratie pris par le Portugal;

Convaincue néanmoins que la défense européenne ne peut avoir une autre base que l'OTAN, que ce soit en Méditerranée ou ailleurs,

RECOMMANDE AU CONSEIL

D'inviter instamment les gouvernements membres:

1. A demander la création d'une capacité d'observation par satellite des Nations Unies placée sous l'autorité du Secrétaire général;
2. A veiller à ce que l'étude approfondie à laquelle se livre actuellement l'OTAN, en ce qui concerne les enseignements que l'organisation pourrait tirer du déroulement et de l'issue du conflit du Moyen-Orient, traite d'une manière approfondie de l'utilisation des missiles antichars et antiaériens ainsi que des satellites d'observation; des conclusions que l'on peut en tirer pour l'équipement des forces de l'OTAN, et de la dévalorisation de la notion d'avertissement politique en cas d'imminence d'un conflit;
3. A demander à tous les pays de l'U.E.O., qui sont en mesure de déployer des forces navales dans l'Océan Indien de s'accorder des droits d'accès réciproques à toutes les bases disponibles et de coordonner leurs plans de telle sorte que le nombre global des unités navales maintenues par les pays de l'OTAN, dans cette zone soit proportionnel à celui des unités soviétiques;
4. A faire les représentations appropriées pour que la Convention de Montreux de 1936 soit dûment respectée, et, notamment, pour que des porte-avions ne franchissent pas les Détroits turcs;
5. A insister pour que les dispositions de défense de l'OTAN en Méditerranée soient améliorées, notamment en demandant que la France reprenne son ancienne responsabilité de commandement en Méditerranée occidentale et en transformant l'actuelle „Force sur appel" en une force navale permanente de la Méditerranée, par le biais d'une importante contribution européenne et d'un financement international dans les conditions appropriées.

RECOMMENDATION 254
ON SECURITY AND THE MEDITERRANEAN

The Assembly,

Deploring the resumption of hostilities in the Near and Middle East in 1973, and expressing its sympathy with all the peoples involved;

Considering that Europe should make its views known and its voice heard through the European Community, and endorsing therefore the communiqué issued by the nine governments on 13th October and the resolution adopted by the European Parliament on 17th October, 1973;

Expressing its full support for Security Council Resolutions 338, 339 and 340;

Recalling paragraph 8 of its Recommendation 227;

Concerned at the possible strategic consequences of Soviet involvement in the Middle East;

Having considered the security problems of the Mediterranean area as a whole, the attitudes of the western Mediterranean countries in particular and hoping that at an appropriate time it will be possible to associate Spain with the defence of Europe;

Welcoming in this connection the decisive step on the road to democracy taken by Portugal;

Convinced however that there is no alternative to NATO as the basis of European defence both in the Mediterranean and elsewhere,

RECOMMENDS THAT THE COUNCIL

Urge member governments:

1. To call for the establishment of a United Nations observation satellite capability under the authority of the Secretary-General;
2. To ensure that the intensive study being carried out in NATO of the lessons which that organisation might learn from the conduct and outcome of the Middle East conflict covers fully the use of anti-tank and anti-aircraft missiles and observation satellites; the conclusions to be drawn for the equipment of NATO forces; and the downgrading of the concept of political warning of impending hostilities;
3. To call on all W.E.U. countries able to deploy naval forces in the Indian Ocean to provide reciprocal access to all available bases, and to coordinate their plans to ensure that the total naval presence maintained by NATO countries in the Ocean is commensurate with that of the Soviet Union;
4. To make appropriate representations to ensure that the Montreux Convention of 1936 is correctly applied, in particular so that aircraft carriers do not pass through the Turkish Straits;
5. To press for improvements in NATO defence arrangements in the Mediterranean, especially through the resumption by France of its former command responsibility in the western Mediterranean and by transforming the present on-call force into a Standing Naval Force, Mediterranean, with a substantial European contribution and with international financing in appropriate circumstances.

REPONSE

A LA RECOMMANDATION NO 254

Les problèmes soulevés par la recommandation No 254 sur la sécurité et la Méditerranée ont fait l'objet de réflexions et d'études de la part de tous les pays membres de l'U.E.O. et de l'Alliance atlantique.

Il est à noter, toutefois, que l'évolution dans certains secteurs des situations politiques et militaires dans la zone méditerranéenne suggère des mises au point des études déjà effectuées et, parfois, l'adoption de nouveaux critères d'appréciation ou de jugement de faits et de données considérés jusqu'à présent comme acquis.

Les motifs de fond qui conduisent les gouvernements membres à exercer leur vigilance sur les éventuels développements de la situation de la sécurité restent cependant valables.

Le Conseil estime donc fondé le souci exprimé dans la recommandation de voir mettre pleinement à profit les expériences fournies par le dernier conflit au Moyen-Orient pour compléter l'étude, dont il est question dans la même recommandation, de missiles antichars et antiaériens et de satellites d'observation.

A ce propos, toutefois, on peut exprimer la conviction que l'usage de missiles n'a pas modifié au fond la valeur du char d'assaut et du chasseur bombardier, surtout si l'on se refère à la particulière conformation géographique européenne. Tout en admettant que le problème de l'utilisation des satellites d'observation mérite d'être étudié d'une manière approfondie, le Conseil doute qu'il lui appartienne de demander la création d'une capacité d'observation par satellite des Nations Unies.

L'océan Indien n'étant ni dans la zone de l'Union de l'Europe Occidentale ni dans celle de l'Alliance atlantique, le Conseil, tout en prenant note des vues de l'Assemblée, ne croit pas être en mesure de formuler des observations sur le nombre et la disposition des unités navales maintenues dans cette région par certains pays membres de l'Alliance.

La recommandation que l'actuelle „force sur appel" de la Méditerranée (NAVOC FORMED) soit transformée en une force permanente est soumise, depuis un certain temps déjà, à l'examen des autorités militaires compétentes; des difficultés existent quant aux limites des budgets de défense de quelques-uns des pays intéressés mais la solution est en vue.

Dans une perspective plus générale, le Conseil estime utile de rappeler que dans le contexte des liens étroits existant entre la sécurité dans le continent européen et la sécurité dans le bassin méditerranéen, la C.S.C.E. a été saisie d'un projet de Déclaration sur la Méditerranée, mis au point d'un commun accord entre les neuf pays membres de la C.E.E. et approuvé par tous les pays membres de l'Alliance atlantique. Ce projet répond à l'intention de donner à la Conférence, où pour la première fois 35 Etats sont réunis afin d'examiner les problèmes de la sécurité et de la coopération en Europe, l'occasion d'indiquer aux Etats méditerranéens non participants que les implications pour la sécurité en Méditerranée n'ont pas été ignorées.

La proposition d'éviter le passage à travers les détroits turcs de porte-avions d'Etats riverains de la mer Noire exige un examen attentif des délicates questions juridiques que pose l'interprétation de la Convention de Montreux, à laquelle neuf Etats au total sont parties. Le Conseil a été assuré par les deux Etats membres intéressés que cette question sera étudiée avec soin.

Finalement, en ce qui concerne la suggestion que la France reprenne son ancienne responsabilité de commandement en Méditerranée occidentale, le Conseil n'est pas en mesure de se prononcer sur un point qui touche aux relations de la France avec l'organisation militaire de l'Alliance atlantique.

REPLY

TO RECOMMENDATION 254

The problems raised by Recommendation 254 on security and the Mediterranean have been considered and studied by all the member countries of W.E.U. and the Atlantic Alliance.

However, changes in some aspects of the political and military situations in the Mediterranean area would suggest that studies already completed will have to be brought up to date and that, in some cases, new criteria will have to be adopted for assessing and evaluating facts and data previously accepted as definite.

Nevertheless, the basic reasons which lead the member governments to watch over any developments in the security situation remain valid.

The Council therefore accept the soundness of the point made in the Recommendation, that full use should be made of the lessons learned from the latest conflict in the Middle East to complement the study, referred to in the Recommendation, of anti-tank and anti-aircraft missiles and observation satellites.

In this context, however, the Council are convinced that the use of missiles has not basically affected the value of the tank and the fighter bomber, particularly in view of Europe's special geographical configuration. While agreeing that the problem of the use of observation satellites is worthy of detailed study, the Council doubt whether it would be appropriate for them to call for the establishment of a United Nations observation satellite capability.

As the Indian Ocean is outside the area both of Western European Union and of the Atlantic Alliance, the Council, while taking note of the Assembly's views, do not feel able to comment on the strength or disposition of naval forces maintained there by certain member countries of the Alliance.

The recommendation that the present on-call force in the Mediterranean (NAVOCFORMED) should be transformed into a standing force has already been under consideration by the competent military authorities for some time; there are difficulties arising from the limitation of the defence budgets of some of the countries concerned but there is hope of an early solution.

More generally, the Council wish to recall that a draft Declaration on the Mediterranean, prepared jointly by the nine member countries of the E.E.C. and approved by all the member countries of the Atlantic Alliance has been submitted to the C.S.C.E., in the context of the close links which exist between security on the mainland of Europe and in the Mediterranean area. This draft is intended to provide an opportunity to the conference, 35 states meeting for the first time to discuss problems of security and co-operation in Europe, to indicate to the non-participating Mediterranean states that the implications for security in the Mediterranean have not been ignored.

The proposal that the passage of aircraft carriers from Black Sea states through the Turkish Straits should be prevented necessitates a close examination of complicated legal issues relating to the interpretation of the Montreux Convention to which nine States in all are party. The Council have been assured by the two W.E.U. member governments concerned that this matter will be given careful consideration.

Finally, as regards the suggestion that France should resume its former command responsibility in the western Mediterranean, the Council are not in a position to express an opinion on a point concerning France's relations with the military command structure of the Atlantic Alliance.

RECOMMANDATION NO 255
SUR LES OBSTACLES A L'UNION POLITIQUE DE L'EUROPE

L'Assemblée,

Rappelant que les chefs d'Etat et de gouvernement européens se sont assignés pour objectif l'élaboration d'une identité européenne;

Regrettant que les étapes fixées par les conférences au sommet, notamment dans le domaine monétaire et dans celui de la politique régionale, n'aient pas été réalisées dans les délais prévus, et que le passage à l'union européenne ne soit pas activement préparé;

Considérant que l'U.E.O., reste la seule organisation européenne compétente en matière de politique de défense et est, en tant que telle, appelée à constituer le cadre défensif d'une Europe unie, sans toutefois mettre en cause l'Alliance atlantique;

Déplorant plus spécialement que, dans le domaine de l'énergie, l'Europe des Neuf n'ait pas su définir, en temps utile, les lignes directrices d'une politique commune;

Redoutant que l'absence d'une coordination suffisante des politiques étrangères des pays membres aboutisse à une remise en cause de l'acquis communautaire;

Craignant, en outre, que l'absence d'une harmonisation des points de vue européenne dans le domaine de la sécurité n'affaiblisse la position de l'Europe dans les négociations internationales en cours,

RECOMMANDE AU CONSEIL

1. De promouvoir la création, dans le cadre de l'union européenne, d'un centre de décisions politiques soumis au contrôle parlementaire ayant compétence en matière de politique étrangère;
2. De définir, compte tenu du lien étroit entre la politique extérieure et la défense, une conception de la sécurité européenne dont toute politique de l'Europe des Neuf devrait tenir compte;
3. De promouvoir, dans les cadres appropriés, une politique visant à définir l'identité européenne, tant dans le domaine politique que dans ceux de la défense, de l'économie, de la monnaie et de l'énergie;
4. D'établir un lien permanent avec les consultations politiques auxquelles participent l'ensemble de ses membres, notamment en assurant que le Secrétaire général de l'U.E.O., assiste à toutes les consultations politiques, tant dans le cadre des Neuf que dans celui de l'Alliance atlantique;
5. De rappeler aux deux pays membres de la C.E.E., non membres de l'U.E.O., que le Traité de Bruxelles modifié leur reste ouvert.

REPONSE

A LA RECOMMANDATION NO 255

1. Les institutions de la Communauté européenne ayant été chargées par la Conférence au sommet réunie à Paris en 1972 d'élaborer un rapport sur l'Union européenne, le Conseil ne croit pas utile de faire des commentaires à ce sujet pour le moment.

2. Le Conseil note avec satisfaction qu'au paragraphe 9 de la Déclaration sur les relations atlantiques signée à Bruxelles le 26 juin 1974, les Alliés ont reconnu ,,que le progrès ultérieur vers l'unité que les Etats membres de la Communauté européenne sont déterminés à faire devraient, le moment venu, avoir un effet bénéfique sur la contribution à la défense commune de l'Alliance de ceux d'entre eux qui en sont membres." Dans

RECOMMENDATION 255
ON OBSTACLES TO EUROPEAN POLITICAL UNION

The Assembly,

Recalling that an aim set by the European Heads of State and of Government is to establish a European identity;

Regretting that the stages decided on at the summit conferences, particularly in the monetary and regional policy fields, have not been achieved within the agreed time limits, and that the introduction of the European union is not being actively prepared;

Considering that W.E.U. is still the only European organisation with responsibilities in the field of defence policy and that as such its role is to provide the defence framework of a united Europe without however calling in question the Atlantic Alliance;

Particularly deploring the fact that in energy matters nine-power Europe has been unable to draw up guidelines for a common policy in time;

Fearing that without adequate co-ordination of the foreign policies of the member countries progress already achieved in the Community may be jeopardised;

Fearing further that if European views on security matters are not harmonised Europe's position may be weakened in the current international negotiations,

RECOMMENDS THAT THE COUNCIL

1. Promote the creation, in the framework of the European union, of a political decision-taking centre subject to parliamentary control with responsibilities in the foreign policy field;

2. In view of the close connection between foreign policy and defence, define a concept of European security which should be taken into account in any policy pursued by nine-power Europe;

3. In the appropriate framework, promote a policy aimed at defining Europe's identity in the political, defence, economic, currency and energy fields;

4. Establish a permanent link with the political consultations in which all its members take part, inter alia by ensuring that the Secretary-General of W.E.U. attends all political consultations whether in the framework of the Nine or of the Atlantic Alliance;

5. Remind the two E.E.C. member countries which are not members of W.E.U. that the modified Brussels Treaty is still open to them.

REPLY

TO RECOMMENDATION 255

1. The institutions of the European Community having been instructed by the 1972 Paris summit conference to prepare a report on European Union, the Council see no purpose in commenting on this matter at the present time.

2. The Council note with satisfaction that in paragraph 9 of the Declaration on Atlantic Relations signed in Brussels on 26th June, 1974, the Allies recognised "that the further progress towards unity, which the member states of the European Community are determined to make, should in due course have a beneficial effect on the contribution to the common defence of the Alliance of those of them who belong to it." In an-

un autre paragraphe de la Déclaration, il est réaffirmé que le Traité de l'Atlantique nord fournit la base indispensable de la sécurité de ses membres.

3. Le Conseil note également avec satisfaction les progrès accomplis par les Neuf dans le cadre de la coopération européenne en d'importants domaines de la politique étrangère. Il y voit une confirmation de la déclaration faite dans le document de décembre 1973 sur l'identité européenne, selon laquelle celle-ci est appelée à évoluer en fonction de la dynamique de la construction de l'Europe. Il en va de même des autres domaines mentionnés par l'Assemblée.

4. Le Conseil estime qu'il n'est pas indiqué que le Secrétaire général de l'U.E.O. prenne part à la coopération politique des Neuf ou à des consultations politiques au sein de l'Alliance atlantique. En effet, ainsi qu'il a été explicitement souligné par l'Assemblée, tous les Etats membres de l'U.E.O. prennent part à ces procédures à tous les niveaux où elles se poursuivent.

5. Le Conseil garde présentes à l'esprit les possibilités offertes par l'Article XI du Traité de Bruxelles modifié.

RECOMMANDATION NO 256
SUR LA SECURITE EUROPEENNE ET LA SITUATION EN MEDITERRANEE ORIENTALE

L'Assemblée,

Déplorant les pertes en vies humaines et les souffrances endurées à Chypre;

Estimant que toute solution de la crise dans l'île dépend d'une amélioration des relations entre la Grèce et la Turquie, ainsi qu'entre les communautés chypriotes, ce qui implique des concessions mutuelles sur plusieurs points;

Rappelant l'accroissement continu de la puissance militaire soviétique, notamment sur le plan maritime;

Consciente de ce que la sécurité européenne est compromise par tout affaiblissement des liens entre l'OTAN et ses pays membres et par toute détérioration des relations entre pays membres de l'OTAN;

Estimant que le maintien des installations de défense britanniques à Chypre, conformément aux accords internationaux auxquels les représentants des communautés chypriotes sont parties, contribue à la défense de l'Europe tout entière;

Convaincue que la force des Nations Unies à Chypre, à laquelle ont participé trois pays membres de la Communauté européenne, joue un rôle capital dans le rétablissement d'une situation normale dans l'île;

Demandant qu'une capacité d'observation par satellite soit mise à la disposition du Secrétaire général des Nations Unies;

Rappelant ses recommandations antérieures concernant le respect de la Convention de Montreux afin que les porte-avions ne franchissent pas les Dardanelles.

RECOMMANDE AU CONSEIL

1. De demander aux gouvernements membres de l'U.E.O. d'examiner, d'une part, dans quelle mesure pourrait être étendue l'aide humanitaire apportée aux réfugiés de Chypre et, notamment, si l'on pourrait assurer la survie des intéressés au cours de l'hiver en effectuant des livraisons rapides à partir des stocks de réserve; et de lancer, d'autre part, un appel aux Etats responsables pour qu'ils ferment les camps de réfugiés et abritent ces derniers dans des logements décents;

2. De s'efforcer de faire en sorte que le recours aux bons offices de leurs

other paragraph of the Declaration it is reaffirmed that the North Atlantic Treaty provides the indispensable basis for the security of its members.

3. The Council also note with satisfaction the progress made by the Nine within the framework of European co-operation in important areas of foreign policy. They regard this as a confirmation of the statement contained in the document on the European Identity of December 1973 that the European Identity will evolve in a dynamic way as the construction of a united Europe proceeds. The same applies to the other fields referred to by the Assembly.

4. In the opinion of the Council, it is not appropriate for the W.E.U. Secretary-General to take part in the political co-operation of the Nine or in political consultations within the Atlantic Alliance. For, as has been explicitly emphasised by the Assembly, all W.E.U. member states are taking part in these procedures on all operative levels.

5. The Council bear in mind the possibilities offered by Article XI of the modified Brussels Treaty.

RECOMMENDATION 256
ON EUROPEAN SECURITY AND THE SITUATION IN THE EASTERN MEDITERRANEAN

The Assembly,

Deploring the loss of life and human suffering in Cyprus;

Believing that any solution to the crisis in the island depends on improved relations between Greece and Turkey and between the communities in Cyprus involving mutual concessions on several issues;

Recalling the continued increase in Soviet military power, especially at sea;

Aware that European security is endangered by any weakening of the links between NATO and its member countries and by any deterioration in relations between NATO countries;

Believing that the continued presence of British defence installations in Cyprus, in accordance with international agreements to which representatives of the Cyprus communities are parties, contributes to the defence of Europe as a whole;

Convinced that the United Nations Force in Cyprus, to which three members of the European Community have contributed, is playing an essential role in the return to normal conditions in the island;

Calling for satellite observation capability to be made available to the Secretary-General of the United Nations;

Reiterating its earlier recommendation for the correct application of the Montreux Convention to prevent the passage of aircraft carriers through the Dardanelles,

RECOMMENDS THAT THE COUNCIL

1. Request member governments of W.E.U. to examine to what extent humanitarian aid for the refugees on Cyprus could be enhanced, particularly, whether through rapid deliveries from reserve defence stocks the survival of those concerned through the winter could be ensured; furthermore to appeal to the responsible states to dissolve the refugee camps and to house the refugees in civilised quarters;

2. Endeavour to ensure that the good offices of their partners and allies and, in particular, of the members of the European Community, continue

partenaires et alliés, et notamment des membres de la Communauté européenne reste possible pour toutes les parties, afin de parvenir à un règlement général du problème de Chypre par des négociations entre les deux communautés;

3. D'insister auprès de toutes les parties au conflit sur les multiples avantages qu'une participation active à l'OTAN apporte à chacun de ses membres et à l'ensemble d'entre eux;

4. De reconnaître l'importance du maintien des installations de défense britanniques à Chypre;

5. De développer les accords d'association de la Grèce et de la Turquie à la Communauté européenne en vue de favoriser l'adhésion de ces deux pays à la C.E.E.

REPONSE

A LA RECOMMANDATION NO 256

1. Le Conseil partage la vive préoccupation exprimée par l'Assemblée à l'égard des pertes en vies humaines et des souffrances endurées à Chypre. Il estime lui aussi que toute solution durable de la crise actuelle dépend d'une amélioration des relations entre la Grèce et la Turquie, ainsi qu'entre les deux communautés chypriotes. Le Conseil a également conscience des conséquences de l'instabilité de la situation actuelle à Chypre pour la sécurité de la Méditerranée orientale.

2. Le Conseil tient à signaler que plusieurs gouvernements membres de l'U.E.O. ont déjà contribué d'une manière substantielle à l'aide humanitaire apportée aux réfugiés à Chypre, en réponse notamment à deux appels lancés à l'automne 1974 par le Comité international de la Croix-Rouge et par le Haute Commissariat des Nations Unies pour les réfugiés. Ce dernier a lancé un nouvel appel de fonds en janvier 1975 et certains gouvernements membres de l'U.E.O. y ont déjà répondu. Le Conseil espère que des négociations entre les deux communautés à Chypre aboutiront à un accord qui conduira à une solution durable du problème des réfugiés et à la réinstallation de ces derniers.

3. Le Conseil confirme son attachement à la souveraineté, à l'indépendance et à l'intégrité territoriale de la République de Chypre. Il souhaite appeler l'attention de l'Assemblée sur le fait que, lors de leur réunion à Dublin le 13 février 1975, dans le cadre de la coopération politique, les ministres des affaires étrangères des neuf pays des Communautés européennes ont examiné les évènements récents à Chypre. Rappelant leurs déclarations précédentes sur le sujet et notamment l'importance qu'ils attachent à l'indépendance et à l'intégrité territoriale de Chypre, ainsi que les résolutions pertinentes des Nations Unies, ils ont décidé de prendre contact par l'entremise du Président avec les gouvernements de Chypre, de Grèce et de Turquie pour leur faire savoir:

- qu'ils continuent à estimer hautement souhaitable la recherche d'une solution négociée, à la fois durable et équitable, par la voie de consultation entre les deux communautés à Chypre;
- que, pour faciliter la réalisation de cet objectif, les Neuf sont prêts à s'entretenir avec les représentants de toutes les parties intéressées.

4. Le Conseil est convaincu que tous les membres de l'Alliance atlantique ont pleinement conscience de l'importance de l'Alliance pour la sécurité de l'Europe. Cependant la République de Chypre, comme on le sait, n'est pas membre de l'Alliance.

5. Des forces britanniques se trouvent dans les bases de souveraineté britannique de Chypre depuis 1960. Mais, à la suite du récent réexamen de la défense, ces forces vont être réduites; les réductions porteront sur l'efectif des soldats britanniques et sur le nombre d'avions de combat station-

to be available to all parties in order to secure a general settlement of the Cyprus problem through negotiations between the two communities;

3. Impress upon all parties to the conflict the manifold advantages which active membership of NATO bestows on each and every member;

4. Recognise the importance of the continued presence of British defence installations in Cyprus;

5. Develop the association agreements of Greece and Turkey towards the objective of their full membership of the European Community.

REPLY

TO RECOMMENDATION 256

1. The Council share the deep concern expressed by the Assembly about the loss of life and human suffering in Cyprus. They agree that a lasting solution to the present crisis depends on an improvement in the relations between Greece and Turkey and between the two communities in Cyprus. The Council are also aware of the implications for the security of the eastern Mediterranean of the present unstable situation in Cyprus.

2. The Council would like to point out that several member governments of W.E.U. have already contributed substantially to the humanitarian aid being provided for refugees in Cyprus, particularly in response to two appeals issued by the International Committee of the Red Cross and the United Nations High Commissioner for Refugees in Autumn 1974. The U.N.H.C.R. issued a further appeal for funds in January 1975 and certain member governments of W.E.U. have already responded to this latest request. It is the hope of the Council that negotiations between the two communities in Cyprus will eventually result in an agreement which will permit a long term solution to the refugee problem and the rehabilitation of the refugees themselves.

3. The Council affirm their continuing concern for the sovereignty, independence and territorial integrity of the Republic of Cyprus. They wish to draw the Assembly's attention to the fact that, at their meeting in Dublin on 13th February, 1975, in the framework of political co-operation, the Foreign Ministers of the nine countries of the European Communities considered recent events in Cyprus. Recalling their previous statements on the subject and particularly the importance they attach to the independence and territorial integrity of Cyprus, as well as the relevant United Nations resolutions, they decided to approach the Governments of Cyprus, Greece and Turkey, through the Chairman, to inform them:

– that they continue to regard as highly desirable the search for a just and lasting negotiated settlement through consultation between the two communities in Cyprus;

– that, in order to facilitate the achievement of this aim, the Nine are ready to hold talks with the representatives of all the interested parties.

4. The Council have no doubt that all members of the North Atlantic Alliance are fully aware of the importance of the Alliance to European security. The Republic of Cyprus is not, of course, a member of the Alliance.

5. British forces have been in the Sovereign Base Areas in Cyprus since 1960. But as a result of the recent Defence Review, these forces will be reduced; there will be cuts both in the number of British soldiers and in the number of strike aircraft stationed there in support of CENTO. In deciding these cuts, due account has however been taken of common se-

nés dans l'île dans le cadre du CENTO. En décidant de ces réductions, il a été tenu compte des intérêts de la sécurité commune en Méditerranée orientale. Les bases elles-mêmes seront évidemment maintenues.

6. La proposition de développer les accords d'association de la Grèce et de la Turquie à la Communauté européenne en vue de favoriser l'adhésion de ces deux pays à la C.E.E. est de la compétence du Conseil des Communautés européennes. Néanmoins, ayant signé le traité d'Athènes et celui d'Ankara, les pays membres de l'U.E.O. ont fait leur objectif d'un développement croissant des relations entre la C.E.E. d'une part, la Grèce et la Turquie d'autre part, qui devrait mener à l'adhésion de ces deux pays aux Communautés en tant que membres à part entière.

RECOMMANDATION NO 257
SUR L'ETAT DES ACTIVITES EUROPEENNES EN MATIERE AERONAUTIQUE

L'Assemblée,

Inquiète des conséquences de la crise du pétrole pour le marché européen du transport aérien civil et, par conséquent, pour l'industrie aéronautique;

Consciente du rôle joué par le transport aérien dans la prospérité de l'Europe et le progrès de sa technologie de pointe;

Considérant l'interdépendance des marchés militaire et civil.

RECOMMANDE AU CONSEIL

D'inviter les pays membres:

1. A s'entendre sur des spécifications communes pour tous les achats de matériels aéronautiques militaires;

2. A tenir compte tout particulièrement, dans la formulation de ces spécifications, de la capacité des constructeurs européens en matière d'avions, de moteurs et d'équipements;

3. A veiller à ce que les exigences du marché à l'exportation soient incorporées à ces spécifications;

4. A donner la préférence, chaque fois que cela est raisonnable et possible, aux produits des constructeurs européens, de façon à ce que l'Europe puisse conserver un potentiel autonome de conception et de construction capable de soutenir la concurrence sur les marchés mondiaux;

5. A s'entendre avec le gouvernement américain sur l'égalité des chances à accorder aux exportations et aux importations de matériels aérospatiaux civils et militaires entre les pays membres et les Etats-Unis et, en attendant la conclusion d'un tel accord, à assurer au marché européen la protection commerciale nécessaire pour protéger l'emploi des travailleurs de l'industrie aérospatiale européenne et la balance des paiements des pays membres;

6. A considérer l'Europe occidentale comme un marché unifié, un marché unique en ce qui concerne les opérations de transport, aérien et les ventes d'avions et à traduire cette réalité dans les faits;

7. A établir un programme cohérent et coordonné, bénéficiant de l'appui des gouvernements et de la C.E.E., en vue de faciliter sur les plans commercial, financier et diplomatique, toutes les exportations de matériels aéronautiques.

curity interests in the eastern Mediterranean. The Bases themselves will of course remain.

6. The proposal that the association agreement of Greece and Turkey with the Community should be developed towards full membership of the E.E.C. is a matter for the Council of the European Communities. Nonetheless the member countries of W.E.U. by their signature of the Treaty of Athens and the Treaty of Ankara are committed to the objective of increasing development of relations between the E.E.C. on the one hand and Greece and Turkey on the other, which should lead to full membership of the Communities for these two countries.

RECOMMENDATION 257
ON THE STATE OF EUROPEAN AVIATION ACTIVITIES

The Assembly,

Concerned about the consequences of the oil crisis for the European civil air transport market and, hence, for the aviation industry;

Aware of the part played by air transport in Europe's prosperity and the development of its advanced technology;

Considering the interdependence of military and civil markets,

RECOMMENDS THAT THE COUNCIL

Invite the member countries to:

1. Agree on joint specifications for all military aviation procurement;
2. Take particular account in the formulation of these specifications of the aircraft, engine and equipment capability of European aviation companies;
3. Ensure that export market requirements are incorporated in the specifications;
4. Give preference, wherever reasonable and possible, to the products of European aviation factories so that a self-sustaining design and manufacturing capability able to compete in world markets can be retained in Europe;
5. Agree with the United States Government on equality of opportunity for the export and import of civil and military aerospace products between member countries and the United States and, until such agreement is reached, establish such commercial protection of the European market as is necessary to protect the jobs of European aerospace workers and the balance of payments of member countries;
6. Recognise and establish western Europe as a unified, single market for air transport operations and aircraft sales;
7. Establish a strong and co-ordinated government and E.E.C.-backed programme of commercial, financial and diplomatic support for all aviation export sales.

REPONSE

A LA RECOMMANDATION NO 257

Le Conseil rappelle les réponses qu'il a données précédemment à la recommandation No 244 sur une politique de l'aéronautique pour l'Europe et à la question écrite No 151.

Les vues exprimées dans la présente recommandation No 257 ont été portées à la connaissance des gouvernements membres. Le Conseil peut assurer l'Assemblée qu'ils continuent de prêter toute leur attention aux différents aspects de l'important problème dont elle se préoccupe.

RECOMMANDATION NO 258
SUR LES ASSEMBLEES NATIONALES
ET L'ASSEMBLEE DE L'U.E.O.

L'Assemblée,

Regrettant la méconnaissance des travaux de l'U.E.O. par les parlements des pays membres;

Soucieuse de développer le sens de la solidarité européenne dans les parlements des pays membres.

RECOMMANDE AU CONSEIL

De prier instamment les gouvernements des pays membres de faire connaître par un rapport lors des débats de politique étrangère, leur position sur les questions examinées au Conseil ou à l'Assemblée de l'U.E.O. et les suites qu'ils entendent donner aux recommandations de l'Assemblée.

REPONSE

A LA RECOMMANDATION NO 258

Le Conseil attache une grande importance aux relations de l'Assemblée avec les parlements nationaux. Celles-ci contribuent en effet au renforcement de l'esprit de solidarité européen.

Les gouvernements des pays membres continueront, comme par le passé, et suivant l'usage établi, à informer leur parlement des problèmes internationaux examinés par le Conseil ou par l'Assemblée de l'U.E.O., et des progrès de la coopération au sein de l'U.E.O. D'autre part, les membres de l'Assemblée de l'U.E.O. ont toujours la possibilité de poser des questions à leur gouvernement, lorsqu'ils souhaitent voir examiner de façon plus approfondie des questions de politique étrangère intéressant particulièrement l'U.E.O.

Enfin, il est loisible aux membres de l'Assemblée de faire des communications à leur Parlement national et de se référer le cas échéant à leurs interventions ou à celles de leurs collègues au sein de l'Assemblée de l'U.E.O.

REPLY

TO RECOMMENDATION 257

The Council refer to their earlier replies to Recommendation 244 on an aviation policy for Europe, and to written question 151.

The views expressed in Recommendation 257 have been brought to the notice of member governments. The Council can assure the Assembly that all aspects of the important problem about which it is concerned continue to receive their fullest attention.

RECOMMENDATION 258 ON NATIONAL PARLIAMENTS AND THE W.E.U. ASSEMBLY

The Assembly,

Regretting that the work of W.E.U. is little known in the parliaments of member countries;

Anxious to develop a sense of European solidarity in the parliaments of member countries,

RECOMMENDS THAT THE COUNCIL

Urge the governments of member countries to present a report, during debates on foreign policy, on their position on matters considered by the Council or Assembly of W.E.U. and the action they intend to take on Assembly recommendations.

REPLY

TO RECOMMENDATION 258

The Council attach great importance to the Assembly's relations with national parliaments. These relations contribute indeed to strengthening the spirit of European solidarity.

Member governments will as in the past and in accordance with their established practice inform their parliaments on international developments considered by the Council or the Assembly of W.E.U. and on the progress of co-operation in W.E.U. Furthermore W.E.U. parliamentarians are at liberty to question their governments whenever they want a more detailed consideration of foreign policy matters which are of particular concern to W.E.U.

Finally, members of the Assembly may make statements in their national parliaments and may refer, as necessary, to their own or their colleagues' statements at the W.E.U. Assembly.

RECOMMANDATION NO 259 SUR LES TECHNIQUES DE POINTE AU CANADA – CONSEQUENCES POUR L'EUROPE

L'Assemblée,

Partageant les regrets concernant l'absence de coopération internationale formulés par le Comité spécial de la politique scientifique du Sénat canadien dans son rapport sur la politique scientifique du Canada;

Considérant la proposition du Sénat canadien de créer une association interparlementaire pour les questions scientifiques et techniques qui serait ouverte à tous les pays membres de l'O.C.D.E. et son désir de recevoir des avis à ce sujet;

Considérant également le désir du Canada de développer dans de nouvelles directions sa politique étrangère et ses échanges extérieures;

Consciente de la nécessité de collaborer avec le Canada dans les domaines:

(*a*) du développement des A.D.A.C. et des A.D.A.V.;

(*b*) de la recherche et du développement nucléaires;

(*c*) des autres ressources énergétiques dans le cadre d'une politique énergétique globale;

(*d*) de la téléinformatique.

RECOMMANDE AU CONSEIL

D'inviter les gouvernements membres:

1. A accorder, à l'association interparlementaire préconisée par le Sénat canadien, leur aide dans l'étude des questions mentionnées ci-dessus;

2. A charger l'Agence Spatiale Européenne de rechercher avec le Canada une coopération portant sur:

(*a*) les systèmes de télésenseurs montés à bord des satellites en vue de développer la surveillance de l'environnement, l'océanographie, les nouvelles méthodes de reboisement et l'évaluation des récoltes mondiales;

(*b*) les systèmes intérieurs de télécommunications par satellites.

REPONSE

A LA RECOMMANDATION NO 259

1. Si des recherches ont été entreprises dès la fin de la seconde guerre mondiale pour tenter de trouver dans le domaine de la recherche et du développement de l'énergie nucléaire une solution d'appoint aux problèmes énergétiques qui risquaient de se poser à la communauté internationale, l'évolution des évènements et la crise actuelle de l'énergie font que les solutions de ces problèmes sont aujourd'hui devenues un véritable défi dont dépend, dans une large mesure, l'avenir économique de notre continent.

2. Les progrès accomplis tant au Canada qu'en Europe depuis deux décennies dans le domaine de la recherche et du développement de l'énergie nucléaire apparaissent en conséquence comme une contribution majeure à la solution de ces problèmes. Ils rendent d'autant plus souhaitable une coopération telle que la préconise la recommandation No 259.

3. Cette préoccupation n'est cependant pas nouvelle: il existe déjà entre les organismes canadiens compétents et les commissions nationales de certains pays européens des coopérations bilatérales visant à développer des programmes communs de recherches concernant les utilisations pacifi-

RECOMMENDATION 259
ON ADVANCED TECHNOLOGY IN CANADA – THE CONSEQUENCES FOR EUROPE

The Assembly,

Sharing the regrets expressed by the Canadian Senate Special Committee on Science Policy in its report on science policy for Canada regarding the absence of international co-operation;

Considering the Canadian Senate's proposal to create an interparliamentary association for scientific and technological affairs open to all O.E.C.D. member countries and its wish to hear opinions on this proposal;

Considering also Canada's wish to develop its foreign policy and overseas trade in new directions;

Aware of the need to collaborate with Canada on:

(*a*) the development of V-STOL aircraft;

(*b*) nuclear research and development;

(*c*) other energy resources within the framework of the overall energy policy;

(*d*) computer communications,

RECOMMENDS THAT THE COUNCIL

Invite member governments:

1. To afford the interparliamentary association – as proposed by the Canadian Senate – their assistance in the study of the abovementioned subjects;

2. To instruct the European Space Agency to seek co-operation with Canada on:

(*a*) remote sensing systems in satellites to further environmental monitoring, oceanography, new reforestation methods and worldwide crop assessment;

(*b*) domestic satellite communications systems.

REPLY

TO RECOMMENDATION 259

1. Immediately after the Second World War, attention was directed to the research and development of nuclear energy as a possible auxiliary solution for the energy problems which seemed to be threatening the international community; but the subsequent progress of events and the present energy crisis have transformed solutions for these problems into a pressing need on which the economic future of our continent largely depends.

2. Consequently, the progress achieved in the field of nuclear research and development over the last twenty years, in both Canada and Europe, represents a major contribution to solving these problems. Co-operation along the lines urged in Recommendation 259 is therefore even more to be desired.

3. This is not, however, a new issue; the Canadian agencies concerned and national commissions in a number of European countries are already co-operating bilaterally for the development of joint research programmes

ques de l'énergie nucléaire. Le problème de l'énergie en général fait l'objet d'une concertation étroite dans diverses instances internationales.

4. Quant à la coopération entre l'Europe et le Canada dans le domaine de l'espace, il convient de noter qu'elle se manifeste déjà. En effet, le gouvernement d'Ottawa s'est associé au programme, adopté en 1971 par l'Organisation Européenne de Recherches Spatiales, concernant l'expérimentation et la mise au point d'un système de contrôle de la navigation aérienne par satellites (programme Aérosat).

En outre, le Canada possède le statut d'observateur au sein de la Conférence spatiale européenne et de ses agences subordonnées. Le Canada a donc la possibilité de faire connaître son point de vue au sein du groupe de travail de la C.S.E. chargé de suivre les travaux des Nations Unies. C'est dans ce groupe que se concertent les politiques des Etats membres dans le domaine spatiel, vis-à-vis d'autres organisations. Le Canada peut ainsi, chaque fois qu'il le juge opportun, coordonner et harmoniser sa propre politique spatiale avec celle des Etats européens.

C'est notamment le cas en ce qui concerne les activités du Comité pour l'utilisation pacifique de l'espace extra-atmosphérique et de ses deux souscomités, où sont étudiés en ce moment les problèmes de la radio-diffusion directe par satellite et de la télédétection des ressources terrestres par satellite, aussi bien sur le plan politique et juridique que sur le plan économique et technique.

Les liens qui se sont ainsi créés de part et d'autre de l'Atlantique devraient faciliter la conclusion éventuelle de nouveaux accords entre la future Agence Spatiale Européenne, héritière du CECLES/ELDO et du CERS/ESRO, et son partenaire canadien pour le développement de systèmes spatiaux de télédétection et de télécommunications.

D. RAPPORT ANNUEL DU CONSEIL A L'ASSEMBLEE

Extrait du Chapitre I sur les relations entre le Conseil et l'Assemblée

,,En 1974 comme lors des années précédentes, le Conseil a fait tous ses efforts pour développer des relations étroites et constructives avec l'Assemblée. Comme suite au voeu souvent exprimé par l'Assemblée, le Conseil s'est employé à répondre plus rapidement à ses recommandations et questions écrites.

Le Dix-neuvième rapport annuel a pu être transmis à l'Assemblée dans les plus courts délais compatibles avec les procédures du Conseil.

Quant au fond des réponses données par le Conseil à l'Assemblée, le Conseil est parfaitement conscient de ce que les voeux et l'attente de l'Assemblée ne sont pas toujours satisfaits. Les raisons de cet état de choses se sont manifestées plus clairement en 1974 que par le passé.

Lorsque l'Assemblée a demandé au Conseil des renseignements et des prises de position sur des questions politiques d'actualité, le Conseil a dû, plus souvent que par le passé, se référer aux autres instances où ces sujets sont traités, ses activités en ces domaines ayant diminué au fur et à mesure que s'est développé par ailleurs la coopération politique à Neuf. Il s'est révélé plus nettement encore que, dans le domaine qui, aux yeux de l'Assemblée comme du Conseil, correspond à la vocation profonde de l'U.E.O., à savoir la politique de défense, le Conseil n'a pu répondre à l'Assemblée comme il eût été souhaitable, la coopération dans le domaine de la politique européenne de défense n'étant pas parvenue au stade où les gouvernements seraient en mesure de faire état devant l'Assemblée de prises de position communes.

Ces différentes considérations expliquent que le Conseil n'ait pu répondre favorablement à la requête de la Commission des affaires générales de on the peaceful uses of nuclear energy. The whole energy problem is the subject of close collaboration in various international bodies.

4. Co-operation is already taking place with Canada on space matters. The Canadian Government joined in the programme, adopted by the European Space Research Organisation in 1971 for the testing and development of a satellite air-navigation control system (Aerosat Programme).

Canada also has observer status with the European Space Conference and its subordinate agencies, She is therefore in a position to make her views known within the E.S.C. working group which keeps in touch with the work of the United Nations. This group is the forum in which the member states concert their space policies for their relations with other organisations. Consequently, Canada can co-ordinate and harmonise her own space policy with that of the European states, whenever she considers this desirable.

This applies particularly to the activities of the Committee on the peaceful use of outer space and its two sub-committees, which are at present considering the problems of direct radio transmission by satellite and prospecting the earth's resources by satellite, not only from the political and legal points of view, but also on the economic and technical level.

The transatlantic links so established should facilitate the conclusion of any new agreements between the future European Space Agency, successor to ELDO/CECLES and ESRO/CERS, and its Canadian partners for the development of space monitoring and communications systems.

D. ANNUAL REPORT OF THE COUNCIL TO THE ASSEMBLY

Extract from Chapter I on relations between the Council and the Assembly

"In 1974, as in previous years, the Council made every effort to develop close and constructive relations with the Assembly. In response to the frequently expressed wishes of the Assembly, the Council succeeded in arranging for it to receive replies to its recommendations and written questions sooner than previously.

The Nineteenth Annual Report was sent to the Assembly at the earliest possible dates compatible with the Council's procedures.

As to the substance of their replies to the Assembly, the Council are well aware that the Assembly's wishes and expectations are not always fulfilled. The reasons for this were more clearly apparent in 1974 than in the past.

When asked by the Assembly to provide information or state their attitude on current political questions, the Council had to refer, more often than in the past, to other agencies dealing with these matters, because their own activities in these fields have diminished as political co-operation between the Nine has developed. In the case of defence policy, which both the Assembly and the Council look upon as W.E.U.'s essential concern, it was even more apparent that the Council could not reply to the Assembly in the desired manner because co-operation in European defence policy had not yet reached a stage at which governments could state a joint view to the Assembly.

This explains why the Council were unable to comply with the request from the General Affairs Committee for a joint meeting to consider a large number of questions on the whole of European policy, and particularly on defence. The Council did, however, state that they would be prepared to tenir une réunion commune en vue d'examiner un nombre important de questions touchant l'ensemble de la politique européenne, particulièrement en matière de défense. Le Conseil a toutefois indiqué qu'il serait prêt à envisager qu'un entretien informel ait lieu avec des membres de la Commission à l'occasion de la prochaine réunion du Conseil au niveau ministériel, si la Commission considérait un tel entretien comme utile.

Quoi qu'il en soit de ces aspects de la situation, le Conseil continue de reconnaître pleinement que les recommandations adressées par l'Assemblée au Conseil constituent des initiatives utiles."

Interventions de ministres de gouvernements membres au cours de la Vingtième session ordinaire de l'Assemblée

Première partie (18–20 juin 1974):

M. Roy Hattersley, ministre d'Etat britannique pour les affaires étrangères et le Commonwealth, représentant le Président en exercice du Conseil;

M. Alex Eadie, sous-secrétaire, d'Etat parlementaire du Royaume-Uni à l'énergie;

Deuxième partie (2–6 décembre 1974)

M. Hans Matthöfer, ministre fédéral de la recherche et de la technologie de la République Fédérale d'Allemagne;

M. Renaat van Elslande, ministre belge des affaires étrangères et de la coopération au développement;

M. H. Vredeling, ministre de la défense des Pays-Bas;

M. Bernard Destremau, secrétaire d'Etat auprès du ministre français des affaires étrangères;

Lord Goronwy-Roberts, sous-secrétaire d'Etat parlementaire aux Affaires étrangères et au Commonwealth du Royaume-Uni.

Extrait du chapitre II relatif aux activités du Conseil

La réunion du Conseil du 23 octobre a coïncidé avec le vingtième anniversaire de la signature en 1954, à Paris, des Protocols modifiant et complétant le Traité de Bruxelles; à cette occasion, le représentant permanent du Royaume-Uni, Sir John Killick, intervenant au nom du Président en exercice du Conseil, M. James Callaghan, secrétaire d'Etat aux affaires étrangères et au Commonwealth, a donné lecture de la déclaration suivante:

„Les vingt années qui viennent de s'écouler ont vu d'importants changements dans l'Europe et dans le monde. L'Union de l'Europe Occidentale, elle aussi, a changé. Elle a montré une remarquable capacité à s'adapter aux besoins nouveaux et aux circonstances nouvelles. En vérité, l'Organisation doit son existence, dans sa forme actuelle, aux exigences de circonstances nouvelles. Le Traité de Bruxelles révisé reste aussi valable aujourd'hui que lorsqu'il fut signé il y a vingt ans. Il unit nos sept pays pour cinquante ans en une alliance dans laquelle ils acceptent l'obligation la plus contraignante qu'un pays puisse souscrire à l'égard d'un autre: l'engagement de défense mutuelle. De surcroît, il est à l'origine de la création de l'Assemblée, dont la contribution à nos travaux a été depuis lors si importante. Puisse l'U.E.O. prospérer dans l'avenir comme elle l'a fait dans le passé."

Le représentant permanent de l'Italie, M. l'Ambassadeur Raimondo Manzini, doyen du Conseil permanent, a déclaré:

„Je désire m'associer, et j'espère interpréter les sentiments des autres membres du Conseil, aux paroles de Sir John Killick à l'occasion du vingtième anniversaire de l'Union de l'Europe Occidentale.

Les idéaux qui avaient inspiré les sept pays en 1954 au moment de leur adhésion aux Protocoles de Paris sont sans doute aujourd'hui encore pleinement valables.

consider informal discussions with members of the Committee on the occasion of the next Ministerial Council meeting, provided the Committee would regard such an arrangement as useful.

Despite these aspects of the situation, the Council continue to attach the greatest value to the recommendations initiated by the Assembly.

Speeches by Ministers of member governments made during the Twentieth Ordinary Session of the Assembly

First Part (18th–20th June, 1974):

Mr. Roy Hattersley, United Kingdom Minister of State for Foreign and Commonwealth Affairs, representing the Chairman in Office of the Council;

Mr. Alex Eadie, United Kingdom Parliamentary Under-Secretary of State, Department of Energy;

Second Part (2nd–6th December, 1974):

Mr. Hans Matthöfer, Federal Minister for Research and Technology of the Federal Republic of Germany;

M. Renaat van Elslande, Belgian Minister for Foreign Affairs and Development Co-operation;

Mr. H. Vredeling, Netherlands Minister of Defence;

M. Bernard Destremau, French Secretary of State for Foreign Affairs;

Lord Goronwy-Roberts, United Kingdom Parliamentary Under-Secretary of State for Foreign and Commonwealth Affairs.

Extract from Chapter II on the activities of the Council

The Council's meeting of 23rd October coincided with the twentieth anniversary of the signing in Paris in 1954 of the Protocols modifying and completing the Brussels Treaty; on this occasion, the United Kingdom Permanent Representative, Sir John Killick, speaking for the Chairman in Office of the Council, Mr. James Callaghan, Secretary of State for Foreign and Commonwealth Affairs, read the following statement:

"The last twenty years have seen vast changes in Europe and the world. There have also been changes in Western European Union, which has shown a remarkable capacity to adapt itself to new requirements and circumstances. Indeed, the Organisation owes its existence in its present form to the challenge of such circumstances. The revised Brussels Treaty remains as valid today as when it was signed twenty years ago. It brings our seven countries together in a 50-year alliance in which we accept the most binding obligation any country can assume with regard to another: the commitment to mutual defence. Not least, it is the origin of the Assembly which has since made such an important contribution to our work. May W.E.U. flourish in the future as it has in the past."

The Permanent Representative of Italy, Ambassador Raimondo Manzini, made the following statement in his capacity as doyen of the Permanent Council:

"In associating myself with Sir John Killick's remarks on the occasion of the twentieth anniversary of Western European Union, I trust that I am also expressing the views of the other members of the Council.

The ideals which inspired the seven countries when they signed the Paris Protocols in 1954 undoubtedly still hold good today.

Just as they did twenty years ago, our common culture and our countries' attachment to the vital principles of freedom and democracy impose upon us tasks which cannot be set aside. Some of these tasks have been

Comme il y a vingt ans, notre civilisation commune et l'attachement de nos pays aux principes essentiels de la liberté et de la démocratie nous imposent des tâches qui ne peuvent être négligées. Plusieurs de ces tâches ont été accomplies: le fait même d'avoir pu défendre notre liberté et consolider notre collaboration est une réalisation de la plus grande importance.

Je voudrais également rappeler le rôle accompli par l'U.E.O. lorsque la Grande-Bretagne n'était pas encore dans le Marché Commun: pendant plusieurs années notre Organisation a représenté à cet égard le trait d'union entre les Six et le Royaume-Uni dans l'attente que ce dernier devienne membre de plein droit de la Communauté Economique Européenne.

De nombreux événements ont eu lieu entretemps et une évolution considérable s'est produite dans la situation internationale mais, sans doute, même dans cette nouvelle perspective, nos anciens accords restent un témoignage valable d'une vocation unitaire. Notre Organisation est l'expression de l'esprit de coopération des pays qui font partie de l'Europe Occidentale. Ceci a été bien prouvé par le grand nombre de matières et de problèmes que le Conseil ainsi que l'Assemblée parlementaire ont examinés et profitablement débattus.

En célébrant le vingtième anniversaire de l'Union, nous exprimons donc le voeu que pendant les prochains trente ans elle puisse continuer de représenter pour les pays membres un centre vital, non seulement de consultations et de coopération politique, mais aussi de réalisations pratiques.

Dans ce but, il est évident qu'il appartiendra à ces mêmes pays membres d'employer l'U.E.O. et ses organes de la façon la plus efficace et de coordonner leur activité d'une façon rationnelle avec celle des autres institutions communes.

C'est ainsi que l'U.E.O. pourra, comme nous le désirons sincèrement, continuer d'occuper la place qu'elle mérite à côté des autres grandes organisations occidentales comme les institutions européennes et l'Alliance atlantique."

E. PUBLICATIONS DE L'ASSEMBLEE DE L'UNION DE L'EUROPE OCCIDENTALE EN 1974

1. Actes officiels de la XXème session ordinaire:
- Première partie (juin 1974)
  I. Documents de séance
  II. Procès-verbaux; comptes rendus des débats
- Deuxième partie (décembre 1974)
  III. Documents de séance
  IV. Procès-verbaux; comptes rendus des débats

2. Dix-neuvième rapport annuel du Conseil à l'Assemblée, portant sur les activités du Conseil en 1973 (le vingtième rapport, concernant les activités du Conseil en 1974, sera publié en 1975).

3. Bulletin mensuel d'information sur l'activité parlementaire européenne des sept Etats membres de l'U.E.O. (Nos 114 à 125).
- Note mensuelle sur les principaux événements intéressant l'U.E.O. (Nos 1 à 4).

4. L'année politique en Europe, rétrospective pour 1973. (publié en avril 1974).

fulfilled; the fact that we have succeeded in defending our freedom and in strengthening our co-operation is in itself an achievement of the greatest importance.

I should also like to recall the role played by W.E.U. when the United Kingdom was still not in the Common Market; for a number of years, our Organisation provided the link between the Six and the United Kingdom until she became a full member of the European Economic Community.

Much has happened in the meantime and the international situation has changed considerably, but even in this new context, our old agreements are still genuine evidence of a unity of purpose. Our Organisation embodies the spirit of co-operation between the countries of western Europe. This has been clearly proved by the many subjects and problems which the Council and the parliamentary Assembly have studied and debated to advantage.

In celebrating the twentieth anniversary of the Union, we therefore express the hope that over the next thirty years, it will continue to provide an important forum for the member countries, not only for consultation and political co-operation, but also for achievements of a practical nature.

To achieve this purpose, the member countries will clearly have to use W.E.U. and its agencies in the most effective manner possible and to coordinate their activities rationally with those of other joint institutions.

W.E.U. will then, as we all sincerely hope, be able to retain its rightful place alongside the other leading western organisations, such as the European institutions and the Atlantic Alliance."

E. PUBLICATIONS OF THE ASSEMBLY OF WESTERN EUROPEAN UNION IN 1974

1. Proceedings of the XXth Ordinary Session:
- First Part (June 1974)
I. Assembly documents
II. Minutes; Official Report of debates
- Second Part (December 1974)
III. Assembly documents
IV. Minutes; Official Report of debates

2. Nineteenth Annual Report of the Council to the Assembly on the Council's activities in 1973 (the Twentieth Report, covering the Council's activities in 1974 will be published in 1975).

3. Monthly Information Bulletin on European parliamentary activity in the seven member states of W.E.U. (Nos. 114 to 125)
- Monthly Note on main events of interest to W.E.U. (Nos. 1 to 4)

4. A Retrospective View of the Political Year in Europe 1973. (Published April 1974).

E. ORGANISATION PRINCIPAUX FONCTIONNAIRES

(*31 décembre 1974*)

Secrétariat général
Secrétaire général: S. E. M. G. Heisbourg[1]
Secrétaire général délégué: M. F.-K. von Plehwe[2]
Secrétaire général adjoint: M. P. B. Fraser
Conseiller juridique: M. J. Westhof

Comité permanent des armements
Secrétaire général adjoint et chef du Secrétariat international du C.P.A.: M. Alain Plantey

Agence pour le contrôle des armements
Directeur: Amiral G. Cantù
Directeur adjoint: Général H. Rodrigo
Chef de la Division information et études: Général G. Philibert
Chef de la Division inspections et contrôles:
Général R. Stockdale (jusqu'au 30.4.74)
Air Vice Marshal C. S. Betts (à partir du 1.5.74)
Chef de la Division administration et affaires juridiques: M. H.-J. Osthus

Greffe de l'Assemblée
Greffier: M. F. Humblet
Greffier adjoint: M. G. Moulias

Adresses
Secrétariat général: 9, Grosvenor Place Londres SW1X 7HL
Tel. 01-235.5351

Secrétariat international du Comité permanent des armements Agence pour le contrôle des armements Greffe de l'Assemblée	43, Avenue du Président Wilson 75116 – Paris Tél.: 723 5432

[1] La démission du Secrétaire général, S.E. M. G. Heisbourg, a été acceptée par le Conseil à la date du 30.9.1974.
[2] Le Secrétaire général délégué, M. F.-K. von Plehwe a assuré les fonctions de Secrétaire général p.i. à la date du 1.10.1974.

F. ORGANISATION PRINCIPAL OFFICERS

(31st December, 1974)

Secretariat-General

Secretary-General: S. E. Mr. G. Heisbourg[1]
Deputy Secretary-General: Mr. F.-K. von Plehwe[2]
Assistant Secretary-General: Mr. P. B. Fraser
Legal Adviser: Mr. J. Westhof

Standing Armaments Committee

Assistant Secretary-General and Head of the International Secretariat of the S.A.C.: Mr. Alain Plantey

Armaments Control Agency

Director: Admiral G. Cantù
Deputy Director: General H. Rodrigo
Head of Information and Research Division: General G. Philibert
Head of Inspection and Control Division:
General R. Stockdale until 30.4.1974
Air Vice-Marshal C. S. Betts from 1.5.1974
Head of Administrative and Legal Division: Mr. H. J. Osthus

Office of the Clerk of the Assembly

Clerk: Mr. P. Humblet
Clerk Assistant: Mr. G. Moulias

Addresses

Secretariat-General: 9, Grosvenor Place, London, SWIX 7HL. Tel.: 01-235 5351.

International Secretariat of the Standing Armaments Committee Arnaments Control Agency Office of the Clerk of the Assembly	43, Avenue du Président Wilson 75116 – Paris Tel.: 723-5432

[1] The Council accepted the resignation of S.E. M. G. Heisbourg as Secretary-General as from 30.9.1974.

[2] The Deputy Secretary-General, Mr. F.-K. von Plehwe, assumed the duties of Acting Secreatry-General as from 1.10.1974.

CHAPITRE IV

ORGANISATION DE COOPERATION ET DE DEVELOPPEMENT ECONOMIQUES

A. CHRONOLOGIE DES PRINCIPAUX EVENEMENTS DE L'ANNEE 1974

17–18 janvier: Le Secrétaire Général prend part à la réunion du Comité des Vingt, créé dans le cadre du Fonds Monétaire International, qui se tient à Rome au niveau ministériel.

23 janvier: Dans une allocution prononcée devant l'Assemblée parlementaire du Conseil de l'Europe, le Secrétaire Général présente le rapport sur les activités de l'OCDE en 1972; il passe notamment en revue les derniers développements survenus à la suite de la hausse des prix pétroliers.

1er février: M. Charles G. Wootton (Etats-Unis) prend ses fonctions de Secrétaire Général Adjoint de l'Organisation, poste où il succède à M. Benson E. L. Timmons III.

11–12 février: Sur l'invitation du Président des Etats-Unis, le Secrétaire Général prend part à la réunion de la Conférence sur l'Energie, qui se tient à Washington, et y fait une déclaration.

14–15 février: Le Comité de Politique Economique se réunit sous la présidence de Sir Douglas Allen (Royaume Uni).

27 février–1er mars: Un colloque „sur les problèmes des zones physiquement défavorisées avec référence spéciale aux régions montagneuses" se tient à Paris dans le cadre du Salon international de l'Agriculture; l'Organisation a accordé son patronage à ce colloque.

18–23 mars: Un séminaire international sur l'élaboration des programmes d'étude, organisé par le Centre pour la Recherche et l'Innovation dans l'Enseignement (CERI) de l'OCDE, se tient à Tokyo.

5 avril: M. François-Xavier Ortoli, Président de la Commission des Communautés Européennes, s'entretient avec le Secrétaire Général au siège de l'Organisation.

9 avril: Décès, à Bruxelles, de l'Ambassadeur Roger Ockrent, Représentant permanent de la Belgique auprès de l'OCDE, et doyen des Chefs de Délégation et Président du Comité Exécutif.

23–24 avril: Le Comité Exécutif tient sa sixième Session Spéciale sous la présidence de l'Ambassadeur Jolles (Suisse).

1er mai: Pour permettre à l'OCDE de faire face à l'accroissement de ses tâches dans le domaine énergétique, le Secrétaire Général nomme un Conseiller spécial, M. Ulf Lantzke (Allemagne), chargé de coordonner les travaux de l'Organisation dans ce domaine et le place à la tête de la nouvelle Direction de l'Energie.

3 Mai: M. Takeo Miki, Vice-Premier Ministre du Japon, s'entretient avec le Secrétaire Général au siège de l'Organisation.

6 mai: Le Secrétaire Général assiste à Strasbourg à la cérémonie célébrant le vingt-cinquième anniversaire de la fondation du Conseil de l'Europe.

10 mai: Le Comité Exécutif tient sa Septième Session Spéciale sous la présidence de l'Ambassadeur Jolles (Suisse).

13–15 mai: Un séminaire de l'OCDE sur „la migration internationale des travailleurs en relation avec les politiques d'ajustement industriel et agricole des pays moins développés" se tient à Vienne.

CHAPTER IV

ORGANISATION FOR ECONOMIC COOPERATION AND DEVELOPMENT

A. CHRONOLOGY OF MAIN EVENTS IN 1974

17th–18th January: The Secretary General attended the meeting of the Committee of Twenty established under the International Monetary Fund. This meeting was held in Rome at Ministerial Level.

23rd January: The Secretary-General addressed the Parliamentary Assembly of the Council of Europe and presented the 1972 OECD Activities Report; the Secretary-General reviewed in particular the latest developments resulting from the rise of prices affecting oil products.

1st February: Mr Charles G. Wootton (United States) took up his duties as Deputy Secretary-General of the Organisation, succeeding Mr. Benson E. L. Timmons III.

11th–12th February: Upon invitation by the President of the United States, the Secretary-General attended the meeting of the Washington Energy Conference, where he made a statement.

14th–15th February: The Economic Policy Committee met under the chairmanship of Sir Douglas Allen (United Kingdom).

27th February to 1st March: A symposium on the "Problems of Naturally Handicapped Zones, with special reference to Mountain Zones" was held in Paris in the framework of the International Agricultural Fair; the Organisation had granted its patronage to this symposium.

18th–23rd March: An International Seminar on Curriculum Development, organised by the OECD Centre for Educational Research and Innovation (CERI) was held in Tokyo.

5th April: Mr. François-Xavier Ortoli, President of the Commission of the European Economic Communities, had a conversation with the Secretary-General at the Organisation's Headquarters.

9th April: Ambassador Roger Ockrent, Permanent Representative of Belgium to the OECD, Dean of the Heads of Delegations and Chairman of the Executive Committee, died in Brussels.

23rd–24th April: The Executive Committee held its Sixth Special Session under the chairmanship of Ambassador Jolles (Switzerland).

1st May: To meet OECD's enlarged responsibilities in the field of energy, the Secretary-General appointed a Special Counsellor – Mr. Ulf Lantzke (Germany) – to coordinate the Organisation's work in this sector and to head the newly-created Directorate for Energy.

3rd May: Mr. Takeo Miki, Deputy Prime Minister of Japan, had a conversation with the Secretary-General at the Organisation's Headquarters.

6th May: The Secretary-General attended the ceremony commemorating the 25th Anniversary of the Council of Europe's foundation, in Strasbourg.

10th May: The Executive Committee held its Seventh Special Session under the chairmanship of Ambassador Jolles (Switzerland).

13th–15th May: An OECD Seminar on International Migration of Workers and its Relation to Industrial and Agricultural Policies in Developing Countries was held in Vienna.

14 mai: L'Ambassadeur François Valéry, Représentant permanent de la France auprès de l'OCDE, est élu Président du Comité Exécutif.

20–22 mai: Une réunion organisée par le Centre pour la Recherche et l'Innovation dans l'Enseignement (CERI) de l'OCDE se tient à La Haye, sur le thème suivant: „Le soutien professionnel apporté aux écoles à l'échelon régional et local."

29–30 mai: Le Conseil de l'Organisation tient sa treizième réunion au niveau des Ministres sous la présidence de M. Antonio Giolitti, Ministre du budget et de la programmation économique de l'Italie. Il adopte, entr'autre, une déclaration en vertu de laquelle les pays Membres s'engagent à ne prendre, pendant un an, aucune mesure protectionniste unilatérale quelqu'en soit la nature, notamment celles visant à restreindre les importations ou les exportations ou, au contraire, à stimuler ces dernières. Cette déclaration ainsi que les conclusions de cette réunion font l'objet d'un communiqué de presse (reproduit plus loin).

4–7 juin: Une conférence internationale, organisée par le Centre pour la Recherche et l'Innovation dans l'Enseignement (CERI) de l'OCDE, se tient à Rungsted (Danemark), sur le thème: „L'enseignement de l'environnement au niveau post-secondaire." Le Secrétaire Général y prononce une allocution. S.A.R. le Prince Henrik de Danemark prend part à la séance d'ouverture.

6 juin: M. Emile van Lennep, Secrétaire Général de l'Organisation depuis octobre 1969, est réélu pour une nouvelle période de cinq ans, à partir du 1er octobre 1974.

6 juin: Le Secrétaire Général prononce une allocution au Symposium sur l'énergie et les matières premières, qui se tient à Paris sous l'égide d'un comité composé d'industriels et d'hommes d'affaires.

11 juin: Lors d'une réunion du Comité d'Aide au Développement de l'OCDE, huit Membres de ce Comité (Allemagne, Danemark, Etats-Unis, Italie, Japon, Norvège, Pays-Bas, Suède) concluent un accord sur un déliement partiel de l'aide au développement.

18 juin: Le Conseil adopte une Recommendation sur „les directives en vue d'une action ayant pour but de réduire les émissions d'oxyde de soufre et de particules résultant de l'emploi de combustibles dans les installations fixes" (texte reproduit plus loin).

21–22 juin: Le Secrétaire Général se rend en visite officielle à Londres, où il est reçu par M. Callaghan, Secrétaire d'Etat aux Affaires Etrangères M. Healey, Chancelier de l'Echiquier, et M. Richardson, Gouverneur de la Banque d'Angleterre.

22–23 juin: Le Secrétaire Général assiste à la cérémonie du centenaire de la Banque d'Espagne et s'entretient avec le Gouverneur de la Banque, ainsi qu'avec M. A. Barrera de Irimo, Ministre des Finances.

24–25 juin: Le Comité de Politique Economique se réunit sous la présidence de Sir Douglas Allen (Royaume Uni).

24–26 juin: Un séminaire de l'OCDE sur „les questions d'ordre politique soulevées par la protection des données" se tient à Paris.

11 juillet: M. Maurice Williams, Président du Comité d'Aide au Développement (CAD) tient, au siège de l'OCDE, une conférence de presse où il commente les tendances récentes de l'aide au développement observées en 1973.

18 juillet: Le Conseil adopte deux Résolutions concernant les conditions auxquelles peuvent être accordés les crédits à l'exportation de navires et de stations terrestres pour satellites de communication (texte reproduit plus loin).

24 juillet: M. William Simon, Secrétaire au Trésor des Etats-Unis, s'entretient avec le Secrétaire Général au siège de l'Organisation.

14th May: Ambassador François Valéry, Permanent Representative of France to the OECD, was elected Chairman of the Executive Committee.

20th–22nd May: A meeting was held in The Hague on Regional and Local Professional Support to Schools, organised by the OECD Centre for Educational Research and Innovation (CERI).

29th–30th May: The Council of the Organisation held its 13th Meeting at Ministerial Level under the chairmanschip of Mr. Antonio Giolitti, Minister of the Budget and Economic Planning of Italy. It adopted, among other things, a Declaration by virtue of which the Member Governments committed themselves to take no unilateral protectionist measures, whatever their nature, for a period of one year, notably those aiming at restricting imports or exports or, on the contrary, stimulating the latter. The text of this Declaration as well as the other conclusions of this meeting were issued as a Press Release (reproduced below).

4th–7th June: An international conference, organised by the OECD Centre for Educational Research and Innovation on Environmental Education at Post-Secondary Level was held at Rungsted, Denmark. The Secretary-General addressed the participants. H.R.H. Prince Henrik of Denmark attended the opening session.

6th June: Mr. Emile van Lennep, Secretary-General of the Organisation since October 1969, was re-elected for a further five-year term with effect from 30th September, 1974.

6th June: The Secretary-General addressed the Symposium on Energy and Raw Materials organised in Paris under the aegis of a committee composed of industrialists and businessmen.

11th June: At a session of the OECD Development Assistance Committee, eight of the Committee's Members (Denmark, Germany, Italy, Japan, the Netherlands, Norway, Sweden and the United States) agreed on a further partial untying of development aid.

18th June: The Council adopted a Recommendation setting out "Guidelines for Action to Reduce Emissions of Sulphur Oxides and Particulate Matter from Fuel Combustion in Stationary Sources" – text reproduced below.

21st–22nd June: The Secretary-General paid an official visit to London where he was received by Mr. Callaghan, Foreign Secretary, Mr. Healy, Chancellor of the Exchequer and Mr. Richardson, Governor of the Bank of England.

22nd–23rd June: The Secretary-General attended the ceremony commemorating the Centenary of the Bank of Spain and had conversations with the Governor of the Bank and the Minister of Finance, Mr. A. Barrera de Irimo.

24th–25th June: The Economic Policy Committee met under the chairmanship of Sir Douglas Allen (United Kingdom).

24th–26th June: An OECD seminar was held in Paris dealing with Policy Issues in Data Protection.

11th July: The Chairman of the Development Assistance Committee (DAC), Mr. Maurice Williams, held a press conference at the OECD headquarters to assess recent trends in development aid as observed in 1973.

18th July: The Council adopted two Resolutions concerning the terms under which export credits for ships and ground satellite communications' stations can be granted – text reproduced below.

24th July: Mr. William Simon, Secretary of the U.S. Treasury, had a conversation with the Secretary-General at the Organisation's headquarters.

5–31 août: Le neuvième cours-séminaire international sur la formation professionnelle et l'enseignement agricoles du niveau secondaire se déroule à Gwatt et Zollikofen (Suisse). Le patronage de l'OCDE a été accordé à cette manifestation.

9–10 août: Une réunion internationale des directeurs d'instituts de recherche et de formation en matière de développement se tient à Abidjan, sous l'égide du Centre de Développement de l'OCDE et de la Banque Mondiale. Cette réunion est suivie par la 14ème Conférence mondiale de la Société internationale de développement, tenue du 12 au 16 août, sous la présidence de M. Paul-Marc Henry, Président du Centre de Développement de l'OCDE.

19–30 août: Plusieurs représentants de l'OCDE assistent à la Conférence mondiale sur la population, organisée par les Nations Unies, à Bucarest. Cette délégation est conduite par M. Paul-Marc Henry, Président du Centre de Développement de l'OCDE.

30 août–8 septembre: Le Secrétaire Général se rend en visite officielle en Australie et y rencontre un certain nombre de personnalités, notamment le Premier Ministre, M. Whitlam, plusieurs ministres et le Gouverneur de la Banque de Réserve d'Australie.

4 septembre: Le Gouvernement danois ratifie deux Conventions, élaborées dans le cadre de l'Agence de l'OCDE pour l'Energie Nucléaire et signées respectivement en 1960 et 1968, qui régissent la responsabilité civile dans le domaine nucléaire et la réparation des dommages en cas d'accident nucléaire. De ce fait, la seconde Convention entre en vigueur le jour même.

9–10 septembre: Le Secrétaire Général se rend en visite officielle en Nouvelle-Zélande, où il est reçu par le Premier Ministre, M. Rowling, ainsi que par plusieurs ministres.

19 septembre: Un groupe de parlementaires suédois, membres de la Commission permanente de la sécurité sociale, visite l'OCDE et rencontre plusieurs hauts fonctionnaires du Secrétariat.

20 septembre: M. John Turner, Ministre des Finances du Canada, s'entretient avec le Secrétaire Général au siège de l'Organisation.

26 septembre: M. Gamani Corea, Secrétaire Général de la Conférence des Nations Unies pour le Commerce et le Développement, s'entretient avec le Secrétaire Général au siège de l'Organisation.

29 septembre–4 octobre: Le Secrétaire Général assiste à Washington aux assemblées annuelles du Fonds Monétaire International et de la Banque Mondiale.

5–10 octobre: Le Secrétaire Général se rend en visite au Japon, où il est reçu par le Ministre des Affaires Etrangères, M. Kimura, ainsi que par d'autres ministres et par le Gouverneur de la Banque du Japon. Le 7 octobre, M. van Lennep prononce une allocution lors d'un Symposium organisé pour marquer le dizième anniversaire de l'adhésion du Japon à l'OCDE.

15–18 octobre: Une Conférence de l'OCDE ,,sur le travail dans une nouvelle société industrielle" se tient au siège de l'Organisation, avec la participation de quelque cent-cinquante experts appartenant aux milieux patronaux, syndicaux, universitaires et gouvernementaux de tous les pays Membres. La conférence est ouverte par M. R. K. Andras, Ministre de la Main-d'Oeuvre et de l'immigration du Canada.

16 octobre: Le Comité d'Aide au Développement étudie avec M. Maurice F. Strong, Directeur exécutif du Programme des Nations Unies pour l'Environnement, des problèmes d'intérêt commun.

22 octobre: Le Secrétaire Général s'entretient avec M. Pierre Elliott Trudeau, Premier Ministre Canadien, lors d'une visite officielle de ce dernier à Paris.

5th–31st August: The Ninth International Study Course on Problems of Training and Secondary Education in Agriculture was held at Gwatt and Zollikofen (Switzerland); OECD had granted its patronage to this event.

9th–10th August: A meeting, sponsored jointly by the OECD Development Centre and the World Bank, of directors of research and training institutes in the field of social and economic research was held in Abidjan. This meeting was followed, from 12th–16th, by the 14th World Conference of the Society of International Development under the chairmanship of Mr. P.-M. Henry, President of the OECD Development Centre.

19th–30th August: An OECD delegation, headed by Mr. P.-M. Henry, President of the OECD Development Centre, attended the World Population Conference in Bucharest.

30th August to 8th September: The Secretary-General paid an official visit to Australia, in the course of which he met with a number of personalities both at Federal and State level, notably the Prime Minister, Mr. Whitlam, several ministers as well as the Governor of the Reserve Bank of Australia.

4th September: The Danish Government ratified two Conventions – elaborated in the framework of the OECD Nuclear Energy Agency signed in 1960 and 1968 respectively – governing nuclear third-party liability and compensation for damage resulting from a nuclear accident. As a consequence, the second Convention came into force on that date.

9th–10th September: The Secretary-General paid an official visit to New Zealand in the course of which he was received by the Prime Minister, Mr. Rowling, and several ministers.

19th September: A group of Swedish Parliamentarians, members of the Standing Committee on Social Insurance, visited the OECD and met with senior officials of the Secretariat.

20th September: Mr. John Turner, Canadian Minister of Finance, had a conversation with the Secretary-General at the Organisation's headquarters.

26th September: Dr. Gamani Corea, Secretary General of the United Nations Conference on Trade and Development, had a conversation with the Secretary-General at the Organisation's headquarters.

29th September to 4th October: The Secretary-General attended the annual meetings of the International Monetary Fund and the World Bank held in Washington.

5th–10th October: The Secretary-General visited Japan where he was received by Mr. Kimura, Minister of Foreign Affairs, several other Ministers and the Governor of the Bank of Japan.

On 7th October, Mr. van Lennep addressed a Tokyo Symposium commemorating the 10th Anniversary of Japan's membership in OECD.

15th–18th October: An OECD Conference on Work in a Changing Industrial Society was held at the Organisation's headquarters with the participation of about 150 management, trade union, university and government experts from all Member countries. The meeting was opened by Mr. R. K. Andras, Canadian Minister for Manpower and Immigration.

16th October: The Development Assistance Committee discussed with Mr. Maurice F. Strong, Executive Director of the UN Environment Programme, issues of common interest.

22nd October: The Secretary-General had a conversation with Mr. Pierre Elliott Trudeau, Canadian Prime Minister, on the occasion of his official visit to Paris.

22–23 octobre: Le Comité d'Aide au Développement tient sa treizième réunion annuelle à haut niveau, présidée pour la première fois par M. Maurice Williams (Etats-Unis). Il considère avec une attention particulière les conséquences pour les pays en développement de la récente hausse des prix du pétrole et de certains autres produits de base essentiels, et convient qu'il est nécessaire que les Membres du CAD et les autres pays qui sont en mesure de le faire apportent d'urgence une aide spéciale de soutien. Le Portugal annonce qu'il a décidé de se retirer du CAD.

5 novembre: Le Secrétaire Général fait une visite officielle à la Commission des Communautés Européennes, à Bruxelles; il est reçu par M. Ortoli, Président de la Commission, et Sir Christopher Soames, Vice-Président.

6 novembre: Le Secrétaire Général prend part, à Rome, à la Conférence Mondiale de l'Alimentation des Nations Unies, où il prononce une allocution.

8 novembre: La Commission des Questions Economiques et du Développement de l'Assemblée parlementaire du Conseil de l'Europe se réunit au siège de l'Organisation. Elle procède, avec le Secrétaire Général et de hauts fonctionnaires du Secrétariat, à un large échange de vues sur les principaux problèmes posés par la situation économique.

13–14 novembre: Le Comité de l'Environnement se réunit au niveau ministériel sous la présidence de Mme. Gro Harlem Brundtland, Ministre de l'Environnement de la Norvège. La réunion adopte une déclaration sur la politique d'environnement. Le Conseil de l'OCDE adopte ensuite dix Recommandations (dont le texte est reproduit plus loin), concernant les actions à mener pour résoudre les problèmes d'environnement urgents qui ont été examinés par les Ministres.

15 novembre: Le Conseil décide de créer, dans le cadre de l'OCDE, l'Agence Internationale de l'Energie, qui aura pour tâche de mettre en oeuvre un vaste programme de coopération dans le domaine énergétique (texte de la Décision reproduit plus loin). Seize pays décident de participer aux travaux de l'Agence dès sa création: l'Allemagne, l'Autriche, la Belgique, le Canada, le Danemark, l'Espagne, les Etats-Unis, l'Irlande, l'Italie, le Japon, le Luxembourg, les Pays-Bas, le Royaume Uni, la Suède, la Suisse et la Turquie.

18 novembre: Les représentants des pays indiqués ci-dessus signent un Accord relatif à un programme international de l'énergie (texte reproduit plus loin).

18 novembre: Lors de sa première réunion, le Comité Directeur de l'Agence Internationale de l'Energie élit à sa présidence l'Ambassadeur Etienne Davignon (Belgique) et nomme au poste de Directeur exécutif de l'Agence, M. Ulf Lantzke (Allemagne).

18–19 novembre: Le Comité de Politique Economique se réunit sous la présidence de Sir Douglas Allen (Royaume Uni).

25–26 novembre: Le Comité Exécutif tient sa huitième Session Spéciale sous la présidence de l'Ambassadeur Jolles (Suisse).

2–5 décembre: Une Conférence organisée par le Centre pour la Recherche et l'Innovation dans l'Enseignement de l'OCDE se tient à Liège (Belgique), sur le thème „les nouvelles méthodes d'évaluation de programmes d'enseignement."

9–13 décembre: Un symposium organisé conjointement par l'Agence de l'OCDE pour l'Energie Nucléaire et par l'Agence Internationale de l'Energie Atomique se tient à Vienne, sur le thème du choix des sites d'installations nucléaires.

17–18 décembre: Le Conseil de direction de l'Agence Internationale de l'Energie tient sa seconde réunion.

22nd–23rd October: The Development Assistance Committee held its 13th Annual High-Level Meeting, chaired for the first time by Mr. Maurice Williams (U.S.) Special attention was given to the implications for developing countries of the recent increase in oil prices and some other essential commodities and the Committee agreed that there was an urgent need for special relief assistance from DAC members and other countries in a position to help. Portugal announced its decision to withdraw from the DAC.

5th November: The Secretary-General paid an official visit to the Commission of the European Communities in Brussels. He was received by Mr. Ortoli, President of the Commission and Sir Christopher Soames, Vice-President.

6th November: The Secretary-General attended the United Nations World Food Conference in Rome where he delivered an address.

8th November: The Committee on Economic Affairs and Development of the Parliamentary Assembly of the Council of Europe met at the Organisation's headquarters. A large exchange of views took place with the Secretary-General and senior Secretariat officials regarding the main issues of the current economic situation.

13th–14th November: The Environment Committee met at Ministerial Level under the chairmanship of Mrs. Gro Harlem Brundtland, Norwegian Minister of Environment. The meeting adopted a Declaration on Environmental Policy. The OECD Council then adopted ten Recommendations regarding action to be taken on urgent environmental issues which had been discussed between Ministers (texts of Recommendations reproduced below).

15th November: The Council decided to set up an International Energy Agency within the Organisation with the task of carrying out a comprehensive programme of cooperation in the energy field (the text of the Decision is reproduced below). Countries initially participating in the work of the Agency were: Austria, Belgium, Canada, Denmark, Germany, Ireland, Italy, Japan, Luxembourg, the Netherlands, Spain, Sweden, Switzerland, Turkey, the United Kingdom and the United States.

18th November: An Agreement on an International Energy Programme was signed by the Representatives of the abovementioned countries (text reproduced below).

18th November: The Governing Board of the International Energy Agency, holding its first meeting, elected Ambassador Etienne Davignon (Belgium) as its Chairman and appointed Dr. Ulf Lantzke (Germany) as Executive Director of the Agency.

18th–19th November: The Economic Policy Committee met under the chairmanship of Sir Douglas Allen.

25th–26th November: The Executive Committee held its 8th Special Session under the chairmanship of Ambassador Jolles (Switzerland).

2nd–5th December: A conference, organised by the OECD Centre for Educational Research and Innovation, on new approaches to the evaluation of educational programmes was held at Liège (Belgium).

9th–13th December: A symposium on the choice of sites for nuclear installations, jointly organised by the OECD Nuclear Energy Agency and the International Atomic Energy Agency, was held in Vienna.

17th–18th December: The Governing Board of the International Energy Agency held its second meeting.

B. PRINCIPAUX ACTES DE L'ORGANISATION (1974)

1. Recommandation du Conseil concernant les fournitures de combustibles de soutes pour les transports maritimes et la pêche [10 janvier 1974].

2. Recommendation du Conseil concernant la fourniture de carburant aux aéronefs civils [10 janvier 1974].

3. Recommendation du Conseil concernant l'action contre les pratiques commerciales restrictives relatives à l'usage des brevets et des licences [22 janvier 1974].

4. Décision du Conseil relative à l'établissement d'un Système de l'OCDE pour le contrôle des matériels forestiers de reproduction destinés au commerce international [5 mars 1974].

5. Résolution du Conseil relative aux relations de travail avec les Nations Unies dans le domaine de l'environnement [12 mars 1974].

6. Arrangement de coopération entre les Secrétariats de l'Organisation de Coopération et de Développement Economiques et de l'Organisation Intergouvernementale Consultative de la Navigation Maritime [26 mars 1974].

7. Communiqué de presse du Conseil au niveau des Ministres [30 mai 1974].

8. Recommendation du Conseil sur des directives en vue d'une action ayant pour but de réduire les émissions d'oxyde de soufre et de particules résultant de l'emploi de combustibles dans des installations fixes [18 juin 1974].

9. Décision du Conseil sur l'adoption de normes provisoires de radioprotection applicables à la conception, à la construction, aux essais et au contrôle des stimulateurs cardiaques radioisotopiques [18 juin 1974].

10. Résolution du Conseil relative à un Arrangement concernant les crédits à l'exportation de stations terrestres pour satellites de télécommunications [27 juin 1974].

11. Recommendation du Conseil concernant l'examen de toutes les restrictions imposées par les pays Membres sur le placement en titres non cotés ou non inscrits à la cote [18 juillet 1974].

12. Résolution du Conseil relative à un Arrangement concernant les crédits à l'exportation des navires [18 juillet 1974].

13. Recommendation du Conseil concernant les normes de divulgation et procédures devant être appliquées à toutes les offres publiques de titres [18 juillet 1974].

14. Recommendation du Conseil concernant la réglementation des offres publiques et de l'admission à la cote out de la cotation de titres étrangers [18 juillet 1974].

15. Décision du Conseil relative à l'établissement d'un Système de l'OCDE pour la certification variétale des semences de trèfle souterrain et d'espèces similaires destinées au commerce international [24 octobre 1974].

16. Recommendation du Conseil sur l'évaluation des effets potentiels des composés chimiques sur l'environnement [14 novembre 1974].

17. Recommendation du Conseil sur l'analyse des effets sur l'environnement des projets publics et privés importants [14 novembre 1974].

18. Recommendation du Conseil sur la prévention et la réduction des nuisances acoustiques [14 novembre 1974].

19. Recommandation du Conseil sur la limitation de la circulation et sur les moyens peu coûteux d'améliorer l'environnement urbain [14 novembre 1974].

20. Recommendation du Conseil sur les mesures requises en vue du renforcement de la lutte contre la pollution atmosphérique [14 novembre 1974].

21. Recommendation du Conseil sur la lutte contre l'eutrophisation des eaux [14 novembre 1974].

B. MAIN ACTS OF THE ORGANISATION (1974)

1. Recommendation of the Council on the Supply of Bunker Fuels for Shipping and Fishing [10th January, 1974].
2. Recommendation of the Council on the Supply of Fuel for Civil Aircraft [10th January, 1974].
3. Recommendation of the Council concerning Action Against Restrictive Business Practices Relating to the Use of Patents and Licences [22nd January, 1974].
4. Decision of the Council Establishing an OECD Scheme for the Control of Forest Reproductive Material moving in International Trade [5th March, 1974].
5. Resolution of the Council on Working Relations with the United Nations in Regard to the Environment [12th March, 1974].
6. Arrangement of Co-operation Between the Secretariats of the Organisation for Economic Co-operation and Development and the Inter-Governmental Maritime Consultative Organisation [26th March, 1974].
7. Press Communiqué of the Ministerial Council [30th May, 1974].
8. Recommendation of the Council on Guidelines for Action to Reduce Emissions of Sulphur Oxides and Particulate Matter from Fuel Combustion in Stationary Sources [18th June, 1974].
9. Decision of the Council on the Adoption of Interim Radiation Protection Standards for the Design, Construction, Testing and Control of Radioisotopic Cardiac Pacemakers [18th June, 1974].
10. Resolutions of the Council concerning an Understanding on Export Credits for Ground Satellite Communications Stations [27th June, 1974].
11. Recommendation of the Council concerning the Review of any Restrictions which Member Countries Impose on Portfolio Investment in Unlisted or Unquoted Securities [18th July, 1974].
12. Resolution of the Council concerning an Understanding on Export Credits for Ships [18th July, 1974].
13. Recommendation of the Council concerning Disclosure Requirements and Procedures to be Applicable to all Publicly Offered Securities [18th July, 1974].
14. Recommendation of the Council concerning Regulations for the Public offer and for Stock Exchange Listing or Quotation of Foreign Securities [18th July, 1974].
15. Decision of the Council Establishing an OECD Scheme for the Varietal Certification of Seed of Subterranean Clover and Similar Species Moving in International Trade [24th October 1974].
16. Recommendation of the Council on the Assessment of the Potential Environmental Effects of Chemicals [14th November, 1974].
17. Recommendation of the Council on the Analysis of the Environmental Consequences of Significant Public and Private Projects [14th November, 1974].
18. Recommendation of the Council on Noise Prevention and Abatement [14th November, 1974].
19. Recommendation of the Council on Traffic Limitation and Low-Cost Improvement of the Urban Environment [14th November, 1974].
20. Recommendation of the Council on Measures Required for Further Air Pollution Control [14th November, 1974].
21. Recommendation of the Council on the Control or Eutrophication of Waters [14th November, 1974].
22. Recommendation of the Council on Strategies for Specific Water Pollutants Control [14th November, 1974].
23. Recommendation of the Council on Energy and the Environment [14th November, 1974].

22. Recommandation du Conseil sur les stratégies de lutte contre les polluants spécifiques des eaux [14 novembre 1974].

23. Recommendation du Conseil sur l'énergie et l'environnement [14 novembre 1974].

24. Recommendation du Conseil sur la mise en oeuvre du principe pollueur payeur [14 novembre 1974].

25. Recommendation du Conseil concernant des principes relatifs à la pollution transfrontière [14 novembre 1974].

26. Décision du Conseil portant création d'une Agence Internationale de l'Energie de l'Organisation [15 novembre 1974].

27. Accord relatif à un Programme international de l'Energie [18 novembre 1974].

Les Actes no. 5 à 7, 17 à 20 et 23 à 27 sont réproduits ci-dessous. Les autres peuveut être obtenus en écrivant au Secrétariat de l'OCDE, 2 rue André Pascal, 75775 Paris Cedex.

RESOLUTION DU CONSEIL RELATIVE AUX RELATIONS DE TRAVAIL AVEC LES NATIONS UNIES DANS LE DOMAINE DE L'ENVIRONNEMENT

(*adoptée par le Conseil à sa 352ème Séance, le 12 mars 1974*)

Le Conseil,

Vu l'article 12 (b) de la Convention relative à l'Organisation de Coopération et de Développement Economiques, en date du 14 décembre 1960;

Vu l'article 10 du Règlement de Procédure de l'Organisation;

Considérant qu'il existe de multiples relations entre le Programme mis en oeuvre par les Nations Unies dans le domaine de l'environnement et les tâches effectuées par le Comité de l'Environnement dans le cadre du mandat qu'il a reçu du Conseil;

Considérant qu'un échange régulier de documents sur l'accomplissement des programmes respectifs et la participation d'observateurs aux réunions tenues de part et d'autre sont de nature à assurer une liaison utile entre les deux Organisations en matière d'environnement;

DECIDE:

1. Le Secrétaire général est autorisé à transmettre au Directeur Exécutif du Programme des Nations Unies pour l'environnement les documents du Comité de l'Environnement, ou de ses sous-groupes, qu'il jugerait bon de lui communiquer.

2. Le Secrétaire général peut inviter le Directeur Exécutif du Programme des Nations Unies pour l'environnement ou son représentant à assister en qualité d'observateur à des réunions du Comité de l'Environnement, ou de ses sous-groupes, dans les conditions prévues à l'article 10 du Règlement de Procédure.

24. Recommendation of the Council on the Implementation of the Polluter-Pays Principle [14th November, 1974].

25. Recommendation of the Council on Principles concerning Transfrontier Pollution [14th November, 1974].

26. Decision of the Council Establishing an International Energy Agency of the Organisation [15th November, 1974].

27. Agreement on an International Energy Program [18th November, 1974].

Nos. 5–7, 17–20 and 23–27 of these Acts are reproduced below. The remainder can be obtained by direct application to the OECD Secretariat, 2 rue André Pascal, 75775 Paris Cedex.

RESOLUTION OF THE COUNCIL ON WORKING RELATIONS WITH THE UNITED NATIONS IN REGARD TO THE ENVIRONMENT

(adopted by the Council at its 352nd meeting on 12th March, 1974)

The Council,

Having regard to Article 12(b) of the Convention on the Organisation for Economic Co-operation and Development of 14th December, 1960;

Having regard to Rule 10 of the Rules of Procedure of the Organisation;

Considering the close relationship between the United Nations Environment Programme and the activities of the Environment Committee under the terms of reference assigned to it by the Council;

Considering that a regular exchange of documents on the execution of the respective programmes and the attendance of observers at meetings held on either side are calculated to ensure valuable liaison between the two Organisations in regard to the environment;

DECIDES:

1. The Secretary-General is authorised to transmit to the Executive Director of the United Nations Environment Programme such documents of the Environment Committee or of its sub-groups as the Secretary-General deems suitable.

2. The Secretary-General may invite the Executive Director of the United Nations Environment Programme or his representative to attend with observer status meetings of the Environment Committee or its sub-groups under the conditions laid down in Rule 10 of the Rules of Procedure.

ARRANGEMENT DE COOPERATION ENTRE LES SECRETARIATS DE L'ORGANISATION DE COOPERATION ET DE DEVELOPPEMENT ECONOMIQUES ET DE L'ORGANISATION INTERGOUVERNEMENTALE CONSULTATIVE DE LA NAVIGATION MARITIME

Echange de Lettres

Lettre du Secrétaire général de l'OMCI au Secrétaire général de l'OCDE

Ref: A1/A/5 – OECD

Organisation Intergouvernementale
Consultative de la Navigation Maritime
101–104 Piccadilly
Londres W1V OAE

Londres, le 5 février 1974

Monsieur le Secrétaire général,

J'ai l'honneur de vous informer que l'Assemblée de l'Organisation Intergouvernementale Consultative de la Navigation Maritime (OMCI) a approuvé la décision du Conseil de cette Organisation autorisant le Secrétaire général à conclure avec le Secrétariat de l'Organisation de Coopération et de Développement Economiques (OCDE) un Arrangement de Coopération pour les questions d'intérêt commun aux deux Organisations.

En vertu de cette autorisation et eu égard aux consultations qui ont eu lieu à ce sujet entre les Secrétariats de l'OMCI et de l'OCDE, je propose maintenant la conclusion, entre les Secrétariats de nos deux Organisations, d'un Arrangement de Coopération s'établissant comme suit:

1. Les Secrétariats de l'OMCI et de l'OCDE coopéreront et se consulteront sur les questions d'intérêt commun aux deux Organisations, conformément aux arrangements qu'elles concluront périodiquement.

2. Les Secrétariats de l'OMCI et de l'OCDE procéderont à des échanges d'informations et de documents sur les questions d'intérêt commun, conformément aux règles et réglementations de leurs Organisations respectives.

3. Le Secrétariat de l'OMCI, lorsqu'il y est autorisé par les règles propres à cette Organisation, invitera le Secrétariat de l'OCDE à se faire représenter aux conférences organisées par l'OMCI, ainsi qu'aux réunions des instances de l'OMCI qui peuvent avoir une incidence sur les sujets qui intéressent l'OCDE. Le Secrétariat de l'OCDE, lorsqu'il est habilité à le faire dans le cadre des règles applicables à l'OCDE, invitera le Secrétariat de l'OMCI à se faire représenter aux réunions traitant de sujets qui intéressent l'OMCI.

4. Ces arrangements seront réexaminés toutes les fois que les Secrétariats de l'OMCI et de l'OCDE le jugeront nécessaire.

5. Le Secrétariat de l'OMCI ou le Secrétariat de l'OCDE peuvent, conformément aux procédures de leurs Organisations respectives, mettre fin à ces arrangements en donnant un préavis de six mois à l'autre partie.

Je vous serais reconnaissant de bien vouloir confirmer que ces arrangements sont également acceptables pour vous. Je considère que la présente lettre et votre réponse à celle-ci constitueront la base des arrangements de coopération entre le Secrétariat de l'OMCI et le Secrétariat de l'OCDE. L'Arrangement prendra effet à la date de votre réponse à la présente lettre.

Je vous prie d'agréer, Monsieur le Secrétaire général, les assurances de ma très haute considération.

(*signé*) C. P. Srivastava
(*dactylographié*) (C. P. Srivastava)
Secrétaire général

ARRANGEMENT OF CO-OPERATION BETWEEN THE SECRETARIATS OF THE ORGANISATION FOR ECONOMIC CO-OPERATION AND DEVELOPMENT AND THE INTER-GOVERNMENTAL MARITIME CONSULTATIVE ORGANIZATION

Exchange of Letters

Letter from the Secretary-General of IMCO to the Secretary-General of OECD

Ref: A1/A/5-OECD

Inter-Governmental Maritime
Consultative Organization
101–104 Piccadilly
London W1V OAE

5 February, 1974

Dear Mr. van Lennep,

I have the honour to inform you that the Assembly of the Inter-Governmental Maritime Consultative Organization (IMCO) has endorsed the decision of the Council of the Organization authorising the Secretary-General to conclude an Arrangement of Co-operation with the Secretariat of the Organisation for Economic Co-operation and Development (OECD) in matters of mutual interest to the two Organizations.

Acting on this authority and in the light of the consultations which have taken place between the Secretariats of IMCO and the OECD on this subject, I now have the honour to propose the conclusion of an Arrangement of Co-operation between our two Secretariats on the following terms:

1. The Secretariats of IMCO and the OECD shall co-operate and consult with each other on matters of common interest to the two Organizations in accordance with arrangements to be made from time to time between them.

2. The Secretariats of IMCO and the OECD shall exchange information and documentation on matters of mutual interest, in accordance with the rules and regulations of their respective Organizations.

3. The Secretariat of IMCO shall, when authorized by the relevant IMCO rules, invite the Secretariat of OECD to send representatives to conferences convened by IMCO and to meetings of IMCO organs which may have a bearing on subjects of interest to OECD. The Secretariat of OECD shall, when authorized to do so in accordance with applicable OECD rules, invite the Secretariat of IMCO to send representatives to attend meetings dealing with subjects of concern to IMCO.

4. These arrangements shall be reconsidered as and when the Secretariats of IMCO and the OECD deem it to be necessary.

5. The Secretariat of IMCO or the Secretariat of the OECD may, in accordance with their respective procedures terminate these arrangements by giving six months' notice to the other party.

I should be grateful if you would confirm that these arrangements are equally acceptable to you. It is my understanding that this letter and your reply to it will constitute the basis of the arrangements of co-operation between the Secretariat of IMCO and the Secretariat of the OECD. The arrangement shall enter into force on the date of your reply to this letter.

Yours sincerely,
(signed) C. P. Srivastava
(typed) (C. P. Srivastava)
Secretary-General

Réponse du Secrétaire général de l'OCDE au Secrétaire général de l'OMCI

E1-1525 Paris, le 26 mars 1974

Monsieur le Secrétaire général,

J'ai l'honneur d'accuser la réception de votre lettre A1/A/5-OECD en date du 5 février 1974, rédigée dans ces termes:

,,J'ai l'honneur de vous informer que l'Assemblée de l'Organisation Intergouvernementale Consultative de la Navigation Maritime (OMCI) a approuvé la décision du Conseil de cette Organisation autorisant le Secrétaire général à conclure avec le Secrétariat de l'Organisation de Coopération et de Développement Economiques (OCDE) un Arrangement de Coopération pour les questions d'intérêt commun aux deux Organisations.

En vertu de cette autorisation et eu régard aux consultations qui ont eu lieu à ce sujet entre les Secrétariats de l'OMCI et de l'OCDE, je propose maintenant la conclusion entre les Secrétariats de nos deux Organisations d'un Arrangement de Coopération s'établissant comme suit:

1. Les Secrétariats de l'OMCI et de l'OCDE coopéreront et se consulteront sur les questions d'intérêt commun aux deux Organisations, conformément aux arrangements qu'elles concluront périodiquement.

2. Les Secrétariats de l'OMCI et de l'OCDE procéderont à des échanges d'informations et de documents sur les questions d'intérêt commun, conformément aux règles et aux réglementations de leurs Organisations respectives.

3. Le Secrétariat de l'OMCI, lorsqu'il y est autorisé par les règles propres à cette Organisation, invitera le Secrétariat de l'OCDE à se faire représenter aux conférences organisées par l'OMCI, ainsi qu'aux réunions des instances de l'OMCI qui peuvent avoir une incidence sur les sujets qui intéressent l'OCDE. Le Secrétariat de l'OCDE, lorsqu'il est habilité à le faire dans le cadre des règles applicables à l'OCDE, invitera le Secrétariat de l'OMCI à se faire représenter aux réunions traitant de sujets qui intéressent l'OMCI.

4. Ces arrangements seront réexaminés toutes les fois que les Secrétariats de l'OMCI et de l'OCDE le jugeront nécessaire.

5. Le Secrétariat de l'OMCI ou le Secrétariat de l'OCDE peuvent, conformément aux procédures de leurs Organisations respectives, mettre fin à ces arrangements en donnant un préavis de six mois à l'autre partie.

Je vous serais reconnaissant de bien vouloir confirmer que ces arrangements sont également acceptables pour vous. Je considère que la présente lettre et votre réponse à celle-ci constitueront la base des arrangements de coopération entre le Secrétariat de l'OMCI et le Secrétariat de l'OCDE. L'Arrangement prendra effet à la date de votre réponse à la présente lettre.''

J'ai l'honneur de vous informer que j'ai soumis cette communication au Conseil de l'OCDE qui, le 26 mars 1974, m'a autorisé à accepter les propositions qu'elle contient. En conséquence, ainsi que vous le suggérez dans le dernier paragraphe de votre lettre, cette lettre et la présente réponse constituent la base de l'Arrangement de Coopération entre le Secrétariat de l'OMCI et le Secrétariat de l'OCDE et l'Arrangement prend effet à compter de ce jour.

Je vous prie d'agréer, Monsieur le Secrétaire général, les assurances de ma très haute considération.

(*signé*) E. van Lennep
(*dactylographié*) (E. van Lennep)
Secrétaire général

Reply by the Secretary-General of OECD to the Secretary-General of IMCO

EL-1525 26th March, 1975

Dear Mr. Srivastava,

I have the honour to acknowledge receipt of your letter A1/A/5-OECD of 5th February, 1974 in the following terms:

"I have the honour to inform you that the Assembly of the Inter-Governmental Maritime Consultative Organization (IMCO) has endorsed the decision of the Council of the Organization authorising the Secretary-General to conclude an Arrangement of Co-operation with the Secretariat of the Organisation for Economic Co-operation and Development (OECD) in matters of mutual interest to the two Organizations.

Acting on this authority and in the light of the consultations which have taken place between the Secretariats of IMCO and the OECD on this subject, I now have the honour to propose the conclusion of an Arrangement of Co-operation between our two Secretariats on the following terms:

1. The Secretariats of IMCO and the OECD shall co-operate and consult with each other on matters of common interest to the two Organizations in accordance with arrangements to be made from time to time between them.

2. The Secretariats of IMCO and the OECD shall exchange information and documentation on matters of mutual interest, in accordance with the rules and regulations of their respective Organizations.

3. The Secretariat of IMCO shall, when authorized by the relevant IMCO rules, invite the Secretariat of OECD to send representatives to conferences convened by IMCO and to meetings of IMCO organs which may have a bearing on subjects of interest to OECD. The Secretariat of OECD shall, when authorized to do so in accordance with applicable OECD rules, invite the Secretariat of IMCO to send representatives to attend meetings dealing with subjects of concern to IMCO.

4. These arrangements shall be reconsidered as and when the Secretariats of IMCO and the OECD deem it to be necessary.

5. The Secretariat of IMCO or the Secretariat of the OECD may, in accordance with their respective procedures, terminate these arrangements by giving six months' notice to the other party.

I schould be grateful if you would confirm that these arrangements are equally acceptable to you. It is my understanding that this letter and your reply to it will constitute the basis of the arrangements of cooperation between the Secretariat of IMCO and the Secretariat of the OECD. The arrangement shall enter into force on the date of your reply to this letter."

I have the honour to inform you that I submitted this communication to the Council of OECD and that on 26th March, 1974 the Council authorised me to accept the proposals therein contained. Accordingly, as suggested in the last paragraph of your letter, that letter and the present reply will constitute the basis of the Arrangement of Co-operation between the Secretariat of IMCO and the Secretariat of OECD, and the Arrangement shall enter into force as from today's date.

Yours sincerely,
(*signed*) E. van Lennep
(*typed*) (E. van Lennep)
Secretary-General

COMMUNIQUE

Approuvé par le Conseil à sa 359ème Séance le 30 mai 1974

1. Le Conseil de l'OCDE, siégeant au niveau des Ministres, s'est réuni à Paris les 29 et 30 mai 1974, sous la présidence de M. Antonio Giolitti, Ministre du Budget et de la Programmation Economique de l'Italie. Les Ministres se sont félicités de cette occasion de procéder à un échange de vues à la lumière des problèmes économiques qui se posent actuellement sur le plan international, et ils ont souligné le rôle constructif que la coopération au sein de l'OCDE peut jouer en contribuant à résoudre ces problèmes.

Les problèmes

2. Les Ministres ont identifié, au premier rang des préoccupations, trois principaux problèmes dont la solution exige une coordination internationale plus poussée des politiques nationales:

- Le problème généralisé de l'inflation, qui avait déjà pris des proportions préoccupantes, s'est trouvé aggravé par la forte augmentation des prix du pétrole; les mesures anti-inflationnistes doivent être soigneusement choisies de façon à éviter de graves problèmes de chômage.
- La situation des paiements internationaux s'étant profondément modifiée du fait de la hausse des prix du pétrole, la balance des paiements courants de la plupart des pays de l'OCDE est devenue largement déficitaire.
- Certains pays en développement, dont quelques-uns des plus pauvres du monde, voient leur situation économique et financière cruellement aggravée.

Les solutions

3. Les gouvernements sont résolus à aborder tous ces problèmes en commun et simultanément, et les Ministres ont souligné leur détermination de mettre au point un ensemble cohérent de mesures à cette fin. Ils reconnaissent notamment que les problèmes particuliers d'équilibre intérieur et extérieur des différents pays ne sauraient être résolus de façon acceptable par une action qui ne ferait qu'exporter ces problèmes vers d'autres pays.

4. *Inflation et emploi.* Les Ministres reconnaissent que, dans tous les pays de l'OCDE, les taux actuels d'inflation constituent une menace pour le progrès économique et social. Leurs gouvernements considèrent par conséquent comme un objectif hautement prioritaire de réduire le taux de hausse des prix. Ils s'efforceront de maintenir l'activité économique à des niveaux satisfaisants et s'abstiendront de mener des politiques qui auraient pour effet de transférer les problèmes d'emploi d'un pays à l'autre. Mais les Ministres sont convenus qu'il faut, à l'heure actuelle, veiller avec le plus grand soin à éviter l'apparition d'un excès de demande dans la zone de l'OCDE, et que les politiques budgétaires et monétaires doivent être adaptées à cette fin. Ils ont aussi souligné la nécessité de recourir, dans les cas où c'est possible, à d'autres mesures, de caractère plus sélectif, visant à accroître l'offre et à tempérer les anticipations inflationnistes. Et ils sont convenus que l'OCDE devrait, en tenant compte des travaux d'autres organisations internationales, chercher à définir des politiques propres à assurer une plus grande stabilité des marchés des produits de base ainsi que des approvisionnements suffisants à des prix qui soient équitables tant pour les pays producteurs que pour les pays consommateurs.

5. *Politique en matière d'échanges et de paiements.* La nécessité pour les pays de l'OCDE de s'adapter à la nouvelle situation de leurs balances des

COMMUNIQUE

Approved by the Council at its 359th Meeting on 30th May, 1974

1. The Council of the OECD met at Ministerial level in Paris on 29th and 30th May, 1974, under the Chairmanship of Mr. Antonio Giolitti, Minister for the Budget and Economic Planning of Italy. Ministers welcomed this opportunity to have an exchange of views in the light of the present international economic problems and underlined the constructive role which co-operation in the OECD can play in helping to solve these problems.

The Problems

2. Ministers identified three main outstanding problems which need further international co-ordination of national policies if they are to be solved:

- The widespread problem of inflation, already of serious proportions, has been aggravated by the sharp increase in the price of oil; anti-inflationary policies must be carefully chosen so as to avoid serious unemployment problems.
- For most OECD countries the international payments situation, radically altered by the oil price increase, has moved into substantial deficit on current account.
- Certain developing countries, including some of the poorest nations in the world, are facing a grievously worsened economic and financial situation.

The Response

3. Governments are resolved to approach all these problems jointly and concurrently, and Ministers emphasized their determination to develop a coherent set of measures to this end. In particular, they recognise that no acceptable solution to individual countries' problems of internal and external balance can be found in action which only shifts those problems across frontiers.

4. *Inflation and Employment*. Ministers recognise that, in all OECD countries, the present rates of inflation constitute a threat to economic and social progress. Their Governments therefore accord high priority to reducing the rate of price increases. They will seek to maintain economic activity at satisfactory levels and avoid policies that would transfer employment problems from one country to another. But Ministers agreed that great care is at present needed to avoid the emergence of excess demand in the OECD area, and that fiscal and monetary policies have to be shaped to this end. They also emphasized the need to use, where feasible, other, more selective, measures to increase supply and reduce inflationary expectations. And they agreed that OECD, taking account of work in other international bodies, should seek to identify policies conducive to better market stability of primary products with adequate supplies at prices equitable both for producing and for consuming countries.

5. *Trade and Payments Policy*. The need for OECD countries to adapt to the new balance of payments situation is a problem that, particularly, has to be tackled on an international basis. Governments are determined to take all appropriate action to limit the size and duration of the weakening of their current account positions. But they recognise that, in the years immediately ahead, a deterioration has to be accepted because of the oil price-rises. Ministers have also recognised that the financing of external

paiements est un problème qu'il importe tout particulièrement de traiter au plan international. Les gouvernements sont résolus à prendre toutes mesures appropriées pour limiter l'ampleur et la durée de l'affaiblissement de leurs balances des paiements courants. Mais ils reconnaissent que, dans le proche avenir, il leur faudra accepter une certaine détérioration de leur position du fait de la hausse des prix du pétrole. Les Ministres ont aussi reconnu que le financement des déficits extérieurs qui persisteraient en dépit de la mise en œuvre de mesures d'ajustement appropriées constituera un problème difficile pour certains pays Membres.

6. Dans ces circonstances, les Ministres ont conscience du danger que pourraient comporter des politiques visant à améliorer les positions compétitives respectives de leurs pays, mais dont les effets seraient préjudiciables pour tous, et ils sont convenus qu'il est nécessaire de prévenir toute nouvelle action unilatérale qui pourrait nuire aux relations économiques internationales. Ils ont, dans le cadre d'une action globale pour faire face à la situation actuelle, publié la Déclaration ci-jointe dans laquelle ils affirment la détermination de leurs gouvernements de s'abstenir, pendant une période d'un an, de recourir à de nouvelles restrictions portant sur les échanges et les autres opérations courantes ainsi qu'à des mesures visant à stimuler artificiellement les exportations visibles ou invisibles, qui seraient contraires aux objectifs de la Déclaration.

7. Parallèlement, dans cette Déclaration, les gouvernements conviennent de coopérer pleinement pour faciliter le financement des déficits décrits ci-dessus, et indiquent qu'ils sont prêts à considérer les arrangements appropriés qui pourraient se révéler nécessaires à cet égard.

8. En outre, les Ministres ont réaffirmé leur soutien aux négociations commerciales multilatérales dans le cadre du GATT et ont insisté pour que ces négociations reçoivent toute la priorité voulue. Ils ont souligné l'importance que revêtent, dans la situation présente, ces nouveaux efforts pour libérer les échanges.

9. Les Ministres ont noté avec satisfaction l'intensification des travaux de l'Organisation sur les questions ayant trait aux investissements internationaux et aux entreprises multinationales, en vue d'améliorer la coopération sur ces questions.

10. *Coopération pour le développement.* Les Ministres ont noté que les Membres du Comité d'Aide au Développement (CAD) ainsi que certains autres pays Membres de l'OCDE feront tous les efforts possibles pour maintenir et accroître leur aide publique au développement en vue de continuer à promouvoir les progrès économiques et sociaux des pays en développement.

11. Les Ministres se sont déclarés particulièrement préoccupés par les graves problèmes économiques que connaissent ceux des pays en développement à faible revenu qui sont les plus durement touchés par la hausse des prix du pétrole et d'autres importations essentielles. Bien qu'il n'existe pas encore d'estimation généralement acceptée quant au montant de l'aide spéciale nécessaire à ces pays, ils ont noté que, d'après les études préliminaires de certaines organisations internationales, ces besoins pourraient être de l'ordre de 3 à 4 milliards de dollars d'ici la fin de 1975.

12. Les Ministres des pays qui sont Membres du CAD et de certains autres pays Membres de l'OCDE, reconnaissant la nécessité de contribuer de façon constructive à la suite à donner à la Sixième Session spéciale de l'Assemblée générale des Nations Unies sur les matières premières et le développement, sont convenus de faire tous les efforts possibles pour contribuer d'une manière appropriée, tant à titre bilatéral que dans le cadre des institutions multilatérales compétentes, à l'aide spéciale nécessaire aux pays en développement les plus durement touchés. Le CAD examinera les progrès des efforts d'assistance entrepris par ses Membres ainsi que toutes autres mesures additionnelles qui pourraient se révéler appropriées. Les Ministres ont de nouveau exprimé l'avis que tous les pays du monde qui

deficits persisting despite the implementation of appropriate adjustment policies will constitute a difficult problem for some Member countries.

6. In these circumstances, Ministers are conscious of the special danger of mutually conflicting policies to improve national competitive positions and agreed on the need to prevent new unilateral action which may have a detrimental impact on international economic relations. They have, as part of an overall response to the current situation, issued the attached Declaration, stating the determination of their Governments, for a period of a year, to avoid recourse to new restrictions on trade or other current account transactions and the artificial stimulation of visible and current invisible exports, which would be contrary to the objectives of the Declaration.

7. The Declaration, at the same time, also expresses the agreement of Governments to co-operate fully to facilitate the financing of the deficits described above, and their readiness to consider appropriate arrangements which may prove necessary in this respect.

8. In addition, Ministers reaffirmed their support for the multilateral trade negotiations in the framework of the GATT and urged that these negotiations be regarded as a matter of priority. They stressed the importance in the present situation of these new efforts to liberalise trade.

9. Ministers welcomed the intensification of the Organisation's work on the issues related to international investment and to multinational enterprises, with a view to improving cooperation on these issues.

10. *Development Co-operation.* Ministers noted that Members of the Development Assistance Committee (DAC) and some other Member countries of the OECD will make strenuous efforts to maintain and enlarge the flow of their official development assistance with a view to promoting further economic and social progress of developing countries.

11. Ministers expressed particular concern at the acute economic problems of those developing countries with low income which are most seriously affected by the increase in the prices of oil and other essential imports. Although there is as yet no generally agreed estimate as to the amount of special assistance required by these countries, they noted the preliminary studies made by certain international organisations indicating that these requirements might amount, as an order of magnitude, to some $3–$4 billion up to the end of 1975.

12. Ministers of the countries which are Members of the DAC and some other OECD Members, recognising the need to contribute constructively to the follow-up of the Sixth Special Session of the General Assembly of the United Nations on Raw Materials and Development, agreed to make every effort to contribute in an appropriate manner to the special relief needed by the most seriously affected developing countries, bilaterally and within the framework of the appropriate international institutions. The DAC will review the progress of its Members' relief efforts under way and any further steps which may be appropriate. Ministers reiterated the view that all countries throughout the world in a position to do so should share the responsibility to contribute to the special relief of the most seriously affected developing countries.

13. Ministers agreed that all possible efforts should be made to ensure that shipments of fertilizers to developing countries with urgent needs are maintained at their previous level and that, through financial and technical assistance, encouragement should be given to increased production of fertilizers in developing countries.

14. *Energy.* Ministers discussed the consequences of recent developments in the world energy market. They agreed that a strong co-operative effort is needed if serious damage to the economic and social welfare of the OECD community as well as to the world economy is to be avoided. Ministers underlined their will to intensify international co-operation on energy problems and to strengthen OECD capability in this field.

sont en mesure de le faire devraient partager la responsabilité de contribuer à l'aide spéciale aux pays en développement les plus durement touchés.

13. Les Ministres sont convenus que tous les efforts possibles devraient être faits pour assurer que les livraisons d'engrais aux pays en développement qui en ont un besoin urgent soient maintenus à leur niveau antérieur, et qu'il faudrait encourager, au moyen d'une assistance financière et technique appropriée, l'accroissement de la production d'engrais dans les pays en développement.

14. *Energie*. Les Ministres ont examiné les conséquences de l'évolution intervenue récemment sur le marché mondial de l'énergie. Ils sont convenus qu'un vigoureux effort de coopération est indispensable si l'on veut éviter que le bien-être économique et social de la communauté des pays de l'OCDE ainsi que l'économie mondiale ne soient gravement affectés. Les Ministres ont souligné leur volonté d'intensifier la coopération internationale sur les problèmes énergétiques et de renforcer la capacité de l'OCDE dans ce domaine.

15. Les Ministres ont noté que les travaux relatifs à l'Evaluation des problèmes et des politiques énergétiques à long terme entrepris par l'OCDE ont été accélérés et que cette évaluation sera à la disposition des gouvernements en octobre 1974 au plus tard. Ils ont souligné la nécessité d'assurer l'approvisionnement en énergie en évitant autant que possible de porter atteinte à l'environnement.

16. Les Ministres ont souligné l'importance des travaux de l'OCDE, déjà en cours, dans les domaines de la conservation de l'énergie et de la limitation de la demande, du développement accéléré des sources d'énergie classiques, de la répartition du pétrole en temps de crise et de pénuries graves et de la recherche et du développement énergétiques. Les travaux consacrés à ces questions ont été accélérés afin que des décisions politiques puissent être prises sans retard.

DECLARATION

Adopteé par les gouvernements de pays Membres de l'OCDE le 30 mai 1974

LES GOUVERNEMENTS DES PAYS MEMBRES DE L'OCDE, *

Considérant que, parmi d'autres facteurs, la hausse des prix du pétrole aggrave les problèmes économiques auxquels les pays Membres se trouvent confrontés, notamment le problème de l'inflation, en même temps qu'elle engendre de nouveaux problèmes structurels, et qu'elle provoque une modification sans précédent dans la structure des balances des paiements, et en particulier une dégradation de la balance courante de l'ensemble des pays Membres;

Considérant que les pays Membres sont tous affectés, encore qu'à des degrés divers, par cette évolution;

CONVIENNENT:

que la nature et l'ampleur des problèmes, mentionnés ci-dessus, auxquels doivent faire face les pays Membres, ainsi qu'un certain nombre de pays en développement, appellent une vaste action en coopération dans les domaines des politiques concernant l'économie, les échanges, les finances, la monnaie, les investissements et le développement;

que le financement des déficits des paiements internationaux constitu-

* La mention de gouvernements est réputée valoir aussi pour les Communautés Européennes.

15. Ministers noted that the work on the Long-Term Assessment of energy and related policies being prepared by the OECD has been accelerated and that the assessment will be at the disposal of Governments in October 1974 at the latest. They underlined the necessity to ensure energy supplies without undue, adverse impact on environmental conditions.

16. Ministers stressed the importance of OECD's work, already under way, in the fields of energy conservation and demand restraint, accelerated development of conventional energy sources, allocation of oil supplies in times of emergency and severe shortages, and energy research and development. The work on these subjects has been speeded up in order to permit early policy decisions.

DECLARATION

Adopted by the Governments of OECD Member countries on 30th May, 1974

GOVERNMENTS OF OECD MEMBER COUNTRIES*

Considering that, among other factors, the rise in oil prices is aggravating the economic problems confronting Member countries, and notably the problem of inflation, as well as causing additional structural problems, and that it is creating an unprecedented change in the structure of the balance of payments and, in particular, a deterioration of current accounts of Member countries as a whole;

Considering that all Member countries are affected by these developments though in varying degrees;

AGREE:

that the nature and size of the above-mentioned problems facing Member countries as well as a number of developing countries call for wide co-operative action in the fields of economic, trade, financial, monetary, investment and development policies;

that the financing of international payments deficits will constitute a difficult problem for certain Member countries and that, accordingly,

* Including the European Communities.

era un problème délicat pour certains pays Membres, et que, en conséquence, les pays Membres coopéreront pleinement pour faciliter ce financement et sont prêts à considérer les arrangements appropriés qui pourraient se révéler nécessaires à cet égard;

que des mesures commerciales ou des mesures visant les autres opérations courantes prises unilatéralement par un ou plusieurs pays Membres pour remédier à cette situation aggraveraient les problèmes des autres pays et que, si elles étaient généralisées, elles iraient à l'encontre du but recherché et auraient un effet déprimant sur l'économie mondiale;

que les pays ont la responsabilité, tant comme importateurs que comme exportateurs, d'éviter que les courants d'échanges réguliers soient perturbés;

qu'il est donc nécessaire de prendre d'urgence, et sans préjuger l'issue des négociations monétaires et commerciales, un engagement commun ayant pour objectif de prévenir toute nouvelle action unilatérale qui pourrait avoir un effet préjudiciable sur les relations économiques internationales;

DECLARENT LEUR DETERMINATION, en ayant à l'esprit ce qui précède et pour une période d'un an,

(*a*) d'éviter de prendre des mesures unilatérales, de caractère général ou spécifique, visant à restreindre les importations ou des mesures analogues concernant les autres opérations courantes, qui seraient contraires aux objectifs de la présente Déclaration;

(*b*) d'éviter de prendre des mesures pour stimuler artificiellement les exportations ou d'autres opérations courantes; et notamment ne se livreront pas à une concurrence destructrice dans les aides officielles au crédit à l'exportation et chercheront à entreprendre, en coopération, des actions appropriées à cet effet dans l'avenir immédiat;

(*c*) d'éviter d'imposer des restrictions à l'exportation qui seraient contraires aux objectifs de la présente Déclaration;

(*d*) de se consulter mutuellement, en utilisant pleinement les procédures générales de consultation au sein de l'OCDE, pour s'assurer que la présente Déclaration est appliquée de façon adéquate;

(*e*) de mettre en œuvre la présente Déclaration conformément à leurs obligations internationales, en tenant dûment compte des besoins spécifiques des pays en développement.

RECOMMANDATION DU CONSEIL SUR L'ANALYSE DES EFFETS SUR L'ENVIRONNEMENT DES PROJETS PUBLICS ET PRIVES IMPORTANTS

(*Adoptée par le Conseil à sa 372ème séance, le 14 novembre 1974*)

Le Conseil,

Vu l'article 5(b) de la Convention relative à l'Organisation de Coopération et de Développement Economiques, en date du 14 décembre 1960;

Vu la Recommandation du Conseil, en date du 26 mai 1972, sur les Principes directeurs relatifs aux aspects économiques des politiques de l'environnement sur le plan international [C (72) 128];

Considérant que dans l'élaboration de leurs programmes d'action les gouvernements devraient tenir compte des objectifs concernant l'environnement au même titre que des objectifs économiques et sociaux;

Considérant que le moyen le plus efficace de réaliser les objectifs concernant l'environnement est de prévenir les effets nuisibles à l'environnement, soit dans le territoire du pays même, soit au-delà de ses frontières;

Considérant que le fait de prévoir et d'analyser les conséquences possibles sur l'environnement des décisions et des actions envisagées par les

Member countries will co-operate fully to facilitate such financing and are ready to consider appropriate arrangements which may prove necessary in this respect;

that unilateral trade or other current account measures by one or more Member countries to deal with this situation would aggravate the problems of other countries and, if generalised, would be self-defeating and have a depressing effect on the world economy;

that countries have responsibilities both as importers and exporters to avoid disruption of regular trade flows;

that, as a matter of urgency and without prejudice to the outcome of the monetary and trade negotiations, there is therefore a need for a joint undertaking having as its objective to prevent new unilateral action which may have a detrimental impact on international economic relations;

DECLARE THEIR DETERMINATION, in the light of the foregoing and for a period of one year.

(*a*) to avoid having recourse to unilateral measures, of either a general or a specific nature, to restrict imports or having recourse to similar measures on the other current accounts transactions, which would be contrary to the objectives of the present Declaration;

(*b*) to avoid measures to stimulate exports or other current account transactions artificially; and, inter alia, abstain from destructive competition in official support of export credit and aim at taking appropriate co-operative actions to this effect in the immediate future;

(*c*) to avoid export restrictions which would be contrary to the objectives of the present Declaration;

(*d*) to consult with each other, making full use of the general procedures of consultation within OECD, in order to assure that the present Declaration is properly implemented;

(*e*) to implement the present Declaration in accordance with their international obligations and with due regard to the special needs of developing countries.

RECOMMENDATION OF THE COUNCIL OF THE ANALYSIS OF THE ENVIRONMENTAL CONSEQUENCES OF SIGNIFICANT PUBLIC AND PRIVATE PROJECTS

(*Adopted by the Council at its 372nd Meeting on 14th November, 1974*)

The Council,

Having regard to Article 5(b) of the Convention on the Organisation for Economic Co-operation and Development of 14th December, 1960;

Having regard to the Recommendation of the Council of 26th May, 1972, on Guiding Principles concerning International Economic Aspects of Environmental Policies [C(72)128];

Considering that environmental goals should be considered equally with other economic and social goals in the establishment of government programmes;

Considering that the prevention of adverse environmental effects is the most effective way of realising environmental policy goals either within a country's territory or beyond its boundaries;

Considering that one helpful way to realise environmental goals is through the forecasting and description of significant consequences to the secteurs public et privé peut contribuer à la réalisation des objectifs concernant l'environnement;

Sur la proposition du Comité de l'Environnement;

I. RECOMMANDE que les gouvernements Membres:

1. mettent au point des procédures et des méthodes pour prévoir et analyser les conséquences sur l'environnement des projets publics et privés importants susceptibles d'avoir une incidence notable sur la qualité de l'environnement;

2. échangent des informations en matière d'environnement qui puissent les aider à prévoir et analyser les conséquences sur l'environnement des programmes ou des projets envisagés.

II. CHARGE le Comité de l'Environnement d'évaluer les actions entreprises en application de la présente Recommandation et de faire rapport au Conseil à ce sujet.

RECOMMANDATION DU CONSEIL SUR LA PREVENTION ET LA REDUCTION DES NUISANCES ACOUSTIQUES

(*Adoptée par le Conseil à sa 372ème Séance, le 14 novembre 1974*)

LE CONSEIL,

Vu l'article 5 b) de la Convention relative à l'Organisation de Coopération et de Développement Economiques, en date du 14 décembre 1960;

Vu la Recommandation du Conseil, en date du 26 mai 1972, sur les Principes directeurs relatifs aux aspects économiques des politiques de l'environnement sur le plan international [C(72) 128];

Considérant que, parmi les nombreux problèmes liés à la qualité de l'environnement urbain, les nuisances acoustiques constituent l'un des plus importants;

Considérant que ces nuisances s'étendent rapidement dans l'espace et dans le temps, affectant la vie d'un nombre sans cesse croissant d'individus, en particulier dans les zones urbaines;

Considérant qu'un excès d'émission sonore présente un danger pour la santé et le bien-être des populations des pays Membres;

Considérant qu'une planification appropriée peut atténuer dans une large mesure les nuisances acoustiques;

Considérant que de nombreux produits, donnant lieu à des échanges internationaux, notamment les véhicules et les aéronefs qui traversent les frontières nationales, constituent des sources sonores;

Considérant qu'une prise de conscience plus poussée de la part du public quant à la nécessité de réduire les émissions sonores évitables peut présenter de grands avantages;

Considérant la nécessité d'une action énergique par les pouvoirs publics afin de restaurer un environnement exempt de nuisances acoustiques excessives;

Sur la proposition du Comité de l'Environnement;

I. RECOMMANDE:

1. Que les gouvernements des pays Membres intensifient leurs efforts en vue de prévenir les nuisances acoustiques et de lutter contre elles par une planification préalable et par l'application des meilleurs techniques existantes, compte tenu du coût de leur mise en oeuvre.

2. Que ces efforts portent notamment sur les points suivants:

(*a*) la promulgation de normes limitant l'émission sonore des produit-qui constituent des sources sonores importantes et, en particulier, les vés environment resulting from proposed decisions and actions, both at public and private levels.

On the proposal of the Environment Committee;

I. RECOMMENDS that Member Governments:

1. establish procedures and methodologies for forecasting and describing the environmental consequences of significant public and private projects likely to have a major impact on the quality of the environment;

2. exchange information on environmental matters which would help them to forecast and describe the environmental effects of proposed programmes or projects.

II. INSTRUCTS the Environment Committee to assess the action taken pursuant to this Recommendation and to report thereon to the Council.

RECOMMENDATION OF THE COUNCIL ON NOISE PREVENTION AND ABATEMENT

(*Adopted by the Council at its 372nd Meeting on 14th November, 1974*)

The Council,

Having regard to Article 5(b) of the Convention on the Organisation for Economic Co-operation and Development of 14th December, 1960;

Having regard to the Recommendation of the Council of 26th May, 1972, on Guiding Principles concerning International Economic Aspects of Environmental Policies [C(72)128];

Considering that among the many problems related to the quality of the urban environment, the nuisance caused by noise is one of the most significant;

Considering that noise nuisance is rapidly extending in space and time, affecting the lives of ever growing numbers of people, particularly in urban areas;

Considering that excessive noise presents a danger to the health and welfare of the Member countries' populations;

Considering that careful planning can mitigate the impact of noise to a significant extent;

Considering that noise is caused by numerous products entering international trade and notably is caused by vehicles and aircraft which cross national frontiers;

Considering the benefits to be gained from making the public more aware of the need to act in a manner conducive to reducing unneccesary noise;

Considering the need for forceful action by public authorities to restore an environment free from excessive noise;

On the proposal of the Environment Committee;

I. RECOMMENDS:

1. That Member Governments strengthen their noise prevention and abatement efforts through advance planning and through the application of the best available technology, taking into account the cost of implementation.

2. That these efforts include the following elements:

(*a*) the promulgation of noise emission standards for products which are major sources of noise, and in particular, transportation equipment, conhicules de transport, les engins de chantier et les moteurs à combustion interne de tous types;

(*b*) la nécessité de considérer l'incidence des nuisances acoustiques et la reconnaissance qu'il convient de réduire et de prévenir ces nuisances lors de la planification, de la conception, de l'approbation, de la construction et de l'exploitation de tous les grands ouvrages, tels que les logements, les routes, les réseaux de transports en commun, les aéroports, les zones industrielles, etc.;

(*c*) des programmes d'enseignement et des campagnes d'information appropriés, destinés à mieux faire comprendre au public la nécessité de se comporter de façon à éviter la production de nuisances acoustiques superflues.

II. CHARGE le Comité de l'Environnement de poursuivre, afin d'appuyer les actions ci-dessus, son aide auprès des gouvernements Membres lors de la préparation et de la mise en oeuvre des politiques et programmes visant à prévenir et à réduire les nuisances acoustiques, en considérant par exemple:

(*a*) l'utilité éventuelle, pour compléter la réglementation directe concernant les émissions sonores par les aéronefs, de divers autres moyens de lutte, tels que les redevances sur les aéronefs bruyants, l'institution de politiques de zonage autour des aéroports associées à un système de planification et de contrôle de l'utilisation des sols, etc.; à cet égard, on tiendra compte des travaux entrepris au sein de l'Organisation de l'Aviation Civile Internationale;

(*b*) certaines formes de compensation, y compris des mesures de protection, lorsque des travaux entrepris par des autorités publiques produisent des effets nuisibles et lorsque les individus lésés n'ont pas la possibilité d'obtenir une réparation légale;

(*c*) l'étiquetage informatif indiquant les caractéristiques acoustiques des produits qui, dans l'environnement urbain, produisent des émissions sonores susceptibles d'avoir des effets nuisibles sur la santé et le bien-être de la population.

III. CHARGE le Comité de l'Environnement d'évaluer les actions entreprises en application de la présente Recommandation et de faire rapport au Conseil à ce sujet.

RECOMMANDATION DU CONSEIL SUR LA LIMITATION DE LA CIRCULATION ET SUR LES MOYENS PEU COUTEUX D'AMELIORER L'ENVIRONNEMENT URBAIN

(*Adoptée par le Conseil à sa 372ème séance, le 14 novembre 1974*)

Le Conseil,

Vu l'article 5 b) de la Convention relative à l'Organisation de Coopération et de Développement Economiques, en date du 14 décembre 1960;

Vu la Recommandation du Conseil, en date du 26 mai 1972, sur les Principes directeurs relatifs aux aspects économiques des politiques de l'environnement sur le plan international [C (72) 128];

Considérant que les zones urbaines constituent le lieu d'habitation d'une proportion de plus en plus importante de la population des pays Membres;

Considérant que la pollution de l'air, le bruit, les encombrements et les accidents qui résultent de la circulation des véhicules automobiles entravent sérieusement les efforts visant à améliorer la qualité de la vie urbaine;

Considérant que la nécessité de réduire la dépendance à l'égard de la struction equipment, and internal combustion engines of all kinds;

(*b*) the requirement to consider the impact of noise and the desirability of reducing existing noise levels and of avoiding the creation of new noise conditions in the planning, design, approval, construction and operation of all major facilities including housing, highways, public transportation systems, airports, industrial developments, etc.;

(c) adequate education programmes and information campaigns designed to make the public more aware of the need to behave in such a manner as to avoid producing unnecessary noise.

II. INSTRUCTS the Environment Committee, in support of the above action, to continue its assistance to Member Governments in the development and implementation of policies and programmes for the prevention and abatement of noise, by considering for example:

(*a*) as a supplement to direct noise emission regulations, and taking into account the work of the International Civil Aviation Organisation, the possible value of various other means of aircraft noise control, such as charges on noisy aircraft, the institution of zoning policies around airports and of associated land use planning and control;

(*b*) some form of compensation, including the provision ot protective measures, where works undertaken by public authorities result in injurious affection and where the individuals concerned lack means of legal redress;

(*c*) the labelling of the noise characteristics of products which, in the urban environment, emit noise capable of adversely affecting the public health and welfare.

III. INSTRUCTS the Environment Committee to assess the action taken pursuant to this Recommendation and to report thereon to the Council.

RECOMMENDATION OF THE COUNCIL ON TRAFFIC LIMITATION AND LOW-COST IMPROVEMENT OF THE URBAN ENVIRONMENT

(*Adopted by the Council at its 372nd Meeting on 14th November 1974*)

The Council,

Having regard to Article 5(b) of the Convention on the Organisation for Economic Co-operation and Development of 14th December, 1960;

Having regard to the Recommendation of the Council of 26th May, 1972, on Guiding Principles concerning International Economic Aspects of Environmental Policies [C(72)128];

Considering that urban areas are the home of a vast and ever growing proportion of the Member countries' populations;

Considering that air pollution, noise, congestion and accidents which result from motorised traffic severely hinder attempts to improve the quality of urban life;

Considering that the need to lessen dependence on private automobiles is reinforced by the necessity to conserve energy resources;

voiture particulière est renforcée par la nécessité d'économiser l'énergie;

Considérant que certaines mesures propres à diminuer les effets nuisibles de la circulation peuvent être mises en oeuvre dans des délais relativement courts, sans requérir nécessairement d'importants investissements en capital;

Considérant que les problèmes d'environnement urbain ne peuvent être réglés par des solutions partielles mais seulement dans le cadre d'une politique urbaine globale;

Sur la proposition du Comité de l'Environnement;

I. RECOMMANDE que les pays Membres:

1. s'efforcent de parvenir à un meilleur équilibre entre les transports collectifs et les transports individuels, en encourageant les autorités locales et autres organismes responsables, en particulier dans les villes encombrées, à développer les services de transport collectif et à en améliorer la qualité, ainsi qu'à encourager l'utilisation de moyens autres que la voiture particulière dans tous les cas où des moyens de remplacement existent ou peuvent être créés;

2. englobent dans les efforts évoqués ci-dessus des mesures d'exploitation et d'autres mesures relativement peu coûteuses telles que la priorité accordée aux autobus, la création de pistes cyclables, l'utilisation collective de véhicules individuels (car pools), les systèmes de régulation de la circulation et du stationnement et l'établissement de zones interdites à la circulation automobile;

3. complètent les mesures ci-dessus par des actions peu coûteuses d'amélioration de l'environnement local comme, par exemple la création de jardins publics, d'espaces verts, d'aires piétonnières et la défense du paysage urbain;

4. appuient et encouragent de nouveaux projets expérimentaux visant à démontrer les possibilités de réalisation et à déterminer les implications financières et les conséquences sur l'environnement et le développement urbain des mesures visées ci-dessus; unissent leurs efforts pour diffuser ces expériences sur le plan international;

5. s'attachent, à plus long terme, à réduire les besoins de transport grâce à une utilisation rationnelle des sols, à une planification des transports et à d'autres mesures influant sur les modes d'activité de l'homme.

II. CHARGE le Comité de l'Environnement:

1. de poursuivre l'examen ainsi que l'évaluation des coûts et de l'efficacité des politiques et des programmes nationaux visant à limiter la circulation automobile en mettant l'accent sur les dispositions dont la mise en oeuvre est relativement peu coûteuse;

2. d'évaluer les actions entreprises en application de la présente Recommandation et de faire rapport au Conseil à ce sujet;

3. d'entreprendre ces travaux en liaison avec d'autres organes appropriés de l'Organisation ainsi qu'avec la Conférence Européenne des Ministres des Transports.

RECOMMANDATION DU CONSEIL SUR LES MESURES REQUISES EN VUE DU RENFORCEMENT DE LA LUTTE CONTRE LA POLLUTION ATMOSPHERIQUE

(*Adoptée par le Conseil à sa 372ème séance, le 14 novembre 1974*)

Le Conseil,

Vu l'article 5 b) de la Convention relative à l'Organisation de Coopération et de Développement Economiques, en date du 14 décembre 1960;

Considering that certain measures to reduce the adverse effects of traffic can be implemented on a relatively short time scale and do not necessarily require large capital investment;

Considering that solutions to urban environmental problems cannot be found on a piecemeal basis but require a comprehensive urban policy approach;

On the proposal of the Environment Committee;

I. RECOMMENDS that Member countries:

1. seek to strike a better balance between private and public transportation by encouraging local authorities and other responsible bodies, particularly in congested cities, to expand and improve the quality of transportation services, and to encourage the use of means of transport other than private automobiles whenever these alternative means are or can be made available;

2. include in the above efforts, traffic management and other measures which can be implemented at relatively low cost – such as bus priority measures, provision of bicycle-ways, car pooling, traffic signal systems, parking control and establishment of car-free areas;

3. complement the above policies with low-cost measures to improve the quality of the local environment, for example through the creation of small parks and open spaces, pedestrian areas, and conservation of the urban landscape;

4. support and encourage further experimental projects aimed at demonstrating the feasibility and financial, environmental and urban development implications of the measures referred to above and co-operate in the international dissemination of this experience;

5. in the longer run, seek to reduce the need for transportation through comprehensive land use and transportation planning and through other measures affecting the patterns of human activities.

II. INSTRUCTS the Environment Committee:

1. to continue its examination of national policies and programmes for traffic limitation and its assessments of their costs and effectiveness with emphasis on measures which can be implemented at relatively low cost;

2. to assess the action taken pursuant to this Recommendation and to report thereon to the Council;

3. to carry out this work in conjunction with other appropriate bodies of the Organisation and with the European Conference of Ministers of Transport.

RECOMMENDATION OF THE COUNCIL ON MEASURES REQUIRED FOR FURTHER AIR POLLUTION CONTROL

(Adopted by the Council at its 372nd Meeting on 14th November, 1974)

The Council,

Having regard to Article 5(b) of the Convention on the Organisation for Economic Co-operation and Development of 14th December, 1960;

Vu la Recommendation du Conseil, en date du 18 juin 1974, sur des directives en vue d'une action ayant pour but de réduire les émissions d'oxyde de soufre et de particules résultant de l'emploi de combustibles dans des installations fixes [C(74) 16 (Final)];

Considérant que l'atmosphère est une ressource essentielle nécessitant une gestion prudente du fait de sa capacité limitée à disperser les nombreuses substances qui y sont rejetées et à s'en épurer;

Considérant qu'il existe des différences parmi les pays et les régions quant aux conditions socio-économiques et aux structures législatives et administratives;

Considérant que le transport des polluants issus des sources d'émission importantes peut affecter les conditions des régions relativement peu polluées, aussi bien à l'intérieur qu'à l'extérieur des frontières nationales;

Considérant que peuvent s'avérer nécessaires des mesures différentes dans le cas de l'amélioration des conditions prévalant dans les zones urbaines industrialisées et dans celui de la protection des zones relativement peu polluées;

Sur la proposition du Comité de l'Environnement;

I. RECOMMANDE que les gouvernements des pays Membres s'efforcent aussi rapidement que possible:

(*a*) de réduire les émissions d'oxydes de soufre et de particules;

(i) par l'application des meilleures techniques disponibles permettant la réduction des émissions de ces polluants;

(ii) par l'encouragement d'une production accrue et plus efficace de combustibles propres, ainsi que de leur utilisation plus efficace;

(*b*) de développer et d'appliquer des mesures destinées à réduire les émissions d'oxydes d'azote et d'hydrocarbures;

(*c*) d'encourager l'utilisation de systèmes de contrôle et d'observation, y compris les systèmes de contrôle des émissions, en tant que parties intégrantes des mesures de mise en oeuvre de la lutte contre la pollution atmosphérique;

(*d*) de contrôler et d'évaluer les effets associés au dépôt de composés soufrés et à l'acidité des précipitations.

II. CHARGE le Comité de l'Environnement d'évaluer les actions entreprises en application de la présente Recommandation et de faire rapport au Conseil à ce sujet.

RECOMMANDATION DU CONSEIL SUR L'ENERGIE ET L'ENVIRONNEMENT

(*Adoptée par le Conseil à sa 372ème Séance, le 14 novembre 1974*)

Le Conseil,

Vu l'article 5 b) de la Convention relative à l'Organisation de Coopération et de Développement Economiques, en date du 14 décembre 1960;

Vu la Recommandation du Conseil, en date du 26 mai 1972, sur les Principes directeurs relatifs aux aspects économiques des politiques de l'environnement sur le plan international [C(72)128];

Reconnaissant l'importance pour le bien-être économique et social des pays Membres d'une sécurité satisfaisante des approvisionnements en énergie;

Reconnaissant que la consommation d'énergie augmentera probablement au cours de la prochaine décennie;

Reconnaissant que le développement, l'obtention sous quelque forme que ce soit des matières premières énergétiques, la production, le trans-

Having regard to the Recommendation of the Council of 18th June, 1974, on Guidelines for Action to Reduce Emissions of Sulphur Oxides and Particulate Matter from Fuel Combustion in Stationary Sources [C(74)16 (Final)];

Considering that the atmosphere is an essential resource requiring careful management due to its limited capability to disperse and cleanse itself of the many substances rejected to it;

Considering the difference in socio-economic conditions and in legislative and administrative structures in different countries and regions;

Considering that transport of pollution from major sources of emission may affect conditions in relatively unpolluted regions, both within and beyond national frontiers;

Considering that different measures may be required to improve conditions in the urban industrialised regions from those necessary for the protection of relatively unpolluted areas;

On the proposal of the Environment Committee;

I. RECOMMENDS that the Governments of Member countries should strive with all practicable speed:

(*a*) to reduce emissions of sulphur oxides and particulate matter;

(i) by applying the best available abatement techniques for these pollutants;

(ii) by encouraging the expanded and more efficient production, as well as the more effective use of clean fuels;

(*b*) to develop and apply measures for reducing emissions of nitrogen oxides and hydrocarbons;

(*c*) to encourage the utilisation of monitoring and surveillance systems, including monitoring of emissions, as an integral aspect of implementing air pollution control policies;

(*d*) to monitor and assess the effects associated with deposition of sulphur compounds and acidity of precipitation.

II. INSTRUCTS the Environment Committee to assess the action taken pursuant to this Recommendation and to report thereon to the Council.

RECOMMENDATION OF THE COUNCIL ON ENERGY AND THE ENVIRONMENT

(*Adopted by the Council at its 372nd Meeting on 14th November, 1974*)

The Council,

Having regard to Article 5(b) of the Convention on the Organisation for Economic Co-operation and Development of 14th December, 1960;

Having regard to the Recommendation of the Council of 26th May, 1972, on Guiding Principles Concerning International Economic Aspects of Environmental Policies [C(72)128];

Recognising the importance of an adequately secure supply of energy for economic and social welfare of Member countries:

Recognising that the consumption of energy is likely to increase in the next decade;

Recognising that development, the extraction of all forms of primary energy recourses, the production, transportation, storage, conversion and use of energy have potential impacts on the environment and, that given port, le stockage, la conversion et l'utilisation de l'énergie ont des incidences potentielles sur l'environnement et, qu'avec une allocation des ressources suffisante, le contrôle des incidences préjudiciables sur l'environnement pourra en général être mis en oeuvre d'une manière harmonieuse;

Reconnaissant qu'il importe de conserver leur impulsion aux politiques de l'environnement malgré les changements des conditions d'approvisionnement en énergie;

Reconnaissant que les efforts entrepris par les gouvernements Membres, étant donné la disponibilité limitée des ressources énergétiques, pour économiser l'énergie et éviter le gaspillage dans son utilisation et pour promouvoir une utilisation plus efficace des ressources énergétiques auront en général des effets bénéfiques pour l'environnement.

Sur la proposition du Comité de l'Environnement;

I. RECOMMANDE que les gouvernements des pays Membres:

1. veillent à ce que les politiques de l'environnement et de l'énergie soient intégrées et adoptent ainsi une approche de l'utilisation de l'énergie propre à garantir une protection adéquate de l'environnement;

2. examinent systématiquement les incidences potentielles de la production et de l'utilisation de l'énergie sur l'environnement ainsi que l'interdépendance des politiques de l'énergie et de l'environnement, échangent des informations et mettent en oeuvre une politique d'information publique appropriée en la matière;

3. mettent au point des pratiques opératoires efficaces du point de vue de la protection de l'environnement, tenant compte notamment des implications relatives aux coûts, pour toutes les opérations intervenant dans la production et l'utilisation d'énergie;

4. encouragent, sur la base, notamment, d'objectifs de qualité de l'environnement, l'élaboration de stratégies visant à assurer une utilisation rationnelle de l'énergie et à éviter les gaspillages, qui soient compatibles avec la poursuite de l'amélioration du bien-être économique et social.

II. INVITE le Comité de l'Environnement, en coopération étroite avec d'autres Comités responsables des politiques de l'énergie, et en tenant compte de toutes les activités pertinentes de l'OCDE et d'autres organisations internationales:

(i) à entreprendre des études spécifiques* sur des problèmes d'environnement prioritaires concernant:

(*a*) tous les stades de la production d'énergie provenant de sources diverses;

(*b*) les utilisations diverses de l'énergie;

(*c*) les mesures et les moyens techniques propres à économiser l'énergie et à promouvoir une plus grande efficacité dans son utilisation;

(ii) à rassembler des données, en relation avec les sujets d'étude mentionnés en (i), sur:

(*a*) les incidences probables sur l'environnement;

(*b*) les divers moyens de protection de l'environnement qui sont disponibles ou susceptibles de le devenir;

(*c*) les coûts de différentes options possibles en ce qui concerne les mesures de protection de l'environnement;

(iii) à procéder, dans tous les cas où c'est possible, à des échanges d'informations et d'expérience concernant les incidences potentielles sur l'environnement des programmes d'approvisionnement en énergie, y compris

---

* Des sujets d'études spécifiques seront déterminés par un Groupe d'experts à la lumière d'autres études entreprises dans le cadre de l'OCEE, notamment l'évaluation des problèmes énergétiques à long terme, et en tenant compte de tous les travaux menés au niveau gouvernemental sur le plan international.

a sufficient allocation of resources, the control of adverse environmental effects could be generally assured in a harmonious manner;

Recognising the importance of maintaining the impetus of environmental policies under changing conditions of energy supply;

Recognising that the efforts of the Member governments in view of the limitation on the availability of energy resources, to improve energy conservation and avoid waste in use of energy and promote more efficient use of energy resources, will generally have beneficial effects for the environment.

On the proposal of the Environment Committee;

I. RECOMMENDS that Member Governments:

1. ensure that environmental and energy policies are integrated and thus develop an approach to the usage of energy which will provide adequate environmental protection;

2. examine systematically, exchange information and develop appropriate public information services on the potential environmental impacts of energy generation and use as well as the interrelationship between environmental and energy policies;

3. develop effective operating practices from the environment protection standpoint, taking into account, amongst others, cost implications for all operations involved in energy generation and use;

4. encourage, on the basis of, amongst others, environmental quality objectives, the development of strategies for rational use of energy and avoidance of waste commensurate with continued improvement in economic and social welfare.

II. INVITES the Environment Committee in close co-operation with other Committees responsible for energy policies, and taking account of all relevant work in the O.E.C.D. and other international organisations:

(i) to undertake specific studies* on priority environmental issues in relation to:

(*a*) all stages in energy production from various sources;

(*b*) different uses of energy;

(*c*) policies and technical means for reducing energy demand, improvement in energy conservation and greater efficiency in the use of energy;

(ii) to collect data in relation to the subjects chosen for study in (i) above on the following:

(*a*) the probable environmental impacts;

(*b*) the various environmental protective measures that exist or can reasonably be expected to become available;

(*c*) the costs of various options in environmental protection measures;

(iii) whenever possible to exchange information about, and experience in examining, the potential environmental impacts of energy supply, including new energy sources, and conservation or demand reduction programmes;

(iv) to work towards agreement between Member countries on guidelines for environmental protection within and beyond national frontiers

* Specific topics for study will be identified by a Group of Expdrts in the light of other work undertaken within the framework of OECD, especially the Long-Term Energy Assessment, and taking into account all work at international governmental level.

ceux relatifs aux nouvelles sources d'énergie, ainsi que des programmes visant à économiser l'énergie ou à réduire la demande d'énergie;

(iv) à chercher à parvenir à un accord entre pays Membres sur des directives de protection de l'environnement applicables à l'intérieur et à l'extérieur des frontières nationales en ce qui concerne la production, le transport, le traitement et l'utilisation des ressources énergétiques dans des zones appropriées.

III. CHARGE le Comité de l'Environnement de faire rapport au Conseil sur les mesures prises par les gouvernements Membres en application de la présente Recommandation.

RECOMMANDATION DU CONSEIL SUR LA MISE EN OEUVRE DU PRINCIPE POLLUEUR-PAYEUR

(*Adoptée par le Conseil à sa 372ème séance, le 14 novembre 1974*)

Le Conseil,

Vu l'article 5 b) de la Convention relative à l'Organisation de Coopération et de Développement Economiques, en date du 14 décembre 1960;

Vu les dispositions de l'Accord Général sur les Tarifs Douaniers et le Commerce;

Vu la Recommandation du Conseil, en date du 26 mai 1972, sur les Principes directeurs relatifs aux aspects économiques des Politiques de l'environnement sur le plan international [C(72) 128];

Vu la note du Comité de l'Environnement sur la mise en oeuvre du Principe Pollueur-Payeur [ENV(73) 32 (Final)];

Vu la possibilité, reconnue par le Conseil, de recourir à des consultations officieuses sur les Principes Directeurs dans le cadre de l'OCDE [C/M(74) 16 (Final), point 157];

Sur la proposition du Comité de l'Environnement;

I. REAFFIRME que:

1. Le Principe Pollueur-Payeur constitue pour les pays Membres un principe de base pour l'allocation des coûts des mesures de prévention et de lutte contre la pollution décidées par les autorités des pays Membres.

2. Le Principe Pollueur-Payeur, tel qu'il est défini par les Principes directeurs relatifs aux aspects économiques des politiques de l'environnement sur le plan international [C(72) 128], qui tiennent compte du fait que des problèmes particuliers peuvent éventuellement se poser dans le cas des pays en voie de développement, signifie que le pollueur devrait se voir imputer les dépenses relatives aux mesures visées au paragraphe précédent, pour faire en sorte que l'environnement soit dans un état acceptable. En d'autres termes, le coût de ces mesures devrait être répercuté dans le coût des biens et services qui sont à l'origine de la pollution du fait de leur production et/ou de leur consommation.

3. Une application uniforme de ce principe, en fondant les politiques de l'environnement des pays Membres sur les mêmes bases, encouragerait l'utilisation rationnelle et l'allocation la meilleure des ressources rares de l'environnement et éviterait l'apparition de distorsions dans les échanges et les investissements internationaux.

II. NOTE:

1. qu'il existe une relation étroite entre la politique de l'environnement d'un pays et sa politique socio-économique globale;

2. que, dans des circonstances exceptionnelles telles que la mise en oeuvre rapide d'un système contraignant et particulièrement sévère de

in relation to production, transportation, processing and use of energy in appropriate areas.

III. INSTRUCTS the Environment Committee to report to the Council on action taken by Member Governments pursuant to this Recommendation.

RECOMMENDATION OF THE COUNCIL
ON THE IMPLEMENTATION OF THE POLLUTER-PAYS PRINCIPLE

(Adopted by the Council at its 372nd Meeting on 14th November, 1974)

The Council,

Having regard to Article 5(b) of the Convention on the Organisation for Economic Co-operation and Development of 14th December, 1960;

Having regard to the provisions of the General Agreement on Tariffs and Trade;

Having regard to the Recommendation of the Council of 26th May, 1972 on Guiding Principles Concerning International Economic Aspects of Environmental Policies [C(72)128];

Having regard to the Note by the Environment Committee on Implementation of the Polluter-Pays Principle [ENV(73)32(Final)];

Having regard to the possibility, approved by the Council, of holding informal consultations on the Guiding Principles within the OECD [C/M(74)16(Final), Item 157];

On the proposal of the Environment Committee;

I. REAFFIRMS that:

1. The Polluter-Pays Principle constitutes for Member countries a fundamental principle for allocating costs of pollution prevention and control measures introduced by the public authorities in Member countries.

2. The Polluter-Pays Principle, as defined by the Guiding Principles concerning International Economic Aspects of Environmental Policies [C(72)128], which take account of particular problems possibly arising for developing countries, means that the polluter should bear the expenses of carrying out the measures, as specified in the previous paragraph, to ensure that the environment is in an acceptable state. In other words, the cost of these measures should be reflected in the cost of goods and services which cause pollution in production and/or consumption.

3. Uniform application of this principle, through the adoption of a common basis for Member countries' environmental policies, would encourage the rational use and the better allocation of scarce environmental resources and prevent the appearance of distortions in international trade and investment.

II. NOTES that:

1. there is a close relationship between a country's environmental policy and its overall socio-economic policy;

2. in exceptional circumstances, such as the rapid implementation of a compelling and especially stringent pollution control regime, socio-eco-

lutte contre la pollution, des problèmes socio-économiques assez importants, pour justifier la prise en considération d'une aide publique, peuvent surgir si les objectifs de l'environnement d'un pays Membre doivent être atteints dans un délai obligatoire et spécifié;

3. que les aides destinées à promouvoir l'expérimentation de nouvelles technologies de lutte contre la pollution et la mise au point de nouveaux équipements de lutte contre la pollution ne sont pas nécessairement incompatibles avec le Principe Pollueur-Payeur;

4. que lorsque les mesures prises pour favoriser les objectifs socio-économiques particuliers des pays, tels que l'atténuation de graves déséquilibres interrégionaux, auraient l'effet accessoire de constituer une aide pour le contrôle de la pollution, l'octroi de cette aide ne serait pas incompatible avec le Principe Pollueur-Payeur.

III. RECOMMANDE:

1. que les pays Membres continuent à travailler ensemble en étroite collaboration en vue d'aboutir à un respect uniforme du Principe Pollueur-Payeur et donc qu'en règle générale ils n'aident pas les pollueurs à supporter des coûts de la lutte contre la pollution que ce soit au moyen de subventions, avantages fiscaux ou autres mesures;

2. que l'octroi de toute aide de cette nature pour la lutte contre la pollution soit strictement limité et, en particulier, respecte chacune des conditions suivantes:

(*a*) l'aide devrait être sélective et limitée aux parties de l'économie telles que les industries, zones ou installations qui, faute de quoi, se trouveraient confrontées à des difficultés sévères;

(*b*) l'aide devrait être limitée à des période transitoires bien définies, précisées à l'avance et adaptées aux problèmes socio-économiques spécifiques liés à la mise en oeuvre des programmes d'environnement d'un pays;

(*c*) l'aide ne devrait pas créer de distorsions importantes dans les échanges et les investissements internationaux;

3. que si, dans des cas exceptionnellement difficiles, un pays Membre consent une aide à des installations nouvelles, les conditions d'octroi de cette aide soient encore plus strictes que celles applicables aux installations existantes et que des critères destinés à servir de base à cette différenciation soient mis au point;

4. que, conformément à des procédures appropriées à élaborer, tous les systèmes d'aides soient notifiés aux pays Membres par l'intermédiaire du Secrétariat de l'OCDE. Dans la mesure du possible, ces notifications s'effectueraient avant la mise en oeuvre de ces systèmes;

5. que des consultations sur la mise en oeuvre de ces systèmes, ainsi qu'il est dit dans les Principes Directeurs [C(72) 128], aient lieu à la demande de tout pays Membre, qu'il y ait eu ou non notification.

IV. INVITE le Comité de l'Environnement à faire rapport au Conseil sur les mesures prises en application de la présente Recommandation.

RECOMMANDATION DU CONSEIL CONCERNANT DES PRINCIPES RELATIFS A LA POLLUTION TRANSFRONTIERE

(*Adoptée par le Conseil à sa 372ème séance, le 14 novembre 1974*)

Le Conseil,

Vu l'Article 5 b) de la Convention relative à l'Organisation de Coopération et de Développement Economiques, en date du 14 décembre 1960;

Considérant que la protection et l'amélioration de l'environnement sont des objectifs communs des pays Membres;

nomic problems may develop of such significance as to justify consideration of the granting of governmental assistance if the environmental policy objectives of a Member country are to be realised within a prescribed and specified time;

3. aid given for the purpose of stimulating experimentation with new pollution-control technologies and development of new pollution-abatement equipment is not necessarily incompatible with the Polluter-Pays Principle;

4. where measures taken to promote a country's specific socio-economic objectives, such as the reduction of serious inter-regional imbalances, would have the incidental effect of constituting aid for pollution-control purposes, the granting of such aid would not be inconsistent with the Polluter-Pays Principle.

III. RECOMMENDS that:

1. Member countries continue to collaborate and work closely together in striving for uniform observance of the Polluter-Pays Principle, and therefore that as a general rule they should not assist the polluters in bearing the costs of pollution control whether by means of subsidies, tax advantages or other measures;

2. the granting of any such assistance for pollution control be strictly limited, and in particular comply with every one of the following conditions:

(*a*) it should be selective and restricted to those parts of the economy, such as industries, areas or plants, where severe difficulties would otherwise occur;

(*b*) it should be limited to well-defined transitional periods, laid down in advance and adapted to the specific socio-economic problems associated with the implementation of a country's environmental programme;

(*c*) it should not create significant distortions in international trade and investment;

3. that if a Member country, in cases of exceptional difficulty, gives assistance to new plants, the conditions be even stricter than those applicable to existing plants and that criteria on which to base this differentiation be developed;

4. in accordance with appropriate procedures to be worked out, all systems to provide assistance be notified to Member countries through the OECD Secretariat. Wherever praticable these notifications would occur prior to implementation of such systems;

5. regardless of whether notification has taken place, consultations, as mentioned in the Guiding Principles [C(72)128] on the implementation of such systems, will take place at the request of any Member State.

IV. INVITES the Environment Committee to report to the Council on action taken pursuant to this Recommendation.

RECOMMENDATION OF THE COUNCIL ON PRINCIPLES CONCERNING TRANSFRONTIER POLLUTION

(*Adopted by the Council at its 372nd Meeting on 14th November, 1974*)

The Council,

Having regard to Article 5(b) of the Convention on the Organisation for Economic Co-operation and Development of 14th December, 1960;

Considering that the protection and improvement of the environment are common objectives of Member countries;

Considérant que les intérêts communs des pays concernés par la pollution transfrontière devraient les conduire à coopérer plus étroitement dans un esprit de solidarité internationale, et à engager des actions concertées pour prévenir et combattre la pollution transfrontière;

Vu les Recommandations de la Conférence des Nations Unies sur l'environnement humain réunie à Stockholm en juin 1972 et, en particulier, les Principes de la Déclaration sur l'environnement humain relatifs à la pollution transfrontière;

Sur la proposition du Comité de l'Environnement;

I. RECOMMANDE que les pays Membres, sans préjudice de l'évolution ultérieure du droit international et de la coopération internationale en matière de pollution transfrontière, s'inspirent dans leur politique de l'environnement des principes relatifs à la pollution transfrontière énoncés dans la présente Recommandation et son Annexe qui en fait partie intégrante.

II. CHARGE le Comité de l'Environnement d'établir sans délai, en tenant compte des travaux entrepris dans d'autres organisations internationales, un programme d'activités destiné à élaborer plus avant ces principes et à en faciliter la mise en oeuvre pratique.

III. RECOMMANDE que les pays Membres coopèrent pour développer le droit international applicable à la pollution transfrontière.

IV. CHARGE le Comité de l'Environnement, dans le cadre de son mandat, d'examiner ou d'approfondir, selon le cas, les questions liées aux Principes de la Déclaration de Stockholm concernant le ,,devoir'' et la ,,responsabilité'', en tenant compte des travaux entrepris dans d'autres organisations internationales, de soumettre un premier rapport au Conseil sur ses travaux pour le 1er mars 1976 et de chercher à formuler aussitôt que possible des Projets de Recommandations.

V. CHARGE le Comité de l'Environnement d'approfondir l'étude des problèmes concernant l'égalité d'accès, de formuler aussitôt que possible des Projets de Recommandations et de faire rapport au Conseil sur ses travaux pour le 1er juillet 1975.

ANNEXE

QUELQUES PRINCIPES RELATIFS A LA POLLUTION TRANSFRONTIERE

TITRE A – INTRODUCTION

La présente annexe énonce quelques principes qui sont destinés à faciliter l'élaboration de politiques harmonisées de l'environnement en vue de résoudre les problèmes de pollution transfrontière. Leur mise en oeuvre devrait se fonder sur un juste équilibre des droits et obligations entre les pays concernés par la pollution transfrontière.

Ces principes devraient être complétés et développés ultérieurement à la lumière des travaux entrepris par l'OCDE ou par d'autres organisations internationales appropriées.

Aux fins de ces principes, on entend par pollution, l'introduction par l'homme, directement ou indirectement, de substances ou d'énergie dans l'environnement, qui entraîne des conséquences préjudiciables de nature à mettre en danger la santé humaine, à nuire aux ressources biologiques et aux systèmes écologiques, à porter atteinte aux agréments ou à gêner les autres utilisations légitimes de l'environnement.

Considering that the common interests of countries concerned by transfrontier pollution should induce them to co-operate more closely in a spirit of international solidarity and to initiate concerted action for prevening and controlling transfrontier pollution;

Having regard to the Recommendations of the United Nations Conference on the Human Environment held in Stockholm in June 1972 and in particular those Principles of the Declaration on the Human Environment which are relevant to transfrontier pollution;

On the proposal of the Environment Committee;

I. RECOMMENDS that, without prejudice to future developments in international law and international co-operation in relation to transfrontier pollution, Member countries should be guided in their environmental policy by the principles concerning transfrontier pollution contained in this Recommendation and its Annex, which is an integral part of this Recommendation.

II. INSTRUCTS the Environment Committee to prepare without delay, taking account of the work undertaken by other international organisations, a programme of work designed to elaborate further these principles and to facilitate their practical implementation.

III. RECOMMENDS Member countries to co-operate in developing international law applicable to transfrontier pollution.

IV. INSTRUCTS the Environment Committee, within the framework of its mandate, to examine or investigate further, as the case may be, the issues related to the Principles of the Stockholm Declaration regarding responsibility and liability, taking into account the work undertaken by other international organisations, to submit a first report to the Council on its work by 1st March, 1976 and to seek to formulate as soon as possible Draft Recommendations.

V. INSTRUCTS the Environment Committee to investigate further the issues concerning equal right of hearing, to formulate as soon as possible Draft Recommendations and to report to the Council on its work by 1st July, 1975.

ANNEX

SOME PRINCIPLES CONCERNING TRANSFRONTIER POLLUTION

TITLE A – INTRODUCTION

This Annex sets forth some principles designed to facilitate the development of harmonized environmental policies with a view to solving transfrontier pollution problems. Their implementation should be based on a fair balance of rights and obligations among countries concerned by transfrontier pollution.

These principles should subsequently be supplemented and developed in the light of work undertaken by the OECD or other appropriate international organisations.

For the purpose of these principles, pollution means the introduction by man, directly or indirectly, of substances or energy into the environment resulting in deleterious effects of such a nature as, to endanger human health, harm living resources and ecosystems, and impair or interfere with amenities and other legitimate uses of the environment.

A moins d'indications contraires, ces principes concernent la pollution qui trouve son origine dans un pays et qui a des effets dans d'autres pays.

TITRE B* – SOLIDARITE INTERNATIONALE

1. Les pays devraient définir une politique concertée à long terme tendant à la protection et à l'amélioration de l'environnement dans les zones susceptibles d'être affectées par la pollution transfrontière.

Sans préjudice de leurs droits et obligations au regard du droit international et conformément au devoir que leur assigne le Principe 21 de la Déclaration de Stockholm, les pays devraient, autant que possible, rechercher un équilibre équitable de leurs droits et obligations en ce qui concerne les zones concernées par la pollution transfrontière.

Dans la mise en oeuvre de leur politique concertée, les pays devraient entre autres:

(*a*) prendre en considération:
- les niveaux de pollution existants et la qualité actuelle du milieu concerné,
- la nature et les quantités de polluants,
- la capacité d'assimilation du milieu, telle qu'établie d'un commun accord par les pays concernés, compte tenu des caractéristiques et de la vocation particulières de la zone affectée par la pollution,
- les activités à l'origine de la pollution et les activités et usages sensibles à cette pollution;
- la situation, la vocation et le développement socio-économiques des zones concernées;

(*b*) définir:
- les objectifs de qualité de l'environnement et les mesures de protection correspondantes;

(*c*) promouvoir:
- les lignes directrices d'une politique d'aménagement compatible avec les impératifs de la protection de l'environnement et du développement socio-économique;

(*d*) établir et mettre à jour:

(i) des listes de substances particulièrement dangereuses pour lesquelles des efforts devraient être faits afin d'éliminer, au besoin par étapes, les rejets polluants, et

(ii) des listes de substances en rapport avec lesquelles les rejets polluants devraient être soumis à un contrôle très strict.

2. En attendant la définition de telles politiques concertées à long terme, les pays devraient prendre, individuellement et conjointement, toutes les mesures appropriées pour prévenir et contrôler la pollution transfrontière et pour harmoniser, dans toute la mesure du possible, leurs politiques à cet égard.

3. Les pays devraient s'efforcer de prévenir tous accroissements de la pollution transfrontière, y compris ceux dus à des substances et à des activités nouvelles ou additionnelles, de réduire et, autant que possible,d'éliminer, dans des délais à déterminer, la pollution transfrontière existant entre eux.

TIRTE C – PRINCIPE DE NON-DISCRIMINATION

4. Les pays devraient initialement fonder leur action sur le principe de non-discrimination en vertu duquel:

(*a*) les pollueurs à l'origine d'une pollution transfrontière devraient être soumis à des dispositions de nature législative ou réglementaire qui

---

* Le Délégué de l'Espagne a réservé sa position sur le Titre B.

Unless otherwise specified, these principles deal with pollution originating in one country and having effects within other countries.

TITLE B* – INTERNATIONAL SOLIDARITY

1. Countries should define a concerted long-term policy for the protection and improvement of the environment in zones liable to be affected by transfrontier pollution.

Without prejudice to their rights and obligations under international law and in accordance with their responsibility under Principle 21 of the Stockholm Declaration, countries should seek, as far as possible, an equitable balance of their rights and obligations as regards the zones concerned by transfrontier pollution.

In implementing this concerted policy, countries should among other things:

(*a*) take account of:

- levels of existing pollution and the present quality of the environment concerned;
- the nature and quantities of pullutants;
- the assimilative capacity of the environment, as established by mutual agreement by the countries concerned, taking into account the particular characteristics and use of the affected zone;
- activities at the source of pollution and activities and uses sensitive to such pollution;
- the situation, prospective use and development of the zones concerned from a socio-economic standpoint;

(*b*) define:

- environmental quality objectives and corresponding protective measures;

(*c*) promote:

- guidelines for a land-use planning policy consistent with the requirements both of environmental protection and socio-economic development;

(*d*) draw up and maintain up to date:

(i) list of particularly dangerous substances regarding which efforts should be made to eliminate polluting discharges, if necessary by stages, and

(ii) lists of substances regarding which polluting discharges should be subject to very strict control.

2. Pending the definition of such concerted long-term policies countries should, individually and jointly, take all appropriate measures to prevent and control transfrontier pollution, and harmonize as far as possible their relevant policies.

3. Countries should endeavour to prevent any increase in transfrontier pollution, including that stemming from new or additional substances and activities, and to reduce, and as far as possible eliminate any transfrontier pollution existing between them within time limits to be specified.

TITLE C – PRINCIPLE OF NON-DISCRIMINATION

4. Countries should initially base their action on the principle of non-discrimination, whereby:

(*a*) polluters causing transfrontier pollution should be subject to legal or statutory provisions no less severe than those which would apply for

* The Delegate for Spain reserved his position on Title B.

ne soient pas moins sévères que celles qui s'appliqueraient à une pollution équivalente ayant lieu à l'intérieur de leur pays dans des conditions et des zones comparables, compte tenu, le cas échéant, du caractère et des besoins particuliers en matière d'environnement de la zone affectée;

(*b*) en particulier, sans préjudice des objectifs de qualité ou des normes concernant la pollution transfrontière agréés d'un commun accord par les pays concernés, les niveaux de la pollution transfrontière qui pénètre dans les zones susceptibles d'être affectées par une telle pollution ne devraient pas dépasser ceux considérés comme acceptables dans des conditions et des zones comparables à l'intérieur du pays d'où provient cette pollution, compte tenu, le cas échéant, de l'état particulier de l'environnement dans le pays affecté par la pollution;

(*c*) un pays lorsqu'il met en oeuvre le Principe Pollueur-Payeur devrait l'appliquer à l'égard de tous les pollueurs à l'intérieur de ce pays sans établir de différences selon que la pollution affecte ce pays ou un autre;

(*d*) les personnes affectées par la pollution transfrontière ne devraient pas recevoir un traitement moins favorable que celui qui est réservé aux personnes affectées par une pollution semblable dans le pays d'où provient la pollution transfrontière.

TITRE D* – PRINCIPE D'EGALITE D'ACCES

5. Les pays devraient tendre, dans toute la mesure du possible, vers l'établissement, s'il n'existe déjà, d'un régime d'égalité d'accès, selon lequel:

(*a*) Lorsqu'un projet, une activité nouvelle ou un comportement est susceptible de créer un risque sensible de pollution transfrontière et fait l'objet d'un examen des autorités publiques, ceux qui sont susceptibles d'être affectés par cette pollution devraient être recevables à utiliser les mêmes procedures juridictionnelles ou administratives dans le pays d'où elle provient que ceux de ce pays;

b) Lorsque la pollution transfrontière donne lieu à des dommages dans un pays, ceux qui sont affectés par cette pollution devraient être recevables à utiliser les mêmes procédures juridictionnelles ou administratives dans le pays d'où provient cette pollution que ceux de ce pays, et devraient jouir, en matière de procédure, de droits équivalents à ceux dont jouissent ceux de ce pays.

TITRE E* – PRINCIPE D'INFORMATION ET DE CONSULTATION

6. Avant le début de travaux ou d'activités qui seraient susceptibles de créer un risque sensible de pollution transfrontière, le pays d'origine de ces travaux ou activités devrait informer assez tôt les autres pays qui sont ou qui pourraient être affectés par la pollution transfrontière. Il devrait fournir à ces pays des informations et données pertinentes dont la communication n'est pas interdite par les dispositions législatives ou réglementaires ou les conventions internationales applicables, et les inviter à faire connaître leurs commentaires.

7. Les pays devraient, à la requête du pays qui est ou pourrait être directement affecté, entrer en consultations sur un problème de pollution transfrontière existant ou prévisible et devraient poursuivre avec diligence dans un délai raisonnable de telles consultations sur ce problème particulier.

8. Les pays devraient éviter de mettre en oeuvre des projets ou activités qui seraient susceptibles de créer un risque sensible de pollution trans-

---

* Le Délégué de l'Espagne a réservé sa position sur le Titre D.
* Le Délégué de l'Espagne a réservé sa position sur le Titre E.

any equivalent pollution occurring within their country, under comparable conditions and in comparable zones, taking into account, when appropriate, the special nature and environmental needs of the zone affected;

(*b*) in particular, without prejudice to quality objectives or standards applying to transfrontier pollution mutually agreed upon by the countries concerned, the levels of transfrontier pollution entering into the zones liable to be affected by such pollution should not exceed those considered acceptable under comparable conditions and in comparable zones inside the country in which it originates, taking into account, when appropriate, the special state of the environment in the affected country;

(*c*) any country whenever it applies the Polluter-Pays Principle should apply it to all polluters within this country without making any difference according to whether pollution affects this country or another country;

(*d*) persons affected by transfrontier pollution should be granted no less favourable treatment than persons affected by a similar pollution in the country from which such transfrontier pollution originates.

TITLE D* – PRINCIPLE OF EQUAL RIGHT OF HEARING

5. Countries should make every effort to introduce, where not already in existence, a system affording equal right of hearing, according to which:

(*a*) whenever a project, a new activity or a course of conduct may create a significant risk of transfrontier pollution and is investigated by public authorities, those who may be affected by such pollution should have the same rights of standing in judicial or administrative proceedings in the country where it originates as those of that country;

(*b*) whenever transfrontier pollution gives rise to damage in a country, those who are affected by such pollution should have the same rights of standing in judicial or administrative proceedings in the country where such pollution originates as those of that country, and they should be extended procedural rights equivalent to the rights extended to those of that country.

TITLE E* – PRINCIPLE OF INFORMATION AND CONSULTATION

6. Prior to the initiation in a country of works or undertakings which might create a significant risk of transfrontier pollution, this country should provide early information to other countries which are or may be affected. It should provide these countries with relevant information and data, the transmission of which is not prohibited by legislative provisions or prescriptions or applicable international conventions, and should invite their comments.

7. Countries should enter into consultation on an existing of foreseeable transfrontier pollution problem at the request of a country which is or may be directly affected and should diligently pursue such consultations on this particular problem over a reasonable period of time.

8. Countries should refrain from carrying out projects or activities which might create a significant risk of transfrontier pollution without first informing the countries which are or may be affected and, except in cases of extreme urgency, providing a reasonable amount of time in the

---

* The Delegate for Spain reserved his position on Title D.

* The Delegate for Spain reserved his position on Title E.

frontière sans avoir préalablement informé les pays qui sont ou qui pourraient être affectés et sans prévoir, à moins qu'il n'y ait urgence extrême, un délai raisonnable, compte tenu des circonstances, pour des consultations diligentes. De telles consultations, menées dans le meilleur esprit de coopération et de bon voisinage, n'habilitent pas un pays quelconque à retarder de manière déraisonnable ou à entraver les activités ou projets sur lesquels porte cette consultation.

TITRE F – ALERTE ET ACCIDENTS

9. Les pays devraient rapidement avertir les autres pays susceptibles d'être affectés de toute situation de nature à faire croître soudainement le niveau de pollution dans des régions situées en dehors du pays à l'origine de la pollution et prendre toutes les mesures appropriées pour réduire les effets d'une telle augmentation soudaine.

10. Les pays devraient se prêter mutuellement assistance, en tant que de besoin, pour prévenir les accidents susceptibles de conduire à une pollution transfrontière, pour minimiser et, si possible, éliminer les effets de tels accidents et ils devraient à cette fin mettre sur pied des plans d'urgence.

TITRE G – ECHANGE D'INFORMATIONS SCIENTIFIQUES, OBSERVATIONS ET RECHERCHES

11. Les pays concernés devraient se transmettre toutes les informations et données scientifique appropriées relatives à la pollution transfrontière lorsque ceci n'est pas interdit par les dispositions législatives ou réglementaires ou les conventions internationales applicables. Ils devraient mettre au point et adopter des méthodes de mesures de la pollution donnant des résultats compatibles.

12. Ils devraient, le cas échéant, collaborer à des programmes de recherche scientifique et technique destinés entre autres à identifier l'origine et les voies de cheminement de la pollution transfrontière, les dommages causés et les meilleures méthodes de prévention et de lutte contre la pollution, et ils devraient se communiquer mutuellement toutes les informations et données ainsi obtenues.

En cas de besoin, ils devraient envisager d'établir conjointement, dans les zones concernées par la pollution transfrontière, un système ou un réseau d'observation permanente de paramètres permettant d'apprecier les niveaux de la pollution et de vérifier l'efficacité des mesures de réduction de cette pollution qu'ils auront prises.

TITRE H – INSTITUTIONS

13. Les pays concernés par un problème particulier de pollution transfrontière devraient prendre en considération les avantages d'une coopération par la création de commissions internationales ou autres organismes, ou par le renforcement d'institutions existantes, pour traiter plus efficacement des aspects particuliers de ce problème.

De telles institutions pourraient être autorisées à réunir les données nécessaires présentant un intérêt pour une évaluation correcte du problème et de ses causes et présenter aux pays concernés des propositions pratiques relatives à des actions concertées contre la pollution transfrontière. Avec le consentement des Etats concernés, elles pourraient aussi effectuer toutes recherches complémentaires requises sur l'origine et le degré de la pollution, examiner l'efficacité des mesures de prévention et de lutte contre la pollution qui auront été adoptées et publier des rapports sur leurs constatations.

light of circumstances for diligent consultation. Such consultations held in the best spirit of co-operation and good neighbourliness should not enable a country to unreasonably delay or to impede the activities or projects on which consultations are taking place.

TITLE F – WARNING SYSTEMS AND CONSULTATION

9. Countries should promptly warn other potentially affected countries of any situation which may cause any sudden increase in the level of pollution in areas outside the country of origin of pollution, and take all appropriate steps to reduce the effects of any such sudden increase.

10. Countries should assist each other, wherever necessary, in order to prevent incidents, which may result in transfrontier pollution, and to minimise, and if possible eliminate, the effects of such incidents, and should develop contingency plans to this end.

TITLE G – EXCHANGE OF SCIENTIFIC INFORMATION, MONITORING MEASURES AND RESEARCH

11. Countries concerned should exchange all relevant scientific information and data on transfrontier pollution, when not prohibited by legislative provisions or prescriptions or by applicable international conventions. They should develop and adopt pollution measurement methods providing results which are compatible.

12. They should when appropriate, co-operate in scientific and technical research programmes inter alia for identifying the origin and pathways of transfrontier pollution, any damage caused and the best methods of pollution prevention and control, and should share all information and data thus obtained.

They should, where necessary, consider setting up jointly, in zones affected by transfrontier pollution, a permanent monitoring system or network for assessing, the levels of pollution and the effectiveness of measures taken by them to reduce pollution.

TITLE H – INSTITUTIONS

13. Countries concerned by a particular problem of transfrontier pollution should consider the advantages of co-operation, by setting up international commissions or other bodies, or by strengthening existing institutions, in order to deal more effectively with particular aspects of such problems.

Such institutions could be authorised to collect any data needed for a proper evaluation of the problem and its causes, and make to the countries concerned practical proposals for concerted efforts to combat transfrontier pollution. With the consent of the States concerned, they could also carry out any necessary additional investigations into the origin and degree of pollution, review the effectiveness of any pollution prevention and control measures which have been taken, and publish reports of their findings.

TITRE I – DIFFERENDS

14. Au cas où les négociations et autres moyens de règlement diplomatique des différends relatifs à la pollution transfrontière échoueraient, les pays devraient avoir la possibilité de soumettre ce différend à une procédure de règlement juridique rapide, efficace et obligatoire.

TITRE J – ACCORDS INTERNATIONAUX

15. Les pays devraient chercher à conclure, en cas de besoin, des accords bilatéraux ou multilatéraux relatifs à la réduction de la pollution transfrontière, conformément aux principes énoncés ci-dessus, et à mettre rapidement en vigueur les accords qu'ils auraient déjà signés.

16. Dans le cadre de la négociation de nouveaux accords bilatéraux ou multilatéraux, les pays devraient, tout en tenant compte des principes énoncés ci-dessus, s'efforcer d'appliquer des mesures efficaces de prévention et de lutte contre la pollution en accord avec le Principe Pollueur-Payeur.

De tels accords pourraient, entre autres, inclure des dispositions relatives à des procédures pratiques destinées à assurer l'indemnisation rapide et équitable des personnes affectées par la pollution transfrontière, et pourraient aussi inclure des procédures destinées à faciliter la fourniture de l'information et de la consultation.

DECISION DU CONSEIL PORTANT CREATION D'UNE AGENCE INTERNATIONALE DE L'ENERGIE DE L'ORGANISATION

(adoptée par le Conseil à sa 373ème séance, le 15 novembre 1974)
(Les Délégués de la Finlande, de la France et de la Grèce se sont abstenus)

Le Conseil,

Vu la Convention relative à l'Organisation de Coopération et de Développement Economiques en date du 14 décembre 1960 (appelée ci-dessous la „Convention") et, en particulier, ses articles 5(a), 6, 9, 12, 13 et 20;

Vu le Règlement financier de l'Organisation et, en particulier, ses articles 5, 10, 14(b) et 16(b);

Vu les Status, Règlement et Instructions applicables aux experts du Conseil et aux consultants de l'Organisation;

Notant que les Gouvernements de certains pays Membres ont déclaré leur intention de conclure un Accord distinct relatif à un Programme International de l'Energie dont le texte figure dans le document [C(74)204 et Corrigendum] en date du 6 novembre 1974 diffusé pour information, et appelé ci-dessous l'„Accord";

Vu la Recommandation du Conseil en date du 29 juin 1971 relative à la constitution de stocks de pétrole [C(71)113(Final)];

Vu la Décision du Conseil en date du 14 novembre 1972 concernant les plans et mesures d'urgence et la répartition des approvisionnements de pétrole dans la zone européenne de l'OCDE en cas de crise [C(72)201(Final)];

Vu la Recommandation du Conseil en date du 10 janvier 1974 concernant les fournitures de combustibles de soutes pour les transports maritimes et la pêche [C(73)257(Final)];

Vu la Recommandation du Conseil en date du 10 janvier 1974 concernant la fourniture de carburant aux aéronefs civils [C(73)258(Final)];

Vu la Note du Secrétaire général, en date du 6 novembre 1974, relatif au Programme International de l'Energie [C(74)203 et Corrigendum].

TITLE I – DISPUTES

14. Should negotiations and other means of diplomatically settling disputes concerning transfrontier pollution fail, countries should have the opportunity to submit such a dispute to a procedure of legal settlement which is prompt, effective and binding.

TITLE J – INTERNATIONAL AGREEMENTS

15. Countries should endeavour to conclude, where necessary, bilateral or multilateral agreements for the abatement of transfrontier pollution in accordance with the above principles, to bring promptly into force any agreements which may already have been signed.

16. When negotiating new bilateral or multilateral agreements countries should, while taking into account the principles set out above, strive for the application of efficient pollution prevention and control measures in accordance with the Polluter-Pays Principle.

Such agreements could, inter alia, include provisions for practical procedures promoting the prompt and equitable compensation of persons affected by transfrontier pollution, and could also contain procedures facilitating the provision of information and consultation.

DECISION OF THE COUNCIL ESTABLISHING AN INTERNATIONAL ENERGY AGENCY OF THE ORGANISATION

(*Adopted by the Council at this 373rd Meeting on 15th November, 1974*)
(The Delegates for Finland, France and Greece abstained)

The Council,

Having regard to the Convention on the Organisation for Economic Co-operation and Development of 14th December, 1960 (hereinafter called the "Convention") and, in particular, Articles 5(a), 6, 9, 12, 13 and 20 of the Convention;

Having regard to the Financial Regulations of the Organisation and, in particular, to Articles 5, 10, 14(b) and 16(b) thereof;

Having regard to the Regulations, Rules and Instructions for Council Experts and Consultants of the Organisation;

Noting that the Governments of certain Member countries have declared their intention to enter into a separate Agreement on an International Energy Program which is attached to document C(74)204 of 6th November, 1974, and Corrigendum 1 thereto, which is circulated for reference and is hereinafter referred to as the "Agreement";

Having regard to the Recommendation of the Council of 29th June, 1971 on Oil Stockpiling [C(71)113(Final)];

Having regard to the Decision of the Council of 14th November, 1972 on Emergency Plans and Measures and Apportionment of Oil Supplies in an Emergency in the OECD European Area [C(72)201(Final)];

Having regard to the Recommendation of the Council of 10th January, 1974 on the Supply of Bunker Fuels for Shipping and Fishing [C(73)257 (Final)];

Having regard to the Recommendation of the Council of 10th January, 1974 on the Supply of Fuel for Civil Aircraft [C(73)258(Final)];

Having regard to the Note by the Secretary-General of 6th November, 1974 concerning the International Energy Program [C(74)203 and Corrigendum 1];

DECIDE:

Article 1

Il est créé une Agence Internationale de l'Energie (appelée ci-dessous l'„Agence") en tant qu'organe autonome dans le cadre de l'Organisation.

Article 2

Les Pays Participants à l'Agence sont les suivants:

(*a*) Allemagne, Autriche, Belgique, Canada, Danemark, Espagne, Etats-Unis, Irlande, Italie, Japon, Luxembourg, Pays-Bas, Royaume-Uni, Suède, Suisse et Turquie.

(*b*) Les autres pays Membres de l'Organisation qui adhèrent à la présente Décision et à l'Accord conformément aux dispositions de celui-ci.

Article 3

La présente Décision est ouverte à l'adhésion des Communautés Européennes à dater de leur adhésion à l'Accord conformément aux dispositions de celui-ci.

Article 4

Un Comité de Direction, qui comprend tous les Pays Participants à l'Agence, est l'organe duquel émanent tous les actes de l'Agence; il est habilité à faire des recommandations et à prendre des décisions qui, sauf disposition contraire, ont force obligatoire pour les Pays Participants, et à déléguer ses pouvoirs à d'autres organes de l'Agence. Le Comité de Direction adopte ses propres règlements et procédure et règles de vote.

Article 5

Le Comité de Direction crée tout organe et institue toute procédure nécessaires au bon fonctionnement de l'Agence.

Article 6

(*a*) Le Comité de Direction définit et applique un Programme International de l'Energie prévoyant une coopération dans le domaine de l'énergie, et dont les objectifs sont les suivants:

(i) assurer un niveau commun d'autonomie des approvisionnements pétroliers en cas d'urgence;

(ii) instituer des mesures communes de restriction de la demande de pétrole en cas d'urgence;

(iii) instituer et mettre en oeuvre des mesures de répartition du pétrole disponible en période d'urgence;

(iv) élaborer un système d'informations relatives au marché pétrolier international et un mécanisme de consultation avec les compagnies pétrolières internationales;

(v) élaborer et appliquer un programme de coopération à long terme en vue de réduire la dépendance à l'égard des importations de pétrole, ayant notamment pour objet la conservation de l'énergie, la mise en oeuvre de sources d'énergie de substitution, la recherche et le développement dans le domaine de l'énergie ainsi que l'approvisionnement en uranium naturel et enrichi;

DECIDES:

Article 1

An International Energy Agency (hereinafter called the "Agency") is hereby established as an autonomous body within the framework of the Organisation.

Article 2

Participating Countries of the Agency are:

(*a*) Austria, Belgium, Canada, Denmark, Germany, Ireland, Italy, Japan, Luxembourg, the Netherlands, Spain, Sweden, Switzerland, Turkey, the United Kingdom and the United States;

(*b*) other Member countries of the Organisation which accede to this Decision and to the Agreement in accordance with its terms.

Article 3

This Decision will be open for accession by the European Communities upon their accession to the Agreement in accordance with its terms.

Article 4

A Governing Board composed of all the Participating Countries of the Agency shall be the body from which all acts of the Agency derive, and shall have the power to make recommendations and to take decisions which shall, except as otherwise provided, be binding upon Participating Countries, and to delegate its powers to other organs of the Agency. The Governing Board shall adopt its own rules of procedure and voting rules.

Article 5

The Governing Board shall establish such organs and procedures as may be required for the proper functioning of the Agency.

Article 6

(*a*) The Governing Board shall decide upon and carry out an International Energy Program for co-operation in the field of energy, the aims of which are:

(i) development of a common level of emergency selfsufficiency in oil supplies;

(ii) establishment of common demand restraint measures in an emergency;

(iii) establishment and implementation of measures for the allocation of available oil in time of emergency;

(iv) development of a system of information on the international oil market and a framework for consultation with international oil companies;

(v) development and implementation of a long-term co-operation programme to reduce dependence on imported oil, including: conservation of energy, development of alternative sources of energy, energy research and development, and supply of natural and enriched uranium;

(vi) promotion of co-operative relations with oil producing countries and with other oil consuming countries, particularly those of the developing world.

(vi) promouvoir des relations de coopération avec les pays producteurs de pétrole et avec les autres pays consommateurs de pétrole, notamment ceux qui appartiennent au monde en développement.

Le Comité de Direction est habilité à adopter d'autres mesures de coopération dans le domaine de l'énergie qu'il peut juger nécessaires, et à modifier de toute autre manière le Programme en se prononçant à l'unanimité, en tenant compte des procédures constitutionnelles des Pays Participants.

(b) Sur la proposition du Comité de Direction de l'Agence, le Conseil peut conférer des responsabilités supplémentaires à l'Agence.

Article 7

(*a*) Les organes de l'Agence sont assistés par un Directeur exécutif et par le personnel nécessaire; le Directeur exécutif et le personnel font partie du Secrétariat de l'Organisation et dans l'exécution de leurs fonctions au titre du Programme International de l'Energie sont responsables envers les organes de l'Agence auxquels ils sont rapport.

(*b*) Le Directeur exécutif est nommé par le Comité de Direction sur la proposition ou avec l'assentiment du Secrétaire général.

(*c*) Les consultants de l'Agence peuvent être engagés pour une durée supérieure à celle qui est prévue à l'Article 2(b) des Statut, Règlement et Instructions applicables aux experts du Conseil et aux consultants de l'Organisation.

Article 8

Le Comité de Direction fait rapport chaque année au Conseil sur les activités de l'Agence. A la demande du Conseil ou de sa propre initiative, le Comité de Direction soumet d'autres communications au Conseil.

Article 9

L'Agence coopère avec les autres organes compétents de l'Organisation dans les domaines d'intérêt commun. Ces organes et l'Agence se consultent mutuellement au sujet de leurs activités respectives.

Article 10

(*a*) Le budget de l'Agence fait partie du Budget de l'Organisation et les dépenses de l'Agence sont imputées sur les crédits ouverts à cette fin à la deuxième partie du Budget où figurent les prévisions et dispositions budgétaires appropriées visant toutes les dépenses nécessaires au fonctionnement de l'Agence. La part respective des Pays Participants dans le financement de ces dépenses est fixée par le Comité de Direction. Les dépenses spéciales engagées par l'Agence à l'occasion d'activités visées à l'Article 11 sont réparties entre les Pays Participants dans des proportions dont les pays conviennent à l'unanimité. Un organe de l'Agence désigné par le Comité de Direction donne, chaque fois qu'il est nécessaire, son avis au Comité de Direction sur l'administration financière de l'Agence et fait connaître son avis sur les propositions budgétaires, annuelles et autres, soumises au Comité de Direction.

(*b*) Le Comité de Direction soumet pour adoption les propositions budgétaires, annuelles et autres, de l'Agence au Conseil par accord des Pays

The Governing Board may adopt other measures of co-operation in the energy field which it may deem necessary and otherwise amend the Program by unanimity, taking into account the constitutional procedures of the Participating Countries.

(*b*) Upon the proposal of the Governing Board of the Agency, the Council may confer additional responsibilities upon the Agency.

Article 7

(*a*) The organs of the Agency shall be assisted by an Executive Director and such staff as is necessary who shall form part of the Secretariat of the Organisation and who shall, in performing their duties under the International Energy Program, be responsible to and report to the organs of the Agency.

(*b*) The Executive Director shall be appointed by the Governing Board on the proposal or with concurrence of the Secretary-General.

(*c*) Consultants to the Agency may be appointed for a period exceeding that provided in Regulation 2(b) of the Regulations and Rules for Council Experts and Consultants of the Organisation.

Article 8

The Governing Board shall report annually to the Council on the activities of the Agency. The Governing Board shall submit, upon the request of the Council or upon its own initiative, other communications to the Council.

Article 9

The Agency shall co-operate with other competent bodies of the Organisation in areas of common interest. These bodies and the Agency shall consult with one another regarding their respective activities.

Article 10

(*a*) The budget of the Agency shall form part of the Budget of the Organisation and expenditure of the Agency shall be charged against the appropriations authorised for it under Part II of the Budget which shall include appropriate Budget estimates and provisions for all expenditure necessary for the operation of the Agency. Each Participating Country's share in financing such expenditure shall be fixed by the Governing Board. Special expenses incurred by the Agency in connection with activities referred to in Article 11 shall be shared by the Participating Countries in such proportions as shall be determined by unanimous agreement of those countries. The Governing Board shall designate an organ of the Agency to advise the Governing Board as required on the financial administration of the Agency and to give its opinion on the annual and other budget proposals submitted to the Governing Board.

(*b*) The Governing Board shall submit the annual and other budget proposals of the Agency to the Council for adoption by agreement of those

Participants à l'Agence qui ont voté au Comité de Direction pour que les propositions soient soumises au Conseil.

(*c*) Nonobstant les dispositions de l'Article 14(b) du Règlement financier, le Comité de Direction peut accepter les contributions volontaires et les dons ainsi que les paiements des services rendus par l'Agence.

(*d*) Nonobstant les dispositions de l'Article 16(b) du Règlement financier de l'Organisation, les crédits relatifs aux activités spéciales visées à l'Article 11 de la présente Décision, qui n'ont pas donné lieu à un engagement à la clôture de l'année financière au titre de laquelle ils ont été ouverts, sont automatiquement reportés sur le budget de l'année suivante.

Article 11

Deux Pays Participants, au moins, peuvent décider d'entreprendre dans le cadre du Programme des activités spéciales autres que celles qui doivent l'être nécessairement par l'ensemble des Pays Participants en vertu de l'Accord. Les Pays Participants qui ne souhaitent pas prendre part à ces activités s'abstiennent de prendre part à ces décisions et ne sont pas liés par celles-ci. Les Pays Participants qui poursuivent de telles activités en tiennent le Comité de Direction informé.

Article 12

En vue d'atteindre les objectifs du Programme, l'Agence est habilitée à établir les relations appropriées avec des pays autres que les Pays Participants, des organisations internationales, gouvernementales ou non gouvernementales, d'autres entités et des personnes physiques.

Article 13

(*a*) Un Pays Participant à l'égard duquel l'Accord a cessé d'être en vigueur ou de s'appliquer à titre provisoire est censé s'être retiré de l'Agence.

(*b*) Nonobstant les dispositions du paragraphe (a), un Pays dont le Gouvernement a signé l'Accord peut, en notifiant par écrit au Comité de Direction et au Gouvernement du Royaume de Belgique que l'adoption du Programme par le Comité de Direction a pour lui force exécutoire en vertu de la présente Décision, rester Pays Participant à l'Agence après que l'Accord ait cessé de s'appliquer à son égard, sous réserve de décision contraire du Comité de Direction. Un tel pays a les mêmes obligations et les mêmes droits qu'un Pays Participant à l'Agence à l'égard duquel l'Accord est entré définitivement en vigueur.

Article 14

La présente Décision entrera en vigueur le 15 novembre 1974.

Participating Countries of the Agency which voted in the Governing Board to submit the proposals to the Council.

(*c*) Notwithstanding the provisions of Article 14(b) of the Financial Regulations, the Governing Board may accept voluntary contributions and grants as well as payments for services rendered by the Agency.

(*d*) Notwithstanding the provisions of Article 16(b) of the Financial Regulations of the Organisation, appropriations in respect of the special activities referred to in Article 11 of this Decision, for which no commitment has been entered into before the end of the Financial Year for which they were appropriated, shall be automatically carried forward to the budget for the ensuing year.

Article 11

Any two or more Participating Countries may decide to carry out within the scope op the Program special activities, other than activities which are required to be carried out by all Participating Countries under the Agreement. Participating Countries who do not wish to take part in such activities shall abstain from taking part in such decisions and shall not be bound by them. Participating Countries carrying out such activities shall keep the Governing Board informed thereof.

Article 12

In order to achieve the objectives of the Program, the Agency may establish appropriate relationships with countries which are not Participating Countries, international organisations, whether Governmental or non-Governmental, other entities and individuals.

Article 13

(*a*) A Participating Country for which the Agreement shall have ceased to be in force or to apply provisionally shall be deemed to have withdrawn from the Agency.

(*b*) Notwithstanding the provisions of paragraph (a), a Country whose Government shall have signed the Agreement may, upon written notice to the Governing Board and to the Government of Belgium to the effect that the adoption of the Program by the Governing Board is binding on it pursuant to this Decision, remain a Participating Country of the Agency after the Agreement shall have ceased to apply for it, unless the Governing Board decides otherwise. Such a Country shall have the same obligations and the same rights as a Participating Country of the Agency for which the Agreement shall have entered definitively into force.

Article 14

The present Decision shall enter into force on 15th November, 1974.

ACCORD
RELATIF A UN PROGRAMME INTERNATIONAL DE L'ENERGIE

LES GOUVERNEMENTS DE LA REPUBLIQUE FEDERALE D'ALLEMAGNE, DE LA REPUBLIQUE D'AUTRICHE, DU ROYAUME DE BELGIQUE, DU CANADA, DU ROYAUME DE DANEMARK, DE L'ESPAGNE, DES ETATS-UNIS D'AMERIQUE, DE L'IRLANDE, DE LA REPUBLIQUE ITALIENNE, DU JAPON, DU GRAND-DUCHE DE LUXEMBOURG, DU ROYAUME DES PAYS-BAS, DU ROYAUME-UNI DE GRANDE-BRETAGNE ET D'IRLANDE DU NORD, DU ROYAUME DE SUEDE, DE LA CONFEDERATION SUISSE ET DE LA REPUBLIQUE TURQUE,

DESIREUX de promouvoir la sécurité des approvisionnements en pétrole à des conditions raisonnables et équitables,

RESOLUS à prendre des mesures communes efficaces pour faire face aux crises d'approvisionnement pétrolier, en assurant une autonomie des approvisionnements pétroliers en cas d'urgence, en restreignant la demande et en répartissant entre lesdits pays, sur une base équitable, les quantités de pétrole disponibles,

DESIREUX de promouvoir des relations de coopération avec les pays producteurs de pétrole et avec les autres pays consommateurs de pétrole, notamment ceux qui appartiennent au monde en voie de développement, par un dialogue constructif ainsi que par d'autres formes de coopération, afin de développer les possibilités d'une meilleure compréhension entre pays consommateurs et producteurs.

SOUCIEUX des intérêts des autres pays consommateurs de pétrole et notamment ceux qui appartiennent au monde en voie de développement,

DESIREUX de jouer un rôle plus actif par rapport à l'industrie pétrolière en établissant un large système international d'information ainsi qu'un cadre permanent de consultation avec les compagnies pétrolières,

RESOLUS à réduire leur dépendance à l'égard des importations de pétrole en entreprenant en coopération des efforts à long terme visant la conservation de l'énergie, la mise en œuvre accélérée de sources d'énergie de substitution, la recherche et le développement dans le domaine de l'énergie ainsi que l'enrichissement de l'uranium,

CONVAINCUS que ces objectifs ne peuvent être atteints que par des efforts soutenus entrepris en coopération au sein d'institutions efficaces,

EXPRIMANT leur intention que de telles institutions soient établies dans le cadre de l'Organisation de Coopération et de Développement Economiques,

RECONNAISSANT que d'autres Pays Membres de l'Organisation de Coopération et de Développement Economiques peuvent souhaiter se joindre à leurs efforts,

CONSIDERANT la responsabilité spéciale qui incombe aux gouvernements en matière d'approvisionnements énergétiques,

CONCLUENT qu'il est nécessaire d'établir un Programme International de l'Energie dont la mise en œuvre sera assurée par une Agence Internationale de l'Energie, et, à cette fin,

SONT CONVENUS de ce qui suit:

Article 1

1. Les Pays Participants mettent en oeuvre le Programme International de l'Energie tel que défini dans le présent Accord, par le moyen de l'Agence Internationale de l'Energie, appelée ci-après l',,Agence'', qui fait l'objet du Chapitre IX.

2. Par ,,Pays Participants'', il faut entendre les Etats auxquels le pré-

AGREEMENT ON AN INTERNATIONAL ENERGY PROGRAM

THE GOVERNMENTS OF THE REPUBLIC OF AUSTRIA, THE KINGDOM OF BELGIUM, CANADA, THE KINGDOM OF DENMARK, THE FEDERAL REPUBLIC OF GERMANY, IRELAND, THE ITALIAN REPUBLIC, JAPAN, THE GRAND DUCHY OF LUXEMBOURG, THE KINGDOM OF THE NETHERLANDS, SPAIN, THE KINGDOM OF SWEDEN, THE SWISS CONFEDERATION, THE REPUBLIC OF TURKEY, THE UNITED KINGDOM OF GREAT BRITAIN AND NORTHERN IRELAND, AND THE UNITED STATES OF AMERICA,

DESIRING to promote secure oil supplies on reasonable and equitable terms,

DETERMINED to take common effective measures to meet oil supply emergencies by developing an emergency self-sufficiency in oil supplies, restraining demand and allocating available oil among their countries on an equitable basis,

DESIRING to promote co-operative relations with oil producing countries and with other oil consuming countries, including those of the developing world, through a purposeful dialogue, as well as through other forms of co-operation, to further the opportunities for a better understanding between consumer and producer countries,

MINDFUL of the interests of other oil consuming countries, including those of the developing world,

DESIRING to play a more active role in relation to the oil industry by establishing a comprehensive international information system and a permanent framework for consultation with oil companies,

DETERMINED to reduce their dependence on imported oil by undertaking long term co-operative efforts on conservation of energy, on accelerated development of alternative sources of energy, on research and development in the energy field and on uranium enrichment,

CONVINCED that these objectives can only be reached through continued co-operative efforts within effective organs,

EXPRESSING the intention that such organs be created within the framework of the Organisation for Economic Co-operation and Development.

RECOGNISING that other Member countries of the Organisation for Economic Co-operation and Development may desire to join in their efforts,

CONSIDERING the special responsibility of governments for energy supply,

CONCLUDE that it is necessary to establish an International Energy Program to be implemented through an International Energy Agency, and to that end,

HAVE AGREED as follows:

Article 1

1. The Participating Countries shall implement the International Energy Program as provided for in this Agreement through the International Energy Agency, described in Chapter IX, hereinafter referred to as the "Agency".

2. The term "Participating Countries" means States to which this

sent Accord s'applique à titre provisoire et les Etats pour lesquels l'Accord est entré et demeure en vigueur.

3. Par „groupe", il faut entendre les Pays Participants considérés en tant que groupe.

Chapitre I

Autonomie énergétique en cas d'urgence

Article 2

1. Les Pays Participants établissent une autonomie commune des approvisionnements pétroliers en cas d'urgence. A cette fin, chaque Pays Participant maintient des réserves d'urgence suffisantes pour couvrir la consommation pendant au moins 60 jours sans importations nettes de pétrole. La consommation et les importations nettes de pétrole sont calculées sur la base du niveau quotidien moyen de l'année civile précédente.

2. Le Conseil de Direction décidera, le 1er juillet 1975 au plus tard, à la majorité spéciale, de la date à compter de laquelle l'engagement en matière de réserves d'urgence de chaque Pays Participant, sur la base duquel est calculé son droit d'approvisionnement visé à l'Article 7, sera censé être porté à un niveau correspondant à 90 jours. Chaque Pays Participant porte le niveau effectif de ses réserves d'urgence à 90 jours en s'efforçant d'y parvenir pour la date ainsi décidée.

3. Par „engagement en matière de réserves d'urgence", il faut entendre les réserves d'urgence équivalentes à 60 jours d'importations nettes de pétrole conformément à l'alinéa 1 et, à compter de la date qui sera décidée selon les dispositions de l'alinéa 2, à 90 jours d'importations nettes de pétrole conformément à l'alinéa 2.

Article 3

1. L'engagement en matière de réserves d'urgence visé à l'Article 2 peut être rempli au moyen:
- de stocks de pétrole,
- d'une capacité de commutation de combustible,
- d'une production pétrolière de réserve,

conformément aux dispositions de l'Annexe qui fait partie intégrante du présent Accord.

2. Le Conseil de Direction décidera, le 1er juillet 1975 au plus tard, à la majorité, de la mesure dans laquelle l'engagement en matière de réserves d'urgence peut être rempli par les divers éléments mentionnés au paragraphe 1.

Article 4

1. Le Groupe Permanent sur les questions urgentes vérifie en permanence l'efficacité des mesures prises par chaque Pays Participant pour remplir son engagement en matière de réserves d'urgence.

2. Le Groupe Permanent sur les questions urgentes fait rapport au Comité de Gestion qui soumet, s'il y a lieu, des propositions au Conseil de Direction. Celui-ci peut adopter à la majorité des recommandations aux Pays Participants.

Agreement upplies provisionally and States for which the Agreement has entered into and remains in force.

3. The term "group" means the Participating Countries as a group.

Chapter I

Emergency Self-Sufficiency

Article 2

1. The Participating Countries shall establish a common emergency selfsufficiency in oil supplies. To this end, each Participating Country shall maintain emergency reserves sufficient to sustain consumption for at least 60 days with no net oil imports. Both consumption and net oil imports shall be reckoned at the average daily level of the preceding calendar year.

2. The Governing Board shall, acting by special majority, not later than 1st July, 1975, decide the date from which the emergency reserve commitment of each Participating Country shall, for the purpose of calculating its supply right referred to in Article 7, be deemed to be raised to a level of 90 days. Each Participating Country shall increase its actual level of emergency reserves to 90 days and shall endeavour to do so by the date so decided.

3. The term "emergency reserve commitment" means the emergency reserves equivalent to 60 days of net oil imports as set out in paragraph 1 and, from the date to be decided according to paragraph 2, to 90 days of net oil imports as set out in paragraph 2.

Article 3

1. The emergency reserve commitment set out in Article 2 may be satisfied by:

- oil stocks,
- fuel switching capacity,
- stand-by oil production,

in accordance with the provisions of the Annex which forms an integral part of this Agreement.

2. The Governing Board shall, acting by majority, not later than 1st July, 1975, decide the extent to which the emergency reserve commitment may be satisfied by the elements mentioned in paragraph 1.

Article 4

1. The Standing Group on Emergency Questions shall, on a continuing basis, review the effectiveness of the measures taken by each Participating Country to meet its emergency reserve commitment.

2. The Standing Group on Emergency Questions shall report to the Management Committee, which shall make proposals, as appropriate, to the Governing Board. The Governing Board may, acting by majority, adopt recommendations to Participating Countries.

Chapitre II

Restriction de la demande

Article 5

1. Chaque Pays Participant tient prêt en permanence un programme d'éventuelles mesures de restriction de la demande de pétrole lui permettant de réduire son taux de consommation finale conformément au Chapitre IV.

2. Le Groupe Permanent sur les questions urgentes vérifie et évalue en permanence:

- le programme de mesures de restriction de la demande établi par chaque Pays Participant,
- l'efficacité des mesures effectivement prises par chaque Pays Participant.

3. Le Groupe Permanent sur les questions urgentes fait rapport au Comité de Gestion qui soumet, s'il y a lieu, des propositions au Conseil de Direction. Celui-ci peut adopter à la majorité des recommandations aux Pays Participants.

Chapitre III

Répartition

Article 6

1. Chaque Pays Participant prend les mesures nécessaires afin que la répartition du pétrole soit effectuée conformément au présent Chapitre et au Chapitre IV.

2. Le Groupe Permanent sur les questions urgentes vérifie et évalue de façon continue:

- les mesures prises par chaque Pays Participant en vue de répartir le pétrole conformément au présent Chapitre et au Chapitre IV,
- l'efficacité des mesures effectivement prises par chaque Pays Participant.

3. Le Groupe Permanent sur les questions urgentes fait rapport au Comité de Gestion qui soumet, s'il y a lieu, des propositions au Conseil de Direction. Celui-ci peut adopter à la majorité des recommandations aux Pays Participants.

4. Le Conseil de Direction détermine sans délai, à la majorité, les procédures pratiques de répartition du pétrole ainsi que les procédures et modalités de participation des compagnies pétrolières dans cette répartition, dans le cadre du présent Accord.

Article 7

1. Lorsque la répartition du pétrole est effectuée conformément aux Articles 13, 14 ou 15, chaque Pays Participant a droit à un approvisionnement égal à sa consommation autorisée, diminuée de son obligation d'abaissement des réserves d'urgence.

2. Un Pays Participant, dont le droit d'approvisionnement dépasse le total de sa production intérieure normale et de ses importations nettes réelles disponibles pendant une période d'urgence, a un droit d'allocation représentant le montant des importations nettes supplémentaires égal à cet excédent.

Chapter II

Demand Restraint

Article 5

1. Each Participating Country shall at all times have ready a program of contingent oil demand restraint measures enabling it to reduce its rate of final consumption in accordance with Chapter IV.

2. The Standing Group on Emergency Questions shall, on a continuing basis, review and assess:
- each Participating Country's program of demand restraint measures,
- the effectiveness of measures actually taken by each Participating Country.

3. The Standing Group on Emergency Qusstions shall report to the Management Committee, which shall make proposals, as appropriate, to the Governing Board. The Governing Board may, acting by majority, adopt recommendations to Participating Countries.

Chapter III

Allocation

Article 6

1. Each Participating Country shall take the necessary measures in order that allocation of oil will be carried out pursuant to this Chapter and Chapter IV.

2. The Standing Group on Emergency Questions shall, on a continuing basis, review and assess:
- each Participating Country's measures in order that allocation of oil will be carried out pursuant to this Chapter and Chapter IV,
- the effectiveness of measures actually taken by each Participating Country.

3. The Standing Group on Emergency Questions shall report to the Management Committee, which shall make proposals, as appropriate, to the Governing Board. The Governing Board may, acting by majority, adopt recommendations to Participating Countries.

4. The Governing Board shall, acting by majority, decide promptly on the practical procedures for the allocation of oil and on the procedures and modalities for the participation of oil companies therein within the framework of this Agreement.

Article 7

1. When allocation of oil is carried out pursuant to Article 13, 14 ,or 15, each Participating Country shall have a supply right equal to its permissble consumption less its emergency reserve drawdown obligation.

2. A Participating Country whose supply right exceeds the sum of its normal domestic production and actual net imports available during an emergency shall have an allocation right which entitles it to additional net imports equal to that excess.

3. A Participating Country in which the sum of normal domestic production and actual net imports available during an emergency exceeds its

3. Un Pays Participant, dont le total de la production normale intérieure et des importations nettes réelles disponibles pendant une période d'urgence dépasse son droit d'approvisionnement, a une obligation de répartition en vertu de laquelle il est tenu de fournir, directement ou indirectement, une quantité de pétrole égale à cet excédent à d'autres Pays Participants. Cette obligation n'empêche pas un Pays Participant de maintenir ses exportations de pétrole vers des pays non participants.

4. Par ,,consommation autorisée'', il faut entendre le taux quotidien moyen de consommation finale admis lorsque des restrictions d'urgence de la demande ont été mises en vigueur au niveau approprié; d'éventuelles restrictions supplémentaires de la demande volontairement effectuées par un Pays Participant n'affectent pas son droit d'allocation ou son obligation de répartition.

5. Par ,,obligation d'abaissement des réserves d'urgence'', il faut entendre l'engagement en matière de réserves d'urgence d'un Pays Participant divisé par l'engagement total du groupe en matière de réserves d'urgence et multiplié par le déficit d'approvisionnement du groupe.

6. Par ,,déficit d'approvisionnement du groupe'', il faut entendre le déficit du groupe, tel qu'il résulte de la consommation autorisée globale du groupe, diminuée du taux quotidien des approvisionnements en pétrole dont il dispose pendant une période d'urgence.

7. Par ,,approvisionnements en pétrole dont dispose le groupe'', il faut entendre:
- la totalité du pétrole brut dont dispose le groupe,
- la totalité des produits pétroliers importés de l'extérieur du groupe, et
- la totalité des produits finis et des approvisionnements des raffineries, obtenus par l'utilisation de gaz naturel et du pétrole brut, et dont dispose le groupe.

8. Par ,,consommation finale'', il faut entendre la consommation intérieure totale de tous les produits pétroliers finis.

Article 8

1. Lorsque du pétrole est alloué à un Pays Participant conformément à l'Article 17, ce Pays Participant:
- impute la réduction de ses approvisionnements en pétrole sur sa consommation finale à concurrence de 7% de sa consommation finale pendant la période de référence,
- a un droit d'allocation égal au montant de la réduction de ses approvisionnements en pétrole, réduction qui a pour conséquence une réduction de sa consommation finale au-delà de ce niveau.

2. L'obligation d'allouer cette quantité de pétrole est partagée entre les autres Pays Participants sur la base de leur consommation finale pendant la période de référence.

3. Les Pays Participants peuvent remplir leurs obligations d'allocation par toutes mesures de leur choix, y compris par des mesures de restriction de la demande ou par l'utilisation des réserves d'urgence.

Article 9

1. Pour donner effet aux droits d'allocation et aux obligations d'allocation, les éléments suivants sont pris en considération:
- la totalité du pétrole brut,
- la totalité des produits pétroliers,
- la totalité des approvisionnements des raffineries, et

supplyright shall have an allocation obligation which requires it to supply, directly or indirectly, the quantity of oil equal to that excess to other Participating Countries. This would not preclude any Participating Country from maintaining exports of oil to non-participating countries.

4. The term "permissible consumption" means the average daily rate of final consumption allowed when emergency demand restraint at the applicable level has been activated; possible further voluntary demand restraint by any Participating Country shall not affect its allocation right or obligation.

5. The term "emergency reserve drawdown obligation" means the emergency reserve commitment of any Participating Country divided by the total emergency reserve commitment of the group and multiplied by the group supply shortfall.

6. The term "group supply shortfall" means the shortfall for the group as measured by the aggregate permissible consumption for the group minus the daily rate of oil supplies available to the group during an emergency.

7. The term "oil supplies available to the group" means
- all crude oil available to the group,
- all petroleum products imported from outside the group, and
- all finished products and refinery feedstocks which are produced in association with natural gas and crude oil and are available to the group.

8. The term "final consumption" means total domestic consumption of all finished petroleum products.

Article 8

1. When allocation of oil to a Participating Country is carried out pursuant to Article 17, that Participating Country shall
- sustain from its final consumption the reduction in its oil supplies up to a level equal to 7 per cent of its final consumption during the base period,
- have an allocation right equal to the reduction in its oil supplies which results in a reduction of its final consumption over and above that level.

2. The obligation to allocate this amount of oil is shared among the other Participating Countries on the basis of their final consumption during the base period.

3. The Participating Countries may meet their allocation obligations by any measures of their own choosing, including demand restraint measures or use of emergency reserves.

Article 9

1. For purposes of satisfying allocation rights and allocation obligations, the following elements will be included:
- all crude oil,
- all petroleum products,
- all refinery feedstocks, and

– la totalité des produits finis obtenus par l'utilisation de gaz naturel et de pétrole brut.

2. Pour calculer le droit d'allocation d'un Pays Participant, les produits pétroliers normalement importés par ce Pays, en provenance d'autres Pays Participants ou de pays non participants, sont convertis en équivalents de pétrole brut et considérés comme des importations de pétrole brut dans ce Pays Participant.

3. Dans la mesure du possible, les circuits normaux d'approvisionnement sont maintenus ainsi que la proportion normale des approvisionnements entre pétrole brut et produits, et entre les diverses catégories de pétrole brut et de produits.

4. Lorsque la répartition est mise en oeuvre, le Programme a notamment pour objectif de répartir le pétrole brut et les produits disponibles, dans la mesure du possible, entre les secteurs du raffinage et de la distribution ainsi qu'entre les compagnies de raffinage et de distribution, conformément aux structures d'approvisionnement traditionnelles.

Article 10

1. Les objectifs du Programme consistent notamment à assurer un traitement équitable à tous les Pays Participants et à baser le prix du pétrole réparti entre eux sur les conditions de prix en vigueur pour des opérations commerciales comparables.

2. Les questions relatives au prix du pétrole alloué en cas d'urgence sont examinées par le Groupe Permanent sur les questions urgentes.

Article 11

1. Le Programme n'a pas pour objectif de chercher à accroître, en cas d'urgence, la part de l'approvisionnement mondial en pétrole dont le groupe disposait dans les conditions normales du marché. Les structures traditionnelles du commerce pétrolier devraient être maintenues dans toute la mesure raisonnable et il devrait être dûment tenu compte de la situation des différents pays non participants.

2. Afin d'assurer le respect des principes prévus à l'alinéa 1, le Comité de Gestion soumet, le cas échéant, des propositions au Conseil de Direction qui prend à la majorité une décision sur ces propositions.

Chapitre IV

Mise en vigueur des mesures

Mise en vigueur des mesures

Article 12

Lorsque le groupe dans son ensemble ou un Pays Participant subit, ou est raisonnablement susceptible de subir, une réduction de ses approvisionnements en pétrole, les mesures d'urgence – à savoir la restriction obligatoire de la demande visée au Chapitre II et la répartition du pétrole disponible visée au Chapitre III – sont mises en vigueur conformément au présent Chapitre.

– all finished products produced in association with natural gas and crude oil.

2. To calculate a Participating Country's allocation right, petroleum products normally imported by that Participating Country, whether from other Participating Countries or from non-participating countries, shall be expressed in crude oil equivalents and treated as though they were imports of crude oil to that Participating Country.

3. Insofar as possible, normal channels of supply will be maintained as well as the normal supply proportions between crude oil and products and among different categories of crude oil and products.

4. When allocation takes place, an objective of the Program shall be that available crude oil and products shall, insofar as possible, be shared within the refining and distributing industries as well as between refining and distributing companies in accordance with historical supply patterns.

Article 10

1. The objectives of the Program shall include ensuring fair treatment for all Participating Countries and basing the price for allocated oil on the price conditions prevailing for comparable commercial transactions.

2. Questions relating to the price of oil allocated during an emergency shall be examined by the Standing Group on Emergency Questions.

Article 11

1. It is not an objective of the Program to seek to increase, in an emergency, the share of world oil supply that the group had under normal market conditions. Historical oil trade patterns should be preserved as far as is reasonable, and due account should be taken of the position of individual non-participating countries.

2. In order to maintain the principles set out in paragraph 1, the Management Committee shall make proposals, as appropriate, to the Governing Board, which, acting by majority, shall decide on such proposals.

Chapter IV

Activation

Activation

Article 12

Whenever the group as a whole or any Participating Country sustains or can reasonably be expected to sustain a reduction in its oil supplies, the emergency measures, which are the mandatory demand restraint referred to in Chapter II and the allocation of available oil referred to in Chapter III, shall be activated in accordance with this Chapter.

Article 13

Lorsque le groupe subit, ou est raisonnablement susceptible de subir, une réduction du taux quotidien de ses approvisionnements en pétrole égale à 7 % au moins du taux quotidien moyen de sa consommation finale pendant la période de référence, chaque Pays Participant met en oeuvre des mesures de restriction de la demande suffisantes pour réduire sa consommation finale d'un volume égal à 7 % de sa consommation finale pendant la période de référence; la répartition du pétrole disponible entre les Pays Participants s'effectue conformément aux Articles 7, 9, 10 et 11.

Article 14

Lorsque le groupe subit, ou est raisonnablement susceptible de subir, une réduction du taux quotidien de ses approvisionnements en pétrole égale à 12 % au moins du taux quotidien moyen de sa consommation finale pendant la période de référence, chaque Pays Participant met en oeuvre des mesures de restriction de la demande suffisantes pour réduire sa consommation finale d'un volume égal à 10 % de sa consommation finale pendant la période de référence; la répartition du pétrole disponible entre les Pays Participants s'effectue conformément aux Articles 7, 9, 10 et 11.

Article 15

Lorsque les obligations quotidiennes cumulées d'abaissement des réserves d'urgence, telles qu'elles sont définies à l'Article 7, atteignent 50 % des engagements en matière de réserves d'approvisionnements d'urgence et qu'une décision a été prise conformément à l'Article 20, chaque Pays Participant prend les mesures ainsi décidées; la répartition du pétrole disponible entre les Pays Participants s'effectue conformément aux Articles 7, 9, 10 et 11.

Article 16

Lorsque la restriction de la demande est mise en vigueur conformément au présent Chapitre, un Pays Participant peut, au lieu d'appliquer des mesures de restriction de la demande, utiliser la fraction des réserves d'urgence qu'il détient en plus de son engagement en matière de réserves d'urgence tels qu'il est défini dans le Programme.

Article 17

1. Lorsqu'un Pays Participant subit, ou est raisonnablement susceptible de subir, une réduction du taux quotidien de ses approvisionnements en pétrole ayant pour conséquence une réduction du taux quotidien de sa consommation finale d'un volume supérieur à 7 % du taux quotidien moyen de sa consommation finale pendant la période de référence, une allocation de pétrole disponible à ce Pays Participant s'effectue conformément aux Articles 8 à 11.

2. Une allocation de pétrole disponible intervient également lorsque les conditions énumérées à l'alinéa 1 sont réunies dans une région importante d'un Pays Participant dont le marché pétrolier n'est pas complètement intégré. En ce cas, l'obligation d'allocation des autres Pays Participants sera réduite de l'obligation d'allocation théorique applicable à une ou plusieurs autres régions importantes du Pays Participant considéré.

Article 13

Whenever the group sustains or can reasonably be expected to sustain a reduction in the daily rate of its oil supplies at least equal to 7 per cent of the average daily rate of its final consumption during the base period, each Participating Country shall implement demand restraint measures sufficient to reduce its final consumption by an amount equal to 7 per cent of its final consumption during the base period, and allocation of available oil among the Participating Countries shall take place in accordance with Articles 7, 9, 10 and 11.

Article 14

Whenever the group sustains or can reasonably be expected to sustain a reduction in the daily rate of its oil supplies at least equal to 12 per cent of the average daily rate of its final consumption during the base period, each Participating Country shall implement demand restraint measures sufficient to reduce its final consumption by an amount equal to 10 per cent of its final consumption during the base period, and allocation of available oil among the Participating Countries shall take place in accordance with Articles 7, 9, 10 and 11.

Article 15

When cumulative daily emergency reserve drawdown obligations as defined in Article 7 have reached 50 per cent of emergency reserve commitments and a decision has been taken in accordance with Article 20, each Participating Country shall take the measures so decided, and allocation of available oil among the Participating Countries shall take place in accordance with Articles 7, 9, 10 and 11.

Article 16

When demand restraint is activated in accordance with this Chapter, a Participating Country may substitute for demand restraint measures use of emergency reserves held in excess of its emergency reserve commitment as provided in the Program.

Article 17

1. Whenever any Participating Country sustains or can reasonably be expected to sustain a reduction in the daily rate of its oil supplies which results in a reduction of the daily rate of its final consumption by an amount exceeding 7 per cent of the average daily rate of its final consumption during the base period, allocation of available oil to that Participating Country shall take place in accordance with Articles 8 to 11.

2. Allocation of available oil shall also take place when the conditions in paragraph 1 are fulfilled in a major region of a Participating Country whose oil market is incompletely integrated. In this case, the allocation obligation of other Participating Countries shall be reduced by the theoretical allocation obligation of any other major region or regions of the Participating Country concerned.

Article 18

1. Par „période de référence", il faut entendre les quatre derniers trimestres précédant la période d'un trimestre nécessaire pour recueillir les informations voulues. La période de référence reste la même aussi longtemps que les mesures d'urgence sont appliquées au groupe ou à un Pays Participant.

2. Le Groupe Permanent sur les questions urgentes examine la période de référence définie à l'alinéa 1, en tenant compte en particulier de facteurs tels que la croissance, les variations saisonnières de la consommation et les évolutions cycliques, et fait rapport, le 1er avril 1975 au plus tard, au Comité de Gestion. Le Comité de Gestion soumet, s'il y a lieu, des propositions au Conseil de Direction qui prend à la majorité une décision sur ces propositions, le 1er juillet 1975 au plus tard.

Article 19

1. Lorsqu'une réduction des approvisionnements en pétrole se produit ou est raisonnablement susceptible de se produire dans les conditions prévues aux Articles 13, 14 ou 17, le Secrétariat procède à une constatation et évalue le montant de la réduction effective ou à prévoir pour chaque Pays Participant et pour le groupe. Le Secrétariat tient le Comité de Gestion informé de ses délibérations, soumet immédiatement sa constatation aux membres du Comité et en informe aussitôt les Pays Participants. Le rapport comprend des informations sur la nature de la réduction.

2. Dans les 48 heures suivant la communication de la constatation du Secrétariat, le Comité de Gestion se réunit pour vérifier l'exactitude des données recueillies et des informations fournies. Le Comité de Gestion fait rapport au Conseil de Direction dans les 48 heures suivant sa réunion. Son rapport expose les vues exprimées par ses membres, notamment toutes opinions quant à la conduite à suivre face à la situation d'urgence.

3. Dans les 48 heures suivant la réception du rapport du Comité de Gestion, le Conseil de Direction se réunit pour examiner la constatation faite par le Secrétariat à la lumière de ce rapport. La mise en vigueur des mesures d'urgence est considérée comme confirmée et les Pays Participants doivent les appliquer dans un délai de 15 jours suivant cette confirmation, à moins que le Conseil de Direction, se prononçant à une majorité spéciale, ne décide, dans un nouveau délai de 48 heures, de ne pas mettre en vigueur les mesures d'urgence, de ne les mettre que partiellement en vigueur, ou de fixer une nouvelle date pour leur mise en vigueur.

4. Si, conformément à la constatation du Secrétariat, les conditions prévues par deux au moins des Articles 14, 13 et 17 sont remplies, toute décision de ne pas mettre en vigueur les mesures d'urgence doit être prise séparément pour chaque article et dans l'ordre indiqué ci-dessus. Si les conditions prévues à l'Article 17 sont remplies dans le cas de deux Pays Participants au moins, toute décision de ne pas mettre en vigueur le système d'allocation doit être prise séparément pour chaque pays.

5. Les décisions prises en application des alinéas 3 et 4 peuvent en tout temps être annulées par le Conseil de Direction se prononçant à la majorité.

6. Pour procéder à la constatation prévue au présent article, le Secrétariat consulte les compagnies pétrolières afin de recueillir leurs avis sur la situation et sur le caractère approprié des mesures à prendre.

7. Un comité consultatif international émanant de l'industrie pétrolière sera réuni, au plus tard au moment de la mise en vigueur des mesures d'urgence, afin d'aider l'Agence à assurer l'application effective de ces mesures.

Article 18

1. The term "base period" means the most recent four quarters with a delay of one quarter necessary to collect information. While emergency measures are applied with regard to the group or to a Participating Country, the base period shall remain fixed.

2. The Standing Group on Emergency Questions shall examine the base period set out in paragraph 1, taking into account in particular such factors as growth, seasonal variations in consumption and cyclical changes and shall, not later than 1st April, 1975, report to the Management Committee. The Management Committee shall make proposals, as appropriate, to the Governing Board, which, acting by majority, shall decide on these proposals not later than 1st July, 1975.

Article 19

1. The Secretariat shall make a finding when a reduction of oil supplies as mentioned in Article 13, 14 or 17 has occurred or can reasonably be expected to occur, and shall establish the amount of the reduction or expected reduction for each Participating Country and for the group. The Secretariat shall keep the Management Committee informed of its deliberations, and shall immediately report its finding to the members of the Committee and inform the Participating Countries thereof. The report shall include information on the nature of the reduction.

2. Within 48 hours of the Secretariat's reporting a finding, the Committee shall meet to review the accuracy of the data compiled and the information provided. The Committee shall report to the Governing Board within a further 48 hours. The report shall set out the views expressed by the members of the Committee, including any views regarding the handling of the emergency.

3. Within 48 hours of receiving the Management Committee's report, the Governing Board shall meet to review the finding of the Secretariat in the light of that report. The activation of emergency measures shall be considered confirmed and Participating Countries shall implement such measures within 15 days of such confirmation unless the Governing Board, acting by special majority, decides within a further 48 hours not to activate the emergency measures, to activate them only in part or to fix another time limit for their implementation.

4. If, according to the finding of the Secretariat, the conditions of more than one of the Articles 14, 13 and 17 are fulfilled, any decision not to activate emergency measures shall be taken separately for each Article and in the above order. If the conditions in Article 17 are fulfilled with regard to more than one Participating Country any decision not to activate allocation shall be taken separately with respect to each Country.

5. Decisions pursuant to paragraphs 2 and 4 may at any time be reversed by the Governing Board, acting by majority.

6. In making its finding under this Article, the Secretariat shall consult with oil companies to obtain their views regarding the situation and the appropriateness of the measures to be taken.

7. An international advisory board from the oil industry shall be convened, not later than the activation of emergency measures, to assist the Agency in ensuring the effective operation of such measures.

Article 20

1. Le Secrétariat procède à une constatation, lorsque les obligations quotidiennes cumulées d'abaissement des réserves d'urgence atteignent, ou sont raisonnablement susceptibles d'atteindre 50 % des engagements en matière de réserves d'urgence. Il communique immédiatement sa constatation aux membres du Comité de Gestion et en informe les Pays Participants. Ce rapport comprend des informations relatives à la situation pétrolière.

2. Dans les 72 heures suivant la communication de la constatation établie par le Secrétariat, le Comité de Gestion se réunit pour examiner les données recueillies et les informations fournies. Sur la base des informations disponibles, le Comité de Gestion fait rapport au Conseil de Direction dans les 48 heures qui suivent et propose les mesures requises pour faire face aux nécessités de la situation, y compris le relèvement du niveau des restrictions obligatoires de la demande qui peut s'avérer nécessaire. Ce rapport expose les vues exprimées par les membres du Comité de Gestion.

3. Le Conseil de Direction se réunit dans les 48 heures suivant la réception du rapport et des propositions du Comité de Gestion. Il examine la constatation faite par le Secrétariat et le rapport du Comité de Gestion et, dans un nouveau délai de 48 heures, décide à la majorité spéciale des mesures requises pour faire face aux nécessités de la situation, y compris le relèvement du niveau des restrictions obligatoires de la demande qui peut s'avérer nécessaire.

Article 21

1. Tout Pays Participant peut demander au Secrétariat de procéder à une constatation conformément aux Articles 19 ou 20.

2. Si, dans les 72 heures suivant une telle demande, le Secrétariat n'a pas procédé à cette constatation, le Pays Participant peut demander au Comité de Gestion de se réunir et d'examiner la situation conformément aux dispositions du présent Accord.

3. Le Comité de Gestion se réunit dans les 48 heures suivant une telle demande afin d'examiner la situation. A la demande de tout Pays Participant, il fait rapport au Conseil de Direction dans un nouveau délai de 48 heures. Le rapport expose les vues exprimées par les membres du Comité de Gestion et par le Secrétariat, y compris toutes opinions quant à la conduite à suivre face à la situation.

4. Le Conseil de Direction se réunit dans un délai de 48 heures suivant la réception du rapport du Comité de Gestion. S'il constate, par un vote à la majorité, que les conditions stipulées aux Articles 13, 14, 15 ou 17 sont remplies, les mesures d'urgence sont mises en vigueur en conséquence.

Article 22

Le Conseil de Direction peut à tout moment décider à l'unanimité de mettre en vigueur toutes mesures d'urgence appropriées non prévues dans le présent Accord, si la situation l'exige.

Levée des mesures

Article 23

1. Le Secrétariat procède à une constatation, lorsqu'une réduction des approvisionnements, telle que mentionnée aux Articles 13, 14 out 17, a

Article 20

1. The Secretariat shall make a finding when cumulative daily emergency reserve drawdown obligations have reached or can reasonably be expected to reach 50 per cent of emergency reserve commitments. The Secretariat shall immediately report its finding to the members of the Management Committee and inform the Participating Countries thereof. The report shall include information on the oil situation.

2. Within 72 hours of the Secretariat's reporting such a finding, the Management Committee shall meet to review the data compiled and the information provided. On the basis of available information the Committee shall report to the Governing Board within a further 48 hours proposing measures required for meeting the necessities of the situation, including the increase in the level of mandatory demand restraint that may be necessary. The report shall set out the views expressed by the members of the Committee.

3. The Governing Board shall meet within 48 hours of receiving the Committee's report and proposal. The Governing Board shall review the finding of the Secretariat and the report of the Management Committee and shall within a further 48 hours, acting by special majority, decide on the measures required for meeting the necessities of the situation, including the increase in the level of mandatory demand restraint that may be necessary.

Article 21

1. Any Participating Country may request the Secretariat to make a finding under Article 19 or 20.

2. If, within 72 hours of such request, the Secretariat does not make such a finding, the Participating Country may request the Management Committee to meet and consider the situation in accordance with the provisions of this Agreement.

3. The Management Committee shall meet within 48 hours of such request in order to consider the situation. It shall, at the request of any Participating Country, report to the Governing Board within a further 48 hours. The report shall set out the views expressed by the members of the Committee and by the Secretariat, including any views regarding the handling of the situation.

4. The Governing Board shall meet within 48 hours of receiving the Management Committee's report. If it finds, acting by majority, that the conditions set out in Article 13, 14, 15 or 17 are fulfilled, emergency measures shall be activated accordingly.

Article 22

The Governing Board may at any time decide by unanimity to activate any appropriate emergency measures not provided for in this Agreement, if the situation so requires.

Deactivation

Article 23

1. The Secretariat shall make a finding when a reduction of supplies as mentioned in Article 13, 14 or 17 has decreased or can reasonably be ex-

atteint, ou est raisonnablement susceptible d'atteindre un niveau inférieur à celui stipulé dans l'Article concerné. Il tient le Comité de Gestion informé de ses délibérations, fait immédiatement rapport sur sa constatation aux membres du Comité et en informe les Pays Participants.

2. Dans les 72 heures suivant la communication de la constatation établie par le Secrétariat, le Comité de Gestion se réunit pour examiner les données recueillies et les informations fournies. Il fait rapport au Conseil de Direction dans un nouveau délai de 48 heures suivant sa réunion. Ce rapport expose les vues exprimées par les membres du Comité de Gestion, y compris toutes opinions quant à la conduite à suivre face à la situation d'urgence.

3. Dans les 48 heures suivant la réception du rapport du Comité de Gestion, le Conseil de Direction se réunit pour examiner la constatation établie par le Secrétariat à la lumière de ce rapport. La levée des mesures d'urgence ou la réduction applicable au niveau de restriction de la demande est considérée comme confirmée à moins que le Conseil de Direction ne décide à la majorité spéciale et dans un nouveau délai de 48 heures de maintenir les mesures d'urgence ou de ne les lever que partiellement.

4. En procédant à sa constatation conformément au présent article, le Secrétariat consulte le comité consultatif international mentionné à l'Article 19, alinéa 7, afin de recueillir ses vues sur la situation et sur le caractère approprié des mesures à prendre.

5. Tout Pays Participant peut demander au Secrétariat de procéder à une constatation en vertu du présent article.

Article 24

Lorsque des mesures d'urgence sont en vigueur, et que le Secrétariat n'a pas effectué la constatation prévue à l'Article 23, le Conseil de Direction peut à tout moment décider à la majorité spéciale de lever les mesures en totalité ou en partie.

Chapitre V

Système d'informations relatives au marché pétrolier international

Article 25

1. Les Pays Participants établissent un système d'informations comprenant deux sections:
- une section générale relative à la situation sur le marché pétrolier international et aux activités des compagnies pétrolières,
- une section spéciale visant à assurer le fonctionnement efficace des mesures décrites aux Chapitres I à IV.

2. Le système fonctionne de façon permanente, en période normale comme en cas d'urgence, et de manière à préserver le caractère confidentiel des informations fournies.

3. Le Secrétariat est responsable du fonctionnement du système d'informations et il met les informations recueillies à la disposition des Pays Participants.

Article 26

Par ,,compagnies pétrolières'', il faut entendre les compagnies internationales, les compagnies nationales, les compagnies non intégrées ainsi que d'autres entités jouant un rôle important dans l'industrie pétrolière internationale.

pected to decrease below the level referred to in the relevant Article. The Secretariat shall keep the Management Committee informed of its deliberations and shall immediately report its finding to the members of the Committee and inform the Participating Countries thereof.

2. Within 72 hours of the Secretariat's reporting a finding, the Management Committee shall meet to review the data compiled and the information provided. It shall report to the Governing Board within a further 48 hours. The report shall set out the views expressed by the members of the Committee, including any views regarding the handling of the emergency.

3. Within 48 hours of receiving the Committee's report, the Governing Board shall meet to review the finding of the Secretariat in the light of the report from the Management Committee. The deactivation of emergency measures or the applicable reduction of the demand restraint level shall be considered confirmed unless the Governing Board, acting by special majority, decides within a further 48 hours to maintain the emergency measures or to deactivate them only in part.

4. In making its finding under this Article, the Secretariat shall consult with the international advisory board, mentioned in Article 19, paragraph 7, to obtain its views regarding the situation and the appropriateness of the measures to be taken.

5. Any Participating Country may request the Secretariat to make a finding under this Article.

Article 24

When emergency measures are in force, and the Secretariat has not made a finding under Article 23, the Governing Board, acting by special majority, may at any time decide to deactivate the measures either wholly or in part.

Chapter V

Information System on the International Oil Market

Article 25

1. The Participating Countries shall establish an Information System consisting of two sections:
- a General Section on the situation in the international oil market and activities of oil companies,
- a Special Section designed to ensure the efficient operation of the measures described in Chapters I to IV.

2. The System shall be operated on a permanent basis, both under normal conditions and during emergencies, and in a manner which ensures the confidentiality of the information made available.

3. The Secretariat shall be responsible for the operation of the Information System and shall make the information compiled available to the Participating Countries.

Article 26

The term "oil companies" means international companies, national companies, non-integrated companies and other entities which play a significant role in the international oil industry.

Section générale

Article 27

1. Dans le cadre de la section générale du système d'informations, les Pays Participants mettent régulièrement à la disposition du Secrétariat des informations relatives aux données précises identifiées conformément à l'Article 29 sur les sujets énumérés ci-après et visant les compagnies pétrolières dont les activités relèvent de leur juridiction respective:

(*a*) Structure de la compagnie;

(*b*) Structure financière, y compris bilans, comptes de profits et pertes, et impôts payés;

(*c*) Investissements réalisés;

(*d*) Conditions des arrangements donnant accès aux principales sources de pétrole brut;

(*e*) Taux de production courants et évolution prévue;

(*f*) Allocation de pétrole brut disponible à des filiales et à d'autres clients (critères et réalisations);

(*g*) Stocks;

(*h*) Coût du pétrole brut et des produits pétroliers;

(*i*) Prix, y compris les prix de cession interne aux filiales;

(*j*) Autres sujets choisis par décision unanime du Conseil de Direction.

2. Chaque Pays Participant prend les mesures appropriées pour faire en sorte que toutes les compagnies pétrolières dont l'activité relève de sa juridiction mettent à sa disposition les informations nécessaires pour lui permettre de remplir les obligations qui lui incombent aux termes de l'alinéa 1, compte tenu des informations pertinentes qui sont déjà à la disposition du public ou des gouvernements.

3. Chaque Pays Participant fournit des informations qui ne font pas l'objet de droits de propriété, ventilées par compagnie et/ou par pays, suivant les cas, d'une manière et avec une précision qui ne portent pas préjudice à la concurrence ni n'aillent à l'encontre des prescriptions légales en matière de concurrence en vigueur dans l'un des Pays Participants.

4. Aucun Pays Participant n'est habilité à obtenir, dans le cadre de la section générale, des informations sur les activités d'une compagnie dont les opérations relèvent de sa juridiction, qu'il ne pourrait obtenir de cette compagnie en vertu de ses lois ou par ses institutions et coutumes, si les opérations de la compagnie ne relevaient que de sa seule juridiction.

Article 28

Par informations „qui ne font pas l'objet de droits de propriété", il faut entendre les informations qui ne constituent ni ne concernent des brevets, marques de fabrique ou de commerce, procédés ou applications scientifiques ou industriels, ventes individuelles, déclarations d'impôt, listes de clients ou informations géologiques et géophysiques, y compris les cartes.

Article 29

1. Dans un délai de 60 jours suivant le premier jour de l'application provisoire du présent Accord, et ultérieurement si cela s'avère approprié, le Groupe Permanent sur le marché pétrolier soumet au Comité de Gestion un rapport précisant les données visées dans la liste des sujets de l'Article 27, alinéa 1, nécessaires au fonctionnement efficace de la section générale, et spécifiant les procédures à suivre pour obtenir régulièrement ces informations.

2. Le Comité de Gestion examine le rapport et soumet des propositions

General Section

Article 27

1. Under the General Section of the Information System, the Participating Countries shall, on a regular basis, make available to the Secretariat information on the precise data identified in accordance with Article 29 on the following subjects relating to oil companies operating within their respective jurisdictions:

(*a*) Corporate structure;

(*b*) Financial structure, including balance sheets, profit and loss accounts, and taxes paid;

(*c*) Capital investments realised;

(*d*) Terms of arrangements for access to major sources of crude oil;

(*e*) Current rates of production and anticipated changes therein;

(*f*) Allocations of available crude supplies to affiliates and other customers (criteria and realisations);

(*g*) Stocks;

(*h*) Cost of crude oil and oil products;

(*i*) Prices, including transfer prices to affiliates;

(*j*) Other subjects, as decided by the Governing Board, acting by unanimity.

2. Each Participating Country shall take appropriate measures to ensure that all oil companies operating within its jurisdiction make such information available to it as is necessary to fulfil its obligations under paragraph 1, taking into account such relevant information as is already available to the public or to Governments.

3. Each Participating Country shall provide information on a non-proprietary basis and on a company and/or country basis as appropriate, and in such a manner and degree as will not prejudice competition or conflict with the legal requirements of any Participating Country relating to competition.

4. No Participating Country shall be entitled to obtain, through the General Section, any information on the activities of a company operating, within its jurisdiction which could not be obtained by it from that company by application of its laws or through its institutions and customs if that company were operating solely within its jurisdiction.

Article 28

Information provided on a "non-proprietary basis" means information which does not constitute or relate to patents, trademarks, scientific or manufacturing processes or developments, individual sales, tax returns, customer lists or geological and geophysical information, including maps.

Article 29

1. Within 60 days of the first day of the provisional application of this Agreement, and as appropriate thereafter, the Standing Group on the Oil Market shall submit a report to the Management Committee identifying the precise data within the list of subjects in Article 27, paragraph 1, which are required for the efficient operation of the General Section, and specifying the procedures for obtaining such data on a regular basis.

2. The Management Committee shall review the report and make proposals to the Governing Board which, within 30 days of the submission of

au Conseil de Direction qui, dans les 30 jours de la présentation du rapport au Comité de Gestion, prend à la majorité les décisions nécessaires à la mise en place et au fonctionnement efficace de la section générale.

Article 30

En établissant ses rapports prévus à l'Article 29, le Groupe Permanent sur le marché pétrolier
- consulte les compagnies pétrolières pour s'assurer de la compatibilité du système avec les activités de l'industrie;
- identifie les problèmes et les questions spécifiques dont se préoccupent les Pays Participants;
- identifie les données particulières utiles et nécessaires à la solution de tels problèmes et de telles questions;
- élabore des normes précises pour harmoniser les informations requises de manière à assurer la comparabilité des données;
- élabore des procédures assurant le caractère confidentiel des informations.

Article 31

1. Le Groupe Permanent sur le marché pétrolier vérifie en permanence le fonctionnement de la section générale.

2. En cas de modification de la situation du marché pétrolier international, le Groupe Permanent sur le marché pétrolier fait rapport au Comité de Gestion. Celui-ci soumet au Conseil de Direction des propositions sur les modifications appropriées; le Conseil de Direction prend à la majorité une décision au sujet de ces propositions.

Section spéciale

Article 32

1. Dans le cadre de la section spéciale du système d'informations, les Pays Participants mettent à la disposition du Secrétariat toutes les informations nécessaires au fonctionnement efficace des mesures d'urgence.

2. Chaque Pays Participant prend les mesures appropriées pour faire en sorte que toutes les compagnies pétrolières dont l'activité relève de sa juridiction mettent à sa disposition les informations nécessaires pour lui permettre de remplir les obligations qui lui incombent aux termes de l'alinéa 1 et de l'Article 33.

3. Sur la base de ces informations et des autres informations disponibles, le Secrétariat examine de façon continue les approvisionnements en pétrole et la consommation de pétrole au sein du groupe et dans chaque Pays Participant.

Article 33

Dans le cadre de la section spéciale, les Pays Participants mettent régulièrement à la disposition du Secrétariat des informations relatives aux données précises identifiées conformément à l'Article 34 et se rapportant aux sujets suivants:

(*a*) Consommation de pétrole et approvisionnement en pétrole;
(*b*) Mesures de restriction de la demande;
(*c*) Niveaux des réserves d'urgence;
(*d*) Disponibilité et utilisation de moyens de transport;

the report to the Management Committee, and acting by majority, shall take the decisions necessary for the establishment and efficient operation of the General Section.

Article 30

In preparing its reports under Article 29, the Standing Group on the Oil Market shall
- consult with oil companies to ensure that the System is compatible with industry operations;
- identify specific problems and issues which are of concern to Participating Countries;
- identify specific data which are useful and necessary to resolve such problems and issues;
- work out precise standards for the harmonization of the required information in order to ensure comparability of the data;
- work out procedures to ensure the confidentiality of the information.

Article 31

1. The Standing Group on the Oil Market shall on a continuing basis review the operation of the General Section.

2. In the event of changes in the conditions of the international oil market, the Standing Group on the Oil Market shall report to the Management Committee. The Committee shall make proposals on appropriate changes to the Governing Board which, acting by majority, shall decide on such proposals.

Special Section

Article 32

1. Under the Special Section of the Information System, the Participating Countries shall make available to the Secretariat all information which is necessary to ensure the efficient operation of emergency measures.

2. Each Participating Country shall take appropriate measures to ensure that all oil companies operating within its jurisdiction make such information available to it as is necessary to enable it to fulfil its obligations under paragraph 1 and under Article 33.

3. The Secretariat shall, on the basis of this information and other information available, continuously survey the supply of oil to and the consumption of oil within the group and each Participating Country.

Article 33

Under the Special Section, the Participating Countries shall, on a regular basis, make available to the Secretariat information on the precise data identified in accordance with Article 34 on the following subjects:

(*a*) Oil consumption and supply;
(*b*) Demand restraint measures;
(*c*) Levels of emergency reserves;
(*d*) Availability and utilisation of transportation facilities;

(*e*) Niveaux actuels et prévus de l'offre et de la demande internationales;
(*f*) Autres sujets choisis par décision unanime du Conseil de Direction.

Article 34

1. Dans les 30 jours suivant le premier jour de l'application provisoire du présent Accord, le Groupe Permanent sur les questions urgentes soumet au Comité de Gestion un rapport identifiant les données précises visées dans la liste des sujets de l'Article 33 nécessaires dans le cadre de la section spéciale à l'application efficace des mesures d'urgence, et indiquant les procédures à suivre pour obtenir régulièrement ces données, y compris les procédures accélérées pour les périodes d'urgence.
2. Le Comité de Gestion examine le rapport et soumet des propositions au Conseil de Direction qui, dans les 30 jours de la présentation du rapport au Comité de Gestion, prend à la majorité les décisions nécessaires à la mise en place et au fonctionnement efficace de la section spéciale.

Article 35

En établissant ses rapports conformément à l'Article 34, le Comité Permanent sur les questions urgentes
– consulte les compagnies pétrolières pour s'assurer de la compatibilité du système avec les activités de l'industrie:
– élabore des normes précises pour harmoniser les informations requises de manière à assurer la comparabilité des données;
– élabore des procédures assurant le caractère confidentiel des informations.

Article 36

1. Le Groupe Permanent sur les questions urgentes examine en permanence le fonctionnement de la section spéciale et, s'il y a lieu, fait rapport au Comité de Gestion. Le Comité de Gestion soumet au Conseil de Direction des propositions sur des modifications appropriées; le Conseil de Direction prend à la majorité une décision au sujet de ces propositions.

Chapitre VI

Cadre de consultation avec les compagnies pétrolières

Article 37

1. Les Pays Participants établissent au sein de l'Agence un cadre permanent de consultation dans lequel un ou plusieurs Pays Participants peuvent, de façon appropriée, consulter individuellement des compagnies pétrolières et leur demander des informations sur tous les aspects importants de l'industrie pétrolière, et dans lequel les Pays Participants peuvent mettre en commun les résultats de ces consultations.
2. Le cadre de consultation est placé sous les auspices du Groupe Permanent sur le marché pétrolier.
3. Dans les 60 jours suivant le premier jour de l'application provisoire du présent Accord, et ultérieurement s'il y a lieu, le Groupe Permanent sur

(*e*) Current and projected levels of international supply and demand;
(*f*) Other subjects, as decided by the Governing Board, acting by unanimity.

Article 34

1. Within 30 days of the first day of the provisional application of this Agreement, the Standing Group on Emergency Questions shall submit a report to the Management Committee identifying the precise data within the list of subjects in Article 33 which are required under the Special Section to ensure the efficient operation of emergency measures and specifying the procedures for obtaining such data on a regular basis, including accelerated procedures in times of emergency.
2. The Management Committee shall review the report and make proposals to the Governing Board which, within 30 days of the submission of the report to the Management Committee, and acting by majority, shall take the decisions necessary for the establishment and efficient operation of the Special Section.

Article 35

In preparing its report under Article 34, the Standing Group on Emergency Questions shall
- consult with oil companies to ensure that the System is compatible with industry operations;
- work out precise standards for the harmonization of the required information in order to ensure comparability of the data;
- work out procedures to ensure the confidentiality of the information.

Article 36

The Standing Group on Emergency Questions shall on a continuing basis review the operation of the Special Section and shall, as appropriate, report to the Management Committee. The Committee shall make proposals on appropriate changes to the Governing Board, which, acting by majority, shall decide on such proposals.

Chapter VI

Framework for Consultation with Oil Companies

Article 37

1. The Participating Countries shall establish within the Agency a permanent framework for consultation within which one or more Participating Countries may, in an appropriate manner, consult with and request information from individual oil companies on all important aspects of the oil industry, and within which the Participating Countries may share among themselves on a co-operative basis the results of such consultations.
2. The framework for consultation shall be established under the auspices of the Standing Group on the Oil Market.
3. Within 60 days of the first day of the provisional application of this Agreement, and as appropriate thereafter, the Standing Group on the Oil

le marchè pétrolier, après consultation des compagnies pétrolières, soumet au Comité de Gestion un rapport sur les procédures à suivre pour ces consultations. Le Comité de Gestion examine le rapport et soumet des propositions au Conseil de Direction qui, dans les 30 jours suivant la présentation du rapport au Comité de Gestion, prend à la majorité une décision au sujet de ces procédures.

Article 38

1. Le Groupe Permanent sur le marché pétrolier présente au Comité de Gestion un rapport sur ses consultations avec toute compagnie pétrolière dans les 30 jours suivant ces consultations.
2. Le Comité de Gestion examine le rapport et peut faire au Conseil de Direction des propositions d'action appropriée à entreprendre en coopération; le Conseil de Direction prend une décision au sujet de ces propositions.

Article 39

1. Le Groupe Permanent sur le marché pétrolier évalue en permanence les résultats des consultations avec les compagnies pétrolières et les renseignements recueillis auprès de ces dernières.
2. Sur la base de ces évaluations, le Groupe Permanent peut examiner et évaluer la situation pétrolière internationale ainsi que la position de l'industrie pétrolière; il fait rapport au Comité de Gestion.
3. Le Comité de Gestion examine ces rapports et présente au Conseil de Direction des propositions d'action appropriée à entreprendre en coopération; le Conseil de Direction prend une décision au sujet de ces propositions.

Article 40

Le Groupe Permanent sur le marché pétrolier présente chaque année au Comité de Gestion un rapport général relatif au fonctionnement du cadre de consultation avec les compagnies pétrolières.

Chapitre VII

Coopération à long terme dans le domaine de l'énergie

Article 41

1. Les Pays Participants sont résolus à réduire à plus long terme leur dépendance à l'égard des importations de pétrole en vue de couvrir la totalité de leurs besoins énergétiques.
2. A cette fin, et dans les domaines définis à l'Article 42, les Pays Participants entreprendront des programmes nationaux et favoriseront l'adoption de programmes de coopération y compris, s'il y a lieu, le partage des moyens et des efforts, tout en se concertant sur leurs politiques nationales.

Article 42

1. Le Groupe Permanent sur la coopération à long terme examine l'action à entreprendre en coopération et fait rapport au Comité de Gestion. Les domaines suivants sont en particulier pris en considération:

Market, after consultation with oil companies, shall submit a report to the Management Committee on the procedures for such consultations. The Management Committee shall review the report and make proposals to the Governing Board, which, within 30 days of the submission of the report to the Management Committee, and acting by majority, shall decide on such procedures.

Article 38

1. The Standing Group on the Oil Market shall present a report to the Management Committee on consultations held with any oil company within 30 days thereof.

2. The Management Committee shall consider the report and may make proposals on appropriate co-operative action to the Governing Board, which shall decide on such proposals.

Article 39

1. The Standing Group on the Oil Market shall, on a continuing basis, evaluate the results of the consultations with and the information collected from oil companies.

2. On the basis of these evaluations, the Standing Group may examine and assess the international oil situation and the position of the oil industry and shall report to the Management Committee.

3. The Management Committee shall review such reports and make proposals on appropriate co-operative action to the Governing Board, which shall decide on such proposals.

Article 40

The Standing Group on the Oil Market shall submit annually a general report to the Management Committee on the functioning of the framework for consultation with oil companies.

Chapter VII

Long Term Co-operation on Energy

Article 41

1. The Participating Countries are determined to reduce over the longer term their dependence on imported oil for meeting their total energy requirements.

2. To this end, the Participating Countries will undertake national programs and promote the adoption of co-operative programs, including, as appropriate, the sharing of means and efforts, while concerting national policies, in the areas set out in Article 42.

Article 42

1. The Standing Group on Long Term Co-operation shall examine and report to the Management Committee on co-operative action. The following areas shall in particular be considered:

(*a*) Conservation de l'énergie et notamment programmes de coopération visant

- des échanges d'expériences nationales et d'informations en matière de conservation de l'énergie;
- des voies et moyens propres à limiter, par la conservation, l'augmentation de la consommation d'énergie.

(*b*) Développement de sources d'énergie de substitution, telles que pétrole d'origine nationale, charbon, gaz naturel, énergie nucléaire et énergie hydro-électrique et, notamment, programmes de coopération visant

- des échanges d'informations sur des sujets tels que les ressources, l'offre et la demande, les prix et la fiscalité;
- des voies et moyens propres à limiter l'augmentation de la consommation de pétrole importé grâce au développement de sources d'énergie de substitution;
- des projets concrets et notamment des projets financés en commun;
- des critères, objectifs de qualité et normes pour la protection de l'environnement.

(*c*) Recherche et développement en matière d'énergie et notamment, en priorité, programmes de coopération dans les domaines suivants

- technologie du charbon;
- énergie solaire;
- gestion des déchets radio-actifs;
- fusion thermonucléaire contrôlée;
- production d'hydrogène à partir de l'eau;
- sécurité nucléaire;
- utilisation des rejets thermiques;
- conservation de l'énergie;
- utilisation des déchets urbains et industriesl aux fins de conservation de l'énergie;
- analyse du système énergétique global et études de caractère général.

(*d*) Enrichissement de l'uranium et, notamment, programmes de coopération visant

- à surveiller l'évolution de l'approvisionnement en uranium naturel et enrichi;
- à faciliter le développement des ressources en uranium naturel et des services d'enrichissement;
- à encourager les consultations qui peuvent être nécessaires pour régler les problèmes internationaux que peut soulever l'accroissement des approvisionnements en uranium enrichi;
- à organiser les opérations nécessaires de collecte, d'analyse et de diffusion de données relatives à la planification des services d'enrichissement.

2. Pour examiner les domaines d'action à entreprendre en coopération, le Groupe Permanent tient dûment compte des activités poursuivies ailleurs.

3. Les programmes mis en oeuvre en vertu de l'alinéa 1 peuvent être financés en commun. Ce financement en commun peut être régi par l'Article 64, alinéa 2.

Article 43

1. Le Comité de Gestion examine les rapports du Groupe Permanent et soumet des propositions appropriées au Conseil de Direction, qui prendra une décision au sujet de ces propositions le 1er juillet 1975 au plus tard.

2. Le Conseil de Direction prend en considération les possibilités de coopération qui peuvent se présenter dans un cadre plus large.

(*a*) Conservation of energy, including co-operative programs on

- exchange of national experiences and information on energy conservation;
- ways and means for reducing the growth of energy consumption through conservation.

(*b*) Development of alternative sources of energy such as domestic oil, coal, natural gas, nuclear energy and hydro-electric power, including co-operative programs on

- exchange of information on such matters as resources, supply and demand, price and taxation;
- ways and means for reducing the growth of consumption of imported oil through the development of alternative sources of energy;
- concrete projects, including jointly financed projects;
- criteria, quality objectives and standards for environmental protection.

(*c*) Energy research and development, including as a matter of priority co-operative programs on

- coal technology;
- solar energy;
- radioactive waste management;
- controlled thermonuclear fusion;
- production of hydrogen from water;
- nuclear safety;
- waste heat utilisation;
- conservation of energy;
- municipal and industrial waste utilisation for energy conservation;
- overall energy system analysis and general studies.

(*d*) Uranium enrichment, including co-operative programs

- to monitor developments in natural and enriched uranium supply;
- to facilitate development of natural uranium resources and enrichment services;
- to encourage such consultations as may be required to deal with international issues that may arise in relation to the expansion of enriched uranium supply;
- to arrange for the requisite collection, analysis and dissemination of data related to the planning of enrichment services.

2. In examining the areas of co-operative action, the Standing Group shall take due account of ongoing activities elsewhere.

3. Programs developed under paragraph 1 may be jointly financed. Such joint financing may take place in accordance with Article 64, paragraph 2.

Article 43

1. The Management Committee shall review the reports of the Standing Group and make appropriate proposals to the Governing Board, which shall decide on these proposals not later than 1st July, 1975.

2. The Governing Board shall take into account possibilities for co-operation within a broader framework.

Chapitre VIII

Relations avec les pays producteurs et les autres pays consommateurs

Article 44

Les Pays Participants s'efforceront de promouvoir des relations de coopération avec les pays producteurs de pétrole et avec les autres pays consommateurs de pétrole, notamment les pays en développement. Ils suivront l'évolution de la situation dans le domaine de l'énergie en vue de déterminer les possibilités d'établir et en vue de promouvoir un dialogue constructif ainsi que d'autres formes de coopération avec les pays producteurs et avec les autres pays consommateurs.

Article 45

Pour atteindre les objectifs définis à l'Article 44, les Pays Participants prendront pleinement en considération les besoins et les intérêts d'autres pays consommateurs et, en particulier, des pays en développement.

Article 46

Les Pays Participants procéderont, dans le cadre du Programme, à des échanges de vues sur leurs relations avec les pays producteurs de pétrole. A cette fin, les Pays Participants devraient s'informer mutuellement des actions qu'ils ont entreprises en coopération avec les pays producteurs et qui présentent un intérêt au regard des objectifs du Programme.

Article 47

Les Pays Participants, dans le contexte du Programme,

- rechercheront, à la lumière de l'examen permanent de l'évolution de la situation énergétique internationale et de ses effets sur l'économie mondiale, les possibilités et les moyens d'encourager la stabilité des échanges pétroliers internationaux et de promouvoir la sécurité des approvisionnements pétroliers à des conditions raisonnables et équitables pour chaque Pays Participant;
- considéreront, à la lumière des travaux en cours dans d'autres organisations internationales, d'autres domaines possibles de coopération, notamment les perspectives de coopération en matière d'industrialisation accélérée et de développement socio-économique des principales régions productrices ainsi que les conséquences à en attendre pour les échanges et les investissements internationaux;
- examineront en permanence les perspectives de coopération avec les pays producteurs de pétrole sur les questions énergétiques d'interêt commun telles que la conservation de l'énergie, le développement de sources de substitution, la recherche et le développement.

Article 48

1. Le Groupe Permanent sur les relations avec les pays producteurs et les autres pays consommateurs examinera les questions décrites dans le présent chapitre et fera rapport à ce sujet au Comité de Gestion.

Chapter VIII

Relations with Producer Countries and with Other Consumer Countries

Article 44

The Participating Countries will endeavour to promote co-operative relations with oil producing countries and with other oil consuming countries, including developing countries. They will keep under review developments in the energy field with a view to identifying opportunities for and promoting a purposeful dialogue, as well as other forms of co-operation, with producer countries and with other consumer countries.

Article 45

To achieve the objectives set out in Article 44, the Participating Countries will give full consideration to the needs and interests of other oil consuming countries, particularly those of the developing countries.

Article 46

The Participating Countries will, in the context of the Program, exchange views on their relations with oil producing countries. To this end, the Participating Countries should inform each other of co-operative action on their part with producer countries which is relevant to the objectives of the Program.

Article 47

The Participating Countries will, in the context of the Program

- seek, in the light of their continuous review of developments in the international energy situation and its effect on the world economy, opportunities and means of encouraging stable international trade in oil and of promoting secure oil supplies on reasonable and equitable terms for each Participating Country;
- consider, in the light of work going on in other international organisations, other possible fields of co-operation including the prospects for co-operation in accelerated industrialisation and socio-economic development in the principal producing areas and the implications of this for international trade and investment;
- keep under review the prospects for co-operation with oil producing countries on energy questions of mutual interest, such as conservation of energy, the development of alternative sources, and research and development.

Article 48

1. The Standing Group on Relations with Producer and other Consumer Countries will examine and report to the Management Committee on the matters described in this Chapter.

2. Le Comité de Gestion peut, sur ces questions, présenter au Conseil de Direction des propositions d'action appropriée à entreprendre en coopération; le Conseil de Direction prend une décision sur lesdites propositions.

Chapitre IX

Dispositions institutionnelles et générales

Article 49

1. L'Agence comprend les organes suivants:
- un Conseil de Direction
- un Comité de Gestion
- des Groupes Permanents sur
  - les questions urgentes
  - le marché pétrolier
  - la coopération à long terme
  - les relations avec les pays producteurs et les autres pays consommateurs.

2. Le Conseil de Direction ou le Comité de Gestion, se prononçant à la majorité, peuvent créer tout autre organe nécessaire à la mise en oeuvre du Programme.
3. L'Agence dispose d'un Secrétariat qui assiste les organes mentionnés aux alinéas 1 et 2.

Conseil de direction

Article 50

1. Le Conseil de Direction est composé d'un ou de plusieurs Ministres de chaque Pays Participant, ou de leurs délégués.
2. Le Conseil de Direction adopte à la majorité son propre règlement de procédure. Sauf s'il en est décidé autrement dans ce règlement de procédure, ce règlement s'applique aussi au Comité de Gestion et aux Groupes Permanents.
3. Le Conseil de Direction élit à la majorité son président et ses vice-présidents.

Article 51

1. Le Conseil de Direction adopte les décisions et fait les recommandations nécessaires au bon fonctionnement du Programme.
2. Le Conseil de Direction examine périodiquement l'évolution de la situation énergétique internationale, notamment les problèmes relatifs aux approvisionnements en pétrole d'un ou de plusieurs Pays Participants, ainsi que les conséquences économiques et monétaires qui en découlent; il prend les mesures appropriées. Dans ses activités se rapportant aux conséquences économiques et monétaires de l'évolution de la situation énergétique internationale, le Conseil de Direction tient compte des compétences et des activités des institutions internationales responsables des questions économiques et monétaires générales.
3. Le Conseil de Direction, se prononçant à la majorité, peut déléguer l'une quelconque de ses fonctions à tout autre organe de l'Agence.

2. The Management Committee may make proposals on appropriate co-operative action regarding these matters to the Governing Board, which shall decide on such proposals.

Chapter IX

Institutional and general provisions

Article 49

1. The Agency shall have the following organs:
- a Governing Board
- a Management Committee
- Standing Groups on
  - Emergency Questions
  - The Oil Market
  - Long Term Co-operation
  - Relations with Producer and Other Consumer Countries.

2. The Governing Board or the Management Committee may, acting by majority, establish any other organ necessary for the implementation of the Program.

3. The Agency shall have a Secretariat to assist the organs mentioned in paragraphs 1 and 2.

Governing Board

Article 50

1. The Governing Board shall be composed of one or more ministers or their delegates from each Participating Country.

2. The Governing Board, acting by majority, shall adopt its own rules of procedure. Unless otherwise decided in the rules of procedure, these rules shall also apply to the Management Committee and the Standing Groups.

3. The Governing Board, acting by majority, shall elect its Chairman and Vice-Chairmen.

Article 51

1. The Governing Board shall adopt decisions and make recommendations which are necessary for the proper functioning of the Program.

2. The Governing Board shall review periodically and take appropriate action concerning developments in the international energy situation, including problems relating to the oil supplies of any Participating Country or Countries, and the economic and monetary implications of these developments. In its activities concerning the economic and monetary implications of developments in the international energy situation, the Governing Board shall take into account the competence and activities of international institutions responsible for overall economic and monetary questions.

3. The Governing Board, acting by majority, may delegate any of its functions to any other organ of the Agency.

Article 52

1. Sous réserve de l'Article 61, alinéa 2, et de l'Article 65, les décisions adoptées conformément au présent Accord par le Conseil de Direction, ou par tout autre organe ayant à cet effet reçu délégation de ce Conseil, ont force obligatoire pour les Pays Participants.

2. Les recommandations n'ont pas force obligatoire.

Comité de gestion

Article 53

1. Le Comité de Gestion est composé d'un ou de plusieurs représentants de haut niveau désignés par le gouvernement de chaque Pays Participant.

2. Le Comité de Gestion exerce les fonctions qui lui sont assignées par le présent Accord, ainsi que toute autre fonction qui lui est déléguée par le Conseil de Direction.

3. Le Comité de Gestion peut examiner toute question entrant dans le champ d'application du présent Accord et, s'il y a lieu, soumettre au Conseil de Direction des propositions à ce sujet.

4. Le Comité de Gestion se réunit à la demande de tout Pays Participant.

5. Le Comité de Gestion élit à la majorité son président et ses vice-présidents.

Groupes permanents

Article 54

1. Chaque Groupe Permanent est composé d'un ou de plusieurs représentants du gouvernement de chaque Pays Participant.

2. Le Comité de Gestion élit à la majorité les présidents et vice-présidents des Groupes Permanents.

Article 55

1. Le Groupe Permanent sur les questions urgentes exerce les fonctions qui lui sont assignées par les Chapitres I à V et par l'Annexe, ainsi que toute autre fonction qui lui est déléguée par le Conseil de Direction.

2. Le Groupe Permanent peut examiner toute question entrant dans le champ d'application des Chapitres I à V et de l'Annexe et faire rapport au Comité de Gestion à ce sujet.

3. Le Groupe Permanent peut consulter les compagnies pétrolières sur tout sujet relevant de sa compétence.

Article 56

1. Le Groupe Permanent sur le marché pétrolier exerce les fonctions qui lui sont assignées par les Chapitres V et VI, ainsi que toute autre fonction qui lui est déléguée par le Conseil de Direction.

2. Le Groupe Permanent peut examiner toute question entrant dans le champ d'application des Chapitres V et VI et faire rapport au Comité de Gestion à ce sujet.

3. Le Groupe Permanent peut consulter les compagnies pétrolières sur tout sujet relevant de sa compétence.

Article 52

1. Subject to Article 61, paragraph 2, and Article 65, decisions adopted pursuant to this Agreement by the Governing Board or by any other organ by delegation from the Board shall be binding on the Participating Countries.
2. Recommendations shall not be binding.

Management Committee

Article 53

1. The Management Committee shall be composed of one or more senior representatives of the Government of each Participating Country.
2. The Management Committee shall carry out the functions assigned to it in this Agreement and any other function delegated to it by the Governing Board.
3. The Management Committee may examine and make proposals to the Governing Board, as appropriate, on any matter within the scope of this Agreement.
4. The Management Committee shall be convened upon the request of any Participating Country.
5. The Management Committee, acting by majority, shall elect its Chairman and Vice-Chairmen.

Standing Groups

Article 54

1. Each Standing Group shall be composed of one or more representatives of the Government of each Participating Country.
2. The Management Committee, acting by majority, shall elect the Chairmen and Vice-Chairmen of the Standing Groups.

Article 55

1. The Standing Group on Emergency Questions shall carry out the functions assigned to it in Chapters I to V and the Annex and any other function delegated to it by the Governing Board.
2. The Standing Group may review and report to the Management Committee on any matter within the scope of Chapters I to V and the Annex.
3. The Standing Group may consult with oil companies on any matter within its competence.

Article 56

1. The Standing Group on the Oil Market shall carry out the functions assigned to it in Chapters V and VI and any other function delegated to it by the Governing Board.
2. The Standing Group may review and report to the Management Committee on any matter within the scope of Chapters V and VI.
3. The Standing Group may consult with oil companies on any matter within its competence.

Article 57

1. Le Groupe Permanent sur la coopération à long terme exerce les fonctions qui lui sont assignées par le Chapitre VII, ainsi que toute autre fonction qui lui est déléguée par le Conseil de Direction.
2. Le Groupe Permanent peut examiner toute question entrant dans le champ d'application du Chapitre VII et faire rapport au Comité de Gestion à ce sujet.

Article 58

1. Le Groupe Permanent sur les relations avec les pays producteurs et les autres pays consommateurs exerce les fonctions qui lui sont assignées par le Chapitre VIII, ainsi que toute autre fonction qui lui est déléguée par le Conseil de Direction.
2. Le Groupe Permanent peut examiner toute question entrant dans le champ d'application du Chapitre VIII et faire rapport au Comité de Gestion à ce sujet.
3. Le Groupe Permanent peut consulter les compagnies pétrolières sur tout sujet relevant de sa compétence.

Secrétariat

Article 59

1. Le Secrétariat se compose d'un Directeur exécutif et du personnel nécessaire.
2. Le Directeur exécutif est nommé par le Conseil de Direction.
3. Dans l'exercice des fonctions qui leur sont assignées par le présent Accord, le Directeur exécutif et le personnel sont responsables envers les organes de l'Agence auxquels ils font rapport.
4. Le Conseil de Direction prend à la majorité toutes les décisions nécessaires à la création et au fonctionnement du Secrétariat.

Article 60

Le Secrétariat exerce les fonctions qui lui sont assignées par le présent Accord et toute autre fonction que lui assigne le Conseil de Direction.

Procédure de vote

Article 61

1. Le Conseil de Direction adopte comme suit les décisions et recommandations qui, dans le présent Accord, ne font l'objet d'aucune disposition expresse relative à la procédure de vote:
(*a*) à la majorité:
- les décisions relatives à la gestion du Programme, notamment les décisions appliquant des dispositions du présent Accord qui imposent déjà des obligations spécifiques aux Pays Participants;
- les décisions relatives aux questions de procédure;
- les recommandations;

(*b*) à l'unanimité:
- toutes les autres décisions, notamment, en particulier, les décisions qui imposent aux Pays Participants des obligations nouvelles non encore stipulées dans le présent Accord.

Article 57

1. The Standing Group on Long Term Co-operation shall carry out the functions assigned to it in Chapter VII and any other function delegated to it by the Governing Board.
2. The Standing Group may review and report to the Management Committee on any matter within the scope of Chapter VII.

Article 58

1. The Standing Group on Relations with Producer and other Consumer Countries shall carry out the functions assigned to it in Chapter VIII and any other function delegated to it by the Governing Board.
2. The Standing Group may review and report to the Management Committee on any matter within the scope of Chapter VIII.
3. The Standing Group may consult with oil companies on any matter within its competence.

Secretariat

Article 59

1. The Secretariat shall be composed of an Executive Director and such staff as is necessary.
2. The Executive Director shall be appointed by the Governing Board.
3. In the performance of their duties under this Agreement the Executive Director and the staff shall be responsible to and report to the organs of the Agency.
4. The Governing Board, acting by majority, shall take all decisions necessary for the establishment and the functioning of the Secretariat.

Article 60

The Secretariat shall carry out the functions assigned to it in this Agreement and any other function assigned to it by the Governing Board.

Voting

Article 61

1. The Governing Board shall adopt decisions and recommendations for which no express voting provision is made in this Agreement, as follows:
(*a*) by majority:
- decisions on the management of the Program, including decisions applying provisions of this Agreement which already impose specific obligations on Participating Countries
- decisions on procedural questions
- recommendations

(*b*) by unanimity:
- all other decisions, including in particular decisions which impose on Participating Countries new obligations not already specified in this Agreement.

2. Les décisions mentionnées à l'alinéa 1, lettre b, peuvent prévoir:
(*a*) qu'elles n'auront pas force obligatoire pour un ou plusieurs Pays Participants;
(*b*) qu'elles n'auront force obligatoire que dans certaines conditions.

Article 62

1. L'unanimité requiert l'ensemble des voix des Pays Participants présents et votants. Les pays qui s'abstiennent sont comptés comme non votants.
2. Lorsque la majorité ou la majorité spéciale est requise, les droits de vote des Pays Participants sont pondérés comme suit:

	Droits de vote généraux	Droits de vote afférents à la consommation de pétrole	Droits de vote combinées
Allemagne	3	8	11
Autriche	3	1	4
Belgique	3	2	5
Canada	3	5	8
Danemark	3	1	4
Espagne	3	2	5
Etats-Unis	3	48	51
Irlande	3	0	3
Italie	3	6	9
Japon	3	15	18
Luxembourg	3	0	3
Pays-Bas	3	2	5
Royaume-Uni	3	6	9
Suède	3	2	5
Suisse	3	1	4
Turquie	3	1	4
Totaux	48	100	148

3. La majorité requiert 60 % du total des droits de vote combinés et 50 % des droits de vote généraux exprimés.
4. La majorité spéciale requiert:
(*a*) 60 % du total des droits de vote combinés et 36 droits de vote généraux pour
- la décision visée à l'Article 2, alinéa 2, relative à l'accroissement de l'engagement en matière de réserves d'urgence;
- les décisions visées à l'Article 19, alinéa 3, de ne pas mettre en vigueur les mesures d'urgence prévues par les Articles 13 et 14;
- les décisions visées à l'Article 20, alinéa 3, relatives aux mesures requises pour faire face aux nécessités de la situation;
- les décisions visées à l'Article 23, alinéa 3, de maintenir les mesures d'urgence prévues par les Articles 13 et 14;
- les décisions visées à l'Article 24, de lever les mesures d'urgence prévues par les Articles 13 et 14.

(*b*) 42 droits de vote généraux pour:
- les décisions visées à l'Article 19, alinéa 3, de ne pas mettre en vigueur les mesures d'urgence prévues par l'Article 17;
- les décisions visées à l'Article 23, alinéa 3, de maintenir les mesures d'urgence prévues par l'Article 17;

2. Decisions mentioned in paragraph 1 (*b*) may provide:
(*a*) that they shall not be binding on one or more Participating Countries;
(*b*) that they shall be binding only under certain conditions.

Article 62

1. Unanimity shall require all of the votes of the Participating Countries present and voting. Countries abstaining shall be considered as not voting.
2. When majority or special majority is required, the Participating Countries shall have the following voting weights:

	General voting weights	Oil consumption voting weights	Combined voting weights
Austria	3	1	4
Belgium	3	2	5
Canada	3	5	8
Denmark	3	1	4
Germany	3	8	11
Ireland	3	0	3
Italy	3	6	9
Japan	3	15	18
Luxembourg	3	0	3
The Netherlands	3	2	5
Spain	3	2	5
Sweden	3	2	5
Switzerland	3	1	4
Turkey	3	1	4
United Kingdom	3	6	9
United States	3	48	51
Totals	48	100	148

3. Majority shall require 60 per cent of the total combined voting weights and 50 per cent of the general voting weights cast.
4. Special majority shall require:
(*a*) 60 per cent of the total combined voting weights and 36 general voting weights for:
- the decision under Article 2, paragraph 2, relating to the increase in the emergency reserve commitment;
- decisions under Article 19, paragraph 3, not to activate the emergency measures referred to in Articles 13 and 14;
- decisions under Article 20, paragraph 3, on the measures required for meeting the necessities of the situation;
- decisions under Article 23, paragraph 3, to maintain the emergency measures referred to in Articles 13 and 14;
- decisions under Article 24 to deactivate the emergency measures referred to in Articles 13 and 14.

(*b*) 42 general voting weights for:
- decisions under Article 19, paragraph 3, not to activate the emergency measures referred to in Article 17;
- decisions under Article 23, paragraph 3, to maintain the emergency measures referred to in Article 17;

– les décisions visées à l'Article 24 de lever les mesures d'urgence prévues par l'Article 17.

5. Le Conseil de Direction décide à l'unanimité de l'accroissement, de la réduction et de la redistribution nécessaires dont les droits de vote mentionnées à l'alinéa 2 font l'objet ainsi que des amendements à apporter aux conditions de vote stipulées aux alinéas 3 et 4 dans le cas où

– un pays adhère au présent Accord conformément à l'Article 71, ou
– un pays se retire du présent Accord conformément à l'Article 68, alinéa 2, ou à l'Article 69, alinéa 2.

6. Le Conseil de Direction examine chaque année le nombre et la répartition des droits de vote prévus à l'alinéa 2 et, sur base de cet examen, décide à l'unanimité s'il y a lieu d'accroître ou de réduire, de redistribuer ces droits de vote ou de combiner ces deux opérations en raison d'un changement dans la part prise par un Pays Participant dans la consommation totale de pétrole, ou pour toute autre raison.

7. Toute modification aux alinéas 2, 3 ou 4 doit être fondée sur les principes qui sont à la base de ces alinéas et de l'alinéa 6.

Relations avec d'autres entités

Article 63

En vue de réaliser les objectifs du Programme, l'Agence peut établir des relations appropriées avec des pays non participants, des organisations internationales, gouvernementales ou non gouvernementales, et d'autres entités et personnes physiques.

Dispositions financières

Article 64

1. Les dépenses du Secrétariat et toutes les autres dépenses communes sont réparties entre tous les Pays Participants suivant un barème de contributions élaboré conformément aux principes et règles énoncés dans l'Annexe à la ,,Résolution du Conseil de l'OCDE relative à l'établissement du barème des contributions des pays Membres au Budget de l'Organisation" du 10 décembre 1963. A l'issue de la première année d'application du présent Accord, le Conseil de Direction examinera ce barème des contributions et décidera à l'unanimité de toute modification appropriée, conformément à l'Article 73.

2. Les dépenses spéciales engagées à l'occasion d'activités spéciales entreprises conformément à l'Article 65 sont réparties entre les Pays Participants qui prennent part à ces activités spéciales dans les proportions que ces pays conviennent à l'unanimité d'appliquer entre eux.

3. Le Directeur exécutif soumet au Conseil de Direction, conformément au règlement financier adopté par celui-ci, le 1er octobre de chaque année au plus tard, un projet de budget comprenant les besoins en personnel. Le Conseil de Direction adopte le budget à la majorité.

4. Le Conseil de Direction adopté à la majorité toute autre décision nécessaire relative à l'administration financière de l'Agence.

5. L'exercice financier commence le 1er janvier et se termine le 31 décembre de chaque année. A la fin de chaque exercice financier, les recettes et les dépenses sont soumises à vérification comptable.

– decisions under Article 24 to deactivate the emergency measures referred to in Article 17.

5. The Governing Board, acting by unanimity, shall decide on the necessary increase, decrease, and redistribution of the voting weights referred to in paragraph 2, as well as on amendment of the voting requirements set out in paragraphs 3 and 4 in the event that

– a Country accedes to this Agreement in accordance with Article 71, or
– a Country withdraws from this Agreement in accordance with Article 68, paragraph 2, or Article 69, paragraph 2.

6. The Governing Board shall review annually the number and distribution of voting weights specified in paragraph 2, and, on the basis of such review, acting by unanimity, shall decide whether such voting weights should be increased or decreased, or redistributed, or both, because a change in any Participating Country's share in total oil consumption has occurred or for any other reason.

7. Any change in paragraph 2, 3 or 4 shall be based on the concepts underlying those paragraphs and paragraph 6.

Relations with Other Entities

Article 63

In order to achieve the objectives of the Program, the Agency may establish appropriate relations with non-participating countries, international organisations, whether governmental or non-governmental, other entities and individuals.

Financial Arrangements

Article 64

1. The expenses of the Secretariat and all other common expenses shall be shared among all Participating Countries according to a scale of contributions elaborated according to the principles and rules set out in the Annex to the "OECD Resolution of the Council on Determination of the Scale of Contributions by Member Countries to the Budget of the Organisation" of 10th December, 1963. After the first year of application of this Agreement, the Governing Board shall review this scale of contributions and, acting by unanimity, shall decide upon any appropriate changes in accordance with Article 73.

2. Special expenses incurred in connection with special activities carried out pursuant to Article 65 shall be shared by the Participating Countries taking part in such special activities in such proportions as shall be determined by unanimous agreement between them.

3. The Executive Director shall, in accordance with the financial regulations adopted by the Governing Board and not later than 1st October of each year, submit to the Governing Board a draft budget including personnel requirements. The Governing Board, acting by majority, shall adopt the budget.

4. The Governing Board, acting by majority, shall take all other necessary decisions regarding the financial administration of the Agency.

5. The financial year shall begin on 1st January and end on 31st December of each year. At the end of each financial year, revenues and expenditures shall be submitted to audit.

Activités spéciales

Article 65

1. Deux ou plusieurs Pays Participants peuvent décider d'entreprendre, dans le cadre du présent Accord, des activités spéciales différentes de celles qui doivent être entreprises par l'ensemble des Pays Participants en vertu des dispositions des Chapitres I à V. Les Pays Participants qui ne souhaitent pas prendre part à ces activités spéciales s'abstiennent de prendre part à ces décisions et ne sont pas liés par ces dernières. Les Pays Participants qui poursuivent des activités de ce genre en tiennent le Conseil de Direction informé.

2. Pour la mise en oeuvre de ces activités spéciales, les Pays Participants intéressés peuvent se mettre d'accord sur des procédures de vote différentes de celles prévues aux Articles 61 et 62.

Mise en oeuvre de l'accord

Article 66

Chaque Pays Participant prend les mesures nécessaires, y compris toute mesure législative requise en vue de mettre en oeuvre le présent Accord et les décisions prises par le Conseil de Direction.

Chapitre X

Dispositions finales

Article 67

1. Chaque Etat Signataire notifiera, au plus tard le 1er mai 1975, au Gouvernement du Royaume de Belgique que, s'étant conformé à ses procédures constitutionnelles, il consent à être lié par le présent Accord.

2. Le dixième jour suivant le dépôt de cette notification ou d'un instrument d'adhésion par six Etats au moins détenant 60 % au moins des droits de vote combinés auxquels se réfère l'Article 62, le présent Accord entrera en vigueur à l'égard de ces Etats.

3. Pour chaque Etat Signataire qui dépose son instrument de notification ultérieurement, le présent Accord entrera en vigueur le dixième jour suivant la date du dépôt.

4. A la demande de tout Etat Signataire, le Conseil de Direction peut décider à la majorité de proroger le délai de notification au-delà du 1er mai 1975 en ce qui concerne cet Etat.

Article 68

1. Nonobstant les dispositions de l'Article 67, le présent Accord sera appliqué à titre provisoire par tous les Etats Signataires, dans toute la mesure compatible avec leur législation, à compter du 18 novembre 1974, après la première réunion du Conseil de Direction.

2. L'application provisoire de l'Accord se poursuivra:

- jusqu'à ce que l'Accord entre en vigueur à l'égard de l'Etat considéré conformément à l'Article 67, ou
- pendant 60 jours après réception par le Gouvernement du Royaume de Belgique de la notification par laquelle l'Etat considéré fait savoir qu'il ne consent pas à être lié par l'Accord, ou

Special Activities

Article 65

1. Any two or more Participating Countries may decide to carry out within the scope of this Agreement special activities, other than activities which are required to be carried out by all Participating Countries under Chapters I to V. Participating Countries which do not wish to take part in such special activities shall abstain from taking part in such decisions and shall not be bound by them. Participating Countries carrying out such activities shall keep the Governing Board informed thereof.

2. For the implementation of such special activities, the Participating Countries concerned may agree upon voting procedures other than those provided for in Articles 61 and 62.

Implementation of the Agreement

Article 66

Each Participating Country shall take the necessary measures, including any necessary legislative measures, to implement this Agreement and decisions taken by the Governing Board.

Chapter X

Final Provisions

Article 67

1. Each Signatory State shall, not later than 1st May, 1975, notify the Government of the Kingdom of Belgium that, having complied with its constitutional procedures, it consents to be bound by this Agreement.

2. On the tenth day following the day on which at least six States holding at least 60 per cent of the combined voting weights mentioned in Article 62 have deposited a notification of consent to be bound or an instrument of accession, this Agreement shall enter into force for such States.

3. For each Signatory State which deposits its notification thereafter, this Agreement shall enter into force on the tenth day following the day of deposit.

4. The Governing Board, acting by majority, may upon request from any Signatory State decide to extend, with respect to that State, the time limit for notification beyond 1st May, 1975.

Article 68

1. Notwithstanding the provisions of Article 67, this Agreement shall be applied provisionally by all Signatory States, to the extent possible not inconsistent with their legislation, as from 18th November, 1974 following the first meeting of the Governing Board.

2. Provisional application of the Agreement shall continue until:

- the Agreement enters into force for the State concerned in accordance with Article 67, or
- 60 days after the Government of the Kingdom of Belgium receives notification that the State concerned will not consent to be bound by the Agreement, or

– jusqu'à l'expiration du délai dans lequel l'Etat considéré peut notifier son consentement en vertu de l'Article 67.

Article 69

1. Le présent Accord restera en vigueur pendant une durée de dix ans à compter de la date de son entrée en vigueur et demeurera ensuite en vigueur aussi longtemps que le Conseil de Direction n'aura pas décidé à la majorité d'y mettre fin.

2. Tout Pays Participant peut mettre fin, en ce qui le concerne, à l'application du présent Accord moyennant un préavis écrit de douze mois au Gouvernement du Royaume de Belgique, ce préavis ne pouvant toutefois être donné au plus tôt que trois ans après le premier jour de l'application à titre provisoire du présent Accord.

Article 70

1. Tout Etat peut, au moment de la signature, de la notification de son consentement à être lié par l'Accord conformément à l'Article 67, de son adhésion ou à toute autre date ultérieure déclarer par notification adresseé au Gouvernement du Royaume de Belgique que le présent Accord s'applique à l'ensemble ou à l'un des territoires dont il est chargé d'assurer les relations internationales ou à tout territoire situé à l'intérieur de ses frontières et dont l'approvisionnement en pétrole lui incombe légalement.

2. Toute déclaration faite en vertu de l'alinéa 1 peut, pour tout territoire mentionné dans ladite déclaration, être retirée conformément aux dispositions de l'Article 69, alinéa 2.

Article 71

1. Le présent Accord est ouvert à l'adhésion de tout Membre de l'Organisation de Coopération et de Développement Economiques en mesure d'observer les obligations du Programme et disposé à le faire. Le Conseil de Direction décide à la majorité de la suite à donner à toute demande d'adhésion.

2. Le présent Accord entrera en vigueur à l'égard de tout Etat dont la demande d'adhésion a été agréée le dixième jour suivant le dépôt par cet Etat de son instrument d'adhésion auprès du Gouvernement du Royaume de Belgique ou à la date d'entrée en vigueur de l'Accord en vertu de l'Article 67, alinéa 2, si celle-ci est postérieure.

3. Jusqu'au 1er mai 1975, l'adhésion peut intervenir sur une base provisoire dans les conditions prévues à l'Article 68.

Article 72

1. Le présent Accord est ouvert à l'adhésion des Communautés Européennes.

2. Le présent Accord ne fait en aucune manière obstacle à la poursuite de l'exécution des traités instituant les Communautés Européennes.

Article 73

Le présent Accord peut à tout moment être amendé par le Conseil de Direction se prononçant à l'unanimité. Ces amendements entreront en

– the time limit for notification of consent by the State concerned referred to in Article 67 expires.

Article 69

1. This Agreement shall remain in force for a period of ten years from the date of its entry into force and shall continue in force thereafter unless and until the Governing Board, acting by majority, decides on its termination.

2. Any Participating Country may terminate the application of this Agreement for its part upon twelve months' written notice to the Government of the Kingdom of Belgium to that effect, given not less than three years after the first day of the provisional application of this Agreement.

Article 70

1. Any State may, at the time of signature, notification of consent to be bound in accordance with Article 67, accession or at any later date, declare by notification addressed to the Government of the Kingdom of Belgium that this Agreement shall apply to all or any of the territories for whose international relations it is responsible, or to any territories within its frontiers for whose oil supplies it is legally responsible.

2. Any declaration made pursuant to paragraph 1 may, in respect of any territory mentioned in such declaration, be withdrawn in accordance with the provisions of Article 69, paragraph 2.

Article 71

1. This Agreement shall be open for accession by any Member of the Organisation for Economic Co-operation and Development which is able and willing to meet the requirements of the Program. The Governing Board, acting by majority, shall decide on any request for accession.

2. This Agreement shall enter into force for any State whose request for accession has been granted on the tenth day following the deposit of its instrument of accession with the Government of the Kingdom of Belgium, or on the date of entry into force of the Agreement pursuant to Article 67, paragraph 2, whichever is the later.

3. Until 1st May, 1975, accession may take place on a provisional basis under the conditions set out in Article 68.

Article 72

1. This Agreement shall be open for accession by the European Communities.

2. This Agreement shall not in any way impede the further implementation of the treaties establishing the European Communities.

Article 73

This Agreement may at any time be amended by the Governing Board, acting by unanimity. Such amendment shall come into force in a manner vigueur dans les conditions déterminées à l'unanimité par le Conseil de Direction qui prendra les dispositions permettant aux Pays Participants de se conformer à leurs procédures constitutionnelles respectives.

Article 74

Le présent Accord fera l'objet d'un examen général après le 1er mai 1980.

Article 75

Le Gouvernement du Royaume de Belgique notifiera à tous les Pays Participants le dépôt de chaque instrument notifiant le consentement à être lié par l'accord conformément à l'Article 67 et de chaque instrument d'adhésion, l'entrée en vigueur du présent Accord ou de tout amendement qui lui serait apporté, toute dénonciation du présent Accord et toute autre déclaration ou notification reçues.

Article 76

L'original du présent Accord, dont les textes en allemand, en anglais et en français font également foi, sera déposé auprès du Gouvernement du Royaume de Belgique, qui en communiquera une copie certifiée conforme à chacun des autres Pays Participants.

C. OUVRAGES DE L'OCDE MIS EN VENTE EN 1974

1. POLITIQUE ECONOMIQUE

Perspectives économiques de l'OCDE. No 15 (juillet 1974, 138 pages) No 16 (décembre 1974, 132 pages)

Etudes économiques de l'OCDE, Séries 1974:
Allemagne (mai 1974, 102 pages), Australie (avril 1974, 92 pages), Autriche (juillet 1974, 76 pages), Canada (décembre 1973, 60 pages), Danemark (juillet 1974, 72 pages), Espagne (avril 1974, 70 pages), Etats-Unis (juillet 1974, 62 pages), Finlande (août 1974, 74 pages), France (février 1974, 100 pages), Irlande (mars 1974, 60 pages), Japon (juillet 1974, 100 pages), Norvège (mars 1974, 82 pages), Pays-Bas (juin 1974, 76 pages), Portugal (juillet 1974, 60 pages), Suède (juillet 1974, 76 pages), Suisse (mars 1974, 84 pages), Turquie (novembre 1974, 90 pages), U.E.B.L. (juillet 1974, 86 pages), Yougoslavie (avril 1974, 86 pages).
Implications économiques du contrôle de la pollution: Appréciation Gènérale (avril 1974, 92 pages).
La politique monétaire en allemagne (mars 1974, 148 pages).
La politique monétaire aux Etats-Unis (novembre 1974, 240 pages).
Comptes nationaux des pays de l'OCDE, 1961–1972, (septembre 1974, 486 pages, bilingue).

---

* Les ouvrages de l'OCDE sont publiés dans les deux langues de l'Organisation – l'Anglais et le Français – Certains d'entre eux sont bilingues.

determined by the Governing Board, acting by unanimity and making provision for Participating Countries to comply with their respective constitutional procedures.

Article 74

This Agreement shall be subject to a general review after 1st May, 1980.

Article 75

The Government of the Kingdom of Belgium shall notify all Participating Countries of the deposit of each notification of consent to be bound in accordance with Article 67, and of each instrument of accession, of the entry into force of this Agreement or any amendment thereto, of any denunciation thereof, and of any other declaration or notification received.

Article 76

The original of this Agreement, of which the English, French and German texts are equally authentic, shall be deposited with the Government of the Kingdom of Belgium, and a certified copy thereof shall be furnished to each other Participating Country by the Government of the Kingdom of Belgium.

C. OECD PUBLICATIONS AND DOCUMENTS* PUT ON SALE IN 1974

1. ECONOMIC POLICY

OECD Economic Outlook. No 15 (July 1974, 124 pages) No 16 (December 1974, 120 pages).

OECD Economic Surveys, 1974 Series:
Australia (April 1974, 84 pages), Austria (July 1974, 74 pages), BLEU (July 1974, 82 pages), Canada (December 1973, 56 pages), Denmark (July 1974, 68 pages), Finland (August 1974, 72 pages), France (February 1974, 92 pages), Germany (May 1974, 98 pages), Ireland (March 1974, 52 pages), Japan (July 1974, 90 pages), Netherlands (June 1974, 70 pages), Norway (March 1974, 76 pages), Portugal (July 1974, 58 pages), Spain (April 1974, 70 pages), Sweden (July 1974, 72 pages), Switzerland (March 1974, 82 pages), Turkey (November 1974, 84 pages), United States (July 1974, 58 pages), Yugoslavia (April 1974, 78 pages).
Economic Implications of Pollution Control: A General Assessment (April 1974, 80 pages).
Monetary Policy in Germany (March 1974, 132 pages).
Monetary Policy in the United States (November 1974, 208 pages).
National Accounts of OECD Countries, 1961–1972 (September 1974, 486 pages, bilingual).

---

* OECD publications and documents are issued in the two official languages of the Organisation – English and French – and some are bilingual.

Principaux indicateurs économiques (mensuel) (12 numéros publiés de janvier à décembre 1974).

Bulletins statistiques du commerce exterieur
Série A, bulletin mensuel. Parution antérieurement trimestrielle, mensuelle depuis juin 1974.

Série B, échanges par produits, tableaux analytiques (trimestriel).
Janvier/septembre 1972 (no 3–6, nos 1 + 2 publiés en 1973).
Janvier/décembre 1972 (nos 5 + 6, nos 1–4 publiés en 1973).
Janvier/mars 1973 (nos 1–4; les suivants sont à paraître en 1975).
Janvier/juin 1973 (nos 1–4; les suivants sont à paraître en 1975).
Janvier/septembre 1973 (nos 1–4 suivants à paraître en 1975).
Janvier/décembre 1973 (nos 1–3 suivants à paraître en 1975).
Janvier/mars 1974 (nos 1–3 suivants à paraître en 1975).
Janvier/juin 1974 (no 1; suivants à paraître en 1975).

Série C, échanges par produits, résumé par marchés (annuel).
Janvier/décembre 1972. Exportation (3 volumes). Importation (2 volumes).
Statistiques de la population active 1961–1972 (juillet 1974, 414 pages, bilingue).
L'évolution démographique de 1970 à 1985 dans les pays membres de l'OCDE (octobre 1974, 456 pages, bilingue).
Statistiques de l'énergie 1958–1972 (mars 1974, 254 pages, bilingue).

2. MOUVEMENTS DE CAPITAUX, AFFAIRES FINANCIERES ET FISCALES

Statistiques financières de l'OCDE (annuelles avec des suppléments bimensuels, bilingue).
No 7 Volumes I et II (déjà publiés en 1973). Suppléments 7A (janvier 1974), 7B (mars 1974), 7C (avril 1974), 7D (juillet 1974), 7E (septembre 1974).
No 8 Volume I (volume II et suppléments à paraître en 1975).
No 7 Volumes I et II, ou suppléments 1–5.
Indexation des valeurs à revenu fixe (janvier 1974, 64 pages).
Les investissements étrangers en Yougoslavie (juillet 1974, 68 pages).
Le financement du logement: problèmes actuels (décembre 1974, 112 pages).
L'impot négatif sur le revenu: un instrument de coordination des politiques fiscales et sociales (Juin 1974, 64 pages).
Aspects théoriques et empiriques de l'imposition des sociétés (septembre 1974, 84 pages).
Rapports annuels sur la politique de concurrence dans les pays membres de l'OCDE – No 1/1974 (mai 1974, 102 pages).
Etiquetage obligatoire des produits de consommation pré-emballés (octobre 1974, 52 pages)
Protection des consommateurs contre la toxicité des cosmétiques et des produits ménagers (octobre 1974, 84 pages).
Ententes à l'exportation (novembre 1974, 104 pages).
Guide de la législation sur les pratiques commerciales restrictives.
7ème série de suppléments de mise à jour:
Supplément no 2, 1973 (mai 1974).
Les transports maritimes, 1973 (août 1974, 174 pages).
Politique du tourisme et tourisme international dans les pays de l'OCDE, 1974 (novembre 1974, 170 pages).

Main Economic Indicators (monthly) (12 issues publihed from January to December 1974).

Statistics of Foreign Trade
Series A. Monthly bulletin. Previously issued quarterly, monthly as from June 1974).

Series B. Trade by Commodities. Country Summaries (quarterly).
January/September 1972 (Nos 3–6, Nos 1 + 2 published in 1973).
January/December 1972 (Nos 5 + 6, Nos 1–4 published in 1973).
January/March 1973 (Nos 1–4; others to be published in 1975).
January/June 1973 (Nos 1–4; others to be published in 1975).
January/September 1973 (Nos 1–4; others to be published in 1975).
January/December 1973 (Nos 1–3; others to be published in 1975).
January/March 1974 (Nos 1–3; others to be published in 1975).
January/June 1974 (No. 1; others to be published in 1975).
One quarterly issue (6 booklets).

Series C. Trade by Commodities. Market Summaries (annual).
January/December 1972. Exports (3 volumes); Imports (2 volumes).
Labour Force Statistics 1961–1972 (July 1974, 414 pages, bilingual).
Demographic Trends 1970–1985 in OECD Member Countries (October 1974, 456 pages, bilingual).
Statistics of Energy 1958–1972 (March 1974, 254 pages, bilingual).

2. CAPITAL MOVEMENTS, FINANCIAL AND FISCAL AFFAIRS

OECD Financial Statistics (yearly with bi-monthly supplements) Bilingual.
No 7. Volumes I and II (already published in 1973). Supplements 7A (January 1974), 7B (March 1974), 7C (April 1974), 7D (July 1974), 7E September 1974).
No 8. Volume I (Volume II and supplements to be published in 1975).
No 7, Volumes I and II, or supplements 1–5.
Indexation of Fixed-Interest Securities (January 1974, 52 pages).
Foreign Investment in Yugoslavia (July 1974, 60 pages).
Housing Finance: Present Problems (December 1974, 100 pages).
Negative Income Tax: an Approach to the Co-ordination of Taxation and Social Welfare Policies (June 1974, 58 pages).
Theoretical and Empirical Aspects of Corporate Taxation (September 1974, 80 pages).
Annual Reports on Competition Policy in OECD Member Countries – No 1/1974 (May 1974, 96 pages).
Compulsory Labelling of Prepackaged Consumer Products (October 1974, 44 pages).
Consumer Protection against the Toxicity of Cosmetics and Household Products (October 1974, 68 pages).
Export Cartels (November 1974, 92 pages).
Guide to Legislation on Restrictive Business Practices
7th series of up-dating supplements:
Supplement No 2, 1973 (May 1974)
Subscription to the 7th Series of Supplements
Maritime Transport, 1973 (August 1974, 158 pages)
Tourism Policy and International Tourism in OECD Member Countries, 1974 (November 1974, 164 pages).

3. AGRICULTURE ET PECHERIES

La politique agricole de la communauté économique européenne (mai 1974, 132 pages).

La politique agricole au Danemark (septembre 1974, 72 pages).

La politique agricole en Espagne (mai 1974, 54 pages).

La politique agricole aux États-Unis (février 1974, 120 pages).

La politique agricole en France (septembre 1974, 92 pages).

La politique agricole en Irlande (juin 1974, 70 pages).

La politique agricole en Italie (janvier 1974, 56 pages).

La politique agricole au Japon (septembre 1974, 88 pages).

La politique agricole en Nouvelle-Zélande (septembre 1974, 108 pages).

La politique agricole aux Pays-Bas (janvier 1974, 72 pages).

La politique agricole au Royaume-Uni (avril 1974, 76 pages).

La politique agricole en Turquie (septembre 1974, 68 pages).

Les produits azotés d'origine industrielle dans l'alimentation animale (avril 1974, 62 pages).

Bilans de la viande dans les pays membres de l'OCDE 1959–1972 (janvier 1974, 124 pages, bilingue).

Situation prévisionnelle des produits laitiers et de la viande bovine en 1975 et 1978 (août 1974, 176 pages).

Bilans du lait et des produits laitiers dans les pays membres de l'OCDE, 1959–1972 (août 1974, 164 pages, bilingue).

La transformation des fruits et légumes dans les pays membres de l'OCDE (novembre 1974, 44 pages).

Examen des pêcheries dans les pays membres de l'OCDE, 1973 (juillet 1974, 248 pages).

4. INDUSTRIE ET ENERGIE

Statistiques pétrolieres provisoires par trimestre (bilingue) 1973, no 3/no 4.

1974, no 1.

L'industrie de l'électricité, 23e Enquête (décembre 1974, 108 pages, bilingue).

L'industrie chimique, 1972–1973 (septembre 1974, 190 pages, bilingue).

L'industrie sidérurgique en 1972 et tendances en 1973 (avril 1974, 96 pages, bilingue).

La prévision de la consommation d'acier. Approches synchroniques et chronologiques (août 1974, 146 pages).

L'industrie des pâtes et papiers, 1972–1973 (mars 1974, 246 pages, bilingue).

L'industrie des pâtes et papiers, 1973–1974 (novembre 1974, 194 pages, bilingue).

Pâtes et papiers. Statistiques trimestrielles (bilingue) 1974, no 1/no 2.

L'industrie des cuirs et peaux et de la chaussure dans les pays de l'OCDE, 1972–1973 (août 1974, 96 pages, bilingue).

L'industrie du ciment. Statistiques 1973, Tendance 1974 (décembre 1974, 40 pages, bilingue).

La politique industrielle de la France (octobre 1974, 140 pages).

5. MAIN-D'OEUVRE ET AFFAIRES SOCIALES

Politique de main-d'oeuvre en Allemagne (mai 1974, 184 pages).

Politique de main-d'oeuvre au Danemark (juillet 1974, 66 pages).

Politique de main-d'oeuvre en Irlande (septembre 1974, 80 pages).

3. AGRICULTURE AND FISHERIES

Agricultural Policy in Denmark (September 1974, 64 pages).
Agricultural Policy of the European Economic Community (May 1974, 122 pages).
Agricultural Policy in France (September 1974, 88 pages).
Agricultural Policy in Ireland (June 1974, 64 pages).
Agricultural Policy in Italy (January 1974, 56 pages).
Agricultural Policy in Japan (September 1974, 82 pages).
Agricultural Policy in the Netherlands (January 1974, 62 pages).
Agricultural Policy in New Zealand (September 1974, 94 pages).
Agricultural Policy in Spain (May 1974, 52 pages).
Agricultural Policy in Turkey (September 1974, 62 pages).
Agricultural Policy in the United Kingdom (April 1974, 68 pages).
Agricultural Policy in the United States (February 1974, 108 pages).
Nitrogenous Products of Industrial Origin for Animal Feeding (April 1974, 56 pages).
Meat Balances in OECD Member Countries, 1959–1972 (January 1974, 124 pages, bilingual).
Forecasts of the Dairy and Beef Situations in 1975 and 1978 (August 1974, 158 pages).
Milk and Milk Products Balances in OECD Member Countries, 1959–1972 (August 1974, 164 pages, bilingual).
Fruit and Vegetable Processing in OECD Member Countries (November 1974, 42 pages).
Review of Fisheries in OECD Member Countries, 1973 (July 1974, 232 pages).

4. INDUSTRY AND ENERGY

Provisional Oil Statistics by Quarters (bilingual) 1973, No 3/No 4. 1974, No 1.
The Electricity Supply Industry. 23rd Enquiry (December 1974, 108 pages, bilingual).
The Chemical Industry, 1972–1973 (September 1974, 190 pages, bilingual).
The Iron and Steel Industry in 1972 and trends in 1973 (April 1974, 96 pages, bilingual).
Forecasting Steel Consumption. Cross-section and time series approaches. (August 1974, 136 pages).
The Pulp and Paper Industry, 1972–1973 (March 1974, 246 pages, bilingual).
Pulp and Paper Industry, 1973–1974 (November 1974, 194 pages, bilingual).
Pulp and Paper. Quarterly statistics (bilingual) 1974, No 1/No 2.
The Hides, Skins and Footwear Industry in OECD Countries, 1972–1973 (August 1974, 96 pages, bilingual).
The Cement Industry. Statistics 1973, Trend 1974 (December 1974, 40 pages, bilingual).
The Industrial Policy of France (October 1974, 136 pages).

5. MANPOWER AND SOCIAL AFFAIRS

Manpower Policy in Denmark (July 1974, 62 pages).
Manpower Policy in Germany (May 1974, 160 pages).
Manpower Policy in Ireland (September 1974, 70 pages).

Détermination des salaires. Documents présentés à une Conférence Internationale, Paris 3–6 juillet 1973 (octobre 1974, 416 pages).

Programme d'élaboration des indicateurs sociaux de l'OCDE 2. Eléments subjectifs du bien-être (décembre 1974, 226 pages).

Mesure des conflits du travail et de leurs répercussions économiques (janvier 1974, 256 pages).

Etude des comportements sur le marché du travail (juin 1974, 162 pages).

Les effets de l'emploi des travailleurs étrangers (juillet 1974, 230 pages).

La politique suédoise de salaires fondée sur le principe de solidarité (novembre 1974, 44 pages).

Série ,,Séminaires Internationaux''

1972–2 Perspectives de la coopération employeurs/travailleurs dans l'entreprise. Séminaire Régional Mixte, Paris, 24–27 octobre 1972. Rapport Final. (octobre 1974, 312 pages).

1972–3 Séminaire syndical régional sur la politique des prix. Paris, du 21 au 24 novembre 1972. Rapport Final. (mai 1974, 194 pages).

1973–1 Les progrès dans l'organisation du travail. Séminaire Patronal International. Paris, 3 au 6 avril 1973. Rapport final (octobre 1974, 72 pages).

6. COOPERATION EN MATIERE DE DEVELOPPEMENT

Coopération pour le développement. Examen 1974. (décembre 1974, 356 pages).

Les apports de ressources aux pays en voie de développement 1961–1971 (janvier 1974, 486 pages).

Comptabilité nationale et planification du développement économique dans les pays à faible revenu, (mai 1974, 570 pages, bilingue).

Programmation distribution des revenus. Investissements privés étrangers (août 1974, 256 pages).

Le choix et l'adaptation de la technologie dans les pays en voie de développement. Un tour d'horizon sur les principaux problèmes de politique (avril 1974, 276 pages).

Etudes sur l'emploi no 10.

Etudes sur l'emploi dans l'industrie mexicaine de logement (mai 1974, 328 pages).

Etudes sur l'emploi no 11.

Conditions de travail et relations professionnelles dans l'industrie du bâtiment au Mexique (mai 1974, 164 pages).

Etude sur les conférences en matière de population exemple de l'Afrique (juin 1974, 82 pages).

Bulletin de liaison entre instituts de recherche et de formation en matière de développement (semestriel) nos 1–3/1974.

7. COOPERATION TECHNIQUE

Aspects de la gestion urbaine (mars 1974, 104 pages).

8. ENVIRONNEMENT

Energie et environnement (mai 1974, 394 pages, bilingue).

Problèmes de la pollution transfrontière (mars 1974, 330 pages).

Problèmes majeurs concernant la pollution de l'air. L'expérience Japonaise (novembre 1974, 186 pages).

Le Mércure et l'environnement (mars 1974, 210 pages).

Wage Determination. Papers presented at an International Conference, Paris 3rd–6th July 1973 (October 1974, 368 pages).

The OECD Social Indicator Development Programme 2. Subjective Elements of Well-Being (December 1974, 204 pages).

Measurement of Labour Disputes and their Economic Effects (January 1974, 240 pages).

Research into Labour Market Behaviour (June 1974, 150 pages).

The Effects of Employment of Foreign Workers (July 1974, 190 pages).

Solidaristic Wage Policy in Sweden (November 1974, 50 pages).

"International Seminars" series

1972–2 Prospects for labour/management co-operation in the enterprise. Regional Joint Seminar, Paris, 24th–27th October 1972. Final Report. (October 1974, 280 pages).

1972–3 Regional trade union seminar on prices policy. Paris, 21st–24th November 1972. Final Report. (May 1974, 184 pages).

1973–1 Advances in work organisation. International Management Seminar, Paris, 3rd–6th April 1973. Final Report (October 1974, 60 pages).

6. DEVELOPMENT CO-OPERATION

Development Co-operation. 1974 Review (December 1974, 328 pages).

Flow of Financial Resources to Developing Countries, 1961–1971 (January 1974, 450 pages).

National Accounts and Development Planning in Low-Income Countries (May 1974, 570 pages, bilingual).

Planning Income Distribution. Private Foreign Investment (August 1974, 234 pages).

Choice and Adaptation of Technology in Developing Countries: an Overview of Major Policy Issues (April 1974, 240 pages).

Employment Series No 10

Studies on Employment in the Mexican Housing Industry (May 1974, 324 pages).

Employment Series No 11

Labour Conditions and Industrial Relations in the Building Industry in Mexico (May 1974, 152 pages).

An Assessment of Population Conferences with Particular Reference to Africa (June 1974, 70 pages).

Liaison Bulletin between Development Research and Training Institutes (quarterly) Nos 1–3/1974.

7. TECHNICAL CO-OPERATION

Aspects of Urban Management (March 1974, 100 pages).

8. ENVIRONMENT

Energy and Environment (May 1974, 394 pages, bilingual).

Problems in Transfrontier Pollution (March 1974, 316 pages).

Major Air Pollution Problems. The Japanese Experience (November 1974, 176 pages).

Mercury and the Environment (March 1974, 196 pages).

9. POLITIQUE SCIENTIFIQUE ET TECHNOLOGIQUE

La société et la maîtrise de la technologie (janvier 1974, 454 pages).
OCDE études d'informatique no 6: L'évaluation de l'efficacité des systèmes informatiques (décembre 1974, 180 pages).
OCDE études d'informatique no 7: L'informatique et les collectivités locales (décembre 1974, 182 pages).

10. EDUCATION

Les modèles mathématiques du secteur enseignement (janvier 1974, 300 pages, bilingue).
Les modèles mathématiques du secteur enseignement annexes: Données de base de l'enquête (mai 1974, 174 pages, bilingue).
Les indicateurs de résultats des systèmes d'enseignement (janvier 1974, 122 pages).
Recherche et développement en matière d'enseignement (mars 1974, 66 pages).
La situation de l'enseignement dans les pays de l'OCDE. Tendances et priorités (août 1974, 76 pages).
Annuaire des statistiques de l'enseignement, volume I: *Tableaux internationaux* (décembre 1974, 66 pages).
L'enseignant face à l'innovation, volume I: *Rapport général* (octobre 1974, 618 pages).
L'enseignant face à l'innovation, volume II: *Evolution récente du recrutement des enseignants* (octobre 1974, 224 pages).;

Conférence sur les Structures Futures de l'Enseignement Post-Secondaire, Paris 26–29 juin 1973

Politiques de l'enseignement supérieur. Rapport général (novembre 1974, 252 pages).
Vers un enseignement supérieur de masse. Nouvelles tendances et options (août 1974, 242 pages).
Structure des études et place de la recherche dans l'enseignement supérieur de masse (novembre 1974, 164 pages).

Tendances nouvelles de la formation et des tâches des enseignants: Rapports de synthèse (novembre 1974, 134 pages).
Acquisition d'une identité professionnelle chez les élèves-professeurs. Etude comparée (novembre 1974, 122 pages).
Expériences nationales: Belgique, France, Royaume-Uni (novembre 1974, 118 pages).
Expériences nationales: Suède (novembre 1974, 174 pages).
Expériences nationales: Etats-Unis (novembre 1974, 192 pages).
Les nouveaux systèmes collégiaux au Canada (janvier 1974, 152 pages).

11. CENTRE POUR LA RECHERCHE ET L'INNOVATION DANS L'ENSEIGNEMENT

Etudes de cas d'innovation dans l'enseignement, Volume I: *Au niveau central* (février 1974, 662 pages).
Etudes de cas d'innovation dans l'enseignement, Volume IV: *Stratégies d'innovation dans l'enseignement* (janvier 1974, 348 pages).
L'enseignement de l'environnement au niveau post secondaire, Volume I: *La formation des généralistes et spécialistes* (mai 1974, 248 pages).

9. SCIENCE AND TECHNOLOGICAL POLICY

Society and the Assessment of Technology (January 1974, 422 pages).

OECD Informatics Studies No 6: The Evaluation of the Performance of Computer Systems (December 1974, 166 pages).

OECD Informatics Studies No 7: Information Technology in Local Government (December 1974, 170 pages).

10. EDUCATION

Mathematical Models for the Education Sector (January 1974, 300 pages, bilingual).

Mathematical Models for the Education Sector Annexes: Supporting Material to the Survey (May 1974, 174 pages, bilingual).

Indicators of Performance of Educational Systems (January 1974, 104 pages).

Research and Development in Education. A Survey (March 1974, 60 pages).

The Educational Situation in OECD Countries. A Review of Trends and Priority Issues for Policy (August 1974, 70 pages).

Educational Statistics Yearbook, Volume I: *International Tables* (December 1974, 66 pages).

The Teacher and Educational Change: A new role, Volume I: *General Report* (October 1974, 600 pages).

The Teacher and Educational Change, Volume II: *Recent Trends in Teacher Recruitment* (October 1974, 218 pages).

Conference on Future Structures of Post-Secondary Education, Paris 26th–29th June, 1973

Policies for Higher Education. General Report (November 1974, 190 pages).

Towards Mass Higher Education. Issues and Dilemmas (August 1974, 228 pages).

Structure of Studies and Place of Research in Mass Higher Education (November 1974, 146 pages).

New Patterns of Teacher Education and Tasks: General Analysis (November 1974, 120 pages).

The Development of Student-Teachers: A Comparative Study of Professional Socialization (November 1974, 90 pages).

Country Experience: Belgium, France, United Kingdom (November 1974, 110 pages).

Country Experience: Sweden (November 1974, 170 pages).

Country Experience: United States (November 1974, 156 pages).

New College Systems in Canada (January 1974, 138 pages).

11. CENTRE FOR EDUCATIONAL RESEARCH IN INNOVATION

Case Studies of Educational Innovation.
Volume I: *At the central level* (February 1974, 618 pages).

Case Studies of Educational Innovation.
Volume IV: *Strategies for Innovation in Education* (January 1974, 300 pages).

Environmental Education at Post-Secondary Level.
Volume I: *The Training of Generalists and Specialists* (May 1974, 208 pages).

L'enseignement de l'environnement au niveau post secondaire ,Volume II: *La formation des enseignants, des responsables de prises de décisions et des catégories professionnelles concernées par l'environnement* (mai 1974, 162 pages).

La créativité de l'école (novembre 1974, 152 pages).

L'éducation recurrente. Politiques et évolution: Rapports par pays. Australie (novembre 1974, 104 pages).

L'éducation recurrente. Politiques et évolution: Rapports par pays. Royaume-Uni (novembre 1974, 32 pages).

12. RECHERCHE ROUTIERE

Eau dans les chaussées: Méthodes de détermination de la teneur en eau et de la tension interstitielle des sols (janvier 1974, 68 pages).

Action du gel sur les chaussées (novembre 1974, 240 pages).

Modèles de circulation urbaine: Possibilités de simplification (novembre 1974, 140 pages).

Recherches sur l'application de la réglementation en matière de circulation (mai 1974, 118 pages).

13. AGENCE POUR L'ENERGIE NUCLEAIRE DE L'OCDE

Normes provisoires de radioprotection applicables à la conception, à la construction, aux essais et au contrôle des stimulateurs cardiaques radioisotopiques (août 1974, 58 pages).

Contrôle des effluents radioactifs. Compte rendu du Séminaire de l'AEN, Karlsruhe 1974 (septembre 1974, 448 pages, bilingue).

Bulletin de droit nucléaire No 13 (avril 1974) no 14 (à paraître).

14. INFORMATION

Activités de l'OCDE en 1973 (mai 1974, 118 pages).

L'observateur de l'OCDE (bimestriel) Cinq numéros (68–72) publiés en 1974.

D. RAPPORTS MIS EN DIFFUSION GENERALE DURANT L'ANNEE 1974

1. AGRICULTURE

- Rapport sur les perspectives du marché des céréales, des autres aliments du bétail et de la production animale, et sur l'incidence de la situation de l'énergie sur l'agriculture.

2. DEVELOPPEMENT

- Repartition géographique des ressources financières mises à la disposition des pays moins développés, 1972 (bilingue).
- Données de base de l'aide aux programmes démographiques 1969–1972 (bilingue).
- Progrès accomplis dans l'élaboration de principes directeurs pour les investissements internationaux dans les pays en développement.

Environmental Education at Post-Secondary Level.
Volume II: *Course for educators, decision-makers and members of professions concerned with the environment* (May 1974, 184 pages).
Creativity of the School (November 1974, 136 pages).
Recurrent Education. Policy and Development in OECD Member Countries. Australia (November 1974, 96 pages).
Recurrent Education. Policy and Development in OECD Member Countries. United Kingdom (November 1974, 30 pages).

12. ROAD RESEARCH

Water in roads: Methods for determining soil moisture content and pore water tension (January 1974, 64 pages).
Frost Action on Roads (November 1974, 232 pages).
Urban traffic models: Possibilities for Simplification (Novembre 1974, 128 pages).
Research on Traffic Law Enforcement (May 1974, 112 pages).

13. OECD NUCLEAR ENERGY AGENCY

Interim radiation protection standards for the design, construction, testing and control of radioisotopic cardiac pacemakers (August 1974, 54 pages).
Monitoring of radioactive effluents. Proceedings of the NEA Seminar, Karlsruhe 1974 (September 1974, 448 pages, bilingual).
Nuclear Law Bulletin No 13 (April 1974) No 14 (to be published).

14. INFORMATION

Activities of OECD in 1973 (May 1974, 114 pages).
OECD Observer (bi-monthly) Five issues (68–72) published in 1974.

D. REPORTS DERESTRICTED IN 1974

1. AGRICULTURE

- Report on the Market Outlook for Cereals, other Animal Feed and Livestock Production, and on the Impact of the Energy Situation on Agriculture.

2. DEVELOPMENT

- Geographical Distribution of Financial Flows to Less-Developed Countries – 1972 (bilingual).
- Basic Figures on Aid to Population Programmes 1969–1972 (bilingual).
- Progress in Elaboration of Guidelines for International Investment in Developing Countries.
  New Trends in Technical Co-operation. Personnel Policies.

- Nouvelles orientations de la politique du personnel de la coopération technique.
- Engagements totaux des pays en développement vis-à-vis l'étranger.
- Les problèmes d'endettement des pays en développement.
- Investissements par le secteur privé des pays membres du Comité de l'aide au développement dans les pays en voie de développement – état des actifs à la fin de 1972.
- L'aide alimentaire.

3. EDUCATION

- Les politiques en faveur de l'innovation, de la recherche et du développement dans l'enseignement.

4. ENVIRONNEMENT

- Note sur la mise en oeuvre du principe pollueur-payeur.
- Les procédés de traitement des eaux usées pour l'élimination du phosphore et de l'azote.
- Rapport du groupe sectoriel sur la gestion de l'eau sur le contrôle de l'eutrophisation.
- Problèmes majeurs concernant la pollution de l'air: l'expérience japonaise (Rapport de la Session technique spéciale du Groupe sectoriel sur la gestion de l'air).
- Le cadmium et l'environnement: Toxicité, économie, contrôle.
- The Price of Land and Land Use Planning: Policy instruments in the urban land market (anglais seulement).
- Les problèmes d'environnement dans la planification des aéroports.
- Modèles de circulation urbaine: possibilités de simplification.
- Capacité des carrefours plans.
- Conférence sur l'enseignement de l'environnement au niveau post-secondaire: bilan et perspective, organisée par le Centre pour la Recherche et l'Innovation dans l'Enseignement qui s'est tenue du 4 au 7 juin 1974 à Rungsted au Danemark.
- Les normes relatives à l'environnement: définitions et besoins d'harmonisation internationale.

5. INDUSTRIE

- Rapport intérimaire du Comité de l'Industrie sur les entreprises internationales.
- Les investissements dans l'industrie sidérurgique – problèmes et perspectives.
- Caractéristiques de la politique de développement régionale de l'Autriche.

6. TOURISME

- La politique gouvernementale du développement du Tourisme.

7. SCIENCE ET TECHNOLOGIE

- La coopération internationale en astronomie.
- Exchange international de chercheurs entre laboratoires gouvernementaux et inventaire d'équipements exceptionnels.

- Total External Liabilities of Developing Countries.
- Debt Problems of Developing Countries.
- Stock of Private Investment by Member Countries of the DAC in Developing Countries – End 1972.
- Food Aid.

3. EDUCATION

- Policies for Innovation and Research and Development in Education.

4. ENVIRONMENT

- Notes on the Implementation of the Polluter-Pays Principle.
- Waste Water Treatment Processes for Phosphorus and Nitrogen Removal.
- Report of the Water Management Sector Group on Eutrophication Control.
- Major Air Pollution Problems: The Japanese Experience (Report of the Special Technical Session of the Air Management Sector Group).
- Cadmium and the Environment: Toxicity, Economy, Control.
- The Price of Land and Land Use Planning: Policy Instruments in the Urban Land Market.
- Environmental Impact of Airport Development.
- Urban Traffic Models: Possibilities for Simplification.
- Capacity of at-grade junctions.
- Conference on Environmental Education at post-secondary level: Review of Experience, Future Action, organised by the Centre for Educational Research and Innovation in Rungsted, Denmark, from 4th to 7th June, 1974.
- Environmental Standards: Definitions and the Need for International Harmonization.

5. INDUSTRY

- Interim Report of the Industry Committee on International Enterprises.
- Investment in the Iron and Steel Industry – Problems and Prospects.
- Salient Features of Regional Development Policy in Austria.

6. TOURISM

- Government Policy in the Development of Tourism.

7. SCIENCE AND TECHNOLOGY

- International Co-operation in Astronomy.
- International exchange of research workers among Government laboratories, and inventories of outstanding facilities.

8. ENERGIE NUCLEAIRE

- Guide relatif aux conteneurs de déchets radioactifs destinés au rejet en mer.
- Rapport d'activité (1973) de l'Agence pour l'Energie Nucléaire de l'Organisation de Coopération et de Développement Economiques.

E. REPRESENTANTS PERMANENTS AUPRES DE L'OCDE EN 1974

Allemagne	S. Exc. le Dr. Egon Emmel
Australie	S. Exc. M. R. J. Cameron
Autriche	S. Exc. le Dr. Carl H. Bobleter
Belgique	S. Exc. M. Roger Ockrent (jusqu'au 9 avril 1974*) S. Exc. M. Herman Noppen (du 16 au 23 septembre 1974*) M. Luc Ceyssens, Chef de la Délégation a.i. (à partir du 24 septembre 1974)
Canada	S. Exc. M. Peter M. Towe
Danemark	S. Exc. M. Vagn Aage Korsbaek
Espagne	S. Exc. M. Francisco Javier Vallaure
Etats-Unis	M. Weir M. Brown, Chef de la Délégation a.i. (jusqu'au 27 mai 1974) S. Exc. M. William C. Turner (à partir du 28 mai 1974)
Finlande	S. Exc. M. Ralph Enckell
France	S. Exc. M. François Valery
Grèce	S. Exc. M. Jean Apostolidis (jusqu'au 13 août 1974) S. Exc. M. Dimitri Athanassopoulos (à partir du 17 septembre 1974)
Irlande	S. Exc. M. Eamonn L. Kennedy (jusqu'au 25 mars 1974) S. Exc. M. Hugh J. McCann (à partir du 7 mai 1974)
Islande	S. Exc. M. Henrik Sv. Björnsson
Italie	S. Exc. M. Luciano Conti
Japon	S. Exc. M. Bunroku Yoshino
Luxembourg	S. Exc. M. Camille Dumont
Norvège	M. Egil Winsnes, Chef de la Délégation a.i. (jusqu'au 28 février 1974) S. Exc. M. Georg Kristiansen (à partir du 7 mars 1974)
Nouvelle-Zélande	S. Exc. M. Paul Gabites
Pays-Bas	S. Exc. M. Johan Kaufmann (jusqu'au 5 mars 1974) S. Exc. M. K. Westerhoff (à partir du 11 mars 1974)
Portugal	S. Exc. M. João Rodrigues Simões Affra (jusqu'au 6 novembre 1974)

* décédé ce jour-là.

8. NUCLEAR ENERGY

- Guidelines for Sea Disposal Packages of Radioactive Waste.
- Activity Report (1973) of the Nuclear Energy Agency of the Organisation for Economic Co-operation and Development.

E. PERMANENT REPRESENTATIVES TO THE OECD IN 1974

Australia	H. E. Mr. R. J. CAMERON
Austria	H. E. Dr. Carl H. BOBLETER
Belgium	H. E. Mr. Roger OCKRENT (up to 9th April, 1974*)
	H. E. Mr. Herman NOPPEN (from 16th to 24th September, 1974*)
	Mr. Luc CEYSSENS a.i. Acting Head of Delegation (from 24th September, 1974)
Canada	H. E. Mr. Peter M. TOWE
Denmark	H. E. Mr. Vagn Aage KORSBAEK
Finland	H. E. Mr. Ralph ENCKELL
France	H. E. Mr. François VALERY
Germany	H. E. Dr. Egon EMMEL
Greece	H. E. Mr. Jean APOSTOLIDIS (up to 13th August, 1974)
	H. E. Mr. Dimitri ATHANASSOPOULOS (from 17th September, 1974)
Iceland	H. E. Mr. Henrik Sv. BJÖRNSSON
Ireland	H. E. Mr. Eamonn L. KENNEDY (up to 25th March, 1974)
	H. E. Mr. Hugh McCANN (from 7th May, 1974)
Italy	H. E. Mr. Luciano CONTI
Japan	H. E. Mr. Bunroku YOSHINO
Luxembourg	H. E. Mr. Camille DUMONT
Netherlands	H. E. Mr. Johan KAUFMANN (up to 5th March, 1974)
	H. E. Mr. K. WESTERHOFF (from 11th March, 1974)
Norway	Mr. Egil WINSNES, Head of Delegation a.i. (up to 28 February, 1974)
	H. E. Mr. Georg KRISTIANSEN (from 7 March, 1974)
New Zealand	H. E. Mr. Paul GABITES
Portugal	H. E. M. João Rodrigues Simões AFFRA (until 6 November 1974)
	H. E. Mr. Manuel de Almeida BELLO (from 7 November 1974)
Spain	H. E. Mr. Francisco Javier VALLAURE
Sweden	H. E. Mr. Leif BELFRAGE
Switzerland	H. E. Mr. Marcel HEIMO (until 14 February 1974)

* deceased on that date

	S. Exc. M. Manuel de Almeida BELLO (à partir du 7 novembre 1974)
Royaume-Uni	S. Exc. M. F. G. K. GALLAGHER
Suède	S. Exc. M. Leif BELFRAGE
Suisse	S. Exc. M. Marcel HEIMO (jusqu'au 14 février 1974)
	S. Exc. M. Albert GRÜBEL (à partir du 5 avril 1974)
Turquie	S. Exc. M. Memduh AYTÜR
Commission des Communautés Européennes*	M. Adolphe de BAERDEMAEKER
Yougoslavie**	S. Exc. M. Jožef KOROŠEC

F. HAUTS FONCTIONNAIRES DU SECRETARIAT EN 1974

Secrétaire général	Emile van Lennep (Pays-Bas)
Secrétaires généraux adjoints	Charles G. Wootton (Etats-Unis)
	Gérard Eldin (France)
Secrétaires généraux suppléants	Rinieri Paulucci di Calboli (Italie)
	Frederick J. Atkinson (Royaume-Uni)
	Helmut Abramowski (Allemagne)
Conseiller spécial auprès du Secrétaire général pour la coordination des questions relatives à l'énergie	Ulf Lantzke (Allemagne)
Affaires Economiques et Statisques	Frederick J. Atkinson Secrétaire général suppléant
Echanges	Erhard Poincilit, Directeur (Allemagne)
Affaires Financières et Fiscales	Raymond Bertrand, Directeur (France)
Développement	André Vincent, Directeur (France)
Environnement	Hilliard Roderick, Directeur (Etats-Unis)
Affaires Sociales, Main d'Oeuvre et Education	James R. Gass, Directeur (Royaume-Uni)
Science, Technologie et Industrie	Keichi Oshima, Directeur (Japon)
Energie	Ulf Lantzke, Directeur (Allemagne)
Agriculture	Albert Simantov, Directeur (Grèce)
Direction Exécutive	Maurice Jacomet, Directeur général (France)
Information	James R. West, Directeur (Etats-Unis)
Centre de Développement	Paul-Marc Henry, Président (France)
Agence Internationale de l'Energie	Ulf Lantzke, Directeur exécutif (Allemagne)
Agence pour l'Energie Nucléaire	Einar Saeland, Directeur général (Norvège)

* En vertu du Protocole Additionnel n° 1 de la Convention relative à l'OCDE, la Commission des Communautés Européennes participe aux travaux de l'Organisation.

** La Yougoslavie participe aux travaux de l'OCDE en vertu d'un Accord, conclu le 30 septembre 1961, entre l'Organisation et le Gouvernement yougoslave.

	H. E. Mr. Albert GRÜBEL (from 5 April 1974)
Turkey	H. E. Mr. Memduh AYTÜR
United Kingdom	H. E. Mr. F. G. K. GALLAGHER
United States	Mr. Weir M. BROWN Head of Delegation a.i. (until 27 May 1974) H. E. Mr. William C. TURNER (from 28 May 1974)
Commission of the European Communities*	Mr. Adolphe de BAERDEMAEKER
Yugoslavia**	H. E. Mr. Jožef KOROŠEC

F. SENIOR SECRETARIAT OFFICIALS, 1974

Secretary-General	Emile van Lennep (Netherlands)
Deputy Secretaries-General	Charles G. Wootton (USA) Gérard Eldin (France)
Assistant Secretaries-General	Rinieri Paulucci di Calboli (Italy) Frederick J. Atkinson (UK) Helmut Abramowski (Germany)
Special Counsellor to the Secretary-General for the Coordination of Energy Matters	Ulf Lantzke (Germany)
Economic and Statistic Affairs	Frederick J. Atkinson, Assistant Secretary-General (UK)
Trade	Erhard Poincilit, Director (Germany)
Financial and Fiscal Affairs	Raymond Bertrand, Director (France)
Development	André Vincent, Director (France)
Environment	Hilliard Roderick, Director (USA)
Social Affairs, Manpower and Education	James R. Gass, Director (UK)
Science, Technology and Industry	Keichi Oshima, Director (Japan)
Energy	Ulf Lantzke, Director (Germany)
Agriculture	Albert Simantov, Director (Greece)
Executive Directorate	Maurice Jacomet, Director-General (France)
Information	James R. West, Director (USA)
Development Centre	Paul-Marc Henry, President (France)
International Energy Agency	Ulf Lantzke, Executive-Director (Germany)
Nuclear Energy Agency	Einar Saeland, Director-General (Norway)

* By virtue of the First Protocol to the OECD Convention, the Commission of the European Communities takes part in the work of the Organisation.

** Yugoslavia takes part in the work of OCDE by virtue of an Agreement between the Organisation and the Yugoslav Government of 30 September 1961.

Centre pour la Recherche et l'Innovation dans l'Enseignement	James R. Gass, Directeur (Royaume-Uni)

Adresse: Organisation de Coopération et de Développement Economiques.
2, rue André Pascal, 75775 Paris Cédex 16 (France).
Tél.: 524.82.00
Télégrammes: DEVELOPECONOMIE
Télex: 62.160 OCDE PARIS

Centre for Educational Research and Innovation — James R. Gass, Director (UK)

Address: Organisation for Economic Co-operation and Development
2, rue André Pascal
75775 Paris Cedex (France)
Tel.: 524.82.00
Cable: DEVELOPECONOMIE
Telex: 62.160 OCDE PARIS

CHAPITRE V

CONSEIL DE L'EUROPE

A. EPHEMERIDES 1974

21–25 janvier: 3ème partie de la 25ème session de l'Assemblée Consultative. M. Ionnis Christophides, Ministre des affaires étrangères de Chypre, M. Christian Bonnet, Secrétaire d'Etat français, le Jonkheer Emile van Lennep, Secrétaire Général de l'OCDE et des parlementaires du Canada et des Etats-Unis interviennent dans les débats.

24 janvier: 53ème session du Comité des Ministres, Strasbourg. Adoption de la Résolution (74) 4 sur le rôle futur du Conseil de l'Europe.

25 janvier: Colloque entre le Comité des Ministres et des représentants de l'Assemblée Consultative, Strasbourg: la solidarité des Etats membres du Conseil de l'Europe face à la crise provoquée par les événements du Proche-Orient.

3 mai: Ratification par la France de la Convention européenne des droits de l'homme.

6 mai: Le Conseil de l'Europe célèbre son 25ème anniversaire. M. Alain Poher, Président de la République française par interim, rend hommage au travail de „la plus ancienne et la plus large des institutions européennes."

6 mai: 54ème session du Comité des Ministres, Strasbourg. Décision de créer un Bureau de liaison du Conseil de l'Europe à Bruxelles et ouverture à la signature des Etats membres d'une Convention européenne relative à la protection sociale des agriculteurs.

6–10 mai: 1ère partie de la 26ème session de l'Assemblée Consultative. M. Giuseppe Vedovato est réélu Président. M. Georg Kahn-Ackermann est élu Secrétaire Général. M. Ionnis Christophides, Ministre des affaires étrangères de Chypre intervient dans le débat.

7 mai: Table ronde entre parlementaires du Conseil de l'Europe et les présidents et greffiers des parlements des Etats membres: les progrès de l'unification européenne et les difficultés de la démocratie parlementaire, Strasbourg.

30–31 mai: 9ème Conférence des Ministres européens de la justice, Vienne.

24–26 juin: Colloque de parlementaires et d'experts sur le rôle et la gestion des télécommunications dans une société démocratique, Munich.

3 juillet: Commission permanente de l'Assemblée, Lucerne. L'appellation „Assemblée parlementaire" sera désormais utilisée pour l'Assemblée Consultative.

18 juillet: Déclaration du Président Vedovato à la presse condamnant le renversement du régime constitutionnel de Chypre.

29 juillet: Commission permanente de l'Assemblée, Paris. Adoption de la Recommandation 734 qui demande au Comité des Ministres d'inscrire la question de Chypre à son ordre du jour et de convoquer le Comité mixte au niveau des Ministres; de la Résolution 573 qui demande notamment la conclusion rapide d'un accord apportant un règlement juste, durable et pacifique du problème chypriote, tenant compte des besoins et des droits légitimes des deux communautés de l'Ile, insiste sur la nécessité d'associer pleinement les deux communautés ethniques aux négociations sur l'avenir de l'Ile et exprime l'espoir que les gouvernements turc et grec coopéreront étroitement pour trouver des solutions communes à ce problème.

21–22 août: Les Délégués des Ministres chargent le Représentant spécial pour les réfugiés de leur soumettre un programme d'aide aux populations éprouvées de Chypre.

CHAPTER V

COUNCIL OF EUROPE

A. MAIN EVENTS 1974

21–25 January: 3rd part of the 25th Session of the Consultative Assembly. Mr. Ionnis Christophides, Cyprus Foreign Minister, Mr. Christian Bonnet, French Secretary of State, Jonkheer Emile van Lennep, Secretary General of OECD and Parliamentarians from Canada and the United States took part in the debates.

24 January: 53rd Session of the Committee of Ministers, Strasbourg. Resolution (74) 4 on the future role of the Council of Europe was adopted.

25 January: Colloquy between the Committee of Ministers and Representatives of the Consultative Assembly: Solidarity among Council of Europe member States in the face of the crisis provoked by events in the Middle-East.

3 May: Ratification by France of the European Convention on Human Rights.

6 May: The Council of Europe celebrated its 25th Anniversary. The interim President of the French Republic, Mr. Alain Poher, paid tribute to the work of "the oldest and most broadly based of the European institutions".

6 May: 54th Session of the Committee of Ministers, Strasbourg. The Committee decided to set up a Council of Europe Liaison Office in Brussels. A European Convention on the social protection of farmers was opened for signature by Member States.

6–10 May: 1st part of the 26th Session of the Consultative Assembly. Mr. Giuseppe Vedovato was re-elected President. Mr. Georg Kahn-Ackermann was elected Secretary General. Mr. Ionnis Christophides, Cyprus Foreign Minister, took part in the debates.

7 May: Round Table meeting of Council of Europe Parliamentarians with Speakers and Clerks of national parliaments of Member States: Progress towards European unity and difficulties confronting parliamentary democracy, Strasbourg.

30–31 May: 9th Conference of European Ministers of Justice, Vienna.

24–26 June: Symposium of parliamentarians and experts on the role and management of telecommunications in a democratic society, Munich.

3 July: Standing Committee of the Assembly, Lucerne. The Consultative Assembly should in future be referred to as the "Parliamentary Assembly."

18 July: Press statement by the President of the Assembly, Mr. Vedovato, deploring the overthrow of constitutional rule in Cyprus.

29 July: Standing Committee of the Assembly, Paris. Adoption of Recommendation 734, asking the Committee of Ministers to include the Cyprus question on its agenda and convene the Joint Committee at ministerial level; of Resolution 573, calling for early agreement on a fair, lasting and peaceful settlement of the Cyprus problem with due respect for the legitimate needs and rights of the island's two ethnic communities; stressing that both communities should be fully associated with negotiations on the island's future; and expressing the hope that the Governments of Turkey and Greece would co-operate closely in seeking common solutions to the Cyprus problem.

21–22nd August: Request by the Ministers' Deputies to the Special Representative for Refugees to submit them an aid programme for the stricken populations of Cyprus.

5 septembre: Le Bureau de l'Assemblée décide de charger un groupe de travail restreint de se rendre à Nicosie, Ankara, Athènes et Londres, et de lui faire rapport.

6 septembre: Création, par le Comité des Ministres, d'un fonds d'urgence du Conseil de l'Europe pour l'aide aux populations de Chypre.

16–21 septembre: 10ème session de la Conférence européenne des pouvoirs locaux, Strasbourg. Présidence: M. R. Laan Jr. Bourgmestre de Zaanstad (Pays-Bas).

17 septembre: M. Georg Kahn-Ackermann prend officiellement ses fonctions de Secrétaire Général.

20 septembre: Le rapporteur de la Commission politique rencontre à Chypre les dirigeants des communautés grecque et turque.

23 septembre: M. Rauf Denktash, Vice-Président, Leader de la Communauté cypriote turc, et M. Tassos Papadopoulos, Président cypriote grec du Parlement participent à une réunion jointe du Bureau et de la Commission des questions politiques.

24–30 septembre: 2ème partie de la 26ème session de l'Assemblée parlementaire. M. Karl Moersch, Ministre d'Etat aux affaires étrangères d'Allemagne, M. Evangelos Averoff, Ministre de la défense et Ministre des affaires étrangères par interim de Grèce, M. Mario Soares, Ministre des affaires étrangères du Portugal, Mme Françoise Giroud, Secrétaire d'Etat chargée de la condition féminine auprès du Premier Ministre de France et une délégation parlementaire japonaise interviennent dans les débats.
Adoption de la Recommandation 736 qui demande notamment que soient facilitées les conversations directes entre les dirigeants de la communauté cypriote grecque et cypriote turque; de la Résolution 574 qui exprime l'espoir que les Etats garants des accords de Zurich et de Londres faciliteront le déroulement des négociations intercommunautaires; de la Recommandation 737 relative à l'aide humanitaire aux populations en détresse à Chypre.

26–27 septembre: Table ronde de parlementaires, experts et journalistes sur les conseils de presse, Stockholm.

22–26 octobre: Confrontation entre parlementaires, urbanistes, conservateurs et architectes sur le coût social de la conservation des centres historiques, Bologne.

23–24 octobre: Colloque de parlementaires et d'experts sur la protection des eaux douces, Strasbourg.

8–9 novembre: Conférence intergouvernementale sur l'éducation des migrants et de leurs familles, Strasbourg.

25–28 novembre: Conférence de directeurs d'instituts de recherches criminologiques sur l'importance des stupéfiants par rapport à la criminalité, Strasbourg.

28 novembre: 55ème session du Comité des Ministres, Paris. Dépôt par M. Dimitri Bitsios, Ministre des affaires étrangères, de l'instrument d'adhésion de la Grèce au Conseil de l'Europe et de l'instrument de ratification de la Convention européenne des droits de l'homme. Dépôt de l'instrument de ratification par la Suisse de la même Convention.

29 novembre: Colloque entre le Comité des Ministres et des représentants de l'Assemblée parlementaire, Paris: la situation en Méditerranée, la CSCE et l'avenir du Conseil de l'Europe.

4–6 décembre: Confrontation entre parlementaires, maires et experts: l'ordinateur au service de l'administration locale, Lausanne.

5 September: Decision by the Bureau of the Assembly to appoint a small working party to go to Nicosia, Ankara, Athens and London and report back.

6 September: The Committee of Ministers set up an emergency fund of the Council of Europe to aid the distressed populations in Cyprus.

16–21 September: 10th Session of the European Conference of Local Authorities, Strasbourg, Mr. R. Laan Jr., Burgomaster of Zaanstad, Netherlands, was in the Chair.

17 September: Mr. Georg Kahn-Ackermann took up his duties as Secretary General.

20 September: Meeting in Cyprus between the Political Affairs Committee's rapporteur and the leaders of the Greek- and Turkish-Cypriot communities.

23 September: Participation by Mr. Rauf Denktash, Vice-President, Leader of the Turkish-Cypriot community, and Mr. Tassos Papadopoulos, Greek Cypriot, speaker of the Cyprus Parliament, in a joint meeting of the Bureau and Political Affairs Committee.

24–30 September: 2nd part of the 26th Session of the Parliamentary Assembly. Mr. Karl Moersch, German Foreign Minister of State, Mr. Evangelos Averoff, Greek Minister of Defence and interim Foreign Minister, Mr. Mario Soares, Portuguese Foreign Minister, Mrs. Françoise Giroud, French Secretary of State for women's Affairs, and a Japanese parliamentary delegation took part in the debates.
Adoption of Recommendation 736, calling for efforts to facilitate direct talks between the leaders of the Greek- and Turkish-Cypriot communities; Resolution 574, expressing the hope that the States acting as guarantors of the Zürich and London Agreements would facilitate the holding of inter-community negotiations; and Recommendation 737 on humanitarian aid to the distressed populations in Cyprus.

26–27 September: Round Table of parliamentarians, experts and journalists on press councils, Stockholm.

22–26 October: Symposium of parliamentarians with townplanners, conservation experts and architects on the social cost of conserving historic centres, Bologna.

23–24 October: Symposium of parliamentarians with experts on the protection of fresh water, Strasbourg.

8–9 November: Intergovernmental Conference on the education of foreign workers and their families, Strasbourg.

25–28 November: Conference of Directors of Criminological Research Institutes on the importance of narcotics in relation to criminality, Strasbourg.

28 November: 55th Session of the Committee of Ministers, Paris. The Greek Foreign Minister, Mr. Dimitri Bitsios deposited his country's instrument of accession to the Council of Europe and the instrument of ratification by Greece of the European Convention on Human Rights. Deposit of the Swiss instrument of ratification of the same Convention.

29 November: Colloquy between the Committee of Ministers and Representatives of the Parliamentary Assembly, Paris: the situation in the Mediterranean, the ECSC and the future of the Council of Europe.

4–6 December: Symposium of parliamentarians with mayors and experts on the use of computers in local government, Lausanne.

B. ACCORDS EUROPEENS

1. CONVENTION EUROPEENNE SUR L'IMPRESCRIPTIBILITE DES CRIMES CONTRE L'HUMANITE ET DES CRIMES DE GUERRE

(25 janvier 1974)

Les Etats membres du Conseil de l'Europe, signataires de la présente Convention,

Considérant la nécessité de sauvegarder la dignité humaine en temps de guerre comme en temps de paix;

Constatant que les crimes contre l'humanité et les violations les plus graves des lois et coutumes de la guerre constituent une atteinte sérieuse à cette dignité;

Soucieux d'éviter en conséquence que la répression de ces crimes soit entravée par la prescription de la poursuite et de l'exécution des peines;

Considérant l'intérêt essentiel de promouvoir dans ce domaine une politique pénale commune, le but du Conseil de l'Europe étant de réaliser une union plus étroite entre ses membres,

Sont convenus de ce qui suit:

Article 1

Tout Etat contractant s'engage à prendre les mesures nécessaires afin que la prescription soit inapplicable à la poursuite des infractions suivantes et à l'exécution des peines prononcées pour de telles infractions, pour autant qu'elles sont punissables dans sa législation nationale:

1. les crimes contre l'humanité prévus par la Convention pour la prévention et la répression du crime de génocide, adoptée le 9 décembre 1948 par l'Assemblée générale des Nations Unies;

2. (*a*) les infractions prévues aux articles 50 de la Convention de Genève de 1949 pour l'amélioration du sort des blessés et des malades dans les forces armées en campagne, 51 de la Convention de Genève de 1949 pour l'amélioration du sort des blessés, des malades et des naufragés des forces armées sur mer, 130 de la Convention de Genève de 1949 relative au traitement des prisonniers de guerre et 147 de la Convention de Genève de 1949 relative à la protection des personnes civiles en temps de guerre,

(*b*) toutes violations analogues des lois de la guerre en vigueur lors de l'entrée en application de la présente Convention et des coutumes de la guerre existant à ce moment, qui ne sont pas déjà prévues par les dispositions susvisées des Conventions de Genève,

lorsque l'infraction considérée en l'espèce revêt une particulière gravité, soit en raison de ses éléments matériels et intentionnels, soit en raison de l'étendue de ses conséquences prévisibles;

3. toutes autres infractions aux lois et coutumes du droit international tel qu'il sera établi à l'avenir, considérées par l'Etat contractant intéressé, aux termes d'une déclaration faite conformément à l'article 6, comme étant de nature analogue à celles prévucs aux paragraphes 1 ou 2 du présent article.

Article 2

1. Dans chaque Etat contractant, la présente Convention s'applique aux infractions commises après son entrée en vigueur à l'égard de cet Etat.

2. Elle s'applique également aux infractions commises avant cette en-

B. EUROPEAN AGREEMENTS

1. EUROPEAN CONVENTION ON THE NON-APPLICABILITY OF STATUTORY LIMITATION TO CRIMES AGAINST HUMANITY AND WAR CRIMES

(25 January 1974)

The member States of the Council of Europe, signatory hereto,

Considering the necessity to safeguard human dignity in time of war and in time of peace;

Considering that crimes against humanity and the most serious violations of the laws and customs of war constitute a serious infraction of human dignity;

Concerned in consequence to ensure that the punishment of those crimes is not prevented by statutory limitations whether in relation to prosecution or to the enforcement of the punishment;

Considering the essential interest in promoting a common criminal policy in this field, the aim of the Council of Europe being to achieve a greater unity between its members,

Have agreed as follows:

Article 1

Each Contracting State undertakes to adopt any necessary measures to secure that statutory limitation shall not apply to the prosecution of the following offences, or to the enforcement of the sentences imposed for such offences, in so far as they are punishable under its domestic law:

1. the crimes against humanity specified in the Convention on the Prevention and Punishment of the Crime of Genocide adopted on 9 December 1948 by the General Assembly of the United Nations;

2. (*a*) the violations specified in Article 50 of the 1949 Geneva Convention for the Amelioration of the Condition of the Wounded and Sick in Armed Forces in the Field, Article 51 of the 1949 Geneva Convention for the Amelioration of the Condition of Wounded, Sick and Shipwrecked Members of Armed Forces at Sea, Article 130 of the 1949 Geneva Convention relative to the Treatment of Prisoners of War and Article 147 of the 1949 Geneva Convention relative to the Protection of Civilian Persons in Time of War,

(*b*) any comparable violations of the laws of war having effect at the time when this Convention enters into force and of customs of war existing at that time, which are not already provided for in the above-mentioned provisions of the Geneva Conventions,

when the specific violation under consideration is of a particularly grave character by reason either of its factual and intentional elements or of the extent of its foreseeable consequences;

3. any other violation of a rule or custom of international law which may hereafter be established and which the Contracting State concerned considers according to a declaration under Article 6 as being of a comparable nature to those referred to in paragraph 1 or 2 of this Article.

Article 2

1. The present Convention applies to offences committed after its entry into force in respect of the Contracting State concerned.

2. It applies also to offences committed before such entry into force in

trée en vigueur dans les cas où le délai de prescription n'est pas encore venu à expiration à cette date.

Article 3

1. La présente Convention est ouverte à la signature des Etats membres du Conseil de l'Europe. Elle sera ratifiée ou acceptée. Les instruments de ratification ou d'acceptation seront déposés près le Secrétaire Général du Conseil de l'Europe.

2. La Convention entrera en vigueur trois mois après la date du dépôt du troisième instrument de ratification ou d'acceptation.

3. Elle entrera en vigueur à l'égard de tout Etat signataire qui la ratifiera ou l'acceptera ultérieurement, trois mois après la date du dépôt de son instrument de ratification ou d'acceptation.

Article 4

1. Après l'entrée en vigueur de la présente Convention, le Comité des Ministres du Conseil de l'Europe pourra inviter tout Etat non membre du Conseil de l'Europe à adhérer à la présente Convention. La résolution concernant cette invitation devra recevoir l'accord unanime des Membres du Conseil ayant ratifié la Convention.

2. L'adhésion s'effectuera par le dépôt, près le Secrétaire Général du Conseil de l'Europe, d'un instrument d'adhésion qui prendra effet trois mois après la date de son dépôt.

Article 5

1. Tout Etat peut, au moment de la signature ou au moment du dépôt de son instrument de ratification, d'acceptation ou d'adhésion, désigner le ou les territoires auxquels s'applique la présente Convention.

2. Tout Etat peut, au moment du dépôt de son instrument de ratification, d'acceptation ou d'adhésion ou à tout autre moment par la suite, étendre l'application de la présente Convention, par déclaration adressée au Secrétaire Général du Conseil de l'Europe, à tout autre territoire désigné dans la déclaration et dont il assure les relations internationales ou pour lequel il est habilité à stipuler.

3. Toute déclaration faite en vertu du paragraphe précédent pourra être retirée, en ce qui concerne tout territoire désigné dans cette déclaration, aux conditions prévues à l'article 7 de la présente Convention.

Article 6

1. Tout Etat contractant peut, à tout moment, par déclaration adressée au Secrétaire Général du Conseil de l'Europe, étendre l'application de la présente Convention aux infractions prévues à l'article 1, paragraphe 3, de la présente Convention.

2. Toute déclaration faite en vertu du paragraphe précédent pourra être retirée aux conditions prévues à l'article 7 de la présente Convention.

Article 7

1. La présente Convention demeurera en vigueur sans limitation de durée.

those cases where the statutory limitation period had not expired at that time.

Article 3

1. This Convention shall be open to signature by the member States of the Council of Europe. It shall be subject to ratification or acceptance. Instruments of ratification or acceptance shall be deposited with the Secretary General of the Council of Europe.

2. The Convention shall enter into force three months after the date of deposit of the third instrument of ratification or acceptance.

3. In respect of a signatory State ratifying or accepting subsequently, the Convention shall come into force three months after the date of the deposit of its instrument of ratification or acceptance.

Article 4

1. After the entry into force of this Convention, the Committee of Ministers of the Council of Europe may invite any non-member State to accede thereto, provided that the resolution containing such invitation receives the unanimous agreement of the Members of the Council who have ratified the Convention.

2. Such accession shall be effected by depositing with the Secretary General of the Council of Europe an instrument of accession which shall take effect three months after the date of its deposit.

Article 5

1. Any State may, at the time of signature or when depositing its instrument of ratification, acceptance or accession, specify the territory or territories to which this Convention shall apply.

2. Any State may, when depositing its instrument of ratification, acceptance or accession or at any later date, by declaration addressed to the Secretary General of the Council of Europe, extend this Convention to any other territory or territories specified in the declaration and for whose international relations it is responsible or on whose behalf it is authorised to give undertakings.

3. Any declaration made in pursuance of the preceding paragraph may, in respect of any territory mentioned in such declaration, be withdrawn according to the procedure laid down in Article 7 of this Convention.

Article 6

1. Any Contracting State may, at any time, by declaration addressed to the Secretary General of the Council of Europe, extend this Convention to any violations provided for in Article 1, paragraph 3 of this Convention.

2. Any declaration made in pursuance of the preceding paragraph may be withdrawn according to the procedure laid down in Article 7 of this Convention.

Article 7

1. This Convention shall remain in force indefinitely.

2. Any Contracting State may, insofar as it is concerned, denounce this

2. Tout Etat contractant pourra, en ce qui le concerne, dénoncer la présente Convention en adressant une notification au Secrétaire Général du Conseil de l'Europe.

3. La dénonciation prendra effet six mois après la date de la réception de la notification par le Secrétaire Général.

Article 8

Le Secrétaire Général du Conseil de l'Europe notifiera aux Etats membres du Conseil et à tout Etat ayant adhéré à la présente Convention:

(*a*) toute signature;

(*b*) le dépôt de tout instrument de ratification, d'acceptation ou d'adhésion;

(*c*) toute date d'entrée en vigueur de la présente Convention conformément à son article 3;

(*d*) toute déclaration reçue en application des articles 5 ou 6;

(*e*) toute notification reçue en application des dispositions de l'article 7 et la date à laquelle la dénonciation prendra effet.

2. CONVENTION EUROPEENNE RELATIVE A LA PROTECTION SOCIALE DES AGRICULTEURS

(6 mai 1974)

Les Etats membres du Conseil de l'Europe, signataires de la présente Convention,

Considérant que le but du Conseil de l'Europe est de réaliser une union plus étroite entre ses Membres, notamment en vue de favoriser leur progrès économique et social;

Considérant qu'une amélioration des conditions de vie des exploitants agricoles mise en oeuvre par des mesures appropriées est de nature à contribuer au progrès social en Europe;

Rappelant que la Charte sociale européenne, élaborée également au sein du Conseil de l'Europe et ouverte à la signature des Etats membres le 18 octobre 1961, a pour objectif l'amélioration du niveau de vie et la promotion du bien-être social de toutes les catégories de leurs populations tant rurales qu'urbaines;

Considérant que les conditions particulières et les caractères spécifiques des activités agricoles ainsi que les mutations affectant le monde agricole exigent que des mesures appropriées soient prises en faveur des exploitants agricoles afin de favoriser leur bien-être social;

Estimant dès lors qu'il convient de compléter et de renforcer la protection sociale des exploitants agricoles, des membres de leurs familles et, le cas échéant, des salariés qu'ils emploient, en tenant compte des besoins sociaux de ces personnes et des conditions particulières des activités agricoles,

Sont convenus de ce qui suit:

TITRE I

Article 1

Toute Partie Contractante s'engage à appliquer les dispositions de la présente Convention à ses ressortissants résidant sur son territoire.

Convention by means of a notification addressed to the Secretary General of the Council of Europe.

3. Such denunciation shall take effect six months after the date of receipt by the Secretary General of such notification.

Article 8

The Secretary General of the Council of Europe shall notify the member States of the Council and any State which has acceded to this Convention of:

(*a*) any signature;

(*b*) any deposit of an instrument of ratification, acceptance or accession;

(*c*) any date of entry into force of this Convention in accordance with Article 3 thereof;

(*d*) any declaration received in pursuance of the provisions of Article 5 or Article 6;

(*e*) any notification received in pursuance of the provisions of Article 7 and the date on which the denunciation takes effect.

2. EUROPEAN CONVENTION ON THE SOCIAL PROTECTION OF FARMERS

(6 May 1974)

The member States of the Council of Europe, signatory hereto,

Considering that the aim of the Council of Europe is to achieve greater unity between its Members, in particular for the purpose of facilitating their economic and social progress;

Considering that the improvement of living conditions of farmers through the implementation of appropriate measures can contribute to social progress in Europe;

Recalling that the aim of the European Social Charter, also drawn up within the Council of Europe and opened to signature by Member States on 18 October 1961, is to improve the standard of living and to promote the social well-being of both their urban and rural populations;

Considering that the special conditions and characteristics of farming as well as the changes taking place in the farming world require the adoption of appropriate measures to promote the social well-being of farmers;

Considering, in consequence, that measures should be taken to extend and to reinforce the social protection of farmers, the members of their families and, where appropriate, their paid employees, with due regard to the social needs of these persons and to the special conditions of farming,

Have agreed as follows:

PART I

Article 1

Each Contracting Party undertakes to apply the provisions of this Convention to its nationals, resident in its territory.

Article 2

Aux fins de la présente Convention, le terme ,,exploitant agricole'' vise toute personne qui, en qualité de travailleur indépendant, consacre exclusivement ou principalement son activité à une profession agricole, sylvicole, horticole, viticole ou similaire, étant entendu qu'elle peut être secondée dans ses travaux par des membres de sa famille et/ou par des salariés.

TITRE II

Article 3

Toute Partie Contractante assurera aux exploitants agricoles, aux membres de leurs familles et, le cas échéant, aux salariés qu'ils emploient, une protection sociale comparable à celle dont jouissent d'autres groupes de la population, compte tenu des dispositions des articles 4 à 13 de la présente Convention.

Article 4

1. Toute Partie Contractante appliquera, dans toute la mesure appropriée, aux exploitants agricoles et à leurs ayants-droit, les normes de sécurité sociale prévues par sa législation pour les autres catégories protégées de la population.

2. Sans préjudice des dispositions du paragraphe 1 du présent article, toute Partie Contractante accordera aux exploitants agricoles, dans les conditions et délais appropriés, la protection de la sécurité sociale pour au moins quatre des éventualités suivantes: maladie, maternité, invalidité, vieillesse, décès, accidents du travail, maladies professionnelles et charges familiales.

Article 5

1. Toute Partie Contractante fera en sorte que lorsqu'un exploitant agricole cesse son activité agricole pour des raisons d'ordre structurel ou autres qu'elle déterminera, cet exploitant, les membres de sa famille et, le cas échéant, les salariés qu'il emploie, bénéficient de mesures appropriées.

Ces mesures comprendront:

(*a*) la mise à disposition de facilités en vue de leur permettre de prendre une nouvelle activité, de préférence dans leur région, notamment des facilités pour l'orientation, la formation et la réadaptation professionnelles;

(*b*) le versement d'allocations temporaires afin de permettre la préparation à une autre activité;

(*c*) le maintien des droits acquis et des droits en cours d'acquisition en matière de sécurité sociale;

(*d*) le versement d'indemnités équitables ou de primes appropriées à un exploitant agricole qui, pour des raisons d'âge, a des difficultés à entreprendre une autre activité, et à condition que la cessation de l'activité agricole apporte une amélioration structurelle.

2. Aux fins du présent article, la notion de cessation d'activité ne doit pas être interprétée comme excluant la possibilité pour l'exploitant de conserver un terrain agricole de superficie limitée à ses besoins personnels.

3. Toute Partie Contractante fera en sorte que lorsqu'un exploitant agricole cesse partiellement son activité pour des raisons d'ordre structurel ou

Article 2

For the purposes of this Convention, the term "farmer" means any self-employed person occupied exclusively or mainly in agriculture, horticulture, forestry, viticulture or other similar work, it being understood that he may be assisted in such work by members of his family and/or paid employees.

PART II

Article 3

Each Contracting Party shall ensure to farmers, the members of their families and, where appropriate, their paid employees, social protection comparable to that enjoyed by other groups of the population, account being taken of the provisions of Articles 4 to 13 of this Convention.

Article 4

1. Each Contracting Party shall apply, as far as appropriate, to farmers and persons entitled through them, the social security standards laid down by its laws for the other protected categories of the population.

2. Without prejudice to the provisions of paragraph 1 of this Article, each Contracting Party shall grant farmers, within appropriate conditions and time-limits, social security protection in respect of at least four of the following contingencies: sickness, maternity, invalidity, old age, death, occupational injuries and diseases and family commitments.

Article 5

1. Each Contracting Party shall ensure that when a farmer ceases farming for structural or other reasons to be determined by the Contracting Party, he, the members of his family and, where appropriate, any of his paid employees, shall benefit from appropriate measures.

These measures shall include:

(*a*) the provision of facilities to enable them to take up a new activity preferably in their own region, in particular, arrangements for vocational guidance, training and re-training;

(*b*) the payment of temporary allowances to enable them to prepare for another activity;

(*c*) the maintenance of acquired rights and of rights in the course of acquisition with regard to social security;

(*d*) the payment of fair compensation or appropriate grants to a farmer who, because of his age, has difficulty in taking up another activity, provided that his ceasing farming contributes towards structural improvement.

2. Cessation of farming is not to be interpreted, for the purposes of this Article, as excluding the retention by the farmer of a limited area of land for his personal needs.

3. Each Contracting Party shall ensure that when a farmer only partially ceases farming for structural or other reasons to be determined by

autres qu'elle déterminera, cet exploitant, les membres de sa famille et, le cas échéant, les salariés qu'il emploie bénéficient des mesures mentionnées aux alinéas (*a*), (*b*) et (*c*) du paragraphe 1 ci-dessus, adaptées aux besoins.

Article 6

Toute Partie Contractante prendra des mesures appropriées en vue de tenir les exploitants agricoles au courant des objectifs de sa politique agricole, de consulter, en tant que de besoin, les milieux agricoles sur cette politique, et de tenir les exploitants agricoles informés des développements internationaux les intéressant dans le domaine agricole.

Article 7

Dans la formulation de sa politique d'aménagement du territoire, toute Partie Contractante tiendra compte des problèmes posés par les disparitions d'emploi dans les zones agricoles, notamment en y facilitant la création d'emplois nouveaux.

Article 8

1. Toute Partie Contractante prendra les mesures appropriées en vue

(*a*) d'assurer, dans les zones agricoles, un équipement socio-culturel adéquat;

(*b*) d'encourager l'amélioration des conditions de vie et d'hygiène dans les exploitations agricoles, au bénéfice de l'exploitant agricole, des membres de sa famille et, le cas échéant, des salariés qu'il emploie;

(*c*) d'octroyer certains avantages, tels que prêts à long terme, subventions ou taux d'intérêts réduits aux exploitants agricoles pour faciliter entre autres la mise en oeuvre des mesures visées à l'alinéa (*b*) ci-dessus.

2. Toute Partie Contractante prendra également les mesures appropriées afin de permettre aux exploitants agricoles, dans des zones qu'elle déterminera, de continuer leurs activités agricoles et de contribuer, en même temps, à la sauvegarde et à la protection du paysage, à la conservation de de la nature, au développement des possibilités de loisirs et au maintien équilibre démographique approprié dans ces zones.

Article 9

Toute Partie Contractante prendra ou encouragera toutes mesures appropriées afin d'assurer aux enfants vivant dans les zones agricoles une formation et une éducation d'un niveau équivalent à celui assuré dans les zones urbaines. Ces mesures porteront notamment sur

(*a*) l'octroi d'aides qui permettront de construire les locaux scolaires nécessaires pour abolir progressivement l'enseignement en classes uniques;

(*b*) le ramassage scolaire;

(*c*) l'affectation aux écoles des zones agricoles, d'un personnel enseignant qualifié, en nombre suffisant.

Article 10

Toute Partie Contractante prendra ou encouragera des mesures en faveur des jeunes des zones agricoles afin notamment the Contracting Party, he, the members of his family, and, where appropriate, any of his paid employees, shall benefit from the measures mentioned in sub-paragraphs (*a*), (*b*) and (*c*) of paragraph 1 above, suitably modified to meet needs.

Article 6

Each Contracting Party shall take appropriate measures to make farmers aware of the objectives of its farming policy, to consult, where appropriate, with farming interests in relation to this policy and to keep farmers informed of relevant international developments in farming.

Article 7

In the formulation of its regional development policy, each Contracting Party shall take account of the problems caused by the loss of employment in farming areas, in particular with a view to creating new employment here.

Article 8

1. Each Contracting Party shall take appropriate measures with a view to:

(*a*) assuring the provision of adequate socio-cultural facilities in farming areas;

(*b*) encouraging the improvement of living and sanitary conditions in farm buildings for the benefit of farmers, the members of their families and, where appropriate, their paid employees;

(*c*) granting advantages such as long-term loans, subsidies or low interest loans to farmers, to facilitate, inter alia, the implementation of the measures referred to in sub-paragraphs (*b*) above.

2. Each Contracting Party shall also take appropriate measures to make it possible for farmers in areas to be specified by it, to continue farming and to contribute, at the same time, to the upkeep and protection of the countryside, nature conservation, the development of recreational facilities and the maintenance of a suitable demographic balance in those areas.

Article 9

Each Contracting Party shall take or encourage appropriate measures to guarantee to children resident in farming areas an education and a training of a level equivalent to that enjoyed by children in urban areas. These measures shall relate particularly to:

(*a*) grants for the construction of such school buildings as are necessary for the gradual abolition of classes comprising children of all ages;

(*b*) transport to and from schools;

(*c*) the appointment of sufficient qualified teachers to schools in farming areas.

Article 10

Each Contracting Party shall take or encourage measures to benefit young persons in farming areas, particularly with a view to:

(*a*) de leur garantir une orientation professionnelle adaptée à leurs besoins et dispensée par des personnes qualifiées, même avant la fin de la scolarité;

(*b*) de leur assurer une formation générale et professionnelle adéquate leur donnant des chances égales à celles offertes aux autres jeunes en ce qui concerne leur insertion dans la vie professionnelle;

(*c*) de créer ou d'aménager, en tant que de besoin, des écoles professionnelles, des centres de formation et de perfectionnement professionnels ou des écoles supérieurs d'agriculture;

(*d*) de leur accorder des bourses d'enseignement dans des conditions leur donnant des chances égales à celles dont jouissent les autres jeunes.

Article 11

Toute Partie Contractante encouragera la mise à la disposition de la population des zones agricoles, de services d'information et de consultation sur les questions agricoles et sur l'évolution du marché de l'emploi dans d'autres secteurs économiques.

Article 12

En vue d'assurer dans les exploitations agricoles des conditions de travail aussi favorables que possible, toute Partie Contractante facilitera et encouragera les diverses formes de coopération, d'entraide entre exploitants agricoles et, le cas échéant, de mise à disposition de main-d'oeuvre de remplacement.

Article 13

En vue de faciliter l'exécution des tâches inhérentes à la vie familiale dans les exploitations agricoles, toute Partie Contractante encouragera

(*a*) l'utilisation d'équipements destinés à simplifier et alléger les travaux domestiques;

(*b*) la mise à disposition de services d'aide familiale à domicile.

Article 14

Les dispositions de la présente Convention ne portent pas atteinte aux dispositions d'autres conventions ou accords internationaux qui sont ou entreront en vigueur, et qui seraient plus favorables aux personnes visées par la présente Convention.

TITRE III

Article 15

1. La présente Convention est ouverte à la signature des Etats membres du Conseil de l'Europe. Elle sera ratifiée, acceptée ou approuvée. Les instruments de ratification, d'acceptation ou d'approbation seront déposés près le Secrétaire Général du Conseil de l'Europe.
2. La Convention entrera en vigueur trois mois après la date du dépôt du troisième instrument de ratification, d'acceptation ou d'approbation.
3. Elle entrera en vigueur à l'égard de tout Etat signataire qui la rati-

(*a*) securing that qualified counsellors are available to give vocational guidance appropriate to their needs, including before school leaving age;

(*b*) ensuring that they receive such general education and vocational training as will give them opportunities equal to those enjoyed by other young persons as regards integration into working life;

(*c*) creating or improving, as necessary, vocational schools, training and further training centres and farming colleges;

(*d*) providing them with educational grants under such conditions as will afford them opportunities equal to those enjoyed by other young persons.

Article 11

Each Contracting Party shall encourage the provision, in farming areas, of advisory and information services dealing with farming matters and the evolution of the labour market in other sectors of the economy.

Article 12

Each Contracting Party, in order to ensure as favourable working conditions on farms as possible, shall facilitate and encourage various forms of co-operation, mutual assistance between farmers and, where appropriate, supply of temporary helpers.

Article 13

With a view to facilitating the tasks inherent in family life on farms, each Contracting Party shall encourage:

(*a*) the use of facilities intended to simplify and lighten household tasks;

(*b*) the provision of home aid and family help services.

Article 14

The provisions of this Convention shall not prejudice the provisions of any international conventions or agreements which are already in force or may come into force under which more favourable treatment would be accorded to the persons referred to in this Convention.

PART III

Article 15

1. This Convention shall be open to signature by the member States of the Council of Europe. It shall be subject to ratification, acceptance or approval. Instruments of ratification, acceptance or approval shall be deposited with the Secretary General of the Council of Europe.

2. This Convention shall enter into force three months after the date of the deposit of the third instrument of ratification, acceptance or approval.

fiera, l'acceptera ou l'approuvera ultérieurement, trois mois après la date du dépôt de son instrument de ratification, d'acceptation ou d'approbation.

Article 16

1. Après l'entrée en vigueur de la présente Convention, le Comité des Ministres du Conseil de l'Europe pourra inviter tout Etat non membre du Conseil de l'Europe à adhérer à la présente Convention.

2. L'adhésion s'effectuera par le dépôt, près le Secrétaire Général du Conseil de l'Europe, d'un instrument d'adhésion qui prendra effet trois mois après la date de son dépôt.

Article 17

1. Tout Etat peut, au moment de la signature ou au moment du dépôt de son instrument de ratification, d'acceptation, d'approbation ou d'adhésion, désigner le ou les territoires auxquels s'appliquera la présente Convention.

2. Tout Etat peut, au moment du dépôt de son instrument de ratification, d'acceptation, d'approbation ou d'adhésion ou à tout autre moment par la suite, étendre l'application de la présente Convention, par déclaration adressée au Secrétaire Général du Conseil de l'Europe, à tout autre territoire désigné dans la déclaration et dont il assure les relations internationales ou pour lequel il est habilité à stipuler.

3. Toute déclaration faite en vertu du paragraphe précédent pourra être retirée, en ce qui concerne tout territoire désigné dans cette déclaration. Le retrait prendra effet six mois après la date de réception de la déclaration de retrait par le Secrétaire Général du Conseil de l'Europe.

Article 18

Tout Etat peut, au moment de la signature, au moment du dépôt de son instrument de ratification, d'acceptation, d'approbation ou d'adhésion ou à tout autre moment par la suite, étendre, par déclaration adressée au Secrétaire Général du Conseil de l'Europe, le bénéfice de la présente Convention, ou de celles des dispositions de cette Convention qu'il spécifiera, à d'autres personnes que ses ressortissants, résidant sur le ou les territoires définis conformément à l'article 17 et désignées dans la déclaration.

Article 19

1. Tout Etat peut, au moment de la signature ou au moment du dépôt de son instrument de ratification, d'acceptation, d'approbation ou d'adhésion, déclarer faire usage de l'une ou plusieurs réserves figurant à l'Annexe à la présente Convention. Aucune autre réserve ne sera admise.

2. Tout Etat peut retirer en tout ou en partie une réserve formulée par lui en vertu du paragraphe précédent, au moyen d'une déclaration adressée au Secrétaire Général du Conseil de l'Europe et qui prendra effet à la date de sa réception.

Article 20

1. Aucune Partie Contractante ne pourra dénoncer la présente Convention avant l'expiration d'une période de quatre ans après la date à laquelle

3. In respect of a signatory State ratifying, accepting or approving subsequently, the Convention shall enter into force three months after the date of the deposit of its instrument of ratification, acceptance or approval.

Article 16

1. After the entry into force of the Convention, the Committee of Ministers of the Council of Europe may invite any non-member State to accede thereto.
2. Such accession shall be effected by depositing with the Secretary General of the Council of Europe an instrument of accession which shall take effect three months after the date of its deposit.

Article 17

1. Any State may, at the time of signature or when depositing its instruments of ratification, acceptance, approval or accession, specify the territory or territories to which this Convention shall apply.
2. Any State may, when depositing its instrument of ratification, acceptance, approval or accession or at any later date, by declaration addressed to the Secretary General of the Council of Europe, extend this Convention to any other territory or territories specified in the declaration and for whose international relations it is responsible or on whose behalf it is authorised to give undertakings.
3. Any declaration made in pursuance of the preceding paragraph may, in respect of any territory mentioned in such declaration, be withdrawn. Such withdrawal shall take effect six months after the date of receipt by the Secretary General of the Council of Europe of the declaration of withdrawal.

Article 18

Any State may, at the time of signature or when depositing its instrument of ratification, acceptance, approval or accession or at any later date, by declaration addressed to the Secretary General of the Council of Europe, extend the benefit of this Convention, or of those provisions thereof which it shall specify, to persons other than its nationals, resident in the territory or territories specified in accordance with Article 17 and designated in the declaration.

Article 19

1. Any State may, at the time of signature or when depositing its instrument of ratification, acceptance, approval or accession, declare that it avails itself of one or more of the reservations provided for in the Annex to this Convention. No other reservation shall be admissible.
2. Any State may wholly or partly withdraw a reservation it has made in accordance with the foregoing paragraph by means of a declaration addressed to the Secretary General of the Council of Europe which shall become effective as from the date of its receipt.

Article 20

1. No Contracting Party may denounce this Convention before the end of a period of four years from the date on which the Convention entered

la Convention est entrée en vigueur en ce qui la concerne, ou avant l'expiration de toute autre période ultérieure de trois ans.

2. La dénonciation s'effectuera par une notification adressée au Secrétaire Général du Conseil de l'Europe et prendra effet six mois après la date de la réception de cette notification par le Secrétaire Général.

Article 21

Le Secrétaire Général du Conseil de l'Europe notifiera aux Etats membres du Conseil et à tout Etat ayant adhéré à la présente Convention:

(*a*) toute signature;

(*b*) le dépôt de tout instrument de ratification, d'acceptation, d'approbation ou d'adhésion;

(*c*) toute date d'entrée en vigueur de la présente Convention conformément à l'article 15;

(*d*) toute déclaration reçue en application des dispositions des paragraphes 2 et 3 de l'article 17;

(*e*) toute déclaration reçue en application des dispositions de l'article 18;

(*f*) toute réserve formulée en application des dispositions du paragraphe 1 de l'article 19;

(*g*) le retrait de toute réserve effectué en application des dispositions du paragraphe 2 de l'article 19;

(*h*) toute notification reçue en application des dispositions de l'article 20 et la date à laquelle la dénonciation prendra effet.

ANNEXE

RESERVES

(Article 19, paragraphe 1)

Chacune des Parties Contractantes peut déclarer qu'elle se réserve:

1. d'exclure du champ d'application de la présente Convention une ou plusieurs des catégories de personnes suivantes:

- les personnes qui, en qualité de travailleurs indépendants, consacrent exclusivement ou principalement leur activité à une profession agricole, sylvicole, horticole, viticole ou similaire, mais qui ne tirent pas la principale partie de leur revenu de cette activité;
- les personnes qui consacrent exclusivement leur activité à la sylviculture;

2. de ne pas appliquer la disposition de l'article 5, paragraphe 1, alinéa (*b*);

3. de ne pas appliquer la disposition de l'article 5, paragraphe 1, alinéa (*c*);

4. de ne pas appliquer la disposition de l'article 5, paragraphe 1, alinéa (*d*);

5. de ne pas appliquer la disposition de l'article 5, paragraphe 3.

3. AUTRES ACCORDS OUVERTS A LA SIGNATURE DES ETATS MEMBRES EN 1974 (*résumé*)

Protocole additionnel au Protocole à l'Arrangement européen pour la protection des émissions de télévision (14.1.1974) – Voir Arrangement, vol. VIII, 1960 et Protocole, vol. XIII, 1965 into force for it or before the end of any successive period of three years.

2. Such denunciation shall be effected by means of a notification addressed to the Secretary General of the Council of Europe and shall take effect six months after the date of receipt by the Secretary General of such notification.

Article 21

The Secretary General of the Council of Europe shall notify member States of the Council of Europe and any State which has acceded to this Convention of:

(*a*) any signature;

(*b*) any deposit of an instrument of ratification, acceptance, approval or accession;

(*c*) any date of entry into force of this Convention in accordance with Article 15 thereof;

(*d*) any declaration received in pursuance of the provisions of paragraphs 2 and 3 of Article 17;

(*e*) any declaration received in pursuance of the provisions of Article 18;

(*f*) any reservation made in pursuance of the provisions of paragraph 1 of Article 19;

(*g*) the withdrawal of any reservation carried out in pursuance of the provisions of paragraph 2 of Article 19;

(*h*) any notification received in pursuance of the provisions of Article 20 and the date on which denunciation takes effect.

ANNEX

RESERVATIONS

(Article 19, paragraph 1)

Each of the Contracting Parties may declare that it reserves the right:

1. to exclude from the field of application of this Convention one or several of the following categories of persons:

- self-employed persons occupied exclusively or mainly in agriculture, horticulture, forestry, viticulture or other similar work, but not deriving the major part of their income from these activities,
- persons occupied exclusively in forestry;

2. not to apply the provisions of Article 5, paragraph 1, sub-paragraph (*b*);

3. not to apply the provisions of Article 5, paragraph 1, sub-paragraph (*c*);

4. not to apply the provisions of Article 5, paragraph 1, sub-paragraph (*d*);

5. not to apply the provisions of Article 5, paragraph 3.

3. OTHER AGREEMENTS OPENED FOR THE SIGNATURE OF MEMBER STATES IN 1974 (*Summary*)

Additional Protocol to the Protocol to the European Agreement on the protection of television broadcasts (14.1.1974) – See Agreement, vol. VIII, 1960, and Protocol, vol. XIII, 1965.

Le chiffre 2 de l'article 3 du Protocole à l'Arrangement est remplacé par le texte suivant:

„2. Toutefois, à partir du 1er janvier 1985, aucun Etat ne pourra demeurer ou devenir partie au présent Arrangement à moins d'être également partie à la Convention internationale sur la protection des artistes interprètes ou exécutants, des producteurs de phonogrammes et des organismes de radiodiffusion, signée à Rome le 26 octobre 1961."

Accord européen sur l'échange de réactifs pour la détermination des groupes tissulaires (17.9.1974)

Cet accord règle les facilités et exemptions nécessaires à l'importation des réactifs pour la détermination des groupes tissulaires afin de rendre possible une assistance mutuelle entre pays européens.

C. RESOLUTIONS DU COMITE DES MINISTRES

1. RESOLUTION (74) 3 SUR LE TERRORISME INTERNATIONAL

(24 janvier 1974)

Le Comité des Ministres,

Considérant les recommandations de l'Assemblée Consultative relatives au terrorisme international et notamment la Recommandation 703 (1973);

Conscient de l'inquiétude croissante causée par la multiplication des actes de terrorisme international qui compromettent la sécurité des personnes;

Souhaitant que des mesures efficaces soient prises pour que les auteurs de tels actes n'échappent pas à toute répression;

Convaincu que l'extradition est un moyen particulièrement efficace de parvenir à ce résultat et que le mobile politique allégué par les auteurs de certains actes de terrorisme ne doit pas avoir pour résultat que ceux-ci ne soient ni extradés, ni punis,

Recommande aux gouvernements des Etats membres de s'inspirer des principes suivants:

1. Lorsqu'ils sont saisis d'une demande d'extradition concernant des infractions visées par les Conventions de La Haye pour la répression de la capture illicite d'aéronefs et de Montréal pour la répression d'actes illicites dirigés contre la sécurité de l'aviation civile, des infractions dirigées contre les agents diplomatiques et autres personnes ayant droit à une protection internationale, des prises d'otages, ou tout autre acte terroriste, ils devraient prendre en considération, lors de l'application des accords ou conventions internationaux en la matière, et spécialement de la Convention européenne d'extradition, ou lors de l'application de leur droit national, le caractère de particulière gravité de ces actes, entre autres:

- lorsque ceux-ci créent un danger collectif pour la vie, la liberté ou la sécurité humaine;
- lorsqu'ils atteignent des personnes innocentes étrangères aux mobiles qui les ont inspirés;
- lorsque des moyens cruels ou perfides sont utilisés pour leur réalisation.

2. S'il refuse l'extradition dans un cas ayant le caractère ci-dessus mentionné, et si ses règles de compétence juridictionnelle le permettent, le gouvernement de l'Etat requis devrait soumettre l'affaire aux autorités compétentes pour l'exercice de l'action pénale. Ces autorités devraient prendre leur décision dans les mêmes conditions que pour toute infraction de droit commun de caractère grave conformément aux lois de cet Etat.

3. Les gouvernements des Etats membres où une telle compétence juridictionnelle fait défaut devraient envisager la possibilité de l'instituer.

Paragraph 2 of Article 3 of the Protocol to the Agreement is substituted by the following:

"2. Nevertheless, as from 1 January 1985, no State may remain or become a Party to this Agreement unless it is also a Party to the International Convention for the Protection of Performers, Producers of Phonograms and Broadcasting Organisations, signed in Rome on 26 October 1961."

European Agreement on the exchange of tissue-typing reagents (17.9.1974)

This agreement determines import facilities and exemptions for tissue-typing reagents in order to make mutual assistance possible among European countries.

C. RESOLUTIONS OF THE COMMITTEE OF MINISTERS

1. RESOLUTION (74) 3 ON INTERNATIONAL TERRORISM

(24 January 1974)

The Committee of Ministers,

Considering the recommendations of the Consultative Assembly on international terrorism and in particular Recommendation 703 (1973);

Aware of the growing concern caused by the multiplication of acts of international terrorism which jeopardise the safety of persons;

Desirous that effective measures be taken in order that the authors of such acts do not escape punishment;

Convinced that extradition is a particularly effective measure for achieving this result and that the political motive alleged by the authors of certain acts of terrorism should not have as a result that they are neither extradited nor punished,

Recommends that governments of member states be guided by the following principles:

1. When they receive a request for extradition concerning offences covered by the Conventions of The Hague for the suppression of unlawful seizure of aircraft and of Montreal for the suppression of unlawful acts against the safety of civil aviation, offences against diplomatic agents and other internationally protected persons, the taking of hostages or any terrorist act, they should, when applying international agreements or conventions on the subject, and especially the European Convention on Extradition, or when applying their domestic law, take into consideration the particularly serious nature of these acts, inter alia:

– when they create a collective danger to human life, liberty or safety;
– when they affect innocent persons foreign to the motives behind them;
– when cruel or vicious means are used in the commission of those acts.

2. If it refuses extradition in a case of the kind mentioned above and if its jurisdiction rules permit, the government of the requested state should submit the case to its competent authorities for the purpose of prosecution. Those authorities should take their decision in the same manner as in the case of any ordinary offence of a serious nature under the law of that state.

3. The governments of member states in which such jurisdiction is lacking should envisage the possibility of establishing it.

2. RESOLUTION (74) 4
SUR LE ROLE FUTUR DU CONSEIL DE L'EUROPE

(24 janvier 1974)

Le Comité des Ministres,

1. Considérant que l'évolution en Europe exige une étude du rôle futur du Conseil de l'Europe et, partant, de ses domaines d'activité;

2. Rappelant qu'il a décidé le 14 mai 1973 de faire procéder à une telle étude dans le cadre du Statut;

3. Ayant pris en considération la Recommandation 704 de l'Assemblée Consultative et le rapport soumis aux Délégués des Ministres le 31 octobre 1973 par le groupe de travail, composé de six Représentants permanents, créé en vertu de la décision du 14 mai 1973;

4. Constatant avec satisfaction que, depuis sa création, le Conseil de l'Europe apporte une contribution importante à la réalisation en Europe d'une union plus étroite entre pays démocratiques à régime parlementaire;

5. Convaincu que les objectifs et principes énoncés dans le Statut conservent toute leur valeur et que le Conseil de l'Europe restera une pierre angulaire de la construction européenne;

6. Soulignant que l'approche par le Conseil de l'Europe des problèmes pratiques dans ses domaines d'activité, empreinte d'un respect tout particulier des droits et de la dignité de l'individu, est un trait marquant de l'Organisation que les Etats membres ont intérêt à maintenir et à renforcer;

7. Convaincu que le Conseil de l'Europe sera mieux en mesure de jouer son rôle spécifique et de s'acquitter de sa mission si ses possibilités d'action politique sont pleinement utilisées;

8. Conscient du fait que l'utilisation plus poussée des mécanismes existants du Conseil et leur sensible amélioration permettraient de poursuivre avec plus d'efficacité les buts et principes du Conseil et les tâches qu'il s'assigne;

9. Considérant que les caractéristiques actuelles de la coopération en Europe rendent le développement des contacts entre le Conseil de l'Europe et les autres organisations et institutions internationales européennes particulièrement souhaitable;

10. Constatant qu'une répartition des tâches entre ces organisations et institutions serait peu réaliste, et qu'il est en conséquence essentiel de coordonner leurs activités en accroissant et en systématisant les échanges d'informations afin de créer entre elles une complémentarité de fait,

I. En ce qui concerne les domaines d'activité, les structures et les méthodes de travail

(*a*) décide de concentrer les activités intergouvernementales du Conseil de l'Europe dans les domaines suivants:

- la sauvegarde et le développement des droits de l'homme et des libertés fondamentales;
- les problèmes sociaux et socio-économiques, tels que les questions relatives aux travailleurs migrants;
- la coopération dans le domaine de l'éducation et de la culture;
- les questions relatives à la jeunesse;
- la protection et la promotion de la santé publique;
- la protection de la nature et la gestion des ressources naturelles; l'environnement humain et l'aménagement du territoire;
- les pouvoirs locaux; les questions relatives à la coopération régionale et municipale;

2. RESOLUTION (74) 4
ON THE FUTURE ROLE OF THE COUNCIL OF EUROPE

(24 January 1974)

The Committee of Ministers,

1. Considering that the evolution in Europe calls for a study of the future role of the Council of Europe and consequently of its fields of activity;

2. Recalling its decision of 14 May 1973 for such a study to be undertaken within the framework of the Statute;

3. Having taken into consideration Recommendation 704 of the Consultative Assembly and the report submitted to the Ministers' Deputies on 31 October 1973 by a working party composed of six Permanent Representatives, set up by their decision of 14 May 1973;

4. Appreciating the contribution which the Council of Europe has made since its creation in promoting greater unity in Europe between democratic countries with parliamentary systems;

5. Convinced that the aims and principles expressed in the Statute retain their validity and that the Council of Europe will remain a cornerstone of European cooperation;

6. Emphasising that the Council of Europe's approach to the practical problems in its fields of activities, characterised as it is by a particular regard for the rights of the individual and the dignity of man, is a distinctive feature of the organisation which it is in the interest of the member states to further promote;

7. Convinced that the Council of Europe will be better able to play its specific role and fulfil its mission if full use is made of its political potential;

8. Conscious that a more intensive utilisation as well as a considerable improvement of the existing mechanisms in the Council would allow it to pursue its aims and principles and carry out its tasks with greater efficiency;

9. Considering that the present state of co-operation in Europe makes it particularly desirable to develop contacts between the Council of Europe and the other European and international organisations and institutions;

10. Noting that it would be unrealistic to share out tasks among these organisations and institutions, and that it is therefore necessary to coordinate their activities and to increase the amount of information exchanged and the regularity of such interchanges, so that these organisations and institutions may in practice complement one another,

I. With regard to the fields of activity, structures and working methods

(*a*) decides to concentrate for the near future the intergovernmental activities of the Council of Europe in the following fields:

- safeguard and promotion of human rights and fundamental freedoms;
- social and socio-economic problems, such as those concerning migrant workers;
- educational and cultural co-operation;
- questions relating to youth;
- protection and promotion of public health;
- protection of nature and the management of natural resources; the manmade environment and regional planning;
- local authorities; matters relating to regional and municipal co-operation;

- la coopération dans le domaine du droit, y compris l'harmonisation des législations et pratiques nationales dans des secteurs juridiques spécifiques, la prévention des crimes et le traitement des délinquants;

(*b*) charge les Délégués des Ministres et le Secrétaire Général de définir dans le cadre de ces domaines des secteurs et objectifs précis, ceux-ci devant être revus périodiquement pour tenir compte de l'évolution et des nécessités nouvelles;

(*c*) charge les Délégués des Ministres d'examiner dans quelle mesure il peut être tenu compte dans les différents domaines d'activité du Programme de travail énumérés ci-dessus de la préoccupation de l'Assemblée Consultative à l'égard des problèmes que pose le progrès scientifique et technologique aux sociétés démocratiques;

(*d*) charge les Délégués des Ministres d'examiner quelles sont celles des activités actuellement entreprises qui pourraient être terminées avec profit pour l'Organisation;

(*e*) charge les Délégués des Ministres d'établir des critères généraux pour le choix des différentes activités dans chacun des secteurs du projet de Programme de travail et pour l'attribution d'un degré de priorité à chacune de ces activités;

(*f*) décide:

- de continuer à se réunir deux fois par an, étant entendu que dès que le nouveau bâtiment sera achevé ces réunions auront normalement lieu à Strasbourg;
- de prévoir pour ces réunions des échanges de vues approfondis sur les questions de politique internationale qui présentent un intérêt commun pour tous les Membres du Conseil de l'Europe;

(*g*) prend note de l'avis exprimé par une majorité que – afin d'accroître l'efficacité du travail des Délégués des Ministres et de l'Organisation dans son ensemble – les gouvernements membres devraient, dans la mesure du possible, désigner des Représentants permanents résidant à Strasbourg;

(*h*) charge les Délégués des Ministres d'examiner la possibilité de renforcer la coopération pratique entre le Comité des Ministres et l'Assemblée Consultative;

(*i*) prend note avec satisfaction de la haute utilité des conférences européennes de ministres spécialisés, avec lesquelles le Conseil de l'Europe est amené à établir ou à poursuivre des rapports particuliers de travail;

- constate que les principes énoncés dans la Résolution (71) 44 gardent toute leur valeur;
- charge les Délégués des Ministres, dans le cadre de l'étude en cours, d'examiner la possibilité de faire en sorte que la préparation et les suites de ces conférences s'intègrent, de la manière la plus efficace, aux procédures du Conseil de l'Europe afin de leur donner leur plein effet;

(*j*) charge les Délégués des Ministres d'étudier les mesures à prendre afin de donner à la Conférence européenne des pouvoirs locaux une fonction plus importante dans le contexte européen;

(*k*) charge les Délégués des Ministres d'examiner les structures des comités, groupes de travail, etc., leurs mandats et leurs méthodes de travail, ceci en vue d'une rationalisation et d'une amélioration de leur rendement en fonction des programmes de travail;

(*l*) charge les Délégués des Ministres:

- d'étudier l'opportunité de remplacer dans certains cas l'élaboration de conventions par un mécanisme plus efficace;
- d'étudier s'il convient d'adopter une politique sélective quant aux suites détaillées à donner aux résolutions;

(*m*) charge les Délégués des Ministres d'examiner la politique de recrutement des fonctionnaires du Secrétariat, en vue d'atteindre le meilleur rendement possible;

- co-operation in the legal field, including the harmonisation of national legislation and practice in specific legal sectors; the prevention of crime and the treatment of offenders;

(*b*) instructs the Ministers' Deputies and the Secretary General to define within these fields precise sectors and objectives to be periodically reviewed in the light of new developments and requirements;

(*c*) instructs the Ministers' Deputies to examine to what extent account can be taken, in the various fields of activity in the Work Programme listed above, of the concern of the Consultative Assembly with problems confronting democratic societies as a result of scientific and technological progress;

(*d*) instructs the Ministers' Deputies to consider what items of work at present being undertaken could with benefit to the organisation be brought to an early conclusion;

(*e*) instructs the Ministers' Deputies to define general criteria for the selection of the various activities in each sector of the draft Work Programme and for the attribution of priority degrees to each of these activities;

(*f*) decides

- to continue to meet twice a year, on the understanding that when the new building is completed, the meetings will normally be held in Strasbourg;
- to plan for those meetings extensive exchanges of views on international political questions of common interest to all the Members of the Council of Europe;

(*g*) takes note of a majority opinion that – in order to increase the efficiency of the Ministers' Deputies' work and of the organisation as a whole – member governments should, as far as possible, appoint Permanent Representatives resident in Strasbourg;

(*h*) instructs the Ministers' Deputies to examine the possibilities of strengthening the current co-operation between the Committee of Ministers and the Consultative Assembly;

(*i*) notes with satisfaction the extreme usefulness of the European Conferences of specialised Ministers with which the Council is called upon to establish or to continue a special working relationship;

- notes that the principles stated in Resolution (71) 44 retain their significance;
- instructs the Ministers' Deputies, in the framework of their ongoing study, to examine how the preparation and follow-up to these conferences might be integrated in the most efficient way possible into the Council of Europe procedures so as to give them their full effect;

(*j*) instructs the Ministers' Deputies to consider ways and means of giving the European Conference of Local Authorities a more important function in the European context;

(*k*) instructs the Ministers' Deputies to examine the structures, terms of reference and working methods of committees, working parties etc. with a view to rationalising them and improving their efficiency in relation to their work programmes;

(*l*) instructs the Ministers' Deputies

- to study the advisability of replacing in certain cases the elaboration of conventions by a more efficient machinery;
- to study the desirability of a selective policy regarding the detailed follow-up to resolutions;

(*m*) instructs the Ministers' Deputies to examine the staff recruitment policy with a view to achieving the greatest possible efficiency;

II. En ce qui concerne les relations extérieurs du Conseil de l'Europe

1. avec les Communautés européennes

(*a*) charge le Secrétaire Général:

- de développer un échange d'informations adéquat entre le Conseil de l'Europe et les Communautés;
- d'organiser dans ce contexte des réunions et contacts réguliers aux niveaux appropriés afin notamment de rechercher les zones d'intérêt commun tant par l'examen périodique des programmes en présence, que par la détermination de dossiers précis se prêtant à un travail commun;

(*b*) décide de donner leur plein effet aux dispositions de l'Arrangement conclu en 1959 entre le Comité des Ministres du Conseil de l'Europe et la Commission des Communautés;

(*c*) charge les Délégués des Ministres d'examiner les moyens de renforcer la coopération entre le Conseil de l'Europe et les Communautés;

(*d*) charge le Secrétaire Général, notamment la Direction des Affaires juridiques, d'examiner avec les services compétents des Communautés les possibilités procédurales et autres d'étendre certaines réalisations communautaires à l'ensemble des Etats membres du Conseil de l'Europe;

(*e*) souligne l'utilité des réunions jointes entre l'Assemblée Consultative et l'Assemblée parlementaire européenne pour débattre des relations entre Etats membres des Communautés et Etats membres du Conseil de l'Europe non membres des Communautés, notamment dans les domaines où les deux institutions ont une activité rendant la concertation nécessaire;

(*f*) envisage favorablement l'installation d'un Bureau de liaison du Conseil de l'Europe avec les Communautés européennes à Bruxelles, afin de faciliter les contacts et les échanges d'informations et charge les Délégués d'en étudier sans délai les modalités et le coût financier;

2. Avec l'Organisation de coopération et de développement économiques

charge le Secrétaire Général de veiller au maintien de contacts réguliers et étroits entre les secrétariats du Conseil de l'Europe et de l'OCDE en vue notamment de tenir compte des activités respectives des deux organisations lors de l'établissement de leurs programmes de travail;

3. Avec l'Office des Nations Unies à Genève

recommande le maintien de relations et de liaisons régulières entre les deux secrétariats dans le cadre de l'échange de lettres mis à jour en novembre 1971;

4. Avec le secrétariat de la Commission économique pour l'Europe des Nations Unies

charge le Secrétaire Général de veiller à ce qu'il y ait entre les secrétariats du Conseil de l'Europe et de la Commission économique pour l'Europe des Nations Unies des contacts plus fréquents et plus systématiques, notamment dans les domaines d'intérêt commun, tels que la démographie, l'environnement et les statistiques;

5. Avec d'autres organisations internationales

demande au Secrétaire Général de garder présentes à l'esprit les décisions qui précèdent, dans ses relations régulières avec des organisations telles que l'Unesco et l'AELE ainsi que dans ses contacts avec d'autres organisations dont les activités se prêtent à une coopération avec le Conseil de l'Europe comme l'OIT et l'OMS;

6. Avec les Etats non membres

charge les Délégués des Ministres d'examiner les possibilités qu'offre le

II. With regard to the external relations of the Council of Europe

1. *With the European Communities*

(*a*) instructs the Secretary General:

- to organise an adequate exchange of information between the Council of Europe and the Communities;
- to organise in this context regular meetings and contacts at appropriate levels in order inter alia to find areas of common interest by periodically examining current programmes and by identifying projects which lend themselves to co-operation;

(*b*) decides to give full effect to the provisions of the arrangement concluded in 1959 between the Committee of Ministers of the Council of Europe and the Commission of the European Communities;

(*c*) instructs the Ministers' Deputies to examine means of reinforcing co-operation between the Council of Europe and the Communities;

(*d*) instructs the Secretary General, and in particular the Directorate of Legal Affairs, to investigate with the competent departments of the Communities the possibilities of extending individual Community achievements to all the member states of the Council of Europe;

(*e*) emphasises the value of the Joint Meetings of the Consultative Assembly and the European Parliamentary Assembly for debates on relations between member states of the Communities and those Council of Europe member states that are not Members of the Communities, particularly in fields where the two organisations are pursuing activities necessitating mutual consultation;

(*f*) favours the setting up of a Council of Europe office in Brussels for liaison with the Communities in order to facilitate contacts and the exchange of information and instructs the Deputies to study without delay the practical arrangements and the expense involved;

2. *With the Organisation for Economic Co-operation and Development*

instructs the Secretary General to ensure that close regular contact is maintained between the Secretariats of the Council of Europe and OECD, particularly in order that account may be taken of the respective activities of the two organisations when their work programmes are being drawn up;

3. *With the United Nations Office in Geneva*

recommends that relations and regular contacts be maintained between the two Secretariats within the framework of the exchange of letters as brought up to date in November 1971;

4. *With the Secretariat of the Economic Commission for Europe*

instructs the Secretary General to see that more frequent and systematic contacts are maintained between the Secretariats of the Council of Europe and of the Economic Commission for Europe, particularly in matters of common concern such as demography, the environment and statistics;

5. *With other international organisations*

instructs the Secretary General to bear the above decisions in mind in his regular relations with organisations such as UNESCO and EFTA, and in his contacts with other organisations, such as ILO and WHO, whose activities lend themselves to co-operation with the Council of Europe;

6. *With non-member states*

instructs the Ministers' Deputies to examine the possibilities the Council

Conseil de l'Europe en vue de développer dans des domaines techniques d'intérêt général une coopération utile avec les pays européens non membres;

7. *Recommandation d'ordre général*

convient que les membres individuels du Comité des Ministres, chacun pour les organisations internationales auxquelles son pays appartient, donneront les instructions appropriées afin d'assurer dans les limites de leur compétence la mise en oeuvre des points énoncés sous II;

8. *Rapport au Comité des Ministres*

charge le Secrétaire Général de lui faire régulièrement rapport sur des développements intervenus ou envisagés entre secrétariats dans le domaine considéré, en application des dispositions qui précèdent;

III. Procédure à suivre

(*a*) charge les Délégués de lui faire rapport à sa 54e Session sur les conclusions auxquelles ils seront parvenus en application du mandat qui leur est donné aux paragraphes *j* du titre I et 1. *f* du titre II et, à la 55e Session, sur le paragraphe *m* du titre I;

(*b*) charge les Délégués de lui proposer, à sa 54e Session, un calendrier precis pour la mise en oeuvre des autres paragraphes du dispositif de la présente résolution.

3. RESOLUTION (74) 15

ELATIVE AR L'EGALITE DE TRAITEMENT ENTRE TRAVAILLEURS NATIONAUX ET TRAVAILLEURS MIGRANTS DANS LES DOMAINES SUIVANTS: CONDITIONS DE TRAVAIL, REMUNERATION, LICENCIEMENT, MOBILITE GEOGRAPHIQUE ET PROFESSIONNELLE

(*29 mai 1974*)

Le Comité des Ministres,

Considérant que le but du Conseil de l'Europe est de réaliser une union plus étroite entre ses membres afin de favoriser leur progrès social;

S'inspirant des dispositions de la Charte sociale européenne concernant l'exercice effectif du droit au travail et l'exercice du droit des travailleurs migrants et de leurs familles à la protection et à l'assistance;

Considérant que l'égalité de traitement entre travailleurs nationaux et travailleurs migrants ne peut être atteinte sans un effort constant des autorités responsables des Etats d'immigration et des Etats d'émigration;

Constatant que la situation des travailleurs migrants peut être, dans certains cas, plus précaire que celle des travailleurs nationaux, notamment en matière de conditions de travail, de rémunération, de licenciement et de mobilité professionnelle et géographique et que, par conséquent, l'égalité de traitement peut difficilement être réalisée sans une action spécifique,

Recommande aux gouvernements des Etats membres de prendre, le cas échéant, des mesures dans les domaines énumérés ci-dessous sans préjudice des dispositions plus favorables aux travailleurs migrants prévues dans leur droit interne ou dans des accords internationaux:

i. Contrat de travail

Prévoir, lors de l'immigration de tout travailleur migrant, la conclusion d'un contrat de travail d'une durée suffisante pour lui permettre d'apprécier clairement sa situation avant la fin de l'emploi et d'effectuer un choix responsable pour l'avenir;

of Europe provides for developing useful co-operation in technical fields. of general interest with European non-member states;

7. General recommendation

agrees that the individual members of the Committee of Ministers, each in respect of the international organisations to which his country belongs, should give the appropriate instructions, within the limits of their competence, to ensure that the various points in Section II are acted on;

8. Report to the Committee of Ministers

instructs the Secretary General to report regularly on any developments that have occurred or are envisaged by the Secretariats in the field under review, in pursuance of the above provisions;

III. With regard to the procedure to be followed

(*a*) instructs the Ministers' Deputies to report to it at its 54th Session on their findings according to their mandate given them in paragraph *j* of Section I and 1. *f* of Section II and at its 55th Session on paragraph *m* of Section I;

(*b*) instructs the Ministers' Deputies to propose for its 54th Session a precise schedule for the implementation of the other paragraphs of the operative part of the present resolution.

3. RESOLUTION (74) 15 ON EQUAL TREATMENT OF NATIONAL AND MIGRANT WORKERS IN THE FOLLOWING SECTORS: WORKING CONDITIONS, REMUNERATION, DISMISSAL, GEOGRAPHICAL AND OCCUPATIONAL MOBILITY

(29 May 1974)

The Committee of Ministers,

Considering that the aim of the Council of Europe is to achieve greater unity among its Members for the purpose of facilitating their social progress;

Guided by the provisions of the European Social Charter concerning the effective exercise of the right to work and the effective exercise of the migrant workers and their families to protection and assistance;

Considering that equal treatment of national and migrant workers cannot be achieved without a sustained effort by the relevant authorities in the immigration and emigration states;

Noting that the position of migrant workers may, in certain cases, be more insecure than that of nationals in particular in respect of working conditions, remuneration, dismissal and occupational and geographical mobility and that special measures are therefore required to ensure equal treatment,

Recommends the governments of member states to take action where appropriate in the following sectors, reserving, however, any provision more favourable to migrant workers that may be laid down in their domestic law, or in international agreement:

i. Work contract

To ensure that on entry all migrant workers benefit from a work contract whose duration is sufficiently long to enable them to take stock of their situation before the end of their employment, and come to a responsible decision for the future;

ii. Conditions de travail

Veiller à ce que le travailleur migrant bénéficie de conditions de travail non moins favorables que celles du travail national;

Promouvoir des mesures en vue de protéger le travailleur migrant qui pourrait être sollicité par une entreprise de location de main-d'oeuvre, en l'informant entre autres des conditions particulières de ce type d'emploi;

iii. Détermination des qualifications professionnelles

Evaluer les aptitudes et les connaissances du travailleur migrant avant la conclusion du contrat de travail, en se référant à des critères fonctionnels, correspondant aux différents niveaux de qualification reconnus dans la pratique de l'Etat d'accueil. Cette évaluation devrait être assurée par une coopération étroite entre les Etats d'émigration et d'immigration, éventuellement par les bureaux de recrutement ouverts dans les Etats d'émigration, aidés, le cas échéant, par les services de l'emploi et les partenaires sociaux des Etats d'immigration;

Encourager les efforts entrepris sur le plan international en vue d'arriver à une harmonisation de certains titres professionnels;

iv. Réemploi

Assurer au travailleur migrant se trouvant régulièrement dans l'Etat d'immigration l'accès aux services de placement dans les mêmes conditions que le travailleur national, notamment lorsqu'il a perdu son emploi sans faute de sa part, à cause d'une récession ou crise économique, ou par suite d'une reconversion industrielle;

Permettre au travailleur migrant dont le contrat arrive à échéance d'accéder à ces mêmes services, s'il désire demeurer dans cet Etat et s'il y est autorisé;

Veiller, dans la mesure du possible, au réemploi des travailleurs migrants déjà sur place, avant de procéder au recrutement de nouveaux étrangers ayant des qualifications professionnelles analogues, compte tenu des emplois disponibles sur le marché national du travail. A cet effet, il faudrait accroître la coordination entre les services de placement dans l'Etat d'immigration, d'une part, et les services éventuels de recrutement, d'autre part;

v. Réadaptation professionnelle

Permettre au travailleur migrant de bénéficier, au même titre que le travailleur national, des facilités de réadaptation professionnelle offertes par les organismes compétents de l'Etat d'immigration;

vi. Litiges en matière d'emploi

Porter à la connaissance du travailleur migrant les procédures et les mécanismes légaux et administratifs, ainsi que le concours du syndicat, susceptibles de lui fournir une protection en cas de litige en matière d'emploi. Les informations utiles pourraient lui être communiquées par des services spécialisés, publics ou privés (services sociaux, greffes des tribunaux, prud'hommes, etc.), ou dans les brochures qui lui sont remises, soit à l'occasion du premier recrutement, soit ultérieurement;

vii. Promotion sociale et professionnelle

Favoriser la promotion sociale et professionnelle, ainsi que l'intégration du travailleur migrant au sein des entreprises;

Encourager dans la mesure du possible sa participation effective à la vie de l'entreprise et notamment aux activités des organes représentatifs des travailleurs;

Encourager les entreprises à admettre à leurs cours de perfectionnement professionnel les travailleurs migrants;

ii. Working conditions

To ensure that migrant workers have working conditions not less favourable than those of national workers;

To promote measures for the protection of migrant workers who may be approached by an undertaking which hires out labour, by informing them inter alia of the special conditions of that kind of job;

iii. Assessment of vocational skills

To assess the skills and knowledge of the migrant worker before concluding the labour contract, by referring to "functional" criteria corresponding to the various levels of qualification recognised in practice by the receiving state. Such skills and knowledge should be assessed by means of close co-operation between the emigration and immigration states, possibly through recruiting centres which exist in some emigration states, assisted, where appropriate, by the employment services and the social partners in the immigration states;

To encourage the efforts made at an international level to achieve the harmonisation of certain vocational qualifications;

iv. Re-employment

To ensure that a migrant worker who is residing legally in the immigration states should have access to the employment services on the same footing as national workers, particularly if loss of employment has occurred involuntarily, through a recession, economic crisis or industrial reorganisation;

To enable the migrant worker whose contract expires to avail himself of the services if he wishes to remain in the state, and if he is authorised to do so;

To ensure, as far as possible, that migrant workers already in the country are re-employed, before recruiting other national workers with similar qualifications, having regard to the jobs available on the national labour market. To that end, coordination should be intensified between employment services in the immigration state and recruiting centres when they exist;

v. Occupational rehabilitation

To enable the migrant worker to enjoy on the same footing as the national worker the vocational occupational rehabilitation facilities provided by the competent services in the immigration states;

vi. Disputes concerning employment

To inform migrant workers of legal and administrative machinery, as well as of the assistance of trade unions, which can afford them protection when disputes arise on questions of employment. Relevant information might be provided through specialised public or private services (social services, court registries, labour conciliation boards etc.), or in leaflets distributed to them when they are first recruited or at a later stage;

vii. Social and vocational promotion

To facilitate social and vocational promotion, as well as the integration of the migrant worker within his firm;

To encourage to the greatest extent possible his effective participation in the life of the firm, and especially in the activities of bodies representing the workers;

To encourage firms to include migrant workers in their vocational training courses;

Permettre aux travailleurs migrants d'apprendre la langue du pays d'accueil;

viii. Rémunération

Dans la mesure où cette question est réglée par des dispositions législatives, réglementaires ou par l'action des autorités administratives, veiller à ce que le travailleur migrant reçoive une rémunération non moins favorable que celle du travailleur national compte tenu de la nature de l'emploi occupé, des aptitudes et des connaissances déterminées conformément au point iii de la présente résolution;

Dans la mesure où cette question est réglée seulement par voie conventionnelle, encourager les partenaires sociaux à faire en sorte que cette égalité de rémunération soit assurée au travailleur migrant;

Dans tous les autres cas, adopter selon les méthodes adaptées aux circonstances nationales des moyens destinés à assurer cette égalité de traitement;

ix. Autres avantages

Encourager les employeurs à tenir compte de l'ancienneté professionnelle acquise par le travailleur migrant auprès d'autres employeurs dans la mesure où une telle ancienneté auprès d'autres employeurs est prise en considération pour la détermination des avantages salariaux accessoires accordés au travailleur national;

x. Non-discrimination en matière de licenciement

Eviter par des moyens correspondant à la situation nationale toute discrimination entre travailleur migrant et travailleur national en matière de licenciement;

xi. Droits de recours

Garantir au travailleur migrant, dans les mêmes conditions qu'au travailleur national, l'exercice du droit de recours auprès des organes compétents, en cas de litige relatif au licenciement;

xii. Aide en cas de licenciement

Etendre au travailleur migrant, dans toute la mesure du possible, le bénéfice de toutes les formes d'assistance et d'aide, notamment en matière de chômage, dans les mêmes conditions qu'au travailleur national;

Encourager toute mesure appropriée en vue d'assister le travailleur migrant se trouvant en chômage pour des raisons indépendantes de sa volonté et qui désire soit être rapatrié, soit être employé dans un autre Etat;

xiii. Mobilité géographique et professionnelle

Réduire au minimum des délais qui limitent la mobilité du travailleur migrant, et prendre toutes les mesures nécessaires pour lui permettre de changer d'employeur, de région, de travail ou de profession s'il le désire.

4. RESOLUTION (74) 26
SUR LE DROIT DE REPONSE – SITUATION DE L'INDIVIDU A L'EGARD DE LA PRESSE

(2 juillet 1974)

Le Comité des Ministres,

Considérant que le droit à la liberté d'expression comprend la liberté de recevoir et de communiquer des informations ou des idées sans qu'il puisse y avoir ingérence d'autorité publique et sans considération de frontières,

To enable migrant workers to learn the language of the receiving country;

viii. Remuneration

To the extent in which these matters are governed by legislative provisions, or by the action of administrative authorities, to ensure that the migrant worker receives a remuneration not less favourable than that of the national worker taking into account the nature of the job held, the skills and the knowledge as assessed in conformity with point iii of the present resolution;

Where these matters are only regulated by collective agreements, to encourage the social partners to arrange the equality of treatment in remuneration;

In all other cases, to adopt according to methods adapted to national circumstances, the necessary means of ensuring this equality of remuneration;

ix. Other benefits

To encourage employers to take into account service in his occupation by the migrant worker with other employers in so far as such services with other employers are taken into account in determining increments accorded to national workers;

x. Non-discrimination with regard to dismissal

To prevent by means appropriate to the national situation, discrimination between migrant workers and national workers in the matter of dismissal;

xi. Right of appeal

To guarantee the migrant worker the use of a right of appeal to competent bodies under the same conditions as the national worker, in the event of a dispute over a dismissal;

xii. Aid in the event of dismissal

To extend to the migrant worker, to the fullest extent possible, the benefit of all forms of assistance and aid, especially in case of unemployment, under the same conditions as the national worker;

To encourage the provision of facilities to the migrant worker involuntarily unemployed, who wishes to be repatriated or to take up employment in a third state;

xiii. Freedom to move and change occupation

To reduce as much as possible any time-limits which restrict the mobility of the migrant worker and to take such steps as are necessary to give the migrant worker the opportunity to change employer, region of employment or occupation if he so wishes.

4. RESOLUTION (74) 26
ON THE RIGHT OF REPLY – POSITION OF THE INDIVIDUAL IN RELATION TO THE PRESS

(2 July 1974)

The Committee of Ministers,

Considering that the right to freedom of expression includes the freedom to receive and to impart information and ideas without interference ainsi que le prévoit l'article 10 de la Convention européenne des Droits de l'Homme;

Considérant qu'aux termes de la même disposition, l'exercice de cette liberté comporte des devoirs et des responsabilités pour ce qui est notamment de la protection de la réputation ou des droits d'autrui;

Considérant qu'il est souhaitable de mettre à la disposition de l'individu des moyens adéquats pour le protéger contre les informations contenant des faits inexacts le concernant et de le doter d'un recours contre la publication des informations, y compris les faits et les opinions, qui constituent une ingérence dans sa vie privée ou une atteinte à sa dignité, à son honneur ou à sa réputation, que ces informations aient été mises à la disposition du public par la presse écrite, par la radio, par la télévision ou par tout autre moyen de communication de masse à caractère périodique;

Considérant qu'il est également de l'intérêt de l'individu et du public de recevoir des informations de différentes sources qui garantissent ainsi la possibilité de disposer d'une information complète;

Considérant qu'il convient par conséquent qu'à cet égard, les mêmes principes s'appliquent à tous les moyens de communication de masse, étant entendu que les moyens qui seront mis à la disposition de l'individu pourraient varier selon qu'il s'agit de la presse écrite, de la radio ou de la télévision;

Considérant qu'il convient à ce stade de tenir compte seulement de la situation de l'individu vis-à-vis des moyens de communication à caractère périodique tels que la presse, la radio et la télévision et qu'il convient en particulier d'examiner la protection de l'individu contre les ingérences dans sa vie privée ou contre les atteintes à sa dignité, à son honneur ou à sa réputation,

Recommande aux gouvernements membres que la situation de l'individu à l'égard des moyens de communication soit conforme aux principes minimaux suivants;

1. En ce qui concerne les informations relatives aux individus publiées par un moyen de communication, l'individu concerné disposera d'une possibilité réelle d'obtenir la rectification, sans délai excessif, des faits, inexacts le concernant et pour la rectification desquels il peut justifier d'un intérêt, cette rectification bénéficiant, autant que possible, de la même importance que la publication initiale.

2. En ce qui concerne les informations relatives aux individus publiées dans les moyens de communication, l'individu concerné disposera d'un recours effectif contre la publication des faits et des opinions, qui constituent:

i. une ingérence dans sa vie privée sauf si un intérêt public légitime et primordial le justifie, si l'individu a consenti expressément ou tacitement à la publication ou si la publication est conforme en l'occurrence à une pratique généralement admise et qui n'est pas contraire à la loi;

ii. une atteinte à sa dignité, à son honneur ou à sa réputation, à moins que l'information ne soit publiée avec le consentement exprès ou tacite de l'individu concerné, ou que la publication ne soit justifiée par un intérêt public primordial et légitime et qu'il s'agisse d'une critique loyale basée sur des faits exacts.

3. Aucun des principes qui précèdent ne peut être interprété comme justifiant la censure.

4. Dans les principes énoncés ci-dessus:

i. le terme ,,individu'' s'entend de toute personne physique et morale ainsi que de toute autre entité sans considération de nationalité ou de résidence, à l'exclusion de l'Etat et d'autres autorités publiques;

ii. le terme ,,moyen de communication'' s'applique à tous moyens de communication à caractère périodique destinés à la diffusion des informations au public, comme la presse, la radio et la télévision;

iii. le terme ,,possibilité réelle d'obtenir la rectification'' signifie toute by public authority and regardless of frontiers, as laid down in Article 10 of the European Convention on Human Rights:

Considering that under this provision the exercise of this freedom carries with it duties and responsibilities, in particular in connection with the protection of the reputation or rights of others;

Considering that it is desirable to provide the individual with adequate means of protection against the publication of information containing inaccurate facts about him, and to give him a remedy against the publication of information, including facts and opinions, that constitutes an intrusion in his private life or an attack on his dignity, honour or reputation, whether the information was conveyed to the public through the written press, radio, television or any other mass media of a periodical nature;

Considering that it is also in the interest of the public to receive information from different sources, thereby guaranteeing that they receive complete information;

Considering that for these purposes the same principles should apply in respect of all media, although the means available to the individual might vary depending on whether the written press, the radio or television were involved;

Considering that at the present stage only the position of the individual in relation to media of a periodical character, such as newspapers, broadcasting and television should be taken into account and that the protection of the individual against interferences with his privacy or against attacks upon his honour, dignity or reputation should be particularly dealt with,

Recommends to member governments, as a minimum, that the position of the individual in relation to media should be in accordance with the following principles:

1. In relation to information concerning individuals published in any medium, the individual concerned shall have an effective possibility for the correction, without undue delay, of incorrect facts relating to him which he has a justified interest in having corrected, such corrections being given, as far as possible, the same prominence as the original publication.

2. In relation to information concerning individuals published in any medium, the individual concerned shall have an effective remedy against the publication of facts and opinions which constitute:

(i) an interference with his privacy except where this is justified by an overriding, legitimate public interest, where the individual has expressly or tacitly consented to the publication or where publication is in the circumstances a generally accepted practice and not inconsistent with law;

(ii) an attack upon his dignity, honour or reputation, unless the information is published with the express or tacit consent of the individual concerned or is justified by an overriding, legitimate public interest and is a fair criticism based on accurate facts.

3. Nothing in the above principles should be interpreted to justify censorship.

4. In the above principles:

(i.) the term "individual" is to include all natural and legal persons as well as other bodies irrespective of nationality or residence, with the exclusion of the state and other public authorities;

(ii) the term "medium" covers any means of communication for the dissemination to the public of information of a periodical character, such as newspapers, broadcasting or television;

(iii) the term "effective possibility for the correction" means any possibility which can be used as a means of redress, whether legal or otherwise, such as a right of correction, or a right of reply, or a complaint to press councils;

(iv) the term "remedy" means a form of redress, whether legal or otherwise, such as provided under the law of defamation or a complaint to press possibilité qui peut être utilisée comme un moyen de recours, soit juridique, soit d'une autre nature, comme le droit de réponse, le droit de correction, ou le droit de recours aux conseils de presse;

iv. le terme „recours" s'entend d'une forme de réparation soit juridique, soit d'une autre nature, comme en prévoit la loi sur la diffamation, ou tel que le droit de recours devant les conseils de presse, dont dispose tout individu sans limitation injustifiée, comme, par exemple, des frais exorbitants.

5. Les principes ci-dessus s'appliqueront à tous les moyens de communication sans distinction. Ceci n'exclut pas de différences dans l'application de ces principes à des moyens de communication particuliers, tels que la radio et la télévision, lorsque cela est nécessaire ou justifié par des différences de nature.

Recommande aux gouvernements membres, lorsqu'ils procéderont à l'adoption de mesures législatives concernant le droit de réponse, de prévoir un droit de réponse à la presse, à la radio et à la télévision et à l'égard de tout autre moyen de communication à caractère périodique, en accord avec les principes susmentionnés, sur le modèle des règles minimales annexées à la présente résolution.

ANNEXE

Règles minimales relatives au droit de réponse à la presse, à la radio, à la télévision et à l'égard d'autres moyens de communication à caractère périodique

1. Toute personne physique ou morale, ainsi que toute autre entité sans considération de nationalité ou de résidence, désignée dans un journal, un écrit périodique, dans une émission de radio ou de télévision, ou par tout autre moyen de communication à caractère périodique, et au sujet de laquelle des informations contenant des faits qu'elle prétend inexacts ont été rendus accessibles au public, peut exercer le droit de réponse afin de corriger les faits la concernant.

2. A la demande de la personne concernée, le moyen de communication de masse est tenu de rendre publique la réponse que cette personne lui aura fait parvenir.

3. La loi nationale peut prévoir, à titre d'exception, que la publication de la réponse pourra être refusée par le moyen de communication dans les cas suivants:

i. lorsque la demande de publication de la réponse n'est pas adressée au moyen de communication dans un délai raisonnablement bref;

ii. lorsque la longueur de la réponse excède ce qui est nécessaire pour corriger l'information contenant les faits prétendument inexacts;

iii. lorsque la réponse ne se limite pas à la correction des faits incriminés;

iv. lorsqu'elle constitue une infraction punissable;

v. lorsqu'elle est contraire aux intérêts juridiquement protégés des tiers;

vi. lorsque l'individu concerné ne justifie pas de l'existence d'un intérêt légitime.

4. La publication de la réponse doit intervenir sans délai excessif et recevoir, autant que possible, la même importance que l'information contenant les faits prétendument inexacts.

5. La loi nationale désignera la personne à qui, en vue d'assurer l'exercice effectif du droit de réponse, la demande de publication de la réponse devra être adressée pour le compte de toute publication ou entreprise de presse, de radio ou de télévision ou de tout moyen de communication concerné. De la même manière sera désignée la personne qui sera responsable

councils, which is available to every individual without undue limitation such as unreasonable costs.

5. The above principles shall apply to all media without any distinction. This does not exclude differences in the application of these principles to particular media, such as radio and television, to the extent that this is necessary or justified by their different nature.

Recommends that member governments, when adopting legislation concerning the right of reply, make provision for the right of reply in the press and on radio and television and any other periodical media on the pattern of the minimum rules annexed to this resolution.

APPENDIX

Minimum rules regarding the right of reply to the press, the radio and the television and to other periodical media

1. Any natural and legal person, as well as other bodies, irrespective of nationality or residence, mentioned in a newspaper, a periodical, a radio or television broadcast, or in any other medium of a periodical nature, regarding whom or which facts have been made accessible to the public which he claims to be inaccurate, may exercise the right of reply in order to correct the facts concerning that person or body.

2. At the request of the person concerned, the medium in question shall be obliged to make public the reply which the person concerned has sent in.

3. By way of exception the national law may provide that the publication of the reply may be refused by the medium in the following cases:

(i) if the request for publication of the reply is not addressed to the medium within a reasonably short time;

(ii) if the length of the reply exceeds what is necessary to correct the information containing the facts claimed to be inaccurate;

(iii) if the reply is not limited to a correction of the facts challenged;

(iv) if it constitutes a punishable offence;

(v) if it is considered contrary to the legally protected interests of a third party;

(vi) if the individual concerned cannot show the existence of a legitimate interest.

4. Publication of the reply must be without undue delay and must be given, as far as possible, the same prominence as was given to the information containing the facts claimed to be inaccurate.

5. In order to safeguard the effective exercise of the right to reply, the national law shall determine the person who shall represent any publication, publishing house, radio, television or other medium for the purpose of addressing a request to publish the reply. The person who shall be responsible for the publication of the reply shall be similarly determined and this person shall not be protected by any immunity whatsoever.

pour la publication de la réponse, et cette personne ne sera protégée par aucune immunité.

6. Les principes ci-dessus s'appliqueront à tous les moyens de communication sans distinction. Ceci n'exclut pas des différences dans l'application de ces principes à des moyens de communication particuliers tels que la radio et la télévision, lorsque cela est nécessaire ou justifié par des différences de nature.

7. Toute contestation sur la mise en oeuvre des règles qui précèdent sera portée devant le tribunal qui pourra ordonner la publication immédiate de la réponse.

5. RESOLUTION (74) 29
RELATIVE A LA PROTECTION DE LA VIE PRIVEE DES PERSONNES PHYSIQUES VIS-A-VIS DES BANQUES DE DONNEES ELECTRONIQUES DANS LE SECTEUR PUBLIC

(20 septembre 1974)

Le Comité des Ministres,

Considérant que le but du Conseil de l'Europe est de réaliser une union plus étroite entre ses Etats membres;

Désireux de contribuer à la compréhension et la confiance du public à l'égard des nouvelles techniques administratives que les autorités publiques mettent en oeuvre dans les Etats membres en vue d'assurer une meilleure exécution des missions dont elles sont chargées;

Conscient que l'utilisation des banques de données électroniques par les autorités publiques a provoqué dans l'opinion une prise de conscience accrue de la nécessité de protéger la vie privée des individus;

Considérant que l'adoption de principes communs dans ce domaine est de nature à contribuer à la solution de ces problèmes dans les Etats membres et tend à éviter que des divergences injustifiées entre les droits des Etats membres ne se créent en la matière;

Rappelant sa Résolution (73) 22 relative à la protection de la vie privée des personnes physiques vis-à-vis des banques de données électroniques dans le secteur privé;

Ayant à l'esprit les dispositions de l'article 8 de la Convention européenne de Sauvegarde des Droits de l'Homme et des Libertés fondamentales,

Recommande aux gouvernements des Etats membres:

(*a*) de prendre toutes les mesures qu'ils estiment nécessaires pour appliquer les principes énoncés dans l'annexe à la présente résolution;

(*b*) d'informer, en temps utile, le Secrétaire Général du Conseil de l'Europe de toutes mesures prises dans ce domaine.

ANNEXE

à la Résolution (74) 29

Les principes énoncés ci-dessous sont applicables aux informations relatives aux personnes enregistrées dans les banques de données électroniques du secteur public.

Au sens de la présente résolution, on entend par „informations relatives aux personnes" les informations concernant les personnes physiques, et par „banques de données électroniques" tout système de traitement électronique de l'information qui est utilisé pour gérer de telles informations.

6. The above rules shall apply to all media without any distinction. This does not exclude differences in the application of these rules to particular media such as radio and television to the extent that this is necessary or justified by their different nature.

7. Any dispute as to the application of the above rules shall be brought before a tribunal which shall have power to order the immediate publication of the reply.

5. RESOLUTION (74) 29
ON THE PROTECTION OF THE PRIVACY OF INDIVIDUALS VIS-A-VIS ELECTRONIC DATA BANKS IN THE PUBLIC SECTOR

(20 September 1974)

The Committee of Ministers,

Considering that the aim of the Council of Europe is to achieve a greater unity between its Members;

Desiring to contribute to public understanding and confidence with regard to new administrative techniques which public authorities in the member states are using in order to ensure the optimal performance of the tasks entrusted to them;

Recognising that the use of electronic data banks by public authorities has given rise to increasing concern about the protection of the privacy of individuals;

Considering that the adoption of common principles in this field can contribute towards a solution of these problems in the member states and can help to prevent the creation of unjustified divergencies between the laws of the member states on this subject;

Recalling its Resolution (73) 22 on the protection of privacy of individuals vis-à-vis electronic data banks in the private sector;

Bearing in mind Article 8 of the European Convention for the Protection of Human Rights and Fundamental Freedoms,

Recommends the governments of member states:

(*a*) to take all steps which they consider necessary to give effect to the principles set out in the annex to the present resolution;

(*b*) to inform the Secretary General of the Council of Europe in due course of any action taken in this field.

ANNEX

to Resolution (74) 29

The following principles apply to personal information stored in electronic data banks in the public sector.

For the purposes of this resolution, "personal information" means information relating to individuals (physical persons) and "electronic data bank" means any electronic data processing system which is used to handle such information.

1.

D'une manière générale, le public doit être régulièrement informé de la création, du fonctionnement et du développement des banques de données électroniques dans le secteur public.

2.

Les informations enregistrées doivent être:
(*a*) obtenues par des moyens licites et loyaux,
(*b*) exactes et tenues à jour,
(*c*) adéquates et pertinentes par rapport à la finalité recherchée.
Toute diligence doit être faite pour corriger les informations inexactes et pour effacer les informations inadéquates, non pertinentes ou périmées.

3.

Particulièrement lorsque des banques de données électroniques traitent des informations concernant l'intimité de la vie privée des personnes, ou lorsque le traitement des informations peut être à l'origine de discriminations,

(*a*) leur création doit être prévue par la loi ou par une réglementation spéciale ou leur existence doit être rendue publique dans une déclaration ou un document, en conformité avec le système juridique de chaque Etat membre;

(*b*) ces loi, réglementation, déclaration ou document doivent préciser la finalité de l'enregistrement et de l'utilisation de telles informations ainsi que les conditions dans lesquelles elles peuvent être communiquées à l'intérieur du secteur public ou à des personnes ou organismes privés;

(*c*) les informations enregistrées ne doivent pas être utilisées à d'autres fins que celles qui ont été définies, à moins qu'une dérogation ne soit expressément autorisée par la loi ou accordée par une autorité compétente ou que les règles régissant l'utilisation de la banque de données électroniques ne soient modifiées.

4.

Des règles doivent être établies pour déterminer le délai au-delà duquel certaines catégories d'informations ne pourront plus être conservées ou utilisées.

Toutefois, il peut être dérogé à ce principe lorsque l'utilisation de ces informations à des fins statistiques, scientifiques ou historiques requiert leur conservation pendant une durée indéterminée. Des mesures doivent alors être prises afin de ne pas porter préjudice à la vie privée des intéressés.

5.

Chaque personne a le droit de connaître les informations enregistrées sur elle.

Toute exception à ce principe ou limitation à l'exercice de ce droit doit être strictement réglementée.

6.

Des précautions doivent être prises contre tout abus ou mauvais usage des informations. Pour cette raison:

1.

As a general rule the public should be kept regularly informed about the establishment, operation and development of electronic data banks in the public sector.

2.

The information stored should be:
(*a*) obtained by lawful and fair means,
(*b*) accurate and kept up to date,
(*c*) appropriate and relevant to the purpose for which it has been stored.
Every care should be taken to correct inaccurate information and to erase inappropriate, irrelevant or obsolete information.

3.

Especially when electronic data banks process information relating to the intimate private life of individuals or when the processing of information might lead to unfair discrimination,

(*a*) their existence must have been provided for by law, or by special regulation or have been made public in a statement or document, in accordance with the legal system of each member state;

(*b*) such law, regulation, statement or document must clearly state the purpose of storage and use of such information, as well as the conditions under which it may be communicated either within the public administration or to private persons or bodies;

(*c*) that data stored must not be used for purposes other than those which have been defined unless exception is explicitly permitted by law, is granted by a competent authority or the rules for the use of the electronic data bank are amended.

4.

Rules should be laid down to specify the time-limits beyond which certain categories of information may not be kept or used.

However, exceptions from this principle are acceptable if the use of the information for statistical, scientific or historical purposes requires its conservation for an indefinite duration. In that case, precautions should be taken to ensure that the privacy of the individuals concerned will not be prejudiced.

5.

Every individual should have the right to know the information stored about him.

Any exception to this principle or limitation to the exercise of this right should be strictly regulated.

6.

Precautions should be taken against any abuse or misuse of information. For this reason:

(*a*) quiconque intervient dans la mise en oeuvre d'une banque de données électroniques doit être lié par des règles de conduite destinées à prévenir le mauvais usage des informations et en particulier être tenu au secret;

(*b*) les banques de données électroniques doivent être munies de systèmes de sécurité empêchant les personnes n'ayant pas le droit d'obtenir les informations d'y avoir accès, et permettant de détecter les détournements d'informations, intentionnels ou non.

7.

L'accès aux informations qui ne peuvent être librement communiquées au public doit être également limité aux personnes qui sont habilitées à en prendre connaissance pour l'exercice de leurs fonctions.

8.

Lorsque les données sont utilisées à des fins statistiques, elles ne peuvent être diffusées que de manière qu'il soit impossible de les attribuer à une personne déterminée.

6. RESOLUTION (74) 33
RELATIVE A LA PLANIFICATION ET A LA PROGRAMMATION DES ACTIVITES INTERGOUVERNEMENTALES DU CONSEIL DE L'EUROPE

(*20 novembre 1974*)

Le Comité des Ministres,

1. Vu la Résolution (74) 4 sur le rôle futur du Conseil de l'Europe;

2. Vu le rapport du groupe de travail des Délégués des Ministres chargé de l'étude de la mise en oeuvre du paragraphe *e* du titre I de la Résolution (74) 4, relatif à l'établissement de critères généraux pour le choix des différentes activités dans chacun des secteurs du projet de Programme de travail et pour l'attribution d'un degré de priorité à chacune de ces activités (Doc. CM (74) 167),

Convient de ce qui suit:

3. Le Programme de travail intergouvernemental sera établi à partir d'un plan à moyen terme;

4. Le plan couvrira une période de cinq ans et sera revu tous les deux ans en tenant compte de l'évolution politique, des progrès de la coopération européenne et des réalisations obtenues dans le cadre du Conseil de l'Europe pendant la période écoulée;

5. Le premier plan à moyen terme aura comme point de départ les huit domaines d'activité retenus dans le paragraphe *a* du titre I de la Résolution (74) 4, à savoir:

- la sauvegarde et le développement des droits de l'homme et des libertés fondamentales;
- les problèmes sociaux et socio-économiques, tels que les questions relatives aux travailleurs migrants;
- la coopération dans le domaine de l'éducation et de la culture;
- les questions relatives à la jeunesse;
- la protection et la promotion de la santé publique;
- la protection de la nature et la gestion des ressources naturelles, l'environnement humain et l'aménagement du territoire;
- les pouvoirs locaux, les questions relatives à la coopération régionale et municipale;
- la coopération dans le domaine du droit, y compris l'harmonisation des

(*a*) everyone concerned with the operation of electronic data processing should be bound by rules of conduct aimed at preventing the misuse of data and in particular by a duty to observe secrecy;

(*b*) electronic data banks should be equipped with security systems which bar access to the data held by them to persons not entitled to obtain such information and which provide for the detection of misdirections of information, whether intentional or not.

7.

Access to information that may not be freely communicated to the public should be confined to the persons whose functions entitle them to take cognisance of it in order to carry out their duties.

8.

When information is used for statistical purposes it should be released only in such a way that it is impossible to link information to a particular person.

6. RESOLUTION (74) 33 ON THE PLANNING AND PROGRAMMING OF THE INTERGOVERNMENTAL ACTIVITIES OF THE COUNCIL OF EUROPE

(*20 November 1974*)

The Committee of Ministers,

1. Having regard to Resolution (74) 4 on the future role of the Council of Europe;

2. Having regard to the report of the working party of Ministers' Deputies set up to study the implementation of Section I, paragraph *e*, of Resolution (74) 4 concerning the establishment of general criteria for the selection of the various activities in each sector of the draft Work Programme and for the attribution of priority degrees to each of those activities (Doc. CM (74) 167),

Resolves as follows:

3. The Intergovernmental Work Programme shall be drawn up on the basis of a medium-term plan;

4. The plan shall cover a period of five years and shall be reviewed every two years in the light of political development, progress in European co-operation and achievements within the framework of the Council of Europe during the intervening period;

5. The first medium-term plan shall be based on the eight spheres of activity specified in Section I, paragraph *a* of Resolution (74) 4, viz.:

- safeguard and promotion of human rights and fundamental freedoms;
- social and socio-economic problems, such as those concerning migrant workers;
- educational and cultural co-operation;
- youth questions;
- protection and promotion of public health;
- protection of nature and the management of natural resources, the man-made environment and regional planning;
- local authorities, matters relating to regional and municipal co-operation;
- co-operation in the legal field, including the harmonisation of national

législations et pratiques nationales dans des secteurs juridiques spécifiques, la prévention des crimes et le traitement des délinquants;

6. A l'intérieur du plan à moyen terme et conformément au dispositif du paragraphe *b* du titre I de la Résolution (74) 4, des secteurs et des objectifs précis seront définis selon les modalités et critères prévus dans la présente résolution;

7. Pour la réalisation des objectifs fixés dans le plan le Comité des Ministres adoptera, sur proposition du Secrétaire Général, un programme annuel d'activités dans la limite d'un plafond budgétaire préalablement fixé;

8. Pour ce qui est des critères généraux qui devront régir le choix des secteurs et objectifs à l'intérieur du plan à moyen terme et le choix des différentes activités dans le projet de programme annuel d'activités, le Comité des Ministres adopte les lignes directrices qui figurent en annexe à la présente résolution et invite les Etats membres, l'Assemblée Consultative, le Secrétaire Général, les comités relevant de l'article 17 du Statut et tout autre organe concerné à en tenir compte lors de la formulation des propositions concernant le Programme de travail intergouvernemental;

9. Pour ce qui est de l'attribution des degrés de priorité à l'intérieur du programme annuel d'activités, le Comité des Ministres estime qu'un moyen efficace d'indiquer l'importance relative et la priorité d'un domaine, d'un secteur, d'un objectif ou d'une activité, réside dans la répartition des moyens disponibles;

Décide:

10. d'adopter à la 57e Session du Comité des Ministres en novembre 1975, un plan à moyen terme couvrant la période de 1976 à 1980;

11. de solliciter, avant d'adopter le plan, l'avis de l'Assemblée Consultative;

12. de réexaminer les activités actuellement inscrites au Programme de travail à la lumière des critères généraux figurant en annexe à la présente résolution et de terminer celles qui ne répondent plus à ces critères, en application du paragraphe *d* du titre I de la Résolution (74) 4;

13. de préciser au niveau du plan à moyen terme les priorités et de donner des indications sur l'importance relative des moyens disponibles à affecter aux différents domaines et secteurs;

14. de préciser au niveau du programme annuel d'activités les dégres de priorité en donnant des indications portant sur:

1. le taux d'expansion admissible pour le budget annuel;

2. des directives de caractère général concernant le taux d'accroissement ou de réduction des programmes;

3. la répartition globale et indicative des masses budgétaires disponibles par grands secteurs d'activité;

4. la fixation préalable d'un taux de croissance et/ou décroissance à l'intérieur de chaque secteur d'activité;

Charge le Secrétaire Général:

15. d'établir pour soumission aux Délégués des Ministres, au cours du premier semestre de 1975, un avant-projet de plan à moyen terme couvrant la période de 1976 à 1980, en tenant compte entre autres des vues que les principaux comités d'experts intergouvernementaux auront la faculté d'exprimer à cette fin;

16. de garder à l'esprit que l'avant-projet du plan à moyen terme ne reflète nécessairement ni les structures administratives existantes qu'il s'agisse du Secrétariat ou des comités relevant de l'article 17 du Statut, ni les programmes en cours;

17. de préparer, en temps utile, à l'intention du Comité des Ministres, un programme annuel d'activités pour 1976, en vue de la réalisation des objectifs retenus dans le plan à moyen terme et dans la limite d'un plafond budgétaire préalablement fixé, conformément au paragraphe 14 de la présente résolution;

18. de soumettre dorénavant un rapport intérimaire en même temps

legislation and practice in specific legal sectors, the prevention of crime and treatment of offenders;

6. Within the medium-term plan, and in accordance with Section I, paragraph *b*, of Resolution (74) 4, precise sectors and objectives shall be defined according to the procedure and criteria specified in this resolution;

7. For the purpose of achieving the objectives specified in the plan, the Committee of Ministers shall, at the Secretary General's proposals, adopt an annual programme of activities within a previously determined budgetary ceiling;

8. With regard to the general criteria governing the choice of sectors and objectives within the medium-term plan and the selection of activities from the draft annual programmes, the Committee of Ministers adopts the guidelines set forth in the appendix to this resolution and invites the member states, the Consultative Assembly, the Secretary General, the committees set up under Article 17 of the Statute and such other bodies as may be concerned, to bear them in mind when formulating proposals concerning the Intergovernmental Work Programme;

9. As regards the attribution of priority degrees within the annual programme of activities, the Committee of Ministers considers that one effective means of indicating the relative importance and priority of any field, sector, objective or activity lies in the apportionment of available resources;

Decides:

10. to adopt at the 57th Session of the Committee of Ministers in November 1975 a medium-term plan for the period 1976–80;

11. to request the opinion of the Consultative Assembly in good time before the adoption of the plan;

12. to review the activities currently entered in the Work Programme in the light of the general criteria set out in the appendix to this resolution and to discontinue those that no longer conform to those criteria, in accordance with Section I, paragraph *d*, of Resolution (74) 4;

13. to specify priorities at the level of the medium-term plan by indicating the relative scale of resources to be allocated to the different fields and sectors;

14. to specify degrees of priority at the level of the annual programme of activities by giving particulars concerning:

1. the permissible growth rate of the annual budget;
2. general directives regarding the rate of programme increase or decrease;
3. the overall indicative apportionment of the budgetary resources available for major sectors of activity;
4. prior establishment of a rate of increase or decrease within each sector of activities;

Instructs the Secretary General:

15. to prepare for submission to the Ministers' Deputies during the first half of 1975 a preliminary draft medium-term plan for the period 1976–80, taking account *inter alia* of the views which the main intergovernmental committees will have the opportunity to express for this purpose;

16. to keep in mind that the preliminary draft medium-term plan does not necessarily have to reflect the present administrative structure of the Secretariat or the committees set up in virtue of Article 17 of the Statute, nor those of the current programmes;

17. to prepare, in due course, for the Committee of Ministers, an annual programme of activities for 1976 for the purpose of achieving the objectives specified in the medium-term plan, within a previously determined budgetary ceiling, in accordance with paragraph 14 of this resolution;

18. to submit henceforth a progress report at the same time as the draft annual programme of activities and the draft budget. The progress report shall specify all relevant information concerning the progress of activities,

que le projet de programme annuel d'activités et le projet de budget. Le rapport intérimaire devra donner toutes les indications utiles en ce qui concerne l'avancement des activités, les résultants déjà obtenus et prévisibles, et les difficultés rencontrées;

Invite les gouvernements des Etats membres:

19. à indiquer par écrit, en temps utile avant la discussion du projet de plan à moyen terme et du projet de programme d'activités, l'ordre de priorité qu'ils souhaitent donner aux différentes propositions contenues dans ces deux projets précités.

ANNEXE

à la résolution (74) 33

Critères généraux pour le choix des secteurs, objectifs et activités dans le programme de travail intergouvernemental

1. Les objectifs poursuivis et les activités entreprises dans le cadre du Programme de travail intergouvernemental doivent répondre aux dispositions de l'article 1 du Statut et s'insérer dans les domaines retenus pour l'action de l'organisation par le Comité des Ministres dans le paragraphe *a* du titre I de la Résolution (74) 4. Ils doivent servir l'intérêt de l'ensemble des Etats membres et contribuer de la sorte au renforcement de la cohésion de ceux-ci.

Quant aux objectifs et activités qui intéressent plutôt un nombre restreint ou un groupe distinct d'Etats, il importe de recourir plus que par le passé aux possibilités offertes par le système d'accords partiels.

2. Le Conseil de l'Europe devra établir son programme en tenant compte des travaux réalisés ou entrepris par d'autres organisations et notamment par les Communautés européennes.

3. Les travaux entrepris devront être orientés vers des résultats d'un intérêt concret pour les Etats membres et leurs résidents. Les activités inscrites au Programme de travail doivent donc présenter un intérêt pratique et non théorique. La notion de l'importance politique intervient au moment du choix des secteurs et des objectifs, le choix des activités se faisant à partir de considérations techniques d'opportunité et de possibilité de réalisation effective.

4. L'analyse du coût, du rendement et de l'efficacité doit intervenir comme élément important lors de la sélection d'activités à inclure dans le programme. Il doit exister en particulier une relation adéquate entre les moyens et les méthodes choisies d'une part, et l'objet de l'activité de l'autre.

En outre, le coût d'une activité ou d'un groupe d'activités ne doit pas être disproportionné par rapport à l'intérêt que celle-ci présente pour l'ensemble des Etats membres et ne doit pas être de nature à déséquilibrer le reste du programme.

7. RESOLUTION (74) 34

(28 novembre 1974)

INVITATION A LA GRECE A REDEVENIR MEMBRE DU CONSEIL DE L'EUROPE

Le Comité des Ministres,

Considérant le désir exprimé par la Grèce de redevenir Membre du Conseil de l'Europe;

the results already obtained or expected and the difficulties encountered;
Invites the governments of member states:
19. to state in writing, in good time before discussion of the draft medium-term plan and the draft programme of activities, the order of priority they wish to assign to the various proposals contained in those two drafts.

APPENDIX

to resolution (74) 33

General criteria governing the choice of sectors, objectives and activities in the intergovernmental work programme

1. The objectives pursued and activities undertaken in the framework of the Intergovernmental Work Programme must conform to the provisions of Article 1 of the Statute, and fall within the scope of the organisation's activities as decided by the Committee of Ministers in Resolution (74) 4, Section I, paragraph *a*. They must serve the interests of all member states and thus help to strengthen their mutual cohesion.

As for those objectives and activities which are of more especial interest to a limited number or a clearly defined group of states, it is important that greater use should be made than in the past of the possibilities of the partial agreement system.

2. The Council of Europe must take account, when drawing up its own programme, of the work achieved or undertaken by other organisations, and especially the European Communities.

3. The work undertaken must be directed towards results of practical value for member states and their residents. The activities in the Work Programme must therefore be of practical interest, not theoretical. The political aspect appears when sectors and objectives are being decided, activities being selected in accordance with considerations of desirability and feasibility.

4. A cost-effectiveness analysis should be an important factor in selecting activities for inclusion in the programme. In particular, an adequate relationship should exist between the means and methods employed on the one hand and the purpose of each activity on the other.

In addition, the cost of an activity or group of activities must not be out of proportion to its value to all the member states, and must not be such as to unbalance the rest of the programme.

7. RESOLUTION (74) 34

(28 November 1974)

INVITATION TO GREECE TO REJOIN THE COUNCIL OF EUROPE

The Committee of Ministers,

Considering the wish expressed by Greece to resume membership of the Council of Europe;

Rappelant ses Résolutions (74) 27 et (74) 32;

Constatant avec satisfaction que la Grèce remplit à nouveau les conditions prévues à l'article 4 du Statut;

Ayant consulté, conformément aux dispositions de la Résolution statutaire (51) 30, l'Assemblée Consultative, qui a exprimé un avis favorable (Résolution 578 (1974) et Avis n° 69),

Décide:

i. d'inviter la Grèce à redevenir Membre du Conseil de l'Europe et à adhérer à nouveau au Statut,

ii. de fixer à sept le nombre de représentants de la Grèce à l'Assemblée Consultative,

iii. de fixer, avec effet au 1er janvier 1975, la quote-part des diverses contributions financières de la Grèce au Conseil de l'Europe selon le tableau ci-annexé qui fait partie intégrante de la présente résolution;

Charge le Secrétaire Général de porter ces décisions à la connaissance du Gouvernement de la Grèce et de prendre pour leur application toutes dispositions utiles.

ANNEXE

1. Le Comité des Ministres, conformément à la Résolution (74) 25, fixe à 2,33% la quote-part de la Grèce au budget général.

2. La participation de la Grèce au Fonds de roulement, calculée selon le même pourcentage que pour le budget général, s'élève à 139 800 F qui s'ajoutent au montant actuel de ce Fonds.

3. Le Comité des Ministres, conformément à la Résolution (71) 1, fixe à 1,47% la quote-part de la Grèce au remboursement de l'emprunt pour les nouveaux bâtiments du Conseil de l'Europe.

8. RESOLUTION (74) 43
SUR LES CONCENTRATIONS DE PRESSE

(*16 décembre 1974*)

Le Comité des Ministres,

1. Considérant la nécessité d'assurer le respect du droit à la liberté d'expression garanti par l'article 10 de la Convention européenne des Droits de l'Homme, y compris celui de recevoir et de communiquer librement des informations;

2. Persuadé de l'importance capitale que revêt, à cet égard, la possibilité pour le public de disposer d'une grande diversité de sources d'informations et d'opinions;

3. Conscient du rôle primordial qui revient à la presse écrite dans la sauvegarde de cette diversité d'informations et d'opinions à l'usage du public;

4. Partageant les inquiétudes souvent exprimées selon lesquelles une diminution du nombre total de journaux possédant leur propre unité rédactionnelle complète ou une concentration du contrôle effectif d'un nombre croissant de tels journaux entre les mêmes mains, risque de porter atteinte aux droits garantis par l'article 10 de la Convention européenne des Droits de l'Homme;

5. Convaincu qu'une telle diversité des informations et des opinions dépend dans une mesure non négligeable du bon fonctionnement de la concurrence entre les journaux, sans contester pour autant que dans certains cas une évolution vers des entreprises de plus grande taille puisse consolider la situation économique de la presse et améliorer sa position et sa tenue;

Recalling its Resolutions (74) 27 and (74) 32;

Observing with satisfaction that Greece now again complies with the conditions laid down in Article 4 of the Statute;

Having, in accordance with the provisions of Statutory Resolution (51) 30, consulted the Consultative Assembly, which has expressed a favourable opinion (Resolution 578 (1974) and Opinion No. 69),

Resolves

(i) to invite Greece to rejoin the Council of Europe and to reaccede to the Statute,

(ii) to fix at seven the number of Greece's Representatives in the Consultative Assembly;

(iii) to determine Greece's various contributions to the Council of Europe, as from 1 January 1975, according to the appended table, which forms an integral part of this resolution;

Instructs the Secretary General to notify the Greek Government of these decisions and to make all necessary arrangements for their implementation.

APPENDIX

1. The Committee of Ministers, in accordance with Resolution (74) 25, fixes the proportion of Greece's contribution to the general budget at 2.33%.
2. The amount which Greece is to contribute to the Working Capital Fund, calculated in accordance with the same percentage as for the general budget, is 139 800 F, which is added to the Fund's present total.
3. The Committee of Ministers, in accordance with Resolution (71) 1, fixes the proportion of Greece's contribution to repayment of the loan for the new Council of Europe buildings at 1.47%.

8. RESOLUTION (74) 43 ON PRESS CONCENTRATIONS

(16 December 1974)

The Committee of Ministers.

1. Considering the need to ensure the implementation of the right to freedom of expression including that of freely receiving and imparting information guaranteed by Article 10 of the European Convention on Human Rights;
2. Believing that the existence of a large diversity of sources of news and views available to the general public is of capital importance in this respect;
3. Conscious of the special role of newspapers in ensuring such diversity of news and views available to the general public;
4. Sharing the concern frequently expressed as to the possible prejudice to the rights guaranteed by Article 10 of the European Convention on Human Rights as a result of a diminution in the total number of newspapers with their own complete editorial units, or of the concentration of the effective control of an increasing number of such newspapers in the same hands;
5. Convinced that such large diversity of news and views depends to no small degree on the existence of properly functioning competition within the press, whilst not denying however that in certain cases a move towards bigger enterprises could consolidate the economic situation of the press and improve its performance;

6. Conscient toutefois du danger que pourrait présenter pour la liberté de la presse et le libre exercice du choix du public le fait de figer d'une manière durable la structure existante de la presse;

7. Reconnaissant que la situation de la presse n'est pas du tout la même dans les différents pays membres en raison notamment de facteurs tenant à la géographie, à l'histoire, aux habitudes de pensée et aux conditions économiques;

8. Persuadé néanmoins que s'offrent aux pouvoirs publics plusieurs formes d'action, notamment les différentes formes d'aides – générales, spécifiques ou sélectives – telles qu'elles ont été définies à l'annexe I du rapport mentionné ci-dessous, lesquelles si elles sont judicieusement adaptées, pourraient dans certains cas et pour un certain temps contribuer à limiter ou freiner le phénomène de concentration;

9. Vu le rapport du Comité d'experts qui accompagne la présente résolution,

Recommande aux gouvernements des Etats membres d'examiner les propositions qui suivent à la lumière de leurs possibilités d'application, dont ils demeurent seuls juges, compte tenu de la situation particulière de chacun des Etats membres:

1. Certaines mesures d'aide publique à la presse, si elles sont judicieusement adaptées, peuvent assurer, dans les limites indiqués plus loin, la survie de journaux, possédant leur propre unité rédactionnelle complète, menacés de disparition ou de rachat par suite de difficultés financières;

2. Lorsqu'une aide revêt un caractère sélectif, elle devrait être limitée à la fois en volume et dans le temps, accordée sur la base de critères objectifs, et réservée en principe aux seuls journaux dont les difficultés peuvent être, quant à leur cause, éliminées par l'octroi d'une telle aide;

3. Sans préjudice de dispositions dont les gouvernements des pays membres conservent l'initiative, eu égard à la structure et à la situation particulière de la presse dans leur pays, une aide capable d'atteindre l'objectif défini ci-dessus semble pouvoir résulter de mesures telles que:

(*a*) l'institution d'un fonds de presse, permettant à des journaux relativement mal placés sur le marché d'obtenir des subventions ou des prêts à des conditions particulièrement favorables en vue d'améliorer leur position concurrentielle;

(*b*) l'octroi à certaines catégories de journaux en position défavorable et donc contraintes de s'adapter à des changements de conditions structurelles, d'aides spécifiques résultant par exemple d'une modulation des aides décrites au chapitre V du rapport ci-annexé;

4. Les gouvernements qui accordent déjà une aide économique à la presse sous une forme ou sous une autre devraient en réexaminer les modalités afin d'éviter tout ce qui pourrait constituer un encouragement involontaire et fortuit au processus de concentration, sans cependant perdre de vue que, là où elle existe, une telle aide fait partie intégrante des conditions d'existence de la presse et qu'une diminution subite de cette aide risque de précipiter la disparition ou le rachat de journaux en proie à des difficultés financières;

5. Lorsqu'un gouvernement est habilité à interdire la prise de contrôle d'un quotidien par un groupe de presse contrôlant déjà plusieurs autres journaux, et au cas où il apparaîtrait clairement qu'un rachat de cette sorte menacerait gravement la liberté d'expression et le droit à l'information, ledit gouvernement, s'il n'a pas déjà qualité pour accorder une assistance financière au journal dont le rachat a été refusé dans l'intérêt public, devrait prendre les dispositions nécessaires pour se doter de pouvoirs qui lui permettent le cas échéant d'en décider l'octroi;

6. Les gouvernements devraient encourager toute action destinée à rationaliser les méthodes de production et de distribution des journaux en vue de réduire les coûts de publication, sous réserve que les journaux les moins bien placés sur le marché puissent également en bénéficier et que,

6. Conscious that a lasting freeze of the existing structure of the press could present a threat to press freedom and public choice;

7. Recognising that there are wide differences between the situations of the press in different member countries inter alia because of factors of geography, history, habits of thought and economic circumstances;

8. Believing however that there exist several possible forms of action open to the public authorities, including the different forms of aid – general, specific, or selective – as defined in Annex I of the report referred to below, which, if suitably adapted, might in certain cases and for a certain time contribute towards some limitation or slowing down of the phenomenon of press concentration;

9. Having regard to the report of the committee of experts accompanying this resolution,

Recommends the governments of member states to examine the following proposals in the light of their applicability, of which they (the governments of member states) remain the sole judge, to the circumstances prevailing in the member state concerned:

2. That certain measures of public aid to the press, if suitably adapted, could ensure within the limits indicated below, the survival of newspapers with their own complete editorial units threatened with disappearance or with being taken over as a result of financial difficulties;

2. That aid given in a selective form should be limited in time and in amount, should be granted on the basis of objective criteria, and should be confined in principle to newspapers whose difficulties can be eliminated by the assistance in question;

3. That, without prejudice to initiatives of which the governments of member states remain the sole judge having regard to the structure and the particular situation of the press in their country, assistance capable of fulfilling the objective referred to above would seem to be possible by means of measures such as:

(*a*) the institution of a press fund enabling less favourably placed newspapers to obtain subsidies or loans on particularly favourable terms with a view to developing their ability to compete on the market;

(*b*) the grant of specific aids, for example those resulting from a modulation of the aids described in Chapter V of the accompanying report, designed to give assistance to certain categories of newspapers finding themselves in underprivileged situations and being forced to adapt themselves to changing structural circumstances;

4. That governments already according economic assistance to the press in one form or another should review the structure of those existing arrangements with a view to avoiding any unintended and unforeseen *de facto* encouragement given thereby to the process of press concentration, nevertheless bearing in mind that, where already accorded, such assistance has become part of the climate in which the press lives and that any sudden diminution of such assistance might precipate the closure or takeover of newspapers in a weak financial position;

5. That, where governments dispose of statutory powers enabling them to forbid the take-over of a daily newspaper by a press group already controlling several other newspapers, and where it may clearly appear that a take-over of this sort would gravely threaten the liberty of expression and the right to information, the governments in question – if they do not already dispose of powers to give financial assistance to the newspaper whose take-over has been refused in the public interest – should take the necessary steps to provide themselves with powers enabling them in appropriate cases to accord such financial assistance;

6. That governments encourage efforts to rationalise the methods of production and distribution of newspapers with a view to diminishing publishing costs subject to the reservation that those newspapers least well placed in the market should equally be able to benefit from such ef-

dans le cas d'ententes particulières ou d'accords de coopération technique entre différents journaux, l'indépendance de chacun d'eux puisse être garantie et respectée;

7. Enfin, les gouvernements devraient stimuler les efforts d'adaptation déployés par la profession elle-même pour trouver les moyens de surmonter ses difficultés, notamment en opérant les changements qu'exige la complémentarité devenue nécessaire avec l'audio-visuel.

D. RECOMMANDATIONS ET RESOLUTIONS DE L'ASSEMBLEE PARLEMENTAIRE

1. RECOMMANDATION 726[1] RELATIVE A LA COOPERATION POLITIQUE ENTRE LES ETATS DE L'EUROPE DE L'OUEST

L'Assemblée,

1. Vu le rapport de sa commission des questions politiques sur la coopération politique entre les Etats de l'Europe de l'Ouest (Doc. 3387);

2. Se référant à sa Recommandation 704 (1973), relative à la mission du Conseil de l'Europe;

3. Réaffirmant son attachement aux valeurs consacrées par le Statut et au rôle du Conseil de l'Europe en tant que seule organisation politique où se retrouvent les Etats démocratiques d'Europe;

4. Considérant que l'article 1er du Statut précise que le but du Conseil de l'Europe sera poursuivi au moyen des organes du Conseil de l'Europe par l'examen des questions d'intérêt commun;

5. Rappelant qu'elle a à maintes reprises invité le Comité des Ministres et les gouvernements des dix-sept Etats membres à mettre en oeuvre une coopération politique effective sur les problèmes qui intéressent l'Europe dans son ensemble;

6. Se référant notamment à ses Résolutions sur les relations entre l'Europe et les Etats-Unis (524 (1973)), et sur l'état des négociations Est-Ouest et des négociations transatlantiques actuellement en cours (556 (1973)), et à sa Recommandation 692 (1973) relative aux relations Est-Ouest en Europe;

7. Regrettant que le Comité des Ministres n'ait pas jusqu'à présent donné des suites satisfaisantes à ses initiatives, et considérant que le cadre de consultation et de coopération politique que sont les institutions du Conseil de l'Europe n'a pas été suffisamment utilisé par les dix-sept Etats membres;

8. Se réjouissant à ce propos de ce que „les Neuf entendent resserrer, dans les cadres existants, leurs liens avec les pays membres du Conseil de l'Europe";

9. Plus convaincue que jamais, après les carences et les défaillances de l'Europe révélées à l'occasion des crises récentes, qu'il convient de renforcer la coopération politique entre Etats membres au sein du Conseil de l'Europe,

10. Recommande au Comité des Ministres:

(*a*) d'inviter les gouvernements membres à prendre l'engagement d'utiliser le Conseil de l'Europe et ses structures pour leurs consultations et leur coopération sur les questions d'intérêt commun;

(*b*) de prendre les mesures appropriées pour empêcher le démembrement

---

[1] *Discussion par l'Assemblée* le 24 janvier 1974 (24e séance) (voir Doc. 3387, rapport de la commission des questions politiques).
Texte adopté par l'Assemblée le 24 janvier 1974 (24e séance).

forts, and that, in the case of particular arrangements or technical co-operation agreements between different newspapers, the independence of each newspaper in question can be guaranteed and respected;

7. That finally, governments stimulate efforts by the industry itself to find appropriate measures of adaptation to meet the difficulties the latter is facing – in particular by making the changes which are called for by the complementarity necessary with audio-visual media.

D. RECOMMENDATIONS AND RESOLUTIONS OF THE PARLIAMENTARY ASSEMBLY

1. RECOMMENDATION 726[1] ON POLITICAL CO-OPERATION BETWEEN THE STATES OF WESTERN EUROPE

The Assembly,

1. Having regard to the report of its Political Affairs Committee on political co-operation between the states of Western Europe (Doc. 3387);

2. Recalling its Recommendation 704 (1973), on the mission of the Council of Europe;

3. Reiterating its faith in the values enshrined by the Statute and in the role of the Council of Europe as the only political organisation that brings together the democratic states of Europe;

4. Considering that according to Article 1 of the Statute, the Council of Europe's aim is to be pursued through the organs of the Council of Europe by discussion of questions of common concern;

5. Recalling its repeated invitations to the Committee of Ministers and governments of the seventeen member states to establish effective political co-operation on problems of concern to Europe as a whole;

6. Recalling its resolutions on relations between Western Europe and the United States (524 (1973)), and the state of current East-West and transatlantic negotiations (556 (1973)), and Recommendation 692 (1973) on East-West relations in Europe;

7. Regretting the failure of the Committee of Ministers so far to provide satisfactory follow-up to the Assembly's initiatives, and considering that insufficient use has been made by the seventeen member states of the framework for political consultation and co-operation provided by the Council of Europe institutions;

8. Welcoming in this connection the intention of the Nine "to strengthen their links, in the present institutional framework, with the member countries of the Council of Europe";

9. More convinced than ever, following Europe's shortcomings and inadequacies in recent crises, that political co-operation between member states within the Council of Europe needs to be reinforced,

10. Recommends that the Committee of Ministers:

(*a*) invite the member governments to give an undertaking that they will make use of the Council of Europe and of its institutions for the purpose of consultations and co-operation on questions of common concern;

(*b*) take appropriate measures to prevent the political dismembering of Europe by devising effective procedures enabling the Council of Europe

---

[1] *Assembly debate* on 24 January 1974 (24th Sitting) (see Doc. 3387, report of the Political Affairs Committee).

Text adopted by the Assembly on 24 January 1974 (24th Sitting).

politique de l'Europe, en mettant au point des procédures efficaces permettant au Conseil de l'Europe de faire office d'instrument de liaison entre les Etats membres de la Communauté et les autres Etats membres du Conseil de l'Europe;

(*c*) de donner plein effet à l'arrangement passé le 18 août 1959 entre le Comité des Ministres du Conseil de l'Europe et la Communauté économique européenne;

(*d*) de revaloriser le rôle et les fonctions du Comité Mixte, afin de le réunir – au niveau ministériel – dans les plus brefs délais en cas de crise.

2. RESOLUTION 561[1]
RELATIVE AUX PETITIONS A L'ASSEMBLEE
(*article 56 du Règlement*)

L'Assemblée,

1. Considérant la nécessité de mettre à jour et de mieux préciser les dispositions de son Règlement relatives aux pétitions, qui datent de 1949;
2. Ayant été informée de l'échange de vues qui a eu lieu à ce sujet au Comité Mixte le 4 juillet 1973;
3. Vu le rapport de sa commission du Règlement (Doc. 3370),
4. Décide de remplacer l'article 56 du Règlement par le texte suivant:

,,Article 56

Pétitions à l'Assemblée

1. Les pétitions à l'Assemblée sont adressées au Président.
2. Elles doivent:

(*a*) mentionner le nom, la qualité et l'adresse de chacun des signataires, dont les signatures doivent être légalisées conformément à la législation interne de leurs pays de résidence respectifs;

(*b*) avoir un objet qui entre dans le cadre des activités du Conseil de l'Europe, conformément aux dispositions de l'article 1er du Statut.

3. Le Bureau de l'Assemblée examine la recevabilité des pétitions.
4. Les pétitions déclarées recevables sont transmises par le Bureau, pour examen, aux commissions respectivement compétentes.
5. Après examen, la commission saisie informe le Président des conclusions auxquelles elle est parvenue et, le cas échéant, des suites qu'il lui paraît opportun de donner à la pétition, notamment en ce qui concerne sa publication totale ou partielle.
6. Le Président soumet ces informations au Bureau de l'Assemblée qui se prononce, s'il y a lieu, sur les mesures à prendre et sur la réponse à adresser au pétitionnaire."

3. RECOMMANDATION 729[2]
RELATIVE A LA POLITIQUE GENERALE DU CONSEIL DE L'EUROPE – APRES VINGT-CINQ ANS DE COOPERATION EUROPEENNE ET ATLANTIQUE

L'Assemblée,

1. Ayant pris connaissance du rapport de sa commission des questions

[1] *Discussion par l'Assemblée* le 22 janvier 1974 (21e séance) (voir Doc. 3370, rapport de la commission du Règlement).
Texte adopté par l'Assemblée le 22 janvier 1974 (21e séance).

[2] *Discussion par l'Assemblée* les 8 et 9 mai 1974 (4e et 5e séances) (voir Doc. 3424, rapport de la commission des questions politiques).
Texte adopté par l'Assemblée le 9 mai 1974 (5e séance).

to function as a liaison instrument between the member states of the Community and the other member states of the Council of Europe;

(*c*) give full effect to the arrangement concluded on 18 August 1959 between the Committee of Ministers of the Council of Europe and the Commission of the European Economic Community;

(*d*) enhance the role and the function of the Joint Committee so that meetings can be called (at ministerial level) at the earliest possible juncture if a crisis occurs.

2. RESOLUTION 561[1]

ON PETITIONS TO THE ASSEMBLY

(*Rule 56 of the Rules of Procedure*)

The Assembly,

1. Considering the need to bring up to date the provisions of the Rules relating to petitions, adopted in 1949, and make them more explicit;

2. Having been informed of the exchange of views on this matter in the Joint Committee on 4 July 1973;

3. Having regard to the report of its Committee on Rules of Procedure (Doc. 3370),

4. Resolves to amend the present Rule 56 as follows:

"Rule 56"

Petitions to the Assembly

1. Petitions must be addressed to the President.

2. They must:

(*a*) show the names, attributes and address of petitioners; the petitioners must cause their signatures to be authenticated in accordance with the internal legislation of the state in which they reside;

(*b*) bear on questions which fall within the competence of the Council of Europe, in accordance with the provisions of Article 1 of the Statute.

3. The Bureau of the Assembly shall examine the admissibility of petitions.

4. Petitions declared admissible shall be transmitted by the Bureau to the competent committees for examination.

5. Upon completion of its examination of a petition, the committee shall inform the President of the conclusions it has reached and of what action, if any, it deems appropriate, in particular publication of all or part of the petition.

6. The President shall submit this information to the Bureau of the Assembly for advice, if necessary, on measures to be taken and on the reply to be addressed to the petitioner."

3. RECOMMENDATION 729[2]

ON THE GENERAL POLICY OF THE COUNCIL OF EUROPE – AFTER TWENTY-FIVE YEARS OF EUROPEAN AND ATLANTIC CO-OPERATION

The Assembly,

1. Having noted the report by its Political Affairs Committee on

---

[1] *Assembly debate* on 22 January 1974 (21st Sitting) (see Doc. 3370, report of the Committee on Rules of Procedure).

Text adopted by the Assembly on 22 January 1974 (21st Sitting).

[2] *Assembly debate* on 8 and 9 May 1974 (4th and 5th Sittings) (see Doc. 3424, report of the Political Affairs Committee).

Text adopted by the Assembly in 9 may 1974 (5th Sitting).

politiques sur vingt-cinq années de coopération européenne et atlantique (Doc. 3424);

2. Considérant le rôle de pionnier joué par le Conseil de l'Europe au cours des vingt-cinq années écoulées pour l'amélioration de la coopération internationale, ainsi que pour le rapprochement des Etats européens;

3. Convaincue que le Conseil de l'Europe conservera une mission de première importance, dans les années à venir, pour la réalisation d'une coopération plus étroite entre les Etats membres;

4. Considérant que le Conseil de l'Europe doit apporter un apport spécifique à la solution des problèmes de la coopération internationale contemporaine, en tant que porte-parole de l'ensemble des Etats démocratiques de l'Europe;

5. Fortement préoccupée par la stagnation continue de l'unification européenne, et prenant acte des développements particulièrement graves qui portent actuellement atteinte au Traité de Rome et qui menacent de ce fait de provoquer l'éclatement de la Communauté européenne;

6. Préoccupée par les symptômes d'une crise de la démocratie parlementaire qui à la longue pourrait menacer la stabilité politique intérieure et peser sur le bon déroulement des relations internationales;

7. Convaincue, aujourd'hui comme hier, de la nécessité d'une coopération étroite et équilibrée entre les Etats de l'Europe occidentale et les Etats de l'Europe occidentale et les Etats d'Amérique du Nord dans tous les domaines d'intérêt commun;

8. Persuadée qu'une meilleure coopération avec les Etats du bassin méditerranéen serait de nature à contribuer à l'amélioration de la situation politique dans cette région;

9. Considérant que la poursuite d'une politique de détente par les Etats membres dans le cadre de la Conférence sur la sécurité et la coopération en Europe devrait avoir pour effet d'améliorer les relations des Etats de l'Europe de l'Ouest avec les Etats de l'Europe de l'Est, sans toutefois que les pressions exercées en vue de parvenir à un accord l'été prochain puissent affaiblir les principes défendus par les pays d'Europe occidentale qui visent essentiellement à accroître la liberté de mouvement des personnes, des idées et des informations à travers les frontières de l'Europe;

10. Se référant à ses Recommandations 704 (1973) et 726 (1974), relatives au rôle politique du Conseil de l'Europe en tant que seule organisation réunissant l'ensemble des Etats de l'Europe démocratique,

11. Recommande au Comité des Ministres, après avoir discuté des principaux problèmes qu'affrontent présentement les Etats européens dans le contexte international:

(*a*) de relancer le processus d'unification européenne, en prenant notamment des initiatives permettant aux Etats européens de se concerter et de confronter leurs positions respectives dans les discussions internationales, et en poursuivant l'approfondissement et le renforcement des activités du Conseil de l'Europe dans le domaine de la coopération intergouvernementale;

(*b*) de contribuer au renforcement de la démocratie européenne:

i. en faisant mieux connaître et en faisant mieux valoir le rôle que le Conseil de l'Europe joue dans les divers domaines de la coopération européenne,

ii. en étudiant les causes de la crise que traversent actuellement les institutions démocratiques et en proposant des remèdes;

(*c*) d'activer la coopération avec les Etats de l'Amérique du Nord:

i. en contribuant à l'élaboration de procédures de consultations transatlantiques,

ii. en faisant ressortir l'intérêt européen dans certains domaines spécifiques, comme l'approvisionnement en énergie, d'une importance vitale, tant pour le monde industrialisé que pour les pays en voie de développement;

twenty-five years of European and Atlantic co-operation (Doc. 3424);

2. Having regard to the pioneer role played by the Council of Europe throughout the past twenty-five years in improving international co-operation and bringing together the states of Europe;

3. Convinced that the Council of Europe will continue to exercise a highly important mission during the coming years in bringing about closer co-operation among its member states;

4. Considering that the Council of Europe, as the spokesman for all European democracies, must make its specific contribution to the solution of the problems confronting international co-operation today;

5. Deeply concerned at the continuing stalemate in European unification, and taking note of the particularly serious developments now affecting the Treaty of Rome and thereby threatening to break up the European Community proper;

6. Concerned at the symptoms of a crisis in parliamentary democracy which in the long run would threaten internal political stability and strain international relations;

7. Convinced, now as in the past, that close and balanced co-operation between the states of Western Europe and North America is necessary in all sectors of mutual interest;

8. Taking the view that closer co-operation with the Mediterranean countries would help to improve the political situation in this area;

9. Considering that the pursuit of a policy of détente by the member states in the framework of the Conference on Security and Co-operation in Europe should bring about improved relations between the countries of Western and Eastern Europe, although pressures to reach agreement this summer must not be permitted to dilute the Western case, which is, in essence, the advocacy of freer movement of people, ideas and information across the frontiers of Europe;

10. Referring to its Recommendations 704 (1973) and 726 (1974) on the political role of the Council of Europe, as the only organisation comprising all the democratic states of Europe,

11. Recommends that the Committee of Ministers, after considering the major international problems with which European states have now to contend:

(*a*) give renewed impetus to the process of European unification by taking steps to encourage European states to get together and discuss their respective positions at international talks, and by continuing to expand and strengthen the Council of Europe's activities in the field of intergovernmental co-operation;

(*b*) help to seek ways of strengthening European democracy:

(i) by arranging for the part played by the Council of Europe in the various sectors of European co-operation to be better known and appreciated,

(ii) by studying the causes of the crisis at present sweeping democratic institutions and suggesting corrective measures;

(*c*) to activate co-operation with the nations of North America:

(i) by helping to devise forms of transatlantic consultations,

(ii) by stressing the European interest in certain specific sectors, such as energy supplies, which are of vital importance for the industrialised and developing countries alike;

(*d*) offer the Council of Europe's help in implementing plans for co-operation with the states bordering on the Mediterranean;

(*e*) consider new initiatives for co-operating with the states of Eastern Europe:

(i) by consulting each other with a view to presenting common positions at the Conference on Security and Co-operation in Europe and stressing at the same time that the three negotiation baskets cannot be separated from each other, (*d*) d'offrir les bons offices du Conseil de l'Europe dans la réalisation de projets de coopération avec les Etats riverains de la Méditerranée;

(*e*) d'envisager de nouvelles initiatives de coopération avec les Etats de l'Europe de l'Est:

i. en se concertant à cet effet en vue de présenter des positions communes à la Conférence sur la sécurité et la coopération en Europe, tout en insistant sur le caractère indivisible des trois corbeilles de négociations,

ii. en refusant la création d'organismes nouveaux et permanents si le déroulement et les résultats de la conférence n'apportent pas de justification pour de telles institutions,

iii. en proposant pour commencer aux Etats de l'Europe de l'Est qui en manifesteraient le désir la possibilité d'accéder à certaines formes de coopération technique dans le cadre du Programme de travail intergouvernemental du Conseil de l'Europe.

4. RESOLUTION 563[1]
RELATIVE A LA SITUATION AU PORTUGAL

L'Assemblée,

1. Se félicitant de l'abolition de la dictature au Portugal et de l'initiative prise par les nouvelles autorités en vue de rétablir la démocratie et de mettre fin à la guerre coloniale;
2. Se félicitant de la suppression de la censure et du démantèlement de la police politique;
3. Se félicitant de l'annonce de la formation d'un gouvernement civil dans les prochaines semaines et de l'organisation d'élections totalement démocratiques dans un délai d'un an;
4. Soulignant l'importance de régler l'avenir des territoires africains conformément au principe d'autodétermination et de décolonisation énoncé par les Nations Unies;
5. Espérant voir le Portugal adhérer au Conseil de l'Europe,
6. Fait appel aux gouvernements des Etats membres pour qu'ils apportent une aide économique au Portugal, étant donné que l'existence de problèmes économiques non résolus menacerait la liberté nouvellement conquise.

5. RESOLUTION 571[2]
RELATIVE A LA PROTECTION DES SECRETS DE FABRICATION ET DE COMMERCE

L'Assemblée,

1. Considérant la nécessité d'une protection juridique adéquate des secrets de fabrication et de commerce et la nécessité de combattre l'espionnage industriel, c'est-à-dire le détournement de tels secrets;
2. Considérant que l'espionnage industriel peut non seulement être gravement préjudiciable à une entreprise industrielle, mais aussi porter atteinte à des intérêts économiques nationaux d'importance vitale;
3. Considérant que les secrets de fabrication et de commerce, qui sont parfois le fruit de longues et coûteuses recherches, d'années d'expérience ou de compétences spéciales, ne bénéficient pas en règle générale de la pro-

---

[1] *Discussion par l'Assemblée* le 9 mai 1974 (5e séance) (voir Doc. 3435, rapport de la commission des pays européens non membres).
Texte adopté par l'Assemblée le 9 mai 1974 (5e séance).

[2] *Texte adopté par la Commission Permanente*, agissant au nom de l'Assemblée, le 3 juillet 1974. Voir Doc. 3440, rapport de la commission des questions juridiques.

(ii) by refusing the setting up of new and permanent organisations unless the developments and results of the conference provide justification for such institutions,

(iii) by offering, to begin with, Eastern European states that so wish the opportunity of participating in certain areas of technical co-operation in the framework of the Inter-governmental Work Programme of the Council of Europe.

4. RESOLUTION 563[1]
ON THE SITUATION IN PORTUGAL

The Assembly,

1. Welcoming the removal of dictatorship in Portugal and the initiative taken by the new authorities to restore democracy and end the colonial war;
2. Welcoming the fact that censorship has been abolished and that the political police has been disbanded;
3. Welcoming the announcement that a civilian government will be formed in the next few weeks and that fully democratic elections will be held within a year;
4. Underlining the importance of settling the future of the territories in Africa in accordance with the principle of self-determination and de-colonisation as expressed by the United Nations;
5. Looking forward to the adherence of Portugal to the Council of Europe,
6. Appeals to the governments of member states to provide economic assistance to Portugal in view of the fact that unresolved economic problems would endanger the newly-won freedom.

5. RESOLUTION 571[2]
ON THE PROTECTION OF MANUFACTURING AND COMMERCIAL SECRETS

The Assembly,

1. Considering the need for adequate legal protection of manufacturing and commercial secrets, and the need to combat industrial spying, i.e. the misappropriation of such secrets;
2. Considering that industrial spying may not only cause serious damage to an industrial enterprise, but also harm vital national economic interests;
3. Considering that manufacturing and commercial secrets, which sometimes are the fruit of long and costly research, years of experience or special skills, are not, as a rule, covered by the protection accorded to the traditional components of industrial property;

---

[1] *Assembly debate* on 9 May 1974 (5th Sitting) (see Doc. 3425, report of the Committee on European Non-Member Countries).
Text adopted by the Assembly on 9 May 1974 (5th Sitting).

[2] *Text adopted by the Standing Committee*, acting on behalf of the Assembly, on 3 July 1974. See Doc. 3440, report of the Legal Affairs Committee.

tection accordée aux composantes traditionnelles de la propriété industrielle;

4. Considérant que tous les Etats membres du Conseil de l'Europe ont promulgué une législation punissant sévèrement l'espionnage militaire et politique qui s'accompagne souvent d'espionnage industriel (lorsqu'il s'agit par exemple de production militaire), tandis que la législation sur l'espionnage industriel est en général insuffisante et inadéquate par rapport aux besoins actuels;

5. Considérant qu'une protection adéquate est impossible au niveau national sans une législation harmonisée à l'échelon international ou un accord international sur l'espionnage industriel;

6. Considérant qu'il est souhaitable de mettre en place un dispositif juridique dans le cadre duquel il serait possible de combattre efficacement l'espionnage industriel au moyen de dispositions de droit pénal et civil;

7. Se félicitant du travail considérable accompli dans ce domaine par sa commission des questions juridiques et estimant qu'il n'est pas nécessaire d'élaborer une convention européenne ou un autre accord dans le cadre du Conseil de l'Europe,

8. Adopte la loi type annexée sur la protection des secrets de fabrication et de commerce;

9. Invite les parlementaires à présenter cette loi type comme une proposition de loi dans leurs parlements respectifs et à prendre toutes mesures jugées nécessaires pour introduire les dispositions de la loi type dans leur législation nationale;

10. Invite sa commission chargée des relations avec les parlements nationaux et le public à prendre les mesures nécessaires pour promouvoir et coordonner l'action envisagée au paragraphe 9 ci-dessus.

ANNEXE

TEXTE DE LA LOI TYPE

Article 1

Objet de la protection

1.1. Au regard de la présente loi, on entend par ,,secret'' toute information de fabrication ou de commerce ayant valeur pour l'entreprise ou le particulier qui la détient de façon non publique, à l'exception des informations déjà protégées.

Article 2

Conditions de protection

2.1. Ne peut invoquer la protection d'un secret au regard de la présente loi que le titulaire dudit secret.

2.2 Pour bénéficier de la protection prévue par la présente loi, le secret ne doit pas être accessible à des tiers non autorisés.

Article 3

Actes réprimés par la présente loi

3.1. Sont punis des peines prévues à l'article 5 tous actes commis par une personne non régulièrement autorisée par le titulaire d'un secret et

4. Considering that all the Council of Europe member states have enacted legislation severely punishing military and political spying, which frequently involve industrial spying (e.g. where military production is concerned), whereas the legislation governing industrial spying is generally insufficient and inadequate to present needs;

5. Considering that adequate protection is impossible nationally without internationally harmonised legislation or an international agreement on industrial spying;

6. Considering that it is desirable to establish a legal framework in which industrial spying could be combated effectively by provisions of penal and civil law;

7. Welcoming the substantial work which its Legal Affairs Committee has done in this field, and considering that there is no need to elaborate a European convention or other agreement in the framework of the Council of Europe.

8. Adopts the appended model law on the protection of manufacturing and commercial secrets;

9. Invites members of parliaments to present this model law as a private members' bill in their national parliaments and to take whatever action may be necessary to introduce the provisions of the model law in their national legislation;

10. Instructs its Committee on Parliamentary and Public Relations to take the necessary steps in order to promote and co-ordinate the action envisaged in paragraph 9 above.

APPENDIX

TEXT OF THE MODEL LAW

Article 1

Subject-matter to be protected

1.1. For the purpose of this act, a secret means any manufacturing or commercial information which is of value to a firm or private person in their non-public possession, with the exception of information already protected.

Article 2

Conditions for protection

2.1. No person may claim protection of a secret in accordance with this act, unless he is entitled to the secret.

2.2. A secret can only be protected in accordance with this act if it is not accessible to outside persons.

Article 3

Offences punishable under this act

3.1. Any act committed for the purpose of unlawful investigation, appropriation, communication or utilisation of a secret, by a person not ayant pour objet l'exploration, l'appropriation, la communication ou l'utilisation illégale dudit secret.

3.2. Est considéré comme acte d'exploration au regard de la présente loi tout acte tendant à obtenir la connaissance d'un secret ou à en aider l'obtention.

3.3. Est considéré comme acte d'appropriation au regard de la présente loi tout acte qui permet à une personne, par quelque moyen que ce soit, d'avoir connaissance d'un secret.

3.4. Est considéré comme acte de communication au regard de la présente loi toute transmission de la connaissance d'un secret à un tiers.

3.5. Est considéré comme acte d'utilisation au regard de la présente loi tout usage d'un secret.

Article 4

Employés et anciens employés

4.1. Est assimilée au cas prévu à l'article 3, alinéa 5, l'utilisation d'un secret par un employé ou ancien employé du titulaire d'un secret ou par toute autre personne ayant eu connaissance du secret.

4.2. Néanmoins, si l'ancien employé a personnellement mis au point un secret ou joué personnellement un rôle essentiel dans son élaboration pendant la période où le titulaire du secret l'employait, l'obligation de conserver ledit secret expire deux ans après la rupture du contrat le liant à son employeur.

Article 5

Peines

5.1. Les délits énumérés à l'article 3 sont punis de (1 mois à) 2 ans de prison ou de (... à) ... d'amende, ou des deux.

(5.2. Les mêmes peines frapperont quiconque aura tenté de commettre l'un des délits énumérés à l'article 3 ou y aura participé comme complice.)

(5.3. Si l'auteur de l'un des délits énumérés à l'article 3 est une entreprise, elle est passible d'une amende de (... à) 1 million d'unités de compte européennes.)

5.4. N'est pas considéré comme un délit au sens de la présente loi le fait, pour toute personne agissant de bonne foi, d'informer le public ou les utilisateurs de l'usage par un fabricant ou un commerçant d'un secret dont elle sait ou dont elle a des raisons sérieuses de croire qu'il soit ou pourrait être nocif.

Article 6

Plaintes

6. Les poursuites ne peuvent être entamées que sur plainte de la personne qui se considère lésée par l'un des actes délictueux énumérés à l'article 3.

authorised to do so by the person entitled to such secret, shall be liable to the penalties prescribed in Article 5.

3.2. For the purpose of this act, investigation means any act committed for the purpose of acquiring knowledge of a secret or of helping the acquisition of such knowledge.

3.3. For the purpose of this act, appropriation means any act, carried out by whatever means, through which a person acquires knowledge of a secret.

3.4 For the purpose of this act, communication means the transmission of a secret to another person.

3.5. For the purpose of this act, utilisation means any use of a secret.

Article 4

Employee or former employee

4.1. Utilisation, as defined in Article 3, paragraph 5, shall also be deemed to include the use of a secret by an employee or former employee of the person entitled to the secret, or by any other person having had knowledge of the secret.

4.2. If a former employee has himself developed a secret or himself played an essential role in the development of a secret during the period of his employment by the person entitled to the secret, no obligation whatsoever to keep the secret shall exist after two years have elapsed since the termination of his contract of employment.

Article 5

Penalties

5.1. Any of the offences listed in Article 3 shall be punishable by a term of imprisonment of (one month to) two years or a fine of (... to) ... or both.

(5.2. Attempt to commit any of the offences listed in Article 3 and complicity in their commission shall be liable to the same penalties.)

(5.3. If any one of the offences listed in Article 3 has been committed by a firm, the firm shall be punishable by a fine of (... to) 1000000 European units of account.)

5.4. A person who, acting in good faith, informs the public or users that a manufacturer or commercial enterprise is using a secret which he knows, or has good reason to believe, is or might be harmful shall not be deemed to commit an offence within the meaning of this act.

Article 6

Complaint

6. Prosecution may take place only upon complaint by the person regarding himself as having been injured by any of the offences listed in Article 3.

Article 7

Action civile

7.1. La présente loi n'exclut pour personne la possibilité d'engager une action civile.
7.2. Outre les dommages-intérêts, le titulaire d'un secret peut exiger que le détenteur illégitime cesse d'en faire quelque usage que ce soit.

Article 8

Intitulé et entrée en vigueur

8.1. Cette loi pourra être intitulée „Loi sur les secrets de fabrication et de commerce n° . . .".
8.2. Elle entrera en vigueur le . . . .

6. RECOMMANDATION 734[1]
RELATIVE A LA SITUATION A CHYPRE ET EN MEDITERRANEE ORIENTALE

L'Assemblée,
1. Rappelant sa Résolution 573;
2. Convaincue que les gouvernements membres ont le devoir, à la lumière des idéaux politiques énoncés dans le Statut, d'apporter d'urgence une contribution collective à la solution du problème de Chypre,
3. Recommande au Comité des Ministres:
(*a*) d'inscrire cette question, ainsi que le situation en Grèce, à l'ordre du jour de sa prochaine session;
(*b*) de se servir de la proposition concernant la procédure à suivre en cas de crise, faite par le Président de l'Assemblée parlementaire, M. Vedovato, lors de la réunion du Comité Mixte de janvier 1974, et de faciliter la convocation d'une réunion du Comité Mixte au niveau des ministres dans les plus brefs délais pour examiner les problèmes causés par le récent conflit de Chypre;
4. Recommande au Comité des Ministres, à la lumière de la Résolution (54) 16 du Comité des Ministres, d'inviter les gouvernements membres à tenir le Secrétaire Général informé des initiatives qu'ils prennent dans d'autres organisations internationales sur des questions qui intéressent directement le Conseil de l'Europe.

7. RESOLUTION 573[2]
RELATIVE A LA SITUATION A CHYPRE ET EN MEDITERRANEE ORIENTALE

L'Assemblée,
1. Rappelant que le Conseil de l'Europe a pour but „de réaliser une union plus étroite entre ses membres afin de sauvegarder et de promouvoir les idéaux et les principes qui sont leur patrimoine commun et de favoriser

---

[1] *Texte adopté par la Commission Permanente*, agissant au nom de l'Assemblée, le 29 juillet 1974. Voir Doc. 3464, rapport de la commission des questions politiques.
[2] *Texte adopté par la Commission Permanente*, agissant au nom de l'Assembléele, 29 juillet 1974. Voir Doc. 3464, rapport de la commission des questions politiques.

Article 7

Civil proceedings

7.1. Nothing in this act shall preclude a person from taking civil proceedings.

7.2. In addition to compensation of damages, a person entitled to a secret may demand that a person in unlawful possession of a secret cease to make any use whatsoever of it.

Article 8

Short title and commencement

8.1. This act may be cited as the "Manufacturing and Commercial Secrets Act 19 . .".

8.2. This act shall come into force at . . . .

6. RECOMMENDATION 734[1] ON THE SITUATION IN CYPRUS AND IN THE EASTERN MEDITERRANEAN AREA

The Assembly,

1. Recalling its Resolution 573;

2. Believing that member governments have an urgent duty, in the light of the political ideals enshrined in the Statute, to make a collective contribution to the solution of the Cyprus problem.

3. Recommends that the Committee of Ministers:

(*a*) include this question as well as the situation in Greece in the agenda of its next session;

(*b*) make use of the proposal concerning the procedure to follow in case of crises, submitted by the President of the Parliamentary Assembly, Mr Vedovato, during the meeting of the Joint Committee in January 1974, and facilitate a meeting of the Joint Committee at Ministers' level as soon as possible in order to examine the problems created by the recent Cyprus conflict;

4. Recommends that the Committee of Ministers invite the member governments, in the light of Resolution (54) 16 of the Committee of Ministers, to keep the Secretary General informed of initiatives they take in other international organisations on matters of direct concern to the Council of Europe.

7. RESOLUTION 573[2] ON THE SITUATION IN CYPRUS AND IN THE EASTERN MEDITERRANEAN AREA

The Assembly,

1. Recalling that the aim of the Council of Europe is to "achieve a greater unity between its Members for the purpose of safeguarding and realising the ideals and principles which are their common heritage and

[1] *Text adopted by the Standing Committee* acting on behalf of the Assembly, on 29 July 1974. See Doc. 3464, report of the Political Affairs Committee.

[2] *Text adopted by the Standing Committee,* acting on behalf of the Assembly, on 29 July 1974. See Doc. 3464, report of the Political Affairs Committee.

leur progrès économique et social," et de promouvoir une coopération pacifique entre toutes les nations;

2. Condamnant le coup d'Etat exécuté à Chypre par des officiers liés à la dictature militaire grecque;

3. Regrettant l'échec des tentatives de règlement politique, qui a conduit le Gouvernement turc à exercer son droit d'intervention en vertu de l'article 4 du Traité de garantie de 1960;

4. Tenant compte de la résolution adoptée par le Conseil de sécurité des Nations Unies le 20 juillet 1974, ainsi que des réactions des pays directement intéressés par le conflit qui ont accepté de se réunir à Genève, et de la position commune prise par les Etats membres de la Communauté européenne et du Conseil de l'OTAN,

5. Exprime l'espoir que les trois Etats signataires du Traité de garantie concluront rapidement à Geneve un cessez-le-feu permanent et un accord apportant un règlement juste, durable et pacifique de problème chypriote, accord qui devrait tenir compte des besoins et des droits légitimes des deux communautés de l'île et des intérêts vitaux des pays concernés par le conflit et qui contribuerait à la suppression des principales causes de friction entre les deux communautés, ainsi qu'entre la Turquie et la Grèce;

6. Considère que les deux communautés ethniques de Chypre doivent être pleinement associées à toutes les négociations sur l'avenir de l'île;

7. Appelle les Etats signataires à garantir la souveraineté, l'intégrité territoriale et la sécurité de Chypre, notamment au moyen d'un statut amélioré, assurant la sécurité et les droits de la communauté turque, ainsi qu l'indépendance politique de l'île sous un gouvernement démocratique, conformément aux dispositions prises lorsque Chypre a acquis son indépendance en 1960;

8. Demande notamment:

- le rétablissement des droits de l'homme et des libertés fondamentales;
- le respect et la garantie formelle des droits des communautés ethniques, pour une paix durable entre les Grecs et les Turcs de l'île;
- l'organisation d'élections libres et démocratiques aussitôt que possible;

9. Espère en particulier que le Gouvernement de la Turquie et le futur Gouvernement démocratique de la Grèce coopéreront étroitement pour trouver des solutions communes aux problèmes de l'avenir politique de Chypre et à d'autres problèmes concernant la Méditerranée orientale;

10. Serait heureuse de recevoir dans un avenir très proche une délégation parlementaire comprenant des représentants grecs et turcs de la population chypriote;

11. Se félicite du remplacement de la dictature militaire grecque par un gouvernement civil, de la libération des prisonniers politiques, de la liquidation des camps de concentration et de l'abolition de la censure, qu'elle considère comme des progrès importants vers la restauration d'une démocratie parlementaire;

12. Aimerait accueillir à nouveau la Grèce au Conseil de l'Europe dès que la démocratie aura été restaurée dans ce pays, conformément au contenu de sa Résolution 558 de janvier 1974.

8. RECOMMANDATION 737[1] RELATIVE A L'AIDE HUMANITAIRE AUX POPULATIONS EN DETRESSE A CHYPRE

L'Assemblée,

1. Vivement préoccupée par les conséquences des récents conflits à

[1] *Discussion par l'Assemblée* le 25 septembre 1974 (9e séance) (voir Doc. 3490, rapport de la commission de la population et des réfugiés).
Texte adopté par l'Assemblée le 25 septembre 1974 (9e séance).

facilitating their economic and social progress," and to promote peaceful co-operation among all nations;

2. Condemning the coup d'état carried out in Cyprus by officers owing allegiance to the Greek military dictatorship;

3. Regretting the failure of the attempt to reach a diplomatic settlement which led the Turkish Government to exercise its right of intervention in accordance with Article 4 of the Guarantee Treaty of 1960;

4. Bearing in mind the resolution passed by the United Nations Security Council on 20 July 1974, the reactions of the countries directly involved in the conflict, which have agreed to meet in Geneva, and the common position adopted by the member states of the European Community and the NATO Council,

5. Expresses the hope that the three signatory states of the Treaty of Guarantee can reach early agreement in Geneva on a permanent ceasefire and a fair, lasting and peaceful settlement of the Cyprus problem, which should take account of the legitimate needs and rights of the two communities of the island and of the vital interests of the countries concerned by the conflict, and would contribute to the elimination of the main causes of friction between the two communities, as well as between Turkey and Greece;

6. Considers that the two ethnic communities in Cyprus should be fully associated with all negotiations concerning the future of the island;

7. Calls upon the signatory states to guarantee the sovereignty, territorial integrity and security of Cyprus, including an improved status, guaranteeing the security and the rights of the Turkish community, as well as the political independence of a democratically governed Cyprus, as laid down when Cyprus became independent in 1960;

8. Calls in particular for:

– the re-establishment of human rights and fundamental freedoms;

– respect and a formal guarantee of the rights of the ethnic communities, in order to assure a lasting peace between the Greeks and Turks of the island;

– the holding of free and democratic elections as soon as possible;

9. Hopes, in particular, that the Government of Turkey and a future democratic Government of Greece will co-operate closely in finding common solutions for the political future of Cyprus as well as for other problems in the Eastern Mediterranean area;

10. Looks forward to welcoming in the very near future a parliamentary delegation including Greek and Turkish representatives of the Cypriot population;

11. Warmly welcomes the replacement of the Greek military dictatorship by a civilian government, the liberation of political prisoners, the liquidation of concentration camps and the abolishing of censorship as important steps towards a restoration of parliamentary democracy;

12. Looks forward to welcoming Greece back into the Council of Europe as soon as she has returned to democracy in accordance with the Assembly's Resolution 558 of January 1974.

8. RECOMMENDATION 737[1]
ON HUMANITARIAN AID TO THE DISTRESSED POPULATIONS IN CYPRUS

The Assembly,

1. Gravely concerned at the consequences of the recent conflicts in Cy-

---

[1] *Assembly debate* on 25 September 1974 (9th Sitting) (see Doc. 3490, report of the Committee on Population and Refugees).
Test adopted by the Assembly on 25 September 1974 (9th Sitting).

Chypre, et en particulier par le très grand nombre de personnes qui ont fui leurs foyers ou en ont été chassées, et qui ont perdu leurs moyens d'existence;

2. Considérant que la perte de la récolte et l'effondrement de l'économie menacent de prolonger pendant des mois la pénurie de produits de première nécessité, et que les combats et les déplacements de population ont créé un grave problème de logement et une crise de l'emploi;

3. Se félicitant des opérations d'urgence entreprises par le Comité international de la Croix-Rouge et le Haut-Commissaire des Nations Unies pour les réfugiés;

4. Notant que les Etats membres du Conseil de l'Europe sont ceux qui ont donné jusqu'ici les garanties les plus substantielles d'aide à cette action;

5. Approuvant la création par le Conseil de l'Europe d'un fonds d'urgence auquel contribueront les gouvernements membres et qui servira aux premiers secours;

6. Convaincue que le Conseil de l'Europe a l'obligation morale de prendre une part importante dans tous les domaines de la reconstruction de Chypre;

7. Reconnaissant que cette reconstruction ne sera possible qu'après le rétablissement d'un certain degré de stabilité et d'administration normale;

8. Faisant valoir néanmoins que les travaux de préparation et les opérations financières nécessaires à un tel programme doivent être entrepris immédiatement;

9. Soulignant que toute assistance doit, avant tout, bénéficier effectivement à ceux qui en ont besoin, sans considération de communauté ou de groupe ethnique,

10. Recommande au Comité des Ministres:

(*a*) d'inviter les gouvernements des Etats membres, en ce qui concerne *l'aide immédiate* aux populations en détresse de Chypre, à verser des contributions financières importantes dans les plus brefs délais au *fonds d'urgence du Conseil de l'Europe* créé par le Comité des Ministres, et à appuyer l'oeuvre humanitaire entreprise par le Comité international de la Croix-Rouge et le Haut-Commissaire des Nations Unies pour les réfugiés qui agit en tant que coordonnateur de l'assistance humanitaire des Nations Unies;

(*b*) d'élaborer dès maintenant, avec le concours du Représentant Spécial du Conseil de l'Europe pour les réfugiés nationaux et les excédents de population, un plan d'*aide à moyen et à long terme* en vue de faciliter la reconstruction et le développement des régions qui ont souffert des conséquences du conflit armé;

(*c*) d'inviter les gouvernements des Etats membres à s'engager à mettre en oeuvre le plan mentionné au paragraphe *b* ci-dessus en fournissant notamment au Représentant Spécial du Conseil de l'Europe chaque année, de 1975 à 1978, une somme à fonds perdus correspondant au moins à un dixième de la contribution de chaque Etat membre au budget du Conseil de l'Europe;

(*d*) d'inviter le Représentant Spécial du Conseil de l'Europe à solliciter du *Fonds de réétablissement* l'octroi aux populations cypriotes de prêts à long terme et à des taux d'intérêts peu élevés;

(*e*) d'informer régulièrement l'Assemblée des résultats du programme d'aide à moyen et à long terme.

prus, and in particular by the very large number of persons who have been made homeless or lost their livelihoods;

2. Considering that the loss of the harvest and dislocation of the economy threaten to prolong for many months the crisis in essential supplies, while the fighting and displacement of the population have created a serious problem of shelter and housing, and a crisis in the employment situation;

3. Expressing its satisfaction at the emergency operation being carried out by the International Committee of the Red Cross and the United Nations High Commissioner for Refugees;

4. Noting that Council of Europe member states have so far provided the most substantial pledges of support for this work;

5. Welcoming the setting up by the Council of Europe of an emergency fund to receive financial contributions from member governments to support the work of immediate relief;

6. Convinced that the Council of Europe is morally obliged to play a prominent part in all aspects of reconstruction in Cyprus;

7. Recognising that the putting into practice of this reconstruction must await the re-establishment of a certain degree of stability and orderly administration;

8. Emphasising nevertheless that the planning and financial operations entailed by any scheme for reconstruction must be undertaken immediately;

9. Stressing that any aid or assistance must above all be such as to benefit effectively all those in need irrespective of their community or ethnic group;

10. Recommends that the Committee of Ministers:

(*a*) invite member governments, as regards *immediate aid* to the distressed populations in Cyprus, to make substantial financial contributions as soon as possible to the *Council of Europe emergency fund* set up by the Committee of Ministers, and to support the humanitarian work being carried out by the International Committee of the Red Cross and by the United Nations High Commissioner for Refugees who is acting as co-ordinator of UN humanitarian aid;

(*b*) begin immediately to work out, with the help of the Special Representative of the Council of Europe for National Refugees and Over-Population, a ***medium- and long-term aid*** plan to facilitate reconstruction and development in regions which have suffered as a result of the fighting;

(*c*) invite member governments to undertake to put into effect the plan mentioned in paragraph *b*, in particular by providing the Special Representative of the Council of Europe each year, from 1975 to 1978, with an outright contribution, the equivalent of at least one tenth of each member state's contribution to the Council of Europe budget;

(*d*) invite the Special Representative of the Council of Europe to request the *Resettlement Fund* to grant long-term low-interest loans to the Cypriot populations;

(*e*) make regular progress reports to the Assembly on the programme of medium- and longterm aid.

9. RESOLUTION 575[1]
RELATIVE A LA SITUATION EN ESPAGNE

L'Assemblée,

1. Rappelant sa Résolution 278 (1964) sur la situation en Espagne et sa Recommendation 314 (1962) sur la possibilité d'une certaine forme d'accord économique entre l'Espagne et la CEE;

2. Considérant la contribution que l'Espagne apporte aux travaux du Conseil de l'Europe dans certains domaines techniques;

3. Constatant avec regret que l'Espagne est encore loin de remplir les conditions nécessaires pour pouvoir adhérer comme membre de plein droit au Conseil de l'Europe, étant donné qu'elle n'est pas dotée d'institutions démocratiques et représentatives;

4. Profondément préoccupée par des faits tels que:

(*a*) la censure qui frappe les critiques à l'égard de l'actuel régime espagnol demeure sévère;

(*b*) les adversaires de l'actuel Gouvernement espagnol – des organisations aussi bien que des individus – sont exposés à une dure répression;

(*c*) les partis politiques et les syndicats démocratiquement constitués ne sont pas autorisés à fonctionner, et il ne leur est même pas reconnu d'existence légale;

(*d*) des élections véritablement démocratiques n'ont pas été autorisées par les autorités espagnoles depuis la guerre civile,

5. Exprime l'espoir que les autorités espagnoles s'engageront en faveur d'une représentation démocratique reflétant la volonté populaire et dotée de vrais pouvoirs de décision;

6. Tout en condamnant les actes de terrorisme perpétrés par certains groupes séparatistes, fait appel au Gouvernement espagnol pour qu'il donne satisfaction, par une législation adéquate, aux aspirations légitimes des régions à une plus grande autonomie;

7. Prie instamment le Chef d'Etat espagnol de déclarer une amnistie générale s'appliquant à toute personne emprisonnée ou exilée pour des raisons politiques, particulièrement en vue de l'Année Sainte 1975;

8. Affirme que l'adhésion d'une Espagne démocratique aux organisations européennes à vocation politique serait à la fois conforme à l'intérêt de ce pays et de nature à renforcer l'influence de l'Europe dans le monde;

9. Déclare que, si l'Espagne pouvait s'engager dans la voie de la démocratisation, les pays et les organisations de l'Europe démocratique devraient lui prêter toute aide et assistance dont elle pourrait avoir besoin;

10. Formule l'espoir que le jour viendra où l'Espagne prendra sa place dans la famille des nations démocratiques européennes réunies au sein du Conseil de l'Europe;

11. Charge sa commission des pays européens non membres et sa commission des questions politiques de continuer à suivre l'évolution de la situation en Espagne.

---

[1] *Discussion par l'Assemblée* le 25 septembre 1974 (8e et 9e séances) (voir Doc. 3466, rapport de la commission des pays européens non membres).
Texte adopté par l'Assemblée le 25 septembre 1974 (9e séance).

9. RESOLUTION 575[1]
ON THE SITUATION IN SPAIN

The Assembly,

1. Recalling its Resolution 278 (1964) on the situation in Spain and its Recommendation 314 (1962) on the possibility of some form of economic agreement between Spain and EEC;

2. Considering Spain's contribution to the work of the Council of Europe in certain technical fields;

3. Observing with regret that Spain is still a long way from meeting the conditions necessary for full membership of the Council of Europe, as she has no democratic and representative institutions;

4. Deeply concerned by such facts inter alia as that:

(*a*) censorship applied to criticism of the present Spanish regime is still severe;

(*b*) political opponents – organisations and individuals – to the presen Spanish Government are exposed to harsh repression;

(*c*) democratically constituted political parties and trade unions are neither permitted to function, nor even legally to exist;

(*d*) no truly democratic elections have been permitted by the Spanish authorities since the Civil war,

5. Expresses the hope that the Spanish authorities will firmly commit themselves to achieving a democratic form of representation reflecting the popular will and exercising real powers of decision;

6. While condemning the acts of terrorism perpetrated by certain separatist groups, appeals to the Spanish Government to satisfy by appropriate legislation the legitimate aspirations of the country's regions to greater autonomy;

7. Urges the Spanish head of state to declare a general amnesty for all persons imprisoned or exiled for political reasons especially in view of Holy Year 1975;

8. Affirms that accession by a democratic Spain to European political organisations would be in that country's interests as well as being likely to strengthen Europe's influence in the world;

9. Declares that, if Spain were able to commit herself to democracy, the countries and organisations of democratic Europe should give her all necessary aid and assistance;

10. Hopes that the day will come when Spain takes her place among the family of European democratic nations in the Council of Europe;

11. Instructs its Committee on European Non-Member Countries and its Political Affairs Committee to continue to follow developments in Spain.

---

[1] *Assembly debate* on 25 September 1974 (8th and 9th Sittings) (see Doc. 3466, report of the Committee on European Non-Member Countries).
Text adopted by the Assembly on 25 September 1974 (9th Sitting).

10. RECOMMANDATION 739[1]
RELATIVE A LA CONFERENCE SUR LA SECURITE ET LA COOPERATION EN EUROPE – PERSPECTIVES ET CONSEQUENCES POUR L'EUROPE

L'Assemblée,

1. Se félicitant de la tenue de la Conférence sur la sécurité et la coopération en Europe qui doit consacrer sur le plan européen une démocratisation de fait de la vie internationale, et dont l'objectif premier doit être la consolidation de la paix et de la coopération européenne fondées sur la prééminence du droit et le patrimoine commun de civilisation et de libertés des peuples européens;

2. Rappelant ses positions de principe, exprimées dans sa Recommandation 692 (1973);

3. Déplorant que l'opinion publique des Etats occidentaux n'est pas suffisamment informée des négociations qui se déroulent à Genève dans le cadre de la deuxième phase de la conférence;

4. Tenant compte de l'état actuel de la négociation, et estimant que le Conseil de l'Europe doit faire connaître sa position avant la clôture de la deuxième phase des négociations;

5. Estimant que la mise en oeuvre d'une politique de détente en Europe doit avoir une dimension humaine, et apporter des bénéfices réels aux populations de tous les Etats européens;

6. Estimant que la paix et la sécurité en Europe ne pourront être que renforcées par l'amélioration des communications entre les Européens et par une diminution des tensions idéologiques,

7. Recommande au Comité des Ministres:

(*a*) de poursuivre ses concertations intergouvernementales et ses échanges de vues avec l'Assemblée tant sur la Conférence sur la sécurité et la coopération en Europe que sur l'évolution de la coopération en Europe que sur l'évolution de la coopération entre l'Europe de l'Ouest et l'Europe de l'Est;

(*b*) d'adopter une position de principe suivant laquelle les gouvernements des Etats membres du Conseil de l'Europe:

i. se concertent pendant le stade final de la deuxième phase de la conférence pour que le mandat de celle-ci, tel qu'il a été défini par les recommandations finales de la réunion préparatoire d'Helsinki, soit largement exécuté;

ii. insistent pour que soient dissipées avant la conclusion de la conférence les équivoques au sujet des principes relatifs à la sécurité en Europe et à la coopération humanitaire entre l'Est et l'Ouest;

(*c*) de s'opposer, dans le cadre de la conférence, à la création de nouvelles organisations internationales si les résultats de la conférence ne fournissent pas une justification précise pour la création de tels organes, et d'étudier dans ce contexte la possibilité d'utiliser les structures du Conseil de l'Europe comme cadre de concertation pour la surveillance des suites de la conférence dans certains domaines, par exemple le domaine culturel.

11. RESOLUTION 578[2]
RELATIVE A LA SITUATION EN GRECE

L'Assemblée,

1. Rappelant sa Résolution 558 (janvier 1974), dans laquelle elle ex-

---

[1] *Discussion par l'Assemblée* le 27 septembre 1974 (13e séance) (voir Doc. 3478, rapport de la commission des questions politiques).
Texte adopté par l'Assemblée le 27 septembre 1974 (13e séance).

[2] *Discussion par l'Assemblée* le 27 septembre 1974 (12e et 13e séances) (voir Doc. 3492, rapport de la commission des questions politiques).
Texte adopté par l'Assemblée le 27 septembre 1974 (13e séance).

10. RECOMMENDATION 739[1]
ON THE CONFERENCE ON SECURITY AND CO-OPERATION IN EUROPE – PROSPECTS AND CONSEQUENCES FOR EUROPE

The Assembly,

1. Welcoming the holding of the Conference on Security and Co-operation in Europe, which should give formal sanction at European level to a *de facto* democratisation of international affairs, and whose primary aim should be to consolidate peace and co-operation in Europe on the basis of the rule of law and the common heritage of civilisation and freedom of the European nations;

2. Recalling the statement of its basic position in Recommendation 692 (1973);

3. Deploring the inadequate state of knowledge among the public in Western states about the current second phase of the negotiations in Geneva;

4. Bearing in mind the present stage of negotiations, and considering that the Council of Europe should make known its position before completion of their second phase;

5. Considering that a policy of détente in Europe should find expression in human terms, and produce real benefit for the populations of all European states;

6. Considering that peace and security in Europe cannot but be strengthened by the improvement of communications between Europeans and by a reduction in ideological tension,

7. Recommends that the Committee of Ministers:

(*a*) continue its intergovernmental consultations and its exchanges of views with the Assembly on the Conference on Security and Co-operation in Europe and on the progress of co-operation between Eastern and Western Europe;

(*b*) agree to a position of principle according to which the member states of the Council of Europe:

i will harmonise their action during the final stage of the second phase of the conference in order that the terms of reference of the conference, as determined by the final recommendations of the preparatory meeting in Helsinki, will be substantially carried out;

ii will insist that before the conclusion of the conference the ambiguities over the principles relating to security in Europe and to humanitarian co-operation between East and West will be dispelled;

(*c*) oppose the setting up in connection with the conference of any additional international organisations not specifically warranted by its outcome and, in this context, investigate the possibility of using the Council of Europe machinery for co-ordinating supervision of the follow-up to the conference in fields such as culture.

11. RESOLUTION 578[2]
ON THE SITUATION IN GREECE

The Assembly,

1. Recalling its Resolution 558 (January 1974), in which it expressed

---

[1] *Assembly debate* on 27 September 1974 (13th Sitting) (see Doc. 3478, report of the Political Affairs Committee).

Text adopted by the Assembly on 27 September 1974 (13th Sitting).

[2] *Assembly debate* on 27 September 1974 (12th and 13th Sittings) (see Doc. 3492, report of the Political Affairs Committee).

Text adopted by the Assembly on 27 September 1974 (13th Sitting).

primait le souhait de pouvoir de nouveau accueillir la Grèce au Conseil de l'Europe dès le retour de ce pays à la démocratie, et sa Résolution 573 (juillet 1974), où elle se félicitait du remplacement de la dictature militaire grecque par un gouvernement civil;

2. Approuvant et encourageant vivement les efforts faits par le Gouvernement grec en vue de restaurer les droits de l'homme et la prééminence du droit, de mettre en oeuvre une constitution démocratique et d'organiser des élections libres en novembre 1974,

3. Exprime la conviction que la Grèce, qui a été un membre du Conseil de l'Europe, répondra ainsi bientôt aux conditions statutaires qui lui restent à remplir pour redevenir membre du Conseil de l'Europe, notamment en ce qui concerne les élections parlementaires libres;

4. Note avec satisfaction que son Président s'est déclaré prêt, dès qu'un nouveau Parlement aura été élu en Grèce, à convoquer d'urgence la Commission Permanente pour qu'elle puisse donner, conformément à la Résolution statutaire (51) 30, son avis sur la réadmission de la Grèce au Conseil de l'Europe, comme le demande la Résolution (74) 27 du Comité des Ministres.

12. RECOMMANDATION 740[1]
RELATIVE A LA SITUATION AU PORTUGAL

L'Assemblée,

1. Suivant avec la plus grande attention l'évolution de la situation au Portugal;

2. Ayant entendu M. Soares, ministre des Affaires étrangères du Portugal,

3. Formule le vif espoir que le processus de démocratisation engagé au Portugal se poursuivra sans heurts et sans entraves, comme cela était le cas depuis le 25 avril 1974;

4. Maintient ses encouragements et son plein soutien à ce processus et à tous ceux qui se sont attelés à cette difficile entreprise;

5. Lance un pressant appel aux gouvernements de tous les Etats démocratiques de l'Europe pour qu'ils apportent d'urgence au Gouvernement provisoire portugais toute l'aide possible sur le plan économique, technologique et technique, afin de faciliter le processus d'un retour à des institutions démocratiques et stables:

6. Recommande au Comité des Ministres de se mettre sans délai en rapport avec les autorités portugaises, en vue de préciser les activités auxquelles le Portugal pourrait, d'ores et déjà, souhaiter participer, à titre permanent ou *ad hoc*, jusqu'au moment où toutes les conditions seront remplies pour qu'il devienne membre de plein droit du Conseil de l'Europe.

E. COMMISSION EUROPEENNE DES DROITS DE L'HOMME

1. MEMBRES DE LA COMMISSION

(*au 31 décembre 1974*)

(Par ordre de préséance)

M. James E. S. FAWCETT, Président
M. Giuseppe SPERDUTI, Vice-Président

[1] *Discussion par l'Assemblée* le 28 septembre 1974 (14e séance) (voir Doc. 3501, projet de recommandation présenté par la commission des pays européens non membres).
Texte adopté par l'Assemblée le 28 septembre 1974 (14é séance).

the wish to welcome Greece back into the Council of Europe as soon as she had returned to democracy, and its Resolution 573 (July 1974), in which it welcomed the replacement of the Greek military dictatorship by a civilian government;

2. Wholeheartedly welcoming and encouraging the recent efforts of the Greek Government towards the restoration of human rights and the rule of law, the installation of a democratic constitution and the announcement of free elections for November 1974,

3. Expresses the conviction that in this way Greece, which was a member state of the Council of Europe, will soon fulfil the remaining statutory requirements for joining the Council of Europe again, particularly the holding of free parliamentary elections;

4. Notes with satisfaction that the President of the Assembly has declared his intention of calling, as soon as a new parliament is elected in Greece, an urgent meeting of the Standing Committee in order that it may give, in accordance with Statutory Resolution (51) 30, its opinion on Greece's readmission to the Council of Europe, as requested in Resolution (74) 27 of the Committee of Ministers.

12. RECOMMENDATION 740[1]
ON THE SITUATION IN PORTUGAL

The Assembly,

1. Following developments in Portugal with the utmost attention;
2. Having heard Mr Soares, Minister for Foreign Affairs of Portugal,
3. Expressed the profound hope that the process of democratisation under way in Portugal will continue smoothly and without hindrance, as has been the case since 25 April 1974;
4. Maintains its encouragement and full support for this process and for all who are engaged in this difficult task;
5. Earnestly appeals to the governments of all democratic European countries to provide the provisional government in Portugal, as a matter of urgency, with all possible economic, technological and technical aid, so as to facilitate the return to democratic and stable institutions;
6. Recommends that the Committee of Ministers approach the Portuguese authorities without delay with a view to ascertaining in what activities Portugal may wish to take part forthwith, on either a permanent or an ad hoc basis, until such time as it qualifies for full membership of the Council of Europe.

E. EUROPEAN COMMISSION OF HUMAN RIGHTS

1. MEMBERS OF THE COMMISSION

(at 31 December 1974)

(in order of precedence)

Mr. James E. S. FAWCETT, President
Mr. Giuseppe SPERDUTI, Vice-President

---

[1] *Assembly debate* on 28 September 1974 (14th Sitting) (see Doc. 3501, draft recommendation presented by the Committee on European Non-Member Countries).
Text adopted by the Assembly on 28 September 1974 (14th Sitting).

M. Felix ERMACORA
M. Michael A. TRIANTAFYLLIDES[1]
M. Felix WELTER
M. Edwin BUSUTTIL
M. Love KELLBERG
M. Bülent DAVER
M. Torkel OPSAHL
M. Kevin MANGAN
M. Jozef CUSTERS
M. Carl Aage NØRGAARD
M. Carel H. F. POLAK
M. Jochen A. FROWEIN
M. Gaukur JÖRUNDSSON
M. René Jean DUPUY

2. STATISTIQUES RELATIVES AUX TRAVAUX DE LA COMMISSION EUROPEENNE DES DROITS DE L'HOMME

	en 1974
Nombre de requêtes enregistrées	445
Nombre de requêtes communiquées aux gouvernements intéressés pour observations à donner sur la recevabilité conformément à l'article 45 du Règlement intérieur de la Commission	21
Nombre de requêtes déclarées recevables	6
Nombre de requêtes déclarées irrecevables et rayées du rôle	394

F. COUR EUROPEENNE DES DROITS DE L'HOMME

1. MEMBRES DE LA COUR

(au 31 décembre 1974)

(Par ordre de préséance)

M. Giorgio BALLADORE-PALLIERI, Président
M. Hermann MOSLER, Vice-Président
M. René CASSIN
M. Alfred VERDROSS
M. Eugène RODENBOURG
M. Mehmed ZEKIA[2]
M. Antoine FAVRE
M. John CREMONA
M. Gérard WIARDA
M. Philip O'DONOGHUE
Mme Helga PEDERSEN
M. Thor H. VILHJALMSSON
M. Sture PETREN
M. Rolv RYSSDAL
M. Ali BOZER
M. Walter J. GANSHOF VAN DER MEERSCH
Sir Gerald FITZMAURICE

[1] M. Triantafyllides continue à siéger comme membre de la Commission en vertu de l'article 22, par. (6) 1.
[2] Conformément aux dispositions de l'article 40, par. 6, première phrase, M. Zekia continue à siéger comme membre titulaire de la Cour, bien que son mandat soit formellement expiré.

Mr. Felix ERMACORA
Mr. Michael A. TRIANTAFYLLIDES[1]
Mr. Felix WELTER
Mr. Edwin BUSUTTIL
Mr. Love KELLBERG
Mr. Bülent DAVER
Mr. Torkel OPSAHL
Mr. Kevin MANGAN
Mr. Jozef CUSTERS
Mr. Carl Aage NØRGAARD
Mr. Carel H. F. POLAK
Mr. Jochen A. FROWEIN
Mr. Gaukur JÖRUNDSSON
Mr. René Jean DUPUY

2. STATISTICS OF THE WORK OF THE EUROPEAN COMMISSION OF HUMAN RIGHTS

	in 1974
Number of applications registered	445
Number of applications communicated to respondent Governments for observations on admissibility under Rule 45 of the Commission's Rules of Procedure	21
Number of applications declared admissible	6
Number of applications declared inadmissible and struck of the list	394

F. EUROPEAN COURT OF HUMAN RIGHTS

1. MEMBERS OF THE COURT

(*at 31 December 1974*)

(in order of precedence)

Mr. Giorgio BALLADORE-PALLIERI, President
Mr. Hermann MOSLER, Vice-President
Mr. René CASSIN
Mr. Alfred VERDROSS
Mr. Eugène RODENBOURG
Mr. Mehmed ZEKIA[2]
Mr. Antoine FAVRE
Mr. John CREMONA
Mr. Gérard WIARDA
Mr. Philip O'DONAGHUE
Mrs. Helga PEDERSEN
Mr. Thor H. VILHJALMSSON
Mr. Sture PETREN
Mr. Rolv RYSSDAL
Mr. Ali BOZER
Mr. Walter J. GANSHOF VAN DER MEERSCH
Sir Gerald FITZMAURICE

---

[1] M. Triantafyllides is still sitting as a member of the Commission in accordance with Article 22, paragraph (6), first sentence.

[2] In accordance with the provision of Article 40 (6), first sentence, Mr. Zekia still sits as a full member of the Court, although his term of office has formally expired.

2. AUDIENCES PUBLIQUES

Au cours de l'année 1974, la Cour européenne des Droits de l'Homme a tenu deux audiences publiques, qui étaient consacrées au débat et au prononcé des arrêts de la Cour dans les affaires suivantes:
- Affaire Neumeister (7 mai 1974)
- Affaire Golder (11 et 12 octobre 1974)

G. ASSEMBLEE PARLEMENTAIRE

BUREAU DE L'ASSEMBLEE

(au 31 décembre 1974)

Président de l'Assemblée parlementaire	M. G. VEDOVATO, Italien
Vice-Présidents	M. X. LEU, Suisse M. R. RADIUS, Français M. R. FLETCHER, Britannique M. T. FEYZIOGLU, Turc M. K. RICHTER, Allemand M. H. LETSCHERT, Néerlandais M. S. ALEMYR, Suédois M. I. GISLASON, Islandais Mme. M. T. GODINACHE-LAMBERT, Belge M. E. COLLINS, Irlandais

Présidence des commissions de l'assemblée:

Commission des questions politiques:	M. K. CZERNETZ (Autrichien)
Commission des questions économiques et du dévéloppement	M. S. ALEMYR (Suédois)
Commission des questions sociales et de la santé:	M. F. GRUSSENMEYER (Français)
Commission des questions juridiques:	M. G. Margue (Luxembourgeois)
Commission de la culture et de l'éducation:	M. F. KARASEK (Autrichien)
Commission de la science et de la technologie:	M. K. RICHTER (Allemand)
Commission de l'aménagement du territoire et des pouvoirs locaux	M. R. RADIUS (Français)
Commission du règlement:	M. P. GRIEVE (Britannique)
Commission de l'agriculture:	M. A. DEQUAE (Belge)
Commission des pays européens non membres:	M. W. HOFER (Suisse)
Commission chargée des relations avec les parlements nationaux et le public:	M. J. HUNT (Britannique)
Commission du budget et du programme de travail intergouvernemental:	M. S. ALBER (Allemand)
Commission de la population et des refugiés:	M. W. RENSCHLER (Suisse)

2. PUBLIC HEARINGS

In the course of 1974, the European Court of Human Rights held two public hearings, which were devoted to the hearing and the pronouncement of the Court's judgments in the following cases:
- Neumeister Case (7 May 1974)
- Golder Case (11 and 12 October 1974)

G. PARLIAMENTARY ASSEMBLY

BUREAU OF THE ASSEMBLY

(at 31 December 1974)

President of the Parliamentary Assembly	Mr. G. Vedovato, Italian
Vice-Presidents	Mr. X. Leu, Swiss Mr. R. Radius, French Mr. R. Fletcher, British Mr. T. Feyzioglu, Turk Mr. K. Richter, German Mr. H. Letschert, Dutch Mr. S. Alemyr, Swedish Mr. I. Gislason, Icelandic Mrs. M. T. Godinache-Lambert, Belgian Mr. E. Collins, Irish

Chairmen of Assembly Committees:

Political Affairs Committee:	Mr. K. Czernetz (Austrian)
Committee on Economic Affairs and Development:	Mr. S. Alemyr (Swedish)
Committee on Social and Health Questions:	Mr. F. Grussenmeyer (French)
Legal Affairs Committee:	Mr. G. Margue (Luxemburger)
Committee on Culture and Education:	Mr. F. Karasek (Austrian)
Committee on Science and Technology:	Mr. K. Richter (German)
Committee on Regional Planning and Authorities:	Mr. R. Radius (French)
Committee on Rules of Procedure:	Mr. P. Grieve (British)
Committee on Agriculture:	Mr. A. Dequae (Belgian)
Committee on European Non-Member Countries:	Mr. W. Hofer (Swiss)
Committee on Parliamentary and Public Relations:	Mr. J. Hunt (British)
Committee on the Budget and the Intergovernmental Work Programme:	Mr. S. Alber (German)
Committee on Population and Refugees:	Mr. W. Renschler (Swiss)

H. REPRESENTANTS PERMANENTS DES ETATS MEMBRES EN 1974

Autriche	M. Heinz LAUBE
Belgique	M. Joseph Jacques LODEWYCK Jusqu'au 9 octobre M. Jean BOUHA
Chypre	M. Polys MODINOS
Danemark	M. Troels MUNK Jusqu'au 14 avril M. ROSENSTAND HANSEN du 15 avril au 15 juillet M. Frode SCHØN
France	M. Albert FEQUANT
Allemagne	Mme E. von PUTTKAMER Jusqu'au 31 mars M. Carl-Heinz LUDERS
Grèce	M. Nicolas KAMBALOURIS depuis le 28 novembre
Islande	M. Arni TRYGGVASON
Irlande	M. Seán Ò HEIDEÀIN
Italie	M. Gherardo CORNAGGIA MEDICI CASTIGLIONI
Luxembourg	M. Paul MERTZ
Malte	M. Carmel MALLIA
Pays-Bas	M. Joseph I. M. WELSING
Norvège	M. Mague REED Jusqu'au 27 mars M. Leif EDWARDSEN
Suède	M. Arne FÄLTHEIM
Suisse	M. Alfred WACKER
Turquie	M. Rahmi GÜMRÜKÇÜOGLU
Royaume-Uni	M. D. J. B. ROBEY Jusqu'au 6 octobre M. Peter Martin FOSTER

I. SECRETARIAT

(à la fin de 1974)

M. G. KAHN-ACKERMANN, Secrétaire Général
M. S. G. SFORZA, Secrétaire Général adjoint
M. S. C. HUNT, Chef de Cabinet du Secrétaire Général

Greffe de l'Assemblée
M. John D. PRIESTMAN, Greffier de l'Assemblée, ayant rang de Secrétaire Général adjoint
M. G. ADINOLFI, Greffier adjoint de l'Assemblée

Affaires administratives
M. A. DAUSSIN, Directeur Général
M. R. CLAMER, Chef de Service, chargé de la Division des Services Techniques et des Conférences

Contrôle financier
M. E. Lucas, Directeur

H. PERMANENT REPRESENTATIVES OF MEMBER STATES IN 1974

Austria	Mr. Heinz LAUBE
Belgium	Mr. Joseph Jacques LODEWYCK Until 9 October Mr. Jean BOUHA
Cyprus	Mr. Polys MODINOS
Denmark	Mr. Troels MUNK Until 14 April Mr. ROSENSTAND HANSEN From 15 April to 15 July Mr. Frode SCHØN
France	Mr. Albert FEQUANT
Germany	Mrs. E. von PUTTKAMER Until 31 March Mr. Carl-Heinz LUDERS
Greece	Mr. Nicolas KAMBALOURIS Since 28 November
Iceland	Mr. Arni TRYGGVASON
Ireland	Mr. Seán Ò HEIDEÀIN
Italy	Mr. Gherardo CORNAGGIA MEDICI CASTIGLIONI
Luxembourg	Mr. Paul MERTZ
Malta	Mr. Carmel MALLIA
Netherlands	Mr. Joseph I. M. WELSING
Norvay	Mr. Mague REED Until 27 March Mr. Leif EDWARDSEN
Sweden	Mr. Arne FÄLTHEIM
Switzerland	Mr. Alfred WACKER
Turkey	Mr. Rahmi GÜMRÜKÇÜOGLU
United-Kingdom	Mr. D. J. B. ROBEY Until 6 October Mr. Peter Martin FOSTER

I. SECRETARIAT

(at the end of 1974)

Mr. G. KAHN-ACKERMANN, Secretary General
Mr. S. G. SFORZA, Deputy Secretary General
Mr. S. C. HUNT, Head of the Secretary General's Private Office

Office of the Clerk of the Assembly
Mr John D. PRIESTMAN, Clerk of the Assembly, with rank of Deputy Secretary General
Mr. G. ADINOLFI, Deputy Clerk of the Assembly

Administration
Mr. A. DAUSSIN, Director General
Mr. R. CLAMER, Head of Department, in charge of the Works and Conferences Division

Financial Control
Mr. E. LUCAS, Director

Affaires politiques
M. H. LELEU, Directeur
M. H. KLEBES, Secrétaire du Comité des Ministres

Affaires économiques et sociales
M. F. H. SUR, Directeur
M. O. MESSER, Directeur adjoint
M. F. CATALANO, Directeur adjoint

Enseignement, Affaires culturelles et scientifiques
M. N. BORCH-JACOBSEN, Directeur
M. H. BEESLEY, Directeur adjoint, Chef du Département I
M. L. de ROULET, Directeur adjoint, Chef du Département II

Environnement et pouvoirs locaux
M. S. RENBORG, Directeur
M. G. BALOUP, Directeur adjoint

Affaires juridiques
M. H. GOLSONG, Directeur
M. R. MULLER, Directeur adjoint

Presse et information
M. G. LÖFDAHL, Directeur

Droits de l'Homme (Direction)
M. R. MULLER, a.i.

Secrétariat de la Commission Européenne des Droits de l'Homme
M. A. B. McNULTY, Secrétaire de la Commission

Greffe de la Cour Européenne des Droits de l'Homme
M. M. A. EISSEN, Greffier de la Cour

Political Affairs
Mr. H. LELEU, Director
Mr. H. KLEBES, Secretary of the Committee of Ministers

Economic and Social Affairs
Mr. F. H. SUR, Director
Mr. O. MESSER, Deputy Director
Mr. F. CATALANO, Deputy Director

Education, Cultural and Scientific Affairs
Mr. N. BORCH-JACOBSEN, Director
Mr. H. BEESLEY, Deputy Director, Head of Department I
Mr. L. de ROULET, Deputy Director, Head of Department II

Environment and Local Authorities
Mr. S. RENBORG, Director
Mr. G. BALOUP, Deputy Director

Legal Affairs
Mr. H. GOLSONG, Director
Mr. R. MULLER, Deputy Director

Press and Information
Mr. G. LÖFDAHL, Director

Human Rights (Directorate)
Mr. R. MULLER, a.i.

Secretariat of the European Commission on Human Rights
Mr. A. B. McNULTY, Secretary of the Commission

Registry of the European Court of Human Rights
Mr. M. A. EISSEN, Registrar of the Court.

CHAPITRE VI

COMMISSION INTERNATIONALE DE L'ETAT CIVIL

A. CHRONOLOGIE 1974

La Commission Internationale de l'Etat Civil se réunit deux fois par an, l'Assemblée Générale en septembre, le Bureau en avril et lors de la réunion de l'Assemblée Générale.

En 1974 les réunions ont eu lieu du 13 au 15 mars à Francfort (Bureau) et du 10 au 13 septembre à Paris (Bureau et Assemblée Générale).

B. TEXTES FONDAMENTAUX

Statuts et Conventions: voir Vol. II p. 462; Vol. III p. 318; Vol. IV p. 328; Vol. V p. 404; Vol. VI p. 260; Vol. IX p. 342; Vol. X p. 696; Vol. XIII pp. 402, 405, 408; Vol. XIV p. 256; Vol. XV p. 398.

C. ORGANISATION

(au 31 mars 1975)

Président: M. le Professeur MONACO
Secrétaire Général: M. le Professeur SIMITIS

La Commission Internationale de l'Etat Civil a une section nationale dans chaque Etat adhérent. Les sections nationales font fonction de commission permanente pour les affaires de l'état civil dans chacun des pays.

La Commission compte actuellement douze sections nationales, à savoir:

Rép. Féd. d'Allemagne:	*Président:* M. le professeur M. FERID
Autriche	*Président:* M. le professeur F. SCHWIND
Belgique	*Président:* M. P. VAN LANGENAEKEN
Espagne	
France	*Président:* M. Guy DELTEL
Grèce	*Président:* M. ALEXANDROPOULOS
Italie	
Luxembourg	*Président:* M. Henri DELVAUX
Pays-Bas	*Président:* M. VAN RIJN VAN ALKEMADE
Portugal	*Président:* M. Joao de DEUS PINHEIRO FARINHA
Suisse	*Président:* M. Ernst GÖTZ
Turquie	*Président:* M. ESENER

Adresse: 6 Frankfurt/Main, Université, Senckenberganlage 31, Rép. Féd. d'Allemagne.

Téléphone: (0611) 798 2186.

CHAPTER VI

INTERNATIONAL COMMISSION ON CIVIL STATUS

A. CHRONOLOGY, 1974

The International Commission on Civil Status meets twice a year, the General Assembly in September and the Bureau in April and at the same time as the General Assembly.

In 1974 the meetings took place from 13 to 15 March in Frankfurt (Bureau) and from 10 to 13 September in Paris (Bureau and General Assembly).

B. BASIC TEXTS

Statute and Conventions: see vol. II p. 462; Vol. III p. 318; Vol. IV p. 328; Vol. V p. 404; Vol. VI p. 260; Vol. IX p. 342; Vol. X p. 696; Vol. XIII pp. 402, 405, 408; Vol. XIV p. 256; Vol. XV p. 398.

C. ORGANISATION

(at 31 March 1975)

President: Professor MONACO
Secretary General: Professor SIMITIS

The International Commission on Civil Status has a national section in each member State. The national sections act as standing commissions for matters of civil status in each country.

The Commission has at present twelve national sections:

Fed. Rep. of Germany:	*Chairman:* Professor M. FERID
Austria	*Chairman:* Professor F. SCHWIND
Belgium	*Chairman:* Mr. P. VAN LANGENAEKEN
France	*Chairman:* Mr. Guy DELTEL
Greece	*Chairman:* Mr. ALEXANDROPOULOS
Italy	
Luxembourg	*Chairman:* Mr. Henri DELVAUX
Netherlands	*Chairman:* Mr. VAN RIJN VAN ALKEMADE
Portugal	*Chairman:* Mr. Joao de DEUS PINHEIRO FARINHA
Switzerland	*Chairman:* Mr. Ernst GÖTZ
Turkey	*Chairman:* Mr. ESENER
Spain	

Address: 6 Frankfurt/Main, Université, Senckenberganlage 31, Fed. Rep. of Germany.

Telephone: (0611) 798 2186.

CHAPITRE VII

LES COMMUNAUTES EUROPEENNES

(*Extraits du Huitième Rapport Général sur l'Activité des Communautés Européennes*)

A. EVOLUTION DE LA COMMUNAUTE EUROPEENNE EN 1974

A. SITUATION POLITIQUE GENERALE DANS LA COMMUNAUTE EUROPEENNE

1. Au début de l'année 1974, la Communauté européenne s'est trouvée en situation de crise. Des difficultés économiques et politiques, surgies de toutes parts, ont trouvé une Communauté insuffisamment préparée pour y faire face. Reculs ou refus devant la mise en oeuvre des orientations des „sommets" de Paris et de Copenhague ont marqué le début de l'année: impossibilité de mettre en place le Fonds européen de développement régional, hésitation devant le passage à la deuxième étape de l'Union économique et monétaire, désaccord fondamental sur la politique à suivre pour faire face à la crise énergétique dans le monde et dans la Communauté.

Ainsi, à la recherche de l'intérêt commun par l'application stricte des dispositions et procédures prévues par les traités s'est substituée une tendance à la coopération basée sur la réalisation d'un intérêt national.

La réalité de la politique nationale dans les États membres, accentuée par des changements gouvernementaux entraînant des mutations parfois profondes, a favorisé ce repli sur soi-même. Ce n'est que lentement que la Communauté s'est relevée de cette dangereuse situation.

2. La Commission, dès le 31 janvier, a adressé aux chefs de gouvernement, et à travers eux, aux citoyens de la Communauté, une déclaration sur l'état de la Communauté. Dans cette déclaration, la Commission a insisté sur une relance de la construction communautaire, sur la nécessité de donner une réponse commune au défi commun par une convergence de politiques nationales et la définition de politiques communes, et sur l'urgence d'une amélioration des institutions indispensable pour assurer un fonctionnement efficace de la Communauté.

Le Parlement a fait siennes les préoccupations de la Commission. Au début de la session de février, le président du Parlement, M. Berkhouwer, dans une déclaration sur la situation de la Communauté, a souligné que le point de non-retour n'était pas dépassé, la construction européenne reposant exclusivement sur une volonté commune. Dans une résolution sur l'état actuel de la Communauté, le Parlement a estimé que l'unité de l'Europe ne pourra être réalisée que si les institutions communautaires sont mises en mesure de mener sans retard une politique fondée sur une véritable solidarité européenne, et a lancé un appel pressant aux institutions, aux gouvernements et aux forces politiques des États membres pour qu'ils éliminent les obstacles qui compromettent l'évolution vers l'Union européenne en apportant une solution aux problèmes immédiats.

Le 2 avril, une déclaration commune du président du Conseil et du président de la Commission sur l'état de la Communauté a été présentée au Conseil par le président en exercice. La déclaration souligne la nécessité de garantir l'acquis communautaire, de prévenir la désintégration et de relancer la Communauté notamment dans les secteurs pour lesquels d'importantes décisions sont en attente. Se limitant volontairement aux ques-

CHAPTER VII

EUROPEAN COMMUNITIES

(*Extracts from the Eighth General Report on the Activities of the European Communities*)

A. DEVELOPMENT OF THE EUROPEAN COMMUNITY IN 1974

A. GENERAL POLITICAL SITUATION IN THE EUROPEAN COMMUNITY

1. Early in 1974 a crisis had developed in the Community. Economic and political difficulties had arisen in many areas, and the Community was not sufficiently equipped to cope with these properly. The year opened with reticence or refusal as regards the implementation of the policy guidelines emerging from the Paris and Copenhagen Summit Conferences: it was impossible to set up the European Regional Development Fund, there was hesitation over the transition to the second stage of economic and monetary union, and there was total disagreement on the policy to be followed in dealing with the energy crisis besetting the worlds and the Community.

In place of endeavours to act for the common benefit by strictly applying the arrangements and procedures laid down in the Treaties, there emerged a trend towards inter-State cooperation based on the achievement of national interests.

In the Member States, difficult political conditions were rendered more delicate by changes of government, some of which involved far-reaching innovation, and this was a factor encouraging a mood of introversion. It took a long time for the Community to recover from this dangerous situation.

2. On 31 January the Commission addressed a Declaration on the state of the Community to the Heads of Government, and through them to the Community's citizens. The Declaration stressed the need to get Europe moving again and to evolve a common response to the challenge facing us all, by bringing national policies closer into line and by working out common policies; it emphasized the urgent need for an improvement in the functioning of its institutions, without which the Community could not work efficiently.

Parliament shared the Commission's concern. Its President, Mr Berkhouwer, opened the February session with a statement on the current situation in the Community, stressing that the point of no return had not yet been reached; the construction of Europe depended exclusively on a common resolve. In a Resolution on the present situation in the Community the Parliament declared that the unity of Europe could only be realized if the Community institutions were enabled to pursue forthwith a policy founded on real European solidarity and launched an urgent appeal to the institutions of the Community, the governments and political forces in the Member States to eliminate obstacles to progress towards European union by providing a solution to the most pressing problems.

On 2 April the Council received a Joint Declaration from its President and the President of the Commission on the state of the Community. This Declaration stressed the need to consolidate what the Community had already achieved, to prevent all possibility of disintegration and to get the Community moving again, particularly in areas where major decisions had to be made. Deliberately covering concrete issues only, the Declaration tions concrètes, la déclaration mentionne les points également évoqués par la Commission et le Parlement, insiste particulièrement sur la nécessité de donner vie aux principaux instruments d'une politique communautaire pour lutter ensemble contre l'inflation, et fait une large place au problème de l'amélioration des mécanismes de décision.

Par ailleurs, la situation de la Communauté a fait l'objet de plusieurs grands débats au Parlement lors de presque chacune des sessions plénières de l'année 1974.

3. Comme pour illustrer la gravité de la situation, deux faits politiques importants étaient entre temps venus s'ajouter au dossier.

Tous les États membres avaient décidé de participer à Washington, au mois de février, à la conférence sur l'énergie, organisée à l'initiative du gouvernement des États-Unis. Des efforts avaient été entrepris pour que la Communauté puisse participer aux travaux en tant que telle.

Une décision en ce sens fut prise par le Conseil, mais des divergences de vues se sont fait jour pendant la conférence, un État membre n'ayant pu se rallier à l'établissement d'un groupe de coordination particulier chargé de préparer un programme d'action d'ensemble, en l'absence d'une politique énérgétique communautaire.

Le 1er avril, le secrétaire d'État britannique aux affaires étrangères et au Commonwealth a fait une déclaration au Conseil concernant la politique du gouvernement britannique, nouvellement venu au pouvoir, à l'égard de la Communauté. Dans cette déclaration, M. Callaghan a confirmé les termes du manifeste électoral du parti travailliste qui, notamment, exige des modifications majeures de la politique agricole commune, demande un ,,financement plus équitable'' du budget communautaire, voit la solution des problèmes monétaires dans un cadre mondial et réclame que le Parlement britannique conserve ,,les pouvoirs sur l'économie britannique.''

4. L'attente de développements politiques internes avait contribué assez largement aux difficultés. Aussi, la clarification politique intervenue dans plusieurs États membres, par rapport à la situation existant au début de l'année, a-t-elle permis aux gouvernements de reprendre la discussion des problèmes européens avec une assurance nouvelle. Une reprise progressive de l'activité communautaire à partir du mois de juin en est résultée.

5. Ainsi les délibérations du Conseil, de juin 1974, ont permis de définir les modalités d'examen des problèmes posés par le Royaume-Uni. La politique de la coopération au développement et de l'association a été marquée par les importants résultats de la conférence de Kingston. Le Conseil a entamé la discussion sur l'amélioration de ses procédures. La Commission avait pris l'initiative de ces développements et elle a assumé ses responsabilités dans la révision des mesures commerciales et monétaires italiennes.

A l'automne, sont intervenus un accord sur le lancement d'emprunts communautaires pour faire face à la hausse des prix pétroliers ainsi que des décisions en matière de protection de l'environnement et de la politique commerciale à l'égard des pays à commerce d'État. Un accord a également été atteint sur d'importantes mesures à prendre pour faire face à la situation conjoncturelle en agriculture.

Le problème de la politique énergétique communautaire a été abordé dans un esprit positif. Sa complexité a cependant rendu malaisé de trouver la voie vers une formule acceptable englobant tous les aspects du problème, mais certains volets ont reçu un début de solution en cours d'année.

Un accord de principe s'est dégagé de réunir vers la fin de l'année la conférence tripartite avec les partenaires sociaux.

Vers l'extérieur, la Communauté s'est déclarée disposée à engager des conversations avec le Conseil d'assistance économique mutuelle (CAEM) pour préparer une éventuelle collaboration.

La cadence des réunions du Conseil, qui s'était accélérée depuis mai 1974, confirme qu'un mouvement s'est engagé vers une reprise de l'activité des institutions communautaires.

mentioned points also raised by the Commission and Parliament and particularly underlined the need to vitalize the main instruments of Community policy so that inflation could be tackled by a united front; considerable attention was paid in the Declaration to the need to improve decision-making machinery.

The state of the Community was the subject of major debates in Parliament at virtually all the 1974 plenary sessions.

3. As if to illustrate the gravity of the situation, two major political events had occurred in the meantime.

In February all the Member States decided to attend the Washington Energy Conference convened by the United States Administration. Efforts were made to enable the Commission itself to take part in the Conference.

A Council decision was taken for this purpose, but at the Conference itself differences of opinion arose when one Member State, in the absence of a Community energy policy, felt unable to support the establishment of a special coordinating group with the task of preparing an overall action programme.

On 1 April, following a change of Government in the United Kingdom, the Secretary of State for Foreign and Commonwealth Affairs made a statement to the Council on the new Government's policy on the Community. Mr Callaghan confirmed certain points in the Labour Party election manifesto calling, among other things, for major changes in the common agricultural policy, "fairer methods of financing the Community budget," solutions to monetary problems in a worldwide framework and the retention by Westminster of "powers over the British economy."

4. The Community's difficulties early in the year had been considerably aggravated by the need to await political developments in the countries. Conversely, once the political situation had become clearer in several Member States the governments were in a position to tackle European problems with renewed vigour. As a result, Community activities gradually gathered momentum again from June onwards.

5. In June the Council considered what procedures it should adopt for the examination of problems raised by the United Kingdom. The results of the Kingston Conference brought a major contribution to the policy on development cooperation and on association. The Council began discussing ways of improving its procedures. The Commission had taken the initiative in these areas, and it also discharged to the full its responsibilities in the matter of the review of the trade and monetary measures which Italy had adopted.

In the autumn, agreement was reached on raising Community loans to help face up to oil price increases and decisions were taken on environmental protection and on a policy on trade with the State-trading countries. Agreement was also reached on an important round of measures to deal with the current situation in agriculture.

The problem of the Community energy policy was tackled in a constructive spirit. The problem was too complex for an acceptable formula covering all aspects to be found easily, but a number of points were dealt with by the end of the year.

Towards the end of the year there was agreement on the principle of holding a tripartite conference with the two sides of industry.

In its external relations, the Community has expressed willingness to open talks with the Council for Mutual Economic Assistance (Comecon) with a view to preparing for cooperation.

The rhythm of Council meetings, which had been picking up since May, confirmed that the Community institutions were intensifying their activities again.

Deuxième réunion des chefs de gouvernement à Paris

6. C'est dans ces conditions qu'est intervenue la réunion des chefs de gouvernement des neuf États de la Communauté qui s'est tenue à Paris les 9 et 10 décembre 1974, avec la participation du président de la Commission. Le communiqué final publié à l'issue de la conférence[1] reflète une discussion approfondie sur les problèmes de l'heure, et certaines décisions ont pu être prises. Le jugement d'ensemble porté sur la conférence, à l'issue de celle-ci, par les participants a été généralement positif.

La première réaction du Parlement au cours d'un débat lors de la session de décembre a été également positive, mais plusieurs orateurs ont souligné la nécessité pour les institutions de la Communauté de continuer sur l'impulsion donnée. Au nom du Conseil, M. FitzGerald a, devant le Parlement, estimé qu'un progrès considérable a été fait, en rassemblant dans un seul cadre les problèmes politique et économique à l'intérieur et à l'extérieur. Il a souligné l'importance que revêt à son avis l'engagement pris par sept pays de procéder à l'élection directe du Parlement et à l'accroissement des pouvoirs de ce dernier. Il a constaté un certain progrès vers l'identification, en la rendant plus spécifique, de la notion d'Union européenne. M. FitzGerald a noté l'issue positive des discussions, notamment en matière économique et financière, régionale et énergétique. Enfin, il a remarqué que le résultat de la conférence a encouragé tous ceux qui sont soucieux de voir la Communauté rester à Neuf.

De l'avis de la Commission, la réunion des chefs de gouvernement, qui avait des objectifs limités, a conduit à des résultats limités, mais positifs, qui ouvrent des perspectives de progrès pour le développement de la Communauté. Elle attache de l'importance à des réunions futures des chefs de gouvernement dans le cadre du Conseil et compte veiller à la pleine application de la décision sur l'abandon de la pratique de l'unanimite. Quant aux questions de fond, la Commission a plus particulièrement mis en lumière l'importance des engagements pris en vue d'une meilleure convergence des politiques économiques des États membres.

De l'avis de la Commission, il est nécessaire que la volonté exprimée par les chefs de gouvernement, en matière énergétique, conduise maintenant à la définition d'une véritable politique énergétique commune.

7. Depuis la réunion des chefs de gouvernement, le Conseil a tenu des réunions qui ont confirmé l'impulsion donnée.

Plus particulièrement dans le domaine de l'énergie, le Conseil a adopté, sur proposition de la Commission, d'une part, une résolution sur les objectifs de la politique énergétique communautaire pour 1985 et, d'autre part, les premières décisions d'application dans le cadre de la nouvelle stratégie en matière de politique énergétique, ainsi que certaines autres décisions. La Commission, pour sa part, a décidé de participer aux travaux de l'Agence internationale de l'énergie, au même titre qu'elle est associée aux autres travaux de l'OCDE.

D'une façon générale, la fin de l'année 1974 voit ainsi apparaître une Communauté en mesure d'apporter de vraies solutions aux problèmes.

Préparation du rapport sur l'Union européenne

8. Au cours de l'année 1974, les travaux préparatoires du rapport sur l'Union européenne demandé par les conférences au sommet de Paris et de Copenhague se sont poursuivis au sein des institutions communautaires.

Dans une ***résolution sur l'Union européenne*** adoptée le 17 octobre 1974, le *Parlement* s'est engagé à présenter son rapport sur l'Union européenne

---

[1] Voir ci-dessous pour le texte intégral.

Second meeting of the Heads of Government in Paris

6. This, then, was the situation when the Heads of Government of the nine Member States met in Paris on 9 and 10 December, at a meeting in which the President of the Commission also took part. The final communiqué published after the conference[1] shows that there was detailed discussion on current issues and that a number of decisions were taken. Those present looked back on the conference in a generally favourably light.

Parliament's initial reaction expressed in a debate at the December session was also favourable, although a number of members stressed the need for the Community institutions to make the most of the new impetus provided by the Paris meeting. Addressing Parliament on behalf of the Council, Mr FitzGerald felt that considerable progress had been made in that all the economic and political problems of the day, both internal and external, had been dealt with in an all-embracing framework. He drew attention to the importance he attached to the undertaking given by seven countries to have Parliament elected directly and to increase its powers. He noted that progress had been made towards deciding what European union meant, particularly by clarifying certain specific aspects. He noted that the discussions had produced positive results, particularly on economic, financial, regional and energy policy. Finally, he remarked that all those who wished the Community to remain a Community of nine had been encouraged by the results of the conference.

The Commission feels that this meeting, which had limited objectives, had produced limited results, but that these are positive in that they open the way to further progress in developing the Community. It attaches importance to the meetings which the Heads of Government are to hold in the future in a Council framework and intends to ensure that the decision to give up unanimous voting is fully applied. On substantive matters, it has particularly highlighted the importance of the undertaking by the Member States to achieve a fuller convergence of their economic policies.

The Commission believes that the determination of the Heads of Government to act together on energy problems must now lead to the elaboration of a genuine common energy policy.

7. Since Paris, the Council has held meetings the results of which confirmed the strength of the new impetus.

On energy in particular, the Council has adopted the Commission's proposals for a resolution on the 1985 objectives of the Community energy policy, for the first decisions implementing the new energy policy strategy and for a number of other decisions. The Commission has decided that it will take part in the work of the International Energy Agency just as it is involved in other activities within the OECD framework.

In general terms, then, the end of 1974 saw a Community at last able to provide real solutions to the problems confronting it.

Preparation of the report on European Union

8. In 1974 the Community institutions continued their work on preparing the report on European Union called for by the Paris and Copenhagen Summit Conferences.

In a *Resolution on European Union* adopted on 17 October 1974 Parliament undertook to draw up and submit its report on European Union

[1] The full text of the final communiqué is given below.

avant le 30 juin 1975 et se déclare prêt à établir en étroite coopération avec les autres institutions communautaires un rapport unique pour l'échéance fixée par le sommet de Paris.

A la suite de la conférence au sommet de Copenhague qui avait décidé l'accélération des travaux nécessaires à la définition de l'Union européenne, le *Conseil*, le 5 février 1974, a chargé le Comité des représentants permanents d'entreprendre sans délai la préparation du projet de rapport du Conseil. Ces travaux ont abouti à la rédaction d'un *questionnaire relatif à la mise en place de l'Union européenne*. Le Conseil, le 25 juin 1974, l'a approuvé et a décidé de le transmettre aux gouvernements des États membres et aux autres institutions communautaires.

La *Commission* a poursuivi et approfondi ses travaux sur l'Union européenne au cours de l'année 1974. Elle souhaite les conduire à leur terme en recherchant la convergence avec le Parlement.

La *Cour de justice*, dans un document transmis le 15 juillet 1974 aux autres institutions communautaires, a exposé ses suggestions sur l'Union européene.

Le *Comité économique et social*, dans son avis du 28 mars 1974 sur la place et le rôle du Comité dans le système institutionnel communautaire et la perspective d'une évolution de celui-ci, s'est également prononcé sur l'Union européenne.

Les *chefs de gouvernement*, réunis à Paris les 9 et 10 décembre 1974, ont estimé qu'il est opportun que les Neuf se mettent d'accord au plus tôt sur une conception d'ensemble de l'Union européenne. A cet égard et conformément aux demandes de la conférence présidentielle de Paris d'octobre 1972, ils ont confirmé l'importance qu'ils attachent aux rapports des institutions de la Communauté. Ils ont demandé au Parlement, à la Commission et à la Cour de justice d'avancer le dépôt de leurs rapports avant la fin du premies semestre 1975. Ils sont convenus de charges M. Tindemans, premier ministre belge, de faire aux chefs de gouvernement, avant la fin de 1975, un rapport de synthèse sur la base des rapports des institutions, et des consultations qu'il mènera avec les gouvernements et les milieux représentatifs de l'opinion publique au sein de la Communauté.

B. COOPERATION POLITIQUE

9. Les travaux de la coopération politique des Neuf visant à harmoniser leurs points de vue en matière de politique internationale se sont poursuivis en 1974, conformément aux dispositions du deuxième rapport sur la coopération politique. En adoptant ce rapport, les gouvernements étaient convenus de se consulter sur toutes les questions importantes de politique étrangère et de dégager les priorités dans le respect des principes suivants: la consultation a pour objet la recherche de lignes communes dans des cas concrets; les sujets doivent toucher aux intérêts de l'Europe, sur notre continent ou en dehors de celui-ci, dans des domaines où une prise de position commune devient nécessaire ou souhaitable.

Les institutions de la Communauté avaient été associées progressivement à plusieurs des activités de la coopération politique, en partant des décisions prises par les gouvernements en 1970 et 1973. Depuis 1974, la Commission a été invitée à participer de plus en plus largement à ces activités; elle est maintenant intégralement associée à pratiquement tous les travaux de la coopération politique.

Comme le président en exercice du Conseil et de la coopération politique l'a souligné devant le Parlement, les liens entre les deux domaines de la Communauté et de la coopération politique sont évidents et le deviennent de plus en plus. Il s'agit en effet de deux aspects extrêmement liés de l'Union européenne en train de se construire.

by 30 June 1975 and declared its readiness to draw up, in close cooperation with the other Community institutions, a single report on European Union by the date set by the Heads of Government at the October 1972 Paris Summit Conference.

Following the decision at the Copenhagen Summit Conference to speed up the work on defining European Union, the *Council* instructed the Committee of Permanent Representatives on 5 February 1974 to begin work without delay on preparing the draft Council Report. This led to the drafting of a *questionnaire of the establishment of European Union*. On 25 June the Council approved the questionnaire and decided to send it to the Member Governments and to the other Community institutions.

The *Commission* has continued and broadened its work on European Union. It hopes to work more and more closely with Parliament as this project nears completion.

The *Court of Justice* set out its suggestions on European Union in a paper sent to the other Community institutions on 15 July.

In its Opinion of 28 March 1974 on the position and function of the Committee in the Community institutional system and on the outlook for future developments in the system, the *Economic and Social Committee* also set out its views on European Union.

At their meeting in Paris on 9 and 10 December, the *Heads of Government* stated that the Nine should agree as soon as possible on an overall view of European Union. As requested by the October 1972 Summit Conference, they confirmed the importance which they attached to the reports by the Community institutions. They asked Parliament, the Commission and the Court of Justice to bring forward the deadline for their reports to the end of June 1975. They instructed Mr Tindemans, Belgian Prime Minister, to produce a summary report for the Heads of Government by the end of 1975, on the basis of the reports by the institutions, consultations with the Member Governments and soundings of public opinion within the Community.

B. POLITICAL COOPERATION

9. Work on political cooperation to harmonize the nine Member States' approaches to international relations continued this year as envisaged by the second report on political cooperation. In adopting this report, the Governments agreed to consult each other on all major questions of foreign policy and to establish priorities on the basis of the following principles: the aim of the consultations was to produce a common line in individual cases; the subjects of consultation should be related to the interests of Europe, whether on this continent or elsewhere in the world, in areas where a common approach was desirable or necessary.

The Community institutions had gradually been involved in several areas of political cooperation, following the decisons taken by the Governments in 1970 and 1973. In 1974 the Commission was invited to play an increasing role in this work; it is now fully involved in almost all the political cooperation work being carried out.

As the President of the Council, who also takes the chair at the political cooperation meetings, stressed in a statement to Parliament, the relationship between the Community as such and the political cooperation system is already clear and is becoming more and more so. These indeed are the two corner stones of the European union towards which we are now moving.

The steady development of political cooperation and the general agree-

Le développement constant de la coopération politique et le consensus en matière de consultations ont contribué à l'examen, dans un esprit communautaire, de plusieurs dossiers. Ainsi, les représentants de la Commission ont participé aux travaux de la Conférence sur la sécurité et la coopération en Europe, selon la formule convenue au Conseil, au sein de la Commission économique et de ses sous-commissions.

Le dialogue euro-arabe a été engagé et des rencontres préparatoires ont eu lieu. Les problèmes politiques méditerranéens ont été examinés, notamment les développements au Portugal, en Grèce et à Chypre. La concertation des positions à prendre dans les débats au sein de l'organisation des Nations unies a fait l'objet de discussions.

Lors de la séance du 16 octobre 1974, le président en exercice des ministres des affaires étrangères a présenté au Parlement la quatrième communication annuelle sur les progrès dans les domaines de la coopération politique.

Les colloques trimestriels entre les ministres et la commission politique du Parlement ont eu lieu le 2 avril à Bonn, le 11 juin à Strasbourg, le 18 septembre à Paris et le 3 décembre à Bruxelles.

10. Les chefs de gouvernement, lors de leur réunion tenue à Paris les 9 et 10 décembre 1974, ont réaffirmé leur volonté, dans la perspective de l'unification européenne, d'arrêter progressivement des positions communes et de mettre en oeuvre une diplomatie concertée dans tous les domaines de la politique internationale qui affectent les intérêts de la Communauté européenne. Ils ont décidé que la présidence exerce la fonction de porte-parole des Neuf et se fait leur interprète sur le plan diplomatique, et qu'elle veille à ce que la concertation nécessaire ait toujours lieu en temps utile.

Compte tenu du rôle croissant de la coopération politique dans la construction européenne, les chefs de gouvernement ont souligné l'importance d'associer plus étroitement le Parlement européen à ses travaux, entre autres par voie de réponse aux questions adressées à la présidence par les parlementaires sur les activités de la coopération politique.

B. TEXTES FONDAMENTAUX

1. DISCOURS PRONONCE LE 18 FEVRIER 1975 DEVANT LE PARLEMENT EUROPEEN PAR M. FRANÇOIS-XAVIER ORTOLI, PRESIDENT DE LA COMMISSION

La Commission ne s'autorisera aucune complaisance en vous présentant le bilan de l'Europe.

Sans doute, refusant de céder à une morosité facile, elle doit reconnaître que les six derniers mois ont vu s'améliorer un état d'aveugle et coupable inertie. Il est juste aujourd'hui de recenser quatre zones de progrès.

En matière économique tout d'abord, l'interdépendance est désormais perçue comme une réalité; un renforcement des mécanismes de concertation ouvre, bien que timidement, la voie à un rapprochement des politiques économiques internes, dont la compatibilité et la complémentarité sont plus systématiquement recherchées; il ouvre aussi, comme en ont témoigné les récents entretiens de Washington, la voie à une attitude commune vers l'extérieur en matière économique et monétaire.

En deuxième lieu, la création d'un Fonds régional, celle d'un mécanisme d'emprunts communautaires, le développement du Fonds social donnent un début de contenu aux politiques d'équilibre économique et social, et de solidarité active, à l'intérieur de la Communauté – politiques qui inspiraient jusqu'ici surtout des exercices de rhétorique.

ment on the need for consultation enabled a number of matters to be dealt with in a Community spirit. For instance, Commission representatives took part in the Conference on Security and Cooperation in Europe, as agreed by the Council, working on the Economic Committee and its subcommittees.

The Euro-Arab dialogue has got under way and preparatory talks have been held. Questions of Mediterranean policy have been considered, particular attention being paid to developments in Portugal, Greece and Cyprus. Discussions have been held to harmonize the points of view to be expressed at debates in the United Nations.

On 16 October the Minister of Foreign Affairs chairing the Council sent Parliament the fourth annual memorandum on progress in political cooperation.

Quarterly meetings between the Ministers and Parliament's Political Affairs Committee took place in Bonn on 2 April, Strasbourg on 11 June, Paris on 18 September and Brussels on 3 December.

10. Meeting in Paris on 9 and 10 December, the Heads of Government reaffirmed their determination, with a view to progress towards European unity, gradually to adopt common positions and coordinate their diplomatic action in all areas of international affairs which affect the interests of the European Community. They decided that the President of the Council would be the spokesman for the Nine and would set out their views in international diplomacy: he would ensure that the necessary concertation always took place in good time.

In view of the increasing role of political cooperation in the construction of Europe, the Heads of Government underlined the importance of associating Parliament more closely with the work of the President's office – for example through replies to questions on political cooperation put by Members.

B. BASIC TEXTS

1. ADDRESS BY MR. FRANÇOIS-XAVIER ORTOLI, PRESIDENT OF THE COMMISSION OF THE EUROPEAN COMMUNITIES, TO THE EUROPEAN PARLIAMENT, STRASBOURG, 18 FEBRUARY 1975

The Commission has no intention of painting you a rosy picture of Europe today.

But it refuses to be unduly pessimistic. In the last six months Europe has become a little less blind, a little less lethargic. I feel that it is only right to begin by listing four areas where progress has been made:

Firstly, the reality of economic interdependence has been recognized. The strengthening of our consultation arrangements is a precursor, however timid, of the harmonization of national economic policies, of a systematic effort to make them compatible and complementary. It marks the beginnings too, as was recently shown in Washington, of a united stand on economic and monetary matters.

Secondly, the creation of a Regional Fund, the establishment of Community loan machinery and the development of the Social Fund have put some flesh on the bones of the Community's economic and social policies, given some form to the idea of solidarity to which little more than lip-service has been paid in the past.

Thirdly, Europe now has a policy on development in the Third and Fourth Worlds. It is a real policy, with clear aims, ambitious and versatile

Ensuite, l'Europe a désormais une politique du développement à l'égard du tiers et du quart monde; une vraie politique, claire dans ses objectifs, ambitieuse et diversifiée dans ses moyens; une politique dont la mise en place obstinée constitue notre plus satisfaisante manifestation extérieure.

Enfin, le sommet de Paris a marqué la volonté de réagir contre l'affaiblissement institutionnel de l'Europe et contre le vide politique que crée l'absence d'autorité, d'une part, l'absence de perspectives mobilisatrices, d'autre part. Je vois, dans l'impulsion qu'il a donnée, une raison de l'efficacité nouvelle que semble montrer le Conseil.

L'objectivité veut que ces progrès soient reconnus. Grâce à eux commence à renaître un certain espoir.

Cependant, je dis clairement, avec la même absence de complaisance, que l'Europe a besoin de réussites d'une autre ampleur pour atteindre ses objectifs d'unité et d'indépendance. Car, sur l'essentiel, nous rencontrons reculs et échecs. Recul de notre indépendance; rétrécissement de nos ambitions; semi-échec institutionnel.

L'indépendance – c'est-à-dire la maîtrise de son propre destin – est la grande affaire de l'Europe. Or, là, depuis quinze mois, nous avons reculé.

Ce recul a des causes objectives.

Nous avons échappé pendant trente ans aux conséquences de notre pauvreté en énergie et en matières premières. Aujourd'hui, nous sommes face à la vérité. Centres de décision et puissance financière se sont brutalement déplacés. Notre dépendance est physique – l'embargo nous l'a montré –, mais elle n'est pas que physique. Elle est aussi économique, par les modifications de nos structures que cette évolution radicale nous impose. Elle est aussi monétaire, puisque d'un seul coup les sommes en cause ne peuvent être payées que par un transfert de nos ressources, c'est-à-dire de notre travail, transfert qu'un endettement – d'ailleurs dangereux – peut seulement étaler dans le temps. Ce sont là de rudes contraintes.

Cette situation a d'autres conséquences qu'il faut tout aussi objectivement constater, par exemple le renforcement de la position dominante des États-Unis, qui ont la richesse en énergie et en matières premières d'un continent, et la volonté, naturelle dans une conjoncture mouvante et grave, d'exercer pleinement l'influence dont ils peuvent disposer.

Mais ne nous y trompons pas: l'accroissement de notre dépendance et la réduction de notre liberté d'allure sont d'abord notre fait. C'est de notre seule responsabilité que découle notre incapacité à suivre une politique claire et à peser notre poids dans la gigantesque et confuse activité diplomatique où se définissent les conditions de notre avenir. De même est-ce essentiellement notre propre faute si nos rapports avec les États-Unis n'arrivent pas à s'établir sur une base d'égalité. Notre tentative de parler d'une seule voix a, dans des cas essentiels, échoué pitoyablement – je pense à la conférence de l'énergie de Washington en février 1974 – et pour certaines circonstances où nous sommes arrivés à nous entendre, sur le recyclage par exemple, combien de domaines où notre dispersion, parfois même notre mésentente, nous retirent tout rôle dans un jeu qui concerne pourtant nos intérêts et prépare notre avenir!

L'Europe n'a pas la place qui devrait être la sienne là où se prennent les décisions qui comptent, qu'elles engagent la paix du monde, ou notre développement économique; cela je le ressens profondément et avec tristesse.

Plus grave peut-être est le rétrécissement de nos ambitions. Nous avons, au fil des années, perdu la ligne directrice qui inspire le traité de Rome: celle qui consiste à mettre en commun des compétences, lorsque cette mise en commun permet d'assumer mieux, à un meilleur niveau, nos responsabilités dans le monde et vis-à-vis de nos peuples. Nos entreprises instruments. Our stubborn determination to get it off the ground is one of the most satisfying features of our public image.

Finally, the Paris Summit Conference provided evidence of a firm desire to fight against the debilitation of Europe's institutional structure and to fill the political vacuum created by a lack of authority, by a lack of any real motivating force. It is a direct cause, to my mind, of the new vigour the Council seems to have acquired.

Progress has been made; daylight is beginning to show at the end of the tunnel.

But let me say, clearly and unequivocally, that it is vital for Europe to aim for success of a different kind if it is to achieve the unity and independence it is seeking. On the real issues Europe stumbles and slips downhill. We are losing our independence; we are lowering our sights; our institutions are failing in important areas.

Europe's real problem is independence, control of its own destiny. And it has been losing ground on this front for the last fifteen months.

There are of course reasons for this.

For thirty years or so Europe was happily able to ignore the unpleasant fact that its energy and raw material resources were limited. There is no avoiding the truth today. The centres of political and financial power have shifted. Our dependence is physical, as the embargo showed us, but it is more than that. It is economic, since our structures have undergone a radical transformation. It is monetary, since we discovered overnight that we can only pay our bills by a transfer of resources, of the fruits of our labour. Borrowing, a hazardous process in itself, can only postpone the evil day. These are hard facts to face.

And there is another aspect which must be recognized. The United States has energy and raw material resources on a continental scale. It is natural that it should want to exert all the influence of its increased dominance in a difficult and unstable situation.

But we must not deceive ourselves; if we have become more dependent, if our freedom of action has been curtailed, we ourselves are the main culprits. It is our fault that we are unable to pursue a clear policy, unable to make our presence felt in the enormous diplomatic jungle where our future way of life is being evolved. Again, it is essentially our own fault that it has not proved possible to establish relations with the United States on an equal footing. Our attempts to speak with a single voice on vital issues – I am thinking in particular of the Washington energy conference last February – have failed miserably. For every area of agreement – the recycling of petrodollars for example – there are many others in which dissension, indeed quarrelsomeness, have ruled us out of a game in which the stakes are Europe's interests and Europe's future.

Europe has not taken her rightful place in the forums where decisions – on world peace, on economic development – are taken. This pains and saddens me.

But more serious perhaps is the fact that we have abandoned our ambitions. Over the years we have lost sight of the ideal which inspired the Treaty of Rome: the pooling of sovereignty where this would allow us to shoulder our responsibilities more effectively at home and abroad. Our joint endeavours are now marginal; our commitments to each other are more and more superficial, more and more ephemeral.

How far have we got with a common energy policy, with harmonization of tax systems, with the pooling of recources, with a single approach to communes sont désormais marginales, et nous engagent de moins en moins profondément et durablement les uns vis-à-vis des autres.

Où en sommes-nous de la politique énergétique commune, du rapprochement des fiscalités, de la mise en commun des réserves, de la représentation unique vers l'extérieur dans les affaires économiques et monétaires? Déciderions-nous aujourd'hui, comme nous avons su le faire en d'autres temps, de donner à l'Europe le soin de fixer les prix agricoles et de gérer les marchés, celui d'assumer la politique commerciale, celui de conduire une politique de concurrence? Dois-je, pour mieux rendre visible notre recul, rappeler que ces accomplissements considérables sont ceux d'une époque où, plus vivement qu'aujourd'hui, on discutait, sur le plan des principes, des structures de l'Europe, et de ses compétences? Nous avons perdu, et en hardiesse, et en capacité de vision.

Je vois un troisième fait majeur dans le semi-échec, que vous avez souvent analysé, de nos institutions. A ce semi-échec, la décision prise à Paris au mois de décembre dernier de tenir régulièrement des conseils de ministres au niveau des chefs de gouvernement ambitionne d'apporter un remède. Mais ce remède, s'il respecte l'économie du système original, en modifie l'esprit et le contenu et risque, si l'on n'y prend garde, d'ébranler toutes les structures institutionnelles établies par le traité.

Si cette novation considérable nous donne, comme il le faut, une nouvelle capacité à décider; si elle nous donne une vraie politique inspirée par une vue d'ensemble, où s'effaceront les distinctions artificielles entre domaine communautaire et coopération intergouvernementale; si elle nous apporte un développement du champ d'action de l'Europe; si, enfin, elle respecte de nos règles communautaires la rigueur qui fait leur vigueur, alors comme nous y aurons gagné!

Mais ne méconnaissons pas le danger que les circonstances ou le manque d'audace, la confusion des compétences ou la commodité conduisent, avant tout, au renforcement de la coopération intergouvernementale au détriment de la voie royale de l'intégration, lorsque celle-ci est nécessaire.

Il faut donc saisir la chance et éviter le danger. Et pour cela il faut que la Commission exerce pleinement sa vocation retrouvée d'institution politique.

La Commission doit hisser son action au niveau qu'exige un système où l'impulsion se situe désormais au sommet. Elle doit prévenir les risques, qui existent, en communiquant aux États membres sa conviction qu'il n'y a pas de solution réelle aux principaux problèmes avec lesquels ils sont confrontés en dehors des solutions communautaires ou collectives qu'implique la construction européenne. Elle doit utiliser de manière vigoureuse et incisive son pouvoir de proposition, sans transiger sur sa propre vision, dans les choix déterminants pour l'Europe.

Cette conscience de notre rôle, cette attitude profondément politique, cette ambition de donner un autre rythme et une autre ampleur à la réalisation de l'Europe inspirent le programme que je vais vous soumettre. Il s'agit d'un programme d'ensemble qui peut, dans notre esprit, ouvrir la voie à une nouvelle évolution de la construction européenne.

Je vais vous en exposer, en cinq points, les lignes d'action principales, laissant au mémorandum complémentaire qui vous a été distribué le soin de détailler l'action que nous envisageons.

Premier objectif: réduire la dépendance de l'Europe.

La maîtrise de notre avenir nous échappe, parce que se multiplient les centres de décision, économiques, financiers et politiques, extérieurs à nos États membres et à notre Communauté.

Cette dépendance accrue est d'une double nature.

economic and monetary issues at international level? If we were starting from scratch today would we be prepared, as we were in 1958, to allow Europe to fix agricultural prices, to manage agricultural markets, to handle commercial policy, to control competition policy? Need I remind you that these major achievements date from a time when the principles, structures and powers of Europe were debated with greater vigour than they are today? We have lost our nerve, we have lost our vision.

There is a third important factor in the near-collapse of our institutions, analysed by this House on many occasions. The decision taken by the Heads of our Governments in Paris last December to meet regularly as the European Council is an attempt to remedy the situation. It may respect the letter of our system but it represents a major change in spirit and may, if we are not careful, shake the institutional structures set up by the Treaties to their foundations.

If this major innovation increases Europe's ability to take decisions; if it produces real policies which eliminate the artificial distinction between the Community approach and political cooperation approach; if it widens Europe's field of action; if it respects the strictness of Community rules which is the very source of their dynamism, then we will have gambled and won!

But we could lose. Let us not close our eyes to the danger that force of circumstances, a lack of courage, confusion as to who is responsible for what, expediency, may tempt us to choose the low road of inter-governmental cooperation when we should be taking the high road of integration.

We must therefore take a chance and shorten the odds. But this means that the Commission must be true to its refound political vocation.

The Commission must adapt its *modus operandi* to the new system in which ideas will come from the top. It must insure against the risks involved – for risks are involved – by converting Member States to its conviction that the real answer to the major problems facing them lies in the collective Community solutions implicit in the construction of Europe. It must make vigorous and incisive use of its power of initiative when choices which are decisive for Europe's future are being made. It must not betray its own ideals.

This awareness of our role, this profoundly political attitude, this ambition to get Europe to change gear and direction, have inspired the programme I am about to present to you. It is an overall programme which we believe could herald a new phase in the construction of Europe.

I propose to indicate the main lines of action under five main headings; the memorandum you have already received will fill in the details.

Our *first objective* must be to make Europe less dependent.

Europe is losing control of its future since the number of economic, financial and political centres of decision outside our Member States and outside our Community is growing apace.

Our dependence is increasing on two points.

D'une part, nous n'avons plus aucune maîtrise, ou seulement une maîtrise insuffisante des facteurs essentiels de notre vie économique: il en va ainsi de notre approvisionnement en énergie, mais aussi, pour plusieurs États membres, et globalement pour la Communauté, des problèmes financiers que pose la couverture de nos besoins vitaux.

Nous devons tout faire pour réduire progressivement mais rapidement cette première forme de dépendance. A côté de la monnaie, qui appelle une action complexe, le point central de cette dépendance est, actuellement, de toute évidence, le problème de l'énergie. Aussi est-ce sur ce point que la Commission entend concentrer son effort. L'année 1975 doit être celle de la politique commune de l'énergie.

Alors que dès mai 1973, avant la crise, la Commission proposait une action à trois niveaux: coopération avec les consommateurs, coopération et établissement de liens d'intérêts avec les producteurs, organisation commune du marché, les progrès réalisés ont été tardifs, hésitants, non significatifs.

Or, le temps qui passe n'est pas du temps gagné. Notre dépendance vis-à-vis de l'extérieur risque de se cristalliser dans un renoncement peint aux couleurs du réalisme.

Il convient que l'Europe se ressaisisse. Pour sa part, la Commission défendra les actions suivantes:

- fixation d'objectifs communs, globaux et par sources d'énergie, et mise en place du dispositif permettant de les atteindre.
- a l'intérieur de ce cadre, développement de nos ressources propres par tous les moyens raisonnables; la Commission proposera:
- le ou les mécanismes communautaires d'incitation, de soutien, ou de garantie (le ou les, car la situation des différentes sources d'énergie n'est pas forcément identique) qui permettront d'assurer continûment aux investissements une rentabilité convenable sur un marché correspondant à des conditions économiques raisonnables;
- la fixation d'une base d'appréciation pour des interventions communautaires à long terme, par exemple la fixation de prix de référence;
- les financements communs qui pourraient s'avérer nécessaires, soit au titre de ces mécanismes, soit pour faciliter la réalisation des investissements, comme c'est le cas pour l'emprunt de 500 millions d'UC qui vient d'être proposé dans le cadre du traité Euratom.
- Programme européen de recherche.

Il n'y a pas dans ce programme d'éléments de confrontation avec les producteurs et notre politique extérieure de l'énergie doit être une politique ouverte. Au contraire, il s'agit de questions d'intérêt commun à eux et à nous, qui doivent être débattues entre eux et nous, comme nous n'avons jamais cessé de le proposer. La conférence dont la préparation s'engagera en mars, avec une Communauté parlant d'une seule voix, nous fournira, je l'espère, l'occasion d'un tel débat; la négociation d'accords de coopération avec certains États nous en donnera une seconde.

Il n'y a pas non plus de contradiction entre ce programme et la concertation entre pays consommateurs, telle qu'elle se déroule au sein de l'Agence internationale de l'énergie, ou plutôt il nous appartient de faire qu'il n'y en ait pas, et pour notre part nous agirons dans ce sens.

La concertation est l'intérêt de la Communauté et de tous ses membres.

Malgré les obstacles de procédure, elle doit se réaliser, et la Commission s'y emploiera, à sa place.

Mais cette concertation implique une appréciation exacte de nos intérêts et la volonté de les défendre. La Communauté, pauvre en énergie, n'a pas les mêmes problèmes que les pays qui disposent d'une quasi-autonomie. Par exemple, et réfléchissons-y bien, certains niveaux de prix qui, aux États-Unis, stimuleraient la production et donc permettraient de tendre vers l'autosuffisance, ne conduiraient pour nous qu'à une charge en devises supplémentaire, et de quel poids.

Firstly, we have little or no control over the main factors of our economic life. This is true of energy supplies but, for a number of Member States and for the Community as a whole, it is also true of the monetary resources needed to cover our essential requirements.

We must do all in our power to reduce this first form of dependence. This can be done in stages if necessary but there is no time to lose. If the monetary problem, which calls for complex action, is left aside it is quite clear that energy is the crux of the matter, which is why the Commission proposes to concentrate on energy. 1975 must be the year of the common energy policy.

In May 1973, before the crisis began, the Commission had already proposed three-pronged action: cooperation with consumers, cooperation and relations with producers, and a common market organization. But whatever hesitant progress was made was too little and too late.

We are gaining nothing by letting time slip by. There is a danger that our depencence on the outside world will harden into resignation masquerading as realism. Europe must act and act now. The Commission therefore proposes the following course of action:

- we must fix common targets, both global targets and targets for each type of energy, and we must do something about attaining them;
- in this context, we must develop our resources by all available means; the Commission will propose:
- a Community mechanism or mechanisms (I say a mechanism or mechanisms since the situation is not necessarily the same for all energy sources) to provide incentives, support and guarantees to ensure an adequate return on investment under reasonable economic conditions;
- we must decide on a basis for assessing long-term Community intervention, for instance by fixing reference prices;
- finance must be made available from joint sources, either to support these mechanisms or to promote investment – witness the recent proposal for a 500 million u.a. loan under the Euratom Treaty.
- a European research programme.

Our external energy policy must be an open one and there is nothing here to provoke a confrontation with producers. Indeed the issues are of interest to both sides and must be debated by both sides. The Commission has always advocated this. The conference for which preparations are to begin in March, a conference at which the Community is to speak with a single voice, will, I hope, provide an opportunity for such a debate; the negotiation of cooperation agreements with a number of countries will provide another.

Nor does this programme conflict with the regular consultations between consumer countries now taking place within the International Energy Agency. Or perhaps I should say that we intend to make it our business to ensure that it does not conflict.

Concertation is in the interests of the Community and of the Member States. Despite procedural difficulties concertation must become a reality and the Commission intends to work towards this goal.

But concertation implies a correct assessment of our interests and a willingness to defend them. The Community, with its limited energy resources, does not have the same problems as countries which are virtually self-sufficient. Let us take one example and think about it: the price levels which, in the United States, would stimulate production and thus help to achieve self-sufficiency would in our case simply create a new burden, a considerable burden, on our currency reserves.

I am not saying that our views cannot be reconciled. But our interests are such that there are limits to reconciliation; we must define these limits and stay within them. If we are to reconcile diverging points of view while respecting our diverging interests, we must acquire political influence and credibility; we must defend a single point with a single voice.

Ceci ne veut pas dire que les points de vue ne peuvent pas être harmonisés. Mais nos intérêts fixent à cette harmonisation des limites qu'il nous faut bien préciser, et ne pas franchir. Pour cela – pour rechercher une conciliation des points de vue qui assure le respect des intérêts –, donnons-nous force politique et crédibilité, en défendant une seule position d'une seule voix.

C'est une partie difficile à jouer. Nous la jouerons, pour notre part, en suivant la ligne que je viens de définir, et avec l'intention de la gagner.

La dépendance a un second aspect: parce qu'il existe un ordre économique international, nous sommes parties d'une organisation mondiale complexe, dont les règles écrites ou non écrites limitent les compétences nationales ou communautaires. Lorsqu'on parle de souveraineté, voyons la réalité: outre les cas où le pouvoir est purement et simplement ailleurs, il est désormais une forme de souveraineté collective, transnationale, dont il faut non pas nier, mais au contraire reconnaître l'existence, soit pour en réduire les effets, soit pour s'assurer qu'elle n'ignore pas nos intérêts.

Notre deuxième grand objectif – et ici je dépasse le cadre de la seule politique de l'énergie – doit donc être d'exercer pleinement notre part dans la souveraineté collective qui s'exerce au travers de l'ordre économique et monétaire mondial en mutation.

Nous sommes dans un monde où s'affrontent les intérêts et où se mesurent les forces. Si nous défendons mal nos intérêts et n'usons pas de toutes nos forces, les règles, les équilibres, les situations de fait s'établiront à notre détriment.

Parce qu'aucun de nos États n'est assuré d'exercer une influence réelle au moment où se redéfinissent les mécanismes et les pouvoirs, l'Europe, bien loin de réduire des souverainetés déjà diminuées, est un instrument de reconquête de la souveraineté. Elle est un facteur d'exercice plein de la part de pouvoir qui nous est reconnue dans les nouveaux centres de décisions. C'est vrai en matière d'énergie, en matière monétaire, en matière de commerce international. C'est vrai dans les organisations internationales, et c'est vrai dans nos relations avec tous nos grands partenaires et notamment avec les États-Unis.

Le débat sur ce dernier point mérite d'être clarifié. L'amitié, l'alliance, la reconnaissance de grands intérêts communs, n'empêchent pas de voir la réalité: celle d'une puissance propre des États-Unis qui leur confère un poids particulier dans leurs relations avec nous; celle d'une volonté de régler les problèmes qui, devant nos faiblesses, ou nos hésitations, prend volontiers, sans se cacher, l'allure d'un leadership.

Nous établirons nos relations avec les États-Unis sur des bases plus égales et plus saines et, je le crois, nous les renforcerons si, attachant tout son prix à notre alliance, et déterminés à agir conjointement avec nos amis américains là où c'est leur intérêt et le nôtre, nous nous décidons à prendre une double attitude:

- celle d'une défense de nos intérêts propres, ou des positions conjointes qui nous paraissent les meilleures, qui soit assurée avec la même détermination, la même constance, la même absence de complexes, et la même franchise salubre que les États-Unis y mettent eux-mêmes;
- celle d'un esprit d'initiative dans les grandes affaires du monde, qui comblerait une lacune – car nous avons des choses à dire, et nous sommes capables de proposer des solutions – et qui romprait avec un comportement trop souvent de pure réaction, lequel traduit à mes yeux une pusillanimité politique.

Cette attitude doit être celle de l'Europe. Seule elle peut nous permettre, dans des relations évidemment déséquilibrées, de réduire la part d'inégalité qui résulte de notre infériorité objective.

Ainsi, nous devons désormais, pour assurer une meilleure défense de nos peuples, choisir dans les affaires internationales une politique qui soit celle de l'Europe, arrêter systématiquement des positions communes, décider,

It will not be an easy contest. But we will play the game in the way I have indicated and we will play to win.

Our dependence has a second facet: since there is an international economic order, we form part of a complex world organization whose written and unwritten rules limit our ability to act as individual nations or as a Community. Let us be realistic about sovereignty: except in instances where power clearly lies elsewhere a form of a new pooled sovereignty has emerged which transcends national frontiers. We must not close our eyes to this; we must accept it as a fact with a view to mitigating its effects or at least making sure that our interests are not overlooked.

For this reason our second major objective – and here I am not just thinking of energy policy – must be to make full use of our share of this pooled sovereignty which finds its expression in a changing economic and monetary world order.

We are living in a world where interests conflict, where strength is being tested. If we fail to defend our interests, if we fail to show our strength then the rules will be drawn up, balances of power established and situations created which are to our disadvantage.

Since none of our Member States is in a position to exercise any real influence when systems are overhauled and powers rebalanced, Europe, far from eroding a sovereignty which is already diminished opens the way to sovereignty regained. Europe offers us an opportunity of exercising to the full the modicum of power allowed us in the new centres of decision. This is true of energy, monetary matters and world trade. It holds good for international organizations and for our relations with our larger partners, notably the United States.

Perhaps I might make myself quite clear on this last point. We may be friend we may be allies and we may recognize that we have interests in common. But this must not blind us to reality: to the power of the United States which weighs on our relations; to its willingness to tackle problems which, contrasted with our weakness, our confusion, marks it as a world leader.

I believe that in the end we will succeed in putting our relations with the United States on a healthier, more equal footing. I believe that we can strengthen our relations with the United States if we learn to value our alliance; if we determine to act with our American friends where both have something to gain; and if we adopt the following two-fold approach:

- we must defend our own interests or the common viewpoint which seems best to us, with the same determination, the same firmness, the same lack of complexes, and the same wholesome sincerity that the United States displays;
- we must use our initiative in all important international affairs, thereby filling a gap, for we have something to say, we have solutions to offer, and it is high time that we abandoned what has too often been a reactionary approach, an approach which to my mind is evidence of political cowardice.

This is the spirit which must guide Europe. Only then, in a situation where our relations are visibly unbalanced can we compensate for that inequality which stems from our intrinsic inferiority.

We must henceforth come to the defence of the people's interests by choosing a European response to international events, by adopting a common stance as a matter of course and by deciding that the Community should speak for all of us on issues which are too big for an individual State to handle. This is our objective at a time when the rules are being changed, when the balance of power is shifting and, let us not forget this, when our future way of life is being evolved.

partout où l'enjeu dépasse les forces de nos États, la représentation de tous par la seule Communauté. Voici notre objectif au moment où se définissent de nouvelles règles, où s'établissent de nouveaux pouvoirs, où, prenons-y garde, s'arrêtent les conditions de notre avenir.

Deuxième objectif: rétablir l'équilibre économique et social de l'Europe, grâce à une croissance fondée sur des bases nouvelles.

Pour cela nous avons arrêté quatre axes d'action:

- développement de politiques économiques complémentaires, et renforcement de la solidarité;
- reprise d'une croissance fondée sur l'investissement;
- mise en place d'instruments de réflexion et d'action nouveaux, renforçant, concrètement, l'Union économique et monétaire;
- une politique faite pour les hommes et les femmes de l'Europe, et avec eux.

Le chômage, l'inflation, le décifit des balances de paiements appellent normalement des politiques conjoncturelles différentes. Comment, sans relance, inverser la tendance qui a porté le nombre des chômeurs à 3 millions et demi environ? Mais comment, alors que nous sommes absolument contraints de redresser nos balances de paiements, affaiblir la vigueur de la lutte contre l'inflation? Il nous faut cependant surmonter ces contradictions, car si l'on ne résout pas les trois problèmes en même temps, il n'y aura pas de retour à un équilibre durable. C'est ma conviction qu'une telle réussite est à la portée de l'Europe.

Tout d'abord, nous avons un magnifique atout: c'est l'existence même de la Communauté. Utilisons à plein cet atout: la Commission et les États membres devront – profitant, une fois n'est pas coutume, des disparités dans les situations économiques – accentuer, je dirai même rechercher systématiquement, la complémentarité des politiques suivies par les États membres qui sont en excédent et par ceux qui sont en déficit. Par là, ils faciliteront la reprise. Ils devront en même temps renforcer les instruments de solidarité qui évitent la contrainte du repliement sur soi-même. Ce n'est que grâce à cette complémentarité et à cette solidarité que le maintien de la liberté des échanges pourra être assuré dans la Communauté et dans le commerce international; or, l'expansion du commerce international est une des clés du rétablissement de la situation de la Communauté comme du retour à un meilleur équilibre mondial. Le retour au protectionnisme serait un détonateur de crise.

Nous avons là une première ligne de conduite pour la Commission.

Nous nous devons également de tenir compte d'un second élément d'une importance capitale. Cette conjoncture d'une exceptionnelle gravité s'accompagne de fortes évolutions structurelles dans la production et la consommation. Que nous le voulions ou non, l'orientation de la consommation se modifie, les conditions de la division internationale du travail changent; il faut investir plus dans le secteur énergétique, plus dans les industries tournées vers l'exportation. Ces mutations sont inévitables, soit que les nouvelles données économiques nous les imposent, soit que sans elles nous ne puissions pas résoudre nos problèmes, notamment d'exportation.

Notre seconde ligne d'action sera donc que la politique économique doit non pas contrarier, mais préparer et encourager les mutations nécessaires.

J'ai la certitude que c'est par la croissance que l'Europe réglera ses problèmes, mais une croissance fondée sur des bases nouvelles. Nous avons à choisir une stratégie et elle passe par l'investissement. Sur le plan de la conjoncture, la relance doit se faire par l'investissement et non par l'accroissement massif de la demande globale. A moyen et long terme, la transformation des structures nécessitera une politique durable de transfert d'une certaine fraction de nos ressources de la consommation vers l'équipement.

Our *second objective* must be to reestablish economic and social equilibrium in Europe by aiming for growth based on new foundations.

We have chosen four axes here:

- development of complementary economic policies and strengthening of solidarity;
- resumption of growth based on investment;
- creation of new aids to decision and action – a practical step towards economic and monetary union;
- a policy made for the men and women of Europe with their help.

Unemployment, inflation and balance of payments deficits are usually met by different types of economic policy. How, without reflation, are we to reverse the trend which has raised the level of unemployment to nearly three and a half million? But how, since we must correct our balance of payments, can we ease up on the fight against inflation? We must resolve the contradiction because unless we attack all three problems at once, we will fail to restore lasting equilibrium. But I am convinced that success is within Europe's grasp.

For one thing, we have a trump card up our sleeve: the Community exists. Let us use this card to best effect. The Commission and the Member States should, exceptionally, take advantage of the present disparities between our economies to make a determined systematic effort to find some means of ensuring that the policies of surplus countries complement those of deficit countries. Success would favour recovery. At the same time they should impart new vigour to the instruments of solidarity to counteract a return to isolationism. Only if they do so will it be possible to maintain free trade in the Community and throughout the world. And the expansion of world trade provides a key to a healthier Community and world equilibrium. A return to protectionism would sow the seeds of a new crisis.

This, then, will be the Commission's first line of action.

But we must also take a second factor of capital importance into consideration. The present exceptionally serious situation is accompanied by structural changes in both production and consumption. Whether we like it or not, the pattern of consumption is changing, the international division of labour is changing. We must step up investment in energy production, we must step up investment in export industries. These changes are inevitable being imposed on us by the new economic order or by our inability in the absence of change to solve our problems, notably our export problems.

Our second line of action will thus be to ensure that our economic policies do not hinder change but rather prepare for and encourage change. I am convinced that Europe will solve its problems through growth but I am equally convinced that growth must be based on new foundations. We must decide on a strategy, a strategy centred on investment. Economic recovery must be based on investment, not on a massive increase in overall demand. In the medium and long term, structural change will call for steady transfers of resources from consumption to investment.

Here, too, Europe has a role to play. To further these new objectives the Commission will be proposing three types of action:

- We must have a better idea of where we are going. To provide a valid scientific basis for forecast and proposals, to ensure a more reliable picture of the economic future, the Commission will shortly be proposing that the Community set up a medium-term research institute.

Là aussi l'Europe a son rôle à jouer. Pour donner toute leur valeur à ces objectifs nouveaux, trois types d'action de caractère différent seront proposés par la Commission.

- Nous devons nous donner les moyens d'une plus grande lucidité. Pour fonder les prévisions et les réflexions sur des bases scientifiques valables, pour prendre une vision mieux assurée de l'avenir économique, la Commission proposera prochainement la création d'un institut du moyen terme de la Communauté.
- Nous devons tirer profit de la complémentarité des industries européennes pour rendre plus efficace notre effort de développement des échanges. A l'échelle de l'Europe, nous devons engager résolument vers l'extérieur une politique de coopération économique et industrielle – cette politique de coopération qui est la manière moderne de définir, au bénéfice des deux parties, au-delà des accords commerciaux traditionnels et du simple mercantilisme, des engagements réciproques, conçus dans un cadre d'ensemble. La Commission en fait un de ses objectifs principaux.
  Pour mener une telle politique, il faut que l'Europe en ait les instruments, et notamment les instruments financiers qu'exigent la nouveauté des risques économiques, leur importance et leur durée. La Commission examine donc le principe et les structures d'une banque européenne d'exportation. Elle envisage de faire les propositions nécessaires au Conseil avant la fin de ce semestre.
- Nous devons mettre les possibilités de la Communauté au service de notre effort d'investissement pour l'accélérer et l'équilibrer. Comme ailleurs, la Communauté peut agir comme multiplicateur, et son intervention permettra plus que la simple addition des possibilités nationales. Comme ailleurs aussi, l'action collective de la Communauté peut rendre effective la solidarité entre États membres aux moyens différents.

C'est ainsi que, en matière d'énergie, nous avons pris l'initiative, je l'ai déjà signalé, de proposer au Conseil l'émission d'un emprunt Euratom de 500 millions d'UC et nous réalisons déjà, dans le cadre de la CECA, des emprunts importants, dont le plus récent de 150 millions de dollars a été conclu le 6 février. Dois-je rappeler que la Communauté est une ,,première adresse," sur les marchés financiers mondiaux, et qu'elle bénéficie de très bonnes conditions par rapport aux conditions générales?

Forts de ces précédents, nous avons mis à l'étude la possibilité de développer notre capacité d'emprunt, soit par un emploi plus large des instruments existants, soit par la création d'instruments nouveaux du même type. Nous examinons aussi la destination la plus utile pour les fonds ainsi rassemblés, investissements dans l'énergie ou aussi restructuration de l'appareil industriel de la Communauté.

Toute cette action veut contribuer à la résorption de la crise, et au retour au plein emploi par une croissance entièrement saine. Faite pour les hommes, elle ne peut ignorer les problèmes qui naissent pour eux du profond changement de notre société. Elle peut les ignorer d'autant moins que ce rééquilibrage ordonné ne se fera pas sans leur concours actif et sans leur adhésion.

Dès lors trois exigences s'imposent à la Communauté et à ses États membres:

- Une exigence de vérité: les risques de la situation présente, et les moyens du rétablissement doivent être présentés clairement, sans dissimuler les sacrifices qu'ils entraîneront – et qui tiennent au transfert de ressources qui nous est imposé –, mais aussi sans oublier les avantages de progrès et de sécurité qui s'attachent aux réponses nouvelles que nous pouvons apporter aux problèmes. Cet éclairage, nos institutions peuvent aider à le fournir, avec l'objectivité et la sérénité qui vont avec notre mission.
- Une exigence de justice, qui appelle le renforcement de la protection sociale, le développement des moyens qui faciliteront l'adaptation, une répartition équitable des revenus. La responsabilité de ce changement

- We must take advantage of the fact that different industries are at work in different Community countries, and make trade promotion more effective. At European level we must resolutely commit ourselves to basing our relations with the rest of the world on a policy of economic and industrial cooperation; this is the modern way of defining commitments in a broader context, leaving the traditional trade agreement, and pure mercantilism behind. The Commission is taking this as one of its main objectives.

If this policy is to be pursued Europe must have the backing, notably the financial backing, made necessary by the novelty, scale and duration of the economic risks involved. For this reason the Commission is considering the possibility of creating a European export bank of some kind. It hopes to put proposals to the Council by June.

- We must harness Community resources to our investment drive to add speed and balance. Here, as elsewhere, the Community can act as a multiplier and make it possible to achieve more than could be achieved by the sum of national efforts. Here, as elsewhere, common action by the Community can make solidarity between Member States a reality.

On the energy issue we have, as I have already said, proposed to the Council that a 500 million units of account loan be launched under the Euratom Treaty. We have already floated loans under the ECSC Treaty; the most recent one, for 150 million dollars, closed on 6 February. Need I remind you that on the world's financial markets the Community has a first class credit rating and that it can borrow money on exceptionally favourable terms?

With this success behind us, we have begun to examine the possibility of expanding our borrowing capacity, either by making greater use of existing instruments or by creating new instruments of a similar kind. We are also considering the best way of using the funds raised, whether they should be invested in energy or used to restructure the Community's industrial base.

The purpose of these measures is to soften the crisis and promote a return to full employment by encouraging healthy growth. Designed with people in mind, they must also deal with the human problems created by the radical transformation of our society. Indeed, an orderly return to equilibrium is inconceivable without the active support of the people.

Accordingly, the Community and its Member States have three needs to fill:

- The need for honesty; the dangers inherent in the present situation and the remedies we propose must be made as clear as possible to the public; there can be no attempt to play down the sacrifices involved in the inevitable transfer or resources; but it will be permissible to stress the benefits to be derived from the progress and security resulting from our new response to problems. Our institutions can help here with the calm, objective outlook which goes hand in hand with our job;
- The need for justice, which means that there must be more protection for the needy, that people must be given more help to adapt; that incomes must be distributed more equitably. Responsibility for this lies primarily with the Member States; but the Community can help by making the need more clearly understood; by developing the means at its disposal, notably the Social Fund, it can help the Member States to succeed;
- The need for involvement: a happy outcome to this imposed process of change will depend on each and every one of us, irrespective of where we work. This is true of society in general but particularly true of the firm where industrial relations and arrangements for participation by workers and management staff in major economic decisions need a complete overhaul.

For this reason the Commission attached great importance to re-opening incombe au premier chef aux États membres; la Communauté peut toutefois aider à en faire comprendre la nécessité et, par le développement des moyens dont elle dispose, notamment le Fonds social, à en permettre la réalisation.

– Une exigence de participation: la réussite du changement, puisqu'il travaille. C'est vrai au-delà du niveau de l'entreprise, mais c'est vrai aussi et d'abord au niveau de l'entreprise où doivent se transformer les relations sociales et les conditions de participation des travailleurs et des cadres aux choix économiques importants.

La Commission attache donc une grande importance à la relance de la discussion sur la participation, au niveau de la Communauté. Elle en fait un élément prioritaire du programme d'action pour l'Union économique.

Dans cette perspective elle présentera au Conseil, dans le courant du printemps, une proposition révisée de statut de la société européenne, reprenant largement les amendements de votre Assemblée. Plus généralement la Commission entend donner une impulsion vigoureuse aux travaux d'harmonisation du droit de société, où elle entend faire valoir les mêmes orientations.

Elle a engagé, parallèlement, la rédaction d'un ,,livre vert'' faisant le point des tendances actuelles de l'évolution des relations industrielles dans les différents États membres dans l'espoir de présenter complètement et objectivement tous les éléments du dossier, d'alimenter la discussion dans votre enceinte, et de dégager des convergences qui permettront de mieux orienter les travaux futurs au niveau de l'Europe ou dans nos États.

Troisième objectif: établir des rapports nouveaux avec le tiers monde.

Il est une politique que l'Europe a engagée hardiment: c'est l'établissement de rapports nouveaux avec le tiers monde fondés sur une coopération à long terme inspirée par l'égalité et la justice. Rapports nouveaux, car faits nouveaux: nous voyons nos propres problèmes, mais il nous faut ressentir tout aussi fortement les bouleversements que connaît cet autre monde.

Un certain nombre de pays en voie de développement qui disposaient, avant les récents événements, de la population, des ressources naturelles et de l'environnement sociologique nécessaires au développement rapide qu'ils ambitionnaient, ont désormais les moyens financiers de ces ambitions. Ils ont conquis la puissance économique.

D'autres pays dépendent des possibilités d'écoulement de leurs produits sur les marchés des pays industrialisés, pour la poursuite de leur développement. D'autres, enfin, se trouvent, du fait des nouveaux rapports de prix, dans une situation plus dramatique encore qu'auparavant: leur objectif principal, pour le moment, est de survivre.

De son côté l'Europe, plus encore que d'autres régions industrialisées, a besoin de pouvoir continuer à importer énergie et matières premières pour soutenir son expansion, et donc besoin d'exporter plus et autrement que par le passé et notamment là où les nouveaux marchés se créent.

Mais bien sûr notre politique vers le tiers monde a une tout autre dimension: parce qu'elle a été, plus que d'autres grands pays industrialisés, impliquée dans l'histoire des peuples d'Asie, d'Afrique et d'Amérique, mais plus encore, parce que l'Europe c'est la démocratie, avec son inspiration de justice et de fraternité, l'Europe ne saurait se désintéresser du destin de la plus grande partie du monde, qui cherche aujourd'hui à conquérir sa dignité.

Dès lors se dessine la stratégie que la Commission propose à la Communauté, laquelle peut jouer un rôle original par rapport aux États membres, car plus libre d'attaches héritées du passé, car plus large par ses dimensions.

Il s'agit, tout en poursuivant l'aide financière si nécessaire vis-à-vis de the debate on participation at Community level. This will be accorded top priority in its action programme for economic union.

With this in mind it will be sending the Council this spring a revise proposal on the Statute of the European Company, incorporating most of the amendments called for by this House. More generally the Commission hopes to give vigorous encouragement to work on the harmonization of company law, emphasizing the same principles.

Side by side with this it has begun drafting a Green Paper outlining current trends in industrial relations in the various Member States; its purpose is to produce a complete, objective survey, to provide this House with a basis for discussion and to establish points of agreement on which future discussions in Europe and Member States can draw.

Our *third objective* is to establish a new relationship with the third world.

Europe has embarked here on a bold policy: the establishment of relations with the third world based on long-term cooperation guided by principles of fair and equal treatment. A new relationship is needed because a new situation has arisen: we are conscious of our own problems, but we must become just as keenly aware of what the profound changes they are going through signify for the countries of the third world.

A number of developing countries which a short time ago possessed the population, natural resources and sociological environment necessary for rapid growth now also possess the financial resources with which to realize their ambitions. They have acceded to economic power.

Other countries depend for their development on their ability to find outlets for their products on the markets of the industrialized nations. Then again, there are others which, given the new price relationships, face an even more critical situation than before: for the time being, their only ambition is survival.

Europe, for its part must, even more than other industrial areas, remain in a position to import energy and raw materials in order to keep up its expansion. It therefore needs to export more than in the past, with a different market pattern giving more prominence to new, emerging markets.

But Europe's policy towards the third world has, of course, a completely different dimension: because the countries of Europe, more than the other large industrialized countries, have been involved in the history of Asia, Africa and America, and even more because Europe stands for democracy, inspired by principles of fairness and brotherhood, it cannot look on with indifference as the greater part of the world's population struggles to achieve decent living conditions.

This is the background to the strategy which the Commission is proposing for the Community, which can play a role of its own, beyond those played by the Member States, since it is less encumbered by the events of the past and has a much broader base.

While continuing the financial aid which is indispensable for certain certains, de s'engager, partout où c'est possible, dans une coopération fondée sur la recherche d'interdépendances économiques à long terme, qui garantissent mieux que tout traité le progrès et la solidarité. Nous voulons, en respectant les options de nos partenaires, conjuguer, dans un dessein commun, nos capacités en technologie et en savoir-faire, nos marchés, parfois notre capital et nos productions, notamment agricoles, avec les ressources dont nos partenaires disposent, et leur volonté de mettre la nouvelle situation à profit pour construire leur développement.

Les pays les plus démunis pourraient être intégrés dans ce schéma de coopération par un effort commun des pays industrialisés, et notamment de l'Europe, et de leurs partenaires, producteurs de matières premières et d'énergie, dans une action triangulaire dont il faudra imaginer en commun les modalités et les règles.

La politique d'association de la Communauté, jadis avec 19 États africains au sein de la convention de Yaoundé, aujourd'hui élargie à toute l'Afrique et même au-delà dans la convention de Lomé et dans les accords qui sont sur le point d'être signés avec les pays qui bordent la Méditerranée, constitue l'exemple le plus complet et le plus réussi de cette politique: aide financière sans doute, mais aussi et surtout accès à de larges marchés, stabilisation de leurs recettes les prémunissant contre les chutes soudaines des cours mondiaux, coopération systématique pour accélérer l'industrialisation, sans oublier les institutions politiques qui font travailler sur pied d'égalité parlementaires et gouvernements d'Europe et des pays en voie de développement concernés. Nous mettrons tout notre coeur à développer nos liens nouveaux avec l'Afrique, les Caraïbes et le Pacifique. Cette politique d'association, encadrée dans notre politique mondiale d'aide au développement, est un signe éclatant de la vitalité de l'Europe.

Le Parlement et la Commission ont été, depuis l'origine, des éléments moteurs de la politique européenne d'aide au développement. Le Parlement a su recommander, ou soutenir avec une force particulière, les solutions les plus audacieuses; la Commission a pris sans cesse l'initiative, et a assumé pleinement ses responsabilités de gestion et de négociation. Est-il présomptueux de dire que le rôle particulier de nos deux institutions explique en partie la cohérence et le dynamisme dont la Communauté fait preuve? C'est ce dynamisme dont la Commission entend pour sa part ne pas se départir.

Je vous ai proposé jusqu'ici des réponses aux problèmes de l'heure. Elles entrent dans un dessein plus ample. Les chefs de gouvernement ont eux-mêmes ressenti cette nécessité en rouvrant la discussion sur les finalités politiques de l'Europe. Leurs délibérations ont remis en marche deux processus convergents – l'Union économique et monétaire et l'Union européenne. En se prononçant pour l'élection directe de votre Assemblée, ils ont en même temps voulu donner à l'Europe le souffle populaire qui lui manque encore.

Dans ce réveil de la construction européenne, nous entendons assumer notre pleine responsabilité. La Commission va se retrouver, dans les deux années qui viennent, au coeur de sa mission politique. Elle la remplira ardemment, avec vous.

Mais comment imaginer une réflexion sur l'avenir de la Communauté en ignorant la consistance géographique de celle-ci? Nous avons toujours eu une attitude claire sur la présence de la Grande-Bretagne dans la Communauté. Cette présence est d'un intérêt majeur, fondamental, pour nous, et aussi, à notre avis, pour la Grande-Bretagne elle-même.

L'Europe sans la Grande-Bretagne serait incomplète. Elle n'aurait pas la même place dans le monde, et n'apporterait pas autant à nos peuples, si elle devait être à nouveau privée de l'apport original britannique qui a tant contribué, entre autres progrès, à lui donner une dimension interna-countries, we must wherever possible work for cooperation based on long-term economic links, which are a better instrument of progress and solidarity than any treaty. With proper respect for our partners' own objectives, we should associate, with a view to joint benefit, our technology and knowhow, our markets, and in certain cases our capital and our products, in particular agricultural, with our partners' resources and their desire to take advantage of the new situation to press forward their own development.

The poorest countries could be included in this cooperation scheme by a joint effort on the part of the industrialized countries, especially Europe, and their partners, the producers of raw materials and energy, in a three-sided arrangement governed by rules drawn up jointly.

The Community's association policy, which began with nineteen African states in the Yaoundé Convention and has now been extended to the whole of Africa and beyond by the Lomé Convention and the agreements which are about to be signed with the Mediterranean countries, is the most complete and most successful example of this strategy. Although financial aid is an important aspect, what really matters is that these agreements provide access to large markets, income stabilization cushioning the associates against a sudden fall in world prices, systematic cooperation to speed up industrialization, and political institutions in which statesmen and Governments from Europe and the developing countries can work together on an equal footing. We shall make every effort to strengthen our new links with Africa, the Caribbean and the Pacific. The Community's association policy, fitted into our world development aid policy, bears striking witness to the vitality of Europe.

From the very outset, Parliament and the Commission have been the driving forces behind Europe's policy on development aid. Parliament has originated – or given vigorous backing – to imaginative strategies, while the Commission has again and again taken the initiative, neglecting no aspect of its responsibilities for implementation and negotiation. Is it too much to claim that the special part played by these two institutions goes far to account for the Community's drive and the strength of its internal bonds? The commission is determined to maintain this dynamic momentum in tackling the problems which lie ahead.

So far I have proposed solutions to our present problems. But these are only part of a larger plan. The Heads of Governments themselves realized this need when they reopened the discussion on Europe's political goals. This discussion brought into movement again two converging processes – economic and monetary union and the unification of Europe. By endorsing the principle of direct election of this Parliament, they also took a step towards establishing that close link with ordinary people which our great venture still lacks.

We intend to play our full part in the revival of interest in building Europe. In the next two years, the Commission's political mission will once again occupy a major place in its work. Working with you, the Commission will spare no effort to achieve success.

But how can we consider the future of the Community without reference to its geographical outline? Our views on Britain's membership of the Community have always been clear. British membership is a fundamental Community interest, and in our opinion is also a British interest.

Without Britain, the Community would be incomplete. It would not have the same position in the world and would not give as much to our people if it were once more deprived of the British contribution which has done so much to give it a wider international dimension, for example in its relations with Asia and the developing countries.

tionale supplémentaire, et par exemple, dans ses relations avec l'Asie et les pays en voie de développement.

Les citoyens britanniques, depuis deux ans, ont pu prendre conscience de l'apport de la Communauté et de l'originalité du système communautaire. Même si nous la voulons plus étendue encore, l'action commune a déjà aidé la Grande-Bretagne, comme ses huit partenaires, dans les difficultés économiques, voire alimentaires, que nous traversons.

Même si nous voulons ce poids plus significatif encore, elle lui a déjà donné, à elle comme aux huit autres, un supplément de poids politique dans les affaires du monde.

Le système communautaire a prouvé sa capacité de prendre en compte les difficultés objectives d'un partenaire et ceci en respectant un cadre, c'est-à-dire des règles et des objectifs, qu'il ne faut pas laisser affaiblir. Cette double exigence a guidé la Commission dans les discussions sur les points soulevés par le gouvernement britannique en avril et en juin derniers, et, tout récemment encore, lorsqu'elle a établi son mémorandum sur le „mécanisme correcteur" appelé à prévenir d'éventuelles „situations inacceptables" pour un pays membre.

Tel est le vrai visage de la Communauté – progrès commun, solidarité, supplément d'influence et de dignité dans les affaires du monde – que la participation quotidienne à ses travaux, à ses succès comme à ses échecs doit permettre à nos peuples de découvrir. Nous connaîtrons dans quelques mois le choix de la Grande-Bretagne et de ses citoyens. Nous espérons qu'ils seront à nos côtés pour élaborer avec nous les structures et les institutions d'une Europe politiquement et économiquement unie.

Quatrième objectif: reprendre la voie de l'Union économique et monétaire.

Nos neuf pays ont confirmé leur volonté d'établir entre eux une Union économique et monétaire. Nous attendons de cette unité un supplément de croissance et de progrès social, un équilibre économique et social plus satisfaisant à l'intérieur de la Communauté, une meilleure représentation de nos intérêts vers l'extérieur. Nous savons aussi que l'Union européenne n'est pas possible sans une telle base. L'objectif est donc ambitieux, mais il est clair. Quelle stratégie définir pour s'en rapprocher, en partant de la situation actuelle où prévalent les éléments de divergence, et les risques de désunion?

L'inflation, la crise de l'énergie et la crise monétaire nous ont laissés sans programme et sans doctrine. Nous nous proposons donc, en 1975:
- de choisir, pour une action à nouveau convaincante, des points d'application limités mais significatifs,
- de redéfinir les conditions et les moyens de réalisation de l'objectif final.

2. Tout d'abord, il n'est pas nécessaire d'attendre les résultats d'une réflexion d'ensemble pour agir. C'est le sens du programme que je viens d'esquisser et qui est de nature à compléter, sur quelques points, la mosaïque de l'Union économique et monétaire.

Ainsi la politique commune de l'énergie, sur laquelle je ne reviendrai pas, et de l'agriculture font partie de la substance de l'Union. Notre politique agricole, malgré les difficultés monétaires, est vivante et conserve son unité. L'inventaire que nous sommes en train de terminer permettra de juger à la fois les résultats atteints et les améliorations possibles à l'intérieur des mécanismes du traité, conformément au processus de création continue sans lequel il n'est pas de politique. De même la politique régionale – politique d'équilibre et de solidarité – est un élément important du parallélisme entre l'Union économique et l'Union monétaire, et la Commission en entreprend la mise en place avec la plus grande diligence. Enfin, les nouveaux instruments que nous envisageons: fonds de coopération monétaire renforcé, institut du moyen terme, banque européenne d'exportation, mé-

Over the past two years, the people of Britain had an opportunity to assess the benefits of membership and the nature of the Community. Although the scope of this action is not yet wide enough, the fact of working together has already aided Britain and its eight partners in the economic difficulties, even in matters of food supplies, which we are undergoing.

Although here, too, more can be achieved, working together has also already given Britain as well as its eight partners more influence in world affairs.

The Community system has proved that the objective difficulties facing a Member State can be accommodated without damage to a structural framework – rules and policy-goals - whose strength must not be impaired. This fact and this condition guided the Commission in its discussion of the points raised by the British Government in April and June of last year and, even more recently, when it prepared its memorandum on the "corrective machinery" used to forestall "unacceptable situations" for Member States.

This is the true face of the Community – joint progress, solidarity, increased influence and prestige in world affairs – which our people will learn to appreciate through daily involvement in its work, its successes and its failures. We will know the decision of the British people in a few months. We hope that they will remain with us to make their contribution to designing the structures and developing the institutions of a politically and economically united Europe.

Our *fourth objective* is to resume progress towards Economic and Monetary Union.

Our nine countries have confirmed their intention to establish an Economic and Monetary Union. We believe that union will yield further growth and social progress, a more satisfactory economic and social balance within the Community and an improved representation of our interests in the outside world. We know, too, that European Union is not possible without such a basis. The objective is therefore ambitious, but is clear. What strategy must we then adopt to move away from the present situation, in which factors tending to drive us apart and to create dissension between us are all too strong, and move towards our goal?

Inflation, the energy crisis and the monetary crisis have left us without a programme and without a doctrine. We therefore propose in 1975:

- To select limited but significant fields for measures which will, as was once the case, carry real conviction;
- To establish what should be done, and how it should be done, to attain the ultimate objective.

1. First of all, we do not have to complete a comprehensive review of all problems before taking action. That is the meaning of the programme I have just outlined, which will fill in certain aspects of the general design for Economic and Monetary Union.

For example, the common energy policy, to which I will not return here, and the common agricultural policy are part of the substance of the Union. Our agricultural policy, in spite of the monetary difficulties, is vigorous and has maintained its unity. The stocktaking operation which we are now completing will enable us to assess both the results achieved and the improvements possible within the machinery of the Treaty in accordance with the process of continuous development without which no policy is possible. The regional policy, too, reflecting the desire for equilibrium and solidarity, is an important factor in the parallel drive towards Economic Union and Monetary Union, and the Commission is devoting the greatest attention to the establishment of this policy. Lastly, the new instruments canismes d'incitation, de soutien ou de développement en matière d'énergie, donneraient, si le Conseil nous suit, un peu plus de matière à la trame encore fragile de notre Union.

Je retrace en quelques mots ces différentes actions, engagées ou proposées, pour montrer que si ce programme se réalise, l'Union aura un peu progressé, avant même que d'autres objectifs plus ambitieux ou plus complets aient été fixés. C'est pour nous et pour vous un encouragement à l'action.

2. Mais il faudra des progrès plus fondamentaux pour assurer l'existence de l'Union économique et monétaire.

La stratégie du passé, développée dans le rapport Werner et adoptée ensuite par nos institutions, a été celle des étapes. Au cours de chaque étape devaient être prises concurremment un ensemble de mesures dans les principaux domaines, pour assurer la convergence des économies et une solidarité monétaire croissante et pour affirmer de plus en plus la présence européenne dans les relations économiques et monétaires internationales.

Les objectifs qui avaient été fixés dans ce cadre, n'ont pu être tenus. Les circonstances ont été contre nous: trop d'entre eux demandaient un environnement international à la fois expansionniste et relativement calme.

Mais prendre acte de ce fait ne signifie pas accepter que notre action se développe désormais sans vue d'ensemble et sans programme. La Commission a donc décidé de reprendre le problème, de faire un bilan des résultats atteints, d'apprécier et de décrire les nouvelles perspectives de l'Union et d'indiquer les actions et les instruments qui permettront de les atteindre.

Nos réflexions en vue de dégager une voie nouvelle sont en cours. Nous les compléterons, le moment venu, par de larges consultations, et nous vous en saisirons. Il serait donc prématuré de vous livrer des conclusions alors que le travail n'est pas achevé.

Je voudrais cependant vous formuler deux réflexions personnelles. D'abord, je suis convaincu que, dans la phase de formation de l'Union, la coordination au sens fort – l'effort patient et parfois mal récompensé que nous devons faire pour tirer parti de la complémentarité de nos économies dans le sens d'une croissance saine – devra être renforcée et systématisée.

J'ai une deuxième certitude: il faut à l'Europe plus d'instruments communs, d'abord destinés à répondre à des besoins immédiats, mais qui développant et s'amplifiant, contribueront à la convergence des économies, et constitueront des éléments du nouvel ordre économique que nous établissons. Ceux qui existent, et ceux que nous voulons susciter, ne disposent encore ou ne disposeront au début que de moyens réduits. Passée la période expérimentale, s'ils font la preuve de leur utilité, et si la volonté politique de nos États est suffisante, ils devront recevoir des moyens et des missions à la dimension de l'économie européenne.

A cet égard, dans la réflexion d'ensemble que nous engageons, l'étude de la création d'une unité de compte européenne qui prépare la voie à l'Union monétaire, a une valeur capitale. Nous vous livrerons, le moment venu, nos réflexions et nos propositions sur ce sujet, mais c'est déjà ma conviction qu'il y a là un pas qu'il faut franchir, et j'espère que nos travaux en démontreront l'utilité et la possibilité.

Une telle démarche nous conduirait à une action à la fois inscrite dans une vue d'ensemble et aussi pragmatique, ce qui ne veut pas dire dépourvue d'ambition. D'ores et déjà, ne sous-estimons pas le pouvoir d'entraînement de premières expériences réussies, puis la capacité d'auto-accélération d'un processus bien engagé.

of action we are planning: a strengthened Monetary Cooperation Fund, a medium-term institute, European export bank and incentive, support or development machinery for the energy field would, if the Council accepts our proposals, give a little more substance to the still fragile framework of our Union.

I have given a brief outline of these various actions, begun or proposed, to show that if this programme is carried out, the Union will have made some progress even before other more ambitious or more complete objectives have been fixed. This is an incentive to us both – Commission and Parliament – to further action.

2. However, more fundamental progress will be required to ensure that Economic and Monetary Union is achieved.

The strategy followed in the past, as developed in the Werner Report and subsequently adopted by our institutions, consisted in a stage-by-stage approach. During each stage, a series of measures were to be taken concurrently in the main fields to ensure the convergence of the economies and growing solidarity in the monetary field and to provide increasing strength to European action in world economic and monetary relations.

The objectives that were set in this way have not been attained. Circumstances were against us, and too many of the objectives required an international climate that was both expansionist and relatively untroubled.

But acknowledging this fact does not mean accepting that our action will develop in future without an overall view or without a programme. The Commission has therefore decided to tackle this problem again, and to make an assessment of the results achieved, to evaluate and report on the present prospects for the Union and to spell out the actions and instruments which will help in attaining objectives.

We have already begun our policy review in this field, the aim being to find a new approach. At the right time, we shall conduct wide-ranging consultations, and we shall submit our ideas to you. But it is too early now to submit conclusions before the review work is finished.

I should like, however, to make two personal points. First of all, I am convinced that while the Union is being formed, coordination in the positive sense of the word – the patient and sometimes poorly rewarded effort we must make to use the complementary nature of our economies to achieve sound growth – will have to be reinforced and made more systematic.

There is a second point, of which I am quite sure: Europe needs more common instruments. These instruments will be intended first of all to meet the immediate requirements but, as they develop and expand, will help bring our economies closer together and will become part of the new economic order we are establishing. Those already in existence, and those we wish to establish, as yet only have or, in the early stages, will only have, limited resources. After the experimental period, if these instruments prove their usefulness and if the political will of our States is strong enough, they must be given resources and tasks commensurate with the scale of the European economy.

In this respect, the study of the creation of a European unit of account to prepare the way for Monetary Union is of capital importance in the overall review we are initiating. When the time comes, we will let you have our ideas and proposals on this subject, but I am already convinced that this is a step we must take and I hope that our research will show that it is feasible and worthwhile.

Such a step would lead on to action in line with overall policy but also pragmatic in nature, which is not the same as devoid of ambition. Let us not forget that initial successes can generate other successes or that a process that has got off to a good start can gather further momentum without additional stimulation.

Cinquième objectif: préparer l'Union européenne.

Telle que nous la vivons, l'Europe manque des perspectives qui pourraient mobiliser nos citoyens. Il faut lui rendre ces perspectives, si nous voulons vraiment achever la tâche historique entreprise il y a vingt-cinq ans. Il faut d'autres visions, et un autre élan, une autre image de l'avenir, pour que nos peuples mettent derrière l'Europe la capacité d'ambition, la ténacité, la passion créatrice, qui, par moments, nous ont portés si haut.

En dessinant l'Union européenne, nous pouvons recréer cet élan. N'oublions pas que le premier Parlement européen élu au suffrage universel se réunira en 1978, c'est-à-dire dans trois ans. Comme il est proche le moment où nous devrons dire à nos citoyens pour quoi ils vont voter. Par ce seul fait, le dialogue sur l'avenir va s'ouvrir avec eux. Nous devons nous y préparer.

Deux échéances proches jalonneront le processus qui vient de s'engager: le dépôt des rapports de l'Assemblée et de la Commission; la mission que les chefs d'État et de gouvernement ont confiée à M. Tindemans, premier ministre de Belgique.

La Commission attache une importance politique majeure à la contribution qu'elle prépare. Elle la considère comme une des grandes tâches de cette année, où, comme vous le voyez, sur tous les points, elle entend jouer son rôle d'initiative et d'inspiration. Notre travail est très engagé et nous respecterons l'échéance de fin juin qui nous a été fixée.

Chacun de nous, Assemblée et Commission, a son rapport à établir, et le fera suivant son jugement. Mais nous sommes évidemment prêts à garder, avec votre commission politique et avec votre Assemblée, tous les contacts qui nous permetttront, le moment venu, de confronter et rapprocher nos points de vue, même si nos démarches restent autonomes et nos contributions originales.

Je le redis, nous espérons que nos travaux aux uns et aux autres aideront à ouvrir enfin le grand dialogue sur l'Europe – ce débat imaginatif et créateur auquel doivent s'associer toutes les forces qui se réclament de notre entreprise; nous espérons que notre rapport tiendra assez compte et des nécessités de nos peuples, et des hautes ambitions qu'ils doivent se fixer ensemble, pour être utiles à M. Tindemans dans la grande mission de celuici.

La Communauté européenne a été la réponse originale apportée, il y aura demain vingt-cinq ans, au défi que constituait pour nos peuples l'obligation de surmonter leurs rivalités et de reconstituer leurs économies dans un univers profondément divisé par la guerre froide. Vingt-cinq ans, c'est une génération. C'est une nouvelle génération, la nôtre, qui est placée aujourd'hui devant de nouveaux défis: celui de dégager les raisons de vivre et d'espérer d'une société etouffée par son propre progrès, celui d'établir, entre l'Europe et les pays tu tiers monde, des rapports nouveaux fondés sur la coopération et la solidarité, celui enfin de redonner à l'Europe la maîtrise de son destin. Nous ne nous sommes pas privés de critiquer et de regretter les timidités, les insuffisances, les échecs des vingt-cinq années écoulées. Notre génération saura-t-elle faire autant et mieux? Nous disposons d'institutions, nous sommes mieux conscients des objectifs et des obstacles, mais notre volonté doit surmonter la lassitude née de la répétition d'initiatives et d'échecs, née aussi de la bureaucratisation inévitable de ce qui a été au début la grande aventure européenne.

Une impulsion a été donnée par nos gouvernements en décembre. Le mois qui suivait, vous l'avez, Mesdames et Messieurs, confirmée en créant les conditions de l'élection directe de votre Assemblée. Ce que la Commission se propose de faire cette année se situe dans cette perspective. Pour elle aussi, le chantier européen s'ouvre à nouveau. Vous l'y verrez présente, active, et courageuse, prête à prendre sa part dans ce nouvel élan pour l'Europe qui est notre grande tâche. Puisse-t-elle, éclairée par vos

Our *fifth objective* is to prepare the way for European Union.

The Europe we live in at the present time lacks a vision of the future of a kind that can win popular enthusiasm. We must restore this vision if we really wish to bring to a successful conclusion the historic task undertaken twenty-five years ago. We need new hearings, a new sense of purpose, a new outlook if our peoples are to commit to the European venture that ambition, that tenacity and that creative passion which at times have taken us to such heights.

In planning the European Union, we can restore this sense of purpose. Let us not forget that the first European Parliament elected by universal suffrage will meet in 1978, that is in three years time. The time will soon come when we will have to tell our citizens what they are voting for. For this reason alone, our debate with the Community's citizens on the Community's future must get under way. We must prepare ourselves for this.

Two tasks are an important part of the process which has now begun: the presentation of the reports of Parliament and the Commission, and the mission which the Heads of State or of Government entrusted to Mr Tindemans, the Prime Minister of Belgium.

The Commission attaches major political importance to the contribution it is preparing. It considers this to be one fo the major tasks of 1975 during which, as you have seen, it intends to play its role as a source of initiative and inspiration on every question. Our work is well in hand and we will meet the deadline at the end of June which we have been set.

Parliament and the Commission both have to make reports, and each will of course do this according to its own judgment. But ,we are naturally prepared to maintain every contact with your Political Affairs Committee and with Parliament itself to enable us, when the time comes, to compare and bring closer together our viewpoints, although our action will remain independent and our contributions our own.

Let me stress once again how much I hope that our work and yours will help finally to open the great dialogue on Europe, this imaginative and constructive debate which must involve all the forces associated in our enterprise. We hope that our report will come close enough to the real needs of our peoples and interpret accurately enough the high ambitions they must share to be of assistance to Mr Tindemans in his great mission.

The European Community was the bold response, made almost twenty-five years ago, to the challenge facing our peoples as a result of the obligation to overcome their rivalries and rebuild their economies in a world deeply divided by the Cold War. Twenty-five years is a whole generation. Ours is a new generation, faced by new challenges: to find reasons for life and hope in a society suffocated by its own progress, to forge new links between Europe and the countries of the Third World based on cooperation and solidarity, and finally to make Europe once again master of its own destiny. We have been quick to criticize and bemoan the lack of courage, the shortcomings and failures of the last twenty-five years. But will our generation do better, or even as well? We have the institutions, we are more aware of the objectives and obstacles, but we must have the will to overcome the lassitude borne of repeated initiatives and failures, borne too of the inevitable bureaucratization of what was, at the beginning, the great European adventure.

New impetus was given by our Governments in December. The following month, you confirmed this, Ladies and Gentlemen, by making the arrangements concerning the direct election of the members of your institution. The action that the Commission is proposing to take this year fits in with this outline for the future. For the Commission too, the work of building Europe is beginning again. You will find us active and courageous in this work, ready to play our part in this new effort for Europe which constitutes our great task. I hope that, enlightened by your criticism, but critiques, mais surtout appuyée sur notre conviction commune, trouver assez d'enthousiasme pour surmonter les scepticismes et aider à rendre les citoyens européens plus conscients des chances que leur promet l'Europe.

2. COMMUNIQUE PUBLIE A LA FIN DE LA REUNION DES CHEFS DE GOUVERNEMENT DE LA COMMUNAUTE PARIS 9 ET 10 DECEMBRE 1974

1. Les chefs de gouvernement des neuf États de la Communauté et les ministres des affaires étrangères, ainsi que le président de la Commission, réunis à Paris à l'invitation du président de la République française, ont procédé à un examen des divers problèmes qui se posent à l'Europe. Il a été pris acte, à cette occasion, des rapports préparés par les ministres des affaires étrangères. L'accord intervenu entre ces derniers sur divers points évoquées dans ces rapports a été enregistré.

2. Reconnaissant la nécessité d'une approche globale des problèmes internes que pose la construction européenne et de ceux avec lesquels l'Europe est confrontée à l'extérieur, les chefs de gouvernement estiment qu'il y a lieu d'assurer le développement et la cohésion d'ensemble des activités des Communautés et des travaux de la coopération politique.

3. Les chefs de gouvernement ont, en conséquence, décidé de se réunir, accompagnés des ministres des affaires étrangères, trois fois par an et chaque fois que nécessaire, en Conseil de la Communauté et au titre de la coopération politique.

Compte tenu des pratiques et procédures en vigueur, le secrétariat administratif sera assuré de manière appropriée.

En vue d'assurer la cohérence des activités communautaires et la continuité du travail, les ministres des affaires étrangères, en Conseil de la Communauté, sont chargés d'un rôle d'impulsion et de coordination. Ils peuvent se réunir à la même occasion au titre de la coopération politique.

Ces dispositions n'affectent, en aucune manière, les règles et procédures arrêtées par les traités ni celles prévues par les rapports de Luxembourg et de Copenhague en ce qui concerne la coopération politique. La Commission exerce les compétences et joue le rôle qui lui est dévolu par ces textes dans les diverses réunions mentionnées aux paragraphes ci-dessus.

4. Les chefs de gouvernement réaffirment, dans la perspective de l'unification européenne, leur volonté d'arrêter progressivement des positions communes et de mettre en oeuvre une diplomatie concertée dans tous les domaines de la politique internationale qui affectent les intérêts de la Communauté européenne. La présidence exerce la fonction de porte-parole des Neuf et se fait leur interprète sur le plan diplomatique. Elle veille à ce que la concertation nécessaire ait toujours lieu en temps utile.

Compte tenu du rôle de la coopération politique dans la construction européenne, il importe d'associer plus étroitement l'Assemblée à ces travaux, entre autres par voie de réponses aux questions adressées à la présidence par les parlementaires sur les activités de la coopération politique.

5. Les chefs de gouvernement jugent nécessaire de renforcer la solidarité des Neuf tant par l'amélioration des procédures communautaires que par le développement de nouvelles politiques communes, dans des secteurs à déterminer, et par l'octroi aux institutions des pouvoirs d'action qui seraient requis à cet effet.

6. Pour améliorer le fonctionnement du Conseil de la Communauté, ils estiment qu'il convient de renoncer à la pratique qui consiste à subordonner au consentement unanime des États membres la décision sur toute question, quelle que puisse être leur position respective à l'égard des conclusions arrêtées à Luxembourg le 28 janvier 1966.

7. Une plus grande latitude sera donnée aux représentants permanents de manière à n'évoquer devant le Conseil que les problèmes politiques les

above all supported by our common conviction, we may find sufficient enthusiasm to overcome scepticism and to make the peoples of Europe more keenly aware of the opportunities Europe holds out to them.

2. COMMUNIQUE OF THE MEETING OF THE HEADS OF GOVERNMENT OF THE COMMUNITY, PARIS 9–10 DECEMBER 1974

1. The Heads of Government of the nine States of the Community, the Ministers of Foreign Affairs and the President of the Commission, meeting in Paris at the invitation of the French President, examined the various problems confronting Europe. They took note of the reports drawn up by the Ministers of Foreign Affairs and recorded the agreement reached by these Ministers on various points raised in the reports.

2. Recognizing the need for an overall approach to the internal problems involved in achieving European unity and the external problems facing Europe, the Heads of Government consider it essential to ensure progress and overall consistency in the activities of the Communities and in the work on political cooperation.

3. The Heads of Government have therefore decided to meet, accompanied by the Ministers of Foreign Affairs, three times a year and, whenever necessary, in the Council of the Communities and in the context of political cooperation.

The administrative secretariat will be provided for in an appropriate manner with due regard for existing practices and procedures.

In order to ensure consistency in Community activities and continuity of work, the Ministers of Foreign Affairs, meeting in the Council of the Community, will act as initiators and coordinators. They may hold political cooperation meetings at the same time.

These arrangements do not in any way affect the rules and procedures laid down in the Treaties or the provisions on political cooperation in the Luxembourg and Copenhagen Reports. At the various meetings referred to in the preceding paragraphs the Commission will exercise the powers vested in it and play the part assigned to it by the above texts.

4. With a view to progress towards European unity, the Heads of Government reaffirm their determination gradually to adopt common positions and coordinate their diplomatic action in all areas of international affairs which affect the interests of the European Community. The President-in-office will be the spokesman for the Nine and will set out their views in international diplomacy. He will ensure that the necessary concertation always takes place in good time.

In view of the increasing role of political cooperation in the construction of Europe, the European Assembly must be more closely associated with the work of the Presidency, for example through replies to questions on political cooperation put to him by its Members.

5. The Heads of Government consider it necessary to increase the solidarity of the Nine both by improving Community procedures and by developing new common policies in areas to be decided on and granting the necessary powers to the institutions.

6. In order to improve the functioning of the Council of the Community, they consider that it is necessary to renounce the practice which consists of making agreement on all questions conditional on the unanimous consent of the Member States, whatever their respective positions may be regarding the conclusions reached in Luxembourg on 28 January 1966.

7. Greater latitude will be given to the Permanent Representatives so that only the most important political problems need be discussed in the Council. To this end, each Member State will take the measures it considers

plus importants. A cet effet, les dispositions que chaque État membre estimera nécessaires seront prises pour renforcer le rôle des représentants permanents et les associer à la préparation des positions nationales sur les affaires européennes.

8. Par ailleurs, ils conviennent de l'intérêt de faire usage des dispositions du traité de Rome, en vertu desquelles les compétences d'exécution et de gestion qui découlent des règlements communautaires peuvent être conférées à la Commission.

9. La coopération entre les Neuf dans des domaines dépassant le champ d'application des traités sera poursuivie dans les secteurs où elle a été engagée. Elle devrait être étendue à de nouveaux domaines par la réunion de représentants des gouvernements, réunis au sein du Conseil chaque fois que cela est possible.

10. Un groupe de travail sera constitué pour étudier la possibilité d'établir une union des passeports, et par anticipation, l'introduction d'un passeport uniforme.

Ce projet devrait être soumis aux gouvernements des États membres si possible avant le 31 décembre 1976. Dans ce projet seront notamment prévus une harmonisation par étapes de la législation sur les étrangers ainsi que l'abolition du contrôle des passeports à l'intérieur de la Communauté.

11. Un autre groupe de travail sera chargé d'étudier les conditions et les délais dans lesquels on pourrait attribuer aux citoyens des neuf États membres des droits spéciaux comme membres de la Communauté.

12. Les chefs de gouvernement ont constaté que l'objectif fixé par le traité, de l'élection au suffrage universel de l'Assemblée, devrait être réalisé le plus tôt possible. Sur ce point, ils attendent avec intérêt les propositions de l'Assemblée, sur lesquelles ils souhaitent que le Conseil statue en 1976. Dans cette hypothèse, l'élection au suffrage universel direct devrai intervenir à partir de 1978.

L'Assemblée se composant de représentants des peuples des États unis dans la Communauté, il est nécessaire que chaque peuple soit représenté d'une manière appropriée.

L'Assemblée est associée au développement de la construction européenne. Les chefs de gouvernement ne manqueront pas de prendre en considération les vues qu'ils lui ont demandé, en octobre 1972, d'exprimer à ce sujet.

Les compétences de l'Assemblée seront élargies notamment par l'octroi de certains pouvoirs dans le processus législatif des Communautés.

Déclaration de la délégation britannique

Le premier ministre britannique a déclaré que son gouvernement ne désirait pas empêcher les gouvernements des huit autres États membres de progresser dans la voie de l'élection de l'Assemblée au suffrage universel. Quant à lui, le gouvernement britannique ne peut pas prendre position sur la proposition en cause avant que le processus de renégociation n'ait été achevé et que les résultats de cette renégociation n'aient été soumis à l'approbation du peuple britannique.

Déclaration de la délégation danoise

La délégation danoise ne peut pas à ce stade s'engager à introduire l'élection au suffrage universel en 1978.

13. Les chefs de gouvernement constatent que le processus de transformation de l'ensemble des relations entre les États membres, conformément aux décisions prises en octobre 1972 à Paris, a déjà commencé, et ils sont déterminés à faire de nouveaux progrès dans cette voie.

Dans cette optique, ils estiment qu'il est opportun que les Neuf se mettent d'accord au plus tôt sur une conception d'ensemble de l'Union européenne. A cet égard et conformément aux demandes de la conférence necessary to strengthen the role of the Permanent Representatives and involve them in preparing the national positions on European affairs.

8. Moreover, they agree on the advantage of making use of the provisions of the Treaty of Rome, whereby the powers of implementation and management arising out of Community rules may be conferred on the Commission.

9. Cooperation between the Nine in areas outside the scope of the Treaty will be continued where it has already begun. It should be extended to other areas by bringing together the representatives of the Governments, meeting within the Council whenever possible.

10. A working party will be set up to study the possibility of establishing a Passport Union and, in anticipation of this, the introduction of a uniform passport.

If possible, this draft should be submitted to the Governments of the Member States before 31 December 1976. It will, in particular, provide for stage-by-stage harmonization of legislation affecting aliens and for the abolition of passport control within the Community.

11. Another working party will be instructed to study the conditions and the timing under which the citizens of the nine Member States could be given special rights as members of the Community.

12. The Heads of Government note that the election of the European Assembly by universal suffrage, one of the objectives laid down in the Treaty, should be achieved as soon as possible. In this connection, they await with interest the proposals of the European Assembly, on which they wish the Council to act in 1976. On this assumption, elections by direct universal suffrage could take place at any time in or after 1978.

Since the European Assembly is composed of representatives of the peoples of the States united within the Community, each people must be represented in an appropriate manner.

The European Assembly will be associated with the achievement of European unity. The Heads of Government will not fail to take into consideration the points of view which, in October 1972, they asked it to express on this subject.

The competence of the European Assembly will be extended, in particular by granting it certain powers in the Communities' legislative process.

Statement by the United Kingdom delegation

The Prime Minister of the United Kingdom explained that Her Majesty's Government did not wish to prevent the Governments of the other eight Member States from making progress with the election of the European Assembly by universal suffrage. Her Majesty's Government could not themselves take up a position on the proposal before the process of renegotiation had been completed and the results of renegotiation submitted to the British people.

Statement by the Danish delegation

The Danish delegation is unable at this stage to commit itself to introducing elections by universal suffrage in 1978.

13. The Heads of Government note that the process of transforming the whole complex of relations between the Member States, in accordance with the decision taken in Paris in October 1972, has already started. They are determined to make further progress in this direction.

In this connection, they consider that the time has come for the Nine to agree as soon as possible on an overall concept of European Union. Consequently, in accordance with the request made by the Paris meeting of présidentielle de Paris d'octobre 1972, ils confirment l'importance qu'ils attachent aux rapports des institutions de la Communauté. Ils demandent à l'Assemblée, à la Commission et à la Cour de justice d'avancer le dépôt de leurs rapports avant la fin du premier semestre 1975. Ils sont convenus de charger M. Tindemans, premier ministre du royaume de Belgique, de faire aux chefs de gouvernement, avant la fin de 1975, un rapport de synthèse sur la base des rapports des institutions, et des consultations qu'il mènera avec les gouvernements et les milieux représentatifs de l'opinion publique au sein de la Communauté.

Union économique et monétaire

14. Les chefs de gouvernement ayant constaté que les vicissitudes internes et internationales n'ont pas permis d'accomplir l'ensemble des progrès escomptés sur la voie de l'Union économique et monétaire, affirment qu'à cet égard leur volonté n'a pas fléchi et que leur objectif demeure celui qu'ils s'étaient fixé lors de la conférence de Paris.

Convergence des politiques économiques

15. Les chefs de gouvernement ont délibéré de la situation économique dans le monde et dans la Communauté.

16. Ils ont constaté que l'augmentation du prix de l'énergie aggrave les tendances inflationnistes et les déficits de balances de paiements, et accentue la menace d'une récession générale. Les mutations ainsi introduites dans les termes de l'échange imposent aux États membres une réorientation de leurs structures de production.

17. Les chefs de gouvernement confirment que l'objectif de la politique économique reste la lutte contre l'inflation et la défense de l'emploi. La coopération des partenaires sociaux constituera un élément essentiel pour le succès d'une telle politique. Ils soulignent que, dans les circonstances présentes, une haute priorité doit être accordée à une relance dans la stabilité, c'est-à-dire à une action qui vise à la fois la prévention d'une récession économique générale et la restauration de la stabilité. Il importe que cette action exclue tout recours au protectionnisme qui, par ses effets en chaîne, pourrait compromettre la relance économique.

Les États membres qui se trouvent dans la situation d'excédent de balance des paiements doivent mener une politique économique de stimulation de la demande interne et de maintien de l'emploi à un haut niveau sans toutefois créer de nouvelles conditions inflationnistes. Une telle attitude permettrait plus facilement aux pays qui connaissent des déficits importants de balance de paiements de poursuivre une politique qui permette, sans recourir à des mesures protectionnistes, d'assurer un niveau d'emploi satisfaisant, une stabilisation des coûts et l'amélioration de leurs comptes extérieurs.

18. Dans la perspective de l'effort à accomplir par les pays excédentaires, les chefs de gouvernement se félicitent des mesures de politique économique déjà adoptées par le gouvernement néerlandais, comme allant dans la direction souhaitée. Ils ont, en outre, pris connaissance avec satisfaction du programme conjoncturel envisagé par le gouvernement de la république fédérale d'Allemagne, notamment en ce qui concerne la relance de l'investissement privé et public, et de l'intention du gouvernement belge de s'engager également dans cette voie.

Ils ont également noté avec satisfaction les efforts entrepris par les pays déficitaires pour maintenir leur compétitivité afin de parvenir à un meilleur équilibre de la balance de paiements et d'améliorer le niveau de l'emploi.

19. Tout en tenant compte de la situation spécifique de chacun des États membres de la Communauté – qui rendrait inadaptée une politique

Heads of Government in October 1972, they confirm the importance which they attach to the reports to be made by the Community institutions. They request the European Assembly, the Commission and the Court of Justice to bring the submission of their reports forward to before the end of June 1975. They agreed to invite Mr Tindemans, Prime Minister of the Kingdom of Belgium, to submit a comprehensive report to the Heads of Government before the end of 1975, on the basis of the reports received from the institutions and of consultations which he is to have with the Governments and with a wide range of public opinion in the Community.

Economic and monetary union

14. The Heads of Government having noted that internal and international difficulties have prevented in 1973 and 1974 the accomplishment of expected progress on the road to EMU affirm that in this field their will has not weakened and that their objective has not changed since the Paris Conference.

Convergence of economic policies

15. The Heads of Government discussed the economic situation in the world and in the Community.

16. They noted that the increase in energy prices is adding to inflationary tendencies and balance of payments deficits and intensifying the threat of general recession. The resulting alterations in the terms of trade are forcing the Member States to redirect their production structures.

17. The Heads of Government reaffirm that the aim of their economic policy continues to be to combat inflation and maintain employment. The cooperation of both sides of industry will be essential if this policy is to succeed. They emphasize that in the present circumstances high priority must be given to economic revival in conditions of stability, i.e. action aimed both at preventing a general economic recession and restoring stability. This must not involve any recourse to protectionist measures which, by setting up a chain reaction, could jeopardize economic revival.

Member States which have a balance of payments surplus must implement an economic policy of stimulating domestic demand and maintaining a high level of employment, without creating new inflationary conditions. Such an attitude would make it easier for countries which have considerable balance of payments deficits to follow a policy which will ensure a satisfactory level of employment, stabilization of costs and an improvement in their external trade balance without resorting to protectionist measures.

18. In the context of the effort to be made by countries having a surplus, the Heads of Government greet the economic policy measures already adopted by the Netherlands Government as a step in the right direction. They also note with satisfaction the short-term economic programme which the Government of the Federal Republic of Germany intends to follow, particularly as regards stimulating public and private investment, and the fact that the Belgian Government intends to follow suit.

They also express satisfaction at the efforts made by the countries having a balance of payments deficit to maintain their competitive position so as to achieve a more satisfactory balance of payments and to improve the level of employment.

19. While acknowledging the special situation of each of the Member States of the Community – which makes a uniform policy inappropriate – the Heads of Government stress that it is absolutely necessary to agree on the policies to be adopted. This convergence will be meaningful only if it works towards Community solidarity and is based on effective permanent

uniforme – les chefs de gouvernement ont insisté sur l'urgente nécessité qu'il y avait à convenir en commun des politiques à entreprendre. Ces politiques convergentes ne prendront leur sens que si elles répondent à un objectif de solidarité communautaire et si elles s'appuient sur des mécanismes permanents et efficaces de consultation. Les ministres de l'économie et des finances sont chargés, dans le cadre des procédures communautaires, de mettre en oeuvre ces orientations.

20. Il est clair que l'ensemble de ces politiques n'aura toute sa portée que dans la mesure où les principaux pays industrialisés du monde sauront faire échec aux tendances naissantes à la récession.

A cet égard, ils ont pris note du compte rendu que le chancelier de la république fédérale d'Allemagne a présenté à l'issue de ses entretiens avec le président des États-Unis.

Ils souhaitent que le président de la république française, lors de sa prochaine rencontre avec le président Ford, souligne, au nom de la Communauté, l'importance d'une convergence des politiques économiques de l'ensemble des pays industrialisés selon les orientations indiquées ci-dessus.

Ils souhaitent également que la Communauté et ses pays membres agissent de même lors des consultations internationales à venir ainsi que dans les organismes internationaux compétents.

21. La Communauté continuera à contribuer au développement harmonieux du commerce mondial, notamment vis-à-vis des pays en développement et, à cet effet, prendra part dans un esprit constructif aux négociations commerciales du GATT, dont elle espère qu'elles seront bientôt poursuivies activement.

Politique régionale

22. Les chefs de gouvernement décident que le Fonds européen de développement régional, destiné à corriger les déséquilibres régionaux principaux dans la Communauté, résultant notamment d'une prédominance agricole, des mutations industrielles et d'un sous-emploi structurel, sera mis en oeuvre par les institutions de la Communauté à compter du 1er janvier 1975.

23. Le Fonds sera doté de 300000000 d'UC en 1975, de 500000000 d'UC pour chacune des années 1976 et 1977, soit 1300000000 d'UC, pour une période triennale d'essai.

24. Ce montant total de 1300000000 d'UC sera financé, à concurrence de 150000000 d'UC, par des crédits actuellement non utilisés du FEOGA (section ,,orientation").

Les ressources du Fonds seront réparties selon le schéma prévu par la Commission:

Belgique	1,5 %
Danemark	1,3 %
France	15 %
Irlande	6 %
Italie	40 %
Luxembourg	0,1 %
Pays-Bas	1,7 %
République fédérale d'Allemagne	6,4 %
Royaume-Uni	28 %

L'Irlande toutefois se verra, en outre, attribuer 6000000 d'UC, qui viendront en déduction de la quote-part des autres États membres, exception faite de l'Italie.

consultation machinery. The Ministers for Economic Affairs and Finance will be responsible, within the framework of Community procedures, for implementing these guidelines.

20. It is obvious that all these policies will be really effective only in so far as the world's major industrialized countries succeed in arresting incipient recessionary tendencies.

In this connection, they note the account given by the Chancellor of the Federal Republic of Germany of his talks with the President of the United States.

They desire that, at his forthcoming meeting with President Ford, the President of the French Republic should, on behalf of the Community, stress the importance of convergence between the economic policies of all industrialized countries along the lines indicated above.

They also wish the Community and its Member States to do the same during the forthcoming international consultations and in the appropriate international bodies.

21. The Community will continue to contribute to the harmonious expansion of world trade, especially in relation to developing countries, and in order to do so will take a constructive part in the GATT trade negotiations which it hopes to see actively continued in the near future.

Regional Policy

22. The Heads of Government decide that the European Regional Development Fund, designed to correct the principal regional imbalances in the Community resulting notably from agricultural predominance, industrial change and structural under-employment will be put into operation by the institutions of the Community with effect from 1 January 1975.

23. The Fund will be endowed with 300 million u.a. in 1975, with 500 million u.a. for each of the years 1976 and 1977, i.e. 1 300 million u.a., for a trial period of three years.

24. This total sum of 1 300 million u.a. will be financed up to a level of 150 million u.a. by credits not presently utilized from the EAGGF (Guidance Section).

The resources of the Fund will be divided along the lines envisaged by the Commission:

Belgium	1.5%
Denmark	1.3%
France	15 %
Ireland	6 %
Italy	40 %
Luxembourg	0.1%
Netherlands	1.7%
Federal Republic of Germany	6.4%
United Kingdom	28 %

Ireland will in addition be given another 6 million u.a. which will come from a reduction in the shares of the other Member States with the exception of Italy.

Problèmes de l'emploi

25. L'effort requis pour faire face à l'inflation, aux risques de récession et au chômage, tel qu'il a été décrit ci-dessus, doit respecter les impératifs d'une politique sociale de progrès et d'équité, faute de quoi il ne pourrait bénéficier de l'adhésion et de la participation des partenaires sociaux, tant au plan national qu'au plan communautaire.

A cet égard, les chefs de gouvernement soulignent que le Comité économique et social peut jouer un rôle important en vue d'associer les partenaires sociaux à la définition des objectifs économiques et sociaux de la Communauté.

Il importe, en premier lieu, d'entreprendre une action vigoureuse et coordonnée au niveau communautaire dans le domaine de l'emploi. Cette action implique que les États membres procèdent, en liaison avec les organisations intéressées, à la concertation appropriée de leurs politiques de l'emploi et arrêtent les objectifs prioritaires à atteindre.

26. Le Conseil de la Communauté examinera, le moment venu, à la lumière de l'expérience, en tenant compte des problèmes des régions et des catégories de travailleurs les plus touchés par les difficultés d'emploi, si et dans quelle mesure il s'avère nécessaire d'augmenter les moyens du Fonds social.

27. Convaincus que, dans cette période de difficultés économiques, un accent particulier doit être mis sur les mesures sociales, les chefs de gouvernement confirment l'importance qu'ils accordent à la réalisation des mesures inscrites dans le programme d'action sociale que le Conseil a approuvé par sa résolution du 21 janvier 1974.

28. Les chefs de gouvernement se fixent pour objectif l'harmonisation dans le progrès de la protection sociale assurée par chaque État membre sans que cela implique l'identité des systèmes sociaux en vigueur.

Energie

29. Les chefs de gouvernement ont discuté le problème de l'énergie et, dans ce contexte, les problèmes financiers essentiels qui se posent de ce fait à la Communauté et, au-delà de celle-ci, au monde.

30. Ils ont en outre noté que les ministres de l'énergie des pays de la Communauté se rencontreront le 17 décembre.

31. Les chefs de gouvernement, conscients de l'importance fondamentale du problème de l'énergie pour l'économie mondiale, ont discuté des possibilités de coopération entre pays exportateurs et pays importateurs de pétrole, et ont entendu un exposé du chancelier fédéral à ce sujet.

32. Les chefs de gouvernement attachent une très grande importance à la prochaine rencontre du président des États-Unis et du président de la République française.

33. Les chefs de gouvernement, se référant à la résolution du Conseil du 17 septembre 1974, ont invité les institutions communautaires à élaborer et à mettre en oeuvre, dans les délais les plus brefs, une politique énergétique commune.

Maintien de l'appartenance de la Grande-Bretagne à la Communauté

34. Le premier ministre du Royaume-Uni a indiqué „la base sur laquelle le gouvernement de Sa Majesté abordait les négociations concernant le maintien de l'appartenance de la Grande-Bretagne à la Communauté," et a exposé les problèmes spécifiques auxquels le gouvernement britannique attachait la plus haute importance.

35. Les chefs de gouvernement rappellent la déclaration faite, lors des négociations d'adhésion, par la Communauté, selon laquelle „si des situations inacceptables devaient apparaître, la vie même de la Communauté exigerait que les institutions y trouvent des solutions équitables."

36. Ils confirment que le système des ressources propres constitue un

Employment problems

25. The effort needed to combat inflation and the risks of recession and unemployment as described above must accord with the imperatives of a progressive and equitable social policy if it is to receive support and cooperation from both sides of industry, both at national and Community level.

In this respect, the Heads of Government emphasize that the Economic and Social Committee can play an important role in associating both sides of industry in the definition of the Community's economic and social aims.

Above all, vigorous and coordinated action must be taken at Community level to deal with the problem of employment. This will require the Member States, in conjunction with the organizations concerned, to coordinate their employment policies in an appropriate manner and to set priority targets.

26. When the time is ripe, the Council of the Community will consider, in the light of experience and with due regard to the problem of the regions and categories of workers most affected by employment difficulties, whether and to what extent it will be necessary to increase the resources of the Social Fund.

27. Being convinced that in this period of economic difficulty special emphasis should be placed on social measures, the Heads of Government reaffirm the importance which they attach to implementation of the measures listed in the Social Action Programme approved by the Council in its Resolution of 21 January 1974.

28. The Heads of Government make it their objective to harmonize the degree of social security afforded by the various Member States, while maintaining progress but without requiring that the social systems obtaining in all Member States should be identical.

Energy

29. The Heads of Government discussed the energy problem and in this connection the related major financial problems created for the Community and for the wider world.

30. They further noted that the Ministers of Energy of the Community countries are due to meet on 17 December 1974.

31. The Heads of Government, aware of the paramount importance which the energy problem has in world economy, have discussed the possibilities for cooperation between oil exporting and oil importing countries, on which subject they heard a report from the Federal Chancellor.

32. The Heads of Government attach very great importance to the forthcoming meeting between the President of the United States and the President of the French Republic.

33. The Heads of Government, referring to the Council Resolution of 17 September 1974, have invited the Community institutions to work out and to implement a common energy policy in the shortest possible time.

Britain's membership of the Community

34. The Prime Minister of the United Kingdom indicated the basis on which Her Majesty's Government approached the negotiations regarding Britain's continued membership of the Community, and set out the particular issues to which the Government attached the highest importance.

35. The Heads of Government recall the statement made during the accession negotiations by the Community to the effect that "if unacceptable situations were to arise, the very life of the Community would make it imperative for the institutions to find equitable solutions."

36. They confirm that the system of "own resources" represents one of the fundamental elements of the economic integration of the Community.

des éléments fondamentaux de l'intégration économique de la Communauté.

37. Ils invitent les institutions de la Communauté (le Conseil et la Commission) à élaborer le plus tôt possible un mécanisme correcteur, ayant une application générale, qui, dans le cadre du système et du fonctionnement des ressources propres, en s'inspirant de critères objectifs, prenant en considération en particulier les suggestions faites à cet égard par le gouvernement britannique, puisse éviter, pendant le processus de convergence des économies des États membres, l'apparition éventuelle de situations inacceptables pour un État membre et incompatibles avec le bon fonctionnement de la Communauté.

C. ORGANISATION INTERNE

1. DEVELOPPEMENT DES STRUCTURES INSTITUTIONNELLES

11. Les chefs de gouvernement, lors de la réunion du sommet de Copenhague, étaient convenus de rendre plus efficace le fonctionnement des institutions de la Communauté.

Dans sa déclaration sur l'état de la Communauté du 31 janvier 1974, la Commission a souligné que les reculs et échecs constatés à la fin de 1973 et au début de 1974 avaient fait douter de la capacité des institutions communautaires de remplir leur mission et que, devant le défi des difficultés monétaires et de la crise énergétique, les institutions actuelles de la Communauté touchaient à leurs limites.

La Commission, d'une part, a notamment attiré l'attention sur le fait que le blocage des mécanismes de décision de la Communauté était dû au fait que le principe d'unanimité, même lorsqu'il n'était pas invoqué, présidait en réalité à toute l'activité communautaire, et cela jusque dans les détails. Dans ces conditions, la Commission avait mis en évidence la nécessité d'une réhabilitation du mécanisme institutionnel.

D'autre part, elle a estimé que l'acheminement vers l'Union européenne et sa réalisation impliqueraient une modification profonde du rôle des institutions – Parlement, Conseil, Commission – qu'il faudrait préparer attentivement.

Dans une déclaration commune sur l'état de la Communauté, présentée au Conseil le 2 avril 1974, les présidents du Conseil et de la Commission ont estimé indispensable que la capacité de fonctionnement des institutions soit améliorée. Ils ont notamment reconnu qu'il n'est possible de faire des progrès sur les décisions de fond et de garantir durablement la capacité de fonctionnement de la Communauté qu'en améliorant les mécanismes de décision. Dans cette optique, ils ont formulé un certain nombre de propositions concrètes. A la suite de ces suggestions, le problème du fonctionnement des institutions communautaires a fait l'objet de délibérations du Conseil lors de ses sessions des 4 et 26 juin 1974. Une certaine convergence de vues au sujet des améliorations à apporter aux mécanismes de décision a trouvé expression notamment dans quelques décisions d'ordre organisationnel.

12. Les chefs de gouvernement, lors de leur séance des 9 et 10 décembre 1974, ont estimé qu'il y a lieu d'assurer le développement et la cohésion d'ensemble des activités des Communautés et des travaux de la coopération politique. Ils ont en conséquence décidé de se réunir, accompagnées des ministres des affaires étrangères, trois fois par an et chaque fois que nécessaire, en Conseil de la Communauté et au titre de la coopération politique. Compte tenu des pratiques et procédures en vigueur, le secrétariat administratif sera assuré de manière appropriée.

En vue d'assurer la cohérence des activités communautaires et la con-

37. They invite the institutions of the Community (the Council and the Commission) to set up as soon as possible a correcting mechanism of a general application which, in the framework of the system of "own resources" and in harmony with its normal functioning, based on objective criteria and taking into consideration in particular the suggestions made to this effect by the British Government, could prevent during the period of convergence of the economies of the Member States, the possible development of situations unacceptable for a Member State and incompatible with the smooth working of the Community.

C. INTERNAL ORGANISATION

1. INSTITUTIONAL DEVELOPMENTS

11. At the Copenhagen Summit Conference, the Heads of Government agreed to make the functioning of the Community institutions more effective.

In its Declaration on the state of the Community of 31 January 1974, the Commission commented that the setbacks and disappointments of late 1973 and early 1974 had cast grave doubt on the ability of the Community institutions to carry out properly the tasks assigned to them and that, in view of the monetary crisis and the energy crisis, the institutions in their existing form were now carrying a maximum burden.

The Commission pointed out that the deadlock in the Community decision-making system was due to the fact that the principle of unanimity – even when not explicitly invoked – overshadowed the entire range of Community activity down to the smallest details. The Commission therefore felt that the institutional machinery must be reviewed.

It also considered that progress towards and attainment of European union would involve a far-reaching transformation of the role of the existing institutions (Parliament, Council and Commission) and that this change should be prepared for carefully in advance.

In a Joint Declaration on the state of the Community, submitted to the Council on 2 April, the Presidents of the Council and of the Commission stated that the functioning of the institutions must be improved. In particular, they recognized that the decision-making machinery would have to be improved if any progress was to be made on substantive matters and if the ability of the Community to work was to be guaranteed in the long-term.

In this context, they made a number of practical proposals. In the light of these proposals the Council discussed the way the Community institutions worked at its sessions of 4 and 26 June. Some measure of agreement was reached on the improvements to be made to the decision-making machinery, and this was reflected, in particular, in a number of decisions adopted on organizational matters.

12. At their meeting of 9 and 10 December the Heads of Government stated that progress and overall consistency in the activities of the Communities and in the work on political cooperation must be ensured. They therefore decided to meet, accompanied by the Ministers of Foreign Affairs, three times a year and whenever otherwise necessary, in the Council of the Communities and in the context of political cooperation. The administrative Secretariat would be provided in an appropriate manner with due regard for existing practices and procedures.

In order to ensure the consistency of Community activities and continuity of work, the Ministers of Foreign Affairs, meeting in the Council of the tinuité de travail, les ministres des affaires étrangères, en Conseil de la Communauté, sont chargés d'un rôle d'impulsion et de coordination. Ils peuvent se réunir à la même occasion au titre de la coopération politique.

Ces dispositions n'affectent en aucune manière les règles et procédures arrêtées par les traités, ni celles prévues par les rapports de Luxembourg et de Copenhague en ce qui concerne la coopération politique. La Commission exerce dans les diverses réunions les compétences et joue le rôle qui lui est dévolu par ces textes.

Pour améliorer le fonctionnement du Conseil, les chefs de gouvernement ont estimé ,,qu'il convient de renoncer à la pratique qui consiste à subordonner au consentement unanime des États membres la décision sur toute question, quelle que puisse être leur position respective à l'égard des conclusions arrêtées à Luxembourg le 28 janvier 1966."

Par ailleurs, les chefs de gouvernement sont convenus de l'intérêt de faire usage des dispositions du traité de Rome, en vertu desquelles les compétences d'execution et de gestion qui découlent des règlements communautaires peuvent être conférées à la Commission.

Election du Parlement européen

13. En ce qui concerne l'élection du Parlement européen au suffrage universel direct, une résolution concernant un projet de convention instituant l'élection des membres du Parlement a été préparée au sein de la commission politique du Parlement. Par ailleurs, dans plusieurs États membres, des projets de lois portant élection directe des représentants de ces pays au Parlement européen sont à l'examen dans les instances législatives.

Les chefs de gouvernement ont constaté, lors de leur réunion des 9 et 10 décembre 1974, que l'objectif fixé par le traité, de l'élection au suffrage universel du Parlement européen, devrait être réalisé le plus tôt possible. Sur ce point, ils ont invité le Parlement à formuler des propositions sur lesquelles ils souhaitent que le Conseil statue en 1976. Dans cette hypothèse, l'élection au suffrage universel direct devrait intervenir à partir de 1978.

Les chefs de gouvernement sont également convenus que les compétences du Parlement seront élargies, notamment par l'octroi de certains pouvoirs dans le processus législatif des Communautés.

Le premier ministre britannique a déclaré que son gouvernement ne désirait pas empêcher les gouvernements des huit autres États membres de progresser dans la voie de l'élection du Parlement européen. Cependant, quant à lui, le gouvernement britannique ne peut pas prendre position sur la proposition en cause avant que le processus de renégociation n'ait été achevé et que les résultats de cette renégociation n'aient été soumis à l'approbation du peuple britannique. La délégation danoise a déclaré qu'à ce stade, elle ne pouvait pas s'engager à introduire l'élection au suffrage universel en 1978.

Cour de justice

14. Le Conseil, lors de sa 315e session du 26 novembre 1974, a décidé une adaptation des dispositions des traités relatives à la Cour de justice, permettant d'améliorer le fonctionnement de celle-ci pour tenir compte de l'accroissement de ses charges. Désormais la Cour pourra renvoyer à ses chambres l'examen de certaines questions préjudicielles, qui ont un caractère essentiellement technique ou qui concernent des questions pour lesquelles existe déjà une jurisprudence établie, et pour autant qu'aucun membre n'intervienne ou qu'une institution ne demande que l'affaire soit traitée en séance plénière.

Communities, will act as initiators and coordinators. They may hold political cooperation meetings at the same time.

These arrangements do not in any way affect the rules and procedures laid down in the Treaties or those on political cooperation contained in the Luxembourg and Copenhagen reports. At all these meetings, the Commission will exercise the powers vested in it and play the part assigned to it by the above texts.

In order to improve the functioning of the Council, the Heads of Government stated that "it is necessary to renounce the practice which consists of making agreement on all questions conditional on the unanimous consent of the Member States, whatever their respective positions may be regarding the conclusions reached in Luxembourg on 28 January 1966."

They also agreed on the advantage of making use of the provisions of the Treaty of Rome whereby the powers of implementation and management arising out of Community rules may be conferred on the Commission.

Election of the European Parliament

13. On the question of the election of the European Parliament by direct universal suffrage, a resolution concerning a draft Convention on the election of Members to Parliament has been prepared by the Political Affairs Committee of Parliament itself. Furthermore, draft laws providing for the direct election of representatives in Parliament are now being considered by the legislative bodies of a number of Member States.

On 9 and 10 December the Heads of Government placed on record their view that the election of the European Parliament by universal suffrage, one of the objectives laid down by the Treaty, should be achieved as soon as possible. They invited Parliament to make proposals, and expressed the wish that the Council would reach a decision on these proposals in 1976. On this assumption elections by direct universal suffrage could take place at any time in or after 1978.

The Heads of Government also agreed that the powers of Parliament should be extended, in particular by giving it certain powers in the Communities' legislative process.

The United Kingdom Prime Minister declared that Her Majesty's Government did not with to prevent the other eight Member States from making progress wish the elections. However, the Government could not take up a position on the proposal before the process of renegotiation had been completed and the results submitted to the British people. The Danish delegation stated that it was unable at that stage to commit itself to introducing elections by universal suffrage in 1978.

Court of Justice

14. At its 315th meeting, held on 26 November, the Council decided to adjust the Treaty provisions relating to the Court of Justice, with a view to improving the Court's procedural machinery so as to enable it to cope with an increased workload. Henceforth, certain requests for preliminary rulings concerning matters which are of an essentially technical nature or forwhich there is already an established body of case law may be assigned by the Court to its Chambers provided that no Member State objects and no institution asks for the case to be heard by the full Court.

Comité économique et social

15. La conférence au sommet de Paris de 1972 avait invité les institutions de la Communauté à reconnaître au CES le droit de rendre des avis de sa propre initiative sur toutes les questions touchant au travail communautaire. Ce droit, dont le Comité avait déjà fait usage en 1973, a été formellement reconnu au Comité par le Conseil lors de sa session des 11 et 12 février 1974. A cette occasion, le Conseil a également marqué son accord pour que le Comité publie lui-même les avis rendus par lui.

Pouvoirs budgétaires du Parlement européen

16. Les propositions de la Commission tendant au renforcement des pouvoirs budgétaires du Parlement européen ont été discutées au Conseil dès la fin de l'année 1973 et pendant tout le premier semestre 1974. Lors de sa session du 4 juin 1974, le Conseil a été en mesure de dégager des orientations communes sur les trois projets.

Ces orientations communes reprenaient dans une large mesure les propositions de la Commission.

17. Répondant au désir formulé par le Parlement, le Conseil lui a transmis, le 7 juin 1974, les différents textes sur lesquels il avait dégagé des orientations communes.

Deux rencontres ont eu lieu entre le Conseil et des délégations du Parlement, en présence de la Commission. Au cours de ces rencontres, les délégations du Parlement ont présenté les observations et critiques que ces orientations communes appelaient de leur part. Les discussions auxquelles ont participé non seulement le président en exercice, mais aussi plusieurs membres du Conseil, ainsi que la Commission, ont permis de rapprocher les positions des institutions sur plusieurs points.

18. Le 3 décembre 1974, le Conseil s'est mis d'accord sur le contenu du projet de traité concernant les pouvoirs budgétaires du Parlement et la création d'une Cour des comptes.

Ce texte sera transmis au Parlement et le Conseil demandera, conformément à la procédure de révision des traités, l'avis du Parlement sur la convocation d'une conférence des représentants des gouvernements des États membres. Lors de cette conférence seront arrêtées d'un commun accord les modifications à apporter aux traités.

Par ailleurs, à la suite d'une initiative de la Commission, le Conseil a approuvé le texte d'un projet de déclaration commune du Parlement, du Conseil et de la Commission relative à l'instauration d'une procédure de concertation entre le Conseil et le Parlement.

2. COMPOSITION ET FONCTIONNEMENT DES INSTITUTIONS COMMUNAUTAIRES

A. PARLEMENT EUROPEEN

Présidence

19. Lors de sa séance constitutive, le 12 mars 1974, le Parlement a procédé à l'élection de son président et de son bureau pour l'année parlementaire 1974–1975. M. Cornelis Berkhouwer (groupe des libéraux et apparentés, néerlandais) a été réélu président du Parlement. Ont été élus vice-présidents MM. Giovanni Bersani (groupe démocrate-chrétien, italien), Walter Behrendt (groupe socialiste, allemand), Lord Bessborough (groupe conservateur européen, britannique), Pierre-Bernard Cousté (groupe des

Economic and Social Committee

15. The Paris Summit Conference of 1972 called upon the Community institutions to recognize the right of the ESC to issue Opinions on its own initiative on any matter relating to Community life. The Committee had already exercised this right in 1973 and the Council formally recognized it at its session of 11 and 12 February this year. On this occasion, the Council also agreed that the Committee should publish its own Opinions.

Budgetary powers of the European Parliament

16. Late in 1973 and during the first half of 1974, the Council discussed the Commission's proposals for strengthening the budgetary powers of the European Parliament. A joint approach to the three proposals emerged from the Council session of 4 June.

This joint approach largely followed the same line as the Commission's proposals, though there were a number of points of divergence.

17. On 7 June, in response to a request from Parliament, the Council sent it the various texts on which a joint approach had been worked out.

There have been two meetings between the Council and delegations from Parliament, attended by the Commission. At these meetings, Parliament's delegations have presented their observations and criticisms on the joint approach. These discussions, in which both the President and a number of other members of the Council took part along with the Commission, enabled the views of the institutions to be brought into line on several points.

18. On 3 December the Council reached agreement on the content of a draft Treaty on the budgetary powers of the Parliament and the setting up of a Court of Auditors.

The draft will be sent to Parliament and, as required by the procedure for amending the Treaties, the Council will consult Parliament on the convening of a Conference of the Representatives of the Governments of the Member States. This Conference would determine by common accord the amendments to be made to the Treaties.

At the Commission's initiative, the Council has also approved a draft joint declaration by Parliament, the Council and the Commission on the introduction of a procedure for concertation between the Council and Parliament.

2. COMPOSITION AND FUNCTIONING OF THE INSTITUTIONS OF THE COMMUNITIES

A. EUROPEAN PARLIAMENT

President, officers, composition

19. At its constituent session on 12 March, Parliament elected its President and officers for the 1974/75 parliamentary year. Mr Cornelis Berkhouwer (Netherlands, Liberal and Allies Group) was re-elected President. The Vice-Presidents elected were Mr Giovanni Bersani (Italy, Christian Democratic Group), Mr Walter Behrendt (Germany, Socialist Group), Lord Bessborough (United Kingdom, European Conservative Group), Mr Pierre-Bernard Cousté (France, Group of European Progressive Democrats), Mr

démocrates européens de progrès, français), Gérard Bordu (groupe communiste et apparentés, français), Fritz Burgbacher (groupe démocrate-chrétien, allemand), Egidio Ariosto (groupe socialiste, italien), Charles McDonald (groupe démocrate-chrétien, irlandais), Poul Christian Dalsager (groupe socialiste, danois), Maurice Dewulf (groupe démocrate-chrétien, belge) et Joseph Wohlfart (groupe socialiste, luxembourgeois). Le même jour le Parlement a constitué ses douze commissions parlementaires. Au cours de l'année 1974, MM. Dalsager, Dewulf et Wohlfart ont été remplacés, en tant que vice-présidents, par MM. Ivar Nørgaard (groupe socialiste, danois), Lucien Martens (groupe démocrate-chrétien, belge) et Franckie Hansen (groupe socialiste, luxembourgeois).

Par ailleurs, le Parlement a nommé M. André Rossi rapporteur général sur le Septième Rapport général sur l'activité des Communautés en 1973 présenté par la Commission le 12 février 1974.

20. A la fin de l'année 1974, le Parlement a compté 183 membres, au lieu de 198, du fait que le parti travailliste britannique refuse toujours d'occuper les sièges qui lui reviennent.

Le Parlement compte six groupes politiques: le groupe démocrate-chrétien (51 membres), le groupe socialiste (49 membres), le groupe des libéraux et apparentés (29 membres), le groupe conservateur européen (20 membres), le groupe des démocrates européens de progrès (16 membres), le groupe communiste et apparentés (SF, Ind. sin.) (15 membres), ainsi que 7 membres non inscrits.

Activités

21. Le Parlement a tenu, en 1974, 14 sessions plénières dont 1 session extraordinaire, totalisant 56 jours de séance (contre 49 en 1973 et 46 en 1972). 8 de ces sessions (38 jours de séance) ont eu lieu à Strasbourg et 6 sessions (18 jours de séance) à Luxembourg.

Au cours de l'année 1974 le Parlement a voté 240 résolutions, dont 164 portant avis sur des propositions ou projets présentés par la Commission. Pour la première fois, le budget général des Communautés a été définitivement arrêté par le Parlement. Le nombre total des documents de séance s'est élevé, pendant l'année 1974, à 532, dont 187 consultations, 235 rapports, 31 propositions de résolution et 79 autres documents.

22. Des travaux très approfondis se sont déroulés au sein des commissions parlementaires qui ont tenu au total 299 réunions. A ces activités s'ajoutent les travaux des groupes politiques: le groupe démocrate-chrétien a tenu 59 réunions et 2 journées d'étude, le groupe socialiste 55 réunions et 2 journées d'étude, le groupe des libéraux et apparentés 30 réunions et 2 journées d'étude, le groupe conservateur européen 56 réunions et 1 journée d'étude, le groupe des démocrates européens de progrès 22 réunions et 2 journées d'étude, le groupe communiste et apparentés (SF, Ind. sin.) 19 réunions et 2 journées d'étude.

23. Au cours de l'année 1974, 801 questions écrites ont été posées par les membres du Parlement, dont 123 au Conseil et 678 à la Commission.

84 questions orales avec débat ont été posées (28 au Conseil et 56 à la Commission) ainsi que 12 questions orales sans débat (3 au Conseil, 9 à la Commission). Dans le cadre de l'heure des questions, le Conseil a répondu à 37 questions et la Commission à 90.

Par ailleurs, le Parlement a été saisi de 10 pétitions.

24. L'année 1974 a été dominée, pour le Parlement, par les affaires budgétaires. Le Parlement a fait preuve de pugnacité pour obtenir de nouveaux pouvoirs budgétaires. En ce qui concerne l'établissement du budget général des Communautés, c'est pour la première fois qu'a été appliquée la nouvelle procédure budgétaire selon laquelle le Parlement a le „dernier mot" sur les dépenses „non obligatoires" et arrête définitivement

Gérard Bordu (France, Communist and Allies Group), Mr Fritz Burgbacher (Germany, Christian Democratic Group), Mr Egidio Ariosto (Italy, Socialist Group), Mr Charles McDonald (Ireland, Christian Democratic Group), Mr Poul Christian Dalsager (Denmark, Socialist Group), Mr Maurice Dewulf (Belgium, Christian Democratic Group) and Mr Joseph Wohlfart (Luxembourg, Socialist Group). On the same day Parliament constituted its twelve Committees. In the course of the year Mr Ivar Nørgaard (Denmark, Socialist Group), Mr Lucien Martens (Belgium, Christian Democratic Group) and Mr Franckie Hansen (Luxembourg, Socialist Group) were elected Vice-Presidents in succession to Mr Dalsager, Mr Dewulf and Mr Wohlfart.

Mr André Rossi was appointed general rapporteur on the Seventh General Report on the Activities of the Communities in 1973, presented by the Commission on 12 February.

20. At the end of 1974, Parliament had 183 members, instead of 198, since the British Labour Party had still abstained from designating the members it is entitled to.

Parliament now has six political groups: the Christian Democratic Group (51 members), the Socialist Group (49 members), the Liberal and Allies Group (29 members), the European Conservative Group (20 members), the Group of European Progressive Democrats (16 members) and the Communist and Allies Group (15 members); seven members are not affiliated to any group.

Activities

21. Parliament held fourteen part-sessions, one of them an extraordinary session, totalling 56 days of meetings (as against 49 in 1973 and 46 in 1972). Eight of these sessions (38 days) took place in Strasbourg and six (18 days) in Luxembourg.

In the course of 1974 Parliament adopted 240 Resolutions, 164 of them embodying Opinions on Commission proposals or drafts. For the first time, the general budget of the Communities was finally adopted by Parliament. Working documents produced during the year totalled 532, of which 187 were in response to requests for opinions, 235 were reports, 31 were motions for resolutions and 79 were other documents.

22. The parliamentary committees carried out a considerable amount of very detailed work, and held 299 meetings in all. In addition there is the work done by the political groups: the Christian Democratic Group held 59 meetings and 2 seminars, the Socialist Group 55 meetings and 2 seminars, the Liberal and Allies Group 30 meetings and 2 seminars, the European Conservative Group 56 meetings and 1 seminar, the Group of European Progressive Democrats 22 meetings and 2 seminars, the Communist and Allies Group 19 meetings and 2 seminars.

23. In the course of the year the members of Parliament tabled 801 written questions, of which 123 were to the Council and 678 to the Commission.

Eighty-four oral questions with debate were put (28 to the Council and 56 to the Commission), and there were 12 oral questions without debate (3 to the Council, 9 to the Commission). At question time, the Council replied to 37 questions and the Commission to 90.

Ten petitions were submitted to Parliament in 1974.

24. Budgetary matters dominated the year for Parliament, which put up a determined fight to secure new budgetary powers. When the general budget of the Communities was being drawn up, the new budgetary procedure was applied for the first time. This gives Parliament the last word on other than necessary expenditure and makes it responsible for final adoption of the budget. Parliament made the most of its opportunities

le budget. Le Parlement a tiré le maximum des possibilités que lui offre cette nouvelle procédure et a obtenu un certain nombre de concessions de la part du Conseil. Lors de sa séance du 12 décembre 1974, le Parlement a définitivement arrêté le budget.

Par ailleurs le Parlement a été extrêmement vigilant à propos du développement de la Communauté et de la situation de crise et a organisé à plusieurs reprises des débats politiques.

B. CONSEIL

25. La présidence du Conseil a été exercée au cours du premier semestre 1974 par la république fédérale d'Allemagne, au cours du second semestre par la République française. En 1974, le Conseil a tenu 51 sessions dont 24 au cours du premier et 27 au cours du deuxième semestre. 17 sessions se sont tenues à Luxembourg.

26. 13 sessions ont été consacrées aux *relations extérieures*. Le Conseil, ayant poursuivi son examen des problèmes essentiels des relations avec les pays du Bassin méditerranéen dans le cadre de l'approche globale, a, lors de sa 302e session du 17 septembre 1974, marqué son approbation formelle sur les textes des directives complémentaires pour les négociations d'accords globaux avec l'Espagne, Israël et les pays du Maghreb ainsi que l'extension de l'accord actuel avec Malte à la coopération et l'agriculture.

Lors de sa 294e session du 25 juin 1974, il a approuvé le 9e rapport annuel d'activité 1973 du conseil d'association à la commission parlementaire mixte CEE-Turquie. Au cours de sa 302e session du 17 septembre 1974, le Conseil est convenu d'examiner de manière ouverte et positive l'ensemble des questions qui résultent, pour le bon fonctionnement de l'accord avec la Grèce, des développements intervenus pendant les sept dernières années.

Le Conseil a discuté plusieurs fois des relations avec les pays de l'AELE; il a pris diverses décisions lors de sa 308e session tenue le 15 octobre 1974 et a en outre procédé, lors de sa 312e session du 12 novembre 1974, à un échange de vues sur l'avenir des relations avec le Portugal, à la lumière des changements intervenus dans ce pays en avril 1974.

L'accord de 1965 sur les échanges commerciaux et la coopération technique entre la Communauté et les États membres d'une part, et le Liban, d'autre part, a été prorogé par décision du Conseil le 25 juin 1974.

Lors de sa 299e session des 22 et 23 juillet 1974, le Conseil et les représentants des États membres de la CECA réunis au sein du Conseil ont formellement approuvé deux décisions portant approbation des listes de concessions de la CEE et de la CECA, résultant de la conclusion des négociations au titre de l'article XXIV/6 du GATT. A la suite de plusieurs débats, le Conseil a arrêté, lors de cette même session, la décision instaurant une procédure de consultation pour les accords de coopération des États membres avec des pays tiers.

Lors de sa 317e session des 2 et 3 décembre 1974, le Conseil a adopté la décision arrêtant les régimes applicables dans les États membres, à partir du 1er janvier 1975, à l'égard des pays à commerce d'État pour des produits soumis à des restrictions quantitatives.

27. 5 sessions ont été tenues dans le cadre de la *coopération au développement*. Lors de la 284e session le 30 avril 1974, le Conseil est parvenu à un accord sur les résolutions concernant le volume de l'aide au développement, les conditions de l'aide et la répartition géographique. D'autre part, le Conseil a confirmé son approbation définitive des cinq résolutions adoptées lors de la 259e session en 1973. En juin, il a pris acte du mémorandum de la Commission relatif aux différentes formes d'aide communautaire au développement convenues au cours de négociations ou proposées par la Commission, et à l'évaluation de leur coût prévisible.

under the new procedure and succeeded in obtaining a number of concessions from the Council. The budget was finally adopted by Parliament at its 12 December sitting.

Parliament kept a close watch on developments in the Community and the current critical situation and organized a number of political debates.

B. COUNCIL

25. Germany was in the chair at the Council for the first half of 1974 and France for the second. The Council held 51 meetings in all: 24 during the first half of 1974 and 27 during the second half. Seventeen meetings were held in Luxembourg.

26. Thirteen meetings were concerned with *external relations*. The Council pursued its discussion of relations with the countries of the Mediterranean basin within the framework of the Community's overall approach to this area and, at its 302nd meeting, on 17 September, formally approved supplementary directives for the negotiation of comprehensive agreements with Spain, Israel, Algeria, Morocco and Tunisia and the extension of the present agreement with Malta to cover cooperation and agriculture.

At its 294th meeting, on 25 June, the Council approved the 9th annual report for 1973 by the Association Council to the EEC-Turkey Joint Parliamentary Committee.

During its 302nd meeting, the Council agreed to examine in an open and positive spirit the whole range of problems, resulting from developments over the last seven years, which affect the proper functioning of the Agreement with Greece.

Relations with EFTA countries were discussed on several occasions: a number of decisions were adopted at the Council's 308th meeting (15 October) and future relations with Portugal in the light of the changes that took place there in April were discussed at its 312th meeting (12 November).

The 1965 agreement on trade and technical cooperation between the Community and the Member States on the one hand, and Lebanon on the other was renewed by a decision of 25 June 1974.

At its 299th meeting, on 22 and 23 July, the Council and the Representatives of the ECSC Member States meeting within the Council formally adopted two decisions approving EEC and ECSC lists of concessions emerging from negotiations under Article XXIV(6) of the GATT. After a series of discussions, the same Council meeting approved a decision introducing a consultation procedure for cooperation agreements between Member States and non-member countries.

At its 317th meeting, on 2 and 3 December, the Council adopted a decision on the treatment to be accorded, as from 1 January 1975, to products subject to quantitative restrictions imported into the Member States from State-trading countries.

27. Five meetings dealt with *development cooperation*. At its 284th meeting, on 30 April, the Council reached agreement on resolutions concerning the volume, terms and geographical distribution of development aid. It also gave final approval to five resolutions adopted at its 259th meeting in 1973. In June the Council took note of the Commission's memorandum on the various forms of Community aid agreed upon, under negotiation or proposed by the Commission together with estimates of their probable cost.

At its 307th meeting, on 3 October, the Council agreed on the Community's initial contribution to the emergency operations undertaken by the

Il a décidé, au cours de sa 307e session du 3 octobre 1974, du montant de la première contribution communautaire aux opérations d'urgence des Nations unies en faveur des pays les plus affectés par la hausse des prix internationaux.

Le Conseil a marqué son accord sur la prorogation, pour un an, de la convention relative à l'aide alimentaire et a arrêté des décisions portant conclusion des accords entre la Communauté économique européenne et de nombreux pays en voie de développement.

Lors de sa 317e session tenue les 2 et 3 décembre 1974, il a arrêté les règlements et décisions relatifs à l'application pour l'année 1975 des préférences généralisées en faveur des pays en voie de développement.

Lors de la même session, le Conseil a adopté trois décisions autorisant la Commission à ouvrir des négociations avec le Pakistan, le Bangladesh et le Sri Lanka, en vue de la conclusion d'accords de coopération commerciale.

Il a en outre procédé à un échange de vues au sujet des orientations à retenir dans les relations de la Communauté avec l'Iran.

Le Conseil a examiné à plusieurs reprises l'état des négociations en vue de la conclusion d'une convention d'association avec les États d'Afrique, des Caraïbes et du Pacifique. Il a arrêté des directives complémentaires de négociations dans les domaines essentiels du futur accord (coopération commerciale, financière et technique, régime des produits agricoles, institutions).

Il a également préparé, lors de sa 299e session des 22/23 juillet, la conférence ministérielle tenue à Kingston (Jamaïque) les 25/26 juillet par les représentants des États ACP et de la Communauté en vue de faire le point des négociations et de leur donner une nouvelle impulsion. Dans cette perspective, il a pris position sur la stabilisation des recettes d'exportations des États ACP, sur les questions relatives au montant global de l'aide financière et technique que la Communauté envisage de prendre à sa charge, ainsi que sur la coopération industrielle. Il en a été de même pour le régime des importations de sucre en provenance des ACP à des conditions préférentielles.

Le Conseil s'est également penché sur les relations avec les EAMA et les PTOM. Il a notamment arrêté, lors de sa 312e session du 12 novembre 1974, la décision fixant l'échéancier des contributions des États membres à appeler en 1975 pour le Fonds européen de développement.

28. Dans le domaine de l'*agriculture*, il y a eu 14 sessions du Conseil dont plusieurs ont été consacrées aux problèmes des prix agricoles que le Conseil a fixés lors de sa 281e session tenue du 21 au 23 mars 1974. Toutefois, à la lumière de l'évolution rapide de la situation économique et de ses incidences sur les revenus des agriculteurs, le Conseil a marqué finalement son accord en octobre sur un ensemble de mesures de redressement comportant notamment une augmentation générale des prix communs de 5 %.

Tenant compte de l'évolution de certaines monnaies sur les marchés de change, le Conseil a arrêté des règlements modifiant le taux de conversion, utilisé dans la politique agricole commune, de la lire italienne, la livre anglaise et la livre irlandaise.

Le marché de la viande bovine a retenu l'attention du Conseil qui a pris une série de mesures dans le cadre d'un plan communautaire d'urgence en vue de stabiliser ce marché. La situation du marché du vin a fait l'objet de plusieurs sessions aboutissant lors de la 314e session, le 19 novembre, à un accord de principe sur le déclenchement d'une opération de distillation dans certaines régions. Les problèmes de l'approvisionnement et du futur régime du sucre dans la Communauté ont été examinés.

En janvier 1974, le Conseil a arrêté la directive sur l'agriculture de montagne et de certaines zones défavorisées; toutefois, cette directive ne prendra effet que lorsqu'auront été arrêtées, d'une part, la liste des régions concernées et, d'autre part, certaines dispositions relatives à la participation financière de la Communauté.

United Nations to assist the countries most affected by international price increases.

The Council agreed to a year's extension of the Food Aid Convention and adopted decisions concluding agreements between the European Economic Community and numerous developing countries.

At its 317th meeting (2 and 3 December) the Council adopted regulations and decisions relating to the application of generalized preferences in favour of developing countries in 1975.

At the same meeting the Council adopted three decisions authorizing the Commission to open negotiations with Pakistan, Bangladesh and Sri Lanka for the conclusion of trade cooperation agreements.

It also discussed the guidelines to be adopted in relations between the Community and Iran.

The Council reviewed progress in the negotiations for the conclusion of an association convention with the African, Caribbean and Pacific States on a number of occasions. It adopted additional negotiating directives concerning major aspects of the future agreement (commercial, financial and technical cooperation, agricultural products, institutions).

At its 299th meeting, on 22 and 23 July, the Council prepared for the ministerial conference of representatives of the ACP countries and the Community held in Kingston, Jamaica, on 25 and 26 July to assess progress and give fresh impetus to the negotiations. The Council worked out its position on stabilization of the ACP countries' export earnings, questions relating to the total amount of financial and technical aid which the Community intends to provide, industrial cooperation and arrangements for imports of sugar from the ACP on preferential terms.

The Council also considered relations with the AASM and the OCT. At its 312th meeting, on 12 November, it adopted a decision laying down the schedule of due dates for Member States' contributions to the European Development Fund to be called up in 1975.

28. In the field of *agriculture*, there were 14 meetings of the Council, several of them dealing with problems arising in connection with the agricultural prices fixed by the Council at its 281st meeting on 21–23 March. However, in view of the effect that the rapidly changing economic situation was having on farmers' incomes, the Council finally agreed in October to a series of remedial measures, the most important of these being a 5% increase in all common prices.

The movement of certain currencies on foreign exchange markets led the Council to adopt regulations modifying the exchange rate applied in agriculture for the Italian lira, the pound sterling and the Irish pound.

The Council devoted considerable time to discussion of the beef and veal market and adopted a series of measures in the context of an emergency Community plan to stabilize it. The situation on the wine market was reviewed at a number of meetings, and on 19 November (314th meeting) agreement in principle was reached on the launching of a distilling operation in certain regions. Sugar supplies and future Community arrangements for sugar were also examined.

In January 1974 the Council adopted a directive on hill farming and farming in certain less-favoured areas. The directive will not take effect, however, until a list of affected regions is agreed and provisions concerning Community financing approved.

29. In 1974 seven Council meetings were devoted exclusively to *economic and financial* affairs. The Council first adopted a decision adjusting the economic policy guidelines for 1974 to take account of the new requirements of the economic situation and then the annual report on the situation in the Community, which laid down the economic policy guidelines to be followed by the Member States in 1975. To assist Member States experiencing balance of payments difficulties as a result of higher oil prices, the Council approved a regulation authorizing the floating of Community

29. 7 sessions du Conseil ont été entièrement consacrées, au cours de l'année 1974, aux questions *économiques et financières*. En matière de politique économique, le Conseil a adopté successivement une décision portant adaptation des orientations de politique économique pour 1974, afin de tenir compte des nécessités nouvelles de l'évolution économique, et le rapport annuel sur la situation de la Communauté fixant les orientations de politique économique à suivre par chaque État membre en 1975. Pour contribuer aux besoins de financement des États membres éprouvant des difficultés de balance des paiements provoquées par le renchérissement des produits pétroliers, le Conseil a approuvé un règlement permettant l'émission d'emprunts communautaires, ainsi qu'un premier règlement d'application. Ayant constaté l'opportunité pour la Communauté de contribuer aux besoins de financement à moyen terme de l'Italie, le Conseil a approuvé une directive accordant à ce pays un concours financier à moyen terme.

Par ailleurs, le Conseil s'est penché sur diverses autres questions dans le domaine des relations monétaires et financières internationales.

30. En matière *sociale*, le Conseil a arrêté, lors de sa 274e session des 21/22 janvier 1974, la résolution concernant le programme d'action sociale; en vue de la mettre en oeuvre il a marqué, au cours de sa 291e session du 10 juin 1974, son accord sur la décision relative à l'intervention du Fonds social en faveur des travailleurs migrants et sur un règlement concernant une aide financière nouvelle pour l'enseignement aux enfants de ces travailleurs. Par ailleurs, le Conseil a décidé d'instituer un comité consultatif pour la sécurité, l'hygiène et la protection de la santé sur le lieu de travail. En outre, il a marqué son accord sur un premier programme d'action communautaire pour la réadaptation professionnelle des handicapés ainsi que sur la décision relative à l'intervention du Fonds social européen en faveur de l'intégration sociale et professionnelle de ces personnes.

Par ailleurs, au cours de sa 320e session du 17 décembre 1974, le Conseil a poursuivi son action tendant à la mise en oeuvre du programme social. Il a ainsi marqué son accord sur une directive concernant l'application du principe de l'égalité des rémunérations entre les hommes et les femmes, sur une directive concernant le licenciement collectif; il a enfin approuvé la création d'un centre européen pour la formation professionnelle ainsi qu'un fondation pour l'amélioration des conditions de vie et de travail.

En matière *régionale*, le Conseil a poursuivi ses travaux relatifs à la création d'un Fonds européen de développement régional.

31. La 290e session des 6 et 7 juin 1974 a été consacrée aux problèmes de l'*éducation*. Le Conseil a pris note d'un rapport sur la mise en route de l'Institut universitaire européen. Deux résolutions ont été prises: la première, par le Conseil, visant à accélérer les travaux relatifs à la reconnaissance mutuelle des diplômes, certificats et autres titres, et la deuxième, par les ministres de l'éducation réunis au sein du Conseil, concernant la coopération dans le domaine de l'éducation. Pour élaborer des actions dans ces domaines, les ministres ont instauré un comité de l'éducation.

32. En matière *énergétique*, le Conseil a décidé, lors de sa 275e session du 30 janvier 1974, la création d'un comité de l'énergie et a adopté le règlement concernant l'établissement de bilans énergétiques exhaustifs pour la Communauté. Les 4/5 février, le Conseil a chargé les présidents du Conseil et de la Commission de représenter la Communauté à la conférence de Washington sur les problèmes de l'énergie et a fixé leur mandat.

Le Conseil a débattu, lors de sa 308e session du 15 octobre 1974, de certains problèmes liés à la conclusion de l'accord résultant des travaux du groupe de coordination créé par cette conférence.

En mai 1974, le Conseil a donné des directives à la Commission pour la négociation d'un accord de garanties entre la CEEA, le Royaume-Uni et loans and adopted a first implementing regulation. The Council also felt that the Community should help to meet Italy's medium-term financing needs and approved a directive granting Italy medium-term financial assistance.

The Council also discussed various other aspects of international monetary and financial relations.

30. At its 274th meeting, on 21 and 22 January, the Council adopted a resolution on the *social* action programme. A first step towards implementing this resolution was taken at its 291st meeting, on 10 June, when agreement was reached on a decision concerning action by the Social Fund to assist migrant workers and a regulation on financial assistance for courses geared to the needs of migrant workers' children. The Council also decided to set up an Advisory Committee on Safety, Hygiene and Health Protection at Work, approved an initial Community action programme for the occupational rehabilitation of the handicapped and adopted a decision on action by the European Social Fund to promote the social and occupational integration of the handicapped.

At its 320th meeting, on 17 December, the Council moved ahead with the implementation of the social action programme. It approved a directive on equal pay for men and women and a directive on mass dismissals; lastly, it endorsed the establishment of a European Vocational Training Centre and a Foundation for the Improvement of Living and Working Conditions.

On *regional* policy, the Council continued its discussions on the creation of a European Regional Development Fund.

31. The Council's 290th meeting, on 6 and 7 June, was devoted to *educational* matters. A progress report on the launching of the European University Institute was noted. Two Resolutions were adopted, the first by the Council on the speeding up of work on the mutual recognition of diplomas, certificates and other evidence of formal qualifications, and the second by the Ministers of Education meeting within the Council on cooperation in this field of education. The Council set up an Education Committee to prepare measures in these fields.

32. As far as *energy* is concerned, the Council at its 275th meeting, on 30 January, decided to set up an Energy Committee and adopted a regulation on the compilation of detailed energy balance sheets for the Community. On 4/5 February it instructed the Presidents of the Council and the Commission to represent the Community at the Washington Conference on international oil policy and fixed their terms of reference.

At its 308th meeting on 15 October the Council discussed a number of problems relating to the conclusion of the Agreement emanating from the Coordination Group set up at the Conference.

In May 1974 the Council gave the Commission a mandate to negotiate an agreement on safeguards between the EAEC, the United Kingdom and the IAEA. In November it gave the Commission a brief to negotiate an agreement on nuclear cooperation between the EAEC and Sweden.

A Resolution on enriched uranium supplies for the Community was adopted at the Council's 287th meeting, on 4 June.

A resolution on the new energy policy strategy proposed by the Commission was approved at its 302nd meeting, on 17 September. In December the Council went on to lay down the 1985 objectives of the Community energy policy; in this connection it approved a resolution on a Community programme of action for the rational utilization of energy. It also adopted a new Community research programme on plutonium recycling in light-water reactors.

33. In January the Council adopted four resolutions on the action programme on *scientific and technological policy* proposed by the Commission, an important step towards the development of common policy in this field.

The 319th Council meeting, on 11 December, was devoted to *transport*.

l'AIEA. En novembre 1974, il a donné des directives à la Commission pour négocier un accord de coopération nucléaire entre la CEEA et la Suède.

Au cours de sa 287e session du 4 juin 1974, le Conseil a adopté une résolution concernant l'approvisionnement en uranium enrichi de la Communauté.

Lors de sa 302e session du 17 septembre 1974, le Conseil a adopté une résolution relative à la „nouvelle stratégie de politique énergétique" proposée par la Commission. Par la suite, il a défini, en décembre, les objectifs pour 1985 de la politique énergétique communautaire et, dans le cadre de ces objectifs, il a marqué son accord sur une résolution relative à un programme d'action communautaire dans le domaine de l'utilisation rationnelle de l'énergie. En outre, le Conseil a arrêté un nouveau programme de recherche communautaire concernant le recyclage du plutonium dans les réacteurs à eau légère.

33. En janvier, le Conseil a arrêté quatre résolutions relatives au programme d'action en matière de *politique scientifique et technologique* proposé par la Commission, marquant ainsi une étape importante en ce qui concerne le développement d'une politique commune dans ce domaine.

La 319e session du Conseil, tenue le 11 décembre 1974, a été consacrée aux questions de transport. Le Conseil a marqué son accord sur une directive relative à l'établissement de règles communes pour certains transports combinés rail/route de marchandises entre États membres. Il a adopté deux règlements modifiant et prorogeant les règlements relatifs au système de tarifs à fourchettes et au contingent communautaire pour les transports de marchandises par route entre États membres. Il a pris acte d'un rapport relatif à l'aménagement des systèmes nationaux de taxes sur les véhicules utilitaires. Le Conseil a marqué son accord de principe sur une décision relative à l'assainissement des entreprises de chemins de fer et aux relations financières entre ces entreprises et les États. Le Conseil a marqué son accord sur une décision modifiant et complétant les directives de négociations d'un accord visant l'immobilisation temporaire de bateaux affectés aux transports de marchandises, notamment dans le bassin rhénan.

34. Lors de sa 287e session du 4 juin 1974, le Conseil a arrêté la directive sur la réalisation de la *liberté d'établissement et la libre prestation des services* pour les activités d'intermédiaires relevant du commerce et de la distribution des produits toxiques, aussi bien que les mesures transitoires permettant également l'utilisation professionnelle de ces produits.

35. Outre diverses décisions de gestion en matière d'*union douanière*, le Conseil a adopté, en juin, une résolution relative aux mesures à prendre en vue de simplifier les tâches des administrations douanières. Le règlement relatif au régime commun applicable aux importations a été arrêté également en juin.

Le Conseil a par ailleurs pris diverses décisions intéressant le domaine des conventions internationales en matière douanière. Il a ainsi autorisé, le 4 juin, la conclusion et la signature de la convention internationale pour la simplification et l'harmonisation des régimes douaniers et décidé à cette même occasion l'acceptation, au nom de la Communauté, d'une annexe à cette convention. Il a adopté également plusieurs décisions autorisant la Commission à négocier, au nom de la Communauté, et selon une procédure ad hoc de coordination avec les États membres, diverses annexes à la convention susvisée, et à mener, au nom de la Communauté et selon cette même procédure, des négociations en vue de la révision de la convention TIR et de l'élaboration, au sein du Conseil de coopération douanière, d'un système harmonisé de désignation et de codification des marchandises.

36. Dans le domaine de la politique *industrielle*, le Conseil a arrêté, en janvier, une résolution concernant une politique communautaire de l'informatique et a poursuivi ses travaux en vue de l'élimination des entraves techniques aux échanges de produits industriels par l'adoption, au cours de l'année 1974, de plus de 10 directives en la matière.

The Council adopted a directive on common action on the combined rail/road carriage of goods between States. It adopted two regulations amending and extending the regulations on the bracket tariff system and on the Community quota for the carriage of goods by road between Member States. It noted a report on the adjustment of national provisions for taxing commercial vehicles. It approved the principle of a decision on measures to place railway undertakings on a sound footing and on the harmonization of financial relations between those undertakings and the States. It approved a decision amending and supplementing the negotiating directives relating to the agreement on the temporary laying-up of inland waterway goods vessels, with particular reference to the Rhine.

34. At its 287th meeting, on 4 June, the Council adopted a directive on the attainment of *freedom of establishment and freedom to provide services* in respect of activities of self-employed persons and of intermediaries engaging in the trade in and distribution of toxic products and transitional measures to facilitate the professional use of these products.

35. Apart from a number of routine decisions relating to the *customs union*, the Council adopted a resolution in June on measures to be taken to simplify the task of the customs administrations and a regulation on common import arrangements.

A number of decisions were also taken in respect of international customs conventions. For instance, on 4 June, the Council authorized the conclusion and signature of the International Convention for the Simplification and Harmonization of Customs Procedures and, at the same time, decided to accept an annex to the Convention on behalf of the Community. The Council also adopted several decisions authorizing the Commission to negotiate a number of annexes to the same Convention on behalf of the Community and in accordance with an *ad hoc* procedure for coordination with the Member States and to conduct negotiations on the same basis for the revision of the TIR Convention and for the elaboration, within the Customs Cooperation Council, of a harmonized system for the description and classification of goods.

36. Turning to *industrial* policy, the Council adopted a resolution in January on a Community data-processing policy, and has continued its work on the removal of technical barriers to trade in industrial products by adopting ten directives in the course of the year.

37. At its 311th meeting, on 7 November, the Council adopted a recommendation to Member States concerning the allocation of the cost of action by public authorities in *environmental* matters – the "polluter pays" principle. The Community's action programme on the environment was discussed at length and a directive on the disposal of waste oils and a resolution on energy and the environment were adopted.

38. On 26 November the Ministers of Justice held a second meeting; the first was in June 1971. They considered a series of questions relating to Community law. These included: the penalties which may be imposed by Community institutions for infringements of the law relating to competition and transport; the rules of procedure and functioning of the Court of Justice; the consolidation or codification and presentation of Community regulations and the establishment of a data retrieval system for Community law. They also noted progress on a number of current proposals and drafts, particularly in areas such as company law, the legal profession, cooperation in economic criminal law and private international law.

39. The Council participated in Question Time at each session of Parliament and was associated with major debates or oral questions with or without debate. It studied the question of increasing Parliament's budgetary powers in great detail and succeeded in reaching agreement on this issue at its 317th meeting on 2 and 3 December.

At its 277th meeting, on 11 and 12 February, the Council approved a series of measures to streamline decision-making.

37. Le Conseil a adopté la recommandation aux États membres concernant l'imputation des coûts de l'intervention des pouvoirs publics en matière d'*environnement* – dit principe „pollueur payeur," lors de sa 311e session du 7 novembre 1974. Le programme d'action communautaire sur le plan de l'environnement a fait l'objet d'un large échange de vues et le Conseil a adopté la directive concernant l'élimination des huiles usagées et la résolution sur l'énergie et l'environnement.

38. Les ministres de la justice des États membres ont tenu une deuxième réunion le 26 novembre, la première ayant eu lieu en juin 1971. Ils ont examiné une série de dossiers touchant au droit communautaire telles: les sanctions que peuvent appliquer les institutions dans les domaines de la concurrence et des transports; les règles de procédure et de fonctionnement de la Cour de justice; la codification et la présentation des actes réglementaires et l'automatisation de la documentation juridique. En outre, ils ont pris acte de l'état d'avancement de plusieurs propositions ou projets en cours d'élaboration et concernant notamment le droit des sociétés, la profession de l'avocat, la coopération en matière de droit pénal économique, ainsi que le droit international privé.

39. Le Conseil a participé à chaque session à l'heure réservée aux questions et à d'autres travaux du Parlement, soit à l'occasion de débats importants, soit par le biais de questions orales avec ou sans débat. Il a longuement examiné le problème de l'accroissement des pouvoirs budgétaires du Parlement et ses travaux lui ont permis, lors de sa 317e session des 2 et 3 décembre 1974, de dégager un accord en la matière.

Lors de sa 277e session des 11 et 12 février 1974, le Conseil a approuvé un ensemble de mesures tendant à améliorer la procédure de prise de décision au sein du Conseil.

40. Le budget général des Communautés européennes pour l'exercice 1975 a été adopté pour la première fois selon les dispositions des articles 78 CECA, 203 CEE et 177 CEEA modifiés par le traité du 22 avril 1970 portant modification de certaines dispositions budgétaires. Lors de sa 304e session du 23 septembre 1974, le Conseil a établi le projet de budget et lors de sa 316e session du 28 novembre 1974, il a statué sur le projet de budget amendé et assorti de propositions de modification par le Parlement.

C. COMMISSION

Composition

41. Par décision des représentants des gouvernements des États membres, M. Guido Brunner a été nommé, le 11 novembre 1974, membre de la Commission jusqu'au 5 janvier 1977 inclus, en remplacement de M. Ralf Dahrendorf, démissionnaire.

Les représentants des gouvernements des États membres de la Communauté, après consultation de la Commission, ont décidé, le 19 décembre 1974, de proroger le mandat de président de la Commission de M. François-Xavier Ortoli jusqu'au 5 janvier 1977.

Liste des membres de la commission

(indiquant leur compétences)

Président	François-Xavier Ortoli	Secrétariat général Service juridique Groupe du porte-parole Bureau de securité

40. The general budget of the European Communities for 1975 was adopted for the first time under Articles 78 of the ECSC Treaty, 203 of the EEC Treaty and 177 of the EAEC Treaty as amended by the Budget Treaty of 22 April 1970. The Council drew up the draft budget at its 304th meeting (23 September) and approved the new draft budget based on Parliament's amendments and proposed modifications at its 316th meeting (28 November).

C. COMMISSION

Composition

41. On 11 November the Representatives of the Governments of the Member States appointed Mr Guido Brunner a Member of the Commission until 5 January 1977, to replace Mr Ralf Dahrendorf following the latter's resignation.

The Representatives of the Governments of the Member States, after consulting the Commission, decided on 19 December to extend until 5 January 1977 the term of office of the President of the Commission, Mr François-Xavier Ortoli.

List of the Members of the Commission

(indicating their special responsibilities)

President	François-Xavier ORTOLI	Secretariat Legal Service Spokesman's Group Security Office

Vice-président	Wilhelm HAFERKAMP	Affaires économiques et financières Crédit et investissements
Vice-président	Carlo SCARASCIA MUGNOZZA	Suit avec le président les affaires parlementaires Politique de l'environnement Protection des intérêts du consommateur Transports Presse et information
Vice-président	Sir Christopher SOAMES	Relations extérieures
Vice-président	Patrick John HILLERY	Affaires sociales
Vice-président	Henri SIMONET	Institutions financières et fiscalité Energie Agence d'approvisionnement d'Euratom
Membre	Altiero SPINELLI	Affaires industrielles et technologiques
Membre	Albert BORSCHETTE	Concurrence Personnel et administration
Membre	George THOMSON	Politique régionale
Membre	Petrus Josephus LARDINOIS	Agriculture
Membre	Finn Olav GUNDELACH	Marché interieur et gestion de l'union douanière
Membre	Claude CHEYSSON	Affaires de développement et coopération Budgets et contrôle financier
Membre	Guide BRUNNER	Recherche, science et éducation Centre commun de recherches Office statistique Diffusion de connaissances scientifiques et techniques

Activités

42. En 1974, la Commission a tenu 44 réunions. En application des traités, elle a transmis au Conseil, en cours d'année, 500 propositions, 169 projets et recommandations, 10 demandes d'avis conforme au titre du traité CECA, 48 actes de nature budgétaire, 135 communications et mémorandums et 56 rapports.

Vice-President	Wilhelm HAFERKAMP	Economic and financial affairs Credit and investments
Vice-President	Carlo SCARASCIA MUGNOZZA	Watching brief for parliamentary affairs in conjunction with the President Environment policy Protection of consumer interests Transport Information
Vice-President	Sir Christopher SOAMES	External relations
Vice-President	Patrick John HILLERY	Social affairs
Vice-President	Henri SIMONET	Taxation and financial institutions Energy Euratom Supply Agence
Member	Altiero SPINELLI	Industrial and technological policy
Member	Albert BORSCHETTE	Competition Personnel and administration
Member	George THOMSON	Regional policy
Member	Petrus Josephus LARDINOIS	Agriculture
Member	Finn Olav GUNDELACH	Internal market and customs union
Member	Claude CHEYSSON	Development and cooperation policy Budgets and financial control
Member	Guido BRUNNER	Research, science and education Joint Research Centre Statistical Office Scientific and technical information and information management

Activities

42. The Commission held 44 meetings in the course of the year. In pursuance of the Treaties it sent to the Council 500 proposals, 169 drafts and recommendations, 10 request for assent under the ECSC Treaty, 48 budget instruments, 135 communications and memoranda and 56 reports.

Relations de la Commission avec les partenaires sociaux

43. Poursuivant les efforts entrepris afin d'associer toujours davantage les partenaires sociaux aux affaires communautaires[1], la Commission a établi des contacts systématiques avec les organisations des travailleurs et des employeurs groupées sur le plan européen. Au niveau du collège, des membres de la Commission, des directeurs généraux et, au niveau inter-services, des réunions d'information et de consultation ont permis aux partenaires sociaux de présenter leurs points de vue sur les diverses politiques en cours d'élaboration.

Depuis le début de 1974, un service ,,Bureau partenaires sociaux'' est chargé d'assurer un contact permanent avec les organisations syndicales et patronales.

Personnel

44. L'organigramme de lz Commission pour 1974 comprend 7 204 emplois permanents et 171 emplois temporaires.

La Commission a procédé à un examen approfondi des structures et du fonctionnement de ses services. Le résultat de cette étude devrait aboutir, en fonction des objectifs et des priorités que la Commission s'est fixés, à une répartition mieux équilibrée des effectifs au sein des services et partant à une meilleure utilisation de son personnel.

Les activités de formation que la Commission organise au profit de son personnel sont d'autre part de nature à faciliter ce type d'opérations.

Dans le cadre des relations entre l'institution et les représentants de son personnel, un accord a été le 20 septembre 1974 entre la Commission et les organisations syndicales et professionnelles de son personnel.

Cet accord porte sur la reconnaissance des organisations syndicales et professionelles et prévoit notamment le moyen de la concertation entre la Commission et les représentants des organisations syndicales et professionnelles. Il fixe les modalités relatives à l'exercice des droits syndicaux au sein de la Commission et prévoit également la répartition des compétences entre le comité du personnel et les organisations syndicales ou professionnelles.

Statut des fonctionnaires

45. La Commission a introduit, le 13 juin 1974, un troisième train de modifications du statut des fonctionnaires des Communautés européennes portant plus particulièrement sur des aspects d'organisation et des améliorations de caractère social: le travail en équipe, les conditions et la durée du travail, le droit de grève et la réglementation de son exercice. Le Parlement, le 15 octobre 1974, et la Cour de justice ont émis leur avis. Le Conseil est désormais appelé à statuer sur cette proposition.

D. COUR DE JUSTICE

Composition de la Cour

46. La Cour de justice a élu pour la durée d'un an à partir du 7 octobre 1974 M. Cearbhall Ó Dálaigh président de la première chambre, et Lord MacKenzie Stuart, président de la deuxleme chambre M. Ó Dálaigh ayant été élu président d'Irlande, a été remplacé comme juge à la Cour de justice par M. Aindrias (Ó Keeffe) Ó Caoimh qui a prêté serment le 12 décembre 1974. Ce même jour, la Cour a élu M. Josse Mertens de Wilmars président

---

[1] Point 6 du communiqué final de la conférence au sommet de Paris de 1972; Sixième Rapport général n° 5.

Relations between the Commission and the two sides of industry

43. Continuing its efforts to involve labour and management more closely in Community activities, the Commission has established systematic relations with European workers' and employers' associations. Meetings for the provision of information and for consultation with the Commission itself, its Members and its Directors-General, and interdepartmental meetings, have given workers and employers the opportunity of stating their views on various planned policies.

Since early 1974 a "Social Partners Office" has been responsible for keeping permanently in touch with unions and employers' associations.

Staff

44. The 1974 establishment plan of the Commission contains 7 204 permanent posts and 171 temporary posts.

The Commission has undertaken an in-depth review of the structures and operation of its departments. In line with the priorities and other objectives which the Commission has set itself, this should help to provide a better balance in the staffing of the various departments and to ensure that members of the staff are deployed more efficiently.

The Commission's staff training programmes will also be of value here.

On 20 September the Commission signed an agreement with the trade unions and staff associations whereby the latter are given formal recognition and provision is made for a consultation procedure between their representatives and the Commission. The agreement regulates the exercise of trade unions functions in the Commission and the division of responsibilities between the Staff Committee and the trade unions and staff associations.

Staff Regulations

45. On 13 June the Commission initiated a third round of amendments to the Staff Regulations of Officials of the European Communities, dealing particularly with organizational points and improvements of a social nature: team work, working conditions and hours, and the right to strike. Parliament and the Court of Justice have delivered their Opinions, the former on 15 October. The proposal is now awaiting a decision by the Council.

D. COURT OF JUSTICE

Composition

46. The Court of Justice elected Mr Cearbhall ÓDálaigh President of the First Chamber and Lord Mackenzie Stuart President of the Second Chamber for the year commencing 7 October 1974. On his election as President of Ireland Mr Ó Dálaigh was succeeded as judge at the Court by Mr Aindrias (Ó Keeffe) Ó Caoimh. Mr Ó Caoimh was sworn in on 12 December 1974. On the same day, the Court elected Mr Josse Mertens de

de la première chambre et M. Alberto Trabucchi premier avocat général.

En conséquence, au 31 décembre 1974, la composition de la Cour était la suivante:

Président de la Cour:	M. Robert Lecourt
Première chambre:	M. Josse Mertens de Wilmars, président
	M. André Donner, juge
	M. Riccardo Monaco, juge
	M. Aindrias (Ó Keeffe) Ó Caoimh, juge
	M. Jean-Pierre Warner, avocat général
	M. Gerhard Reischl, avocat général
Deuxième chambre:	Lord Alexander John MacKenzie Stuart, président
	M. Pierre Pescatore, juge
	M. Hans Kutscher, juge
	M. Max Sørensen, juge
	M. Albert Trabucchi, premier avocat général
	M. Henri Mayras, avocat général
Greffier:	M. Albert Van Houtte

Activités judiciaires

47. En 1974, les activités judiciaires de la Cour de justice, de même que les contacts entre la juridiction européenne et les juridictions nationales des neuf États membres, ont continué à se développer.

L'année écoulée a été par ailleurs celle du premier recours direct (Irlande) et du premier renvoi à titre préjudiciel (Royaume-Uni) de nouveaux États membres.

48. Pendant l'année 1974, la Cour de justice a été saisie de 102 nouvelles affaires, dont 39 demandes de décisions préjudicielles, 41 recours de fonctionnaires et 22 autres recours directs. Au cours de cette même année, elle a rendu des arrêts dans 146 affaires, dont 42 sur des demandes de décisions préjudicielles, 95 sur recours de fonctionnaires et 9 sur autres recours directs. 14 affaires ont été rayées du registre. Au 31 décembre 1974, 103 affaires étaient encore en instance devant la Cour.

49. Le 15 juillet, la Cour de justice a remis aux autres institutions de la Communauté un document sur l'*Union européenne*. Elle est ainsi la première des institutions qui ait répondu à l'invitation de la conférence au sommet de Paris en 1972.

E. ORGANES CONSULTATIFS

Comités

Comité économique et social

50. Le mandat des membres du Comité, pour le quatrième exercice quadriennal, est arrivé à échéance le 22 août 1974. Le 17 septembre, le Conseil a procédé au renouvellement des membres du Comité. Le Comité compte actuellement 133 membres du fait que le nombre de membres britanniques ne s'élève qu'à 13 au lieu de 24. Lors de la session constitutive (7 au 9 octobre 1974), M. Henri Canonge (France – activités diverses) a été élu président du Comité, il succède à M. Alfons Lappas (Allemagne – travailleurs). M. Louis Ameye (Belgique – employeurs) et M. John Carroll (Irlande – travailleurs) ont été élus vice-présidents.

En 1974, le Comité a tenu dix sessions plénières, il a rendu 99 avis dont quatre de sa propre initiative, et élaboré six études. Lors de la session de juillet, le Comité a pour la première fois procédé à un échange de vues avec

Wilmars President of the First Chamber and Mr Alberto Trabucchi first Advocate-General.

The composition of the Court on 31 December 1974 was as follows:

President of the Court:	Mr Robert Lecourt
First Chamber:	Mr Josse Mertens de Wilmars, President
	Mr André Donner, Judge
	Mr Riccardo Monaco, Judge
	Mr Aindrias (Ó Keeffe) Ó Caoimh, Judge
	Mr Jean-Pierre Warner, Advocate-General
	Mr Gerhard Reischl, Advocate-General
Second Chamber:	Lord Alexander John Mackenzie Stuart, President
	Mr Pierre Pescatore, Judge
	Mr Hans Kutscher, Judge
	Mr Max Sørensen, Judge
	Mr Albert Trabucchi, First Advocate-General
	Mr Henri Mayras, Advocate-General
Registrar:	Mr Albert Van Houtte

Activities

47. The Court's activities, and contacts between the Court and Courts in the nine Member States, continued to expand.

The past year saw the first direct law suit (Ireland) and the first reference for a preliminary ruling (United Kingdom) from the new Member States.

48. In the course of the year 102 new cases were brought before the Court, 39 of them requests for preliminary rulings, 41 applications by Community civil servants and 22 other direct applications. The Court gave judgment in 146 cases, 42 of them relating to requests for preliminary rulings, 95 to applications by Community civil servants and 9 to other direct applications. 14 were removed from the register. At 31 December there were 103 actions pending before the Court.

49. On 15 July, the Court transmitted a paper on European Union to the other Community institutions. It was thus the first institution to respond to the invitation made by the 1972 Summit Conference in Paris.

E. CONSULTATIVE BODIES

Committees

Economic and Social Committee

50. On 22 August the fourth four-year term of office of the members of the Committee expired. On 17 September the Council appointed the new Committee. The Committee now has 133 actual members, the United Kingdom having filled only 13 of its 24 seats. At the constituent session (7 to 9 October) Mr Henri Canonge (France, various interests group) was elected Chairman to succeed Mr Alfons Lappas (Germany, workers' group). Mr Louis Ameye (Belgium, employers' group) and Mr John Carroll (Ireland, workers' group) were elected Vice-Chairmen.

This year the Committee held ten plenary sessions, issued 99 Opinions, four of them on its own initiative, and published six studies. At its July session, the Committee had its first discussion with the President of the Council on the general situation of the Community.

le président en exercice du Conseil sur la situation générale de la Communauté.

Après son approbation par le Conseil, le nouveau règlement intérieur du Comité est entré en vigueur le 13 juin 1974.

Comité consultatif CECA

51. En 1974, le Comité a tenu sept sessions, dont six à Luxembourg et une à Ajaccio. Parmi les nombreuses consultations du Comité en application du traité CECA, il convient de citer notamment l'avis sur la nouvelle stratégie de politique énergétique pour la Communauté, adopté lors de la session des 3 et 4 octobre 1974. Par ailleurs, le Comité a entendu et débattu des exposés de membres de la Commission sur la situation générale de la Communauté, les activités communautaires relevant du traité CECA et les politiques de l'énergie et des transports. Le 25 juin, le Conseil a procédé à la nomination des membres du Comité consultatif pour la période du 26 juin 1974 au 25 juin 1976. Deux membres britanniques ayant refusé leur mandat, le Comité compte actuellement 79 membres.

Lors de la session constitutive, M. Michel Arnaud (France, catégorie „utilisateurs, acier") a été élu président. Le président sortant, Sir David Davies (Royaume-Uni, catégorie „travailleurs, acier"), et M. Marcel Peeters (Belgique, catégorie „producteurs, charbon") ont été élus vice-présidents.

Comité monétaire

52. Le Comité monétaire a tenu 13 sessions en 1974. Il a renouvelé son bureau vers le milieu de l'année, élisant M. Cort comme président, MM. Emminger et de Strycker comme vice-présidents.

Il a poursuivi régulièrement ses tours d'horizon sur la politique monétaire des États membres. Il a en particulier procédé à une consultation sur la décision, prise en janvier par le gouvernement français, de laisser flotter isolément le franc. En outre, il a été amené à différentes reprises à émettre des avis au sujet du fonctionnement de l'unité de compte du marché agricole commun.

Le Comité a été chargé par le Conseil d'étudier, en coopération avec le comité des gouverneurs des banques centrales, „la possibilité de modifier les règles relatives aux transferts d'or entre autorités monétaires des États membres." En conséquence, le Comité a adopté un rapport qui a permis aux ministres des finances réunis à Zeist en avril 1974 d'arrêter certains éléments d'une position commune. Il a également été chargé d'examiner les problèmes liés à la mise au point d'un dispositif d'emprunts communautaires. Il a émis un avis écrit à ce sujet.

En application de l'article VII de l'accord instituant un soutien monétaire à court terme entre les banques centrales de la Communauté et à la suite de l'octroi d'un tel crédit à la Banca d'Italia, le Comité a procédé à deux reprises à l'examen de la situation économique et financière de l'Italie, il a en outre étudié, à la demande du Conseil, les conditions financières et de politique économique dont serait assorti l'octroi à l'Italie d'un concours financier à moyen terme; il a développé des conclusions dans un avis écrit.

Le Conseil a également demandé au Comité de procéder aux études techniques qu'impliquent les propositions faites par M. Fourcade, ministre français des finances, lors de la session du 16 septembre. Ayant exécuté ce travail, le Comité a adopté des rapports sur l'unité de compte européenne et sur le système communautaire de change.

Enfin, conformément à l'usage qui es'st instauré depuis plusieurs années, le Comité a consacré une large part de ses travaux aux problèmes monétaires internationaux, en contribuant à la mise au point d'une position commune des Neuf sur certaines questions qui se sont posées dans le cadre du comité des Vingt et lors de l'assemblée annuelle du Fonds monétaire international.

Following approval by the Council, the Committee's new rules of procedure came into force on 13 June.

ECSC Consultative Committee

51. The Committee met seven times, six times in Luxembourg and once in Ajaccio. Of the various matters on which the Committee was consulted in accordance with the ECSC Treaty, particular attention should be paid to its Opinion on a new energy policy strategy for the Community, adopted at its meeting on 3 and 4 October. The Committee also heard and discussed statements by members of the Commission on the general situation of the Community, Community activities covered by the ECSC Treaty, energy policy and transport policy. On 25 June the Council appointed the members of the Consultative Committee for the period from 26 June 1974 to 25 June 1976. As two United Kingdom members refused to accept their appointments, the Committee is currently composed of 79 members.

At the constituent session Mr Michel Arnaud (France, steel users' group) was elected Chairman. The retiring Chairman, Sir David Davies (United Kingdom, steel workers' group), and Mr Marcel Peeters (Belgium, coal producers' group) were elected Vice-Chairmen.

Monetary Committee

52. The Monetary Committee met thirteen times in 1974. Towards the middle of the year it appointed its officers: Mr Cort was elected Chairman, with Mr Emminger and Mr de Strycker as Vice-Chairmen.

It continued its regular general discussions on the monetary policies of the Member States. It held consultations on the French Government's decision in January to allow the franc to float independently. On a number of occasions it also issued Opinions on the way the unit of account for the common agricultural policy was operating.

The Committee received instructions from the Council to work with the Committee of Governors of Central Banks on studying the possibility of changing the rules governing gold transfers between monetary authorities at international level or between the monetary authorities of the Member States. Accordingly, the Committee adopted a report which enabled the Ministers of Finance, meeting at Zeist in April, to decide on a number of points for a common approach. It was also instructed to examine problems relating to the establishment of Community loan machinery. It issued a written Opinion on this.

Under Article VII of the Agreement establishing short-term monetary support between the central banks of the Community and following the grant of a loan of this type to the Banca d'Italia, the Committee twice reviewed the economic and financial situation in Italy. At the Council's request it studied the financial and economic-policy conditions to be imposed if Italy was granted medium-term financial assistance and presented its conclusions in a written Opinion.

The Council also asked the Committee to undertake the technical studies implied in the proposals made by Mr Fourcade, the French Finance Minister, at the Council meeting held on 16 September. On completion of these studies the Committee adopted reports on the European unit of account and the Community exchange system.

Finally, in line with its practice over several years, the Committee devoted a good part of its discussions to international monetary problems, and helped with the development of a common approach by the Nine to a number of questions raised in the Committee of Twenty and at the annual meeting of the International Monetary Fund.

Comité de politique économique

53. Par décision du 18 février 1974, le Conseil a institué un Comité de politique économique. Celui-ci exerce toutes les fonctions attribuées jusque-là aux Comités de politique conjoncturelle, de politique budgétaire et de politique économique à moyen terme. Cette décision a été pour assurer une meilleure coordination des politiques économiques à court et à moyen terme.

Toutefois, avant la mise en place de ce nouvel organe, les anciens comités ont poursuivi leurs travaux:

- le Comité de politique conjoncturelle s'est réuni en janvier pour procéder à l'examen des répercussions de la crise pétrolière sur l'évolution conjoncturelle des États membres;
- le Comité de politique économique à moyen terme a tenu une réunion le 13 février 1974 pour infléchir, à la suite de la menace de limitation quantitative des approvisionnements pétroliers et de la hausse de leurs prix, le rapport sur les perspectives économiques de la Communauté dont il avait entrepris la préparation au second semestre de 1973;
- le Comité de politique budgétaire a poursuivi son examen des budgets des États membres par l'analyse de l'exécution des budgets 1973 et des perspectives pour 1974; en outre, il a organisé en mai un séminaire à Luxembourg.

54. Le Comité de politique économique s'est réuni pour la première fois en juin 1974. Il a procédé à la désignation de son bureau. Il a également adopté son règlement intérieur et défini un programme de travail. Au total six réunions du Comité ont eu lieu en 1974. Elles ont été consacrées à l'achèvement des travaux du rapport sur les perspectives économiques de la Communauté – rapport que le Comité a décidé de transmettre au Conseil et à la Commission –, à la définition de la politique budgétaire devant être suivie par les pays membres en 1975, ainsi qu'à l'examen des budgets économiques préliminaires pour 1975, examen dont les conclusions ont été résumées dans un avis écrit. En outre, conformément à la procédure prévue par le traité, le Comité a adressé à la Commission un avis sur le taux maximum d'augmentation des dépenses non obligatoires du budget de la Communauté pour 1975.

3. SECRETARIAT GENERAL DE LA COMMISSION

Rue de la Loi 200, 1049 Bruxelles
Wetstraat 200, 1049 Brussel

Secrétaire général	Emile NOËL
Secrétaire général adjoint	Klaus MEYER
Secrétaire général adjoint	Christopher AUDLAND

Service juridique

Directeur général	
Directeur général adjoint	Giancarlo OLMI

Groupe du porte-parole

Porte-Parole	Beniamino OLIVI

Office statistique (Luxembourg)

Directeur général	Jacques MAYER

Economic Policy Committee

53. The Economic Policy Committee was set up by a Council decision dated 18 February 1974. It carries out all the functions hitherto exercised by the Short-term Economic Policy Committee, the Budgetary Policy Committee and the Medium-term Economic Policy Committee. Under the decision the Committee may meet with reduced composition for the purpose of dealing with specific problems in the fields of short-term economic policy, budgetary policy or medium-term economic policy.

However, before this new committee actually got down to work, its predecessors continued theirs:

- the Short-term Economic Policy Committee met in January to consider the effects of the oil crisis on economic trends in the Member States;
- the Medium-term Economic Policy Committee held a meeting on 13 February to modify, in response to the threat of cutbacks in oil supplies and of increased prices, the report on the economic outlook for the Community which it had begun preparing in the second half of 1973;
- the Budgetary Policy Committee continued its review of the Member States' budgets by examining how 1973 budgets had been implemented and the outlook for 1974; in May it organized a seminar in Luxembourg.

54. The Economic Policy Committee met for the first time in June and appointed its officers. It also adopted its rules of procedure and decided on its programme of work. In all it met six times this year. The meetings were held to complete the work on the report on the economic outlook for the Community (which the Committee decided to transmit to the Council and the Commission), to determine the budgetary policy to be followed by the Member States in 1975 and to review the preliminary economic budgets for 1975 (its conclusions on this last item being set down in a written Opinion). Moreover, in accordance with the procedure laid down in the Treaty, the Committee addressed an Opinion to the Commission on the maximum rate of increase for "other than necessary" expenditure in the Community budget for 1975.

3. SECRETARIAT-GENERAL OF THE COMMISSION

Rue de la Loi 200, 1049 Bruxelles
Wetstraat 200, 1049 Brussel

Secretary-General	Emile NOËL
Deputy Secretary-General	Klaus MEYER
Deputy Secretary-General	Christopher AUDLAND

Legal Service

Director-General	
Deputy Director-General	Giancarlo OLMI

Spokesman's Group

Spokesman	Beniamino OLIVI

Statistical Office (Luxembourg)

Director-General	Jacques MAYER

Gestion de l'Union Douanière

Directeur Klaus PINGEL

Service de l'environnement et de la protection des consommateurs

Directeur Michel CARPENTIER

	Directions Générales	*Directeur Général*
I.	Relations extérieures	Edmond WELLENSTEIN
II.	Affaires économiques et financières	Ugo MOSCA
III.	Affaires industrielles et technologiques	
IV.	Concurrence	Willy SCHLIEDER
V.	Affaires sociales	Michael SHANKS
VI.	Agriculture	Louis-Georges RABOT
VII.	Transports	Raymond LE GOY
VIII.	Développement et coopération	Hans-Broder KROHN
IX.	Personnel et administration	Pierre BAICHERE
X.	Information	Sean RONAN
XI.	Marché intérieur	Fernand BRAUN
XII.	Recherche, science et éducation	Günter SCHUSTER
XIII.	Information scientifique et technique	Raymond APPLEYARD
XV.	Institutions financières et fiscalité	Erik ALBAN-HANSEN
XVI.	Politique régionale	Renato RUGGIERO
XVII.	Energie	Fernand SPAAK
XVIII.	Crédit et investissements	Antonio NICOLETTI
XIX.	Budgets	Josef van GRONSFELD
XX.	Contrôle financier	Carlo FACINI

D. SECTEURS D'UN INTERET SPECIAL

1. POLITIQUE REGIONALE

Fonds européen de développement régional
et Comité de politique régionale

206. A la conférence au sommet de Paris d'octobre 1972, les chefs de gouvernement des neuf États membres de la Communauté européenne avaient accordé une haute priorité à l'objectif de remédier, dans la Communauté, aux déséquilibres structurels et régionaux, susceptibles d'affecter la réalisation de l'Union économique et monétaire. Faisant suite à l'invitation de la conférence au sommet, la Commission a présenté, en mai 1973, un rapport sur les problèmes régionaux dans la Communauté élargie et, en juillet de la même année, elle a soumis au Conseil des propositions pour la création d'un Comité de politique régionale et d'un Fonds européen de développement régional.

207. Au cours des débats sur ces propositions au Conseil, l'attention s'est principalement concentrée sur le montant et la répartition géographique des ressources à attribuer au Fonds européen de développement régional et, malgré l'engagement réitéré des chefs de gouvernement à la conférence au sommet de Copenhague, l'échéance du 31 décembre 1973 fixée au sommet de Paris en octobre 1972 pour la mise en place de ce Fonds n'a pu être respectée. Les négociations se sont poursuivies au cours des premiers mois de l'année 1974 mais en dépit des efforts déployées,

Administration of the Customs Union

Director — Klaus PINGEL

Environment and Consumer Protection Service

Director — Michel CARPENTIER

	Directorates General	*Director General*
I.	External Relations	Edmond WELLENSTEIN
II.	Economic and Financial Affairs	Ugo MOSCA
III.	Industrial and Technological Affairs	
IV.	Competition	Willy SCHLIEDER
V.	Social Affairs	Michael SHANKS
VI.	Agriculture	Louis-Georges RABOT
VII.	Transport	Raymond LE GOY
VIII.	Development and Cooperation	Hans-Broder KROHN
IX.	Personnel and Administration	Pierre BAICHERE
X.	Information	Sean RONAN
XI.	Internal Market	Fernand BRAUN
XII.	Research, Science and Education	Günter SCHUSTER
XIII.	Scientific and Technical Information	Raymond APPLEYARD
XV.	Financial Institutions and Taxation	Erik ALBAN-HANSEN
XVI.	Regional Policy	Renato RUGGIERO
XVII.	Energy	Fernand SPAAK
XVIII.	Credit and Investments	Antonio NICOLETTI
XIX.	Budgets	Josef van GRONSFELD
XX.	Financial Control	Carlo FACINI

D. SECTORS OF SPECIAL INTEREST

1. REGIONAL POLICY

European Regional Development Fund and Committee for Regional Policy

206. At the Paris Summit Conference of October 1972 the Heads of Government of the nine Member States of the European Communities gave high priority to the aim of correcting, in the Community, the structural and regional imbalances which might affect the realization of economic and monetary union. In May 1973 the Commission presented the report on regional problems in the enlarged Community which the Summit Conference has asked it to prepare, and in July it put proposals to the Council to set up a Committee for Regional Policy and a European Regional Development Fund.

207. When these proposals were discussed by the Council, attention was paid mainly to the amount and the geographical distribution of the resources to be allocated to the Regional Development Fund; although the Heads of Government repeated their commitment at the Copenhagen Summit Conference, the 31 December 1973 deadline fixed at Paris in October 1972 for the setting up of this Fund was not met. Negotiations continued in the first few months of this year, but despite considerable effort, particularly on the part of the Commission, to bring the various views into line, no agreement has been reached.

notamment par la Commission, pour rapprocher les positions en présence, aucun accord n'est intervenu.

208. Les négociations ont été suspendues à la fin du mois de mars à la suite de la déclaration du secrétaire d'État britannique aux affaires étrangères et au Commonwealth, concernant la politique du gouvernement britannique à l'égard de la Communauté.

Lors de sa réunion du 4 juin, le Conseil a cependant confirmé la priorité à donner aux décisions en matière de politique régionale et, au cours de sa réunion du 27 juin, il a pris acte d'une déclaration du président de la Commission selon laquelle celle-ci réexaminerait dans une série de contacts bilatéraux l'ensemble du problème avec les États membres dans le but de présenter au Conseil, au moment approprié, une communication contenant, le cas échéant, des perspectives de solution.

Entre temps, le Parlement, dans sa résolution du 13 décembre 1973, confirmée le 13 mars 1974, avait exprimé le souhait d'une plus grande concentration des interventions du Fonds sur les régions affectées par les déséquilibres les plus graves. Le CES, réuni en session plénière les 26 et 27 juin 1974, avait de sa propre initiative émis un avis sur les mesures provisoires à mettre en oeuvre en attendant la création du Fonds européen de développement régional.

209. Fin octobre, les contacts bilatéraux ayant eu lieu, la Commission a, dans le cadre de la préparation de la réunion des chefs de gouvernement des 9 et 10 décembre 1974, élaboré un document de travail dans lequel elle a souligné, en se référant à la situation inflatoire et au chômage croissant en Europe, la nécessité de la mise en oeuvre d'une politique régionale globale, et cela:

- par la création sans délai du Comité de politique régionale appelé à faciliter la coordination des politiques régionales nationales et l'amélioration des incidences régionales des politiques communautaires;
- en cherchant les moyens pour promouvoir le flux d'investissements directs créateurs d'emplois vers les régions les moins favorisées;
- en créant dans les trois mois le Fonds européen de développement régional.

Sur la base de ce document de travail de la Commission, les chefs de gouvernement ont pris une décision opérationnelle. Selon cette décision, le Fonds européen de développement régional, destiné à corriger les déséquilibres régionaux principaux dans la Communauté, résultant notamment d'une prédominance agricole, des mutations industrielles et d'un sous-emploi structurel, sera mis en place pour une période triennale d'essai à compter du 1er janvier 1975.

Pour cette période triennale, le Fonds sera doté de 1 300 millions d'UC, soit 300 millions d'UC pour la première année et 500 millions d'UC pour chacune des deux années suivantes. Ce montant total de 1 300 millions d'UC sera financé à concurrence de 150 millions d'UC par des crédits non utilisés du Fonds européen d'orientation et de garantie agricole, section „orientation."

Les ressources du Fonds seront réparties de la façon suivante: 1,5 % pour la Belgique, 1,3 % pour le Danemark, 15 % pour la France, 6 % pour l'Irlande, 40 % pour l'Italie, 0,1 % pour le Luxembourg, 1,7 % pour les Pays-Bas, 6,4 % pour la république fédérale d'Allemagne, 28 % pour le Royaume-Uni.

L'Irlande toutefois se verra, en outre, attribuer 6 millions d'UC qui viendront en déduction de la quote-part des autres États membres exception faite de l'Italie.

210. Au cours de ces derniers mois, le Parlement a témoigné un grand intérêt envers les régions situées de part et d'autre des frontières intérieures de la Communauté et envers les problèmes particuliers que la frontière pose à ces régions. Les services de la Commission procèdent actuellement à une analyse des problèmes frontaliers et des formes de coopération

208. Negotiations were suspended at the end of March following the statement by the United Kingdom Secretary of State for Foreign and Commonwealth Affairs on the United Kingdom Government's policy concerning the Community.

On 4 June, however, the Council confirmed that priority was to be given to matters of regional policy, and on 27 June it noted a statement by the President of the Commission to the effect that the Commission would hold a series of bilateral meetings to review the problem as a whole with the Member States and would present the Council in due course with a communication, possibly containing proposed solutions.

In the meantime Parliament, in its Resolution of 13 December 1973, confirmed on 13 March 1974, called for the activities of the Fund to be more strongly concentrated on the regions which suffered from the most serious imbalances. At its plenary session of 26 and 27 June the ESC, acting on its own initiative, issued an Opinion on provisional measures to be put into effect pending creation of the European Regional Development Fund.

209. At the end of October, bilateral contacts having taken place, the Commission produced a working paper as part of the preparations for the meeting of Heads of Government on 9 and 10 December, in which, referring to the inflationary situation and growing unemployment in Europe, it stressed the need to implement a comprehensive regional policy:

- by setting up without delay the Committee for Regional Policy, whose task would be to facilitate the coordination of national regional policies and the improvement of the regional aspects of Community policies;
- by finding the means to encourage a flow of direct investment to create employment in the less-favoured regions;
- by setting up within three months the European Regional Development Fund.

On the basis of this Commission paper, the Heads of Government reached an operational decision. In accordance with this decision, the European Regional Development Fund, whose purpose will be to correct the main regional imbalances within the Community resulting from a predominance of agriculture, industrial change and structural underemployment, will be set up for a three-year trial period beginning on 1 January 1975.

For this period the Fund will have at its disposal 1 300 million u.a. (300 million u.a. for the first year and 500 million u.a. for each of the following years). Of this 1 300 million u.a., 150 million u.a. will be drawn from unused appropriations for the Guidance Section of the European Agricultural Guidance and Guarantee Fund.

The resources of the Fund will be shared out as follows:

1.5% for Belgium, 1.3% for Denmark, 15% for France, 6.4% for Germany, 6% for Ireland, 40% for Italy, 0,1% for Luxembourg, 1.7% for the Netherlands and 28% for the United Kingdom.

Ireland, however, will also receive 6 million u.a., this sum to be deducted from the share of the other Member States, with the exception of Italy.

210. In recent months Parliament has shown great interest in the regions which lie across the frontiers between Community countries and in the special problems which the frontiers pose for such regions. The Commission is now making an analysis of frontier problems and the existing forms of cooperation across frontiers so that the responsibilities of the Community in this matter may be defined.

transfrontalière existantes, afin d'essayer de situer les responsabilités de la Communauté en la matière.

Reconversion (CECA)

214. En 1974, le nombre des demandes de prêts de reconversion adressées à la Commission ainsi que leurs montants ont considérablement augmenté par rapport à l'année précédente. Ceci est dû aux demandes provenant du Royaume-Uni et de la république d'Irlande, mais également à une légère augmentation des demandes des autres pays membres.

On ne peut toutefois pas baser sur ces demandes un jugement sur le rythme des opérations de restructuration des industries CECA dans les pays membres; en effet, la corrélation entre ces opérations et les demandes de prêts est relativement faible.

Dans la même période, la Commission a pris 16 décisions d'octroi de prêts représentant un montant de 92,5 millions d'UC, qui, en partie, doivent encore recevoir l'avis conforme du Conseil.[1]

13 de ces décisions concernent des prêts directs pour un montant de 68,3 millions d'UC, qui doivent permettre la réalisation d'investissements de l'ordre de 319 millions d'UC et la création d'environ 7 500 emplois nouveaux, dont environ la moitié seront offerts en priorité aux anciens travailleurs des industries CECA rendus disponibles. Le Royaume-Uni a bénéficié, pour la première fois, de deux prêts directs, représentant 37,6 millions d'UC, soit 55 % du montant total des prêts directs accordés.

3 décisions concernent des crédits-cadres respectivement en France, au Royaume-Uni et en Irlande, pour un montant total de 24,2 millions d'UC, crédits que la Commission ouvre en faveur d'organismes financiers de développement regional ou de reconversion afin de faciliter le financement de programmes d'investissements des entreprises de petite et moyenne dimensions qui créent des nouvelles activités ou étendent leurs activités existantes, dans les régions charbonnières et sidérurgiques et, de ce fait, favorisent le réemploi des travailleurs des industries CECA rendus disponibles.

Ci-après figure la liste par régions CECA des prêts décides par la Commission en 1974. Quelques-uns de ces prêts ont déjà reçu l'avis conforme du Conseil; pour les autres, cet avis n'interviendra que dans les premiers mois de 1975.

Allemagne (RF)
Sarre: deux prêts pour un montant de 11,5 millions d'UC.

France
Nord, Pas-de-Calais: un prêt pour un montant de 0,9 million d'UC.
Lorraine: trois prêts pour un montant de 9,9 millions d'UC.
Savoie: un prêt pour un montant de 3,8 millions d'UC.
Centre-Midi: un crédit-cadre pour un montant de 3,2 millions d'UC.

Royaume-Uni
Écosse: un prêt pour un montant de 28,0 millions d'UC.
Nord-Ouest: un prêt pour un montant de 9,6 millions d'UC.
Pays de Galles, Écosse, Nord: un crédit-cadre pour un montant de 19,0 millions d'UC.

Pays-Bas
Limbourg: quatre prêts pour un montant de 4,6 millions d'UC.

---

[1] Les tableaux 3 et 4 ci-après donnent respectivement le résultat des décisions d'octroi des prêts par pays et par année et la répartition par secteurs d'activités selon la classification NACE.

Conversion (ECSC)

214. The number of applications for conversion loans received by the Commission and the amounts involved rose sharply in 1974 over 1973. This was mainly due to applications from the United Kingdom and Ireland, although there was also a slight increase in those from other Member States.

These applications cannot, however, serve as a basis for a judgment on the rate at which restructuring operations are progressing in the ECSC industries in the Member States, for the correlation between such operations and applications for loans is relatively insignificant.

In the course of the year the Commission took sixteen decisions to grant loans amounting to 92.5 million u.a., some of which are still awaiting the assent of the Council.

Thirteen of these decisions relate to direct loans totalling 68.3 million u.a., which should lead to investments of the order of 319 million u.a. and the creation of about 7 500 new jobs, approximately half of which will be offered in the first place to former workers in ECSC industries who have become redundant. The United Kingdom received, for the first time, two direct loans totalling 37.6 million u.a. (55% of the total granted in direct loans).

Three decisions were taken to grant framework loans to France, the United Kingdom and Ireland respectively, for a total sum of 24.2 million u.a. The credits were made available by the Commission to bodies involved in financing regional development or conversion in order to facilitate the financing of investment programmes by small and medium-sized firms starting new activities or extending their existing activities in coalmining and steel-working regions and thus contributing to the re-employment of redundant workers from the ECSC industries.

There follows a list setting out for each region the loans granted by the Commission from ECSC funds in 1974. A number of these loans have already received the assent of the Council; in the case of the others this will not be given until early in 1975.

Germany
Saar: two loans – 11.5 million u.a.

France
Nord, Pas-de-Calais: one loan – 0.9 million u.a.
Lorraine: three loans – 9.9 million u.a.
Savoie: one loan – 3.8 million u.a.
Centre-Midi: one framework loan – 3.2 million u.a.

United Kingdom
Scotland: one loan – 28 million u.a.
North West: one loan – 9.6 million u.a.
Wales, Scotland, North: one framework loan – 19 million u.a.

Netherlands
Limburg: four loans – 4.6 million u.a.

Irlande
Tipperary: un crédit-cadre pour un montant de 2,0 millions d'UC.

2. POLITIQUE SOCIALE

Aspects généraux

216. L'année sociale a été dominée par la préparation d'un certain nombre de propositions concrètes destinées à être soumises au Conseil, conformément au calendrier prévu par le programme d'action sociale, objet de la résolution du Conseil du 21 janvier 1974.

La réunion des ministres des affaires sociales au mois de juin a été la première occasion offerte au Conseil de statuer sur ces propositions. Il a décidé d'approuver trois propositions relatives à l'extension de l'article 4 du Fonds social aux travailleurs handicapés et aux travailleurs migrants, à la création d'un Comité général pour la sécurité du travail et à l'adoption d'un programme visant a réaliser une intégration fructueuze des travailleurs handicapés dans la vie active normale.

D'autres décisions ont été prises vers la fin de l'année lors d'une seconde réunion du Conseil, où il a été décidé d'adopter une directive prévoyant l'harmonisation des législations en matière d'égalité des salaires entre hommes et femmes, ainsi qu'une directive concernant les licenciements collectifs visant à améliorer la protection des travailleurs menacés de chômage. Le Conseil a également approuvé la création de deux nouveaux organes – un Centre européen pour le développement de la formation professionnelle et un Institut pour l'amélioration des conditions de vie et de travail.

Les décisions intervenues dans ces divers secteurs ont quasiment mis un point final à la première partie du programme d'action sociale. Au stade suivant, la Commission a soumis des propositions sur un certain nombre d'autres actions considerées comme prioritaires par le Conseil. Il s'agissait notamment du très important programme d'action en faveur des travailleurs migrants, qu'ils soient ressortissants de la Communauté ou ressortissants de pays tiers. Ce programme contient un certain nombre de propositions d'actions spécifiques de la Communauté.

Le programme envisage d'octroyer, pour 1980, le droit de vote à tous les migrants lors des élections locales se déroulant dans les États membres et d'améliorer la situation, sur le plan de la sécurité sociale, des migrants des pays tiers, en vue de réaliser progressivement l'égalité de traitement de toutes les personnes vivant et travaillant dans la Communauté.

Conformément aux priorités définies par le Conseil, la Commission met actuellement la dernière main à la préparation d'un certain nombre d'actions sur lesquelles le Conseil pourra se prononcer en 1975. Il s'agit notamment d'un programme d'ensemble concernant l'égalité de traitement des hommes et des femmes au travail. Au nombre des mesures en préparation figure un nouvel instrument communautaire visant à supprimer la discrimination dont souffrent les femmes en ce qui concerne l'accès à l'emploi et la formation professionnelle.

De même on s'active, dans d'autres domaines, à étendre la protection sociale dans le cadre de la politique de la sécurité sociale et un programme de projet pilote visant à soulager la pauvreté a été élaboré en vue d'encourager les efforts faits par les États membres dans ce domaine.

L'évolution de la situation économique pendant l'année, résultant de l'augmentation du coût de l'énergie, a posé aux États membres de sérieux problèmes d'emploi.

Il fallait, en priorité, examiner l'incidence que ce déséquilibre économique aurait sur la Communauté et, plus particulièrement, sur les couches

Ireland
Tipperary: one framework loan – 2 million u.a.

2. SOCIAL POLICY

General aspects

216. The social year has been dominated by the preparation of a number of concrete proposals for submission to the Council in accordance with the timetable set out in the Social Action Programme adopted by the Council in its Resolution of 21 January 1974.

The Council took its first opportunity to take decisions on these proposals at a meeting of Social Ministers in June. It was decided to approve three proposals relating to the opening up of Article 4 of the Social Fund for handicapped workers and migrant workers; the establishment of a General Safety Committee; and the adoption of a programme aimed at the successful integration of handicapped workers into normal working life.

Further decisions were taken at a second Council meeting towards the end of the year when the Council agreed to adopt a directive calling for the harmonization of legislation on equal pay for men and women and a directive on mass dismissals aimed at offering greater protection to workers when threatened with unemployment. The Council also agreed to the establishment of two new bodies, one a European Vocational Training Centre, the other a European Foundation for the Improvement of Living and Working Conditions.

Decisions in all these areas virtually completed the first part of the Social Action Programme. The next stage was the submission by the Commission of proposals on a number of other actions which the Council established as priorities. These include the vitally important action programme for all migrant workers whether they are Community nationals or citizens of non-member countries. This programme contains a number of specific proposals for action by the Community.

The programme envisages the implementation of voting rights by 1980 for all migrants in the local elections of Member States and improvements in the social security situation of migrants from non-member countries aimed at progressively bringing about equality of treatment of all people who live and work in the Community.

In accordance with the Council priorities the Commission is now in the final stages of preparing a number of actions that will be ready for decision by the Council during 1975. These include a comprehensive programme on equality of treatment for men and women at work. Among the measures being prepared is a new Community instrument aimed at eliminating discrimination against women in access to employment and vocational training.

Similarly, in other fields work has begun on extending social protection within the framework of social security policy, and a programme of pilot projects to promote the alleviation of poverty has been prepared to act as a stimulus to the efforts of Member States in this field.

Developments in the economic situation during the year brought about by the increased cost of energy posed serious problems for employment in the Member States.

The first need was to examine the effects that such economic disruptions would have on the Community and more particularly on the more vulnerable sections of the population. Early in the year the Commission drew up a report on the possible repercussions of the energy crisis on employment, drawing attention to the role of the Social Fund in providing les plus vulnérables de la population. Au début de l'année, la Commission a élaboré un rapport sur les répercussions éventuelles de la crise de l'énergie sur l'emploi, et a souligné le rôle du Fonds social dans l'amélioration, par la formation et la rééducation, des perspectives d'emploi offertes aux travailleurs. Durant toute l'année, l'accent n'a cessé d'être mis sur l'importance croissante du Fonds social résultant non seulement de l'augmentation du volume des aides fournies dans le domaine de la formation, mais également de l'élargissement de ses activités.

L'emploi a également été l'un des principaux thèmes de la conférence des chefs d'État, qui s'est tenue à Paris les 9 et 10 décembre et qui a réaffirmé l'importance constante que revêt une politique sociale énergique.

Ce même thème a été repris par l'importante conférence tripartite qui s'est tenue à Bruxelles le 16 décembre, et où le rapport de la Commission sur les „Perspectives d'une politique sociale européenne" a été au centre d'un débat constructif entre les représentants des gouvernements, la Commission et les partenaires sociaux européens.

Il est clair que le problème du chômage est un sujet qui concerne l'ensemble des milieux de la Communauté, et la participation des partenaires sociaux à la recherche de solution revêt une importance toute particulière. A cet égard, la Commission accueille favorablement la décision de relancer le comité permanent de l'emploi, dont la première réunion est prévue début 1975.

Aspects sociaux des politiques communautaires dans d'autres domaines

217. Dans le domaine de la politique économique, la Commission s'est préoccupée, en premier lieu, des problèmes liés à l'inflation et de l'incertitude qui pèse sur l'evolution de l'activité économique et de l'emploi, problèmes aggravés par la crise de l'énergie. A plusieurs reprises, la Commission a souligné que la lutte contre l'inflation était l'objectif prioritaire de la politique économique et que tous les milieux économiques et sociaux devraient y contribuer. Étant donné, cependant, que le niveau de vie atteint sera vraisemblablement affecté par cette situation, il importe que les sacrifices soient répartis équitablement entre les différentes couches de la population. C'est pourquoi on a estimé opportun d'améliorer la protection contre les risques de chômage et les actions spécifiques en faveur des travailleurs dont l'emploi est menacé.

Ds propositions ont été soumises au Conseil dans le domaine de la politique industrielle, dans des secteurs connaissant des problèmes sociaux graves (par exemple papier, textile). De même, des propositions ont été faites relevant du programme de l'environnement et de la protection des consommateurs dans le but d'assurer aux peuples de la Communauté une meilleure qualité de vie.

Promotion de l'emploi

218. L'accentuation générale de l'inflation et les premières répercussions de la crise énergétique ont, au cours du second semestre, renversé les tendances de l'évolution de l'emploi, qui a été marquée par le ralentissement des recrutements de travailleurs salariés et un accroissement du chômage. La Commission a entrepris l'étude de la situation des marchés et s'est employée à promouvoir une politique de concertation des mesures nationales, déjà prises par l'Allemagne, la France et l'Italie.

Des études sur les prévisions d'emploi à moyen terme ont été faites par branche d'activité dans la perspective de travaux permettant également une ventilation par niveau de qualification. Les experts des pays membres ont discuté des résultats de ces études. Des travaux se sont également poursuivis en ce qui concerne l'exploitation des statistiques conjoncturelles de l'emploi et des prévisions d'emploi à court terme. Par ailleurs, les better employment opportunities for workers through training and retraining. The increasing importance of the Social Fund has been underlined throughout the year not only by the growing volume of assistance it provides in training but in the widening scope of its activities.

Employment was also a major issue at the Conference of Heads of Government which met in Paris on 9 and 10 December, where the continuing importance of a vigorous social policy was reaffirmed.

This theme was again taken up by the important Tripartite Conference held in Brussels on 16 December, when the Commission's paper on "Prospects for a European Social Policy" became the focal point for a constructive debate between representatives of the Governments, Commission and the two sides of industry.

The problem of unemployment is clearly a matter for the involvement of all interests within the Community, and particularly important is the active involvement of the two sides of industry in the search for solutions. In this respect the Commission welcomes the decision to reconvene the Standing Committee on Employment, the first meeting of which is expected early in the new year.

Social aspects of Community policies in other areas

217. As regards economic policy the Commission was primarily concerned with the problems associated with inflation and the uncertainty surrounding developments in the economy and the employment situation, these problems having been aggravated by the energy crisis. On several occasions the Commission stressed that the fight against inflation had priority over other economic policy objectives and that all sections of the economy and society would have to help in the fight. Since, however, standards of living will probably be affected by the present situation, it is important that sacrifices should be spread equitably among the various sections of the population. For this reason it was considered advisable to improve protection against unemployment risks and to adopt specific measures on behalf of workers whose jobs are threatened.

Proposals have therefore been submitted in the field of industrial policy relating to sectors with serious social problems (e.g. paper, textiles). Likewise, initial proposals have been made for the implementation of the environmental action programme and the consumer protection programme, which both aim to achieve a better quality of life for the people of the Community.

The promotion of employment

218. In the second half of the year further general inflation and the first repercussions of the energy crisis reversed employment trends, which were thereafter characterized by a slowing down of the recruitment of workers and by increased unemployment. The Commission undertook a study of the market situation and actively promoted coordination of the national measures already taken in Germany, France and Italy.

Sector-by-sector studies of medium-term employment forecasts were carried out, with provision for a statistical breakdown according to levels of qualification. The results of these studies have been discussed by experts from the Member States. Work also continued on the processing of current employment statistics and short-term employment forecasts. Furthermore, the senior officials concerned with employment in the Member States met to lay the foundations for concerting employment policies, in hauts fonctionnaires de l'emploi des États membres se sont réunis pour jeter les bases d'une concertation des politiques de l'emploi, afin de déterminer les priorités et notamment d'éclairer l'action du Fonds social européen.

Fonds social européen

219. Les crédits disponibles pour le nouveau Fonds social européen avaient été initialement fixés à 168,4 millions d'UC. Sur la proposition de la Commission, le Conseil a accepté, par une décision prise en septembre 1974, de reporter à l'année budgétaire en cours le crédit exceptionnel de 40,7 millions d'UC accordé en 1973 pour l'article 4, et de le transférer, pour 1974, à l'article 5.

	Article 4	Article 5	Expériences pilotes	Total
Dotation initiale	98,8	168,4	0,60	267,8
Dotation complémentaire	—	40,7	—	40,7
Total	98,8	209,1	0,60	308,5

Le second rapport d'activité du nouveau Fonds social, concernant l'année 1973, a été transmis au Conseil et au Parlement, conformément à la décision créant ce Fonds.

Le 10 juin 1974, le Conseil a, sur proposition de la Commission, pris deux décisions d'octroi du concours du Fonds, au titre de l'article 4 de la décision du 1er février 1971, pour certaines actions spécifiques en faveur des personnes handicapées et des travailleurs migrants.

Les demandes de concours du nouveau Fonds introduites pour les opérations à réaliser en 1974, au titre des articles 4 et 5 de la décision du Conseil du 1er février 1971, ont atteint un montant total de 406,8 millions d'UC, dont 46,7 millions d'UC au titre de l'article 4 (agriculture: 31,0 millions d'UC; textile: 6,3 millions d'UC; travailleurs migrants: 8,0 millions d'UC; handicapés: 1,4 million d'UC) et 207,7 millions d'UC au titre de l'article 5 (dont 164,1 millions d'UC pour des actions en faveur de régions en déclin, d'industries affectées par les exigences du progrès technique ou de groupes d'entreprises en difficulté, et le reliquat, d'un montant de 43,6 millions d'UC, en faveur des handicapés).

Au cours de l'exercice considéré, la Commission a examiné des demandes portant sur un montant d'environ 406,8 millions d'UC et agrée celles-ci, après consultation du comité du Fonds social européen, dans la limite des crédits disponibles. Le montant des concours ainsi octroyés est de 254,5 millions d'UC se répartissant comme suit:

order to define the priorities and, in particular, clarify the operation of the European Social Fund.

European Social Fund

219. The appropriations for the new European Social Fund had been initially set at 168.4 million units of account. However, acting on a proposal from the Commission, the Council agreed, by a decision taken in September, to carry forward to the current budgetary year the special appropriation of 40.7 million units of account which had been made available in 1973 for the purposes of Article 4 and to transfer this sum to Article 5 for 1974:

	Art. 4	Art. 5	Pilot schemes	Total
Initial endowment	98.8	168.4	0.60	267.8
Supplementary endowment	—	40.7	—	40.7
Total	98.8	209.1	0.60	308.5

The second report on the activities of the new Social Fund, covering 1973, was forwarded to the Council and to Parliament, in accordance with the decision setting up the Fund.

On 10 June 1974 the Council, acting on a proposal from the Commission, took two decisions on the granting of assistance from the Fund, under Article 4 of the Decision of 1 February 1971, towards certain specific measures on behalf of handicapped persons and migrant workers.

The amount of assistance applied for from the new Fund for operations to be carried out in 1974 under Articles 4 and 5 of the Council Decision of 1 February 1971 totalled 406.8 million u.a., of which 46.7 million u.a. was granted under Article 4 (agriculture 31.0 million u.a., textile industry 6.3 million u.a., migrant workers 8.0 million u.a., handicapped persons 1.4 million u.a.), and 207.7 million u.a. under Article 5 (of which 164.1 million u.a. was earmarked for assistance to declining regions, industries affected by technical progress, or groups of undertakings in difficulties, and the remainder, amounting to 43.6 million u.a., for handicapped persons).

During the financial year under consideration the Commission examined applications involving a total of approximately 406.8 million u.a. and, after consulting the Committee of the European Social Fund, approved these applications as far as the financial resources available permitted. The total amount of assistance thus granted is 254.5 million u.a., allocated as shown in the following table:

Tableau 5

Ensemble des engagements décidés pour l'exercice 1974

(*en millions d'UC*)

	Article 4					Article 5		
	Agriculture	Industrie textile	Travailleurs migrants	Handicapés	Total Art. 4	Régions et progrès technique	Handicapés	Total Art. 5
Belgique	0,3	0,6	—	—	0,9	4,1	1,5	5,6
Danemark	—	—	—	—	—	3,3	8,9	2,2
Allemagne (RF)	6,6	2,6	0,1	—	9,3	6,5	12,2	18,7
France	14,9	0,7	0,4	0,2	16,3	27,9	5,2	33,2
Irlande	6,0	1,2	—	—	7,2	8,7	1,0	9,6
Italie	2,2	0,5	1,2	0,3	4,3	65,3	3,2	68,5
Luxembourg	—	—	—	—	—	—	0,01	0,01
Pays-Bas	0,9	—	—	—	0,9	3,7	2,1	5,8
Royaume-Uni	0,2	0,6	6,4	0,8	7,9	44,5	9,6	54,1
Total	31,0	6,3	8,0	1,4	46,8	164,1	43,7	207,7

220. En ce qui concerne l'ancien Fonds social, son activité s'est poursuivie en application de l'article 125 du traité CEE, conformément au règlement général d'application (CEE) 2396/71. Les remboursements intervenus ont atteint 52,77 millions d'UC, se répartissant comme suit:

Tableau 6

Ancien Fonds – Concours octroyés en 1974

(*en UC*)

Pays	Rééducation	Réinstallation	Total
Belgique	1 727 785,70	219,36	1 728 005 06
Allemagne (RF)	21 074 433,61	640 614,13	21 715 047,74
France	3 821 296,25	86 922,76	3 908 219,01
Italie	23 198 060,75	62 666,49	23 260 727,24
Luxembourg	—	—	—
Pays-Bas	2 138 133,18	19 725,02	2 157 858,20

En ce qui concerne les aides communautaires aux travailleurs italiens licenciés des mines de soufre, un montant de 146 492,78 UC a été versé au gouvernement italien au cours de l'exercice 1974.

Il est à noter enfin que, au titre de l'exercice 1975, le Fonds social européen dispose d'un budget de 320 millions d'UC, dont 110 millions d'UC affectés aux concours à octroyer au titre de l'article 4 et 210 millions d'UC à ceux relevant de l'article 5. A la suite de la délibération du Parlement, un montant supplémentaire de 35 millions d'UC a été ajouté au titre de l'article 5, portant ainsi le montant total du Fonds à 355 millions d'UC. A ce montant s'ajoutent 13,4 millions d'UC pour les opérations „ancien Fonds" et 0,9 million d'UC pour la réalisation d'études ou expériences pilotes.

Table 5

Total commitments decided for 1974

(*million u.a.*)

Country	Article 4					Article 5		
	Agriculture	Textiles	Migrant Workers	Handicapped	Total under Article 4	Regions and Technical Progress	Handicapped	Total under Article 5
Belgium	0.3	0.6	—	—	0.9	4.1	1.5	5.6
Denmark	—	—	—	—	—	3.3	8.9	12.2
Germany	6.6	2.6	0.1	—	9.3	6.5	12.2	18.7
France	14.9	0.7	0.4	0.2	16.3	27.9	5.2	33.2
Ireland	6.0	1.2	—	—	7.2	8.7	1.0	9.6
Italy	2.2	0.5	1.2	0.3	4.3	65.3	3.2	68.5
Luxembourg	—	—	—	—	—	—	0.01	0.01
Netherlands	0.9	—	—	—	0.9	3.7	2.1	5.8
United Kingdom	0.2	0.6	6.4	0.8	7.9	44.5	9.6	54.1
Total	31.0	6.3	8.0	1.4	46.8	164.1	43.7	207.7

220. The former Social Fund has continued its activities under Article 125 of the EEC Treaty, in accordance with the general implementing Regulation (EEC) No 2396/71. Assistance granted totalled 52.77 million u.a., allocated as shown in the following table:

Table 6

Old Fund – Assistance granted in 1974

(*u.a.*)

Country	For retraining	For resettlement	Total
Belgium	1 727 785.70	219.36	1 728 005.06
Germany	21 074 433.61	640 614.13	21 715 047.74
France	3 821 296.25	86 922.76	3 908 219.01
Italy	23 198 060.75	62 666.49	23 260 727.24
Luxembourg	—	—	—
Netherlands	2 138 133.18	19 725.02	2 157 858.20

Community assistance for redundant workers from the Italian sulphur mines totalled 146 492.8 u.a. paid to the Italian Government in 1974.

Finally, for 1975 the European Social Fund has a budget of 320 million u.a., of which 110 million u.a. have been allocated for assistance under Article 4 and 210 million u.a. for assistance under Article 5. Following consideration by Parliament an additional 35 million u.a. for Article 5 was added, bringing the total of resources for the Fund to 355 million u.a. There are also 13.4 million u.a. for the operations of the "old Fund" and 0.9 million u.a. for the carrying out of studies or pilot schemes.

221. More than 95% of the assistance granted from the European Social Fund is for the creation and development of vocational training pro-

221. Plus de 95 % des crédits accordés par le Fonds social européen sont consacrés à la création et au développement de programmes de formation professionnelle dans les États membres. En vue d'assurer le plein rendement des ressources croissantes du Fonds, la Commission a commencé à définir des critères d'évaluation de leur efficacité; elle est assistée dans ce travail par un groupe d'experts nationaux, qui ont analysé une série de projets du Fonds social.

222. La Commission a proposé de nouvelles interventions par le Fonds social, et le Conseil a pris des décisions spécifiques en vertu de l'article 4, en faveur des travailleurs migrants et des handicapés. Ces décisions sont entrées en vigueur le 14 juillet.

Par ailleurs, au titre de l'article 7 du règlement d'application de la décision réformant le Fonds social, elle a engagé un certain nombre d'expériences pilotes et une série d'études. Ces travaux ont trait essentiellement à l'intégration des travailleurs migrants, à la réadaptation des handicapés, à la formation dans le secteur de l'informatique, à la formation polyvalente dans certains secteurs et à la réinsertion des femmes de plus de 35 ans dans l'activité économique.

La Commission a organisé, en fin d'année, un séminaire sur l'informatique et la formation des adultes. Le thème central en était les problèmes de formation du personnel posés par le passage au système informatique et le développement de ses applications. Ce séminaire avait pour but de fournir à la Commission les éléments lui permettant de décider s'il y avait lieu d'envisager des interventions spécifiques du Fonds social dans ce secteur.

Réadaptation des travailleurs

223. Le gouvernement britannique et la Commission ont conclu au titre de l'article 56, 2, § b, du traité CECA une convention portant sur l'aide aux mineurs touchés par les fermetures de houillères au Royaume-Uni. Cette convention prévoit les mêmes types d'aides à la réadaptation que les accords conclus avec les autres pays de la Communauté.

La pénurie de jeunes mineurs fait que, parmi toutes les aides existantes, seules sont utilisées les aides qui permettent le transfert de jeunes mineurs vers d'autres puits et les aides aux travailleurs sans emploi, qui permettent la mise à la retraite anticipée des mineurs plus âgés dont le réemploi pose de graves problèmes. Bien que le montant de l'aide par mineur augmente avec l'évolution des salaires, le montant total des aides s'est stabilisé du fait du ralentissement des fermetures résultant de la pénurie d'énergie.

Reconversion d'entreprises et réemploi

224. Au cours de l'année 1974, la Commission a favorisé, par des prêts de reconversion s'élevant à 92,5 millions d'UC, la création de quelque 7 500 emplois dans différentes régions où sont implantées des industries relevant du traité CECA. L'obligation faite aux bénéficiaires de ces prêts de reconvertir d'anciens travailleurs des industries houillère et sidérurgique garantit le reclassement par priorité de quelque 3 750 personnes dans les entreprises financées de la sorte.

3. POLITIQUE AGRICOLE

261. L'année 1974 a été marquée par la poursuite des tendances inflationnistes dues essentiellement à la crise énergétique et à la hausse généra-

grammes in the Member States. In order to ensure a full return on the growing resources of the Fund, the Commission has set about defining criteria for the assessment of their effectiveness; in this task the Commission has the help of a group of national experts, who have analysed a number of Social Fund projects.

222. New interventions by the Social Fund were also proposed by the Commission during 1974 and specific decisions under Article 4, the one relating to migrant workers and the other to handicapped persons, were taken by the Council. Both decisions came into force on 14 July.

Pursuant to Article 7 of the Regulation implementing the Council Decision on the reform of the European Social Fund, the Commission has initiated a number of pilot schemes and studies mainly concerned with the integration of migrant workers, the readaptation of handicapped persons, training in the data-processing field, multi-skill training in certain sectors and the reintegration into employment of women aged over 35.

Towards the end of the year the Commission organized a seminar on data processing and the training of adults. Discussion centred mainly on staff training problems posed by the changeover to computerized systems and the development of computer applications. The purpose of this seminar was to provide the Commission with a factual basis on which to decide whether specific intervention by the Social Fund in this sector would be appropriate.

Retraining and re-employment of workers

223. The United Kingdom Government and the Commission concluded an agreement under Article 56(2) (b) of the ECSC Treaty providing for assistance to miners affected by pit closures in the United Kingdom. The agreement provides for the same type of assistance towards retraining and re-employment as the agreements concluded with other Member States of the Community.

The shortage of young miners has meant that, of all the forms of assistance available, only those have been used which make possible the transfer of young miners to other collieries and those available for unemployed workers, which enable elderly miners, whose re-employment would pose serious problems, to retire early. Although the assistance granted per miner is linked to wage trends, the total amount of assistance has levelled off because of the slowing down of pit closures as a result of the energy shortage.

Conversion of undertakings and re-employment

224. During 1974 the Commission granted conversion loans to the amount of 92.5 million u.a. in order to help create about 7 500 jobs in various regions where ECSC industries are located. The obligation incumbent upon the recipients of these loans to retrain former workers in the coal and iron and steel industries guarantees that priority will be given to resettling about 3 750 people in the undertakings financed in this way.

3. AGRICULTURAL POLICY

261. The year 1974 was marked by continuing inflationary trends resulting basically from the energy crisis and the general increase in the

lisée des prix des matières premières importées. L'agriculture européenne a subi le contrecoup de ces événements qui lui sont extérieurs, sans pouvoir profiter des prix élevés pratiqués sur les marchés internationaux. C'est ainsi que l'on peut dire que l'agriculture européenne a été durement touchée par la crise économique, mais que la politique agricole commune a apporté une contribution non négligeable à la lutte contre l'inflation (notamment par l'institution de prélèvements à l'exportation pour les céréales, le sucre, l'huile d'olive et le riz et par l'interdiction d'exportation pour le froment dur).

262. L'inflation généralisée a eu plusieurs conséquences en agriculture:

Au niveau des coûts de production: Outre les prix des biens et des services achetés par l'agriculture, qui ont suivi le mouvement inflationniste général, les prix de deux catégories de produits ont fortement grevé les coûts de production agricoles: il s'agit des produits énergétiques (carburants, combustibles et engrais) et des produits destinés à l'alimention animale (non seulement le soja, mais aussi le maïs, dont la Communauté importe chaque année plus de 10 millions de t). Face à une telle situation le Conseil a décidé la création d'une organisation commune de marché pour les fourrages déshydratés et la mise en place de mesures spéciales pour les graines de soja. En ce qui concerne les problèmes énergétiques, la Commission a demandé aux États membres de n'accorder, et ce jusqu'au 30 juin 1975 seulement, que des aides aux secteurs les plus concernés par la hausse du coût de l'énergie; en outre, elle a transmis au Conseil un mémorandum relatif aux modifications des conditions de concurrence dans certains secteurs agricoles résultant de la situation nouvelle existant sur les marchés énergétiques.

Au niveau des marchés: Lors de la fixation annuelle des prix agricoles communs, en mars 1974, le Conseil de ministres avait décidé d'accorder une hausse moyenne de 8,8 % des prix communs pour la campagne 1974–1975. Mais les tensions inflationnistes persistantes l'ont amené à rouvrir le dossier ,,prix'' en cours même de campagne, au mois de septembre, et à décider une hausse linéaire de 5 % appliquée aux prix communs décidés en mars 1974.

Au cours de l'année 1974 certains marchés ont spécialement retenu l'attention du Conseil de ministres. En effet, si le marché des produits laitiers n'a pas occasionné trop d'inquiétude en 1974, par contre le marché de la viande bovine a connu une augmentation sensible de l'offre, ce qui a fortement perturbé le marché et, pour la première fois dans son histoire, la Communauté a été presque autosuffisante en viande bovine. Il ne faut cependant en tirer aucune conclusion en ce sens pour l'avenir, cette situation étant due à un concours de circonstances particulières (hausse importante des prix des aliments du bétail; retour des prix de marché à une situation plus normale après la hausse exceptionnelle de 1972–1973, phase haute de production du cycle porcin). Le Conseil de ministres a été amené à prendre un certain nombre de mesures dans ce secteur ainsi que dans d'autres secteurs, notamment ceux du vin et du sucre.

Au niveau économique général: Face à l'inflation généralisée, des mesures ont été adoptées, qui ont influencé fortement l'agriculture européenne. Suite au flottement du franc français, il a été nécessaire d'introduire, à partir du 28 janvier 1974, des montants compensatoires monétaires pour les échanges agricoles de ou vers la France. En Italie, en mai 1974, le gouvernement a décidé le dépôt préalable d'une caution bancaire représentant 50 % de la valeur des importations, bloquée en espèces à la banque d'Italie pour six mois et sans intérêt. Cette mesure, qui touchait la plupart des produits industriels et agricoles, parmi lesquels notamment la viande bovine, les produits laitiers, les produits de la pêche et les oeufs, a été partiellement levée, grâce à une décision de la Commission, en juillet, et presque totalement le 23 octobre 1974. Par ailleurs, le taux représentatif de la lire italienne retenu pour les actes de la politique agricole commune a été prices of imported commodities. European agriculture suffered the repercussions to these external events without being able to profit from the increased prices on international markets. Because of this it can be said that although European agriculture was hard hit by the economic crisis, the common agricultural policy made a not insignificant contribution to the struggle against inflation (in particular by the introduction of export levies for cereals, sugar, olive oil and rice and by the ban on exports of durum wheat).

262. Widespread inflation has had several consequences for agriculture:

As regards production costs. Apart from the prices of goods and services purchased by agriculture, which have been subject to the general inflationary trend, the prices of two categories of product have seriously affected the costs of agricultural production: these are the energy products (motor fuel, fuel oil and fertilizer) and animal feedingstuffs (not only soya, but also maize, of which the Community imports more than 10 million tonnes each year). Faced with such a situation, thc Council decided to establish a common organization of the market in dehydrated fodder and to introduce special measures for soya beans. As regards the energy problem the Commission asked Member States – up to 30 June 1975 only – to grant aid only to the sectors most affected by the increased cost of energy, and in addition it sent a memorandum to the Council relating to changes in the conditions of competition in certain agricultural sectors resulting from the new situation on the energy markets.

As regards markets. When fixing this year's common agricultural prices in March the Council decided to make an average increase of 8.8% in common prices for 1974/75. But continuing inflationary pressures led the Council, in September, to reconsider the prices fixed in March and to apply an across-the-board increase of 5%. During 1974 certain markets attracted the special attention of the Council. Indeed, whereas the markets in milk products did not cause too much concern in 1974, on the other hand the market in beef and veal was considerably disturbed by a major increase in supplies and, for the first time in its history, the Community was almost self-sufficient in beef and veal. However, no conclusion in this sense should be drawn for the future, the situation being due to a combination of special circumstances (considerable rise in the prices of animal feedingstuffs, the return of market prices to a more normal situation after the exceptional rise of 1972/73, a high production point in the pigmeat cycle). The Council decided on several measures in this and other sectors, such as wine and sugar.

As regards the economy as a whole. In view of the general inflation, measures were adopted which had a considerable impact on European agriculture. The floating of the French franc from 28 january 1974 necessitated the introduction of monetary compensatory amounts for agricultural trade with France. In May the Italian Government decided to introduce advance cash deposits amounting to 50% of the value of imports to be held without interest for six months by the Bank of Italy. This measure, which affected most industrial and agricultural products, including beef and veal, milk products, fisheries products and eggs was withdrawn in part in July – as a result of a Commission decision – and almost completely on 23 October. In addition, changes in the representative rate of the Italian lira for purposes of the common agricultural policy brought about a "devaluation" of the agricultural lira totalling 21.1% for 1974/75. The British and Irish pounds were similarly readjusted. In Denmark, the consumption of certain agricultural products was also affected by tax measures taken by the Danish Government at the beginning of May.

263. In this situation, the common agricultural policy has demonstrated its great flexibility and vitality, for not only has it met these successive challenges, it has also extended its work of integration both in range and in depth (proposal for a directive on forestry measures; Directive of 21

modifié de sorte que, pour la campagne 1974–1975, la ,,dévaluation'' de la lire verte a atteint au total 21,1 %. De même, la livre anglaise et la livre irlandaise ont été réajustées. Au Danemark, la consommation de certains produits agricoles a été également frappée par les mesures fiscales prises au début de mai par le gouvernement danois.

263. En présence d'une telle situation, la politique agricole commune a pu faire la preuve de sa grande souplesse et de son dynamisme, car non seulement elle a su faire face à cette série de défis successifs, mais elle a encore poursuivi ses efforts d'intégration aussi bien au niveau de l'élargissement qu'à celui de l'approvisionnement (proposition de directive sur les mesures forestières; directive du 21 janvier 1974 sur l'agriculture de montagne et de certaines zones défavorisées; proposition de directive du 18 décembre 1974 sur l'agriculture de montagne et de certaines zones défavorisées; proposition de directive concernant une aide spéciale aux jeunes exploitants installés depuis moins de cinq ans et réalisant un plan de développement), tout en maintenant la sécurité des approvisionnements et une certaine stabilité des prix en faveur des consommateurs.

Certes, si l'on a critiqué certains aspects de la politique agricole commune, il n'en reste pas moins qu'on n'a pas remis en question ses principes fondamentaux. La Commission elle-même, dans son mémorandum sur l'aménagement de la politique agricole commune, avait présenté des propositions d'aménagement de cette politique; quelques-unes de ses propositions ont été reprises par le Conseil au mois de mars ou d'octobre; d'autres sont encore pendantes devant le Conseil. Dans cette optique, le Conseil de ministres a demandé à la Commission d'établir pour le 1er mars 1975 un inventaire complet de la politique agricole commune en fonction notamment des objectifs de l'article 39 du traité; cet inventaire sera discuté au Conseil et au Parlement en 1975.

4. POLITIQUE ENERGETIQUE

334. Lors de la conférence au sommet de Paris en 1972, les chefs de gouvernement avaient chargé les institutions communautaires d'élaborer dans les meilleurs délais une politique énergétique qui garantisse un approvisionnement sûr et durable dans des conditions économiques satisfaisantes. Au cours de leur conférence de Copenhague, les 14 et 15 décembre 1973, ils avaient consacré une grande partie de leurs discussions à la situation créée par la crise énergétique, discussions dont les résultats ont été reflétés dans un document annexé à la communication finale de cette conférence. Les intentions qui se sont exprimées au cours de ces conférences et qui ont été réaffirmées lors de la conférence au sommet de Paris des 9/10 décembre 1974, ont connu certaines concrétisations au cours de l'année 1974: la Commission qui, dans un mémorandum complémentaire au discours-programme 1974, avait indiqué les lignes directrices de son programme de travail dans ce domaine, a en effet pris plusieurs initiatives importantes qui touchent aux aspects essentiels de la politique énergétique.

Politique énergétique

335. Les problèmes soulevés par la nouvelle situation sur le marché énergétique sont restés au premier plan des préoccupations des institutions communautaires, au cours de l'année 1974. La Commission a présenté au Conseil, les 10 et 16 janvier 1974, une série de propositions tendant à résoudre de manière concertée les problèmes posés par l'évolution de la crise énergétique et à assurer que tous les États membres prennent sur des bases concertées et harmonisées des mesures en vue de restreindre la consommation d'énergie. Ces propositions n'ont pas été approuvées par le

January 1974 on hill farming and farming in less-favoured areas, proposal for a diective of 18 December 1974 on hill farming and farming in less-favoured areas; proposal for a directive on special aid for young farmers who have been farming for less than five years and are carrying out a development plan) while maintaining supplies and price stability for consumers.

Although here and there voices were raised in criticism of certain aspects of the common agricultural policy, they never called into question its fundamental principles. The Commission itself presented a memorandum containing proposals for the improvement of the common agricultural policy; some of these were adopted by the Council in March and October; others are still pending. In this connection, the Council asked the Commission to draw up by 1 March 1975 a complete inventory of the common agricultural policy in relation to the objectives set out in Article 39 of the Treaty; this inventory will be discussed by the Council and Parliament in 1975.

4. ENERGY POLICY

334. At the Paris Summit Conference in 1972 the Heads of Government gave the Community institutions the task of formulating as soon as possible an energy policy guaranteeing reliable and lasting supplies on satisfactory terms. Much of the Copenhagen Conference on 14 and 15 December 1973 was devoted to the situation arising from the energy crisis. The results of the discussions were recorded in a document annexed to the final Communiqué of the Conference. Some of the intentions expressed at these conferences – and reaffirmed at the Paris Summit Conference on 9 and 10 December 1974 – were given substance in the course of 1974. The Commission, which had indicated the broad lines of what it intended to do in this area in the Memorandum annexed to the address on the programme for 1974, took several important steps in respect of the essential points of the energy policy.

The energy policy

335. The problems caused by the new situation on the energy market remained one of the Community institutions' main concerns in the early months of 1974. On 10 and 16 January the Commission presented to the Council a set of proposals aimed at resolving the problems raised by developments in the energy crisis and at ensuring that all Member States take steps to cut down energy consumption in accordance with uniform criteria worked out in concert. These proposals have not been approved by the Council even though Parliament came out in favour of them in a

Conseil, malgré l'avis favorable du Parlement, exprimé dans une résolution sur les mesures à prendre en matière de politique énergétique, à la suite des décisions arrêtées lors de la conférence au sommet de Copenhague. Par lettre du 13 mai 1974 au Conseil, la Commission les a retirées.

Lors de sa 275e session du 30 janvier 1974, le Conseil a approuvé un règlement concernant des informations destinées à l'établissement de bilans exhaustifs pour la Communauté. Se fondant sur les renseignements transmis par les gouvernements des États membres, sur une base volontaire, la Commission avait déjà établi auparavant des bilans sommaires décrivant les aspects importants de la situation énergétique dans la Communauté au cours du dernier trimestre 1973 et du premier trimestre 1974. Les bilans établis conformément au règlement du 30 janvier 1974 ont servi de base à un premier rapport sur les répercussions actuelles et prévisibles de la situation de l'approvisionnement en énergie, sur la production, l'emploi, les prix, les balances de paiements et l'évolution des réserves monétaires, rapport qui a été transmis au Conseil le 1er février 1974.

Lors de la même session, le Conseil, sur proposition de la Commission datant du 17 décembre 1973, a en outre pris une décision portant création d'un Comité de l'énergie. Composé de représentants des États membres et présidé par un membre de la Commission, ce comité a pour tâche d'assurer l'application coordonnée par les États membres des mesures prises par la Communauté, de permettre l'information et la consultation entre les États membres et la Commission sur les conditions de l'approvisionnement et son évolution prévisible, ainsi que d'assister la Commission dans l'élaboration des propositions qu'elle a l'intention de formuler. Son secrétariat est assuré par le secrétariat du Conseil avec le concours d'experts de la Commission sur les questions techniques.

Le comité s'est depuis lors réuni à dix reprises; ces réunions ont permis notamment de larges échanges d'informations sur la situation énergétique, et les membres du Comité ont donné leur avis sur les projets de la Commission qui ont ensuite fait l'objet de communications et propositions au Conseil.

336. La Commission, répondant au vœu exprimé par les chefs de gouvernement lors de leur conférence de Copenhague, a transmis au Conseil, le 5 juin 1974, une communication intitulée „Vers une nouvelle stratégie de politique énergétique pour la Communauté". Dans cette communication, elle tire les conséquences de la crise pétrolière qui, mettant en évidence les points faibles de l'approvisionnement énergétique de la Communauté, a démontré la nécessité pour celle-ci de se doter d'une politique commune à long terme. La stratégie proposée vise à changer profondément la structure de l'approvisionnement énergétique de la Communauté afin de réduire la dépendance vis-à-vis du pétrole. La réalisation d'un tel objectif nécessite, de l'avis de la Commission, une réduction de la consommation d'énergie par l'élimination des gaspillages et par une utilisation plus rationelle, un encouragement de la consommation d'électricité permettant l'accélération du développement de l'énergie nucléaire, qui représente pour la Communauté la seule alternative acceptable à la dépendance pétrolière, une augmentation de la consommation de combustibles solides de production indigène – dont le niveau devra au moins être stabilisé – ou importés, ainsi qu'une augmentation de l'offre du gaz naturel. On peut espérer réduire ainsi progressivement la consommation de produits pétroliers et faire passer plus de 60 % à environ 40 % la part de l'énergie importée dans le total de la consommation. Les objectifs indiqués par la Commission seront susceptibles de révision, selon les circonstances, et leur application dans les États membres s'adaptera aux situations particulières. Leur réalisation nécessite une politique communautaire pour chaque source énergétique, dont le document contient les lignes directrices.

Lors de sa session des 22 et 23 juillet 1974, le Conseil a procédé à une

Resolution on energy policy measures to be taken following the decisions adopted at the Copenhagen Summit Conference. On 13 May the Commission wrote to the Council withdrawing these proposals.

At its 275th meeting, on 30 January, the Council approved a Regulation on information for the establishment of comprehensive energy balance sheets for the Community. The Commission had already used information supplied by the governments of the Member States to draw up summary balance sheets covering the main aspects of the energy situation in the Community in the last quarter of 1973 and the first quarter of 1974. These balance sheets, drawn up pursuant to the Regulation of 30 January 1974, served as a basis for an initial report on the present and foreseeable repercussions of the energy supply situation on production, employment, prices, the balances of payments and the trends of monetary reserves; this report was sent to the Council on 1 February.

At the same meeting the Council, on a proposal from the Commission dated 17 December 1973, also took a Decision setting up an Energy Committee. This Committee, consisting of representatives of the Member States and chaired by a Member of the Commission, has the task of ensuring the coordinated application by Member States of measures taken by the Community, facilitating information and consultation between Member States and the Commission regarding supply and foreseeable trends in supply, and helping the Commission to prepare the proposals which it intends to put forward. Secretarial services are provided by the Council Secretariat and assistance regarding technical questions is given by Commission experts.

The Committee has met on ten occasions; these meetings made it possible to exchange a great deal of information on the energy situation, and the Committee gave its opinion on the Commission drafts which were subsequently embodied in Communications and proposals to the Council.

336. In accordance with the wishes expressed by the Heads of Government at the Copenhagen Conference, the Commission transmitted to the Council on 5 June 1974 the Communication entitled "Towards a new energy policy strategy for the Community." In this Communication the Commission analyses the implications of the oil crisis; in showing up the vulnerable points of the Community energy supply pattern, the crisis demonstrated the need for the Community to have a common long-term policy. The aim of the proposed strategy is to bring about a fundamental change in the structure of the Community's energy supplies in order to reduce the extent of dependence on oil. In the Commission's opinion, to attain this target energy consumption must be reduced by eliminating waste and by using energy in a more rational fashion. by promoting the consumption of electricity and hence speeding up the development of nuclear energy (which is the only acceptable alternative to oil open to the Community), by increasing the consumption both of solid fuels produced within the Community (the level of solid fuel production must be at least stabilized) and of imported solid fuels, and by increasing the supply of natural gas. It is to be hoped that the consumption of petroleum products will be progressively reduced as a result of these measures and that the share of imported energy in total consumption will be reduced from more than 60% to about 40%. The targets indicated by the Commission are subject to revision as dictated by circumstances, and their application in each of the Member States will be adapted to the particular situations existing there. To attain them a Community policy must be implemented for each source of energy; the broad lines of these policies are contained in the Communication.

At its meeting on 22 and 23 July the Council held an initial discussion on this Communication, which had already been enthusiastically endorsed by Parliament, the ESC and the ECSC Consultative Committee, but was unable to reach agreement on a draft resolution proposed by the Com-première discussion de cette communication qui avait déjà fait l'objet des avis très favorables du Parlement, du CES et du Comité consultatif CECA, mais sans pouvoir se mettre immédiatement d'accord sur un projet de résolution proposé par la Commission. Cet accord a pu être réalisé lors de la 302e session du Conseil du 17 septembre 1974. Dans la résolution approuvée à l'unanimité, le Conseil affirme sa volonté politique d'élaborer et de mettre en oeuvre une politique énergétique communautaire qui implique une coordination étroite des positions des États membres de la Communauté, permettant à cette dernière d'exprimer progressivement un point de vue commun sur les problèmes énergétiques vis-à-vis de l'extérieur. En outre, le Conseil fait siennes les principales orientations de la nouvelle stratégie et décide de tenir avant la fin de 1974 une session consacrée aux problèmes énergétiques, pour pouvoir se prononcer sur des objectifs chiffrés pour la production et la consommation de la Communauté d'ici à 1985, sur les orientations et actions nécessaires au développement de chaque source d'énergie, ainsi que sur les conditions d'un fonctionnement ordonné du marché commun de l'énergie.

En vue de préparer cette session, la Commission, après consultation du Comité de l'énergie, a transmis au Conseil, par lettre du 29 novembre 1974, un ensemble de communications concernant la politique énergétique commune. Dans le document intitulé ,,Politique énergétique communautaire – objectifs pour 1985,'' elle présente les objectifs chiffrés de la nouvelle strategie révisée, en tenant compte de leur cohérence et de leurs possibilités de réalisation et à la lumière des perspectives des États membres dans ce domaine, ainsi que les principales actions qui devraient permettre leur réalisation. Ces actions sont développées en détail dans les communications sectorielles qui sont accompagnées de projets de résolutions du Conseil. L'ensemble des communications a également été transmis au Parlement et au CES, qui en ont commencé l'examen au mois de décembre 1974.

Sur la base de ces communications, le Conseil, lors de sa 321e session du 17 décembre 1974, a adopté une résolution sur les objectifs de la politique énergétique communautaire pour 1985 qui constituent des lignes directrices pour les politiques nationales et, en même temps, des orientations importantes pour les producteurs et consommateurs d'énergie dans la Communauté.

Dans cette résolution, le Conseil approuve l'objectif visant à modifier la structure de l'approvisionnement de la Communauté d'ici à 1985, afin de réduire à moins de 50 %, et si possible à 40 %, la dépendance de la Communauté à l'égard de l'énergie importée (63 % en 1973). Il indique les objectifs particuliers à poursuivre en ce qui concerne la demande et l'offre de différentes formes d'énergie. La Commission devra lui faire rapport semestriellement, et pour la première fois le 30 juin 1975, sur les progrès accomplis dans la réalisation de ces objectifs communautaires, notamment sur les mesures prises aux plans communautaire et national. Elle soumettra des propositions pour la mise en oeuvre de la résolution.

Le Conseil a en outre approuvé une résolution concernant un programme d'action communautaire dans le domaine de l'utilisation rationnelle de l'énergie, dans laquelle il fait sien l'objectif d'une réduction du taux de croissance moyen à long terme de la consommation d'énergie, pour l'ensemble de la Communauté. Il s'agira d'atteindre, en 1985, un niveau de consommation de 15 % inférieur à celui qui était prévu pour cette date dans les perspectives initiales de la Commission, établies en janvier 1973, sans pour autant compromettre les objectifs de développement économique et social. Le Conseil a pris acte du programme d'action en la matière défini par la Commission et de la procédure envisagée pour sa mise en oeuvre. Le Conseil s'est réservé enfin de fixer, selon les circonstances et sur proposition de la Commission, des objectifs particuliers d'économie d'énergie à plus courte échéance: la possibilité est ainsi ouverte, suivant les némission. Agreement on the draft resolution was reached at the 302nd Council meeting, on 17 September. In the resolution, which was unanimously approved, the Council affirms its political resolve to formulate and implement a Community energy policy implying the close coordination of the positions of the Member States of the Community, which will enable it progressively to express a common viewpoint on energy problems *vis-à-vis* the outside world. In addition, the Council adopted the main guidelines contained in the new strategy and decided to hold a meeting on energy problems before the end of 1974 at which it will state its position on the target figures for Community energy production and consumption until 1985, the guidelines and action needed to develop each energy source and the requirements for the orderly functioning of the common market for energy.

In preparation for this meeting the Commission consulted the Energy Committee and, by letter on 29 November 1974, transmitted to the Council a series of communications on the common energy policy. In the document entitled "Community Energy Policy – Aims for 1985," the Commission sets out the revised target figures of the new strategy, with due allowance for their mutual compatibility and the possibility of achieving them; these figures are based on the relevant forecasts made by the Member States. The principal actions required to achieve these targets are also set out, and are treated in greater detail in the separate communications for each sector, to which are annexed draft resolutions for submission to the Council. All these documents were also sent to Parliament and the ESC, which began to study them in December.

At its 321st meeting, on 17 December, the Council took these Documents as a basis in adopting a Resolution on the objectives of Community energy policy for 1985; they constitute guidelines for national policies at the same time as providing important guidance for producers and consomers of energy in the Community. In the Resolution the Council approved the aim of changing the pattern of the Community's energy supplies between now and 1985 in order to reduce its dependence on imported energy (which stood at 63% in 1974) to below 50% and, if possible, to 40%. The Council also set out specific objectives regarding the supply of and demand for various forms of energy. The Commission will be required to report to the Council on 30 June 1975, and thereafter at six-monthly intervals, on progress towards attaining the Community objectives, in particular steps taken at Community and national levels, and will submit proposals for implementing the Resolution.

The Council also approved a Resolution on a Community action programme for the rational use of energy, with the objective of reducing the average long-term rate of growth in energy consumption in the Community as a whole. The aim will be to achieve in 1985 a level of consumption 15% below the level forecast for them in the Commission's original projections drawn up in January 1973, yet without jeopardizing economic and social development objectives. The Council took note of the action programme formulated by the Commission and the planned implementing procedure. The Council also reserved the right – according to the circumstances and on proposals from the Commission – to set specific, shorter-term objectives for energy conversation, thus opening the way, should the need arise, for action designed to cut demand more rapidly.

The Council's other decisions taken on 17 December related to oil and gas and the use of natural gas in thermal power stations.

cessités, d'entreprendre des actions en vue de réduire plus rapidement la demande.

Les autres décisions du Conseil du 17 décembre 1974 concernent le secteur de hydrocarbures ainsi que l'utilisation du gaz naturel dans les centrales électriques thermiques.

Relations de la Communauté avec les pays exportateurs d'énergie

337. Répondant au voeu exprimé par la conférence des chefs de gouvernement, la Commission a transmis au Conseil, le 23 janvier 1974, une communication sur les relations de la Communauté avec les pays producteurs d'énergie. Dans cette communication, elle demande au Conseil de l'autoriser à faire connaître à ces pays que la Communauté et ses Etats membres sont disposés à ouvrir des négociations sur des accords de coopération économique, industrielle, technique, technologique et commerciale, et à ouvrir des conservations exploratoires avec les pays qui manifesteraient leur intérêt.

Le Conseil ne s'est pas encore prononcé sur cette communication, mais dans sa résolution du 17 septembre 1974, il confirme que les aspects mondiaux des problèmes énergétiques rendent nécessaire une coopération entre pays consommateurs et pays producteurs, à laquelle la Communauté en tant que telle et les Etats membres entendent participer.

Le 11 juin 1974 déjà, la Communauté avait envoyé un aide-mémoire aux pays membres de l'Organisation des pays exportateurs de pétrole (OPEP) concernant les intentions de cette organisation d'accroître la fiscalité du pétrole brut de concession.

En vue d'une meilleure information réciproque, une première rencontre entre l'Organisation des pays arabes exportateurs de pétrole (OPAEP) représentée par le Dr Attiga, secrétaire général de cette organisation, et la Commission représentée par MM. Simonet et Cheysson, a eu lieu le 7 octobre 1974 à Bruxelles. Il a été décidé de développer des relations périodiques afin d'échanger les informations techniques concernant les activités des deux institutions.

Relations avec les autres pays importateurs

338. Lors de sa session du 15 janvier 1974, le Conseil a marqué l'accord de la Communauté pour participer en tant que telle à la conférence de Washington prévue pour les 11–13 février 1974, et à laquelle elle avait été invitée par le président des Etats-Unis. La Commission a ensuite adressé au Conseil, le 24 janvier 1974, une recommandation pour une position communautaire à prendre lors de cette conférence, en évoquant les principes de coopération énergétique internationale, l'organisation de cette coopération ainsi que les implications de la situation énergétique sur l'économie générale dans le monde, notamment dans le domaine monétaire.

Le Conseil est parvenu, lors de sa session du 4/5 février 1974, à se mettre d'accord sur une position communautaire, qui a ensuit été présentée à la conférence de Washington par le pésident en exercice du Conseil et par le président de la Commission.

Les résultats de cette conférence, à laquelle ont participé, outre la Communauté, tous les Etats membres, les Etats-Unis, le Canada, le Japon et la Norvège, sont évoqués dans un communiqué final auquel tous les participants ont intégralement souscrit, à l'exception de la France qui a émis des réserves au sujet d'un certain nombre de points et qui, par la suite, n'a pas participé aux travaux du Groupe de coordination de l'énergie (ECG) créé par la conférence.

La Commission, qui n'était pas associée aux travaux du ECG, les a at-

The Community's relations with the energy-exporting countries

337. In response to a wish expressed by the Conference of Heads of Government, the Commission sent to the Council on 23 January a Communication on the Community's relations with the energy-producing countries. In this Communication the Commission asked the Council for authorization to inform these countries that the Community and its Member States were prepared to open negotiations with a view to economic, industrial, technical, technological and trade cooperation agreements and to start exploratory talks with interested countries.

The Council has not yet stated its attitude to this Communication, but in its Resolution of 17 September it confirms that the worldwide aspects of energy problems necessitate cooperation between consuming countries and producing countries and that the Community as such and the Member States intend to participate in this cooperation.

As early as 11 June, the Commission sent an *aide-mémoire* to the member countries of OPEC (Organization of the Petroleum Exporting Countries) regarding the intention of that organization to increase the level of taxation on concession crude. On 7 October a first meeting – with a view to better bilateral exchanges of information – was held in Brussels between OAPEC (Organization of Arab Petroleum Exporting Countries), represented by Dr Attiga, its Secretary-General, and the Commission, represented by Mr Simonet and Mr Cheysson. It was decided to arrange further periodic meetings for the exchange of technical information regarding the activities of the two institutions.

Relations with the other importing countries

338. At its meeting on 15 January the Council agreed that the Community should participate as such at the Washington Conference on 11–13 February, to which it had been invited by the President of the United States. The Commission subsequently addressed to the Council, on 24 January, a Recommendation for a Community position to be adopted at this Conference; the Recommendation refers to the principles of international energy cooperation, the organization of this cooperation and the implications of the energy situation for the general world economy, particularly in the monetary sphere.

At its meeting on 4/5 February the Council reached agreement on a Community position, which was then presented at the Washington Conference by the Presidents of the Council and of the Commission.

The results of this Conference, which, in addition to the Community, was attended by all the Member States, the United States, Canada, Japan and Norway, are discussed in the final Communiqué. This was signed by all the countries taking part except France, which expressed reservations about a number of points and which, as a result, did not participate in the work of the Energy Coordination Group (ECG) set up by the Conference.

The Commission was not directly involved in the work of the ECG but followed its progress attentively. The Commission was informed of the ECG's findings by a letter from the Belgian Government dated 9 October tentivement suivis. Elle a été saisie du résultat final de ces travaux par une lettre du gouvernement belge du 9 octobre, lui demandant de porter une appréciation sur ce résultat sous l'angle des dispositions des traités instituant les Communautés européennes.

Dans une lettre adressée au gouvernement belge le 25 octobre, la Commission a reconnu que cet accord peut constituer une première concrétisation de l'attitude commune des États membres en matière de politique énergétique, mais souligne la nécessité d'une définition précise et rapide de cette politique. C'est dans cette perspective que la Commission a proposé au Conseil que la Communauté adhère à l'accord.

Elle a en outre insisté pour que les États membres qui souscriraient à l'accord prennent les mesures nécessaires afin que la solidarité communautaire et les dispositions des traités soient respectées en cas d'application du système de répartition des approvisionnements pétroliers prévu par l'accord.

Cette position de la Commission a été appuyée par le Parlement qui, lors de sa session plénière du 11 décembre 1974, a approuvé une résolution dans laquelle il invite entre autres le Conseil à agir sans délai pour que les Communautés européennes, dotées d'une politique énergétique commune, puissent adhérer dès que possible à l'accord international sur l'énergie.

Par ailleurs, répondant à l'invitation que lui avait adressée le président du comité directeur de l'Agence internationale de l'énergie créée au sein de l'OCDE, la Commission a décidé, le 11 décembre 1974, de participer aux travaux de cette agence au même titre qu'elle est associée aux autres activités de l'OCDE.

E. RELATIONS EXTERIEURES

A. EN GENERAL

361. Si l'on examine l'ensemble de l'activité extérieure de la Communauté pendant l'année 1974, année où l'Europe a subi d'une manière particulièrement lourde les effets d'une situation entièrement nouvelle, notamment dans le domaine de l'énergie, on peut faire les constatations suivantes:

Au plan des échanges, l'ouverture traditionnelle de la Communauté sur l'extérieur s'est manifestée une nouvelle fois par un accroissement très sensible de ses importations (+ 61,4 % de croissance en valeur constante pour les six premiers mois de 1974 par rapport au premier semestre de 1973; les importations en provenance des PVD ont atteint un taux annuel d'accroissement record de 108,1 % sur la même base semestrielle, en partie à cause du renchérissement des matières premières). Les exportations de la Communauté ont connu elles aussi une augmentation notable (+ 41,9% pour les six premiers mois de 1974 par rapport au premier semestre de 1973; l'accroissement vers les pays a commerce d'État et vers les PVD a été substantiel: + 50,0 % et 49,9 %).

Le déficit de la balance commerciale de la Communauté, qui était de moins de 5 milliards d'UC en 1973, s'est considérablement aggravé: il est de plus de 12 milliards d'UC pour les seuls six premiers mois de 1974.

Au plan général on est frappé par la continuité de l'ensemble de la politique extérieure de la Communauté, qu'il s'agisse de celle poursuivie bilatéralement ou dans le cadre des négociations multilatérales dans lesquelles la Communauté a continué à jouer un rôle important.

- En ce qui concerne la négociation commerciale multilatérale, seuls les travaux préparatoires ont pu être effectués dans l'attente du vote par le Congrès américain du „Trade Reform Act." Un certain nombre de conwhich asked the Commission to assess the findings in the light of the Treaties establishing the European Communities. In a letter to the Belgian Government dated 25 October, the Commission recognized that this agreement could constitute a first step towards giving substance to the common attitude of the Member States regarding energy policy, but emphasized the need to define this policy in precise fashion as rapidly as possible. With this aim in view the Commission proposed to the Council that the Community approve the agreement. It also emphasized that Member States signing the agreement should take steps to ensure that Community solidarity and the provisions of the Treaties are respected in the event of applying the arrangements for sharing oil supplies provided for in the agreement.

This position taken up by the Commission was supported by Parliament, which at its plenary session of 11 December approved a resolution in which it invites the Council, *inter alia,* to take prompt action to ensure that the European Communities, equipped with a common energy policy, are able to become a party to the international energy agreement.

Moreover, in response to the invitation issued to the Commission by the Chairman of the Governing Board of the International Energy Agency, which has been set up in OECD, the Commission decided on 11 November to take part in the work of the Agency on the same basis as for its links with the other OECD activities.

E. EXTERNAL RELATIONS

A. IN GENERAL

361. The following remarks may be made concerning the Community's external activities as a whole in the course of 1974, a year in which Europe was particularly hard hit by a wholly new situation, especially in respect of energy.

As regards trade, the Community's traditional openness to the outside world was reflected once again in a very substantial increase in imports (61.4% up in the first half of 1974 on the first half of 1973, at constant prices; imports from the developing countries running at a record annual growth rate of 108.1% on the same comparison, mainly owing to the increase in the price of raw materials). The Community's exports also went up considerably (41.9% up in the first six months of 1974 on the first half of 1973, with a substantial 50.9% and 49.9% increase in exports to State-trading and developing countries respectively).

The Community's deficit on trade, which was less than 5 000 million u.a. in 1973, worsened considerably: it was over 12 000 million u.a. in the first six months of 1974 alone.

In more general terms, a striking feature has been the continuity of the Community's external policy – both in its bilateral aspects and in the context of the multilateral negotiations in which the Community continued to play an important part.

- In the multilateral trade negotiations, no more than preparatory work could be done pending enactment of the trade reform bill by the United States Congress. A number of points were cleared up at Geneva, but the real negotiations will not get under way until 1975.
- The Community made great progress in negotiating with the African, Caribbean and Pacific (ACP) States. These negotiations are not only

cepts ont pu être clarifiés dans les travaux de Genève, mais ce n'est qu'en 1975 que la véritable négociation se nouera.

- La Communauté a fortement avancé la négociation avec les États d'Afrique, des Caraïbes et du Pacifique (ACP), négociation comportant non seulement un régime commercial rénové et un volume d'aide fortement augmenté, mais encore une innovation: un régime de stabilisation des recettes provenant des exportations de certains produits de base originaires des États ACP.
- La Communauté a poursuivi sa participation active à la conférence sur la sécurité et la coopération en Europe. Les travaux dans l'ordre économique sont très avancés, et le passage à la phase finale dépend surtout des décisions politiques relatives aux deux autres domaines.
- Les relations de la Communauté avec les Nations unies sont devenues plus étroites:
  * elle est devenue observateur à l'Assemblée générale;
  * a poursuivi une active participation aux travaux de la CNUCED (notamment dans le domaine des préférences généralisées), à la conférence alimentaire mondiale, à celle de la population ainsi qu'à celle sur le droit de la mer;
  * a participé de bout en bout aux travaux d'élaboration de la Charte des droits et devoirs des États.
- En ce qui concerne les pays développés à économie libérale, d'une part, des conversations souvent tres approfondies ont eu lieu avec les États-Unis, le Canada, l'Australie, la Nouvelle-Zélande et avec le Japon, portant non seulement sur les relations réciproques, mais encore sur celles des uns et des autres avec l'ensemble des partenaires mondiaux et, d'autre part, avec les sept pays de l'AELE (Autriche, Finlande, Islande, Norvège, Portugal, Suède, Suisse), ce dialogue s'est poursuivi dans le cadre des commissions mixtes prévues dans les accords conclus en 1973 avec ses pays. Il y a lieu de souligner l'intérêt tout particulier que la Communauté a porté à ses relations avec la Grèce et le Portugal à la suite des événements politiques de l'année écoulée, qui a marqué la fin de régimes non démocratiques.
- Avec toute une série de pays en voie de développement qui ont conclu avec la Communauté des accords bilatéraux (Argentine, Brésil, Inde, Uruguay, Yougoslavie), le dialogue régulier intervient également dans le cadre de commissions mixtes qui ont commencé à se réunir en 1974; avec d'autres, des négociations sont en cours (Pakistan, Bangladesh, Sri Lanka).
- Enfin, avec les pays à commerce d'État, des dialogues bilatéraux sont susceptibles de résulter de l'offre formulée à leur égard par la Communauté et destinée à entreprendre des négociations après le 1er janvier 1975, date où les accords individuels des États membres avec ces pays deviennent caducs.

362. Mais la Communauté a aussi pris une série d'initiatives ayant pour but d'adopter à l'égard des circonstances nouvelles une attitude dynamique, constructive et non purement défensive.

- C'est ainsi que la Communauté a pris l'initiative de proposer à l'ensemble des pays arabes, qu'ils soient ou ne soient pas producteurs de pétrole ou d'autres matières premières, un dialogue de type nouveau, qui permette de concrétiser une coopération fondée sur l'échange des ressources existant de part et d'autre, compte tenu des différences de structure, de niveau de développement et de besoins.
  En même temps, les négociations propres à l' ,,approche méditerranéenne'' d'ensemble ont été poussées (Maghreb) ou commencées (Machrak).
- Dans le domaine de la politique de développement, la Communauté n'a pas, à l'instar d'autres pays développés, effectué un mouvement de repli. Bien au contraire, elle a pris des initiatives dans différentes directions et ce malgré les contraintes de sa situation extérieure. Elle a aussi fait

renewed trade arrangements and a large increase in the volume of aid: there is also an innovation – a scheme for stabilizing export earnings from a number of commodities originating in the ACP States.

- The Community continued to take an active part in the Conference on Security and Cooperation in Europe. The work in the economic field is well advanced, and the move to the final stage depends mainly on political decisions relating to the two other fields.
- The Community's relations with the United Nations became closer still:
  * the Community was granted observer status in the General Assembly;
  * the Community took an active part in the proceedings of UNCTAD (particularly on the generalized preferences), the World Food Conference, the World Population Conference and the Conference on the Law of the Sea;
  * the Community took part from start to finish in the drafting of the Charter of Economic Rights and Duties of States.
- As regards the developed countries with free market economies, talks were held (in some cases very detailed talks) with the United States, Canada, Australia, New Zealand and Japan, covering relations not only between the two sides involved but also between them and their other trading partners throughout the world; and the Community's dialogue with the seven EFTA countries (Austria, Finland, Iceland, Norway, Portugal, Sweden and Switzerland) was continued in the joint committees set up under the agreements concluded in 1973. The Community paid particular attention to its relations with Greece and Portugal following political events in the course of the year which terminated the non-democratic régimes in those two countries.
- Regular contacts were also kept up in joint committees which began to meet this year with a number of developing countries having concluded bilateral agreements with the Community (Argentina, Brazil, India, Uruguay and Yugoslavia); negotiations with certain other countries (Pakistan, Bangladesh and Sri Lanka) are still in progress.
- Lastly, bilateral contacts with the State-trading countries are liable to result from the offer made by the Community for negotiations to be started after 1 January 1975, the date when individual agreements between Member States and these countries lapse.

362. But the Community has also made several moves with a view to taking up a dynamic, constructive and not purely defensive attitude to changed circumstances.

- For instance, the Community has proposed a new type of dialogue with all the Arab countries, whether or not producers of oil or other raw materials, which will make it possible to give practical form to cooperation based on the exchange of resources available to one side or the other, with due regard for differences of structure, level of development and needs. Negotiations as part of the overall approach to the Mediterranean countries have at the same time been pursued (in the case of the Maghreb countries) or begun (the Mashrek countries).
- Unlike other developed countries, the Community has refrained from cutting back on its development policy. On the contrary, it has taken varying initiatives despite the limitations imposed by its external position. It has also pressed on with the negotiations with the ACP States and has actively worked on the preparation and implementation of the United Nations emergency operation to assist the countries most seriously affected by the recent price increases. The generalized preferences scheme was extended and liberalized during the year in respect both of processed agricultural products and of industrial products.
- The Community took the first steps to give technical assistance to non-associated countries in promoting theirex ports and helping economic integration.
- The Commission's food aid proposals to the Council involved a sub-

progresser la négociation avec les États ACP d'une manière active, la conception et la mise en oeuvre de l'opération d'urgence des Nations unies en faveur d'un certain nombre de pays particulièrement affectés par les récentes hausses de prix. Le régime des préférences généralisées a encore été développé et libéralisé en 1974 dans le domaine des produits agricoles transformés et dans celui des produits industriels.

- La Communauté a fait les premiers pas sur la voie de l'assistance technique avec des pays non associés dans le domaine de la promotion de leurs exportations et de l'aide à leur intégration économique.
- La Commission a proposé au Conseil une aide alimentaire nettement accrue tenant compte des conditions de famine endémique sévissant dans différentes parties du monde, notamment en Asie, et formulé une politique de coopération au développement à l'échelle mondiale.

363. Une autre observation, de caractère général, significative de l'évolution actuelle de la politique extérieure de la Communauté, permet de dire que la notion de coopération apparaît de plus en plus souvent dans les instruments de cette politique en raison notamment du fait que la politique commerciale classique, fondée sur les instruments douaniers et contingentaires, ne peut avoir qu'un faible impact sur le développement des relations économiques de la Communauté avec les pays tels que l'Inde, le Mexique, le Pakistan et Sri Lanka.

364. Enfin, cette année a vu le rapprochement des deux formes que prenait jusqu'ici l'action extérieure commune des neuf pays: la politique extérieure communautaire, d'une part, et la coopération politique, de l'autre. Les buts poursuivis étant communs, les circonstances économiques identiques, il est normal que, malgré les différences institutionnelles, il y ait un rapprochement entre ces deux structures. Le dialogue euro-arabe en a été le premier exemple; les décisions prises à la conférence de Paris de décembre 1974 ont sanctionné ce rapprochement.

B. NEGOCIATIONS COMMERCIALES MULTILATERALES (GATT)

365. Le Comité des négociations commerciales, créé par la „déclaration ministérielle" adoptée à Tokyo en septembre 1973, a poursuivi ses travaux sous la présidence de M. Olivier Long, directeur général du GATT. En effet, pendant toute l'année 1974, les parties aux négociations se sont bornées en fait à continuer leurs travaux et discussions préparatoires pour la phase effective de négociation, puisque les principaux gouvernements ne disposaient pas des pouvoirs nécessaires. Les perspectives pour 1975, maintenant que le Trade Act est voté aux États-Unis, sont que les négociations vont s'engager dans un très bref délai.

Ainsi, laissant de côté le problème du cadre institutionnel pour les négociations, dont il avait discuté à sa première session en octobre 1973, le Comité a adopté en février 1974 un programme de travaux analytiques à entreprendre durant la phase préparatoire des négociations. Ce programme a été réparti entre six groupes de travail établis selon l'architecture du paragraphe 3 de la déclaration de Tokyo.

Au cours du printemps, quatre de ces groupes ont activement progressé dans leurs travaux analytiques: ceux responsables pour les produits tropicaux, l'agriculture, les obstacles non tarifaires et, enfin, les tarifs. Les deux derniers groupes, chargés d'étudier l'approche „sectorielle" et le système multilatéral de sauvegarde, ont eu en octobre une première discussion sur des problèmes de méthodologie et sur la préparation d'une documentation de base. Ils ont été mis en activité au cours de la troisième réunion du Comité des négociations commerciales en juillet, qui a été par ailleurs consacrée à une revue des travaux effectués par les quatre premiers groupes.

Le groupe chargé du „secteur spécial et prioritaire" des produits tropistantial increase because of the famine conditions which are endemic in various parts of the world, especially Asia, and the Commission has also formulated a global policy of development cooperation.

363. Another general observation of significance for current trends in the Community's external policy is that the idea of cooperation is appearing more and more frequently in policy instruments, chiefly because traditional trade policy, based on tariffs and quotas, can have no more than a slight impact on the development of the Community's economic relations with countries such as India, Mexico, Pakistan and Sri Lanka.

364. To conclude, the past year has seen a coming-together of the two forms which the common external policy of the nine Community countries has hitherto taken – the Community's external policy on the one hand and political cooperation on the other. Since the aims are the same and the economic circumstances identical, it is natural that there should be some alignment despite the institutional differences. The European-Arab dialogue was the first instance of this, and it was endorsed by the decisions taken at the Paris conference in December.

B. MULTILATERAL TRADE NEGOTIATIONS (GATT)

365. The Trade Negotiations Committee, established by the Declaration issued at the end of the Ministerial Meeting in Tokyo in September 1973, has continued its work under the chairmanship of Mr Olivier Long, Director-General of GATT. Throughout 1974 the parties to the negotiations simply carried on with their talks and other work in preparation for the negotiating phase proper, since the principal governments concerned had not been given the necessary powers. Now that the Trade Act has passed into law in the United States, the 1975 outlook suggests that negotiations themselves can quickly be set in train.

Thus, leaving aside the problem of the institutional framework for the negotiations, which it had discussed at its first session in October 1973, the Committee adopted in February 1974 a programme of analytical work to be undertaken during the preparatory phase of the negotiations. This programme was divided up between six subgroups along the lines set out in paragraph 3 of the Tokyo Declaration.

Four of these groups made active progress in their analytical work during the spring – those concerned with tropical products, agriculture, non-tariffbarriers, and tariffs. The last two groups – those on the "sectoral" approach and the multilateral safeguard system – held a preliminary discussion in October on methods and the preparation of basic documentation; they had been activated during the third meeting of the Negotiations Committee in June, at which the work of the first four groups was reviewed.

The subgroup dealing with tropical products ("a special and priority sector") was able to assemble and analyse statistical information on trade caux a pu réunir et analyser une documentation statistique sur le commerce de ces produits. La délégation de la Communauté a souligné à cet égard que les fluctuations parfois brutales des prix et des volumes des exportations de ces produits posent aux pays en voie de développement des problèmes graves et elle a obtenu que l'analyse porte également sur ces aspects.

Dans le cadre des travaux du groupe responsable de l'agriculture, la délégation de la Communauté a fait valoir qui la situation sur les marchés mondiaux s'est en quelque sorte inversée, ces deux dernières années, passant d'un excédent de l'offre par rapport à la demande solvable à une insuffisance de l'offre par rapport à la demande, sous l'effet de facteurs conjoncturels et structurels, climatologiques et économiques.

Le groupe resonsable de l'examen des obstacles non tarifaires a réuni une documentation de base sur des questions telles que les méthodes d'évaluation douanière, les règles d'étiquetage et d'emballage, les restrictions quantitatives ou les subventions à l'exportation.

Dans le domaine plus spécifique des droits compensateurs, le but recherché par la CEE est d'obtenir que les législations et les pratiques de certains pays, les États-Unis notamment, soient rendues conformes aux principes et règles du GATT. La délégation de la Communauté ayant posé la question d'une étude des restrictions à l'exportation, le groupe est convenu d'en référer au Comité des négociations commerciales.

Le groupe chargé des travaux préparatoires sur les tarifs a procédé à la mise à jour de sa documentation de base concernant les structures des principaux tarifs en cause et les statistiques commerciales des pays correspondants. Il a entamé par ailleurs une discussion préliminaire sur la base de départ à partir de laquelle seraient prévues les réductions tarifaires à négocier, c'est-à-dire les taux de base, l'année de référence, la monnaie de compte à utiliser dans les comparaisons statistiques, etc. De son cøté, la Commission a soumis en octobre au Conseil un document qui explicite et rend plus opérationnelles les thèses contenues dans sa „conception d'ensemble" en ce qui concerne ces négociations, que la Commission considère dans le contexte économique actuel plus que jamais nécessaires.

C. NEGOCIATIONS AVEC LES PAYS D'AFRIQUE, DES CARAIBES ET DU PACIFIQUE

Déroulement des négociations

407. La conférence ministérielle conjointe, tenue à Kingston (Jamaïque) les 25/26 juillet 1974, a marqué un tournant capital dans les négociations.[1]

Le premier résultat important de Kingston est d'avoir donné l'occasion de souligner la volonté politique des États ACP et de la Communauté d'adopter la convention dans les délais imposés notamment par l'expiration de la convention de Yaoundé et de l'accord d'Arusha.

En deuxième lieu, des orientations politiques ont été convenues qui ont permis de débloquer un certain nombre de points de désaccord, ou d'approfondir des matières à peine abordées à défaut de directives.

408. A travers les différentes phases, les États ACP ont su consolider leur cohésion et leur unité: l'ensemble des États ACP ne forme qu'un seul groupe aux négociations, avec un porte-parole unique.

Depuis la conférence de Kingston, leur entente a permis de créer des sous-comités spécialisés au niveau des ambassadeurs, au sein desquels l'en-

---

[1] Aux 43 Etats mentionnés dans le Septième Rapport général, n° 527, se sont jointes Grenade, devenue indépendante en février 1974, et la Guinée-Bissau.
(La Guinée équatoriale a fait connaître son intérêt pour l'issue des négociations).

in these products. The Community delegation emphasized that the sometimes abrupt fluctuations in the price and volume of exports of tropical products present serious problems to the developing countries, and it has managed to get the analysis to cover these aspects too.

In the agriculture subgroup, the Community delegation remarked that over the past two years the situation on world markets has to some extent been reversed, changing from a supply surplus in relation to effective demand to a supply shortfall in relation to demand as a result of market conditions and structural, climatic and economic factors.

The subgroup concerned with the examination of non-tariff barriers has assembled a core of basic information on matters such as customs valuation methods, labelling and packaging rules, quantitative restrictions and export subsidies.

With particular reference to countervailing duties, the EEC's objective is to see that the legislation and practices of certain countries, notably the United States, are made to conform with the principles and rules of GATT. The Community delegation raised the question of studying export restrictions, and the subgroup agreed to refer this to the Trade Negotiations Committee.

The subgroup engaged in preparatory work on tariffs updated its basic documentation on the structure of the principal tariffs involved and the trade statistics of the relevant countries. It also began a preliminary discussion concerning the basis on which tariff cuts are to be negotiated, i.e., base rates, reference year, accounting currency for statistical purposes, etc. In October the Commission sent the Council a paper clarifying and putting on a more practical basis the ideas behind its overall approach to these negotiations, which in the Commission's view are now more necessary than ever in the current economic situation.

C. NEGOTIATIONS WITH THE AFRICAN, CARIBBEAN AND PACIFIC COUNTRIES

Progress of the negotiations

407. The Joint Ministerial Conference held in Kingston, Jamaica, on 25/26 July 1974 marked a turning point in the negotiations.[1]

The first major result of Kingston was that it provided the opportunity to emphasize the political resolve of the ACP States and the Community to adopt the convention within the time limits imposed by the expiry of the Yaoundé Convention and the Arusha Agreement.

Secondly, political guidelines were agreed which made further progress possible on a number of points of disaccord and permitted matters which, for lack of negotiating directives, had hardly been touched upon to be examined in greater detail.

408. Throughout the various phases the ACP States were able to consolidate their cohesion and their unity: all the ACP States formed one group in the negotiations, with a single spokesman.

Since the Kingston Conference their agreement has enabled specialized subcommittees to be set up at ambassadorial level on which the ACP as a

[1] Grenada, which became independent in February 1974, and Guinea-Bissau have joined the 43 States mentioned in the Seventh General Report, point 527. Equatorial Guinea has expressed its interest in the outcome of the negotiations.

semble des ACP se faisaient représenter par un nombre limité d'entre eux: sur le plan de la procédure de négociation, cette innovation a été très importante: elle a permis d'abandonner la méthode, suivie jusqu'alors au sein du Comité plénier des ambassadeurs, des échanges de déclarations préétablies et écrites de part et d'autre au profit de pourparlers véritables, et de négocier simultanément plusieurs sujets au sein de souscomités différents.

Cette procédure accélérée compense partiellement le démarrage relativement lent des négociations. Il fallait du temps aux pays partenaires pour coordonner leur position et leurs travaux afin d'aborder les questions de fond dans l'esprit d'unité voulu. L'entente des États ACP a permis à la Communauté d'être confrontée avec un négociateur unique, situation que la Commission, pour sa part, a toujours souhaitée.

409. Les travaux au sein du Comité plénier des ambassadeurs et plénipotentiaires ont abouti à l'établissement, lors de la dernière séance du 9 décembre, d'un projet de convention couvrant l'ensemble des matières de la future coopération CEE-ACP. Ce texte comporte encore un certain nombre de points ouverts. Parmi ceux-ci figurent notamment les questions réservées au niveau ministériel au stade final des négociations, notamment le volume de l'aide financière. Sur d'autres questions politiques, les États ACP et la Communauté doivent encore se concerter chacun de leur côté; certaines d'entre elles sont importantes et touchent au caractère même de la future convention. Mais, dans l'ensemble, la Commission peut confirmer que les résultats des négociations consignés dans le projet de convention reflètent les aspirations de part et d'autre.

Contenu de la future convention CEE-ACP

410. L'objet des négociations est de définir les futurs rapports de coopération de la Communauté avec l'ensemble des pays concernés: la totalité des pays indépendants d'Afrique noire, six pays antillais et trois pays de l'océan Pacifique. Elles visent à l'adoption de formules de coopération originales dans le cadre d'un ,,partnership" équitable.

Les États ACP entendent placer leurs relations futures avec la Communauté sous le signe général de la ,,coopération économique" et, dans ce contexte plus large, ils attachent un intérêt particulier à la coopération industrielle. En faisant siens cette conception et l'objectif poursuivi, la Communauté a rappelé que sa proposition de départ de négocier un ,,accord global" était faite dans cette même optique. A la conférence de Kingston, les deux parties ont confirmé que l'objet visé était de poser un premier jalon d'un nouvel ordre économique mondial, en définissant les principes d'un nouveau modèle de relations entre les pays industrialisés et les pays en voie de développement fondés sur le principe de la justice sociale internationale.

Cette approche novatrice des relations futures CEE/ACP a dominé tout au long des négociations et se reflète dans les principaux domaines du projet de convention CEE/ACP.

Coopération commerciale

411. Basée sur la reconnaissance de l'asymétrie qui caractérise la situation économique des États ACP par rapport à leurs partenaires européens, la coopération commerciale comprendra pour l'essentiel le libre accès des produits des États ACP au marché de la Communauté, y compris la quasitotalité des produits agricoles pour lesquels ils ont un intérêt économique, tandis que les États ACP ne seront pas tenus d'accepter d'obligation correspondante. De leur côté, les États ACP assureront un régime non discriminatoire entre les États membres de la Communauté et appliqueront à cette dernière la clause de la nation la plus favorisée, sauf lorsqu'il s'agit d'avan-

whole appointed a limited number of members to represent their interests. From the angle of negotiating procedure this innovation has been very important: it has enabled the method, followed until then within the Plenary Committee of Ambassadors, of exchanges of prepared written statements between the two sides to be abandoned for negotiations proper, with a number of subjects being negotiated simultaneously within different subcommittees.

This accelerated procedure partly compensated for the relatively slow start to the negotiations. The partner countries needed time to coordinate their position and their work in order to deal with the substantive issues in the desired spirit of unity. Agreement among the ACP States enabled the Community to deal with a single negotiator, a situation which the Commission has for its part always desired.

409. The work of the Plenary Committee of Ambassadors and Plenipotentiaries led, at the last meeting on 9 December, to a draft convention covering all the subjects of the future EEC-ACP cooperation. The text still contains a number of outstanding points. Among these are the matters reserved for the ministers in the final stage of the negotiations, in particular the volume of financial aid. On other political issues the ACP States and the Community still have to concert their respective positions; some of these matters are important and touch upon the very character of the future convention. On the whole, however, the Commission is able to confirm that the results of the negotiations recorded in the draft convention reflect the aspirations of both sides.

Content of the future EEC-ACP convention

410. The purpose of the negotiations is to define the Community's future relations of cooperation with all the countries concerned: all the independent countries in Black Africa, six Caribbean countries and three Pacific countries. The goal is the adoption of original formulas for cooperation within the framework of an equitable partnership.

The ACP States intend to make economic cooperation the general theme for their future relations with the Community and, in this wider context, they attach particular importance to industrial cooperation. In also adopting this conception and the objective pursued, the Community recalled that its initial proposal to negotiate a "global agreement" was made with the same aim in mind. At the Kingston Conference the two parties confirmed that the object in view was to take the first step towards a new world economic order by defining the principles of a new model for relations between industrialized countries and developing countries based on the principle of international social justice.

This innovatory approach for future relations between the EEC and the ACP predominated throughout the negotiations and was reflected in the main areas of the draft EEC-ACP Convention.

Trade cooperation

411. Based on recognition of the disparity between the economic situation of the ACP States and that of their European partners, trade cooperation will mainly include free access to the Community market for ACP products, including virtually all the agricultural products which are of economic importance to the, while them ACP States will not discriminate between the Member States of the Community and will apply to the latter most-favoured-nation treatment except as regards advantages which they accord to other developing countries. Promotion of the ACP States' trade will be stepped up.

tages qu'ils accordent à d'autres pays en voie de développement. La promotion commerciale des États ACP sera intensifiée.

Quant aux règles d'origine, certaines d'entre elles ont été assouplies et permettent notamment le „cumul intégral," les États ACP étant considérés comme un seul territoire douanier pour les produits transformés à l'intérieur de celui-ci. Il faut toutefois constater que les revendications ACP vont au-delà de ce régime; la Communauté ne pourra pas y réprondre favorablement dans la mesure où elles dépassent le régime intracommunautaire.

Système de stabilisation de recettes d'exportation

412. Ce système, qui est un des éléments les plus novateurs de la coopération future, est destiné à pallier les effets nocifs sur l'économie des pays intéressés des chutes de prix ou de quantité des principaux produits exportés. A la demande des États ACP, le nombre de produits pouvant bénéficier du système sera plus élevé que celui proposé initialement par la Commission, et englobera notamment certains produits de première transformation.

Dans ce contexte, en ce qui concerne le sucre, bien qu'un large consensus se soit établi fin décembre 1974 sur les principes généraux des arrangements futurs, un accord n'était pas encore intervenu sur la question centrale des prix.

Coopération industrielle

413. Cette coopération vise notamment la promotion du développement et de la diversification industrielle et l'établissement de relations nouvelles dans ce domaine entre les États ACP, la Communauté et ses États membres; elle facilitera le transfert de la technologie, son adaptation aux conditions et besoins spécifiques des États ACP, la recherche et la formation y afférente. A cet effet, un comité de coopération industrielle veillera notamment à la mise en oeuvre de cette partie de la convention et un centre pour le développement industriel sera chargé de l'information et des contacts nécessaires entre responsables des politiques industrielles, leurs promoteurs et opérateurs de part et d'autre.

Coopération financière et technique

414. En cette matière aussi, la coopération a été améliorée, tant dans ses procédures que dans les domaines d'intervention. Les améliorations concernent notamment le processus de décision, la gestion et l'administration de l'aide. Dans le contexte de la coopération financière et technique, la Communauté apportera un concours efficace à la coopération régionale et interrégionale, objectifs auxquels une part des moyens financiers sera réservée. Une dotation spéciale du futur FED sera consacrée aux aides exceptionnelles; en outre, des mesures particulières seront prévues en faveur des États les moins développés.

Institutions

415. L'aspect novateur réside dans la possibilité d'assurer des contacts et des consultations avec les milieux économiques et sociaux des États membres et des États ACP, dans la mesure où l'institution de décision et de gestion au niveau des ministres et des ambassadeurs les juge utiles. En plus de ses compétences de décision, de consultation et de gestion, cette institution pourra également procéder notamment à des échanges de vues sur les questions ayant une incidence directe sur les domaines visés par la convention.

Il est proposé de créer une assemblée consultative composée, sur une

As for the rules of origin, some of them have been made more flexible and permit in particular 'full cumulation', the ACP States being considered a single customs territory for products processed whithin that territory. It must however be noted that the ACP are pressing their claims, further; the Community will not be able to give a favourable response where they go beyond intra-Community treatment.

System of stabilizing export earnings

412. This system, which is one of the chief innovations of future cooperation, is intended to remedy the harmful effects on the economies of the countries concerned of falls in price or quantity of the main exports. At the request of the ACP States the number of products to which the system may apply will be higher than that initially proposed by the Commission and will take in a number of products having undergone a first stage of processing. In regard to sugar, although a broad consensus was achieved at the end of December 1974 on the general principles of the future arrangements, an agreement had not yet been reached on the central question of prices.

Industrial cooperation

413. The main purpose of this form of cooperation is to promote industrial development and diversification and the establishment of new relations in this field between the ACP States and the Community and its Member States; it will facilitate the transfer of technology, its adaptation to the specific conditions and requirements of the ACP States, research and related training. To this end, an Industrial Cooperation Committee will see that this part of the convention is implemented and an Industrial Development Centre will be responsible for providing information and making the necessary contacts between those responsible for industrial policies, the promoters of those policies, and firms and nationals on both sides.

Financial and technical cooperation

414. Here too, cooperation has been improved as regards both procedures and areas of action. The improvements involve mainly the decision-making process and aid management and administration. In the context of financial and technical cooperation the Community will make a real contribution to regional and inter-regional cooperation, objectives for which part of the financial resources will be earmarked. A special appropriation in the future EDF will be devoted to exceptional aid; special measures will also be planned to help the least developed States.

Institutions

415. The novel aspect is the possibility of providing contacts and consultations with business and labour in the Member States and the ACP States where the decisionmaking and management institution at ministerial and ambassadorial levels considers them to be of use. Apart from its decision-making, consultation and management powers this institution will also be able to have exchanges of views on matters directly affecting the areas covered by the convention.

It is proposed to set up a Consultative Assembly, composed of an equal base paritaire, de membres du Parlement pour la Communauté, et de représentants désignés par les États ACP.

Mesures transitoires

416. Entre temps, la Commission a présenté au Conseil ses propositions relatives aux mesures transitoires à prendre, à partir du 1er février 1975, dans les relations entre la Communauté et les États ACP. Basées sur la mise en application de certaines dispositions de la future convention CEE/ACP dans le cadre d'un accord intérimaire, les mesures transitoires devraient, de l'avis de la Commission, consister, pour une première phase, en un régime de statu quo prorogeant les régimes en vigueur pendant quelques mois, afin de permettre la préparation pratique nécessaire sur le plan réglementaire et technique de la mise en application d'un tel accord intérimaire.

D. RELATIONS AVEC D'AUTRES PAYS ET REGIONS

i. Relations avec les pays membres de l'AELE

424. L'accord entre la Finlande et la CEE est entré en vigueur le 1er janvier 1974. Ainsi, les accords conclus entre la Communauté et chacun des sept pays de l'AELE sont désormais tous en vigueur, avec le même calendrier de désarmement tarifaire.

Le Comité mixte CEE/Finlande a tenu sa première réunion en janvier 1974 en vue d'arrêter un certain nombre de décisions en matière de coopération administrative et douanière. Par la suite, chacun des sept comités mixtes a tenu deux autres réunions, qui ont eu lieu en mai/juin 1974 et en novembre/décembre 1974. Le Comité mixte CEE/Portugal présente chaque fois un caractère particulier et sera décrit plus loin.

A l'occasion de chacune de leurs réunions, les comités mixtes ont examiné le fonctionnement des accords dans le contexte de l'évolution économique mondiale. Si l'on a pu constater le bon fonctionnement de tous les accords, sauf en ce qui concerne le protocole no 6 annexé à l'accord avec l'Islande qui n'est pas encore en vigueur faute d'un règlement du litige entre l'Islande et la république fédérale d'Allemagne au sujet des zones de pêche, l'attention a été attirée sur les problèmes pouvant résulter des difficultés de balances de paiements, aggravés par les prix du pétrole, l'inflation et l'approvisionnement en matières premières. Les mesures de balance de paiements prises par la Communauté en vue de protéger l'économie d'un État membre, au sujet desquelles les pays membres de l'AELE ont exprimé l'espoir qu'elles ne remettraient pas en cause le libre-échange, ont également retenu l'attention.

Au cours de l'année 1974, les comités douaniers ont soumis des propositions, qui ont été approuvées par les comités mixtes, visant une simplification considérable des formalités douanières entre la Communauté et les pays de l'AELE et l'introduction de certaines modifications dans les listes A et B des règles d'origine, ainsi que la propagation pour un an du système de remboursement des droits d'importation. La première de ces mesures, la simplification, a pris effet le 1er septembre 1974, et les deux autres entreront en vigueur le 1er janvier 1975.

Les relations entre la Communauté et le Portugal ont été marquées par la récente évolution politique dans ce pays. Dès mai 1974, M. Mario Soares, devenu peu après ministre des affaires étrangères du Portugal, s'était entretenu avec des membres de la Commission. Les discussions avaient porté sur la nouvelle situation politique du pays et sur le soutien économique, financier et technique que la Communauté et les États membres number of members of Parliament for the Community and of representatives designated by the ACP States.

Transitional measures

416. In the meantime the Commission has presented the Council with its proposals for transitional measures to be taken with effect from 1 February 1975 in respect of relations between the Community and the ACP States. Based on the implementation of certain provisions of the future EEC-ACP convention under an interim agreement, the transitional measures should in the Commission's opinion initially consist of a *status quo* arrangement extending for a few months the arrangements in force so as to enable the necessary practical preparations to be made – adoption of regulations and technical arrangements – for the implementation of such an interim agreement.

D. RELATIONS WITH OTHER COUNTRIES AND REGIONS

i. Relations with EFTA countries

424. The Agreement between Finland and the EEC came into force on 1 January 1974. and thus the Agreements between the Community and each of the seven EFTA countries are now all in force with a common schedule of tariff dismantling.

The EEC-Finland Joint Committee held its first meeting in January in order to take a number of decisions on administrative and customs cooperation. Subsequently there were two further meetings of each of the seven Joint Committees, the first round of meetings taking place in May-June and the second in November-December. On each of these occasions, the EEC-Portugal Joint Committee meeting was of a special nature (see below).

The Joint Committees at each of their meetings considered the functioning of the Agreements against the background of world economic developments. While the Agreements were all functioning smoothly (except for Protocol No 6 to the Iceland Agreement, which is not in force since there is still no settlement in the fishing dispute between Iceland and the Federal Republic of Germany), attention was drawn to the problems which might arise from balance of payments difficulties accentuated by oil prices, inflation and the supply of raw materials. Consideration was also given to the balance of payments measures taken by the Community in order to protect the economy of one Member State, which the EFTA countries hoped would not impede free trade.

During the year the Customs Committees submitted proposals, which the Joint Committees approved, for a considerable measure of simplification in customs procedures between the Community and the EFTA countries and for certain changes in Lists A and B of the rules of origin and the continuation of drawback for a further year. The first of these measures (simplification) came into force on 1 September 1974, and the last two will come into force on 1 January 1975.

Relations between the Community and Portugal were marked by the recent political developments in that country. In May 1974 Mr Mario Soares, who shortly after became Portugal's Minister of Foreign Affairs, had talks with Commission members. The discussions dealt with the new political situation in Portugal and the economic, financial and technical support which the Community and the Member States would be able to give to help Portugal in its desire to restore democracy and effect an economic recovery. Before Parliament the Commission confirmed its desire pourraient apporter à la volonté de redressement démocratique et économique du Portugal. Devant le Parlement, la Commission a confirmé le désir de voir s'établir des relations plus étroites entre le Portugal et la CEE. La nature de ces relations a ensuite été au centre des échanges de vues entre le président de la Commission, M. Adelino da Palma Carlos, premier ministre de la République portugaise, et M. Mario Soares, ministre des affaires étrangères, en visite à Bruxelles le 26 juin 1974.

Ces thèmes ont été repris lors de la 3e réunion du comité mixte, le 27 juin 1974. La délégation portugaise a fait part du souhait de son gouvernement d'aller au-delà des accords signés en 1972. Elle a réaffirmé l'entière adhésion de son pays aux principes démocratiques et aux objectifs fondamentaux de la Communauté; elle a souligné la nécessité de développer les liens de coopération entre les deux parties, notamment en exploitant les possibilités offertes par la clause évolutive des accords. Elle a exprimé l'espoir que la Communauté serait en mesure d'apporter rapidement à l'économie portugaise l'aide et la coopération à la reconversion nécessaire pour permettre au Portugal de jouer pleinement son propre rôle dans une Europe démocratique.

La délégation de la Communauté s'est félicitée des possibilités que l'évolution politique actuelle du Portugal ouvre au développement des relations de la Communauté avec le Portugal. Elle a tenu à souligner son attitude positive en la matière et sa volonté de mettre tout en oeuvre pour répondre aux souhaits que pourrait exprimer le Portugal dans les domaines où celui-ci voudrait voir s'instaurer ou se développer la coopération établie par l'accord de 1972.

Accords CECA

425. Les accords conclus entre la CECA, l'Autriche, le Portugal, la Suisse et la Suède sont entrés en vigueur le 1er janvier 1974; les comités mixtes prévus dans ces accords ont tenu leur première réunion en mai/juin 1974. Les accords conclus entre la CECA et la Norvège et entre la CECA et la Finlande ayant été ratifiés par tous les États membres de la Communauté au 30 novembre 1974, ces deux accords entreront en vigueur le 1er janvier 1975.

ii. Relations avec les pays du Bassin méditerranéen

Association avec la Grèce

426. Les relations entre la Grèce et la Communauté se sont poursuivies jusqu'en juillet 1974 dans le cadre de la „gestion courante", depuis 1967, de l'accord d'association conclu en 1961.

C'est ainsi que la Grèce a procédé, le 1er mai 1974, à une nouvelle réduction de ses droits de douane sur certains produits industriels des États membres originaires de la CEE. Cette réduction a été opérée après celle du 1er novembre 1972 et correspond à 36 % des droits de base grecs en vigueur le 1er novembre 1962.

Le Comité d'association a pris une décision relative au désarmement douanier concernant les produits industriels à partir du 1er mai 1974. Le Conseil a décidé, en juin 1974, de proroger jusqu'au 30 juin 1974 la durée de validité du règlement concernant l'importation dans la Communauté, en provenance de Grèce, de certaines marchandises issues de la transformation de produits agricoles. Il a prorogé, pour la campagne de commercialisation 1974–1975, le montant forfaitaire applicable aux importations d'huile d'olive non raffinée entièrement fabriquée en Grèce et transportée directement du pays vers la Communauté.

427. En mars et mai 1974, la Communauté avait encore marqué son indignation à la suite de l'internement de M. Georges Mavros et de l'aggravation de la dictature.

to see closer relations established between Portugal and the EEC. The nature of these relations was subsequently the central issue in the exchanges of views which took place between the President of the Commission and Mr Adelino da Palma Carlos, Prime Minister of Portugal, accompanied by Mr Mario Soares, Minister of Foreign Affairs, during their visit to Brussels on 26 June.

These subjects were taken up again at the third meeting of the Joint Committee on 27 June. The Portuguese Delegation indicated its Government's desire to go beyond the Agreements signed in 1972. It reaffirmed Portugal's total adherence to democratic principles and to the basic objectives of the Community; it emphasized the need to develop cooperation between the two parties, particularly by exploiting the possibilities offered by the clause in the Agreements permitting extension to further fields. It expressed the hope that the Community would soon be able to give the Portuguese economy the aid and cooperation for redevelopment required to enable Portugal to play to the full a role of its own in a democratic Europe.

The Community Delegation welcomed the possibilities which the present political trend in Portugal opened for developing the Community's relations with that country. It was anxious to stress its positive attitude on this matter and its intention to do everything within its power to meet any wishes which Portugal might express with regard to the fields where it would like to see the cooperation established by the 1972 Agreement launched or developed.

ECSC Agreements

425. The Agreements between the ECSC and Austria, Portugal, Switzerland and Sweden came into force on 1 January 1974, and Joint Committees provided for in these Agreements held their first meetings in May-June. The Agreements between the ECSC and Norway and between the ECSC and Finland were ratified by all Member States of the Community by 30 November, and these two Agreements will therefore come into force on 1 January 1975.

ii. Relations with the Mediterranean countries

The Association with Greece

426. Up to July 1974 relations between Greece and the Community remained governed by the "routine business" approach applied since 1967 to the Association Agreement concluded in 1961.

On 1 May Greece made another reduction in its customs duties on certain industrial products from the original Member States of the EEC. This followed the reduction of 1 November 1972 and brought the aggregate tariff cuts to 36% of the basic duties applying in Greece on 1 November 1962.

The Association Committee took a decision to modify the customs duties on industrial products with effect from 1 May. In June the Council decided to extend until 30 June the regulation on the import into the Community from Greece of certain goods resulting from the processing of agricultural products. It extended to the 1974/75 marketing year the standard amount applicable to imports of unrefined olive oil wholly obtained in Greece and transported direct from Greece to the Community.

427. In March and May the Community again expressed strong indignation at the internment of Mr Georges Mavros and the further intensification of the dictatorship.

However, the political changes that took place in Greece on 24 July will reshape the context of relations between Greece and the Community.

Cependant, les changements politiques intervenus en Grèce le 24 juillet 1974 vont modifier le contexte des relations entre la Grèce et la Communauté.

Dès le 30 août 1974, la Commission a adressé une communication au Conseil dans laquelle elle proposait une série de mesures que la Communauté pourrait prendre immédiatement en vue de la ,,réactivation'' de l'association.

Ce thème a été au centre des entretiens entre la Commission et M. Mavros, vice-président du Conseil et ministre des affaires étrangères de Grèce, accompagné par M. Pesmazoglou, ministre des finances.

La Commission s'est félicitée de voir la Grèce engagée sur la voie du rétablissement des institutions démocratiques et s'est penchée sur les perspectives de développement de l'association. M. Mavros a fait part de l'intention de son gouvernement de soumettre bientôt à la Communauté une demande visant l'accélération de l'intégration de la Grèce dans la Communauté, en vue de rendre son adhésion possible dans un délai rapproché. En effet, la date du 31 octobre 1974 marquera la fin de la phase transitoire normale de l'association et l'achèvement de l'union douanière pour l'essentiel des échanges de marchandises entre les deux parties.

La Commission a assuré ses interlocuteurs qu'elle mettra tout en oeuvre pour que les travaux nécessaires à la réactivation de l'association, tels qu'ils seront décidés par les instances compétentes de la Communauté et de la Grèce, soient menés avec toute la célérité possible.

Par la suite, le Conseil a rendu publique une décalaration dans laquelle il marque de la façon la plus nette sa détermination de reprendre sans délai le processus de développement de l'association.

De même, le Parlement s'est prononcé, le 26 septembre 1974, pour le dégel immédiat des aspects économiques et commerciaux de l'association.

Le premier Comité d'association CEE-Grèce, après le rétablissement de la démocratie en Grèce, a eu lieu à Bruxelles le 22 novembre 1974. Ses travaux ont été consacrés à la préparation du Conseil d'association, qui s'est tenu le 2 décembre 1974.

Le 26 novembre 1974, le gouvernement grec a remis un aide-mémoire à la Communauté, dans lequel il a fait état de ses intentions de voir la Grèce adhérer à la Communauté dans l'avenir le plus proche. D'après le gouvernement grec l'adhésion de la Grèce devrait être assortie d'une période de transition et de certaines dispositions spéciales, comme ce fut le cas pour les États qui ont déjà adhéré à la Communauté.

Le Conseil d'association s'est tenu à Bruxelles le 2 décembre 1974, la Grèce y étant représentée par M. Papalygouras, ministre de la coopération du gouvernement formé à la suite des élections du 17 novembre dernier.

Le Conseil a abouti notamment à la décision du côté hellénique de signer le protocole additionnel étendant l'association aux trois nouveaux Etats membres de la Communauté et à la reprise des négociations d'harmonisation dans le secteur agricole.

Les rouages de l'association ont donc été remis en marche le 2 décembre 1974.

Association avec la Turquie

428. Les relations entre la Turquie et la CEE ont été marquées par l'entrée en vigueur, le 1er janvier 1974, de l'accord intérimaire CEE-Turquie signé à Ankara le 30 juin 1973. Cet accord sera applicable jusqu'à l'entrée en vigueur du protocole complémentaire et au plus tard jusqu'au 31 décembre 1974, date à laquelle il sera reconduit tacitement d'année en année jusqu'à l'entrée en vigueur du protocole. Ainsi. les dispositions en vigueur entre la Communauté et la Turqui sont désormais applicables à la Communauté élargie dans le domaine des échanges.

Ces développements de l'association CEE-Turquie se sont accompagnés

On 30 August the Commission sent the Council a communication proposing a series of measures which the Community could take as an immediate first step to "unfreeze" the Association.

This was the main theme discussed when the Commission received a visit from Mr Mavros, Deputy Prime Minister and Minister of Foreign Affairs, accompanied by Mr. Presmazoglou, Minister of Finance.

The Commission welcomed the fact that Greece had begun to restore democratic institutions and once again began considering how the Association could develop further. Mr Mavros took the opportunity to state that his government would shortly be presenting the Community with a request to speed up the process of integrating Greece into the Community so that it could rapidly become a full member. On 31 October the normal transitional stage of the Association was to come to an end and customs union to be completed as regards trade in most goods.

The Commission assured its Greek visitors that it would do all it could to ensure that work on unfreezing the Association, in whatever manner decided on by the appropriate authorities in the Community and Greece, would be carried out as quickly as possible.

Thereafter the Council issued a declaration clearly stating that it intended to waste no time in resuming work on the development of the Association.

Likewise, on 26 September, Parliament spoke out in favour of getting the economic and trade sides of the Association moving again.

The first meeting of the EEC-Greece Association Committee since Greece's return to democracy was held in Brussel on 22 November, when preparations were made for the 2 December meeting of the Association Council.

On 26 November the Greek Government delivered an *aide-mémoire* to the Community, stating its intention that Greece should become a full member of the Community in the very near future. The Greek Government would like provision to be made for a transitional period and certain special arrangements – as in the case of the States which have already become new members of the Community.

The Association Council met in Brussels on 2 December. Greece was represented by Mr Papalygouras, Minister for Cooperation in the government formed after the 17 November elections.

One of the results of the meeting was that Greece decided to sign the additional protocol extending the Association to the three new Member States of the Community and to resume negotiations on harmonization in the agricultural sector.

The machinery of the Association was thus set in motion again on 2 December 1974.

The Association with Turkey

428. The highlight in relations between Turkey and the EEC was the entry into force on 1 January 1974 of the interim agreement signed in Ankara on 30 June 1973. This agreement will apply until the entry into force of the Additional Protocol – though not later than 31 December 1974, after which it will be automatically renewed from year to year until the Protocol does enter into force. Thus the rules governing relations between the Community and Turkey henceforth apply to trade involving the whole of the enlarged Community.

In addition to these developments in the EEC-Turkey Association, Mr de la visite officielle de M. Ortoli en Turquie, du 25 avril au 28 avril 1974, de la visite de M. Ecevit, premier ministre, à M. Ortoli en juin 1974, et de l'entretien de ce dernier avec M. Gunes, ministre des affaires étrangères de Turquie, le 19 septembre à Bruxelles.

La Commission parlementaire mixte CEE-Turquie a étudié, entre autres, la situation des travailleurs turcs dans la Communauté. Elle s'est félicitée de ce que le Conseil ait adopté, le 10 juin 1974, sur proposition de la Commission, un projet de décision du Conseil d'association CEE-Turquie relative aux prestations de sécurité sociale pour les travailleurs turcs qui se déplacent dans la Communauté et pour les membres de leur famille qui y résident.

Association avec Chypre

429. La Commission a exprimé sa vive préoccupation au sujet des événements qui se sont déroulés à Chypre en juillet 1974, et elle a rappelé que l'association entre la Communauté et la république de Chypre est fondée sur l'indépendance et l'intégrité territoriale de ce pays et sur le principe que les avantages de l'association doivent profiter à toute la population de l'île.

Sur l'initiative de la Commission, la Communauté a participé en automne dernier aux mesures d'urgence d'aide alimentaire en faveur des réfugiés cypriotes.

Association avec Malte

430. Après l'adoption par le Conseil de deux règlements douaniers, la visite officielle de Sir Christopher Soames, du 11 au 13 juillet 1974, a été l'élément essentiel des relations entre la Communauté et Malte. Dans un discours devant le Conseil national de la foire commerciale internationale de Malte, Sir Christopher Soames a situé l'association dans le cadre de la politique communautaire d'approche globale pour le Bassin méditerranéen.

Le Conseil des Communautés a arrêté, lors de sa session des 22/23 juillet 1974, les directives concernant la négociation que la Commission devra conduire au nom de la Communauté avec la délégation maltaise. Les négociations sur l'extension de l'accord d'association ont été engagées.

Accord avec l'Espagne

431. Le Conseil des Communautés a adopté les directives complémentaires pour le poursuite des négociations avec l'Espagne, lors de sa session du 17 septembre 1974. Ces négociations ont eu lieu les 20 et 21 novembre 1974 et n'ont pas abouti à la conclusion d'un accord.

Relations avec la Yougoslavie

432. La Commission mixte prévue par l'accord commercial non préférentiel pour assurer le fonctionnement de l'accord s'est réunie en avril 1974 en séance extraordinaire à la demande de la Yougoslavie. La délégation yougoslave a exprimé son inquiétude à propos de la mise en oeuvre par la Communauté d'une clause de sauvegarde frappant la viande bovine. La Communauté a justifié le recours à cette mesure et a clarifié la portée des modifications du régime d'importation de la viande bovine qu'elle envisageait.

Sir Christopher Soames, en visite officielle en Yougoslavie les 29 et 30 avril 1974, a eu une série d'entretiens avec les dirigeants yougoslaves et notamment avec M. Bijedic, président du Conseil exécutif fédéral yougoslave, et MM. Ludviger et Snuderl, membres du Conseil exécutif fédéral yougoslave.

La situation particulière de la Yougoslavie, pays non aligné au carrefour des pays industrialisés et des pays en voie de développement, a permis des

Ortoli made an official visit to Turkey from 25 to 28 April; Mr Ecevit, Turkey's Prime Minister, visited Mr Ortoli in June and Mr Gunes, Turkish Minister of Foreign Affairs, had talks with Mr Ortoli in Brussels on 19 September.

The Parliamentary Joint Committee for the EEC-Turkey Association has considered, among other things, the position of Turkish workers in the Community. It welcomed the fact that on 10 June, on a proposal from the Commission, the Council adopted a draft decision of the EEC-Turkey Association Council on social security benefits for Turkish workers moving within the Community and for the members of their family residing in the Community.

The Association with Cyprus

429. The Commission expressed grave concern at July's events in Cyprus; it recalled that the Association was based on the assumption that Cyprus retained full independence and territorial integrity and on the principle that its benefits were to be felt by the whole population of the island.

At the Commission's initiative the Community took part in an emergency food aid operation for Cyprus refugees in the autumn.

The Association with Malta

430. Apart from the Council's adoption of two customs regulations, Sir Christopher Soames's official visit from 11 to 13 July was the main point to be noted in the Community's relations with Malta. Addressing the National Council of the International Trade Fair in Malta, Sir Christopher set the Association within the general context of the Community's policy on an overall approach to the Mediterranean.

At its meeting on 22 and 23 July the Council adopted directives for negotiations to be conducted by the Commission on behalf of the Community with a Maltese Delegation. Negotiations for the extension of the Association Agreement have begun.

The Agreement with Spain

431. On 17 September the Council adopted additional directives for continuing the negotiations with Spain. A negotiating session took place on 20 and 21 November but failed to lead to the conclusion of an agreement.

Relations with Yugoslavia

432. The Joint Committee set up by the non-preferential trade agreement to monitor its operation held an extraordinary session in April at the request of Yugoslavia. The Yugoslav Delegation expressed concern at the implementation by the Community of a safeguard clause affecting beef and veal. The Community explained why it had taken this step and clarified the scope of the changes it proposed to make in the treatment of imports of beef and veal.

During his official visit to Yugoslavia on 29 and 30 April, Sir Christopher Soames had a series of talks with leading Yugoslav personalities, including Mr Bijedic, Chairmain of the Federal Executive Council, and Mr Ludviger and Mr Snuderl, Members of the Council.

The special situation of Yugoslavia, a non-aligned country lying at the crossroads between the industrialized and the developing countries, meant that highly fruitful discussions were held on a number of matters of common interest.

conversations très fructueuses sur de nombreux sujets d'intérêt commun.

L'opportunité d'un renforcement des liens entre les parties et de l'extension progressive de la coopération, prévue par le nouvel accord non préférentiel, a été reconnue de part et d'autre.

Par ailleurs, M. P. Hillery, vice-président de la Commission, au cours d'un voyage officiel en Yougoslavie du 9 au 13 octobre 1974, a eu l'occasion notamment de s'entretenir avec les autorités yougoslaves du problème de la main-d'oeuvre de ce pays employée dans la Communauté.

Enfin, le 22 novembre 1974, le président de la Commission, M. Ortoli, et le vice-président, Sir Christopher Soames, ont reçu M. Minic, vice-président du Conseil exécutif fédéral et socialiste et secrétaire pour les affaires étrangères de la RFS de Yougoslavie.

C'était la première fois qu'une personnalité politique yougoslave exerçant de si hautes responsabilités rendait visite à la Communauté.

Relations avec les pays du Maghreb

433. Une nouvelle session de négociations avec chacun de ces trois pays a eu lieu au cours du dernier trimestre de 1974.

Elle a permis de constater une très large concordance de vues des partenaires du Maghreb sur les objectifs de la coopération proposée par la Communauté ainsi que sur la gamme des moyens à mettre en oeuvre.

Divers problèmes soulevés en négociation devront encore trouver une solution, notamment dans le domaine des échanges agricoles et de la main-d'oeuvre, mais la Commission espère pouvoir tenir vers la fin de janvier une session conclusive avec chacun de ces trois pays.

Entre temps, les accords d'association avec le Maroc et la Tunisie, qui sont entrés en vigueur le 1er septembre 1969 pour une durée de 5 ans, ont été prorogés en attendant la conclusion des nouveaux accords. En outre, les protocoles complémentaires en raison de l'adhésion des nouveaux États membres à la Communauté sont entrés en vigueur le 1er janvier 1974 pour le Maroc et le 1er août 1974 pour la Tunisie.

Relations avec la RAE

434. A la suite de l'entrée en vigueur de l'accord préférentiel entre la Communauté et la RAE le 1er novembre 1973, la première réunion de la Commission mixte s'est tenue au Caire en mai 1974.

Au cours de cette réunion, les premiers effets de l'accord sur les échanges entre la Communauté et la RAE ont été examinés. Le gouvernement égyptien a réitéré à l'occasion de cette réunion sa demande de conclure le plus rapidement possible avec la Communauté un accord sur des bases élargies dans le cadre de l'approche globale méditerranéenne.

Relations avec le Liban

435. En attendant l'entrée en vigueur de l'accord préférentiel signé en décembre 1972, l'accord sur les échanges commerciaux et la coopération technique de 1965 a été reconduit pour une année à partir du 1er juillet 1974.

Relations avec la Syrie

436. Manifestant l'intérêt croissant qu'il porte à des relations étroites entre la Communauté et la Syrie, le gouvernement syrien a fait part, en mars 1974, de son désir d'ouvrir dès que possible des négociations en vue de la conclusion avec la Communauté d'un accord dans le cadre de l'approche globale méditerranéenne.

Relations avec la Jordanie

437. Des conversations exploratoires avaient eu lieu en 1973, suite à la demande de la Jordanie de conclure un accord préférentiel avec la Com-

Both sides agreed that links should be strengthened and that the cooperation provided for by the new non-preferential agreement should be extended stage by stage.

During an official visit to Yugoslavia from 9 to 13 October, Dr Hillery, Vice-President of the Commission, had an opportunity to talk over with the Yugoslav authorities the problem of Yugoslavs employed in the Community.

On 22 November Mr Ortoli, President of the Commission, and Sir Christopher Soames, Vice-President, received Mr Minic, Vice-Chairman of the Federal Executive Council and Secretary for Foreign Affairs of Yugoslavia. This was the first time that so eminent a member of the Yugoslav Government had visited the Community.

Relations with the Maghreb countries

433. A further session of negotiations with each of the three Maghreb countries was held during the last quarter of 1974.

This showed that the Maghreb countries held very similar views on what should be the objectives of the cooperation proposed by the Commission and on what measures should be brought into play.

Various problems raised during negotiation remain to be solved, in particular as regards agricultural trade and workers, but the Commission hopes to have a final session with each country towards the end of January.

The Association Agreements with Morocco and Tunisia which entered into force on 1 September 1969 for a period of five years were renewed pending the conclusion of new agreements. Additional protocols to take account of the accession of the new Member States to the Community entered into force for Morocco on 1 January and for Tunisia on 1 August.

Relations with the Arab Republic of Egypt

434. Following the entry into force on 1 November 1973 of the preferential agreement between the Community and the Arab Republic of Egypt, the Joint Committee held its first meeting in Cairo in May.

At this meeting the initial effects of the trade agreement between the Community and Egypt were reviewed. The Egyptian Government took the opportunity at this meeting to repeat its request for the rapid conclusion of an agreement with the Community on an extended basis as part of the overall approach to the Mediterranean.

Relations with Lebanon

435. Pending the entry into force of the preferential agreement signed in December 1972, the 1965 agreement on trade and technical cooperation was renewed for one year from 1 July.

Relations with Syria

436. As a sign of the growing interest which it attaches to close relations with the Community, the Syrian Government in March stated that as soon as possible it would like to open negotiations for the conclusion of an agreement with the Community under the overall approach to the Mediterranean.

Relations with Jordan

437. In 1973 exploratory talks were held at Jordan's request with a view to concluding a preferential agreement. This was not followed up in 1974.

munauté. Cette première prise de contact n'a pas eu de suite en 1974. Cependant, la Commission envisage de recommander au Conseil, en 1975, l'ouverture de négociations avec la Jordanie, en vue de la conclusion d'un accord global de coopération dans le cadre de l'approche globale méditerranéenne, initiative qui comprendra également la RAE, le Liban et la Syrie.

Aide aux réfugiés palestiniens

438. La Communauté a accordé à l'Office de secours et de travaux des Nations unies pour les réfugiés de Palestine (UNRWA) une aide s'élevant à 6,55 millions d'UC destinée à couvrir une partie des dépenses de fonctionnement de l'Office en 1974 dans le domaine de l'enseignement. Cette contribution de la Communauté a été décidée afin de permettre à l'UNRWA de maintenir dans son intégralité son programme d'éducation en faveur des réfugiés palestiniens.

Relations avec Israël

439. Les négociations en vue de conclure un nouvel accord préférentiel avec Israel ont repris en octobre. Dans la session des 9 et 10 décembre, les parties ont pratiquement atteint, à l'exception d'une question, un accord sur tous les points restés en suspens.

La Commission envisage, dans le cadre de l'approche globale méditerranéenne, de recommander au Conseil, au début de l'année 1975, d'entamer des négociations avec Israël, en vue de la conclusion d'un protocole complémentaire visant a établir une coopération économique et financière.

iii. Dialogue euro-arabe

440. L'engagement dans le dialogue euro-arabe a résulté de la déclaration des Neuf du 6 novembre 1973, du sommet arabe de novembre 1973 et de la rencontre à Copenhague, le 14 décembre 1973, entre les chefs de gouvernement de la Communauté et les envoyés de la Ligue arabe.

En février 1974, le Conseil a décidé d'habiliter son président d'engager, de concert avec la Commission, les pourparlers avec la partie arabe dans les domaines relevant de la compétence des Communautés. D'autre part, sur le plan de la coopération politique, un accord est intervenu en mars 1974, sur une action d'ensemble associant étroitement les États membres au sein de la coopération politique et de la Communauté en vue de situer la coopération euro-arabe dans un cadre politique général. La décision de s'engager dans cette voie a été prise lors de la réunion ministérielle sur la coopération politique du 10 juin. Dans la réponse européenne à l'offre arabe de coopération, a été suggérée une coopération à long terme, notamment dans les domaines économique, technique et culturel.

Du côté européen, le dialogue est mené d'une manière combinée par les États membres dans le cadre de la coopération politique et la Communauté. Il a été instauré un groupe de coordination composé d'ambassadeurs désignés par les neuf pays et d'un représentant de la Commission de rang équivalent.

Une première rencontre euro-arabe s'est tenue à Paris le 31 juillet 1974, les Neuf étant représentés par M. Sauvagnargues, en sa double qualité de président du Conseil des Communautés et de la conférence ministérielle de la coopération politique, et par M. Ortoli, président de la Commission. A cette occasion, il a été convenu de créer une commission générale euro-arabe et un certain nombre de commissions de travail. Une réunion préparatoire à la première réunion de la commission générale a eu lieu au Caïre le 20 octobre 1974 entre hauts fonctionnaires représentant la présidence française et la Commission ainsi que la présidence et le secrétariat général de la Ligue arabe.

However, the Commission proposes recommending to the Council in 1975 that negotiations be opened with Jordan for the conclusion of a comprehensive cooperation agreement under the overall approach to the Mediterranean countries; Egypt, the Lebanon and Syria will also be affected.

Aid to Palestine refugees

438. The Community granted the United Nations Relief and Works Agency for Palestine Refugees (UNRWA) 6.55 million u.a. to cover part of the Agency's operating expenditure in 1974 on education. The Community decided to make this contribution because it wished UNRWA to maintain its full programme on education for Palestine refugees.

Relations with Israel

439. Negotiations for the conclusion of a new preferential agreement with Israel were resumed in October. At the session of 9 and 10 December the parties reached agreement to all intents and purposes on all but one of the items still outstanding.

As part of the overall approach to the Mediterranean, the Commission proposes recommending to the Council early in 1975 that negotiations be opened with Israel for an additional protocol concerning economic and financial cooperation.

iii. Euro-Arab dialogue

440. The Euro-Arab dialogue got under way as a result of the Declaration made by the nine Member States on 6 November 1973, the Arab Summit held in November 1973 and the meeting in Copenhagen on 14 December, between the Heads of Government and envoys from the Arab League.

In February 1974 the Council authorized its President to open talks with the Arab countries, in concert with the Commission, on matters falling within Community jurisdiction. In march a political cooperation meeting reached agreement on an overall plan of action whereby the Member States would work out a general political approach to Euro-Arab cooperation, within the political cooperation and Community contexts. The decision to do this was taken at the ministerial meeting on political cooperation on 10 June. Europe's response to the Arab offer of cooperation was to suggest long-term arrangements, particularly in economic, technical and cultural matters.

On the European side, the Member States are treating the dialogue jointly within the political cooperation and Community contexts. A coordinating group composed of ambassadors from the nine Member States and a Commission representative of equivalent rank has been set up.

A first Euro-Arab meeting was held in Paris on 31 July, when the Nine were represented by Mr Sauvagnargues, acting both as President of the Council and as chairman of the political cooperation conference, and by Mr Ortoli, President of the Commission. It was agreed that a Euro-Arab General Commission and a number of working parties would be set up. Preparatory talks for the first meeting of the General Commission were held in Cairo on 20 October between senior officials representing the country then in the chair at Council meetings, the Commission of the Communities and the Chairmanship and Secretariat of the Arab League.

iv. Relations avec les pays en voie de développement en Asie et en Amérique latine

Asie

441. Poursuivant des objectifs définis lors des sommets des chefs de gouvernement, la Communauté s'est employée à nouer et à développer des liens de plus en plus étroits avec les pays en voie de développement du continent asiatique.

442. Depuis l'échéance, le 30 novembre 1973, de l'accord entre la CEE et l'Iran du 14 octobre 1963, le Conseil a examiné les orientations à retenir dans les relations avec ce pays. Il a marqué l'importance politique et économique que la Communauté attache à ses relations avec l'Iran et son désir de rechercher les solutions appropriées dans l'intérêt mutuel des deux parties. Le Conseil a reconnu que la solution d'un accord commercial classique n'est plus appropriée et il s'est déclaré disposé à envisager la négociation d'un accord sur des bases élargies, susceptible de permettre un développement harmonieux de relations économiques et commerciales futures.

Des conversations exploratoires ont eu lieu à Bruxelles pour définir le type d'accord souhaité par les parties.

En revanche, l'accord de coopération commerciale conclu avec l'Inde en 1973 est entré en vigueur le 1er avril 1974, après approbation par le Conseil des Communautés. La Commission mixte s'est réunie les 27 et 28 mai 1974. Elle a défini son programme de travail pour 1974 et a créé deux sous-commissions spécialisées, l'une pour veiller au fonctionnement des accords en vigueur entre l'Inde et la CEE dans le domaine de produits de jute et de coco, des textiles de coton et des produits de l'artisanat, l'autre pour étudier des mesures à prendre dans les domaines de l'assistance technique et de la coopération commerciale.

Les résultats positifs obtenus dans le cadre de la coopération avec l'Inde ont conduit la Commission à proposer au Conseil l'ouverture de négociations en vue de la conclusion d'accords de coopération commerciale avec le Pakistan, le Sri Lanka et le Bangladesh.

En date du 15 octobre 1974, le Conseil a approuvé le mandat de négociation à confier à la Communauté. Les négociations avec deux de ces pays – le Pakistan et le Sri Lanka – ont débuté respectivement les 4 et 5 novembre 1974.

En février 1974, le président de la Commission, M. François-Xavier Ortoli, a eu des entretiens à Djakarta avec le président indonésien, M. Suharto. La crise énergétique, la coopération économique entre l'Indonésie et la Communauté et les perspectives de relations commerciales entre la Communauté et les pays de l'ASEAN ont été au centre des discussions.

En septembre 1974, une délégation de la Commission, présidée par Sir Christopher Soames, s'est rendue en visite en Indonésie, en Malaisie, à Singapour et aux Philippines, pays membres de l'ASEAN (Association des pays du Sud-Est asiatique). A Djakarta, les 24 et 25 septembre, la délégation a procédé à un échange de vues sur les problèmes d'intérêt mutuel avec les représentants de l'ASEAN. A cette occasion, Sir Christopher Soames a exposé les lignes directrices de la nouvelle politique de la Communauté en matière de coopération à l'égard des PVD non associables, en soulignant en particulier les possibilités d'actions existant dans le domaine de la promotion commerciale et de l'aide à l'intégration régionale. A cette fin, et en vue d'approfondir le dialogue déjà existant entre la Communauté et l'ASEAN, les deux parties sont convenues, en outre, de créer un groupe d'étude formé par des représentants de la Commission et de l'ASEAN.

iv. Relations with the developing countries of Asia and Latin America

Asia

441. In pursuit of objectives laid down at the Summit conferences of Heads of Government, the Community has been working on establishing and developing ever closer relations with developing countries in Asia.

442. Since the expiry on 30 November 1973 of the 14 October 1963 Agreement between the EEC and Iran, the Council has been considering what guidelines should be laid down for relations with that country. It has stressed the political and economic importance that the Community attaches to its relations with Iran and its intent to find appropriate solutions which would be in the joint interest of both parties. The Council has recognized that the classical trade agreement is no longer appropriate and has stated its willingness to consider the negotiation of a broader-based agreement which would promote the harmonious development of economic and commercial relations in the future. Exploratory talks have been held in Brussels to determine what type of agreement would suit the parties.

The trade cooperation agreement concluded with India in 1973 entered into force on 1 April 1974 after being approved by the Council of the Communities. The Joint Commission met on 27 and 28 May. It decided on its programme of work for 1974 and set up two specialist subcommissions, one to monitor the operation of agreements between India and the EEC relating to jute and coir products, cotton textiles and handcrafts, the other to study measures relating to technical assistance and trade cooperation.

In view of the success achieved in cooperation with India, the Commission has proposed to the Council that negotiations be opened on trade cooperation agreements with Pakistan, Sri Lanka and Bangladesh.

On 15 October the Council approved the negotiating directives to be given to the Commission. Negotiations were started with Pakistan on 4 November and with Sri Lanka on 5 November.

In February the President of the Commission, Mr François-Xavier Ortoli, met the Indonesian President Mr Suharto, for talks in Djakarta. The energy crisis, economic cooperation between Indonesia and the Community and the outlook for trade relations between the Community and the ASEAN countries were the main topics touched on.

In September a Commission delegation led by Sir Christopher Soames visited Indonesia, Malaysia, Singapore and the Philippines – all members of ASEAN (Association of South East Asian Nations). On 24 and 25 September the delegation had talks on matters of common interest with ASEAN representatives in Djakarta. Sir Christopher Soames outlined the Community's new policy on cooperation with non-associable developing countries; he particularly stressed the possibilities for action to promote trade and to assist regional integration. With this in mind and with a view to taking the existing dialogue between the Community and ASEAN a stage further, the two sides agreed to set up a study group composed of Commission and ASEAN representatives.

Amérique latine

Relations bilatérales

443. A la même date, le 1er août 1974, sont entrés en vigueur l'accord commercial entre la Communauté et l'Uruguay, signé le 2 avril 1973, et l'accord commercial entre la Communauté et le Brésil, signé le 19 décembre 1973.

Les conversations exploratoires commencées en 1973 avec une délégation mexicaine se sont terminées en juin 1974. La Commission a présenté une recommandation au Conseil en vue de l'ouverture de négociations devant conduire à la conclusion d'un accord bilatéral entre la Communauté et le Mexique. Un accord de coopération visant au développement et à la diversification des échanges peut être envisagé dans un premier temps; il serait susceptible d'être progressivement étendu.

Les chefs des missions d'Argentine, du Paraguay et de l'Uruguay ont eu des entretiens avec la Commission, le 20 mars 1974, à propos des problèmes que connaît le secteur de la viande bovine. Les délégués sud-américains ont exprimé le souhait de voir leurs pays assurer un approvisionnement régulier de la Communauté en viande bovine, et de parvenir, grâce à une coopération renforcée, à de meilleures conditions d'accès au marché de la Communauté. Par une démarche collective faite en juin 1974, ces trois pays et la Colombie, qui s'était jointe à eux, ont demandé la négociation d'un accord à long terme en matière de viande bovine.

Ce même problème a été évoqué, parmi d'autres, lors de la deuxième session annuelle de la Commission mixte CEE-Argentine créée par l'accord commercial conclu entre les deux parties. A cette occasion, la délégation argentine a manifesté le souhait de son gouvernement de voir élargi, à l'avenir, l'accord commercial conclu en 1971 et venant à échéance à la fin de 1974. Une demande officielle à ce sujet a été présentée peu de temps après la session de la Commission mixte. Le nouvel accord devrait, de l'avis des Argentins, redéfinir et orienter à long terme les dispositions relatives à la coopération dans le domaine de la viande bovine, afin de contribuer à la stabilité des exportations argentines et à celle du marché communautaire. Il devrait aussi inclure des clauses de coopération dans les secteurs économico-commercial, industriel et technologique, agricole, financier et des investissements. En attendant que l'examen de ces demandes par la Communauté soit terminé, l'accord commercial de 1971 sera reconduit jusqu'au 31 décembre 1975.

Relations multilatérales

444. Une délégation du secrétariat exécutif de l'Association latino-américaine de libre-échange (ALALC) a été reçue du 22 au 26 avril 1974 à la Commission, à la Cour de justice et à la Banque européenne d'investissement. Cette visite, organisée à l'initiative de la Commission, a permis aux représentants de l'ALALC de confronter certains de leurs projets avec les conceptions et les réalisations communautaires correspondantes. La Commission espère avoir ainsi apporté à cette organisation, sur le plan pratique, des éléments concrets, notamment en vue de la restructuration de ses secteurs d'activité qu'elle est en train d'étudier.

Dans le cadre de la mise en oeuvre de la résolution du Conseil du 30 avril 1974 concernant l'aide à l'intégration régionale des pays en voie de développement, la Commission maintient un contact étroit avec ce même secrétariat de l'ALALC, la Junta de l'accord de Cartagène (groupe andin) et la SIECA (Secrétariat pour l'intégration économique de l'Amérique centrale) du marché commun centre-américain. Un plan d'action communautaire de soutien à ces trois organismes est en route depuis fin 1974.

En mars 1974, la Commission a organisé des séminaires d'information sur le schéma des préférences généralisées de la Communauté, en Uruguay,

Latin America

Bilateral relations

443. On 1 August 1974 the trade agreement between the Community and Uruguay, signed on 2 April 1973, and the trade agreement between the Community and Brazil, signed on 19 December 1973, both entered into force.

The exploratory talks with a Mexican Delegation which began in 1973 were completed in June 1974. The Commission has put before the Council a recommendation concerning the opening of negotiations for the conclusion of a bilateral agreement between the Community and Mexico. A co-operation agreement designed to expand and diversify trade is envisaged as a first step; this could then be extended by stages.

On March the Heads of the Missions of Argentina, Paraguay and Uruguay met the Commission to discuss problems relating to beef and veal. They stated that their countries would like to supply the Community with beef and veal on a regular basis and to obtain better terms for access to the Community market through increased cooperation. In June these three countries and Colombia together asked that negotiations be started with a view to a long-term agreement on beef and veal.

This problem was raised again, along with others, at the second annual meeting of the Joint Committee set up under the trade agreement between the EEC and Argentina, when the Argentine Delegation stated that its Government would like the trade agreement concluded in 1971, and due to expire at the end of 1974, to be given a broader basis in the future. An official request to this effect was made shortly after the Joint Committee meeting. Argentina felt that the new agreement should redefine the arrangements on cooperation in beef and veal and put them on a long-term footing so as to stabilize Argentina's exports and at the same time the Community market. Clauses shoud also be inserted on cooperation in economic and commercial matters, industrial and technological questions, agriculture, finance and investment. While these points are being examined by the Commission, the 1971 agreement will be extended to 31 December 1975.

Multilateral relations

444. A delegation from the Executive Committee of the Latin American Free Trade Association (LAFTA) visited the Commission, the Court of Justice and the European Investment Bank from 22 to 26 April. This visit, which was made at the Commission's suggestion, enabled the LAFTA representatives to compare certain of their plans with what the Community was contemplating and actually doing in the same fields. In this way the Commission hopes to have made a practical contribution to LAFTA's plans to restructure the spheres in which it is active.

As one of the measures to implement the Council Resolution of 30 April 1974 on assistance for the regional integration of developing countries, the Commission is maintaining close contacts both with the LAFTA Executive Committee and with the Junta of the Cartagena Agreement (Andean Group) and SIECA (Permanent Secretariat of the General Treaty of Central American Economic Integration). A Community plan of action to support these organizations has been under way since the end of 1974.

In March the Commission organized seminars in Uruguay, El Salvador and Colombia to provide information on the Community's generalized preferences scheme. The object of the seminars, which were aimed at the en el Salvador et en Colombie. Destinés aux pays membres de groupements régionaux d'amérique latine – respectivement l'ALALC (Association latino-américaine de libre-échange), le MCCA (Marché commun centre-américain) et le groupe andin –, ces séminaires ont eu pour but de familiariser les autorités et les exportateurs locaux avec le mécanisme complexe du schéma de la Communauté et de leur permettre de retirer le maximum possible d'avantages des préférences octroyées.

D'autre part, dans le cadre des procédures prévues par la déclaration commune adoptée par la conférence du 18 juin 1971, a eu lieu à Bruxelles, le 28 juin 1974, entre la Communauté et les pays d'Amérique latine membres de la Commission spéciale de coordination latino-américaine (CECLA), la première session de la cinquième rencontre Communauté-Amérique latine.

Cette session a été consacrée à un échange de vues sur les principaux problèmes du moment; du côté de la Communauté, les commentaires ont porté, entre autres, sur les aspects récents du commerce international, sur la coopération au développement et sur la politique d'association, tandis que les pays latino-américains évoquaient principalement le système communautaire et les problèmes liés aux exportations de viande bovine à destination de la Communauté.

La seconde session, tenue le 6 décembre 1974, a porté plus particulièrement sur les travaux poursuivis durant l'année par le groupe mixte CEE/Amérique latine des questions commerciales, en matière de fonctionnement technique des préférences généralisées et de promotion commerciale. Dans ce dernier secteur, la mise en oeuvre de la résolution du Conseil du 30 avril 1974 sur la promotion des exportations des pays en voie de développement s'est traduite – vis-à-vis de l'Amérique latine – par la préparation d'un premier programme d'actions concrètes de promotion à exécuter par la Communauté en 1975.

Enfin, le programme de stages de fonctionnaires latino-américains auprès des services de la Commission s'est poursuivi durant toute l'année 1974.

v. Relations avec les Etats-Unis, le Japon, le Canada, l'Australie et la Nouvelle-Zélande

Etats-Unis

445. Sir Christopher Soames a déclaré devant le Parlement en janvier 1974 que les relations de l'Europe avec les États-Unis ,,sont, doivent rester et resteront d'une importance primordiale pour les deux parties.'' Cet objectif a été concrétisé par la conclusion des négociations avec les États-Unis au titre de l'article XXIV, 6, du GATT, qui a sensiblement amélioré le climat des relations CEE/États-Unis.

La huitième consultation entre la Commission, représentée par Sir Christopher Soames, et l'administration américaine, représentée par M. Eberle, a eu lieu à Bruxelles les 6 et 7 juin. La neuvième s'est tenue à Washington les 5 et 6 décembre et a porté sur toute une série de sujets, notamment les problèmes énergétiques, l'agriculture et les négociations multilatérales. En outre, les membres de la Commission et les dirigeants américains ont eu de nombreux contacts.

Les questions de fond n'ont pas pu être abordées lors des négociations commerciales multilatérales au GATT, vu le retard pris par l'adoption du Trade Reform Bill au Congrès américain.

Quant à la politique préférentielle à l'égard des pays en voie de développement, les positions se sont sensiblement rapprochées entre la Communauté et les États-Unis.

Les discussions sur l'agriculture qu'a eues la Commission avec l'administration américaine ont fait apparaître une volonté commune d'améliorer member countries of regional groupings in Latin America – LAFTA, CACM (Central American Common Market) and the Andean Group – was to familiarize local authorities and exporters with the complex machinery of the Community scheme and to enable them to derive optimum benefit from the preferences themselves.

On 28 June the Community and those Latin American countries which are members of the Special Committee on Latin American Coordination (CECLA) held the first session of the fifth Community/Latin America meeting in Brussels in accordance with the procedural arrangements in the Joint Declaration adopted by the Conference of 18 June 1971.

The purpose of the meeting was to discuss the main problems of the day; on the Community side, the subjects dealt with included recent aspects of international trade, development cooperation and association policy- while the Latin American countries were mainly concerned with the Community's arrangements and with problems of exporting beef and veal to the Community.

The second session of the meeting was held on 6 December, when the main point on the agenda was the year's work of the Joint EEC/Latin America Working Party on Trade concerning trade promotion and the technical operation of the generalized preferences. As regards trade promotion, the Council Resolution of 30 April 1974 on the promotion of developing countries' exports was translated into action as far as Latin America is concerned by the preparation of an initial programme of measures to be carried through by the Community in 1975.

Finally, the programme of in-service training in the Commission for Latin American civil servants continued to operate throughout 1974.

v. Relations with the United States, Japan, Canada, Australia and New Zealand

United States

445. Addressing Parliament in January, Sir Christopher Soames stated that relations between Europe and the United States were, must be and always would be of the utmost importance to both sides. One practical illustration of this was the conclusion of negotiations with the United States under Article XXIV (6) of the GATT, which appreciably improved the climate of relations between the EEC and the USA.

The eighth round of consultations between the Commission, represented by Sir Christopher Soames, and the United States Administration, represented by Mr Eberle, was held in Brussels on 6 and 7 June. The ninth round took place in Washington on 5 and 6 December, when the items discussed included energy, agriculture and the multilateral negotiations. Apart from this, members of the Commission have regularly met American officials.

Delay in approval of the trade reform bill by Congress made it impossible to deal with matters of substance in the multilateral trade negotiations in GATT.

As regards policy on preferential treatment for the developing countries, substantial convergence of views has been obtained between the Community and the United States.

The Commission's discussions on agriculture with the US Administration revealed the desire of both sides to step up the two-way exchange of l'information réciproque sur la situation de l'approvisionnement, notamment pour les céréales et la viande bovine. Les deux parties ont souligné l'importance qu'elles attachaient à la coordination préalable de leurs positions lors de rencontres internationales, comme elles en ont fait la démonstration lors de la Conférence mondiale de l'alimentation.

Dans le domaine de l'énergie, la Commission et l'administration américaine ont poursuivi leurs échanges de vues sur tous les aspects de la consommation et de la situation de l'approvisionnement, y compris le développement de nouvelles sources d'énergie. Sur le plan pratique, les experts des deux parties se sont rencontrés pour s'informer de leurs programmes respectifs dans le domaine de la recherche énergétique.

Par ailleurs, des procédures de consultations et des échanges d'informations ont également été prévus entre la Commission et les services américains chargés des problèmes de l'environnement.

Les contacts entre des délégations du Parlement européen et du Congrès américain se sont poursuivis selon le rythme semestriel convenu.

Le nouveau chef de la délégation de la Commission aux États-Unis, M. Jens Otto Krag, a pris ses fonctions au mois de janvier. A cette occasion, il a été reçu par le secrétaire d'État américain, M. Kissinger, auquel il a remis sa lettre d'introduction.

Japon

446. Le président de la Commission a fait un séjour au Japon du 18 au 23 février 1974. Après avoir été reçu par l'empereur, M. François-Xavier Ortoli a rencontré M. Tanaka, premier ministre, avec qui il a passé en revue tous les problèmes de l'heure. Les entretiens se sont poursuivis avec M. Ohira, ministre des affaires étrangères, et avec d'autres membres du gouvernement. Ils ont porté sur les développements de la crise énergétique. En accord avec le président de la Commission, le Japon souhaite renforcer la coopération avec les Communautés en matière de recherche et de développement en ce qui concerne l'énergie de substitution et notamment l'énergie atomique.

La même volonté de coopération s'est manifestée lors de l'analyse de l'évolution future dans le cadre des négociations multilatérales au GATT.

Par ailleurs, le dialogue avec le Japon a été élargi par d'autres rencontres entre des membres de la Commission et des membres du gouvernement japonais, ainsi qu'entre des hauts fonctionnaires des deux parties.

Ces relations se sont concrétisées plus particulièrement par l'établissement d'une délégation de la Commission à Tokyo, initiative accueillie avec satisfaction par le Japon. Un accord sur l'établissement ainsi que les privilèges et immunités de la délégation a été paraphé le 22 février 1974 à Tokyo et signé à Bruxelles le 11 mars 1974; il est entré en vigueur le 31 mai 1974 après sa ratification par la Diète japonaise en juin dernier. W. Wolfgang Ernst, directeur général adjoint aux relations extérieures, a été nommé chef de la délégation.

Sur le plan des relations commerciales, l'année a été caractérisée par un accroissement sensible des courants d'échanges dans les deux sens, les exportations de la Communauté ayant enregistré une progression plus sensible que les importations en provenance du Japon. La balance commerciale du Japon reste toutefois excédentaire.

Canada

447. Le Canada, cherchant à diversifier ses relations extérieures, s'efforce depuis quelque temps de resserrer ses liens avec l'Europe. La Communauté s'est à son tour employée à concrétiser le ,,dialogue constructif'' avec le Canada, préconisé par la coopération plus étroite entre la Commission et les autorités canadiennes.

Dans ce contexte, les relations entre la Communauté et le Canada en information on the supply situation, particularly for grain and beaf and veal. Both sides have stressed the importance they attach to advance coordination of their approach at international meetings, as evidenced at the World Food Conference.

On energy matters, the Commission and the US Administration continued their discussions on all aspects of consumption and the supply situation, including the development of new energy sources. From the practical point of view, experts from the two sides have met to inform each other of what they are doing in energy research.

Consultation procedures and exchanges of information have also been organized between the Commission and the American government departments with responsibilities for environmental matters.

Contacts between delegations of the European Parliament and of the United States Congress have continued following the agreed six-monthly pattern.

The new Head of the Commission's Delegation in the United States, Mr Jens Otto Krag, took up his post in January. He was received by the Secretary of State, Mr Kissinger, to whom he handed his letter of introduction

Japan

446. The President of the Commission visited Japan from 18 to 23 February. After being received by the Emperor, Mr Ortoli met Mr Tanaka, the Prime Minister, with whom he discussed the major problems of the day. The talks continued with Mr. Ohira, the Minister of Foreign Affairs, and with other members of the Government. They dealt with developments in the energy crisis. In agreement with the President of the Commission, Japan wishes to strengthen its cooperation with the Communities on research and development concerning substitute energy sources, particularly atomic energy.

The same desire for cooperation was expressed when talks were held to analyse the outlook for the multilateral negotiations in GATT.

The dialogue with Japan was further extended by other meetings between members of the Commission and members of the Japanese Government and between senior officials on both sides.

One concrete manifestation of these relations was the establishment of a Commission Delegation in Tokyo; this was warmly welcomed by Japan. An agreement on the establishment and on the privileges and immunities of the Delegation was initialled in Tokyo on 22 February and signed in Brussels on 11 March; it entered into force with effect from 31 May following ratification by the Japanese Diet in June. Mr. Wolfgang Ernst, Deputy Director-General for External Relations, was appointed Head of the Delegation.

To turn to trade relations, this year saw a substantial expansion of trade in both directions, Community exports having increased more sharply than imports from Japan. Nevertheless, Japan still has a surplus on trade with the Community.

Canada

447. Canada, in an endeavour to diversify its external relations, has in recent times sought to strengthen its links with Europe. The Community has, in its turn, endeavoured to give substance to the "constructive dialogue" with Canada called for at the Community Summit of October 1972 in Paris, notably through a closer working relationship between the Commission and the Canadian authorities.

1974 ont pris une nouvelle dimension. Deux événements se détachent en particulier: premièrement, la remise par le Canada au Conseil et à la Commission d'un aide-mémoire du 20 avril 1974 proposant „que des négociations soient entreprises avec les institutions compétentes de la Communauté en vue de la conclusion d'un accord commercial entre le Canada et la Communauté européenne"; deuxièmement, la visite de M. Pierre-Elliott Trudeau, premier ministre canadien, aux Communautés en octobre, suivie par celle de M. Allan MacEachen, ministre des affaires étrangères, en décembre.

L'aide-mémoire canadien a donné lieu à une série de contacts exploratoires informels entre des représentants de la Commission et du gouvernement et, le 12 septembre, à une communication de la Commission au Conseil, exposant les premières réactions de la Commission à la suite de la démarche canadienne. Dans cette communication, la Commission a exprimé sa préférence pour l'établissement d'un accord-cadre de coopération entre la Communauté et le Canada. Sur la base de ces discussions, le Conseil des ministres du 15 octobre s'est prononcé en faveur d'un resserrement des liens entre la Communauté et le Canada.

La proposition canadienne en vue de la conclusion d'un accord commercial a été au centre des entretiens que le premier ministre canadien a eus avec le président Ortoli, Sir Christopher Soames et d'autres membres de la Commission. A la lumière de ces discussions, il a été décidé de procéder à un examen exploratoire pour déterminer le contenu et la forme du lien de la Communauté avec le Canada. La Commission a également été en mesure d'informer M. Trudeau de son intention d'ouvrir une représentation à Ottawa dans le courant de l'année 1975.

Le désir de resserrer les liens entre la Communauté et le Canada s'est également manifesté au niveau provincial canadien, comme l'a montré la visite officielle effectuée en avril 1974 par M. Bourassa, premier ministre du Québec. Dans ses discussions avec le président Ortoli et avec Sir Christopher Soames, M. Bourassa a évoqué la structure des courants commerciaux entre la Communauté et le Québec, ainsi que les investissements européens dans la province canadienne.

Dans le cadre des consultations bilatérales qui ont eu lieu régulièrement entre la Communauté et le Canada, une quatrième série d'entretiens a été organisée à Bruxelles les 11 et 12 juin 1974. Poursuivant leur examen des problèmes tant bilatéraux que multilatéraux d'intérêt commun, les deux parties ont notamment discuté de la politique commerciale, de la coopération dans les secteurs de l'industrie et de l'énergie ainsi que des relations avec les pays en voie de développement.

A la suite des consultations, une mission, composée de représentants de la Commission et des milieux industriels des États membres, a visité le Canada en octobre 1974 en vue d'explorer les possibilités de coopération dans le secteur forestier.

Australie et Nouvelle-Zélande

448. Les relations entre la CEE, d'une part, et l'Australie et la Nouvelle-Zélande, d'autre part, ont été marquées par plusieurs visites officielles.

Sir Christopher Soames s'est rendu en Australie et en Nouvelle-Zélande en septembre. A cette occasion, a été mise en place une procédure de „dialogue" comportant des conversations à l'instar de ce qui se fait déjà avec d'autres pays industrialisés. M. Walding, ministre néo-zélandais du commerce extérieur, et le premier ministre d'Australie, M. Gough Whitlam, ont rendu visite à la Commission respectivement en mars et en décembre. Une délégation du Trade Development Council d'Australie a eu des entretiens avec des hauts fonctionnaires de la Commission en mars.

Lors de ces visites, ont été examinés dans un esprit constructif et avec franchise tant les problèmes internationaux du moment que les questions bilatérales interessant les deux pays en cause.

Against this background, Community/Canada relations in 1974 took on a new dimension. Two events in particular stand out: firstly, the transmission of a Canadian *aide-mémoire*, dated 20 April, to the Council and to the Commission, which proposed "that negotiations be initiated with the appropriate Community institutions with a view to concluding a trade agreement between Canada and the European Community"; secondly, the visits to the Community of the Prime Minister of Canada, Mr Pierre-Elliott Trudeau, in October and of the Secretary of State for External Affairs, Mr Allan MacEachen, in December.

The Canadian *aide-mémoire* gave rise to a series of informal exploratory contacts between the Commission and Canadian Government representatives and, on 12 September, a communication from the Commission to the Council setting out the Commission's initial reactions to the Canadian *démarche*. In this communication the Commission expressed a preference for an outline agreement on Community/Canada cooperation. On the basis of these deliberations, the Council on 15 October called for a strengthening of the Community's links with Canada.

The Canadian proposal for a trade agreement formed the centrepiece of the talks which the Canadian Prime Minister had with President Ortoli, Sir Christopher Soames and other Members of the Commission. In the light of these discussions it was decided that a process of exploration should be initiated to determine what should be the substance and the form of the Community's link with Canada. Also, the Commission was able to inform Mr Trudeau of its intention to open a delegation in Ottawa in the course of 1975.

The momentum towards closer Community/Canada relations is also reflected at Canadian Provincial level, as was apparent when the Prime Minister of Quebec, Mr Bourassa, paid an official visit in April 1974. In discussions with President Ortoli and Sir Christopher Soames, Mr Bourassa reviewed the structure of trade flows between the Community and Quebec, as well as European investment in Quebec.

In the series of regular bilateral consultations between the Community and Canada, the fourth round of talks took place in Brussels on 11 and 12 June. Continuing their review of bilateral and multilateral issues of mutual interest, the two sides discussed commercial policy matters, cooperation in the industrial and energy sectors, and relations with developing countries.

In the aftermath of these consultations a mission made up of Commission representatives and industrialists from the Member States visited Canada in October in order to explore the potential for cooperation in the forestry sector.

Australia and New Zealand

448. Relations between the EEC and Australia and New Zealand were highlighted by a number of official visits.

Sir Christopher Soames went to Australia and New Zealand in September, when a dialogue procedure was instituted providing for talks on the same lines as those which are already held with other industrialized countries.

The New Zealand Minister of Overseas Trade, Mr Walding, and the Australian Prime Minister, Mr Gough Whitlam, visited the Commission in March and December respectively. A delegation from the Australian Trade Development Council had talks with senior Commission officials in March.

In the course of these visits the international problems of the day and bilateral questions affecting Australia and New Zealand were examined in a constructive and frank atmosphere.

En ce qui concerne l'Australie, les mesures de limitation des importations de viande appliquées par la Communauté ont constitué un point de discussion important. La Commission, pour sa part, s'est intéressée aux possibilités d'exportations de matières premières, notamment énergétiques, de l'Australie vers la CEE, et à la politique australienne dans le secteur industriel, ainsi qu'aux perspectives de réduction tarifaire dans ce secteur dans le cadre des prochaines négociations multilatérales.

En ce qui concerne la Nouvelle-Zélande, le point le plus important dans les relations avec ce pays a trait aux importations dans le Royaume-Uni de produits laitiers, dans le cadre des dispositions du protocole 18.

vi. Conférence sur la sécurité et la coopération en Europe – Relations avec les pays à commerce d'Etat

Conférence sur la sécurité et la coopération en Europe

449. Le problème de la forme de la participation de la Communauté à la CSCE avait été réglé par une décision du Conseil de septembre 1973. Aussi les représentants de la Commission participent-ils aux travaux de la „deuxième corbeille" chargée des questions économiques (commerce, coopération, science et technologie, environnement, transports, main-d'oeuvre, tourisme, etc.). Mais c'est en particulier dans la sous-commission d'„échanges commerciaux", où sont traitées le plus directement les questions relevant des compétences existantes de la Communauté, que cette participation a été particulièrement active, car les représentants de la Commission ont à y défendre la position de la Communauté.

Un autre problème non moins important était celui de la coordination des États membres. C'est grâce à cette coordination systématique des Neuf, en particulier sur les questions économiques, que la Communauté a fourni, à la CSCE, un modèle de cohésion et de solidarité.

Les Neuf ont pu ainsi se présenter à la conférence en tant que communauté solidaire et y apporter une contribution constructive, souvent décisive quant au fond. C'est le cas en particulier pour les questions économiques, où la rédaction des documents finals s'inspire largement des propositions des Neuf.

Ainsi la CSCE constitue une facette importante du dialogue entre la Communauté et les pays à commerce d'État à un moment où ces relations sont entrées dans une nouvelle phase.

Relations générales avec les pays à commerce d'Etat

450. Mise à part la continuation du dialogue avec les pays à commerce d'État dans les cadres multilatéraux, l'année 1974 a marqué de nouvelles étapes dans les relations avec ces pays dans plusieurs domaines. L'échéance des accords commerciaux bilatéraux des États membres a suscité la mise au point par le Conseil d'un régime autonome pour les échanges avec ces pays au cours de l'année 1975 et la communication aux pays à commerce d'État concernés d'un aide-mémoire assorti d'un schéma pour esquisser le contenu éventuel d'un accord communautaire avec chacun d'eux.[1] En même temps une certaine évolution s'est fait sentir dans le domaine des relations avec le CAEM.

Contacts avec le CAEM

451. Au mois d'août 1973, M. Fadeyev, secrétaire du Conseil d'assistance économique mutuelle (CAEM), s'était rendu auprès de M. Nørgaard, qui assurait à cette époque la présidence du Conseil des Communautés, en suggérant officieusement l'organisation d'un contact entre son organisa-

---

[1] N° 452 du présent Rapport.

As regards Australia, the measures taken by the Community to restrict imports of meat were a major point of discussion. The Commission expressed interest in the possibility of importing Australian raw materials, particularly energy, into the EEC and in Australia's industrial policy and the prospects for tariff reductions in this sector as part of the coming multilateral negotiations.

The main point at issue in the Commuinty's relations with New Zealand relates to imports of dairy products into the United Kingdom under Protocol No 18.

vi. Conference on Security and Cooperation in Europe and relations with State-trading countries

Conference on Security and Cooperation in Europe

449. The problem of how the Community should participate in the CSCE was settled by a Council decision in September 1973. Commission representatives were therefore sent to the Second Committee on economic matters (trade, cooperation, science and technology, environment, manpower, tourism, etc.). It was in Subcommittee D (Trade) that Commission representatives were particularly active, since this is where questions falling within Community jurisdiction were most directly concerned and where the Community's position had to be defended.

Another problem, just as important, was that of internal coordination of the positions taken by the Member States. Thanks to this systematic coordination, particularly on economic matters, the Community was able to set the CSCE an example of consistency and solidarity.

This enabled the Nine to appear before the Conference as a Community speaking with one voice and thus to make a constructive contribution, often a decisive one. This is the case particularly of economic questions, where the final documents were largely drafted in line with the proposals of the Nine.

Thus the CSCE is an important element in the dialogue between the Community and the State-trading countries as their relations embark on a new phase.

General relations with State-trading countries

450. Apart from the continued dialogue with the State-trading countries in multilateral contexts, this year saw a number of significant events in relations with these countries in a number of fields. Expiry of the bilateral trade agreements with the Member States led the Council to lay down autonomous trade arrangements for 1975 and to send the relevant countries an *aide-mémoire* with a model for a possible agreement which the Community might conclude with each of them. At the same time relations with Comecon have also been changing.

Contacts with Comecon

451. In August 1973 Mr Fadeyev, Secretary-General of the Council for Mutual Economic Assistance (Comecon), approached Mr Nørgaard, who at the time was President of the Council of the Communities, and suggested unofficially that contacts be organized between Comecon and the Com-

tion et la Communauté. La présidence danoise a fait savoir à M. Fadeyev, au nom de la Communauté, que celle-ci avait pris connaissance de sa démarche et que, si le CAEM désirait approcher la Communauté, la Commission était prête à recevoir toute communication en la matière. Le Conseil des Communautés a estimé nécessaire, en mai 1974, de réaffirmer son attitude positive à l'égard de la démarche de M. Fadeyev. Il a chargé l'ambassade de la république fédérale d'Allemagne à Moscou, qui assurait alors la présidence, de confirmer à nouveau à M. Fadeyev que la Commission était ouverte à tout contact.

A la suite de cette démarche, M. Fadeyev a adressé au président de la Commission, le 16 septembre, une invitation à Moscou pour une prise de contact avec le CAEM. Une réponse a été donnée le 14 novembre qui, tout en acceptant cette invitation, suggère qu'il serait opportun de faire précéder ce contact à haut niveau par des conversations préparatoires menées par des fonctionnaires; ces conversations auraient pour but de définir dans quels domaines relevant de leurs compétences respectives les deux organisations peuvent trouver des intérêts communs pouvant donner lieu à une éventuelle collaboration.

Mise en oeuvre de la politique commerciale commune à l'égard des pays à commerce d'Etat

Politique commerciale contractuelle

452. La plupart des accords commerciaux à long terme négociés par les États membres avec les pays à commerce d'État sont venus à échéance le 31 décembre 1974.

Un nombre très limité d'accords à long terme existant entre les nouveaux États membres et certains pays à commerce d'État resteront exceptionnellement encore en vigueur, car leur échéance avait été initialement fixée au 31 décembre 1975. C'est ainsi que les États membres intéressés ont été autorisés à proroger encore une fois, pour une année, conformément aux dispositions du titre I de la décision du 16 décembre 1969, les protocoles commerciaux qu'ils avaient négociés pour l'année 1973 dans le cadre de ces accords à long terme, et qui avaient déjà fait l'objet d'une prorogation pour l'année écoulée.

En outre, le Conseil, après avoir réitéré sa volonté de conclure des accords commerciaux avec chacun des pays à commerce d'État ayant des relations contractuelles avec l'un ou l'autre des États membres, a mis au point un schéma d'accord commercial indiquant les conceptions de la Communauté quant au contenu possible de tels accords éventuels. Bien entendu, ce contenu, pour pouvoir répondre aux exigences des situations concrètes, devra tenir compte des demandes que voudront faire connaître les pays intéressés. Le schéma envisage des accords à long terme non préférentiels, fondés sur une réciprocité assurant l'équivalence des advantages et des obligations. La Communauté prévoit d'inclure dans les accords l'octroi du traitement de la nation la plus favorisée dans le domaine tarifaire, compte tenu des exceptions traditionnelles; des dispositions en matière agricole ne seraient pas davantage exclues. Comme c'est l'usage pour ces accords, le schéma prévoit la création d'un comité mixte et de mécanismes de sauvegarde appropriés.

Au mois de novembre 1974 la Commission, à la demande du Conseil, a transmis ce schéma aux pays en cause avec un aide-mémoire indiquant que la Communauté est disposée à entamer avec ces pays des négociations dont le contenu pourrait s'inspirer des indications retenues dans le schéma.

munity. Mr. Nørgaard informed Mr. Fadeyev on behalf of the Community that the Community had noted this, and that if Comecon wished to approach the Community the Commission was open to any further moves. In May the Council felt it was necessary to confirm its positive reaction to Mr Fadeyev's *démarche*. It asked the Moscow Embassy of the Federal Republic of Germany, which by then had replaced Denmark in the Chair of the Council, to reiterate to Mr Fadeyev that the Commission was open to any move.

On 16 September Mr Fadeyev responded by inviting the President of the Commission to visit Moscow for preliminary talks with Comecon. The Commission's reply of 14 November, although accepting the invitation, suggested that it would be a good idea for high-level contacts to be preceded by preparatory talks by officials; the aim would be to find out in what areas of their respective jurisdictions the two organizations have matters of common interest on which cooperation might be possible.

The common commercial policy and State-trading countries

Contractual commercial policy

452. Most of the long-term trade agreements between Member States and State-trading countries expired on 31 December 1974.

A very limited number of long-term agreements between the new Member States and certain State-trading countries are still in force, exceptionally, as they are not to expire until 31 December 1975. Accordingly, the relevant Member States have been authorized, under Title I of the Decision of 16 December 1969, to renew for another year the trade protocols which they had negotiated for 1973 under these long-term agreements, which had already been renewed for the past year.

In addition, having reiterated its desire to conclude trade agreements with each of the State-trading countries which already have agreements with one or more Member States, the Council has finalized a model trade agreement setting out the principles which might be contained in them. Naturally, if these agreements are to be of any practical value, they will have to reflect the preoccupations of the other side too. The model envisages a long-term non-preferential agreement based on reciprocity ensuring that both sides have equal rights and obligations. The Community is considering granting most-favoured-nation treatment on tariff matters, subject to the usual exceptions; there will also be provisions on agriculture. There will be the customary Joint Committee and appropriate safeguard arrangements.

In November the Commission, at the request of the Council, sent the model agreement to the relevant countries together with an *aide-mémoire* stating that the Commission was willing to enter into negotiations, and that they could be guided by the points made in the model.

Politique commerciale autonome

Libération des importations

453. Par règlement (CEE) no 238/74 du 21 janvier 1974, le Conseil a décidé une nouvelle extension (16 positions entières, 26 positions partielles) de la liste annexée au règlement no 109/70 portant sur l'établissement d'un régime commun d'importations applicable à l'égard des pays à commerce d'État en ce qui concerne les produits libérés au niveau communautaire.

Produits soumis à des restrictions quantitatives

454. En attendant la négociation d'accords commerciaux communautaires avec les pays à commerce d'État, la Communauté applique à ces pays tiers, depuis le 1er janvier 1975, une politique commerciale intégralement autonome en ce qui concerne les produits non libérés.

C'est ainsi que, par sa décision no 74/652/CEE du 2 décembre 1974, le Conseil a arrêté le régime d'importation applicable dans les États membres, à titre provisoire, à partir du 1er janvier 1975, à l'égard des pays à commerce d'État en ce qui concerne les produits soumis à des restrictions quantitatives.

Application des arrangements techniques dans le secteur agricole entre la Commission et certains pays à commerce d'État

455. Au cours de l'année 1974, l'application des arrangements techniques conclus entre la Commission et la Bulgarie, la Hongrie, la Pologne et la Roumanie n'a donné lieu à aucun problème particulier.

Relations avec les pays à commerce d'État au GATT

456. Le groupe de travail chargé de l'examen annuel prévu par le protocole d'accession de la Pologne au GATT a été saisi d'une proposition polonaise visant à mettre un terme à la période transitoire à l'issue de laquelle toutes les restrictions quantitatives spécifiquement appliquées à l'égard de la Pologne devront être supprimées.

Le représentant de la Communauté a soulevé le problème de la formation des prix à l'exportation de la Pologne, et a attiré l'attention sur le lien étroit existant entre les diverses formes de ,,subventions'' en Pologne et le maintien de restrictions quantitatives à l'Ouest.

La Communauté a participé activement aux travaux du groupe spécial chargé d'examiner le nouveau tarif douanier que la Roumanie entend mettre en vigueur dés le 1er janvier 1975.

Commission économique pour l'Europe

457. Les services de la Commission ont participé aux travaux de la session plénière de la Commission économique pour l'Europe des Nations unies (ECE), qui s'est déroulée en 1974 à Bucarest, ainsi qu'à la 23e session du Comité pour le développement du commerce et au deuxième séminaire sur la promotion des échanges. Le représentant de la Commission a fait part aux délégues de la 23e session des raisons et des grandes lignes de la décision du Conseil de septembre 1974 relative à la négociation des accords commerciaux avec chacun des pays à commerce d'État.

Autonomous commercial policy

Liberalization of imports

453. By Regulation (EEC) No 238/74 of 21 January 1974, the Council made a further extension (sixteen full items, twenty-six sub-items), to the list annexed to Regulation No 109/70 laying down common rules for imports from State-trading countries of products liberalized in the Community.

Products subject to quantitative restrictions

454. Pending the negotiation of Community trade agreements with the State-trading countries, the Community will, from 1 January 1975, apply a fully autonomous commercial policy as regards products which are not yet liberalized.

Thus, by Decision No 74/625/EEC of 2 December 1974 the Council laid down the provisional arrangements applicable from 1 January 1975 in the Member States to imports from State-trading countries of products subject to quantitative restrictions.

Implementation of technical arrangements on agriculture between the Commission and certain State-trading countries

455. In 1974 there were no particular difficulties in applying the technical arrangements concluded by the Commission with Bulgaria, Hungary, Poland and Romania.

Relations with the State-trading countries in GATT

456. The working party responsible for the annual review provided for by the Protocol on the Accession of Poland to GATT has received a Polish proposal to terminate the transitional period at the end of which all quantitative restrictions specifically applied to Poland are to be removed.

The Community representative raised the problem of export price formation in Poland and drew attention to the close relationship between the various forms of "subsidies" in Poland and the maintenance of quantitative restrictions in the West. The Community took an active part in the Working party on the customs tariff which Romania is to introduce on 1 January 1975.

Economic Commission for Europe

457. The Commission sent officials to the plenary session of the UN Economic Commission for Europe in Bucharest and to the twenty-third session of the Committee on the Development of Trade and the Second Seminar on East-West Trade Promotion. The Commission representative informed the Committee of the reasons for and main points of the Council decision taken in September on the negotiation of trade agreements with each of the State-trading countries.

F. DROIT COMMUNAUTAIRE

Introduction

458. L'année 1974, comme d'ailleurs l'année 1973, est caractérisée par le dynamisme remarquable de la jurisprudence de la Cour de justice. Les arrêts rendus témoignent, une nouvelle fois, de la volonté constante et très ferme de la Cour d'assurer leurs pleins effets intégrateurs à toutes les dispositions du droit communautaire. Ainsi, comme les années précédentes, la Cour s'est, à plusieurs reprises, appuyée sur les principes qui forment la base de la Communauté, tels que la libre circulation des personnes et des biens ou le principe de non-discrimination pour en déduire les conséquences concrètes. Dans le même sens, plusieurs arrêts ont été rendus, qui confirment et renforcent la jurisprudence relative à l'applicabilité directe de certaines dispositions du droit communautaire.

On doit néanmoins regretter, en revanche, que les efforts de la Cour de justice, en vue de garantir l'application uniforme du droit communautaire dans tous les États membres, ne trouvent pas toujours leur correspondant dans les décisions des juridictions nationales. On déplorera plus particulièrement la réticence de certains tribunaux à faire usage de la procédure de renvoi préjudiciel ou la volonté de telle Cour suprême de se réserver le dernier mot quant au contrôle de certains aspects des dispositions communautaires.

Sur le plan des institutions, en dépit des incertitudes dues à la situation économique qui ont pesé sur la vie des Communautés, on a pu déceler, au cours de l'année écoulée, des progrès importants, qu'il s'agisse, entre autres, des bonnes conditions du déroulement de la nouvelle procédure budgétaire ou des initiatives concrètes qui ont trouvé l'approbation des chefs de gouvernement lors de la conférence de Paris des 9 et 10 décembre 1974 en vue de l'amélioration des procédures de décision et du renforcement des institutions de la Communauté.

ELEMENTS CARACTERISTIQUES DE L'ORDRE JURIDIQUE COMMUNAUTAIRE

EVOLUTION INSTITUTIONNELLE

459. Deux innovations importantes caractérisent l'évolution institutionnelle au cours de l'année 1974. Il s'agit de:

- la concertation qui s'est instaurée entre le Conseil et le Parlement en ce qui concerne les propositions de révision des traités formulées par la Commission en vue de renforcer les pouvoirs budgétaires du Parlement;
- l'entrée en vigueur de l'article 203 du traité CEE et des dispositions correspondantes des traités CECA (article 78) et Euratom (article 177).

460. Consulté sur les propositions de la Commission, le Parlement avait expressément demandé au Conseil, dans sa résolution du 5 octobre 1973, de ne pas arrêter sa décision sans s'être concerté au préalable avec lui. Dans sa session des 17–18 décembre 1973, le Conseil avait accepté cette demande.

Effectivement, le Conseil, après avoir dégagé des „orientations communes" sur les propositions de la Commission, au cours de sa session du 4 juin 1974, a communiqué les textes résultant de ces orientations au Parlement, en lui demandant de lui faire connaître ses observations éventuelles.

Cette communication a été suivie d'une véritable concertation entre le Conseil et une délégation de membres du Parlement, au cours de deux ren-

F. COMMUNITY LAW

Introduction

458. In 1974, as in 1973, the Court of Justice displayed remarkable vigour in its decisions. Its judgments once again reveal its constant and firm determination to give the provisions of Community law their full effect as an instrument of integration. As in previous years the Court on a number of occasions based its judgments on the founding principles of the Community, such as free movement of persons and goods and the principle of non-discrimination. Likewise, a number of judgments have confirmed and indeed reinforced the rules applied by the Court as to the direct applicability of certain provisions of Community law.

Nevertheless it must be regretted that the endeavours of the Court of-Justice to ensure that Community law is uniformly applied in all the Member States have not always been paralleled by decisions of national courts. Particularly to be regretted is the reluctance of certain courts to use the preliminary ruling procedure and the desire of one particular superior court to retain the last word in reviewing certain aspects of Community legislation.

Turning to the Community institutions, despite the uncertainty created by the economic situation, which has weighed so heavily on Community life, considerable progress has been made, for instance in the smooth operation of the new budgetary procedure and in the practical measures approved by the Heads of Government at the Paris Conference on 9 and 10 December to improve decision-making procedures and to strengthen the Community institutions.

CHARACTERISTICS OF THE COMMUNITY LEGAL ORDER

INSTITUTIONAL DEVELOPMENTS

459. 1974 saw two major institutional developments:

- the holding of joint discussions between the Council and Parliament on the Commission's proposals for revision of the Treaties to strengthen Parliament's budgetary powers;
- the putting into effect of the new Article 203 of the EEC Treaty and of the corresponding provisions in the ECSC Treaty (Article 78) and the Euratom Treaty (Article 177).

460. Having been consulted on the Commission proposals, Parliament adopted a Resolution on 5 October 1973 expressly requesting that the Council should not take its decision without first consulting it. At its meeting of 17 and 18 December 1973, the Council agreed to this.

Thus, at its meeting of 4 June 1974 the Council, after adopting "common guidelines" on the Commission proposals, sent Parliament the texts formulated on the basis of these guidelines and asked it for its views.

This was followed by full joint discussions between the Council and a Parliament delegation at two meetings held in Luxembourg on 25 June and 14 October. In the intervening period the Presidents of the Council and Parliament were able to clarify their respective positions by means of an exchange of correspondence.

Although the resulting dialogue has not yet brought the two sides into agreement on all the points on which they differ, it has nevertheless been fruitful. First, it has shown that, going beyond the legal forms used, views contres qui ont eu lieu à Luxembourg les 25 juin et 14 octobre 1974. Entre temps, un échange de lettres avait permis au président du Conseil et au président du Parlement de mieux préciser leurs positions respectives.

Si le dialogue qui s'est ainsi engagé n'a pas permis d'aboutir à un accord sur tous les points de divergence existant entre les deux institutions, il n'en a pas moins été fructueux. D'une part, il a permis de constater que, au-delà des formules juridiques utilisées, les positions sont parfois très proches et, d'autre part, il préfigure la façon dont pourrait se développer la concertation que la Commission a proposé d'instaurer entre les trois institutions pour „l'adoption des actes communautaires de portée générale ayant des implications financières notables et dont l'adoption ne s'impose pas en vertu d'actes préexistants."

461. Le budget de l'exercice 1974 a été adopté en 1973 sur la base des articles 203 bis CEE, 78 A CECA, 177 bis Euratom. D'après ces textes, le Parlement disposait certes de pouvoirs accrus dans l'adoption du budget par rapport au régime initial prévu par les traités, mais ce rôle restait, en définitive, essentiellement consultatif. Ces dispositions ont fait place, pour l'adoption du budget de l'exercice 1975, aux articles 203 CEE, 78 CECA et 177 Euratom dans leur version résultant du traité du 22 avril 1970, qui confère au Parlement le dernier mot sur les dépenses ne découlant pas obligatoirement du traité ou des actes arrêtés en vertu de celui-ci.

Pour apprécier l'importance de ce pouvoir, il faut signaler que, alors que les auteurs du traité du 22 avril 1970 avaient évalué les dépenses non obligatoires à un chiffre oscillant entre 4 et 5 % du montant total du budget, cette proportion s'établit en définitive, dans le budget de l'exercice 1975, à près de 15 %.

De plus, la difficulté de distinguer les dépenses obligatoires des dépenses non obligatoires, c'est-à-dire en définitive de délimiter les compétences respectives du Parlement et du Conseil, a amené les deux institutions à intensifier le dialogue qui avait commencé à s'instaurer entre elles lors de la préparation du budget de 1974.

S'appuyant enfin sur les termes mêmes des traités qui disposent que „l'Assemblée... arrête en conséquence le budget," le Parlement a confirmé son interprétation selon laquelle cette disposition lui conférait également, de façon implicite, le pouvoir de rejeter le buudget. En adoptant, le 25 septembre 1974, une résolution sur ses dispositions réglementaires internes pour l'examen du projet de budget général des Communautés européennes relatifs à l'exercice 1975, il a donc notamment réglementé l'exercice de ce pouvoir (article 6).

PUBLICITE ET PRESENTATION DU DROIT COMMUNAUTAIRE

462. L'abondance de la réglementation communautaire ainsi que les fréquentes modifications qu'il est nécessaire d'y apporter en fonction de l'évolution de la situation économique imposent à la Communauté de se préoccuper des questions concernant la publicité et la présentation du droit communautaire.

C'est ainsi que, depuis le 1er janvier 1974, le sommaire de chaque fascicule du Journal officiel permet, grâce à une présentation typographique spéciale, de distinguer immédiatement, parmi les actes publiés, les actes de gestion courante pris dans le cadre de la politique agricole commune et ayant une durée de validité limitée. Le 5 octobre 1973, la Commission a, d'autre part, transmis au Conseil une proposition de règlement tendant à instaurer une procédure de codification, selon laquelle elle serait autorisée à publier, à titre déclaratoire, la version codifiée d'actes du Conseil plusieurs fois modifiés.

Par ailleurs, les institutions ont entrepris des efforts concourant au même but et visant à rationaliser et à simplifier les réglementations com-are very close on many points; secondly, it is a model for the "conciliation procedure" which the Commission has proposed establishing between the three institutions in respect of "Community acts of general application which have appreciable financial implications, and of which the adoption is not required by virtue of acts already in existence".

461. The 1974 budget was adopted in 1973 under Articles 203a EEC, 78A ECSC and 177a Euratom. Under these Articles Parliament admittedly had greater powers than originally, but ultimately its role was still only consultative. For the 1975 budget, these Articles have been replaced by Articles 203 EEC, 78 ECSC and 177 Euratom, as amended by the Treaty of 22 April 1970, so that Parliament now has the last word on expenditure not necessarily resulting from the Treaty or from instruments adopted under it.

To understand the importance of this power, it should be pointed out that, whereas the draftsmen of the 1970 Treaty estimated that expenditure "not necessarily resulting" would account for between 4 and 5% of the total budget, the percentage finally appearing in the 1975 budget is substantially higher at nearly 15%.

Moreover, the difficulty of distinguishing between expenditure "necessarily" and "not necessarily" resulting, in other words of establishing a demarcation line between Parliament's and the Council's powers, means that the dialogue between the institutions, which began with the preparation of the 1974 budget, has had to be intensified.

Finally, basing itself on the express words of the Treaties, which provide that "the Assembly... shall adopt the budget accordingly," Parliament has reiterated its view that this provision by implication also confers the power to reject the budget. In its Resolution adopted on 25 September 1974 on the internal rules of procedure for consideration of the draft general budget of the European Communities for the 1975 financial year, provisions were adopted (Article 6) for the exercise of this power.

PUBLICATION AND PRESENTATION OF COMMUNITY LAW

462. The volume of Community legislation and the frequent amendments required by changes in the economic situation mean that the Community has had to review the publication and presentation of Community law.

Thus, since 1 January 1974 the use of different kinds of type on the cover page of each issue of the Official Journal has enabled acts which relate to the day-to-day management of agricultural matter and are generally valid for a limited period to be distinguished at a glance from other acts. On 5 October 1973 the Commission submitted to the Council a proposal for a Regulation to introduce a consolidation and codification procedure, under which it (the Commission) would be authorized to publish, by way of information, consolidated texts of Council instruments which have been frequently amended.

Moreover, the institutions have taken other measures to achieve the same objective of rationalizing and simplifying Community legislation. In the customs field, a practical example of this is the Council Resolution of munautaires. Dans le domaine des dispositions douanières, cette volonté trouve expression dans la résolution du Conseil du 27 juin 1974, relative aux mesures à prendre en vue de simplifier les tâches des administrations douanières.

463. Le Conseil (ministres de la justice), en sa 315e session le 26 novembre 1974, a traité de ces deux problèmes. En ce qui concerne la présentation du droit communautaire et la subdivision du Journal officiel, il a chargé le comité de direction de l'Office des publications officielles de lui faire rapport au plus tard le 1er mai 1975. En matière de codification du droit communautaire il s'est, par une résolution, prononcé en faveur d'une codification constitutive entraînant l'abrogation des actes antérieurs et s'est engagé à adopter rapidement, sans discussion au fond, les propositions de textes codifiés que la Commission pourrait lui transmettre.

RAPPORTS ENTRE LE DROIT COMMUNAUTAIRE ET LE DROIT NATIONAL

Protection juridique des droits fondamentaux

Jurisprudence communautaire

464. La Cour de justice a concrétisé et précisé sa jurisprudence relative à la protection des droits fondamentaux dans le droit communautaire. La Cour avait déjà affirmé que les droits fondamentaux font partie intégrante des principes généraux du droit dont elle assure le respect.[1]

La garantie de ces droits a été confirmée de façon nette et catégorique par la Cour de justice dans son arrêt du 14 mai 1974.[2] Les éléments nouveaux dans cet arrêt résident dans une référence plus précise aux droits fondamentaux reconnus et garantis par les constitutions des États membres ainsi que dans la constatation que les instruments internationaux concernant la protection des droits de l'homme auxquels les États membres ont coopéré ou adhéré, peuvent également fournir des indications dont il convient de tenir compte dans le cadre du droit communautaire. Comme instrument international immédiat, les institutions devront respecter les principes de la convention sur la protection des droits de l'homme et des libertés fondamentales conclue le 4 novembre 1950 par les États membres du Conseil de l'Europe. Maintenant que tous les États membres l'ont ratifiée, cette convention peut être considérée comme faisant partie du droit commun des États membres.

Dans l'affaire dont elle avait à connaître, la Cour de justice a donné clairement à entendre que la propriété ainsi que la liberté du travail, le libre exercice du commerce et d'autres activités professionnelles constituent des droits fondamentaux qui jouissent également d'une protection dans le cadre du droit communautaire. Cependant, cette protection n'est pas illimitée. De même que dans le droit constitutionnel des États membres, la protection de ces biens et de ces activités est appréciée en considération de leur „fonction sociale," de même ces droits font l'objet dans l'ordre communautaire de certaines limitations justifiées par les objectifs d'intérêt général poursuivis par la Communauté, dès lors qu'il n'est pas porté atteinte à la substance de ces droits.

Jurisprudence nationale

465. Dans sa décision du 29 mai 1974,[3] la Cour constitutionnelle fédérale (Deuxième Chambre) de la république fédérale d'Allemagne, saisie

---

[1] Aff. 29–69 (Stauder/Ville d'Ulm) – Recueil 1969, et aff. 11–70 (Internationale Handelsgesellschaft/Einfuhr- und Vorratsstelle Getreide) – Recueil 1970. Deuxième Rzpport général, n° 633 et Quatrième Rapport général, n° 550.

[2] Aff. 4–73 (Nold/Commission) – Receuil 1974.

[3] Neue Juristische Wochenschrift, 1974. p. 1697 à 1704, qui reproduit, avec la décision, l'opinion dissidente de trois juges.

27 June 1974 concerning measures to be adopted to simplify the task of the customs administrations.

463. At the 315th Council meeting held in Brussels on 26 November, the Ministers of Justice considered both these questions. It instructed the Managing Board of the Official Publications Office to report to it by 1 May 1975 on the presentation of Community law and the possibility of subdividing the Official Journal. As regards the consolidation and codification of Community law, it adopted a Resolution in favour of a form of constitutive codification involving the repeal of the original instruments, and agreed that the proposals for consolidated or codified texts put forward by the Commission would be adopted expeditiously and without debate as to the substance of the measures concerned.

RELATIONSHIP BETWEEN COMMUNITY LAW AND NATIONAL LAW

Legal protection of fundamental rights

Community case law

464. The Court of Justice has confirmed and clarified its judicial approach to the protection of fundamentel rights in Community law. It had already stated that fundamental rights formed an integral part of the general principles of law, the observance of which it ensured.[1]

Its judgment of 14 May[2] was a firm and categorical confirmation that these rights are to be protected. The novel elements here were the more precise reference to the fundamental rights recognized and guaranteed by the Member States' constitutions and the statement that international treaties on the protection of human rights on which the Member States had collaborated or to which they were signatories could provide guidelines which should be followed within the framework of Community law. As an immediate example, the institutions must henceforth follow the principles of the Convention for the Protection of Human Rights and Fundamental Freedoms concluded by the Member States of the Council of Europe on November 1950. Now that all the Community countries have ratified the Convention, it can be regarded as part of the law common to all the Member States.

In the case before it, the Court stated in no uncertain terms that rights of ownership and the right freely to choose and practise a trade or profession were among the fundamental rights also protected by Community law. However, this protection was not unlimited. As was the case under the constitutional law of the Member States, where protection of these rights and activities was generally viewed in the light of their "social function", the protection given by Community law was also subject to certain limits justified by the overall objectives pursued by the Community, although the basic substance of these rights could not be attacked.

National case law

465. In a judgment of 29 May[3] on a reference from the Frankfurt Administrative Court, the Second Chamber of the German Federal Consti-

[1] Case 29/69 (Stauder v Stad Ulm): [1969] Recueil; Case 11/70 (Internationale Handelsgesellschaft v Einfuhr- und Vorratsstelle Getreide): [1970] Recueil. See also Second General Report, point 633, and fourth General Report, point 550.

[2] Case 4/73 (Nold v Commission): [1974] ECR.

[3] [1974] Neue Juristische Wochenschrift 1697–1704 which reproduces both the judgment and the dissenting opinions of the three judges.

d'une ordonnance de renvoi par le tribunal administratif de Francfort, s'est déclarée compétente pour contrôler la compatibilité entre le droit communautaire dérivé – en l'espèce, le régime des cautions prévu dans le cadre de l'organisation de marché des céréales – et les droits fondamentaux inscrits dans la constitution allemande, et pour déclarer éventuellement inapplicable, en République fédérale, une disposition du droit communautaire dérivé qui serait contraire à ces derniers.

Dans le cas dont elle avait à connaître, la Cour constitutionnelle n'a cependant pas constaté, au fond, de violation d'un droit fondamental, suivant en cela la Cour de justice qui avait statué précédemment dans la même affaire.[1]

La Cour constitutionnelle prescrit aux tribunaux allemands qui éprouveraient à l'avenir des doutes sur la compatibilité d'une disposition du droit communautaire dérivé avec les droits fondamentaux inscrits dans la loi fondamentale, de demander d'abord une décision préjudicielle au titre de l'article 177 du traité CEE; un renvoi à la Cour constitutionnelle fédérale serait recevable et nécessaire au cas où il subsisterait des doutes après cette décision préjudicielle. La Cour constitutionnelle fédérale entend maintenir cette position tant que le processus d'intégration n'aura pas atteint un stade suffisamment avancé pour que le droit communautaire comporté également un catalogue de droits fondamentaux adopté par un Parlement directement élu, et mis en application.

Cette décison de la Cour constitutionnelle fédérale est contraire au droit communautaire – notamment aux principes d'autonomie et de primauté de celui-ci sur le droit des États membres, y compris sur leur droit constitutionnel – et à la jurisprudence constante de la Cour de justice des Communautés européennes. Elle est donc dangereuse pour l'unité du droit communautaire, et nuit à la sécurité juridique quant à l'application uniforme de ce droit.

En se reconnaissant un pouvoir de contrôle sur la compatibilité du droit communautaire dérivé avec les droits fondamentaux énumérés dans la loi fondamentale allemande, la Cour constitutionnelle fédérale a mis en cause le pouvoir exclusif de la Cour de justice chargée d'assurer le respect du droit dans l'interprétation et l'application des traités (voir l'article 164 du traité CEE).

La Commission a saisi le gouvernement allemand des graves préoccupations exprimées ci-dessus.[2]

Applicabilité directe du droit communautaire

466. Au cours de l'année 1974, la Cour de justice a eu l'occasion à plusieurs reprises de confirmer et de renforcer sa jurisprudence relative à l'applicabilité directe de dispositions du droit communautaire.

Dans plusieurs espèces, la Cour a fortement insisté sur la conséquence de l'expiration de la période de transition pour la reconnaissance de l'applicabilité directe à des articles du traité CEE prévoyant une élimination progressive de restrictions incompatibles avec le marché commun. La Cour a en conséquence clairement réaffirmé que, en présence d'une règle fondamentale du traité, le fait que la progressivité n'a pas été respectée laisse entière l'obligation elle-même au-delà du terme prévu pour son exécution; selon la Cour, cette conséquence est renforcée par l'article 8, § 7, du traité qui prévoit que l'expiration de la période de transition constitue le terme extrême pour l'entrée en vigueur de l'ensemble des règles du

[1] Aff. 11-70 (Internationale Handelsgesellschaft/Einfuhr- und Vorratsstelle Getreide) – Recueil 1971.

[2] Voir, par ailleurs, la question écrite n° 414/74 posée par M. Cousté à la Commission.

tutional Court declared by a five-to-three majority that it had jurisdiction to rule on the compatibility of the law of the European Communities – in this case, the arrangements for the lodging of security under the rules governing the organization of the market in cereals – with the fundamental rights enshrined in the German Constitution, and to declare inapplicable in Germany any provision of Community secondary legislation which should be found to conflict with these rights.

In the case before it, the Constitutional Court in the event followed the Court of Justice, which had already given a preliminary ruling in the same case,[1] in finding that no fundamental rights had been violated.

It stated that German courts which had any doubts as to whether a provision of secondary Community law was compatible with the fundamental rights enshrined in the German Basic Law (*Grundgesetz*) should first request a preliminary ruling under Article 177 of the EEC Treaty; if, after such a ruling, doubt should still remain then the matter could and indeed must be referred to the Federal Constitutional Court. The Court intends to maintain this approach until such time as the process of integration is far enough advanced for Community law to contain and enforce a similar "Bill of Rights" enacted by a directly elected parliament.

This ruling is contrary to Community law – and in particular to the principle of its autonomy and of its primacy over national law, including constitutional law – and to all the relevant case law of the European Court. Accordingly it is a dangerous threat to the unity of Community law and creates uncertainty as to the latter's uniform application.

By claiming the power to verify the compatibility of Community secondary legislation with the fundamental rights in the Basic Law, the Constitutional Court is impugning the exclusive jurisdiction of the Court of Justice to ensure that in the interpretation and application of the treaties the law is observed (Article 164 of the EEC Treaty).

The Commission has informed the German Government of its grave concern.[2]

Direct applicability of Community law

466. This year gave the Court of Justice numerous opportunities to confirm and strengthen the principles it has evolved as to the direct applicability of Community law.

In a number of cases the Court has firmly stressed the consequences of the expiration of the transitional period for the direct applicability of EEC Treaty Articles providing for the progressive removal of restrictions which are incompatible with the common market. It has clearly stated that, in the case of a basic rule of the Treaty, in spite of the fact that the timetable has not been complied with, the obligation concerned will continue to exist after the expiry of the period prescribed for its execution. The Court found support for this view in Article 8(7) of the Treaty, which provides that the expiry of the transitional period is to constitute the latest date by which all the rules laid down must enter into force and all the measures required for establishing the common market must be implemented.

---

[1] Case 11/70 (Internationale Handelsgesellschaft v Einfuhr- und Vorratsstelle Getreide): [1971] Recueil.

[2] See also Written Question No 414/74 by Mr Cousté to the Commision.

traité et pour la mise en place de l'ensemble des réalisations que comporte l'établissement du marché commun.

467. La Cour a fait application de ces principes dans le domaine de la libre circulation des personnes. Après avoir déclaré dans un arrêt du 4 avril 1974[1] que l'article 48 est directement applicable et qu'en conséquence ses dispositions engendrent, dans le chef des intéressés, les droits que les autorités nationales doivent respecter et sauvegarder, elle a également affirmé ce caractère directement applicable pour les articles 52, 59 et 60, alinéa 3, du traité.

S'agissant de l'article 52, la Cour, dans un arrêt du 21 juin 1974,[2] constate que cette disposition du traité prescrit une obligation de résultat précise dont l'exécution devait être facilitée mais non conditionnée par la mise en oeuvre d'un programme de mesures progressives au cours de la période de transition. Elle en déduit qu'il importe peu que, dans un domaine déterminé, le Conseil n'ait pas encore arrêté les directives prévues par l'article 54.

S'agissant des articles 59, alinéa 1, et 60, alinéa 3, relatifs à la libre prestation des services, la Cour a, dans un arrêt du 3 décembre 1974,[3] également déclaré que ces dispositions ont un effet direct et peuvent dès lors être invoquées par les intéressés devant les juridictions nationales, dans la mesure où elles visent à l'élimination de toute discrimination à l'encontre du prestataire, en raison de sa nationalité ou de la circonstance qu'il réside dans un État membre autre que celui où la prestation doit être fournie.

Ces deux arrêts de la Cour peuvent être considérés comme marquant une nouvelle étape dans sa jurisprudence en ce qui concerne les droits que l'ordre juridique communautaire confère aux justiciables dans les États membres. En effet, dans les cas précédents, les articles du traité déclarés directement applicables ne prévoyaient pas pour leur mise en oeuvre l'intervention d'actes des institutions de la Communauté, si ce n'est simplement pour fixer le calendrier d'application de ces dispositions. A la différence de ce qui s'est passé pour l'article 48, dont la mise en oeuvre avait été assurée en temps utile par un règlement spécifique, toutes les directives prévues pour la mise en oeuvre de la liberté d'établissement et de la liberté de prestation de services n'étaient pas arrêtées à la fin de la période de transition. Ainsi donc, la carence des institutions communautaires à intervenir dans le délai prescrit, pas plus que celle des États membres, ne peut empêcher les particuliers d'invoquer les droits qu'ils trouvent directement dans le traité; cette intervention est devenue superflue pour supprimer les discriminations visées par ces dispositions concernant la libre circulation des personnes et des services.

Également dans le domaine de la libre circulation des personnes, la Cour a déclaré que l'article 3, § 1, de la directive 64/221 du Conseil, du 25 février 1964, pour la coordination des mesures spéciales aux étrangers en matière d'établissement et de séjour justifiées par des raisons d'ordre public, de sécurité publique etde santé publique, est une disposition directement applicable.[4]

L'arrêt de la Cour peut ici aussi être considéré comme un nouveau pas dans la conception du droit communautaire directement applicable: jusqu'à présent, la Cour n'avait eu l'occasion de se prononcer que sur des dispositions de droit communautaire dérivé qui mettent en oeuvre des objectifs nettement définis par le traité CEE lui-même quant au résultat à atteindre ainsi qu'à leur délai de réalisation.[5] L'article 3 de la directive pré-

---

[1] Aff. 167-73 (Commission/République française) - Recueil 1974.
[2] Aff. 2-74 (Reyner/Etat belge) - Recueil 1974.
[3] Aff. 33-74 (Van Binsbergen/Bestuur van de Bedrijfsvereniging voor de Metaalnijverheid).
[4] Aff. 41-74 (Van Duyn/Home Office).
[5] Aff. 9-70 (Grad/Finanzant Traunstein) - Recueil 1970, et aff. 33-70 (SACE/Ministère des Finances italien) - Recueil 1970.

467. The Court has applied these principles in cases concerning free movement of persons. After declaring in a judgment given on 4 April 1974[1] that Article 48 was directly applicable and that accordingly its provisions created rights in those concerned which national authorities must respect and protect, it also stated that Articles 52 and 59 and the third paragraph of Article 60 of the Treaty were likewise directly applicable.

Dealing with Article 52, a ruling of 21 June[2] states that this Article imposes obligations with precise effects whose performance must be facilitated but not conditioned by the implementation of a programme of progressive measures throughout the transitional period. It concluded that it was of little importance that in a given field the Council had not yet adopted the directives called for by Article 54.

As regards the first paragraph of Article 59 and the third paragraph of Article 60, relating to freedom to provide services, a Court ruling of 3 December[3] declared that these provisions also have direct effect and can therefore be invoked by parties before national courts to the extent that the object of the said provisions is to abolish all discrimination against the person providing services on the basis of his nationality or of the fact that he resides in another Member State rather than the one where the services are to be provided.

These two decisions of the Court of Justice can be regarded as a landmark in the evolution of its rules of law relating to the rights conferred by the Community legal order on individuals in the Member States. In earlier cases, the Treaty Articles declared directly applicable were those which did not require intervention by the Community institutions to implement them except as regards the fixing of timetables. Article 48 was brouht into operation at the appropriate time by a specific Regulation; in contrast, not all the directives for attaining freedom of establishment and freedom to provide services had been adopted by the end of the transitional period. Thus neither the failure of the Community institutions to act before the prescribed time limit nor that of the Member States can preclude individuals from relying upon rights which they can find directly in the Treaty; action by the institutions or by the Member States is no longer required in order to end discrimination of the kind which the provisions in question seek to remove as regards the free movement of persons and services.

Still dealing with the free movement of persons, the Court declared that Article 3(1) of Council Directive No 64/221 of 25 February 1964 on coordination of special measures concerning the movement and residence of foreign nationals which are justified on grounds of public policy, public security and public health is also directly applicable.[4]

This ruling too can be regarded as a landmark in the evolution of the concept of directly applicable Community law: hitherto the only provisions of Community secondary legislation which the Court has had to interpret have been those implementing objectives clearly defined by the Treaty itself, both as regards the results to be obtained and the time limit for doing so.[5] In contrast, Article 3 of the Directive in question imposes re-

[1] Case 167/73 (Commission v French Republic): [1974] ECR.
[2] Case 2/74 (Reyners v Belgium): [1974] ECR.
[3] Case 33/74 (Van Binsbergen v Bestuur van de Bedrijfsvereniging voor de Metaalnijverheid).
[4] Case 41/74 (Van Duyn v Home Office).
[5] Case 9/70 (Grad v Finanzamt Traunstein): [1970] Recueil; Case 33/70 (SACE v Italian Minister of Finance): [1970] Recueil.

citée contient, par contre, une limitation du pouvoir des États membres de prendre des mesures d'ordre public et de sécurité publique à l'égard des ressortissants des États membres, limitation énoncée de façon précise mais qui ne peut pas être déduite telle quelle des dispositions du traité.

APPLICATION UNIFORME DU DROIT COMMUNAUTAIRE: LE RENVOI PREJUDICIEL

468. Le Conseil (ministres de la justice), en sa 315e session du 26 novembre 1974, a, dans le souci d'améliorer les procédures et d'alléger la tâche de la Cour de justice, arrêté une décision portant adaptation des articles 32 du traité CECA, 165 du traité CEE et 137 du traité CEEA, et approuvé une modification consécutive du règlement de procédure afin de permettre que soient déférées à des chambres de celle-ci certaines catégories de questions préjudicielles visées à l'article 41 du traité CECA, à l'article 177 du traité CEE et à l'article 150 du traité CEEA. Cette faculté vaut pour les litiges ayant un caractère essentiellement technique ou concernant des questions pour lesquelles existe déjà une jurisprudence établie, et à condition qu'aucun État membre n'intervienne et qu'une institution ne demande pas que l'affaire soit jugée en séance plénière.

469. La Cour de justice a toujours souligné l'importance capitale d'une application uniforme du droit communautaire grâce à la procédure de renvoi préjudiciel. L'efficacité de cette procédure, destinée à assurer en toutes circonstances le même effet au droit communautaire dans tous les États de la Communauté, dépend non seulement de l'obligation faite aux juridictions de dernière instance de former une demande de décision préjudicielle, mais aussi du droit donné aux juridictions de degré inférieur de faire de même. Dans ses arrêts du 16 janvier 1974 et du 12 février 1974,[1] la Cour a vigoureusement affirmé ce droit. En l'espèce, la question était de savoir si un *Finanzgericht* allemand, tribunal de degré inférieur, saisi d'un litige renvoyé par l'instance de révision, le *Bundesfinanzhof*, après cassation, est tenu de suivre l'appréciation portée en droit dans la décision du *Bundesfinanzhof*, comme prévu par les règles internes de procédure, et se trouve ainsi privé de son droit de demander à la Cour de statuer à titre préjudiciel, au cas où il ne serait pas d'accord sur l'interprétation du droit communautaire donnée par le *Bundesfinanzhof*. Selon la Cour de justice, l'existence en droit interne d'une règle liant les juridictions à l'appréciation portée en droit par une juridiction de degré supérieur ne saurait, de ce seul fait, les priver de la faculté prévue à l'article 177 de saisir la Cour.

La Cour, par ailleurs, a confirmé sa jurisprudence antérieure selon laquelle elle reste valablement saisie d'un recours préjudiciel aussi longtemps que la décision de renvoi n'est pas retirée ou mise à néant, alors même qu'elle fait l'objet d'une voie de recours interne.[2]

Soucieuse d'assurer à la procédure préjudicielle une large portée, la Cour a reconnu, dans son arrêt du 30 avril 1974,[3] que les accords internationaux conclus par le Conseil, conformément aux articles 228 et 238 du traité CEE, sont des actes pris par une des institutions de la Communauté, au sens de l'article 177, alinéa 1, b. En tant que tels, ils font partie intégrante de l'ordre juridique communautaire. La Cour de justice est donc compétente pour statuer à titre préjudiciel sur l'inter prétation de ces accords, sur demande des juridictions nationales.

470. La Cour a été saisie, pour la première fois, d'une question d'interprétation d'une disposition d'une directive ne présentant aucun caractère

---

[1] Aff. 166–73 et 146–73 (Rheinmühlen Düsseldorf/Einfuhr- und Vorratsstelle Getreide) – Recueil 1974.
[2] Aff. 127–73 (BRT-I/Sabam) – Recueil 1974.
[3] Aff. 181–73 (Haegeman/Etat belge) – Recueil 1974.

strictions on the power of Member States to take measures justified by considerations of public policy and public security in respect of nationals of the Member States; the restriction is made quite clear but cannot be deduced as such from the Treaty itself.

UNIFORM APPLICATION OF COMMUNITY LAW: PRELIMINARY RULINGS

468. At the 315th Council meeting on 26 November, the Ministers of Justice, with a view to improving the procedures and lightening the workload of the Court of Justice, adopted a decision amending Article 165 of the EEC Treaty, Article 32 of the ECSC Treaty and Article 137 of the Euratom Treaty and approved consequential amendments to the Court's Rules of Procedure to enable requests for preliminary rulings under Article 177 of the EEC Treaty, Article 41 of the ECSC Treaty and Article 150 of the Euratom Treaty to be assigned by the Court to its Chambers. This will apply to disputes which are of an essentially technical nature or concern matters for which there is already an established body of case law, provided that no Member State objects and no institution asks for the case to be heard by the full Court.

469. The Court of Justice has constantly stressed the capital importance of a uniform application of Community law, by means of the preliminary ruling procedure. The effectiveness of this procedure, the purpose of which is to ensure that Community law is at all times applied uniformly in all the Member States, depends not only on the obligation upon courts of final appeal to request preliminary rulings but also on the option open to inferior courts to do so as well. In its judgments of 16 January and 12 February[1] the Court vigorously reaffirmed this right. In this case the question was whether a German *Finanzgericht*, an inferior court, to which a case is referred back by a court of review, the *Bundesfinanzhof*, after its decision has been quashed on appeal, must in accordance with the procedural rules of domestic law apply the law as interpreted by the *Bundesfinanzhof*, thus being deprived, where it is not in agreement with the *Bundesfinanzhof's* interpretation of Community law, of the right to request a preliminary ruling from the Court of Justice. The Court of Justice held that the fact that domestic law contained a rule that inferior courts were bound by the findings in law of superior courts could not in itself deprive the inferior court of its power under Article 177 to refer questions to the Court of Justice.

The Court also confirmed previous decisions to the effect that it remains validly seized of a request for a preliminary ruling as long as the decision to refer is not withdrawn or quashed, even if an appeal against such decision is pending in proceedings before a national court.[2]

In a judgment of 30 April[3] the Court, desirous of giving Article 177 the largest passible scope, held that international agreements entered into by the Council under Articles 228 and 238 of the EEC Treaty are acts of a Community institution within the meaning of subparagraph (b) of the first paragraph of Article 177. As such they are an integral part of the Community legal order. The Court of Justice accordingly has jurisdiction to give preliminary rulings on the interpretation of such agreements at the request of national courts.

470. For the first time the Court has had to deal with interpreting a provision in a directive which can in no sense be considered to be directly

---

[1] Cases 166/73 and 146/73 (Rheinmühlen-Düsseldorf v Einfuhr- und Vorratsstelle Getreide(: [1974] ECR.

[2] Case 127/73 (BRT-I v SABAM): [1974] ECR.

[3] Case 181/73 (Haegeman v Belgium): [1974] ECR.

d'applicabilité directe. Sur recours préjudiciel du *Bundesgerichtshof*, la Cour a en effet, par son arrêt du 12 novembre 1974,[1] été amenée à interpréter le texte d'un article de la première directive en matière d'harmonisation du droit des sociétés.[2] Cet arrêt revêt un intérêt particulier sur le plan du rôle de l'article 177 dans le maintien de l'uniformité des règles de droit national coordonnées au niveau communautaire. On constate, en effet, que c'est pour pouvoir appliquer correctement sa législation nationale, modifiée expressément pour mettre en oeuvre une directive, que le juge de renvoi a été amené à se poser la question de la signification exacte de la directive, source de droit pour la législation nationale.

471. Pour la première fois également, la Cour de justice a été saisie d'une procédure préjudicielle introduite par une juridiction anglaise, en l'espèce, la *High Court*; elle s'est prononcée par arrêt du 4 décembre 1974.[3]

472. Dans un sens moins positif, il faut faire mention d'un arrêt interlocutoire rendu le 22 mai 1974 par la *Court of Appeal* anglaise dans l'affaire Bulmer Ltd. and Showerings Ltd./Bollinger et Champagne Lanson Père et Fils.[4] Certaines considérations émises par Lord Denning, Master of the Rolls, traitent, sur un plan général, de questions relatives à l'application de l'article 177 du traité CEE telles que la notion de juridiction de dernière instance, l'effet juridique obligatoire d'une décision préjudicielle de la Cour de justice et des éléments d'interprétation à prendre en considération par les juridictions nationales dans l'application des dispositions du droit communautaire. L'affirmation selon laquelle seule la Chambre des lords constituerait une juridiction de dernière instance tenue de saisir la Cour de justice au titre de l'article 177, alinéa 3, appelle de sérieuses réserves.

EXECUTION PAR LES ETATS MEMBRES DE LEURS OBLIGATIONS

473. Le nombre de procédures engagées de manière formelle a légèrement diminué pendant la période de référence. Alors qu'une trentaine de nouvelles procédures ont été engagées, plus de quarante procédures ont pu être closes en 1974. Les nouvelles procédures concernent à nouveau exclusivement le traité CEE, à l'exception d'une procédure fondée à la fois sur l'article 169 de ce traité et sur l'article 141 du traité CEEA.

474. La Cour de justice n'a été saisie en 1974 que d'une seule procédure en constatation d'un manquement.[5] Cette affaire (loi allemande sur le vin) est encore pendante.

Sur les quatre cas d'infraction mentionnés dans le précédent Rapport général, la Commission a pu renoncer à poursuivre la procédure devant la Cour de justice dans trois affaires,[6] les États intéressés ayant mis fin aux infractions en cause.

Dans la quatrième affaire, la Cour de justice a rendu, le 4 avril 1974, un arrêt[7] qui présente un intérêt de principe dans la mesure où la Cour s'est prononcée sur „l'intérêt à agir" de la Commission à l'encontre du maintien, dans l'ordre juridique national d'un État membre, d'une disposition légale contraire à des dispositions communautaires directement applicables.

Sur le plan de la recevabilité, la Cour a précisé que, dans l'exercice des compétences qu'elle tient des articles 155 et 169 du traité CEE, la Commission n'a pas à démontrer l'existence d'un intérêt à agir puisque, dans l'intérêt général communautaire, elle a, d'office, pour mission de veiller à

---

1 Aff. 32-74 (HAAGA).
2 Directive n° 68/151 du Conseil du 9.3.1968 (JO L 65 du 14.3.1968).
3 Aff. 41-74 (Van Duyn/Home Office).
4 Common Market Law Reports, 1974, p. 91-126.
5 Aff. 12-74; JO C 31 du 21.3.1974.
6 Aff. 156-73, 173-73 et 174-73; Septième Rapport général, n° 589, note 2.
7 Aff. 167-73 (Commission/République française) - Recueil 1974.

applicable. In a judgment delivered on 12 November[1] on a request for a preliminary ruling from the *Bundesgerichtshof* the Court had to interpret an Article in the first Directive on harmonization of company law.[2] The judgment is particularly significant as regards the role of Article 177 in preserving the uniformity of rules of national law which have been coordinated at Community level. The referring court was seeking to apply national legislation correctly, and as national legislation had been amended to implement the directive, it was now seeking the exact meaning of the directive, which was the source of the national legislation.

471. This year the Court also received its first request for a preliminary ruling from an English court, the High Court; judgment was given on 4 December.[3]

472. Another case worth mentioning is the interlocutory judgment given on 22 May by the English Court of Appeal in *Bulmer Ltd and Showerings Ltd v Bollinger and Champagne Lanson Pére et Fils*.[4] A number of the statements in the speech by Lord Denning MR deal in general terms with questions relating to the application of Article 177 of the EEC Treaty, such as what constitutes a court of final appeal, the binding legal effect of a preliminary ruling by the Court of Justice and the rules of interpretation to be applied by English courts in applying Community law. The view that only the House of Lords can be regarded as a court of final appeal obliged to refer cases to the Court of Justice under the third paragraph of Article 177 must be treated with reservation.

PERFORMANCE BY THE MEMBER STATES OF THEIR OBLIGATIONS

473. The number of proceedings formally initiated fell slightly this year. Although thirty or so new proceedings were initiated, more than forty were terminated. The new proceedings again concern exclusively the EEC Treaty, with the exception of one which is based both on Article 169 of the EEC Treaty and on Article 141 of the Euratom Treaty.

474. The Court of Justice had to deal with only one proceeding for non-application.[5] This case (German Law on wine) is still before the Court. Of the four infringements mentioned in the Seventh General Report, the Commission has been able to abandon proceedings in three cases[6] as the Member States concerned had terminated the infringements.

In the fourth case the Court gave judgment on 4 April;[7] this judgment is interesting in that the Court considered the Commission's "legal interest" as regards the maintenance within the national legal order of one Member State of a provision in conflict with directly applicable Community provisions.

As to the admissibility of the action, the Court stated that the Commission, in the exercise of the powers which it has under Articles 155 and 169 of the EEC Treaty, does not have to show the existence of a legal interest since, in the general interest of the Community, its function is to ensure that provisions of the Treaty are applied by the Member States and to note the existence of any failure to fulfil the obligations deriving therefrom, with a view to bringing it to an end. As to the actual existence of a default giving rise to action under Article 169, the Court held that where

---

1 Case 32/74 (HAAGA).
2 Council Directive No 68/151 of 9.3.1968 (OJ L 65 of 14.3.1968).
3 Case 41/74 (Van Duyn v Home Office).
4 [1974] Common Market Law Reports.
5 Case 12/74; OJ C 31 of 21.3.1971.
6 Cases 156/73, 172/73 and 174/73 (cited in Seventh General Report, p. 462, footnote 1).
7 Case 167/73 (Commission v French Republic): [1974] ECR.

l'application du traité par les États membres et de faire constater, en vue de leur cessation, l'existence de manquements éventuels aux obligations qui en dérivent. Quant à l'existence même d'un manquement justifiant un recours fondé sur l'article 169, la Cour a relevé que, lorsqu'une contestation juridique existe en droit à propos de l'applicabilité directe et de la primauté d'une disposition communautaire dans l'ordre juridique national d'un État membre, le maintien dans cet État de dispositions légales nationales contraires à cette disposition communautaire donne lieu à une situation de fait ambiguë en maintenant, pour les sujets de droit concernés, un état d'incertitude quant aux possibilités de faire appel au droit communautaire, et que l'insécurité qui en résulte constitue une entrave à l'application correcte de la disposition communautaire en cause. Il s'ensuit que, dans de telles conditions, la Commission est fondée à exiger, pour des motifs de sécurité juridique, la suppression formelle de dispositions nationales incompatibles avec des dispositions de droit communautaire, alors même que celles-ci sont directement applicables.

475. Le problème, déjà évoqué l'an dernier,[1] de l'application des directives s'est aggravé, comme en témoigne le fait que la plupart des délais fixés aux nouveaux États membres dans les documents d'adhésion pour l'insertion, dans leur ordre juridique, des directives en vigueur au moment de l'adhésion n'ont pas été respectés. Il est apparu que les nouveaux États membres n'étaient pas plus en mesure que jadis les membres originaires de respecter les engagements souscrits lors de l'adoption des directives au Conseil en ce qui concerne leur insertion dans l'ordre juridique national dans les délais prévus. Compte tenu du grand nombre de directives arrêtées depuis la création des Communautés, le problème du retard apporté à l'application des directives finit par prendre des dimensions considérables et même inquiétantes.

Il est évident que la mise en oeuvre des directives dépend d'abord de l'effort soutenu des pouvoirs publics nationaux. Pour sa part, la Commission a pris des mesures pour accélérer et améliorer les procédures du contrôle de l'application des directives.

G. PUBLICATIONS

BULLETIN DES COMMUNAUTES EUROPEENNES: SUPPLEMENTS 1974

Hors série:
- Annuaire de la Commission des Communautés européennes (janvier 1974)
- Annuaire de la Commission des Communautés européennes (août 1974)

1/74 Groupement européen de coopération (GEC)
2/74 Programme d'action sociale
3/74 L'éducation dans la Communauté européenne
4/74 Vers une nouvelle stratégie de politique énergétique pour la Communauté
5/74 De l'énergie pour l'Europe: Recherche et développement
6/74 Les comptes annuels des sociétés de capitaux (proposition modifiée de quatrième directive)
7/74 Situation économique et financière dans la Communauté depuis l'élargissement: Inventaire et aperçu de l'évolution future
8/74 L'aide au développement: Fresque de l'action communautaire, demain

[3] Septième Rapport général, n° 590.

there is legal dispute as to the direct applicability and primacy of a Community provision in the national legal order of a Member State, the maintenance in that State of legal provisions conflicting with the Community provision would create an ambiguous state of affairs where persons subject to the relevant law would be kept in a state of uncertainty as to the possibilities available to them of relying on Community law. Accordingly the Commission, on grounds of certainty in the law, can demand the formal repeal of national provisions which are incompatible with Community provisions even where the latter are directly applicable.

475. The problem mentioned in last year's Report[1] of the application of directives has become more serious, as can be seen from the fact that most of the time limits set for incorporation of directives into the national legal systems of the new Member States have not been observed. It has been found that the new Member States have been no more capable than the original Member States of meeting commitments, entered into when Council directives are adopted, to incorporate them into their national legal systems within a set time limit. In view of the number of directives adopted since the Community was created, the problem of delay in implementing them is growing to substantial proportions and becoming a source of preoccupation.

It is clear that the implementation of directives depends primarily on a sustained effort on the part of national public authorities. For its part the Commission has taken measures to speed up and improve the procedures for monitoring the application of directives.

G. PUBLICATIONS

BULLETIN OF THE EUROPEAN COMMUNITIES: SUPPLEMENTS 1974

Special Supplements:

Directory of the Commission of the European Communities (January 1974)

Directory of the Commission of the European Communities (August 1974)

1/74 European cooperation grouping (ECG)
2/74 Social Action Programme
3/74 Education in the European Community
4/74 Towards a new energy policy strategy for the European Community
5/74 Energy for Europe: research and development
6/74 The annual accounts of limited liability companies (Amended proposal for a fourth Directive)
7/74 Community's economic and financial situation since enlargement
8/74 Development aid: "Fresco" of Community action tomorrow

[1] Seventh General Report, point 590.

CHAPITRE VIII

CONSEIL NORDIQUE ET CONSEIL MINISTERIEL NORDIQUE

A. STRUCTURE ET FONCTIONS

1. CONSEIL NORDIQUE

Le Conseil Nordique est un organe consultatif au service des Parlements et des Gouvernements des Etats nordiques. C'est en 1952 qu'il a été fondé par le Danemark, l'Islande, la Norvège et la Suède et en 1955 que la Finlande y a adhéré. Les dispositions fondamentales le régissant sont énoncées par le Traité d'Helsinki signé en 1962 et révisé en 1971 et 1974. Le Conseil connaît des problèmes relatifs à la coopération entre Etats nordiques en matières économiques, juridiques, sociales et culturelles et dans les domaines de la protection de l'environnement, des transport et des communications. Il agit en adoptant des recommendations dans le cadre de ses sessions annuelles et en émettant des déclarations d'opinion. Ses recommendations proposent la mise en oeuvre de modalités de coopération par les Gouvernements concernés. A la suite de la révision du Traité d'Helsinki en 1971, il a été instauré un *Conseil de Ministres des Pays Nordiques* chargé d'assurer la coopération entre les Gouvernements ainsi qu'entre eux et le Conseil Nordique.

Outre les représentants gouvernementaux désignés pour chaque session plénière annuelle, l'Assemblée plénière, qui constitue l'organe central du Conseil Nordique comprend 78 membres élus chaque année par les cinq Parlements des Etats nordiques, à raison de 16 pour le Danemark, de 17 pour la Finlande, de 6 pour l'Islande, de 18 pour la Norvège et de 18 pour la Suède; en outre, la délégation danoise comprend deux membres élus par l'Assemblée législative des Iles Féroé et la délégation finlandaise un membre désigné par l'Assemblée législative des Iles d'Åland. La composition de chaque délégation reflète l'importance des effectifs de chaque parti politique au sein des Parlements nationaux, qui désignent également un suppléant pour chacun de leurs délégués au Conseil Nordique.

Chaque Gouvernement désigne parmi ses membres le nombre qui lui convient de délégués auprès du Conseil Nordique, les Gouvernements provinciaux des Iles d'Åland et Féroé en désignant chacun un. Normalement 50 à 60 représentants des Gouvernements participent à la Session plénière annuelle du Conseil Nordique en prenant part à ses travaux mais non à ses scrutins, seuls les 78 délégués parlementaires ou leurs suppléants pouvant y exercer le droit de vote.

Chaque année, le Conseil Nordique se réunit en Assemblée plénière dans une des capitales nordiques. Les Commissions permanentes respectives préparent les affaires dont il sera débattu au cours de la session. Chacun des 78 délégués parlementaires siège dans l'une des cinq Commissions permanentes à raison de 13 dans chacune des trois Commissions juridique, de politique sociale et des communications, de 17 dans la Commission culturelle et de 22 dans la Commission économique. En dehors de ses réunions à l'occasion des sessions annuelles du Conseil, chacune de ces Commissions se réunit trois ou quatre fois par an.

Les travaux du Conseil Nordique se déroulent selon la procédure suivante:

Chacun de ses 78 membres élus et les cinq Gouvernements agissant de concert ou séparément ont le droit d'émettre des propositions, lesquelles sont examinées par la Commission compétente du Conseil, qui recueille au

CHAPTER VIII

NORDIC COUNCIL AND NORDIC COUNCIL OF MINISTERS

A. STRUCTURE AND FUNCTIONS

1. NORDIC COUNCIL

The Nordic Council is an advisory body to the Nordic Parliaments and Governments. It was founded in 1952 between Denmark, Iceland, Norway and Sweden. Finland joined in 1955. The fundamental provisions regarding the Nordic Council are laid down in the Treaty of Helsinki, signed in 1962 and revised in 1971 and 1974. The Council deals with questions concerning cooperation between the Nordic countries in the economic, legislative, social and cultural fields and regarding environmental protection and communications. The Council acts through adopting recommendations at the annual sessions and by passing declarations of opinion. The recommendations propose cooperation activities to be carried through by the Governments of the countries concerned. By the revision of the Treaty of Helsinki in 1971 a *Nordic Council of Ministers* was founded, with responsibility for cooperation between the Governments and for that between the Governments and the Nordic Council.

The plenary assembly, which is the central body of the Nordic Council, is composed of 78 members elected annually by the five Parliaments and furthermore of Government representatives appointed to each annual plenary session of the Council. The Danish Parliament elects 16 members, the Finnish Parliament 17, the Icelandic Parliament 6 and the Norwegian and Swedish Parliaments each elect 18 members. The Danish delegation further includes 2 members elected by the legislature of the Faroe Islands and the Finnish delegation includes 1 member elected by the legislature of the Åland Islands. The national delegations represent the political parties within each Parliament on a proportional basis. The Parliaments also elect Deputies for the members of the delegations.

Each Government appoints among its members as many Government representatives as it wishes. The Faroese landsstyre and the Åland landskapsstyrelse (provincial governments) each appoint one representative among their members. Normally, 40–50 Government representatives take part in the annual plenary session of the Council, participating in the work of the Council but not in the voting. Only the 78 elected members (or their deputies) have voting rights.

The Nordic Council meets annually for a plenary session in one of the Nordic capitals. The respective standing committees prepare the items to be dealt with at the session. Each of the 78 Council members belongs to one of the five standing committees. Thus there are 13 members in the Committees for Legal questions, Social Policy and Communications, 17 members in the Cultural Committee and 22 in the Economic Committee. Apart from meetings in connection with the plenary sessions the Committees meet 3–4 times a year.

The working procedure of the Nordic Council may be described as follows: Each of the 78 elected members of the Council has the right to make proposals and so have the five Nordic Governments, jointly or separately. The proposals are dealt with by the standing committee concerned; other bodies are asked for their opinion prior to the Committee discussions. On the proposal of the Committee, the Nordic Council then decides either upon a recommendation or a declaration of opinion to the préalable l'avis des divers organismes consultés à ce sujet. Sur proposition de ses Commissions, le Conseil Nordique se prononce ensuite au sujet d'une recommandation ou d'une déclaration d'opinion à l'attention du Conseil de Ministres des Pays Nordiques ou des Gouvernements concernés. Des rapports sur les mesures adoptées à la suite des recommandations doivent être soumis aux session ultérieures du Conseil Nordique. Depuis 1972, le Conseil des Ministres adresse un vaste rapport sur la coopération internordique au Conseil Nordique, qui reçoit également des rapports annuels émanant de divers organismes internordiques permanents et de certains autres organismes de coopération et qui se trouve ainsi en mesure de surveiller la suite donnée aux recommandations qu'il a émises précédemment.

Le Praesidium du Conseil examine les affaires courantes dans l'intervalle des sessions et se réunit environ six ou huit fois par an. Elu chaque année, cet organisme comprend cinq membres, un Président et quatre vice-Présidents, le premier appartenant à la Délégation nationale, dont il est généralement le Président, chargée d'organiser la session de l'année. Le Praesidium comporte un Secrétariat installé à Stockholm et auquel sont rattachés les Secrétaires des cinq Commissions permanentes. Chaque délégation nationale au Conseil Nordique est assistée d'un Secrétariat rattaché au Parlement.

Nordic Council of Ministers or to the Governments concerned. Reports on action taken on the basis of the recommendations are submitted to later sessions of the Nordic Council. Since 1972, a general report on Nordic cooperation is delivered to the Nordic Council by the Nordic Council of Ministers. A number of permanent joint institutions and other permanent cooperation bodies also submit annual reports to the Council, thus enabling it to follow up the recommendations previously adopted.

The Council Presidium attends to current matters between the sessions and meets approximatelly 6–8 times a year. The Presidium is elected annually and consists of five members, one president and four vice presidents. The President is a member (normally the chairman) of the delegation organizing the ordinary session that year. The Presidium has a Secretariat in Stockholm to which also the secretaries of the five standing committees belong. Each national delegation of the Nordic Council has a Secretariat attached to the national Parliament.

ORGANIGRAMME DU CONSEIL NORDIQUE

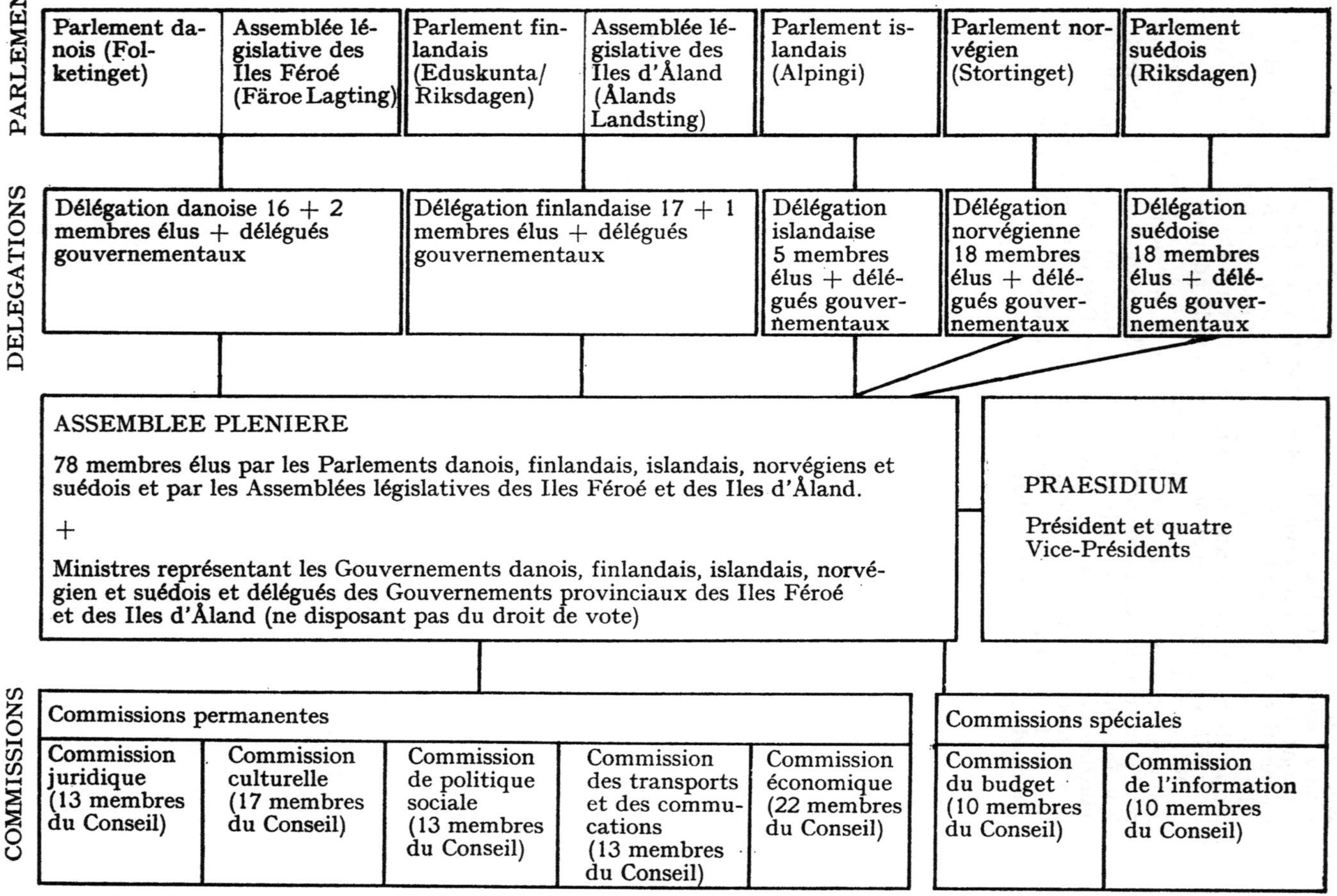

ORGANISATION CHART OF THE NORDIC COUNCIL

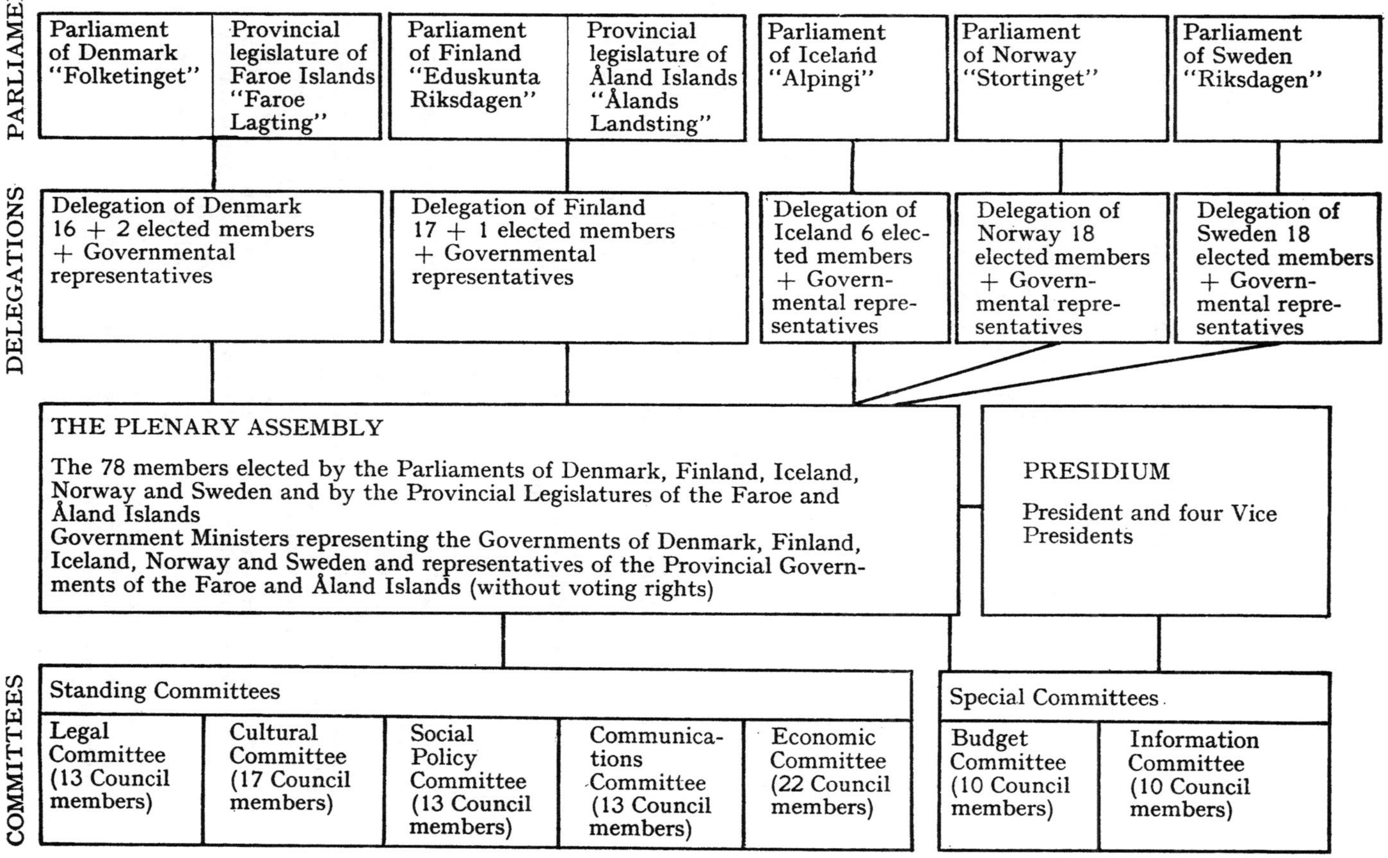

PRAESIDIUM ET SECRETARIATS

Praesidium du Conseil Nordique

Président M. Kåre Willoch, Norvège (Janvier-Février 1974)
M. Johannes Antonsson, Suède (Février 1974–Février 1975)
Mme Ragnhildur Helgadottir, Islande (à partir de février 1975)

Vice-Présidents M. Anker Jørgensen, Danemark (Jan. 1974–Fév. 1975)
M. Knud Enggaard (à partir de fév. 1975)
M. V. J. Sukselainen, Finlande
M. Jon Skaftason, Islande (jusqu'à fév. 1974)
M. Matthías A. Mathiesen (jusqu'à nov. 1974)
Mme Ragnhildur Helgadottir (Nov. 1974–fév. 1975)
M. Odvar Nordli, Norvège (à partir de fév. 1974)
M. Johannes Antonsson, Suède (Janv. 1974, à partir de fév. 1975)

Secrétariats du Conseil Nordique

Secrétariat du Praesidium du Conseil Nordique
Fack, S–103 10 Stockholm 2
Tél. 08–14 10 00
Telex 10887
Secrétaire du Praesidium: M. Helge Seip
Secrétaires adjoints: M. Pär Kettis (jusqu'en avril 1974)
M. Arnold Willén (à partir de fév. 1974)
M. Lasse Lindhard (depuis sept. 1974)
Chef du Service d'information: M. Sten-Olof Westman jusqu'à sept. 1974)
M. Harry Granberg (depuis sept. 1974)
Chargé des publications: M. Åke Edwall
Secrétaire d'information: Mlle Anita Söderman

Secrétariats nationaux

Délégation danoise, Christiansborg Ridebane 10, DK–1218 Copenhague K. Tél. 01–11 66 00
Secrétaire Général: M. Frantz Wendt
Secrétaire adjoint: M. Axel Gormsen

Délégation finlandaise, Eduskuntatalo, SF–00102 Helsinki 10. Tél. 90–49 67 98, 44 81 28, 44 00 51. Telex 121464.
Secrétaire Général: M. Eiler Hultin (jusqu'en févr. 1975)
M. Håkan Branders (depuis avril 1975)
Secrétaire adjoint: M. Håkan Branders (jusqu'en avril 1975)
Service d'information: Mlle Anna-Maija Korpi (jusqu'à mars 1974, depuis avr. 1975)
Mlle Nina Björkell (mars 1974–mars 1975)

Délégation islandaise, Altinget, Reykjavik. Tél. 11560.
Secrétaire Général: M. Fridjon Sigurdsson

Délégation norvégienne, Stortinget, N–Oslo 1. Tél. 02–41 38 10.
Secrétaire Général: M. Gudvin Låder Ve
Secrétaire adjoint: M. Olof Vefald

PRESIDIUM AND SECRETARIATS

Presidium of the Nordic Council

President Mr Kåre Willoch, Norway (Jan-Febr 74)
Mr Johannes Antonsson, Sweden (Febr 74–Febr 75)
Mrs Ragnhildur Helgadottir, Iceland (from Febr 75)
Vice Presidents Mr Anker Jørgensen, Denmark (Jan 74–Febr 75)
Mr Knud Enggaard (from Febr 75)
Mr V. J. Sukselainen, Finland
Mr Jon Skaftason, Iceland (until Febr 74)
Mr Matthías A. Mathiesen (Febr–Nov 74)
Mrs Ragnhildur Helgadottir (Nov 74–Febr 75)
Mr Odvar Nordli, Norway (from Febr 74)
Mr Johannes Antonsson, Sweden (Jan 74, from Febr 75)

Nordic Council Secretariats

Secretariat of the Presidium of the Nordic Council
Fack, S–103 10 Stockholm 2
Tel 08–14 10 00
Telex 10887
Secretary of the Presidium: Mr Helge Seip
Deputy Secretaries: Mr Pär Kettis (until April 74)
Mr Arnold Willén (from Febr 74)
Mr Lasse Lindhard (from Sept 74)
Head of Information: Mr Sten-Olof Westman (until Sept 74)
Mr Harry Granberg (from Sept 74)
Editor: Mr Åke Edwall
Information Secretary: Miss Anita Söderman

National Secretariats

Delegation of Denmark, Christiansborg Ridebane 10, DK–1218 Copenhagen K. Tel 01–11 66 00
Secretary General: Mr Frantz Wendt
Assistant Secretary: Mr Axel Gormsen
Delegation of Finland, Eduskuntatalo, SF–00102 Helsinki 10. Tel 90–49 67 98, 44 81 28, 44 00 51.
Secretary General: Mr Eiler Hultin (until Febr 75)
Mr Håkan Branders (from April 75)
Assistant Secretary: Mr Håkan Branders (until April 75)
Information Secretary: Miss Anna-Maija Korpi (until March 74, from April 75)
Miss Nina Björkell (March 74–March 75)
Delegation of Iceland, Altinget, Reykjavik. Tel 11560.
Secretary General: Mr Fridjon Sigurdsson
Delegation of Norway, Stortinget, N–Oslo 1. Tel 02–41 38 10
Secretary General: Mr Gudvin Låder Ve
Assistant Secretary: Mr Olav Vefald
Delegation of Sweden, Fack, S–103 10 Stockholm 2. Tel 08–14 10 00

Délégation suédoise, Fack, S–103 10 Stockholm 2. Tél. 08–14 10 00.
Secrétaire Général: M. Christer Jacobson
Secrétaires adjoints: Mme Birgitta Malmros
M. Eric Hultén
Mme Eva Smekal
Service d'information: Mlle Anita Söderman

Secrétaires des Commissions

Commission juridique	M. Peter Lilholt Ministère de la Justice Slotsholmsgade 10 DK–1216 Copenhague K Tél. 01–14 36 15
Commission culturelle	M. Dag Lindberg Secrétariat de la Délégation finlandaise (*cf.* plus haut)
Commission de politique sociale	M. Claes Wiklund Secrétariat du Praesidium (*cf.* plus haut)
Commission des transports et des communications	M. Hubert Jensen (jusqu'en juillet 1974) Secrétariat de la Délégation danoise (*cf.* plus haut) M. Olav Vefald (remplissant les fonctions de Secrétaire depuis juillet 1974) Secrétariat de la Délégation norvégienne (*cf.* plus haut) M. Olafur Petursson (depuis avr. 1975) Secrétariat du Praesidium (*cf.* plus haut)
Commission économique	M. Lars Blaaflat Ministère du Commerce et de la Navigation Fr. Nansens plass 4 N–Oslo Depl. 02–20 51 10

2. CONSEIL MINISTERIEL NORDIQUE

Le Conseil Ministériel Nordique est un organe de coopération au service des Gouvernements des Pays nordiques. Il a été institué en 1971 en application d'une révision du Traité de coopération du 23 mars 1962 entre le Danemark, la Finlande, l'Islande, la Norvège et la Suède (Traité d'Helsinki), aux termes duquel il incombe aux parties contractantes de s'efforcer de poursuivre et de développer la coopération entre leurs pays en matières juridiques, culturelles, sociales et économiques ainsi que dans les domaines de la protection de l'environnement, des transports et des communications.

Le Conseil Ministériel Nordique répond de la coopération engagée entre les Gouvernements des Etats nordiques ainsi qu'entre eux et le Conseil Nordique. Il prend des décisions dans la mesure prévue par le Traité d'Helsinki et par d'autres accords conclus entre les Etats nordiques.

Chaque Etat désigne un membre de son Gouvernement dit Ministre chargé de la coordination de la coopération internordique, lequel, assisté d'un haut fonctionnaire, est responsable dans son pays de la coordination des questions relatives à la coopération internordique.

Comprenant des membres des Gouvernements à raison d'un seul ou de plusieurs de chaque Etat, le Conseil de Ministres peut ainsi se composer de ministres chargés de la coordination ou de ministres spécialisés ou encore d'une combinaison des uns et des autres.

Secretary General: Mr Christer Jacobson
Assistant Secretaries: Mrs Birgitta Malmros
Mr Eric Hultén
Mrs Eva Smekal
Information Secretary: Miss Anita Söderman

Secretaries of the Committees

Legal Committee	Mr Peter Lilholt Justitsministeriet, Slotsholmsgade 10 DK–1216 Copenhagen K. Tel 14 36 15
Cultural Committee	Mr Dag Lindberg Secretariat of the Finnish delegation, (see above) *Social Policy Committee*
Social Policy Committee	Mr Claes Wiklund Secretariat of the Presidium, (see above)
Communications Committee	Mr Hubert Jensen (until July 74) Mr Olav Vefald (acting Secretary from July 74) Secretariat of the Norwegian delegation, (see above) Mr Olafur Petursson (from April 75) Secretariat of the Presidium, (see above)
Economic Committee	Mr Lars Blaaflat Departementet for handel og skipsfart Fr. Nansens plass 4, N–Oslo Dep. Tel 205110

2. NORDIC COUNCIL OF MINISTERS

The Nordic Council of Ministers (NMR) is the co-operation organ of the Nordic Governments. The Council of Ministers was set up in 1971 by amending the Treaty of Co-operation of March 23, 1962, between Denmark, Finland, Iceland, Norway and Sweden, the so-called "Helsinki Treaty." According to the terms of this treaty the Contracting Parties shall endeavour to maintain and further develop co-operation between the countries in the juridicial, cultural, social and economic fields and also in questions of communications and environmental protection.

The Nordic Council of Ministers is responsible for the co-operation between the governments of the Nordic countries and also between the governments and the Nordic Council. The Council of Ministers takes decision to the extent stipulated in the Helsinki Treaty and in other agreements between the Nordic countries.

Each country appoints a Member of Government, Minister for Nordic Co-operation, who, with the assistance of an official, is responsible for the co-ordination of Nordic co-operation questions.

In the Council of Ministers are included one or more Members of Government from each country. Consequently, the Council of Ministers can be composed of Ministers for Nordic Co-operation, or of Cabinet Ministers or of a combination of such Ministers.

Les décisions prises par le Conseil Ministériel sont obligatoires pour chacun des Etats. Cependant, les décisions portant sur des questions qui, aux termes de la Constitution de l'un des Etats, requièrent une approbation parlementaire, n'obligeront cet Etat que lorsque son Parlement les aura approuvées.

Le Conseil Ministériel est chargé:

a) d'accomplir les tâches qui lui incombent en application du Traité de coopération conclu le 23 mars 1962 entre le Danemark, La Finlande, l'Islande, la Norvège et la Suède, compte tenu des amendements qui y ont été apportés en 1971 (Traité d'Helsinki);

b) d'accomplir les autres tâches incombant au Conseil Ministériel en application des accords conclus entre les Etats nordiques;

c) d'examiner d'autres questions intéressant la coopération internordique, et, ce faisant, de préparer et de diriger les travaux visant à approfondir cette coopération, en particulier dans les domaines prévus à l'article 1er du Traité d'Helsinki.

Les ministres désignés pour répondre de la coordination des questions de coopération internordique (Ministres chargés de la coordination), doivent, après avoir dûment consulté les autres membres des Gouvernements qui au sein de ceux-ci sont responsable des diverses questions de coopération (Ministres spécialisés):

a) agir en faveur d'un élargissement de la coopération internordique;

b) coordonner les travaux entre les divers domaines de coopération;

c) établir s'il y a lieu, un ordre pertinent de priorités relatif aux efforts qu'appelle la coopération internordique;

d) prendre des décisions portant sur des questions d'organisation et ayant trait à plusieurs domaines de coopération;

e) délibérer des questions dont les ministres chargés de la coordination seront saisis par les ministres spécialisés, ou des questions étant d'une importance fondamentale pour la coopération internordique.

Dans ses activités, le Conseil Ministériel est assisté par son secrétariat et par des comités des agents gouvernementaux.

Dans les principaux domaines de coopération, le Conseil Ministériel a institué des comités de hauts fonctionnaires, lesquels préparent ses réunions et dirigent les enquêtes servant de base à ses décisions. Dans ces comités siègent de hauts fonctionnaires de chacun des Etats nordiques, agissant selon des directives données par les Ministres spécialisés concernés, et sous la direction desquels travaillent des commissions et de groupes de travail.

Le Comité de hauts fonctionnaires relevant des Ministres chargés de la coordination (Comité des Suppléants) répond de la coordination de la coopération internordique au niveau des agents gouvernementaux.

Pour ce qui est des autres comités de hauts fonctionnaires, se reporter à l'organigramme.

Decisions by the Council of Ministers are binding on the individual countries. Decisions on questions which, according to the Constitution of any of the countries, require the approval of the national parliament are not binding on that country until the parliament has approved the decision.

It is incumbent on the Council of Ministers to:

a) fulfil the assignments which rest upon the Council of Ministers in accordance with the Treaty of Co-operation of March 23, 1962, between Denmark, Finland, Iceland, Norway and Sweden dated March 23, 1962, (Helsinki Treaty) as amended in 1971;

b) fulfil the other assignments which rest upon the Council of Ministers in accordance with agreements between the Nordic countries, and

c) in other respects deal with questions of importance for Nordic co-operation and prepare and conduct the work on intensified Nordic co-operation, particularly in the fields mentioned in Article 1 of the Helsinki Treaty.

Those Members of Government who have been appointed to be responsible for the co-ordination of Nordic co-operation questions (Ministers for Nordic Co-operation) are required, after necessary consultation with the other Members of Government who are responsible within the Governments for the various co-operation questions (Cabinet Ministers):

a) to work for an expansion of Nordic co-operation;

b) to co-ordinate the work between the different fields of co-operation;

c) when necessary to arrange for a proper priority of the achievements made in the fields of Nordic co-operation;

d) to take decisions on questions of organization which affect several fields of co-operation; and

e) to decide questions which the Cabinet Ministers have referred to the Ministers for Nordic Co-operation or which are of fundamental importance for Nordic co-operation.

The Council of Ministers is assisted in its acrivities by Committees of Senior Officials and by the Secretariat of the Council of Ministers.

In the more important fields of co-operation the Council of Ministers has appointed Committees of Senior Officials which prepare the meetings of the Council of Ministers and conduct the research which forms the basis for decisions by the Council of Ministers. These Committees include officials from the Nordic countries who act on instructions from the relevant Cabinet Ministers. Committees and working groups operate under the supervision of the Committees of Senior Officials.

The Committee of Senior Officials of the Ministers for Nordic Co-operation (Committee of Deputies) is responsible for the co-ordination of Nordic co-operation on the level of Senior Officials.

With regard to the other Committees of Senior Officials reference is made to the organization chart.

CONSEIL MINISTERIEL NORDIQUE

Ministres chargés de la coordination de la coopération internordique	Ministres de la Justice	Ministres des Finances, du Commerce, de l'Industrie; Ministres chargés des questions de politique régionale	Ministres du Travail, des Affaires Sociales et de la Santé Publique, de l'Environnement et de l'Environnement du Travail	Ministres des Transports et des Communications, du Tourisme et de la Consommation	Ministres des Affaires Culturelles et de l'Education Nationale
Comité des Suppléants	Comité de hauts fonctionnaires pour les questions juridiques	Comités de hauts fonctionnaires pour les questions de politique commerciale, monétaires et des finances, de politique régionale, de politique industrielle et énergétique, de coopération en matière de bâtiment	Comités de hauts fonctionnaires pour les questions de politique sociale, de marché de l'emploi, de protection de l'environnement, d'environnement du travail	Comités de hauts fonctionnaires pour les questions de consommation, de transports et de communications	Comité de hauts fonctionnaires pour les questions de coopération culturelle nordique

SECRETARIAT D'OSLO DU CONSEIL MINISTERIEL NORDIQUE

Secrétaire Général

Section de coordination
- questions juridiques
- budget
- personnel
- information

Section des affaires administratives

Section des questions de coopération économique, de politique industrielle et énergétique, de politique régionale et de coopération en matière de bâtiment

Section des questions de coopération dans les domaines de la politique sociale et de la santé publique, du marché de l'emploi et de l'environnement

Section des questions de coopération dans les domaines des transports et des communications, du tourisme et de la consommation

SECRETARIAT DE COPENHAGUE DE LA COOPERATION CULTURELLE NORDIQUE

Directeur

Sections en matière
- d'enseignement
- de recherche
- d'autres activités culturelles

NORDIC COUNCIL OF MINISTERS

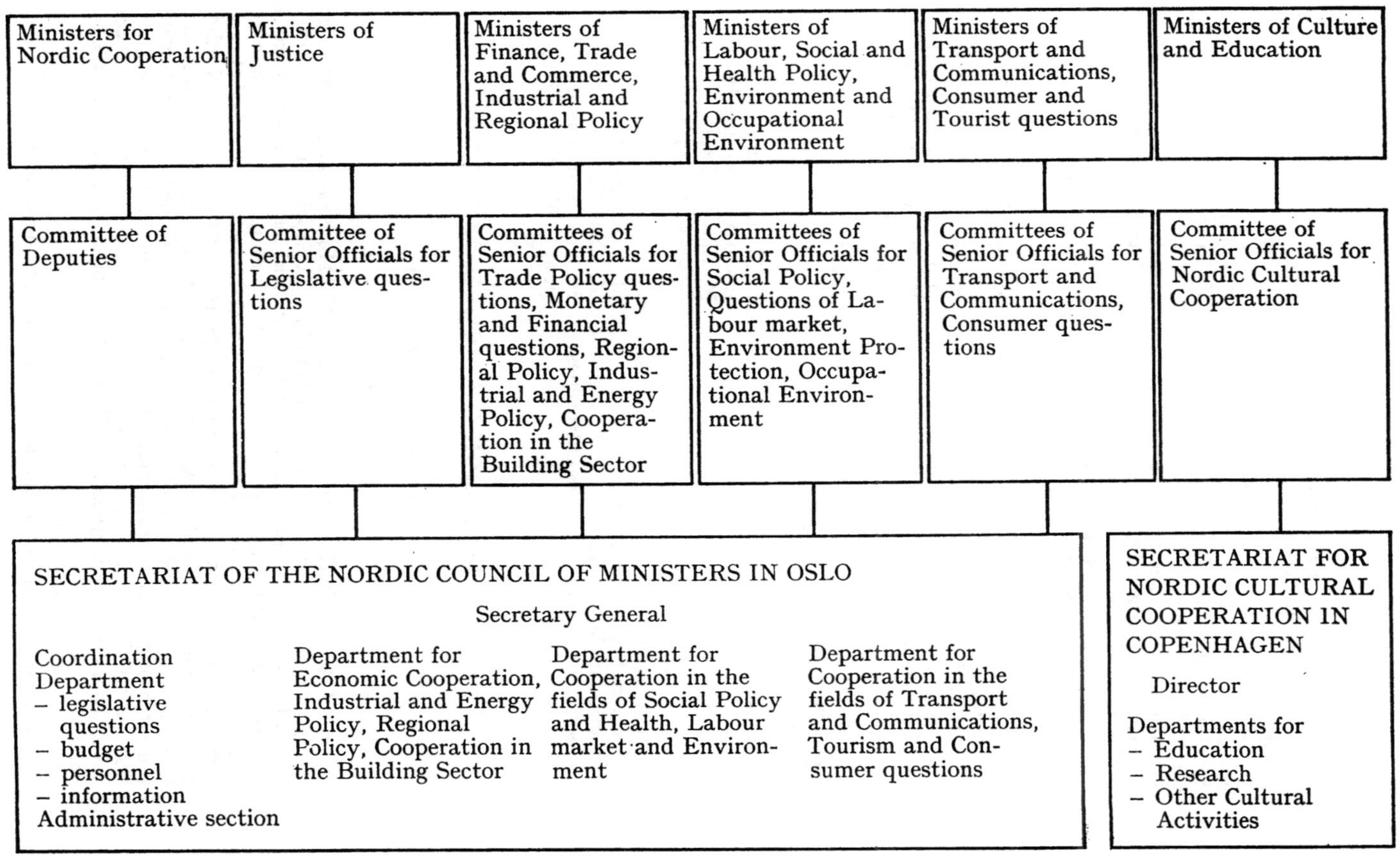

Secrétariats du Conseil Ministériel Nordique
Postboks 1477 Vika
N–Oslo 1
Tél. 02–11 10 52. Télex 19646

Secrétaire Général	M. Olli Bergman
Secrétaire Générale adjoint	M. Gudmund Saxrud
Chefs de Sections	
– Section des questions de coordination, juridiques budgétaires et de personnel	M. Carl Ivar Öhman
– Section des questions de coopération économique, de politique industrielle, énergétique et régionale	M. Gudmund Saxrud
– Section des questions de coopération en matière de politique sociale, du marché de l'emploi et de l'environnement	M. Sven Holmstedt
– Section des questions de coopération en matière de transports et de communications, de consommation et de tourisme	M. Niels Ove Gottlieb (à partir de février 1974)
Service d'information	M. Tom Westergård (à partir d'août 1974)

Secrétariat de la coopération culturelle internordique
Snaregade 10
DK–1205 Copenhague K
Tél. 01–11 47 11

Directeur	M. Magnus Kull jusqu'à septembre 1975) M. Clas Olofsson (à partir de septembre 1975)
Chefs de Sections	
– Section de l'enseignement	M. J. J. Engelhardt
– Section de la recherche	M. Hans Näslund
– Section des autres activités culturelles	M. Niels Matthiasen (mai 1974–février 1975)

B. XXIIe SESSION DU CONSEIL NORDIQUE

1. ACTIVITES EN 1974

Réunions

En 1974, le Conseil Nordique a tenu sa XXIIe Session plénière, qui a comporté deux assemblées, la première réunie à Stockholm (Suède) du 16 au 20 février et la seconde à Ålborg (Danemark) les 7 et 8 novembre. Le Praesidium s'est réuni huit fois, trois de ces réunions ayant été consacrées à des délibérations avec le Conseil Ministériel (Ministres chargés de la coordination). De plus les cinq Commissions permanentes du Conseil Nordique (pour les questions juridiques, culturelles, économiques, de politique sociale et celles relatives aux communications) se sont réunies chacune de trois à cinq fois en dehors de leurs réunions à l'occasion des deux assemblées de la Session plénière. Lors d'une ou deux de ses réunions, chacune de ces commissions a délibéré de questions d'intérêt commun avec les Ministres concernés.

Au cours de l'année, il a été constitué un Groupe de travail chargé d'étudier certaines matières budgétaires et certaines questions de contrôle. Un

Secretariat of the Nordic Council of Ministers Postboks 1477 Vika N–Oslo 1 Tel 02–11 10 52. Telex 19646	
Secretary General	Mr Olli Bergman
Deputy Secretary General	Mr Gudmund Saxrud
Heads of Division	
– Coordination Department Legislative questions, budget and personnel	Mr Carl Ivar Öhman
– Department for Economic Co-operation, Industrial and Energy Policy, Regional Policy	Mr Gudmund Saxrud
– Department for Co-operation in the fields of Social Policy, Labour market Policy and Environmental Policy	Mr Sven Holmstedt
– Department for Co-operation in Transport and Communications, Consumer questions and Tourism	Mr Niels Ove Gottlieb (from Febr 1974)
Information Scretary	Mr Tom Westergård (from August 1974)

Secretariat for Nordic Cultural Cooperation Snaregade 10 DK–1205 Copenhagen K Tel 01–11 47 11	
Director	Mr Magnus Kull (until Sept 1975) Mr Clas Olofsson (from Sept 1975)
Heads of Division	
– Department for Education	Mr J. J. Engelhardt
– Department for Research	Mr Hans Näslund
– Department for other Cultural Activities	Mr Niels Matthiasen (March 1974–Febr 1975)

B. 22nd SESSION OF THE NORDIC COUNCIL

1. ACTIVITIES IN 1974

Meetings

During 1974 the Nordic Council held its 22nd plenary session. The session was divided into two assemblies, the first one being held in Stockholm, Sweden, on February 16–20, and the second one in Ålborg, Denmark, on November 7–8. The Presidium of the Council had eight meetings and at three meetings discussions took place between the Presidium and the Nordic Council of Ministers (Ministers for coordination). Furthermore, the five standing Committees (for legal, cultural, social policy, communications and economic questions) of the Council held three to five meetings each, apart from the meetings held in connection with the two assemblies. Each Committee held joint discussions with the Government Ministers concerned at one or two of the Committee meetings.

During the year, a special working group was set up to study matters concerning budget and control questions. An interim report was presented to the second assembly of the Council in Ålborg. On the basis of the final

Rapport intérimaire a été présenté à la seconde assemblée du Conseil Nordique réunie à Ålborg. Sur la base du Rapport final présenté à la XXIIIe Session tenue à Reykjavik en 1975, il a été institué une Commission chargée d'assumer le rôle d'organisme particulier du Conseil Nordique pour les questions budgétaires et de contrôle relatives aux mesures projetées à l'échelon gouvernemental.

Un Groupe de travail a été spécialement chargé d'étudier les questions touchant les règles à appliquer en matière de communication au public des documents relatifs à la coopération internordique. Le rapport émanant de ce Groupe a fait l'objet d'une discussion préliminaire au cours de l'assemblée tenue à Ålborg et d'un débat terminal dans le cadre de la Session plénière de Reykjavik, au cours de laquelle le Conseil Nordique a adopté des résolutions au sujet de ce rapport.

La Commission de l'Information du Conseil Nordique a concentré ses efforts sur une planification à court et à long terme des activités du Conseil en matière d'informations.

Conférences et contacts internationaux

Une conférence sur la coopération en matière d'enseignement a été organisée en collaboration avec le Secrétariat pour la Coopération culturelle internordique. Ses travaux ont porté sur l'harmonisation des systèmes d'enseignement des Pays nordiques et sur l'éducation permanente des adultes. Le Conseil était représenté dans plusieurs conférences tenues dans la Zone nordique et dont les délibérations ont porté sur différents problèmes de coopération, notamment en ce qui concerne les populations lapones des Etats nordiques, l'environnement maritime de la Baltique et la coordination de certaines activités en matière de santé publique et de prévoyance sociale.

Le Conseil entretient des contacts réguliers avec différentes organisations internationales. Il était représenté par un observateur à une réunion de l'Assemblée consultative du Conseil de l'Europe, à une conférence organisée par le Comité International Socialiste Consultatif, à une réunion organisée par la Commission Economique pour l'Europe et par l'UNEP sur les problèmes de l'environnement. De même que les années précédentes, l'Association Européenne de Libre-Echange était représentée à la première assemblée de la Session plénière du Conseil Nordique, et en décembre une délégation de l'Association des Nations de l'Asie du Sud-Est, venue en Europe pour étudier diverses organisations régionales a été informée de la structure et des fonctions du Conseil Nordique.

Matières à l'ordre du jour

Entre la XXIIe et la XXIIIe Sessions, 2 propositions émanant des Gouvernements et 39 de membres du Conseil Nordique ont été inscrites à l'ordre du jour du Conseil Nordique (*cf.* ci-après Recommandations et déclarations d'opinion).

Le Conseil de Ministres des Pays Nordiques (ou les Gouvernements respectifs) ont porté à la connaissance de la XXIIe Session les mesures qui avaient été prises à la suite de recommandations adoptées précédemment par le Conseil Nordique et dont l'Assemblée plénière a considéré que vingt-quatre d'entre elles pouvaient être considérées comme classées. Au cours de cette session, les Gouvernements ont répondu à dix-sept questions particulières émanant des membres du Conseil Nordique.

Chaque session s'ouvre par un débat au cours duquel les délégués abordent les questions d'actualité. Au cours de la XXIIe Session, les délibérations ont porté notamment sur les questions de coopération en matières report presented at the 23rd session in Reykjavik in 1975 a special Committee was formed, to act as a special Council body for budget and control questions with respect to actions planned at the governmental level.

Questions concerning the rules to be followed regarding the public's right of access to documents at joint Nordic co-operation bodies was studied by a special working group. The report of this group was subject to a preliminary discussion at the Ålborg assembly and the final debate and decisions by the Council took place at the Reykjavik meetings. The Council Committee for Information worked with emphasis on efficient short and long term planning of the Council's information activities.

Conferences and international contacts

A conference on cooperation in education was arranged jointly with the Secretariat for Nordic Cultural Co-operation. The conference dealt with harmonisation of the educational systems of the Nordic countries and with adult education. The Council was represented at several conferences within the Nordic region where various co-operation questions were discussed, i.e. conferences relating to the Samic population of the countries, to the marine environment of the Baltic and to coordinated activities in health and social care. Joint meetings are regularly held with the League of Norden Associations and the Council of Nordic Trade Unions.

The Council has regular contacts with various international organisations as well. The Nordic Council was represented by an observer at a meeting in the Consultative Assembly of the Council of Europe, at a conference arranged by the CMEA and at ECE and UNEP meetings on questions of environment. EFTA was represented, as during previous years, at the first assembly of the Nordic Council session; in December a delegation from the Association of South-East Asian Nations, which was in Europe studying various regional organisations, was briefed on the structure and functions of the Nordic Council.

Items on the agenda

Between the 22nd and the 23rd sessions 39 Members' Proposals and two Government' Proposals were put on the agenda of the Council. (See below for Recommendations and Declarations of Opinion adopted).

Furthermore, the Nordic Council of Ministers (or the respective Governments) reported to the 22nd session on action taken on Recommendations adopted at previous sessions of the Council. The plenary assembly found that twenty four of these Recommendations could be regarded as concluded. At the session, the Governments answered seventeen specific questions put by the Council members.

Every session starts with a general debate in which the delegates take up questions of current interest. At the 22nd session the debate concentrated on questions of energy and industrial co-operation, multinational enter-énergétiques et industrielles, sur les entreprises multinationales, sur la Convention Nordique en matière de protection de l'environnement et sur les activités de coopérations dans le domaine culturel.

Ci-après une liste des propositions inscrites à l'ordre du jour du Conseil Nordique.

Questions juridiques

- Mesures législatives communes aux Etats nordiques sur les entreprises multinationales.
- Coordination et extension des droits reconnus au public d'accéder pour ses loisirs à des terres en friche.
- Changement de la dénomination de la Commission de politique sociale en „Commission de la politique sociale et de l'environnement."
- Révision du nombre des commissions permanentes et de leur champ de compétence.
- Elaboration d'un plan commun d'action visant à limiter et à briser le pouvoir des entreprises multinationales dans les Pays nordiques.
- Extension de la coopération internordique en matière d'activités des comités officiels.
- Question d'une représentation lapone au sein du Conseil Nordique.
- Questions relatives à aménagements de traduction simultanée dans le cadre des réunions du Conseil Nordique.
- Révision de l'Accord sur le Fonds culturel nordique.

Questions culturelles

- Enseignement linguistique des enfants finnois vivant en Suède.
- Amélioration de la distribution internordique du matériel audiovisuel.
- Efforts internordiques en vue d'améliorer les possibilités culturelles à la disposition des enfants.
- Séminaires internordiques de perfectionnement pédagogique à l'intention des enseignants des Instituts universitaires de journalisme.
- Mesures en faveur de la culture lapone.
- Co-production et co-distribution de programmes télévisés à l'intention des gens de mer.
- Programme nordique d'études du futur.
- Recherche internordique en matière de mass media.
- Ouvrage d'histoire sur la Femme nordique.

Questions de politique sociale

- Centre internordique de soins pour personnes âgées.
- Formation internordique complémentaire des infirmières.
- Conseil internordique pour les problèmes concernant le rôle des sexes et l'égalité entre hommes et femmes.
- Uniformisation des règles nordiques en matière de préparations pharmaceutiques dites naturelles.
- Protection légale de l'égalité entre hommes et femmes.
- Organisation d'une exposition sur „Les Femmes dans les Pays nordiques."
- Efforts en vue de limiter et d'empêcher l'utilisation de substances toxiques ou dangereuses dans l'environnement du travail.
- Réduction du nombre des heures de travail.
- Plan commun visant à protéger certains types de paysages et de biotopes présentant un intérêt commun pour les Pays nordiques.

Questions relatives aux communications

- Utilisation obligatoire de dispositifs réfléchissants pour les piétons.
- Libéralisation de la réglementation des vols charter dans la Zone nordique.

prises, the Nordic convention on the protection of the environment and on cultural co-operation activities.

The following is a list of the new Proposals on the Council agenda:

Legal questions

- Joint Nordic legislation on multinational enterprises.
- Co-ordination and widening of the right of the public's access to non-cultivated land for recreation purposes.
- Changing the name of the Committee for questions of Social Policy to the Committee for questions of Social Policy and Environment.
- Review of the number of standing Committees and their fields of competence.
- Working out a joint plan of action to limit and break the power of the multinational enterprises in the Nordic countries.
- Enlarged Nordic co-operation in the field of official committee work.
- Question of Samic representation in the Nordic Council.
- Questions of facilities for simultaneous interpretation at the meetings of the Nordic Council.
- Revision of the Agreement of the Nordic Cultural Fund.

Cultural questions

- Language tuition for Finnish children in Sweden.
- Improved distribution of AV-material across the borders.
- Joint Nordic efforts to improve cultural facilities for children.
- Joint seminars for teachers at university colleges of journalism for pedagogical development work.
- Measures to strengthen the Samic culture.
- Joint production and distribution of TV programmes to seamen.
- Nordic programme for future studies.
- Joint Nordic research in mass media.
- A book on the history of the Nordic woman.

Questions of Social Policy

- A joint Nordic center for the care of the aged.
- Joint advanced training of nurses.
- A joint Nordic council for matters relating to the role of the sexes and equality between them.
- Similar Nordic rules on natural pharmaceutical preparations.
- Protection under the law for equality between men and women.
- Setting up of an exhibition "Women in the Nordic countries."
- Efforts to limit and hinder the use of poisonous and dangerous substances in he working environment.
- Reduction of working hours.
- A common plan to protect types of landscape and biotopes of joint Nordic interest.

Questions of traffic and communications

- Compulsory use of reflex devices for pedestrians.
- More liberal regulations for charter flights within the Nordic area.

- Billets „Nordtourist" visant à abaisser pour les jeunes le coût des voyages internordiques.
- Validité internordique des permis de conduire pour la circulation des véhicules à titre professionnel.
- Liaisons maritimes entre l'Islande, les Iles Féroé et le reste de la Zone nordique.
- Validité internordique des permis de conduire.
- Billets „Nordtourist" à prix réduits pour les retraités.
- Mesures visant à faciliter, en particulier pour les émigrants, le trafic aérien à l'intérieur de la Zone nordique.

Questions économiques
- Institut Nordique en matières énergétiques.
- Coopération internordique en matières énergétiques.
- Stratégie internordique dans le domaine de l'énergie.
- Programme d'action pour un accroissement de l'approvisionnement alimentaire.
- Législation internordique sur les pratiques commerciales limitatives de la concurrence.
- Majoration des subventions allouées à „Nordtest."
- Uniformité du régime fiscal du commerce frontalier.

2. RECOMMANDATIONS ET DECLARATIONS D'OPINION

Au cours de sa XXIIe session, le Conseil Nordique a adopté 28 recommandations préconisant l'adoption de différentes mesures de coopération par le Conseil Ministériel Nordique ou par deux ou plusieurs des Gouvernements. Par ailleurs, le Rapport principal annuel du Conseil Ministériel a constitué la base de 8 déclarations d'opinion de la part du Conseil Nordique et aux termes desquelles celui-ci présente des listes alternatives de priorités ou exprime sa satisfaction au sujet des mesures de coopération à sa connaissance.

La suite du présent rapport rend compte de la teneur de ces recommandations et déclarations d'opinion, présentées sous cinq titres correspondant aux attributions respectives des Commissions permanentes.

a. Questions juridiques

Recommandations

No. 1. Le Conseil Nordique énonce quatre principes à appliquer par le Conseil Ministériel comme base d'une plus vaste coopération internordique en matière de législation.

No. 2. Il est recommandé aux Gouvernements d'interdire la publicité en faveur de la consommation des spiritueux et de lancer une campagne efficace relative à leurs effets nuisibles.

No. 7. Il est recommandé au Conseil Ministériel d'élaborer le projet d'amendements et d'additifs à apporter au Traité d'Helsinki.

No. 24. Il est recommandé au Conseil Ministériel d'élaborer un programme internordique de protection et de sauvegarde de l'environnement dans les principales zones habitées par le Lapons.

No. 25. Il est recommandé au Conseil Ministériel d'étudier le rôle des entreprises multinationales dans l'économie des Pays nordiques et d'envisager une législation nordique commune ou d'autres mesures appropriées.

Déclaration d'opinion

No. 1. Il incombe au Conseil Ministériel de communiquer au Conseil Nordique avant l'adoption de toute décision définitive le rapport émanant

- Cheaper inter Nordic travel for young people through a system of Nordtourist tickets.
- Nordic validity for driving licenses for professional vehicle traffic.
- Connection by boat between Iceland, the Faroe Islands and the rest of the Nordic region.
- Nordic validity for driving licences.
- A system of cheap Nordtourist tickets for pensioners.
- Measures to facilitate the air traffic in the Nordic area with special reference to migrants.

Economic questions
- A Nordic institute for energy matters.
- Nordic co-operation in energy questions.
- Common strategy for the Nordic countries in the energy sphere.
- Action programme for increased food supplies.
- Joint Nordic legislation on restrictive trade practices.
- Increased grants to Nordtest.
- Uniform system for commodity taxation in frontier commerce.

2. RECOMMENDATIONS AND DECLARATIONS OF OPINION

At its 22nd session, the Nordic Council adopted 28 Recommendations which advocate various co-operation measures to be carried through by the Nordic Council of Ministers or by two or more of the Governments. Furthermore, the main yearly report from the Council of Ministers formed the basis for eight Declarations of Opinion by the Nordic Council, where the Council put forward alternative lists of priorities or stated its satisfaction with the co-operation measures reported upon.

In the following summary, there is a presentation of the contents of these recommendations and declarations of opinion. They are presented under five headings, in accordance with the Committee concerned.

a. Legal questions

Recommendations

No 1. The Nordic Council lays down four principles to be followed by the Nordic Council of Ministers as the basis of a greater degree of Nordic co-operation in the field of legislation.

No 2. The Governments are urged to introduce a ban on the advertising of alcoholic liquors and to launch an effective campaign concerning the detrimental effects of alcoholic liquors.

No 7. The Council of Ministers is urged to implement the draft amendments and additions to the Helsinki Treaty.

No 24. The Council of Ministers is urged to draft a joint programme for the protection and preservation of the environment in the basic areas of the Lapp population.

No 25. The Council of Ministers is urged to investigate the rôle played by multinational enterprises in the economy of the Nordic countries and to consider joint Nordic legislation or other appropriate measures.

Declaration of Opinion

No 1. The Council of Ministers is asked to submit the report presented by the working-group to examine the principle of the public's right of du Groupe de travail chargé d'examiner le principe de droit public relatif au libre accès aux documents existant au sein des organes de coopération internordique et de soumettre au Conseil Nordique avant qu'ils ne soient déposés sur le Bureau des Parlements nationaux les projets de futurs accords concernant les organes internordique et leur statut juridique.

b. Questions culturelles

Recommandations

No. 17. Il est recommandé au Conseil Ministériel de renforcer et de développer les recherches entreprises à l'échelon national en matière de paix et de conflits et d'accroître les ressources financières mises à la disposition du Comité internordique compétent en la matière pour lui permettre de réaliser en toute indépendance des projets de recherche.

No. 18. Il est recommandé au Conseil Ministériel de constituer un comité d'enquête et d'élaborer un projet de mesures communes destinées à améliorer l'approvisionnement de la Finlande en documents d'enseignement et d'information relatifs aux autres Pays nordiques. Il est particulièrement fait mention de l'activité des lecteurs itinérants, des cours de langues scandinaves et d'un Centre d'information.

Déclarations d'opinion

No. 5. Le Conseil Nordique exprime le souhait qu'à l'avenir le Rapport du Conseil Ministériel rende également expressément compte des mesures de planification qui, sans avoir abouti à un nouveau programme d'action, impliquent néanmoins la révision du programme préexistant, rende compte de la réaction du Conseil Ministériel aux déclarations d'opinion adoptées par le Conseil Nordique et fournisse un décompte sommaire des sommes consacrées à la coopération culturelle internordique au cours de l'exercice ayant précédé l'année sur laquelle porte ce rapport. Par ailleurs, le Conseil Nordique y constate un certain manque de clarté dans l'exposé de sa collaboration avec le Conseil Ministériel en matières budgétaires et de discussions mutuelles. De plus, il considère qu'il devrait être procédé à une étude commune en vue de la rationalisation des rapports et communications qui lui sont adressés.

No. 7. Le Conseil Nordique considère qu'il conviendrait de résoudre au plus tôt le problème de communication automatique à sa Commission culturelle de certains documents élaborés au sein d'organismes gouvernementaux. Il se prononce par ailleurs en faveur d'une majoration substantielle des crédits alloués au Fonds culturel nordique.

c. Questions de politique sociale

Recommandations

No. 3. Il est recommandé au Conseil Ministériel d'organiser la formation internordique spécialisée d'enseignants en matière de physiothérapie.

No. 4. Il est recommandé au Conseil Ministériel d'étudier les possibilités d'organiser la formation de spécialistes de radiothérapie.

No. 5. Il devrait être procédé à titre expérimental pendant une période de cinq ans à des recherches concernant les états de stress provenant de l'environnement du travail.

No. 6. Il conviendrait de trouver des manières adéquates de sauvegarder les droits légaux des patients et de répondre à leurs besoins d'information au sujet des traitements dont ils font l'objet.

No. 8. Il devrait être organisé sans délai une étude des modalités adéquates d'une recherche coordonnée et intégrée relative à l'usage des produits toxiques.

No. 27. Le Conseil Nordique recommande l'étude des problèmes relaaccess to documents in joint Nordic co-operation bodies to the Nordic Council prior to any final decisions, and to submit to the Nordic Council the drafts of future agreements concerning the joint Nordic bodies and their legal position, before they are put before the national parliaments.

b. Cultural questions

Recommendations

No 17. The Council of Ministers is asked to strengthen and develop peace and conflict research in the Nordic countries on a national plane, as well as to put increased funds at the disposal of the Joint Nordic Committee in this field to carry out research projects independently.

No 18. The Council of Ministers is asked to make an inquiry and work out proposals for joint measures to improve the supply in Finland of educational and information material on the other Nordic countries. The scheme of visiting teachers and courses in the Nordic languages, as well as the establishing of a Nordic language and information centre, are especially mentioned.

Declarations of Opinion

No 5. The Nordic Counsil wishes to find in the Report by the Council of Ministers an explicit account of planning which has not resulted in a new programme of action but involves a revision of the current programme; an account of the Council of Ministers' reaction to the Declarations of opinion adopted by the Nordic Council, and a summarised audit statement concerning the funds used for Nordic cultural co-operation in the year preceeding the year that the Report covers. It is also stated that there is some lack of clarity in the presentation of the collaboration between the Nordic Council and the Council of Ministers on budgetary questions and mutual discussions. Also, a joint study should be carried out on how to rationalise the methods of reporting to the Council through communications regarding steps taken to implement earlier Council recommendations and through reports from Nordic institutions.

No 7. The question of an automatic communication of certain types of documents produced within government organs to the Cultural Committee of the Council should be solved as soon as possible. It is also stated that the Nordic Cultural Fund should be allotted substantially increased funds.

c. Questions concerning Social Policy

Recommendations

No 3. The Council of Ministers is asked to carry out joint Nordic specialised training in the teaching of physiotherapy.

No 4. The Council of Ministers is asked to examine the feasibility of arranging joint Nordic courses for the training of specialists in radiotherapy.

No 5. A joint Nordic research project concerning stress in the occupational environment should be carried out, on a trial basis during a five-year period.

No 6. Suitable forms should be found to safeguard the security of patients through legal regulations and to implement measures suitable to cover their need of information on their treatment.

No 8. A study should be commissioned, without delay, of suitable forms for co-ordinated and integrated research into the use of intoxicants.

tifs à la création d'un Institut nordique de recherche en matière d'archipèles.

No. 28. Il est recommandé au Conseil Ministériel de poursuivre l'élaboration des suggestions visant à sa sauvegarde des types de nature et de biotopes d'intérêt internordique et partant d'une division de la région nordique en zones naturelles homogènes tout en tenant compte des intérèts existant aux échelons local et régional.

Déclarations d'opinion

No. 2. C'est avec satisfaction que le Conseil Nordique constate l'inauguration des travaux du Comité nordique de fonctionnaires en matière d'environnement du travail. Il souligne que l'aspect législatif de la coopération ne doit pas être négligé dans ce domaine. En considération de la Convention en matière de protection de l'environnement qui doit être signée au cours de sa XXIIe session et de la Conférence d'Helsinki ayant réuni en mars 1974 des représentants de tous les Etats riverains de la Baltique, le Conseil Nordique déclare qu'une fois ratifiées les conventions internationales doivent être complétées par des accords bilatéraux. Les pourparlers dano-suédois en vue de la conclusion d'un accord sur la protection de l'Oeresund contre les pollutions doivent être menés à bien le plus tôt possible et des mesures pratiques doivent être prises pour parer à la pollution du Skagerack et du Kattegat. Il convient d'envisager à nouveau les possibilités de recherche internordique en matière de protection de l'environnement. Par ailleurs, le Conseil Nordique désire recevoir un rapport sur les mesures prises en vue de réduire les émanations dans l'atmosphère de dioxyde de soufre et autres matières polluantes.

No. 8. Le Conseil Ministériel devrait soumettre aux commentaires du Conseil Nordique le projet de révision de la Convention nordique de 1965 en matière de sécurité sociale. Il convient de développer davantage les échanges de vues entre la Commission de politique sociale et les Ministres concernés par ses travaux. Le Conseil Nordique et le Conseil Ministériel doivent délibérer de concert avec les partenaires du marché de l'emploi. Le Conseil Nordique désire être informé au sujet des observations recueillies à la lumière de l'accord sur la canalisation de la main-d'oeuvre finno-suédoise par les bureaux de placement. Il souhaite délibérer le plus tôt possible avec le Conseil Ministériel au sujet d'un programme internordique d'action en matière de politique de l'emploi. Les possibilités d'instaurer un marché internordique du travail pour les vétérinaires doivent également faire l'objet d'un nouvel examen.

d. Questions relatives aux transports et aux communications

Recommandations

No. 9. Une étude doit être consacrée au plus tôt à la question du marquage des médicaments et autres substances contribuant à réduire les facultés des usagers de la route.

No. 10. Le Conseil Nordique recommande aux Gouvernements finlandais et norvégien de construire au plus tôt un pont sur le Tana à Utsjoki (Utsjoki kyrkby).

No. 11. Il conviendrait d'organiser une recherche internordique en matière de bruits de la circulation et de rechercher la possibilité de recourir à des critères uniformes touchant la limitation de ces bruits.

No. 12. Des mesures devraient être prises aux fins de rendre obligatoire dans les Pays Nordiques l'usage des ceintures de sécurité à bord des véhicules automobiles.

No. 13. Il devrait être procédé à une enquête au sujet de la formation internordique des cadres de la profession des hôtels et restaurants.

No. 14. Il est recommandé aux Gouvernements finlandais et suédois de construire au plus tôt un pont sur le Muonio à Kolari.

No 27. The questions of the establishment of a Nordic institute for archipelagic research should be investigated.

No 28. The Council of Ministers is asked to continue the work on drafting proposals for the protection of types of nature and biotopes of common Nordic interest, based on a division of the countries into homogenous natural geographical zones and with special consideration shown to the existing interests at local and regional level.

Declarations of Opinion

No 2. The Nordic Council notes with satisfaction that a Committee has been set up and work begun on occupational environmental problems. The Council emphasizes that the legislative side of co-operation should not be neglected in this field. With reference to the Convention on Protection of the Environment to be signed during the 22nd session, and to the Helsinki Conference of all the Baltic coastal states, March 1974, the Council states that international agreements should, when warranted, be supplemented by bilateral ones. Denmark and Sweden should conclude negotiations on an agreement to protect the Sound, steps should be taken to deal with pollution in the Skagerack and the Kattegatt. The possibilities of joint Nordic research projects in the environmental field should be reviewed. Furthermore, the Nordic Council wishes to receive a report on the steps taken to reduce the emission into the air of sulphur dioxide and other pollutants.

No 8. The Nordic Council of Ministers should submit the draft text revising the Nordic Social Security Convention of 1955 to the Nordic Council for consideration. Further development of the existing contacts between the Council Committee on Social Policy questions and the ministers concerned is called for. Joint discussions should be held between the representative parties of the labour market, on the one hand, and the Nordic Council and the Council of Ministers, on the other. The Council also wishes to have a report on the experience gained after the agreement on canalisation of the Finnish-Swedish labour through labour exchange offices. The Nordic Council also askes for discussions with the Council of Ministers on the draft of a Nordic programme regarding labour market policy. Also, the question of a joint Nordic labour market for veterinary surgeons should be subject to renewed consideration.

d. Traffic and Communications questions

Recommendations

No 9. The question of the marking of medicines and other substances that impede the functions of road-users should be subject to a study without delay.

No 10. The Finnish and Norwegian Governments are urged to construct a bridge over the River Tana at Utsjoki church village.

No 11. Joint Nordic research into road-traffic noise and an examination of the feasibility of employing uniform Nordic criteria in regard to the abatement of road-traffic noise should be undertaken.

No 12. Steps should be taken to make the use of seat-belts in motorcars compulsory in the Nordic countries.

No 13. An investigation should be conducted in respect of joint Nordic training for senior hotel and restaurant staff.

No 14. The Finnish and Swedish Governments are urged, without delay, to construct a bridge over the River Muonio at Kolari.

No. 26. Des mesures devraient être prises au plus tôt en vue de rendre obligatoire l'usage des casques de protection pour la conduite des motocycles.

Déclarations d'opinion

No. 3. Le Conseil Nordique déclare désirer en matiére de coopération des rapports plus détaillés en ce qui concerne la sécurité de la circulation routière. Il désire également que le Conseil Ministériel réponde à ses déclarations d'opinion et qu'il lui soit donné la possibilité de suivre les travaux portant sur les projets STINA (analyse des structures et coûts du système routier) et NORDKOLT (transport collectif dans les zones urbaines) et de s'en entretenir avec le Conseil Ministériel. Les enquêtes relatives à la politique des transports doivent réserver une place importante aux problèmes énergétiques. Le programme en dix points élaboré par la Commission des communications faisant ressortir un rapport étroit entre le développement des communications et la politique régionale, les Gouvernements devraient poursuivre leurs travaux à ces sujets plus activement que ne le propose le rapport du Conseil Ministériel. Le Conseil Nordique demande par ailleurs l'exploitation dans les zones nordiques en voie de développement de lignes aériennes pendant une période expérimentale et rappelle que les critères traditionnels de rentabilité ne peuvent être retenus avant la poursuite de cette exploitation pendant une période suffisamment longue. Il demande également un rapport annuel sur l'état d'avancement des différents projets routiers et désire recevoir du Conseil Ministériel des propositions au sujet de la poursuite des travaux inaugurés par NORDTRANS concernant les problèmes de transport; il désire également qu'il soit procédé à une enquête sur les possibilités d'harmonisation des tarifs de transport.

No. 6. Vu le rapport du Conseil Ministériel sur la coopération en matière de tourisme, le Conseil Nordique en approuve les principes et déclare que l'extension des services touristiques doit prendre en considération l'intérêt de la population locale tant au niveau régional qu'au point de vue de l'environnement. Il souhaite également délibérer avec le Conseil Ministériel au sujet de la future coopération touristique et il attire l'attention de celui-ci sur la Conférence sur le tourisme que le Conseil Nordique organisera en mai 1975.

e. Questions économiques

Recommandations

No. 15. Il est recommandé au Gouvernements d'engager des négociations avec la CEE en vue de la reconnaissance mutuelle des résultats d'essais.

No. 16. Il est recommandé aux Gouvernements d'oeuvrer en faveur d' une harmonisation internationale des conditions d'octroi de crédits à l'exportation, en tenant particulièrement compte du crédit dans les échanges avec les Etats de l'Europe de l'Est.

No. 19. Des consultations régulières entre Etats nordiques devraient avoir lieu avant l'élaboration de règles en matière d'impositon des personnes physiques.

No. 20. Les Gouvernements devraient étudier les possibilités qu'ont les salariés d'entreprises internordiques de jouir en matière de démocratie industrielle des mêmes droits que ceux des entreprises nationales des secteurs privé et public.

No. 21. Il est recommandé au Conseil Ministériel de présenter une estimation des modalités possibles de coopération internordique en matières industrielles et énergétiques et notamment une étude de la situation à venir concernant l'approvisionnement en pétrole brut et en produits pétroliers.

No 26. Prompt measures should be taken to initiate regulations on the use of protective helmets when driving motor cycles and mopeds.

Declarations of Opinion

No 3. The Council states that road-traffic safety is an area of co-operation where further reports are necessary. The Council also asks for replies from the Council of Ministers to the Council statements in former Declarations of Opinion. It wishes to be given an opportunity to follow the work on the two projects STINA (analysis of road structures and costs) and NORDKOLT (collective transport in urban areas) and to discuss with the Council of Ministers matters arising in this context. Considerable regard should be paid to energy questions in the framing of transport policy. The 10-point programme from the Traffic Committee pointed out a close connection between the expansion of communications and regional policy – the Governments should go further into these questions than proposed in the report. The Council further asks for a programme of regular airline connections for a trial period in the Nordic development areas, and states that traditional profitability criteria cannot be applied until after a sufficiently long trial period. The Council in addition requires an annual report on the current state of various interstate highway projects. The Council further states its wish to receive follow-up plans from the Council of Ministers regarding the far-reaching study of the NORDTRANS committee on transport problems, and asks that an inquiry should be commenced into the feasibility of harmonising the tariffs of transport charges.

No 6. With regard to the Council of Ministers' report on co-operation in the field of tourism, the Council supports the basic ideas expressed in it and further states that, when extending tourist services, attention should be given to the interests of the local population as well as to regional and environmental viewpoints. The Council also wishes to discuss with the Council of Ministers future touristic co-operation, and draws the Council of Ministers' attention to the conference on tourism of the Nordic Council, May 1975.

e. Economic questions

Recommendations

No 15. The Governments are urged to start discussions with the EEC on the reciprocal recognition of test results.

No 16. The Governments are urged to work for a global co-ordination of the terms of export credits, with special attention given to credits in trade with the East European countries.

No 19. There should be regular consultations between the Nordic countries before the framing of rules on the taxation of private individuals.

No 20. The Governments should study the possibilities for employees of joint Nordic enterprises to have the same rights in respect to industrial democracy as employees of enterprises organised on a national basis.

No 21. The Council of Ministers is requested to present an evaluation of possible forms for Nordic co-operation in the fields of industry and energy, including the question of future supply situation for crude oil and oil products.

No 22. The possibilities of a joint utilisation of resources within the field of surface chemistry and colloidal research should be investigated.

No. 22. Il conviendrait d'étudier les possibilités d'une utilisation en commun des ressources en matière de recherche dans la domaine de la chimie des surfaces et des colloïdes.

No. 23. Il conviendrait d'étudier la création d'un Fonds de coopération en matière de politique régionale dans les régions dans les régions septentrionales des Pays nordiques.

Déclaration d'opinion

No. 4. Le Conseil Nordique suppose que l'extension du cadre institutionnel de la coopération internordique permettra l'adoption de mesures plus importantes de coopération. Il demande au Conseil Ministériel d'émettre en novembre ou en décembre une déclaration préliminaire au sujet de son rapport à venir. Il conviendrait de délibérer au sujet de la procédure à suivre lors de l'examen du budget. Le Conseil se déclare satisfait de la coopération internordique touchant les règles d'origine énoncées dans les conventions conclues avec la CEE et avec l'AELE. Il désire souligner l'importance d'une libéralisation sans cesse croissante du commerce mondial. En ce qui concerne la réforme du système monétaire, il se déclare d'accord avec les directives élaborées par les Gouvernements nordiques. C'est avec intérêt qu'il a pris note de l'allocation supplémentaire proposée en faveur du Fonds de Développement technologique et industriel; il n'a aucune objection à formuler en ce qui concerne les priorités proposées pour les différents secteurs du programme mais souhaite que les projets adoptés dans le cadre de ce dernier soient portés à sa connaissance. Il déclare que le NORDTEST devrait faire fonction d'organisme de recherche dans l'éventualité de négociations avec la CEE au sujet de l'élaboration de normes et de la reconnaissance mutuelle des résultats d'essais. Il approuve l'extension de la coopération dans le domaine de la météorologie. Il prend note de la déclaration du Conseil Ministériel au sujet de l'approvisionnement énergétique et de la possibilité d'une coopération en matière d'énergie. Il prend également note de l'intensification des travaux visant à l'intégration des marchés nordiques du bâtiment. Il se déclare satisfait de l'élaboration à venir d'un projet d'accord en matière de politique régionale. Il recommande l'organisation d'une enquête sur le financement d'une coopération internationale plus étroite entre services publics locaux, enquête dont les résultats devraient lui être communiqués. Il renvoie à la proposition émanant d'un de ses membres et aux délibérations au sein de son Assemblée plénière touchant la coordination institutionnelle des problèmes intéressant les consommateurs. Il exprime le désir d'être tenu au courant des résultats de l'enquête sur la poursuite de la coopération internordique en matière d'aide au développement, et si nécessaire, d'avoir la possibilité d'exprimer son opinion au sujet de ces résultats.

C. ACTIVITES DU CONSEIL MINISTERIEL NORDIQUE EN 1974

Réunions

En 1974, le Conseil Ministériel Nordique (Ministres chargés de la coordination de la coopération internordique) s'est composé des ministres suivants:

Danemark: M. Ove Guldberg, Ministre des Affaires Etrangères
Finlande: M. Pekka Tarjanne, Ministre des Transports et des Communications
Islande: M. Olafur Jóhannesson, Premier Ministre (jusqu'à août)
M. Geir Hallgrímsson, Premier Ministre (à partir de septembre)

No 23. The question of a regional policy fund for the Northern regions of the Nordic countries should be investigated.

Declaration of Opinion

No 4. The Council assumes, *inter alia*, that the enlargement of the organisational framework for Nordic co-operation will lead to greater measures of co-operation. The Council of Ministers is asked to give a preliminary statement on the coming Report by November-December. The procedure used in budget questions should be discussed. The Council states its satisfaction with the co-operation between the countries with respect to rules of origin in the agreements with the EEC and EFTA. The Council wishes to emphasize the importance of a steadily increasing liberalisation of world trade. With respect to a reformed currency system, the Council agrees with the guidelines put forward by the Nordic governments. The Council has noted with interest the additional funds proposed for the Fund for Technological and Industrial Development, and has no objection to the priority ratings of the various programme sectors, but wishes to be kept informed of the projects approved in the framework of the programme. It is also stated that Nordtest should be the responsible Nordic research body, if there are to be discussions with the EEC on the framing of standards and the approval of test results. The Council further agrees to widened co-operation in metrology. The Council takes note of the statement on energy supplies and the feasibility of co-operation in energy. The Council also takes note of the intensified work on integration of the building markets. The Council is satisfied that a draft agreement on regional policy is to be drawn up. Furthermore, there should be an inquiry into the financing of a greater degree of co-operation over the frontiers between local authorities, the findings should then be submitted to the Nordic Council. The Council also makes reference to a members' proposal and to the discussions in the plenary assembly, as regards the new organisational set-up in consumer questions. The Council wishes to be informed about the findings of the inquiry into continued Nordic co-operation in development assistance, and would, if necessary, express an opinion on these findings.

C. ACTIVITIES OF THE NORDIC COUNCIL OF MINISTERS IN 1974

Meetings

In 1974, the Nordic Council of Ministers (Ministers for Nordic Co-operation) consisted of the following Ministers:

Denmark: Minister for Foreign Affairs Mr Ove Guldberg
Finland: Minister for Transport and Communications Mr Pekka Tarjanne
Iceland: Prime Minister Mr Olafur Jóhannesson (until August)
Prime Minister Mr Geir Hallgrímsson (from September)

Norvège: M. Bjartmar Gjerde, Ministre des Affaires Culturelles et de l'Education Nationale
Suède: M. Kjell-Olof Feldt, Ministre du Commerce

Dans sa composition de ministres chargés de la coordination, le Conseil Ministériel s'est réuni en 1974 comme suit: à Reykjavik le 31 janvier, à Stockholm les 15 et 17 février, à Copenhague le 11 mars, à Oslo le 21 mai, à Helsinki le 20 septembre, à Copenhague le 30 octobre, à Ålborg le 6 novembre et à Stockholm le 5 décembre.

En outre, les ministres chargés de la coordination se sont réunis en commun, d'abord à Stockholm le 17 février, avec les Ministres des Finances, le Praesidium et les Présidents de Commission du Conseil Nordique, ensuite, à Ålborg le 8 novembre, avec le Praesidium du Conseil Nordique et le Groupe de travail constitué par ce dernier en vue d'étudier des questions budgétaires et de contrôle. Les Ministres chargés de la coordination ont également rencontré à Oslo le 22 mai des représentants des partenaires du marché de l'emploi.

En 1974, le Conseil Ministériel a tenu avec les ministres spécialisés les réunions suivantes:

Ministres des Affaires Culturelles et de l'Education Nationale: Stockholm, les 15 et 19 février; Reykjavik, le 18 mars, les 14 et 15 juin; Helsinki, le 30 septembre; Ålborg, le 8 novembre; Oslo, le 16 décembre

Ministres du Travail: Stockholm, les 2 et 3 octobre

Ministres de l'Industrie et des Affaires Energétiques: Stockholm, le 15 février

Ministres de l'Industrie: Helsinki, le 19 juin; Rold, le 6 novembre

Ministres de la Justice: Stockholm, le 19 février

Ministres de l'Environnement: Stockholm, le 19 février

Ministres des Affaires Sociales: Ålborg, le 9 novembre

Ministres des Transports et des Communications: Stockholm, le 18 février; Ålborg, le 9 novembre

Ministres du Tourisme: Ålborg, le 7 novembre.

En dehors du cadre des réunions du Conseil Ministériel, les consultations gouvernementales se sont poursuivies dans celui des rencontres des différents ministres spécialisés, ceux-ci ayant tenu avec les Commissions du Conseil Nordique les réunions communes suivantes:

Ministres des Affaires Culturelles et de l'Education Nationale/Commission culturelle: Stockholm, le 15 février; Helsinki, le 30 septembre; Ålborg, le 8 novembre

Ministres de l'Industrie et des Affaires Energétiques/Commission economique: Stockholm, le 16 février

Ministres de la Justice/Commission juridique: Stockholm, le 6 février; Helsinki, le 21 août

Ministres de l'Environnement/Commission de politique sociale: Stockholm, le 17 février

Ministres des Affaires sociales/Commission de politique sociale: Ålborg, 9 novembre

Ministres des Transports et des Communications/Commission des transports et des communications: Stockholm, le 18 février; Ålborg, le 9 novembre.

Secteurs de coopération

Au cours de l'année 1974, le Conseil Ministériel Nordique a oeuvré en faveur du développement et de l'intensification du programme nordique d'action, en portant tout particulièrement son attention sur les problèmes

Norway: Minister for Education Mr Bjartmar Gjerde
Sweden: Minister of Trade Mr Kjell-Olof Feldt

The Council of Ministers, consisting of the Ministers for Nordic co-operation, had the following meetings in 1974: January 31 in Reykjavik, February 15 and 17 in Stockholm, March 11 in Copenhagen, May 21 in Oslo September 20 in Helsinki, October 30 in Copenhagen, November 6 in Ålborg and December 5 in Stockholm.

Furthermore, the Ministers for Nordic Co-operation had joint meetings on February 17 in Stockholm with the Ministers of Finance, the Presidium of the Nordic Council and the Chairmen of the Council Committees, and with the Presidium and the Working group of the Nordic Council on budget and control questions on November 8 in Ålborg. The Ministers for Nordic co-operation had also a joint meeting in Oslo May 22 with representatives for the parties of the Labour market.

In 1974, the Council of Ministers had the following meetings of Ministers with portfolio:

Ministers for Culture and Education: February 15 and 19, Stockholm, March 18, June 14–15, Reykjavik, September 30, Helsinki, November 8, Ålborg and December 16, Oslo

Ministers of Labour: October 2–3, Stockholm

Ministers of Industry and Energy: February 15, Stockholm

Ministers of Industry: June 19, Helsinki and November 6, Rold

Ministers of Justice: February 19, Stockholm

Ministers of Environment: February 19, Stockholm

Ministers of Social Policy: November 9, Ålborg

Ministers of Transport: February 18, Stockholm, November 9, Ålborg

Ministers of Tourism: November 7, Ålborg

Apart from the meetings in the Council of Ministers, there have been consultations between the Governments in other meetings with various Ministers with portfolio.

There have been the following joint meetings between the Ministers with portfolio and Committees of the Nordic Council:

Ministers of Culture and Education with the Cultural committee: February 15, Stockholm, September 30, Helsinki and November 8, Ålborg.

Ministers of Industry and Energy with the Economic Committee: February 16, Stockholm

Ministers of Justice with the Legal Committee: February 6, Stockholm and August 21, Helsinki

Ministers of Environment with Social Policy Committee: February 17, Stockholm

Ministers of Social Policy with the Social Policy Committee: November 9, Ålborg

Ministers of Transport with the Communications Committee: February 18, Stockholm and November 9, Ålborg.

Fields of Co-operation

During 1974 the Nordic Council of Ministers developed and intensifed the co-operation coming within the framework of the Nordic Action Programme. It paid particular attention to energy and labour-market ques-en matière d'énergie et de marché de l'emploi. Les points de vue qu'il aura adoptés à la suite de l'enquête nordique en matière d'énergie ainsi qu'un programme de coopération dans le domaine de la politique de l'emploi seront exposés dès qu'ils auront été élaborés.

En 1974, le Conseil Ministériel a étendu ses activités à de nouveaux secteurs, la coopération internordique portant actuellement sur les principaux domaines suivants:

a) législation
b) enseignement, recherche et activités générales d'ordre culturel
c) politique sociale et problèmes d'hygiène et de santé
d) problèmes relatifs au marché de l'emploi
e) problèmes relatifs à l'environnement du travail
f) problèmes relatifs à la protection de l'environnement
g) problèmes de politique commerciale
h) problèmes de politique monétaire et financière
i) politique industrielle et énergétique
j) politique régionale
k) problèmes concernant les consommateurs
l) problèmes de transports et de communications
m) problèmes touristiques
n) problèmes d'aide au developpement.

Le Conseil Ministériel a fait procéder à une enquête au sujet de l'heure d'été et de la nouvelle heure normale (NU 12/74) et dont l'introduction est maintenant envisagée dans les Pays nordiques. Sur sa demande, il a été procédé à une étude du problème touchant l'électorat et l'éligibilité aux assemblées municipales et départementales en faveur des ressortissants nordiques résidant dans un pays autre que celui dont ils possèdent la nationalité. Le rapport portant sur cette étude était achevée en mars 1975.

Le Conseil Ministériel a consacré une attention particulière aux incidences que comporte dans différents domaines la diversité des relations entretenues par les Etats nordiques avec les Communautés Européennes, diversité qui n'a toutefois pas suscité de problèmes majeurs pour la coopération internordique et n'a pas mis obstacle au maintien pour l'essentiel de la liberté des échanges commerciaux entre les Pays nordiques.

Financement de la coopération internordique

Le Conseil Ministériel finance la coopération internordique au moyen de son budget général, de son budget culturel et du Fonds industriel nordique. En vertu d'une décision de portée générale, les dépenses sont réparties entre les différents Etats nordiques en proportion de leur produit national brut, à savoir 22% pour le Danemark, 16% pour la Finlande, 1% pour l'Islande, 16% pour la Norvège et 45% pour la Suède. C'est par ailleurs au Conseil Ministériel qu'il appartient de fixer les crédits alloués aux projets nordiques d'assistance.

Financement des activités du Conseil Ministériel en 1974 et 1975

	1974 (Cr. 1.000)	1975 (Cr. 1.000)
Budget général du Conseil Ministériel (Cr. N)	6.225	13.883
Budget culturel (Cr. D)	33.700	38.656
Fonds industriel nordique (Cr. S)	10.000	10.000

In convient de signaler que la majeure partie de la coopération internordique au sens large de ce terme est financée d'une manière autre que celle exposée ci-dessus, surtout par les budgets nationaux.

tions. The Council of Minister's decision arising from the report of the Nordic Committee of Officials on Energy Questions, and a programme for co-operation in the field of labour-market policy, will be made known as soon as they have been finalised.

During 1974 the Council of Ministers extended its activities to certain fresh areas. The fields of co-operation now comprises the following:

a) legislation
b) education, research and general cultural activities
c) social policy and health questions
d) labour-market questions
e) questions concerning the occupational environment
f) questions concerning the environment
g) trade-policy questions
h) monetary and financial questions
i) industrial policy and energy policy
j) regional policy
k) consumer questions
l) transportation and communications questions
m) tourist questions
n) development-assistance questions

The Council of Ministers has commissioned an inquiry into summer time/new normal time in the Nordic region (NU 12/74), which is now being considered in the Nordic countries. An inquiry, commissioned by the Council of Ministers, too, is also being made into the question of municipal franchise and the eligibility of Nordic nationals who reside in a country other than the Nordic country whose nationals they are, to stand in municipal elections in their country of residence. The findings of this inquiry were available in March 1975.

The Council of Ministers has devoted special attention to the consequences in certain fields of the fact that the Nordic countries are linked to the EEC in different forms. However no major problems for Nordic co-operation have emerged. The free trade established between the Nordic countries has accordingly been maintained in all essential areas.

The Financing of Nordic Co-operation

The Council of Ministers finances its co-operation in the following way: the Council of Minister's general budget, the cultural budget and the Nordic Industrial Fund. According to a general decision, costs are borne by the Nordic countries in relation to their gross national products in the following way: Denmark 22%, Finland 16%, Iceland 1%, Norway 16%, Sweden 45%. In addition, the Council of Ministers authorises funds to be made available for Nordic assistance projects.

The *financing of the work of the Council of Ministers in 1974 and 1975* was as follows:

	1974 (kr. 1.000)	1975 (kr. 1.000)
The Council of Minister's General Budget (Nkr)	6.225	13.883
The Cultural Budget (Dkr)	33.700	38.656
The Nordic Industrial Fund (Skr)	10.000	10.000

It should be noted that the major part of Nordic co-operation in a wider sense is financed in ways other than those recorded above, principally from the national budgets.

Prises de contact avec les partenaires du marché de l'emploi

En 1974, les prises de contact du Conseil Ministériel avec les partenaires du marché de l'emploi en sont restées à la phase introductive. Il a décidé de les inviter à des entretiens annuels portant sur des problèmes d'intérêt commun. L'une de ces rencontres tenue en mai 1974 a réuni des représentants des groupements syndicaux internordiques et notamment les présidents de la plupart des organismes syndicaux centraux des Pays nordiques, le président de la Fédération Nordique des Travailleurs du Bâtiment et du Bois et des délégués occupant des postes de direction dans les associations patronales du Danemark, de la Finlande, de la Norvège et de la Suède. Cet entretien a porté notamment sur les problèmes touchant l'environnement du travail et la démocratie industrielle.

Questions de législation

Au cours de l'année 1974, le Conseil Ministériel a élaboré un programme de législation destiné à compléter celui présenté dans le rapport sur la coopération internordique adressé à la XXIe session (1973) du Conseil Nordique. Le Conseil Ministériel a pris tout particulièrement en considération les points de vue exprimés par la Commission juridique du Conseil Nordique lors de l'élaboration de la recommandation No 1/1974 concernant la coopération internordique en matière de législation et à l'occasion des entretiens qui ont eu lieu entre cette commission et les ministres au sujet de cette recommandation.

Les délibérations du Conseil Ministériel dans le cadre de ce programme ont porté sur les lois régissant le mariage, les contrats d'assurance, la réparation des dommages causés, l'assurance de la circulation, la protection de l'intégrité personnelle, les marques de fabrique et de commerce, le cautionnement, les infractions pénales portant atteinte aux biens et sur les problèmes juridiques afférents aux plateformes de forage pétrolier.

Les agents de liaison pour la coopération internordique en matière de législation ont été remplacés en 1974 par un ,,Comité de fonctionnaires pour les problèmes de législation.''

Coopération en matières culturelles

Les organes instaurés par l'Accord culturel ont adopté des modalités fixes de planification à long terme de la coopération. Dans la limite de ses attributions, chacun des comités consultatifs a élaboré un plan de poursuite de cette coopération, ces plans ayant constitué le point de départ des délibérations que le Conseil Ministériel a tenues à ce sujet en juin 1974. En automne, des entretiens avec la Commission culturelle du Conseil Nordique ont porté sur la planification des activités culturelles. Sur la base de ces travaux préparatoires, le Conseil Ministériel a approuvé au cours de sa réunion du 16 décembre 1974 les lignes directrices de la coopération en matières culturelles (NU 1974: 24).

En matière d'enseignement, cette coopération porte essentiellement sur l'enseignement public obligatoire, visant plus particulièrement à son harmonisation internordique. Toutefois, dans un proche avenir, les initiatives concerneront plus particulièrement l'enseignement professionnel, l'éducation des adultes et l'enseignement supérieur.

En matière de recherche, il sera reconnu une haute priorité au développement des contacts entre chercheurs et organismes nordiques de recherche, à fin de stimuler les échanges de chercheurs et d'apporter un soutien efficace aux rencontres scientifiques internordiques.

Contracts with the parties on the labour-market

Contacts between the Council of Ministers and the parties on the labour market have not yet progressed beyond the introductory stage in 1974.

The Council of Ministers has decided to invite the parties on the labour market to annual discussions on matters of common interest. Such discussions were held in May 1974 and were attended by the Joint Nordic trade union organisations represented by such persons as the chairmen of most trade union central organisations in the Nordic region and by the chairmen of the Nordic Federation of Building and Wood Worker Unions, and of prominent representatives of the employers' associations in Denmark, Finland, Norway and Sweden. There was a discussion of a number of matters, among them the integration of the Nordic building markets, problems concerned with he occupational environment, as well as industrial democracy.

Legislative questions

In 1974 the Council of Ministers drew up a programme of legislation which is intended to supplement the programme presented in the report on Nordic co-operation to the 21st session of the Nordic Council in 1973. When doing so, the Council of Ministers stressed in particular the views put forward by the Legal Standing Committee of the Nordic Council when it was drafting Recommendation No 1/1974 concerning Nordic co-operation on legislation and the discussions that were held between the Standing Committee and the Ministers on the Recommendation.

In conjunction with the work on the programme of legislation, the Council of Ministers has in particular studied the following spheres in 1974: marriage legislation, laws relating to insurance contracts, legislation relating to damages, legislation on road-traffic insurance, the protection of personal integrity, legal problems concerned with oil-drilling platforms, the right to use a trade-mark, personal guarantees and offences against property.

During 1974 the former system for Nordic legislative co-operation was superseded by the creation of a Committee of Senior Officials for Legislative Questions.

Cultural Co-operation

The bodies coming under the Cultural Agreement, have given their co-operation in a long term permanent form. The consultative committees, each in its own field, has drawn up plans for future co-operation. These plans provided one of the bases for the Council of Minister's talks on future co-operation at a meeting held in June 1974. During the autumn conversations were held with the Nordic Council's Cultural Standing Committee on the planning of work in the cultural field. In view of the preparatory work done on the matter, the Council of Ministers, at its meeting on 16th December 1974, approved the guide-lines for Nordic cultural co-operation (NU 1974:24).

In the sphere of education, the main emphasis in this co-operation has been on activities within the comprehensive-school systems. The work to be undertaken has been given priorities so that the main emphasis has been on harmonisation; it will also concern other fields of educational co-operation, above all vocational education, adult education and higher education.

The question of wider scientific contact between research workers and research institutions in the Nordic region are to be given high priority. Measures will be taken to stimulate the exchange of Nordic researchers to support Nordic scientific conferences and symposia.

En matières culturelles générales, l'élément essentiel a été en 1974 l'enquête sur la coopération internordique en matière de radiodiffusion et de télévision. Le rapport final émanant du Comité de la télévision auprès du Conseil Ministériel (NU 1974: 19), qui esquisse les solutions techniques et juridiques visant à une extension de la coopération internordique en matière de télévision. En vue de servir la coopération dans le domaine de la littérature, il a été instauré à partir de 1975 une activité expérimentale hautement prioritaire visant à la traduction en langues scandinaves et finnoise d'ouvrages littéraires nordiques.

Politique sociale

La coopération internordique en matière de politique sociale repose essentiellement sur la Convention nordique de sécurité sociale de 1955, dont il importe que les dispositions, actuellement en cours de révision, soient adaptées aux nouvelles conditions sociales, aux besoins des individus et aux amendements législatifs adoptés dans les différents Pays nordiques au cours de ces dernières années.

Il a été conclu un accord nordique sur les prestations octroyées en cas de maladie, de grossesse et d'accouchement et qui doit en principe entrer en vigueur en 1975, abrogeant l'accord de 1967 sur le transfert des bénéficiaires de l'assurance maladie.

Le Conseil Ministériel a décidé l'instauration à partir de 1975 d'une Commission des produits pharmaceutiques, dont le secrétariat sera installé en Suède pour une période initiale de quatre ans, à l'expiration de laquelle il sera procédé à un examen de l'opportunité d'une poursuite de cette activité. L'Accord sur la Commission nordique de pharmacopée sera dénoncé et, à dater du 1er janvier 1976, les attributions de cette dernière seront transférées à la Commission des produits pharmaceutiques.

Le Conseil a également décidé l'instauration à dater du 1er janvier 1975 d'un organisme nordique de coopération en matière de recherche sur les drogues, dont le secrétariat sera installé à Oslo et qui est destiné à fonctionner pendant une période expérimentale de trois ans.

Il a également octroyé des crédits à un projet concernant un perfectionnement des méthodes d'estimation des besoins et du rendement en matière de soins médicaux, perfectionnement que réclament tous les Pays nordiques. Il est prévu que ce projet portera sur trois ans. Localisées en Islande, ces activités seront menées en liaison avec le Comité Nordique de statistique médicale.

Pour l'année 1975, le Conseil Ministériel a décidé d'affecter sur le budget nordique 1.150.000 couronnes norvégiennes à la coopération en matière de politique sociale, d'hygiène et de santé.

Problèmes relatifs au marché de l'emploi

Les problèmes relatifs au marché de l'emploi revêtent une importance primordiale tant au point de vue national que pour la coopération internordique.

Un important chômage général règne actuellement au Danemark. Dans tous les Pays nordiques se posent des problèmes de chômage de caractère soit local soit structurel. La Norvège en particulier ainsi que la Finlande et la Suède souffrent d'une pénurie de main-d'oeuvre pour certaines professions.

L'accord conclu entre le Danemark, la Finlande, la Norvège et la Suède sur un marché commun internordique du travail est entré en vigueur le 1er juillet 1954, les Pays nordiques constituant ainsi un tel marché depuis 20 ans. En vertu de cet accord, il n'est plus requis de permis de travail pour

In the general cultural sector the feature of main interest in 1974 has been the inquiry into Nordic radio and television co-operation. The final report of the Council of Minister's Television Committee, (NU 1974:19), outlines the technical and legal solutions that would enable Nordic television co-operation to be enlarged in scope. As regards co-operation in the field of literature, high priority has been given to the introduction, from 1975, of a scheme organised on a trial basis for the translation of works of Nordic literature into the Nordic languages.

Social Policy

Social-policy co-operation in the Nordic region has as its main foundation the 1955 Nordic Social Security Convention. It is of prime importance for the Convention to be adapted to changed conditions in the Nordic communities and to the needs of private individuals, as well as to the amendments to the legislation that have been introduced in the Nordic countries during recent years. A general review of the Convention is now being made.

A Nordic agreement on benefits to be paid in the event of illness, pregnancy and childbirth has been concluded and is to enter into force in 1975. It is to supersede the 1967 agreement concerning the transfer of persons insured under the sickness insurance scheme, etc.

The Council of Ministers has decided to set up a joint Nordic Board for Medicines from 1975. For the first four-year period the Board's Secretariat will be located in Sweden; at the end of that time the Board's future work will be reviewed. The agreement on the Nordic Pharmaceutical Board will be terminated and it is intended that its activities will be transferred to the Board for Medicines on 1st January 1976.

In addition, the Council of Ministers has decided to set up a joint Nordic liaison body for research concerning drugs; it has commenced its work in 1975 for a three-year trial period. Its Secretariat is located in Oslo.

Furthermore, funds have been allocated to a project concerned with finding better methods of measuring the requirements and efficiency of medical care. Such methods are sought in all the Nordic countries. It is expected that this project will be extended over a period of three years. It is to be located in Iceland and to be carried out in consultation with the Nordic Committee on Medical Statistics.

The Council of Ministers has resolved to allocate some Nkr 1.150.000 for 1975 from the Nordic budget for co-operation relating to social policy and public health.

Labour-market questions

Labour-market questions are of central importance, both nationally and for Nordic co-operation.

There is at present widespread general unemployment in Denmark. In all the Nordic countries problems concerned with unemployment of a local and/or structural kind have arisen. However there is a shortage of labour, at least of certain types, in Norway, and also in Finland and Sweden.

The agreement on a common Nordic labour market between Denmark, Finland, Norway and Sweden entered into force on 1st July 1954. The Nordic countries have thus constituted such a market for 20 years. This agreement has meant, among other things, that a Nordic national does not have to hold a labour permit when seeking work in another Nordic les ressortissants nordiques en quête d'un emploi dans un autre Pays nordique, ce qui a permis au cours de ces vingt ans le déplacement de quelque 880.000 personnes à travers les frontières nordiques, la plus grande partie d'entre elles venant s'installer en Suède.

Le Conseil Ministériel a décidé l'élaboration d'un programme visant à la poursuite de la coopération en matière de politique du marché de l'emploi, élaboration qui se poursuit à l'heure actuelle au sein des organismes du Conseil Ministériel. Ce programme énoncera probablement des objectifs et des projets de coopération à court, moyen et long termes. Il présentera une certaine souplesse et pourra être révisé en fonction des besoins de coopération qui se manifesteront. Le Conseil Ministériel se propose de le présenter à l'occasion de la XXIIIe session du Conseil Nordique.

Le Centre de formation professionnelle du marché de l'emploi (AMU) pour la Zone septentrionale, exploité à titre expérimental à Overtorneå depuis 1970 en vertu d'un accord entre la Finlande, la Norvège et la Suède, ayant donné des résultats satisfaisant, les Ministres du Travail de ces trois pays ont décidé la poursuite de ses activités à titre permanent à partir de 1975, un accord devant probablement ratifier prochainement cette décision.

Pour l'année 1975, le Conseil Ministériel a affecté environ 330.000 couronnes norvégiennes à cette coopération touchant le marché de l'emploi.

Problèmes relatifs à l'environnement du travail

Au cours de l'année 1974, il a porté une attention particulière aux possibilités d'accroître l'efficacité de la coopération en matière de médecine du travail et de réglementation visant à la protection des travailleurs.

Il attache un grand prix aux échanges d'information et à la coopération des services publics nordiques dans ce domaine. A l'occasion de leur rencontre à Oslo en mai 1975, les ministres compétents en matière d'environnement du travail s'entretiendront des nouvelles lignes directrices de la législation nordique en ces matières ainsi que de l'enseignement s'y rattachant.

Pour l'année 1975, le Conseil Ministériel a décidé d'affecter environ 220.000 couronnes norvégiennes à la coopération en matière d'environnement du travail.

Problèmes relatifs à la protection de l'environnement

Aux termes de la Convention nordique sur la protection de l'environnement signée en février 1974 par le Danemark, la Finlande, la Norvège et la Suède, les services publics de chacun de ces pays appelés à se prononcer sur la tolérance d'une activité nuisible à l'environnement sont tenus de comparer les intérêts des pays voisins en cette matière avec ceux de leur propre pays.

En mars 1974, les sept Etats riverains de la Baltique ont signé une convention sur la protection de l'environnement marin de ce basin. Ce texte, qui régit les déversements opérés à partir des côtes et ceux provenant des navires, énonce également des dispositions en matière de coopération scientifique.

En avril 1974, le Danemark et la Suéde ont conclu sur la protection contre les polutions de l'Oeresund une convention aux termes de laquelle chacun de ces pays s'engage à prendre des mesures efficaces en vue d'assurer la purification des déversements urbains et industriels.

Le Conseil Ministériel a arrêté les directives de la coopération internordique en matière de protection de la nature: méthodes d'analyse des paysages, division de la Zone nordique en régions naturelles, types de nature country. In the past 20-year period it has been possible for, in round figures, 880.000 persons to migrate over the Nordic frontiers, the majority to Sweden.

The Council of Ministers has decided that a programme is to be drawn up with a view to continuing the present co-operation in the field of labour-market policy. A draft programme is being worked out by the bodies coming under the Council of Ministers. This programme will probably contain targets and joint projects for the short, medium and long term. It will be flexible, which will enable it to be renewed as fresh requirements emerge.

The labour-market training centre (AMU) for the northernmost parts of Finland, Norway and Sweden, which was set up by the Governments of the three countries, has functioned on a trial basis at Övertorneå since 1970, in accordance with an agreement between these countries. In view of the positive experience that has been gained from this centre, the Ministers of Labour in the three countries have decided that the centre will be made permanent in 1975. An agreement to that effect is likely to be ratified shortly.

The Council of Ministers has allocated some Nkr 330.000 for 1975 to be used for co-operation in the labour-market sector.

Questions concerning the occupational environment

During 1974 the Council of Ministers has devoted particular attention to the feasibility of making the joint work done on occupational medicine and industrial safety regulations more efficient.

An exchange of information and co-operation between the authorities in the Nordic countries in regard to this matter will be undertaken. At a meeting in Oslo in May 1975 and elsewhere the Ministers of Labour are to discuss new lines of approach in labour-market legislation in the Nordic area, as well as training in labour-market questions.

For 1975 the Council of Ministers has allocated some Nkr 220.000 for the occupational environment sector.

Environmental questions

The Nordic Environmental Convention was signed in February 1974 by Denmark, Finland, Norway and Sweden. By the Convention when the authorities of each country are examining a question to see if they can permit activities that are detrimental to the environment, they must put the environmental protection interests of their neighbours on the same footing as corresponding interests in their own country.

In March 1974 a Convention on the Protection of the Marine Environment in the Baltic was signed by all the seven coastal states. This Convention regulates both air- and land-based discharges, as well as discharges and dumping from ships. In addition, the Convention contains rules on scientific co-operation.

A Danish-Swedish agreement on protection against pollution in the Sound was signed in April 1974. In this agreement Denmark and Sweden pledge themselves to take effective steps to purify both municipal and industrial discharges.

The Council of Ministers has laid down the guide-lines for Nordic co-operation in the field of nature conservation relating to: methods for analysing types of countryside, the regional division of the Nordic region menacés, espèces animales et végétales de la Zone nordique et sauvegarde des terres de culture.

Le projet afférent à 1975 porte sur des questions relatives à la manutention des déchets, à la protection de la nature et à l'élaboration de procédés de mesure à appliquer dans le cadre d'un programme européen de surveillance et d'estimation des pollutions atmosphériques. Le Conseil Ministériel y a affecté environ 440.000 couronnes norvégiennes.

Problèmes de politique commerciale

La communauté d'action en ce qui concerne les problèmes traités au sein des organismes internationaux constitue une part importante de la coopération internordique.

Le régime d'exemption douanière réalisé dans le cadre de l'AELE et qui a notamment contribué à un accroissement des échanges commerciaux et de la coopération économique entre les Pays nordiques, subsiste à quelques exceptions près entre les Etats actuellement et anciennement membre de cette Association. En étroite coopération avec les autres Etats nordiques, le Danemark devenu membres des Communautés Européennes a oeuvré en faveur de la conservation dans toute la mesure du possible du régime de libre-échange. Conformément aux accords, le désarmement douanier s'est poursuivi entre les Etats nordiques et les Communautés Européennes. C'est ainsi qu'au 1er janvier 1974, les droits de douane frappant les produits industriels ont été réduits de 40% des taux de base et qu'une nouvelle réduction de 20% doit entrer en vigueur le 1er janvier 1975. En ce qui concerne la Finlande, la Norvège et la Suède, il est prévu des délais plus longs de désarmement douanier pour certains produits dits ,,sensibles.'' Les concessions faites par la CEE à l'Islande en matière de produits de la pêche ne sont pas encore entrées en vigueur. Ayant décidé de ne pas adhérer à la CEE, les Iles Féroé ont conclu avec celle-ci un accord particulier de libre-échange prévoyant certaines facilités pour leurs exportations de poissons.

Dans le cadre de la Commission Economique pour l'Europe, les Etats nordiques ont pris l'initiative d'une simplification des documents commerciaux. Les problèmes relatifs aux procédures commerciales (documents, etc.) peuvent entraîner des frais notables pour le commerce international. Le Conseil Ministériel considère q'une simplification de ces procédures permettrait d'importantes économies et un notable accroissement de rendement. Il se propose d'apporter au cours de l'année 1975 son appui à tout projet visant à ce but.

La coopération en matière de politique commerciale continuera à constituer une part importante de ses activités. En vue d'accroître l'efficacité de ces dernières, il a été constitué un Comité de fonctionnaires pour les questions de politique commerciale.

Problèmes de politique monétaire

Les problèmes monétaires internationaux ont revêtu une grande importance au cours de l'année 1974 et il y a lieu de prévoir qu'il en sera de même en 1975. Les grandes perturbations affectant les balances des paiements suscitent des difficultés particulières. Aussi le Conseil Ministériel juge-t-il que l'importance d'une étroite communauté internordique d'action en ces matières ne fera que croître. Jusqu'à maintenant, cette communauté a fonctionné de façon satisfaisante et a permis de mieux défendre les intérêts nordiques sur le plan international. Cette coopération s'est poursuivie sous différentes formes, notamment by principles of physical geography, threatened types of natural features, flora and fauna in the Nordic region, as well as the preservation of the cultivated landscape.

The projects in this field during 1975 concern questions related to the handling of wastes and nature conservation, as well as the working out of measurement methods to be used in a European programme for the monitoring and evaluation of air pollution. For these projects the Council of Ministers has allocated some Nkr 440.000.

Trade-policy questions

Collaboration in regard to issues dealt with in various international bodies are an important part of Nordic co-operation.

The free trade established through EFTA, which has been partly instrumental in increasing the economic co-operation between the Nordic countries and in leading to greatly increased trade, has been retained between the present and previous EFTA countries with few exceptions. Denmark, as a member of the EEC, has worked in close consultation with the other Nordic countries for the retention of free trade between them as far as this is possible. Tariffs have been dismantled between the Nordic countries and the EEC according to the agreements. From 1st January 1974 the customs duties for industrial commodities have been reduced by 40% of the basic tariffs and it is intended that a further reduction of 20% will be made from 1st January 1975. In Finland's, Norway's and Sweden's case, a longer tariff dismantling period has been laid down for certain "sensitive" commodities. The EEC concessions to Iceland for fish products have not yet entered into force. The Faroe Islands have decided not to accede to the EEC but they have concluded a special free-trade agreement with the Community which permits, for instance, some relief on the export of fish.

At an earlier date the Nordic countries took an initiative in the ECE for as simplification of trade documents. Problems connected with trade procedures (documents, etc) may involve substantial costs for internationl trade. The Council of Ministers considers that a simplification of these procedures would lead to considerable saving and to an increase in efficiency. The Council of Ministers intends to support concrete projects in this field during 1975.

Trade-policy co-operation accounts for an important part of the work of the Council of Ministers. In order to make work in this sector more efficient, a special Committee of Senior Officials for Trade-Policy Questions has been set up.

Questions concerning monetary policy

International monetary problems have been of central importance during 1974 and it can be expected that they will continue to be during the years to come. Major disturbances in the balance-of-payments create special difficulties. On this account the Council of Ministers considers that the importance of close collaboration between the Nordic countries on these questions will increase. Nordic co-operation has functioned well so far; it has made it easier to satisfy Nordic interest internationally. This co-operation has taken place in various ways, such as by:

- par des délibérations entre les Ministres des Finances,
- par des rencontres à dates régulières entre les Chefs des banques centrales nordiques,
- par une communauté d'action ou dans le cadre des champs d'activité du Fonds monétaire international et de la Banque mondiale, à la fois au sein des Conseils d'administration de ces deux organismes et à l'échelon ministériel dans les nouveaux comités interimaire et de développement,
- par une communauté d'action dans le cadre de l'OCED.

Coopération en matière industrielle

La coopération entre entreprises industrielles nordiques a continué à se développer à un rythme accéléré, les activités petrolières en Norvège ouvrant à cet égard de nouvelles possibilités d'avenir.

Le principal instrument dont il dispose pour financer cette coopération industrielle consiste dans le Fonds Nordique de Technologie et de Développement Industriel ou ,,Fonds industriel," dont les activités ont débuté en 1973 et à la disposition duquel le Conseil Ministériel a mis successivement 10 millions de couronnes suédoises pour la période écoulée jusqu'au 31 décembre 1974 et 10 autres millions pour chacun des exercices 1975 et 1976. Il accordera la priorité aux techniques de l'environnement, des secteurs sanitaires et des transports ainsi que, selon une décision plus récente, aux techniques de l'énergie et des moyens d'action. Jusqu'au 15 novembre 1974, le ,,Fonds industriel" avait subventionné 23 projets pour une somme globale d'environ 10 millions de couronnes suédoises.

Problèmes énergétiques

En 1974, les problèmes énergétiques sont passés au premier plan de l'actualité nordique. Le rapport de l'enquête nordique en matières énergétiques a été déposé en 1975 et la décision prise à son sujet par le Conseil Ministériel fut connue lors de la Session de Reykjavik en 1975.

La coopération dans le cadre du NORDEL ainsi que la communauté d'action en matière de développement de l'énergie nucléaire ont continué à revêtir une grande importance. Les prises de contacts internordiques lors de l'adoption de mesures nationales visant à limiter les effets de la crise énergétique de 1973–1974 se sont révélées utiles. Dans les Pays nordiques, cette crise a renforcé le besoin d'une intervention étatique visant à assurer l'approvisionnement énergétique et une meilleure utilisation de l'énergie, les considérations de prix, d'approvisionnement et de protection de l'environnement jouant à cet égard un rôle important; des mesures d'économie y ont été prises, entraînant déjà un ralentissement de la croissance de la consommation d'énergie.

Secteur du bâtiment

Le rapide accroissement des travaux d'aménagement en Norvège par suite de l'expansion du secteur pétrolier ne fait que souligner le besoin d'une concentration accrue dans l'industrie du bâtiment. Les difficultés résident essentiellement dans les différences internordiques en matière de réglementation de la construction et de la négociation des marchés.

Le programme d'action du Conseil Ministériel souligne l'importance des efforts visant à assurer l'intégration des marchés du bâtiment et à éliminer les obstacles qui s'y opposent encore. Le Conseil poursuit actuellement la réalisation de deux projets de coordination en matière de réglementation

- discussions between Ministers of Finance,
- regular meetings between the heads of the Nordic Central Banks,
- a common front within the province of the International Monetary Fund and of the World Bank by Nordic representatives, on the one hand, on the Boards of Governors of the two bodies and, on the other, at Ministerial level on the recently established interim and development committees,
- co-ordinated action within the framework of the OECD.

Industrial co-operation

Co-operation between firms in the Nordic countries has continued to develop at an increasing speed. The current activity within the Norwegian oil sector has opened up fresh opportunities for co-operation in the future.

The Council of Minister's most important instrument for the financing of co-operation in the industrial sector is the Nordic Fund for Technology and Industrial Development – the Industrial Fund – which began to function on 1st July 1973. For the period up to 31st December 1974 the sum of Skr 10 million has been put at the disposal of the fund. Finally, the Council of Ministers has decided that Skr 10 million is also to be allocated to the Fund for 1976. The following spheres are being given priority: environmental technology, technology for the health sector and transportation technology. In addition, energy and resources technology are also to be given priority. Up to 15th November 1974 the Fund had given financial assistance to 23 projects to the tune of some Skr 10 million.

Energy questions

During the year energy questions have been of great prominence in the Nordic countries. The Nordic Committee of Officials on Energy Questions presented its report in early 1975. A special report on these questions was given by the Council of Ministers to the 23rd session of the Nordic Council in Reykjavik in 1975.

Co-operation through the medium of NORDEL (the Joint Nordic Electricity Producers' Council) has continued to be of great importance, just as has the collaboration established in regard to the development of nuclear power. The Nordic contacts taken up when national measures were being adopted to limit the harmful effects of the oil-supply crisis in the winter of 1973–74 have proved very valuable. The energy crisis in the Nordic countries has given rise to increased demands for State activity and planning to secure the supply of energy and to attain a more effective use of energy. Consideration has to be given to the price, supply and environmental aspects of the problem. Concrete steps have been taken in the Nordic countries to save energy; they have already slowed down the rate of increase in energy consumption.

The building sector

The need for greater integration in the building sector has been underlined by such factors as the rapidly increasing construction of installations in Norway in connection with the expansion of the oil sector. The most pressing problems are largely to be found in the differences in building regulations, purchasing regulations, etc. in the various Nordic countries.

In its Action Programme the Council of Ministers has put special emphasis on the efforts to secure the integration of the building markets and to remove the obstacles that remain. Two co-ordinating projects – on building rules and on purchasing rules – are now being conducted under the de la construction et de la négociation des marchés. Certaines parties de ce programme ont été réalisées au cours de l'année 1974, les travaux ayant porté essentiellement sur une analyse des obstacles à l'intégration.

Les frais engagés en 1974 par le Conseil Ministériel dans le secteur du bâtiment sont estimés à un peu plus de 400.000 couronnes norvégiennes.

Le Conseil Ministériel continuera à accorder une haute priorité aux travaux visant à assurer l'intégration nordique du marché du bâtiment. Pour l'année 1975, il a décidé d'y consacrer environ 1.100.000 couronnes norvégiennes.

Politique régionale

Le programme d'action du Conseil Ministériel en matière de politique régionale vise notamment à un accroissement de la coopération dans les zones frontière et à une coordination des mesures de politique régionale dans les Pays nordiques.

En 1974, les frais afférents aux activités du Conseil dans ce domaine sont estimés à environ 460.000 couronnes norvégiennes, y compris certains crédits affectés à des projets concernant la Zone septentrionale. Ces dépenses ont porté notamment sur une étude des préférences de la population en matière d'environnement, des effets résultant des mesures de politique régionale et des conditions de la planification régionale. Ces projets se poursuivront en 1975.

Parmi les nouveaux projets au titre de l'année 1975, il convient de mentionner une étude des conditions préalables d'une coopération en matière de politique dans les zones frontière à faible densité démographique, un inventaire des conditions régionales dans les Pays nordiques et des méthodes de planification en matière de politique régionale, l'élaboration d'un système d'information pour la planification nationale à l'échelon communal et de procédés d'estimation de différentes solutions alternatives de planification. Par ailleurs, des crédits ont été réservés notamment pour un inventaire des possibilités d'accroissement des échanges commerciaux dans la Zone septentrionale et pour un séminaire industriel concernant cette Zone.

Pour 1975, le Conseil Ministériel a réservé environ 1.700.000 couronnes norvégiennes pour la coopération en matière de politique régionale.

Problèmes concernant les consommateurs

Le Conseil Ministériel considère qu'une intensification de la coopération en ces matières peut entraîner d'importants avantages pour les consommateurs des Pays nordiques. Aussi a-t-il décidé d'étendre son champ d'action à ces problèmes et a constitué un comité de fonctionnaires en la matière. La coopération internordique englobera notamment les examens de produits, les questions de marquage, la publicité et le marketing et les questions touchant à l'enseignement et à l'information. Les résultats d'une étude des mesures possibles de politique des consommateurs en matière de services seront publiés prochainement dans la Série NU.

Le Conseil Ministériel a alloué une subvention de 1.310.000 couronnes norvégiennes à la réalisations du programme au titre de l'année 1975.

Problèmes en matières de transports, de communications et de sécurité de la circulation

Les principes de la coopération en matière de transports et de communications sont énoncés par l'Accord nordique sur les transports, lequel est entré en vigueur en 1973.

Dans le cadre du champ d'action du Conseil Ministériel, il a été inauguré auspices of the Council of Ministers. Certain sections of the Action Programme have been followed up in 1974. Work has been concentrated on an analysis of obstacles to integration.

It is estimated that expenditure in the building sector by the Council of Ministers in 1974 will be rather more than Nkr 400.000.

The Council of Ministers will continue to give high priority to work on securing integration within the Nordic building market. The Council of Ministers has resolved to allocated some Nkr 1.100.000 for this sector in 1975.

Regional policy

The Council of Minister's Action Programme in the field of regional policy aims at, among other things, increasing co-operation in the frontier regions and at co-ordinating regional policy measures in the Nordic countries.

It is estimated that the Council of Minister's regional policy activities in 1974 will cost some Nkr 460.000, this sum including certain expenditure on projects in the region north of the Arctic circle. These funds have been used for such matters as an inquiry into the environmental preferences of the population, into the effects of the regional-policy funds and into administrative conditions for regional planning. This project is to continue in 1975.

New projects in 1975 will include a study of the pre-conditions for co-operation in regard to policy concerned with the sparsely populated areas in the frontier regions, a survey of the regional conditions in the Nordic countries and of methods for regional-policy planning, work on an information system for community planning at municipal level and methods for evaluating the various p anning alternatives. In addition, funds have been set aside for such matters as a survey of the feasibility of increasing trade in the region north of the Arctic Circle and also for an industrial seminar for that area.

For 1975 the Council of Ministers has allocated the sum of about Nkr 1.7 million for regional-policy co-operation.

Consumer questions

The Council of Ministers considers that intensified co-operation in the field can benefit consumers in the Nordic countries very considerably. It has therefore decided to extend its sphere of activity to cover consumer questions and to appoint a committee of senior officials for that field. Nordic co-operation will cover such matters as the examination of goods, marking questions, advertising and marketing, as well as training and information questions. A study of possible consumer measures in the field of services is shortly to be published in the Nordic Official Reports series.

The Council of Ministers has laid down and granted funds (Nkr 1.310. 000) for a project programme in 1975.

Transportation, communications and road-safety questions

The principles for co-operation in the field of transportation and communications are laid down in the Nordic transport agreement, which entered into force in 1973.

In the Council of Minister's field of activity two projects were commencau cours de l'année 1973 un projet STINA concernant l'action exercée sur les chaussées routières par le volume du trafic et les charges sur essieux et un projet NORDKOLT concernant les systèmes à venir de trafic collectif dans les agglomérations nordiques. Dans le cadre de ce dernier projet, il a été déposé un rappport partiel portant sur les besoins actuels et à venir en matière de déplacements, sur le confort de ces déplacements dans les agglomérations nordiques, sur les facteurs touchant à l'environnement en matière de transports dans ces agglomérations et sur les problèmes de sécurité qui s'y rattachent. Les résultats obtenus dans le cadre de ces deux projets peuvent revêtir une importance primordiale pour l'économie et la planification des systèmes de liaison en matière de circulation.

Aide aux pays en voie de développement

Les Etats nordiques coopèrent activement et de différentes manières en matière d'aide aux Pays en voie de développement. Sous le contrôle du Conseil Ministériel, se poursuit au Kénya et en Tanzanie la réalisation d'un certain nombre de projets financés en commun.

Les Etats nordiques ont des représentants communs au sein du groupe de la Banque Mondiale, où le Fonds International de Développement (FID) joue un rôle important en matière d'assistance, ainsi qu'au sein du Fonds Africain de Développement et de la Banque Asiatique de Développement. Ils sont également représentés en commun dans le nouveau Comité de développement instauré au sein de la Banque Mondiale et du Fonds Monétaire International. De plus, ils coopèrent étroitement au sein d'un certain nombre d'organismes internationaux d'assistance, principalement dans le cadre de l'ONU.

Les activités nordiques d'assistance s'inspirent du désir, conforme aux voeux des Pays en voie de développement, de les aider à réaliser une plus grande indépendance économique, une amélioration des conditions d'existence des parties les plus pauvres de leur population, une amélioration des possibilités d'enseignement pour toutes les catégories de cette population et une réduction du nombre des chômeurs et des personnes insuffisamment occupées. Le Conseil Ministériel considère qu'une coopération internordique accroît les possibilités d'oeuvrer sur le plan international en faveur de ces objectifs.

D. CONVENTIONS ET ACCORDS

La coopération repose sur un vaste ensemble d'accords différents dont l'étendue et la dignité varient, et dont, à titre d'exemples, seulement certains sont cités ci-dessous.

1. Traité de coopération du 23 mars 1962 entre le Danemark, la Finlande, l'Islande, la Norvège et la Suède avec amendements ultérieurs (Traité d'Helsinki).

Objet: Les parties contractantes doivent s'efforcer de poursuivre et de développer la coopération entre leurs pays en matières juridiques, culturelles, sociales et économiques ainsi que dans les domaines de la protection de l'environnement, des transports et des communications.

2. Convention du 15 mars 1971 entre le Danemark, la Finlande, l'Islande, la Norvège et la Suède en matière de coopération culturelle.

Objet: De renforcer et d'intensifier entre les parties contractantes, la coopération culturelle, au sens large de ce terme, en vue de développer la communauté culturelle nordique et d'accroître au moyen d'une conmmne planification, d'une coordination, d'une collaboration et d'une division du travail, les effets conjugués résultant des contributions fournies par les ed in 1973 – the STINA project relating to the volume of traffic and the effect of axle pressure on the road pavement and the NORDKOLT project relating to future systems of public transport in Nordic built-up areas. One of the reports on the NORDKOLT project has been presented; it deals with present and future travel needs, the travelling standard in built-up areas, environmental factors connected with transportation systems in built-up areas and security problems inherent in such systems. The findings of these two projects may be of great significance for the finance and planning of communications.

Assistance to developing countries

The Nordic countries are co-operating actively in various ways in regard to assistance to the developing countries. Under the auspices of the Council of Ministers a number of jointly financed assistance projects in Kenya and Tanzania are in progress.

The Nordic countries have joint representatives in the World Bank group, where the International Development Association is important from a purely assistance point of view – and in the African Development Fund and the Asiatic Development Bank. Furthermore, the Nordic countries are jointly represented in the recently establishment Development Committee in the World Bank and the International Monetary Fund. The Nordic countries also co-operate closely within a number of international assistance organisations, primarliy those coming within the UN framework.

The assistance co-operation established by the Nordic countries is based on a desire to aid the developing countries – according to their own priorities – in their efforts to achieve greater economic independence, better conditions for the poorest sections of their populations, better educational openings for all groups of the population and a reduction in the number of unemployed and underemployed. In the opinion of the Council of Ministers Nordic co-operation gives a greater potential for work for these goals internationally.

D. CONVENTIONS AND AGREEMENTS

The co-operation is based on a large number of conventions and agreements of various scope and significance. Only a few examples of such conventions and agreements are given below.

1. Treaty of Co-operation of March 23, 1962 between Denmark, Finland, Iceland, Norway and Sweden with subsequent amendments (Helsinki Treaty.)

Aim: The contracting parties shall endeavour to maintain and further develop co-operation between the countries in the juridical, cultural, social and economic fields and also in questions of communications and environmental protection.

2. Agreement on Cultural Co-operation of March 15, 1971 between Denmark, Finland, Iceland, Norway and Sweden.

Aim: to strengthen and intensify cultural co-operation in a wider sense between the contracting parties in order to further develop the cultural community of the Nordic countries and to expand the accumulated results of the contributions of the countries in education, research and other cultural activity by common planning, co-ordination, co-operation and dis-différents pays, et de créer les conditions pratiques de mise en oeuvre d'une coopération satisfaisante.

3. Convention du 6 novembre 1972 entre le Danemark, la Finlande, l'Islande, la Norvège et la Suède en matière de transports et de communications.

Objet: De consolider et d'élargir la coopération en vue d'une organisation rationelle et efficace des transports et des systèmes de communications, et d'améliorer, au moyen d'une coordination, d'une collaboration et d'une division du travail, la mise à profit des travaux réalisés en matière de transports et de communications ainsi que d'en accroître les effets conjugués.

4. Convention nordique du 15 septembre 1955 en matière de sécurité sociale avec amendements ultérieurs.

Objet: De réaliser l'égalité en droits entre les ressortissants d'un Etat signataire séjournant dans un autre Etat signataire et les nationaux de celui-ci dans tous les domaines de la législation en matière de sécurité sociale.

5. Convention relative au marché commun de l'emploi conclu le 22 mai 1954 entre le Danemark, la Finlande, la Norvège et la Suède.

Objet: De garantir la libre circulation de la main-d'oeuvre entre les Pays nordiques.

6. Convention du 19 février 1974 entre le Danemark, la Finlande, la Norvège et la Suède en matière de protection de l'environnement.

Objet: De préserver et d'améliorer l'environnement au moyen d'une lutte contre l'action nuisible exercée sur l'environnement.

7. Accord du 20 février 1973 entre le Danemark, la Finlande, l'Islande, la Norvège et la Suède portant création d'un Fonds nordique de Technologie et de Développement Industriel.

Objet: Le fonds vise à encourager une mise à profit plus efficace des ressources nordiques en matière de technologie et de développement industriel et, ce faisant, à agir en faveur d'une coopération élargie entre les parties contractantes et à contribuer au financement tant de projets intéressant deux ou plusieurs Pays nordiques que de projets internationaux d'intérêt internordique.

8. Accord relatif au statut juridique du personnel des institutions internordiques conclu entre le Danemark, la Finlande, l'Islande, la Norvège et la Suède.

Objet: De créer des règles analogues relatives au statut juridique, y compris les conditions d'engagement et de travail du personnel des institutions internordiques.

9. Protocole du 22 mai 1954 relatif à l'exemption de passeports et de permis de séjour accordée aux ressortissants du Danemark, de la Finlande, de la Norvège et de la Suède résidant dans un Pays nordique autre que leur pays d'origine.

L'Islande a adhéré à ce Protocole le 14 novembre 1955.

tribution of the work and to create practical pre-requisite conditions for a well-functioning co-operation.

3. Agreement on Co-operation in the field of Transport and Communications of November 6, 1972 between Denmark, Finland Iceland, Norway and Sweden.

Aim: to strenthen and develop co-operation aiming at a simplified and efficient system of transport and communications and to achieve a better use and expanded accumulated result of the work in the field of transport and communications by means of co-ordination, co-operation and distribution of the work.

4. Nordic Convention on Social Security of September 15, 1955 between Denmark, Finland, Iceland, Norway and Sweden with subsequent amendments.

Aim: that citizens from one of the contracting countries shall in another Nordic country enjoy the same privileges as the country's own citizens in all fields of legislation on social security.

5. Agreement on a Common Labour Market of May 22, 1954, between Denmark, Finland, Norway and Sweden.

Aim: to create free migration of workers inside the Nordic countries.

6. The Nordic Agreement on the Protection of the Environment of February 19, 1974 between Denmark, Finland, Norway and Sweden.

Aim: to protect and improve the environment by preventing activities detrimental to the environment.

7. Agreement on a Nordic Fund for Technology and Industry of February 20, 1973 between Denmark, Finland, Iceland, Norway and Sweden.

Aim: The aim of the Fund is to encourage a more efficient use of the Nordic resources for technology and industrial development by promoting increased co-operation between the contracting parties and by supporting the financing of projects of interest to two or more Nordic countries as well as international projects of common Nordic interest.

8. Agreement between Denmark, Finland, Norway and Sweden on the Legal Status of Employees.

Aim: to create uniform rules on the legal status, including employment and working conditions for employees in Nordic institutions.

9. Protocol of May 22, 1954, on the Exemption for citizens of Denmark, Finland, Norway and Sweden to hold passport and residence permit when visiting any other Nordic country than the country of domicile.

Iceland acceded to the Protocol on November 14, 1955.

E. PUBLICATIONS

The Proceedings of the Nordic Council, published after each session, contain a record of the proceedings and all the documents dealt with at the session. The first issue of the Proceedings was published in 1953, after the 1st Council session in Copenhagen. The Council Documents of 1974 were issued in three volumes, the first two covering the 1st and 2nd Assembly of the 22nd Session and the third covering the opinions of the various remit bodies on the different proposals on the agenda.

A series, entitled *Norisk Utredningsserie* (NU), has been published since 1960. It contains reports on investigations carried through by joint committees on various special areas, conference reports, compilation of treaties (since 1970) and a Statistical Yearbook (since 1962). In the 1974 series the following publications were issued which are available in full or in summary form in English. (Publications available only in one of the Nordic languages are not listed.)

Naturorienterande ämnen i grundskolan i Norden, årskurserna 1–6	Teaching of natural science topics in the first six years of the primary school. Joint survey in the framework of harmonization of the educational systems in Nordic countries.	Summary in English
Förslag till Nordisk tentamensgyldighet	Proposals to new guidelines referring to the validity of high school examinations.	Summary in English
Grunnskolen i Norden	The compulsory school in the Nordic countries. Joint survey in the framework of the educational systems in the Nordic countries.	Summary in English
Spesialundervisning i Norden	Special training in the Nordic countries. Joint survey in the framework of harmonization of the educational systems in the Nordic countries.	Summary in English
De gymnasiale utdannelser i Norden	Secondary education in the Nordic countries. A survey in the framework of harmonization of the educational systems.	Summary in English
Nordisk specialpedagogisk terminologi	Terminology within special education. List of Swedish, Danish, Norwegian, Islandic, Finnish and English terminology.	Partly in English
TV över gränserna. Slutrapport	TV across the borders. Final report by a committee to study an expanded distribution of programmes from the neighbour countries.	Summary in English
Utvärdering av universitet	Evaluation of university education. Report from the third Nordic conference on university education.	Partly in English
Yearbook of Nordic Statistic, 1974 (Nordisk statistisk årsbok)	Statistical data on the Nordic countries. Volume XIII.	text in English and Swedish

Since 1955 the Nordic Council publishes a periodical called *Nordisk Kontakt*, which appears fortnightly during the parliament sessions (16 numbers annually) and contains political information from the five Nordic countries. Text in the Nordic languages.

A calendar of Nordic meetings is published regularly. (approx. 15 per year). A pamphlet on Nordic co-operation has been published in the Nordic languages as well as in English, French and German. The main co-operation treaties are also available in English, French and German. A slide film on Nordic co-operation is available in Swedish, Finnish and English.

The Secretariat for Nordic Cultural Co-operation publishes a pamphlet on Nordic cultural co-operation called *Meddelelser*. Text in the Nordic languages, four issues annually since 1973.

Press releases are issued in the Nordic languages by the Nordic Council and the Nordic Council of Ministers' Secretariats.

CHAPITRE IX

CONFERENCE EUROPEENNE DES MINISTRES DES TRANSPORTS

La Conférence Européenne des Ministres des Transports (CEMT) a été créée par un Protocole signé à Bruxelles, le 17 Octobre 1953.

Elle groupe des Ministres des Transports de 18 pays, dont la liste figure ci-après. Ceux-ci se réunissent en Conseil deux fois par an, la session de printemps se tenant dans le pays du Président, sur invitation de ce dernier. Les travaux du Conseil sont préparés par un Comité des Suppléants. Un Secrétariat, dont le siège est à Paris, 33, rue de Franqueville (16ème), assiste ces deux organes.

La Conférence a pour objectifs:

a) de prendre toutes mesures destinées à réaliser, dans un cadre général ou régional, la meilleure utilisation et le développement le plus rationnel des transports intérieurs européens d'importance internationale;

b) de coordonner et de promouvoir les travaux des Organisations internationales s'intéressant aux transports intérieurs européens, compte tenu de l'activité des autorités supra-nationales dans ce domaine.

Dix-huit pays sont membres de la CEMT, à savoir: l'Allemagne, l'Autriche, la Belgique, le Danemark, l'Espagne, la France, la Grèce, l'Irlande, l'Italie, le Luxembourg, la Norvège, les Pays-Bas, le Portugal, le Royaume-Uni, la Suède, la Suisse, la Turquie et la Yougoslavie.

Le Bureau de la CEMT est actuellement composé comme suit:

	Conseil des Ministres	*Comité des Suppléants*
Président	Monsieur N. MATTHIASEN Ministre des Travaux Publics Danemark	M. J. L. HALCK Secrétaire d'Etat Trafikministeriet, Danemark
1er Vice Président	Monsieur M. CAVAILLE Secrétaire d'Etat aux Transports, France	M.G. BILLET Ministère de l'Equipement, France
2ème Vice Président	Monsieur G. VOYATZIS Ministre des Transports et Communications, Grèce	M. J. TZITZIS Conseiller, Délégation de la Grèce auprès de l'OCDE

Parmi les grands problèmes qui ont fait l'objet, dans le passé, des travaux de la CEMT ou qui sont en cours d'examen, on peut citer:

- la politique générale des transports, y compris la coordination et le financement des investissements, la théorie et la pratique dans l'économie des transports;
- problèmes découlant des relations entre les Etats et les entreprises de chemin de fer;
- la prévention des accidents de la route et l'uniformisation, sur le plan européen, des règles de la circulation et de la signalisation routières;
- questions relatives aux transports urbains;
- l'évolution du trafic, les investissements et les prévisions de développement du trafic à long terme;
- le développement du réseau des grandes voies de communication européennes.

CHAPTER IX

EUROPEAN CONFERENCE OF MINISTERS OF TRANSPORT

The European Conference of Ministers of Transport (ECMT) was created by a Protocol signed in Brussels on 17 October 1953.

It consists of the Ministers of Transport of 18 countries listed below. They meet in Council twice a year, the spring session being held in the country of the Chairman, on the invitation of the latter. The work of the Council is prepared by a Committee of Deputies. These two organs are assisted by a Secretariat, the seat of which is in Paris, at 33 Rue de Franqueville (16e).

The aims of the Conference are:

a) to take whatever measures may be necessary to achieve, at general or regional level, the maximum use and most rational development of European inland transport of international importance;

b) to co-ordinate and promote the activities of international organisations concerned with European inland transport, taking into account the work of supranational authorities in this field.

Eighteen countries are members of ECMT: Germany, Austria, Belgium, Denmark, Spain, France, Greece, Ireland, Italy, Luxembourg, Norway, Netherlands, Portugal, United Kingdom, Sweden, Switzerland, Turkey and Yugoslavia.

The Bureau of the ECMT is currently as follows:

	Council of Ministers	*Committee of Deputies*
Chairman	Mr. N. MATTHIASEN Minister of Public Works, Denmark	Mr. J. L. HALCK State Secretary Trafikministeriet, Denmark
1st Vice-Chairman	Mr. M. CAVAILLE Secretary of State for Transport, France	Mr. G. BILLET Ministry of Equipment, France
2nd Vice-Chairman	Mr. G. VOYATZIS Minister of Transport and Communications, Greece	Mr. J. TZITZIS Greek Delegation to OECD

Among the major problems with which the Conference has been concerned in the past, or which are currently being studied, the following may be mentioned:

- general transport policy, including the coordination and financing of investments, the theory and practice of transport economy;
- problems resulting from relations between the State and railways enterprises;
- road safety and standardisation, on a European basis, of traffic rules and road signs;
- questions relating to urban transport;
- the development of traffic, investments and forecasts of long-term traffic development;
- the development of a network of European highways.

En outre, la CEMT constitue un centre de rencontres permettant, avec le concours de personnalités choisies en raison de leur compétence, de discuter sous l'angle économique, les principaux problèmes posés par la politique des transports.

La CEMT publie chaque année un Rapport d'activité, un volume des Résolutions et Rapports adoptés par la Conseil, ainsi qu'un Bulletin semestriel de documentation.

In addition, ECMT affords a meeting place which makes possible, with the assistance of specialists chosen for their competence, the discussion from the economic point of views of the principal problems posed by transport policy.

ECMT publishes every year a Report on its activities, a volume of Resolutions and Reports adopted by the Council and a bi-annual Bulletin of documentation.

CHAPITRE X

ORGANISATION EUROPEENNE POUR LA RECHERCHE NUCLEAIRE

A. ACTIVITES EN 1974

L'année 1974 s'est avérée extrêmement passionnante pour la physique des hautes énergies en raison de l'importance des découvertes qui ont été faites dans le monde entier. Le nombre de laboratoires qui ont contribué à cet afflux de nouveaux résultats relève le caractère véritablement international de la recherche dans ce domaine, ainsi que l'excellent esprit de coopération et d'émulation qui anime les chercheurs.

L'Europe est particulièrement bien équipée en machines de haute énergie de divers types offrant de nombreuses possibilités d'utilisation. Les plus grandes sont installées au CERN, l'Organisation Européenne pour la Recherche Nucléaire dont les deux laboratoires chevauchent la frontière France-Suisse à quelque 8 km à l'ouest de Genève. Le CERN constitue ainsi par la nature même de son organisation et de ses buts un centre européen de collaboration et de coordination des recherches en physique fondamentale. Ce rôle est encouragé par l'accueil et le renouvellement permanent des physiciens visiteurs qui réalisent d'ailleurs la majeure partie de ces recherches.

L'effectif du CERN se stabilise à 3600 personnes parmi lesquelles on dénombre environ 150 chercheurs. Le nombre des attachés scientifiques et des boursiers continue cependant d'augmenter. Ainsi, leur effectif de 1090 en fin d'année n'est que légèrement inférieur au maximum enregistré en période de pointe. La majorité d'entre eux ne sont pas rémunérés par le CERN et restent dépendants de leurs établissements d'origine. Ils assurent ainsi un constant échange de connaissances avec les universités et le laboratoires de recherche des Etats Membres.

La structure de l'Organisation n'a subi aucune modification au cours de l'année, et les pourcentages de contribution des Etats Membres sont restés identiques à ceux des deux années précédentes. Toutefois, comme le prévoit la Convention, un nouveau calcul a été réalisé pour les années 1975, 1976 et 1977 sur la base du revenu national net des Etats Membres durant les années 1971, 1972 et 1973. Pour la première fois, le revenu global de la République fédérale d'Allemagne a dépassé 25% du total et sa contribution a atteint la limite de 25% fixée par la Convention pour le programme de base et ISR (qui peut être considéré comme la partie „exploitation" des activités du CERN) et de 25,4% pour le Programme 300 GeV (qui est doté d'un budget distinct ayant pour objet la construction et la mise en exploitation d'une nouvelle zone de laboratoires axée sur un synchrotron à protons dont l'énergie est maintenant fixée à 400 GeV). Cette différence s'explique par le fait que la Grèce, dont le Conseil a accepté de réduire la contribution au programme de base et ISR, ne participe pas au Programme 300 GeV.

La dernière formalité régularisant sur le plan administratif le Programme 300 GeV a été la signature, le 16 décembre 1974, d'un contrat de superficie avec la Suisse pour la partie du nouveau Laboratoire sise sur le territoire suisse (68 ha sur 480 ha).

En 1974, le Comité des Finances s'est réuni à intervalles réguliers pour approuver les contrats importants de l'Organisation et examiner les incidences financières des nouvelles réalisations. Un Groupe de travail spécial procède actuellement à la révision de la politique des pensions et devrait normalement soumettre son rapport au Conseil en 1975.

CHAPTER X

EUROPEAN ORGANISATION FOR NUCLEAR RESEARCH

A. ACTIVITIES IN 1974

The year 1974 was one of the most exciting of recent times for high energy physics with important discoveries being made all over the world. The number of laboratories contributing to this rush of new data has emphasized the truly international nature of this research and the excellent cooperation – and competition – that prevails.

Europe is particularly well endowed with high energy machines of diverse types and capabilities with the largest examples located at CERN the European Organization for Nuclear Research whose two laboratories straddle the Franco-Swiss frontier some 8 km west of Geneva. CERN provides a centre for European collaboration and coordination, facilitated by the large through-put of physicists carrying out the research.

The staffing of the Laboratories has reached a plateau of 3600 people, including some 150 research physicists. Most of the research is however carried out by scientific associates and fellows the number of whom continues to rise. The end year figure of 1090 is somewhat less than the number at the periods of peak activity. The majority of these are not paid by CERN but remain attached to their base establishments. They thus provide a continuous feed-back into the Universities and research laboratories of the Member States.

There were no changes in the structure of the Organization in the course of the year and the percentage contributions of Member States remained as in the two previous years. As laid down by the Convention, however, a new calculation was made for the years 1975, 6, 7 and the basis of the net national revenues of the Member States for the years 1971, 2, 3. For the first time, the German Federal Republic had an aggregate revenue greater than 25% of the total and its contribution becomes limited by the Convention to 25% for the Basic and ISR Programme (which may be considered to be the operating side of CERN's activities) and to 25.4% for the 300 GeV Programme (which covers, under a separate budget, the construction and first operation of a new laboratory area centred on a proton synchrotron now rated at 400GeV). The difference arises from the fact that Greece while benefiting from a reduced contribution to the Basic and ISR Programme as agreed by Council is not participating in the 300 GeV Programme.

The final administrative act in regularizing the 300 GeV programme was the signing on December 16, 1974 of the "contrat de superficie" with Switzerland for that part of the new Laboratory which is on Swiss territory (68 ha out of 480 ha).

During 1974 the Finance Committee met at regular intervals to adjudicate the major contracts being awarded by the Organization and consider the financial implications of developments. A special working party is reviewing pension policy and is expected to report to Council during 1975.

Fluctuating exchange rates and the run on the Swiss franc in particular posed major problems to the Organization in 1974; the combination of adverse rates and high inflation bears heavily on the Member States who for Laboratory I in 1975, were not able to apply the "Bannier procedure" of updating the provisional estimates of the preceding year by the application of a calculated cost variation index. Instead a set budget of 410 M. Sw. Fr. (representing a reduction of about 10 M. Sw. Fr.) was agreed

Les fluctuations des taux de change et la ruée sur le franc suisse notamment, ont posé de sérieux problèmes en 1974. Les taux de change défavorables joints à la forte inflation imposent de lourdes charges aux Etats Membres qui n'ont pu appliquer au budget du Laboratoire I pour 1975 la „Procédure Bannier", selong laquelle les déterminations provisoires établies l'année précédente sont actualisées par application d'un indice de variation des coûts calculé. Au lieu de cela, un budget fixe de 410 millions de francs suisses (soit une réduction d'environ 10 millions de francs suisses) a été approuvé pour le Laboratoire I. Le budget du Laboratoire II a néanmoins été réévalué par application de l'indice de variation des coûts convenu aux montants qui avaient été prévus pour chacune des huit années du programme lors de l'approbation du projet du nouvel accélérateur en février 1971.

Le Conseil s'est réuni deux fois au cours de l'année, en juin et décembre et a entendu les rapports présentés par les Directeurs généraux sur l'activité des Laboratoires.

Le Professeur Jentschke, Directeur général du Laboratoire I a énuméré les changements qui sont intervenus dans notre interprétation de la nature du monde physique. Pendant de nombreuses années, on a cru que quatre forces distinctes agissaient dans la nature: la force gravitationelle, dont les effets sont familiers mais négligeables à l'échelle des particules, l'interaction faible responsable de la désintégration radioactive, la force électromagnétique qui régit les réactions chimiques et le comportement des solides, l'interaction forte qui lie entre eux les nucléons dans le noyau de l'atome.

Il y a peu de temps encore, chacune de ces trois dernières forces semblait très différente des autres. Il semble désormais, pour la première fois, qu'elles puissent être les diverses facettes d'un même mode d'interaction.

Une partie très importante du programme de recherche du CERN a porté sur l'étude des nombreuses particules qui subissent l'interaction forte – les hadrons – au moyen de détecteurs électroniques et de chambres à bulles. (Ces instruments permettent essentiellement de déterminer la trajectoire des particules porteuses d'une charge électrique.) Une theorie qui rend parfaitement compte de leurs caractéristiques suppose qu'ils sont constitués par différentes combinaisons de trois „quarks." L'utilisation de la chambre à bulles à liquide lourd, Gargamelle, comme détecteur et de neutrinos (particules dépourvues de masse et de charge) comme projectiles, a permis d'obtenir des résultats dont l'explication la plus simple consiste à admettre que le proton – le noyau de l'atome d'hydrogène et l'un des éléments composant tout atome – est formé de 3 constituants ponctuels. Les résultats proviennent de l'analyse des photographies de traces laissées par les collisions et désintégrations dans les chambres à bulles de particules chargées.

Pendant ce temps, dans les Anneaux de stockage à intersections du CERN – une machine unique en son genre où des protons accélérés dans le synchrotron de 25 GeV sont accumulés dans deux anneaux pour former des faisceaux intenses qui sont ensuite soumis à des collisions frontales en plusieurs points où les anneaux se croisent – on constatait que des hadrons se déplaçant à haute vitesse sont émis sous de grands angles en quantité particulièrement inattendue et possèdent des caractéristiques dont la meilleure explication suppose, elle aussi, que le proton est formé de constituants ponctuels durs.

C'est en étudiant des photographies d'interactions provoquées par des neutrinos dans Gargamelle que l'on a découvert le premier indice d'une forme particulière de l'interaction faible que l'on doit nécessairement postuler si l'on veut unifier la force électromagnétique et l'interaction faible. Ces résultats ont maintenant été amplement confirmés et complétés par la mise en évidence d'une forme différente du même phénomène. L'interprétation de deux photographies permet de conclure avec 99% de cerfor Laboratory I. The budget for Laboratory II was nonetheless updated to 237.0 M. Sw. Fr. by applying the agreed cost variation index to the forecast figure which had been laid down, as for each year of the 8-year programme, when the project for the new accelerator was agreed in February 1971.

Council met twice during the year, in June and December and heard reports from the Directors-General on progress at the Laboratories.

Professor W. Jentschke, the Director-General of Laboratory I reviewed the changes that had taken place in our interpretation of the nature of the physical world. For many years it was believed that four separate forces were at work in nature: gravity, the effects of which are familiar but negligible at the individual particle level, the weak force which is responsible for radioactive decay, the electromagnetic force which controls chemistry and the behaviour of solids, the strong force which binds the nucleons together in the nucleus of the atom. Until recently these last three forces have looked very different but now, for the first time, it seems they could be different facets of a single form of interaction.

A very important part of the research programme at CERN has been the study of the large number of particles which interact through the strong force – the hadrons – using both electronic detectors and bubble chambers. (These permit primarily the line of flight of particles carrying an electric charge to be determined.) A theory which has proved to be very powerful in explaining their characteristics supposes them to be made up of different combinations of three "quarks." Using the heavy liquid bubble chamber, Gargamelle, as detector and neutrinos (mass-less, charge-less particles) as projectile, results have been obtained which are most easily explained by assuming that the proton – the nucleus of the hydrogen atom and one of the components of all atoms – contains 3 point-like constituents. The results come from the analysis of photographs of the tracks left by charged particles which are produced by collisions and disintegrations in the bubble chamber.

Meanwhile at the CERN Intersecting Storage Rings – a unique machine where protons accelerated in the 25 GeV synchrotron are built up into intense beams in two rings and made to meet in head-on collision at several points where the rings cross – it has been found that hadrons moving at high speed are emitted at wide angles in unexpectedly large numbers and with characteristics that are again best explained by assuming that the proton contains hard point-like constituents.

It was from studies of pictures of interactions induced by neutrinos in Gargamelle that the first evidence had been found for a particular form of the weak force which would be necessary if the weak and electromagnetic forces were to be unified. These results have now been amply confirmed and supplemented by evidence for a different form of the same effect. Two pictures are interpreted with 99% certainty as being due to a collision between a neutrino and an electron. When it is remembered that a set of 8 pictures is taken every two seconds in the course of a run with the bubble chamber and a run lasts several weeks, it will be appreciated how rare and precious such a discovery is.

Much of modern physics depends upon the identification of attributes which remain on aggregate unchanged when particles interact, even though the particles themselves may be transmuted. These properties are thus the descriptors of nature and evidence has been accumulating to suggest that another, labelled charm, is needed to explain certain anomalies in behaviour. This, in terms of a quark model, means adding a fourth quark. An intensive search is currently under way to prove the existence of "charmed" particles (which would be indicated by the transformation of particles in ways otherwise forbidden) but the evidence is not conclusive and no free quarks of any sort have been found. The discovery in the USA and the measurements at Frascati in Italy and Desy in Germany of two titude à la présence d'une évènement résultant d'une collision entre un neutrino et un électron. Si l'on songe qu'une série de huit clichés est prise toutes les deux secondes au cours d'une période d'expérimentation, laquelle dure plusieurs semaines, on jugera de la rareté et de la valeur d'une telle découverte.

La physique moderne accorde une grande importance à l'identification de propriétés restant totalement inchangées lorsque des particules entrent en interaction, même si ces dernières proprement dites subissent une transformation. Ces propriétés sont donc les descripteurs de la nature et des données se sont accumulées laissant supposer qu'il faut faire intervenir une autre propriété que l'on a nommée ,,charme,'' pour expliquer certaines anomalies de comportement. Cela revient à admettre, dans le cadre du modèle des quarks, l'existence d'un quatrième quark. La preuve de l'existence de particules charmées (dont la transformation de particules selon des modes autrement interdits pourrait être un indice) fait actuellement l'objet d'une recherche active mais à ce jour, les résultats ne sont pas concluants et nul quark libre n'a été observé.

La découverte aux Etats-Unis d'Amérique de deux particules tout à fait nouvelles et leur mesure à Frascati en Italie et à Desy en Allemagne ont ajouté une dernière note de fébrilité à une année marquée par un foisonnement d'idées et de résultats nouveaux.

Les travaux de construction du synchrotron à protons de 400GeV de 2,2 km de diamètre se sont déroulés dans l'ensemble selon le calendrier prévu et en dépit de retards dans la livraison de certaines pièces d'équipement, il est toujours prévu de mettre en service l'accélérateur au cours du second trimestre de 1976, afin que les expériences puissent commencer à la fin de cette même année.

L'excavation du tunnel de l'anneau principal de 6,9 km de circonférence à l'aide d'une machine à forer à pleine section s'est achevée le 31 juillet 1974; au terme de ce cheminement compliqué, l'écart avec la trajectoire idéale ne dépassait pas quelques milimètres. Les travaux d'installation avancent progressivement et au printemps 1975 un sextant complet d'aimants de guidage et de focalisation a été soumis à des essais poussés. La ligne électrique de 380 kV alimentant le Laboratoire a été mise en service et l'installation de la sous-station électrique et du compensateur de puissance est bien avancée. Le système d'alimentation en eau est également en voie d'achèvement.

Une grande partie du système de commande a été livrée, notamment la plupart des ordinateurs qui en font partie intégrante ainsi que l'équipement d'adressage. On procède actuellement à la mise au point des systèmes de visualisation et d'exploitation en mode dialogué qui seront utilisés par le chef opérateur, ainsi qu'au raccordement de l'équipement de la salle de commande. Le premier tronçon des cavités accélératrices est arrivé sur le site et l'installation des alimentations se poursuit.

L'essentiel des travaux de génie civil requis pour les bâtiments de l'accélérateur et les tunnels d'éjection étant maintenant terminé, l'attention se porte sur la construction de la zone d'expérimentation Nord qui devrait être achevée au cours des deux dernières années du programmes. Les plans de la zone (ainsi qu'une bonne partie du programme d'expérimentation) ont été arrêtés d'un commun accord en 1974 et le déblaiement du site a commencé au printemps de 1975.

Lorsqu'il a approuvé le Programme 300 GeV, le Conseil a créé un second Laboratoire, comme indiqué dans la Convention révisée tout en décidant que les deux Laboratoires devraient être unifiés aprés l'achèvement du nouvel accélérateur. Le SPS, sigle qui désigne maintenant le synchrotron de 400 GeV, devrait être mis en service dans le courant de 1976 et le Conseil a décidé lors d'une session tenue en mars 1975 que l'unification des Laboratoires serait effective à partir du 1er janvier 1976, date à laquelle l'actuel Directeur général du Laboratoire I aura achevé son mandat de quite new particles may also be a result of this postulated new property of charm. It added a final touch of fever to a year characterised by a ferment of ideas and new results.

Construction work on the 2.2 km diameter 400 GeV proton-synchrotron has proceeded largely according to schedule and in spite of delays in the delivery of some items of equipment it is still expected that the accelerator will be commissioned in the second half of 1976 so that experiments can begin at the end of that year.

The full-face boring machine excavating the main ring tunnel completed the 6.9 km circuit on July 31, 1974 emerging from its complicated burrow within millimetres of its planned position. Installation work goes on progressively and in the Spring of 1975 a complete sextant of guiding and focusing magnets was given an extended test. The 380 kV supply line to the Laboratory has been put into service and the transformer station with the associated surge suppressor units is well advanced. The water supply is also nearing completion.

Much of the control system has been delivered to site including most of the computers which are an integral part of the sytems and the addressing equipment. The visual display and interactive systems for the chief operator are in an advanced state of development and the control room is being wired. The first section of the accelerating cavities had arrived on site and installation of the power supplies is proceeding.

With the majority of the civil engineering work connected with the accelerator buildings and ejection tunnels now complete, attention is being turned to the construction of the northern experimental zone due to be completed during the last two years of the programme. Full agreement was reached on the design of the zone during 1974 (as well as on much of the experimental programme) and site clearance was started in the Spring of 1975.

When Council approved the 300 GeV programme it set up a second Laboratory as indicated in the revised Convention but resolved that the two Laboratories should be unified when the new accelerator was completed. The SPS, as this 400 GeV synchrotron is now known, is due to be commissioned during 1976 and Council decided at a meeting in March 1975 that the Laboratories should be unified from January 1 of that year when the present Director-General of Laboratory I will have completed his 5-year term. Dr. John B. Adams, presently Director-General of Laboratory II and Professor Léon Van Hove former Head of the Theoretical Physics Department are appointed Directors-General for a period of five years from that date.

The President of Council and Chairman of the CERN committees together with the names of senior staff as at April 1, 1975 are set out below together with a table indicating the contribution of Member States for the next 3 years.

cinq ans. M. John B. Adams, actuellement Directeur général du Laboratoire II, et le Professeur Léon Van Hove, ancien Directeur du Département Physique théorique, ont été nommés Directeurs généraux pour une période de cinq ans à compter de cette date.

On trouvera ci-dessous les noms du Président du Conseil, des Présidents des Comités du CERN et des fonctionnaires supérieurs en fonction au 1er avril 1975 ainsi qu'un tableau indiquant les contributions des Etats Membres pour les trois prochaines années.

B. ORGANISATION

Siège	Genève, Suisse
Téléphone	Genève (022) 41 98 11
Télex	Suisse- 2 36 98
Adresse postale	Laboratoire I: CH–1211 Genève 23 Laboratoire II: Prévessin (France) F–01631 CERN Cedex

Etats membres (12)

Allemagne (République fédérale)	Italie
Autriche	Norvège
Belgique	Pays-Bas
Danemark	Royaume-Uni
France	Suède
Grèce	Suisse

Président du conseil du CERN
P. LEVAUX (Belgique)

Président du comité des finances (FC)
M. LEMNE (Suède)

Président du comité des directives scientifiques (SPC)
W. PAUL/Université de Bonn

Présidents des comités d'expériences
Comité des Expériences Electroniques
A. ASTBURY/Laboratoire de Rutherford, Chilton
Comité des chambres à Traces
D. C. COLLEY/Université de Birmingham
Comité Physique III
V. SOERGEL/Université de Heidelberg
Comité des Anneaux de Stockage à Intersections
H. SCHOPPER/Laboratoire de DESY, Hambourg
Comité des expériences SPS
E. LOHRMANN/Laboratoire de DESY, Hambourg

Président du comité consultatif de la machine 300 GeV
F. AMMAN/Laboratoires de Frascati

Directeurs généraux

CERN Laboratoire I	CERN Laboratoire II
W. K. JENTSCHKE	J. B. ADAMS

B. ORGANISATION

Seat	Geneva, Switzerland
Telephone	Geneva (022) 41 98 11
Telex	Switzerland: 2 36 98
Postal address	Laboratory I: CH–1211 Geneva 23
	Laboratory II: Prévessin (France) F–01631 CERN Cedex

Member States (12)

Austria	Italy
Belgium	Netherlands
Denmark	Norway
France	Sweden
Germany (Federal Republic)	Switzerland
Greece	United Kingdom

President of the council of CERN
P. Levaux (Belgium)

Chairman of the finance committee (FC)
M. Lemne (Sweden)

Chairman of the Scientific policy committee (SPC)
W. Paul/University of Bonn

Chairmen of the experiments committees
Electronic Experiments Committee
A. Astbury/Rutherford Laboratory, Chilton
Track Chamber Experiments Committee
D. C. Colley/University of Birmingham
Physics III Committee
V. Soergel/University of Heidelberg
Intersecting Storage Rings Committee
H. Schopper/DESY Laboratory, Hamburg
SPS Experiments Committee
E. Lohrmann/DESY Laboratory, Hamburg

Chairman of the 300 GeV Advisory Machine Committee
F. Amman/Frascati Laboratories

Directors-General

CERN Laboratory I	CERN Laboratory II
W. K. Jentschke	J. B. Adams

CERN LABORATOIRE I

(Programmes de base et ISR)

Superficie
41 hectares en Suisse et 39,5 hectares en France de part et d'autre de la frontière.

Budget 1975
410 millions de francs suisses.

Effectif (chiffres de décembre 1974)
3172 titulaires et auxiliaires (savants, ingénieurs, techniciens, administrateurs et ouvriers);
195 laborantins
112 boursiers
967 attachés de recherche

CERN LABORATOIRE II

(Programme du Laboratoire du 300 GeV)

Superficie
412 hectares en France et 68 hectares en Suisse de part et d'autre de la frontière (site contigu au Laboratoire I).

Budget 1975
237.9 millions de francs suisses

Effectif (chiffres de décembre 1974)
417 titulaires,
11 attachés de recherche et boursiers

CONTRIBUTIONS DES ETATS MEMBRES

	Lab. I %	Lab. II %		Lab. I %	Lab. II %
Allemagne (Rép. Féd.)	25,00	25,40	Italie	13,33	13,34
Autriche	2,22	2,22	Norvège	1,60	1,60
Belgique	4,01	4,02	Pays-Bas	5,30	5,30
Danemark	2,28	2,29	Royaume-Uni	16,40	16,41
France	21,47	21,49	Suède	4,55	4,55
Grèce	0,46	—	Suisse	3,38	3,38

CERN LABORATORY I

(Basic and ISR programmes)

Area
41 hectares in Switzerland and 39.5 hectares in France on either side of the border.

Budget 1975
410 million Swiss francs.

Staff (December 1974 figures)
3172 staff members and auxiliaries (scientists, engineers, technicians, administrators and workmen)
195 laboratory staff
112 fellows
967 scientific associates

CERN LABORATORY II

(300 GeV Laboratory Programme)

Area
412 hectares in France and 68 hectares in Switzerland on either side of the border, adjacent to Laboratory I.

Budget 1975
237.9 million Swiss francs

Staff (December 1975 figures)
417 staff members
11 scientific associates and fellows

CONTRIBUTIONS OF MEMBER STATES

	Lab. I %	Lab. II %		Lab. I %	Lab. II %
Austria	2.22	2.22	Italy	13.33	13.34
Belgium	4.01	4.02	Netherlands	5.30	5.30
Denmark	2.28	2.29	Norway	1.60	1.60
France	21.47	21.49	Sweden	4.55	4.55
Germany (F.R.)	25.00	25.40	Switzerland	3.38	3.38
Greece	0.46	—	United Kingdom	16.40	16.41

COMMISSION EUROPEENNE DE L'AVIATION CIVILE

A. INFORMATIONS GENERALES

La création d'un organisme européen de transport aérien fut envisagée initialement en 1951, lorsque furent soumises à l'examen de l'Assemblée consultative du Conseil de l'Europe certaines propositions visant à réaliser le plus grand degré possible de coordination des transports aériens intra-européens et à établir à cette fin une institution européenne de l'aviation civile.

Comme suite à une recommandation de l'Assemblée consultative, le Comité des Ministres du Conseil convint qu'une conférence européenne devrait être convoquée et que l'Organisation de l'Aviation Civile Internationale (OACI) devait être invitée à entreprendre cette tâche.

C'est ainsi que se tint à Strasbourg, en avril 1954, la Conférence de coordination des transports aériens européens (CATE) après réunion d'un comité préparatoire en novembre 1953 à Paris. Cette Conférence recommanda l'établissement d'un organe permanent, appelé Commission Européenne de l'Aviation civile (CEAC), dont la première session eut lieu du 29 novembre au 10 décembre 1955 à Strasbourg.

Les dix-neuf Etats européens qui constituèrent la CEAC sont les suivants: Autriche, Belgique, Danemark, Finlande, France, Allemagne (République fédérale), Grèce, Islande, Irlande, Italie, Luxembourg, Pays-Bas, Norvège, Portugal, Espagne, Suède, Suisse, Turquie et Royaume-Uni.

Chypre est devenue en 1969 membre de la Commission, portant ainsi à vingt le nombre total de ses membres.

Depuis sa création, la CEAC jouit d'un statut autonome, c'est-à-dire qu'elle n'est ni une institution totalement indépendante, ni un organe subordonné à l'OACI et intégré à cette organisation. La Commission établit son propre programme de travail, convoque ses propres réunions et prépare leur ordre du jour, tout en travaillant en étroite liaison avec l'OACI et en utilisant les services du Secrétariat de l'OACI en vertu de dispositions administratives et financières particulières.

La Commission, qui se réunissait en session plénière tous les deux ans jusqu'en 1961, tient une telle session tous les trois ans depuis cette date. Toutes ces sessions ont été convoquées à Strasbourg, dans les locaux du Conseil de l'Europe, à l'exception de la deuxième qui s'est tenue en 1957 à Madrid. La Commission plénière se réunit également en session intermédiaire au cours de chacune des années qui ne comportent pas de session triennale, et des sessions intermédiaires spéciales peuvent être convoquées en cas de nécessité ou d'urgence. Les principales décisions de la Commission sont prises en session plénière mais, en cas d'urgence, une procédure particulière permet l'adoption de décisions après un vote par correspondance. Entre les sessions, un Comité de coordination composé du Président, des vice-présidents et des présidents des quatre Comités permanents est habilité à prendre différentes mesures telles que l'établissement du calandrier des réunions et de l'ordre du jour provisoire des sessions, l'examen de la situation financière de la CEAC et la coordination des activités des quatre Comités permanents, à savoir:

Comité économique pour les transports aériens réguliers (ECO-I)
Comité économique pour les transports aériens non réguliers (ECO-II)
Comité technique
Comité de facilitation.

Pour l'exécution de la partie du programme de travail qui leur est assig-

CHAPTER XI

EUROPEAN CIVIL AVIATION CONFERENCE

A. GENERAL INFORMATION

A European air transport body was first envisaged in 1951 when the Consultative Assembly of the Council of Europe considered certain proposals aiming at achieving the greatest possible degree of co-ordination in intra-European air transport and establishing some kind of European civil aviation agency for the purpose.

Following a recommendation of the Consultative Assembly, the Committee of Ministers of the Council agreed that a European conference should be convened and decided that the International Civil Aviation Organization (ICAO) should be asked to undertake the task.

The Conference on Co-ordination of Air Transport in Europe (CATE) accordingly took place in Strasbourg in April 1954, after a preparatory committee had met in Paris in November 1953. This Conference recommended the establishment of a permanent body, called the European Civil Aviation Conference (ECAC), the inaugural session of which was held in Strasbourg on 29 November–10 December 1955.

The nineteen European States which formed ECAC were: Austria, Belgium, Denmark, Finland, France, Federal Republic of Germany, Greece, Iceland, Ireland Italy, Luxembourg, Netherlands, Norway, Portugal, Spain, Sweden, Switzerland, Turkey and United Kingdom.

In 1969, Cyprus joined the Conference, thus bringing the total membership to twenty States.

Since its inception, ECAC has been given an autonomous status, i.e. it is neither a completely independent agency nor a body subordinate to ICAO and integrated with that organization. The Conference formulates its own work programme, calls its own meetings and establishes their agenda, while working in close liaison with ICAO and using the services of the ICAO Secretariat under special administrative and financial arrangements.

The Conference which used to hold a plenary session every second year has been holding since 1961 such sessions every third year. All of them were convened in Strasbourg in the premises of the Council of Europe, with the exception of the Second Session which was held in Madrid in 1957. The Plenary Conference also holds an intermediate session in those years in which no triennial session takes place, and special intermediate cessions can be convened if it appears urgent or necessary to do so. The major decisions of the Conference are taken in plenary session, but a special procedure is resorted to, in cases of emergency, to have such decisions also adopted by mail vote. Between the session a Co-ordinating Committee, composed of the President, the Vice-Presidents and the chairmen of the four Standing Committees, is empowered to take action such as the establishment of the calendar of meetings and provisional agenda for the sessions, review of the financial situation and co-ordination of the activity of the four Standing Committees which are:

Economic Committee for scheduled air transport (ECO-I)
Economic Committee for non-scheduled air transport (ECO-II)
Technical Committee
Facilitation Committee

In order to carry out the part of the work programme assigned to them, the Standing Committees usually establish working groups or groups of experts.

It should be noted that the functions performed by ECAC through this née, les Comités permanents créent habituellement des groupes de travail ou des groupes d'experts.

Il convient de noter que les fonctions remplies par la CEAC selon ces mécanismes sont consultatives et que ses résolutions, recommandations et autres conclusions sont adoptées sous réserve de l'approbation des gouvernements des Etats membres.

Le domaine d'intérêt de la CEAC étant aussi large et aussi varié que celui de l'aviation internationale elle-même, les recommandations et mesures adoptées par la Commission aident les Etats dans la préparation de leurs règlements nationaux et fournissent des éléments d'orientation pour le travail pratique des autorités aéronautiques. Cette coopération, ainsi que la mise en commun des expériences acquises, se sont révélées être de l'intérêt de la communauté aéronautique tout entière et à l'avantage de l'ensemble du public qui voyage.

Aux termes de sa Constitution, adoptée lors de la première Session en 1955 et révisée en 1958, la CEAC a pour objet de suivre d'une façon générale l'évolution des transports aériens européens afin de favoriser la coordination, une meilleure utilisation et de développement ordonné de ces transports et d'examiner tout problème particulier qui pourrait se poser dans ce domaine.

La Commission, en choisissant les problèmes à inscrire à son programme de travail, accorde une attention particulière à l'importance et à l'intérêt qu'ils présentent pour un grand nombre d'Etats membres, à leur caractère spécifiquement européen et à la possibilité d'apporter une contribution réelle aux travaux permanents de l'OACI.

Dans le domaine ECONOMIQUE, la CEAC suit en permanence le développement des transports aériens réguliers et non réguliers effectués tant en provenance et à destination de l'Europe qu'à l'intérieur de l'Europe. Elle recueille, analyse et diffuse des statistiques sur ces transports et publie en outre des prévisions et études préparées à sa demande par des consultants. La CEAC adopte des recommandations visant à l'harmonisation des politiques de ses Etats membres, notamment en ce qui concerne la coopération entre compagnies aériennes (par exemple en facilitant la banalisation des aéronefs), la réglementation des vols affrétés intra-européens et nord atlantiques, le contrôle des tarifs, etc.... Sous l'égide de la Commission, des accords multilatéraux sur les droits commerciaux pour les transports aériens non réguliers en Europe et sur la procédure applicable à l'établissement des tarifs aériens réguliers ont été signés en 1956 et en 1967 respectivement.

Dès sa création, la CEAC a ressenti la nécessité d'une action dans le domaine de la FACILITATION et adopté des recommandations tendant à la suppression des obstacles à la libre circulation des aéronefs, des passagers, des marchandises et de la poste à travers les frontières nationales. La simplification ou même la suppression pur et simple des exigences documentaires par les Etats membres de la CEAC, ainsi que la normalisation des procédures douanières, d'immigration et d'acheminement au sol, non seulement assurent l'écoulement sans entraves du trafic aérien en Europe, mais donnent également l'exemple aux Etats extérieurs à cette région et contribuent efficacement aux efforts déployés sur le plan mondial dans le secteur de la facilitation.

Dans le domaine TECHNIQUE, la CEAC traite une variété de questions, par exemple:

En ce qui concerne la formation du personnel, la CEAC a entrepris l'élaboration d'un répertoire renfermant les informations essentielles sur les établissements de formation du personnel navigant et du personnel au sol, idée que l'OACI a reprise et développée par la suite à l'intention de tous ses Etats membres.

Dans le domaine de la navigabilité, la CEAC examine les problèmes machinery are consultative and its resolutions, recommendations or other conclusions are subject to the approval of Member governments.

The range of interest in ECAC being as wide and as varied as the field of international aviation itself, recommendations and measures adopted by the Conference assist States in the preparation of their national regulations and give guidance to the everyday practical work of the aeronautical authorities. This co-operation and the exchange of experiences have proved to be in the interest of the whole air transport community and to the benefit of the travelling public at large.

Under the terms of its Constitution, which was adopted at its First Session in 1955 and revised in 1968, the objectives of ECAC are to review generally the development of European air transport in order to promote the co-ordination, the better utilization and the orderly development of such air transport, and consider any special problem that may arise in this field.

In selecting the problems to be included in the work programme, the Conference pays particular attention to their importance and interest to a large number of Member States, their peculiarity to Europe or the possibility of making an effective contribution to the continuing work of ICAO.

In the ECONOMIC field ECAC keeps under constant review the development of scheduled and non-scheduled air transport within, to and from Europe. In addition to collecting, analysing and disseminating statistics on such air transport, it publishes forecasts and studies prepared by consultants at its request. Recommendations are adopted by ECAC aiming at the harmonization of policies of its Member States, particularly concerning co-operation between their airlines (e.g. facilitating interchange of aircraft), regulation of charter operations inside Europe and on the North Atlantic, control of fares and rates, etc.... Under the auspices of the Conference, Multilateral Agreements on commercial rights of non-scheduled air services in Europe and on the procedure for the establishment of tariffs for scheduled air services were signed in 1956 and 1967 respectively.

From the beginning ECAC has also seen the need for action in the FACILITATION field and adopted recommendations for the removal of obstacles in the path of free passage of aircraft, passengers, cargo and mail across national boundaries. The implementation by ECAC Member States of the simplified documentary requirements or even their complete abolition as well as the standardization of customs, immigration and ground handling procedures have not merely ensured the smooth and unimpeded flow of air traffic in Europe, but have also set an example to States outside this region and effectively contributed to the worldwide efforts made in the facilitation sector.

In the TECHNICAL field, ECAC has covered various subjects, for instance:

In personnel training ECAC began a Directory containing essential details about training centres for flight and ground personnel, an idea which was later adopted and amplified by ICAO for the use of all Member States.

Regarding airworthiness, ECAC examines problems arising from certification of imported aircraft and spare parts (a Multilateral Agreement was signed in this connection in 1960).

It deals also with problems of communications such as airborne radio aids and performance characteristics of airborne equipment (ECAC issued in 1965 an Information Paper on recommended performance characteristics for airborne equipment which is kept up to date following the progress of technology).

soulevés par la certification des aéronefs et pièces de rechange importes (un Accord multilatéral sur ce sujet a été signé en 1960).

Elle traite élagement de questions de télécommunications telles que celles intéressant les aides radio de bord et les caractéristiques de performanse des équipements de bord (en 1965 la CEAC a publié une Note d'information sur les caractéristiques de performance recommandées pour les équipements de bord, note qui est mise à jour en fonction des progrès de la technologie).

Lse rapports étroits que la CEAC entretient avec plus de vingt organisations internationales gouvernementales et non gouvernementales – notamment le Conseil de l'Europe et l'OACI avec lesquels elle a des liens particuliers – ont été aussi fructueux que la coordination internationale existant parmi ses Etats membres. La CEAC est un exemple de coopération internationale réussie et aucun effort n'est épargné pour la rendre encore plus efficace dans l'avenir afin d'assurer que l'aviation civile en Europe et dans le monde pourra poursuivre son développement de façon sûre et ordonnée.

B. RECOMMANDATIONS ET RESOLUTIONS ADOPTEES LORS DE LA SEPTIEME SESSION INTERMEDIAIRE TENUE A PARIS DU 11 AU 13 SEPTEMBRE 1974

RECOMMANDATION NO 1
DIFFUSION DES ORDRES GOUVERNEMENTAUX EMIS PAR LES ETATS MEMBRES DE LA CEAC

LA COMMISSION

CONSIDERANT

que l'émission unilatérale d'ordres gouvernementaux tend à miner les structures tarifaires multilatéralement convenues et qu'elle est contraire aux dispositions des accords gouvernementaux sur les services aériens;

CONSIDERANT

que si le problème est mondial il n'en est pas moins souhaitable d'en rechercher la solution en premier lieu dans un cadre géopgraphique limité;

CONSIDERANT

que la Recommandation no 1 de la quatrième Session intermédiaire, qui propose une réserve uniforme à la résolution 200 g de l'IATA, constitue un premier pas vers la réduction des ordres gouvernementaux;

CONSIDERANT

la nécessité de déployer de nouveaux efforts en vue de suivre l'émission et l'application des ordres gouvernementaux dans la région européenne;

RECOMMANDE

à chaque Etat membre de communiquer au Secrétariat de la CEAC, pour transmission aux autres Etats membres, le texte complet anglais ou français, de tout ordre gouvernemental émis par ses autorités et ayant des incidences sur les tarifs et conditions applicables sur les routes entre cet Etat et tout autre Etat membre, étant entendu que cette recommandation n'est pas applicable aux ordres gouvernementaux visant un seul voyage ou une seule expédition.

B. RECOMMENDATIONS AND RESOLUTIONS ADOPTED AT THE SEVENTH INTERMEDIATE SESSION HELD IN PARIS, 11–13 SEPTEMBER 1974.

RECOMMENDATION NO. 1
CIRCULATION OF GOVERNMENT ORDERS ISSUED BY ECAC STATES

WHEREAS
the unilateral issue of government orders tends to undermine the multilaterally agreed fares and rates structures and is contrary to the requirements of Government Air Services Agreements;

WHEREAS
the problem of government orders exists throughout the world but it is desirable to seek solutions to these problems in a limited area in the first instance;

WHEREAS
Recommendation No. 1 of the Fourth Intermediate Session concerning a standard reservation to IATA Resolution 200g is a first step towards the reduction of government orders; and

WHEREAS
further efforts are required to monitor the issue and application of government orders in the European region,

THE CONFERENCE RECOMMENDS
that each Member State should submit to the ECAC Secretariat for transmission to all other Member States the full text of the English or French versions of any government order issued by its authorities which affects the tariffs and conditions on the route between that State and any other Member State, it being understood that this recommendation should not apply to any government order concerning a specific individual journey or shipment.

RESOLUTION

TARIFS DES SERVICES REGULIERS ET PRIX MINIMA D'AFFRETEMENT APPLICABLES SUR L'ATLANTIQUE NORD A PARTIR DU 1ER NOVEMBRE 1974

LA COMMISSION

AYANT NOTE
les résultats de la Conférence inter-compagnies tenue du 7 au 10 septembre 1974 à San Diego entre transporteurs réguliers et non réguliers exerçant une activité de transport aérien sur l'Atlantique nord;

AYANT A L'ESPRIT
les problèmes économiques du transport aérien et notamment ceux qui résultent des importantes augmentations de coûts récemment intervenues;

SOULIGNANT
la nécessité de fixer des tarifs qui rétabliront la santé économique des transporteurs dans l'intérêt, à long terme, du public;

ACCUEILLANT AVEC SATISFACTION
le fait que la Conférence inter-compagnies ait donné des résultats positifs qui apportent une contribution à la création d'une situation tarifaire plus stable dans le transport aérien nord atlantique;

CONSIDERANT
que l'efficacité de l'accord conclu entre transporteurs réguliers et non réguliers dépend de son application à l'ensemble du trafic nord atlantique; et

CONSIDERANT
en outre que l'application de l'accord à l'ensemble du trafic aérien nord atlantique est une condition préalable à l'entrée en vigueur de l'accord de l'IATA sur les tarifs des services réguliers;

1) PRIE INSTAMMENT
les gouvernements membres d'accepter et d'appliquer sans retard les dispositions relatives aux tarifs réguliers et aux prix des vols affrétés convenues à la Conférence intercompagnies et à la Conférence de trafic nord atlantique de l'IATA; et

2) INVITE
le Président de la CEAC à faire le nécessaire pour que la présente résolution soit portée à l'attention des gouvernements des Etats-Unis et du Canada, en exprimant le souhait que ces gouvernements arrivent à des conclusions similaires suffissamment à temps pour assurer l'entrée en vigueur des dispositions convenues.

RESOLUTION

TARIFFS FOR SCHEDULED SERVICES, AND MINIMUM CHARTER PRICES, ON THE NORTH ATLANTIC FROM 1 NOVEMBER 1974

HAVING NOTED
the results of the Inter-Carrier Conference held at San Diego from 7 to 10 September 1974 between scheduled and non-scheduled carriers engaged in North Atlantic air transport;

BEARING IN MIND
the economic problems of air transport, especially those resulting from the recent large cost increases;

STRESSING
the necessity of establishing tariffs and rates which will restore the economic health of the carriers in the long-term interests of the travelling public;

WELCOMING
the fact that the Inter-Carrier Conference has produced positive results which contitute a constribution to the establishment of a more stable rates situation in North Atlantic air transport;

CONSIDERING
that the effectiveness of the agreement reached between scheduled and non-scheduled carriers depends on its application to the whole of North Atlantic traffic; and

CONSIDERING
further that the application of the agreement to the whole of North Atlantic traffic is a prerequisite for the coming into effect of the IATA agreement on fares for scheduled services,

THE CONFERENCE
1) URGES
member governments to accept and apply without delay the packages relating to scheduled fares and non-scheduled prices concluded at the Inter-Carrier Conference and the IATA North Atlantic Traffic Conference; and

2) REQUESTS
the President of ECAC to arrange for the present resolution to be brought to the attention of the United States and Canadian governments and to express the hope that they will arrive at similar conclusions in sufficient time to ensure the implementation of the agreed packages.

RECOMMANDATION NO 2
CONTROLE OU SURVEILLANCE DES VOLS AFFRETES POUR VOYAGES A FORFAIT SUR L'ATLANTIQUE NORD

LA COMMISSION

CONSIDERANT
que la Recommandation no 3 de la sixième Session intermédiaire (Spéciale) contient des dispositions relatives aux prix minimaux des voyages à forfait par vols affrétés nord-atlantiques pour la période du 1 avril 1974 au 31 mars 1975;

CONSIDERANT
que depuis cette session les coûts du transport aérien et des prestations au sol composant les forfaits de voyages ont subi des augmentations notables, affectant les prix des voyages à forfait assurés par services réguliers aussi bien que par affrètement;

RECOMMANDE
que jusqu'au 31 mars 1975 les principes sur lesquels est fondé le premier paragraphe de ladite recommandation soient appliqués sur la base des niveaux et conditions IATA en vigueur pour les tarifs GIT au moment du dépø de la demande.

RECOMMANDATION NO 3
ELABORATION DE LA LEGISLATION OU REGLEMENTATION CONCERNANT LES ORGANISATEURS DE VOYAGES

LA COMMISSION

CONSIDERANT
la participation croissante des organisateurs de voyages à la commercialisation du transport aérien;

CONSIDERANT
que leurs activités doivent, comme l'industrie du transport aérien, être soumise au contrôle des pouvoirs publics;

CONSIDERANT
qu'il est souhaitable que les administrations de l'aviation civile de chacun des Etats membres de la CEAC interviennent dans l'élaboration de la réglementation applicable aux organisateurs de voyages;

RECOMMANDE
que les administrations de l'aviation civile de chacun des Etats membres prennent toutes les dispositions utiles pour promouvoir et pour participer à l'élaboration des dispositions législatives ou réglementaires concernant les organisateurs de voyages.

RECOMMENDATION NO. 2

PRICE CONTROL OR SURVEILLANCE OF ITC OPERATIONS ON THE NORTH ATLANTIC

WHEREAS

Recommendation No. 3 of the Sixth Intermediate Session (Special) has made provisions for minimum prices for North Atlantic ITCs for the period from 1 April to 31 March 1975; and

WHEREAS

since that Session there have been marked increases in many costs for the air transport and ground elements of package tours, affecting the prices of inclusive tours both by scheduled services and by charter operations,

THE CONFERENCE RECOMMENDS

that until 31 March 1975 the principles underlying the first paragraph of the said recommendation should be applied, on the basis of the IATA levels and conditions for GIT fares prevailing at the time of application for the proposed charter.

RECOMMENDATION NO. 3

DEVELOPMENT OF STATUTORY OR REGULATORY PROVISIONS CONCERNING TRAVEL ORGANIZERS

WHEREAS

travel organizers are taking an increasing part in air transport marketing;

WHEREAS

their activity should, like the air transport industry, be brought under the control of the authorities; and

WHEREAS

it is desirable for the civil aviation administrations in each ECAC Member State to take a hand in the development of regulations applicable to travel organizers,

THE CONFERENCE RECOMMENDS

that the civil aviation administrations in all Member States take all necessary steps to promote, and to take part in, the development of statutory or regulatory provisions concerning travel organizers.

RECOMMANDATION NO 4
HARMONISATION DES CONDITIONS APPLICABLES AUX VOLS AFFRETES DE VOYAGES A FORFAIT EFFECTUES SUR L'ATLANTIQUE NORD

LA COMMISSION

CONSIDERANT
que parmi les objectifs de la CEAC figure l'harmonisation des règlements et pratiques nationaux en matière de transport aérien non régulier;

CONSIDERANT
que dans l'intérêt du développement ordonné de l'industrie le marché du transport aérien touristique de masse doit être considéré sous tous ses aspects et dans un cadre organisé;

CONSIDERANT
qu'à cet effet il est nécessaire de mettre en oeuvre, pour les vols affrétés de voyage à forfait sur l'Atlantique nord, une série de conditions appropriées, incluant les dispositions des recommandations CEAC en vigueur tant sur le contrôle tarifaire que sur les principes généraux régissant jusqu'ici ce type d'exploitation;

RECOMMANDE
1) que les Etats membres qui autorisent les vols ITC sur l'Atlantique nord prennent des mesures effectives pour réglementer ces vols en leur appliquant les conditions suivantes:

a) un vol ITC s'effectue en exécution d'un contrat d'affrètement aux termes duquel toute la capacité d'un appareil est affrétée par un ou plusieurs organisateurs de voyage pour le transport de passagers qui ont acheté un voyage a forfait;

b) le voyage aérien à forfait est un voyage aller et retour ou circulaire dont tout ou partie est effectué par la voie aérienne, qui est organisé par un organisateur de voyage et qui est offert au puboic pour un prix global publié comprenant, outre le transport aérien, l'hébergement pour la durée du voyage, les transports de surface et, le cas échéant, d'autres prestations. La durée ainsi que la ou les destinations d'un voyage à forfait sont établies et annoncées à l'avance, et le forfait est normalement payé avant le départ;

c) la durée du séjour au(x) lieu(x) de destination n'est pas inférieure à six nuits;

d) les groupes ITC comprennent chacun au moins 40 passagers qui voyagent ensemble à l'aller et au retour. Sur justification d'un cas de force majeure, jusqu'à cinq pour cent des passager d'un groupe pourront être autorisés à effectuer le retour sur un vol différent;

e) l'exploitation de ces vols est soumise à un contrôle des prix d'après les modalités suivantes:

1. l'évolution des prix ITC est suivie attentivement par les Etats membres, tant individuellement que collectivement par le jeu des instances appropriées de la CEAC;

2. les programmes de séries de vols ITC, de même que les prix de gros d'affrètement et les prix de vente au public, sont déposés auprès de l'autorité compétente, si possible 60 jours avant le premier vol de toute série, et en tout cas suffisamment à l'avance pour qu'aucune gêne ne soit occasionnée au public en cas de refus d'autorisation de la part de cette autorité;

3. les instances appropriées de la CEAC établissent périodiquement les prix de vente minimaux applicables aux affrètements de voyage à forfait sur l'Atlantique nord, conformément aux recommandations de la CEAC en la matière;

RECOMMENDATION NO. 4
HARMONIZATION OF CONDITIONS CONCERNING NORTH ATLANTIC INCLUSIVE TOUR CHARTERS

WHEREAS
one of the aims of ECAC is to harmonize national regulations and practices in the field of non-scheduled transport;

WHEREAS
it is in the interest of the orderly development of the industry that the mass air transport tourist market should be considered in all its aspects and in an organized framework; and

WHEREAS
it is necessary to that end to apply a series of appropriate conditions relating to inclusive tour charter flights on the North Atlantic, including the provisions of the ECAC recommendations in force relating both to tariff control and to the general principles governing such operations to date.

THE CONFERENCE RECOMMENDS
1) that Member States which authorize ITC flights on the North Atlantic take effective measures to regulate such flights by applying to them the following conditions:
a) an ITC flight is carried out under a charter contract according to which the entire capacity of the aircraft is chartered by one or more tour organizers for the transport of passengers who have purchased an inclusive tour;
b) an air inclusive tour consists of a round trip or circle trip performed in whole or in part by air, organized by a tour organizer, and offered to the public at a comprehensive published price including, besides air transport, accommodation for the duration of the trip, surface transport, and, where appropriate, other amenities. It is normally paid for before departure, is for a predetermined period and is to an announced destination or destinations;
c) the duration of stay at the destination(s) is not less than six nights;
d) ITC groups have a minimum size of 40 passengers, who travel together on the outward and inward portions of the trip. In proven cases of "force majeure" up to five per cent of the passengers of a group may be authorized to return by a different flight;
e) the operation of such flights is subject to control of prices as set out below:
(i) the development of ITC prices is followed closely by Member States both individually and collectively through appropriate ECAC bodies;
(ii) programmes for series of ITC flights as well as wholesale charter rates and individual selling prices to the public are filed with the authorities concerned if possible 60 days before the first flight of any such series, but in any case sufficiently in advance to avoid inconvenience to the travelling public in the event that the authorities refuse permission for the flights;
(iii) the appropriate ECAC bodies establish periodically minimum prices applicable to ITC operations on the North Atlantic in accordance with the relevant ECAC recommendations;
f) the publicity for an inclusive tour indicates the comprehensive price per passenger, the services offered and the name(s) of the air carrier()s operating the flight;

f) la publicité d'un voyage à forfait indique le prix global par passager, les prestations offertes et le(s) nom(s) du (ou des) transporteur(s) aérien(s) assurant le vol;

g) l'éventuelle annulation d'un vol doit être annoncée dans les meilleurs délais à l'autorité compétente et aux passagers; et

2) que, dans le cadre de la présente recommandation, référence soit faite également aux critères d'une politique commune qui figurent en Annexe aux Recommandations 7 et 8 de la deuxième Session intermédiaire, qui conservent toute leur valeur sauf en ce qui concerne l'indication du niveau tarifaire et la conditions imposant au moins trois escales dans les programmes de voyage à forfait.

MANDAT DU GROUPE D'ETUDE DE L'EXPLOITATION TOUS TEMPS

a) Mise au point des conditions normalisées destinées à être utilisées par les Etats membres de la CEAC pour autoriser les compagnies aériennes étrangères à exploiter en catégorie II et portant au moins sur les aspects suivants:

(1) établissement des minima d'exploitation (HD/RVR);

(2) équipements de bord nécessaires;

(3) vérification de la performance des systèmes de guidage et de pilotage utilisés en exploitation;

(4) procédures d'exploitation et formation correspondante du personnel navigant technique;

(5) promulgation de la catégorie d'exploitation des pistes.

Note: Cette énumération ne comporte aucune idée de priorité d'examen futur.

b) Afin d'éviter une duplication d'efforts, tenir compte de la circulaire OACI 121–AN/90 et des résultats de tout travail correspondant de l'OACI, tel celui que est actuellement mené par les groupes AWOP et OCP.

RECOMMANDATION NO 5
PRIX DU CARBURANT AVIATION

LA COMMISSION

CONSIDERANT

que la clause 2) de la Recommandation no 1 de sa sixième Session intermédiaire (Spéciale) vise à permettre à la CEAC et aux Etats membres d'exercer la surveillance voulue des prix du carburant aviation;

CONSIDERANT

que les informations recueillies sur l'évolution des prix du carburant aviation montrent que des difficultés sont apparues sur certains aéroports en ce qui concerne la fourniture à des prix non discriminatoires du carburant aviation à toutes les compagnies aériennes;

1) RECOMMANDE

que les Etats membres assurent ou, tout au moins, encouragent la fourniture sur leurs aéroports du carburant aviation à des prix non discriminatoires à toutes les compagnies aériennes;

2) PRIE

le Président de la CEAC de porter la présente recommandation à l'attention des organisations et des Etats concernés.

g) the cancellation of any flight must be notified to the appropriate authorities and to the passengers as soon as possible; and

2) that, in connection with this recommendation, reference should also be made to the criteria for a common policy contained in the Annex to Recommendations Nos. 7 and 8 of the Second Intermediate Session which remain fully valid except in respect of the references to the level of fares and to the requirement of at least three stops in the inclusive tours programmes.

TERMS OF REFERENCE FOR THE WORKING GROUP ON ALL-WEATHER OPERATIONS

a) Develop standardized requirements for use by ECAC Member States for the authorization of Category II operations by foreign airlines, covering at least the following:

(1) Establishment of operating minima (DH/RVR)
(2) Airborne equipment requirements
(3) Verification of the performance of the guidance and piloting systems in operational use
(4) Operating procedures and related flight crew training
(5) Promulgation of operational category of runways.

Note: The above are not listed in any sense of priority for future consideration.

b) In order to avoid duplication of effort, take into account ICAO Circular 121–AN/90 and the results of any related ICAO work, such as that currently being carried out by the AWOP and the Obstacle Clearance Panel (OCP).

RECOMMENDATION NO. 5
AVIATION FUEL PRICES

WHEREAS

clause 2) of Recommendation No. 1 of the Sixth Intermediate Session (Special) of the Conference aimed at enabling ECAC and Member States to exercise appropriate surveillance of aviation fuel prices; and

WHEREAS

information obtained on the development of aviation fuel prices shows that difficulties have arisen at certain airports with respect to the supply of aviation fuel at nondiscriminatory prices to all airlines,

THE CONFERENCE

1) RECOMMENDS

that Member States ensure, or at least encourage, the supply at their airports of aviation fuel at non-discriminatory prices to all airlines; and

2) REQUESTS

the President of ECAC to bring this recommendation to the attention of the organizations and States concerned.

MANDAT DU GROUPE DE TRAVAIL SUR DES PROBLEMES DE SURETE

a) Examiner les mesures de sûreté prises actuellement par les services officiels, les administrations d'aéroport et les compagnies aériennes des Etats membres de la CEAC pour prévenir les détournements, les attentats à la bombe, les actes de sabotage et les autres formes de violence sur les aéroports internationaux des Etats de la CEAC.

b) Déterminer les différences qui peuvent exister entre les Etats de la CEAC dans la nature des mesures de sûreté et dans les modalités prévues pour leur mise en oeuvre.

c) Elaborer des propositions pour l'adoption de mesures de sûreté efficaces par les services officiels, les administrations d'aéroport et les compagnies aériennes des Etats membres de la CEAC.

Dans le cadre de son mandat, le groupe de travail devrait être invité à se pencher particulièrement sur les questions suivantes:

(i) Dispositions prévues pour la fouille des passagers et des bagages et leurs modalités d'exécution, entre autres dans quelle mesure un équipement est utilisé et quel personnel est chargé des fouilles.

(ii) Les variations entre les procédures de fouille en fonction de la route et du type de service – par exemple, régulier, charter, intérieur.

(iii) Les dispositions prises en vue d'assurer la sécurité matérielle des aéroports, y compris le contrôle de l'accès côté piste, la garde des aéronefs et dans quelle mesure le personnel militaire, la police et d'autres y participent.

(iv) Le coût et les modalités de financement des fouilles et des autres mesures de sûreté aux aéroports.

APPENDICE

REPONSE AU CONSEIL DE L'EUROPE

traduction

Monsieur,

J'ai l'honneur de vous écrire au sujet de certaines des questions posées dans la Résolution 545 (1973) et dans le document 3275 du Conseil de l'Europe sur des questions relatives à l'aviation civile en Europe. Comme vous le savez, la huitième Session triennale de la Commission européenne de l'aviation civile, tenue à Strasbourg du 25 au 30 juin 1973, a renvoyé ces documents aux Comités permanents (cf. paragraphe 21 – Doc 9062, ECAC/8), dont les rapports viennent d'être examinés par la septième Session intermédiaire tenue à Paris du 11 au 13 septembre 1974.

La Commission accueille avec satisfaction l'intérêt que continue à porter le Conseil au transport aérien et elle se félicite de pouvoir poursuivre le dialogue avec lui en la matière.

La CEAC a noté avec le plus grand intérêt, aux paragraphes 7 de la Résolution, et 25 à 31 du rapport de M. Rivière, les vues de votre Assemblée sur les problèmes que pose la capacité offerte sur l'Atlantique nord, et l'importance qu'elle attache à la nécessité de parvenir, en accord avec les autorités américaines et canadiennes, à un certain contrôle effectif de cette capacité. C'est là une question qui préoccupe de nombreux gouvernements depuis longtemps, et qui ne se pose pas seulement en fonction de la concurrence entre services réguliers et vols d'affrètement.

Toute solution à ce problème qui n'emporterait pas l'adhésion de toutes les parties intéressées n'aurait qu'une portée pratique limitée. Malgré des

TERMS OF REFERENCE FOR THE WORKING GROUP ON SECURITY PROBLEMS

a) Examine the kind of security precautions being taken by government agencies, airport administrations and airlines of ECAC Member States to prevent hijacking, bomb threats, sabotage and other forms of violence at international airports within ECAC States.

b) Identify differences in the security precautions and the arrangements for their implementation among ECAC States.

c) Develop proposals for the adoption of effective common measures of security by government agencies, airport administrations and airlines withing ECAC States.

Within its terms of reference the working group should be invited to consider particularly the following matters:

(i) The arrangements for searching passengers and baggage and the form these take, including the extent to which equipment is used, and the personnel who carry out the searching.

(ii) The way in which searching procedures are varied according to the route and type of service, for example scheduled, charter, domestic.

(iii) The provisions for physical security of the airports, including the control of access to the airside, the guarding of aircraft and the extent to which military forces, police and other personnel are involved.

(iv) The cost of searching and other security measures at airports and how this is financed.

APPENDIX

REPLY TO THE COUNCIL OF EUROPE

Sir,

I have the honour to write to you on certain of the questions raised in Council of Europe Resolution 545 (1973) and document 3275 of the Council on matters relating to civil aviation in Europe. As you know, the Eighth Triennial Session of the European Civil Aviation Conference, held at Strasbourg from 25 to 20 June 1973, referred these documents to the Standing Committees (cf. paragraph 21 of Doc 9062, ECAC/8), and their reports have now been considered by the Seventh Intermediate Session, which met in Paris from 11 to 13 September 1974.

The Conference welcomes the Council's continued interest in air transport and is glad to be able to pursue the dialogue on this subject with the Council.

ECAC has noted with great interest your Assembly's views, expressed in paragraph 7 of the Resolution and paragraphs 25–31 of Mr Rivière's report, on the problems connected with capacity available on the North Atlantic, and the importance which your Assembly attaches to the need to achieve effective control of that capacity in agreement with the Canadian and United States authorities. This question has caused concern to a number of governments for several years, and it has wider implications than those arising from the competition between scheduled services and charter flights.

Any solution to the problem that did not have the whole-hearted supdiscussions sur ce sujet au cours des dernières années, les principes de base et les facteurs économiques qui guident l'attitude des divers partenaires et qui régissent l'application de la plupart des accords bilatéraux dans ce secteur géographique n'ont pas permis jusqu'à présent d'envisager une solution globale satisfaisante. Une évolution s'est cependant fait sentir récemment, sous la pression d'une situation économique et financière difficile, et tout spécialement par suite de la crise du carburant. Certaines compagnies aériennes, appuyées par leur gouvernement, ont ainsi décidé des mesures de réduction ou de coordination des capacités offertes sur des routes déterminées. Il faut souhaiter que les enseignements à tirer de ces mesures seront utiles à long terme. Une délégation de la CEAC a aussi, récemment, eu des entretiens officieux avec des représentants des autorités canadiennes et américaines sur les tarifs passagers des services réguliers nord-atlantiques; certains participants ont estimé qu'il y aurait lieu de retenir, parmi les mesures à envisager pour rétablir la santé économique du transport aérien, un alignement plus étroit de la capacité mise en oeuvre par les compagnies régulières et non régulières sur la demande de transport aérien nord atlantique. Les avantages et inconvénients de toute solution devront cependant être soigneusement pesés avant que puisse être envisagée une évolution des principes qui ont jusqu'à présent régi l'exploitation des services aériens nord-atlantiques.

D'autre part, les autorités des Etats membres de la CEAC apportent toute leur attention à la planification et au développement des infrastructures aéroportuaires, en tenant compte notamment des considérations relatives à l'environnement mentionnées au paragraphe 9 de votre résolution. La responsabilité de base à cet égard appartient tout naturellement aux autorités responsable dans chaque pays. Il y a cependant de bonnes raisons pour que soit formulée une politique commune de la CEAC sur ces problèmes. Les meilleurs moyens d'y parvenir seront étudiés plus à fond dans le cadre d'une étude maintenant envisagée des contraintes qui pourraient affecter l'avenir du transport aérien européen. Nous ne manquerons pas de vous tenir informé des développements de ces études sur des questions dont nous savons qu'elles préoccupent beaucoup votre Assemblée. Le paragraphe 6 de votre résolution, où la question d'une libéralisation multilatérale coordonnée et progressive des droits de trafic est évoquée en liaison avec le rôle que pourraient jouer les Communautés européennes, a déjà été examiné par la CEAC , qui rassemble les autorités compétentes en matière d'aviation civile des Etats européens.

Comme la CEAC l'avait déjà souligné dans sa réponse à la Recommandation 391 (1964) de votre Assemblée, c'est une question aux implications nombreuses et variées, sur les plans technique, commercial, voire politique: dans la réponse mentionnée ci-dessus (cf. note d'information no 11 de la CEAC, paragraphe 10.13), il était suggéré en effet que la division de l'Europe du point de vue politique et les intérêts nationaux divergents avaient pu empêcher jusqu'alors la CEAC de se rallier unanimement aux propositions de libéralisation formulées dans le passé et de réaliser un accord multilatéral par l'échange de droits de trafic. Il était estimé probable (paragraphe 10.14) que si l'Europe était une entité économique et politique, les critères pour l'exploitation des services aériens ne seraient plus fondés sur les cinq libertés de l'air mais sur les données économiques du marché européen. La situation a considérablement évolué à beaucoup d'égards en Europe depuis lors, et la manière de considérer le probleme est elle-même susceptible de changer.

La CEAC a, au cours de ces dernières années, concentré son activité sur les problèmes des vols non réguliers. Elle envisage maintenant d'entreprendre dans un proche avenir l'analyse des problèmes que pose l'exploitation du réseau aérien régulier intra-européen. Nous ne manquerons pas, bien entendu, de vous tenir informé de ces développements.

En ce qui concerne le problème des vols non réguliers, évoqué à diverses port of all the parties concerned would have little practical effect. Although there have been discussions over recent years on this subject, the guiding principles and the economic conditions which influence the attitudes of the different partners and govern the application of most of the bilateral agreements in the North Atlantic sector have not so far permitted those involved to work out a satisfactory overall solution. However, under the recent pressure of economic and financial difficulties, and expecially as a result of the fuel crisis, the situation has been changing. Some airlines have decided, with the support of their governments, to take measures to reduce or to co-ordinate the capacity offered on particular routes. It is hoped that the lessons to be drawn from such measures will be useful in the long term. An ECAC delegation has also recently held informal talks with representatives of the Canadian and United States authorities on North Atlantic scheduled passenger fares; the opinion was expressed by some participants that, among the measures that should be considered for restoring the economic health of air services, attention should be paid to bringing the capacity offered by air carriers, scheduled and non-scheduled, more closely into line with the demand on the North Atlantic. It will nevertheless be necessary to weigh carefully the advantages and the disadvantages of any solution before considering a change in the principles that have so far governed the operation of North Atlantic air services.

In addition, the authorities of ECAC Member States are giving detailed attention to the planning and development of airport infrastructure, taking in to account the environmental considerations mentioned in paragraph 9 of the Resolution. The basic responsibility for this lies of course with the competent authorities in each country. There is nevertheless much to be said for formulating a common ECAC policy on these matters. Further consideration will be given to the best means of pursuing this in the framework of a study now being planned of the constraints that may affect the future of European air transport. We shall continue to keep you informed of the development of these studies on questions that we know are of great concern to your Assembly. Paragraph 6 of the Resolution, which refers to the question of a co-ordinated and progressive multilateral liberalisation of traffic rights in the context of the role which the European Communities might play, has already been considered in ECAC, which comprises the competent civil aviation authorities of the European States concerned.

As ECAC had already emphasized in its reply to Recommendation 391 (1964) of your Assembly, the question of traffic rights has many widely varying implications, technical, commercial and even political. In that reply (cf. ECAC Information Paper No. 11, paragraph 10.13) it was suggested that the political divisions within Europe and the differing national interests had so far prevented ECAC from following unanimously the proposals for liberalization put forward in the past and from achieving a multilateral agreement for the exchange of traffic rights. It was thought likely (see paragraph 10.14) that if Europe were a single political and economic entity the criteria for the operation of air services would be developed from the economic realities of the European market rather than the five freedoms of the air. The situation in Europe has evolved considerably in many respects since then, and the way in which the problem is looked at is also likely to change.

ECAC has in recent years years concentrated its activities on the problems of non-scheduled flights. It now plans to undertake in the near future an analysis of the problems raised in the operation of the intra-European network of scheduled air services. We shall of course keep you informed of developments.

With regard to the problem of non-scheduled flights, to which several references are made in Document 3275, and in particular to the analysis contained in Annex 1, you are no doubt aware of the steps that ECAC has reprises dans le document 3275 et notamment dans l'analyse de l'Annexe 1, vous êtes sans doute au courant des actions que la CEAC a entreprises, en concertation avec le Canada et les Etats-Unis. Ces pays recherchent ensemble les meilleurs moyens de rétablir une certaine cohérence sur le marché nord-atlantique, perturbé depuis de nombreuses années par une concurrence anarchique et par l'inadaptation fréquente des modalités d'affrètement aux nouvelles conditions du marché.

Cette entente avec le Canada et les Etats-Unis a déjà abouti à la mise en application sur l'Atlantique nord, avec quelques variantes inévitables d'un pays à l'autre, d'un nouveau système d'affrètement basé essentiellement sur la notion de réservation à l'avance. On peut expérer que ce système, dont certaines modalités sont déjà en cours de révision à la lumière des premières expériences, contribuera à stabiliser la marché au bénéfice, à long terme, à la fois du public et des transporteurs.

Le Canada, les États-Unis et la CEAC ont en outre décidé d'étudier d'éventuelles dispositions pour un cadre multilatéral pouvant permettre un développement ordonné de tous les types d'affrètement sur l'Atlantique nord.

Sur le plan proprement européen, la CEAC continue son effort d'harmonisation des réglementations et des politiques de ses membres en matière de vols non réguliers. Les progrès dans ce domaine et l'attitude généralement libérale des autorités aéronautiques ne sont certainement pas étrangères au développement rapide de ces vols et ont sans aucun doute fortement contribué à l'essor du tourisme intra-européen. La CEAC procède en permanence au bilan de ces politiques et de leurs conséquences et restera bien entendu attentive à leur future évolution.

VICTOR VERES
Président de la CEAC

C. ORGANISATION

BUREAU DE LA COMMISSION ELU A LA HUITIEME SESSION TRIENNALE

(*CEAC/8: Strasbourg, juin 1973*)

Président de la CEAC	V. VERES (Portugal)
Premier vice-Président	H. RABEN (Pays-Bas)
Deuxième vice-Président	D. HUBBACK (Royaume-Uni)
Troisième vice-Président	W. REHM (Rép. Féd. d'Allemagne)
Président Comité ECO–I (transport aérien régulier)	H. RABEN (Pays-Bas)
Président Comité ECO–II (transport aérien non régulier)	E. WILLOCH (Norvège)
Président Comité technique	K. J. TEMMES (Finlande)
Président Comité de facilitation	W. GULDIMANN (Suisse)
Secrétaire de la CEAC	MAURICE DOZ
Adresse	Commission européenne de l'Aviation civile 3bis, villa Emile Bergerat 92200 – Neuilly-sur-Seine France

undertaken in consultation with Canada and the United States. These countries are together seeking the best means to restore orderly development in the North Atlantic market, for many years upset by inadequately regulated competition and the fact that some of the charter concepts are not always suited to the changing market conditions.

The understanding with Canada and the United States has led to the introduction on the North Atlantic, though inevitably with some differences from country to country, of a new charter system based mainly on the advance booking concept. It is to be hoped that this system, which has already been subject to some modifications in the light of initial experience, will help to stabilize the market, to the long-term benefit both of the travelling public and of the air carriers.

As a further measure Canada, the United States and ECAC have agreed to study possible arrangements for a multilateral framework which should permit the orderly development of all types of charter operations on the North Atlantic.

In respect of intra-European non-scheduled operations, ECAC is continuing its efforts to harmonize the regulations and policies of its Member States. Progress in this field and the generally liberal attitude of the aeronautical authorities have certainly fostered the rapid development of such operations and without doubt are still contributing to the expansion of intra-European tourism. ECAC has these policies and their consequences under constant review and will of course remain on the alert for possible future development.

Yours faithfully,
VICTOR VERES
President of ECAC

C. ORGANISATION

OFFICERS OF THE CONFERENCE ELECTED AT THE EIGHT TRIENNIAL SESSION OF ECAC

(ECAC/8: Strasbourg, June 1973)

President of ECAC	V. VERES (Portugal)
First Vice-President	H. RABEN (Netherlands)
Second Vice-President	D. HUBBACK (United Kingdom)
Third Vice-President	W. REHM (Fed. Rep. Germany)
Chairman ECO-I Committee	H. RABEN (Netherlands)
Chairman ECO-II Committee	E. WILLOCH (Norway)
Chairman Technical Committee	K. J. TEMMES (Finland)
Chairman Facilitation Committee	W. GULDIMANN (Switzerland)
Secretary of ECAC	MAURICE DOZ
Address	European civil aviation conference 3 bis, villa Emile Bergerat 92200–Neuilly-sur-Seine France

D. PUBLICATIONS

DOCUMENTS CEAC

Editions françaises et anglaises

A. Rapports (à partir de septembre 1974)
Septième Session intermédiaire.
Paris, 11–13 septembre 1974.
(Doc ECAC/INT.S/7). 1974. 34 pages

B. Autres documents

ECAC. CEAC Doc No. 1	Recueil des règlements et pratiques des Etats de la CEAC en matière de transports aériens non réguliers (1970) (Diffusion restreinte aux administrations des Etats membres de la CEAC)
ECAC. CEAC Doc No. 2	Manuel de l'état de mise en application des recommandations de la CEAC relatives au au transport aérien non régulier (1970) Révision no. 1 (janvier 1973) Révision no. 2 (mars 1975)
ECAC. CEAC Doc No. 3	Prévision du trafic aérien régulier intra-européen de passagers 1968–1980 (1970)
ECAC. CEAC Doc No. 4	Statistiques du trafic non régulier enregistré dans les Etats de la CEAC Année se terminant le 31/10/70
ECAC. CEAC Doc No. 5	Statistiques du trafic non régulier enregistré dans les Etats de la CEAC Année se terminant le 31/10/71
ECAC. CEAC Doc No. 6	Manuel de l'état de mise en application des recommandations de la CEAC relatives au transport aérien régulier (1973)
ECAC. CEAC Doc No. 7	Statistiques du trafic non régulier enregistré dans les Etats de la CEAC Année se terminant le 31/10/72
ECAC. CEAC Doc No. 8	Statistiques du trafic non régulier enregistré dans les Etats de la CEAC Année se terminant le 31/10/73
ECAC. CEAC Doc No. 9	Manuel des règlements et pratiques des Etats de la CEAC en matière de transports aériens non réguliers (1974)

ACCORDS INTERNATIONAUX ET MULTILATERAUX

Editions trilingues (anglais, français, espagnol)

Accord Multilatéral sur les droits commerciaux pour les transports aériens non réguliers en Europe.
Ouvert à la signature à Paris le 30 avril 1956
(Doc 7695) 8 pages
Accord Multilatéral relatif aux certificats de navigabilité des aéronefs importés.
Ouvert à la signature à Paris le 22 avril 1960
(Doc 8056) 12 pages
Accord International sur la procédure applicable à l'établissement des tarifs des services aériens réguliers.

D. PUBLICATIONS

ECAC DOCUMENTS

English and French editions

A. Report series (commencing September 1974)
Seventh Intermediate Session.
Paris, 11–13 September 1974.
(Doc ECAC/INT.S/7). 1974. 34 pp.

B. Other documents

ECAC. CEAC Doc No. 1	Digest of regulations and practices of ECAC States on non-scheduled air transport (1970) (Not for distribution outside ECAC member administrations)
ECAC. CEAC Doc No. 2	Manual on the status of implementation of ECAC recommendations relating to non-scheduled air transport (1970) Revision No. 1 (January 1973) Revision No. 2 (March 1975)
ECAC. CEAC Doc No. 3	Forecast of intra-European scheduled air passenger traffic 1968–1980 (1970)
ECAC. CEAC Doc No. 4	Statistics of non-scheduled traffic reported in ECAC States Year ending 31/10/70
ECAC. CEAC Doc No. 5	Statistics of non-scheduled traffic reported in ECAC States Year ending 31/10/71
ECAC. CEAC Doc No. 6	Manual on the status of implementation of ECAC recommendations relating to scheduled air transport (1973)
ECAC. CEAC Doc No. 7	Statistics of non-scheduled traffic reported in ECAC States Year ending 31/10/72
ECAC. CEAC Doc No. 8	Statistics of non-scheduled traffic reported in ECAC States Year ending 31/10/73
ECAC. CEAC Doc No. 9	Manual on the regulations and practices of ECAC States on non-scheduled air transport (1974)

INTERNATIONAL AND MULTILATERAL AGREEMENTS

Trilingual editions (English, French, Spanish)

Multilateral Agreement on commercial rights of non-scheduled air services in Europe.
Opened for signature at Paris on 30 April 1956.
(Doc 7695) 8 pp.
Multilateral Agreement relating to certificates of airworthiness for imported aircraft.
Opened for signature at Paris on 22 April 1960.
(Doc 8056 12 pp.
International Agreement on the procedure for the establishment of tariffs for scheduled air services.

Ouvert à la signature à Paris le 10 juillet 1967
(Doc 8681) 11 pages
Les documents peuvent être commandés à l'adresse suivante:
Section des Documents
Organisation de l'Aviation civile international
3 bis Villa Emile Bergerat
92200 Neuilly-sur-Seine
France

Opened for signature at Paris on 10 July 1967.

(Doc 8681) 11 pp.

Orders for documents should be sent to the following address:

Documents Section
International Civil Aviation Organization
3 bis, villa Emile Bergerat
92200 Neuilly-sur-Seine
France

CHAPITRE XII

CONFERENCE EUROPEENNE DES ADMINISTRATIONS DES POSTES ET DES TELECOMMUNICATIONS

A. ACTIVITES DE LA CEPT EN 1974

29 et 30 janvier: Réunion extraordinaire des Chefs des Administrations postales membres de la CEPT à Madrid.
11–21 mars: Réunion extraordinaire de la Commission „Postes" à Las Palmas de Grande Canarie (Espagne).
12 et 13 mars: Réunion du Comité de coordination des Présidents et des Vices-Présidents de la Commission „Télécommunications" (CCPVP) à Puerto de la Cruz (Espagne).
14–22 mai: Réunion extraordinaire de la Commission „Télécommunications" à Puerto de la Cruz (Espagne).
22 mai – 5 juillet: Réunions spéciales de la Commission „Postes" durant le XVIIe Congrès postal universel à Lausanne.
11 et 12 juillet: Réunion du Comité de coordination des télécommunications par satellite (CCTS) à Lausanne.

La réunion des Chefs des Administrations postales membres de la CEPT a permis aux participants de procéder à de larges échanges de vues sur l'attitude que les membres de la CEPT devaient adopter lors de la discussion de problèmes politiques par le Congrès de l'Union postale universelle à Lausanne.

La réunion extraordinaire de la Commission „Postes" à Las Palmas eut pour but d'examiner les propositions introduites au Congrès de l'Union postale universelle. Elle désigna les Administrations qui devaient intervenir lors des débats de ce Congrès, pour appuyer ces propositions ou pour les combatre.

Les réunions spéciales de la Commission „Postes" durant le XVIIe Congrès de l'UPU à Lausanne permirent de maintenir le contact entre les membres de la CEPT et de coordonner leurs points de vue. A cette occasion, six groupes de travail furent constitués pour étudier les nouvelles propositions diffusées par le Bureau international de l'UPU. La préparation minutieuse de ce Congrès par la CEPT eut des résultats positifs pour ses membres. Ainsi, les 330 propositions qu'ils introduisirent ont été acceptées par le Congrès, à l'exception de quelques-unes seulement. Le Conseil exécutif et le Conseil consultatif des études postales seront présidés jusqu'au prochain Congrés (1979) par des membres de la CEPT. Quatre des dix Commissions du Conseil exécutif seront également présidées par des membres de la CEPT. Onze sièges sur les trente-cinq que compte le Conseil consultatif des études postales ont été attribués à des Pays dont les Administrations sont membres de la CEPT.

Le Comité de coordination des Présidents et des Vice-Présidents de la Commission „Télécommunications" (CCPVP) a consacré la plus grande partie de ses travaux à l'examen du fonctionnement de cette Commission. Il a élaboré à son intention des directives pour délimitation des champs d'activité des Groupes de travail. Il lui a demandé de charger les Groupes de travail d'examiner la question de la diffusion des Recommandations et de les classer dans l'une des trois catégories „à usage exclusif de la CEPT," „à diffusion restreinte" ou „à diffusion libre."

La réunion extraordinaire de la Commission „Télécommunications" de Puerto de la Cruz a adopté 19 Recommandations; elle en a revisé 13 et abrogé 7. Elle a mis à l'étude 8 nouvelles questions. La Commission a

CHAPTER XII

EUROPEAN CONFERENCE OF POSTAL AND TELECOMMUNICATIONS ADMINISTRATIONS

A. ACTIVITIES IN 1974

January 29–30: Extraordinary meeting of the Heads of the Postal Administrations of ECPT, Madrid.

March 11–21: Extraordinary meeting of the Postal Commission at Las Palmas, Canary Islands (Spain).

March 12–13: Meeting of the Co-ordinating Committee of the Chairmen and Vice-Chairmen of the Telecommunications Commission (CCPVP) at Puerto de la Cruz (Spain).

May 14–22: Extraordinary meeting of the Telecommunications Commission at Puerto de la Cruz (Spain).

May 22 – July 5: Special meetings of the Postal Commission during the 17th. Universal Postal Congress at Lausanne.

July 11–12: Meeting of the Committee on Co-ordination of Telecommunications by Satellite (CCTS) at Lausanne).

The meeting of the Heads of the Postal Administrations of ECPT enabled the participants to undertake an exchange of views on the attitude which the members of ECPT should adopt during the discussion of policy questions by the Universal Postal Union at Lausanne.

The extraordinary meeting of the Postal Commission at Las Palmas was devoted to an examination of the proposals tabled for discussion at the Congress of the Universal Postal Union. It decided which Administrations should intervene during the debates of the Congress, either to support or oppose these proposals.

The special meetings of the Postal Commission during the 17th. Congress of the U.P.U. enabled the members of the ECPT to keep in touch and co-ordinate their views. On this occasion six working groups were set up to study the new proposals made by the Bureau of the U.P.U. The careful preparation of this Congress by the ECPT had positive results for its members. Thus, the 330 proposals which they introduced were accepted by the Congress, with a few exceptions. The Executive Council and the Consultative Council on Postal Studies will be under the chairmanship of members of ECPT until the next U.P.U. Congress in 1979. Four of the ten Commissions of the Executive Council will also be chaired by members of ECPT. Eleven out of thirty five seats on the Consultative Council on Postal Studies have been allocated to members of ECPT.

The Co-ordinating Committee of the Chairmen and Vice-Chairmen of the Telecommunications Commission (CCPVP) devoted the greater part of its time to an examination of the functioning of this Commission. It worked out for the Commission certain directives to define the fields of Competence of the Working Groups. It asked the Commission to instruct them to examine the question of distribution of its Recommendations, and to classify them in three categories: "only for the use of CEPT," "restricted distribution" and "unrestricted distribution."

The extraordinary meeting of the Telecommunications Commission at Puerto de la Cruz adopted 19 Recommendations: it revised 13 and annulled 7. It inaugurated the study of 8 new questions. The Commission adopted certain directives intended to avoid overlopping between its Working Groups. It discussed its position in regard to certain proposals of the European Economic Community (EEC) for opening up the telecométabli des directives visant à éviter des chevauchements d'activités entre ses Groupes de travail. Elle a étudié sa position face aux projets de la Communauté économique européenne (CEE) d'ouverture des marchés des télécommunications, de même que la manière d'établir des contacts avec les organes compétents en matière de télécommunications aux Etats-Unis.

Le Comité de coordination des télécommunications par satellites (CCTS) a constaté une intense activité dans le domaine des satellites en raison de l'avancement rapide des programmes en cours et de la naissance de nouveaux projets. Afin de faire valoir le point de vue des membres de la CEPT, il a créé un Groupe de travail ,,Satellites de télécommunications maritimes."

Les divers Groupes et Sous-groupes de travail de la CEPT ont tenu de nombreuses réunions pour traiter les problèmes dont l'étude leur avait été confiée par l'Assemblée plénière et les Commissions ,,Postes" ou ,,Télécommunications."

L'Administration gérante de la CEPT pour les années 1972–1975 (Administration des postes et télécommunications d'Espagne) a préparé, organisé et convoqué la VIIIe Session ordinaire de la Conférence et de ses organes, qui siégèrent à Malaga-Torremolinos du 8 au 18 avril 1975.

B. PUBLICATIONS

En 1974, l'Administration gérante de la CEPT a diffusé deux numéros du ,,Bulletin CEPT."

C. ORGANISATION

La Présidence de la CEPT a été assumée par Monsieur Pedro Sanchez Perez, Directeur général des postes et télécommunications d'Espagne, après la nomination de Monsieur Leon Herrera aux fonctions de Ministre de l'information et du tourisme d'Espagne.

La Commission ,,Postes" fut présidée par Monsieur J. Ascandoni, Chef du service international des postes.

La Commission ,,Télécommunications" fut dirigée par Monsieur F. Molina Negro, Chef du service international des télécommunications.

Le Secrétariat fut placé sous la direction de Monsieur J. de Frutos du service international des postes. Un Office de liaison traitant les affaires courantes de secrétariat fonctionna à Berne.

La gérance de la CEPT, après la réunion de l'Assemblée plénière de Malaga-Torremolinos est assumée en commun par l'Administration des postes de Suède et l'Administration des télécommunications de Suède. La nouvelle adresse de l'organisation est la suivante:

Secrétariat CEPT
S–105 00 Stockholm, Suède

munications market and also as regards the methods of establishing contacts with the competent organs for telecommunications in the U.S.A.

The Committee on Co-ordination of Telecommunications by Satellite (CCTS) observed an intense activity in the field of satellites by reason of the rapid progress of current programmes and the birth of new projects. In order to present the point of view of the members of ECPT it set up a Working Group on "Maritime Telecommunications Satellites."

The different Working Groups and Sub-Groups of ECPT held many meetings to deal with the problems entrusted to them by the plenary Assembly and the Commissions on Posts and Telecommunications.

The Administration in charge of ECPT for the years 1972 to 1975 (the Spanish Administration for Posts and Telecommunications) prepared, organised and convened the eighth Ordinary Session of the Conference and its organs, held at Malaga-Torremolinos from April 8 to 18, 1975.

B. PUBLICATIONS

The Administration in charge of ECPT has published two numbers of the ECPT Bulletin.

C. ORGANISATION

The presidency of the ECPT was assumed by Mr. Pedro Sanchez Perez, Director General of the Spanish Posts and telecommunications, after the appointment of Mr. Leon Herrera as Minister of Information and Tourism.

The Postal Commission was presided over by Mr. J. Ascandoni, Head of the International Postal Service.

The Telecommunications Commission was directed by Mr. F. Molina Negro, Head of the International Telecommunications Service.

The Secretariat was placed under the direction of Mr. J. de Frutos, of the International Postal Service. A liaison office for current affairs has been set in Berne.

The management of the ECPT, after the meeting of the plenary Assembly at Malaga-Torremolinos, is assured jointly by the Swedish Postal and Telecommunications Administrations. The new address of the organisation is as follows:

Secretariat ECPT
S–105 00 Stockholm, Sweden

CHAPITRE XIII

ASSOCIATION EUROPEENNE DE LIBRE-ECHANGE

A. DEVELOPPEMENTS EN 1974

Pour les sept pays de l'AELE – Autriche, Finlande, Islande, Norvège, Portugal, Suède et Suisse – 1974 a été une année particulièrement troublée. La crise du pétrole, l'inflation, l'instabilité monétaire internationale et la menace d'une sérieuse récession économique ont pesé lourdement sur les gouvernements et ont été un sujet d'inquiétude pour les nations. Pourtant, le fait d'être tous de petits pays menacés par de événements trop considérables pour être contrôlés par des actions nationales individuelles a contribué à unir les membres de l'AELE et à approfondir les relations au sein de celle-ci. Une volonté générale s'est manifestée de renforcer la coopération dans l'Association et dans tous les forums internationaux qui traitent des graves problèmes économiques de l'heure. Dans ce contexte, il faut citer aussi la solidarité manifestée à l'égard du Portugal; non seulement plusieurs pays de l'AELE ont engagé une action bilatérale pour venir en aide à l'économie portugaise, mais le Conseil au niveau ministériel a décidé d'examiner en priorité quelle action commune pouvait être entreprise dans ce sens au sein de l'AELE. Cette extension de la coopération de l'AELE à des domaines plus larges est un phénomène qu'on a observé non seulement au sein des Conseils, mais également dans les réunions du comité consultatif et des parlementaires de l'AELE.

Etendre et intensifier le libre-échange

Considérés comme un groupe, les sept pays de l'AELE sont davantage tributaires du commerce international que n'importe quelle autre région commerçante comparable. Totalisant seulement 1,2% de la population du globe, ils s'attribuent 7% des exportations mondiales et 9% des importations. Il est donc naturel qu'en 1974 aucun effort n'ait été négligé pour préserver et améliorer le système libéral des échanges qui a tant contribué à la prospérité dans le monde au cours du dernier quart de siècle.

A l'intérieur même de l'AELE, on a commencé à renforcer et à approfondir le libre-échange entre les pays membres; en termes d'exportations, les échanges intrarégionaux représentent à peu près 20% des exportations totales des Sept. Etant donné que les droits de douane et les contingents ont été supprimés dans les échanges de produits industriels à l'intérieur de la Zone, l'attention s'est portée naturellement sur l'amélioration des arrangements destinés à éliminer les obstacles non tarifaires au commerce, en particulier ceux résultant de l'existence de normes et de règlements nationaux différents. Cette action s'est concrétisée de trois manières.

Tout d'abord, on a décidé de rendre plus efficaces les procédures selon lesquelles les pays de l'AELE notifient à l'avance au Secrétariat – et par conséquent à chacun d'eux – toute norme ou règlement nouveau qui va être appliqué et qui est susceptible d'avoir des effets négatifs sur les échanges. La notification anticipée porte également sur toute mesure envisagée par des autorités de normalisation qui ne font pas partie des instances gouvernementales. Il convient d'accorder un délai suffisant pour permettre aux autres pays de l'Association de faire leurs observations et, toute norme nouvelle qui s'écarte d'une règle admise sur le plan international doit être motivée.

Deuxièmement, il a été décidé de ne rien négliger pour engager des pays non membres de l'AELE à participer aux divers arrangements de recon-

CHAPTER XIII

EUROPEAN FREE TRADE ASSOCIATION

A. DEVELOPMENTS IN 1974

For the seven EFTA countries – Austria, Finland, Iceland, Norway, Portugal, Sweden and Switzerland – the year 1974 was an unusually troubled period. The oil crisis, inflation, world monetary instability and the threat of a deep economic recession all pressed on the governments and disturbed the people. However, the awareness that they were all small countries, menaced by events too large to be overcome by separate national action, also served to bring the countries together and to deepen the EFTA relationship. There was a general determination to strengthen co-operation within EFTA and in all other international gatherings which were trying to deal with the grave economic problems affecting the whole world. Another example of EFTA solidarity was the case of Portugal; not only did several EFTA countries begin bilateral action to assist the Portuguese economy, but the EFTA Council at Ministerial level decide that urgent steps must be taken to examine what common action could be taken within the Association to the same end. This extension of EFTA co-operation to wider fields was a phenomenon observed not only in the Councils, but also in the meetings of the Consultative Committee and of the EFTA Parliamentarians.

Widening and deepening free trade

As a group, the seven EFTA countries are more dependent on international trade than any other comparable trading group. With only 1.2% of the world's population, they account for 7% of world exports and 9% of world imports. It was therefore natural that every effort was made during 1974 to preserve and improve the liberal trading system which has made such a large contribution to world prosperity over the past quarter of a century.

This work began within EFTA itself, to strengthen and deepen the free trade between the participating countries; in terms of exports, intra-EFTA trade accounts for about 20% of the total exports of the seven countries. Since there are no longer any tariff or quota barriers to trade in manufactured goods within the Association, attention was concentrated on improving the arrangements to remove non-tariff barriers, particularly those which arise from the existence of differing national standards and regulations. This action took three forms.

Firstly, agreement was reached to tighten up the procedures whereby the EFTA countries give advance notification to the Secretariat – and thereby to each other – of any new standards or regulations which were to be imposed and which might have negative effects on trade, This advance notification is to include proposed action by standards authorities outside the government machine. Sufficient notice is to be given to allow for comments from the other participating countries – and any new standard which departs from an agreed international rule must be explained and justified.

Secondly, it was decided that greater efforts must be made to attract non-EFTA countries to participate in the various schemes for the mutual recognition of tests and inspections which have been developed in EFTA since 1969. These schemes cover a variety of products –electrical equipnaissance réciproque des essais et contrôles qui sont élaborés au sein de l'AELE depuis 1969. Ces arrangements couvrent un grand nombre de produits – les appareils électriques, les appareils à gaz, les appareils à pression, les produits pharmaceutiques, les machines et les tracteurs agricoles, les équipements de sauvetage et de lutte contre l'incendie à bord des navires, le poinçonnement des ouvrages en métaux précieux; on a examiné la possibilité d'étendre ces arrangements à d'autres produits. Il importe évidemment que des pays ne faisant pas partie de l'Association et qui sont d'importants partenaires commerciaux soient invités à s'associer à ces arrangements, afin d'en assurer le maximum d'efficacité.

Troisièmement, il a été décidé de convoquer au début de 1975 une réunion des représentants des ministères du commerce des pays de l'AELE et des représentants des autorités de normalisation qui participent activement aux travaux d'harmonisation internationale des normes, cela afin de permettre aux deux groupes de mieux comprendre leurs problèmes et besoins respectifs.

En 1974, on n'a négligé aucun effort pour assurer le bon fonctionnement et le développement des accords de libre-échange conclus entre les pays de l'AELE et les Communautés européennes. Ces accords sont entrés en vigueur le 1er janvier 1973 et en 1974 les droits de douane sur les produits manufacturés faisant l'objet d'échanges entre les deux parties avaient déjà été réduits de 40%. L'importance de ces accords se mesure au fait que 40% environ des exportations totales des pays de l'AELE sont absorbées par les marchés des neuf pays des Communautés.

En 1974, les sept Comités mixtes ont tenu deux séries de réunions, l'une en mai et l'autre en décembre; les Comités mixtes ont été institués conformément aux accords de libre-échange pour s'occuper de la gestion des accords et veiller à leur bonne exécution et aussi pour servir de forum au sein duquel les pays de l'Association peuvent examiner avec la Commission des Communautés tout problème qui se pose. Comme à l'accoutumée, les pays de l'AELE ont étudié ensemble et à l'avance l'ordre du jour des réunions des Comités mixtes, afin d'assurer une coordination éventuelle de leurs positions.

En fait, les Comités mixtes ont examiné un large éventail de questions. Comme en 1973, les règles d'origine des accords de libre-échange ont subi des modifications qui en ont facilité l'application dans les milieux du négoce, tant au sein de l'AELE que dans les CE. Ces changements ont été élaborés par les comités douaniers institués par les Comités mixtes, qui ont bénéficié pour leur part des travaux du comité AELE des experts en matière d'origine et de douane, cela bien avant que les négociations ne soient entamées avec les Communautés. D'autres questions de détail ont encore été examinées au sein des Comités mixtes; notamment celles touchant les échanges entre les parties contractantes.

Mais les Comités mixtes se sont penchés également sur des questions de plus vaste portée, chacune des parties estimant qu'il ne faut rien négliger par des échanges de vues et d'informations, pour empêcher que les objectifs des accords en matière de libre-échange ne soient compromis sous la pression des difficultés internationales qui pourraient inciter les gouvernements à prendre des mesures nationales dangereuses pour le système libéral des échanges consacré par lesdits accords. Ainsi, dans chaque Comité mixte on a discuté des effets de la conjoncture sur la situation dans les pays respectifs de l'AELE et dans la Communauté. A l'occasion de la réunion de décembre, chaque pays de l'AELE a tenu à soulever la question des difficultés que rencontre l'Islande, dont l'accord de libre-échange est compromis par le refus de la Communauté d'appliquer le régime libéral des échanges aux importations de poisson, du fait qu'un pays de la Communauté, la République fédérale d'Allemagne, n'est pas parvenue à un accord avec l'Islande sur la question de la limite des eaux de pêche.

Toutefois, c'est le Portugal qui a fait le plus largement usage du Comiment, gas stoves, pressure vessels, pharmaceuticals, agricultural tractors, ships' safety and fire-fighting equipment, the hallmarking of articles made of precious metals – and the possibility of adding other products was being studied. It was obviously of importance that outside countries which are important trading partners should be induced to participate, so that the schemes could operate with maximum efficiency.

Thirdly, it was decided to call together early in 1975 a meeting of officials from the Trade Ministries of EFTA with their colleagues from the Standards authorities who are actively engaged in the international effort to arrive at harmonized international standards, so that both groups could arrive at a better understanding of each others' problems and needs.

Every effort was also made during 1974 to ensure the smooth operation and development of the Free Trade Agreements (FTA's) between the EFTA countries and the European Communities. These Agreements came into force on 1 January 1973 and in 1974 had already brought about a 40% reduction in the tariffs on manufactured goods between the parties. Their importance can be guaged from the fact that about 40% of the total exports of the EFTA countries are sold to the markets of the nine countries participating in the Communities.

There were two series of meetings during 1974, one series in May and the second in December, of the seven Joint Committees which were set up under the FTAs to supervice their operation and to serve as a forum in which the EFTA countries could discuss with the Commission of the Communities any problems which arose. As is customary, in EFTA countries studied together in advance the agenda for the Joint Committee meetings, so as to provide for any necessary coordination of their positions.

In fact, the range of matters raised in the Joint Committees was very wide. As in 1973, the origin rules of the FTAs were further amended so as to be more easily operated by the trading community both in EFTA and in the EC. This work was prepared in advance by the Customs Committees set up by the Joint Committees – and they in their turn were served by the EFTA Committee of Origin and Customs Experts, before negotiations were opened with the Communities. There was also discussion of other matters of detail in the Joint Committees, on questions affecting the trade between the parties.

But the Joint Committees also gave attention to much wider questions, the feeling on both sides being that every effort must be made, through open exchanges of views and information, to prevent the free trade objectives of the FTAs from being frustrated by the pressure of world difficulties which might cause governments to take national measures inimical to the liberal trading regime enshrined in the Agreements. Thus in each Joint Committee there was discussion of the impact of the general economic situation on conditions in the EFTA country concerned and in the Community. At the December meetings, each EFTA country also made a point of raising the difficulties of Iceland, whose FTA was frustrated by the refusal of the Community to apply the liberal trading regime for fish imports because one Community country, Germany, had not reached agreement with Iceland on the question of fisheries limits.

However, the most extensive use of the Joint Committee machinery was made by Portugal. In this case the Committee did not confine itself to a discussion only of trade and of the general economic situation. The Portuguese side, against the background of the overthrow in April 1974 of the 40-year-old dictatorship, also made use of Article 35 of the FTA, which could permit the extension of relations with the Communities to fields not covered in the Agreement. Thus Portugal suggested concessions from the Communities concerning investment, technical assistance, sub-contracting and the status and treatment of Portuguese workers in the EC countries. On the trade side, the Portuguese requests included better entry terms into the E.C. for her exports of textiles, paper, wine, tomato paste and sarté mixte. En l'occurrence, le Comité ne s'est pas limité à une discussion portant sur les échanges et la situation économique générale. Les Portugais, à la suite du renversement d'une dictature qui avait duré une quarantaine d'années, ont fait usage de l'article 35 de l'accord de libre-échange qui permet d'étendre les relations établies avec les Communautés à des domaines non couverts par l'accord. C'est ainsi que le Portugal a souhaité des concessions de la part des Communautés en matière d'investissements, d'assistance technique, de sous-traitance et concernant le statut et les conditions des travailleurs portugais dans les CE. Dans le domaine commercial, les Portugais ont demandé l'aménagement des régimes applicables à l'importation dans les Communautés de certains produits dont les textiles, le papier, les vins, les concentrés de tomates et les conserves de sardines. Ils ont également demandé un calendrier plus étendu pour la réduction des droits de douane à l'importation de certains produits manufacturés en provenance des CE, ainsi qu'une plus grande souplesse pour ce qui est de la protection des ,,industries naissantes."

De son côté, la Communauté a affirmé son soutien à une évolution politique qui a ouvert la voie à un ordre démocratique et a décidé que le Comité mixte devait entreprendre le plus rapidement possible l'examen des demandes portugaises.

Les pays de l'AELE ont aussi pris des mesures pour protéger le système libéral des échanges dans des forums plus importants. C'est ainsi que les représentants des pays de l'AELE à l'OCDE ont vivement soutenu la Déclaration aux termes de laquelle tous les pays membres sont convenus en mai 1974 de s'abstenir de recourir, pendant une période déterminée, à des mesures commerciales restrictives. Au sein du GATT également, les pays de L'AELE ont joué un røle à part entière dans les travaux préparatoires qui se sont déroulés en 1974 en vue de la nouvelle série de négociations commerciales multilatérales et ont exprimé le souhait que celles-ci entrent aussi rapidement que possible dans leur phase active. Dans la situation économique difficile que nous connaissons actuellement, il importe surtout, a souligné l'AELE ,que les principales nations commerçantes soient engagées dans des négociations actives pour préserver et améliorer le système libéral des échanges. Cela constituerait en quelque sorte une sauvegarde contre la récession économique.

Des consultations dans d'autres domaines

Mais la coopération dans l'AELE s'est étendue au-delà des questions commerciales. En 1974, on a aussi procédé au sein de l'Association à des échanges de vues sur les problèmes énergétiques, en particulier sur la création de *l'Agence internationale de l'énergie*. Lorsque l'Agence a été instituée, trois pays de l'AEle – l'Autriche, la Suède et la Suisse – en sont devenus membres; la Norvège, pour sa part, en tant que pays producteur de pétrole et futur exportateur, a cherché à établir des relations spéciales avec la nouvelle organisation, différentes de la participation en qualité de membre à part entière. Les ministres et les délégués permanents ont aussi examiné dans le cadre de l'AELE d'autres questions présentant un intérêt commun, comme l'inflation et les problèmes monétaires à l'échelon international, permettant de réaliser ainsi une certaine identité de vues. Etant donné que le pouvoir individuel de négociation de chacun des pays de l'Association est peu considérable, des avantages évidents pouvaient être acquis dans divers forums internationaux à condition que plusieurs pays de l'AELE considèrent dans leur intérêt de s'exprimer d'une seule voix.

dines. A longer timetable was asked for the reduction of Portuguese duties on certain manufactures imported from the E.C.; and more flexibility was requested regarding Portuguese protection for "infant industries."

The Community side stated its support for a democratic political evolution in Portugal and agreed that the Joint Committee should undertake to examine all the Portuguese requests, detailed work to begin without delay.

The EFTA countries also acted to protect the world liberal trading system in wider fields. For example, the EFTA representatives in the OECD gave strong support to the "trade pledge" whereby all the participating countries agreed in May 1974 to refrain for a fixed period of time from restrictive trade measures. In the GATT also, the EFTA countries played their full part in the preparatory work which went on throughout 1974 to prepare for the new "Tokyo Round" of multilateral trade negotiations and urged that the stage of active negotiating should begin as soon as possible. The EFTA view stressed the vital importance, in the existing difficult world economic situation, of the principal trading nations being engaged in active talks to preserve and improve the liberal trading system. Such a situation would itself be some safeguard against regression.

Consultation on other problems

But EFTA cooperation did not stop at trade. The Association was used during 1974 for exchanges of views on energy questions, particularly concerning the establishment of the new *International Energy Agency*. When the Agency was set up, three EFTA countries – Austria, Sweden and Switzerland – became members and Norway, as an oil producer and large potential exporter, sought a special relationship with the new organization, short of full membership. EFTA Ministers and officials also used the EFTA framework for the discussion of other matters of common interest such as inflation and world monetary problems, thus making possible some identity of approach. Since the individual bargaining power of each EFTA country is slight, there were obvious advantages to be gained in various world gatherings if several EFTA countries could find it in their interest to speak with one voice.

Les Conseils de l'AELE

Selon la procédure établie, le Conseil de l'AELE et le Conseil mixte AELE-Finlande se réunissent simultanément au niveau des délégués permanents une fois par semaine, au siège de l'Association à Genève. Les délégués permanents sont les ambassadeurs des pays membres auprès de l'AELE à Genève. Deux fois par an, habituellement en mai et en novembre, les Conseils de l'AELE se réunissent simultanément au niveau ministériel. La plupart de ces réunions ont lieu à Genève; parfois, elles se tiennent dans la capitale d'un autre pays de l'Association, comme la réunion de novembre 1974 à Helsinki.

Toutefois, les décisions ne sont pas prises seulement à l'occasion de ces réunions semestrielles. Aux termes de la Convention de Stockholm, les Conseils ont tous pouvoirs de décision, quel que soit le niveau de représentation. Par conséquent, dans les réunions ministérielles on procède davantage à des échanges de vues en matière de politique générale qu'à des décisions concernant le régime commercial de l'AELE.

Cette constatation ressort en particulier des deux communiqués publiés à l'issue des réunions ministérielles de mai et d'octobre.

Réunion ministérielle des 8 et 9 mai 1974, à Genève

Le Conseil de l'AELE et le Conseil mixte AELE-Finlande se sont réunis au niveau ministériel à Genève, les 8 et 9 mai 1974. La séance était présidée par le chef du Département fédéral de l'économie publique de la Suisse, M. Ernst Brugger, Président de la Confédération.

Tout en constatant avec satisfaction la croissance continue des échanges à l'intérieur de l'AELE, les ministres ont examiné l'évolution au sein de l'Association, au moment où l'économie mondiale se trouve dans une situation difficile caractérisée par des taux d'inflation élevés, une forte augmentation des prix du pétrole et d'autres matières premières et les risques persistants de perturbation monétaires à l'échelon international. Les ministres ont exprimé leur conviction qu'il fallait continuer d'utiliser au maximum les consultations multilatérales pour traiter les problèmes économiques auxquels la plupart des pays sont confrontés actuellement. Ils ont souligné la valeur du forum que l'Association offre aux pays de l'AELE pour des echanges de vues utiles sur ces questions.

Dans le domaine commercial, les ministres sont convenus que les gouvernements feraient tout leur possible, conformément aux accords et dispositions existants, pour éviter, face à des difficultés de balance des paiements ou d'ordre sectoriel, de prendre des mesures qui pourraient en ellesmêmes avoir un effet contraire et qui seraient préjudiciables au système du commerce international. Ils ont donc décidé de soutenir l'idée d'une déclaration des gouvernements de s'abstenir pour une période déterminée de prendre des mesures commerciales restrictives et autres mesures relatives aux opérations courantes et de s'engager dans une concurrence nuisible en matière de soutien officiel des crédits à l'exportation.

Les ministres ont souligné que dans l'AELE la Convention de Stockholm constitue un ensemble de règles très précieuses pour assurer la continuité du libre-échange. Les ministres ont également souligné que les accords de libre-échange conclus entre les pays de l'AELE et les Communautés européennes étaient destinés à jouer un rôle semblable dans les relations commerciales entre les deux groupes de pays. Les règles du GATT servent de cadre pour le maintien du système commercial multilatéral et pour en améliorer le degré de libéralisation; les ministres on réaffirmé la détermination de leurs gouvernements de préserver et de renforcer ce système par les nouvelles négociations commerciales multilatérales et se sont déclarés disposés à s'engager dans la phase des négociations actives.

Les ministres sont convenus qu'une priorité absolue doit être donnée

The EFTA Councils

The procedure in EFTA is for the EFTA Council and the Joint Council of EFTA and Finland to meet simultaneously at official level once a week at the Geneva headquarters of the Association. The officials present are the Ambassadors to EFTA of the participating countries. Twice a year, usually in May and November, there are meetings, also simultaneous, of the Councils at Ministerial level. Most of these are held in Geneva, but on occasion, such as the November 1974 meeting in Helsinki, they take place in the capital of another EFTA country.

However, decisions do not await these semi-annual occasions; under the Stockholm Convention, the Councils have full decisionmaking powers, irrespective of the level of representation. As a result, the Ministerial meetings are more concerned with exchanges of views on high policy than with decisions on the trading regime of EFTA.

This fact is well illustrated by the two Communiqués which were published after the May and October meetings.

Ministerial Meeting of the Councils, 8/9 May 1974, Geneva

The EFTA Council and the Joint Council of EFTA and Finland met at Ministerial level in Geneva on 8th and 9th May 1974. The meeting was chaired by the Head of the Federal Department of Public Economy of Switzerland, Mr. Ernst Brugger, President of the Swiss Confederation.

While welcoming the continued growth of intra-EFTA trade, Ministers discussed developments within the Association against the background of a difficult world economic situation, characterized by high rates of inflation, sharply increased prices for oil and other primary products and continuing risks of international monetary disturbances. Ministers expressed their conviction that maximum use must continue to be made of multilateral consultations to deal with the conomic problems now facing most countries. They emphasized the value to the EFTA countries of the framework which the Association provided for useful exchanges of views on these problems.

In the field of trade, Ministers agreed that governments would do their utmost, consistent with existing agreements and rules, to avoid action in dealing with balance of payments or sectoral difficulties which could be counter-productive in itself and would be prejudicial to the world trading system. They therefore agreed to support the idea of a declaration by governments to refrain for a fixed period of time from restrictive trade and other current account measures, including destructive compettiion in official support of export credit.

Ministers emphasized that within EFTA the Stockholm Convention constituted a most valuable body of rules for the continuation of free trade. Ministers stressed that the Free Trade Agreements between the EFTA countries and the European Communities were intended to play a similar rôle for the trade relations between the two groups of countries. The rules of the GATT provided a framework for the maintenance of the multilateral trading system and for its further liberalization; Ministers reiterated the determination of their governments to preserve and reinforce this system through the new round of multilateral trade negotiations and declared that they were prepared to enter the stage of active negotiation.

Ministers agreed that high priority must be given to national and international efforts to fight inflation, but that governments should avoid policies which might make it more difficult for others to maintain reasonable rates of economic growth. With respect to the international monetary situation, Ministers stressed that continuing co-operation was decisive in aux efforts nationaux et internationaux visant à combattre l'inflation, mais que les gouvernements devraient éviter une politique qui pourrait entraver les possiblités d'autres pays de maintenir un taux de croissance économique raisonnable. S'agissant de la situation monétaire internationale, les ministres ont souligné qu'une coopération continue était déterminante pour assurer un équilibre raisonnable des balances des paiements et des taux de change relativement stables. Les ministres considèrent aussi que la coopération multilatérale est indispensable pour assurer une répartition adéquate des produits de base essentiels. A cet égard, ils ont souligné l'importance d'un dialogue constructif entre pays producteurs et pays consommateurs.

Les ministres ont exprimé leur préoccupation au sujet de la détérioration très sérieuse de la situation économique de nombreux pays en voie de développement affectés par la hausse rapide des prix à l'importation. Ils ont souligné qu'un large effort international supplémentaire était indispensable pour assurer le développement de ces pays. Les gouvernements de l'AELE sont prêts à jouer pleinement leur rôle dans cette coopération. A cet égard, les ministres ont souligné l'importance de la récente session extraordinaire de l'Assemblée générale des Nations Unies.

Les ministres se sont plu à constater l'intensification et l'élargissement des relations économiques Est-Ouest et ont estimé qu'il y avait amplement matière à des efforts continus et réciproques sur le plan bilatéral ainsi que multilatéral pour développer les échanges et autres formes de coopération économique.

Le délégué du Portugal a informé les Conseils des changements de grande portée qui se déroulent acutellement au Portugal. Il a fait état des intentions des autorités portugaises d'apporter des modifications profondes aux structures du pays par l'instauration d'institutions démocratiques. Il a également exprimé la détermination de ses autorités d'établir les fondements d'une nouvelle politique économique à orientation sociale et d'élargir et de diversifier les relations internationales du Portugal sur la base de la coopération et du respect de ses obligations internationales. Les ministres ont fait part de la sympathie avec laquelle ils suivent les événements qui se déroulent maintenant au Portugal; ils espèrent que le processus actuel de transition attaindra des résultats qui serviront au mieux les intérêts du peuple portugais. Ils ont été informés des mesures transitoires prises par l'administration portugaise pour faire face aux difficultés économiques à court terme et ont décidé de les examiner au sein de l'AELE dans un esprit de compréhension pour les circonstances présentes exceptionnelles.

A l'invitation du gouvernement finlandais, la prochaine réunion ministérielle de l'AELE aura lieu à Helsinki, les 31 octobre et 1er novembre 1974.

Réunion ministérielle des 31 octobre et 1er novembre 1974, à Helsinki

Le Conseil de l'AELE et le Conseil mixte AELE-Finlande se sont réunis au niveau ministériel à Helsinki, les 31 octobre et 1er novembre 1974. M. J. Laine, ministre finlandais du commerce, qui préside le Conseil mixte, en assumait la présidence.

En discutant de la situation à l'intérieur de l'Association, les ministres ont exprimé leur satisfaction au sujet du développement des échanges entre pays de l'AELE et quant à la coopération dans l'Association orientée vers la pleine application des dispositions de libre-échange de la Convention de Stockholm.

Les ministres ont passé en revue les activités de l'AELE visant à améliorer les conditions du commerce par la suppression des obstacles techniques aux échanges. Ils sont d'accord pour renforcer encore les ententes existantes. Ils ont aussi souligné l'intérêt qu'il y aurait à rendre plus efficaces les ensuring reasonable equilibrium in balances of payments and relatively stable exchange rates. Ministers believed also that multilateral co-operation was indispensable to achieve an appropriate distribution of essential commodities. In this connection, they stressed the value of a constructive dialogue between producer and consumer countries.

Ministers expressed their concern that the economic situation of many developing countries had been very seriously affected by rapidly rising import prices. They stressed that a broadly-based additional international effort would be essential to ensure the development of those countries. The EFTA Governments were ready to play their full part in this co-operation. In this connection Ministers stressed the importance of the recent special session of the UN General Assembly.

Ministers welcomed the growth and broadening of East-West economic relations and considered that there was ample room for continued mutual efforts on the bilateral as well as multilateral level to develop trade and other economic co-operation.

The Portuguese Delegate informed the Councils about the far-reaching changes now taking place in Portugal. He stated the intention of the Portuguese authorities to promote profound modifications in the structures of the country by means of the establishment of democratic institutions. He also expressed the determination of his authorities to lay down the foundations of a new socially-oriented economic policy and to enlarge and diversify Portugal's international relations on the basis of friendship, co-operation and respect for international obligations. Ministers expressed the sympathy with which they were following the developments now taking place in Portugal and hoped that the present process of transition would achieve results which would serve the best interests of the Portuguese people. They were informed of the transitional measures taken by the Portuguese Administration to meet short-term economic difficulties and decided to examine them in EFTA in a spirit of understanding for the current exceptional circumstances.

At the invitation of the Finnish Government, the next meeting of the EFTA Councils at Ministerial level will take place in Helsinki on 31st October and 1st November 1974.

Ministerial Meeting of the Councils, 31 Oct. & 1 Nov. 1974, Helsinki

The EFTA Council and the Joint Council of EFTA and Finland met at Ministerial level in Helsinki on 31st October and 1st November 1974. Mr. J. Laine, Finnish Minister for Trade, who is Chairman of the Joint Council, was in the chair.

In discussing the situation within the Association, Ministers expressed their satisfaction with the development of trade between EFTA countries and with EFTA cooperation directed at the full application of the free trade provisions of the Stockholm Convention.

Ministers reviewed the work carried out in EFTA to improve trading conditions by the elimination of technical barriers to trade. They agreed that existing arrangements should be further strengthened. They also urged the importance of making more effective the various arrangements for the mutual recognition of tests and inspections by enlarging their memdivers accords de reconnaissance réciproque des essais et contrôles en les ouvrant à la participation d'un plus grand nombre de partenaires commerciaux des pays de l'AELE.

Les ministres ont été informées de la situation économique actuelle au Portugal. Ils ont réaffirmé leur sympathie pour les efforts accomplis en vue d'améliorer la situation du pays et de consolider ses nouvelles institutions. En plus des discussions bilatérales en cours, les ministres ont décidé d'examiner en priorité quelle action pouvait être entreprise au sein de l'-AELE pour aider le Portugal.

Les ministres ont constaté que le démantèlement des barrières aux échanges prévu dans les accords de libre-échange conclus entre les pays de l'AELE et les Communautés européennes progressait selon le calendrier établi. Les Comités mixtes chargés de la gestion des accords, ainsi que leurs comités douaniers, accomplissent un travail utile et des perfectionnements techniques sont à l'étude. Dans le cas de l'Islande, les ministres se sont préoccupés de ce que les concessions les plus importantes faites par la CEE ne sont pas encore entrées en vigueur, faute d'un accord satisfaisant avec tous les Etats membres de la Communauté sur les droits des pêcheries. Les ministres ont également pris note de la déclaration du ministre portugais soulignant l'importance des développements attendus de la prochaine réunion du Comité mixte Portugal-CEE.

Les ministres ont discuté de la situation mondiale actuelle dans les secteurs économique, commercial, monétaire et énergétique. Ils ont réaffirmé leur détermination de renforcer la coopération au sein de l'AELE et dans tous les forums internationaux traitant des difficultés présentes. Bien que chaque pays ait ses politiques et problèmes particuliers, les ministres ont exprimé l'avis que c'est sur la base d'une coopération internationale globale que des progrès décisifs peuvent être accomplis en vue de résoudre ces difficultés.

Les ministres ont exprimé leur conviction qu'une coopération de vaste portée est indispensable pour améliorer le système des paiments et pour préserver et renforcer le régime libéral des échanges, tous deux ayant beaucoup contribué à l'élévation des niveaux de vie dans le monde. Le renforcement de la coopération a déjà donné des resultats. La Déclaration adoptée à l'unanimité par tous les pays de l'OCDE au mois de mai et marquant leur engagement de s'abstenir de recourir à des mesures commerciales restrictives a eu des effets positifs sur le maintien de la structure libérale du commerce.

Les ministres ont à nouveau souligné l'importance du GATT pour maintenir le bon fonctionnement du commerce mondial. A cet égard, ils ont exprimé leur conviction que les négociations commerciales multilatérales, dont le coup d'envoi a été donné a Tokyo il y a plus d'une année, revêtent même une plus grande signification dans les circonstances présentes. Ces négociations sont essentielles non seulement pour réaliser une plus large libéralisation du commerce mondial, question d'une grande importance tant pour les pays développés que pour les pays en développement, mais aussi pour améliorer le cadre international régissant le commerce mondial. Il est urgent que toutes les parties aux nouvelles negotiations obtiennent les pouvoirs nécessaires pour négocier, afin, que celles-ci puissent entrer dans leur phase active.

Les ministres se sont déclarés préoccupés par les difficultés particulières que la hausse des prix a entraînées pour bon nombre de pays en développement et ils ont souligné la nécessité de maintenir à un niveau élevé le flux des ressources réelles destinées à ces pays.

Concernant les relations économiques Est-Ouest, les ministres ont salué les divers efforts faits sur le plan bilatéral et multilatéral pour développer les échanges et élargir la coopération économique; ils ont réaffirmé leur point de vue qu'il y avait matière à développer ces relations dans une plus large mesure encore.

bership to include an increasing number of trading partners of the EFTA countries.

Ministers were informed of the current economic situation in Portugal. They reaffirmed their sympathy for the efforts which were being made to improve the situation of the country and to consolidate its new institutions. In addition to bilateral discussions already in progress, Ministers decided to examine, as a matter of urgency, what action might be taken within the EFTA framework to support Portugal.

Ministers noted that the dismantling of barriers to trade provided for in the Free Trade Agreements between the EFTA countries and the European Communities was progressing according to the agreed timetable. Useful work was being done in the Joint Committees set up to administer the Agreements and in their Customs Committees and further technical improvements were under consideration. Ministers noted with concern that in the case of Iceland the most important concessions by the EEC had not yet entered into force, since satisfactory agreement on fishing rights had not been reached with all Community Member States. Ministers also noted the statement of the Portuguese Minister stressing the importance of the developments to be expected from the forthcoming meeting of the Joint Committee of Portugal and the EEC.

Ministers discussed the present world economic, trade, monetary and energy situation. They reaffirmed their determination to strengthen cooperative action within EFTA and in all international fora dealing with the difficulties involved. While each country had its own problems and policies, Ministers were of the opinion that it was on the basis of comprehensive international cooperation that decisive progress could be made in dealing with these difficulties.

Ministers expressed their conviction that wide-ranging cooperative action was essential to improve the payments system and to preserve and reinforce the liberal trade system, both of which had done so much for world standards of living. Strengthened cooperative action was already producing useful results. The Declaration renouncing national restrictive trade measures, which had been unanimously accepted by all the OECD countries in May, had had positive effects for the maintenance of the liberal trade structure.

Ministers emphasized the continued importance of GATT for maintaining orderly conditions for world trade. In this connection they stated their conviction that the multilateral trade negotiations which had been launched more than a year earlier in Tokyo were even more relevant in present circumstances. They were essential not only for the further liberalization of world trade, a matter of great importance for developed and developing countries alike, but also for the improvement of the international framework for the conduct of world trade. It was therefore urgent that all the partners to the new round should obtain the necessary negotiating authority so that the negotiations could proceed to the active stage.

Ministers expressed concern that the rise in prices had caused particular difficulties for many developing countries and emphasized the necessity of ensuring the flow of real resources to those countries at a high level.

On East-West economic relations, Ministers welcomed the various efforts being made on the bilateral as well as multilateral level to develop trade and broaden other economic cooperation, and reaffirmed the view that there was ample room for further development of these relations.

The next meeting of the Councils at Ministerial level will take place in Geneva on 22nd May 1975.

La prochaine réunion ministérielle de l'AELE aura lieu à Genève, le 22 mai 1975.

Le comité consultatif

Comme à l'accoutumée, le comité consultatif de l'AELE s'est réuni deux fois en 1974, les dates étant proches de celles des deux réunions ministérielles du Conseil de l'AELE et du Conseil mixte AELE-Finlande. En fait, le rôle du comité est de faire connaître aux ministres le point de vue du secteur privé de chacun des pays membres. Le président du Conseil des ministres de l'AELE assume également la présidence des séances du comité consultatif. Il rend compte des débats à la réunion ministérielle qui a lieu quelques jours plus tard.

Des délégations de cinq personnes par pays prennent part aux réunions du comité; elles représentent les fédérations des industries, les organisation syndicales, la paysannerie, etc. Des observateurs peuvent aussi suivre les débats. Les délégués permanents des pays de l'AELE à Genève, qui constituent le Conseil au niveau officiel, assistent en qualité d'observateurs.

Aussi bien à la réunion de mai à Berne (présidée par M. E. Brugger, alors Président de la Confédération suisse et chef du département fédéral de l'économie publique) qu'à celle d'octobre qui s'est tenue à Helsinki (sous la présidence de M. J. Laine, ministre finlandais du commerce) les débats ont commencé par une discussion générale de la situation économique, ouverte par un exposé du président du Conseil des ministres.

A la réunion de *mai*, les débats sur cette question notamment ont fait apparaître des différences selon les pays. La Norvège, par exemple, constitue un cas à part en raison de ses ressources considérables en pétrole. Celles-ci sauvegardent sa balance des paiements, mais l'inflation inférieure reste un sujet de préoccupation sérieuse. En outre, la question de l'exploitation des ressources pétrolières donne lieu à bien des discussions en Norvège. Il y a maintes raisons de „se hâter lentement": il faut notamment préserver une ressource naturelle importante et éviter des changements trop profonds dans la société norvégienne, bien qu'une telle évolution ne soit peut-être pas du goût d'autres pays. La Suède, elle aussi, constitue un cas d'exception: on prévoit que la croissance économique pour 1974 sera légèrement supérieure à celle de l'année précédente ($3^1/_2$ à 4%). Dans l'ensemble pourtant, les déclarations des divers orateurs ont porté davantage sur les appréhensions exprimées par le président.

Considérant la question monétaire, M. G. Winterberger, de l'Union suisse du commerce et de l'industrie, devait déclarer, bien que le flottement de monnaies européennes ait contribué à surmonter des difficultés à court terme, il ne constituait pas une solution à longue échéance. Cette mesure devrait être complétée par des consultations plus étroites en matière de politique économique et par des contrôles plus sévères relatifs aux mouvement de capitaux spéculatifs, tous deux à long et à court terme. Plusieurs orateurs ont souligné la valeur de l'AELE en tant que forum pour un échange de vues sur un grand nombre de problèmes économiques.

Le comité consultatif a abordé ensuite d'autres points importants de l'ordre du jour. Le rapport sur les activités de l'AELE, présenté par le Secrétaire général de l'AELE, M. B. Rabaeus, a donné matière à un certain nombre de commentaires, notamment de la part de M. W. Paues, directeur de la Fédération des industries suédoises.

M. A. Jetzer, de l'Union suisse du commerce et de l'industrie, a présenté un rapport oral sur les travaux du groupe ad hoc du comité consultatif sur les règles d'origine. Ce groupe s'est penché durant l'année écoulée sur les difficultés commerciales provenant des règles d'origine contenues dans les accords de libre-échange conclus avec les Communautés – et dans la Convention de Stockholm revisée – en vue de suggérer des améliorations. Le

The Consultative Committee

As is customary, the EFTA Consultative Committee met twice during 1974, the dates being set in close proximity to those of the two meetings of the EFTA Council and Joint Council of EFTA and Finland at Ministerial level. In fact, the role of the Committee is to advise Ministers of the views of the private sector in the participating countries and the Ministerial Chairman of EFTA also takes the chair at the meetings of the Committee. He makes a report of its proceedings to his Ministerial colleagues when they meet a few days later.

The membership of the Committee consists of five representatives from each EFTA country of the industrial federations, the trades unions, agricultural organizations, etc. Observers may also be present. The permanent representatives of the EFTA countries in Genevea, who make up the Councils at official level, also attend as observers.

Both at its May meeting in Berne (when Mr. Ernst Brugger, President of the Swiss Confederation and Head of the Federal Department of Public Economy was Chairman) and at its October meeting in Helsinki (when Mr. Jermu Laine, Finnish Minister for Trade, took the Chair) the Committee proceedings opened with a general debate on the economic situation, with the Ministerial Chairman making an introductory statement.

At the May meeting this discussion brought out several differences in the situations of the various countries. For example, Norway was, in some ways, an exception to the general rule because of her important oil resources. These sheltered her balance of payments – but internal inflation remained a serious problem. In addition, the question of the exploitation of the oil resources was the subject of much debate in Norway. There were many reasons for "hastening slowly," including conservation of a valuable resource and avoidance of too violent changes in Norwegian society, although such a course might not be pleasing to other countries. Sweden also was an exceptional case, in that economic growth in 1974 was expected to be at a slightly higher rate ($3^1/_2$–4%) than in the previous year. On the whole, however, the contributions of the various speakers lent further to weight the apprehensions voiced by the Chairman.

Referring to the monetary question, Mr. G. Winterberger said that although the floating of European currencies had helped to overcome some short-term difficulties, it did not constitute a long-term solution. It would to be supplemented by much closer consultation on economic policies and by tighter controls over speculative capital movements, both long- and short-term. Tribute was paid by several speakers to the value of EFTA as a framework for useful exchanges of views on a wide range of economic problems.

The Consultative Committee then went on to other substantial agenda items. A Report on EFTA activities, presented by Mr. B. Rabaeus, EFTA Secretary-General, gave rise to a number of comments, particularly by Mr. W. Paues, Director, Federation of Swedish Industries.

There followed an oral report by Mr. A. Jetzer, Swiss Federation of Trade and Industry on the work of the ad hoc group of the Consultative Committee on origin rules. This group has been working for the past year on difficulties for trade arising from the origin rules embodied in the Free Trade Agreements with the Communities – and in the revised EFTA Convention – and to suggest remedies. The group has consulted with the EFTA customs officials engaged with the problems and individual members of the group have been in touch with industrial federations in the Community countries. Mr. Jetzer was confident that the work of the ad hoc group groupe a consulté les fonctionnaires des administrations douanières de l'AELE qui s'occupent de ces questions et des membres individuels du groupe ont été en contact avec des associations industrielles des pays de la Communauté. M. Jetzer est persuadé que les travaux du groupe ad hoc contribueront à améliorer notablement les règles d'origine de l'AELE.

M. G. Dahlström, des syndicats suédois, montra l'importance de l'étude qui vient de paraître sous les auspices du comité de développement économique de l'AELE, intitulée *National Settlement Strategies; a framework for regional development*. Il a fait l'éloge de cette étude, estimant qu'elle était une des contributions les plus originales de l'Association. Elle introduit un cadre nouveau qui pourrait être très utile aux différents pays en matière d'urbanisation, en faisant un tout des fonctions régionales et de la planification. M. Goddard, de la London School of Economics, qui jouait le rôle de conseiller auprès du groupe de travail qui a élaboré cette étude, remercia M. Dahlström de ses considérations et déclara que l'importance de la publication avait été pleinement reconnue dans les milieux administratifs et académiques de plusieurs pays. Elle sert de guide à la formation des fonctionnaires dans le domaine de l'urbanisation et aura sans doute pour effet la revision de dispositions administratives.

Le dernier point figurant à l'ordre du jour de la réunion de mai du comité consultatif était l'examen d'un rapport dû au Secrétariat de l'AELE sur la suppression des barrières techniques aux échanges. Le comité s'est dit satisfait des travaux en cours et exprima l'espoir qu'un plus grand nombre de produits pourraient donner matière à des arrangements de reconnaissance réciproque des essais et contrôles. On a aussi insisté sur l'importance d'élargir le champ d'application de ces accords en obtenant l'adhésion d'autres pays. Si, au lieu d'adhérer aux arrangements existants, des pays tiers essaient de conclure simplement des accords bilatéraux avec plusieurs parties aux arrangements, cela ne saurait être qu'une cause de confusion. Cette constatation vaut surtout pour la convention sur les produits pharmaceutiques. On a aussi exprimé l'idée que les pays de l'AELE devaient coordonner la date d'entrée en vigueur des règlements techniques nouveaux ou modifiés et décider d'intervalles appropriés pour la revision de ceux-ci.

A la réunion *d'octobre* à Helsinki, tous les orateurs étaient d'accord avec le président pour reconnaître qu'aucun pays ne pouvait surmonter les difficultés présentes par ses propres moyens. Aucun pays ne peut progresser si l'économie mondiale est dans une situation difficile, et les mesures prises à des fins nationales sans tenir compte de leurs répercussions extérieures ne peuvent avoir qu'un effet contraire à leur objectif.

L'Autriche, la Norvège et le Portugal ont vu leur monnaie valorisée par rapport à celles de bon nombre de leurs partenaires commerciaux. Alors que cette situation avait pour effet de réduire les taux d'inflation en maintenant les prix à l'importation à un niveau peu élevé, les autres effets ont été négatifs. Les devises provenant des exportations rapportaient moins une fois rapatriées et converties en monnaie nationale, ce qui a entraîné une basse des bénéfices des exportateurs. De plus, en Autriche et en Suisse l'industrie du tourisme a enregistré une nette diminution de recettes, la réévaluation ayant découragé les touristes étrangers – dont le nombre a de toute manière régressé sous l'effet du ralentissement de l'économie. Pour ces deux pays, il s'agit là d'un tournant sérieux. Par le passé et pendant plusieurs années, leurs revenus au titre des services – le tourisme étant le principal facteur – leur ont assuré une balance des paiements excédentaire, malgré les déficits relativement importants du commerce des marchandises.

La plupart des discussions sur ce point ont mis en évidence les effets néfastes de la hausse massive des prix du pétrole sur l'économie et la balance des paiements des pays représentés. La seule délégation à même de considérer l'augmentation de la facture du pétrole avec sérénité était évidemment la délégation norvégienne: la Norvège sera un exportateur net de would result in improvements in the rules of origin of importance to the EFTA countries.

Mr. G. Dahlström, Swedish Trade Unions, then analysed for the Committee the importance of the recently published study, sponsored by the EFTA Economic Development Committee, entitled "National Settlement Strategies; a framework for regional development." He praised the study in the highest terms and said that it was one of the most original contributions of the Association. It introduced a new and comprehensive framework which could be of great benefit to countries by drawing together all planning and regional functions into a comprehensive whole. Mr. Goddard, of the London School of Economics, who was a consultant to the working party which produced the study, thanked Mr. Dahlström for his analysis and said that the importance of the book was fully reconigzed in administrative and academic circles in several countries. It had become a text for the training of officials in the relevant fields and would, no doubt, bring about the re-casting of administrative arrangements concerning many functions which were now divided between different ministries.

The last item on the Consultative Committee agenda was the consideration of a report by the EFTA Secretariat on the elimination of technical obstacles to trade. The Committee expressed satisfaction with the work going on and hoped that more products could be brought within the scope of arrangements for the mutual recognition of tests and inspections. Emphasis was also laid on the importance of widening the operations of these arrangements by obtaining the adherence of other countries. If, instead of adhering to the existing arrangements, outside countries tried to make bilateral agreements with several members only, this would lead only to confusion. This was particularly true of the Pharmaceutical Convention. The view was also put forward that the EFTA countries should coordinate the dates on which new or revised technical regulations were put into effect and agree on appropriate time intervals for the revision of regulations.

At Helsinki in October, all speakers agreed with the Chairman that no single country could face up on its own to the many current difficulties. No country could do well if the world economy does badly; indeed, measures aimed at national goals which took no account of external repercussions would be self-defeating.

Austria, Norway and Portugal had all seen the value of their currencies rise in relation to those of many of their trading partners. While this had had the positive effect of reducing rates of inflation by keeping down the cost of imports, the other effects were negative. The foreign currencies earned abroad by their exports were less valuable when repatriated and converted into the national currency, with the result that exporters' profits were reduced. Moreover, the tourism industries of Austria and Switzerland were experiencing a sharp reduction of earnings because revaaluation of their currencies had discouraged tourists – whose numbers, in any case, had been reduced by the general economic downturn. For both countries this is a serious development; for many years past, their earnings on services, with tourism the main item, have enabled their total balance of payments to be positive, despite relatively large deficits on commodity trade.

Most contributions to the discussion made a particular point of the adverse effects of the greatly increased oil prices on their economies and balances of payments. Indeed the only delegation which could view the increased oil bill with equanimity was Norway, which will become a net oil exporter from 1975 onward – and, consequently, become a capital exporting nation rather than a borrower, as in the past.

The level of employment was another subject touched on by several speakers. While the dangers to employment from a generalized recession were recognized, it was still true that the situation in most EFTA countries pétrole à partir de 1975 et d'importateur deviendra un exportateur de capitaux.

Le niveau de l'emploi a lui aussi été abordé par plusieurs orateurs. Tout en reconnaissant les dangers qu'une récession générale présente pour le plein emploi, il n'en demeure pas moins que la situation dans la plupart des pays de l'AELE est satisfaisante. La Finlande et la Suisse ont davantage d'offres de places vacantes que de demandes. Au Portugal, en revanche, le chômage est en augmentation.

Pour ce qui est de l'inflation, un délégué a émis l'opinion que les salaires avaient suivi les prix, au lieu de les faire monter et que les causes réelles de l'inflation doivent être recherchées ailleurs. On a alors demandé au Secrétariat s'il était possible d'effectuer une étude des problèmes spéciaux qui se posent dans un contexte inflationniste aux petits pays industrialisés, fortement tributaires du commerce extérieur. En réponse à cette question et à d'autres questions connexes posées par divers délégués, le Secrétaire général a déclaré que le comité économique de l'AELE devait se réunir en novembre et que la question de l'inflation figurait à son ordre du jour.

Répondant aux questions qui lui étaient posées, le ministre finlandais du commerce, M. J. Laine, a donné un aperçu des principales caractéristiques des accords sur la suppression réciproque des obstacles aux échanges que son gouvernement a signés ces derniers mois avec la Bulgarie, la Hongrie et la Tchécoslovaquie. Il s'agit là essentiellement d'accords de libre- échange, semblables à ceux actuellement en vigueur entre les pays de l'AELE et les Communautés européennes. Ils prévoient la suppression réciproque des droits de douane sur les produits industriels, selon un calendrier allant de 1975 à 1980. Les règles d'orgine sont semblables à celles appliquées dans les échanges entre l'AELE et la Communauté et des règles de sauvegarde peuvent être introduites en cas de difficultés sectorielles. M. Laine a estimé que ces accords pourraient bien être considérés comme un pas en avant intéressant pour développer le commerce et les relations économiques Est-Ouest.

Les délégués ont discuté également de l'attitude de l'Association face aux propositions faites par la Confédération européenne des syndicats (CES). Celle-ci avait demandé que l'AELE se livre à une activité dans le secteur social pour que ses sept gouvernements puissent remplir le même rôle à l'égard des syndicats et du patronat que la Communauté en ce qui concerne ses neuf États membres. Le Secrétaire général de l'AELE a fait valoir que les chefs des délégations accréditées auprès de l'Association à Genève estiment que les activités proposées par la CES, ne relevant pas de la Convention de Stockholm, devaient de préférence s'exercer au sein d'autres organismes internationaux plus directement concernés par le secteur social et comptant davantage de pays membres que l'AELE.

Les membres des syndicats représentés au comité consultatif ont jugé cette interprétation de la Convention de Stockholm trop formelle et suggéré qu'il fallait avoir recours à l'AELE sur une base pragmatique en matière de coopération dans les questions touchant de près aux échanges. Ils ont exprimé l'espoir que la question serait réexaminée et ont demandé que le document de la CES soit étudié plus avant, non seulement en ce qui concerne une action éventuelle de l'AELE, mais aussi quant au fond. D'autres membres ont soutenu le point de vue des syndicalistes rappelant les avis exprimés lors des précédentes réunions, à savoir que l'AELE devrait envisager dans la mesure du possible une action dans les mêmes domaines que la Communauté.

Dans le contexte des obstacles techniques aux échanges, on a encore discuté de la nécessité d'étendre la participation aux arrangements de reconnaissance réciproque des essais et contrôles. Ces arrangements s'appliquent à un certain nombre de produits importants, dont les produits pharmaceutiques, les ouvrages en métaux précieux, les équipements de navires, les appareils à gaz et les appareils à pression, les apparails élecwas satisfactory. Finland and Switzerland had many more job vacancies than people to fill them. On the other hand, unemployment was on the increase in Portugal.

On the subject of inflation, one delegate suggested that wages had followed prices rather than pushed them and that the real causes of inflation lay elsewhere. The Secretariat was therefore asked if it would be possible to prepare a study of the special problems in an inflationary climate of the smaller industrialized countries, highly dependent on foreign trade. In reply to this and other related questions raised by various delegates, the Secretary-General of EFTA pointed out that the Economic Committee of EFTA was to meet in November and the problem of inflation was on its Agenda.

In response to questions, Minister Laine described the main features of the Agreements on the Reciprocal Removal of Obstacles to Trade which his Government had signed in preceding months with Bulgaria, Hungary and Czechoslovakia. These were essentially Free Trade Agreements, similar to those now in operation between the EFTA countreis and the European Communities. They provided for the reciprocal removal of tariffs on industrial products on a timetable stretching from 1975 to 1980. The origin rules of the Agreements were similar to those used in EFTA-Community trade and there were safeguard clauses to come into operation in the event that the Agreements led to sectoral difficulties. Mr. Laine believed that these Agreements might well become a generally interesting move to develop East-West trade and economic relations.

There was also some discussion of the EFTA attitude to proposals put forward by the European Trades Union Confederation (ETUC). The latter had asked that EFTA undertake work in the social sector, so that the seven EFTA Governments could perform the same role vis-à-vis the trades unions and employers as was played by the European Community for its nine member states. The EFTA Secretary-General had reported to the meeting that the Heads of EFTA delegations in Geneva had taken the view that, since the activities proposed by the ETUC fell outside the Stockholm Convention, they could better be pursued in other international bodies directly competent in the social sector and with a wider membership than EFTA.

The trade unionist members of the Committee found this interpretation of the Stockholm Convention too formal and suggested that EFTA should be used pragmatically for cooperation on questions closely interrelated with trade. They expressed the hope that the matter would be reconsidered and requested that the ETUC statement should be further studied, not only as to possible action by EFTA but also as to its substance. The vieuws of the trade unionist members were supported by some other members, who recalled the strong feeling, expressed in the Committee at previous meetings, that EFTA should consider action in the same fields as the Community, so far as possible.

In the context of technical barriers to trade, there was some discussion of the need to enlarge the memberschip of the various schemes for the mutual recognition of tests and inspections. These schemes apply to a number of important products, including pharmaceuticals, ships' equipment, pressure vessels, electrical applicances, gas stoves and agricultural tractors. Although originally sponsored by EFTA, the various agreements and conventions are open to the membership of other countries. The Committee was informed of the efforts being made to enlist new members, particularly from the European Community, so that the trade effects of the schemes could be increased.

The Committee of Trade Experts had reviewed the implementation of the procedure in EFTA for advance notification by governments of new or revised technical regulations and suggested that it should be maintained, but with further improvements. In this context, Trade Experts had given special consideration to the proposal made in the Consultative triques, les machines et les tracteurs agricoles. Bien qu'ils aient été établis à l'origine sous l'égide de l'AELE, ces conventions et arrangements sont ouverts à la participation d'autres pays. Le comité a été informé des efforts faits en vue de gagner de nouveaux membres, en particulier des pays de la Communauté, afin d'étendre les effets d'ordre commercial de ces arrangements.

D'autre part, le comité des experts commerciaux a étudié l'application de la procédure AELE de notification anticipée des règlements techniques nouveaux ou modifiés et a propose que celle-ci soit maintenue, mais avec quelques retouches. Les experts commerciaux ont aussi considéré avec une attention speciale la proposition du comitee consultatif selon laquelle les pays de l'Association devraient coordonner les dates d'entrée en vigueur des règlements techniques nouveaux ou modifiés. La question était alors devant le Conseil.

D'autre part, les deux rénions du comité consultatif qui se sont tenues en 1974 ont été l'occasion d'entretiens non formels avec les représentants de l'industrie du Danemark et de la Grande-Bretagne, pays qui ont quitté l'AELE à la fin de 1972 pour adhérer aux Communautés européennes. Ces rencontres permettent de procéder à des discussions franches sur des problèmes d'intérêt commun, quelle que soit leur importance, dont le fonctionnement des accords de libre-échange, les règles d'origine, les obstacles non tarifaires aux échanges, la coopération en matière d'énergie, etc. Il est apparu que ces entretiens non formels sont appréciés de tous ceux concernés et ils continueront à se dérouler dans le cadre des réunions du comité consultatif.

Les parlementaires de l'AELE

Pour la première fois dans l'histoire de l'Association, lors de leur 27e réunion, les parlementaires des pays de l'AELE se sont réunis à Genève, les 9 et 10 septembre 1974. Toutes les rencontres précédentes avaient eu lieu à Strasbourg à l'occasion de l'Assemblée consultative du Conseil de l'Europe. Ce changement de lieu de rencontre tient à l'importance des sujets traités qui exigeait une séance séparée au siège de l'Association, où se tiendront dorénavant toutes les réunions des parlementaires de l'AELE.

M. J. Weber (radical démocrate, Suisse) a été élu président, tandis que M. M. Luptowitz (socialiste, Autriche) prenait la place de premier vice-président et M. H. Holkeri (conservateur, Finlande) celle de second vice-président. Une délégation du Portugal, représentant les partis politiques de la coalition provisoire, a suivi les débats en qualité d'observateurs. Leur présence a été chaleureusement accueillie par les autres participants qui ont exprimé leur sympathie et leur volonté d'aider le peuple portugais.

Le débat général a porté sur le rôle présent et futur de l'AELE et de ses activités à la lumière des récents développements économiques; un document préparé par le Secrétaire général et le quatorzième Rapport annuel de l'AELE ont servi de base aux discussions. Bien que la fonction principale de l'Association soit de promouvoir le libre-échange entre ses membres et avec d'autres pays, l'Association est de plus en plus utilisée comme centre de discussions sur des questions économiques plus générales, en l'occurrence, le problème de l'inflation, le coût et l'approvisionnement des matières et les règles régissant le commerce international. Les parlementaires sont convenues que les pays de l'AELE devraient faire davantage usage des possibilités qu'offre l'Association en matière de coopération et de consultation, concernant ces questions d'intérêt commun.

Le second point principal inscrit à l'ordre du jour portait sur les travaux effectués dans l'AELE sur la suppression des barrières techniques aux échanges. L'effet de ces obstacles est plus grand lorsque les droits de douane sont supprimés. C'est pourquoi l'AELE a accordé la priorité à cette

Committee that EFTA countries should co-ordinate the dates on which new or revised technical regulations are to be put into effect. The matter was before the Council.

A feature of both Consultative Committee meetings in 1974 was the holding of an informal gathering with industrial representatives of the two countries, Britain and Denmark, which left EFTA at the end of 1972 to join the European Communities. In this way frank discussions are made possible of common problems, both large and small, such as the functioning of the Free Trade Agreements, the rules of origin, non-tariff barriers, energy cooperation and so on. It was clear that these informal discussions were felt to be of great value by all concerned and will become a regular part of Consultative Committee gatherings.

The EFTA Parliamentarians

For the first time in the history of EFTA, representative Parliamentarians from the participating countries met in Geneva, on 9/10 September 1974. This was in fact the 27th meeting of this group, but all the others had taken place in Strasbourg, taking advantage of the attendance of the Parliamentarians at the Assembly of the Council of Europe. The change of venue was due to the belief of all concerned that the importance of the subject required a separate meeting at the headquarters of EFTA, where all future meetings will be held.

Mr. J. Weber (Swiss Radical Democrat) was elected Chairman, Mr. M. Luptowitz (Austrian Social Democrat) First Vice Chairman and Mr. H. Holkeri (Finnish Conservative) as second Vice Chairman. A delegation from Portugal, representing the political parties included in the provisional coalition, attended the meeting as observers. Their presence was warmly welcomed by the other participants, who expressed their sympathy and their willingness to help the Portuguese people.

The Parliamentarians had a general discussion on the present and future rôle of EFTA and of its activities in the light of recent economic developments, on the basis of a paper presented by the Secretary-General and of the Fourteenth Annual Report of EFTA. Although EFTA's first function is to promote free trade within EFTA and with other countries, increasing use is being made of the Association as a forum for discussions on more general economic questions. These include the problem of inflation, the price and supply of raw materials and the rules governing world trade. The Parliamentarians agreed that the EFTA countries should make a greater use of the possibilities provided by EFTA for cooperation and consultation in the face of these common problems.

The second main item on the Agenda provided for a survey of the work work being done in EFTA on the elimination of technical barriers to trade. Such obstacles have a greater impact when tariffs have been removed. EFTA has therefore given this work a high priority as a further way of activité destinée à apporter une contribution nouvelle au développement harmonieux et à l'expansion du commerce mondial. Un second document émanant du Secrétariat et qui a été soumis aux parlementaires décrivait la manière dont l'AELE procède dans ce domaine.

Le comité économique

Le comité économique, dont le rôle est d'examiner la situation économique des pays de l'AELE, de procéder à un échange de vues sur les derniers développements économiques et monétaires internationaux et de conférer sur l'évolution des travaux effectués par d'autres organisations internationales, s'est réuni deux fois pendant l'année sous revue.

En juin 1974, il a examiné l'évolution récente de la situation économique au Portugal et en Islande et les mesures adoptées par ces pays. Les délégations nationales ont exprimé leur compréhension à l'égard des difficultés spéciales que connaissent ces pays; le comité a exprimé l'espoir que les problèmes actuels pourront être résolus par des interventions qui ne compromettent pas directement le libre-échange et que le Portugal et l'Islande seront à même de renoncer dans un très proche avenir aux mesures d'urgence qu'ils ont été amenés à prendre temporairement. La situation économique et les mesures adoptés en Finlande ont également été examinées.

Le comité a, d'autre part, débattu de la situation économique générale de tous les pays de l'AELE, en se référant plus particulièrement aux effets de la hausse du prix du pétrole. On a reconnu que celle-ci avait grandement contribué à augmenter les pressions inflationnistes, tant directement qu'indirectement, et qu'il pourrait en résulter de graves problèmes de balance des paiements. Le comité devait conclure qu'il serait dangereux de faire accroire que les problèmes énergétiques auraient été surmontés.

Passant en revue les mesures anti-inflationnistes, les participants ont souligné que dans la plupart des cas un mélange de mesures directes et sélectives s'imposait pour contenir les pressions inflationnistes. Il a été décidé qu'il convenait de soutenir les propositions d'intervention d'une vaste portée internationale, qui seraient réalisables, pour empêcher les effets négatifs sur le plan international de mesures prises par des pays individuellement.

La seconde réunion de 1974 du comité économique s'est déroulée les 14 et 15 novembre. Le comité a alors discuté de la nécessité d'une action rapide pour prévenir une grave recession et des problèmes auxquels les petits pays sont confrontés (y compris ceux de l'AELE) dans leurs efforts pour faire échec à une menace de récession et pour financer le déficit de leurs balances des paiements.

Ces discussions se sont déroulées peu avant la réunion du Comité de politique économique de l'OCDE (qui s'est tenue à Paris les 18 et 19 novembre). Les hauts fonctionnaires des banques centrales et les représentants des ministères des finances qui participaient aux délibérations du comité économique de l'AELE sont convenus qu'il était essentiel d'attirer l'attention du Comité de l'OCDE sur deux aspects de ces problèmes.

Tout d'abord, l'attitude des grands pays pourrait poser des problèmes aux petits pays et, à une époque où le principal sujet de préoccupation est la récession, il importe que les grands pays prennent rapidement des mesures. Le second aspect, par rapport aux petits pays, les grands ont financé une plus large part de leur déficit extérieur en recourant à l'emprunt, ce qui pourrait aussi entraîner des difficultés. Il serait peut-être nécessaire, de l'avis du comité économique, de recycler vers de petits pays des fonds en provenance de ceux dont la balance extérieure est moins défavorable.

Le comité a aussi examiné l'évolution récente du secteur monétaire et a exprimé l'opinion qu'étant donné la diversité des effets de la hausse des contributing to the harmonious development and expansion of world trade. A second Secretariat paper presented to the Parliamentarians described how EFTA sets about this task.

The Economic Committee

The Economic Committee, which has the triple task of reviewing the economic situation in the EFTA countries, exchanging views on international economic and monetary developments and consulting on developments in other international organisations, met twice during the year.

In June 1974, the Committee discussed recent developments and policy decisions in Portugal and Iceland. The national delegations from the other countries expressed their understanding of the special difficulties experienced by these countries, and the Committee voiced the hope that the problems could be solved by the use of measures which would not directly interfere with free trade, and that Portugal and Iceland would find it possible in the very near future to abandon their temporary emergency measures. Recent developments and policy decisions in Finland were also reviewed.

The general economic situation in all the EFTA countries, with specific reference to the effects of the rise in the price of oil, was also discussed by the Committee. It was agreed that this had greatly increased inflationary pressures, both directly and indirectly, and that serious balance of payments problems could arise. The Committee concluded that it would be dangerous to allow the impression to gain hold that the energy problems had been overcome.

In a review of anti-inflationary policies it was stressed that in most cases a mix of direct and selective measures was required to contain inflationary pressures. It was agreed that support should be given to workable proposals for action on a wide international level to prevent the negative international effects of measures taken by individual countries.

The second meeting of 1974 was on 14/15 November, when the Economic Committee discussed the need for early action to prevent a serious recession and the problems facing small countries (including all the EFTA countries) in their attempts to counter the threat of recession and to finance their balance of payments deficits.

The discussion took place shortly before a meeting of the OECD Economic Policy Committee (held in Paris on 18th and 19th November), and the senior central bank representatives and finance ministry officials taking part in the EFTA Economic Committee's deliberations agreed that it was essential to draw the OECD Committee's attention to two aspects of these problems.

One was that the behaviour of the larger countries could create problems for the smaller countries, and that at a time when the main cause for concern was recession it was important that the larger countries should take early action. The other point was that the larger countries had financed a greater share of their balance of payments deficits by borrowing than the smaller countries had, and that this could cause difficulties. Some recycling of funds from the countries with a better balance of payments position to the smaller countries might become necessary, in the Economic Committee's view.

The Committee also discussed recent developments in the monetary field and expressed the opinion that, because of the different impact of the rise in oil prices on the balance of payments of different countries, it was necessary to increase the official recycling of oil funds, for example by the creation of an adequate oil facility. It was recognised that a special effort should be made to help the developing countries which are not oil producers.

prix du pétrole sur la balance extérieure des différents pays, il convenait d'intensifier le recyclage officiel des fonds pétroliers, notamment par des arrangements appropriés. On a reconnu qu'un effort spécial devait être fait pour aider les pays en développement non producteurs de pétrole.

Sous un troisième point figurant à l'ordre du jour, le comité a examiné en détail le développement de l'inflation dans les pays de l'AELE et l'évolution de leurs balances extérieures.

Le comité de développement économique

La dernière étude du comité de développement économique de l'AELE – cinquième de la série – sur des aspects de la politique régionale a été publiée par le Secrétariat en novembre 1973 (en anglais) et s'intitule *National Settlement Strategies: a framework for regional development*. Elle a été accueillie avec intérêt, aussi bien en dehors de l'AELE qu'au sein de celle-ci.

A sa réunion de décembre 1973, le comité de développement économique a estimé que l'importance pour les pays de l'AELE des politiques régionales que d'autres organisations internationales commencent à élaborer devait l'inciter à une étude plus approfondie, comme l'avait suggéré le président de son groupe de travail sur les tratégies nationales d'urbanisation. Aussi les Conseils ont-ils décidé que le Secrétariat devrait s'occuper aussi complètement que possible de la préparation d'une nouvelle étude, notamment en rassemblant des informations sur les activités d'autres organisations internationales au sujet du développement régional.

L'administration et les finances

En avril 1974, les Conseils ont décidé d'ajouter un nouveau poste au plan d'organisation de l'AELE, portant ainsi l'effectif total à 68 personnes. Ils ont également adopté de nouvelles règles concernant le personnel du Secrétariat; celles-ci visent essentiellement le recrutement et l'engagement, la cessation des rapports de service, les salaires et allocations, les dispositions en matière de consultation du personnel, la constitution d'un comité consultatif et le droit de recours auprès du Tribunal administratif de l'Organisation internationale du travail. En outre, le principe a été admis d'affilier l'AELE à la caisse de retraite d'une autre organisation.

A la fin juin 1974, le personnel du Secrétariat comptait 65 fonctionnaires dont 29 dans la catégorie des administrateurs et des directeurs et 36 dans les services généraux. Les noms des principaux fonctionnaires pour 1973–1974 figurent ci-dessous.

Le budget net pour l'exercice 1973–1974 s'est élevé à 6 178 051 francs suisses. Celui pour l'année financière 1974–1975, qui commence le 1er juillet 1974, a été fixé à la somme brute de 7 359 316 francs suisses, ce qui, après déduction d'une évaluation des recettes de 371 700 francs suisses, laisse une somme nette de 6 987 616 francs suisses à financier par les contributions des Etats de l'AELE.

Le barème des contributions au budget de l'AELE est établi chaque année en fonction du produit national brut des Etats de l'AELE, au coût des facteurs. Aucun pays n'est tenu de verser une contribution supérieure à 30% des dépenses nettes de l'Association. Voici les contributions de chaque pays pour 1973–1974 (les chiffres pour 1974–1975 figurent entre parenthèses): Suède 30% (30%); Suisse 24,688% (25,169%); Autriche 14,844% (15,101%); Norvège 12,031% (11,640%); Portugal 5,937% (5,820%); Islande 1,562% (1,573%). La contribution de la Finlande, qui est membre associé, s'élève à 10,938% (10,697%).

Under a third item on the agenda the Committee also had a full discussion of the course of inflation in the EFTA countries and of developments in their balances of payments.

The Economic Development Committee

The fifth and most recent EFTA study on aspects of regional policy prepared by EFTA's Economic Development Committee was published by the EFTA Secretariat in November 1973 under the title of "National Settlement Strategies: a framework for regional development." It was received with interest in both EFTA and non-EFTA circles.

At a meeting in December 1973 the Economic Development Committee agreed that the significance for EFTA countries of the emerging regional policies of other international organisations was a worth-while subject for further study by the Committee, as had been suggested by the Chairman of the EDC working party on national settlement strategies. Accordingly the Councils have agreed that the Secretariat should do as much preparatory work as possible for the new study, notably collecting information about the activities of other international organisations regarding regional development.

Administration and Finance

In April 1974, the EFTA Councils agreed to increase the manning table by one post, bringing the total of the staff to 68. They also approved new Regulations for the Secretariat staff which relate mainly to questions of recruitment and appointment, separation from the service of the Association, salaries and allowances, arrangements for consultation of the staff, the establishment of an advisory board and the right of appeal to the Administrative Tribunal of the International Labour Organisation. In addition, the principle of having EFTA affiliate with another organisation's pension scheme was recognised.

At the end of June 1974 the staff of the Secretariat totalled 65: of these 29 were in the Professional category and above and 36 were in the General Service grades. The names of the principal officers during 1973–1974 are given below.

The net budget for the financial year 1973–1974 was 6,178,051 Swiss francs. The budget of the financial year 1974–1975 beginning 1st July 1974 has been established at S. Frs. 7,359,316 gross, which, after deduction of estimated income of S. Frs. 371,700, leaves a net sum of S. Frs. 6,987,616 to be financed by contributions from EFTA States.

The scale of contributions to the EFTA budget is determined each year by reference to the gross national products at factor costs of the EFTA countries, none being required to contribute more than 30 per cent of the net expenditure of the Association. The individual national contributions for 1973–1974 were on the following basis (the figures assessed for 1974–1975 are shown in brackets): Sweden 30 per cent (30 per cent), Switzerland 24.688 per cent (25.169 per cent), Austria 14.844 per cent (15.101 per cent), Norway 12.031 per cent (11.640 per cent), Portugal 5.937 per cent (5.820 per cent), Iceland 1.562 per cent (1.573 per cent). The contribution of Finland, which is an Associate Member, was 10.938 per cent (10.697 per cent).

Les résultats des pays de l'AELE en 1974

Dans l'ensemble, les économies de la plupart des pays de l'AELE ont bien résisté aux tensions qui se sont manifestées en 1974. L'emploi est resté à un niveau élevé; en fait, une pénurie de main-d'oeuvre est apparue en cours d'année dans certains secteurs. De même, la croissance économique s'est maintenue dans la plupart des pays à un niveau supérieur à la moyenne observée par les nations industrialisées du monde. En Autriche, le taux de croissance a été de 5% environ; en Norvège et en Suède de quelque 4,5%.

Plusieurs pays de l'AELE sont également parvenus à maintenir un taux d'inflation inférieur à la moyenne de l'OCDE. L'Autriche, la Norvège, la Suède et la Suisse ont observé des taux voisins de 10%. Cependant, la Finlande, le Portugal et l'Islande ont connu respectivement des hausses de prix de l'ordre de 16,5,30 et 41%.

C'est surtout la balance commerciale des pays de l'AELE qui s'est ressentie intégralement des effets du relèvement des prix du pétrole et d'autres produits de base. L'Autriche s'en est le mieux tirée, avec une dégradation de sa balance extérieure de quelque 150 millions de dollars seulement; cela tient certes, dans une certaine mesure, à ses ressources indigènes de pétrole et de charbon. La balance commerciale de la Suisse s'est détériorée de 33% environ, pourcentage inférieur aux prévisions – la revalorisation du franc suisse par rapport au dollar ayant réduit la note des importations de pétrole dont les prix sont libellés en dollars. La Norvège a aussi enregistré une détérioration de quelque 33% de sa balance commerciale, ce qui tire peu à conséquence étant donné qu'elle sera un important producteur de pétrole dès 1975. L'excédent commercial de la Suède, de 1 milliard 700 millions de dollars en 1973, a fait place à un léger passif en 1974. Le déficit commercial de la Finlande a plus que doublé, totalisant 1 milliard 300 millions de dollars environ. Celui du Portugal s'est accru de près de 50%, soit de 500 millions de dollars. Quant à l'Islande, son déficit a plus que doublé, accusant une augmentation de 80 millions de dollars.

En chiffres ronds, le déficit de la balance commerciale des pays de l'AELE considérés dans leur ensemble est passé de quelque 5 milliards 500 millions en 1973 à 10 milliards environ en 1974. Ces chiffres n'indiquent évidemment pas la situation de la balance des paiements; dans les opérations courantes. le poste des services se soldera, comme à l'accouumtée, par un important excédent compensatoire. Ils donnent néanmoins une idée de l'ampleur des problèmes qu'il faudra résoudre en 1975 et dans les années à venir.

B. HAUTS FONCTIONNAIRES DE L'AELE

Secrétaire général: B. Rabaeus
Sous-secrétaire général: C. Sommaruga

Fonctionnaires supérieures
Bureau du secrétaire général. Directeur: E. Heinrichs
Affaires commerciales. Directeur: I. Stugu
Affaires juridiques. Directeur: A. Gaeta
Affaires économiques. Directeur: J. Lanner
Service de presse et information. Chef: R. Couvreu
Secrétaire du Conseil: Mlle S. Baverstock
Section administrative. Directeur: R. Girod

Adresse du secrétariat de l'AELE
9–11, rue de Varembé, 1211 Genève 20, Suisse
Téléphone (022) 34 90 00 *Télex:* 22 660

Performance of the EFTA countries in 1974

By and large, the economies of most of the EFTA countries held up well against the strains of 1974. Employment remained at a high level; in fact shortages of labour developed during the year in some industrial sectors. Similarly, economic growth continued in most of the participating countries at a higher rate than the average for the world's industrialized nations. Austria registered about 5 per cent and Norway and Sweden about 4.5 per cent.

Several EFTA countries also managed to hold rates of inflation below the OECD average. Austria, Norway, Sweden and Switzerland had rates around 10 per cent. But Finland faced a 16.5 per cent increase in prices, Portugal more than 30 per cent and Iceland no less than 41 per cent.

It was on their trade balances, however, that the EFTA nations felt the full effects of the higher prices for oil and other essential materials. Austria put up the best performance, with a worsening of her trade balance of only the equivalent of about $ 150 million. This was no doubt partially due to the fact that she has domestic resources of oil and coal. Switzerland's trade balance worsened by about 33 per cent, less than had been expected; the result was influenced by the appreciation of the Swiss franc against the dollar, thus reducing the bill for imported oil, which is based on dollar values. Norway's trade balance also worsened by about 33 per cent, but this was regarded as of slight importance in the light of the fact that Norway will be a large oil producer from 1975 onward. The Swedish trade surplus of $ 1,700 million in 1973 was transformed into a small deficit for 1974. The Finnish trade deficit more than doubled to a total of about $ 1,300 million. Portugal's deficit worsened by almost 50 per cent, or $ 500 million. And Iceland's deficit more than doubled, a worsening of about $ 80 million.

In round terms, therefore, the trade deficit of the EFTA countries as a group increased from about $ 5,500 million in 1973 to about $ 10,000 milion in 1974. This was not, of course, a balance of payments result; there will, as usual, be large countervailing surpluses on the services side of the current account. But the figures do indicate the magnitude of the problems to be faced in 1975 and in the years to follow.

B. SENIOR OFFICIALS OF EFTA

Secretary-General: B. Rabaeus
Assistant Secretary-General: C. Sommaruga

Principal Secretariat Officers
Secretary-General's Office. Director: E. Heinrichs
Trade Policy Affairs. Director: I. Stugu
Legal Affairs. Director: A. Gaeta
Economic Affairs. Director: J. Lanner
Press and Information Service. Head: R. Couvreu
Secretary to the Council: Miss S. Baverstock
Administrative Section. Director: R. Girod

EFTA Secretariat Headquarters
9–11, rue de Varembé, 1211 Geneva 20, Switzerland
Telephone: (022) 34 90 00 *Telex:* 22660

C. PUBLICATIONS DE L'AELE DISPONIBLES

Les publications de l'AELE sont distribuées gratuitement mais, à l'exception du Bulletin, pas automatiquement. On peut les obtenir auprès du Service de presse et d'information de l'AELE, 1211 Genève 20, et également auprès des dépositaires indiqués au dos de la page de couverture de l'EFTA Bulletin.

L'AELE, ce qu'elle est, ce qu'elle fait. Ce dépliant donne une description sommaire de l'AELE, son histoire et ses buts. Il est disponible en grandes quantités (Juillet 1973). Anglais, français et allemand.

L'Association européenne de libre-échange. Une brochure de 15 pages sur l'histoire et le fonctionnement de l'AELE. Contient aussi un chapitre consacré aux accords de libre-échange conclus avec les CE. Anglais (octobre 1974), français, allemand, norvègien, portugais et suédois (juin 1973).

Etudes sur les échanges

Echanges de l'AELE 1973. Intéressant surtout les économistes. Cette édition contient une analyse des échanges de l'AELE en 1973 accompagnée d'une importante annexe statistique. Anglais, français et allemand.

Les effets de l'AELE et de la CEE sur les échanges 1959–1967. Intéresse surtout les économistes. 168 pages, avec 77 tableaux (1972). Anglais, français et allemand.

Politique régionale dans l'AELE

An examination of the Growth Centre Idea. Etude du rôle des pôles de croissance comme instrument de politique régionale dans les pays de l'AELE (1968). 232 pages. Anglais seulement.

Industrial Estates. Etude sur le système des zones industrielles (1970). 80 pages. Anglais seulement.

Industrial Mobility. Cette étude analyse les expériences des pays de l'AELE en matière d'encouragement à la mobilité dans l'industrie (1971). 160 pages. Anglais seulement.

National Settlement Strategies: a framework for regional development. Etude sur les nouvelles formes d'urbanisation faite par un groupe de travail du comité de développement économique de l'AELE (1973). 200 pages. Anglais seulement.

Publications officielles

La Convention de Stockholm. Une nouvelle édition bilingue (anglais-français) et brochée de la Convention instituant l'Association européenne de libre-échange.

Edition à feuilles mobiles de *la Convention de Stockholm*

L'édition à feuilles mobiles de la Convention de Stockholm est tenue constamment à jour par l'envoi de tous les amendements aux abonnés. Contrairement à l'édition brochée, elle contient le texte intégral de l'annexe B (sur les règles d'origine). C'est la seule qui reproduit intégralement les règles d'origine.

Cette édition bilingue anglais-français peut être obtenue auprès du Secrétariat de l'AELE au prix de Fr. 60.–. Les abonnés recevront automatiquement tous les amendements qui paraîtront en 1975. Les amendements ultérieurs seront envoyés moyennant un versement de Fr. 20.– par année.

Rapports de l'AELE de 1966 à juin 1974. Anglais, français et allemand.

Les accords de libre-échange signés par les pays de l'AELE avec les Communautés européennes. Le Bulletin de l'AELE No 8 de 1972 présente les accords de libre-échange signés par l'Autriche, l'Islande, le Portugal, la Suède et la Suisse. L'accord signé par la Norvège est examiné dans l'édi-

C. EFTA PUBLICATIONS AVAILABLE

EFTA publications are distributed free of charge but, with the exception of the EFTA Bulletin, not automatically. They can be obtained from the EFTA Press and Information Service, 1211 Geneva 20, or from the distributors listed on the back cover page of the EFTA Bulletin.

EFTA – what it is, what it does. This brief folder leaflet gives general information about the history and purposes of EFTA. Available in bulk or single orders. (July 1974). English, French and German.

The European Free Trade Association. A 14-page booklet outlining the history and working of EFTA. Also contains a section on the Free Trade Agreements with the EC. English (Oct. 1974), French, German, Norwegian, Portuguese and Swedish editions (June 1973).

Trade studies

EFTA Trade 1973. Of interest mainly to economists. Contains an analysis of EFTA trade in 1973 with a substantial statistical appendix. English, French and German.

The trade effects of EFTA and the EEC 1959–1967. Also of interest mainly to economists. Contains 168 pages with 77 tables. English, French and German.

Regional policy in EFTA

An examination of the Growth Centre Idea. A study of the role of growth centres as a means of regional policy in EFTA countries (1968). 232 pages. English only.

Industrial Estates. A study of the industrial estate system (1970). 80 pages. English only.

Industrial Mobility. Analyses the experience of the EFTA countries in encouraging industrial mobility (1971). 160 pages. English only.

National Settlement Strategies: a framework for regional development. Report by a working party of the Economic Development Committee. English only. 200 pages. 1973.

Formal publications

The Stockholm Convention. English-French bilingual paperback edition of the Stockholm Convention.

Loose-leaf edition of *the Stockholm Convention*

The loose-leaf edition of the Stockholm Convention is kept constantly up to date by the issue to subscribers of all amendments. Unlike the paperback edition it also includes the full text of Annex B (on origin rules). It is thus the only edition to reproduce the origin rules in the fullest detail.

This bilingual English-French edition is available from the EFTA Secretariat at the price of 60 Swiss ffancs. Subscribers will automatically receive any amendments issued in 1975. Subsequent amandments will be supplied to subscribers at the price of 20 Swiss francs per annum.

EFTA Annual Reports 1967 to June 1974. English, French and German.

The Free Trade Agreements of the EFTA countries with the European Communities. EFTA Bulletin No 8 of 1972 presented the Free Trade Agreements with the enlarged European Communities signed by Austria, Iceland, Portugal, Sweden and Switzerland. The Agreements of Norway with the Communities were described in the June 1973 issue (No 5/73) and those of Finland in the November issue (No 8/73). English, French and German.

tion de juin 1973 (No 5) et celui signé par la Finlande dans l'édition de novembre 1973 (No 8). Anglais, français et allemand.

Compulsory technical regulations. Liste des autorités nationales compétentes dans chacun des pays de l'AELE (1969). Anglais seulement. Cette brochure peut être obtenue auprès du ministère du commerce des pays de l'AELE.

Conventions et arrangements de reconnaissance réciproque

Le Secrétariat de l'AELE assure les services de secrétariat dans le cadre des Conventions et des Arrangements mentionnés ci-dessous:

Textes officiels

Convention pour la reconnaissance mutuelle des inspections concernant le fabrication des produits pharmaceutiques (1970). Bilingue anglais-français, allemand, italien.

Convention sur le contrôle et le poinçonnement des ouvrages en métaux précieux (1972). Bilingue anglais-français.

Arrangement concernant la reconnaissance réciproque des essais et contrôles effectués sur les appareils à pression (édition revisée en août 1974). Anglais, français et allemand.

Arrangement concernant la reconnaissance réciproque des essais et contrôles effectués sur les appareils à gaz (édition revisée en mars 1973). Anglais, français et allemand.

Arrangement concernant la reconnaissance réciproque des essais effectués sur les machines et les tracteurs agricoles (édition revisée en juillet 1973). Anglais, français et allemand.

Arrangement concernant la reconnaissance réciproque des essais et contrôles effectués sur les équipements de navires (édition revisée en avril 1973). Anglais seulement.

Brochures publiées sous les auspices de la Convention pour la reconnaissance mutuelle des inspections concernant la fabrication des produits pharmaceutiques.

Normes de base relatives aux règles de bonne pratique applicables à la fabrication des produits pharmaceutiques. Edition trilingue anglais, français, allemand (1972).

Directives pour la fabrication de produits stériles. Edition trilingue anglais, français, allemand (1973).

Directives pour le traitement des matières premières. Edition trilingue anglais, français, allemand (1973).

Safety Aspects involved in the Packaging and Labelling of Pharmaceutical Products. Rassemble les travaux présentés lors du séminaire organisé par l'AELE en avril 1971. 172 pages. Anglais seulement.

Sampling and analytical control. Travaux présentés lors d'un séminaire organisé à Edinbourg en septembre 1973. Anglais seulement.

Manufacturing and quality control under contract. Travaux présentés lors d'un séminaire organisé à Berne en juillet 1974.

Compulsory Technical Regulations. Lists the competent national authorities in each EFTA country (1969). English only. This brochure can also be obtained from Trade Ministries in the EFTA countries.

Conventions and mutual recognition schemes

The EFTA Secretariat provides secretariat services for the Conventions and Schemes mentioned below:

Convention for the Mutual Recognition of inspections in respect of the Manufacture of Pharmaceutical Products. (1970). Bilingual English-French, German, Italian.

Convention on the Control and Marking of Articles of Precious Metals. (1972). Bilingual English-French.

Available in stencilled form are texts of the following:

Scheme for the Reciprocal Recognition of Tests and Inspections carried out on Pressure Vessels. (revised August 1974). In English, French and German.

Scheme for the Reciprocal Recognition of Tests and Inspections carried out on Gas Appliances (revised March 1973). English, French and German.

Scheme for the Reciprocal Recognition of Tests carried out on Agricultural Machines and Tractors (revised July 1973). English, French and German.

Scheme for the Reciprocal Recognition of Tests and Inspections carried out on Ships Equipment (revised April 1973). English only.

Brochures published under the auspices of the Convention for the Mutual Recognition of Inspections in respect of the Manufacture of Pharmaceutical Products.

Basic Standards of Good Manufacturing Practice for Pharmaceutical Products. Prepared by EFTA Working Party on Pharmaceutical Inspections (1972). Tri-lingual English, French and German.

Guidelines for the Manufacture of Sterile Products. Guidelines for the Handling of Starting materials. Both of these are annexes to the brochure on basic standards for the manufacture of pharmaceuticals. 1973. Tri-lingual English, French and German.

Safety Aspects involved in the Packaging and Labelling of Pharmaceutical Products. Contains the paper presented at a seminar organised by EFTA in April 1971. 172 pages. English only.

Sampling and Analytical Control. Papers presented at a seminar held in Edingburgh, Scotland, September 1973.

Manufacturing and quality control under contract. Papers presented at a seminar in Berne, July 1974.

CHAPITRE XIV

LES ORGANISATIONS SPATIALES EUROPEENNES[1]

Le CERS/ESRO et le CECLES/ELDO ont célébré en 1974 le dixième anniversaire de leur fondation. Ce dixième anniversaire aurait dû être couronné par l'établissement de facto de l'Agence Spatiale Européenne dans laquelle ces deux organisations se seraient fondues. 1974 se caracterise par un élargissement des programmes et des missions, la mise en route des programmes nouveaux décidés en 1974, par un élargissement du cercle des participants dans les programmes, par un élargissement des moyens. L'Europe spatiale voit son audience s'accroître sur la scène internationale.

A. LE CERS/ESRO

I. Le Programme scientifique commun

Pour la période 1972–1974, le niveau des ressources affectées chaque année à ce programme ne devait pas être inférieur à 27 millions d'unités de compte.

ESRO–IV, le septième satellite du CERS/ESRO après une année d'exploitation en orbite, est rentré dans l'atmosphère le 15 avril 1974. On peut noter que la durée de vie a dépassé les prévisions. Les résultats scientifiques paraissent extrêmement intéressants.

L'enregistreur de bord no 2 du satellite *TD. 1A* qui s'était remis en marche de façon inattendue à la mi-octobre 1973 a acquis depuis lors des données orbitales de haut intérêt.

HEOS–A2, 5ème satellite du CERS/ESRO, achevait en janvier sa deuxième année de séjour dans l'espace. Le satellite est rentré dans l'atmosphère le 2 août 1974. Quant à *HEOS A1*, sa fin de vie en orbite est prévue pour le 28 octobre 1975 et son potentiel scientifique reste très limité.

D'ici à 1980 le CERS/ESRO doit réaliser quatre nouveaux satellites scientifiques: COS–B; GEOS; ISEE B; EXOSAT, et participer à un programme international en collaboration avec la NASA et le Science Research Council du Royaume Uni, le programme IUE (International ultraviolet explorer). Ces nouveaux satellites pèseront entre 160 et 300 kg et emporteront des charges utiles pesant entre 30 et 120 kg.

La première partie du programme de qualifaction du prototype du satellite *COSB* s'est achevée par des essais divers. De même l'intégration du modèle de vol s'est également terminée. Par suite de retards toutefois la date de lancement a dû être reportée au 17 juillet 1975.

Le modèle de structure de *GEOS* a franchi avec succès son programme d'essais. Le modèle de développement a été intégré avec les expériences. Il faut relever que les propulseurs à hydrazine en cours de développement ont donné des résultats prometteurs. Le programme de moteur d'apogée se poursuit sans heurt. Le lancement est prévu en 1976.

Le projet *ISEE B* est passé de la phase d'étude (phase B) à la phase de développement et d'intégration (phase C/D). Le contrat a été attribué au Consortium Star dont le chef de file est la Société Dornier system. Une réunion commune s'est tenue entre le CERS/ESRO, la NASA et des grou-

[1] Chapitre préparé par G. Lafferanderie, Département des Affaires Internationales, OERS. Les vues exprimées sont purement personnelles à l'auteur et n'engagent en aucune façon l'organisation à laquelle il appartient.

CHAPTER XIV

EUROPEAN SPACE ORGANISATIONS[1]

In 1974 ESRO and ELDO celebrated the tenth anniversary of their foundation. This tenth anniversary should have culminated in the de facto establishment of the European Space Agency, into which these two Organisations were intended to merge. The year 1974 has been marked by an expansion of programmes and tasks, the starting up of new programmes decided upon that year, an expansion in the number of participants in the programmes, and an increase in the means made available as well as in international interest in European space activities.

A. ESRO

I. The common scientific programme

Over the period 1972 to 1974, the annual level of resources allotted to the scientific programme did not fall below 27 million units of account.

ESRO-IV, the seventh ESRO satellite, re-entered the atmosphere on 15 april 1974 after seventeen months' exploitation in orbit, a lifetime which exceeded the post-launch expectations. The scientific results appear to be most interesting.

The No. 2 on-board recorder of the *TD-1A* satellite, which reactivated itself unexpectedly in mid-October 1973, has since then recorded orbital data of the highest interest.

HEOS-A2, the fifth ESRO satellite, completed its second year in space in January 1974. This satellite re-entered the atmosphere on 2 August. Re-entry of *HEOS-A1* is expected to take place on 28 October 1975, and its remaining scientific potential is now very limited.

Between now and 1980 ESRO is due to develop four new scientific satellites, namely COS-B, GEOS, ISEE-B, EXOSAT, and to take part, in cooperation with NASA and the United Kingdom Science Research Council, in an international programme going by the name of IUE (International Ultraviolet Explorer). These new satellites will weigh between 160 and 300 kg, and will carry payloads weighing between 30 and 120 kg.

The first part of the *COS-B* prototype satellite qualification programme ended with the completion of various tests. Integration of the flight model has also been completed. Owing to delays, however, the launch date has been postponed to 17 July 1975.

The structural model of *GEOS* has successfully completed its test programmes. The development model has been integrated with the experiments. It should be noted that the hydrazine thrusters under development have given promising results. The apogee motor programme is progressing smoothly. Launch is planned for 1976.

The *ISEE-B* project has moved from the design phase (phase B) to the development and integration phase (phase C/D). The contract has been awarded to the Star Consortium, the leading firm in which is Dornier System. A joint meeting has taken place between ESRO, NASA and the

---

[1] Chapter prepared by G. Lafferanderie, International Affairs Department, ESRO. The views expressed are the author's own and in no way commit his Organisation.

pes de scientifiques ayant proposé des expériences. Un projet de memorandum d'accord entre le CERS/ESRO et la NASA était élaboré.

La mission d'*EXOSAT* doit se dérouler sur deux années (1980 et 1981). Le projet entrera dans sa phase de définition à la fin 1975. Les premières études se poursuivent à l'intérieur du CERS/ESRO. La date de lancement prévue est la fin de décembre 1979.

En ce qui concerne le projet *IUE* le modèle destiné à vérifier et à tester la conception du satellite a été assemblé, et il a été décidé d'implanter la station au sol sur le site de Villafranca del Castillo (près de Madrid).

De nouvelles possibilités de coopération entre le CERS/ESRO et la NASA ont été étudiées lors d'une réunion au début de 1974. Ont été passées en revue les perspectives offertes par les programmes du CERS/ESRO et de la NASA jusqu'en 1980.

II. Les satellites d'applications

1. *Le programme Aérosat.* Le Memorandum d'accord portant sur le Programme commun d'évaluation d'Aérosat entre la FAA (Etats-Unis), le CERS/ESRO et le Gouvernement du Canada était, le 9 mai à Londres, signé par le représentant de la FAA et paraphé à Paris par les représentants du CERS/ESRO et du Gouvernement du Canada. Ces derniers signaient à leur tour le Memorandum d'accord le 2 août à Paris. Le Programme Aérosat est un programme d'expérimentation et d'évaluation préparant la mise en oeuvre d'un système opérationnel mondial de contrôle de la circulation aérienne par satellites dans les années 1980. Le premier des deux satellites doit être lancé ver la fin de 1978.

Le Memorandum d'accord prévoyait que le secteur spatial serait réalisé aux termes d'arrangements contractuels entre le CERS/ESRO, le Gouvernement du Canada et une société américaine. Le choix de cette dernière revenant au CERS/ESRO, un appel d'offres fut lancé auquel cinq sociétés répondirent.

Finalement le Conseil directeur du programme Aérosat choisissait en septembre 1974 la Comsat General Corporation. La dernière main était mise au projet d'arrangement entre le CERS/ESRO, le Gouvernement du Canada et la Comsat General. Cet Arrangement (assez unique, entre une Organisation internationale, un Gouvernement et une société privée), était signé à Washington le 2 décembre 1974. Le lendemain avait lieu la première réunion officielle du Conseil d'Aérosat réunissant les signataires du memorandum d'accord. Ainsi, après bien des vicissitudes le programme Aerosat pouvait démarrer.

L'Australie et le Japon, associés dès le début aux travaux sur l'établissement de ce programme, ont continué à marquer leur intérêt et indiquaient leur souhait d'être tenus au courant des développements.

Restent deux questions pour les Etats membres du CERS/ESRO participant au programme Aérosat; mettre en place une structure de définition et d'éxecution du programme coordonné européen, réviser le texte de l'Arrangement signé en décembre 1971 afin de le mettre en concordance avec le Memorandum d'accord.

2. *Le programme Meteosat* a continué à faire l'objet d'une concertation avec les pays qui participent à la Veille Météorologique Mondiale de l'Organisation Météorologique Mondiale (OMM) en développant des satellites météorologiques stationnaires, c'est-à-dire les Etats-Unis, l'Union Soviétique et le Japon. Le Secrétariat du CERS/ESRO était chargé de tâches de coordination technique et opérationnelle. La quatrième réunion de coordination sur les satellites météorologiques geostationnaires organisée à l'initiative du CERS/ESRO, se tenait du 13 au 18 mai au siège de l'OMM.

La construction du premier modèle d'identification de Météosat est en cours. Le centre d'acquisition de données, de télécommande et de poursuite scientific groups that had proposed experiments. A Memorandum of Understanding between ESRO and NASA was drawn up.

The *EXOSAT* mission is due to take place over two years (1980 and 1981). The project definition phase will beginn at the end of 1975. The first studies are being carried out in ESRO. Launch is planned for the end of December 1979.

As regards the *IUE* project, the satellite design checkout model has been assembled, and it has been decided to set up the ground station at Villafranca del Castillo, near Madrid.

New possibilities cooperation between ESRO and NASA were studied at a meeting early in 1974, during which the prospects offered by ESRO and NASA programmes up to 1980 were reviewed.

II. Applications Satellites

1. *Aeronautical Satellite Programme* (*Aerosat*). The Memorandum of Understanding on the joint Aerosat evaluation programme between the FAA (U.S.A.), ESRO and the Canadian Government was signed in London on 9 May 1974 by the FAA representative and initialled in Paris by the representatives of ESRO and of the Canadian Government. The latter representatives signed the Memorandum of Understanding in Paris on 2 August. The Aerosat Programme is an experimentation and evaluation programme preparing the introduction, in the 1980s, of a world-wide operational system for air traffic control by means of satellites. The first of the two satellites involved is due to be launched towards the end of 1978.

The Memorandum of Understanding provided for the space segment to be developed under contractual arrangements between ESRO, the Canadian Government, and an American firm to be selected by ESRO. Tenders were called for, and five firms answered.

In September, the Aeronautical Satellite Programme Board selected Comsat General Corporation. The draft Arrangement between ESRO, the Canadian Government and Comsat General was finalised. This Arrangement (a rather unusual one, between an international organisation, a government and a private firm) was signed in Washington on 2 December The next day saw the first official meeting of the Aerosat Council, which was attended by the signatories of the Memorandum of Understanding. Thus, after a number of vicissitudes, the Aerosat Programme was able to start.

Australia and Japan, which had from the beginning been associated with the work for the establishment of this programme, showed continued interest and expressed the wish to be kept informed of developments.

The ESRO Member States participating in the Aerosat Programme still have to set up a structure for the definition and execution of the European Coordinated Programme and revise the text of the Arrangement signed in December 1971 in order to bring it into line with the Memorandum of Understanding.

2. The *Meteorological Satellite Programme* (Meteosat) has continued to be the subject of consultations with the countries that take part in the World Weather Watch of the World Meteorological Organisation (WMO) by developing geostationary meteorological satellites, namely the U.S.A., the U.S.S.R. and Japan. The ESRO Secretariat was entrusted with technical and operational coordination tasks. The fourth coordination meeting on geostationary meteorological satellites, organised on ESRO's initiative, was held from 13 to 18 May 1974 at WMO headquarters.

The first Meteosat identification model is under construction. The tracking telemetry and control station will be set up in the Odenwald mountain area (Germany). In view of delays in various sectors it would sera implanté dans le massif de l'Odenwald (Allemagne). En raison de retards constatés dans divers secteurs, il n'aurait pas été possible de procéder au lancement à la date prévue (décembre 1976) et la lancement est maintenant fixé au mois d'avril 1977.

Une campagne d'expérience de propagation multiple menée conjointement par le CERS/ESRO et le Centre Nationale d'Etudes Spatiales (CNES) au large de Cassis en Septembre-Octobre s'est soldée par un grand succès.

3. *Le programme de satellites de télécommunications* est un de ceux dont les caractéristiques sont de nature à satisfaire les besoins de pays ou de groupes de pays qui ont des besoins comparables à ceux de l'Europe dans ce domaine. A partir de 1978 l'Europe disposera à titre expérimental et préopérationnel d'un système de télécommunications par satellites.

Le contrat de phase C/D du satellite OTS (Orbital Test Satellite) était octroyé à la fin de janvier 1974 au consortium MESH. Les études sur le système de télécommunications pour le satellite ECS (European communication satellite) se poursuivent. Des études pratiques ont été menées sur l'atténuation atmosphérique de signaux à 11 G Hz en utilisant des radiomètres installés en plusieurs stations en Europe.

Rappelons que le CERS/ESRO participe au programme canadien CTS.

4. *Le programme de satellite Marots*. L'évènement majeur a été la passation des contrats de phase C/D pour le développement et la fabrication du véhicule spatial. Le contrat pour la plateforme (partie commune à Marots et à OTS) a été attribué à la fin de novembre 1974 à Hawker Siddeley Dynamics et le contrat pour la charge utile à Marconi.

Marots serait lancé par une fusée Thor Delta du type 3914. La date de lancement est maintenant prévue pour Octobre 1977. A la suite de contacts avec le consortium américain Marisat et pour éviter des interférences, le Conseil directeur de programme Marots a décidé de repositionner le satellite qui sera donc à présent mis à poste à 40° de longitude est.

Le 12 novembre 1974, par un accord conclu sous forme d'échange de lettres, la Norvège devenait un participant au programme Marots; pour la première fois un Etat non membre participait à un programme du CERS/ESRO. La Norvège financera 1,5% du coût total du programme. Les pays participants représentent 36% du tonnage mondial. Aussi une grande attention est-elle prêtée aux travaux se déroulant dans le cadre de l'ONU en vue de la mise sur pied d'un système mondial de satellites maritimes par une Organisation Internationale nouvelle (INMARSAT). Le CERS/ESRO participe activement aux travaux préparatoires.

III. Le programme de laboratoire spatial (*Spacelab*)

Les études de définition de la phase B_3 de ce programme exécutées par les deux contractants retenus (ERNO et MBB) se terminaient à la fin février. L'appel d'offres pour la phase C/D était alors lancé. Les deux contractants présentaient dans leurs réponses un concept flexible du Spacelab comportant notamment un module et une plateforme porte instruments.

Le 5 juin 1974 la procédure d'attribution du contrat pour la phase de réalisation du programme s'achevait par l'octroi à l'équipe industrielle VFW/FOKKER/ERNO d'un contrat de 180 millions d'unités de compte. Préalablement au mois de mai le Directeur Général du CERS/ESRO et l'Administrateur de la NASA avaient procédé à une première revue commune du programme Spacelab. Les procédures relatives au choix de la première charge utile du Spacelab étaient approuvées. Le CERS/ESRO invitait les utilisateurs potentiels à proposer des idées, et recevait plus de 200 propositions d'expériences dans les domaines de la science, des applications, de la technologie, à effectuer au cours de la première mission du Spacelab (milieu de 1980). En novembre, le CERS/ESRO effectuait, avec la participation de la NASA et du contractant un examen préliminaire des not have been possible to launch Meteosat at the envisaged time (December 1976), and launch is now planned for April 1977.

A series of multipath propagation experiments conducted jointly by ESRO and the Centre National d'Etudes Spatiales (CNES–France) off the coast near Cassis (France) in September-October was completed with great success.

3. The *Communications Satellite Programme* is one of several programmes whose characteristics can satisfy the needs of countries or groups of countries with requirements similar to those of Europe in this field. As from 1978, Europe will have an experimental and preoperational satellite communications system.

The phase C/D contract for the OTS (Orbital Test Satellite) was awarded to the MESH consortium at the end of January 1974. Studies on the telecommunications systems for the ECS (European Communication Satellite) continue. Practical studies have been carried out on the atmospheric attenuation of 11-GHz signals by means of radiometers set up in several European station.

It should also be remembered that ESRO takes part in the Canadian CTS programme.

4. *Maritime Satellite Programme* (Marots). The major event has been the placing of the phase C/D contracts for the development and construction of the spacecraft. The contract for the platform (common to Marots and to OTS) was awarded at the end of November 1974 to Hawker Siddeley Dynamics, and the payload contract to Marconi.

Marots is intended to be launched by means of a Thor Delta 3914 rocket. The launch is now scheduled for October 1977. Following discussions with the American Marisat consortium the Maritime Satellite Programme Board decided that, in order to preclude electrical interference, the Marots satellite would be repositioned at 40° longitude east.

On 12 November, by virtue of an agreement concluded in the form of an exchange of letters, Norway became a participant in the Marots programme; and thus, for the first time, a non-member state joined an ESRO programme. Norway will fund 1.5% of the total cost of the programme. The participating countries represent 36% of world shipping tonnage. Great attention is therefore paid to the discussions held under UN auspices for a world-wide maritime navigation satellite system to be set up by a new international organisation (Inmarsat). ESRO takes an active part in the preparatory work.

III. Space Laboratory Programme (*Spacelab*)

The phase B_3 definition studies for this programme, carried out by the two selected contractos (ERNO and MBB), were completed at the end of February 1974. A call for tenders for phase C/D was then issued. The two contractors presented in their replies a flexible design for Spacelab, involving in particular a module and an instrument platform.

On 5 June the contract action for the programme development phase ended with the award of a 180-million-accounting-unit contract to the German industrial team VWF/FOKKER/ERNO. Before that, in May, the Director General of ESRO and the Administrator of NASA had carried out a first joint review of the Spacelab programme. The procedures for the choice of the first Spacelab payload were and received more than 200 proposals for experiments in the areas of science, applications and technology to be carried out during the first Spacelab mission (mid-1980). In November a preliminary examination of the requirements was carried out by ESRO together with NASA and the contractor; the purpose was to ascertain that the contractor's plans for implementation of the programme complied with the programme requirements.

impératifs; il s'agissait de vérifier que les plans du contractant pour la mise en oeuvre du programme respectaient les impératifs de celui-ci.

Le 7 février 1975 était signé à Vienne un accord entre le CERS/ESRO et l'Autriche, par lequel l'Autriche devenait un participant au programme· C'était la première fois que l'Autriche se trouvait associée à un projet spatial.

IV. Le programme de lanceur Ariane

En février 1974, le Conseil directeur du programme Ariane approuvait les conclusions de la phase de définition du projet et autorisait le CNES à passer au stade de la réalisation.

Mais à la fin du mois de juillet le CNES, gérant du programme, informait le CERS/ESRO et les contractants industriels que la signature des contrats était reportée à plus tard pour laisser au Gouvernement français le temps de réexaminer l'ensemble de sa politique spatiale. Le Conseil directeur du programme faisait part au Gouvernement français, dans un Résolution, de ses inquiétudes les plus vives. Le 16 octobre le Gouvernement français confirmait sa participation au programme de lanceur Ariane et les contrats principaux pouvaient être signés.

L'étude et la réalisation des sous-systèmes se poursuivent, ainsi que la mise en place des moyens de production et la construction des installations d'intégration et d'essais au sol. L'adaptation des installations de la base de lancement du CECLES à Kourou (Guyane française) connaissait un certain début. Par un échange de lettres les biens du CECLES/ELDO nécessaires pour l'exécution du programme Ariane avaient été mis à la disposition du CERS/ESRO à charge pour ce dernier d'en assurer la maintenance.

Le 18 octobre 1974, le Conseil directeur du programme acceptait un réaménagement du plan de développement du programme de manière à le rendre compatible avec les moyens de financement disponibles. Les examens préliminaires de conception pour tous les systèmes et sous-systèmes débutaient à la fin de l'année. La technologie développée dans le cadre de ce programme présente un intérêt certain pour les Etats. On en trouve un exemple dans l'obtention par le Gouvernement Indien de la licence de fabrication du moteur Viking d'Ariane aux fins de son programme national de lanceur.

V. L'élargissement de la mission et des moyens du CERS/ESRO

Le projet de Convention portant création d'une Agence spatiale européenne prévoit une intégration progressive des programmes spatiaux des Etats Membres. Dans cet esprit le Gouvernement français proposait l'européanisation du programme de satellite GEOLE, programme de localisation geodésique étudié par le CNES. Un groupe de travail était constitué par le Conseil du CERS/ESRO; deux présentations étaient organisées par le CNES et un projet d'arrangement était élaboré.

Les nouveaux programmes de satellites demandaient l'établissement de nouvelles installations au sol. Une station de contrôle de satellites géostationnaires était implantée à Michelstadt/Odenwald (Allemagne) aux termes d'un accord signé le 7 juin, ainsi qu'à Villafranca del Castillo (près de Madrid) sur la base d'un accord signé le 2 août 1974.

On 7 February 1975 an agreement between ESRO and Austria was signed in Vienna, by virtue of which Austria became a participant in the programme. This was the first time that Austria found herself associated in a space project.

IV. Ariane Launcher Programme

In February 1974 the Ariane Launcher Programme Board approved the conclusion of the project definition phase and authorised CNES, the programme manager, to start on development.

However, at the end of July, CNES informed ESRO and the industrial contractors that the signing of the contracts was deferred until a later date in order to allow the French Government to review its space policy as a whole. The Programme Board passed a Resolution informing the French Government of its deepest concern. On 16 October the French Government confirmed its participation in the Ariane Launcher Programme, and the main contracts were signed.

Work is progressing on the design and construction of the subsystems, the installation of production plants and the setting up of integration and ground test facilities. A start has been made on the adaptation of the facilities of the ELDO launch site at Kourou (French Guiana). Through an exchange of letters the ELDO assets required for the execution of the Ariane programme had previously been made available to ESRO, which assumed responsibility for their maintenance.

On 18 October the Ariane Launcher Programme Board agreed to modify the programme development plan in order to make it compatible with the available funds. Preliminary design studies on all systems and subsystems began at the end of the year. The technology developed under this programme is of definite interest for the States. This is illustrated by the Indian Government's obtaining a licence to build the Ariane Viking engine for its own national launcher programme.

V. Extension of ESRO's task, and increased funding

The draft Convention for the establishment of a European Space Agency provides for gradual integration of the Member States' space programmes. Bearing this in mind, the French Government proposed the Europeanisation of the Geole satellite programme, a programme for geodesic position determination drawn up by CNES. A working party was set up by the Council of ESRO; two presentations were organised by CNES and a draft Arrangement was prepared.

The new satellite programmes called for new ground facilities. A geostationary satellite control station was set up at Michelstadt, in the Odenwald (Germany), under an agreement signed on 7 June, and another at Villafranca del Castillo (near Madrid) under an agreement signed on 2 August.

B. LES ACTIVITES DU CECLES/ELDO

La liquidation du programme Europa III était terminée en octobre 1973. Celle du programme Europa II s'est poursuivie. La liquidation „active" s'est achevée en fait en juillet; au-delà ne restait que du travail „passif" consistant principalement à liquider des paiements encore dûs.

Le Conseil du CERS/ESRO acceptait la demande du Conseil du CECLES/ELDO que le personnel du CECLES y compris le „groupe de liquidation" soit transféré au CERS le 1er juillet 1974 si la création de facto de l'ASE était repoussée à une date ultérieure. La liquidation demeurait toutefois la responsabilité du Secrétaire Général du CECLES et le personnel du Groupe de liquidation était mis à sa disposition. Le mandat du Secrétaire Général prenait fin le 1er juillet 1974, date à laquelle les fonctions de Secrétaire Général du CECLES étaient confiées à une autre personne.

Le Conseil du CECLES ayant décidé que la totalité de la documentation technique du CECLES devait être enregistrée et mise en forme pour introduction dans le SDS (Space Documentation Service) du CERS, il a fallu mettre sur pied une équipe de travail. On estime que ce travail sera terminé en 12 mois à compter de septembre 1974.

L'Australie qui n'envisage pas de devenir membre de l'Agence Spatiale européenne, a annoncé son retrait du CECLES/ELDO. Un accord a été conclu entre le CECLES/ELDO et l'Australie dont le retrait a pris effet au 1er janvier 1975.

C. LA CONFERENCE SPATIALE EUROPEENNE ET LE PROJET DE CREATION D'UNE AGENCE SPATIALE EUROPEENNE

Au printemps 1974, le projet de Convention portant création d'une Agence Spatiale Européenne (ASE), de l'Acte final de la Conférence des Plénipotentiaires, ainsi que des Résolutions à adopter par les Conseils du CERS/ESRO et du CECLES/ELDO étaient trés avancées. Le Comité des Suppléants de la Conférence spatiale européenne (C.S.E.) surmontait les dernières réserves identifiées par son Groupe de Travail sur l'Agence Spatiale Européenne et la Conférence des Plénipotentiaires était envisagée pour le mois de juin. Un comité de rédaction sous la conduite du Secrétariat de la CSE se réunissait pour assurer la concordance entre les diverses versions existantes des textes (quatre, puis bientôt sept langues). La Délégation de la France faisait alors savoir qu'elle envisageait de déposer de nouvelles propositions d'amendements au projet de Convention. Un nouveau temps de réflexion fut admis. Les propositions d'amendements étaient présentées au Comité des Suppléants à la fin du mois de novembre. Elles portaient sur des points importants, comme la structure de l'Agence, la politique en matière de lanceurs et en matière d'approvisionnement de matériels. Le Groupe de travail sur l'Agence Spatiale Européenne tenait deux réunions avant la fin de l'année. Un Groupe de travail „Convention" était chargé d'analyser la portée juridique des propositions sur le texte du projet de Convention et faisait rapport au Comité des Suppléants.

Parallèlement à ces travaux relatifs à l'élaboration de la Convention, le Comité des Suppléants étudiait les mesures à prendre en vue de préparer la mise en place des structures de l'Agence ainsi que les dispositions à adopter pour assurer la reprise par l'Agence des droits et obligations du CERS/ESRO et du CECLES/ELDO. L'Irlande devenait membre de la CSE.

Sur la base des travaux du Comité des Suppléants, le Conseil du CERS/

B. ELDO ACTIVITIES

The winding up of the Europa III programme was completed in October 1973. That of the Europa II programme continued. "Active" winding up was in fact completed in July 1974; after that there only remained "passive" work, consisting mainly in attending to payments still outstanding.

At the request of the ELDO Council, the ESRO Council agreed that, if the de facto establishment of the European Space Agency was deferred beyond 1 July 1974 ELDO staff, including the "liquidation group" would be transferred to ESRO on that date. Winding up, however, remained a matter for the Secretary General of ELDO, and the liquidation group was placed at his disposal. The term of office of the Secretary General of ELDO ended on 1 July and on that date his duties were entrusted to another person.

As the ELDO Council had decided that the whole of the ELDO technical documentation should be recorded and prepared for introduction into the ESRO Space Documentation Service (SDS), a work team had to be set up for the purpose. It is estimated that this work will be completed within 12 months from September 1974.

Australia, which does not envisage becoming a member of the European Space Agency, has announced its withdrawal from ELDO. An agreement was concluded between ELDO and Australia, whose withdrawal took effect on 1 January 1975.

C. THE EUROPEAN SPACE CONFERENCE AND THE PROJECTED ESTABLISHMENT OF A EUROPEAN SPACE AGENCY

By the Spring 1974 the draft Convention for the establishment of a European Space Agency (ESA), the draft Final Act of the Conference of Plenipotentiaries, as well as the Resolutions to be adopted by the ESRO and ELDO Councils, had made considerable progress. The Committee of Alternates of the European Space Conference (ESC) overcame the last reservations identified by its Working Group on the European Space Agency, and a Conference of Plenipotentiaries was planned to take place in June. A drafting group arranged by the ESC Secretariat met in order to ensure concordance between the various existing versions of the text (in four languages, soon to become seven). Then the French Delegation made it known that it intended to make new proposals for modifications to the draft Convention. Further time was allowed for reflection. The proposals for amendment were present to the Committee of Alternates at the end of November. They bore on important issues, such as the structure of the Agency and the policy with respect to launchers and supply of materials. The ESA Working Group met twice before the end of the year. The Workking Group of the Convention was instructed to analyse the legal impact of the proposals on the text of the draft Convention, and report on it to the Committee of Alternates.

Concurrently with work on the draft Convention, the Committee of Alternates examined the measures to be taken for the preparation and setting up of the structures of the Agency and the provisions to be adopted to ensure that the Agency could assume the rights and obligations of ESRO and ELDO. Ireland became a member of the ESC.

On the basis of the work done by the Committee of Alternates, the Council of ESRO adopted new staff regulations and new financial regulations.

ESRO adoptait un nouveau statut du personnel et un nouveau règlement financier.

Outre le projet de convention, restaient encore deux problèmes importants à régler – celui des personnalités devant constituer l'équipe dirigeante de la future agence spatiale européenne, ainsi que celui de la participation de l'ASE aux frais de fonctionnement du centre spatial guyanais à la solution duquel la Délégation de la France déclarait attacher une grande importance.

Nota. La Convention établissant l'Agence spatiale européenne fut signée à Paris le 31 mai, 1975. Le texte sera publié dans l'Annuaire Européen vol. XXIII.

D. BIBLIOGRAPHIE

Dr. H. Kaltenecker	La nouvelle Agence Spatiale européenne, Institut international de droit spatial XVIIe Colloque, Amsterdam, octobre 1974.
	– Bulletin ESRO/ELDO No. 26, décembre 1974.
	– Zur Gründung der europaïschen Weltraumorganisation.
	– Zeitschrift für Luftrecht und Weltraumrechtsfragen, Band 23 Nr. 4, 1.10.74.
Dr. Kaltenecker et R. Orye	– L'Accord Ariane – Aspects juridiques et mise en oeuvre, L'Aéronautique et l'Astronautique No. 49, 1976–6.
Bulletin ESRO/ELDO No. 24	– Le Xe Anniversaire du CERS/ESRO et du CECLES/ELDO (articles de M. A. Hocker et du Genl. Aubinière).
L'Europe Spatiale	– Etude préparé par le CERS/ESRO–1974 (Programmes de l'ESRO – Organismes et programmes nationaux – L'industrie et ses compétences).

Apart from the draft Convention, there remained two important problems to be settled, namely the matter of the persons to be appointed as directors of the future European Space Agency and that of ESA participation in the running costs of the Guiana Space Centre, an issue which the French Delegation considered to be of the utmost importance.

Note. The Convention establishing the European Space Agency was signed in Paris on 31 May 1974. The text will be published in European Yearbook Vol. XXIII.

CHAPITRE XV

ORGANISATION EUROPEENNE POUR LA SECURITE DE LA NAVIGATION AERIENNE

Le texte de la convention établissant l'EUROCONTROL a été publié dans *l'Annuaire européen*, Vol. XXI aux pages 690 à 714.

Sont publiés ci-après:

A. L'Annexe I à la Convention: Statuts de l'Agence.
B. Le Protocole de signature du 13 décembre 1960.

A. *ANNEXE I*

STATUTS DE L'AGENCE

Article 1

L',,AGENCE DES SERVICES DE LA CIRCULATION AERIENNE,'' instituée par l'article 1 de la Convention internationale de coopération pour la sécurité de la navigation aérienne en date du 13 décembre 1960, ci-après dénommée la ,,Convention,'' est régie par les présents Statuts.

Article 2

1. L'Agence a pour objet d'assurer, dans tous les espaces définis conformément au paragraphe 2 d) de l'article 6 de la Convention et à l'article 38 de la Convention, les services de la circulation aérienne, c'est-à-dire:

a) d'empêcher les abordages entre aéronefs;

b) d'assurer l'écoulement ordonné et rapide de la circulation aérienne;

c) de fournir les avis et les renseignements utiles à l'exécution sûre et efficace des vols;

d) d'alerter les organes appropriés lorsque les aéronefs ont besoin de l'aide des services de recherche et de sauvetage, et de prêter à ces organes le concours nécessaire.

2. L'Agence met en place les moyens nécessaires à l'exécution des missions énumérées ci-dessus et en assure le bon fonctionnement.

3. A cette fin l'Agence travaille en étroite collaboration avec les autorités militaires afin de satisfaire le plus efficacement et le plus économiquement possible les besoins de la circulation aérienne et les besoins particuliers de l'aviation militaire.

4. Elle peut notamment créer des centres de recherches et d'expérimentation de la circulation aérienne et des écoles servant au perfectionnement et à la spécialisation du personnel des services de la navigation aérienne.

Article 3

Sous réserve des pouvoirs reconnus à la Commission permanente pour la sécurité de la navigation aérienne instituée par la Convention et qui est dénommée ci-après la ,,Commission,'' l'Agence est administrée par un Comité de gestion, ci-après dénommé le ,,Comité'' et par un Directeur. Les pouvoirs propres à ce dernier sont définis à l'Article 13 ci-après.

CHAPTER XV

EUROPEAN ORGANISATION FOR THE SAFETY OF AIR NAVIGATION

The text of the Convention establishing EUROCONTROL was published in *European Yearbook*, Vol. XXI at pp. 691 to 715.

There are published below:

A. Annex I to the Convention: Statute of the Agency.

B. The Protocol of Signature of 13 December 1960.

A. *ANNEX I*

STATUTE OF THE AGENCY

Article 1

The "AIR TRAFFIC SERVICES AGENCY," established by Article 1 of the International Convention relating to Co-operation for the Safety of Air Navigation dated the 13th day of December 1960, hereinafter called "the Convention," shall be governed by the present Statute.

Article 2

1. The purpose of the Agency shall be to provide, within the whole of the air space defined in accordance with paragraph 2 d) of Article 6 of the Convention and with Article 38 of the Convention, air traffic service, that is to say:

a) to prevent collisions between aircraft;

b) to ensure the orderly and rapid flow of air traffic;

c) to provide advice and information useful for the safe and efficient conduct of flights;

d) to notify appropriate organisations regarding aircraft in need of search and rescue aid, and assist such organisations as required.

2. The Agency shall install the necessary facilities for the performance of the tasks enumerated above and shall ensure their satisfactory operation.

3. To that end, the Agency shall work in close collaboration with the military authorities in order to meet as efficaciously and economically as possible the requirements of air traffic and the special requirements of military aviation.

4. The Agency may inter alia establish air traffic research and experimental centres and schools for the advanced and specialised training of personnel of air navigation services.

Article 3

Subject to the powers conferred upon the permanent Commission for the Safety of Air Navigation, established by the Convention and hereinafter called "the Commission," the Agency shall be administered by a Committee of Management, hereinafter called "the Committee," and by a Director. The powers of the Director are defined in Article 13 hereunder.

Article 4

Le Comité est composé de deux représentants de chacun des Parties Contractantes dont l'un seulement a voix délibérative. Ce dernier est un haut fonctionnaire exerçant dans son pays des responsabilités dans le domaine de la navigation aérienne. Chaque représentant est pourvu d'un suppléant, qui le représente valablement en cas d'empêchement.

Article 5

Le Comité élit dans son sein, pour une durée de deux ans, un Président et un Vice-Président. Ceux-ci sont rééligibles. Le Comité désigne un Secrétaire qui peut être pris en dehors de ses membres. En cas d'empêchement du Président, la présidence du Comité est assurée par le Vice-Président ou, à défaut, par le plus âgé des membres présents à la réunion.

Article 6

1. Le Comité délibère valablement lorsque tous les représentants des Parties Contractantes ayant voix délibérative sauf un sont présents.
2. Si ce quorum n'est pas atteint, la délibération est remise à une séance ultérieure, qui fait l'objet d'une nouvelle convocation et ne doit se tenir au plus tôt que dix jours après la précédente. Pour la deuxième délibération le quorum exigé est de la moitié au moins des représentants ayant voix délibérative.

Article 7

1. Les votes ont lieu à la majorité des voix attribuées aux Parties Contractantes, étant entendu que celles-ci sont affectées de la même pondération que celle dont les Parties contractantes disposent au sein de la Commission en application de l'article 9 de la Convention.
2. Toutefois, un vote ne sera acquis que si la majorité visée à l'alinéa précédent représente la moitié au moins des Parties Contractantes.
3. En cas de partage égal des voix le Président décide, soit de procéder à un deuxième scrutin au cours de la même séance, avec ou sans interruption de courte durée, soit d'inscrire la proposition mise en délibération à l'ordre du jour d'une nouvelle séance dont il fixe la date. Si le partage des voix se renouvelle lors de la nouvelle séance, la voix du Président est prépondérante.

Article 8

1. Le Comité élabore son règlement intérieur.
2. Celui-ci doit comporter notamment des dispositions relatives aux incompatibilités. Il doit prévoir en outre que les convocations aux séances seront envoyées par lettre missive ou, en cas d'urgance, par télégramme et comprendront l'ordre du jour.
3. Le règlement est soumis à l'approbation de la Commission.

Article 4

The Committee shall be composed of representatives of each of the Contracting Parties, two representatives for each Party. Only one of the two representatives shall be a highly placed official exercising in his country responsibilities in matters of air navigation. Each representative shall have an alternate who shall validly represent him if he is unable to be present.

Article 5

The Committee shall elect a President and a Vice-President from amongst its members for a term of office of two years. These officers shall be eligible for re-election. The Committee shall appoint a Secretary who need not be one of its members. If the President is unable to be present, the meeting of the Committee shall be presided over by the Vice-President, or, in his absence, by the oldest member present.

Article 6

1. All but one of those representatives of the Contracting Parties who are entitled to vote shall be required to form a quorum for the meetings of the Committee.
2. If there are not sufficient numbers to form the above quorum, the deliberations shall be deferred until a meeting to be held at a later date and not earlier than ten days after the preceding meeting; the Committee shall be re-convened for the second meeting and at least half the representatives entitled to vote shall be required to form a quorum.

Article 7

1. The decisions of the Committee shall be carried by a majority of the votes allotted to the Contracting Parties, it being understood that those votes shall be subject to the same weighting as the votes to which the Contracting Parties are entitled on the Commission in application of Article 9 of the Convention.
2. A proposal shall not be carried, however, unless the majority referred to in the preceding paragraph represents at least half the Contracting Parties.
3. Should an equal number of votes be cast for and against the proposal, the President shall decide either to take a second vote during the same meeting, with or without a short suspension, or to include the proposal under deliberation in the agenda of a fresh meeting of which he shall fix the date. Should an equal number of votes again be cast during the new meeting, the President shall have a casting vote.

Article 8

1. The Committee shall establish its rules of procedure.
2. Those rules shall include inter alia provisions relating to disqualifications. Furthermore, they shall prescribe that notices convening meetings be sent by letter or, in case of urgency, by telegram and include the agenda.
3. The rules shall be subject to the approval of the Commission.

Article 9

1. Le Comité statue sur l'organisation technique de l'Agence qui lui est proposée par le Directeur.

2. Toutefois, il doit soumettre à l'approbation de la Commission statuant à l'unanimité de ses membres:

a) les projets relatifs au nombre et à l'emplacement des centres de contrôle ou d'information de vol et à leur domaine d'action;

b) les mesures portant création des centres de recherches et d'expérimentation et d'écoles de perfectionnement et de spécialisation ou d'autres organismes établis en application du paragraphe 4 de l'article 2 des présents Statuts.

Article 10

Le Comité adresse chaque année à la Commission un compte rendu des activités et de la situation financière de l'Organisation.

Article 11

Le Comité élabore des programmes d'investissement et d'exploitation portant sur plusieurs années à la demande de la Commission. Ils sont soumis à l'approbation de celle-ci.

Article 12

Le Comité élabore un règlement relatif à la passation des marchés et notamment aux conditions d'appel à la concurrence, qui est soumis à l'approbation de la Commission.

Article 13

1. Le Directeur est nommé pour une durée de cinq ans par le Comité statuant dans les conditions prévues aux paragraphes 1 et 2 de l'article 7 des présents Statuts, sou réserve que la majorité calculée conformément au premier paragraphe dudit article atteigne 70% des voix pondérées exprimées. Son mandat est renouvelable dans les mêmes conditions.

2. Il représente l'Organisation en Justice et dans tous les actes de la vie civile.

3. En outre, au nom de l'Organisation, et conformément aux directives générales du Comité, mais sans avoir à en référer à celui-ci pour les cas d'espèce:

a) il nomme les agents dont le traitement brut annuel est inférieur à un montant déterminé par le Comité, approuvé par la Commission, et met fin à leurs services dans les conditions prévues au Statut du personnel;

b) il contracte les emprunts dont la durée n'excède pas un an, sous réserve que le montant cumulé desdits emprunts, compte tenu des remboursements déjà effectués, ne dépasse pas 200.000 nouveaux francs;[1]

---

[1] Les sommes dont il s'agit se rapportent au nouveau franc français constitué par deux cents milligrammes d'or au titre de neuf cent millièmes de fin. La conversion dans chaque monnaie nationale se fera en chiffres ronds.

Article 9

1. The Committee shall give decisions on the technical organisation of the Agency in respect of which proposals shall be submitted to it by the Director.

2. It shall, however, submit for the approval of the Commission, for which approval the unanimous vote of the members of the Commission shall be required:

a) plans relating to the number and location of control or flight information centres and to their spheres of action;

b) measures to establish research and experimental centres and advanced and specialised training schools or other institutions established in application of paragraph 4 of Article 2 of the present Statute.

Article 10

Every year the Committee shall furnish the Commission with a report of the activities and financial position of the Organisation.

Article 11

At the request of the Commission the Committee shall prepare investment and operating programmes extending over several years. The programmes shall be subject to the approval of the Commission.

Article 12

The Committee shall draw up regulations relating to entry into contracts, including the conditions governing invitations for competitive tenders, which regulations shall be subject to the approval of the Commission.

Article 13

1. The Director shall be appointed for a term of office of five years by the Committee by a vote taken under the conditions prescribed in paragraphs 1 and 2 of Article 7 of the present Statute, provided that the majority calculated in accordance with the first paragraph of the aforesaid Article is not less than 70% of the weighted votes cast. His term of office may be renewed under the same conditions.

2. The Director shall represent the Organisation in legal proceedings and for all civil purposes.

3. Furthermore, on behalf of the Organisation and in accordance with the general directives of the Committee, but without being required to refer individual cases to the Committee:

a) He may appoint those officials whose gross annual salary is less than a sum determined by the Committee and approved by the Commission, and may terminate their services under the conditions prescribed in the staff regulations;

b) He may borrow for a term not exceeding one year, provided that the cumulative amount of such borrowing, allowing for repayments already effected, does not exceed 200,000 new francs;[1]

---

[1] The sums indicated are applicable to the new French franc containing 200 milligrams gold millesimal fineness 900. They shall be converted into each national currency in round figures.

c) il passe les contrats dont le montant ne dépasse pas 600.000 nouveaux francs.[1,2] Toutefois lorsqu'il s'agit de cession à titre onéreux de biens mobiliers appartenant à l'Agence, ce montant est limité à 80.000 nouveaux francs.[1,3]

d) il achète ou aliène des immeubles lorsque leur prix ne dépasse pas 200.000 nouveaux francs.[1]

Il tient le Comité informé de toutes les mesures prises en vertu des pouvoirs précités.

Le Comité détermine les conditions dans lesquelles le Directeur est remplacé en cas d'empêchement.

Article 14

1. Le Comité élabore le statut administratif du personnel de l'Agence; celui-ci doit comporter notamment les dispositions touchant la nationalité du personnel, les barêmes des traitements, les incompatibilités, le secret professionnel, la continuité du service, le commissionnement et définir les emplois qui ne peuvent etre cumulés avec aucun autre sans autorisation spéciale du Directeur.

2. Ce statut est soumis à l'approbation de la Commission statuant à l'unanimité.

Article 15

1. L'Agence n'est habilitée à recruter directement le personnel que si les Parties Contractantes ne sont pas en mesure de mettre à sa disposition du personnel qualifié.

2. Durant tout le temps de son emploi par l'Agence, le personnel fourni par les Administrations nationales est soumis au statut régissant le personnel de l'Agence, sans préjudice du maintien des avantages de carrière qui sont garantis par les réglementations nationales au personnel du corps administratif dont il fait partie lorsqu'il est mis à la disposition d'un organisme public national.

3. Le personnel fourni par une Administration nationale peut toujours être remis à la disposition de celle-ci sans que cette mesure ait un caractère disciplinaire.

Article 16

1. Toutes les recettes et les dépenses de l'Agence doivent faire l'objet de prévisions pour chaque exercice budgétaire et être inscrites soit au budget de fonctionnement, soit au budget d'investissement.

2. Chaque budget doit être équilibré en recettes et en dépenses. Les recettes et les dépenses de l'Agence relatives aux centres de recherches et d'expérimentation, écoles et plus généralement à tous organismes créés en application de l'article 2 des présents Statuts, sont détaillés dans un état spécial.

---

[1] Les sommes dont il s'agit se rapportent au nouveau franc français constitué par deux cents milligrammes d'or au titre de neuf cent millièmes de fin. La conversion dans chaque monnaie nationale se fera en chiffres ronds.

[2] Ce montant était à l'origine de 350.000 francs, il a éte relevé à 600.000 francs lors de la 38e session de la Commission permanente le 12 avril 1973.

[3] Ce montant était à l'origine de 50.000 francs, il a été relevé à 80.000 francs lors de cette même session.

c) He may enter into contracts for sums not in excess of 600,000 new francs.[1,2] Nevertheless, in the case of the transfer for valuable consideration of movable property belonging to the Agency, that sum shall be limited to 80,000 new francs.[1,3]

d) He may purchase or transfer immovable property when the price therefore does not exceed 200,000 new francs[1].

He shall keep the Committee informed of all the measures taken in the exercise of the aforesaid powers.

The Committee shall determine the conditions under which a substitute for the Director may be appointed should he be unable to perform his duties.

Article 14

1. The Committee shall draw up the Agency's staff regulations; they shall include inter alia provisions relating to the nationality of personnel, salary scales, disqualifications for office, professional secrecy, continuity of the service and authority to report infringements, and they shall define those posts which may not be held in plurality with any other without the special authorisation of the Director.

2. The aforesaid regulations shall be submitted to the Commission for its approval by unanimous vote.

Article 15

1. The Agency shall be empowered to recruit personnel directly only if the Contracting Parties are unable to make qualified personel available to it.

2. A member of the personnel who is provided by a national Administration shall be subject, throughout the period of his employment by the Agency, to the Agency's staff regulations, without prejudice to the retention of those carreer benefits which are guaranteed by national regulations to members of the administrative group to which he belongs if they are made available to a national public body.

3. Staff provided by a national Administration may always be returned to that Administration without the return being regarded as a disciplinary measure.

Article 16

1. Estimates of all the receipts and expenditure of the Agency shall be prepared for each budgetary financial year and shall be allocated either to the operating budget or to the investment budget.

2. Each budget shall be balanced as between receipts and expenditure. The receipts and expenditure of the Agency which relate to research and experimental centres, schools and more generally to any institutions set up under Article 2 of the present Statute shall be set forth in detail in a special statement.

---

[1] The sums indicated are applicable to the new French franc containing 200 milligrams gold millesimal fineness 900. They shall be converted into each national currence in round figures

[2] This amount was initially 350,000 francs; it was raised to 600,000 francs at the 38th Session of the Permanent Commission on 12 April 1973.

[3] This amount was originally 50,000 francs; it was raised to 80,000 francs at the same session.

3. Les conditions de prévision, d'exécution et de contrôle des recettes et dépenses qui ne sont pas stipulées ci-après sont déterminées par un règlement financier pris en exécution de l'article 30 des présents Statuts.

Article 17

1. L'exercice budgétaire s'étend du 1er janvier au 31 décembre.
2. Les prévisions pour chaque exercice budgétaire sont soumises par le Comité à l'approbation de la Commission au plus tard le 31 octobre* de chaque année.

Article 18

1. Les dépenses figurant au budget de fonctionnement comprennent notamment:

a) les dépenses de personnel, d'entretien et d'exploitation des installations de l'Organisation;

b) les rémunérations des prestations de services à l'Organisation, y compris les frais correspondant à l'utilisation à titre onéreux de matériel ou installations, ou éventuellement à des locations-ventes ou ventes à tempérament;

c) les dépenses correspondant au service des emprunts que l'Organisation serait autorisée à contracter;

d) les dépenses relatives au fonctionnement de la Commission.

2. Les conditions dans lesquelles il pourrait être éventuellement procédé à un amortissement industriel, compte tenu de l'amortissement financier, seront définies les cas échéant pour l'évaluation des dépenses budgétaires ainsi que pour l'évaluation des services rendus au sens du paragraphe 4 de l'article 30 des présents Statuts, par le règlement financier prévu au dit article.

Article 19

Les dépenses figurant au budget d'investissement comprennent les dépenses relatives à l'exécution du programme d'équipement.

Article 20

1. Les dépenses inscrites au budget de fonctionnement sont autorisées pour la durée d'un exercice budgétaire. Les crédits correspondants sont spécialisés par chapitres groupant les dépenses selon leur nature ou leur destination, et subdivisés, pour autant que de besoin, conformément au règlement financier.

2. Dans les conditions et limites qui sont déterminées dans le règlement financier, les crédits de ce budget autres que ceux relatifs aux dépenses de personnel, qui sont inutilisés à la fin de l'exercice budgétaire, peuvent faire l'objet d'un report qui est limité au seul exercice suivant. Le règlement financier fixe notamment le pourcentage et la nature des dépenses pouvant l'objet de reports.

---

* A la signature de cette Convention, la date était le 30 septembré. La Commission permanente a modifié cette date à sa 16e session, le 16 novembre 1966.

3. The conditions, other than those stipulated hereinafter, under which receipts and expenditure shall be estimated, put into effect and controlled shall be determined by financial regulations adopted under Article 30 of the present Statute.

Article 17

1. The budgetary financial year shall begin on 1 January and end on 31 December.

2. The estimates for each budgetary financial year shall be submitted by the Committee for the approval of the Commission by 31 October* every year at the latest.

Article 18

1. The expenditure shown in the operating budget shall comprise inter alia:

a) the expenditure relating to personnel, maintenance and operation of the installations of the Organisation;

b) remuneration for services rendered to the Organisation, including expenditure in respect of the use of equipment or installations for a consideration or, should the case arise, to hirepurchase or payments by instalments;

c) the expenditure corresponding to the service of any loans which the Organisation is authorised to contract;

d) the expenditure relating to the functioning of the Commission.

2. The conditions governing any industrial amortization, taking into account financial amortization, shall be defined, if necessary, for the purpose of determining the value of budgetary expenditure and the value of services rendered within the meaning of paragraph 4 of Article 30 of the present Statute, by the financial regulations referred to in the said Article.

Article 19

The expenditure allocated to the investment budget shall comprise the expenditure relating to the execution of the equipment programme.

Article 20

1. The expenditure allocated to the operating budget shall be authorised for the term of one financial year. The corresponding credits shall be classified into chapters according to the nature or purpose of the expenditure, and sub-divided, in so far as is required, in accordance with the financial regulations.

2. Any credits under this budget, other than those relating to expenditure in respect of personnel, which have not been used by the end of the financial year may be carried forward to the next financial year, but for no longer period, subject to the conditions and limits fixed by the financial regulations. Those regulations shall in particular specify the percentage and nature of the expenditure which may be so brought forward.

* When the Convention was signed, this date was 30 September. It was changed by the Permanent Commission at its 16th Session on 16 November 1966.

Article 21

1. Les dotations applicables aux dépenses d'investissement comprennent:

a) des crédits d'engagement, qui couvrent une trance constituant une unité individualisée et formant un ensemble cohérent;

b) des crédits de paiement, qui constituent la limite supérieure des dépenses susceptibles d'être payées chaque année pour la couverture des engagements contractés au titre du paragraphe a) ci-dessus.

2. L'échéancier des engagements et des paiements figure en annexe au projet de budget correspondant proposé par le Comité.

3. Les crédits ouverts au titre des dépenses d'investissement sont spécialisés par chapitres groupant les dépenses selon leur nature ou leur destination, et subdivisés, pour autant que de besoin, conformément au règlement financier.

4. Les crédits de paiement disponibles en fin d'exercice sont reportés à l'exercice suivant dans les conditions fixées par le règlement financier.

Article 22

Les recettes du budget de fonctionnement comprennent:

a) les contributions des Parties Contractantes déterminées conformément à l'article 23 des présents Statuts;

b) les recettes provenant des Parties Contractantes qui, en application de l'article 2 de la Convention, auraient confié à l'Organisation les services de la circulation aérienne pour tout ou partie de leur espace aérien inférieur;

c) les recettes provenant d'Etats non parties à la Convention qui utiliseraient ses services conformément à l'article 13 de la Convention;

d) les rémunérations des prestations de service par l'Organisation aux Etats, au bénéfice de leurs services de la circulation aérienne dans l'espace inférieur;

e) les recettes qui proviendraient de la rémunération des services rendus par les centres de recherches et d'expérimentation, les écoles ou autres organismes créés en application de l'article 2 des présents Status;

f) les recettes diverses;

g) les redevances éventuelles à la charge des usagers qui seraient établie en application de l'article 20 de la Convention.

Article 23

1. Pour le calcul des contributions annuelles des Parties Contractantes au budget de fonctionnement, le coût global des services de l'Organisation afférent au contrôle de l'espace aérien supérieur est réputé égal à la différence entre les dépenses budgétaires d'un exercice et les recettes, relatives au même exercice, visées aux paragraphes b) à f) inclus de l'article 22 des présents Statuts.

Ce coût global est réparti en deux fractions, au prorata des services rendus aux catégories d'usagers suivantes:

a) aéronefs civils d'Etats non contractants, et aéronefs militaires, de douane et de police;

b) aéronefs civils des Parties Contractantes.

2. Cette répartition est fixée pour chaque exercice par la Commission, en se fondant sur l'importance des services rendus dans l'espace supérieur aux catégories d'usager définies ci-dessus (par référence aux pénultième et antépénultième années).

Article 21

1. The provision for investment expenditure shall comprise:

a) credits for commitments to expenditure, which shall cover an instalment constituting a particular unit and forming a coherent whole;

b) credits for payment, which shall constitute the upper limit of the expenditure in respect of which payments may be made every year to cover the commitments entered into under paragraph a) above.

2. The diary of commitments and payments shall be annexed to the corresponding draft budget proposed by the Committee.

3. The credits opened under the investment expenditure shall be classified into chapters according to the nature or purpose of the expenditure, and subdivided, in so far as is required, in accordance with the financial regulations.

4. Any credits for payment which are available at the end of the financial year shall be carried forward to the next financial year under the conditions fixed by the financial regulations.

Article 22

The receipts of the operating budget shall comprise:

a) the contributions of the Contracting Parties determined in accordance with Article 23 of the present Statute;

b) the receipts collected from the Contracting Parties which, under Article 2 of the Convention, have entrusted to the Organisation the air traffic services for the whole or part of their lower air space;

c) the receipts collected from States which are not parties to the Convention and which use its services in accordance with Article 13 of the Convention;

d) remuneration for services rendered by the Organisation to the States for the benefit of their air traffic services in the lower air space;

e) any receipts in respect of remuneration for services rendered by the research and experimental centres, schools or other institutions set up under Article 2 of the present Statute;

f) miscellaneous receipts;

g) any charges payable by users, established under Article 20 of the Convention.

Article 23

1. For the purpose of calculating the annual contributions of the Contracting Parties to the operating budget, the total cost of the services of the Organisation in respect of upper air space control shall be deemed to be equal to the difference between the budgetary expenditure of one financial year and the receipts, relating to the same financial year, referred to in paragraphs b) to f) inclusive of Article 22 of the present Statute.

That total cost shall be divided into two fractions proportional to the services rendered to the following categories of users:

a) civil aircraft of non-contracting States, and military, customs and police aircraft;

b) civil aircraft of the Contracting Parties.

2. The Commission shall determine the above division for each financial year, on the basis of the extent of the services rendered in the upper air space to the categories of users defined above (by reference to the penultimate and antepenultimate years).

La contribution annuelle de l'ensemble des Parties Contractantes en ce qui concerne la première fraction est déterminée en déduisant de celle-ci le montant global des redevances éventuellement payées à l'Organisation par la catégorie d'usagers correspondante.

3. La part de chacune des Parties Contractants est calculée proportionnellement à l'importance des Produits Nationaux Bruts (P.N.B.) des Parties Contractantes tels qu'ils sont définis à l'article 9 de la Convention.

4. La formule de répartition de la deuxième fraction entre les Parties Contractantes est fondée sur la valeur des services rendus par l'Organisation aux aéronefs civils immatriculés dans le territoire de chacune des Parties Contractantes. Cette formule est fixée par la Commission et révisée tous les cinq ans.

5. La contribution annuelle de chacune des Parties Contractantes est arrêtée en déduisant de sa part, calculée par application de ladite formule, le montant des redevances éventuellemet mises à la charge des exploitants pour les aéronefs civils immatriculés dans son territoire.

Article 24

Les recettes du budget d'investissement comprennent:

a) les emprunts contractés par l'Organisation;

b) d'autres ressources éventuelles, notamment celles résultant, en cas d'adhésion d'un nouvel Etat ou de la ratification par un Etat signataire postérieurement à l'entrée en vigueur de la Convention, de l'application des articles 40 et 41 de la Convention;

c) des contributions financières des Parties Contractantes affectées à ce budget.

Article 25

1. Le règlement financier fixe les procédures selon lesquelles l'Organisation peut contracter et rembourser des emprunts.

2. Chaque budget annuel fixe le montant maximum que l'Organisation peut emprunter au cours de l'année couverte par le budget.

3. L'Organisation peut emprunter sur les marchés financiers internationaux les ressources nécessaires à l'accomplissement de ses tâches.

4. L'Organisation peut emprunter sur les marchés financiers d'une Partie Contractante dans le cadre des dispositions légales s'appliquant aux emprunts intérieurs, où à défaut de telles dispositions quand cette partie Contractante et l'Organisation se sont concertées et se sont mises d'accord sur l'emprunt envisagé par celle-ci.

5. Dans les domaines visés par le présent article, l'Organisation agit en accord avec les autorités compétentes des Parties Contractantes ou avec leur banque d'émission.

Article 26

1. Les contributions des Parties Contractantes au budget d'investissement sont déterminées en application de l'Article 32 de la Convention de façon à couvrir la différence entre les dépenses budgétaires et les recettes visées aux paragraphes a) et b) de l'article 24 des présents Statuts.

2. La répartition de ces contributions entre les Parties Contractantes se fait proportionnellement à l'importance respective de leurs Produits Nationaux Bruts (P.N.B.) évalués comme il est dit à l'article 9 de la Convention.

The annual contribution of all the Contracting Parties in respect of the first fraction shall be determined by deducting from that fraction the total amount of any charges paid to the Organisation by the corresponding category of users.

3. The share of each of the Contracting Parties shall be calculated proportionately to the value of the Gross National Products (G.N.P.), as defined in Article 9 of the Convention, of the Contracting Parties.

4. The formula for sharing the second fraction among the Contracting Parties shall be based on the value of the services rendered by the Organisation to civil aircraft registered in the territory of each of the Contracting Parties. The said formula shall be fixed by the Commission and revised every five years.

5. The annual contribution of each Contracting Party shall be determined by deducting from its share, calculated by means of the above formula, the amount of any charges payable by operators in respect of the civil aircraft registered in its territory.

Article 24

The receipts of the investment budget shall comprise:

a) loans contracted by the Organisation;

b) any other resources, in particular those resulting from the application of Articles 40 and 41 of the Convention, in the case of the adherence of a new State or of ratification by a signatory State after the entry into force of the Convention;

c) financial contributions of the Contracting Parties allocated to the aforesaid budget.

Article 25

1. The financial regulations shall lay down the procedures in accordance with which the Organisation may borrow and repay loans.

2. Each annual budget shall specify the maximum amount which the Organisation may borrow during the year covered by that budget.

3. The Organisation may borrow on the international financial markets in order to obtain the necessary resources for the accomplishment of its tasks.

4. The Organisation may borrow on the financial markets of a Contracting Party in accordance with the statutory provisions relating to internal loans, or, in the absence of such provisions, when the Contracting Party and the Organisation have consulted together and agreed on the loan envisaged by the Organisation.

5. In matters falling within the scope of the present Article, the Organisation shall act in agreement with the competent authorities of the Contracting Parties or with their banks of issue.

Article 26

1. The contributions of the Contracting Parties to the investment budget shall be determined in accordance with Article 32 of the Convention in such manner as to cover the difference between the budgetary expenditure and the receipts referred to in paragraphs a) and b) of Article 24 of the present Statute.

2. The sharing of those contributions among the Contracting Parties shall be proportional to the respective values of their Gross National Products (G.N.P.) calculated in accordance with Article 9 of the Convention.

Article 27

Les budgets de fonctionnement et d'investissement peuvent être révisés en cours d'exercice, si les circonstances l'exigent, suivant les modalités prévues pour leur établissement et leur approbation.

Article 28

1. Les dépenses relatives aux budgets de fonctionnement et d'investissement sont prises en compte au titre du budget de l'année au cours de laquelle les titres de paiement sont visés par le comptable de l'Agence.
2. Les recettes sont prises en compte au titre du budget de l'année au cours de laquelle elles sont encaissées par l'Agence.
3. Les comptes de chaque exercice sont arrêtés par le Comité au plus tard six mois après la clôture de l'exercice et soumis à l'approbation de la Commission qui statue définitivement á leur égard.

Article 29

1. Les comptes de la totalité des recettes et dépenses de chaque budget sont examinés par une mission de contrôle composée de deux fonctionnaires spécialisés appartenant aux administrations des Parties Contractantes. Ces fonctionnaires, qui doivent être de nationalités différentes, sont nommés, pour une période de cinq ans, par la Commission statuant dans les conditions de vote définies au paragraphe 1 de l'article 13 des présents Statuts. Les dépenses relatives à la mission de contrôle sont à la charge de l'Organisation.
2. La vérification, qui a lieu sur pièces et au besoin sur place, a pour objet de constater la légalité et la régularité des recettes et dépenses et de s'assurer de la bonne gestion financière. La mission de contrôle établit un rapport après la clôture de chaque exercice.
3. La Commission donne au Directeur et au Comité décharge de leur gestion relative à chacun des budgets.

Article 30

1. La Commission statuant a l'unanimité de ses membres, sur proposition de l'Agence, arrête le règlement financier de celle-ci.
2. En outre des objets spécifiés aux articles 16,18, 20, 21, 25 et 31 des Statuts, le règlement financier fixe notamment:
a) les modalités d'établissement et d'exécution des budgets et celles afférentes à la reddition et la vérification des comptes;
b) les procédures selon lesquelles les avances et les contributions doivent être mises à la disposition de l'Organisation;
c) les conditions dans lesquelles il pourra être procédé à des virements de crédits soit de chapitre à chapitre, soit de subdivision à subdivision. Toutefois aucune dépense de personnel ne peut être couverte par virement de crédits affectés à d'autres dépenses;
d) les conditions dans les quelles des crédits peuvent être ouverts à l'Organisation dans le cas où les budgets de fonctionnement et d'investissement n'auraient pas été votés au début de l'exercice ainsi que les fonds à mettre à la disposition de l'Organisation par les Parties Contractantes, à valoir sur les contributions.
3. Le règlement financier détermine les règles à suivre par les ordonna-

Article 27

The operating and investment budgets may be revised during the financial year, if circumstances so require, in accordance with the conditions prescribed for their preparation and approval.

Article 28

1. Expenditure under the operating and investment budgets shall be taken into account in the budget for the year during which the documents in proof of payment are passed by the accountant of the Agency.

2. Receipts shall be taken into account in the budget for the year during which they are encashed by the Agency.

3. The accounts for each financial year shall be made up by the Committee not later than six months after the end of the financial year and shall be submitted for the approval of the Commission which shall have the final decision regarding them.

Article 29

1. The accounts for all the receipts and expenditure of each budget shall be examined by a control board consisting of two expert officials belonging to the Administrations of the Contracting Parties. Those officials, who shall have different nationalities, shall be appointed for a period of five years by a vote of the Commission subject to the conditions laid down in paragraph 1 of Article 13 of the present Statute. The expenditure relating to the control board shall be borne by the Organisation.

2. The audit, which shall be made from the vouchers and if necessary in the place where the documents are, shall be designed to establish the authenticity and regularity of the receipts and expenditure and to verify that the financial administration is satisfactory. The control board shall draw up a report after the end of each financial year.

3. The Commission shall give the Director and the Committee discharge of their administration in respect of each of the budgets.

Article 30

1. The financial regulations of the Agency shall be fixed by the Commission, for which purpose proposals submitted by the Agency shall be carried by the unanimous vote of the members of the Commission.

2. In addition to the matters specified in Articles 16, 18, 20, 21, 25 and 31 of the present Statute, the financial regulations shall determine inter-alia:

a) The conditions of establishing and giving effect to the budgets and the conditions of rendering and auditing accounts;

b) The procedures in accordance with which advances of funds and contributions shall be made available to the Organisation;

c) The conditions under which credits may be transferred either from chapter to chapter or from sub-division to sub-division. No expenditure relating to personnel, however, may be covered by the transfer of credits assigned to other expenditure;

d) The conditions under which credits may be opened for the Organisation if the operating and investment budgets have not been voted at the beginning of the financial year, and also the funds to be made available to the Organisation by the Contracting Parties, on account of the contributions.

teurs et les comptables, l'étendue de leurs responsabilités et les contrôles auxquels ils sont assujettis.

4. Il détermine les conditions dans lesquelles l'Agence doit tenir une comptabilité analytique faisant apparaître la valeur des services rendus, et instituer un contrøle budgétaire permettant de suivre régulièrement l'utilisation des crédits en cours d'exercice.

Article 31

1. Les budgets de fonctionnement et d'investissement sont établis dans la monnaie du pays où l'Organisation a son siège.

2. Les contributions financières prévues aux paragraphes a) de l'Article 22 et c) de l'Article 24 des présents Statuts sont payables en cette monnaie. Cependant le règlement financier détermine dans quelles conditions les Parties Contractantes pourront payer une partie de leur contribution en toute monnaie dont l'Organisation aura besoin pour accomplir ses tâches.

3. Le règlement financier précise les bases de référence servant à la détermination des taux de conversion et les mesures d'adaptation reconnues nécessaires à la suite de fluctuations d'ordre monétaire.

Article 32

A titre transitoire, et par dérogation à l'Article 23 des présents Statuts, la répartition des contributions des Parties Contractantes au budget de fonctionnement pour les trois premiers exercices se fait en appliquant à la totalité de la différence définie au paragraphe 1 de l'Article 23 précité, le critère du Produit National Brut tel qu'il est défini à l'article 9 de la Convention.

Article 33

A titre exceptionnel il sera établi, deux mois au plus tard après l'entrée en vigueur de la Convention et au titre du premier exercice, un budget initial couvrant la période allant de la date de cette entrée en vigueur jusqu'à la fin de l'année civile. Les Parties Contractantes seront invitées à faire des avances appropriées au fond de roulement.

Article 34

1. Les services de l'Agence peuvent, à la diligence de la Commission, agissant de sa propre initiative ou sur la demande du Comité ou du Directeur, faire l'objet d'inspections administrative et technique.

2. Ces inspections sont effectuées par des agents appartenant aux Administrations des Parties Contractantes. Chaque mission d'inspection est composée d'au moins deux délégués de nationalité différente. Toute mission d'inspection doit comprendre, autant que possible, un délégué ayant participé à une inspection précédente.

Article 35

1. La langue utilisée pour les opérations de contrôle de la circulation aérienne assurées par l'Agence est l'anglais, sous réserve de l'adoption

3. The financial regulations shall determine the rules to be followed by officers empowered to order disbursements and by accounting officers, the extent of the responsibility of such officers and the controls to which such officers are subject.

4. The financial regulations shall determine the conditions under which the Agency shall keep analytical accounts showing the value of the services rendered, and shall establish a budgetary control by means of which the use of the credits during the financial year can be shown regularly.

Article 31

1. The operating and investment budgets shall be drawn up in the currency of the country in which the Organisation has its seat.

2. The financial contributions provided for in paragraph a) of Article 22 and paragraph c) of Article 24 of the present Statute shall be payable in that currency. The financial regulations shall, however, determine the conditions under which the Contracting Parties may pay part of their contributions in any currency which is required by the Organisation for the accomplishment of its tasks.

3. The financial regulations shall specify the bases to be used in determining the rates of conversion and any measures of adjustment deemed to be necessary as a result of currency fluctuations.

Article 32

As a transitional measure, and by way of exception to Article 23 of the present Statute, the contributions of the Contracting Parties to the operating budget for the first three financial years shall be apportioned by applying the criterion of the Gross National Product, as defined in Article 9 of the Convention, to the whole of the difference defined in paragraph 1 of Article 23 of the aforesaid Statute.

Article 33

By way of exception, an initial budget, covering the period from the date of entry into force of the Convention until the end of the calender year, shall be established, for the first financial year, at latest two months after the entry into force of the Convention. The Contracting Parties shall be invited to make appropriate advances for working funds.

Article 34

1. Administrative or technical inspections of the Services of the Agency may be carried out, if so required by the Commission, acting either on its own initiative or at the request of the Committee or Director.

2. Such inspections shall be made by officers of the Administrations of the Contracting Parties. Each inspection committee shall consist of at least two representatives of different nationalities and shall include as far as possible a representative who has taken part in a previous inspection.

Article 35

1. The language used for the air traffic control operations ensured by the Agency shall be the English language, subject to the subsequent adoption

ultérieure par l'Organisation de l'Aviation Civile Internationale d'une langue aéronautique internationale. Toutefois des dispositions seront prises pour que les pilotes puissent utiliser leur propre langue lors du survol de leur territoire national. Les mesures appropriées devront être mises en oeuvre par l'Agence à la demande des Parties Contractantes intéressées.

2. Le Comité détermine les langues administratives de l'Agence.

Article 36

L'Agence procède aux publications nécessaires à son fonctionnement.

Article 37

Dans les conditions prévues à l'article 34 de la Convention, le Comité soumet à l'approbation de la Commission toutes modifications aux Statuts qui lui paraissent nécessaires.

Article 38

Les présents Statuts entrent en vigueur en même temps que la Convention et dans les mêmes conditions que celle-ci.

B. *PROTOCOLE DE SIGNATURE*

DE LA CONVENTION INTERNATIONALE DE COOPERATION POUR LA SECURITE DE LA NAVIGATION AERIENNE „EUROCONTROL"

Lors de la signature de la Convention internationale de coopération pour la sécurité de la navigation aérienne, ci-après dénommée la „Convention," les plénipotentiaires soussignés de la République Fédérale d'Allemagne, du Royaume de Belgique, de la République Française, du Royaume-Uni de Grande-Bretagne et d'Irlande du Nord, du Grand-Duché de Luxembourg et du Royaume des Pays-Bas reconnaissent s'être mis d'accord sur les déclarations ci-après:

1. *ad Article 2 de la Convention:*
Dans le cas d'un transfert des services de la circulation aérienne en application du paragraphe 1 de l'article 2 de la Convention, la date d'entrée en vigueur du transfert sera fixée par la Partie Contractante qui aura présenté la demande, en accord, suivant le cas, avec l'Organisation ou avec l'autre Partie Contractante.

2. *ad Article 19 de la Convention:*
La rédaction de cette disposition n'implique pas que les procès-verbaux dressés par les agents de l'Agence aient une valeur supérieure à celle des procès-verbaux qui pourront être dressés par les agentsdes Parties Contractantes.

3. *ad Article 38 de la Convention:*
En ce qui concerne les espaces aériens supérieurs contigus visés à l'article 38 de la Convention, il est convenu que:

of an international aeronautical language by the International Civil Aviation Organisation. Nevertheless, provision shall be made for pilots to use their own language during flight over their national territory. The appropriate measures shall be taken by the Agency at the request of the Contracting Parties concerned.

2. The Committee shall determine the administrative language of the Agency.

Article 36

The Agency shall publish such material as is necessary for its operation.

Article 37

The Committee shall submit for the approval of the Commission any modifications of the Statute which are considered to be necessary by the Committee, subject to the conditions prescribed in Article 34 of the Convention.

Article 38

The present Statute shall enter into force at the same time and under the same conditions as the Convention.

B. *PROTOCOL OF SIGNATURE*

OF THE "EUROCONTROL" INTERNATIONAL CONVENTION RELATING TO CO-OPERATION FOR THE SAFETY OF AIR NAVIGATION

At the time of signing the International Convention relating to Co-operation for the Safety of Air Navigation, hereinafter called "the Convention," the undersigned plenipotentiaries of the Federal Republic of Germany, the Kingdom of Belgium, the French Republic, the United Kingdom of Great Britain and Northern Ireland, the Grand Duchy of Luxembourg and the Kingdom of the Netherlands recognise that they have agreed on the following declarations:

1. *ad Article 2 of the Convention:*
In the case of a transfer of air traffic services, under paragraph 1 of Article 2 of the Convention, the date on which the transfer shall take effect shall be fixed by the Contracting Party which has submitted the request, in agreement either with the Organisation or with the other Contracting Party, as the case may be.

2. *ad Article 19 of the Convention:*
The wording of this provision shall not imply that reports drawn up by officers of the Agency have a greater value than those which may be drawn up by officers of the Contracting Parties.

3. *ad Article 38 of the Convention:*
In respect of the contiguous upper air space referred to in Article 38 of the Convention it is agreed that:

a) les services de la circulation aérienne relatifs à l'espace aérien de la Région d'Information de Vol Shannon-Prestwick telle que définie au Plan de Navigation Aérienne de la Région Atlantique-Nord de l'O.A.C.I. et à ses amendements éventuels ne seront pas confiés à l'Agence, sauf demande formelle que le Gouvernement du Royaume-Uni de Grande-Bretagne et d'Irlande du Nord, en accord avec tout autre Gouvernement concourant au fonctionnement de ces services, adresserait ultérieurement à la Commission;

b) les services de la circulation aérienne relatifs aux espaces aériens situés au sud du parallèle 39°30' Nord ne seront pas confiés à l'Agence, sauf demande formelle que le Gouvernement de la République Française adresserait ultérieurement à la Commission.

Dans les deux cas, la Commission aurait à se prononcer sur la demande en conformité des dispositions du paragraphe 2 d de l'article 6 de la Convention.

4. *ad Article 14 des Statuts annexés à la Convention:*

L'expression „barême des traitements" s'entend de l'éventail qui les caractérise et non de la fixation précise de leur montant.

5. Rien dans la Convention ni dans les Statuts y annexés n'a pour effet de restreindre la compétence des tribunaux nationaux en ce qui concerne les différends opposant l'Organisation et le personnel de l'Agence.

FAIT à Bruxelles le 13 décembre 1960, en langue allemande, anglaise, française et néerlandaise, en un seul exemplaire, qui restera déposé aux Archives du Gouvernement du Royaume de Belgique qui en communiquera copie certifiée conforme à tous les Etats signataires. Le texte en langue française fera foi en cas de divergence entre les textes.

Pour la République Fédérale d'Allemagne — K. OPPLER, H. C. SEEBOHM

Pour le Royaume de Belgique — P. WIGNY, P. W. SEGERS

Pour la République Française — R. BOUSQUET, R. BURON

Pour le Royaume Uni de Grande-Bretagne et d'Irlande du Nord — J. NICHOLLS, P. THORNEYCROFT

Pour le Grand-Duché de Luxembourg — N. HOMMEL, P. GREGOIRE

Pour le Royaume des Pays-Bas — E. TEIXEIRA DE MATTOS, E. G. STIJKEL *a*) the air traffic services in the air space of the Shannon-Prestwick Flight Information Region, as defined in the Air Navigation Plan – North Atlantic Region – of the International Civil Aviation Organisation, as from time to time amended, will not be entrusted to the Agency except upon a formal request being made to the Commission by the Government of the United Kingdom of Great Britain and Northern Ireland in agreement with any other government participating in the provision of those services:

b) the air traffic services in the air space to the south of the parallel of latitude 39°30′ North will not be entrusted to the Agency except upon a formal request being made to the Commission by the Government of the French Republic.

In either case the Commission shall make a determination as to the request in accordance with paragraph 2d) of Article 6 of the Convention.

4. *ad Article 14 of the Statute annexed to the Convention:*

The expression "salary scales" shall be understood to refer to the grading of salaries and not to the precise determination of the amounts of those salaries.

5. Nothing in the Convention or the Statute annexed thereto shall be deemed to restrict the jurisdiction of national courts in respect of disputes between the Organisation and the personnel of the Agency.

DONE at Brussels this 13th day of December, 1960, in the German, English, French and Dutch languages, in a single copy which shall remain deposited in the archives of the Government of the Kingdom of Belgium which shall transmit certified copies to all the signatory States. In case of any inconsistency, the text in the French language shall prevail.

For the Federal Republic of Germany	K. Oppler H. C. Seebohm
For the Kingdom of Belgium	P. Wigny P. W. Segers
For the French Republic	R. Bousquet R. Buron
For the United Kingdom of Great Britain and Northern Ireland	J. Nicholls P. Thorneycroft
For the Grand Duchy of Luxembourg	N. Hommel P. Gregoire
For the Kingdom of the Netherlands	E. Teixeira de Mattos E. G. Stijkel

SECTION BIBLIOGRAPHIQUE
BIBLIOGRAPHICAL SECTION

I. LIVRES SUR LA COOPERATION EUROPEENNE

I. BOOKS ON EUROPEAN CO-OPERATION

BEHRENDT (Walter), Das Parlement und die politische Integration Europa's. Internationale Universität für vergleichende Wissenschaften, Luxemburg, Verlag UGA, Heule, Bruxelles, Namur, z.d.

ROSE (Richard), Electing a European Parliament. European Parliament. PE 35.666, u.d.

Both publications, the first by the President of the European Parliament, deal with the relative immobility of the European situation in regard to further integration. It seems clear that Europe has a choice between integration and non-integration but that it cannot stop halfway without achieving its clearly stated goals.

The difficulties seem to lie in the uncertain situation of Europe itself, its relation to the U.S. and the Eastern bloc, its projection of further expansion which begins to lack realism to an increasing degree, etc. One might feel tempted to add the paucity and onesidedness of its "philosophy" which creates no real response in the Europeans, because it is a philosophy which is more negative than positive. It is against communism, foreign demonation, poverty, injustice, etc. but a European identity requires deeper and more farreaching roots.

Walter Behrendt argues that far too much power is concentrated in the Council of Ministers while the role of the Commission has eroded. The increase in the role of the European Parliament is not conform to the increasing complexity of the European situation. Integration is a total concept and the increasing practice of cutting it up in numerous segments only makes it confusing and ineffective.

So far the guiding principles of the Community have been ignored by the member states when the actual situation becomes difficult. It would be logical to strengthen the role of the Parliament in order to make the processes of the Community less technocratic and more democratic.

The hesitancy which prevails in relation to the direct election of the European Parliament is perhaps due to a uncertainty about the attitude of populations which now regard European integration as the concern of the "expert." There is only a road forward or backward; and Behrendt believes that if no real progress is possible, the Community should restrict its activities and not plan for further expansion.

The needed impetus for the Community can only come from the European himself via a fullfledged political system, and if there is not enough courage to embark on this road, the result will be frustration and stagnation. If governments act only on behalf of the citizen but not with his participation and consent, there can be no question of mutual trust and of responsibility. The techniques of the manipulated society rest upon fear, and this fear in turn undermines the society.

For Behrendt democratic controls and parliamentary participation in decision-making is the needed answer.

Richard Rose deals with the technicalities of direct European elections of which he expects no very basic change in the composition of the European parliament. He analyzes the various possibilities; the size of the Parliament; the role of large versus mall countries in its composition, and related problems.

B.L.

KUNDOCH (Harold Giselbert), Die Konstituierung des Europäischen Parlements. Zur Reform des Berufungsverfahrens der Abgeordneten. Mit einem Vorwort von Fernand Dehousse.
Kölner Schriften zum Europarecht. Band 23. Köln, etc., Carl Heymans Verlag, 1974, 193 pp.

In his Preface Fernand Dehousse stresses the inaction which prevails in regard to the election of the European Parliament, particularly since the Treaty of Luxemburg of 1970 increased its powers, mostly in the budgetary field. The essence of the Community in the eyes of Dehousse is not in the economic but in the political realm as was recognised by Robert Schuman already in 1950. "...... il n'est pas aujourd'hui d'autre pouvoir légitime que celui qui trouve sa source dans une large adhésion populaire."

The study of Kundoch is an elaborate and painstaking investigation of the nomination procedures of the members of the European Parliament. It culminates in a plea for direct elections as well as an extension of the competence of the Parliament as an absolutely essential element in the further structuring of the Community.

The author is, however, not optimistic about the possibilities as the unanimity rule of the Council makes it impossible to speed up a process which does not find enough political support while also the increase in "managerial politics" does not augur well for further steps in the direction of political integration.

One might add that the insecure and unstable worldsituation, politically as well as economically, is not a positive factor in a situation in which "economic growth" has been the leading concept. As a great deal of the activities of the Communities are geared to a projection of the future, recent developments, which show a smaller impact of human volition than was anticipated, lead to a general feeling of uncertainty. The future-projections are still maintained but they carry less conviction as reality seems to obey laws which are not those which have been visualised.

This state of affairs does not detract, however, from the merits of Dr. Kundoch's study. His complete survey and juridical analysis of all aspects of the election of the European parliamentary representatives is of great value, especially when further progress might again become possible.

B.L.

PESCATORE (PIERRE), The law of integration. Emergence of a new phenomenon in international relations, based on the European communities. Leiden, A. W. Sijthoff, 1974, 115 pages.

The author bases his study on the recognition that the Treaties establishing the European Communities are "the first attempt on a significant scale to create real structural poles apart from the hitherto dominant one of the representation of states."

In dealing with the Council, Pescatore refers to the Committee of Permanent Representatives which he does not see as an infringement of the powers of the Commission but rather as indicative of the growing complexity of the activities of the Communities.

Under the heading of "structural developments" the author describes the relations between the organs of the Community, stressing the excessive weight of the Council in relation to the Commission and the Parliament. In the structural developments which take place, the Council operates as the inter-governmental agency while the community element as such belongs more to the realm of the Commission.

Special committees like the management committees in the agricultural sector establish a permanent link between the Commission and the Council.

The intriguing role of the Communities lies in their going beyond a customs union and envisaging economic as well as political union. In relation to economic union the programme is a vast one. "Hence, everything concerning freedom of movement for workers and for persons in general, freedom of establishment and services, for individuals as well as for commercial companies, freedom of payments, transport policy, harmonisation of taxes and approximation of laws; all this forms an integral part of the objectives enshrined in the commitments undertaken in the Treaty." The motivation is exclusively economic and egalitarian, and this favors the stronger actors in the system although democratic parliamentary controls could correct the technocratic tendencies.

The author is not optimistic about progress toward political union: ". . . . my conclusions must be negative as regards the prospects for political union: no commitment to this effect; no perceptable, or at least no irresistible, spillover effect from the economic towards the political." If the author is correct, this would make the Community the superstructure of the European sector of the Western industrial system. This means that its European function would need a new evaluation, or, should one say "an agonizing re-appraisal?."

Pescatore considers at length the relation of national sovereignty to the structure of the Community. Sovereignty is a purely abstract legal concept which, in social reality, one can define as a function of state-power or state-capability. This attribute of the state has diminished in relation to an internationalised industrial system, and, in this sense, the Community does no more than give legal expression to an existing situation, with the intent of continuing this prosess of internationalising the industrial system on a European basis.

Pescatore sees the system of the Communities as a new one. "It has shown that limitations on national sovereignty lose their edge when the operation takes the character of a pooling of powers in the hands of independent institutions not identified with the personality or the interests of any of the participants – these concepts of limited, shared, transferred soveriegnty, or pooling are more than theoretical visions –. They are operative legal concepts which include the dynamic perspective of greater union yet to be achieved.

The combination of the three criteria: common objective, reality of power and autonomy establishes the essence of the Community. The difficulty in this structure is the relation between the objectives and the social reality of Europe as this relation seems to be showing an increasing divergence.

B.L.

SEIDL-HOHENVELDERN (Ignaz), Umfang und Intensität einer rechtlichen Einigung Europas. Sonderdruck aus Festschrift für Hermann Jahrreisz 1974.

In 1929 Hermann Jahrreisz signaled the vagueness of efforts for legal unity in Europe although he admitted the many good intentions.

Seidl-Hohenveldern quotes this opinion in the beginning of his analysis of European legal unification which has been hampered by the ongoing debate about global and regional priorities.

The United Nations has given no clear definition of the region, and whether the concept is more geographic or more functional has not been defined and seems to shift with the prevailing conditions.

The author argues that wherever a community of interests exists, as in Western Europe, legal organisation has a better chance than when there is a severe cleavage between law and social reality.

European integration has been upon the basis of common interests and this functional aspect gives a non-geographic value to the term "European." The author points out the differences in "Europeanness" of the various organisations: The Economic Commission for Europe of the U.N., embraces all European nations, the Council of Europe is regional in a more limited sense while the European Community is restricted to its nine European members. OEEC is functional in the sense of representing the states industrialised after the Western model.

Seidl-Hohenveldern is not optimistic about the possible expansion of any of the European organisations into a regional unity. Legal organisation cannot abolish social conflicts but may keep them within the bounds of reason unless situations arise on which rationality has no longer sufficient impact.

B.L.

D. Lasok and J. W. Bridge: Introduction to the Law and Institutions of the European Communities, London, 1973, 314 pp.

Among a number of books about the European Communities published – principally for the benefit of English readers – just after their enlargement, that of Lasok and Bridge constitutes an introduction to the subject, intended mainly for students.

The authors of this book are a professor of law and a senior lecturer at the University of Exeter, whose Faculty of Law was among the first to realise the importance of this subject for English lawyers. This work is the fruit of their experience in teaching European law at Exeter; it will certainly be useful for many students who wish to understand the implications for the United Kingdom of accession to the Communities.

The plan of the book is to tackle the subject in four parts, the first dealing with the nature of the Communities and of Community law. This runs to almost a hundred pages, and will be particularly helpful to those who approach the subject for the first time because, after a brief historical introduction (which contains some minor inaccuracies) it explains clearly the nature of the Communities, against the background of orthodox conceptions of federation and confederation, and the nature of Community law as "neither a national nor an international system of law, but a *sui generis* system" emanating from a political will to create institutions of a novel character. These concepts are analysed not only in theoretical terms but also by citations from decisions of the Luxembourg Court and of national courts in the original member States, with some valuable explanations of the principles of the civil law systems which have been incorporated into Community law – and may well be unfamiliar to most common lawyers. A useful section is included on "the language of Community law" which contains a five-page glossary of terms which "present linguistic as well as conceptual teasers."

Part II describes the institutions of the Communities. It is not limited to a bare legal analysis of the constitutional provisions of the treaties, but also includes a summary of some of the major developments in recent years, including the crisis in 1965 and the Luxembourg Agreement in the following year (though their effect on the Merger Treaty is not mentioned); political co-operation and the Davignon Report are mentioned briefly at pages 121 to 123, which leads to an explanation of the distinction between Community activities and extra-Community action by the foreign ministers. Similarly, the chapter on the European Parliament explains not only its structure and methods of work, but also the 1960 draft convention on direct elections and the Vedel report (1971) on increasing its powers. This reviewer found particularly helpful the chapter on the Court of Justice (pages 146 to 169), which explains clearly the procedure, practice and jurisdiction of the Court, though one is surprised to find here no reference to the competence of the Court to give preliminary rulings under Article 177 of the Treaty – a matter dealt with separately in the following chapter.

Part III of the book deals with the difficult problem of the relationship between Community law and the municipal law of the member States. Chapter 10 explains clearly the different methods of incorporation of international law into municipal law and the practice of the six original members in this respect; this involves consideration of the monist and dualist theories and also of the "hierarchy of legal norms" – problems little known to common lawyers but which they are well advised to study in this context. The procedure of requesting preliminary rulings from the Luxembourg Court under Article 177 of the EEC Treaty is well set out, though one may question the statement that there is "some reluctance" on the part of national courts to have recourse to this procedure. By December 1972 181 out of 319 cases filed with the Court were requests for preliminary rulings under Article 177. The topical question of the impact of Community law in the United Kingdom is dealt with in Chapter 12 which, having been written in 1972, is in some ways prophetic.

The last part of the book is devoted to "the law of the Economy" and examines the provisions of the Treaty of Rome which set out the general principles of the E.E.C., the foundations of the common market and the policy of the Community as regards rules on competition, approximation of laws, economic policy, social policy and so on. The whole work constitutes a comprehensive and, for such a complex subject, very readable survey of the law of the European Communities, which will form a very useful introduction to the subject for common lawyers.

A. H. Robertson

II. BIBLIOGRAPHIE SELECTIVE DES ARTICLES DE PERIODIQUES ET DES BROCHURES 1974

II. SELECTIVE BIBLIOGRAPHY OF PERIODICAL AND PAMPHLET MATERIAL 1974

A. LA COOPERATION EUROPEENNE EN GENERAL
A. EUROPEAN COOPERATION IN GENERAL

APEL (H.), Europa am Scheideweg. Europa-Archiv, no. 29, 25 février 1974, p. 99–104.

BIDAULT (G.), Europe européenne ou Europe atlantique. Revue politique et parlementaire, vol. 76, no. 849, mars–avril 1974, p. 9–21.

BOWEN (R.) et A. PARRY, European patent conventions. The first convention. Common market law review, vol. 11, février 1974, p. 105–113.

BROWN (J. F.), Détente and Soviet policy in Eastern Europe. Survey: a journal of East and West studies, no. 20, printemps-été 1974, p. 46–58.

CHEYSSON (C.), L'Europe, la crise et le tiers monde. Défense nationale, no. 30, mai 1974, p. 11–32.

CRITCHLEY (J.), East-West diplomacy and the European interest (CSCE, MFR and SALT II), The round table, juillet 1974, p. 299–306.

DOCUMENTS et rapports écrits de la XXVIIe table ronde européenne (Bruxelles, avril 1974). Les problèmes de l'Europe, vol. 17, no. 64, 1974, p. 33–80.

DUPUY (R.-J.), La protection et les limites de la liberté d'expression de l'artiste dans la société européenne. Revue des droits de l'homme. Human rights journal. vol. 7, no. 1, 1974, p. 41–59.

EMERGENCE (THE) of a European sovereignty. Government and opposition, no. 9, hiver 1974, p. 79–95.

EUROPE (L') et les régions. Congrès international des économistes de langue française. Montpellier, juin 1973. Revue d'économie politique, no. 84, mars–avril 1974, p. 141–276.

FIESCHI (G.), Europa "comunitaria" o Europa "societaria"? Rivista di studi politici internazionali, no. 41, juillet-septembre 1974, p. 351–364.

FONCTION PARLEMENTAIRE (LA) en Europe. 30 jours d'Europe, octobre 1974, p. 31–36.

GATEAU (E.), Les structures régionales en Europe. Les problèmes de l'Europe, vol. 17, no. 63, 1974, p. 20–24.

GEMEINSCHAFT in der Krise. Wirtschaftsdienst, no. 54, mars 1974, p. 113–120.

GOLDSBOROUGH (J. O.), France, the European crisis and the Alliance. Foreign affairs, no. 52, avril 1974, p. 538–555.

HAERTEL (K.), The Munich diplomatic conference on European patent law, septembre–octobre 1973. International review of industrial property and copyright law, vol. 4, no. 3–4, 1973, p. 271–280.

INSTITUT (L') européen d'écologie. Mineurs de France, no. 268, juin 1974, p. 3–6.

KAPLAN (MARCOS), Möglichkeiten und Grenzen Europas in Lateinamerika. Zeitschrift für Kulturaustausch, np. 4, 1974, p. 10–15.

KENNAN (G. F.), Europe's problems, Europe's choices. Foreign policy, été 1974, p. 3–16.

KIMMINICH (O.), Die internationale Kontrolle der europäischen Atomindustrie. Zeitschrift für ausländisches öffentliches Recht und Völkerrecht no. 33, décembre 1973, p. 636–671.

KORBONSKI (A.), The prospects for change in Eastern Europe. Slavic review, no. 33, juin 1974, p. 219–239.
LUTZ (CHRISTINE), Das unmündige Europa. Bilanz eines Krisenjahres. Europa Archiv, no. 1, janvier 1974, p. 1–8.
LUTZ (C.), Das unmündige Europa – Bilanz eines Krisenjahres. Europa-Archiv, no. 29, 10 janvier 1974, p. 1–8.
MERLE (M.), De quel mal souffre l'Europe? Projet, avril 1974, p. 445–456.
MORGAN (R.), Can Europa have a foreign policy? The world today, no. 30, février 1974, p. 43–50.
MORTIMER (E.), Southern Europe in crisis. The round table, octobre 1974, p. 381–392.
NÖTZOLD (J.), Ost-West-Kooperation und – Kommunikation. Aussenpolitik, no. 25, 3. Quartal 1974, p. 291–301.
PIERRE (Andrew), Was wird aus dem "Jahr Europa?" Europa-Archiv, no. 4, février 1974, p. 131–149.
PIERRE (A. J.), What happened to the year of Europe? The world today, no. 30, mars 1974, p. 110–119.
PRECIGOUT (JEAN DE), L'Europe et la crise. Patronat, no. 346, février 1974, p. 8–15.
PRZETACZNIK, (F.), L'attitude des états socialistes à l'égard de la protection internationale des droits de l'homme. Revue des droits de l'homme. Human rights journal, vol. 7, no. 1, 1974, p. 175–206.
RELATIONS (AMERICAN-EUROPEAN), The round table, juillet 1974, no. 319–330.
ROGNONI (CARLO), Surtout pas l'Europe standard. Vision, no. 40, mars 1974, p. 47–50.
SCHEEL (WALTER), Die politische Einigung und das Gleichgewicht der Kräfte. Bulletin. Presse- und Informationsamt der Bundesregierung, no. 24, février 1974, p. 223–227.
SCHEEL (W.), Europa am Scheideweg. Aussenpolitik, no. 25, 2. Quartal 1974, p. 123–133.
SCHMIDT (HELMUT), Notwendigkeit einer integrierten europäischen Gesamtpolitik. Bulletin. Presse- und Informationsamt der Bundesregierung, no. 12, janvier 1974, p. 105–108.
SCHUMANN (MAURICE), Suffrage universel européen. Vision, no. 39, février 1974, p. 17.
STARK (T.), The admission of refugees in Europe. Migration news, vol. 23, no. 5, 1974, p. 6–16.
VARSANYI (J.), Limited sovereignty or regional integration for East-Central Europe? The international and comparative law quarterly, no. 28, juillet 1974, p. 657–666.
VEDOVATO (G.), Europa e Stati Uniti negli anni '70. Rivista di studi politici internazionali, no. 40, octobre-décembre 1973, p. 609–688.
WELL (G. VAN), Strukturelemente eines neuen europäischen Staatensystems in der Diskussion. Europa-Archiv, no. 29, 10 octobre 1974, p. 643–649.

B. LA COOPERATION ECONOMIQUE
B. ECONOMIC COOPERATION

AIKTKEN (Norman D.), The effect of the EEC and EFTA on European trade: A temporal cross-section analysis. The American economic review, no. 5, décembre 1973, p. 881–892.
ALEKSIC (M.), La Yougoslavie et le CAME, une coopération qui se renforce. La nouvelle revue internationale; problèmes de la paix et du socialisme, no. 17, juillet 1974, p. 30–40.
ARROYO PICHARDO (G.), Análisis causal de la transformación al socialismo

de los países de Europa del Este. Relaciones internacionales (México), no. 1, octobre–décembre 1973, p. 49–74.

ASSEILY (A.), Eurocurrency market at bay. The Bankers' magazine, no. 218, octobre 1974, p. 13–17.

BÄR (H.), Rechtliche Regelung der Zusammenarbeit auf dem Gebiet der Planung im Rahmen des RGW. Staat und Recht, no. 23, juillet 1974, p. 1086–1102.

BEAUDEUX (P.), Le championnat d'Europe des places financières. L'expansion, mai 1974, p. 112–123.

BELL (G.), The Euro-currency markets in 1974. Euromoney, février 1974, p. 4–7.

BELLINI (J.), Europe of regions in the 1980s. Futures; the journal of forecasting and planning, no. 6, juin 1974, p. 183–200.

BENELUXLANDEN (De) gaan hun samenwerking op het gebied van de milieuhygiene intensiveren. Les pays du Benelux vont intensifier leur coopération dans le domaine de l'environnement. Benelux, no. 4, 1974, p. 3–6.

BOGOMOLOV (O.), Dva tipa mezhdunarodnoĭ ékonomischeskoĭ integratsii (SEV i EEC). Mirovaia ékonomika i mezhdunarodnye otnosheniia, no. 11, noiabr' 1974, p. 26–35.

BOLZ (K.) et P. PLÖTZ, East-West cooperation. German experiences. Intereconomics, mai 1974, p. 158–162.

BRENDEL (G.) et H. J. DUBROWSKY, Der Aussenhandel der RGW-Lände unter den Bedingungen der sozialistischen ökonomischen Integration. Deutsche Aussenpolitik, no. 19, Heft 6, 1974, p. 1320–1344.

CAESAR (R.), Politische Aspekte einer europäischen Zentralbank. Europa-Archiv, no. 29, 25 mai 1974, p. 325–343.

CARMOY (G. DE), L'énergie en Europe, demain. Etudes, février 1974, p. 169–182.

COOPERATION INDUSTRIELLE et commerciale inter-européenne Est-Ouest. Revue de l'Est (France), vol. 5, no. 2, 1974, p. 1–144.

COVILLE (G.), Les grandes surfaces en Europe. 30 jours d'Europe, septembre 1974, p. 32–36.

CRAVEN (J. A.), The challenge facing the Eurobond market in 1974. Euromoney, mars 1974, p. 9.

DE CECCO (M.), Optimum currency areas and European monetary integration. Journal of world trade law, no. 8, septembre-octobre 1974, p. 463–474.

DU PRE DE SAINT-MAUR (JEAN), Les Euro-crédits financiers. Le point de vue du banquier. Banque, no. 331, juillet/août 1974, p. 667–688.

EGGER (K.), et B. GLAESER, Die systemverändernde Funktion der Landwirtschaft. Die neue Gesellschaft, no. 6, 1974, p. 487–495.

ENRICHISSEMENT (L') de l'uranium, réalité industrielle d'aujourd'hui. ATEN. Bulletin d'information, mai-juin 1974, p. 5–20.

EUROPE (L') à la recherche d'une nouvelle énergie. 30 jours d'Europe, février 1974, p. 26–36.

EUROPA denkt um – Grünes Licht fuer gemeinsame Energiepolitik. Atomwirtschaft – Atomtechnik, no. 10, octobre 1974, p. I–III.

FREIHANDEL (EUROPÄISCHER) zwischen Währungschaos und Währungsintegration aus schweizerischer und österreichischer Sicht. Aussenwirtschaft, no. 29, juin 1974, p. 5–79.

GESETZE (ÖKONOMISCHE) und sozialistische Leitung. Einheit, vol. 29, no. 3, 1974, p. 262–298.

GOODE (R. M.), A credit law for Europe? The international and comparative law quarterly no. 23, avril 1974, p. 227–291.

GUMPEL (W.), 25 Jahre "sozialistische ökonomische Integration" im RGW. Osteuropa, no. 24, janvier 1974, p. 13–26.

HAYWARD (J.), National aptitudes for planning in Britain, France and Italy. Government and opposition, no. 9, autumn 1974, p. 397–410.

HEWSON (J.) et E. SAKAKIBARA, The Euro-dollar deposit multiplier: a portfolio approach. International monetary fund. Staff papers, no. 21me juillet 1974, p. 307–328.
HEYMANN (P.), Les multinationales et l'Europe. 30 jours d'Europe, décembre 1974, p. 31–36.
JAHRE (25) Rat für gegenseitige Wirtschaftshilfe. Wirtschaftswissenschaft, no. 22, avril 1974, p. 481–543.
JAHRE (25) RGW. Einheit, vol. 29, no. 1, 1974, p. 10–43.
KAMECKI (Z.), CMEA countries' economic integration and the possibilities of developing East-West trade. Studies on international relations (Warsaw), no. 3, 1974, p. 57–80.
KIMMINICH (OTTO), Die internationale Kontrolle der europäischen Atomindustrie. Vorgeschichte und Funktion des Verifikationsabkommens vom 5. April 1973. Zeitschrift für ausländisches öffentliches Recht und Völkerrecht, no. 4, décembre 1973, p. 636–672.
KING (H. T.), Tax aspects of joint ventures and other ways of doing business with the Soviet block countries and Yugoslavia. Tax management international. Journal, juin 1974, p. 5–11.
LADYGIN (B.), The motive forces of socialist integration. International affairs (Moscow), octobre 1974, p. 22–29.
LARRE (R.), Les développements récents du marché des eurodevises. Banque, septembre 1974, p. 775–778.
LEE (B. E.), An introduction to the Euro-currency market. Bank of Canada. Review. Revue de la Banque du Canada, avril 1974, p. 3–18.
LIEBSCH (H.) et G. PROFT, Neue Aspekte bei der Leitung und Planung in der sozialistischen ökonomischen Integration. Wirtschaftswissenschaft, no. 22, septembre 1974, p. 1281–1299.
LUTZ (C.), Nachruf auf die europäische Währungsschlange. Europa-Archiv, no. 29, 10 mai 1974, p. 285–290.
LUTZ (F. A.), The Euro-currency system. Banca nazionale del lavoro. Quarterly review (Roma), septembre 1974, p. 183–200,
MALLY (G.), Regionalism in Western and Eastern Europe. World affairs (Washington), no. 137, été 1974, p. 38–53.
MAYER (H. W.), Some analytical aspects of the intermediation of oil surpluses by the Euro-currency market. Banca nazionale del lavoro. Quarterly review (Roma) septembre 1974, p. 201–226.
MICHAELIS (HANS), Grundlinien einer Rohstoffpolitik. Lage und Aussichten der Versorgung. Rohstoffpolitik in USA, Japan, Sowjetunion und in der EWG. Glückauf, no. 9, mai 1974, p. 348–354.
MOROZOV (V.), CMEA countries. Wide international cooperation (the 25th anniversary of CMEA). International affairs (Moscow), avril 1974, p. 9–15.
NOUËL (E.), La mer du Nord, richesses énormes, dépotoir géant. Nouvelles de l'OTAN, vol. 22, no. 2, 1974, p. 24–29.
NUORTILA (R.), Finnish economic relations with the socialist countries. Bank of Finland. Monthly bulletin, no. 48, octobre 1974, p. 20–26.
O.C.D.E., Coopération pour le développement. „Examen" 1973. Extrait du chapitre VI du rapport annuel sur la Coopération pour le développement, Paris, novembre 1973.
Problèmes politiques et sociaux, no. 249, 10 janvier 1974, p. 45–48.
OPPENHEIMER (P. M.), Monetary union. A survey of the main issues. De economist (Amsterdam), vol. 122, no. 1, 1974, p. 23–48.
PAKENHAM (K.), The flow of funds in the Eurocurrency market in 1974. Euromoney, septembre 1974, p. 17–19.
PLAN (LE) directeur du chemin de fer européen de l'avenir. Revue générale des chemins de fer, no. 93, janvier 1974, p. 12–18.
POLITIQUE (LA) des prix dans les pays du Benelux. Benelux, no. 1, 1974, p. 21–29.

POLITIQUE (LA) des prix dans les pays du Benelux. Benelux, no. 2, 1974, p. 9–23.

RESNICK (S. A.) et E. M. TRUMAN, The distribution of West European trade under alternative tariff policies. The review of economics and statistics, no. 56, février 1974, p. 83–91.

RHODES (R. A. W.), Regional policy and a "Europe of regions"; a critical assessment. Regional studies, no. 8, août 1974, p. 105–114.

RIBOUD (J.), Théorie d'une monnaie européenne à pouvoir d'achat stable. Revue politique et parlementaire, no. 76, juillet-août 1974, p. 1–24.

ROUGEMONT (D. DE), Stratégie de l'Europe des régions. Centre européen de la culture. Bulletin, no. 14, printemps 1974, p. 3–20.

SIMONET (H.), The harmonisation of banking in Europe. Revue de la banque, vol. 38, no. 3, 1974, p. 372–380.

STOCK (WALTER), Brauchen wir einen Europäischen Währungsblock? Zeitschrift für das gesamte Kreditwesen, no. 4, février 1974, p. 121–123.

STRATEGIE di integrazione della CEE e del Comecon e relazioni Est-Ovest. Una tavola rotonda, Trieste, 28–29 settembre 1973. Est-Ovest, vol. 4, no. 3, 1973, p. 7–129.

SZITA (J.), As összeurópai együttmüködés és a keletnyugati kereskedelem egyes kérdései. Közgazdasági i szemle, no. 21, novembre 1974, p. 1245–1263.

TABLE RONDE (UNE) sur l'énergie. Revue française de l'énergie, no. 25, avril 1974, p. 415–422.

TOULEMON (R.), Les perspectives de l'Europe industrielle. Les problèmes de l'Europe, vol. 17, no. 65, 1974, p. 7–16.

TOULEMON (ROBERT) et JEAN FLORY, Une politique industrielle pour l'Europe.
I. L'industrie, les hommes et les régions dans la Communauté européenne.
II. L'Europe et la croissance économique.
France-Forum, no. 131, mars-avril 1974.

TURNER, (J. H.), New trends in Eurodollar agreements. Euromoney, mars 1974, p. 28–31.

VANDAMME (R.), L'unification des droits d'accise au sein du Benelux. Bulletin de documentation fiscale international, no. 28, septembre 1974, p. 373–381.

VAUBEL (R.), Plans for a European parallel currency and SDR reform: the choice of value-maintenance provisions and "Gresham's law." Weltwirtschaftliches Archiv, no. 110, Heft 2, 1974, p. 194–226.

VEL'IAMINOV (G.), Sotsialisticheskaia ékonomicheskaia integratsiia i provo. Vneshniaia torgovlia (USSR), no. 1, 1974, p. 7–12.

WASILKOWSKI (A.), Legal regulation of economic relations within the Council for mutual economic assistance. Polish yearbook of international law, vol. 5, 1972–1973, p. 7–27.

WENNINK (C. J.), The superports of Europe in the era of giant tankers. Petroleum review, no. 28, janvier 1974, p. 33–44.

WILCZYNSKI (J.), Atomic energy for peaceful purposes in the Warsaw pact countries. Soviet studies, no. 26, octobre 1974, p. 568–590.

ZORGBIBE (C.), Comecon. La tentation de l'Occident. Projet, janvier 1974, p. 68–73.

C. CONSEIL DE L'EUROPE
C. COUNCIL OF EUROPE

ANNIVERSAIRE (25ème) du Conseil de l'Europe. Ici l'Europe, no. 2, 1974, p. 18–20.
BAUSCHER (W.), Le vingt-cinquième anniversaire du Conseil de l'Europe. Documents, no. 29, juillet–août 1974, p. 17–25.
BOYLE (K.) et H. HANNUM, Individual applications under the European convention on human rights and the concept of administrative practice: the Donnelly case. American journal of international law, no. 68, juillet 1974, p. 440–453.
DAUBIE (C.), Conciliation et protection européenne des droits de l'homme. Revue belge de droit international. 9, no. 2, 1973, p. 503–546.
EUROPA (L') verso l'unità. Celebrazione del XXV anniversario del Consiglio d'Europa. Rivista di studi politici internazionali, no. 41, avril-juin 1974, p. 163–224.
FAWCETT (J. E. S.), The Council of Europe and integration. International affairs (London), no. 50, avril 1974, p. 242–250.
HALLS (W. D.), L'étude Oxford/Conseil de l'Europe. Education et culture, no. 24, p. 17–22.
HIOU (T.), La Charte sociale européenne. Revue hellénique de droit international, no. 25, janvier-décembre 1972, p. 311–333.
LOEWE (R.), Die Empfehlungen des Europarats zur Vereinheitlichung der Rechtsbegriffe "Wohnsitz" und "Aufenthalt." Österreichische Juristen-Zeitung, no. 29, 22 mars 1974, p. 144–151.
MELCHIOR DE MOLÈNES (C.), 25e anniversaire de sa fondation, l'orginalité du Conseil de l'Europe. Revue de droit international, de sciences diplomatiques et politiques, no. 52, avril-juin 1974, p. 148–166.
MONCONDUIT (FRANÇOIS), Commission européenne des droits de l'homme. Bilan de la Jurisprudence, janvier 1969–mai 1973. Annales de droit, no. 1–2, p. 107–127.
VASAK (K.) et D. COIN, Le Conseil de l'Europe. Notes et études documentaires, no. 4080, avril 1974, p. 1–52.
VEDOVATO (GIUSEPPE), Le rôle du Conseil de l'Europe dans l'intégration européenne. L'Europe en formation, no. 169–170, avril-mai 1974, p. 8–9.

C.

ANNEXE I

INDEX BIBLIOGRAPHIQUE DES ARTICLES ET ETUDES AYANT TRAIT A LA CHARTE SOCIALE EUROPEENNE

APPENDIX I

BIBLIOGRAPHICAL INDEX OF ARTICLES RELATING TO THE EUROPEAN SOCIAL CHARTER

I. LIVRES ET ARTICLES
BOOKS AND ARTICLES

ALKEMA (E. A.), „Het Europees Sociaal Handvest." Nederlands juristenblad, No 18 1967, pp. 484–486.

ALDERS (J. A. G.), „Een Europees Sociaal Handvest?" Lering en Leiding, No 1, Januari 1959, pp. 3–13.
ASBECK (F. M. VAN), „La Charte sociale européenne: sa portée juridique, sa mise en oeuvre." Mélanges offerts à Henri Rolin: Problèmes de Droit des Gens. Paris, A. Pedone, 1964.
„Het Europees Sociaal Handvest" in werking getreden, S.E.W., 1965, p. 131 et sq.
BAKELS (H. L.), „Het Europees Sociaal Handvest" De Vakbeweging, 11e Jaargang, No 1, 6 Januari 1959, pp. 8–10 et 13.
„Het Europees Sociaal Handvest en de democratie" De Vakbeweging, 13e Jaargang, No 23, 21.11.1961.
BALZARINI (R.), "La Carta Sociale Europea e la Costituzione Italiana" Il Diritto dell'Economia, 1962, pp. 286–298.
"La libertà sindacale e il diritto di negoziazione collettiva nella Carta Sociale Europea." In: "La Carta Sociale Europea." A cura di: La Rassegna del Lavoro, Ministero del Lavoro e della Previdenza Sociale. Roma 1961, pp. 165–182.
BARILE (G.), "La Carta Sociale Europea e il diritto internazionale." Rivista di Diritto Internazionale, 1961, pp. 621–644.
"La Carta Sociale Europea e il diritto internazionale." in: "La Carta Sociale Europea." A cura di: La Rassegna del Lavoro, Ministero del Lavoro e della Previdenza Sociale. Roma 1961. pp. 61–82.
BENVENUTI (L.), „Les buts sociaux et politiques de la Charte sociale européenne." Revue belge de Sécurité sociale, Année IV, No 4, mai 1962, pp. 657–666.
„Le finalità sociali e politiche della Carta Sociale Europea." in: „La Carta Sociale Europea." A cura di: La Rassegna del Lavoro, Ministero del Lavoro e della Previdenza Sociale, Roma 1961, pp. 13–24.
BERNARDINI (A.), „ La Carta Sociale Europea" Iniziativa Europea, Anno VI, No 54–55, 1964, pp. 17–20.
BLECKMANN (A.), „Interprétation et application en droit interne de la Charte sociale européenne, notamment du droit de grève." Cahiers de droit européen, 1967, No 4, pp. 388–412.
BORST, „Het Europees Sociaal Handvest en het Stakingsrecht," S.M.A., 1962, p. 89.
BRUGEL (J. W.), „La Charte sociale européenne" Europa-Archiv, 17. Jahrgang, No 11, 10 juin 1962, pp. 399, 404.
La Documentation française, Articles et Documents, Faits et Opinions, No 0.1318, 22.11.1962.
BUCHI (W.), "Die Europäische Sozialcharta von Strassburg.
- Ausgangspunkt und Grundlage
- Inhalt und Gehalt
- Kritische Würdigung
- Bedeutung einer Europäischen Sozialcharta für die Schweiz"
Cahiers du Syndicalisme Chrétien, Avril 1960, pp. 66–70.
CANNELLA (G.), "Il diritto alla sicurezza sociale e i diritti affini nella Carta Sociale Europea," in: "La Carta Sociale Europea." A cura di: La Rassegna del Lavoro, Ministero del Lavoro e della Previdenza Sociale, Roma, 1961, pp. 199–240.
„Le droit à la sécurité sociale et les droits connexes de la Charte sociale européenne." Revue belge de sécurité sociale, Année V. No 1, janvier 1963, pp. 1–45.
CANSACCHI D'AMELIA (G.), "Considerazioni sulla Carta Sociale Europea." Il Diritto dell'Economia, 1962, pp. 263–280.
CLUYSENAER, „De Betekenis van sociale grondrechten," S.M.A., 1961, p. 238.
CONSEIL DE L'EUROPE, „L'Europe des Travailleurs" Direction de l'Information C.E. 1962 (en anglais, allemand, néerlandais et italien).
CONSEIL DE L'EUROPE, La Charte sociale européenne, in: Rapport du Con-

seil de l'Europe à la Conférence Internationale des Droits de l'Homme, 1968, p. 52.
COTTIER (M.), "Die arbeitsrechtlichen Bestimmungen der Europäischen Socialcharta. Rechtsnatur, Inhalt und Vergleich mit dem Schweizerischen Recht." Freiburg/Schweiz. Jur-Diss. 1967 IV. XX. 186 s.
DE FEO (I.), „La Carta Sociale Europea, tutela delle libertà fondamentali" Esteri, No 4, 29 février, 15 mars 1960, pp. 13–14.
DEHOUSSE (F.), „L'Europe et le monde – Recueil d'études, de rapports et de discours, 1945–1960."
pp. 126–132; „Pour la création d'un Conseil économique et social européen." Discours prononcé en qualité de rapporteur à l'Assemblée Consultative du Conseil de l'Europe, Strasbourg, séance du 18 octobre 1955. (Compte rendu des débats, VIIe Session ordinaire, II. pp. 430–434).
pp. 133–137: „Le projet de Charte sociale européenne." Discours inaugural prononcé à la Conférence Tripartite convoquée par l'O.I.T. à la demande du Conseil de l'Europe, Strasbourg, séance du 1er décembre 1958. (Compte rendu des travaux du B.I.T., Genève 1959, pp. 52–57).
pp. 138–151: „Le projet de Charte sociale européenne devant la récente Conférence tripartite...." Conférence prononcée à l'Association belge pour le progrès social, Bruxelles, séance du 11 février 1959. (Le Progrès social, Liège, 1959, No 59, pp. 19–34). Paris, Librairie générale de droit et de jurisprudence, 1960.
DEIRMENZOGLOUPANAYOTOPOULOU (S.), „La Charte sociale européenne et l'influence de la Déclaration universelle des droits de l'homme." In: Revue hellénique de droit international, 1965 (Bd 18), pp. 137–147.
DEL GIUDICE (R.), „La Protezione e l'assistenza dei lavoratori migranti nella Carta sociale europea." In: „La Carta Sociale Europea." A cura di: La Rassegna del Lavoro, Ministero del Lavoro e della Previdenza Sociale, Roma 1961, pp. 271–291.
DELPEREE (A.), „Les droits sociaux et la Charte sociale européenne." In: Revue des droits de l'homme, Vol. I, No 4, 1968, pp. 549–581.
DELPEREE (A.), (et GILON C.), „La Charte sociale européenne.
1. Son élaboration
2. Son objectif et sa justification
3. Les aspects essentiels
– forme
– contenu juridique
– choix des droits sociaux
– niveau des droits sociaux
– mesures de mise en oeuvre de la Charte sociale européenne
– quelques problèmes de ratification."
Revue du travail. Bruxelles. No 10, octobre 1958, pp. 1216–1223.
DIEZ (E.), „Internationales Sozialrecht und Menschenrechtskonvention" Vortrag gehalten am 24. juni 1970, Seelisberg.
DI MARCANTONIO (A.), „La protezione della famiglia, della madre e dei fanciulli nella Carta Sociale europea." In „La Carta Sociale Europea." A curi di: La Rassegna del Lavoro, Ministero del Lavoro e della Previdenza Sociale. Roma 1961, pp. 261–276.
DROST (P. N.), "Human Rights as Legal Rights," Leiden, 1965, p. 65.
ERDMANN (E. G.), „Die Strassburger Konferenz über die Europäische Sozialcharta." Sozialer Fortschritt, No 5, 1959, pp. 100–103.
FABBRI (F.), „Osservazioni sull'efficacia internazionale ed interna della Carta Sociale Europea" Rivista giuridica del lavoro e della previdenza sociale, 1969, p. 213.
FUKS (F.), „Les dispositions de la Charte Européenne à la lumière des revendications des syndicats belges." In: „La Charte sociale européen-

ne," Numéro spécial de la Revue de l'Institut de Sociologie, Bruxelles, No 1, 1966, pp. 29–63.
GELLER (M. G.), „Etude de la Charte sociale du Conseil de l'Europe au regard de l'activité sociale des différents pays." Colloque régional de la C.I.S.S. sur la Coopération sociale en Europe. Introduction et conclusion des travaux de la Commission No 1 (dont M. Geller était Président) Informations sociales U.N.C.A.F., No 2, février 1960, pp. 15–21.
GEORGES (F.), „Europäische Sozialcharta nicht perfekt." Europa Brücke, 8. Jahrgang, No 3, März 1962, pp. 30–31.
GILON (C.) (et DELPEREE A.), „La Charte sociale européenne
1. Son élaboration
2. Son objectif et sa justification
3. Les aspects essentiels
– forme
– contenu juridique
– choix des droits sociaux
– niveaux des droits sociaux
– mesures de mise en oeuvre de la Charte sociale
– quelques problèmes de ratification."
Revue du travail. Bruxelles, No 10, octobre 1958, pp. 1216–1223.
GOETHEM (F. VAN), Overwegingen bij het Europees Sociaal Handvest, in: Festschrift für Nipperdey, 1965, II, p. 745.
GOSSERIES (Ph.) (et TAQUET M.), „La Charte sociale européenne," Journal des Tribunaux, 18.3.1962, pp. 181–188, 25.3.1962, pp. 202–205.
GRAMICCIA (G.) (et MELCHIONNA R.), „La Carta Sociale Europea." Il Mercato Comune. NN. 3/4, 5/6, 7/8, 1962.
GUIDOTTI (F.), „La protezione del lavoro delle donne e dei fanciulli nella Carta Sociale Europea" In: „La Carta Sociale Europea." A cura di La Rassegna del Lavoro, Ministero del Lavoro e della Previdenza Sociale, Roma, 1961, pp. 183–198.
HARRIS (D. J.), "The European Social Charter." The International and Comparative Law Quarterly, Vol. 13, No 3, July 1964, pp. 1076–1087.
HEISE (B.), „Vor der Ratifizierung der Europäischen Sozialcharta durch die BRD." Soziale Sicherheit (Köln), XII. Jahrgang, No 11, November 1963, pp. 329–332.
HEUSKIN (L.), „Le droit à la protection de la santé dans la Charte sociale européenne." In: „La Charte sociale européenne." Numéro spécial de la: Revue de l'Institut de Sociologie, (Bruxelles), No 1, 1966, pp. 65–81.
HEYDE (P.), „Die Europäische Sozialcharta" Arbeit und Recht, 1962, p. 70.
HOLZER (M.), „Die Schweiz und die Europäische Sozialcharta." Schriftenreihe der Schweizerischen Vereinigung für Sozialpolitik, 1968, Heft 1.
ISELE (H. G.), „Die Europäische Sozialcharta." Wiesbaden. Steiner. 1967.
JANSSEN (G.), „Les engagements des Parties Contractantes et la mise en oeuvre de la Charte sociale européenne." In: „La Charte sociale européenne." Numéro spécial de la: Revue de l'Institut de Sociologie, (Bruxelles), No 1, 1966, pp. 9–28.
KAHN-FREUND (O.), "Labour relations and international standards – some reflections on the European Social Charter. In: Mélanges W. J. Ganshof van der Meersch, Paris, 1972.
KARISCH (A.), „Die Europäische Sozialcharta" Oesterreichische Juristenzeitung, No 6, 9.4.1963, pp. 171–176.
KHOL (A.), „Die Europäische Sozialcharta und die Oesterreichische Rechtsordnung" Juristische Blätter, 87 Jahrgang, No 3–4, 13 Februar 1965, pp. 75–82.
„Zwischen Staat und Weltstaat. Die internationalen Sicherungsverfahren zum Schutze der Menschenrechte" Schriftenreihe der öster-

reichischen Gesellschaft für Aussenpolitik und internationale Beziehungen. Wien, 1969.

KISS (A. C.), „Entrée en vigueur de la Convention européenne d'établissement et de la Charte sociale européenne." Annuaire français de droit international. Vol. II. 1965–1966, pp. 686–691.

KNOPP (A.), „Die Europäische Sozialcharta" Recht der Arbeit, 1965.

KRAFT (H.), „Die Europäische Sozialcharta – Dokument des Sozialen Fortschritts?." Zeitschrift für Sozialreform, No 5, 1960, pp. 285–289.

KUKAKOWSKI (J.), „En marge de la Charte sociale européenne." Labor, No 5, 1961, pp. 222–223.

LEGA (C.), „L'orientamento, la formazione e il riadattamento professionale nella Carta Sociale Europea." In: „La Carta Sociale Europea." A cura di: La Rassegna del Lavoro. Ministero del Lavoro e della Previdenza Sociale. Roma, 1961, pp. 241–260.

LUME (G.), „La Carta Sociale Europea." Idea. No 5, 1960, pp. 313–315.

MARYAN-GREEN (N.), „Droits sociaux et normes régionales." (Etude du rapport existant entre les droits sociaux énoncés dans le Pacte international relatif aux droits économiques, sociaux et culturels et les divers instruments régionaux, dont la "Charte sociale européenne"). Journal du Droit international. 96e année, No 1, 1969. pp. 58–71.

MAZZONI (G.), „Il diritto ad eque condizioni di lavoro nella Carta Sociale Europea." In: „La Carta Sociale Europea." A cura di: La Rassegna del Lavoro, Ministero del Lavoro e della Previdenza Sociale, Roma, 1961, pp. 147–156.

MELCHIONNA (R.), „La Carta Sociale Europea
I. Premessa
II. Iter di elaborazione del documento
III. Struttura della Carta
IV. Breve esame dei singoli articoli
V. Conclusioni."
La Previdenza sociale nell'agricoltura, Anno XVI, No 3–4, maggio-agosto 1965, pp. 171–183.

MELCHIONNA (R.) (et GRAMICCIA G.), „La Carta Sociale Europea." Il Mercato Comune, NN. 3/4, 5/6, 7/8, 1962.

MENGONI (L.), „La Carta Sociale Europea e la Serrata." Rivista di Diritto del Lavoro, Vol. 21, p. 20.

MEEUWISSEN (D. H. M.), De Europese Conventie en het Nederlandse Recht, Europese Aspekten, No 8, A. W. Sijthoff, Leiden, 1968, pp. 114–120.

MÜLLER (G.), „Grundrechtsordnung und Sozialcharta." In: Gesellschaft und Politik, No. 1, 1965.

PAPADATOS (P.), „La Charte sociale européenne
I. Le concept de droit social
II. Elaboration et objectifs de la Charte
III. Structure et contenu de la Charte
IV. Conclusions et perspectives pour l'avenir."
Revue de la Commission internationale de Juristes, tome VII. No 2, hiver 1966, pp. 227–257.

PARLEMENT EUROPEEN „Rapport fait au nom de la Commission sociale sur la Charte sociale européenne." Rapporteur: Léon-Eli Troclet. Documents de séance 1963–1964. Doc. 1, 11.3.1963.

PARTMANN (M.), „Probleme des Koalitionsrechts und des Arbeitskampfes in Oesterreich und die Artikel 5 und 6 Ziffer 4 der Europäischen Sozialcharta." Dissertation, Wien, 1967.

PISCHEL (K.), „Die Bedeutung der europäischen Sozialcharta für das Recht in der Bundesrepublik." Deutschland–Würzburg 1966.

PROSPERETTI (U.), „La sicurezza e l'igiene del Lavoro nella Carta Sociale Europea." In: „La Carta Sociale Europea." A cura di: La Rassegna del Lavoro, Ministero del Lavoro e della Previdenza Sociale. Roma, 1961, pp. 157–164.

PUGSLEY (D.), "The European Social Charter." Yearbook of the A.A.A. The Hague, 1969, Vol. 39, pp. 97–100.
PURPURA (R.), ,,La Carta Sociale Europea." Il Giornale del Levante, 28.3. 1962.
,,La Carta Sociale Europea." Roma, Istituto Italiano di Medicina Sociale, 1962, p. 170.
,,L'elaborazione della Carta Sociale Europea." In: ,,La Carta Sociale Europea." A cura di: La Rassegna del Lavoro. Ministero del Lavoro e della Previdenza Sociale, Roma, 1951, pp. 25–60.
RELLINI (G.), ,,La Carta Sociale Europea e il diritto italiano." In: ,,La Carta Sociale Europea." A cura di: La Rassegna del Lavoro. Ministero del Lavoro e della Previdenza Sociale, Roma, 1961, pp. 83–104.
RICHEMONT (J. DE), ,,La Charte sociale européenne." Le Droit européen, 1963, p. 333.
RIVA SANSEVERINO (L.), ,,Il diritto al lavoro nella Carta Sociale Europea." In: ,,La Carta Sociale Europea." A cura di: La Rassegna del Lavoro. Ministero del Lavoro e della Previdenza Sociale. Roma, 1961, pp. 135–146.
,,L'equa retribuzione nella Carta Sociale Europea." Il Diritto dell' Economia, 1962, pp. 280–286.
ROBERTSON (A. H.), "Human Rights in Europe." Manchester, University Press, 1963, pp. 140–150.
RODRIGUEZ-PINERO (M.), ,,Antecedentes, genesis y significado de la Carta Social Europea." Madrid, Instituto de Estudios Politicos, s.d. p. 70 (Separata de la Revista de Politica Social, No 53, 1962).
SCHAMBECK (H.), ,,Grundrechte und Sozialordnung: Gedanken zur Europäischen Sozialcharta." Berlin, 1969.
,,Bild und Recht des Menschen in der Europäischen Sozialcharta." In: Das Arbeitsrecht der Gegenwart. 5. 1967. (1968) pp. 80–95.
SCHEVENELS (W.), ,,Une Charte pour l'Europe." Monde du travail libre, No 106, avril 1959, pp. 162–164 et 171.
SCHOETTER (P.), ,,La Charte sociale européenne: considérations critiques." In: ,,La Charte sociale européenne." Numéro spécial de la: Revue de l'Institut de Sociologie (Bruxelles), No 1, 1966, pp. 109–141.
SCHROEDER (J. W. M.), ,,Le problème des droits fondamentaux dans le domaine social, économique et culturel. Vers une convention européenne des droits sociaux et économiques." Bologna, Cappelli s.d. (tiré à part de la: Rivista di Diritto Internazionale e Comparato del Lavoro, Vol. 2, fasc. 3, 1958, pp. 400–409).
SELA QUINTANA, ,,La Carta Social Europea." Publicaciones de la Escuela Social. Oviedo, 1962.
SMYTH (J. P.), "The Implementation of the European Social Charter." ,,Mélanges Modinos." Paris, A. Pedone, 1968, pp. 290–303.
SPROEDT (B.), ,,Koalitionsfreiheit und Streikrecht in den universellen und europäischen Kollektivabkommen." Dissertation, Heidelberg, 1972.
STEINBACH (F.), ,,Die soziale Sicherheit in Oesterreich und die Europäische Sozialcharta." Soziale Sicherheit (Wien). No 3, 18. März 1970, pp. 78–81.
STRANNER (H.), ,,Les Chambres fédérales ont accepté le ,postulat Muheim': Pouvons-nous signer la Charte sociale européenne?" Europa (Bern), No 4, 1970, pp. 6–7.
Un seul sujet ,,européen" aux Chambres fédérales suisses: Charte sociale: postulat accepté au Conseil des Etats. Europa (Bern). 38e année, No 1, janvier 1971, p. 5.
SULLO (F.), ,,La Carta Sociale Europea." In: ,,La Carta Sociale Europea." A cura di: La Rassegna del Lavoro, Ministero del Lavoro e della Previdenza Sociale, Roma, 1961, pp. 7–12.

TAQUET (M.) (et GOSSERIES Ph.), „La Charte sociale européenne." Journal des Tribunaux, 18.3.1962, pp. 181–188 et 25.3.1962, pp. 202–205.

TENNFJORD (F.), „La Charte des 19 droits." Monde combattant, 14e année, No 153, mai-juin 1965, pp. 7–8.
"The Charter of the 19 rights." World Veteran, 14th year, No 153, May–June 1965.
"The European Social Charter – an instrument of social collaboration in Europe." Annuaire européen, Vol. IX, La Haye, Nijhoff 1962, pp. 71–83.

THOMAS (F.), „Zum Inkrafttreten der Europäischen Sozialcharta. Die Bundesrepublik ratifiziert als 5. Staat." Bundesarbeitsblatt, 1965, p. 223 et suiv.

TRIEBNIGG (E.), „Österreich, die sozialen Grundrechte und die Europäische Sozialcharta." Gesellschaft und Politik, Neue Folge, Heft 1/1965, p. 15 et sq.

TROCLET (L. E.), „Eléments de droit social européen." pp. 95–122: „La Charte sociale européenne." Bruxelles, Université libre, Institut de Sociologie. Edition préliminaire, 1963, p. 361.

TRUYOL Y SERRA (A.), „La Carta Social Europea." Los Derechos Humanos Declaraciones y Convenios internacionales. Madrid, 1968, pp. 52–54, 139–160.

VALENTIN (A.), „La Carta Sociale Europea e il diritto internazionale." Rivista di diritto europeo, Anno II, No 1, 1962, pp. 77–80.

VALTICOS (N.), „La Charte sociale européenne. Sa structure, son contenu, le contrôle de son application." Droit social, 26e Année, No 9, 10 septembre-octobre 1963, pp. 466–482.
„L'influenza delle Convenzioni e delle Raccomandazioni internazionali del lavoro sulla Carta Sociale Europea." In: „La Carta Sociale Europea." A cura di: La Rassegna del Lavoro, Ministero del Lavoro e della Previdenza Sociale, Roma, 1961, pp. 105–134.

VEN (F. VAN DER), „Soziale Grundrechte" pp. 36–44: Kap. I: „Inventarisierung der Sozialen Grundrechte. 7) Die Sozialcharta des Europarates." Köln, J. P. Bachem, 1965, p. 164.

VEN DU VAN (J. J. M.), „Het Europees Sociaal Handvest en Nederland." In: S.M.A., 1965, pp. 386 et sq.

VOGEL-POLSKY (E.), „L'Article 6 de la Charte sociale européenne" In: „La Charte sociale européenne." Numéro spécial de la: Revue de l'Institut de sociologie, (Bruxelles), No 1, 1966, pp. 83–107.

VONTZ (W.), „Europäische Sozialcharta. Nach der Menschenrechtskonvention: Festlegung der sozialen Grundrechte (I), (II)." Deutsches Aerzteblatt, 62. Jahrgang No 4, 23 Januar 1965, pp. 213–216, No 5, 30 Januar 1965, pp. 269–272.

WENGLER (W.), „Die Unanwendbarkeit der Europäischen Socialcharta im Staat." Ein Beitrag zu der Frage des Verhältnisses zwischen Völkerrecht und staatlichem Recht. Bad Homburg – V.D.H. Berlin, Zürich Verlag Gehlen 1969 in 8°, 72 p. (Aktuelles Recht B.d. – 1).

WIEBRINGHAUS (H.), „La Charte sociale européenne." Annuaire français de Droit international, IX Année, 1963, pp. 709–721.
„Première mise en oeuvre du système de contrôle instauré par la Charte sociale européenne." Annuaire français de Droit international, XIVe Année, 1968, pp. 784–789.
„Die Europäische Menschenrechts-Konvention und die Europäische Sozialcharta." Europa – Information 1.2.1969. Gustaf Stresemann Institut.
„Le Champ d'Application ‚ratione personae' de la Charte sociale européenne." Libro-Homenaje al Profesor Luis Sela Sampil Oviedo, 1970, pp. 525–542.
„Jurisprudence du droit social européen." Rivista di Diritto Europeo, Roma, 1972, Anno XII, No 3.

II. AUTRES PUBLICATIONS

OTHER PUBLICATIONS

,,Charte sociale: la coopération sociale en Europe." Informations sociales UNCAF. Février 1960, pp. 1-65.

,,Conférence tripartite sur le projet de Charte sociale européenne. Strasbourg, 1-13 décembre 1958." Informations sociales BIT, 1.4.1959, pp. 260-266.

,,Conferencia tripartita para la preparación de la Carta Social Europea." Revista Ibero-americana de Seguridad Social, (RISS) No 2, 1959, pp. 513-517.

,,Conférence tripartite sur le projet de Charte sociale européenne. Strasbourg, 1-13 décembre 1958." Revue du Travail, (Bruxelles), avril 1959, pp. 466-471.

,,Considerazioni sulla Carta Sociale Europea." Bollettino quindicinale dell'emigrazione, Anno XIX, No 20, 25 ottobre 1965, pp. 297-301.

,,Denkschrift zur Europäischen Sozialcharta." Bundestag-Drucksache, IV/2117.

,,Die Europäische Sozialcharta. Gesetzentwurf der Bundesregierung - Ratifizierung mit Ausnahme von fünf Absätzen." Zeitschrift für Sozialreform, 10. Jahrgang, No 5, Mai 1964, pp. 294-297.

,,Die Europäische Sozialcharta ist in Kraft getreten." Der Europäische Gemeindetag, 1-2, 1965, pp. 52-54.

,,Europees Sociaal Handvest." De Onderneming, No 2, 17.1.1959, pp. 60-64.

,,Europees Sociaal Handvest voorlopig nog een vrome wens?." Ruim Zicht, No 17, 12.1959, pp. 266-270.

,,Goedkeuring Europees Sociaal Handvest." De Onderneming, 16e Jaargang, No 12, 11 Juni 1966, pp. 333-334.

,,Het Europees Sociaal Handvest." De Onderneming, No 22, 28.10.1961, pp. 801-805.

,,Het Europees Sociaal Handvest. Behandeling in Europese Parlement." De Onderneming, Jaargang 13, No 15, 1963, pp. 508-509.

,,La Carta Sociale Europea." A cura di: La Rassegna del Lavoro Ministero del Lavoro e della Previdenza Sociale. Istituto Poligrafico dello Stato, Roma, 1961, pp. 332.

,,La Carta Sociale Europea sarà firmata a Torino" Esteri (l'Europa a Strasburgo). Anno XII, No 14, 31.7-15.8.1961, pp. 1-4.

,,La Charte sociale européenne." Bulletin de la Commission internationale de juristes, No 18, mars 1964, pp. 1-9.

,,La Charte sociale européenne." Le Droit européen, No 53, 4e trimestre 1963, pp. 333-342.

,,La Charte sociale européenne:

I. Janssen G.: Les engagements des Parties Contractantes et la mise en oeuvre de la Charte sociale européenne;

II. Fuks F.: Les dispositions de la Charte européenne à la lumière des revendications des syndicats belges;

III. Heuskin L.: Le droit à la protection de la santé dans la Charte sociale européenne;

IV. Vogel-Polsky E.: L'Article 6 de la Charte sociale européenne.

V. Schoetter P.: La Charte sociale européenne: considérations critiques."

Revue de l'Institut de sociologie, (Bruxelles), No 1, 1966. (Numéro spécial consacré à la Charte sociale européenne). p. 9-141.

,,La Charte sociale européenne et les normes internationales du travail." Revue internationale du Travail, Vol. LXXXIV, No 5, novembre 1961, pp. 388-411 et No 6, décembre 1961, pp. 506-522.

,,La Charte sociale européenne. Historique, clauses, ratifications, entrée

en vigueur (26 février 1965)." Marché Commun européen, nouvelle série VIe Année, No 7, 15 février 1965, pp. D 15/1, - D 15/6.
,,La Conférence tripartite européenne." Revue du travail, Bruxelles, No 11, novembre 1958, pp. 1408–1411.
,,Las Ratificaciones de la Carta Social Europea" (Deutsche Versicherungszeitschrift, No 4, April 1964). Revista Ibero-americana de Seguridad Social (RISS) Año XIV, No 1, enero-febrero 1965, pp. 64–65.
,,Raad van Europa. Europees Sociaal Handvest." De Onderneming, No 3, 6.2.1960, pp. 97–99.
,,Ratificatie Europees Sociaal Handvest. De memorie van antwoord" De Onderneming, 17e Jaargang, No 3, 11 februari 1967, pp. 78–79.
,,Sozialcharta der europäischen Landwirtschaft." Agrarpolitische Revue, 21. Jahrgang, No 2–3, (No 185), Oktober–November 1964, pp. 93–98.
"The European Social Charter." Bulletin of the International Commission of Jurists, No 18, March 1964, pp. 1–9.
,,Une Charte sociale de l'agriculture européenne. (Confédération européenne de l'Agriculture)." Cahiers mensuels de documentation européenne, (Parlement européen), 6e Année, No 11–12, novembre-décembre 1964, (en allemand, anglais, italien et néerlandais).
,,Voorlopig verslag Tweede Kamer nopens ratificatie Europees Sociaal Handvest." De Onderneming, 16e Jaargang, No 25, 10 December 1966 pp. 781.

C.

ANNEXE II

APPENDIX II

LISTE DES PRINCIPALES PUBLICATIONS CONCERNANT LA CONVENTION EUROPEENNE DES DROITS DE L'HOMME

SELECTIVE BIBLIOGRAPHY OF PUBLICATIONS CONCERNING THE EUROPEAN CONVENTION ON HUMAN RIGHTS

ALBERS (H.), Voorlopige hechtenis en het Hof van Straatsburg, in: Rechtskundig Weekblad, 1972–1973, kol. 1745ss.
ALKEMA (E. A.), West Europa en de Rechten van de Mens (Western Europe and Human Rights, in: Civis Mundi, No 13, 1974, pp. 111ss.
AMEKRANE Case, in: Public Law, pp. 77ss. et 336.
BACKER (J. D.), Martelingen (Torture), in: Militair Rechtelijk Tijdschrift, No 67, 1974, pp. 385ss.
BARIE (M.), Das Vermögen als Gegenstand des Gleichheitssatzes und als geschütztes Rechtsgut der Europäischen Menschenrechtskonvention. Jur. Diss. v. 25.5.1974, Heidelberg, 146pp.
BENVENUTI (P.), La ,,ragionevolezza" della detenzione preventiva nell'art. 5, par. 3, della Convenzione europea dei Diritti dell'Uomo, in: Rivista di Diritto Internazionale, Vol. LVII, 1974, pp. 508ss.
BILAN de la Convention européenne des Droits de l'Homme/Stock-taking of the European Convention on Human Rights/Eine Bestandsaufnahme der Europäischen Menschenrechtskonvention, Strasbourg: Conseil de l'Europe, Commission européenne des Droits de l'Homme, octobre 1974 (doc. DH (74) 6).
BOBBIO (N.), Il preambolo della Convenzione Europea dei Diritti dell' Uomo, in: Rivista di Diritto Internazionale, Vol. LVII, 1974, pp. 437ss.

Boes (M.), Enige beschouwingen over de ontvankelijkheidsvereisten van een verzoekschrift bij de Europese Commissie van de Rechten van de Mens, in: Tijdschrift voor bestuurswetenschappen en publiekrecht, No 3, 1973, pp. 155ss.

Capotorti (F.), Contributo allo studio della Convenzione europea dei Diritti dell'Uomo, in: Rivista di Diritto Internazionale, No 3, 1974.

Cassese (A.), Sul funzionamento del sistema dei ricorsi individuali alla Commissione europea dei Diritti dell'Uomo, in: Rivista di Diritto Internazionale, Vol. LVII, 1974, pp. 548ss.

Castberg (F.), The European Convention on Human Rights (translated from the Norwegian edition of 1970, revised and supplemented – as of 1 December 1973, edited by Torkel Opsahl and Thomas Ouchterlony), Leiden: Sijthoff, 1974.

Chiavario (M.), La Convenzione europea dei Diritti dell'Uomo ed il suo contributo al rinnovamento del processo penale italiano, in: Rivista di Diritto Internazionale, Vol. LVII, 1974, pp. 454ss.

Communication à la Commission des Droits de l'Homme des Nations Unies sur les activités du Conseil de l'Europe dans le domaine des droits de l'homme au cours de l'année 1974, Strasbourg: Conseil de l'Europe, 1975 (doc. H (75) 3).

Compte rendu annuel de la Commission européenne des Droits de l'Homme/Annual Review of the European Commission of Human Rights, 1974, Strasbourg: Conseil de l'Europe, janvier 1975.

Convention europeene des Droits de l'Homme: aspects nationaux/ European Convention on Human Rights: national aspects, Strasbourg: Conseil de l'Europe, janvier 1975.

Coolen (G. L.), Het militaire tuchtrecht en het Europees Verdrag voor de Rechten van de Mens (Military discipline law and the European Convention on Human Rights), in: Nederlands Juristenblad, 1974, pp. 519ss.

De Meyer (J.), La situation des ,,personnes physiques," ,,organisations non gouvernementales" et ,,groupes de particuliers" dans la procédure devant la Cour européenne des Droits de l'Homme, in: Annales de Droit, No 1/2, 1974, pp. 65ss.

Doehring (K.) et Isensee (J.), Pflichten und Rechte der Ausländer, in: Die staatsrechtliche Stellung der Ausländer in der BRD – Veröffentlichungen der Vereinigung der deutschen Staatsrechtslehrer, Berlin, New York: De Gruyter, 1974, pp. 1ss.

Dupuy (R. J.), La protection et les limites de la liberté d'expression de l'artiste dans la société européenne, in: Revue des Droits de l'Homme, Vol. VII, No 1, 1974, pp. 41ss.

Eissen (M.-A.), Le limitazioni ratione temporis nelle dichiarazioni di accettazione della competenza della Commissione rispetto ai ricorsi individuali, in Rivista di Diritto Internazionale, Vol. LVII, 1974, pp. 536ss.

Elles The Baroness, Aliens and activities of the United Nations in the field of Human Rights, in: Revue des Droits de l'Homme, Vol. VII, No 2–4, 1974, pp. 291ss.

Ercman (S.), L'année internationale de la Femme, in: Informations Sociales, No 8, 1974, pp. 12ss.

Ermacora (F.), Menschenrechte in der sich wandelnden Welt – I. Band: Historische Entwicklung der Menschenrechte und Grundfreiheiten, Wien: Verlag der ,,Österreichische Akademie der Wissenschaften," 1974.

Europakonventionen och europeiska sociala stadgan (The European Convention and the European Social Charter), in Swedish Government Official Reports, Series No. 1974: 88 (only Swedish).

Frid (A.), De tolk in strafzaken: een goed verstaander ...? (The interpreter in criminal cases: a word to the wise . . . ?), in: Nederlands Tijdschrift voor Criminologie, Vol. 16, 1974, pp. 123ss.

FRIEDMANN (Th.), Conflicting rights and Human Rights, in: Protection of Human Rights in the light of scientific and technological progress in biology and medicine. Proceedings of a Round Table conference organized by CIOMS with the assistance of Unesco and WHO; WHO Headquarters, Geneva, 14, 15 and 16 Nov. 1973, 1974, pp. 160ss.

GANTER (H. G.), Die Spruchpraxis der Europäischen Kommission für Menschenrechte auf dem Gebiet des Strafvollzuges, Bonn: Röhrscheid, 1974 (Rechtsvergl. Untersuchungen z. ges. Strafrechtswissenschaft N.F. 49).

GOOSE (P. E.), Der internationale Pakt über bürgerliche und politische Rechte, in: Neue Juristische Wochenschrift, 1974, pp. 1305ss.

GREMENTIERI (V.), Le garanzie internazionali del processo civile, in: Scritti dedicati ad Antonio Raselli, Milano: Ed. A. Giuffrè, T. I., 1971, pp. 795ss.

HAM (R.), Der gesetzliche Richter und die Ablehnung wegen Besorgnis der Befangenheit unter bes. Berücks. des Strafverfahrens. Rechtswiss. Diss. v. 18.11.1974, Berlin: Freie Universität, XXIX, 222pp.

HANNUNG (H.) and BOYLE (K.), Individual applications under the European Convention on Human Rights and the concept of administrative practice: The Donnelly Case, in: American Journal of International Law, 1974, pp. 440ss.

HARPER (T.), Note on question of a Bill of Rights, in: New Law Journal, 1974, p. 1143.

HELGESEN (J. E.), Rett til augjôrelse ved domstoler (Right to a decision by Tribunals), Institutt for Statsrett og Folkerett, Universitetet, Oslo.

HIRSCH (E. E.), Menschenrechte und Grundfreiheiten im Ausnahmezustand. Eine Fallstudie über die Türkei und die Agitation „strikt unpolitischer" internationaler Organisationen, in: Schriften zum öffentlichen Recht, Berlin: Duncker & Humblot, Bd. 231, 1974.

HONDIUS (F. W.), De Rechten van de Mens in Europa (Human Rights in Europe), in: Civis Mundi, Vol. 15, 1974, pp. 244ss.

HONDIUS (F. W.), WALDECK (P. W.), WIJSENBEEK (F. A.), Nederlanders in het buitenland en het kiesrecht (The voting of the Netherlands citizens abroad), in: Nederlands Juristenblad, 1974, pp. 480ss.

HUYNEN (S.), La protection de la jeunesse, in: Informations Sociales, No 8, 1974, pp. 18ss.

INDEMNISATION pour privation de liberté injustifiée et détention préventive inopérante, in: Journal des Tribunaux, No 4866, 1974, pp. 237ss.

IRELAND v. United Kingdom, East African Asians' Case, Handyside Case, The Sunday Times Case, in: Public Law, 1974, pp. 255ss.

KIMMINICH (O.), Menschenrechtsschutz im geteilten Deutschland, in: Öffentliches Recht und Politik, Festschrift für H. U. Scupin, Hrsg. v. Norbert Achterberg, Berlin: Duncker & Humblot, 1973.

KISS (A. C.) et MARIE (J. B.), Le droit à la vie – dans les instruments internationaux relatifs aux droits de l'homme – in: Revue des Droits de l'Homme, Vol. VII, No 2–4, 1974, pp. 338ss.

KRIELE ( ), Geschichte der Grund- und Menschenrechte, in: Öffentliches Recht und Politik, Festschrift für H. U. Scupin, Hrsg. v. Norbert Achterberg, Berlin: Duncker & Humblot, 1973.

LEANZA (U.), Per una effettiva garanzia dei Diritti dell'Uomo, in: Annuario di Diritto Internazionale, 1967–1968, pp. 414ss., et in: Scritti in onore di Gaspare Ambrosini, Milano: Ed. Giuffrè, 1970, pp. 1157ss.

LES DROITS DE L'HOMME, in: Informations Sociales, Revue de l'action sociale, du travail social et des collectivités, Paris, No 7 et 8, 1974.

MARGIOTTA BROGLIO, F., Interesse religioso, sicurezza collettiva e stato di necessità nella Convenzione europea dei Diritti dell'Uomo, in: Studi in memoria di Carlo Esposito, Padova: Cedam, 1972, pp. 1283ss.

MAYENCE (S.), Les Droits de l'Homme, Présentation, in: Informations Sociales, No 8, 1974, pp. 2ss.
McDOUGAL (M. S), LASSWELL (H. D) and CHU CHEN (L.), Nationality and Human Rights: the protection of the individual in external areas, in: The Yale Law Journal, 1973/74, pp. 900ss.
MEEUWISSEN (D. H. M.), Konstitutionele problematiek in West-Europa (Constitutional problems in Western Europe), in: Civis Mundi, Vol. 13, 1974, pp. 89ss.
MELCHIOR (M.), Les droits de l'homme: aspects juridiques, in: Informations Sociales, No 7, 1974, pp. 4ss.
MELICHAR (E.), Grundrechte und Strafvollzug in der Rechtsprechung des Österreichischen Verfassungsgerichtshofs – Vortrag – Kärtner Juristische Gesellschaft, in: Juristische Blätter, 1974, pp. 364ss.
MEYER (D.), Nochmals: Auslegung des Art. 6 Abs. 3 litt. c) und e) der Menschenrechtskonvention, in: Neue Juristische Wochenschrift, 1974, pp. 1175ss.
MIRIMANOFF-CHILIKINE (J.), Conférence diplomatique sur la réaffirmation et le développement du droit international humanitaire applicable dans les conflits armés (Quelques remarques sur les projets d'instruments juridiques), in: Revue Belge de Droit International, Vol. X, No 1, 1974, pp. 36ss.
MONCONDUIT (F.), Commission européenne des Droits de l'Homme. Bilan de la jurisprudence: janvier 1969 – mai 1973, in: Annales de Droit, No 1/2, 1974, pp. 107ss.
MOSER (B.), Europäische Menschenrechtskonvention als Quelle des internationalen Privatrechts, in: Österreichische Juristen-Zeitung, 1974, pp. 650ss.
MOSLER (H.), Das Institut de Droit International und die völkerrechtliche Stellung der menschlichen Person, in: Justitia e Pace, 1974, pp. 77ss.
MUNRO (H.), Britain and European Human Rights, in: New Law Journal, 1974, pp. 340ss.
NISET (J.), Les droits de l'homme, 25 ans après la Déclaration Universelle, in: Journal des Tribunaux, 1974, pp. 53ss.
NOTE on protection of witnesses before the European Commission of Human Rights, in: New Law Journal, 1974, pp. 422ss.
NOTES sur: Affaire Lawless, Affaire De Becker, Affaires relatives à certains aspects de l'enseignement linguistique en Belgique, Affaire Wemhoff, Affaire Neumeister, Affaire Stögmüller, Affaire Matznetter, Affaire Delcourt, Affaires De Wilde, Ooms et Versyp (vagabondage), Affaire Ringeisen, in: Rivista di Diritto Internazionale, Vol. LVII, 1974, pp. 567ss.
PALADIN (L.), Il divieto di discriminazione e la Convenzione europea dei Diritti dell'Uomo, in: Rivista di Diritto Internazionale, Vol. LVII, 1974, pp. 446ss.
PANZERA (A. F.), Il potere della Corte europea dei Diritti dell'Uomo di accordare un'equa riparazione alla parte lesa, in: Rivista di Diritto Europeo, 1974, pp. 317ss.
PETZOLD (H.), Le règlement de la Cour européenne des Droits de l'Homme, in: Annales de Droit, No 1/2, 1974, pp. 165ss.
RAUCH (E.), The compatibility of the detention of terrorists order (Northern Ireland) with the European Convention for the Protection of Human Rights, in: New York University Journal of International Law and Politics, 1973, pp. 1ss.
ROBERTSON (A. H.), De internationale bescherming van de rechten van de mens, Groningen: Tjeenk Willink, 1974: Dutch version by H. C. Dirkse-Bresters (Original: The international protection of human rights, Manchester: Manchester University Press, 1972).
ROOD (M. G.), Stakingsrecht en internationale verdragen (The right to

strike and international conventions), in: Nederlands Juristenblad, 1974, pp. 661ss.
ROSDORF (L. W.), The framework of legal evolution, Deventer: Kluwer, 1974 (Thesis, 1974, at the University of Utrecht).
SCHMIDT (H.), Zur Auslegung des Art. 6, Abs. 3 c) und e), der Menschenrechtskonvention, in: Neue Juristische Wochenschrift, 1974, pp. 90ss.
SCHUTTER (B.) DE, De strafsanktie als vreedzaam wapen in het humanitair recht 1949–1974, in: Revue Belge de Droit International, Vol. X, No 1, 1974, pp. 73ss.
SHARMA (V. D.) et WOOLDRIDGE (F.), Some legal questions arising from the expulsion of the Ugandan Asians, in: International and Comparative Law Quarterly, 1974, pp. 397ss.
SPERDUTI (G.), Caratteri del sistema europeo di protezione dei diritti dell' uomo, in: Rivista di Diritto Internazionale, Vol. LVII, 1974, pp. 434ss.
TRECHSEL (S.), Die Europäische Menschenrechtskonvention, ihr Schutz der persönlichen Freiheit und die schweizerischen Strafprozessrechte, Bern: Stämpfli, 1974.
VALTICOS (N.), La protection internationale de la liberté syndicale vingt-cinq ans après, in: Revue des Droits de l'Homme, Vol. VII, No 1, 1974, pp. 5ss.
VERDOODT (A.), La protection des droits de l'homme dans les pays plurilingues, Bruxelles: Labor, 1973, pp. 210.
WHITE (R. C. A.), When is a British protected person not a British protected person, in; International and Comparative Law Quarterly, No 4, pp. 866ss.
WILLIAMS (W. D.), British Passports and the right to travel, in: International and Comparative Law Quarterly, 1974, pp. 642ss.
ZANGHI (C.), La protection des droits de l'homme: universalisme ou régionalisme?, in: Revue des Droits de l'Homme, Vol. VII, No 2–4, 1974, pp. 641ss.
ZANGHI (C.), Osservazioni sulla composizione della Commissione europea dei Diritti dell'Uomo, in: Rivista di Diritto Europeo, 1974, pp. 329ss.
ZHARA BUDA (S.), L'adesione dell'Italia alla clausola del ricorso individuale e alla giuridizione obbligatoria della Corte di Diritti dell'Uomo, in: La Giustizia Penale, No 1, 1973, pp. 350ss.

D. COMMUNAUTES EUROPEENNES
D. EUROPEAN COMMUNITIES

1. GENERAL

BAILEY (RICHARD), Britain and a Community energy policy. Colliery Guardian, no. 1, janvier 1974, p. 14–17.
BALASSA (B.), Trade creation and trade diversion in the European common market. The Manchester school of economic and social studies, no. 42, juin 1974, p. 93–135.
BARREAU (HERVE), La recherche scientifique et l'intégration européenne. L'Europe en formation, no. 166, janvier 1974, p. 16–24.
BERGSTEN (FRED C.), Die amerikanische Europa-Politik angesichts der Stagnation des Gemeinsamen Marktes. Europa Archiv, no. 4, février 1974, p. 115–122.
CARSAC (J. B.), Les rapports entre la C.E.E. et le Comecon. Défense nationale, no. 30, mars 1974, p. 69–79.
CICHOVICZ (JÜRGEN A.), Neuere verkehrspolitische Konzeption in der Europäischen Gemeinschaft. New transport policy concept in the

European Community. Stahl und Eisen, no. 11, 23 mai 1974, p. 512–522.

COLENBRANDER (W. S. A.), Engeland één jaar in de EEG. Internationale spectator, no. 21, décembre 1973, p. 743–747.

COLLET (P.), La „redistribution" communautaire. L'économie no. 30, 22 juillet 1974, p. 14–22.

COMMUNITY (THE EUROPEAN): factors of disintegration – DE CECCO (M.), Pressure of economic difficulties. TURNER (L.), Politics of the energy crisis. International affairs (London), no. 50, juillet 1974, p. 404–415.

CONDITIONS (LES) de la relance de la Communauté économique européenne. 30 jours d'Europe, avril 1974, p. 1–36.

DASKALOV (M.), Ikonomicheskite otnosheniia na NR Bŭlgariia sŭs stranitechlenki na Evropeĭskata ikonomicheska obshtnost. Novo vreme, vol. 50, no. 1, janvier 1974, p. 29–40.

FIUMEL (H. DE), Aspects juridiques de la politique commerciale commune de la CEE à l'égard des pays socialistes. Cahiers de droit européen, vol. 10, nos. 3–4, 1974, p. 288–302.

EMPLOI (L') face à une situation nouvelle dans la Communauté. Revue du travail, juin-juillet 1974, p. 321–322.

GLESKE (L.), Stand und Zukunftsperspektiven der Wirtschafts- und Währungsunion. Europarecht, no. 9, janvier-mars 1974, p. 6–24.

GOTTWALD (M. L. C.), Les relations CEE Amérique latine. Realtà economica (Milano), no. 6, mars-avril 1974, p. 29–37.

HARTLEY-BREWER (MICHAEL), Die Labour party, das Volk und die Europäische Gemeinschaft. Die neue Gesellschaft, octobre 1974, p. 871–876.

HERMANN (H. J.), Zur Steuerpolitik gegenüber multinationalen Unternehmen im Bereich der Europäischen Gemeinschaften. Aussenwirtschaftsdienst des Betriebsberaters, no. 20, juin 1974, p. 297–303.

HUFFEL (L. VAN), Ebauche d'une politique portuaire de la CEE. European transport law, vol. 9, no. 2, 1974, p. 234–242.

INTEGRATIONSVERTRÄGE (DIE ÖSTERREICHISCHEN) mit den Europäischen Gemeinschaften. Monatsberichte, Österreichisches Institut für Wirtschaftsforschung, no. 2, 1974, p. 74–94.

KEBSCHULL (DIETRICH), EC policy and developing countries. Monthly review of international trade and development, no. 5, mai 1974, p. 145–153.

KRIER (HENRI), Les incidences du Marché commun sur le développement économique d'une région: le cas de la Bretagne. Revue d'économie politique, no. 2, mars-avril 1974, p. 173-209.

LAGRANGE (M.), L'avenir institutionnel de la Communauté européenne. Revue trimestrielle de droit européen, no. 10, janvier-mars 1974, p. 88–98.

LIPTON (MICHAEL) et PETER TULLOCK, India and the enlarged European Community. International affairs, no. 1, janvier 1974, p. 49–66.

LODGE (J.), The role of EEC summit conferences. Journal of Common market studies, vol. 12, no. 3, 1974, p. 337–345.

LODGE (J.), Parliamentary reform in the EEC. The Parliamentarian, no. 55, octobre 1974, p. 250–257.

MARCHANDISE (H.), La recherche européenne sur les matériaux. Annales des mines, mai-juin, p. 29–36.

MAYER (J.), Comparaison réelle du produit intérieur brut des pays de la Communauté européenne-Analyse et prévision, no. 17, juin 1974, p. 643–781.

MILIĆ (P.), Les perspectives de la coopération entre la Yougoslavie et la C.E.E. Questions actuelles du socialisme (Belgrade), vol. 24, no. 3, 1974, p. 75–87.

MILLER (J. D. B.), The unassociables: the EEC and developed countries overseas. The world today, no. 30, août 1974, p. 327–334.

MORTELMANS (K. J.), The extramural meetings of the member states of the Community. Common market law review, no. 11, février 1974, p. 62–91.

NEGOCIATIONS (Les) entre la C.E.E. et les pays associés ou associables. Marchés tropicaux et méditerranéens, no. 1482, avril 1974, p. 941–943.

NEGOCIATIONS(Les) entre le Marché commun, les états africains et Malgache associés et les pays „associables" du Commonwealth. Patronat, no. 345, janvier 1974, p. 52–55.

PETRILLI (GIUSEPPE), Les structures économiques de la Communauté européenne et les difficultés actuelles de l'Union économique et monétaire. Revue de la Société d'études et d'expansion, no. 260, avril-mai-juin 1974, p. 230–234.

PINDER (JOHN), Kann die Europäische Gemeinschaft eine Ostpolitik betreiben? Europa Archiv, no. 4, février 1974, p. 105–114.

PINDER (J.), A community policy towards Eastern Europe. The world today, no. 30, mars 1974, p. 119–128.

PREFERENZE (Le) generalizzate della Comunità economica europea. Mondo aperto, no. 6, décembre 1974, p. 433–440.

PREWO (W.), Integration and export performance in the European economic community. Weltwirtschaftliches Archiv. Review of world economics, no. 110, 1974, p. 1–35.

PRINCIPES, objectifs et portée d'une politique harmonisée de tarification des prestations documentaires dans la Communauté économique européenne. Documentaliste, no. 2, juin 1974, p. 81–84

REICHERT (KARLHEINZ), Lage und Aussichten des Kohlenbergbaus in der Gemeinschaft. Glückauf, no. 5, mars 1974, p. 179–183.

RELATIONS (EXTERNAL) of the European community. Journal of Common market studies, no. 12, septembre 1973, p. 1–103.

RELAZIONE di Ortoli sui problemi della Comunità europea. Relazioni internazionali, no. 8, février 1974, p. 218–220.

SASSE (C.), Kooperationsabkommen und EG-Handelspolitik. Europa-Archiv, no. 29, 25 octobre 1974, p. 695–706.

SCHERER (F. M.), Europäische Fusionskontrollpolitik, die "Rule of Reason" und die Regel der Geheimhaltung. Wirtschaft und Wettbewerb, no. 2, février 1974, p. 81–90.

SCHMIDT (GEROLD), Schutzmassnahmen des Aussenwirtschaftsrechts der Europäischen Gemeinschaft. Die öffentliche Verwaltung, no. 2, 1974, p. 50–56.

SENTI (R.), Diskriminierungseffekt der Ursprungsregelung. EFTA-EWG? Aussenwirtschaft, no. 29, mars 1974, p. 40–57.

SERRE (FRANÇOISE DE LA,), Problèmes institutionnels: la C.E.E. et les relations Est-Ouest. Studia diplomatica, septembre-novembre 1974, no. 5–6, p. 727–731.

SHLAIM (A.), The Vedel report and the reform of the European parliament. Parliamentary affairs, no. 27, printemps 1974, p. 159–170.

SHLAIM (A.), The role of summittry in E.E.C. decisionmaking. International relations, no. 4, mai 1974, p. 455–471.

SIDJANSKI (D.) et U. AYBERK, Bilan des groupes et du processus de décision dans la Communauté des six. Res publica, vol. 16, no. 1, 1974, p. 33–61.

SIMONET (HENRI), Zur Situation der Kohle in der Europäischen Gemeinschaft. Erdölkrise und Tätigwerden der Kommission. Weltenergiemarkt. Glückauf, no. 5. mars 1974, p. 176–179.

SOAMES (SIR CHRISTOPHER), US-European community relations. Intereconomics, no. 7, juillet 1974, p. 202–203.

SOCIETES (Les) multinationales dans les Communautés européennes. Bruxelles, 24–25 janvier 1974, Bulletin économique et sociale, no. 2 mars-avril 1974, p. 1–11.

„SOMMET" (UN) pour une Europe en crise. 30 jours d'Europe, décembre 1974, p. 7-16.

THIRLWALL (A. P.), Regional economic disparities and regional policy in the Common market. Urban studies, no. 11, février 1974, p. 1-12.

THOMSON (GEORGE M.), Die integrationspolitische Bedeutung europäischer Regionalpolitik im Rahmen der Neun. Europa-Archiv, no. 2, janvier 1974, p. 37-44.

TOURET (D.), Le tarif douanier commun de la CEE et les problèmes posés par son application. Cahiers de droit européen, vol. 10, nos. 3-4, 1974, p. 303-354.

VAN DAMME (JACQUES), Controle van de concentraties in de EEG. Rechtskundig weekblad, no. 38, 18 mai 1974, p. 2190-2204.

VAN STEENBERGE (J.), La sécurité sociale dans la perspective du Marché commun. Documents, no. 5-6, 1973, p. 95-128.

VYGEN (HENDRIK), Ergänzung des EWG-Vertrages im Hinblick auf eine europäische Umweltpolitik. Zeitschrift für Rechtspolitik, no. 3, mars 1974, p. 58-62.

WEGNER (M.) et G. SCHNEIDER, Stabilisierungschancen in der EG. Wirtschaftsdienst no. 54, septembre 1974, p. 443-451.

WOOD (R. S.), The diplomacy of the enlarged European communities. World affairs (Washington), no. 137, été 1974, p. 3-22.

2. AGRICULTURE

BAUDIN (P.), L'agriculture communautaire et l'enchérissement de l'énergie. Revue du Marché commun, septembre 1974, p. 382-389.

CARLES (ROLAND), Les revenus dans l'exploitation agricole: définitions et mesures. Economie et statistique, no. 53, février 1974, p. 41-51.

ENDE des EG.-Agrarmarktes? Wirtschaftsdienst, no. 10, octobre 1974, p. 503-511.

JOHNSTON (R.), Some aspects of the common agricultural policy. Contemporary review, no. 109, octobre 1974, p. 169-176.

PARFITT (T.), CAP, beginning to take stock. The world today, no. 30, novembre 1974, p. 466-471.

PRODUITS (LES) alimentaires transformés. Application du nouveau système de l'AELE. EFTA, no. 2, mars 1974, p. 3-5.

VISTOSI (GIANFRANCO DI), Sviluppi recenti della politica agricola della C.E.E. Aggiornamenti sociali, no. 6, juin 1974, p. 415-440.

3. FINANCE

ASZKENAZY (H.), Les bourses du Marché commun affectées par les incertitudes conjoncturelles. Les problèmes de l'Europe, vol. 17, no. 65, 1974, p. 154-167.

BALLEGOOIJEN (C. W. M. VAN), De vrijheid van vestiging en dienstverlening van financiële instellingen in Europese gemeenschappen. Economisch statistische berichten, no. 2976, novembre 1974.

CAMPET (C.), La libération de l'activité bancaire dans la Communauté économique européenne. Banque, mars 1974, p. 255-263.

CARLI (G.), The problems of international monetary reform and the European community. Quarterly review, no. 1, 1974, p. 9-13.

CHEVALLIER (G.), La politique budgétaire des pays de la Communauté européenne. Notes et études documentaires, nos. 4102-4103, 10 juillet 1974, p. 1-84.

CLAROTTI (P.), The first year of the Nine in the field of financial institutions. Credit (London), no. 15, septembre 1974, p. 54-63.

DOSSER (MAGNIFICO PEETERS), European economic integration and monetary unification. Problèmes de l'Europe, no. 63, 1974, p. 37–74.
EHRING (H.), Zur Abgrenzung des Beihilfeverbots vom Verbot der zollgleichen Abgaben und der inländischen Abgaben, welche die Einfuhr höher belasten als die inländische Erzeugung. Europarecht, no. 9. avril-juin 1974, p. 108–148.
MOHAMMED (A. F.) et F. SACCOMANNI, Short-term banking and Eurocurrency credits to developing countries. International monetary fund. Staff papers, no. 20, novembre 1973, p. 612–638.
PAPI (GIUSEPPE UGO), I tempi lunghi della riforma monetaria. Giornale degli economisti e annali di economia, no. 1–2, janvier- février 1974, p. 54–69.
SCHULER (MANFRED), Die vierte Ebene: Haushalts- und finanzpolitische Probleme der Europäischen Gemeinschaften. Europa-Archiv, no. 2, janvier 1974, p. 45–54.
WOOLEY (P. K.) et J. H. COATES, Debt management in the EEC. National Westminster bank. Quarterly review (London), février 1974, p. 7–20.

4. DROIT/LAW

ABELLÁN HONRUBIA (V.), La profesión de abogado ante la Comunidad económica europea. Rivista jurídica de Cataluña, no. 73, juillet-septembre 1974, p. 603–621.
BARMAN (JOHANNES), Catégories et autonomie du droit communautaire. Revue internationale de droit comparé, no. 1, janvier-mars 1974, p. 33–60.
BEBR (G.), How supreme is Community law in the national courts? Common market law review, vol. 11, février 1974, p. 3–37.
CAHIER (P.), Les articles 169 et 171 du traité instituant la CEE à travers la pratique de la Commission et la jurisprudence de la Cour. Cahiers de droit européen, vol. 10, no. 1–2, 1974, p. 3–38.
CAUWELAERT, (ADGAR VAN), De juridische aard van de Europese gemeenschappen. Rechtskundig weekblad, no. 24, février 1974, p. 1299–1318.
DALTON (C.), Proposals for the unification of corporation law within the European economic community. Effect on the British company. New York university journal of international law and politics, no. 7, printemps 1974, p. 59–102.
DERINGER (ARVED) et JOACHIM SEDEMUND, Europäisches Gemeinschaftsrecht. Die Entwicklung bis Januar 1974. Neue juristische Wochenschrift, no. 10, mars 1974, p. 400–405.
DONNER (A. M.), The constitutional powers of the Court of justice of the European communities. Common market law review, no. 11, mai 1974, p. 127–140.
ECKER (W.), Einige Besorgnisse bei Anrufung des Europäischen Gerichtshofs (Art. 177 EWG-Vertrag). Juristenzeitung, no. 29, 4 octobre 1974, p. 606–609.
ÉLÉMENTS (LES) caractéristiques de l'ordre juridique communautaire. Revue trimestrielle de droit européen, no. 10, janvier-mars 1974, p. 99–118.
ENTREPRISES (LES) multinationales dans le contexte des règlements communautaires. Revue trimestrielle de droit européen, no. 9, novembre-décembre 1973, 0. 647–669.
FIUMEL (H. DE), Aspekty prawne wspólnej polityki handlowej EWG wobec państw socjalistycznych. Państwo i prawo, no. 29, mars 1964, p. 20–32. Legal aspects of EEC common commercial policy with respect to the socialist states; summaries in English, French and Russian.
HAEGEN (MARC VAN DER) et CLAUDE VERBRAEKEN, L'adaptation de la

législation belge à la première directive de la CEE relative aux sociétés. Journal des tribunaux, no. 4860, février 1974, p. 125–136.
HEYNEN (KLAUS-JÖRG), Konzentrationskontrollen für die Europäische Wirtschaftsgemeinschaft. Neue juristische Wochenschrift, 35, août 1974, p. 1526–1529.
JACOBS (F. G.), When to refer to the European court. The law quarterly review, no. 90, octobre 1974, p. 486–493.
KOVAR (R.), Les accords liant les Communautés européennes et l'ordre juridique communautaire. Revue du Marché commun, juillet-août 1974, p. 345–360.
LAGRANGE (M.), L'action préjudicielle dans le droit interne des Etats membres et en droit communautaire. Revue trimestrielle de droit européen, no. 10, avril-juin 1974, p. 268–297.
LANDO (O.), The EC draft convention on the law applicable to contractual and non-contractual obligations. Rabels Zeitschrift für ausländisches und internationales Privatrecht, no. 38, 1. Heft, 1974, p. 6–55.
LANG, (J. T.), Three EEC draft directives on company law: capital, mergers and management. The Irish jurist, no. 7, l'hiver 1972, p. 306–328.
LEIGH (GUY I. F.), Shareholder's pre-merger rights under the European company statute: a comparison with English and German law. Common market law review, no. 4, novembre 1974, p. 425–447.
LIPSTEIN (K.), Some practical comparative law: the interpretation of multi-lingual treaties with special regard to the EEC treaties. Tulane law review, no. 48, juin 1974, p. 907–915.
MALAWER (S. S.), International law, European community law and the rule of reason. Journal of world trade law, no. 8, janvier-février 1974, p. 17–74.
MEIER (GERT), Die Beendigung der Mitgliedstaaten in der Europäischen Gemeinschaft. Neue Juristische Wochenschrift, no. 10, mars 1974, p. 391–394.
MORALES (PAUL L.), La aplicación del derecho comunitario por el juez nacional. Derecho de la integración (Buenos Aires), vol. 7, núm. 15, mars 1974, p. 23–30.
NEGATIVATTEST fuer Zusammenarbeit von Nicht-Konkurrenten. Entscheidung der EG-Kommission vom 23. Februar 1972. Wirtschaft und Wettbewerb, no. 3, mars 1974, p. 205–206.
OVERBECK (A. E. VON) et P. VOLKEN, Das internationale Deliktsrecht im Vorentwurf der EWG. Rabels Zeitschrift für ausländisches und internationales Privatrecht, no. 38, 1. Heft, 1974, p. 56–77.
PESCATORE (P.), Rôle et chance du droit et des juges dans la construction de l'Europe. Revue internationale de droit comparé, no. 26, janvier-mars 1974, p. 5–19.
PRYLES (M.) et F. A. TRINDADE, The Common market (EEC) convention on jurisdiction and enforcement of judgments in civil and commercial matters. The Australian law journal, no. 48, avril 1974, p. 185–195.
RENGELING (H. W.), Nationaler Verwaltungsvollzug von Gemeinschaftsrecht: die Gemeinschaftskompetenzen. Europarecht, no. 9, juillet-septembre 1974, p. 216–237.
RIDEAU (J.), Le contentieux de l'application du droit communautaire par les pouvoirs nationaux. Recueil Dalloz Sirey; chronique, 19 juin 1974, p. 147–156.
RIEGEL (R.), Zum Problem der allgemeinen Rechtsgrundsätze und Grundrechte im Gemeinschaftsrecht. Neue juristische Wochenschrift, no. 27, septembre 1974, p. 1585–1590.
SCHERMERS (H. G.), The European court of justice: promotor of European integration. The American journal of comparative law, no. 22, été 1974, p. 444–464.
TOMUSCHAT (C.), La contribution de la Cour de justice des Communautés

européennes au règlement des conflits entre états membres. Revue générale de droit international public, no. 78, janvier-mars 1974, p. 40–59.
TRABUCCHI (A.), L'effet „erga omnes" des décisions préjudicielles rendues par la Cour de justice des Communautés européennes. Revue trimestrielle de droit européen, vol. 10, janvier-mars 1974, p. 56–87.
VINCENT (J. Y)., Le retrait des actes administratifs unilatéraux. Revue trimestrielle de droit européen, no. 10, janvier-mars 1974, p. 31–55.
VOULGARIS (J.), De la compétence judiciaire internationale en matière de faillite dans le cadre de la CEE. Journal du droit international, no. 101, juillet–septembre 1974, p. 522–561.
WÄLDE (T.), Die „Europäische Aktiengesellschaft" und multinationale Unternehmen. Aussenwirtschaftsdienst des Betriebs-Beraters, no. 20, février 1974, p. 82–87.
WÜRDINGER (H.), Die Konzernregelung im Statut der „Societas Europaea" und die Harmonisierung der nationalen Rechte in den Europäischen Gemeinschaften. Europarecht, no. 9, janvier-mars 1974, p. 25–35.
ZIEGER (G.), Die Rechtsprechung des Europäischen Gerichtshofs. Jahrbuch des öffentlichen Rechts der Gegenwart, no. 22, 1973, p. 298–356.

E. QUESTIONS DE DEFENSE

E. DEFENCE QUESTIONS

BALL (R.), NATO needs a fresh breeze. Fortune, no. 89, février 1974, p. 104–109, 112, 116–117.
BEYOND NATO. International journal, no. 29, spring 1974, p. 155–278.
BIRNBAUM (K. E.), Die Genfer Phase der Konferenz über Sicherheit und Zusammenarbeit in Europa. Europa-Archiv, no. 29, 25 mai 1974, p. p. 305–317.
DÉFENSE (LA) de l'OTAN, les défits du changement. Suite d'articles. Nouvelles de l'OTAN, vol. 22, no. 1, 1974, p. 8–13.
DÉFENSE nationale – sécurité en Europe. Perspectives, no. 1340, mai 1974, p. 1–8.
EHRHARDT (C. A.), Neue Impulse für Europa und NATO. Aussenpolitik, no. 25, 3. Quartal 1974, p. 270–279.
GREENHILL (D.), The future security of Western Europe. International affairs (London), no. 50, janvier 1974, p. 1–14.
GROLL (G. VON), Die Genfer KSZE-Verhandlungen. Aussenpolitik, no. 25, 2. Quartal 1974, p. 159–166.
KIELMANSEGG (J. A.), Les problèmes de la détente militaire et de la réduction des forces en Europe centrale. Politique étrangère, vol. 39, no. 3, 1974, p. 275–290.
LUNS (J.), Perspectives d'alliance, Nouvelles de l'OTAN, vol. 22, no. 1, 1974, p. 3–7.
MARRIOTT (J.), The development of NATO's nuclear potential 1949/74. Nato's fifteen nations, no. 19, février–mars 1974, p. 39–50.
MECHANISM of security and disarmament problems in Europe. Peace and the sciences (Vienna), no. 3, septembre 1974, p. 1–105.
MULTAN (W.) et A. TOWPIK, Die westliche Abrüstungspolitik in Europa und ihre Konsequenzen aus östlicher Sicht. Europa-Archiv, no. 29, 10 avril 1974, p. 223–232.
PALMER (J.), Nato lives or dies by the sea. Nato's fifteen nations, no. 19, octobre–novembre 1974, p. 20–23.
RUEHL (L.), Die Wiener Verhandlungen über Truppenverminderung in Ost und West. Europa-Archiv, no. 29, 10 août 1974, p. 507–518.

SCHOFIELD (B. B.), Problems of NATO 1974. World survey, février 1974, p. 1–8.
STEINHOFF (J.), Der Zwang zur Verteidigungskooperation Westeuropas. Europa-Archiv, no. 29, 25 juillet 1974, p. 473–478.
TALPĂ (L.), Quelques considérations concernant la Conférence sur la sécurité et la coopération en Europe (1re phase). Revue roumaine d'études internationales, vol. 8, no. 1, 1974, p. 29–43.
TOINET (M. F.), Les troupes américaines en Europe. Le débat aux Etats-Unis. Défense nationale, no. 30, février 1974, p. 17–28.
TUNKIN (G. I.), The problem of sovereignty and organisation of European security. Revue belge de droit international, vol. 10, no. 1, 1974, p. 1–10.
VALENTIN (F.), L'Europe de l'Ouest et la défense. Défense nationale, no. 30, août–septembre 1974, p. 31–38.
VIKTOROV (V.), The Vienna talks (on the question of troop and arms cuts in Central Europe). International affairs (Moscow), août 1974, p. 22–30.
WILCZYNSKI (J.), Technology and the NATO-Warsaw pact strategic balance. Australian outlook, no. 27, décembre 1973, p. 286–306.
WINDSOR (P.), Nato's twenty-five years. The world today, no. 30, mai 1974, p. 181–187.

TABLE DES NOMS LIST OF NAMES

INDEX ALPHABETIQUE

GENERAL INDEX

La Résolution du Comité des Ministres du Conseil de l'Europe, en date du 30 juin 1953, stipulait que *l'Annuaire Européen* serait consacré à l'étude objective des organisations internationales européennes et de leurs travaux, sous la responsabilité d'un Comité de Rédaction indépendant, sans caractère officiel ou politique, qui s'interdirait de formuler des opinions sur aucun aspect des affaires internationales.

A maintes reprises, tant dans les revues de presse que dans les journaux spécialisés, *l'Annuaire Européen* a été qualifié d'instrument indispensable à l'étude des institutions européennes. Il semble en effet avoir répondu pleinement au mandat défini par le Comité des Ministres en 1953, et être devenu la source autorisée de toute étude méthodique des organisations européennes et de leurs travaux.

* *
*

The Resolution of the Committee of Ministers of the Council of Europe of 30th June, 1953, laid down that the *European Yearbook* should be devoted to the scientific study of European organisations and their work, under the responsibility of an independent Editorial Committee of an unofficial and non-political character, precluded from expressing an opinion on any aspect of international affairs.

Reviews in the press and in the learned journals have on a number of occasions described the *European Yearbook* as an indispensable instrument for the study of European institutions. It appears to have complied fully with the mandate of the Committee of Ministers in 1953 and to have become the authoritative source for the scientific study of European organisations and their work.

(ISBN 90 247 1892 9)

GPSR Compliance

The European Union's (EU) General Product Safety Regulation (GPSR) is a set of rules that requires consumer products to be safe and our obligations to ensure this.

If you have any concerns about our products, you can contact us on ProductSafety@springernature.com

In case Publisher is established outside the EU, the EU authorized representative is:

Springer Nature Customer Service Center GmbH
Europaplatz 3
69115 Heidelberg, Germany

Batch number: 10823769

Printed by Printforce, the Netherlands